Chauceer to Spenser

BLACKWELL ANTHOLOGIES

Chaucer to Spenser: An Anthology
Edited by Derek Pearsall

Blackwell Anthologies are a series of extensive and comprehensive volumes designed to address the numerous issues raised by recent debates regarding the literary canon, value, text, context, gender, genre and period. While providing the reader with key canonical writings in their entirety, the series is also ambitious in its coverage of hitherto marginalized texts, and flexible in the overall variety of its approaches to periods and movements. Each volume has been thoroughly researched to meet the current needs of teachers and students.

Published titles

BRITISH LITERATURE

British Literature 1640–1789: An Anthology
edited by Robert DeMaria, Jr

Victorian Women Poets: An Anthology
edited by Angela Leighton and Margaret Reynolds

Chaucer to Spenser: An Anthology of Writings in English 1375–1575
edited by Derek Pearsall

Romanticism: An Anthology. Second Edition
edited by Duncan Wu

Romantic Women Poets: An Anthology
edited by Duncan Wu

AMERICAN LITERATURE

Nineteenth-Century American Women Poets
edited by Paula Bernat Bennett

Nineteenth-Century American Women Writers: An Anthology
edited by Karen L. Kilcup

Forthcoming

BRITISH LITERATURE

Renaissance Drama: An Anthology of Plays and Performances
edited by Arthur F. Kinney

Renaissance Literature: An Anthology
edited by Michael Payne and John Hunter

The Victorians: An Anthology of Poetry and Poetics
edited by Valentine Cunningham

Old and Middle English: An Anthology
edited by Elaine Treharne

Restoration Drama: An Anthology
edited by David Womersley

Modernism: An Anthology
edited by Lawrence Rainey

AMERICAN LITERATURE

Native American Women Writers *c.*1800–1925: An Anthology
edited by Karen L. Kilcup

Colonial American Literature
edited by Susan Castillo and Ivy Schweitzer

Early African-American Literature: An Anthology
edited by Phillip M. Richards

Nineteenth-Century American Literature: An Anthology
edited by Kenny J. Williams

CHAUCER TO SPENSER

AN ANTHOLOGY OF WRITINGS IN ENGLISH 1375–1575

EDITED BY **DEREK PEARSALL**

BLACKWELL
Publishers

First published 1999

2 4 6 8 10 9 7 5 3 2 1

Blackwell Publishers Ltd
108 Cowley Road
Oxford OX4 1JF
UK

Blackwell Publishers Inc.
350 Main Street
Malden, Massachusetts 02148
USA

British Library Cataloguing in Publication Data

A CIP catalogue record for this book is available from the British Library.

Library of Congress Cataloging-in-Publication Data

Chauper to Spenser: an anthology / edited by Derek Pearsall.
p. cm. — (Blackwell anthologies)
Includes bibliographical references and index.
ISBN 0-631-19838-5. — ISBN 0-631-19839-3 (pbk.)
1. English literature—Middle English, 1100–1500. 2. Great Britain—Civilization—1066–1485—Sources. 3. Great Britain—Civilization—16th century—Sources. 4. English literature—Early modern, 1500–1700. I. Pearsall, Derek Albert. II. Series.
PR1120.W75 1999
820.8'001—DC21 98-3678
CIP

Commissioning Editor: Andrew McNeillie
Desk Editor: Brigitte Lee
Production Manager: Lisa Eaton
Text Designer: Lisa Eaton
Picture Researcher: Leanda Shrimpton

Typeset in 9½ on 11 pt Garamond 3
by Ace Filmsetting Ltd, Frome, Somerset
Printed in Great Britain by T.J. International, Padstow, Cornwall

This book is printed on acid-free paper.

Contents

Alphabetical List of Authors and Works

Introduction

The aim of this book is to provide substantial reading in the best and most important writers of the two centuries from Chaucer to Spenser – Chaucer himself, Langland, the *Gawain*-poet, Julian of Norwich, Malory, Henryson, Skelton, More, Wyatt – and to surround them with shorter extracts from other writers and texts so that a fuller picture will emerge of the whole culture of the period. Though drama is necessarily, and at some cost to the comprehensiveness of this picture, excluded, the reader will be able to gain from this volume, with its apparatus of headnotes and explanatory notes as well as its texts, some first-hand experience of most of the significant things that were happening in English writing from the late fourteenth century, when English took over from French as the prestige literary language of England and Scotland, until the time of Spenser and Shakespeare.

No attempt is made to define the 'late Middle Ages' nor to draw a line under 'the Middle Ages'. The last text represented is 'January' from Spenser's *Shepherd's Calendar*, not because it marks the end of an era but because one of the ways in which the arbitrariness of periodization can be demonstrated is by seeing the centuries meet in a single writer. Periodization is a practical necessity as an aid to reading and study, but the forms of periodization that we become accustomed to need to be constantly challenged so that they do not become part of the history to which they refer. Changes of profound significance to literary culture took place in the second quarter of the sixteenth century, but every text looks both backward and forward, and continuities are as well worth stressing as changes.

It is for this reason too that the volume reaches back into the fourteenth century. A collection of writing from 1400 to Spenser would have been easier to put together, and more the sort of thing that is usually done, but it would have excluded those writers – Chaucer, and to a lesser extent Langland – whose poetry shaped the discourses of culture, the very terms in which writing in English was thought to be important, during the next two centuries.

An anthology or collection of writing such as this is designed to give the reader a sampling of what is best and most representative in the writing of the period, in prose and poetry – larger samples of what is best and smaller samples of what is more representative. But the two criteria are constantly in operational conflict and in question: if one were aiming to include only the best writing, the whole volume could be devoted to Chaucer and Henryson; if one were to seek only the most representative, many pages would be given over to genres of limited or ephemeral or merely historical interest. So a constant war is waged in the mind of the selector, and many painful battles of choice fought to an unsatisfactory conclusion (*how* could the *Kingis Quair* and the *Flower and the Leaf* possibly get left out?). But it makes one's mind a little easier, in transcribing and editing pieces of verse and prose that are evidently inferior in interest and quality to poems of, say, Chaucer that have been left out, to recall that Chaucer's poetry needs this context of understanding. Taught so frequently now as the sole representative of English writing before Shakespeare, Chaucer is in danger of being read and learnt about in a vacuum, away from the structures of linguistic and cultural meaning that provide the architecture for the understanding of his poetry. So there is good sense in building a causeway back to his poetry, through which we can come to understand it better and also come to understand how it has come to be understood. The two hundred years between the *Parliament of Fowls* and the *Shepherd's Calendar* turn out to be very much bound together by a sense of common cultural tradition, or a series of such traditions. There is no radical break in continuity.

Chaucer is important enough to merit this special attention, and the large share of this volume that he occupies, but there are many other cultural narratives to attend to apart from those for which he gave the signal. 'Writings', in this volume, are not taken to be just the canonical literary texts, in prose and poetry, but also other kinds of writing that have 'literary' value and interest, sometimes in unexpected ways. But the insistence upon 'literary' value is important, even though the term is difficult to define. There can be no question of defining it in exclusively formal terms (though form, metre, style are all important) or of attempting to separate a text from its historical 'field'. It would be possible to talk of various kinds of imaginative power – expressed in language and form, in story-making, in the creation of an authorial presence – but in the end 'literary value' is best defined in a contrast: it is what is left that gives pleasure and interest when historical explanations, and the demand for answers to questions, are exhausted. It is such a definition that makes possible a distinction between a collection of writings such as the present one and another kind of collection that might be imagined, of 'Documents in Cultural History'. Such a collection would be valuable, and someone should do it, but it would be different in its emphasis and interest. It might include pieces of writing that are represented here, such as the Letters of John Ball, or the Testimony of William Thorpe, or the Protestant polemic of Latimer or Foxe, but it would include them for different reasons – because they were of historical importance rather than, as here, because they are of more-than-historical importance.

The many writers and texts represented here are bound together by a multitude of common interests, preoccupations, anxieties, as well as by the circumstances and processes of history in which they participated. Reading them in relation to one another, and within the structures of cross-reference that are provided, sharpens awareness of these cultural and historical patterns of interconnection. The status of English is a recurrent theme: its diversity and precarious stability (Chaucer, *Troilus*; Caxton, *Eneydos*) despite its newly won triumph (Trevisa); the need to encourage and promote it (Lydgate, *Troy-Book*) and to annex Latin to it through translation (Trevisa, the Bible, the *Aeneid*-translations of Douglas and Surrey); the perception of its inferiority, even late in the day, to Latin (More, *Utopia*; Ascham, *Toxophilus*). Associated with this is the debate about poetic style, about the proper language of poetry, to which Lydgate, Caxton, Hawes and Dunbar all contribute, but which is most eloquently concluded among those writers (e.g. Cavendish, Gascoigne) whose ease with prose contrasts with the exhaustion of their poetry and of the poetic high style (Sackville, in the *Mirror for Magistrates*). Every mention of Chaucer (e.g. Lydgate, Hoccleve, Hawes, Dunbar) is an opportunity to talk about the nature and function of poetry, to contribute something to the developing discourse of an English poetic and cultural tradition (Caxton, Leland). For the understanding of such interests and concerns, this volume is at once a representation, an index, and a history.

Other themes can be traced too. The flowering of mysticism (the *Cloud of Unknowing*, Julian) and affective devotion (Nicholas Love, Margery Kempe, 'In a tabernacle') can be observed as it runs parallel to the growth of anticlerical reformism (Langland) and the anticlerical polemic of Lollardy (William Thorpe). Lollard beliefs were tenacious, and the anxiety to suppress them (Hoccleve, Kempe, Pecock) foreshadows their re-emergence in substantially unaltered form at the time of the Reformation (Fish, Latimer), with Langland himself recruited to that same cause (Gascoigne). Powerful continuities are to be observed in attitudes towards death and mortality, as they are announced in the Pardoner's Tale and Langland: early and late there is the impersonal moralization of the inevitability of death (Lydgate, *Dance Macabre*, and *Fall of Princes*; 'Farewell this world'; the *Mirror for Magistrates*), but there is always a more personal sense of what mortality means to the individual (Hoccleve, *Complaint*; Dunbar, *Lament for the Makers*; More, *Dialogue*). The idea of Fame as something that transcends death is not a Renaissance invention: Chaucer is very conscious of the desire for it, as well as Hawes, Dunbar and (incessantly) Skelton.

The immersion of these texts in their social, cultural and political history is an inescapable reality. Both Chaucer and Langland offer to their successors a variety of questions, urgently debated, about the nature of the community and its relation to the individual, about the public good, about authority and its obligations, about law, and these questions are returned to again and again, in old and new ways (Henryson, *Fables*; More, *Utopia*). A sense of the arbitrariness of state power, and its ubiquity – as well as its impotence in the face of spiritual conviction – is present in the interrogations of Thorpe and Kempe and in the martyrdoms of Foxe. The role of monarchs, and the manner in which they are to be ruled by law, remains central to these debates, from Langland through Fortescue to Tyndale, and Henry V makes several appearances as a model king (Hoccleve, *Regement*; the *First English Life*; Elyot, *The Governor*); but there is an increasing awareness of the role of the old class of knights as the new governors in Hawes, Elyot and Gascoigne. Few writers apart from Henryson (e.g. *The Wolf and the Lamb*) pay attention as Langland did to poverty and the oppressions of indigence, though Fish, in the *Supplication*, makes playful rhetoric of them. Women are, inevitably, not largely represented among the authors included (Julian of Norwich, Kempe, the Paston women), though some effort has been made to recognize their possible presence among anonymous writings of the period (the Findern lyrics). But of the investigation and reinvestigation of those themes relating to the representation of women and marriage that Chaucer set at the centre of cultural consciousness in the persons of the Wife of Bath and Criseyde there is no end, whether in Henryson's *Testament of Cresseid* and Dunbar's *Two Married Women*, or in the imagined other of the lyrics of Charles of Orleans and Wyatt, or more slyly and obliquely in More's account of Shore's wife.

Of all the themes that are to be followed out, perhaps the most continuously absorbing is the location and unfolding of the sense of self, of interior subjectivity. It is not that 'personality' is being invented, or that anything could be more subtle than the practice or observation of self-construction in Chaucer, Langland, Gower or the *Gawain*-poet, but there is, in time, a greater complexity of cultural circumstance to which the individual subject must adapt or be fashioned, and a fuller documentation of the record of that process. The idea of 'the self' can be followed out in the figure of the lover, as the extreme case of the (male) person, in Charles of Orleans, Wyatt and Surrey; in the allegorical dreamer of Chaucer's *Parliament of Fowls* or Skelton's *Bowge of Court*; in the guise of the confessional in Chaucer (the Wife of Bath, the Pardoner), Langland, Gower, Hoccleve, or Lydgate's *Testament*; in 'autobiographical' narrative (Hoccleve and Kempe, comically to be set beside Mandeville); in the elaboration of the conflict, in romance-narrative, between the private and the public spheres of conduct (*Gawain*, Malory); and increasingly, in the later period, in the more intimate as well as more self-consciously 'historical' record of the lives of the famous (More's *Richard III*, Roper's *More*, Cavendish's *Wolsey*).

These are some of the lines of thought and connections that will be set up in the reading of this collection of writing. There are many others, including happy conjunctions that are the accident of selection: a little history of the observation (or non-observation) of nature, from the seasons-prologues of Chaucer and Lydgate, of Hawes and Skelton, to the free-standing descriptions of nature in Douglas's *Aeneid*-prologues, to Ascham's naturalist's delight at the play of wind on the snow in *Toxophilus*; or the woman's lament at the absence of her beloved, as spoken by the male poet in Chaucer's Franklin's Tale and Surrey's two poems, but perhaps by a woman in the Findern lyrics; or, most serendipitously, the presence of two versions of Psalm 130 (*De profundis*), Jonah's (in *Patience*) and Wyatt's. There are also some pieces of writing here that, though they could be shown to form part of any number of cultural narratives, are chiefly here because they give such extreme pleasure in themselves – the Miller's Tale, *Patience*, some of the songs and lyrics, parts of Malory, Skelton's *Philip Sparrow*, Lindsay's *Squire Meldrum*, Spenser's precocious 'January'.

The layout of the volume is as broadly chronological as can be managed without excessive fussiness. Headnotes and explanatory notes offer suggestions about interpretation as well as contextual and elucidatory information. The bibliographical information that is provided is basic, and recommendations for further reading are confined to (mostly recent) works that students will find directly useful or where fuller bibliographical information is given.

Editorial practice

Most of the texts in this volume have been newly edited from original sources, though the purposes of the volume make full critical editions inappropriate. Editorial practice will of course vary, with such a wide range of written and printed texts, but generally one manuscript or print is selected to serve as a base text in each case and is emended where necessary in the light of readings from one or two other manuscripts or prints, or conjecturally. All departures from the base text of a substantive nature (that is, excluding correction of mechanical and meaningless scribal or printer's error, elimination of misleading eccentricities of spelling, especially in texts of later provenance, and normalization of the spelling of exotic proper nouns) are recorded in the Textual Notes. The sources of preferred readings are indicated only in the case of those texts that survive in many witnesses and that have a complex editorial history; sigils and other abbreviations, in such cases, are explained in the Headnote to the text. In all texts, obsolete letters are replaced by their modern equivalents: *thorn* is represented as *th*, *yogh* as *gh*, *g*, *y*, *w* or *z* as appropriate. The letters *i/j* and *u/v* are normalized according to modern practice, initial *ff* appears as *F* or *f*, and pronoun *y* as *I*. Abbreviations and contractions are silently expanded; roman numerals in verse texts are rendered as words according to the metrically appropriate practice. Capitalization, word division, punctuation and paragraphing are editorial. The aim is accessibility without loss of authenticity.

Acknowledgements

I should like to thank Andrew McNeillie, at Blackwell Publishers, for his encouragement throughout the planning of this book, and the production staff at Blackwell, especially Lisa Eaton, for cheerfully coping with it. I am grateful to all those who gave helpful advice or encouragement in the early stages, especially Jaques Berthoud, Elizabeth Fowler, Stephen Greenblatt, Anne Middleton, and Lee and Annabel Patterson, when there was still a chance that the project might be shaped for the better. I am deeply indebted to those who read portions of the work in the later stages and helped to save me from many of the mistakes I remained determined to make – David Benson, Julia Boffey, Chris Cannon, Tony Edwards, Barry Windeatt, and especially Peter Nicholson.

List of Abbreviations and Short Titles

AV	Authorized Version (of the Bible)
BN	Bibliothèque Nationale, Paris
Bodl.	Bodleian Library, Oxford
ChauR	*Chaucer Review*
CCCC	Corpus Christi College, Cambridge
CT	Chaucer's *Canterbury Tales*
CUL	Cambridge University Library
E&S	*Essays and Studies*
EC	*Essays in Criticism*
EETS, ES, OS, SS	Early English Text Society, Extra Series, Original Series, Supplementary Series
ELH	*English Literary History*
ELR	*English Literary Renaissance*
Ecclus.	Ecclesiasticus (also called Sirach), apocryphal in AV
FrankT	Chaucer's Franklin's Tale
GP	General Prologue to Chaucer's *Canterbury Tales*
JMRS	*Journal of Medieval and Renaissance Studies*
LSE	*Leeds Studies in English*
M&H	*Medievalia et Humanistica*
MAE	*Medium Aevum*
ME	Middle English
MET	Middle English Texts
Met.	The *Metamorphoses* of Ovid
MillT	Chaucer's Miller's Tale
MLQ	*Modern Language Quarterly*
MLR	*Modern Language Review*
MnE	Modern English
MP	*Modern Philology*
MRTS	Medieval and Renaissance Texts and Studies (Binghamton, NY)
MS	*Medieval Studies*
Neoph.	*Neophilologus*
NLS	National Library of Scotland, Edinburgh
NMS	*Nottingham Medieval Studies*
NQ	*Notes and Queries*

NT	New Testament
OT	Old Testament
PardP, PardT	Chaucer's Pardoner's Prologue and Tale
PBA	*Proceedings of the British Academy*
PF	Chaucer's *Parliament of Fowls*
PMLA	*Publications of the Modern Language Association of America*
PL	*Patrologia Latina*, ed. J.P. Migne
PP	*Piers Plowman*, by William Langland
PQ	*Philological Quarterly*
Ps.	Book of Psalms (OT)
RES	*Review of English Studies*
Rom.	*Romaunt of the Rose*, the Chaucerian translation of *RR*
RR	*Le Roman de la Rose*, by Guillaume de Lorris and Jean de Meun
SAC	*Studies in the Age of Chaucer*
SN	*Studia Neophilologica*
SP	*Studies in Philology*
STS	Scottish Text Society
TC	*Troilus and Criseyde*, by Chaucer
TCBS	*Transactions of the Cambridge Bibliographical Society*
TCC	Trinity College, Cambridge
TSLL	*Texas Studies in Language and Literature*
UL	University Library
UTQ	*University of Toronto Quarterly*
Vg.	Vulgate (Latin) translation of the Bible
WBP, WBT	Chaucer's Wife of Bath's Prologue and Tale
YES	*Yearbook of English Studies*

Short titles

Aers (1986)	D. Aers (ed.), *Medieval Literature: Criticism, Ideology and History* (Brighton, 1986)
Aers (1988)	D. Aers, *Community, Gender and Individual Identity: English Writing 1360–1430* (London, 1988)
Anderson (1984)	J. Anderson, *Biographical Truth: The Representation of Historical Persons in Tudor-Stuart Writing* (New Haven, 1984)
Barratt (1992)	A. Barratt (ed.), *Women's Writing in Middle English* (London, 1992)
Boffey and Cowen (1991)	J. Boffey and J. Cowen (eds), *Chaucer and Fifteenth-Century Poetry*, King's College London Medieval Studies, 5 (1991)
Brewer (1966)	D.S. Brewer (ed.), *Chaucer and Chaucerians* (London and Edinburgh, 1966)
Duffy (1992)	E. Duffy, *The Stripping of the Altars: Traditional Religion in England 1400–1580* (New Haven, 1992)
Gray (1985)	D. Gray (ed.), *The Oxford Book of Late Medieval Verse and Prose* (Oxford, 1985)
Greenblatt (1980)	S. Greenblatt, *Renaissance Self-Fashioning: From More to Shakespeare* (Chicago, 1980)
Greenblatt (1988)	S. Greenblatt (ed.), *Representing the Renaissance* (Berkeley, 1988)
Hadfield (1994)	A. Hadfield, *Literature, Politics and National Identity: Reformation to Renaissance* (Cambridge, 1994)
Halpern (1991)	R. Halpern, *The Poetics of Primitive Accumulation: English Renaissance Culture and the Genealogy of Capital* (Ithaca, 1991)

Hammond (1927)	E.P. Hammond, *English Verse Between Chaucer and Surrey* (Durham, NC, 1927)
Hudson (1988)	A. Hudson, *The Premature Reformation: Wycliffite Texts and Lollard History* (Oxford, 1988)
Klibansky (1964)	R. Klibansky, E. Panofsky and F. Saxl, *Saturn and Melancholy* (London, 1964)
Lerer (1993)	Seth Lerer, *Chaucer and his Readers: Imagining the Author in Later Medieval England* (Princeton, 1993)
Lewalski (1986)	B.K. Lewalski (ed.), *Renaissance Genres: Essays in Theory, History, and Interpretation* (Cambridge, MA, 1986)
Lewis (1936)	C.S. Lewis, *The Allegory of Love* (Oxford, 1936)
Lewis (1954)	C.S. Lewis, *English Literature in the Sixteenth Century, excluding Drama* (Oxford, 1954)
Morse and Windeatt (1990)	R. Morse and B. Windeatt (eds), *Chaucer Traditions: Studies in Honour of Derek Brewer* (Cambridge, 1990)
Patterson (1990)	L. Patterson (ed.), *Literary Practice and Social Change in Britain, 1380–1530* (Berkeley, 1990)
Scanlon (1994)	L. Scanlon, *Narrative, Authority and Power: The Medieval Exemplum and the Chaucerian Tradition* (Cambridge, 1994)
Sisam (1921)	K. Sisam (ed.), *Fourteenth-Century Verse and Prose* (Oxford, 1921)
Spearing (1976)	A.C. Spearing, *Medieval Dream-Poetry* (Cambridge, 1976)
Spearing (1985)	A.C. Spearing, *Medieval to Renaissance in English Poetry* (Cambridge, 1985)
Spearing (1993)	A.C. Spearing, *The Medieval Poet as Voyeur: Looking and Listening in Medieval Love-Narratives* (Cambridge, 1993)
Tilley	M.P. Tilley, *A Dictionary of the Proverbs in England in the Sixteenth and Seventeenth Centuries* (Ann Arbor, 1950)
Whiting	B.J. Whiting, *Proverbs, Sentences and Proverbial Phrases from English Writings Mainly before 1500* (Cambridge, MA, 1968)
Windeatt (1994)	B.A. Windeatt (ed.), *English Mystics of the Middle Ages* (Cambridge, 1994)
Yeager (1984)	R.F. Yeager (ed.), *Fifteenth-Century Studies: Recent Essays* (Hamden, CT, 1984)

Chronological Table of Dates

Historical events	*Literary landmarks*
1377 Death of Edward III. Accession of Richard II.	*c.* 1377 *Langland writing B-text of* Piers Plowman.
1378 Beginning of Papal Schism.	
	c. 1380 *Chaucer's* Parliament of Fowls.
1381 Peasants' Revolt.	
1382 Official condemnation of Wyclif's opinions.	*c.* 1382–5 *Chaucer's* Troilus and Criseyde.
	c. 1385–6 *Chaucer's* Legend of Good Women.
1386 Council of Regency.	*c.* 1386 *Gower begins* Confessio Amantis.
	1387 *Trevisa's prose translation of Higden.*
	c. 1387 *Chaucer begins* Canterbury Tales.
1389 Richard II resumes full royal power.	1389–1418 *Christine de Pizan at French royal court.*
	c. 1390 *BL MS Cotton Nero A.x, containing* Sir Gawain and the Green Knight, Patience, Pearl *and* Cleanness.
	c. 1390 *The Vernon MS (Bodl.MS Eng.poet.a.1), a massive collection of religious and didactic writing in English.*
	c. 1390 *Earliest English version of* Mandeville's Travels.
c. 1395 Second version of the Wycliffite Bible in English.	*c.* 1395 The Cloud of Unknowing.
	1398 *Trevisa's prose translation of Bartholomew's* Encyclopaedia.
1399 Deposition of Richard II. Accession of Henry IV.	
	1400 *Death of Chaucer.*
	c. 1400 *Alliterative* Morte Arthure.
1401 Statute of burning against Lollard heretics.	
1407 The examination of William Thorpe by archbishop Arundel.	
	1408 *Death of Gower.*
	1410 *Nicholas Love's* Mirror of the Blessed Life of Jesus Christ *approved for publication.*
	1411–12 *Hoccleve's* Regement of Princes.
	1412–20 *Lydgate's* Troy-Book.
1413 Death of Henry IV. Accession of Henry V.	1413 *First copying of the long version of Julian's* Revelations.

1415 Battle of Agincourt.

1415–40 Charles of Orleans prisoner in England.

1415 Council of Constance ends Papal Schism (1417).

1419–67 Philip le Bon duke of Burgundy: golden age of Burgundian culture in the Low Countries.

1420 Treaty of Troyes: the dual kingdom of England and France.

1422 Death of Henry V. Accession of Henry VI (9 months old).

1431 Burning of Joan of Arc in Rouen.

1435 Death of the duke of Bedford, regent in France.

1435 First gift of books to Oxford by Humphrey, duke of Gloucester.

1443 Henry VI's first episode of madness.

1443 Henry VI marries Margaret of Anjou.

1450 First Bible printed at Mainz.

1453 Turks take Constantinople: exodus of Greek scholars to the west.

1455 End of Hundred Years' War.

1455 First battle of Wars of Roses, at St Albans.

1457 The abjuration of bishop Reginald Pecock.

1461 Battle of Towton. Henry VI deposed. Edward IV proclaimed king.

1470 Henry VI reinstated by the earl of Warwick.

1471 Henry VI deposed and murdered; Edward IV restored.

1476 Introduction of printing into England by Caxton.

1483 Edward IV dies; Richard, duke of Gloucester, acts as Protector for Edward V; then succeeds as Richard III.

1485 Battle of Bosworth Field. Richard III killed; accession of Henry VII.

1488–1513 James IV king of Scotland.

1492 Christopher Columbus lands in the West Indies.

1413 *Margery Kempe on the road to Bridlington.*

1421–2 *Lydgate's* Siege of Thebes.

1421–2 *Hoccleve's* Series.

c. 1425–50 *John Shirley active as a copyist and publicizer of the writing of Chaucer and Lydgate.*

1426 *Death of Hoccleve.*

1426–32 *Lydgate active as royal propagandist and court poet.*

1431–8 *Lydgate's* Fall of Princes.

c. 1440 *Robert Thornton active in Yorkshire in copying important miscellanies of English writing.*

1449 *Death of Lydgate.*

c. 1460 *CUL MS Ff.i.6 (the Findern anthology), a household compilation of Chaucerian poems and original lyrics.*

1460–80 *Many letters surviving from those exchanged among members of the Paston family of Norfolk.*

1471 *Death of Sir Thomas Malory.*

c. 1475 *Sir John Fortescue,* The Governance of England.

1485 *Caxton's print of Malory's* Morte D'Arthur.

c. 1490 *Robert Henryson active as a poet.*

1497 John Cabot lands in North America.
1498 Erasmus, the Dutch humanist scholar, at Oxford.
1509 Death of Henry VII. Accession of Henry VIII.
1513 Battle of Flodden; James IV killed.
1516 The Greek New Testament of Erasmus.
1517 Martin Luther's Wittenberg theses.
1519–56 Charles V Holy Roman Emperor.
1526 William Tyndale's first English New Testament published in Cologne.
1529 Fall of Cardinal Wolsey. More becomes Lord Chancellor.
1533 Coronation of Anne Boleyn as queen.
1533–9 John Leland, as king's antiquary, journeys through England to inspect the monastic libraries.
1534 Act of Succession; Act of Supremacy; execution of More.
1536 Execution of Anne Boleyn.
1536–9 Suppression of the monasteries.
1540 Execution of Thomas Cromwell, chief minister since 1533.
1543 Copernicus, *De Revolutionibus.*
1547 Death of Henry VIII. Accession of Edward VI.
1549 Act of Uniformity. Thomas Cranmer's Book of Common Prayer.
1553 Death of Edward VI. Accession of Mary.
1555 Burning of Ridley and Latimer.
1558 Death of Mary. Accession of Elizabeth.
1563 First edition of John Foxe's *Acts and Monuments.*

1499 *Skelton's* Bowge of Court.
1506 *Hawes's* Pastime of Pleasure.
1508 *Dunbar's* Golden Targe *and* Two Married Women.
1513 *Douglas completes his translation of the* Aeneid.
1513 *Macchiavelli's* The Prince *published in Italy.*
1516 *Thomas More's* Utopia *(in Latin).*
1516 *Ariosto's* Orlando Furioso.
c. 1516 *Skelton's play of* Magnificence.
1521–3 *Skelton's anti-Wolsey satires and* Garland of Laurel.
1528 *Castiglione's* The Courtier *published in Italy.*
1529 *Simon Fish,* A Supplication for the Beggars.
c. 1530–40 *The Devonshire MS (BL MS Add. 17492), a court album containing many poems by Wyatt.*
1531 *Sir Thomas Elyot,* The Governor.
1532 *Publication of William Thynne's collected Chaucer.*
1532 *Rabelais's* Pantagruel *published in France.*
1540 *Lindsay's* Satire of the Three Estates *(play).*
1542 *Surrey's translation of* Aeneid I–II.
1550 *Robert Crowley's print of* Piers Plowman.
1554 *First plans for* The Mirror for Magistrates.
c. 1555 *Cavendish,* Metrical Visions *and* Life of Wolsey.
1557 *Tottel's* Songs and Sonnets.
1558 *Birth of Shakespeare.*
1570 *First printing of* The Schoolmaster *of Roger Ascham (d. 1568).*
1576 *George Gascoigne's* The Steel Glass.
1579 *Edmund Spenser's* The Shepherd's Calendar.

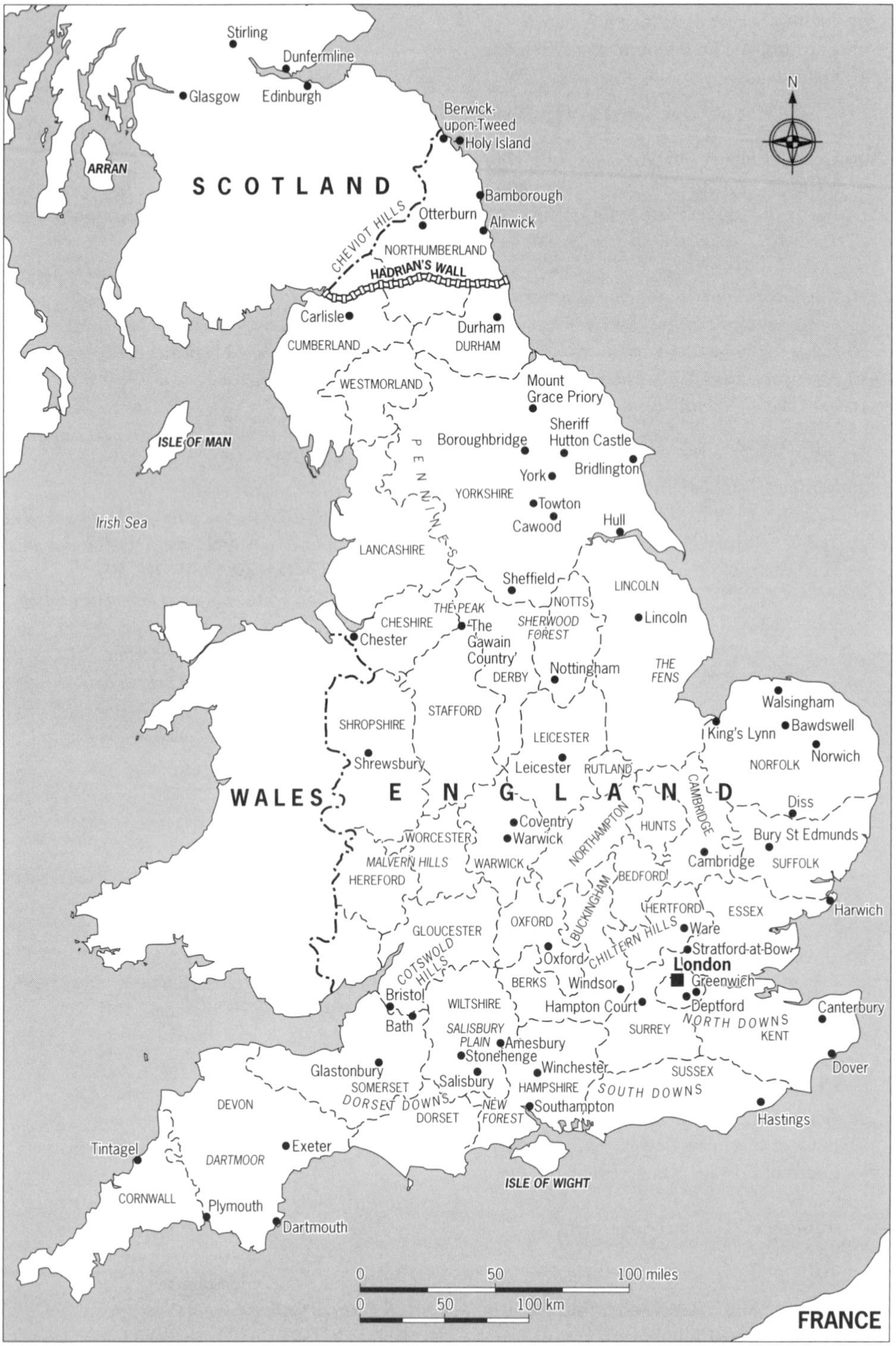

Stirling
Dunfermline
Glasgow
Edinburgh
Berwick-upon-Tweed
Holy Island
ARRAN
SCOTLAND
Bamborough
CHEVIOT HILLS
Otterburn
Alnwick
NORTHUMBERLAND
HADRIAN'S WALL
Carlisle
Durham
CUMBERLAND
DURHAM
WESTMORLAND
Mount Grace Priory
Sheriff Hutton Castle
Boroughbridge
Bridlington
ISLE OF MAN
PENNINES
York
YORKSHIRE
Towton
Cawood
Irish Sea
Hull
LANCASHIRE
Sheffield
LINCOLN
NOTTS
THE PEAK
CHESHIRE
SHERWOOD FOREST
Lincoln
Chester
'The Gawain Country'
Nottingham
DERBY
THE FENS
Walsingham
SHROPSHIRE
STAFFORD
King's Lynn
Bawdswell
LEICESTER
Norwich
Shrewsbury
Leicester
RUTLAND
NORFOLK
WALES
ENGLAND
CAMBRIDGE
Diss
Coventry
Warwick
NORTHAMPTON
HUNTS
Bury St Edmunds
WORCESTER
MALVERN HILLS
WARWICK
Cambridge
SUFFOLK
HEREFORD
BEDFORD
Harwich
BUCKINGHAM
HERTFORD
ESSEX
GLOUCESTER
OXFORD
Ware
CHILTERN HILLS
Stratford-at-Bow
COTSWOLD HILLS
Oxford
London
BERKS
Windsor
Greenwich
Bristol
WILTSHIRE
Hampton Court
Deptford
Canterbury
Bath
NORTH DOWNS
SURREY
SALISBURY PLAIN
Amesbury
KENT
Stonehenge
Dover
Glastonbury
Winchester
SUSSEX
SOMERSET
Salisbury
HAMPSHIRE
SOUTH DOWNS
DORSET DOWNS
NEW FOREST
Southampton
DEVON
DORSET
Hastings
Tintagel
Exeter
DARTMOOR
ISLE OF WIGHT
CORNWALL
Plymouth
Dartmouth
0
50
100 miles
0
50
100 km
FRANCE
N

Geoffrey Chaucer (*c.* 1343–1400)

Geoffrey Chaucer was born about 1343, only son of a wealthy London wine-merchant who grew richer after bequests from relatives who died in the Black Death (1349), and could afford to send his son into service as a page in the household of the countess of Ulster (1357). From there he progressed to service as a *valettus* in the household of Lionel, second son of the king, Edward III. He saw active service in France (1360), was captured and ransomed, and later became a squire in the royal household. He married Philippa de Roet, a *domicella* in the household of Edward III's queen, Philippa, about 1366. She was the sister of Katherine, who after the death in 1368 of Blanche, duchess of Lancaster, became the mistress of the duke of Lancaster, John of Gaunt, third son of the king, the most wealthy and powerful man in England after the king and the 'patron', in some capacity, of Chaucer's first poem, the *Book of the Duchess*. This poem, written in English and thus signalling Chaucer's determination to assert the poetic potential of English in a mainly French-speaking court, is an elegiac celebration of John of Gaunt's love for Blanche. During these years as royal esquire, Chaucer was frequently employed as a junior member of diplomatic and trading missions to France (on many occasions), to Spain (in 1366) and to Italy (in 1372–3 and 1378). He was fluent in French and Italian, and well read in the literatures of those languages; his Latin was good, especially for one who had no formal education beyond grammar school and what he could pick up at court. In 1374 Chaucer was appointed Controller of the Customs of Hides, Skins and Wools in the port of London, an arduous and responsible position that he held until 1386. He was representative of a new class of government officials, neither of 'gentle' birth nor possessed of a university or clerical training; he was one of the first English 'civil servants'. He was deputized at the Customs from time to time in order that he might go on missions abroad; the Italian journey of 1378, where he became further acquainted with the work of Dante, Petrarch and Boccaccio, was a critical moment in the development of his ambitions for an English poetry that should be the servant of neither court nor church. The dream-poem of the *House of Fame* (1378) was a first, somewhat bewildered response. The *Parliament of Fowls* (1380) is a more matured exploration of Chaucer's new Italian inheritance. The early 1380s see Chaucer at the height of his career as a public poet and a poet of the court. As a royal esquire, he was still technically a member of the royal household, and his great poem of *Troilus and Criseyde* (1381–6) is evidently addressed, in the first instance, to a court or courtly audience. The *Legend of Good Women* (1386–7) is very much a court poem, and is associated explicitly with Queen Anne, whom Richard II had married in 1382. Richard suffered a series of political setbacks in the years after 1386, and Chaucer's career, as that of a royal servant, went into decline. He resigned his government post, gave up his annuity, and retired to live outside London. During these quieter years he conceived the plan of and began to write the *Canterbury Tales*, a poem of London, Europe and the world, but emphatically not a court poem. Chaucer was briefly recalled to the royal service in 1389 (after Richard's resumption of his regality) as Clerk of the King's Works, responsible for the maintenance and upkeep of all royal buildings in the vicinity of London, but he resigned this again very arduous post in 1391. His last years were spent in fairly comfortable semi-retirement, while he worked busily on the *Canterbury Tales*. He died on 25 October 1400, and was buried in Westminster Abbey, in the precincts of which he had recently leased a house. He was reburied in 1556 in a grander tomb in the Abbey that subsequently became the nucleus of 'Poets' Corner'. His son Thomas was a highly successful government servant and parliamentarian in the courts of the Lancastrian kings; of his younger son Lewis nothing is known except that his father wrote for him an introduction to astronomy, the *Treatise on the Astrolabe*, when he was eleven years old, in 1391.

For the documentary evidence of Chaucer's life, see M.M. Crow and C.C. Olson, *Chaucer Life-Records* (Oxford, 1966); for a traditional 'life and works', see D. Pearsall, *The Life of Geoffrey Chaucer: A Critical Biography* (Oxford, 1992); P. Strohm, *Social Chaucer* (Cambridge, MA, 1989), sets the poems in their Chaucerian milieu. Classic studies of Chaucer's poetry include D. Brewer, *An Introduction to Chaucer* (rev. edn, London, 1984), C. Muscatine, *Chaucer and the French Tradition: A Study in Style and Meaning* (Berkeley and Los Angeles, 1957), and D.W. Robertson, *A Preface to Chaucer* (Princeton, 1962). Recent important studies include D. Aers, *Chaucer, Langland and the Creative Imagination* (London, 1980), C. Dinshaw, *Chaucer's Sexual Poetics* (Madison, WI, 1989), J. Mann, *Geoffrey Chaucer, New Feminist Readings* (London, 1991), and L. Patterson, *Chaucer and the Subject of History* (Madison, WI, 1991). The *Oxford Guides to Chaucer* published by Oxford University Press (*The Canterbury Tales*, by H. Cooper, 1989; *Troilus and Criseyde*, by B. Windeatt, 1992; and *The Shorter Poems*, by A.J. Minnis, 1995) are generally useful. J. Dillon, *Geoffrey Chaucer* (London, 1993), is a good short introduction. The standard edition of Chaucer (with valuable introduction on language and versification) is L.D. Benson (ed.), *The Riverside Chaucer* (Boston, 1987). A year-by-year Chaucer bibliography is kept up in *SAC*.

METRE. All of Chaucer's poetry represented here is in iambic pentameter, the five-beat line with stress falling on the second syllable of the foot (x/x/x/x/x/) that Chaucer introduced into English verse and that was to become its staple measure. His earlier poems, such as the *Book of the Duchess* and the *House of Fame*, are in the shorter octosyllabic couplet derived from French; the longer line, with its greater amplitude and complexity, was hammered out on the model of the Italians. Chaucer uses it in couplet and, in the *Parliament*, *Troilus* and some of the *Canterbury Tales*, in the seven-line stanza known as 'rhyme royal'. The stanza allowed for an ampler narrative flow, and for a greater degree of emotional expansiveness, lacking the potential crispness and satirical temper of the couplet. Chaucer allows many variations on the basic metrical pattern of the iambic pentameter, including frequent feminine endings, that is, extra syllables after the last stress (GP 1–2), headless lines, lacking the first unstressed syllable (GP 1), occasional 'Lydgate' lines, lacking an unstressed syllable at the caesura (GP 751, 803; *TC* II.588, III.1380), and reversal of stress in the first foot (GP 8) and occasionally elsewhere. Consonantal syllables (e.g. *cloystrer*, GP 259; *motlee*, GP 271; *chauntrye*, GP 510; *borwed*, PardT 871) are not uncommon.

Language. Chaucer's poetry, like that of his contemporaries, needs to be read with some understanding of the nature of late fourteenth-century pronunciation if the full musicality of his versification is to be appreciated. There are two main rules to be remembered. The first is that the long vowels are given their continental rather than their modern English or American values (examples from the opening lines of GP): long *a* (*bathed*) is pronounced like *a* in 'father'; long *e* is pronounced like French *e acute* (not quite [ay]) in words like *sweete* (mostly spelt in modern English with *ee*) or like French *e grave* (not quite [air]) in words like *breeth* (mostly spelt in modern English with *ea*); long *i* (*inspired*) is pronounced [ee] as in 'machine'; long *o* is pronounced like [o] in 'note' in words like *roote* (mostly spelt in modern English with *oo*) and like [oa] in 'broad' in words like *goon* (mostly spelt in modern English with *o* or *oa*); and long *u* (*shoures*) is pronounced [oo] as in 'root'. The second rule is that everything seen should be pronounced, including initial consonant groups like *gn-* and *kn-*, medial and final consonant groups with *gh* (pronounced like *ch* in Scottish 'loch' after *a*, *o* and *u*, and like *ch* in German 'nicht' after *e* and *i*), medial *e* in inflexions such as *-es* and *-en*, and final *-e* in inflexions now lost. The pronunciation of inflexional final *-e* is vital to the understanding of the music of Chaucer's ten-syllable line; it has to be distinguished (probably better by practice in listening to the verse than by learning the complex grammatical rules, with their many exceptions) from redundant final *-e* which is not pronounced. Words of French origin are sometimes pronounced in the French way (e.g. *licour*, GP 3, with accent on the second syllable). There is a good account of Chaucer's language in D. Burnley, *A Guide to Chaucer's Language* (London, 1983).

The Parliament of Fowls

The Parliament of Fowls was written about 1380, perhaps with some allusion, in the final 'parliament', to the rivalry of three suitors for the hand of Anne of Bohemia, who eventually married Richard II in 1382. Such an occasion, like the association with St Valentine's day (386), would be important in reminding us that the *Parliament* is a poem of the court, appealing to a court clientele. But Chaucer loads the conventional form of the French allegorical love-vision with a new weight of significance. It is not just the dream of a lover who sees in his dream the allegorical acting out of his desires; the dreamer here is no lover, is unclear about his desires, and mystified by what unfolds before him. As in the earlier two dream-poems, the device of the guileless narrator allows the opening out of the narrative to a richer array of meanings. The poem's theme is sexual love, as is usual, but the place of love within an ordered moral universe and in relation to the good of the community is put before us as well as the joys and pains of sexual love itself. Those joys and pains are given a new imaginative vividness through borrowings from Boccaccio, who was to be Chaucer's major inspiration at this formative time in his poetic career. As a poem, the *Parliament* is a seeking and exploring, a questioning and doubting, and the effect is to draw the reader into a participation with the dreamer in his search for an answer to his question, or at least to help him find the right question. None of this is a 'cover' for a rationally conducted discourse on the legitimacy of sexuality. Chaucer's poetic techniques are not clever ways of arriving by indirect routes at answers known from other sources to be true. The techniques of indirection, of *not* asserting, are the realities. The second half of the poem explodes out of the frame of the love-vision into the comic framework of the bird-parliament, where Chaucer's ear for the give-and-take of colloquial repartee and gift for brisk character-portrayal are for the first time fully in evidence.

The *Parliament* is Chaucer's first major poem in pentameter, the verse-form of all his subsequent poetry (see headnote to Chaucer above), and in rhyme royal (see headnote to *Troilus* below). There is a study of the poem by J.A.W. Bennett, *The Parlement of Foules* (Oxford, 1957), and valuable description of the dream-poem genre in A.C. Spearing, *Medieval Dream Poetry* (Cambridge, 1976); see also the edition of the poem by D.S. Brewer (London and Edinburgh, 1960; 2nd edn, 1972). For some more recent essays, see D. Aers, in *ChauR* 16 (1981), 1–17; E. Salter, *Fourteenth-Century English Poetry* (Oxford, 1983), pp. 127–40; A.C. Spearing, in *SAC (Proceedings)*, 2 (1986), 169–77; K.L. Lynch, in *ChauR* 25 (1990), 1–16, 85–95.

There are 14 MSS of the *Parliament*, some imperfect and fragmentary. The best text is that contained in CUL MS Gg.4.27 (Gg), an early MS (*c.* 1420–30) probably representing an attempt to do a large collection of Chaucer's poetry (a kind of 'First Folio'). This is the base-text here, though with much normalization of the scribe's eccentric spelling and occasional emendation from Bodl.MS Fairfax 16 (F) or CUL MS Ff.1.6 (Ff) or other MSS as listed in *The Riverside Chaucer*.

(craft or art of love)	The lyf so short, the craft so longe to lerne,
first trial, winning of success	Th'assay so sharp, so hard the conquerynge,
fearful, slides away so quickly	The dredful joye alwey that slit so yerne –
	Al this mene I be Love, that my felynge
Stuns into bewilderment	Astonyeth with his wonderful werkynge
	So sore, iwis, that whan I on hym thynke
whether I float or sink	Nat wot I wel wher that I flete or synke.
in real life	For al be that I knowe nat Love in dede,
pays, reward	Ne wot how that he quiteth folk here hyre,
	Yit happeth me ful ofte in bokes reede
	Of hise myrakles and his crewel yre.
	Ther rede I wel he wol be lord and syre:
so severe (as I have read they are)	I dar nat seyn his strokes been so sore,
	But 'God save swich a lord!' – I sey namoore.
somewhat, pleasure, instruction	Of usage – what for lust and what for lore –
	On bokes rede I ofte, as I yow tolde.
Not long ago	But wherfore that I speke al this? Nat yoore
	Agon it happede me for to beholde
	Upon a bok, was write with lettres olde,
(the 'real meaning of love'?)	And therupon, a certeyn thing to lerne,
intently	The longe day ful faste I redde and yerne.
	For ofte of olde feldes, as men sey,
	Cometh al this newe corn from yer to yere,
faith	And out of olde bokes, in good fey,
knowledge	Cometh al this newe science that men lere.
	But now to purpos as of this matere:
	To rede forth so gan me to delite
only a short time	That al that day me thoughte but a lyte.
	This bok of which I make mencioun
	Entitled was al thus, as I shal telle:

1–3 The opening lines allude to the familiar saying, 'Art is long, life is short'. It is a marvellously artful rhetorical opening that seems to announce a new era in English poetry, but that quickly dissolves, Chaucerian-style, into homely bewilderment.

8–14 Love is Cupid, the God of Love, not a pink boy with chubby cheeks but a feudal lord, as in *RR* 885–917, stern, demanding and quick to chastise. It is not a 'romantic' image of love: the painful and humiliating imperatives of sexual appetite are as well communicated, allegorically, as its miraculous joys. Chaucer hints timidly at the fearful powers of Love but, even as an outsider, finds it most politic to join the chorus of obeisance.

15–16 Chaucer, in his dream-poems, commonly represents himself taking refuge in books from the sometimes painful realities of experience, thereby parodying the motives of the reader of his poem and also opening out his poem to a larger world of literary discourses.

'Tullyus of the Drem of Scipioun.'
Chapitres sevene it hadde, of hevene and helle
And erthe, and soules that therynne dwelle,
Of whiche, as shortly as I can it trete,
meaning, substance Of his sentence I wol yow seyn the greete.

Fyrst telleth it, whan Scipion was come
In Affrike, how he meteth Massynisse,
taken That hym for joie in armes hath inome;
Thanne telleth he here speche and of the blysse
fail That was betwix hem til that day gan mysse,
And how his auncestre, Affrycan so deere,
Gan in his slep that nyght to hym apere.

Thanne telleth it that, from a sterry place,
How Affrycan hath hym Cartage shewed,
future fortune And warnede hym beforn of al his grace,
whatever, ignorant And seyde what man, lerned other lewed,
(and was) endowed with virtues That lovede comoun profyt, wel ithewed,
He shulde into a blysful place wende
There as joye is that last withouten ende.

Thanne axede he if folk that here been dede
Han lyf and dwellynge in another place,
And African seyde, 'Ye, withouten drede,'
And that oure present worldes lyves space
whatever, tread Nys but a maner deth, what weye we trace;
And rightful folk shul gon, after they dye,
the Milky Way To hevene; and shewede hym the Galaxye.

Thanne shewede he hym the lytel erthe that here is,
Compared to, size At regard of the hevenes quantite,
And after shewede he hym the nyne speres,
And after that the melodye herde he
That cometh of thilke speres thryes thre,
That welle is of musik and melodye
In this world here, and cause of armonye.

little Than bad he hym, syn erthe was so lyte,
deceitful, ill fortune And disseyvable and ful of harde grace,
That he ne shulde hym in the world delyte.

31 The 'Dream of Scipio' formed the last book of Cicero's *Republic*, lost to the Middle Ages except for this book as embedded in the commentary of Macrobius (*c.*400). The lengthy discussion of the nature and significance of dreams in this commentary was well known to the Middle Ages and Chaucer. Here, Chaucer makes reference to the embedded text, which tells how Scipio Africanus the Younger, a Roman general, met Massinissa, king of Numidia, in 149 BC. They talked late into the night of Scipio's adoptive grandfather, the famous Scipio Africanus the Elder, whom Massinissa had known well; it is this Scipio who appears that night to his grandson in a dream.

47 **comoun profyt**: 'the good of the community', alluding to language often used in English documents relating to the conduct of public affairs.

59 **the nyne speres**. The round globe was surrounded by nine concentric transparent revolving spheres: in the first seven were set the seven planets and in the eighth the fixed stars, while the ninth was the sphere of the Primum Mobile, or First Mover, which controlled the complexly differential movement of the others. Each revolving sphere gave off a different note, and so was produced 'the music of the spheres', the heavenly model of musical harmony.

64–6 The account of the Ciceronian (pre-Christian) cosmology, which Chaucer is reading partly through Boethius (*Consolation* II, prose 7; see *TC* II.621n), slips momentarily into a commonplace of Christian *contemptus mundi* ('contempt of the world') belief – that this world is a form of exile or imprisonment, from which we emerge into eternal life.

Thanne tolde he hym, in certeyn yeres space — *after a certain period of years*
That every sterre shulde come into his place
Ther it was first, and al shulde out of mynde
That in this world is don of al mankynde.

Thanne preyede hym Scipion to telle hym al
The weye to come into that hevene blisse.
And he seyde, 'Know thyself first immortal,
And loke ay besyly thow werche and wysse — *direct yourself (and others)*
To comoun profit, and thow shalt not mysse
To comen swiftly to this place deere
That ful of blysse is and of soules cleere. — *bright*

'But brekeres of the lawe, soth to seyne,
And lykerous folk, after that they ben dede, — *people devoted to sensual pleasure*
Shul whirle aboute th'erthe alwey in peyne
Tyl manye a world be passed, out of drede, — *many ages*
And that foryeven is hir wikked dede;
Than shul they come into this blysful place,
To whiche to comen God sende us his grace.'

The day gan faylen, and the derke nyght,
That reveth bestes from here besynesse, — *removes*
Berafte me my bok for lak of lyght,
And to my bed I gan me for to dresse, — *get ready*
Fulfyld of thought and busy hevynesse:
For bothe I hadde thyng that I nolde,
And ek I ne hadde thyng that I wolde.

But fynally my spirit at the laste,
For-wery of my labour al the day, — *Very weary*
Tok reste, that made me to slepe faste;
And in my slep I mette, as that I lay, — *dreamed*
How Affrican, ryght in the same aray
That Scipion hym say byfore that tyde, — *saw*
Was come and stod right at my beddes syde.

The wery huntere, slepynge in his bed,
To wode ayen his mynde goth anon;
The juge dremeth how hise plees been sped; — *law-cases*
The cartere dremeth how his carte is gon;
The riche, of gold; the knyght fyght with his fon; — *foes*
The syke met he drynketh of the tunne; — *dreams*
The lovere met he hath his lady wonne.

67–70 The reference is to the 'great year', the period at the end of which all the planets and stars are in the position they were many thousands of years (variously estimated) before. The era thus marked is thought of here as the period of mankind's existence.

84 The mention of God contributes further (cf. 73–7) to the Christian colouring of the pagan cosmology.

90–1 Chaucer alludes here to a passage in the *Consolation of Philosophy* (III, prose 3, 33–6) where Boethius confesses to lady Philosophy that his life, though apparently successful, has always *lacked* something: this turns out to be the 'sovereign good' (true knowledge of self and God). What Chaucer has learnt so far, in this quest for *a certeyn thing* (20), is a grand Roman moral theorem of the universe, concerning good and bad action in relation to the service of the state. It is not exactly what he thought he was looking for, though it is a less peremptory answer to the question (of the place of love in human life) than might have been returned by a strict Christian spokesman (namely, that 'love' is concupiscence).

99–105 Familiar medieval explanations of the origin of dreams.

Can I nat seyn if that the cause were
For I hadde red of Affrican byforn
That made me to mete that he stod theere;
But thus seyde he: 'Thow hast the so wel born
In lokynge of myn olde bok to-torn,
was not a little mindful Of whiche Macrobye roughte nat a lyte,
somewhat, I would like to reward That sumdel of thy labour wolde I quyte.'

Venus Cytherea, thow blysful lady swete,
conquer whom you please That with thy fyrbrond dauntest whom thow lest
dream And madest me this swevene for to mete,
Be thow myn helpe in this, for thow mayst best!
As surely as I saw you As wisely as I seye the north-nor-west,
Whan I began my swevene for to write,
So yif me myght to ryme and ek t'endyte!

took hold of This forseyde Affrican me hente anon
And forth with hym unto a gate broughte,
Ryght of a park walled of grene ston;
And over the gate, with lettres large iwrowhte,
verses There were vers iwriten, as me thoughte,
On eyther side, of ful gret difference,
clear import Of which I shal now seyn the pleyn sentence:

'Thorw me men gon into that blysful place
health Of hertes hele and dedly woundes cure;
fountainhead Thorw me men gon unto the welle of grace,
Theere grene and lusty May shal evere endure.
fortune This is the weye to al good aventure.
Be glad, thow redere, and thy sorwe of-caste;
Al open am I – passe in, and sped the faste!'

'Thorw me men gon,' than spak that other side,
'Unto the mortal strokes of the spere
Of whiche Disdayn and Daunger is the gyde,
Ther nevere tre shal fruyt ne leves bere.
weir (with a fish-trap) This strem yow ledeth to the sorweful were
left high and dry There as the fish in prysoun is al drye:
Th'eschewing is only the remedye!'

These vers of gold and blak iwriten were,
bewildered Of whiche I gan astoned to beholde,
Because For with that oon encresede ay my fere
grow bold And with that other gan myn herte bolde:
heated That oon me hette, that other dede me colde.
because of my confusion No wit hadde I, for errour, for to chese
lose To entre or flen or me to save or lese.

117 **north-nor-west**. Venus appeared in this position, to a London observer, every few years (including 1380).
122 The walled garden is the traditional *locus amoenus* ('pleasant place') of European love-poetry, most famously in the *Roman de la Rose* (136–9), a poem Chaucer knew intimately and had partly translated.
127 **Thorw me men gon** echoes Dante's *Per me si va* inscribed over the portal of Hell (*Inferno* 3.1–9). The two very different inscriptions here, over the same double-doored gateway, allegorically suggest that falling in love is something of a gamble.
136 **Daunger** is the quality of cold reserve in a lady which makes her resist the lover's blandishments.

lode-stones Right as betwixen adamauntes two
equal power Of evene myght, a pece of yren set
Ne hath no myght to meve to ne fro –
attract, repels For what that oon may hale, that other let –
So it was with me, better Ferde I, that nyste whether me was bet
To entre or leve, til Affrycan, my gide,
pushed Me hente and shof in at the gates wide,

And seyde, 'It stant iwriten in thy face,
Thyn errour, thogh thow telle it not to me;
But dred the not to come into this place,
has no relevance to you For this writyng nys nothing ment bi the,
Ne by non but he Loves servaunt be –
For thow of love hast lost thy tast, I gesse,
sick As sek man hath of swet and bytternesse.

'But natheles, althogh that thow be dul,
Yit that thow canst not do, yit mayst thow se.
bout of wrestling For manye a man that may nat stonde a pul
It liketh hym at wrastlyng for to be,
whether this one … or that one And demen yit wher he do bet or he.
And there if thow haddest connyng for t'endite,
I shal the shewe mater for to wryte.'

With that myn hand he tok in his anon,
Of which I confort caughte, and went in faste.
in a happy situation But, Lord, so I was glad and wel begoon!
For overal where that I myne eyen caste
Were trees clad with leves that ay shal laste,
according to its nature Eche in his kynde, of colour fresh and greene
As emeraude, that joye was to seene.

oak for building The byldere ok, and ek the hardy assh;
for posts, corpse The pilere elm, the cofere unto carayne;
for making pipes, holly The box-tre pipere, holm to whippes lash;
for sailing-ships' masts The saylynge fyr; the cipresse, deth to pleyne;
(see n.) The shetere ew; the asp for shaftes pleyne;
'drunken' (for making drink) The olyve of pes, and ek the dronke vyne;
laurel used in divination The victor palm, the laurer to devyne.

A gardyn saw I ful of blosmy bowes
river-bank Upon a ryver, in a grene mede,
There as that swetnesse everemore inow is,

167–8 Chaucer, characterized as Love's outsider, a mere observer, is nevertheless to be given the opportunity to gather material for his poetry.

176–82 The tree-catalogue is a rhetorical *tour de force* of classical poetic tradition, which is sufficient reason for Chaucer to try his hand at it. The evergreen beauty of the trees (173) is part of the theme of the paradisal garden; the emphasis on service to mankind, in the series of unusual and witty epithets, is an unrelated (and somewhat contradictory) topos. The 'luxury of naming', above all, seems to partake in the energy of first creation.

180 'The shooter yew (for making bows), the aspen for smooth-shafted arrows'.

183–210 The garden of love is first viewed as a paradise of natural joy and harmony, imaged in flowers and small fish and clean friendly animals. The procreative impulse is there (192), but the delight and beauty of natural existence seems sufficient to itself. Chaucer borrows heavily (as in the whole description up to 294) from the *Teseida* of Boccaccio (who in turn borrowed from earlier writers), tuning the Italian poet's brilliance to gentler harmonies (204–10 are new).

With floures white, blewe and yelwe and rede,
springs, sluggish And colde welle-stremes, nothyng dede,
darting about That swymmen ful of smale fishes lighte,
With fynnes rede and skales sylver bryghte.

On every bow the bryddes herde I synge
With voys of aungel in here armonye,
So besyede hem here bryddes forth to brynge.
rabbits The litele conyes to here pley gonne hye,
And ferthere al aboute I gan aspye
timid The dredful ro, the buk and hert and hynde,
refined (i.e. not rats, etc.) Squyrels, and bestes smale of gentil kynde.

Of instrumentes of strenges in acord
Herde I so pleye, and ravyshyng swetnesse,
That God that makere is of all and lord
Ne herde nevere beter, as I gesse.
it could hardly be softer Therwith a wynd, unnethe it myghte be lesse,
Made in the leves grene a noyse softe
Acordaunt to the bryddes song alofte.

temperate Th'aire of that place so attempre was
That nevere was grevaunce of hot ne cold.
herb There wex ek every holsom spice and gras;
No man may waxe there sek ne old.
Yit was there joye more a thousandfold
become night Than man can telle; ne nevere wolde it nyghte,
But ay cler day to ony mannes syghte.

saw Under a tre, besyde a welle, I say
Cupide, oure lord, hise arwes forge and file,
And at his fet his bowe al redy lay;
And Wil, his doughter, temperede al this whyle
cunning skill The hevedes in the welle, and with hire wile
filed to a point She touchede hem, after they shulde serve
Some for to sle, and some to wounde and kerve.

Tho was I war of Plesaunce anon-ryght,
And of Aray, and Lust, and Curteysie,
Cunning (devious prompting of sex) And of the Craft that can and hath the myght
To don by force a wyght to don folye –
Disfigurat was she, I nyl nat lye;
And by hemself, under an ok, I gesse,
Saw I Delyt, that stod with Gentilesse.

I saw Beute withouten ony atyr,
And Youthe, ful of game and jolyte;
Foolhardynesse and Flaterye and Desyr,

211–17 With the mention of **Cupide** and the detail of his arrows, a shadow seems to fall across the garden: sexual desire (**Wil**, Italian *Volutta*) is associated only with pain. The single **tre** might recall the tree at the centre of the garden of Eden.

218 **Plesaunce**, etc. The allegorical personifications are sketched in only briefly, like personages in a tableau, standing in attendance upon Venus (and representing the qualities needed and rewards expected in her service).

sending messages, giving bribes	Messagerye and Meede and other thre –
as far as I am concerned	Here names shul not here be told for me–
tall (i.e. the pillars)	And upon pileres greete of jasper longe
	I saw a temple of bras ifounded stronge.
	Aboute that temple daunseden alwey
in plenty	Wemen inowe, of whiche some ther weere
richly dressed	Fayre of hemself, and some of hem were gay;
with hair hanging loose	In kerteles, al dishevele, wente they there:
	That was here offyce alwey, yer be yeere.
	And on the temple, of dowves white and fayre
pair	Saw I syttynge manye an hundrede peyre.
	Byfore the temple-dore ful soberly
	Dame Pes sat, with a curtyn in hire hond,
	And by hire syde, wonder discretly,
	Dame Pacience syttynge there I fond,
	With face pale, upon an hil of sond;
nearest of all	And aldernext, withinne and ek withoute,
Promise (the making of promises)	Byheste and Art, and of here folk a route.
sighs	Withinne the temple, of sykes hoote as fyr
sound as of wind (soughing), run	I herde a swogh that gan aboute renne,
	Whiche sikes were engenderede with desyr,
altar, burn	That maden every auter for to brenne
	Of newe flaume; and wel espyed I thenne
suffer	That al the cause of sorwe that they drye
	Cam of the bittere goddesse Jelosye.
	The god Priapus saw I, as I wente,
	Withinne the temple in sovereyn place stonde,
state, spoilt his plans	In swich aray as whan the asse hym shente
	With cri be nyghte, and with sceptre in his honde.
	Ful besyly men gonne assaye and fonde
	Upon his hed to sette, of sondry hewe,
	Garlondes ful of floures freshe and newe.
	And in a prive corner in desport
	Fond I Venus and hire porter Richesse,
dignified, demeanour	That was ful noble and hautayn of hyre port –
	Derk was that place, but afterward lightnesse
little, hardly	I saw a lyte, unnethe it myghte be lesse –

231 The **temple of bras**, with its pillars of jasper (the walls of the heavenly city are of jasper in Rev. 21:18–19), seems grandly discordant in the garden of natural beauty; yet, allegorically representing heightened and glamorized forms of sexual passion (brass, like copper, is a metal of Venus), it is still *within* the garden.

240 **curtyn**. The lady Peace has in her hand the curtain that conceals the hidden mysteries of the temple, like the veil of the Tabernacle (Ex. 26:1) or the veil of the Temple (Matt. 27:51) in the Bible (such allusions are never far from mind in the cult of the 'religion of love'). When the curtain is drawn, the entry is made to loss of all peace of mind.

243 **an hil of sond**: a little allegory of the uncertainty of love.

253–9 **Priapus**, god of gardens and fertility, was all set, erect penis in hand, to ravish a sleeping nymph when everyone was woken up by the braying of Silenus's ass (Ovid, *Fasti* 1.415–40). It is not a very 'romantic' statue.

260–73 Images of oppressive heat, stifling enclosure, glamorous artifice and voyeuristic pleasure vie with images of Botticellian beauty, simultaneously repelling and attracting, provoking yet silencing rebuke.

And on a bed of gold she lay to reste
sink in the west — Tyl that the hote sonne gan to weste.

golden tresses — Hyre gilte heres with a goldene thred
with her hair loose — Ibounden were, untrussede as she lay,
And naked from the brest up to the hed
Men myghte hire sen; and, sothly for to say,
covered, pleasure — The remenaunte was wel keverede, to my pay,
delicately woven — Ryght with a subtyl covercheif of valence –
that would obstruct the view — Ther nas no thikkere cloth of no defense.

sweet — The place yaf a thousand savoures sote,
And Bachus, god of wyn, sat hire besyde,
remedy — And Ceres next, that doth of hunger boote,
Venus — And, as I seyde, amyddes lay Cypride,
To whom on knees two yonge folk there cryde
To ben here helpe. But thus I let hem lye,
And ferthere in the temple I gan espie

That in dispit of Dyane the chaste
Ful manye a bowe ibroke heng on the wal
Of maydenes swiche as gonne here tymes waste
everywhere — In hyre servyse; ipeyntede were overal
Ful manye a story, of whiche I touche shal
A fewe, as of Calyxte and Athalante,
And many a mayde of whiche the name I wante.

Semyramus, Candace and Hercules,
Biblis, Dido, Thisbe and Piramus,
Isolde — Tristram, Isaude, Paris and Achilles,
Helen — Eleyne, Cliopatre and Troylus,
Silla, and ek the moder of Romulus –
Alle these were peynted on that other syde
And al here love and in what plyt they dyde.

Whan I was come ayen unto the place
That I of spak, that was so sote and grene,
walked — Forth welk I tho, myselven to solace.
Tho was I war wher that ther sat a queene
shining bright — That, as of lyght the someres sonne shene
beyond measure — Passeth the sterre, right so over mesure
She fayrere was than ony creature.

grassy glade — And in a launde, upon an hil of floures,
Was set this noble goddesse of Nature.

272 **valence**: fine cloth made at Valence, in France.

282 **manye a bowe ibroke**. Broken bows of Diana's maidens were hung in Venus's temple as trophies when, like Callisto and Atalanta, they gave up their dedication to chastity.

288–94 Lists of famous unhappy lovers were commonly inscribed, or their stories painted (as here), on the walls of love's temple in medieval poetry, enriching the poems with allusion and evidencing the irresistible power of love. Among the less well known, **Semyramus** was queen of Assyria, usually figured as rapaciously lustful; **Candace** was the Indian queen who fell in love with Alexander (or else *Canace*, who fell in love with her brother); **Biblis** also fell in love with her brother; **Silla** (Scylla) betrayed her father and city for love of king Minos; the mother of Romulus, Rhea Silvia, was beloved of Mars.

303 **Nature** was portrayed in medieval philosophical and love-poetry, and especially by Alain de Lille (see 316 below) and in the *Roman de la Rose*, as a noble queen and goddess, the mediator of God's will (see 379 below) for the continuance and ordered being of his creatures.

Of braunches were here halles and here boures
design Iwrought after here cast and here mesure;
bird, procreation Ne there was foul that cometh of engendrure
eagerly ready That they ne were al prest in here presence
receive her decision To take hire dom and yeve hire audyence.

For this was on Seynt Valentynes day
choose its mate Whan every bryd cometh there to chese his make
Of every kynde that men thynke may,
And that so huge a noyse gan they make
That erthe and eyr and tre and every lake
So ful was that unethe was there space
For me to stonde, so ful was al the place.

And right as Aleyn, in the Pleynt of Kynde,
Devyseth Nature in aray and face,
In swich aray men myghte hire there fynde.
This noble emperesse ful of grace
Bad every foul to take his owene place,
accustomed As they were woned alwey fro yer to yeere,
Seynt Valentynes day, to stonden theere.

birds of prey That is to seyn, the foules of ravyne
Were hyest set, and thanne the foules smale
That eten, as hem Nature wolde enclyne,
As worm or thyng of which I telle no tale;
And water-foul sat lowest in the dale;
But foul that lyveth by sed sat on the grene,
many And that so fele that wonder was to sene.

There myghte men the ryal egle fynde,
That with his sharpe lok perseth the sonne,
And othere egles of a lowere kynde,
know how to Of whiche that clerkes wel devyse conne.
dull-brown feathers Ther was the tiraunt with his federes donne
causes suffering And grey – I mene the goshauk, that doth pyne
ravenousness To bryddes for his outrageous ravyne;

grasps The gentyl faucoun, that with his feet distrayneth
sparrow-hawk The kynges hand; the hardy sperhauk eke,
The quayles foo; the merlioun, that payneth
Hymself ful ofte the larke for to seke.
There was the douve with hire yen meke;

309 **Seynt Valentynes day** was the day when birds (and humans) chose their mates, and the occasion of several poems by Chaucer and his circle, among whom this bit of whimsical 'folk'-lore may have been invented. The date of 14 February grew to be attached to it, but is not specified by Chaucer: a day in spring seems more appropriate (see 680 below). The choice of birds for the allegory of love's choices is in accord with medieval convention, deriving from the association of bird-song with human love, as also from the comparatively discreet and restrained nature of avian sexuality as described in the natural history encyclopaedias (see 323n).

316 **Aleyn**: Alain de Lille (d. 1203), philosopher-poet, author of the *De planctu Naturae*, in which the goddess Nature, elaborately portrayed, complains that her laws (including sexual laws) are not obeyed by men.

323–9 The division of birds into groups according to their eating habits was familiar in medieval encyclopaedias of natural history such as the *Speculum naturale* of Vincent of Beauvais and the *De proprietatibus rerum* of Bartholomaeus Anglicus. The **foules of ravyne** are clearly to be understood to represent the aristocracy, but the other kinds of bird cannot be associated with specific social classes, though it is tempting to try.

(see n.) The jelous swan, ayens hire deth that syngeth;
forewarning The oule ek, that of deth the bode bryngeth;

The crane geaunt, with his trompes soun;
magpie The thef, the chough; and ek the jangelynge pye;
The skornynge jay; the eles fo, heroun;
(see n.) The false lapwynge, ful of trecherye;
The starlyng, that the conseyl can bewrye;
robin redbreast The tame rudok, and the coward kyte;
chronometer, small villages The kok, that orloge is of thorpes lyte;

(because reputed to be so lecherous) The sparwe, Venus sone; the nyhtyngale,
That clepeth forth the grene leves newe;
(bee-eater) The swalwe, mortherere of the foules smale
That maken hony of floures freshe of hewe;
turtledove The wedded turtil, with hire herte trewe;
The pokok, with his aungeles clothes bryghte;
(seducer of hens) The fesaunt, skornere of the cok be nyghte;

watchful, unnatural (see 613 below) The waker goos; the cukkow ever unkynde;
parrot, fancy tastes The popinjay, ful of delicasye;
(in the frenzy of copulation) The drake, stroyere of his owene kynde;
(see n.) The stork, the wrekere of avouterye;
hot (inflamed by appetite) The hote cormeraunt of glotenye;
of 'take care' (warning of rain) The raven wys; the crowe with vois of care;
white-chested (or winter-resident?) The throstil old; the frosty feldefare.

What shulde I seyn? Of foules every kynde
That in this world hath federes and stature
Men myghten in that place assemblede fynde
Byfore the noble goddesse of Nature,
diligence And everiche of hem dede his besy cure
Benygnely to chese or for to take,
female (of bird of prey) By hire acord, his formel or his make.

But to the poynt: Nature held on hire hond
A formele egle, of shap the gentilleste
created That evere she among hire werkes fond,
The moste benygne and the goodlieste.
settled in its proper place In hire was everi vertu at his reste,
So ferforth that Nature hireself hadde blysse
beak To loke on hire, and ofte hire bek to kysse.

appointed deputy Nature, vicarye of the almyghty Lord,
That hot, cold, hevy, lyght, moyst and dreye
in equal and harmonious proportions Hath knyt with evene noumberes of acord,

342 'The swan, jealous (of her territory), that sings at the approach of her death'.

347–8 The lapwing feigns injury to distract pursuers, and the starling can betray secrets because it can be taught to speak.

358 **waker goos**: alluding to the story of the geese whose cackling warned the defenders of the Roman Capitol of the approaching enemy. Like the trees earlier in the poem, the birds are often characterized, following the encyclopaedias of Vincent and Bartholomaeus, in terms of their service to mankind.

361 The stork is the avenger of adultery because unfaithful females are killed.

380 The reference is to the mixing or 'tempering' of the elements in the harmony of the divinely ordered universe (cf. Boethius, *Consolation* III, metre 9).

gentle In esy voys gan for to speke and seye,
decision 'Foules, tak hed of my sentence, I preye,
And for youre ese in fortheryng of youre nede
As faste as I may speke I wol yow speede.

'Ye knowe wel how, Seynt Valentynes day,
By my statut and thorw my governaunce,
Ye come for to cheese – and fle youre wey –
desire Youre makes, as I prike yow with plesaunce;
But natheles, my ryghtful ordenaunce
even to win the whole world May I nat breke for al this world to wynne,
That he that most is worthi shal begynne.

tercel (male eagle or hawk) 'The terslet egle, as that ye knowe ful wel,
The foul ryal, aboven every degre,
discreet The wyse and worthi, secre, trewe as stel,
Whiche I have formed, as ye may wel se,
In every part as it best liketh me –
It nedeth not his shap yow to devyse –
manner He shal first chese and speken in his gyse.

'And after hym by ordere shul ye chese,
According to your nature After youre kynde, everich as yow lyketh,
fortune And as youre hap is shul ye wynne or lese.
entangles But which of yow that love most entriketh,
God sende hym hire that sorest for hym syketh!'
And therwithal the tersel gan she calle,
And seyde, 'My sone, the choys is to yow falle.

'But natheles, in this condicioun
Mot be the choys of everich that is heere,
That she agre to his eleccioun,
mate What-so he be that shulde be hire feere.
This is oure usage alwey fro yer to yeere
And who-so may at this tyme have his grace
In blisful tyme he cam into this place.'

With hed enclyned and with humble cheere
This ryal tersel spak, and tariede noght:
equal partner 'Unto my soverayn lady, and not my fere,
I chese, and ches with wil and herte and thought,
The formel on youre hond, so wel iwrought,
Whos I am al, and evere wol hire serve,
die Do what hire lest, to do me lyve or sterve;

'Besekynge hire of merci and of grace,
As she that is my lady sovereyne,
at once Or let me deye present in this place.
For certes, longe I may nat lyve in payne,

387, 390 **statut** and **ordenaunce** are terms from constitutional law: Nature behaves like the king's Chancellor opening a session of parliament.

cut (and bleeding)
For in myn herte is korven every veyne.
regard
And havynge only reward to my trouthe,
My deere herte, have of my wo som routhe.

'And if that I to hyre be founde untrewe,
Disobeysaunt or wilful necligent,
A boaster, in course of time
Avauntour, or in proces love a newe,
I preye to yow this be my jugement –
torn to pieces
That with these foules be I al to-rent
That ilke day that evere she me fynde
by my fault
To hir untrewe or in my gilt unkynde.

'And syn that hire loveth non so wel as I,
promised
Al be it that she me nevere of love behette,
Thanne ouhte she be myn thorw hire mercy,
fasten
For other bond can I non on hire knette.
stop
Ne nevere for no wo ne shal I lette
To serven hire, how fer so that she wende.
Say what yow leste, my tale is at an ende.'

Ryght as the freshe rede rose newe
In face of
Ayen the somer sonne coloured is,
Ryght so for shame al wexen gan the hewe
Of this formel, whan she herde al this;
favourably, anything unfavourable
She neyther answerde wel ne seyde amys,
So sore abasht was she, tyl that Nature
Seyde, 'Doughter, drede the nought, I yow assure.'

Another tersel egle spak anon,
Of lower kynde, and seyde, 'That shal nat be!
I love hire bet than ye don, be Seynt John,
Or at the leste I love as wel as ye,
And longere have served hire in my degre;
should have
And if she shulde a loved for long lovynge,
granting of the prize
To me ful longe hadde be the gerdonynge.

'I dar ek seyn, if she me fynde fals,
an idle gossip
Unkynde or janglere or rebel ony wyse,
neck
Or jelous, do me hangen by the hals!
And, but I bere me in hire servyse
As wel as that my wit can me suffyse,
beginning to end
From poynt to poynt, hyre honour for to save,
Take she my lif and al the good I have!'

The thredde tercel egle answerde tho,
time to spare
'Now, sires, ye seen the lytel leyser heere,
to depart
For every foul cryeth out to ben ago
Forth with his make or with his lady deere;
And ek Nature hireself ne wol not heere,

449, 463 The arguments of the second and third tercel eagles to some extent match the historical experience of the unsuccessful suitors for the hand of Anne of Bohemia. Their speeches are not bombastic or absurd or excessively high-flown, but they are less fine, to the discriminating observer, than that of the royal eagle.

For taryinge here, not half that I wolde seye; *In order to avoid tarrying*
And but I speke, I mot for sorwe deye.

'Of long servyse avante I me nothing, *boast*
But as possible is to me to deye to-day
For wo as he that hath ben languyssynge
This twenty yeer, and, as wel happen may,
A man may serven bet and more to pay *more satisfactorily*
In half a yer, althogh it were no moore,
Than som man doth that hath served ful yoore.

'I sey not this by me, for I ne can *in my own cause*
Don no servyse that may my lady plese;
But I dar seyn, I am hire treweste man
As to my dom, and fayneste wolde hire ese.
At shorte wordes, til that deth me sese *seize*
I wol ben heres, wher I wake or wynke, *hers, whether*
And trewe in al that herte may bethynke.'

Of al my lyf, syn that day I was born,
So gentil ple in love or other thyng *petition*
Ne herde nevere no man me beforn –
Who that hadde leyser and connyng *Whoever had*
For to reherse hyre chere and hire spekyng;
And from the morwe gan this speche laste
Tyl dounward drow the sonne wonder faste.

The noyse of foules for to ben delyvered *dismissed*
So loude ronge, 'Have don, and lat us wende!'
That wel wende I the wode hadde al to-slyvered. *(see n.)*
'Com of!' they crieden, 'allas, ye wol us shende! *Get a move on!*
Whan shal youre cursede pletynge have an ende? *making of pleas*
How shulde a juge eyther partie leve *believe*
For ye or nay withouten other preve?'

The goos, the cokkow, and the doke also
So cryede, 'Kek kek! kokkow! quek quek!' hye,
That thourw myne eres the noyse wente tho.
The goos seyde, 'Al this nys not worth a flye!
But I can shape herof a remedie,
And I wol seye my verdit fayre and swythe *quickly*
For water-foul, who-so be wroth or blythe!'

'And I for worm-foul,' quod the fol kokkow; *foolish*
'And I wol of myn owene autorite,
For comun profit, take on the charge nowe, *responsibility*
For to delyvere us is gret charite.'
'Ye may abyde a while yit, parde!'

485 **ple**. Many words in these stanzas (e.g. 491, 495, 530–2; cf. 387–90 above) have a legal or parliamentary flavour, and the outbreak of abuse and name-calling that follows is suggestive of a parliamentary atmosphere in which an old world of *noblesse oblige* confronts a new world of loud-mouthed upstart ducks and geese.

493 'That I fully thought the wood would have shattered into fragments (with the noise)'.

the will of you all	Quod the turtel, 'If it be youre wille
(see n.)	A wiht may speke, hym were as fayr ben stylle.
	'I am a sed-foul, oon the unworthieste,
	That wot I wel, and litel of connynge.
	But bet is that a wyhtes tonge reste
interfere in	Than entermeten hym of suche doinge,
speak (with any knowledge)	Of which he neyther rede can ne synge;
takes on sorely too much	And who-so doth ful foule hymself acloyeth,
(see n.)	For offyce uncommytted ofte anoyeth.'
	Nature, which that alwey hadde an ere
ill-bred ignorance	To murmur of the lewednesse behynde,
eloquent	With facound voys seyde, 'Hold youre tonges there!
an advisory formula	And I shal sone, I hope, a conseyl fynde
	Yow to delyvere and from this noyse unbynde:
every bird-group	I juge, of every folk men shul oon calle
	To seyn the verdit for yow foules alle.'
	Assented was to this conclusioun
	The briddes alle; and foules of ravyne
unanimous choice	Han chosen fyrst, by playn eleccioun,
male of the falcon, state exactly	The terselet of the faucoun to diffyne
(see n.)	Al here sentence as hem lest to termyne;
they proceeded to	And to Nature hym gonne to presente,
	And she accepteth hym with glad entente.
	The terslet seyde thanne in this manere:
	'Ful hard were it to prove by resoun
	Who loveth best this gentil formele heere,
skill in reply	For everych hath swich replicacioun
reasonable arguments	That non by skilles may been brought adoun.
	I can not se that argumentes avayle:
trial by battle (judicial duel)	Thanne semeth it there moste be batayle.'
	'Al redy!' quod this egles terslet tho.
	'Nay, sires,' quod he, 'if that I durste it seye,
finished	Ye don me wrong, my tale is not ido!
don't take offence	For, sires – ne taketh not agref, I preye –
	It may not gon as ye wolde in this weye;
(see n.)	Oure is the voys that han the charge on honde,
decision, must abide	And to the juges dom ye moten stonde.
	'And therfore, pes! I seye, as to my wit,
	Me wolde thynke how that the worthieste
	Of knyghthod, and lengest hath used it,
	Most of estat, of blod the gentilleste,
most suitable	Were sittyngest for hire, if that hir leste;
	And of these thre she wot hireself, I trowe,
it is easy for her to know	Which that he be, for hire is light to knowe.'

511 'That one (i.e. myself) might speak, (I would say) that the cuckoo would be as well to keep quiet'.

518 **offyce uncommytted**: doing something one is not asked to do.

530 'All their opinion as it pleased them to articulate (it) in its final form'.

545 'Ours is the voice that has the responsibility for deciding'.

	The water-foules han here hedes leid
after a short deliberation	Togedere, and of a short avysement,
mouthful	Whan everyche hadde his large gole seyd,
	They seyden sothly, al be oon assent,
genteel eloquence	How that the goos, with hire facounde so gent,
what is necessary for us to say	'That so desyreth to pronounce oure nede,
	Shal telle oure tale,' and preyede God hire spede!
	As for these water-foules tho began
	The goos to speke, and in hire kakelynge
	She seyde, 'Pes! Now tak kep every man,
good argument	And herkeneth which a resoun I shal brynge!
	My wit is sharp – I love no taryinge:
advise, though	I seye I rede hym, thogh he were my brother,
	But she wol love hym, lat hym take another!'
	'Lo, here a parfit resoun of a goos!'
prosper	Quod the sperhauk; 'Nevere mot she the!
	Lo, swich it is to have a tonge loos!
fool	Now parde, fol, now were it bet for the
foolishness	Han holde thy pes than shewe thy nycete.
(i.e. the fool's)	It lyth nat in his might ne in his wille,
	But soth is seyd, "a fol can not be stille."'
	The laughtere aros of gentil foules alle,
	And right anon the sed-foul chosen hadde
	The turtil trewe and gonne hire to hem calle
sober truth	And preyede hire for to seyn the sothe sadde
would advise	Of this matere, and axede what she radde.
	And she answerde that pleynly hire entente
	She wolde it shewe and sothly what she mente.
	'Nay, God forbede a lovere shulde chaunge!'
	The turtil seyde, and wex for shame red;
Though ... cold and distant	'Thogh that his lady everemore be straunge,
	Yit lat hym serve hire til that he be ded.
advice	Forsothe, I preyse nat the goses red,
	For thogh she deyede I wolde non other make;
	I wol ben hires til that the deth me take.'
That's a good joke	'Wel borded,' quod the doke, 'by myn hat!
	That men shul loven alwey causeles!
sense	Who can a resoun fynde or wit in that?
	Daunseth he murye that is myrtheles?
care about him who does not care	What shulde I rekke of hym that is recheles?'
	'Kek kek!' yit seith the goos, ful wel and fayre:
	'There been mo sterres, God wot, than a payre!'

558–9 The slithering from indirect to direct speech is not unusual in medieval poetry, which was close still to the more relaxed conventions of oral delivery.

587–8 The turtledove's feelings are so strong that she momentarily takes on the person of the disappointed male lover.

589–95 The duck and the goose speak with a kind of coarse pragmatism. The advantage of the debate-form is that it can accommodate their views alongside those of the turtledove and the falcon without necessarily making the one the measure of the other.

noble 'Now fy, cherl!' quod the gentil terselet,
'Out of the donghil cam that word ful right!
appropriately applied Thow canst nat seen what thyng is wel beset!
behave concerning Thow farst by love as oules don by lyght:
blinds The day hem blent but wel they se by nyght.
Thy kynde is of so low a wrechednesse
That what love is thow canst nat seen ne gesse.'

push himself forward Tho gan the kokkow putte hym forth in pres
briskly For foul that eteth worm, and seyde blyve:
'So I,' quod he, 'may have my make in pes,
care I reche nat how longe that ye stryve.
single Lat eche of hem ben soleyn al here lyve!
This is my red, syn they may nat acorde;
(see n.) This shorte lessoun nedeth nat recorde.'

if the glutton has filled 'Ye, have the glotoun fild inow his paunche,
Thanne are we wel!' seyde thanne a merlioun;
hedge-sparrow 'Thow mortherere of the heysoge on the braunche
most pitiful That broughte the forth, thow reufullest glotoun!
Lyve thow soleyn, wormes corupcioun,
(see n.) For no fors is of lak of thy nature!
stay ill-bred and ignorant Go, lewed be thow whil that the world may dure!'

'Now pes,' quod Nature, 'I comaunde heer!
For I have herd al youre opynyoun
nearer (to a conclusion) And in effect yit be we not the neer.
But fynally, this is my conclusioun,
That she hireself shal han the eleccioun
whoever Of whom hire lest, and, who be wroth or blythe,
immediately Hym that she cheseth, he shal hire han aswithe.

decided 'For syn it may nat here discussed be
Who loveth hire best, as seyth the terselet,
Thanne wol I don hire this favour, that she
Shal han ryght hym on whom hire herte is set,
fastened And he hire that his herte hath on hire knet.
Thus juge I, Nature, for I may not lye:
(see n.) To non estat I have non other ye.

'But as for conseyl for to chese a make,
If I were Resoun, certis thanne wolde I
Conseyle yow the ryal tersel take,
reasonably As seyde the terselet ful skylfully,
As for the gentilleste and most worthi,

609 **recorde**: 'to be recorded' (it's simple enough to be remembered).
613 **broughte the forth**: 'hatched you'. Some cuckoos lay their eggs in the nests of other birds, and the young eject the young of their hosts.
615 'It is no matter if your kind dies out'.
630 'I have no eye (desire) to be anything else' (other than perfectly fair and impartial).
632 **If I were Resoun**. Nature stands for the natural order of creation, including natural desire for a mate, but she seems to appreciate the role of Reason, or rational understanding, as another of God's officers.
633 The **ryal tersel** gets Nature's vote as well as that of the spokesman for the aristocracy (553), which is appropriate if the poem alludes to Richard II's eventually successful candidacy for the hand of Anne of Bohemia.

Which I have wrought so wel to my plesaunce
That to yow oughte to been a suffisaunce.'

fearful With dredful vois the formel tho answerde,
'My rightful lady, goddesse of Nature!
rod (subject to your authority) Soth is that I am evere under youre yerde,
any other As is another lyves creature,
must be yours And mot be youre whil that my lyf may dure;
this first boon that I have asked And therfore graunteth me my firste bone
And myn entent that wol I sey wel sone.'

'I graunte it yow,' quod she, and ryght anon
in this manner This formel egle spak in this degre:
until 'Almyghty queen, unto this yer be gon
period of delay, consider I axe respit for to avise me
And after that to have my choys al fre.
This al and som that I wol speke and seye:
Ye gete no more althogh ye do me deye!

'I wol nat serve Venus ne Cupide
Forsothe as yit, by no manere weye.'
'Now syn it may non otherwise betyde,'
Quod tho Nature, 'heere is no more to seye.
Thanne wolde I that these foules were aweye,
so as to avoid tarrying Eche with his make, for taryinge lengere heere!'
And seyde hem thus, as ye shul after here.

'To yow speke I, ye terslets,' quod Nature:
'Beth of good herte, and serveth alle thre –
A yer nis nat so longe to endure –
taking pains And eche of yow peynynge in his degre
released from obligation For to do wel, for, God wot, quyte is she
As far as you are concerned, whatever For yow this yer, what after so befalle:
between-courses dish is prepared This entermes is dressed for yow alle.'

And whan this werk al brought was to an ende,
To every foul Nature yaf his make
mutual agreement By evene acord, and on here way they wende.
But Lord, the blisse and joye that they make!
For ech gan other in his wynges take,
And with here nekkes eche gan other wynde,
Thankynge alwey the noble queen of Kynde.

But fyrst were chosen foules for to synge,
As yer by yer was alwey the usance
To synge a roundele at here departynge
To don to Nature honour and plesaunce –
tune The note I trow imaked were in Fraunce;

648 **respit**. Poetic debates usually end in a deferred decision (as does the twelfth-century *Owl and the Nightingale*, the most famous bird-debate in English before this one), so that the poem can be removed from too crude a relation to the world of action.

675 **roundele**: a French lyric form, on two rhymes, in which one or more lines from the beginning are repeated as a variable refrain. The form is reconstructed below (680–92) from the evidence of the MSS.

677 **note**. Some MSS insert after 679 the words, 'Qui bien aime a tard oublie', presumably to indicate a tune, familiarly known by the first line of the French song that was sung to it, that could be appropriate for the roundel.

The wordes were swiche as ye may fynde
The nexte vers, as I now have in mynde.

'Nowe welcome, somer, with thy sonne softe,
That hast thes wintres wedres overeshake *storms shaken off*
And drivene away the longe nyghtes blake!

'Saynt Valentyne, that art ful hy o-lofte,
Thus syngen smale foules for thy sake:
[Nowe welcome, somer, with thy sonne softe,
That hast thes wintres wedres overshake.]

'Wel han they cause for to gladen ofte, *be glad*
Sethe ech of hem recoverede hathe hys make. *secured possession of*
Ful blisseful mowe they synge when they wake: *may*
[Nowe welcome, somer, with thy sonne softe,
That hast thes wintres wedres overeshake
And drivene away the longe nyghtes blake!']

And with the shoutyng, whan the song was do,
That the foules maden at here flyght awey, *in their flying away*
I wok, and othere bokes tok me to
To reede upon, and yit I rede alwey
In hope, ywis, to rede so som day
That I shal mete som thyng for to fare *shall find*
The bet, and thus to rede I nyl nat spare.

TROILUS AND CRISEYDE

Chaucer's great poem of *Troilus and Criseyde* was written about 1381–6, when he had acquired some reputation in fashionable court circles as a poet of courtly love. His poem is based on Boccaccio's *Il Filostrato* ('The man stricken down by love'), completed about 1338, though Chaucer makes no acknowledgement of his deep indebtedness; he expands the courtly love theme with material from the *Roman de la Rose* and from the French love-poems of his older contemporary Guillaume de Machaut. What Boccaccio had done was to disentangle from the story of the siege of Troy (as it had been 'romanced' from Latin prose redactions in the *Roman de Troie* of the twelfth-century French poet Benoit de Sainte-Maure) the episode of Criseida's parting from Troilo and subsequent surrender of her affections to the Greek Diomede; to balance the story of loss and betrayal with a lyrical account of the passionate beginning of the love-affair in the wooing and winning of Criseida; to introduce a new character, Pandaro, as go-between; and to cast over the whole a colouring of passionate sensuality and fashionable urban sophistication. Chaucer heightens the courtly tone, raises the emotional stakes, and develops Boccaccio's poem as a more prolonged and luxuriously expansive, infinitely more subtle and poignant narrative of the intensities and frustrations of high courtly passion, the anxious subterfuges of winning, the ecstasies of possession, and the sadness and sad consequence of parting. The role of Pandarus is much extended, so that he is not just the worldly pragmatist and busy manipulator but also guide, priest and confessor of love to Troilus and uncle and trusted advisor to Criseyde. Criseyde herself is given a completely new depth and complexity as a woman of richly realized independent subjectivity, who tries to play the few cards she has – her father, Calchas, is a traitor who has gone over to the Greeks, and she, a young widow, is living on suffrance in Troy – so as to preserve her reputation and independence and yet not be left out of the blissful 'game' of romantic love. In her, Chaucer explores, more deeply and subtly than in any other of his creations, the nature – or even the possibility – of human agency and free will, as a woman finds herself so compromised by inner conflicts and so brutally constrained by circumstance that acquiescence in the choicelessness of the socially determined self seems almost a necessity. The colouring that Chaucer gives to this story of passionate sexual yearning, fulfilment and loss is different from Boccaccio's: he adds much to make the poem into a high Boethian meditation on fate, free will and mutability: he modifies Boccaccio's urbane sensuality in the direction of comedy in the role of Pandarus, with much consequent ironic complication of the love-story; and he portrays the narrator as a mere looker-on of love (unlike Boccaccio's passionately involved young narrator) who follows in a good-natured and bumbling way in the wake of his own narrative. There is a tendency on the narrator's part helplessly to invoke the workings of Fortune at every juncture in the story, and a corresponding tendency on Troilus's part to play the Boethian fatalist, only sure of what is happening when everything is going wrong. The management of these complexly different elements is a miracle of imaginative concentration and fusion. Chaucer's care with this poem, his care to revise and prepare it for 'publication' and to provide for it an ending of unexampled sonorousness, is remarkably to be contrasted with the *insouciance* of his handling of the *Canterbury Tales*. It is, and he knew it was, his masterpiece.

Troilus is written in the seven-line stanza, rhyming *ababbcc*, called 'rhyme royal', the form that Chaucer used for his first experiments with iambic pentameter in the *Parliament of Fowls*. After going over to the couplet, in the *Legend of Good Women* and the *Canterbury Tales*, he still used rhyme royal for religious poems of an affecting kind (e.g. the Man of Law's Tale, the Prioress's Tale and the Clerk's Tale) involving a direct appeal to the readers' emotions. This quality of 'affect' is important in *Troilus*, as well as the greater amplitude in expression that the stanza allows.

The poem survives in 16 MSS, with fragments or extracts in a further 16. The three most important MSS are CCCC MS 61 (Cp) (which has as frontispiece the famous picture of Chaucer reciting his poem to the assembled court), Cambridge, St John's College MS L.1 (J), and New York, Pierpont Morgan Library MS M817 (Cl) (the 'Campsall' MSS, which once belonged to Prince Hal). Another group of MSS seems to represent a first draft of the poem, perhaps never intended to be released as a 'version' of the poem. There is full discussion of these and other textual matters in B.A. Windeatt, *Troilus and Criseyde: A New Edition of 'The Book of Troilus'* (London, 1984), which has a full apparatus, including the Italian of Boccaccio in parallel text with the corresponding English. In the present text, Cp is followed, with corrections and emendations from J, Cl, and other MSS where necessary.

Troilus is discussed in the general works on Chaucer cited above. On *Troilus* specifically, the following are important: C.S. Lewis, *The Allegory of Love* (Oxford, 1936), pp. 176–97 (an enormously influential account of the poem), and 'What Chaucer really did to *Il Filostrato*', *E&S* 17 (1932), 56–75; D.W. Robertson, 'Chaucerian Tragedy', *ELH* 19 (1952), 1–37; E. Salter, '*Troilus and Criseyde*: A Reconsideration', in J. Lawlor (ed.), *Patterns of Love and Courtesy* (London, 1966), pp. 86–106; G. Shepherd, 'Chaucer's *Troilus and Criseyde*', in D. Brewer (ed.), *Chaucer and Chaucerians* (London, 1966), pp. 65–87; A.C. Spearing, *Chaucer's Troilus and Criseyde* (London, 1976); J. Mann, 'Troilus's Swoon', *ChauR* 14 (1980), 319–35. There is valuable translation of the relevant parts of the Italian poem in N. Havely, *Chaucer's Boccaccio* (Woodbridge, 1980), and collections of essays in M. Salu (ed.), *Essays on Chaucer's Troilus and Criseyde* (Woodbridge, 1979); S.A. Barney (ed.), *Chaucer's Troilus: Essays in Criticism* (London, 1980); and C.D. Benson (ed.), *Critical Essays on Chaucer's Troilus and Criseyde and Major Early Poems* (Toronto, 1991).

{The poem is in five books, of which Books II and III, most fully represented here, are freest in their treatment of Boccaccio, with much new and independent material. Book I introduces briefly the story of the siege of Troy, and describes how Criseyde, left alone in Troy after the defection of her father Calchas to the Trojans, is taken under the protection of Hector and allowed to live as a free and independent woman in Troy. Troilus, one of king Priam's younger sons, sees her at a gathering in the temple and falls headlong in love with her but is unable to speak his love because of feelings of unworthiness and fear of rebuff. His friend Pandarus, who is Criseyde's uncle, agrees to act as mediator.}

Proem to Book II

waves — Owt of thise blake wawes for to saylle,
begins to clear — O wynde, O wynde, the weder gynneth clere!
boat, difficulty — For in this see the bote hath swych travaylle
skill, with difficulty — Of my connyng that unneth I it steere –

1–7 In the proems to these early books, Chaucer takes up a lofty poetic posture, using allusion and invocation in emulation of the classical poets and the great Italians. The image here of the **bote** of his **connyng** sailing into calmer waters is from Dante, *Purgatorio* I.1–3 ('la navicella del mio ingegno').

call	This see clepe I the tempestous matere
	Of disespeir that Troilus was inne;
the first day (of the month)	But now of hope the kalendes bygynne.
Clio (muse of History)	O lady myn, that called art Cleo,
helper to succeed	Thow be my speed fro this forth and my Muse
finished	To ryme wel this book til I have do:
	Me nedeth here noon othere art to use.
Wherefore	Forwhi to every lovere I me excuse
out of no personal feeling	That of no sentement I this endite,
	But out of Latyn in my tonge it write.
	Wherfore I nyl have neither thank ne blame
	Of al this werk, but prey yow mekely
	Disblameth me if any word be lame,
author (of authoritative text)	For as myn auctour seyde, so sey I.
	Ek though I speeke of love unfelyngly
there's nothing new about it	No wondre is, for it nothyng of newe is:
colours	A blynd man kan nat juggen wel in hewis.
	Ye knowe ek that in fourme of speche is chaunge
then	Withinne a thousand yeer, and wordes tho
value, foolish	That hadden pris now wonder nyce and straunge
	Us thenketh hem, and yet thei spake hem so –
	And spedde as wel in love as men now do;
	Ek for to wynnen love in sondry ages,
	In sondry londes, sondry ben usages.
	And forthi if it happe in any wyse
	That here be any lovere in this place
	That herkneth, as the storie wol devise,
achieved, lady's	How Troilus com to his lady grace,
would I not	And thenketh, 'So nold I nat love purchace,'
is surprised at	Or wondreth on his speche or his doynge,
I do not know	I noot; but it is me no wonderynge.
goes	For every wight which that to Rome wente
Keeps not to one path	Halt nat o path or alwey o manere;
ruined	Ek in som lond were al the game shente
behaved	If that they ferde in love as men don here,
public actions or behaviour	As thus, in opyn doyng or in chere,
(see n.)	In visityng in forme, or seyde hire sawes;
Which is why	Forthi men seyn, 'Ecch contree hath hise lawes.'

14 **Latyn**. Chaucer's pretence is that he is the slavish translator of the Latin of one 'Lollius' (I.394). Boccaccio, as being of less 'authority', is set aside, as also the passionate personal involvement (**sentement**) of his narrator in the story of the lovers.

30 **in this place**: the image of a listening audience is one that Chaucer cultivates (cf. 43 below) in order to give immediacy to the narrative and ambiguity to his own role as 'performer'. The frontispiece of MS Cp follows out literally the implication of the image (which was not, of course, a total fabrication in an age of oral delivery and recitation and public reading).

40–1 The point of this long apologia for accurately portraying the manners of the ancients (which is as transparently insincere as the similar apologia of GP 725–42) is focused here: Chaucer endeavours to explain that the behaviour of Troilus, in not presenting his suit directly to Criseyde, has to be understood in the light of the social customs of his day. Pseudo-history is invoked for the tactical artistic purpose of rendering the go-between respectable.

41 'In formal visiting, or (if they) spoke openly what they thought'.

	Ek scarsly ben ther in this place thre
said alike and done (alike)	That have in love seide like, and don, in al;
be pleasing to thee	For to thi purpos this may liken the,
And to thee, shall (be said)	And the right nought – yet al is seid or schal;
carve, wood	Ek som men grave in tree, som in ston wal,
happens, since	As it bitit. But syn I have bigonne,
	Myn auctour shal I folwen if I konne.

Book II

	In May, that moder is of monthes glade,
When	That fresshe floures, blew and white and rede,
alive	Ben quike agayn that wynter dede made,
balmy odours, overflowing	And ful of bawme is fletyng every mede,
	Whan Phebus doth his bryghte bemes sprede
Bull (Taurus), happened	Right in the white Bole, it so bitidde,
	As I shal synge, on Mayes day the thrydde,
	That Pandarus for al his wise speche
sharp arrows	Felt ek his parte of loves shotes keene,
however well he might	That, koude he nevere so wel of lovyng preche,
	It made his hewe a-day ful ofte greene.
It was so destined, befell, sorrow	So shop it that hym fil that day a teene
	In love, for which in wo to bedde he wente,
twist and turn (in his bed)	And made er it was day ful many a wente.
	The swalowe Proigne with a sorowful lay
lamentation	Whan morwen com gan make hire waymentyng
transformed	Whi she forshapen was; and evere lay
	Pandare abedde, half in a slomberyng,
	Til she so neigh hym made hire cheteryng
	How Tereus gan forth hire suster take,
	That with the noyse of hire he gan awake,
call (his servants), prepare	And gan to calle, and dresse hym up to ryse,
	Remembryng hym his erand was to doone
task	From Troilus, and ek his grete emprise;
(see n.)	And caste and knew in good plit was the moone
make a journey	To doon viage, and took his way ful soone
	Unto his neces palays ther biside.
	Now Janus, god of entree, thow hym gyde!
	Whan he was come unto his neces place,
	'Wher is my lady?' to hire folk quod he;
pass	And they hym tolde and he forth in gan pace

58 Like any self-respecting *cavaliere sirvente*, Pandarus, despite his years, must suffer the pains of unrequited love, though his **maistresse** (see 98), whom we never see, seems to be a bit of a joke.

64–70 The story of the rape and mutilation of Philomena (transformed into a nightingale) by Tereus, the husband of her sister Procne (transformed into a swallow), is told in Ovid, *Metamorphoses* VI.412–674 (and by Gower, below). It is not, at this point, the happiest allusion that Chaucer could have made.

74 'And made his astrological forecast and knew the moon was in a good position'.

77 Janus was god of thresholds (cf. FrankT 1252n).

78–84 This scene is a famous allusion to a presumably common practice in aristocratic households in Chaucer's time. Criseyde, though ostensibly alone and vulnerable in Troy, seems to live in some style. She is portrayed as higher in rank than Boccaccio's Criseida, so that as a *domina* she can be an appropriate object for Troilus's affections.

seated	And fond two othere ladys sete and she
	Withinne a paved parlour and they thre
story	Herden a mayden reden hem the geste
during their pleasure	Of the siege of Thebes while hem leste.
(God be with you)	Quod Pandarus, 'Madame, God yow see,
	With al youre fayre book and al the compaignie!'
	'Ey, uncle myn, welcome iwis,' quod she,
quickly	And up she roos and by the hond in hye
thrice	She took hym faste, and seyde, 'This nyght thrie –
I hope it bodes well, dreamed	To goode mot it turne – of yow I mette.'
	And with that word she doun on benche hym sette.
get on	'Ye, nece, yee shal faren wel the bet,
	If God wol, al this yeere,' quod Pandarus;
hindered	'But I am sory that I have yow let
	To herken of youre book ye preysen thus.
	For Goddes love, what seith it? telle it us!
learn	Is it of love? O, som good ye me leere!'
	'Uncle,' quod she, 'youre maistresse is nat here.'
	With that thei gonnen laughe, and tho she seyde,
	'This romaunce is of Thebes that we rede,
	And we han herd how that kyng Layus deyde
all those doings	Thorugh Edippus his sone, and al that dede,
(see n.)	And here we stynten at thise lettres rede –
	How the bisshop, as the book kan telle,
	Amphiorax, fil thorugh the grounde to helle.'
	Quod Pandarus, 'Al this knowe I myselve
	And al th'assege of Thebes and the care,
	For her-of ben ther maked bookes twelve.
leave off	But lat be this and telle me how that ye fare:
Get rid of your widow's wimple	Do wey youre barbe and shew youre face bare;
	Do wey youre book, rys up and lat us daunce
	And lat us don to May som observaunce.'
Oh! (= ey, as in 87 above)	'I! God forbede!' quod she. 'Be ye madde?
	Is that a widewes lif, so God yow save?
you absolutely terrify me	By God, ye maken me ryght soore adradde!
	Ye ben so wylde it semeth as ye rave.
It would be much more fitting for me	It satte me wel bet ay in a cave

85–595 The conversation between Pandarus and Criseyde that follows is the high point of Chaucer's dramatic art – all but 35 lines are in direct speech – in the revelation of character and the carrying forward of the action without direct narratorial intervention.

86 **With al youre fayre book**. The preservation of MS **fayre** keeps a certain mild sarcasm in Pandarus's tone, as if suggestive that ladies might find better occupation than *books*.

97 **Is it of love?** Pandarus, with his delicate mission in mind, tries this as an opening gambit. The siege of Thebes (which begins with the story of Oedipus) is unfortunately about as unpromising an opening as could be imagined, as Criseyde, in the relish with which she describes the latest episode (103–5), seems mischievously to realize.

103 **lettres rede**: rubricated letters (in red) used for a chapter heading.

108 **bookes twelve**. Pandarus, thwarted in his first move, is reluctant to let the moment pass without embroidering it with his one bit of information on the subject (apt to the *Thebaid* of Statius, but not to the French version that a fourteenth-century Criseyde would have been listening to). See II.824n.

117–18 Criseyde exaggerates – she doesn't *really* think this – for effect and for fun, and to mock Pandarus's evident earnestness to stir up her attention.

pray	To bidde and rede on holy seyntes lyves;
	Lat maydens gon to daunce, and yonge wyves.'
	'As evere thrive I,' quod this Pandarus,
make you happy	'Yet koude I telle a thyng to doon yow pleye.'
	'Now, uncle deere, quod she, 'telle it us
	For Goddes love: is than th'assege aweye?
	I am of Grekes so fered that I deye.'
	'Nay, nay,' quod he, 'as evere mote I thryve,
five such (pieces of news)	It is a thing wel bet than swyche fyve.'
Yea	'Ye, holy God,' quod she, 'what thyng is that?
	What, bet than swiche fyve? I! Nay, ywys!
work out	For al this world ne kan I reden what
	It sholde ben – som jape I trowe is this,
unless	And but youreselven telle us what it is
too feeble to work it out	My wit is for t'arede it al to leene.
do not know	As help me God, I not nat what ye meene.'
As I am your guarantor (take it from me)	'And I youre borugh, ne nevere shal, for me,
	This thyng be told to yow, as mote I thryve!'
	'And whi so, uncle myn? Whi so?' quod she.
forthwith	'By God,' quod he, 'that wol I telle as blyve!
	For proudder womman is ther noon on lyve,
If	And ye it wiste, in al the town of Troye.
	I jape nought, as evere have I joye!'
	Tho gan she wondren moore than biforne
	A thousand-fold, and down hire eyghen caste,
	For nevere sith the tyme that she was borne
	To knowe thyng desired she so faste;
sigh	And with a syk she seyde hym atte laste,
	'Now, uncle myn, I nyl yow nought displese,
cause you discomfort	Nor axen more that may do yow disese.'
	So after this with many wordes glade
	And frendly tales and with merie chiere
began to go into	Of this and that they pleide and gonnen wade
unfamiliar	In many an unkouth, gladde and depe matere,
met together	As frendes doon whan thei ben mette yfere,
was doing	Tyl she gan axen hym how Ector ferde,
scourge of the Greeks	That was the townes wal and Grekes yerde.
	'Ful wel, I thonk it God,' quod Pandarus,
	'Save in his arme he hath a litel wownde,
	And ek his fresshe brother Troilus,
	The wise, worthi Ector the secounde,
is pleased to abound	In whom that alle vertu list habounde,
nobility of nature	As alle trouthe and alle gentilesse,
generosity	Wisdom, honour, fredom and worthinesse.'

141–7 Though naturally eager to hear it, Criseyde is determined not to beg for the news, whose general purport she must have a shrewd idea of by now.

uncle, I am very pleased to hear 'In good feith, em,' quod she, 'that liketh me
Thei faren wel: God save hem bothe two!
source of satisfaction For trewelich I holde it gret deynte
A kynges sone in armes wel to do
And ben of goode condiciouns therto,
For gret power and moral vertu here
seen, one, together Is selde yseyn in o persone yfeere.'

'In good faith, that is soth,' quod Pandarus.
'But by my trouthe the kyng hath sones tweye –
That is to mene, Ector and Troilus –
That certeynly, though that I sholde deye,
Thei ben as voide of vices, dar I seye,
As any men that lyven undre the sonne:
are capable of Hire myght is wyde i-knowe, and what they konne.

'Of Ector nedeth it namore for to telle:
In al this world ther nys a bettre knyght
source Than he, that is of worthynesse welle,
And he wel moore vertu hath than myght:
This knoweth many a wise and worthi wight.
value, acknowledge The same pris of Troilus I seye:
God help me so, I knowe nat swiche tweye.'

'By God,' quod she, 'of Ector that is sooth.
Of Troilus the same thyng trowe I,
without doubt For dredeles men tellen that he doth
In armes day by day so worthily
And bereth hym here at hom so gentily
praise To everi wight that alle pris hath he
(see n.) Of hem that me were levest preysed be.'

'Ye sey right sooth, ywys,' quod Pandarus;
'For yesterday who-so hadde with hym ben
He myghte han wondred upon Troilus;
bees For nevere yet so thikke a swarm of been
flew, because of him did flee Ne fleigh as Grekes for hym gonne fleen,
And thorugh the feld in everi wightes eere
Ther nas no cry but "Troilus is there!"

'Now here, now ther, he hunted hem so faste
Ther nas but Grekes blood and Troilus.
Now hem he hurte and hem al down he caste;
Everywhere Ay wher he wente it was arayed thus:
He was hire deth, and sheld and lif for us,
as for that day That as that day ther dorste non withstonde
Whil that he held his blody swerd in honde.

169 **In good faith** (cf. 162). The earnestness of their agreement on these banalities suggests that each knows that the other knows that he/she is really thinking of something else.

189 'Of them that people (*me*, 'men') would most like to be praised by'.

	'Therto he is the frendlieste man
in my whole life	Of gret estat that evere I saugh my lyve;
(see n.)	And wher hym lest, best felawshipe kan
worthy of deserving	To swich as hym thynketh able for to thryve.'
with all haste	And with that word tho Pandarus as blyve
hence	He took his leve, and seyde, 'I wol gon henne.'
	'Nay, blame have I, myn uncle,' quod she thenne.
	'What aileth yow to be thus wery soone
particularly, Is that how it is?	And namelich of wommen? Wol ye so?
have occasion	Nay, sitteth down; by God, I have to doone
business	With yow to speke of wisdom er ye go.'
	And everi wight that was aboute hem tho,
	That herde that, gan fer awey to stonde
dealt with all they had in mind to	Whil they two hadde al that hem liste in honde.
discussion	Whan that hire tale al brought was to an ende
	Of hire estat and of hire governaunce,
left	Quod Pandarus, 'Now is it tyme I wende.
	But yet, I say, ariseth, lat us daunce,
to the devil	And cast youre widewes habit to mischaunce!
	What list yow thus youreself to disfigure
befallen, piece of good luck	Sith yow is tid thus faire an aventure?'
I'm glad you thought of that	'A, wel bithought! For love of God,' quod she,
get to know	'Shal I nat witen what ye meene of this?'
requires time	'No, this thing axeth leyser,' tho quod he,
	'And eke me wolde muche greve, iwis,
	If I it tolde and ye it toke amys.
hold still	Yet were it bet my tonge for to stille
	Than seye a soth that were ayeyns youre wille.
	'For, nece, by the goddesse Mynerve
	And Jupiter that maketh the thondre rynge
	And by the blisful Venus that I serve,
	Ye ben the womman in this world lyvynge –
(see n.), knowledge	Withouten paramours, to my wyttynge –
	That I best love and lothest am to greve,
know, believe	And that ye weten wel youreself, I leve.'
many thanks	'Iwis, myn uncle,' quod she, 'grant mercy!
relied upon always up to now	Youre frendshipe have I founden evere yit.
indebted	I am to no man holden, trewely,
repaid	So muche as yow and have so litel quyt;
as far as lies in my power	And with the grace of God, emforth my wit,
By any fault in me	As in my gylt I shall yow nevere offende,
make amends	And if I have er this I wol amende.

206 'And where it pleases him, knows how to show the greatest friendliness'.

208–10 Pandarus gambles that Criseyde will not let him go without reminding him of the great piece of news he is supposed to have brought; Criseyde gets the better of him, in this game of wits, by detaining him, but on another pretext (a discussion of business affairs, where the irony of Pandarus's position, as presumably her interim guardian, is sharply in mind). He finally has to admit defeat, and bring it up himself (224).

236 'Not to speak of sexual love (or, not having a lover?)'.

'But for the love of God I yow biseche,
As ye ben he that I love moost and triste, — *trust*
Lat be to me youre fremde manere speche — *Give over, strange and formal*
And sey to me, youre nece, what yow liste.'
And with that word hire uncle anoon hire kiste,
And seyde, 'Gladly, leve nece dere!
Tak it for good that I shal sey yow here.'

With that she gan hire eighen down to caste
And Pandarus to coghe gan a lite, — *a little*
And seyde, 'Nece, alwey, lo, to the laste, — *in the last analysis*
How so it be that som men hem delite
With subtyl art hire tales for to endite,
Yet for al that in hire entencioun
Hire tale is al for som conclusioun.

'And sithe th'ende is every tales strengthe
And this matere is so bihovely, — *proper*
What sholde I poynte or drawen it on lengthe — *(see n.)*
To yow, that ben my frend so feythfully?'
And with that word he gan right inwardly
Byholden hire and loken on hire face,
And seyde, 'On swich a mirour goode grace!' — *(see n.)*

Than thought he thus: 'If I my tale endite
Aught harde or make a proces any whyle, — *(see n.)*
She shal no savour have therin but lite — *pleasure*
And trowe I wolde hire in my wil bigyle, — *wilfully*
For tendre wittes wenen al be wyle — *(see n.)*
Ther as thei kan nought pleynly understonde;
Forthi hire wit to serven wol I fonde' – — *(see n.)*

And loked on hire in a bysi wyse — *earnest*
And she was war that he byheld hire so,
And seyde, 'Lord! so faste ye m'avise! — *you stare at me so intently!*
Sey ye me nevere er now? What sey ye, no?' — *Saw, say*
'Yis, yys,' quod he, 'and bet wol er I go! — *will do better*
But be my trouthe, I thoughte now if ye — *was just now thinking how you*
Be fortunat, for now men shal it se.

'For to every wight som goodly aventure — *piece of good fortune*
Som tyme is shape if he it kan receyven, — *destined*
But if he wol take of it no cure — *notice*
Whan that it commeth but wilfully it weyven, — *ignore*
Lo, neyther cas ne fortune hym deceyven, — *chance*
But ryght his verray slouthe and wrecchednesse;
And swich a wight is for to blame, I gesse.

262 'Why should I go into details or drag it out at length?'
266 'May good fortune befall such a face (beauty's mirror)'.
268–9 'If I tell my story in any way difficult to comprehend or at any time make a long discourse of it'.
271 'For innocent minds think that everything is a trick'.
273 'Therefore I will try to suit what I have to say to her understanding'.

fair niece 'Good aventure, O beele nece, have ye
easily, if you know how to Ful lightly founden and ye konne it take,
And for the love of God, and ek of me,
lest the chance slip away Cache it anon, lest aventure slake!
discourse What sholde I lenger proces of it make?
Give Yif me youre hond, for in this world is noon –
in such a happy situation If that yow list – a wight so wel bygon.

'And sith I speke of good entencioun,
As I to yow have told wel here-byforn,
And love as wel youre honour and renoun
As creature in al this world yborn,
By alle tho othes that I have yow sworn –
If, think And ye be wrooth therfore or wene I lye,
again Ne shal I nevere sen yow eft with eye.

frightened 'Beth naught agast, ne quaketh naught! Wherto?
Ne chaungeth naught for feere so youre hewe!
truly, is all over For hardely the werst of this is do;
And though my tale as now be to yow newe
Yet trist alwey ye shal me fynde trewe,
unsuitable And were it thyng that me thoughte unsittynge
To yow wolde I no swiche tales brynge.'

'Now, good em, for Goddes love I preye,'
get a move on Quod she, 'come of and telle me what it is!
For both I am agast what ye wol seye
And ek me longeth it to wite, ywis;
For whethir it be wel or be amys
Say on, lat me nat in this feere dwelle.'
'So wol I doon; now herkeneth, I shall telle:

'Now, nece myn, the kynges deere sone,
The goode, wise, worthi, fresshe and free,
wont Which alwey for to don wel is his wone,
The noble Troilus, so loveth the
unless, destruction That but ye helpe it wol his bane be.
Lo, here is al – what sholde I moore sey?
Doth what yow lest to make hym lyve or dey.

die 'But if ye late hym deyen, I wol sterve –
Have here my trouthe, nece, I nyl nat lyen –
Even if I had to Al sholde I with this knyf my throte kerve.'
With that the teris breste out of his eighen,
And seyde, 'If that ye don us bothe dyen
made a fine catch! Thus gilteles, than have ye fisshed fayre!
(see n.) What mende ye though that we booth appaire?

'Allas, he which that is my lord so deere,
That trewe man, that noble gentil knyght,
That naught desireth but youre frendly cheere,

329 'How do you gain by it if we both should perish?'

	I se hym dyen ther he goth upryght
	And hasteth hym with al his fulle myght
	For to ben slayn, if his fortune assente.
	Allas, that God yow swich a beaute sente!
	'If it be so that ye so cruel be
it pleases you to care nothing	That of his deth yow listeth nought to recche,
	That is so trewe and worthi, as ye se,
	Namoore than of a japer or a wrecche –
	If ye be swich, youre beaute may nat strecche
	To make amendes of so cruel a dede;
Careful consideration	Avysement is good byfore the nede.
(see n.)	'Wo worth the faire gemme vertulees!
has no healing power	Wo worth that herbe also that dooth no boote!
	Wo worth that beaute that is routheles!
treads everyone	Wo worth that wight that tret ech undir foote!
(the whole being of beauty)	And ye, that ben of beaute crop and roote,
If with that	If therwithal in yow ther be no routhe,
	Than is it harm ye lyven, by my trouthe!
piece of trickery	'And also think wel that this is no gaude,
	For me were levere thow and I and he
pimp (pander)	Were hanged, than I sholde ben his baude,
	As heigh as men myghte on us alle ysee!
	I am thyn em; the shame were to me,
	As wel as the, if that I sholde assente
abetting, should injure	Thorugh myn abet that he thyn honour shente.
	'Now understond, for I yow nought requere
promise	To bynde yow to hym thorugh no byheste
be nicer to him	But only that ye make hym bettre chiere
(show him) more kind attention	Than ye han doon er this, and moore feste,
	So that his lif be saved atte leeste.
This is the whole matter, fully	This al and som and pleynly oure entente:
	God help me so, I nevere other mente!
not unreasonable	'Lo, this requeste is naught but skylle, ywys,
reasonable fear	Ne doute of resoun, pardee, is ther noon.
Let me suppose as a hypothesis	I sette the worste, that ye dreden this:
would be surprised to see him	Men wolde wondren sen hym come or goon.
In reply to that	Ther-ayeins answere I thus anoon
congenital idiot	That every wight, but he be fool of kynde,
affection between friends	Wol deme it love of frendshipe in his mynde.
think	'What, who wol demen, though he se a man
	To temple go, that he th'ymages eteth?
	Thenk ek how wel and wisely that he kan
	Governe hymself that he nothyng foryeteth,
praise	That where he cometh he pris and thank hym geteth;
	And ek therto he shal come here so selde,
What great matter would it be	What fors were it though al the town byhelde?

344 'Woe befall the fair gem that lacks the power intrinsic to gems!'

affection between friends	'Swych love of frendes regneth al this town:
(see n.)	And wre yow in that mantel evere moo,
As God may surely be	And God so wys be my savacioun,
your best course	As I have seyd, youre beste is to do soo.
assuage	But alwey, goode nece, to stynte his woo,
public aloofness, sweetened	So lat youre daunger sucred ben a lite
blame	That of his deth ye be naught for to wite.'
going on in this way	Criseyde, which that herde hym in this wise,
feel for (try to figure out)	Thoughte, 'I shal felen what he meneth, ywis.'
suggest	'Now, em,' quod she, 'what wolde ye devise?
advice	What is youre rede I sholde don of this?'
	'That is wel seyd,' quod he. 'Certein, best is
in return	That ye hym love ayeyn for his lovynge,
reasonable payment of reward	As love for love is skilful guerdonynge.
age	'Thenk ek how elde wasteth every houre
	In eche of yow a partie of beautee,
	And therfore er that age the devoure
for when you are old	Go love, for old, ther wol no wight of the.
lesson	Lat this proverbe a loore unto yow be:
The realization comes too late	"To late ywar, quod Beaute, whan it paste";
conquers women's primness	And Elde daunteth Daunger at the laste.
(see n.)	'The kynges fool is wont to crien loude
behaves haughtily	Whan that hym thinketh a womman bereth hire heighe,
	"So longe mote ye lyve, and alle proude,
	Til crowes feet be growe under youre eighe,
peer	And sende yow than a myrour in to prye
in the morning	In which that ye may se youre face a-morwe!"
I would not wish you	Nece, I bidde wisshe yow namore sorwe.'
	With this he stynte and caste adown the hede
burst into tears	And she began to breste a-wepe anoon,
	And seyde, 'Allas, for wo! Why nere I deede?
	For of this world the feyth is al agoon.
strangers	Allas, what sholden straunge to me doon
thought to be	When he that for my beste frend I wende
Advises, forbid	Ret me to love, and sholde it me defende?
	'Allas! I wolde han trusted douteles
misfortune	That if that I thorugh my disaventure
	Hadde loved outher hym or Achilles,
creature of man's kind	Ector, or any mannes creature,
restraint (in condemning)	Ye nolde han had no mercy ne mesure
reproach	On me, but alwey had me in repreve.
believe	This false worlde, allas, who may it leve?
	'What, is this al the joye and al the feste?
advice, piece of good fortune	Is this youre reed? Is this my blisful cas?

380 'And conceal yourself in that cloak (of being just good friends) evermore'.

398 Proverbial (Whiting B155).

400 **kynges fool**: fool who has licence to say what everyone knows.

fulfilment, promise	Is this the verray mede of youre byheeste?
elaborate build-up	Is al this paynted proces seyd, allas,
purpose, Pallas Athene (= Minerva)	Right for this fyn? O lady myn, Pallas!
frightening, make provision	Thow in this dredful cas for me purveye,
	For so astoned am I that I deye.'
	Wyth that she gan ful sorwfully to syke.
	'A, may it be no bet?' quod Pandarus;
week	'By God, I shal namore come here this wyke,
And (I swear so) before God	And God aforn, that am mystrusted thus!
set little store by	I se ful wel that ye sette lite of us
	Or of oure deth! Allas, I woful wrecche!
nothing to worry about	Might he yet lyve, of me is nought to recche.
(see n.)	'O cruel god, O dispitous Marte,
	O Furies thre of helle, on yow I crye!
	So lat me nevere out of this hous departe
	If that I mente harm or any vilenye!
	But sith I se my lord mot nedes dye
make my confession	And I with hym, here I me shryve and seye
	That wikkedly ye don us bothe deye.
	'But sith it liketh yow that I be dede,
	By Neptunus, that god is of the see,
	Fro this forth shal I nevere eten brede
	Til I myn owen herte blood may see,
	For certeyn I wol deye as soone as he.'
started out	And up he sterte and on his wey he raughte,
(see n.)	Til she agayn hym by the lappe kaughte.
was dead	Criseyde, which that wel neigh starf for feere,
Being as she was	So as she was the ferfulleste wighte
	That myghte be, and herde ek with hire ere
	And saugh the sorwful ernest of the knyght
nothing wrong	And in his preier ek saugh noon unryght,
	And for the harm that myghte ek fallen moore
have pity and be fearful	She gan to rewe and dredde hire wonder soore,
Misfortunes	And thoughte thus: 'Unhappes fallen thikke
in such kinds of way	Alday for love, and in swych manere cas
in (actions) against themselves	As men ben cruel in hemself and wikke;
	And if this man sle here hymself, allas,
not be very nice for me	In my presence, it wol be no solas.
	What men wolde of hit deme I kan nat seye:
cunningly to play (my cards)	It nedeth me ful sleighly for to pleie.'

435 **dispitous Marte**: 'malicious Mars' (planetary deity of misfortune).

448 'Till she in response caught him by a fold (in the sleeve) of his garment'.

451–4 The tumble of **and**-clauses seems to represent the turmoil of Criseyde's mind, as she turns over and over in her mind the decision she is going to make and works out how it is both for the best and unavoidable.

456–73 The relationship between soliloquy and speech is hard to establish. Is **A, Lord!** what Criseyde **sayde thrie**, and does she then resume her internal meditation until she speaks in 473?

thrice	And with a sorowful sik she sayde thrie,
What a sad fate has befallen me!	'A, Lord! What me is tid a sory chaunce!
position in life, jeopardy	For myn estat lith now in a jupartie
	And ek myn emes lif is in balaunce;
guidance	But natheles with Goddes governaunce
	I shal so doon, myn honour shal I kepe
	And ek his lif' – and stynte for to wepe.
is best to be chosen	'Of harmes two, the lesse is for to chese:
I would rather be pleasant to him	Yet have I levere maken hym good chere
Honourably, lose	In honour than myn emes lyf to lese. –
	Ye seyn, ye nothyng elles me requere?'
indeed (= ywis)	'No, wis,' quod he, 'myn owen nece dere.'
do my utmost	'Now wel,' quod she, 'and I wol doon my peyne;
(see n.)	I shal myn herte ayeins my lust constreyne –
	'But that I nyl nat holden hym in honde,
	Ne love a man ne kan I naught ne may
in all else, try	Ayeins my wyl, but elles wol I fonde,
Saving my honour	Myn honour sauf, plesen hym fro day to day.
	Therto nolde I nat ones han seyd nay
was afraid, my imaginings	But that I dredde, as in my fantasye;
if the cause should cease	But cesse cause, ay cesseth maladie.
	'And here I make a protestacioun
further	That in this proces if ye depper go
	That certeynly, for no salvacioun
	Of yow, though that ye sterven bothe two,
in one day	Though al the world on o day be my fo,
	Ne shal I nevere of hym han other routhe.'
	'I graunte wel,' quod Pandare, 'by my trowthe.
	'But may I truste wel therto,' quod he,
promised	'That of this thyng that ye han hight me here
	Ye wole it holden trewely unto me?'
	'Ye, doutelees,' quod she, 'myn uncle deere.'
	'Ne that I shal han cause in this matere,'
	Quod he, 'to pleyne or after yow to preche?'
	'Why, no, parde; what nedeth moore speche?'
	Tho fellen they in other tales glade,
	Tyl at the laste, 'O good em,' quod she tho,
(i.e. God's)	'For his love which that us bothe made
knew	Tel me how first ye wisten of his wo.
	Woot noon of it but ye?' He seyde, 'No.'
	'Kan he wel speke of love?' quod she; 'I preye
so that, prepare myself	Tel me, for I the bet me shal purveye.'
	Tho Pandarus a litel gan to smyle,
	And seyde, 'By my trouthe I shal yow telle.

476–7 'I shall allow compassion to constrain my own wishes, except that I will not deceive him with false hopes'.

	This other day, naught gon ful longe while,
	In-with the paleis gardyn, by a welle,
	Gan he and I wel half a day to dwelle,
plan	Right for to speken of an ordinaunce
get the better of	How we the Grekes myghten disavaunce.
jump up	'Soon after that bigonne we to lepe
spears	And casten with oure dartes to and fro,
	Tyl at the laste he seyde he wolde slepe
grass	And on the gres adoun he leyde hym tho,
stroll	And I therafter gan romen to and fro,
walked	Til that I herde as that I welk alone
	How he bigan ful wofully to grone.
	'Tho gan I stalke hym softely byhynde,
certainly	And sikirly the sooth for to seyne,
	As I kan clepe ayein now to my mynde,
	Right thus to Love he gan hym for to pleyne:
	He seyde, "Lord, have routhe upon my peyne,
Although	Al have I ben rebell in myn entente;
	Now, *mea culpa*, lord, I me repente!
according as you dispose	'"O god, that at thi disposicioun
(see n.)	Ledest the fyn by juste purveiaunce
humble	Of every wight, my lowe confessioun
graciously	Accepte in gree, and sende me swich penaunce
but against despair	As liketh the, but from disesperaunce,
spirit alienate	That may my goost departe awey fro the,
	Thow be my sheld, for thi benignite.
	'"For certes, lord, so soore hath she me wounded,
	That stood in blak, with lokyng of hire eyen,
plunged	That to myn hertes botme it is ysounded,
	Thorugh which I woot that I moot nedes deyen.
reveal (my love)	This is the werste – I dar me nat bywreyen,
red-hot coals	And wel the hotter ben the gledes rede,
When men cover them	That men hem wrien with asshen pale and dede."
smote his brow and hung his head	'Wyth that he smot his hede adown anon
mutter	And gan to motre, I noot what, trewely.
quietly	And I with that gan stille awey to goon
acted as though	And leet therof as nothing wist had I
	And com ayein anon and stood hym by,
	And seyde, "Awake, ye slepen al to longe!
causes you to pine with longing	It semeth nat that love doth yow longe,

507–53 Some have suggested that Pandarus is recounting an episode we have not been told of; but it seems clear that he has attached a familiar story of the overheard lover's complaint (rather like Chaucer's own *Book of the Duchess*) to Troilus, knowing that it is the very thing to appeal to a disposition nurtured on romances of love.

525 ***mea culpa***: mine is the blame, a formula from the confessional, and an example, like the next stanza, and the brow-beating (540), of the use of Christian terms of penitence in the language of love, a practice to be thought of more as daringly witty than as either a barbed criticism of love or a surreptitious endorsement.

527 'Controllest the destined end by just providence'.

530–1 **disesperaunce**: despair, or loss of hope, was the sin against the Holy Spirit, and the denial and loss of God's grace.

534 **stood in blak**. A reference to Criseyde's attire when Troilus first saw her in the temple (I.177).

'"That slepen so that no man may yow wake.
saw, lethargic Who sey evere or this so dul a man?"
may you lot have your heads ache "Ye, frende," quod he, "do ye youre hedes ake
For love, and lat me lyven as I kan."
But though that he for wo was pale and wan,
put on Yet made he tho as fresshe a countenaunce
As though he sholde have led the newe daunce.

'This passed forth til now this other day
It fel that I com romyng al allone
Into his chaumbre and fond how that he lay
Upon his bed; but man so soore grone
Ne herde I nevere, and what that was his mone
Ne wist I nought, for as I was comyng
Al sodeynly he lefte his complaynyng.

'Of which I took somwat suspecioun
And ner I com and fond he wepte soore,
As God may surely be And God so wys be my savacioun
As nevere of thyng hadde I no routhe moore,
ingenuity, instruction For neither with engyn ne with no loore
Unnethes myghte I fro the deth hym kepe,
That yet fele I myn herte for hym wepe.

'And God woot, nevere sith that I was born
Was I so besy no man for to preche
Ne nevere was to wight so depe isworn
Before, physician Or he me told who myghte ben his leche.
But now to yow rehercen al his speche
repeat Or all his woful wordes for to sowne
unless you want to see me swoon Ne bid me naught, but ye wol se me swowne.

nothing else 'But for to save his lif and elles nought
And to noon harm of yow thus am I dryven,
And for the love of God that us hath wrought
Swich cheer hym dooth that he and I may lyven!
plainly, confessed Now have I plat to yow myn herte shryven,
my purpose is honest And sith ye woot that myn entent is cleene,
Take heede therof, for I non yvel meene.

success, may you have 'And right good thrift, I prey to God, have ye
such a one That han swich oon ykaught withouten net!
And if you are as wise And be ye wis as ye be faire to see,
Wel in the rynge than is the rubie set.
Ther were nevere two so wel ymet
entirely Whan ye ben his al hool as he is youre:
Ther myghty God yet graunte us see that houre!'

'Nay, therof spak I nought, ha, ha!' quod she;
spoil everything 'As helpe me God, ye shenden every deel!'

549 **do ye youre hedes ake**. Pandarus represents Troilus as holding to his former pretence of being fancy-free and scornful of love, as described in Book I.

554–71 This is the episode described at length in Book I.

'O, mercy, dere nece,' anon quod he,
'What-so I spak, I mente naught but wel, *Whatever*
By Mars, the god that helmed is of steel!
Now beth naught wroth, my blood, my nece dere.'
'Now wel,' quod she, 'foryeven be it here!'

With this he took his leve and home he wente,
And, Lord, so he was glad and wel bygon! *very pleased with everything*
Criseyde aros, no lenger she ne stente, *stayed*
But streght into hire closet wente anon
And set hire doun as stylle as any ston
And every word gan up and down to wynde *turn in her mind*
That he had seyd, as it com hire to mynde,

And wax somdel astoned in hire thoughte
Right for the newe cas, but whan that she
Was ful avysed, tho fond she right noughte *Thought about it fully, found*
Of peril why she ought afered be:
For man may love, of possibilite, *it's quite possible*
A womman so his herte may to-breste *break in pieces*
And she naught love ayein but if hire leste. *unless she wanted*

But as she sat allone and thoughte thus,
Ascry aros at scarmuch al withoute, *The outcry arose at a skirmish*
And men criden in the strete, 'Se, Troilus
Hath right now put to flighte the Grekes route!' *army*
With that gan al hire meigne for to shoute, *household attendants*
'A, go we se! Caste up the yates wyde!
For thorwgh this strete he moot to paleys ride,

'For other wey is to the yate noon
Of Dardanus, there opyn is the cheyne.'
With that com he and al his folk anoon
An esy pas rydyng, in routes tweyne, *At a slow pace, in two columns*
Right as his happy day was, sooth to seyne – *day of destined good fortune*
For which, men seyn, may nought destourbed be *prevented*
That shal bityden of necessitee.

This Troilus sat on his baye steede
Al armed save his hede ful richely;
And wownded was his hors, and gan to blede,
On which he rood a pas ful softely. *at a walking pace*
But swich a knyghtly sighte trewely
As was on hym was nought, withouten faille,
To loke on Mars that god is of bataille.

So lik a man of armes and a knyght
He was to seen, fulfilled of heigh prowesse, *to look upon*

621–3 One of several reflections on the inevitability of destiny that Chaucer introduces from the *Consolation of Philosophy* of the fifth-century Christian-Roman philosopher Boethius (V, prose 6, 162–8) – without mentioning Boethius's further argument, that 'Fortune' and 'Destiny' are only names men give to the operations of a divine providence that allows them complete free will but that they choose wilfully not to understand (see also III.617n).

For bothe he hadde a body and a myght
To don that thing as wel as hardynesse, *that deed (of prowess), courage*
And ek to seen hym in his gere hym dresse, *all got up in his armour*
So fressh, so yong, so weldy semed he, *vigorous*
It was an heven upon hym for to see.

His helm to-hewen was in twenty places,
That by a tyssew heng his bak byhynde;
His sheeld to-dasshed was with swerdes and maces,
In which men myghte many an arwe fynde
That thirled hadde horn and nerf and rynde; *(see n.)*
And ay the peple cryde, 'Here cometh oure joye,
And, next his brother, holder up of Troye!'

For which he wex a litel reed for shame
When he the peple upon hym herde cryen,
That to byholde it was a noble game
How sobrelich he caste down his eyen.
Criseyda gan al his chere aspien
And leet so softe it in hire herte synken
That to hireself she seyde, 'Who yaf me drynken?'

For of hire owen thought she wex al reed, *became*
Remembryng hire right thus, 'Lo, this is he
Which that myn uncle swerith he moot be deed
But I on hym have mercy and pitee.'
And with that thought for pure ashamed she *for very shame*
Gan in hire hed to pulle, and that as faste,
While he and alle the peple forby paste,

And gan to caste and rollen up and down
Withinne hire thought his excellent prowesse
And his estat and also his renown, *station in life*
His wit, his shap and ek his gentilesse; *wisdom*
But moost hire favour was for his distresse *was because*
Was al for hire, and thought it was a routhe
To sleen swich oon if that he mente trouthe.

Now myghte som envious jangle thus: *spiteful-minded people*
'This was a sodeyn love! how myght it be
That she so lightly loved Troilus *quickly*
Right for the firste syghte, ye, parde?'
Now who seith so, ne mote he nevere y-the! *may he never thrive*
For every thyng a gynnyng hath it nede *has to have a beginning*
Er al be wrought, withowten any drede. *doubt*

For I sey nought that she so sodeynly
Yaf hym hire love, but that she gan enclyne

642 'That had pierced horn and sinew and skin (of the shield)'.
651 Criseyde's words may recall the episode in which Tristan and Isolde fall in love after drinking the love-potion. She half-consciously distances the movement of desire within herself as something that comes upon her magically, from outside, regardless of her will.

666–79 As has often been remarked, the narrator's intervention here on behalf of Criseyde acts to stir up doubts as much as to dispel them. But Chaucer may have felt that Criseyde's reputation for fickleness needed to be explicitly addressed.

To like hym first, and I have told yow whi;
suffering And after that, his manhod and his pyne
Made love withinne hire herte for to myne,
For which by proces and by good servyse
obtained He gat hire love, and in no sodeyn wyse.

And also blisful Venus, wel arrayed,
Sat in hire seventhe hous of hevene tho,
(see n.) Disposed wel and with aspectes payed
poor innocent To helpe sely Troilus of his woo.
And soth to seyne, she nas nat al a foo
To Troilus in his nativitee:
the better God woot that wel the sonner spedde he.

for a while Now lat us stynte of Troilus a throwe,
That rideth forth, and lat us torne faste
Unto Criseyde, that heng hire hed ful lowe
Ther as she sat allone, and gan to caste
What she would finally decide Where-on she wolde apoynte hire atte laste,
If it so were hire em ne wolde cesse
For Troilus upon hire for to presse.

And Lord! so she gan in hire thought argue
In this matere of which I have yow tolde,
And what to doone best were and what eschuwe –
(see n.) That plited she ful ofte in many folde.
Now was hire herte warm, now was it colde,
And what she thoughte somwhat shal I write,
my author (source for my story) As to myn auctour listeth for t'endite.

Troilus's She thoughte wel that Troilus persone
She knew by syghte and ek his gentilesse,
although, not appropriate And thus she seyde, 'Al were it nat to doone
To graunte hym love, yit for his worthynesse
It were honour with pleye and with gladnesse
Honourably In honestee with swich a lord to deele,
well-being For myn estat and also for his heele.

'Ek wel woot I my kynges sone is he,
And sith he hath to se me swich delite,
utterly and openly If I wolde outreliche his sighte flee
Perhaps Peraunter he myghte have me in dispite,
plight Thorugh whicche I myghte stonde in worse plite.
to bring hatred on myself Now were I wis me hate to purchace,
Withouten nede, ther I may stonde in grace?

677 The medieval siege engineer dug tunnels (mined) under the walls of a castle, shored up the tunnel roofs with timbers, then set light to the timbers and retired hastily before the tunnels collapsed – and with them, it was hoped, the fortifications. It works better as a metaphor than it did in reality.

680–6 Troilus's cause was assisted by Venus, who favoured him in the horoscope of his nativity (684–5), and was also that day in a favourable position (**Disposed wel**) in the seventh **hous** or division of the celestial sphere, with other signs and bodies likewise propitious (**aspectes payed**). Chaucer throws the colouring of judicial astrology over what has already been said (621–3) about the influence of destiny.

697 'That (was something) she turned this way and that'.

moderation 'In every thyng, I woot, ther lith mesure;
forbid For though a man forbede dronkenesse,
requires He naught forbet that every creature
Be drynkeles for alwey, as I gesse.
Ek sith I woot for me is his destresse,
I ne aughte naught for that thing hym despise,
Sith it is so he meneth in good wyse.

'And eke I knowe of longe tyme agon
qualities, foolish His thewes goode and that he is nat nyce;
Nor a boaster N'avantour, seith men, certein is he noon –
To wis is he to doon so gret a vice;
since, never show him such favour Ne als I nyl hym nevere so cherice
That he may make avaunt by juste cause,
(see n.) He shal me nevere bynde in swiche a clause.

let us suppose a certain situation 'Now sette a caas: the hardest is, ywys,
Men myghten demen that he loveth me.
What dishonour were it unto me, this?
stop him doing that May ich hym lette of that? Why, nay, parde!
I knowe also, and alday heere and se,
quite without their permission Men loven wommen al biside hire leve,
(see n.) And whan hem leste namore, lat hem byleve!

'I thenk ek how he able is for to have
worthiest Of al this noble town the thriftieste
provided that To ben his love, so she hire honour save,
For out and out he is the worthieste,
Save only Ector, which that is the beste –
at my disposal And yet his lif al lith now in my cure.
good fortune But swich is love and ek myn aventure.

'Ne me to love a wonder is it nought,
For wel woot I myself, so God me spede –
Al wolde I that noon wiste of this thought –
the very fairest, without doubt I am oon the faireste, out of drede,
And goodlieste, who that taketh hede,
And so men seyn, in al the town of Troie.
What wonder is though he of me have joye?

an independent woman 'I am myn owene womman, wel at ese –
as befits my station in life I thank it God – as after myn estate,
untethered in a pleasant pasture Right yong, and stonde unteyd in lusty leese,
Withouten jalousie or swich debate:
Shal noon housbond seyn to me "Chek-mate!"
For either they ben ful of jalousie
Or maisterfull or loven novelrie.

728 'in terms of such a stipulation (i.e. as to be entitled to boast)'.

735 'And when they've stopped wanting to do that, let them leave off'.

754 **housbond**. Fashionable codes of love tended to exclude husbands, since the power relations of marriage were regarded as incompatible with the idealized relations of lovers (this is the reason for Arveragus's unusual pact with his wife in FrankT V.751, 764). But there were many medieval stories of fashionable courtship ending conventionally in happy marriage, and Criseyde's remark here is not representative of a fixed and universal 'system' of 'courtly love'.

purpose	'What shal I doon? To what fyn lyve I thus?
in a situation such as pleases me	Shal I nat love in cas if that me leste?
(see n.)	What, pardieux! I am naught religious.
	And though that I myn herte sette at reste
	Upon this knyght, that is the worthieste,
	And kepe alwey myn honour and my name,
By all that's proper	By alle right it may do me no shame.'
	But right as when the sonne shyneth bright
	In March, that chaungeth ofte tyme his face,
	And that a cloude is put with wynd to flight,
overspreads	Which oversprat the sonne as for a space,
	A cloudy thought gan thorugh hire soule pace
	That overspradde hire brighte thoughtes alle
	So that for feere almost she gan to falle.
since	That thought was this: 'Allas! syn I am free,
	Sholde I now love and put in jupartie
enslave	My sikernesse and thrallen libertee?
	Allas, how dorst I thenken that folie?
	May I naught wel in other folk aspie
fearful	Hire dredfull joye, hire constreinte and hire peyne?
opportunity (occasion)	Ther loveth noon that she nath wey to pleyne.
	'For love is yet the moste stormy lyf,
	Right of hymself, that evere was bigonne,
	For evere som mystrust or nice strif
	Ther is in love, som cloude is overe that sonne.
	Therto we wrecched wommen nothing konne
	Whan us is wo but wepe and sitte and thinke:
(see n.)	Oure wrecche is this, oure owen wo to drynke.
eager	'Also thise wikked tonges ben so preste
	To speke us harm; ek men ben so untrewe
as soon as, their desire	That right anon as cessed is hire leste
	So cesseth love, and forth to love a newe.
may regret	But harm ydoon is doon, who-so it rewe:
torture themselves at first	For though thise men for love hem first to-rende,
(see n.)	Ful sharp bygynnyng breketh ofte at ende.
	'How ofte tyme hath it yknowen be
done	The tresoun that to wommen hath ben do!
end	To what fyn is swich love I kan nat see
what becomes of it	Or wher bycometh it whan that it is ago.
	Ther is no wight that woot, I trowe so,
trips over it (it's not really there)	Where it bycometh. Lo, no wight on it sporneth;
at first	That erst was nothing into nought it torneth.
	'How bisy, if I love, ek most I be
gossip, imagine things	To plesen hem that jangle of love and dremen,

759 'What, by God! I am not in any way a member of a religious order' (e.g. a nun).

784 'Our wretchedness is this, to endure woes of our own making'.

791 'An eager beginning often leads to a separation in the end'.

talk nicely to them And coye hem, that they seye noon harm of me!
it seems to them For though ther be no cause, yet hem semen
please Al be for harm that folk hire frendes quemen;
And who may stoppen every wikked tonge
Or sown of belles whil that thei ben ronge?'

And after that hire thought gan for to clere,
And seide, 'He which that nothing undertaketh
whether he like it or not Nothyng n'acheveth, be hym looth or deere.'
And with another thought hire herte quaketh,
Than slepeth hope and after drede awaketh,
Now hoot, now cold. But thus, bitwixen tweye,
rises She rist hire up and wente hire for to pleye.

Adown the steyre anon-right tho she wente
Into the gardyn with hire neces thre,
took many a turn (stroll) And up and down ther made many a wente –
Flexippe, she, Tharbe and Antigone –
To pleyen that it joye was to see;
company And other of hire wommen, a gret route,
Hire foloweden in the gardyn al aboute.

(see n.) This yerd was large, and rayled alle th'aleyes,
And shadewed wel with blosmy bowes grene,
(see n.) And benched newe, and sonded alle the weyes,
In which she walketh arm in arm bitwene,
bright Til at the laste Antigone the shene
Gan on a Troian song to singen cleere
That it an heven was hire vois to here.

She seyde, 'O Love, to whom I have and shal
subject Ben humble subgit, trewe in myn entente
I give As I best kan, to yow, lord, yeve ich al
as tribute For everemo myn hertes lust to rente;
For nevere yet thi grace no wight sente
So blisful cause as me my lif to lede
security, without fear In alle joie and seurte out of drede.

bestowed (planted) 'Ye, blisful god, han me so wel byset
In love, iwys, that al that bereth lif
Ymagynen ne kouthe how to be bet;
For, lord, withouten jalousie or strif,
someone, diligent I love oon which that moost is ententif
To serven wel, unweri or unfeyned,
injurious intention stained That evere was, and leest with harm desteyned,

813–931 The garden-scene and Antigone's song are new in Chaucer, with hardly a hint in Boccaccio. Both serve to answer, point by point, the objections to engaging in a love-affair that Criseyde raised in her soliloquy.

820 'The enclosed garden was large, and the paths fenced with low rails'.

822 'And furnished with new turf-topped benches, and all the paths sanded'.

824 **Antigone**. The name was familiar from the story of Thebes, to which Criseyde and her ladies were earlier listening, and in assigning it to Love's votaress Chaucer is adding to the store of allusions (e.g. II.100, V.937, 1486) to the dark history of destruction and tragedy that lies ominously behind his story (see Patterson, *Chaucer and the Subject of History*, pp. 47–164).

He being the one, source (fountain)	'As he that is the welle of worthynesse,
foundation, excellence	Of trouthe grownd, mirour of goodlihede,
wisdom, rock of security	Of wit Apollo, stoon of sikernesse,
beginner and source of pleasure	Of vertu roote, of lust fynder and hede,
slain in me	Thorugh which is alle sorwe fro me dede.
	Iwis, I love hym best, so doth he me:
May he fare well	Now good thrift have he wher-so that he be!
	'Whom shulde I thanken but yow, god of Love,
I begin to bathe	Of al this blisse in which to bathe I gynne?
	And thanked be ye, lord, for that I love!
	This is the righte lif that I am inne,
banish	To flemen alle manere vice and synne:
devote myself	This dooth me so to vertue for t'entende
	That day by day I in my wille amende.
	'And who-so seith that for to love is vice
a form of enslavement	Or thraldom, though he feele in it destresse,
	He outher is envyous or right nyce
unable, wickedness	Or is unmyghty for his shrewednesse
	To loven; for swich manere folk, I gesse,
	Defamen Love as nothing of hym knowe –
never tried it for themselves	Thei speken but thei benten nevere his bowe!
of its very nature	'What is the sonne wers of kynde right
	Though that a man for fieblesse of his eyen
because it is so bright	May nought endure on it to see for bright?
complain about it	Or love the wers though wrecches on it crien?
happiness is worthwhile, endure	No wel is worth that may no sorwe dryen.
glass	And forthi who that hath an hed of verre,
war	Fro caste of stones war hym in the werre!
	'But I with al myn herte and al my myghte,
	As I have seyd, wol love unto my laste
	My deere herte and al myn owen knyghte,
	In which myn herte growen is so faste,
	And his in me, that it shal evere laste.
	Al dredde I first to love hym to bigynne,
	Now woot I wel ther is no peril inne.'
ceased	And of hir song right with that word she stente,
	And therwithal, 'Now nece,' quod Cryseyde,
expressing such admirable sentiments	'Who made this song now with so good entente?'
	Antygone answerde anoon and seyde,
	'Madame, ywys, the goodlieste mayde
	Of gret estat in al the town of Troye,
And that leads	And let hire lif in moste honour and joye.'
	'Forsothe, so it semeth by hire songe,'
	Quod tho Criseyde and gan therwith to sike,

851–4 The idea that love promoted the growth of virtue in the lover is perhaps the fundamental identifying characteristic, if there is one, of the medieval cult of idealized sexual love ('courtly love').

867–8 An earlier version of 'People in glass houses…'

And seyde, 'Lord, is ther swych blisse amonge
(see n.) Thise loveres as they kan faire endite?'
Yes, indeed, fair(-haired) 'Ye, wis,' quod fresshe Antigone the white,
have (been) or are (now) alive 'For alle the folk that han or ben on lyve
Ne konne wel the blisse of love discryve.

'But wene ye that every wrecche woot
The parfit blisse of love? Why, nay, iwys!
(see n.) They wenen all be love if oon be hoot.
Get away (forget it!) Do wey, do wey, they woot nothyng of this!
ask of Men moste axe at seyntes if it is
At all Aught faire in hevene – why? for they kan telle –
And axen fendes is it foule in helle.'

Criseyde unto that purpos naught answerde,
But seyde, 'Ywys, it wol be nyght as faste.'
But every word which that she of hire herde
imprint She gan to prenten in hire herte faste
to frighten And ay gan love lasse hire for t'agaste
Than it dide erst, and synken in hire herte,
That she wex somwhat able to converte.

The dayes honour and the hevenes eye,
The nyghtes foo – al this clepe I the sonne –
turn Gan westren faste and downward for to wrye,
As he that hadde his dayes cours yronne,
dun-coloured And white thynges wexen dymme and donne
For lakke of lyght, and sterres for t'apere,
together That she and alle hire folk in went yfeere.

So whan it liked hire to go to reste
withdrawn And voided weren thei that voiden oughte,
She seyde that to slepen wel hire leste:
Hire wommen soon unto hire bed hire broughte.
hushed Whan al was hust than lay she stille and thoughte
Of al this thing – the manere and the wise
you know already Reherce it nedeth nought, for ye ben wise.

A nyghtyngale upon a cedre grene
Under the chambre wal ther-as she ley
in the face of, bright Ful loude song ayein the moone shene,
Perhaps in its bird's fashion Peraunter in his briddes wise a lay
Of love, that made hire herte fressh and gay.
That herkned she so longe in good entente
deep, overcame Til at the laste the dede slepe hire hente.

slept, she dreamed And as she slep, anon-right tho hire mette
How that an egle, fethered whit as bone,

886 'As these lovers can describe so beautifully in their writing?'
892 'They think it's all love, even if someone is just aflame with passion'.
904–5 For the self-conscious signalling of the figure of *circumlocutio*, cf. FrankT V.1017–18.
925–31 The dream beautifully embodies both Criseyde's fear that love is a certain source of pain (see 771–805 above) and her readiness, encouraged by Antigone, to believe that it will not be so.

Under hire brest his longe clawes sette
And out hire herte he rente, and that anone,
caused — And dide his herte into hire brest to gone –
felt frightened, felt pain — Of which she nought agroos ne nothyng smerte –
flew — And forth he fleigh, with herte left for herte.

{Exchanges of letters follow, but Criseyde, despite Pandarus's urging, is unwilling to allow matters to proceed further. In order for Troilus to present his suit in person, Pandarus organizes a dinner-party at the house of Deiphebus, Troilus's brother, at which Helen will also be present, the pretext being that Criseyde is under attack from people in Troy and needs confirmation of the support of the Trojan nobility, including Troilus. Troilus will be at Deiphebus's house, but ostensibly sick in bed ('sik in ernest', says Troilus, II.1529) in a separate room, so that Pandarus will be able to arrange a private meeting. This first meeting goes well: Criseyde kisses Troilus and grants that he may be her servant in love. This involves constant thought and devotion on his part but only occasional brief meetings, because of the need (enjoined by the code of love and to some extent by their particular circumstances) for secrecy. Criseyde is happy (Troilus is to her 'a wal / Of stiel, and sheld from every displesaunce', III.479–80), Troilus somewhat less so, Chaucer apologetic for not describing every word and look that passed between them, Pandarus determined as always to push the business on.}

Book III

But now to the main point — But to the grete effect: than sey I thus,
That stondyng in concord and in quiete,
Thise ilke two, Criseyde and Troilus,
As I have told, and in this tyme swete –
Save only often myghte they nought mete
leisure, speak fully — Ne leiser have hire speches to fulfelle –
That it bifel right as I shal yow telle

That Pandarus, that evere dide his myght
purpose — Right for the fyn that I shal speke of here,
As for to bryngen to his hows som nyght
His faire nece and Troilus yfere,
Where — Wher as at leiser al this heighe matere
might be fully concluded — Touchyng here love were at the fulle up-bounde,
Hadde out of doute a tyme to it founde.

For he with gret deliberacioun
Hadde every thyng that her-to myght availle
Planned — Forncast and put in execucioun,
left nothing undone, hard work — And neither left for cost ne for travaille.
If it pleased them to come, lack — Come if hem list, hem sholde nothyng faille;
And for to ben in ought aspied there,
That wiste he wel an impossible were.

(see n.) — Dredeles, it clere was in the wynde
chattery magpie and spoil-sport — Of every pie and every lette-game;
Now al is wel, for al the world is blynde
wild and tame (i.e. everyone) — In this matere, bothe fremed and tame.
This tymbur is al redy up to frame;

526 'Without doubt, it was downwind and safe from discovery'.
528–32 These lines could be given to Pandarus or they could be regarded as the narrator's enthusiastic participation in Pandarus's plans.

Us lakketh nought but that we witen wolde
A certeyn houre in which she comen sholde.

And Troilus, that al this purveiaunce, *preparation*
Knew at the fulle and waited on it ay,
Hadde hereupon eke made gret ordinance, *elaborate arrangements*
And found his cause and therto his aray, *worked out his excuse, preparations*
If that he were missed nyght or day
Ther-while he was aboute this servyse, *During the time that, business*
That he was gon to don his sacrifise,

And moste at swich a temple allone wake, *must, keep vigil*
Answered of Apollo for to be,
And first to sen the holy laurer quake *laurel (sacred to Apollo)*
Er that Apollo spak out of the tree
To telle hym next whan Grekes sholde flee –
And forthy lette hym no man, God forbede, *let no one interfere with his plans*
But prey Apollo helpen in this nede.

Now is ther litel more for to doone,
But Pandare up and, shortly for to seyne,
Right sone upon the chaungynge of the moone,
Whan lightles is the world a nyght or tweyne
And that the wolken shop hym for to reyne, *the sky seemed to prepare itself*
He streght o morwe unto his nece wente – *in the morning*
Ye han wel herd the fyn of his entente. *final goal of his intended action*

Whan he was come, he gan anon to pleye
As he was wont, and of hymself to jape, *make fun of himself*
And finaly he swor and gan hire seye
By this and that she sholde hym nought escape,
Ne lenger don hym after hire to cape; *to keep chasing*
But certeynly she moste, by hire leve,
Come soupen in his hous with hym at eve.

At which she lough and gan hire faste excuse,
And seyde, 'It reyneth, lo, how sholde I gon?'
'Lat be,' quod he, 'ne stant nought thus to muse. *don't stand debating the matter*
This moot be don! Ye shal be ther anon.'
So at the laste her-of they fille aton, *fell into agreement*
Or elles, softe he swor hire in hire ere,
He nolde nevere comen ther she were.

Soone after this she to hym gan to rowne *whisper*
And axed hym if Troilus were there.
He swor hire nay, for he was out of towne,
And seyde, 'Nece, I pose that he were – *I put to you the supposition*
Yow thurste nevere han the more fere, *need*
For rather than men myghte hym ther aspie
Me were levere a thousand-fold to dye.'

	Nought list myn auctour fully to declare
	What that she thoughte whan that he seyde so,
gone	That Troilus was out of towne yfare,
	As if he seyde therof soth or no;
without further ado	But that withowten await with hym to go
	She graunted hym, sith he hire that bisoughte,
	And as his nece obeyed as hire oughte.
	But natheles yet gan she hym biseche,
was not a cause of apprehension	Although with hym to gon it was no fere,
goose-like (silly)	For to ben war of goosissh poeples speche,
	That dremen thynges whiche as nevere were,
	And wel avyse hym whom he broughte there;
most (must?) trust in you	And seyde hym, 'Em, syn I moste on yow triste,
	Loke al be wel and do now as yow liste.'
(see n.)	He swor hire 'yes', by stokkes and by stones
	And by the goddes that in hevene dwelle,
	Or elles were hym levere, soule and bones,
(god of the underworld)	With Pluto kyng as depe ben in helle
(see n.)	As Tantalus – what sholde I more telle?
	Whan al was wel he roos and took his leve
	And she to soper com whan it was eve
a certain number	With a certein of hire owen men
	And with hire faire nece Antigone
	And other of hire wommen nyne or ten.
	But who was glad now, who, as trowe ye,
	But Troilus, that stood and myght it se
tiny room or closet	Thoroughout a litel wyndow in a stewe,
shut up, in hiding	Ther he bishet syn mydnyght was in mewe,
Unknown to	Unwist of every wight but of Pandare?
	But to the point: now whan that she was come,
friendly behaviour	With alle joie and alle frendes fare
taken	Hire em anon in armes hath hire nome,
	And after to the soper, alle and some,
	Whan tyme was ful softe they hem sette.
(see n.)	God woot ther was no deynte for to fette!
	And after soper gonnen they to rise,
	At ese wel with herte fresshe and glade,
	And wel was hym that koude best devyse
To please her	To liken hire or that hire laughen made:
(see n.)	He song, she pleyde, he tolde tale of Wade,
	But at the laste, as every thyng hath ende,
	She took hire leve and nedes wolde wende.

575–81 Criseyde's motives are inaccessible to Chaucer – but she also makes them inaccessible to herself, so that she does not have to acknowledge to herself what she is deciding to do. Her duty as a niece (581) comes in very conveniently.

589 i.e. by pagan idols made of wood (tree-stumps) and stone.

593 Tantalus is parched with thirst and tormented for ever in hell with the sight of water he cannot reach.

609 'there was no delicacy that had to be looked for (i.e. was lacking)'.

614 **Wade** is an otherwise virtually unknown hero of Germanic legend: the reference here is famously tantalizing. **He ... she ... he** are impersonal ('one sang, one played...') and do not necessarily refer to Pandarus and Criseyde.

of the decrees of destiny	But O Fortune, executrice of wyerdes,
	O influences of thise hevenes hye!
shepherds	Soth is that under God ye ben oure hierdes,
hidden	Though to us bestes ben the causez wrie.
hasten	This mene I now, for she gan homward hye,
entirely without her permission	But execut was al bisyde hire leve
remain	The goddes wil, for which she moste bleve.
	The bente moone with hire hornes pale,
	Saturne, and Jove, in Cancro joyned were,
come down	That swych a reyn from heven gan avale
	That every maner womman that was there
	Hadde of that smoky reyn a verray feere;
then laughed	At which Pandare tho lough and seyde thenne,
	'Now were it tyme a lady to gon henne!
	'But, goode nece, if I myghte evere plese
	Yow any thyng, than prey ich yow,' quod he,
	'To don myn herte as now so gret an ese
	As for to dwelle here al this nyght with me,
Because	For-whi this is youre owen hous, parde.
as a joke	For by my trouthe – I sey it nought a-game –
leave	To wende as now it were to me a shame.'
knew the best thing to do	Criseyde, which that koude as muche good
	As half a world, took hede of his preiere,
rained	And syn it ron and al was on a flod,
(see n.)	She thoughte, 'As good chep may I dwellen here
	And graunte it gladly with a frendes chere,
complain	And have a thonk, as grucche and thanne abide;
cannot easily happen	For hom to gon it may nought wel bitide.'
dear	'I wol,' quod she, 'myn uncle lief and deere,
is reasonable	Syn that yow list it skile is to be so:
	I am right glad with yow to dwellen here;
	I seyde but a-game I wolde go.'
many thanks	'Iwys, graunt mercy, nece,' quod he tho,
	'Were it a game or no, soth for to telle,
	Now am I glad, syn that yow list to dwelle.'
	Thus al is wel; but tho bigan aright
	The newe joie and al the feste agayn.
if he could decently have done so	But Pandarus, if goodly hadde he myght,
hurried her off gladly	He wolde han hyed hire to bedde fayn,
	And seyde, 'Lord, this is an huge rayn!

617–20 In the Boethian hierarchy of causes (see *Consolation* IV, prose 6, 42–196; V, metre 1, 18–23), human beings perceive their lives as governed by planetary influence and Fortune; these, though, are only the instrumentation of the power of fate or destiny, which in turn is the enactment of divine providence (you hope).

624–5 The conjunction of Saturn and Jupiter with the moon in the zodiacal sign of Cancer was extremely rare: it occurred in May 1385 for the first time in 600 years, while Chaucer was in the midst of his poem, and was an event to which Chaucer and his knowledgeable astrological circle would look forward with keen interest. As one of the **influences** mentioned above, it was assigned a historical role in relation both to the Flood and to the Crucifixion. The invoking of such a majestic wheeling of the heavens as the cause of a rainstorm that obliges a lady to spend the night at her uncle's house (did they predict it? see 551, 562) seems comically overdone.

641 **As good chep**: 'as good a bargain' (i.e. I might as well).

This were a weder for to slepen inne –
And that I rede us soone to bygynne.

have you sleep 'And nece, woot ye wher I wol yow leye,
lie far apart For that we shul nat liggen far asonder,
And for ye neither shullen, dar I seye,
Heren noyse of reyne nor of thonder?
By God, right in my litel closet yonder.
And I wol in that outer hous allone
Be wardein of youre wommen everichone.

'And in this myddel chambre that ye se
Shal youre wommen slepen wel and softe,
And there I seyde shal youreselven be,
And if ye liggen wel to-nyght, com ofte,
And careth nought what weder is alofte.
(He calls for wine) The wyn anon, and whan so that yow leste,
So go we slepe: I trowe it be the beste.'

Ther nys no more, but hereafter soone,
wine taken before retiring, screen The voide dronke and travers drawe anon,
Gan every wight that hadde nought to done
More in the place out of the chaumbre gon.
violently, rained And evere-mo so sterneliche it ron
And blew therwith so wondirliche loude
That wel-neigh no man heren other koude.

Tho Pandarus, hire em, right as hym oughte,
With wommen swiche as were hire most aboute,
Ful glad unto hire beddes syde hire broughte
bow down And took his leve and gan ful lowe loute,
And seyde, 'Here at this closet dore withoute,
Directly opposite (the door) Right overe-thwart, youre wommen liggen alle,
That whom yow list of hem ye may here calle.'

So whan that she was in the closet leyde
as arranged And alle hire wommen forth by ordinaunce
Abedde weren, ther as I have seyde,
no further occasion, traipse about There was no more to skippen nor to traunce,
bidden, with trouble to follow But boden go to bedde with meschaunce
stirring If any wight was steryng anywhere
prevented And lat hem slepen that abedde were.

every bit But Pandarus, that wel koude ech a deel
The old game of love Th'olde daunce and every point therinne,
Whan that he sey that alle thyng was wel,
He thought he wolde upon his werk bigynne,
And gan the stuwe doore al softe unpynne,

663–8 The geography of the sleeping-quarters seems to be as follows: the main hall is divided by a **travers** or screen (674) into an **outer hous** (where Pandarus claims he will sleep, but doesn't) and a **myddel chambre** (where Criseyde's women will sleep), off which opens a **litel closet** where Criseyde will be, presumably in a bed concealed by hangings. The **stewe** where Troilus has been hiding has access to the **closet** by a **trappe** (741).

And stille as stoon withouten lenger lette *delay*
By Troilus adown right he hym sette.

And shortly to the point right for to gon,
Of al this werk he tolde hym word and ende, *from beginning to end*
And seyde, 'Make the redy right anon
For thow shalt into hevene blisse wende.'
'Now, blisful Venus, thow me grace sende!'
Quod Troilus, 'for nevere yet no nede
Hadde ich er now, ne halvendel the drede.' *a half-part*

Quod Pandarus, 'Ne drede the nevere a deel,
For it shal be right as thow wolt desire;
So thryve I, this nyght shal I make it weel
Or casten al the gruwel in the fire.' *(see n.)*
'Yet, blisful Venus, this nyght thow me enspire,'
Quod Troilus, 'as wys as I the serve, *as surely as*
And evere bet and bet shal til I sterve.

'And if ich hadde, O Venus ful of myrthe,
Aspectes badde of Mars or of Saturne, *(see n.)*
Or thow combust or let were in my birthe,
Thy fader prey al thilke harm disturne *Jupiter, turn aside*
Of grace, and that I glad ayein may turne, *may become happy again*
For love of hym thow lovedest in the shawe – *woodlands*
I meene Adoun, that with the boor was slawe. *Adonis, boar, slain*

'O Jove ek, for the love of faire Europe, *Europa*
The which in forme of bole awey thow fette, *bull, abducted*
Now help! O Mars, thow with thi blody cope, *cloak*
For love of Cipris, thow me nought ne lette! *Venus, don't hinder me*
O Phebus, thynk whan Dane hireselven shette *Daphne, enclosed*
Under the bark, and laurer wax for drede – *became a laurel-tree*
Yet for hire love, O help now at this nede!

'Mercurie, for the love of Hierse eke, *Herse*
For which Pallas was with Aglawros wroth, *Aglauros*
Now helpe! And ek Diane, I the biseke
That this viage be nought to the looth! *undertaking, displeasing*
O fatal sustren which, er any cloth *before any clothes*
Me shapen was, my destine me sponne, *Were made for me, spun*
So helpeth to this werk that is bygonne!'

Quod Pandarus, 'Thow wrecched mouses herte,
Artow agast so that she wol the bite?
Why, don this furred cloke upon thy sherte
And folwe me, for I wol have the wite. *take the blame*

711 **gruwel**: gruel (everything we've been cooking up).

715–35 Troilus displays a considerable knowledge of classical lore in his invocations, which Pandarus thinks quite inappropriate to the occasion.

716–17 'Bad influences of Mars or Saturn' (planets of notoriously bad influence).

717 **combust**: 'rendered powerless by the sun'. **let**: 'prevented from exerting good influence'.

733 **fatal sustren**: the Fates, or Parcae.

wait	But bide, and lat me gon biforn a lite.'
trap-door (in the wall)	And with that word he gan undon a trappe,
holding the fold of his garment	And Troilus he brought in by the lappe.
roar	The sterne wynd so loude gan to route
	That no wight oother noise myghte heere,
	And they that layen at the dore withoute
	Ful sikerly they slepten alle yfere;
	And Pandarus with a ful sobre cheere
without anyone stopping him	Goth to the dore anon, withouten lette,
	Ther as they laye, and softely it shette.
back (across the room)	And as he com ayeynward pryvely,
	His nece awook and axed, 'Who goth there?'
	'My dere nece,' quod he, 'it am I.
	Ne wondreth nought, ne have of it no fere.'
	And ner he com and seyde hire in hire ere,
	'No word, for love of God, I yow biseche!
	Lat no wight risen and heren of oure speche.'
	'What, which wey be ye comen, benedicite?'
	Quod she, 'and how thus unwist of hem alle?'
	'Here at this secre trappe-dore,' quod he.
	Quod tho Criseyde, 'Lat me som wight calle!'
Oh! (= ey), happen	'I! God forbede that it sholde falle,'
	Quod Pandarus, 'that ye swich folye wrought!
	They myghte demen thyng they nevere er thought.
	'It is nought good a slepyng hound to wake
make conjectures	Ne yeve a wight a cause for to devyne:
	Youre wommen slepen alle, I undertake,
(see n.)	So that for hem the hous men myghte myne,
they will	And slepen wollen til the sonne shyne.
	And whan my tale brought is to an ende,
Unnoticed	Unwist right as I com so wol I wende.
	'Now, nece myn, ye shul wel understonde,'
	Quod he, 'so as ye wommen demen alle,
(see n.)	That for to holde in love a man in honde
beloved	And hym hire lief and deere herte calle
hood over his cap (i.e. deceive him)	And maken hym an howve above a calle –
	I meene, as love another in this meene while –
deception	She doth hireself a shame and hym a gyle.
	'Now, wherby that I telle yow al this:
	Ye woot youreself as wel as any wight
	How that youre love al fully graunted is
	To Troilus, the worthieste knyght,
(And the worthiest) one	Oon of this world, and therto trouthe yplight
due to him (his fault)	That, but it were on hym alonge, ye nolde
	Hym nevere falsen while ye lyven sholde.

767 'As far as they are concerned, the house might be undermined (as in a siege)'.

773 'to hold off a man, in matters of love, with fair promises'.

stands	'Now stant it thus, that sith I fro yow wente
plainly	This Troilus, right platly for to seyn,
	Is thorugh a goter, by a pryve wente,
	Into my chaumbre come in al this reyn,
	Unwist of every manere wight, certeyn,
as surely as	Save of myself, as wisly have I joye,
owe to	And by the feith I shal Priam of Troie.
	'And he is come in swich peyne and distresse
	That but he be al fully wood by this
	He sodeynly mot falle into wodenesse,
	But if God helpe, and cause whi this is:
	He seith hym told is of a frend of his
(see n.)	How that ye sholden loven oon that hatte Horaste;
	For sorwe of which this nyght shal ben his laste.'
	Criseyde, which that al this wonder herde,
grow cold	Gan sodeynly aboute hire herte colde
	And with a sik she sorwfully answerde,
believed	'Allas! I wende, who-so tales tolde,
	My deere herte wolde me nought holde
	So lightly fals! Allas, conceytes wronge,
	What harm they don! for now lyve I to longe.
	'Horaste! Allas, and falsen Troilus?
	I knowe hym nowt, God helpe me so!' quod she.
	'Allas, what wikked spirit tolde hym thus?
if	Now certes, em, tomorwe and I hym se,
	I shal therof as ful excusen me
	As evere dide womman, if hym like.'
	And with that word she gan ful soore sike.
happiness	'O God,' quod she, 'so worldly selynesse,
	Which clerkes callen fals felicitee,
mixed together	I-medled is with many a bitternesse!
Full of anxiety	Ful angwissous than is, God woot,' quod she,
	'Condicioun of veyn prosperitee,
not unmixed	For either joies comen nought yfeere,
	Or elles no wight hath hem alwey here.
brittle	'O brotel wele of mannes joie unstable!
	With what wight so thow be, or how thow pleye,
mutable	Either he woot that thow, joie, art muable,
	Or woot it nought – it mot ben oon of tweye.
	Now if he woot it nought, how may he seye
	That he hath verray joie and selynesse
	That is of ignoraunce ay in derknesse?

787 Troilus is said, it seems, to have climbed over the roof along the eaves-trough (**goter**) and made his way into Pandarus's bedroom (where Criseyde is, but cannot see Troilus because of the bed-hangings) by a secret passage (**wente**). This is not true, of course.

797 'you are said to love someone called Orestes'.

813–36 Criseyde is so shocked by the story of Troilus's jealousy (which is of course again quite untrue) that she becomes for a while a Boethian philosopher, meditating and concluding, in the appropriate philosophical language, on the mutability of worldly happiness (*Consolation* II, prose 4).

'Now if he woot that joie is transitorie,
As every joye of worldly thyng mot flee, *Seeing that*
Than every tyme he that hath in memorie,
The drede of lesyng maketh hym that he *losing*
May in no perfit selynesse be,
And if to lese his joie he sette a myte *sets only a small value*
Than semeth it that joie is worth ful lite.

'Wherfore I wol diffyne in this matere *conclude*
That trewely, for aught I kan espie,
Ther is no verray weele in this world heere. *true happiness*
But O thow wikked serpent, jalousie,
Thow mysbyleved and envyous folie *misbelieving*
Why hastow Troilus made to me untriste *distrustful*
That nevere yet agylt hym that I wiste?' *did him wrong*

Quod Pandarus, 'Thus fallen is this cas –'
'Why! Uncle myn,' quod she, 'who tolde hym this?
Why doth my deere herte thus, allas?'
'Ye woot, ye, nece myn,' quod he, 'what is.
I hope al shal be wel that is amys,
For ye may quenche al this if that yow leste – *put an end to*
And doth right so, for I holde it the beste.'

'So shal I do to-morwe, ywys,' quod she,
'And God toforn, so that it shal suffise.' *(so I swear) before God*
'To-morwe? Allas, that were a faire!' quod he; *would be a fine thing*
'Nay, nay, it may nat stonden in this wise,
For, nece myn, thus writen clerkes wise
That peril is with drecchyng in ydrawe; *brought in by delaying*
Nay, swiche abodes ben nought worth an hawe. *delays, hawthorn-berry*

'Nece, al thyng hath tyme, I dar avowe;
For whan a chaumbre afire is or an halle
Wel more nede is it sodeynly rescowe *rescue*
Than to disputen and axe amonges alle
How the candele in the strawe is falle.
A, benedicite! For al among that fare *while all that is going on*
The harm is don, and fare-wel feldefare! *(see n.)*

'And nece myn – ne take it naught a-grief – *don't take offence at this*
If that ye suffre hym al nyght in this wo, *allow him to remain*
God help me so, ye hadde hym nevere lief! *never really loved him*
That dar I seyn, now ther is but we two.
But wel I woot that ye wol nat do so;
Ye ben to wys to doon so gret folie
To putte his lif al nyght in jupertie.'

'Hadde I hym nevere lief? by God, I weene
Ye hadde nevere thyng so lief!' quod she.

861 **fare-wel feldefare**: 'good-bye, thrush' (the bird has flown, it's too late).

'Now by my thrift,' quod he, 'that shal be seene! — *upon my word*
For syn ye make this ensaumple of me, — *(see n.)*
If ich al nyght wolde hym in sorwe se,
For al the tresour in the town of Troie,
I bidde God I nevere mote have joie. — *pray to*

'Now loke thanne, if ye that ben his love
Shul putte his lif al night in jupertie
For thyng of nought, now by that God above
Naught oonly this delay comth of folie
But of malice, if that I shal naught lie.
What! platly and ye suffre hym in destresse, — *plainly if*
Ye neyther bounte don ne gentilesse.'

Quod tho Criseyde, 'Wol ye don o thyng — *one thing*
And ye therwith shal stynte al his disese? — *stop, distress*
Have heere and bereth hym this blewe ryng — *blue*
For ther is nothyng myghte hym bettre plese,
Save I myself, ne more his herte apese,
And sey my deere herte that his sorwe
Is causeles; that shal be sene to-morwe.'

'A ryng?' quod he, 'Ye haselwodes shaken! — *(see n.)*
Ye, nece myn, that ryng moste han a stoon — *gem of magical power*
That myghte dede men alyve maken,
And swich a ryng trowe I that ye have non.
Discrecioun out of youre hed is gon:
That fele I now,' quod he, 'and that is routhe.
O tyme ilost, wel maistow corsen slouthe! — *curse*

'Woot ye not wel that noble and heigh corage
Ne sorweth nought, ne stynteth ek, for lite? — *nor stops grieving*
But if a fool were in a jalous rage,
I nolde setten at his sorwe a myte — *a farthing-coin*
But feffe hym with a fewe wordes white — *bestow, specious and pleasing*
Anothir day whan that I myghte hym fynde;
But this thyng stant al in another kynde.

'This is so gentil and so tendre of herte — *This man*
That with his deth he wol his sorwes wreke; — *avenge*
For trusteth wel, how sore that hym smerte, — *however badly he is hurt*
He wol to yow no jalous wordes speke.
And forthi, nece, er that his herte breke,
So speke youreself to hym of this matere,
For with a word ye may his herte stere. — *steer (back to its normal course)*

'Now have I told what peril he is inne,
And his comynge unwist is to every wight,
Ne, parde, harm may ther be non, ne synne:
I wol myself be with yow al this nyght.

872 **ensaumple of me**: 'comparison with me' (as to how much I love him).

890 'My! You hazel-bushes shake!' (what an earth-shattering suggestion!).

Ye knowe ek how it is youre owen knyght
And that bi right ye moste upon hym triste,
ready And I al prest to fecche hym whan yow liste.'

happening This accident so pitous was to here
at first sight And ek so like a sooth at prime face,
And Troilus hire knyght to hir so deere,
His prive comyng, and the siker place,
That though that she did hym as thanne a grace,
Considered alle thynges as they stoode,
No wonder is, syn she did al for goode.

As surely as Criseyde answerde, 'As wisly God at reste
My soule brynge as me is for hym wo!
And em, iwis, fayn wolde I don the beste
If that ich hadde grace for to do so;
But whether that ye dwelle or for hym go,
a more composed mental state I am, til God me bettre mynde sende,
At dulcarnoun, right at my wittes ende.'

Quod Pandarus, 'Yee, nece, wol ye here?
Dulcarnoun called is "flemyng of wrecches":
learn It semeth hard for wrecches wol nought lere,
faults of will For verray slouthe or other wilfull tecches –
vetches (beans) This is seyd by hem that beth nought worth two fecches;
But ye ben wis, and that we han on honde
nor reasonable to oppose Nis neither hard, ne skilful to withstonde.'

Then 'Than, em,' quod she, 'doth her-of as yow liste.
But er he come I wil first up arise,
And, for love of God, syn al my triste
Is on yow two, and ye ben bothe wise,
So werketh now in so discret a wise
That I may have honour and he plesaunce:
For I am here al in youre governaunce.'

'That is wel seyd,' quod he, 'my nece deere,
And may good prosperity attend Ther good thrift on that wise gentil herte!
stay in bed, receive But liggeth stille and taketh hym right here –
move It nedeth nought no ferther for hym sterte –
And ech of yow ese otheres sorwes smerte,
give thee praise For love of God! And Venus, I the herye;
For soone hope I we shul ben alle merye.'

knees This Troilus ful soone on knees hym sette
Ful sobrely right be hyre beddes hede
And in his beste wyse his lady grette.
But Lord, so she wex sodeynliche rede!

918–24 A glimpse of the working of Criseyde's inner consciousness, with the tumble of *and*-phrases conveying the turmoil of her will; cf. II.451n.

931–3 **At dulcarnoun**: completely perplexed, as if faced with the most difficult proposition in Euclid (the 47th, called 'dulcarnon' in Arabic). Pandarus picks up the nickname of another brain-splitting theorem, the 4th, called **flemyng of wrecches** ('banishment of wretches', i.e. it drives away the miserable wretches who cannot demonstrate the proof) and applies it skilfully to refer to Criseyde's superior understanding.

Ne though men sholde smyten of hire hede — *strike off*
She koude nought a word aright out brynge
So sodeynly for his sodeyn comynge.

But Pandarus, that so wel koude feele — *was so sensitive*
In everythyng, to pleye anon bigan,
And seyde, 'Nece, se how this lord kan knele!
Now, for youre trouthe, se this gentil man!'
And with that word he for a quysshen ran, — *cushion*
And seyde, 'Kneleth now while that yow leste,
There God youre hertes brynge soone at reste!' — *And may God*

Kan I naught seyn, for she bad hym nought rise, — *since she*
If sorwe it putte out of hire remembraunce
Or elles that she took it in the wise — *in the manner*
Of dewete as for his observaunce, — *as part of the honour he owed to her*
But wel fynde I she dede hym this plesaunce,
That she hym kiste, although she siked sore,
And bad hym sitte adown withouten more.

Quod Pandarus, 'Now wol ye wel bigynne, — *(see n.)*
Now doth hym sitte, goode nece deere,
Upon youre beddes syde al ther withinne, — *within the bed-curtains*
That eche of yow the bet may oother heere.'
And with that word he drow hym to the feere, — *withdrew, fire*
And took a light and fond his contenaunce — *composed*
As for to looke upon an old romaunce.

Criseyde, that was Troilus lady right, — *truly*
And clere stood on a grounde of sikernesse, — *clear of blame*
Al thoughte she hire servant and hire knyght
Ne sholde of right non untrouthe in hire gesse, — *suspect*
Yet natheles, considered his distresse
And that love is in cause of swich folie, — *the cause of*
Thus to hym spak she of his jalousie:

'Lo, herte myn, as wolde the excellence — *it was because of*
Of love, ayeins the which that no man may — *against*
Ne oughte ek goodly make resistence, — *properly*
And ek bycause I felte wel and say — *perceived and saw*
Youre grete trouthe and servise every day,
And that youre herte al myn was, soth to seyne –
This drof me for to rewe upon youre peyne.

'And youre goodnesse have I founden alwey yit,
Of which, my deere herte and al my knyght,
I thonke it yow, as fer as I have wit, — *understanding to do so*
Al kan I nought as muche as it were right;

964 **quysshen**. The fetching of the cushion is comical, and is often thought to be comically reductive, but Pandarus's intention is to remind Criseyde of the inappropriate posture in which she allows **this lord** to remain.

974 'Now if you want to get off to a good start'.

979 Pandarus puts on an appropriately absorbed and pensive look, but it is not clear that he actually picks up a book.

to the extent of my knowledge
however much pain it causes me

And I, emforth my connyng and my might,
Have and ay shal, how sore that me smerte,
Ben to yow trewe and hool with al myn herte,

doubtless, when put to the test
provided that you don't get upset
holds
put an end to

'And dredeles that shal be founde at preve.
But, herte myn, what al this is to seyne
Shal wel be told, so that ye nought yow greve
Though I to yow right on youreself compleyne,
For therwith mene I fynaly the peyne
That halt youre herte and myn in hevynesse
Fully to slen and every wrong redresse.

my own
wyvern (snake)
crept
deliver you from
all of him (jealousy), a sliver
refuge, worthy
May Jove, root out

'My goode myn, noot I for-why ne how
That jalousie, allas, that wikked wyvere,
Thus causeles is cropen into yow,
The harm of which I wolde fayn delyvere.
Allas, that he, al hool or of hym slyvere,
Shuld han his refut in so digne a place –
Ther Jove hym sone out of youre herte arace!

originator
godhead
quite free
permissible
allows to exist

'But O, thow Jove, O auctour of nature,
Is this an honour to thi deyte
That folk ungiltif suffren hire injure
And who that giltif is al quyt goth he?
O were it lefull for to pleyn on the,
That undeserved suffrest jalousie,
Of that I wolde upon the pleyne and crie!

are now accustomed
a single, shoved into it
more like, anger
according to, its (proper) name

'Ek al my wo is this, that folk now usen
To seyn right thus, "Ye, jalousie is love!"
And wolde a busshel venym al excusen
For that o greyn of love is on it shove.
But that woot heighe God that sit above,
If it be likere love, or hate, or grame,
And after that it oughte bere his name.

some inkling (of this cause)
regard for duty
in a well-behaved way endures

'But certeyn is, som manere jalousie
Is excusable more than som, iwys;
As whan cause is and som swich fantasie
With piete so wel repressed is
That it unnethe doth or seyth amys
But goodly drynketh up al his distresse –
And that excuse I, for the gentilesse;

plight
anxious care

'And som so ful of furie is and despit
That it sourmounteth his repressioun.
But herte myn, ye be nat in that plit,
That thonke I God; for which youre passioun
I wol nought calle it but illusioun
Of habundaunce of love and besy cure,
That doth youre herte this disese endure.

'Of which I am right sory but nought wrothe;
for the sake of my duty
But for my devoir and youre hertes reste,
trial by ordeal or oath
Wher-so yow list, by ordal or by othe,
sortilege (magical divination)
By sort or in what wise so yow leste,
have it brought to the proof
For love of God, lat preve it for the beste,
And if that I be giltif do me deye!
Allas, what myght I more don or seye?'

With that a fewe brighte teris newe
Owt of hire eighen fille, and thus she seyde,
'Now God, thow woost, in thought ne dede untrewe
To Troilus was nevere yet Criseyde.'
With that here heed down in the bed she leyde,
covered, sighed
And with the sheete it wreigh and sighte soore
And held hire pees: nought o word spak she more.

But now help God to quenchen al this sorwe!
So hope I that he shal, for he best may.
seen
For I have seyn of a ful misty morwe
Folowen ful ofte a myrie someris day,
And after wynter foloweth grene May;
Men sen alday and reden ek in stories
fierce conflicts
That after sharpe shoures ben victories.

This Troilus, whan he hire wordes herde,
Don't spend time thinking about it
Have ye no care, hym liste nought to slepe,
(see n.)
For it thought hym no strokes of a yerde
To heere or seen Criseyde, his lady, wepe;
But wel he felt aboute his herte crepe,
escaped from
For everi tere which that Criseyde asterte,
The crampe of deth to streyne hym by the herte.

And in his mynde he gan the tyme acorse
and the time too that
That he com there and that that he was born;
bad
For now is wikke torned into worse
And al that labour he hath don byforn
was as good as lost
He wende it lost, he thought he nas but lorn.
guile
'O Pandarus,' thoughte he, 'allas, thi wile
alas the day!
Serveth of nought, so weylaway the while!'

And therwithal he heng adown the hede
And fil on knees and sorwfully he sighte.
What myghte he seyn? He felte he nas but dede,
lighten
For wroth was she that sholde his sorwes lighte.
But natheles, whan that he speken myghte,
business
Than seyde he thus, 'God woot that of this game,
Whan al is wist, than am I nought to blame.'

1058–9 As throughout the following scene of love's fulfilment, the narrator takes an unexpected role as an enthusiastic participant in the promotion of the happy event; his zeal is bound to make us feel a little uneasy.

1067 'Being beaten with a stick was nothing compared with it'.

constricted Therwith the sorwe so his herte shette
That from his eyen fil ther nought a tere,
withdrew into itself And every spirit his vigour in knette,
So they astoned or oppressed were.
The felyng of his sorwe or of his fere,
Or of aught elles, fled were out of towne,
in a swoon And down he fel al sodeynly a-swowne.

This was no litel sorwe for to se;
hushed But al was hust and Pandare up as faste:
'O nece, pes, or we be lost!' quod he,
'Beth naught agast!' But certeyn, at the laste,
For this or that, he into bed hym caste,
And seyde, 'O thef, is this a mannes herte?'
tore off his clothes And of he rente al to his bare sherte,

And seyde, 'Nece, but ye helpe us now,
Allas, youre owen Troilus is lorn!'
'Iwis, so wolde I, and I wiste how,
Ful fayn,' quod she. 'Allas, that I was born!'
'Yee, nece, wol ye pullen out the thorn
That stiketh in his herte?' quod Pandare.
(see n.) 'Sey "Al foryeve," and stynte is al this fare!'

'Ye, that to me,' quod she, 'ful levere were
Than al the good the sonne aboute gooth.'
And therwithal she swor hym in his ere,
'Iwys, my dere herte, I am nought wroth,
Have here my trouthe!' – and many another othe.
'Now speke to me, for it am I, Criseyde!'
come out of his swoon But al for nought: yit myght he nought abreyde.

pulse (wrists), palms Therwith his pous and paumes of his hondes
rub They gan to frote, and wete his temples tweyne;
And to deliveren hym fro bittre bondes
She ofte hym kiste; and shortly for to seyne,
call back to life Hym to revoken she did al hire peyne;
And at the laste he gan his breth to drawe
swoon, awaken And of his swough sone after that adawe,

And gan bet mynde and reson to hym take;
abashed But wonder soore he was abayst, iwis,
And with a sike, whan he gan bet awake,
He seyde, 'O mercy, God, what thyng is this?
Why do ye with youreselven thus amys?'
Quod tho Criseyde, 'Is this a mannes game?
What, Troilus, wol ye do thus for shame?'

1088–92 The 'spirits' are those that operate most of the body's vital processes; their power withdrawn, the body goes into a coma. Troilus's swoon (see Mann, 'Troilus's Swoon') is not an indication of his feebleness as a lover but of the deep growth within him of those impulses of loving respect and trust which Criseyde has berated him for apparently lacking. Having fallen in with Pandarus's doubtful strategies, he now finds himself in an impossibly difficult position; so he faints.

1106 'Say "All is forgiven", and an end is put to all this fuss'.

And therwithal hire arm over hym she leyde
kissed And al foryaf and ofte tyme hym keste.
He thonked hire and to hire spak and seyde
As fil to purpos for his herte reste,
And she to that answerde hym as hire leste,
cheer him up And with hire goodly wordes hym disporte
She gan, and ofte his sorwes to comforte.

Quod Pandarus, 'For aught I kan aspien,
This light, nor I, ne serven here of nought.
Light is nought good for sike folkes yen!
But for the love of God, syn ye ben brought
In thus good plit, lat now no hevy thought
Ben hangyng in the hertes of yow tweye' –
fireplace And bar the candel to the chymeneye.

no particular need (for oaths) Soone after this, though it no nede were,
pleased to devise Whan she swiche othes as hire leste devyse
(there was) then no cause of fear Hadde of hym take, hire thoughte tho no fere,
Ne cause ek non to bidde hym thennes rise.
Yet lasse thyng than othes may suffise
In many a cas, for every wyght, I gesse,
That loveth wel, meneth but gentilesse.

for information But in effect she wolde wite anon
Of what man and ek wheer and also why
He jalous was, syn ther was cause non;
(see n.) And ek the sygne that he took it by,
She badde hym that to telle hire bisily,
put it to him Or elles certeyn she bar hym on honde
test That this was don of malice hire to fonde.

Withouten more, shortly for to seyne,
lady's command Hym most obeye unto his lady heste,
had to pretend And for the lasse harm he moste feyne.
He seyde hire, whan she was at swiche a feste,
(on Horaste) She myght on hym han loked at the leste –
(see n.) Noot I nought what, al deere ynough a rysshe,
fish for reasons As he that nedes most a cause fisshe.

even if And she answerde, 'Swete, al were it so,
What harm was that, syn I non yvel mene?
For, by that God that bought us bothe two,
In alle thyng is myn entente cleene.
Swiche argumentes ne ben naught worth a beene.
Wol ye the childissh jalous contrefete?
Now were it worthi that ye were ybete.'

1152 'And also the piece of evidence that had convinced him'.

1161 'I don't know what, not worth paying the cost of a rush-light for' (i.e. worthless).

1165 The reference to Christ's redemption of man slips out naturally in this conventional adjuration. Chaucer attends to the 'historicalness' of the story, but it is impossible for him to avoid anachronism of this kind if he is to represent his characters meaningfully, that is, within the context of a coherent medieval world-view.

1169 **ye were ybete**. The scribe of one MS adds in the margin, 'Ye, with a fether'. He got the point.

Tho Troilus gan sorwfully to sike –
Lest she be wroth, hym thoughte his herte deyde –
And seyde, 'Allas, upon my sorwes sike *(that make me) sick*
Have mercy, swete herte myn, Criseyde!
And if that in tho wordes that I seyde
Be any wrong, I wol no more trespace.
Doth what yow list: I am al in youre grace.'

And she answerde, 'Of gilt misericorde! *(see n.)*
That is to seyn, that I foryeve al this;
And evere more on this nyght yow recorde,
And beth wel war ye do namore amys.'
'Nay, dere herte myn,' quod he, 'iwys!'
'And now,' quod she, 'that I have don yow smerte *caused you pain*
Foryeve it me, myn owene swete herte.'

This Troilus, with blisse of that supprised *suddenly overcome*
Putte al in Goddes hand, as he that mente *being one who*
Nothing but wel and, sodeynly avysed, *on a sudden brainwave*
He hire in armes faste to hym hente. *clasped*
And Pandarus with a ful good entente *in a very happy state of mind*
Leyde hym to slepe and seyde, 'If ye be wise,
Swouneth nought now, lest more folk arise!'

What myghte or may the sely larke seye
Whan that the sperhauk hath hym in his foot? *sparrow-hawk*
I kan namore; but of thise ilke tweye –
To whom this tale sucre be or soot – *sugar, soot (i.e. bitter)*
Though that I tarie a yer, somtyme I moot
After myn auctour tellen hire gladnesse
As wel as I have told hire hevynesse.

Criseyde, which that felte hire thus itake,
As writen clerkes in hire bokes olde,
Right as an aspes leef she gan to quake *aspen's*
Whan she hym felte hire in his armes folde.
But Troilus, al hool of cares colde, *wholly recovered*
Gan thanken tho the bryghte goddes sevene: *(i.e. the planets)*
Thus sondry peynes bryngen folk in hevene.

This Troilus in armes gan hire streyne,
And seyde, 'O swete, as evere mot I gon,
Now be ye kaught, now is ther but we tweyne!
Now yeldeth yow, for other bote is ther non!' *remedy*
To that Criseyde answerde thus anon,
'Ne hadde I er now, my swete herte deere,
Ben yolde, iwys, I were now nought heere.' *yielded*

1177 '(A confession) of guilt (calls for) mercy'.
1188–90 Pandarus is not said to leave the room; but perhaps a kind of decorum is preserved by the enclosure of the bed in its hangings.
1210–11 Criseyde's self-possessed reply makes it clear that she wishes it to be understood that she has not been coerced into consent, and that the narrator's sparrowhawks and larks (1191–2) and Troilus's talk of 'surrender' are old-fashioned male wishful thinking on their part. Whether she was actually coerced or not is a different question.

O sooth is seyd that heled for to be
As of a fevre or other gret siknesse
Men moste drynke, as men may ofte se,
Ful bittre drynke; and for to han gladnesse
endure Men drynken ofte peyne and gret distresse –
series of events I mene it here, as for this aventure,
its happy outcome That thorugh a peyne hath founden al his cure.

And now swetnesse semeth more swete,
To the degree that, experienced That bitternesse assaied was byforn;
float For out of wo in blisse now they flete –
Non swich they felten syn they were born.
than that both should be destroyed Now is this bet than bothe two be lorn?
For love of God, take every womman heede
To werken thus if it comth to the neede.

released, trouble Criseyde, al quyt from every drede and tene,
As she that juste cause hadde hym to triste,
Made hym swich feste it joye was to seene,
honourable intention Whan she his trouthe and clene entente wiste;
tendril And as aboute a tree with many a twiste
encircles and wreathes Bytrent and writhe the swote wodebynde,
Gan ech of hem in armes other wynde.

suddenly startled And as the newe abaysed nyghtyngale,
That stynteth first whan she bygynneth to synge
shepherd speak Whan that she hereth any herde tale
Or in the hegges any wyght stirynge,
And after siker doth hire vois out rynge,
Right so Criseyde, whan hire drede stente,
Opned hire herte and tolde hym hire entente.

And right as he that seth his deth yshapen
according to everything that And dyen mot in ought that he may gesse
rescue enables him to escape And sodeynly rescous doth hym escapen
And from his deth is brought in sykernesse,
For al this world in swych present gladnesse
Was Troilus, and hath his lady swete.
With worse hap God lat us nevere mete!

slender Hire armes smale, hire streghte bak and softe
Hire sydes longe, flesshly, smothe and white
(see n.) He gan to stroke, and good thrift bad ful ofte
Hire snowissh throte, hire brestes rounde and lite.
Thus in this hevene he gan hym to delite
And therwithal a thousand tyme hire kiste,
That what to don for joie unnethe he wiste.

Than seyde he thus: 'O Love, O Charite!
Venus Thi moder ek, Citheria the swete,

1249 **good thrift bad**: 'wished health and happiness to' (greeted warmly).

After thiself next heried be she – [*worshipped*]
Venus mene I, the wel-willy planete – [*benevolent*]
And next that, Imeneus, I the grete, [*Hymen (god of marriage)*]
For nevere man was to yow goddes holde [*so beholden*]
As I, which ye han brought fro cares colde.

'Benigne Love, thow holy bond of thynges,
Whoso wol grace and list the nought honouren, [*wishes for grace*]
Lo, his desire wol fle withouten wynges; [*disappear in a flash*]
For noldestow of bownte hem socouren [*if you would not, goodness, help*]
That serven best and most alwey labouren,
Yet were al lost, that dar I wel seyn, certes,
But if thi grace passed oure desertes. [*unless, surpassed*]

'And for thow me, that leest koude disserve
Of hem that noumbred ben unto thi grace,
Hast holpen, ther I likly was to sterve,
And me bistowed in so heigh a place
That thilke boundes may no blisse pace, [*pass beyond*]
I kan namore; but laude and reverence [*I am speechless (with gratitude)*]
Be to thy bounte and thyn excellence!'

And therwithal Criseyde anon he kiste,
Of which certein she felte no disese, [*dis-ease*]
And thus seyde he: 'Now wolde God I wiste,
Myn herte swete, how I yow myght plese!
What man,' quod he, 'was evere thus at ese
As I, on which the faireste and the beste
That evere I say deyneth hire herte reste? [*saw*]

'Here may men seen that mercy passeth right: [*surpasses justice*]
Th'experience of that is felt in me,
That am unworthi to so swete a wight.
But herte myn, of youre benignite,
So thynk that though that I unworthi be
Yet mot I nede amenden in som wyse [*needs*]
Right thorugh the vertue of youre heigh servyse.

'And for the love of God, my lady deere,
Syn God hath wrought me for I shall yow serve –
As thus I mene: he wol ye be my steere, [*steersman*]
To do me lyve, if that yow liste, or sterve – [*make*]
So techeth me how that I may disserve
Youre thonk, so that I thorugh myn ignoraunce
Ne do no thing that yow be displesaunce.

'For certes, fresshe wommanliche wif,
This dar I seye, that trouth and diligence,

1261–7 This lofty invocation is imitated from the address to the Virgin Mary in Dante, *Paradiso* 33.14–18. The blurring of the Christian into the profane (e.g. 1267, cf. 1282), of the God of creation into the god of love (1254), is characteristic of these epithalamion-like stanzas.

1286–8 Troilus refers to the central belief of the ideal code of love (II.851n).

That shal ye fynden in me al my lif,
N'I wol nat, certein, breken youre defence; *go against your forbidding*
And if I do, present or in absence,
For love of God, lat sle me with the dede *may I be slain in the act*
If that it like unto youre wommanhede.'

'Iwys,' quod she, 'myn owen hertes list *heart's desire*
My ground of ese and al myn herte deere,
Gramercy, for on that is al my trist!
But lat us falle awey fro this matere, *turn aside*
For it suffiseth, this that seyd is heere,
And at o word, withouten repentaunce, *regret*
Welcome, my knyght, my pees, my suffisaunce!'

Of hire delit or joies oon the leeste *or of the very least of their joys*
Were impossible to my wit to seye;
But juggeth ye that han ben at the feste
Of swich gladnesse, if that hem liste pleye!
I kan namore, but thus thise ilke tweye
That nyght, bitwixen drede and sikernesse,
Felten in love the grete worthynesse.

O blisful nyght, of hem so longe isoughte,
How blithe unto hem bothe two thow weere!
Why nad I swich oon with my soule ybought, *Why had I not such a one*
Ye, or the leeste joie that was theere?
Awey, thow foule daunger and thow feere, *woman's coldness towards men*
And lat hem in this hevene blisse dwelle
That is so heigh that al ne kan I telle!

But sooth is, though I kan nat tellen al,
As kan myn auctour of his excellence,
Yet have I seyd, and God toforn, and shal *and (I swear so) before God*
In every thyng, al holly his sentence; *meaning*
And if that ich, at Loves reverence *in the reverence of Love*
Have eny word in-eched for the beste, *added in*
Doth therwithal right as youreselven leste. *(see n.)*

For myne wordes, heere and every parte,
I speke hem alle under correccioun
Of yow that felyng han in loves arte, *truly sensitive understanding*
And putte it al in youre discrecioun
To encresse or maken dymynucioun
Of my langage, and that I yow biseche.
But now to purpos of my rather speche. *point, former*

Thise ilke two, that ben in armes laft,
So loth to hem asonder gon it were, *to part from each other*

1306 Is it possible to detect an inclination on Criseyde's part to call a halt to Troilus's prayers and protestations?
1319–20 As usual, the hyperbolically inappropriate intervention of the narrator (who seems to act for Pandarus, while that character is off-stage, as love's business-manager) serves as much to critique as to heighten the ecstasies of the occasion.
1330 i.e. disregard those bits if you don't like them.

That ech from other wenden ben birafte, — *thought it was like being torn apart*
Or elles – lo, this was hir mooste feere –
That al this thyng but nyce dremes were;
For which ful ofte ech of hem seyde, 'O swete,
Clippe ich yow thus or elles I it meete?' — *Embrace, do I dream it*

And Lord! so he gan goodly on hire se — *lovingly, look*
That nevere his look ne bleynte from hire face, — *turned away*
And seyde, 'O deere herte, may it be
That it be soth that ye ben in this place?'
'Yee, herte myn, God thank I of his grace,'
Quod tho Criseyde, and therwithal hym kiste,
That where his spirit was for joie he nyste.

This Troilus ful ofte hire eyen two
Gan for to kisse, and seyde, 'O eyen clere, — *bright*
It weren ye that wroughte me swich wo,
Ye humble nettes of my lady deere!
Though ther be mercy writen in youre cheere, — *in the expression (of your eyes)*
God woot, the text ful hard is, soth, to fynde!
How koude ye withouten bond me bynde?'

Therwith he gan hire faste in armes take
And wel an hundred tymes gan he syke –
Naught swich sorwfull sikes as men make
For wo, or elles when that folk ben sike,
But esy sykes, swiche as ben to like, — *are pleasing*
That shewed his affeccioun withinne:
Of swich sikes koude he nought blynne. — *cease*

Soone after this they spake of sondry thynges
As fel to purpos of this aventure, — *came to mind as being relevant to*
And pleyinge entrechaungeden hire rynges,
Of whiche I kan nought tellen no scripture; — *writing (inscriptions on the rings)*
But wel I woot a broche, gold and asure,
In which a rubye set was lik an herte,
Criseyde hym yaf, and stak it on his sherte. — *pinned*

Lord, trowe ye a coveytous or a wrecche,
That blameth love and halt of it despite, — *holds it in*
That of tho pens that he kan mokre and cretche — *pence, rake in and scrape together*
Was evere yit y-yeven hym swich delite — *given*
As is in love, in o poynt, in som plite? — *in one single detail, in some way*
Nay, douteles, for also God me save,
So perfit joie may no nygard have.

They wol seyn 'Yis,' but Lord, so they lye, — *how they lie*
Tho besy wrecches, ful of wo and drede! — *anxious*
Thei callen love a woodnesse or folie, — *madness*
But it shall falle hem as I shal yow rede: — *befall, tell*
They shal forgon the white and ek the rede — *lose everything (wine?)*
And lyve in wo, ther God yeve hem meschaunce, — *may God give them*
And every lovere in his trouthe avaunce!

Would to God	As wolde God tho wrecches that dispise
ears	Servise of love hadde erys also longe
Midas (see WBP 951)	As hadde Mida, ful of coveytise,
	And therto dronken hadde as hoot and stronge
wrongful desires	As Crassus didde for his affectis wronge,
in the wrong	To techen hem that they ben in the vice
(they *are 'tho wrecches'*)	And loveres nought, although they holde hem nyce.
	Thise ilke two of whom that I yow seye,
	Whan that hire hertes wel assured were,
	Tho gonne they to speken and to pleye
	And ek rehercen how and whan and where
got to know each other	Thei knewe hem first, and every wo or feere
	That passed was; but al swich hevynesse –
	I thank it God – was torned to gladnesse.
they happened	And evere-mo when that hem fel to speke
	Of anythyng of swich a tyme agoon,
should be broken off	With kissyng al that tale sholde breke
	And fallen in a newe joye anoon;
together	And diden al hire myght, syn they were oon,
	For to recoveren blisse and ben at eise,
past unhappiness, counterbalance	And passed wo with joie contrepeise.
It is not reasonable	Resoun wol nought that I speke of slepe,
	For it acordeth nought to my matere.
heed	God woot, they took of that ful litel kepe!
	But lest this nyght that was to hem so deere
	Ne sholde in veyn escape in no manere,
employed, activity	It was byset in joie and bisynesse
has to do with	Of al that souneth into gentilesse.
public	But whan the cok, comune astrologer,
	Gan on his brest to bete and after crowe,
the morning star (Venus)	And Lucyfer, the dayes messanger,
	Gan for to rise and out hire bemes throwe,
recognize	And estward roos (to hym that koude it knowe)
immediately upon that	*Fortuna Major* – that anoon Criseyde
	With herte soor to Troilus thus seyde:
trust	'Myn hertes lif, my trist, al my plesaunce,
	That I was born, allas, what me is wo
	That day of us moot make disseveraunce!
	For tyme it is to ryse and hennes go
	Or ellis I am lost for evere mo!
hover	O nyght, allas, why nyltow over us hove
	As longe as whan Almena lay by Jove?

1390 Crassus was slain by having molten gold poured into his mouth because of his greed.

1420 ***Fortuna Major*** is the name of a sign in geomancy, a magical art of divination, that was used to refer to a particular group of stars. Chaucer fetches his reference from Dante (*Purgatorio* 19.4–5), and seems pleased to draw attention to the unusualness of his allusion.

1422–1533 The lovers' lament at the approach of dawn (the *aube*) is a tradition of European love-poetry from Ovid (*Amores* 1.13) to Donne ('Busy old fool, unruly Sun!...').

1428 **Almena**: Alcmena, mother of Hercules, for whom Jove extended the night.

	'O blake nyght, as folk in bokes rede,
	That shapen art by God this world to hide
garment	At certeyn tymes wyth thi derke wede,
	That under that men myghte in reste abide,
	Wel oughten bestes pleyne and folk the chide
how till we break	That there as day wyth labour wolde us breste
deignest not to grant us	That thow thus fleest and deynest us nought reste.
too briskly	'Thow doost, allas, to shortly thyn office,
hasty, May God, nature	Thow rakle nyght! Ther God, maker of kynde,
Thee, unnatural	The for thyn haste and thyn unkynde vice
	So faste ay to oure hemysperie bynde
turn	That nevere more under the ground thow wynde!
	For now, for thow so hiest out of Troie,
	Have I forgon thus hastili my joie!'
	This Troilus, that with tho wordes felte,
piteous	As thoughte hym tho, for pietous distresse
	The blody teris from his herte melte,
	As he that nevere yet swich hevynesse
Experienced, following upon	Assayed hadde, out of so gret gladnesse,
	Gan therwithal Criseyde, his lady deere,
	In armes streyne, and seyde in this manere:
exposer	'O cruel day, accusour of the joie
hidden	That nyght and love han stole and faste iwryen,
	Acorsed be thi comyng into Troye
chink	For every bore hath oon of thi bryghte yen!
why does it please you	Envyous day, what list the so to spien?
do you seek out	What hastow lost? Why sekestow this place?
May God	Ther God thi light so quenche, for his grace!
how, offended	'Allas, what have thise loveris the agylt,
Cruel	Dispitous day? Thyn be the peyne of helle!
	For many a lovere hastow slayn, and wilt:
staring (poring)	Thy pourynge in wol nowher lat hem dwelle.
Why do you offer	What profrestow thi light here for to selle?
(i.e. who require good light)	Go selle it hem that smale selys grave –
	We wol the nought, us nedeth no day have.'
	And ek the sonne, Titan, gan he chide,
	And seyde, 'O fool, wel may men the dispise
(see n.)	That hast the dawyng al nyght by thi syde
from thee	And suffrest hire so soone up fro the rise
annoy	For to disese loveris in this wyse.
thy Morning-Dawn (Aurora)	What, holde youre bed ther, thow, and ek thi Morwe!
pray	I bidde God so yeve yow bothe sorwe!'
sighed	Therwith ful soore he syghte and thus he seyde:
	'My lady right and of my wele or wo

1466 **the dawyng**: dawn (Aurora, whose lover Tithonus here merges with Titan).

The welle and roote, O goodly myn, Criseyde, *source*
And shal I rise, allas, and shal I so?
Now fele I that myn herte moot a-two, *must break in two*
For how sholde I my lif an houre save
Syn that with yow is al the lif ich have?

'What shal I don? For, certes, I not how *I do not know how*
Ne whan, allas, I shal the tyme see
That in this plit I may ben eft with yow; *situation, again*
And of my lif, God woot how that shal be,
Syn that desire right now so biteth me *holds me in its grip*
That I am ded anon but I retourne.
How sholde I longe, allas, fro yow sojourne?

'But natheles, myn owen lady bright,
Were it so that I wiste outrely *absolutely*
That I, youre humble servant and youre knyght,
Were in youre herte iset so fermely
As ye in myn – the which thyng trewely
Me levere were than thise worldes tweyne – *two such worlds as this*
Yet sholde I bet enduren al my peyne.'

To that Criseyde answerde right anon,
And with a sik she seyde, 'O herte deere,
The game, ywys, so ferforth now is gon *is advanced*
That first shal Phebus fallen fro his speere *sphere*
And everich egle ben the dowves feere *companion*
And everich roche out of his place sterte *rock*
Er Troilus oute of Criseydes herte.

'Ye ben so depe in-with myn herte grave
That though I wolde it torne out of my thought,
As wisly verray God my soule save, *As sure as*
To dyen in the peyne, I koude nought. *Even if I were made to die by torture*
And for the love of God that us hath wrought
Lat in youre brayn non other fantasie
So crepe that it cause me to dye!

'And that ye me wolde han as faste in mynde
As I have yow, that wolde I yow biseche;
And if I wiste sothly that to fynde, *that I would find that to be true*
God myght nought a poynt my joies eche. *in a single detail, add to*
But herte myn, withouten more speche,
Beth to me trewe, or ellis were it routhe,
For I am thyn, by God and by my trouthe!

'Beth glad, forthy, and lyve in sikernesse! *therefore*
Thus seyde I nevere er this ne shal to mo; *to others*
And if to yow it were a gret gladnesse
To torne ayeyn soone after that ye go, *come back again*
As fayn wolde I as ye it were so,
As wisly God myn herte brynge to reste!' *As surely as*
And hym in armes tok and ofte keste.

	Agayns his wil, sith it mot nedes be,
clothed	This Troilus up ros and faste hym cledde
	And in his armes took his lady free
	An hondred tyme and on his wey hym spedde,
	And with swich wordes as his herte bledde
	He seyde, 'Farewel, my dere herte swete:
May God, sound (in health)	Ther God us graunte sownde and soone to mete!'
	To which no word for sorwe she answerde,
affect	So soore gan his partyng hire distreyne;
	And Troilus unto his paleys ferde
	As wo-bygon as she was, soth to seyne.
wrung (tortured)	So harde hym wrong of sharp desire the peyne
	For to ben eft there he was in plesaunce
	That it may nevere out of his remembraunce.
royal	Retorned to his real paleys soone,
	He softe into his bed gan for to slynke,
	To slepe longe as he was wont to doone.
close his eyes	But al for nought: he may wel ligge and wynke,
	But slep ne may ther in his herte synke,
burned	Thynkyng how she for whom desir hym brende
	A thousand-fold was worth more than he wende.
turn over (in his memory)	And in his thought gan up and down to wynde
every look on her face	Hire wordes alle and every countenaunce
	And fermely impressen in his mynde
	The leeste point that to him was plesaunce;
	And verraylich of thilke remembraunce
burnt, desire to increase	Desire al newe hym brende, and lust to brede
(i.e. yet he went on remembering)	Gan more than erst, and yet took he non hede.
	Criseyde also, right in the same wyse,
shut (treasure up)	Of Troilus gan in hire herte shette
eager desire	His worthynesse, his lust, his dedes wise,
	His gentilesse, and how she with hym mette,
	Thonkyng Love he so wel hire bisette,
	Desiryng eft to han hire herte deere
situation as, make him welcome	In swich a plite she dorste make hym cheere.
who in the morning	Pandare o-morwe which that comen was
	Unto his nece and gan hire faire grete,
	Seyde, 'Al this nyght so reyned it, allas,
	That al my drede is that ye, nece swete,
leisure	Han litel laiser had to slepe and mete.
	Al nyght,' quod he, 'hath reyn so do me wake
	That som of us, I trowe, hire hedes ake.'

1555 It is still not entirely clear where Pandarus has been all night.

1561 **hedes ake**. The *double entendre* could hardly be missed, and Criseyde's half-serious accusation and half-pretended shame, and readiness to be intimate again with her uncle, all likewise speak of a close and familiar understanding.

And ner he com and seyde, 'How stant it now
This mury morwe? Nece, how kan ye fare?' *How are you doing?*
Criseyde answerde, 'Nevere the bet for yow,
Fox that ye ben! God yeve youre herte kare!
God help me so, ye caused al this fare. *business*
Trowe I,' quod she, 'for al youre wordes white, *innocent-sounding*
O, who-so seeth yow, knoweth yow ful lite.'

With that she gan hire face for to wrye *cover*
With the shete and wax for shame al reede,
And Pandarus gan under for to prie, *peer*
And seyde, 'Nece, if that I shal be dede,
Have here a swerd and smyteth of myn hede!'
With that his arm al sodeynly he thriste
Under hire nekke and at the laste hire kyste.

I passe al that which chargeth nought to seye. *is not important to talk about*
What! God foryaf his deth, and she al so *in just the same way*
Foryaf, and with here uncle gan for to pleye,
For other cause was ther noon but so. *there was no reason to do otherwise*
But of this thing right to the effect to go: *to the point*
Whan tyme was, hom til here hous she wente,
And Pandarus hath fully his entente. *fully achieved his objective*

{The lovers continue happily in their secret love-affair for three years.}

{Book IV begins with the request of Calchas, Criseyde's father, that his daughter be returned to him in exchange for the captured Antenor. The arrangement is ratified at the Trojan parliament, at which Troilus is present but obliged to remain silent. He is cast into despair, returns home to lament his fate, and is not much comforted by Pandarus's airy consolations, nor impressed by his casual plan to abduct Criseyde by force. His fate, as he tells us at length in a Boethian soliloquy, is predetermined and inescapable. But he meets again with Criseyde, who has heard the news of the exchange and is distracted with grief, and, after he has tentatively suggested they might steal away together, they tearfully agree to her plan that she shall seek to return to Troy after ten days. The exchange with Antenor is made at the beginning of Book V, and Criseyde is handed over to the Greek Diomede, who begins his subtle and accustomed campaign of seduction. Troilus is left to grieve and yearn and hope while the ten days pass.}

Book V

But for to tellen forth of Diomede:
It fel that after, on the tenthe day *befell*
Syn that Criseyde out of the citee yede, *went*
This Diomede, as fressh as braunche in May,
Come to the tente ther as Calkis lay
And feyned hym with Calkas han to doone – *to have business*
But what he mente I shal yow tellen soone.

Criseyde, at shorte wordes for to telle,
Welcomed hym and down hym by hire sette –
And he was ethe ynough to maken dwelle! *easy*

1577 **God foryaf his deth**. This comparison of Criseyde's forgiveness to Christ's forgiveness of those who crucified him (Luke 23:34) may suggest that the narrator's enthusiasm has finally tipped the scales of his sanity, but Christian terms and ideas are often employed in the medieval language of love (in a manner that a modern reader might think improper), and this comparison was commonplace.

delay
spiced cakes, brought
together

And after this, withouten longe lette,
The spices and the wyne men forth hem fette,
And forth they speke of this and that yfeere,
As frendes don, of which som shal ye heere.

fell to talking
manners

He gan first fallen of the werre in speche
Bitwixen hem and the folk of Troie town,
And of th'assege he gan hire ek biseche
To tellen hym what was hire opynyoun;
Fro that demaunde he so descendeth down
To axen hire if that hire straunge thoughte
The Grekis gise and werkes that they wroughte,

understanding

And whi hire fader tarieth so longe
To wedden hire unto som worthy wight.
Criseyde, that was in hire peynes stronge
For love of Troilus, hire owen knyght,
As ferforth as she konnyng hadde or myght
Answerde hym so; but as of his entente,
It semed nat she wiste what he mente.

Grew more sure of himself

But natheles, this ilke Diomede
Gan in hymself assure, and thus he seyde:
'If ich aright have taken of yow hede,
Me thynketh thus, O lady myn Criseyde,
That syn I first hond on youre bridel leyde,
Whan ye out come of Troie by the morwe,
Ne koude I nevere sen yow but in sorwe.

Except that, may be
distress

'Kan I nat seyn what may the cause be
But if for love of som Troian it were,
The which right sore wolde athynken me
That ye for any wight that dwelleth there
Sholden spille a quarter of a tere
Or pitously youreselven so bigile –
For dredeles, it is nought worth the while.

as one might say, one and all

'The folk of Troie, as who seyth, alle and some
In prisoun ben, as ye youreselven se,
Nor thennes shal nat oon on-lyve come
For al the gold atwixen sonne and se.
Trusteth wel and understondeth me
Ther shal nat oon to mercy gon on-lyve,
Al were he lord of worldes twies fyve!

vengeance, abducting
gods of the lower world and of death
destroy

'Swich wreche on hem for fecchynge of Eleyne
Ther shal ben take er that we hennes wende
That Manes, which that goddes ben of peyne,
Shal ben agast that Grekes wol hem shende,
And men shul drede unto the worldes ende
From hennesforth to ravysshen any queene,
So cruel shal oure wreche on hem be seene.

mislead, ambiguities 'And but if Calkas lede us with ambages –
That is to seyn, with double wordes slye,
Swiche as men clepen a word with two visages –
Ye shal wel knowen that I naught ne lye
And al this thyng right sen it with youre eye,
And that anon, ye nyl nat trowe how sone:
what will certainly happen Now taketh hede, for it is for to doone.

'What, wene ye youre wise fader wolde
Han yeven Antenor for yow anon
If he ne wiste that the cite sholde
Destroied ben? Whi, nay, so mote I gon!
He knew ful wel ther shal nat scapen oon
That Troian is; and for the grete feere
He dorste nat ye dwelte lenger there.

'What wol ye more, lufsom lady deere?
Lat Troie and Troian fro youre herte pace!
Drif out that bittre hope and make good cheere
summon back And clepe ayeyn the beaute of youre face
That ye with salte teris so deface,
For Troie is brought in swich a jupartie
That it to save is now no remedie.

'And thenketh wel ye shal in Grekis fynde
lover A moore parfit love, er it be nyght,
Than any Troian is, and more kynde,
And bet to serven yow wol don his myght.
And if ye vouche-sauf, my lady bright,
I wol ben he to serven yow myselve,
Yee, levere than be lord of Greces twelve!'

And with that word he gan to waxen rede
trembled And in his speche a litel wight he quoke
a little bit And caste asyde a litel wight his hede
shook himself as if from a reverie And stynte a while; and afterward he woke,
with an air of seriousness And sobreliche on hire he threw his loke,
And seyde, 'I am, al be it yow no joie,
As gentil man as any wight in Troie.

'For if my fader Tideus,' he seyde,
'Ilyved hadde, ich hadde ben er this
Calydon and Argos Of Calydoyne and Arge a kyng, Criseyde.
And so hope I that I shal yet, iwis.
But he was slayn – allas, the more harm is! –
Unfortunately, all too soon Unhappily at Thebes al to rathe,
Polynices, to the great harm of Polymyte and many a man to scathe.

'But herte myn, syn that I am youre man –
you are And ben the first of whom I seche grace –

939 **herte myn**. Diomede's confidence in the progress of his campaign is accurately measured in his increasingly intimate forms of address.

(your man vowed) to serve — To serve yow as hertely as I kan
And evere shal whil I to lyve have space,
Provided that — So, er that I departe out of this place,
Ye wol me graunte that I may to-morwe
At bettre leyser telle yow my sorwe.'

What sholde I telle his wordes that he seyde?
most — He spak inough for o day at the meeste.
It's well shown in the event — It preveth wel: he spak so that Criseyde
Graunted on the morwe, at his requeste,
For to speken with hym at the leeste –
(see n.) — So that he nolde speke of swich matere.
And thus to hym she seyde, as ye mowe here,

As she that hadde hire herte on Troilus
root out — So faste that ther may it non arace,
as to a stranger — And strangely she spak, and seyde thus:
'O Diomede, I love that ilke place
Ther I was born; and Joves for his grace
Delyvere it soone of al that doth it care!
grant — God, for thy myght, so leve it wel to fare!

'That Grekis wolde hire wrath on Troie wreke
If that they myght I knowe it wel, iwis;
But it shal naught byfallen as ye speke,
I swear in the sight of God — And God toforn! And forther overe this,
full of good counsel — I woot my fader wys and redy is,
And that he me hath bought, as ye me tolde,
beholden — So deere, I am the more unto hym holde.

'That Grekis ben of heigh condicioun
I woot ek wel; but certeyn, men shal fynde
As worthi folk withinne Troie town,
As konnyng and as parfit and as kynde
Orkneys, India (ends of the earth) — As ben bitwixen Orkades and Inde;
And that ye koude wel yowre lady serve,
I trowe ek wel, hire thank for to deserve.

'But as to speke of love, ywis,' she seyde,
'I hadde a lord, to whom I wedded was,
The whos myn herte al was, til that he deyde;
And other love, as help me now Pallas,
Ther in myn herte nys ne nevere was.
family — And that ye ben of noble and heigh kynrede,
I have wel herd it tellen, out of drede.

951 'So long as he would not speak of such matters (as he had just been broaching)'.

956–7 Since she cannot speak of Troilus, Criseyde speaks of her love for Troy, paying her private respect to love's memory in a way that will not compromise her present situation.

960–73 Criseyde takes up Diomede's points one by one.

974–80 Criseyde seems to transfer her love for Troilus to her dead husband, burying the two, so to speak, in the same grave, so as to leave options open for the future. The acknowledgement of Diomede's breeding follows interestingly.

causes | 'And that doth me to han so grete a wonder
treat with such disrespect | That ye wol scornen any womman so.
Ek, God woot, love and I ben fer ysonder!
I am disposed bet, so mot I go,
Unto my deth to pleynen and maken wo.
What I shal after don I kan nat seye;
engage in talk of love | But trewelich, as yet me list nat pleye.

'Myn herte is now in tribulacioun,
And ye in armes bisy day by day.
Herafter, whan ye wonnen han the town,
Perhaps | Peraunter then, so it happen may,
what I never saw before | That whan I se that nevere er I say
Than wol I werke that I nevere wroughte.
This word to yow ynough suffisen oughte.

'To-morwe ek wol I speken with yow fayn,
So that ye touchen naught of this matere.
And whan yow list ye may come here ayayn;
And er ye gon thus muche I sey yow here:
bright hair | As help me Pallas with hire heres clere,
If that I sholde of any Greke han routhe,
It sholde be youreselven, by my trouthe!

'I say nat therfore that I wol yow love,
Nor am I saying | N'I say nat nay; but in conclusioun,
I mene wel, by God that sit above!'
And therwithal she caste hire eyen down,
And gan to sike, and seyde, 'O Troie town,
pray | Yet bidde I God in quiete and in reste
make my heart break | I may yow sen, or do myn herte breste.'

in the event | But in effect, and shortly for to seye,
This Diomede al fresshly new ayeyn
Gan pressen on and faste hire mercy preye;
And after this, the sothe for to seyn,
Hire glove he took, of which he was ful feyn;
had become evening | And finaly, whan it was woxen eve
And al was wel, he roos and tok his leve.

The brighte Venus folwede and ay taughte
The wey ther brode Phebus down alighte,
(see n.) | And Cynthea hire chare-hors overe-raughte
To whirle out of the Leoun, if she myghte,
And Signifer his candels sheweth brighte

986 **What I shal after don**. Criseyde makes it clear that her inclination to spend the rest of her life in lamentation will not last for ever.

990 The winning of the town is now an accepted fact in Criseyde's calculation of the matter.

1006 **Troie town**. Troilus is now incorporated, even in the private thoughts that Criseyde allows herself, into the stones of Troy.

1016–20 **Venus**, the evening star, shows the way for **Phebus**, the sun (**brode**, enlarged in appearance as it sets), to sink to the horizon, while **Cynthea**, the moon, hastens to pass out of the sign of Leo (Criseyde had promised to return before the moon left Leo, IV.1590–6), and **Signifer**, the sign-bearer, or Zodiac, shows forth his **candels** or stars.

1018 'reached over (to urge on) her chariot-horses'.

Whan that Criseyde unto hire bedde wente
Inwith hire fadres faire brighte tente,

Turning over Retornyng in hire soule ay up and down
The wordes of this sodeyn Diomede,
His grete estat, and perel of the town,
And that she was allone and hadde nede
Of frendes help – and thus bygan to brede
The cause whi, the sothe for to telle,
That she took fully purpos for to dwelle.

truthfully The morwen come and, gostly for to speke,
This Diomede is come unto Criseyde;
interrupt (with impatience) And shortly, lest that ye my tale breke,
So wel he for hymselven spak and seyde
made to subside That alle hire sikes soore adown he leyde;
And finaly, the sothe for to seyne,
relieved, the main part He refte hire of the grete of alle hire peyne.

And after this the storie telleth us
That she hym yaf the faire baye stede
The which he ones wan of Troilus;
And ek a broche – and that was litel nede –
That was Troilus's That Troilus was, she yaf this Diomede,
And ek the bet from sorwe hym to releve
(see n.) She made hym were a pencel of hire sleve.

I fynde ek in the stories elleswhere,
Whan thorugh the body hurt was Diomede
Of Troilus, tho wepte she many a teere
Whan that she saugh hise wyde wowndes blede,
And that she took to kepen hym good hede,
painful And for to helen hym of his sorwes smerte,
I don't know Men seyn – I not – that she yaf hym hire herte.

But trewely the storie telleth us
Ther made nevere womman moore wo
Than she whan that she falsed Troilus.
She seyde, 'Allas, for now is clene ago
My name of trouthe in love for everemo!
For I have falsed oon the gentileste
That evere was, and oon the worthieste!

'Allas, of me, unto the worldes ende,
Shal neyther ben ywriten nor ysonge
destroy No good word, for thise bokes wol me shende.
O, rolled shal I ben on many a tonge!

1023–7 The tumble of paratactic clauses (cf. II.451n) conveys something of the overwhelming accumulation of circumstances that Criseyde feels herself faced with, as well as the strategic indeterminacies by which she comes to the conclusion that her decision is inevitable.

1038 **faire baye stede**. Chaucer forgets to explain how Diomede had earlier given this horse to Criseyde.

1043 'She made him wear her sleeve as a pennon (on his lance)'.

Thorughout the world my belle shal be ronge;
And wommen moost wol haten me of alle.
befall Allas, that swich a cas me sholde falle!

as the fault is in me 'Thei wol seyen, in as muche as in me is,
I have hem don dishonour, weylaway!
Al be I nat the first that dide amys,
What helpeth that to don my blame awey?
But syn I se ther is no bettre way
And that to late is now for me to rewe,
at any rate To Diomede algate I wol be trewe.

'But, Troilus, syn I no bettre may,
part And syn that thus departen ye and I,
Yet prey I God, so yeve yow right good day,
As for the gentileste, trewely,
saw That evere I say, to serven feythfully,
And best kan ay his lady honour kepe.'
burst And with that word she brast anon to wepe.

'And certes yow ne haten shal I nevere,
And frendes love, that shal ye han of me,
even if I should live forever And my good word, al sholde I lyven evere.
And trewely I wolde sory be
For to seen yow in adversitee;
And gilteles, I woot wel, I yow leve.
But al shal passe; and thus take I my leve.'

as an interval until But trewely how longe it was bytwene
That she forsok hym for this Diomede,
Ther is non auctour telleth it, I wene.
Take every man now to his bokes heede,
specified period of time He shal no terme fynden, out of drede;
woo For though that he bigan to wowe hire soone,
Er he hire wan yet was ther more to doone.

Ne me ne list this sely womman chyde
Forther than the storye wol devyse.
Hire name, allas, is punysshed so wide
That for hire gilt it oughte ynough suffise.
And if I myghte excuse hire any wise,
For she so sory was for hire untrouthe,
Iwis, I wolde excuse hire yet for routhe.

{Criseyde does not again appear in person, though we read, with Troilus, her letter of glutinous self-exculpation. Troilus, after racking himself with hope, finally sadly acknowledges, when he sees on Diomede's armour the brooch

1062 **my belle shal be ronge**: a proverbial expression, alluding to the way gossip noises abroad a scandalous story. It may have inspired Henryson's cruel sequel, *The Testament of Cresseid*, where Criseyde, already a by-word for fickleness and inconstancy in the pre-Chaucerian story of Troy, is punished with leprosy (lepers had to carry a bell to announce their presence).

1085 **and thus take I my leve**. Criseyde's exit, like her whole performance in these stanzas, is stagey, self-performing, unwinning. What she has lost, through her accommodation with Diomede, understandable as it is in the circumstances, is already evident.

1093–9 The narrator, attendant as ever to *sentement*, attempts to cloud Criseyde's responsibility for her actions in a haze of extenuation, though he succeeds only in making her behaviour seem worse – even he can find no excuse.

that he gave to Criseyde, that all is lost: 'Thorugh which I se that clene out of youre mynde / Ye han me cast – and I ne kan ne may, / For al this world, withinne myn herte fynde / To unloven yow a quarter of a day!' V.1695–8). Pandarus, whose strategies are for fair weather only, has long been reduced to bewildered and cynical irrelevance.}

Gret was the sorwe and pleynte of Troilus,
But forth hire cours Fortune ay gan to holde.
Criseyde loveth the sone of Tideus,
And Troilus moot wepe in cares colde.
Swich is this world, who-so it kan byholde:
In ech estat is litel hertes reste.
grant God leve us for to take it for the beste.

In many cruel bataille, out of drede,
Of Troilus, this ilke noble knyght,
As men may in thise olde bokes rede,
Was seen his knyghthod and his grete myght;
And dredeles, his ire, day and nyght,
paid for Ful cruwely the Grekis ay aboughte;
And alwey moost this Diomede he soughte.

And ofte tyme I fynde that they mette
With blody strokes and with wordes grete,
sharpened Assayinge how hire speres weren whette;
passion of rage And, God it woot, with many a cruel hete
Gan Troilus upon his helm to bete!
But natheles Fortune it naught ne wolde
Of oothers hond that eyther deyen sholde.

undertaken And if I hadde ytaken for to write
The armes of this ilke worthi man,
Than wolde ich of his batailles endite;
But for that I to writen first bigan
Of his love, I have seyde as I kan –
His worthi dedes, who-so list hem heere,
Rede Dares, he kan telle hem alle ifeere –

Bysechyng every lady bright of hewe
And every gentil womman, what she be,
That al be that Criseyde was untrewe
That for that gilt she be nat wroth with me.
Ye may hire giltes in other bokes se;
And gladlier I wol write, yif yow leste,
Penelopes trouthe and good Alceste.

1771 **Dares**: Dares Phrygius, supposedly the original Trojan author of a Latin prose history of Troy very popular in the Middle Ages.

1772–1869 There are many contradictions and cross-currents in this remarkable 'Epilogue', and it has been much discussed. It is hard not to see it as some kind of 'palinode', in which Chaucer, forced to find a meaningful frame for his story of love's joy and loss, can in the end only reject its implied values and lock it into the grid of Christian transcendence.

1778 Penelope was the faithful wife of Odysseus, and Alceste of Admetus. The latter is the heroine of the Prologue to *The Legend of Good Women*, Chaucer's next poem, which he seems to be anticipating. His pretence there that he is called to task and has to do penance for writing ill of women is a charge he addresses here by disclaiming responsibility and attempting to ingratiate himself with women by claiming, rather disingenuously in the circumstances, that it is men who are the real villains.

in relation to men	N'I sey nat this al oonly for thise men,
betrayed	But moost for wommen that bitraised be
	Thorugh false folk – God yeve hem sorwe, amen! –
	That with hire grete wit and subtilite
moves	Bytraise yow. And this commeveth me
	To speke, and in effect yow alle I preye,
	Beth war of men and herkneth what I seye.
	Go, litel boke, go, litel myn tragedye,
And may God	Ther God thi makere yet, er that he dye,
compose	So sende myght to make in som comedye!
no writing of poetry	But litel book, no makyng thow n'envie,
But humble yourself, poetry	But subgit be to alle poyesye,
pass	And kis the steppes where as thow seest pace
Statius	Virgile, Ovide, Omer, Lucan, and Stace.
	And for ther is so gret diversite
	In Englissh and in writyng of oure tonge,
	So prey I to God that non myswrite the,
	Ne the mysmetre for defaute of tonge;
read, or else recited	And red wherso thow be, or elles songe,
understood	That thow be understonde, God I biseche!
earlier	But yet to purpos of my rather speche.
	The wrath, as I bigan yow for to seye,
	Of Troilus the Grekis boughten deere,
	For thousandes his hondes maden deye,
	As he that was withouten any peere
	Save Ector, in his tyme, as I kan heere.
except that it was God's will	But weilawey – save only Goddes wille –
In scornful wrath, slew	Despitously hym slough the fierse Achille.
	And whan that he was slayn in this manere,
light (not heavy with earth) spirit	His lighte goost ful blisfully is went
hollow inner concavity	Up to the holughnesse of the eighthe spere,
(see n.)	In convers letyng everich element;
quite open to his inspection	And ther he saugh with ful avysement
wandering (i.e. the planets)	The erratik sterres, herkenyng armonye
(the music of the spheres)	With sownes ful of hevenyssh melodie.
intently, contemplate	And down from thennes faste he gan avyse
	This litel spot of erthe that with the se
	Embraced is, and fully gan despise

1786–92 The closing address to the **litel boke** is a 'modesty-topos' of great antiquity, and as such enables Chaucer to set his work, with extraordinary audacity, beside that of the great classical writers (two of them, Homer and Lucan, no more than names to him). He imagines them passing in dignified procession, with his book following eagerly and kissing their footprints (**steppes**).

1788 This **comedye** has often been thought to be the earliest premonition of the *Canterbury Tales*.

1793–6 Chaucer imagines scribes miscopying or mistaking the metre because of the deficiency of their own dialect (**for defaute of tonge**). His fears were to be fully realized: the secret of his metre, particularly his use of sounded final *e*, was lost during the fifteenth century and not rediscovered until the eighteenth.

1807–27 It is Arcite who ascends to the eighth (*ottava*) sphere in Boccaccio's epic of Theseus, the *Teseida*. Chaucer does not use the passage in his reworking of the *Teseida* in the Knight's Tale (written before *Troilus*), and therefore has it available to provide an apotheosis of sorts for Troilus. The **eighthe spere** (most MSS read *seventhe*, but an early mistake with roman numerals would account for that) is that of the fixed stars (see *PF* 59n).

1810 'Leaving on the reverse (convex) side every planetary sphere'.

This wrecched world, and held al vanite
In respect of, full | To respect of the pleyn felicite
That is in hevene above; and at the laste,
Ther he was slayn his lokyng down he caste,

laughed | And in hymself he lough right at the wo
Of hem that wepten for his deth so faste,
And dampned al oure werk that foloweth so
desire for earthly pleasure | The blynde lust, the which that may nat laste,
And sholden al oure herte on heven caste,
And forth he wente, shortly for to telle,
assigned | Ther as Mercurye sorted hym to dwelle.

end | Swich fyn hath, lo, this Troilus for love!
Swich fyn hath al his grete worthynesse,
royal | Swich fyn hath his estat real above,
Swich fyn his lust, swich fyn hath his noblesse,
brittleness | Swych fyn hath false worldes brotelnesse.
And thus bigan his lovyng of Criseyde,
As I have told, and in this wise he deyde.

O yonge, fresshe folkes, he or she,
In which that love up groweth with youre age,
Return to (your real) home (heaven) | Repeyreth hom fro worldly vanyte,
And of youre herte up casteth the visage
To thilke God that after his ymage
fair (i.e. a temporary amusement) | Yow made, and thynketh al nys but a faire
This world that passeth soone as floures faire.

And loveth hym the which that right for love
cross, redeem | Upon a crois, oure soules for to beye,
died | First starf, and roos, and sit in hevene above;
For he nyl falsen no wight, dar I seye,
wholly | That wol his herte al holly on hym leye.
And syn he best to love is, and most meke,
counterfeit | What nedeth feynede loves for to seke?

pagans' | Lo here, of payens corsed olde rites!
Lo here, what alle hire goddes may availle!
Lo here, thise wrecched worldes appetites!
end result and reward for effort | Lo here, the fyn and guerdoun for travaille
rascally crew | Of Jove, Appollo, of Mars, of swich rascaille!
the way the old poets wrote | Lo here, the forme of olde clerkis speche
In poetrie, if ye hire bokes seche.

O moral Gower, this book I directe
To the, and to the, philosophical Strode,

1828–32 The insistent repetition, here and in 1849–55, is uncharacteristically strained and uninflected, as if Chaucer were borrowing a rhetorical voice to conceal his unease. These two passages were very popular with and much imitated by fifteenth-century admirers such as Lydgate.

1835–48 The exhortation to love Christ (who at least can be relied upon) and the condemnation of paganism make the preceding narrative into an exemplum of *blynde lust*, which seems a misrepresentation of the poem's own high seriousness.

1856–7 Chaucer dedicates his poem, not to any court figure, but to two London friends: John Gower, the poet, and Ralph Strode, the Oxford logician and London lawyer. The request that they correct his work is a conventional 'modesty-topos'.

To vouchen-sauf, ther nede is, to correcte,
Of youre benignites and zeles goode.
died on the cross And to that sothfast Crist, that starf on rode,
With al myn herte of mercy evere I preye,
And to the Lord right thus I speke and seye:

Thow oon, and two, and thre, eterne on lyve,
That regnest ay in thre, and two, and oon,
(see n.) Uncircumscript, and al maist circumscrive,
Us from visible and invisible foon
Defende, and to thy mercye, everichon,
So make us, Jesus, for thi mercy, digne,
For love of Mayde and Moder thyn benigne.
Amen.

The Canterbury Tales

The *Canterbury Tales*, written between 1387 and 1400, are a new and highly experimental venture in organizing a framework narrative for a series of tales. Chaucer imagines a group of pilgrims gathering at the Tabard Inn in Southwark (on the south bank of the Thames across from London) to begin their journey to the shrine of St Thomas Becket at Canterbury. They agree to tell tales on the journey to pass the time more agreeably; there is to be a competition for the best tale, and a prize. There had been framework narratives for linked series of tales before: *A Thousand and One Nights*, Boccaccio's *Decameron* (which influenced Chaucer profoundly), Chaucer's own *Legend of Good Women* (a string of tales of virtuous women told by Chaucer as a 'penance' for speaking ill of women in *Troilus and Criseyde*). But their design is predictable, and there is rarely any variety in the mode of narration. The plan for the *Canterbury Tales* has the advantage that it allowed for the introduction, because of the social variety of the pilgrims, of all kinds of stories, including stories of low life (attributed to the *cherles*) that might have seemed beneath the attention of a great and fairly famous poet; it also allowed for a degree of dramatic interchange between the pilgrims, and an apparently spontaneous development of the framework narrative – interruptions, arguments, feuds, comments, a completely new character (the Canon's Yeoman); finally, it gave Chaucer the freedom to move behind the scenes, to shed the responsibility for being an *auctor* (a maker of authoritative pronouncements) that he had always found burdensome. It enabled him to make of the *Canterbury Tales* a vast laboratory of narrative experiment, in which any form or genre or type of tale could be tried out – romances, comic tales, *fabliaux*, religious tales, saints' lives, exemplary stories, anecdotes of contemporary life, a beast-fable, a *pourquoi*, a minstrel-parody, a fairy-tale. Though a design was put in place, with a prospective ending, it does not press upon the constituent tales, which are innovative in many ways. The freedom to experiment with narrative that Chaucer sought and found in this way was not of course an end in itself. What it gave Chaucer was a means to explore in many ways and at many levels of seriousness the issues that preoccupied the society of which he was part: questions to do with sexual exploitation, the negotiations within the marriage contract, the 'voicing' of women, the nature of authority and the necessity of obedience, the extent to which human beings control their lives or consent to the manner in which they are controlled, the operation of institutions, including the church, as self-serving and self-perpetuating organs of greed and privilege, the existence of 'the holy' as a transforming agency. Of the 120 tales allowed for in the Host's two-way four-tale plan, Chaucer completed only 20, with a further three left unfinished (including *Sir Thopas*, the first of the two tales attributed to 'Chaucer the pilgrim') and one from a new character who turns up on the road. It seems likely that he had nearly completed an original one-way one-tale plan (to conclude with the arrival at Canterbury, which is anticipated in the last scene of the pilgrimage in the Parson's Prologue) but decided to postpone impending closure by introducing a new and impossibly grandiose scheme. The original plan for the ending was superseded, and the work left inevitably unfinished, which perhaps contributes to the sense of an 'ultimate' open-endedness.

The *Canterbury Tales* survive in 82 manuscripts, of which 55 are complete or near-complete and seven frag-

1863–5 The prayer to the Trinity begins with echoes of Dante, *Paradiso* 14.28–30.

1865 'Uncircumscribed and yet able to circumscribe all things'.

mentary, while the remainder contain excerpts. The number of manuscripts is extraordinarily large, though only the relic of the much larger number that once existed. Caxton printed the *Tales* in 1478 and again in 1485, and the work has remained continuously in print ever since. Chaucer did not complete the *Tales* nor organize the fragmentary groupings of tales into a fixed order. Scribes and modern editors have done their best to arrange the tale-groupings in a sensible order, but there is no ordering of the tales authorized by Chaucer. As to the text, two manuscripts stand out, both copied in the first decade of the fifteenth century by the same scribe. One is the Hengwrt MS in the National Library of Wales in Aberystwyth (MS Peniarth 392D), which has the tales in an 'unordered' state, with many omissions and lacunae, but with a very good text; the other is the Ellesmere MS in the Huntington Library in San Marino, California (MS EL 26.C.9), copied somewhat later when there had been more time to digest the information contained in Chaucer's 'foul papers'. Ellesmere has the tales in the order that has come to be widely accepted, and is complete, but the text is slightly inferior to that contained in Hengwrt. The following texts are based on Hengwrt (Hg), with omissions supplied and corrections introduced from Ellesmere (El) or from the corpus of variants in Manly and Rickert (see below). In both Hg and El the *Tales* survive in a series of unconnected fragments. In the following selections, the line-numbering of the fragments in the *Riverside* Chaucer is kept.

There is a full edition of the *Canterbury Tales*, with variants from all manuscripts, in J.M. Manly and E.M. Rickert (eds), *The Text of the Canterbury Tales, studied on the basis of all known manuscripts* (Chicago, 1940). For general critical studies of the *Tales*, see D. Howard, *The Idea of the Canterbury Tales* (Berkeley and Los Angeles, 1976); H. Cooper, *The Structure of the Canterbury Tales* (London, 1983); D. Pearsall, *The Canterbury Tales* (London, 1985, repr. 1993).

The General Prologue

Chaucer's rash and adventurous first move is to offer to introduce the *dramatis personae* of the *Canterbury Tales* to us in a consecutive series of portraits. It looks a recipe for monotony, but Chaucer plucks triumph from seemingly certain disaster by observing no apparently predictable order, by varying the angle of approach, by concentrating in different portraits on different kinds of detail, by beginning and ending the portraits in different ways. He speaks of the pilgrims with an immediacy and spontaneity that suggests he has just met them, throwing in apparently arbitrary and meaningless detail, like the Cook's *mormal* (386), and frank confession of ignorance, as of the Merchant's name (284), as guarantees of 'authenticity'. He varies the 'voice' of the narrator, so that at times he is the naive 'cub-reporter', overwhelmed by this brave new world of clever and self-confident people like the Monk or starry-eyed at the elegance of the Prioress, while at other times he is a smug know-all, making superior-sounding jokes about the Clerk's poverty (297–8). Sometimes the voice is transparent and unironic, as in the description of the Parson. Above all, Chaucer detaches the pilgrims from their traditional moorings in the moralizing of estates satire (on this see J. Mann, *Chaucer and Medieval Estates Satire* (Cambridge, 1973)) and floats each one free as if on a raft of their own devising. All are superbly good at whatever they do: they write their own recommendations as well as their CV. They are *characters*.

April, sweet	Whan that Averill with his shoures soote
	The droghte of March hath perced to the roote
such liquid	And bathed every veyne in swich lycour
By whose power	Of which vertu engendred is the flour;
	Whan Zephirus eek with his sweete breeth
grove and field	Inspired hath in every holt and heeth
new shoots	The tendre croppes, and the yonge sonne
	Hath in the Ram his half cours yronne,
birds	And smale foweles maken melodye,
eye	That slepen al the nyght with open iye

1–8 These opening lines evoke an English springtime but are also a philosophical evocation of the principle of renewal in nature: the language (**lycour, vertu, engendred**) is the semi-scientific language of medieval natural history, with the addition of classical (**Zephirus**, the west wind) and astronomical allusion.

7–8 The sun is 'young' because its year has just begun at the vernal equinox (12 March in the fourteenth century); it has completed half of its course through the zodiacal sign of Aries, the Ram (12 March–11 April), which would appear to indicate a date in early April, but the second half may be meant, since Chaucer specifies 18 April as the second day of the pilgrimage in the Introduction to the Man of Law's Tale (II.5).

hearts	(So priketh hem nature in hir corages),
	Thanne longen folk to goon on pilgrymages
professional pilgrims, foreign shores	And palmeres for to seeken straunge strondes,
distant shrines, well known	To ferne halwes, kouthe in sondry londes;
	And specially from every shires ende
	Of Engelond to Caunterbury they wende,
	The holy blisful martir for to seke
helped, sick	That hem hath holpen whan that they weere seeke.
It befell	Bifel that in that sesoun on a day,
	In Southwerk at the Tabard as I lay
	Redy to weenden on my pilgrymage
	To Caunterbury with ful devout corage,
	At nyght was come into that hostelrye
	Wel nyne and twenty in a compaignye
fallen by chance	Of sondry folk, by aventure yfalle
	In felaweshipe, and pilgrymes weere they alle,
	That toward Caunterbury wolden ryde.
	The chambres and the stables weeren wyde
accommodated	And wel we weeren esed at the beste.
	And shortly, whan the sonne was to reste,
	So hadde I spoken with hem everichoon
	That I was of hir felaweshipe anoon,
agreement	And maade forward erly for to ryse,
where, tell	To take oure wey ther as I yow devyse.
	But nathelees, while I have tyme and space,
proceed	Er that I ferther in this tale pace,
	Me thynketh it acordant to resoun
	To telle yow al the condicioun
	Of eech of hem, so as it seemed me,
social rank	And whiche they weere and of what degree
	And eek in what array that they weere inne;
	And at a knyght thanne wol I first bigynne.
	A KNYGHT ther was, and that a worthy man,
	That fro the tyme that he first bigan
	To ryden out, he loved chivalrye,
generosity of spirit	Trouthe and honour, fredom and curteisye.
war	Ful worthy was he in his lordes werre,
farther	And therto hadde he ryden, no man ferre,
	As wel in Cristendom as hethenesse,
	And evere honured for his worthynesse.
	At Alisaundre he was whan it was wonne;
headed the table	Ful ofte tyme he hadde the bord bigonne
national companies of knights	Aboven alle nacions in Pruce;
campaigned	In Lettow hadde he reysed and in Ruce,

17 **martir**: St Thomas Becket, archbishop of Canterbury, murdered on the steps of the high altar in Canterbury cathedral in 1170 at the instigation of Henry II, who resented the archbishop's intractability in matters of clerical privilege. His canonization in 1173, Henry's ostentatious repentance, and the establishment of his shrine as the major place of pilgrimage in England, bear witness to the church's determination to demonstrate that its power was not to be slighted.

43 The Knight is portrayed, somewhat nostalgically, as the representative of an idealized crusading chivalry. He has not fought for the English king in the French wars, but chiefly against Moslems on the shores of the Mediterranean (**the grete see**): in Egypt at the siege of Alexandria (1365), in southern Spain at the siege of Algeciras (1344) in Granada, on the Barbary coast at Beni Marin (**Belmarye**) and Tlemcen (**Tramyssene**), in Turkey at Ayash (**Lyeys**) and Antalya (**Satalye**) and in the service of the lord of Balat (**Palatye**). He has also fought in the campaigns in Prussia (**Pruce**), Lithuania (**Lettow**) and Russia (**Ruce**) against the Russian Orthodox Christians of the lands to the east.

No Cristen man so ofte of his degree.
In Gernade at the seege eek hadde he be
Of Algizir, and ryden in Belmarye.
At Lyeys was he and at Satalye
Whan they weere wonne, and in the grete see
military landing — At many a noble arivee hadde he bee.
  At mortal batailles hadde he been fiftene
And foghten for oure feyth at Tramyssene
jousting competitions — In lystes thryes and ay slayn his foo.
  This ilke worthy knyght hadde been also
Somtyme with the lord of Palatye
against — Agayn another hethen in Turkye,
reputation — And everemoore he hadde a sovereyn prys.
And thogh that he weere worthy, he was wys,
demeanour — And of his poort as meke as is a mayde,
rudeness — Ne nevere yet no vileynye he sayde
creature — In al his lyf unto no manere wight.
true — He was a verray parfit gentil knyght.
  But for to tellen yow of his array,
horses — Hise hors weere goode but he ne was nat gay.
Of fustian he wered a gypoun
Al bismotered with his haubergeoun,
journeying — For he was laate comen from his viage
And wente for to doon his pilgrymage.
  With hym ther was his sone, a yong SQUYER,
gallant knight-to-be — A lovere and a lusty bachiler,
curled — With lokkes crulle as they weere leyd in presse;
Of twenty yeer he was of age, I gesse.
moderate height — Of his stature he was of evene lengthe
agile — And wonderly delyvere and of greet strengthe.
on mounted expeditions — And he hadde been somtyme in chivachye
In Flaundres, in Artoys and Picardye,
himself, time — And born hym wel, as in so litel space,
lady's — In hope to stonden in his lady grace.
Embroidered, meadow — Embrouded was he, as it weere a meede
Al ful of fresshe floures, white and reede.
Syngynge he was or floytynge al the day:
He was as fressh as is the monthe of May.
Short was his gowne, with sleves longe and wyde.
Wel koude he sitte on hors and faire ryde.
compose — He koude songes make and wel endite,
Joust — Juste and eek daunce and wel portreye and write.
at night-time — So hoote he loved that by nyghtertale
He slepte namoore than dooth a nyghtyngale.
eager to serve — Curteys he was, lowely and servysable,
carved — And carf biforn his fader at the table.
no more — A YEMAN he hadde and servantz namo
At that tyme, for hym liste ryde so,

75–6 His tunic of coarse cloth was marked with the rust stains of his coat of mail.

86 Places in northern France which saw much fighting in the wars between England and France; the Squire's experience of combat is very different from his father's.

100 To carve before one's knight, still more one's father, was a great honour for a squire.

101 The Yeoman is in the service of the Knight as a forester (110) and master of the hunt.

And he was clad in coote and hood of greene.
A sheef of pecok arwes, bright and keene, — *sharp*
Under his belt he bar ful thriftily — *properly*
(Wel koude he dresse his takel yemanly: — *look after*
His arwes drowped noght with fetheres lowe), — *drooped in flight*
And in his hand he bar a myghty bowe.
A not-heed hadde he, with a broun visage. — *close-cropped ('nut')*
Of wodecraft koude he wel al the usage.
Upon his arm he bar a gay bracer — *archer's arm-guard*
And by his syde a swerd and a bokeler
And on that oother syde a gay daggere
Harneysed wel and sharpe as poynt of spere, — *Ornamented*
A Cristofre on his brest of silver sheene. — *bright*
An horn he bar, the bawdryk was of greene: — *shoulder strap*
A forster was he, soothly, as I gesse.
  Ther was also a Nonne, a PRIORESSE,
That of hir smylyng was ful symple and coy; — *unaffected and demure*
Hir gretteste ooth was but by seinte Loy;
And she was clepyd madame Eglentyne. — *called*
Ful wel she soong the servyce dyvyne, — *sang*
Entuned in hir nose ful semely;
And Frenssh she spak ful faire and fetisly – — *elegantly*
After the scole of Stratford at the Bowe, — *After the fashion of*
For Frenssh of Parys was to hire unknowe.
At mete wel ytaught was she withalle: — *mealtimes*
She leet no morsel from hir lyppes falle
Ne wette hir fyngres in hir sauce deepe.
Wel koude she carye a morsel and wel keepe — *take care*
That no drope ne fille upon hir brest.
In curteisye was set ful muchel hir lest. — *good manners, delight*
Hir over-lyppe wyped she so cleene
That in hir coppe ther was no ferthyng seene — *speck*
Of grece, whan she dronken hadde hir draghte. — *grease*
Ful semely after hir mete she raghte. — *for her food, reached*
And sikerly she was of greet desport — *excellent deportment*
And ful plesaunt and amyable of port — *bearing*
And peyned hire to countrefete chiere — *the manners*
Of court, and been estatlich of manere — *dignified*
And to been holden digne of reverence.
But for to speken of hir conscience, — *moral sensibility*

115 **Cristofre**: an image of St Christopher, worn as a lucky charm.

118 The Prioress is the head of a convent of nuns. There was a prosperous Benedictine nunnery at St Leonard's, near 'Stratford at the Bowe' (125). Chaucer had visited it.

120 *Seinte Loi* (Fr. *Eloi*) had a particular association with Benedictine nunneries and was perhaps further renowned for refusing to take oaths.

121 **Eglentyne**, 'briar rose', is not an obviously suitable name for a nun, but nunneries around London in the late fourteenth century often served to some extent as schools for rich girls, as places of retirement for ladies, and as homes for the unmarried and unmarriageable daughters of the well-off, who, having no urgent vocation, saw no cause to abandon all their courtly customs and manners for the cloister.

123 **Entuned**: 'intoned', an economical rather than an affected way of singing the divine office.

124–6 **Stratford at the Bowe**: two miles east of the city of London. The French typically spoken there was the Anglo-Norman dialect of French long spoken in England but thought of by sophisticated Londoners as provincial and *passé* in comparison with Parisian French.

127–36 The Prioress's concern for table-manners is given an added piquancy if one recalls that Chaucer's immediate source here is a passage in the *Roman de la Rose* (a widely disseminated thirteenth-century poetic allegory of love that had a profound influence on Chaucer), where an old bawd describes to a young woman how to make herself attractive to men (*RR* 13408–32).

She was so charitable and so pitous
She wolde wepe if that she sawe a mous
Caught in a trappe, if it weere deed or bledde.
Of smale houndes hadde she that she fedde
fine white bread With rosted flessh, or mylk and wastel-breed;
But soore wepte she if oon of hem weere deed
stick, painfully Or if men smoot it with a yerde smerte;
And al was conscience and tendre herte.
pleated Ful semely hir wympel pynched was,
well-formed Hir nose tretez, hir eyen greye as glas,
Hir mouth ful smal and therto softe and reed.
But sikerly she hadde a fair forheed,
hand-span It was almoost a spanne brood, I trowe,
certainly For, hardily, she was nat undergrowe.
elegant, aware Ful fetys was hir cloke, as I was war.
Of smal coral aboute hir arm she bar
string (rosary) A peyre of bedes, gauded al with greene,
And theron heeng a brooch of gold ful sheene
On which ther was first writen a crowned A
And after *Amor vincit omnia*.
   Another NONNE with hire hadde she
That was hire chapeleyne, and preestes thre.
a fine one surpassing all others   A MONK ther was, a fair for the maystrye,
An outrydere, that lovede venerye,
A manly man, to been an abbot able.
Ful many a deyntee hors hadde he in stable,
And whanne he rood, men myghte his brydel heere
Gyngle in a whistlynge wynd as cleere
And eek as loude as dooth the chapel belle
There as this lord is kepere of the selle.
The rule of Seint Maure or of Seint Beneyt,
strict Bycause that it was oold and somdeel streyt,
go (hang) This ilke Monk leet oolde thynges pace
the while And heeld after the newe world the space.
plucked He yaf noght of that text a pulled hen
That seith that hunterys been none holy men,
heedless of his rule Ne that a monk, whan he is recchelees,
Is likned til a fissh that is waterlees –
This is to seyn, a monk out of his cloystre.
But thilke text heeld he nat worth an oystre.
And I seyde his opynyon was good.

143–50 The Prioress's care for mice and for her little dogs is touchingly sentimental. Whether it is meant to seem excessively so, or to remind us of the absent poor who might more appropriately have exercised her 'conscience', is a matter for debate.

152–62 The Prioress is described in terms quite appropriate to a romance heroine, though the satire is gentle (her forehead should perhaps have been more discreetly covered). The coral rosary is fashionable, the brooch a touch extravagant, the motto ('Love conquers all') not necessarily ambiguous.

166 As an **outrydere**, that is, a monk licensed to travel alone on the monastery's business, looking after the administration of its estates, the Monk has many opportunities to come into contact with local landowners and enjoy their sport of hunting (**venerye**). His position as the head of a small outlying house or 'cell' (172) of his monastery gives him additional freedoms. He has acquired worldly tastes, and would like the old monastic rule of St Maurus and St Benedict (173) and St Augustine (187) to be adapted to his new lifestyle.

183–8 The comically misplaced enthusiasm for the Monk's self-serving opinion of the monastic rule is an example of the projection upon 'Chaucer the pilgrim', with all his naiveté, of views that no sensible person would share (see the famous essay by E.T. Donaldson, in *PMLA* 69 [1954], 928–36). He practically demolishes the Monk's case single-handed. But this is not the only narrative 'voice' in the General Prologue.

mad	What sholde he studie and make hymselven wood
pore	Upon a book in cloystre alwey to poure
work	Or swynke with his handes and laboure
commands	As Austyn bit? How shal the world be served?
	Lat Austyn have his swynk to hym reserved!
a really enthusiastic huntsman	Therfore he was a prykasour aryght:
	Grehoundes he hadde as swift as fowel in flyght;
coursing	Of prikyng and of huntyng for the haare
delight	Was al his lust, for no cost wolde he spaare.
hemmed with fur	I saugh his sleves purfiled at the hond
grey squirrel fur	With grys, and that the fyneste of a lond,
	And for to festne his hood under his chyn
intricately made	He hadde of gold ywroght a ful curious pyn;
	A love-knotte in the gretter ende ther was.
bald	His heed was balled, that shoon as any glas,
	And eek his face, as he hadde been enoynt.
condition	He was a lord ful fat and in good poynt,
bulging	His eyen steepe, and rollynge in his heed,
(see n.)	That stemed as a fourneys of a leed,
	Hise bootes souple, his hors in greet estaat.
	Now certeynly he was a fair prelat.
	He nas nat paale as is a forpyned goost:
	A fat swan loved he best of any roost.
	His palfrey was as broun as is a berye.
	A FRERE ther was, a wantowne and a merye,
(self-)important	A lymytour, a ful solempne man.
	In alle the ordres foure is noon that kan
	So muche of daliaunce and fair langage:
	He hadde maked ful many a mariage
	Of yonge wommen at his owene cost;
support	Unto his ordre he was a noble post.
	Ful wel biloved and famylier was hee
landowners	With frankeleyns overal in his contree
	And eek with worthy wommen of the town,
	For he hadde power of confessioun,
	As seyde hymself, moore than a curaat,
	For of his ordre he was licenciaat.
	Ful swetely herde he confessioun
	And plesant was his absolucioun:
	He was an esy man to yeve penaunce
offering	Ther as he wiste to have a good pitaunce.
	For unto a povre ordre for to yeve
confessed	Is signe that a man is wel yshryve,
make bold to say	For if he yaf, he dorste make avaunt,
	He wiste that a man was repentaunt.
	For many a man so hard is of his herte
he suffers painfully	He may nat weepe, thogh that he soore smerte:

202 'That gleamed like a furnace-fire under a lead cauldron'.

209 The Friar is licensed to beg, as a **lymytour**, in a specific district, and also, as a **licentiaat** (220), to hear confession. He takes advantage of these freedoms to cultivate the rich people in his area and to give easy absolution to those who make generous offerings (222–4), to play the dignified arbitrator at **love-dayes** (258), days of out-of-court conciliation where the money changing hands often found its way into his, and (possibly) seducing girls and arranging safe marriages for them (212–13).

210 The four orders of friars were Dominicans, Franciscans, Carmelites and Austin friars.

Therfore instede of wepynge and preyeres
Men moote yeve silver to the povre freres.
His typet was ay farsed ful of knyves — *dangling tip of his hood, stuffed*
And pynnes, for to yeven faire wyves.
And certeynly he hadde a murye noote: — *pleasant voice*
Wel koude he synge and pleyen on a roote; — *fiddle*
Of yeddynges he bar outrely the prys. — *songs, absolutely, prize*
His nekke whit was as the flour-de-lys;
Therto he stroong was as a champioun.
He knew the tavernes wel in every town
And every hostiler and tappestere — *innkeeper, barmaid*
Bet than a lazer or a beggestere,
For unto swich a worthy man as he
Acorded nat, as by his facultee, — *official position*
To have with syke lazers aqueyntaunce.
It is nat honeste, it may noght avaunce, — *be of any advantage*
For to deelen with no swich poraille, — *poor people*
But al with riche and sellerys of vitaille. — *victuals (provisions)*
And overal, ther as profit sholde aryse,
Curteys he was and lowely of servyse;
Ther was no man nowheer so vertuous.
He was the beste beggere of his hous,
And yaf a certeyn ferme for the graunt –
Noon of his bretheren cam ther in his haunt.
For thogh a wydwe hadde noght a sho,
So plesant was his '*In principio*'
Yet wolde he have a ferthyng er he wente:
His purchaas was wel bettre than his rente. — *'take', official income*
And rage he koude, as it weere right a whelp. — *lark about, puppy*
In love-dayes koude he muchel help,
For there he was nat lyk a cloystrer
With a threedbare cope, as is a povre scoler,
But he was lyk a maister or a pope. — *university teacher*
Of double worstede was his semycope, — *short cloak*
And rounded as a belle out of the presse.
Somwhat he lypsed for his wantownesse — *affectation*
To make his Englyssh sweete upon his tonge,
And in his harpyng, whan that he hadde songe,
Hise eyen twynkled in his heed aryght — *exactly*
As doon the sterres in the frosty nyght.
This worthy lymytour was cleped Huberd.
  A MARCHANT was ther with a forked berd,
In motlee, and hye on hors he sat, — *parti-coloured cloth*
Upon his heed a Flaundryssh bevere hat, — *Flemish*
His bootes clasped faire and fetisly. — *elegantly*

242 The leper and the poor beggar-woman were of course supposed to be the special charge of the friars, with their roving commission to bring the message of the gospels to the outcast and the parish-less.

252a–b He paid a sum of money for the exclusive privilege of begging in a certain area. The two lines, since they are not in Ellesmere and are therefore omitted in some influential modern editions, are conventionally numbered thus to avoid disruption.

254 '*In principio*', 'in the beginning', is the opening of the book of Genesis and of the gospel of St John; it was a phrase used in solemn devotions, pronouncements and greetings.

270 The Merchant is an export/import trader, with perhaps a special interest in the wool trade (Middelburgh, on the Dutch coast, opposite Orwell in Essex, was the port of staple for wool 1384–8, that is, the only place through which English wool could officially enter Europe); he is also an international dealer in currency.

opinions	Hise resons he spak ful solempnely,
Going on about	Sownyng alwey th'encrees of his wynnyng.
protected above all things	He woolde the see weere kept for anythyng
	Bitwixen Myddelburgh and Orewelle.
	Wel koude he in eschaunge sheeldes selle.
put his mind to things	This worthy man ful wel his wit bisette:
	Ther wiste no wight that he was in dette,
dignified	So estaatly was he of his governaunce
financial dealing	With his bargaynes and with his chevysaunce.
	Forsoothe he was a worthy man withalle,
	But sooth to seyn I noot how men hym calle.
	A CLERC ther was of Oxenford also,
dedicated himself	That unto logyk hadde longe ygo.
	As leene was his hors as is a rake,
	And he was noght right fat, I undertake,
gaunt	But looked holwe and therto sobrely.
top coat	Ful threedbare was his overeste courtepy,
	For he hadde geten hym yet no benefice
	Ne was so worldly for to have office.
he would rather	For hym was levere have at his beddes heed
	Twenty bookes clad in blak or reed
	Of Aristotle and his philosophye
fiddle, psaltery (kind of harp)	Than robes riche or fithele or gay sautrye.
although	But al be that he was a philosophre,
	Yet hadde he but litel gold in cofre;
get	But al that he myghte of his frendes hente,
	On bookes and on lernynge he it spente
	And bisily gan for the soules preye
be a scholar	Of hem that yaf hym wherwith to scoleye.
care	Of studye took he moost cure and moost heede.
	Noght oo word spak he moore than was neede
with due formality	And that was spoke in forme and reverence
serious meaning	And short and quyk and ful of heigh sentence.
All to do with	Sownynge in moral vertu was his speche,
	And gladly wolde he lerne and gladly teche.
prudent	A SERGEAUNT OF LAWE, waar and wys,
	That often hadde been at the Parvys,
	Ther was also, ful ryche of excellence.
	Discreet he was and of greet reverence –
	He seemed swich, hise wordes weeren so wyse.
	Justice he was ful often in assise
royal appointment, full	By patente and by pleyn commissioun.
knowledge	For his science and for his heigh renoun
	Of fees and robes hadde he many oon.
land-buyer	So greet a purchasour was nowher noon:

285 A clerk was a man of learning, whether a student or an ecclesiastic; students at Oxford were normally supposed to be preparing for the priesthood, though many did not take holy orders. Chaucer's Clerk has not been appointed to an ecclesiastical living, or **benefice** (291), nor is he worldly enough to accept secular preferment (**office**, 292). He seems to be the eternal graduate student.

297–8 Chaucer's little joke: the 'philosopher's stone' sought by alchemists was what would turn base metals into gold. One of the *Tales* (the Canon's Yeoman's Tale) is about the kind of scam that resulted.

309 A Sergeant was the highest rank of lawyer, with exclusive rights to plead in certain courts and to act as justice at the county assizes (314). His knowledge of the law makes Chaucer's Sergeant an expert in land-conveyancing, not, it appears, just for the benefit of others.

310 The **Parvys** was the porch of St Paul's cathedral, used as a meeting place for lawyers and their clients.

free from constraints on possession	Al was fee symple to hym in effect;
invalidated on a technicality	His purchasyng myghte nat been infect.
	Nowher so bisy a man as he ther nas
	And yet he seemed bisyer than he was.
(see n.)	In termes hadde he caas and doomes alle
	That from tyme of kyng William weere falle.
compose, draw up a legal document	Therto he koude endite and make a thyng,
find a flaw in	Ther koude no wight pynchen at his writyng;
fully by heart	And every statut koude he pleyn by roote.
parti-coloured	He rood but hoomly in a medlee coote,
belt, narrow stripes	Girt with a ceynt of sylk, with barres smale;
	Of his array telle I no lenger tale.
	A FRANKELEYN was in his compaignye.
	Whit was his berd as is the dayesye;
	Of his complexcion he was sangwyn.
piece of bread	Wel loved he by the morwe a sope in wyn:
wont	To lyven in delyt was evere his wone,
	For he was Epicurus owene sone,
pure pleasure	That heeld opynyoun that pleyn delit
	Was verray felicitee parfit.
	An housholdere, and that a greet, was hee;
(patron saint of hospitality)	Seint Julyan he was in his contree.
of the same high standard	His breed, his ale, was alweys after oon;
stocked with wine	A bettre envyned man was nevere noon.
	Withouten bake mete was nevere his hous,
	Of fressh fissh and flessh, and that so plentevous
	It snewed in his hous of mete and drynke,
	Of alle deyntees that men koude bithynke.
	After the sondry sesons of the yeer
	So chaunged he his mete and his soper.
bird-pen	Ful many a fat partrych hadde he in muwe
pike, fish-pond	And many a breem and many a luce in stuwe.
	Wo was his cook but if his sauce weere
spicy	Poynaunt and sharpe, and redy al his geere!
permanently in place	Hys table dormaunt in his halle alway
	Stood redy covered al the longe day.
	At sessions ther was he lord and sire;
	Ful ofte tyme he was knyght of the shire.
dagger, purse	An anlaas and a gipser al of sylk
	Heeng at his girdel, whit as morne mylk.
sheriff, county tax auditor	A shirreve hadde he been, and countour.
county landowner	Was nowheer swich a worthy vavasour.
	An HABERDASSHERE and a CARPENTER,
weaver, carpet-maker	A WEBBE, a DYERE, and a TAPYCER –
	And they weere clothed alle in oo lyveree

323 'In proper legal written form he had all the cases and decisions'.

333 The 'complexion' or particular 'mix' of the four humours or bodily fluids (blood, phlegm, yellow or red bile, black bile) determined a person's 'temperament'. The Franklin is **sangwyn** because blood is dominant; he is by nature cheerful and generous.

336 **Epicurus** was a Greek philosopher who was popularly believed to advocate that pleasure was the chief goal of existence.

355–6 He presided at the local sessions as a justice of the peace, and had been often returned to parliament as one of the knights of the shire (there were also burgess-members).

363–4 Their **lyveree**, or distinctive costume, is not that of a trade-guild (they would belong to different guilds) but of a parish fraternity of a religious kind such as it was becoming prestigious (and politically more prudent) to belong to in the late fourteenth century.

	Of a solempne and a greet fraternytee.
adorned	Ful fressh and newe hir geere apyked was:
mounted	Hir knyves weere chaped noght with bras
	But al with silver, wroght ful cleene and wel,
	Hir girdles and hir pouches everydel.
tradesman-citizen	Wel seemed eech of hem a fair burgeys
guildhall, dais	To sitten in a yeldehalle on a deys.
	Everych, for the wisdom that he kan,
fit	Was shaply for to been an alderman,
property, income	For catel hadde they ynogh and rente,
	And eek hir wyves wolde it wel assente;
	And ellis certeyn weere they to blame.
	It is ful fair to been yclepyd 'madame'
	And goon to vigilies al bifore
	And have a mantel realliche ybore.
for the occasion	A COOK they hadde with hem for the nones
marrow-bones	To boille the chiknes with the marybones
(spices)	And poudre-marchaunt tart and galyngale.
	Wel koude he knowe a draghte of London ale.
	He koude rooste and seethe and broille and frye,
stews	Maken mortreux and wel bake a pye.
	But greet harm was it, as it thoughte me,
ulcerous sore	That on his shyne a mormal hadde he.
As for thick milky chicken stew	For blankmanger, that maade he with the beste.
dwelling far in the west	A SHIPMAN was ther, wonyng fer by weste;
Dartmouth (in Devon)	For aught I woot he was of Dertemouthe.
nag, as best he could	He rood upon a rouncy, as he kouthe,
coarse cloth	In a gowne of faldyng to the knee.
strap	A daggere hangyng on a laas hadde he
	Aboute his nekke, under his arm adown.
	The hoote somer hadde maad his hewe al brown.
	And certeynly he was a good felawe:
	Ful many a draghte of wyn hadde he drawe
Bordeaux, merchant, slept	Fro Burdeux-ward whil that the chapman sleepe.
	Of nyce conscience took he no keepe:
	If that he faught and hadde the hyer hond
	By watre he sente hem hoom to every lond.
	But of his craft to rekene wel his tydes,
currents	His stremys and his daungers hym bisydes,
harbour, art of navigation	His herberwe and his moone, his lodmenage,
Cartagena (in Spain)	Ther was noon swich from Hulle to Cartage.
prudent in his undertakings	Hardy he was and wys to undertake;
	With many a tempest hadde his beerd been shake.
	He knew alle the havenes, as they weere,
	Fro Gootlond to the cape of Fynysteere,
inlet, Brittany	And every cryke in Britaigne and in Spayne.
sailing-ship	His barge yclepyd was the Mawdelayne.
	With us ther was a DOCTOUR OF PHISYK,
	In al this world ne was ther noon hym lyk,

377–8 They liked going at the head of the procession to church for the service on the eve of a great feast-day, and having the train of their cloak carried as if they were royalty.

387 **For** performs here a famously ambiguous function, as conjunction or preposition, which a modern editor, obliged to punctuate, must disambiguate.

408 Gotland is an island off the coast of Sweden; it was an important trading post.

To speken of phisyk and of surgerye.
For he was grounded in astronomye.
He kepte his pacient a ful greet deel
In houres by his magyk natureel.
Wel koude he fortunen the ascendent
Of hise ymages for his pacient.
He knew the cause of every maladye,
Weere it of hoot or coold or moyste or drye,
And where it engendred and of what humour;
practitioner He was a verray parfit practisour.
The cause yknowe, and of his harm the roote,
remedy Anoon he yaf the sike man his boote.
Ful redy hadde he hise apothecaryes
medicines To senden hym his drogges and his letuaryes,
For eech of hem maade oother for to wynne –
recently begun Hir frendshipe was noght newe to bigynne.
Wel knew he the oolde Esculapyus,
And Deyscorides and eek Rufus,
Olde Ypocras, Haly and Galyen,
Serapion, Razis and Avycen,
Averroys, Damascien and Constantyn,
Bernard and Gatesden and Gilbertyn.
Of his diete mesurable was hee,
For it was of no superfluytee
But of greet norissynge and digestible.
His studye was but litel on the Bible.
rich cloth of red and grey-blue In sangwyn and in pers he clad was al,
(kinds of silk) Lyned with taffata and with sendal,
moderate in spending And yet he was but esy of dispence:
He kepte that he wan in pestilence.
Since, health-giving drink For gold in phisyk is a cordial,
Therfore he loved gold in special.
  A good WYF was ther of bisyde BATHE,
a pity But she was somdel deef, and that was scathe.
skill Of clooth-makynge she hadde swich an haunt
She passed hem of Ipres and of Gaunt.
In al the parysshe wyf ne was ther noon
offertory (offering made at the altar) That to the offrynge bifore hire sholde goon,
And if ther dide, certeyn so wrooth was shee
That she was out of alle charitee.
linen head-coverings, texture Hir coverchiefes ful fyne weere of grownd:
I dorste swere they weyeden ten pownd
That on a Sonday weeren upon hir heed.
Hir hosen weeren of fyn scarlet reed,

414–18 The reading of planets and stars in relation to the patient's horoscope was important in medieval medicine. The Doctor watched over (**kepte**) his patient with particular care during the hours he knew, from his astrological predictions (**magyk natureel**), to be critical. He knew how to calculate the position of the planets (417) so that his talismanic **ymages** would be of particular benefit to the patient.

420 The four 'humours' (see 333n) were different combinations of these four properties, related also to the four elements. For a succinct account of the doctrine of the elements and humours, see Klibansky (1964), pp. 3–15.

429–34 Medical authorities, from the Greek Aesculapius to the contemporary Englishman, Gilbertus Anglicus.

447–8 The area around Bath was the centre for an expanding cloth-industry, using fine Cotswold wool, in the late fourteenth century. It began to rival traditional cloth-making centres in Flanders such as Ypres and Ghent. It was not very common for a single or widowed woman to run an independent business enterprise, but it was not unusual.

Ful streyte yteyd, and shoes ful moyste and newe. — *tightly laced, supple*
Boold was hir face and fair and reed of hewe.
She was a worthy womman al hir lyve:
Housbondes at chirche dore she hadde fyve,
Withouten oother compaignye in yowthe –
But therof nedeth noght to speke as nowthe. — *just now*
And thries hadde she been at Jerusalem;
She hadde passed many a straunge strem. — *foreign*
At Rome she hadde been, and at Boloyne,
In Galyce at Seint Jame, and at Coloyne:
She koude muchel of wandrynge by the weye.
Gat-tothed was she, soothly for to seye. — *(see n.)*
Upon an amblere esily she sat, — *easy-paced horse*
Ywympled wel, and on hir heed an hat
As brood as is a bokeler or a targe, — *shield*
A foot-mantel aboute hir hypes large,
And on hir feet a peyre of spores sharpe.
In felaweshipe wel koude she laughe and carpe. — *chatter*
Of remedies of love she knew, perchaunce, — *as it happened*
For she koude of that art the olde daunce. — *the old tricks*
   A good man was ther of religioun
And was a povre PERSOUN OF A TOUN,
But riche he was of holy thoght and werk.
He was also a lerned man, a clerk,
That Cristes gospel trewely wolde preche;
His parisshens devoutly wolde he teche.
Benygne he was and wonder diligent
And in adversitee ful pacient
And swich he was ypreved ofte sythes. — *times*
Ful looth weere hym to cursen for his tythes, — *he was, excommunicate*
But rather wolde he yeven, out of doute, — *without doubt*
Unto his povre parisshens aboute
Of his offrynge and eek of his substaunce;
He koude in litel thyng have suffisaunce.
Wyd was his parisshe, and houses fer asonder,
But he ne lafte noght, for reyn ne thonder, — *neglected*
In siknesse nor in meschief to visite — *distress*
The ferreste in his parisshe, muche and lyte, — *farthest, great and small*
Upon his feet, and in his hond a staf.
This noble ensample to his sheep he yaf
That first he wroghte and afterward he taughte.
Out of the gospel he tho wordes caughte
And this figure he added eek therto, — *metaphor*
That if gold ruste, what sholde iren do?
For if a preest be foul, on whom we truste,

459 The punctuation here can enliven the suggestiveness of the juxtaposition of the two lines of the couplet.
460 The binding pledge of a marriage was made at the church door, not at the communion service at the altar that sometimes followed.
465–6 Well-known places of pilgrimage: there was a miraculous image of the Virgin at Boulogne, the shrine of St James at Compostela in Galicia, in northern Spain, and the shrines of the Magi, St Ursula and the Eleven Thousand Virgins at Cologne.
468 **Gat-tothed**: with teeth set wide apart ('gate'-toothed).
478 The Parson is the holder of an ecclesiastical living, or benefice, as distinct from a vicar or a curate. One of his ideal attributes is that he does not hire such a deputy (507) and rush off to London to a comfortable job as a chantry-priest, saying masses for the souls of dead rich people (510), or as the chaplain of a religious fraternity (511).

an ignorant layman	No wonder is a lewed man to ruste,
	And shame it is, if a preest take keepe,
dirty	A shiten shepherde and a clene sheepe.
	Wel oghte a preest ensample for to yive
	By his clennesse how that his sheep sholde lyve.
	He sette noght his benefice to hyre
left	And leet his sheep encombred in the myre
	And ran to Londoun unto Seinte Poules
	To seeken hym a chauntrye for soules,
retained (as a chaplain)	Or with a breetherede to been withhoolde,
	But dwelte at hoom and kepte wel his foolde,
	So that the wolf ne maade it noght myscarye:
	He was a sheepherde and noght a mercenarye.
	And thogh he hooly weere and vertuous
contemptuous	He was to synful men noght despitous
disdainful, haughty	Ne of his speche daungerous ne digne
	But in his techyng discreet and benygne.
	To drawen folk to hevene with fairnesse,
	By good ensample, this was his bisynesse.
if there were	But it weere any persone obstynaat,
	What-so he weere, of heigh or lowe estaat,
rebuke	Hym wolde he snybben sharply for the nonys.
	A bettre preest I trowe ther nowher noon ys.
looked for	He wayted after no pompe and reverence
over-fastidious	Ne maked hym a spyced conscience,
	But Cristes loore and hise apostles twelve
	He taughte, but first he folwed it hymselve.
	With hym ther was a PLOWMAN, was his broother,
hauled, cartload	That hadde ylad of donge ful many a foother;
	A trewe swynkere and a good was he,
	Lyvynge in pees and parfit charitee.
	God loved he best with al his hoole herte
whether it pleased or pained him	At alle tymes, thogh hym gamed or smerte,
	And thanne his neighebore right as hymselve.
ditch and dig	He wolde thresshe and therto dyke and delve,
	For Cristes sake, for every povre wight,
pay	Withouten hyre, if it laye in his myght.
	His tythes payde he ful faire and wel,
own, possessions	Bothe of his propre swynk and his catel.
sleeveless tunic, mare	In a tabard he rood upon a mere.
	Ther was also a REVE and a MILLERE,
	A SOMONOUR and a PARDONER also,
	A MAUNCIPLE and myself – ther weere namo.
fellow	The MILLERE was a stout carl for the nones;
muscle	Ful byg he was of brawen and eek of bones –
was very evident, everywhere	That proeved wel, for overal ther he cam
(given as a prize)	At wrastlynge he wolde have alwey the ram.
compactly built, a thick-set fellow	He was short-shuldred, brood, a thikke knarre:
hinge	Ther was no dore that he noolde heve of harre
by running at it	Or breke it at a rennynge with his heed.
	His beerd as any sowe or fox was reed
	And therto brood, as thogh it weere a spaade.
top	Upon the cope right of his nose he haade

hairs	A werte, and theron stood a tuft of heerys,
ears	Reede as the bristles of a sowes eerys;
nostrils	Hise nosethirles blake weere and wyde.
	A swerd and a bokeler baar he by his syde.
	His mouth as greet was as a greet fourneys:
loud-mouth, teller of coarse tales	He was a janglere, a golyardeys,
bawdiness	And that was moost of synne and harlotryes.
extract three times the usual extra levy	Wel koude he stelen corn and tollen thryes,
	And yet he hadde a thombe of gold, pardee.
blue	A whit coote and a blew hood wered hee.
make a noise with	A baggepipe wel koude he blowe and sowne
	And therwithal he broghte us out of towne.
	A gentil MAUNCIPLE was ther of a Temple,
purchasers	Of which achatours myghte take exemple
buying	For to been wyse in byynge of vitaille;
on credit (tally)	For wheither that he payde or took by taille,
(see n.)	Algate he wayted so in his achaat
always ahead of the game	That he was ay biforn and in good staat.
	Now is nat that of God a ful greet grace
surpass	That swich a lewed mannes wit shal pace
	The wysdom of an heepe of lerned men?
	Of maistres hadde he mo than thryes ten,
skilful	That weeren of lawe expert and curious,
	Of whiche ther weere a dozeyne in that hous
	Worthy to been stywardes of rente and lond
	Of any lord that is in Engelond,
own wealth	To make hym lyve by his propre good
unless he were crazy	In honour dettelees (but if he weere wood),
	Or lyve as scarsly as hym lyst desire,
	And able for to helpen al a shire
chance to happen	In any caas that myghte falle or happe –
made fools of them all	And yet this Maunciple sette hir aller cappe.
	The REVE was a sclendre coleryk man.
	His beerd was shave as neigh as ever he kan;
	His heer was by his eerys ful rownd yshorn;
	His top was dokked lyk a preest byforn.
	Ful longe weere hise legges and ful leene,
	Ylik a staf – ther was no calf yseene.
granary, grain-bin	Wel koude he keepe a gerner and a bynne;
get the better of him	Ther was noon auditour koude on him wynne.
	Wel wiste he by the droghte and by the reyn
	The yeldynge of his seed and of his greyn.
oxen, dairy-herd	His lordes sheepe, his neet, his dayerye,
horses, livestock	His swyn, his hors, his stoor and his pultrye

563 Alluding to the proverb, 'An honest miller hath a golden thumb' (i.e. there aren't any).

567 The Manciple is the steward and purchaser of provisions for a **Temple** or inn of court (a place in London where lawyers and law-students lived, learnt and practised).

571 'Always he was so sharply on the look-out in his purchasing'.

587 The Reeve is the foreman or chief bailiff of a large estate, with many supervisory and financial responsibilities. His office encourages him to think well of himself and guard his station jealously. He is **coleryk**, that is, dominated by the humour of choler (see 333n, 420n); such people were thought to be, amongst other things, clever and ill-tempered.

588–90 The close-shaven (therefore stubbly) beard, the hair cut in a round pudding-basin (hemispherical) shape at ear-level, and the hair above the forehead cropped short almost like a priest's tonsure, are signs of the Reeve's clerkly and social aspirations, as well as his 'close' and retentive nature.

Was hoolly in this Reves governynge,
And by his covenant yaf the rekenynge
Syn that his loord was twenty yeer of age.
Ther koude no man brynge hym in arrerage. — *catch him in arrears on his accounts*
Ther nas baillyf, ne hierde, nor oother hyne — *herdsman, servant*
That he ne knew his sleyghte and his covyne: — *cheating*
They weere adrad of hym as of the deeth. — *afraid*
His wonyng was ful faire upon an heeth; — *dwelling*
With greene trees shadwed was his place.
He koude bettre than his lord purchace;
Ful riche he was astoored pryvely. — *provided*
His lord wel koude he plesen subtilly,
To yeve and leene hym of his owene good — *lend, his (master's) own money*
And have a thank and yet a coote and hood.
In youthe he lerned hadde a good mister: — *craft*
He was a wel good wrighte, a carpenter. — *workman*
This Reve sat upon a wel good stot — *horse*
That was a pomely gray and highte Scot. — *dappled, called*
A long surcote of pers upon he haade — *grey-blue cloth*
And by his syde he baar a rusty blaade.
Of Northfolk was this Reve of which I telle,
Bisyde a town men clepyn Baldeswelle. — *Bawdswell (in Norfolk)*
Tukked he was as is a frere aboute — *with his gown tucked up in his belt*
And evere he rood the hyndreste of oure route.
  A somonour was ther with us in that place
That hadde a fyr-reed cherubynnes face,
For sawceflewm he was, with eyen narwe,
And hoot he was and lecherous as a sparwe,
With scaled browes blake and pyled berd. — *scabby, wispy*
Of his visage children weere aferd.
Ther nas quyk-silver, lytarge ne brymstoon, — *lead monoxide nor sulphur*
Borace, ceruce, ne oille of tartre noon, — *borax, white lead*
Ne oynement that wolde clense and byte,
That hym myghte helpen of his whelkes whyte — *pustules*
Nor of the knobbes sittynge on his chekes.
Wel loved he garlek, oynons and eek lekes
And for to drynke strong wyn, reed as blood;
Thanne wolde he speke and crye as he were wood,
And whan that he wel dronken hadde the wyn
Thanne wolde he speke no word but Latyn.
A fewe termes hadde he, two or thre,
That he hadde lerned out of som decree –
No wonder is, he herde it al the day,
And eek ye knowe wel how that a jay
Kan clepen 'Watte!' as wel as kan the pope. — *shout 'Walter!'*
But who-so koude in oother thyng hym grope,
Thanne hadde he spent al his philosophie;

623 The Summoner is a church official responsible for issuing summonses to people to attend the ecclesiastical court, where they would be arraigned for adultery, fornication and other non-criminal acts. There were many opportunities for blackmail (663–5) and accepting bribes (649–51).

624–5 The suggestion is of the fiery red faces of the cherubim, inflamed with divine love, in paintings of the angelic hierarchy. The Summoner's face is covered with pimply red blotches (**sawceflewm**) and swollen up so that his eyes look out of narrow slits.

633 It is not difficult to see a connection between the Summoner's diet and his problems with his complexion (he is suffering from a disease known as *alopicia*).

	Ay '*Questio quid juris*' wolde he crye.
rascal	He was a gentil harlot and a kynde;
	A bettre felawe sholde men noght fynde.
	He wolde suffre for a quart of wyn
	A good felawe to have his concubyn
	A twelf-monthe, and excusen hym at the fulle;
trick someone simple	Ful pryvely a fynch eek koude he pulle.
anywhere	And if he foond owher a good felawe
	He wolde techen him to have noon awe
archdeacon's excommunication	In swich caas of the ercedeknes curs,
	But if a mannes soule were in his purs,
	For in his purs he sholde ypunysshed be.
	'Purs is the ercedeknes helle,' seyde he.
	But wel I woot he lyed right indede:
	Of cursyng oghte ech gilty man him drede,
slay, absolution	For curs wol sle right as assoillyng savyth –
(see n.)	And also war hym of a *Significavit*.
in his power, at his own pleasure	In daunger hadde he at his owene gyse
	The yonge gerles of the diocise
secrets, their only source of advice	And knew hir conseil and was al hir reed.
	A gerland hadde he set upon his heed,
alehouse-sign	As greet as it were for an ale-stake;
round flat loaf	A bokeler hadde he maad hym of a cake.
	With hym ther rood a gentil PARDONER
companion	Of Rouncyval, his freend and his comper,
	That streight was comen fro the court of Rome.
	Ful loude he soong 'Com hyder, love, to me!'
strong bass	This Somonour baar to hym a styf burdoun,
	Was nevere trompe of half so greet a soun.
	This Pardoner hadde heer as yelow as wex,
hank	But smothe it heeng as dooth a stryke of flex;
In thin strands	By ounces henge his lokkes that he hadde
	And therwith he his shuldres overspradde;
in straggling separate strands	But thynne it lay, by colpons oon and oon.
	But hood, for jolitee, wered he noon,
tucked away, pouch	For it was trussed up in his walet.
in the latest fashion	Hym thoughte he rood al of the newe jet;
(see n.)	Dischevelee, save his cappe he rood al bare.
	Swiche glarynge eyen hadde he as an hare.
	A vernycle hadde he sowed upon his cappe,
	His walet biforn hym in his lappe,
Chock-full	Bretful of pardoun comen from Rome al hoot.

646 When really drunk (637), he parrots incessantly a common phrase from the court-room, 'The question is, what point of law (applies)?'.

659–61 Chaucer's voice here seems less elusive than usual.

662 'And also let him beware of an order for imprisonment'.

663–5 **yonge gerles**: young people (not necessarily female) who have fallen foul of the courts and whom the Summoner 'protects' (perhaps by pimping).

669 The Pardoner is licensed by the pope to carry 'indulgences', granting remission of earthly penance (such as fasts, vigils, extra prayers) to those who are truly penitent. Indulgences are a free gift from the church's treasury of merit, but the grateful penitent's offering to the church came to be thought of as part of the transaction. The Pardoner encourages this belief, and also the idea that the indulgences are pardons, that grant *forgiveness* of sin.

670 **Rouncyval** is the hospital of St Mary Rouncesval at Charing Cross in London, a cell of the house of Roncesvalles in the Pyrenees. It is the base from which the Pardoner is said to operate, and was in fact somewhat notorious in the 1380s and 1390s.

683 'With hair hanging down, save for his (skull-)cap he rode all bare-headed'.

685 A **vernycle** was a badge with an image of Christ's face made in imitation of the veil miraculously so imprinted when given by St Veronica to Christ to wipe his face on the way to Calvary.

thin and high-pitched	A voys he hadde as smal as hath a goot.
	No berd hadde he, ne nevere sholde have:
	As smothe it was as it were late yshave –
	I trowe he were a geldyng or a mare.
	But of his craft, fro Berwik into Ware
	Ne was ther swich another pardoner.
bag, pillow-case	For in his male he hadde a pilwe-beer
	Which hat he seyde was Oure Lady veyl;
piece	He seyde he hadde a gobet of the seyl
	That Seint Peter hadde whan that he wente
took up	Upon the see, til Jesu Crist hym hente;
cross, brass alloy	He hadde a cros of latoun ful of stones
	And in a glas he hadde pigges bones.
	But with thise relykes, whan that he foond
parson, in the country	A povre person dwellyng upon lond,
	Upon a day he gat hym moore moneye
	Than that the persoun gat in monthes tweye;
tricks	And thus with feyned flaterye and japes
dupes	He made the person and the peple his apes.
	But trewely to tellen at the laste,
	He was in chirche a noble ecclesiaste.
	Wel koude he rede a lesson and a storie,
(see n.)	But alderbest he soong an offertorie;
	For wel he wiste, whan that soong was songe,
smooth ('file')	He moste preche and wel affyle his tonge
	To wynne silver, as he ful wel koude;
	Therfore he soong the muryerly and loude.
briefly	Now have I told you soothly, in a clause,
	Th'estaat, th'array, the nombre and eek the cause
	Why that assembled was this compaignye
	In Southwerk at this gentil hostelrye
(another pub)	That highte the Tabard, faste by the Belle.
	But now is tyme to yow for to telle
conducted ourselves	How that we baren us that ilke nyght,
	Whan we weere in that hostelrye alyght,
journey	And after wol I telle of oure viage
	And al the remenant of oure pilgrymage.
	But first I pray yow of youre curteisye
attribute to, rudeness	That ye n'arette it noght my vileynye
	Though that I pleynly speke in this matere,
behaviour	To telle yow hir wordes and hir cheere,
exactly	Ne thogh I speke hir wordes proprely.
	For this ye knowen al so wel as I:
	Who-so shal telle a tale after a man

691 The insinuation, whether of eunuchry, effeminacy or homosexuality, or all three, is often taken as a 'fact' about the Pardoner, and much evidence adduced to support the inference, some of it dubious, such as the suggestion of a homosexual relationship with the Summoner in the supposed *double entendre* of **styf burdoun** (673). But clearly, with his glaring eyes, high-pitched voice and beardlessness, there is something odd about him.

692 Berwick, on the Scottish border, and Ware, just north of London, towns at either end of the Great North Road.

710 'But best of all he sang the anthem sung at the offering'.

725–42 The elaborate apology for retelling the pilgrims' tales exactly as they told them, even at the expense of indecorousness, is obviously tongue-in-cheek; but it is also a way of talking obliquely about a kind of 'truth to experience' that Chaucer, within the aesthetic of representation of his day, dominated by the moral demands placed upon the *auctor* to be full of 'sentence', would have found it difficult to speak about more directly.

He moot reherce as neigh as evere he kan — *close*
Everich a word, if it be in his charge, — *be his job*
Al speke he never so rudeliche and large, — *Though he speak, broadly*
Or ellis he moot telle his tale untrewe
Or feyne thyng or fynde wordes newe.
He may noght spare, althogh he weere his brother;
He moot as wel seye o word as another.
Crist spak hymself ful brode in holy writ – — *plainly*
And wel ye woot no vileynye is it.
Ek Plato seith, who-so kan hym rede,
'The wordes mote be cosyn to the dede.'
Also I pray yow to foryeve it me,
Al have I nat set folk in hir degree — *Though I have*
Here in this tale, as that they sholde stonde:
My wit is short, ye may wel understonde.
   Greet cheere made oure Hoost us everichon — *Good cheer*
And to the souper sette he us anon.
He served us with vitaille at the beste;
Strong was the wyn, and wel to drynke us leste. — *it pleased us*
A semely man oure Hoost was withalle — *suitable*
For to been a marchal in an halle. — *master of ceremonies*
A large man he was with eyen stepe – — *prominent*
A fairer burgeys was ther noon in Chepe –
Boold of his speche and wys and wel ytaught,
And of manhode hym lakkede right naught.
Eke therto he was right a murye man,
And after souper pleyen he bigan
And spak of murthe amonges othere thynges
(Whan that we hadde maad oure rekenynges),
And seyde thus: 'Now, lordes, trewely,
Ye been to me right welcome, hertely;
For by my trouthe, if that I shal nat lye,
I seigh noght this yeer so murye a compaignye
Atones in this herberwe as is now. — *place of lodging*
Fayn wolde I doon yow myrthe, wiste I how,
And of a myrthe I am right now bithoght
To doon yow ese, and it shal coste noght. — *pleasure*
   'Ye goon to Caunterbury – God yow spede,
The blisful martir quyte yow youre mede! — *grant, reward*
And wel I woot, as ye goon by the weye,
Ye shapen yow to talen and to pleye, — *tell tales*
For trewely, confort ne murthe is noon
To ryde by the weye domb as stoon;
And therfore wol I maken yow desport,
As I seyde erst, and doon yow som confort. — *first*
And if yow liketh alle by oon assent
For to stonden at my juggement
And for to werken as I shal yow seye,

741–2 A reference to the medieval commonplace that style must be appropriate to content, for which Plato is a mere hearsay authority.

747 The Host is named as Herry Bailly in the Cook's Prologue (I.4358). There was a real innkeeper of this name in the London records for 1381–2.

754 **Chepe** (modern Cheapside) was the main shopping street and market area of London.

Tomorwe, whan ye ryden by the weye,
Now, by my fader soule that is deed, *father's*
But ye be murye I wol yeve yow myn heed! *Unless*
Holde up youre hondes, withouten moore speche.'
  Oure conseil was nat longe for to seche; *seek*
Us thoughte it was nat worth to make it wys *make difficulties*
And graunted hym withouten moore avys *discussion*
And bade hym seye his voirdit as hym leste. *decision*
  'Lordynges,' quod he, 'now herkneth for the beste;
But taketh it noght, I pray yow, in desdeyn.
This is the poynt, to speken short and pleyn,
That ech of yow, to shorte with oure weye,
In this viage shal tellen tales tweye –
To Caunterbury-ward, I mene it so –
And homward he shal tellen othere two,
Of aventures that whilom have bifalle.
And which of yow that bereth hym best of alle –
That is to seyn, that telleth in this cas
Tales of best sentence and moost solas – *(see n.)*
Shal have a souper at oure aller cost *at the expense of all of us*
Here in this place, sittynge by this post,
Whan that we come agayn fro Caunterbury.
And for to make yow the moore mury
I wol myself goodly with yow ryde,
Right at myn owene cost, and be youre gyde;
And who-so wole my juggement withseye *oppose*
Shal paye al that we spende by the weye.
And if ye vouchesauf that it be so, *agree*
Tel me anoon, withouten wordes mo,
And I wol erly shape me therfore.' *prepare*
  This thyng was graunted and oure othes swore
With ful glad herte, and preyden hym also
That he wolde vouchesauf for to do so
And that he wolde been oure governour
And of oure tales juge and reportour *record-keeper*
And sette a souper at a certeyn prys
And we wol ruled been at his devys *wish*
In heigh and logh; and thus by oon assent *in every respect*
We been acorded to his juggement.
And therupon the wyn was fet anoon; *fetched*
We dronken, and to reste wente echon,
Withouten any lenger taryynge.
  A-morwe, whan that day bigan to sprynge,
Up roos oure Hoost and was oure aller cok *of us all*
And gadred us togydres in a flok
And forth we ryden a litel moore than pas *walking pace*
Unto the wateryng of Seint Thomas;
And there oure Hoost bigan his hors areste
And seyde, 'Lordes, herkneth, if yow leste.
Ye woot youre forward and it yow recorde: *call it to your mind*

798 **sentence and ... solas**: 'serious content and power of giving pleasure'.

826 A brook, where horses would be watered, about two miles out of London on the Old Kent Road.

If even-song and morwe-song acorde,
Lat se now who shal telle the firste tale.
As evere mote I drynke wyn or ale,
Who-so be rebel to my juggement
Shal paye for al that by the wey is spent.
(see n.) Now draweth cut, er that we ferrer twynne:
He which that hath the shorteste shal bigynne.
'Sire Knyght,' quod he, 'my mayster and my lord,
decision Now draweth cut, for that is myn acord.
Cometh neer,' quod he, 'my lady Prioresse,
And ye, sire Clerc, lat be youre shamefastnesse,
Ne studieth noght; ley hond to, every man!'
Anoon to drawen every wight bigan,
And shortly for to tellen as it was,
Were it by aventure, or sort, or cas,
The sothe is this: the cut fil to the Knyght,
Of which ful blithe and glad was every wight,
And telle he moste his tale, as was resoun,
agreement By forward and by composicioun,
As ye han herd; what nedeth wordes mo?
And whan this goode man saugh that it was so,
Being one that As he that wys was and obedient
To kepe his forward by his free assent,
He seyde, 'Syn I shal bigynne the game,
What, welcome be the cut, in Goddes name!
Now lat us ryde, and herkneth what I seye.'
And with that word we ryden forth oure weye
And he bigan with right a murye cheere
His tale anoon and seyde as ye may heere.

{The Knight's Tale follows}

The Miller's Prologue and Tale

The Miller's Prologue

The Host has his plans for the management of the tale-telling competition and, after the Knight has finished his noble and tragic philosophical romance of the love of Palamon and Arcite for Emelye, he turns to the Monk, as in some sense the next highest in the social hierarchy, for the next tale. But at this point his well-laid plans begin to come unstuck, and the spontaneous drama of the pilgrimage takes over, as the drunken and unruly Miller claims the stage. His promised tale causes immediate offence to the Reeve, who vows revenge and so provides a dramatic set-up for the next tale following. The pilgrimage begins to generate its own apparently unsupervised drama; the Host stands helplessly by. (Line-numbering from Fragment I, which continues.)

Whan that the Knyght had thus his tale ytoold,
In al the compaignie nas ther yong ne oold
That he ne seyde it was a noble storie
recall And worthy for to drawen to memorie,
specially And namely the gentils everichon.
As I may live Oure Hoost lough and swoor, 'So moot I gon,

835 'Now draw lots (sticks or straws of different lengths), before we go any further'.

844 Chance, luck and destiny may have played less part than the Host's deferential handling of things to ensure that the Knight, as the highest in rank, tells the first story, as is appropriate in the 'nature of things'.

unbuckled, bag	This gooth aright! Unbokeled is the male.
	Lat se now who shal telle another tale,
	For trewely the game is wel bigonne.
	Now telleth ye, sire Monk, if that ye konne,
set against in competition	Somwhat to quite with the Knyghtes tale.'
because of being drunk	The Millere, that for dronken was al pale,
with difficulty	So that unnethe upon his hors he sat,
doff (as a mark of respect)	He nolde avalen neither hood ne hat,
	Ne abiden no man for his curteisye,
	But in Pilates voys he gan to crye,
(Christ's) arms	And swoor, 'By armes, and by blood and bones,
	I kan a noble tale for the nones
	With which I wol now quite the Knyghtes tale.'
	Oure Hoost saugh that he was dronke of ale,
	And seyde, 'Abyde, Robyn, leeve brother;
	Som bettre man shal telle us first another.
properly	Abyde, and lat us werken thriftily.'
	'By Goddes soule,' quod he, 'that wol nat I,
	For I wol speke or elles go my wey.'
in the devil's name	Oure Hoost answerde, 'Tel on, a devele way!
	Thow art a fool, thy wit is overcome.'
one and all	'Now herkneth,' quod the Millere, 'alle and some!
	But first I make a protestacioun
	That I am dronke – I knowe it by my soun.
say amiss	And therfore if that I mysspeke or seye,
Blame it on	Wite it the ale of Southwerk, I preye.
(see n.)	For I wol telle a legende and a lyf
	Bothe of a carpenter and of his wyf,
made a fool of the carpenter	How that a clerk hath set the wrightes cappe.'
Stop your loud mouth	The Reve answerde and seyde, 'Stynt thy clappe!
	Lat be thy lewed dronken harlotrye.
	It is a synne and eek a greet folye
injure	To apeyren any man or hym diffame,
ill-fame	And eek to bryngen wyves in swich fame.
	Thow mayst ynow of othere thynges seyn.'
in reply	This dronken Millere spak ful soone ageyn
	And seyde, 'Leeve brother Osewold,
	Who hath no wyf, he is no cokewold.
	But I sey nat therfore that thow art oon:
	Ther been ful goode wyves many oon
	And evere a thousand goode ayeyns oon badde –
are mad	That knowestow wel thyself, but if thou madde.
	Why artow angry with my tale now?
	I have a wyf, pardee, as wel as thow,
	Yet nolde I, for the oxen in my plough,
	Take upon me moore than ynough,
one (i.e. a cuckold)	As demen of myself that I were oon;

3124 **in Pilates voys**: the loud thick voice in which Pontius Pilate delivered his bombastic speeches in the medieval plays of the Trial of Jesus (such as we know them from the fifteenth-century mystery-play cycles).

3141 **legende**: saint's life (i.e. story with a martyrdom).

3144 The Reeve, in his profession as a farm manager, would not be a friend of millers; but he had also been in his youth, as we are told in GP 614, a carpenter, and he suspects the Miller is getting at him. It may be that we are supposed to understand that they know each other of old: unusually, they address each other by name.

I wol bileeve wel that I am noon. — *(see n.)*
An housbonde shal noght been inquisityf
Of Goddes pryvetee nor of his wyf. — *secrets (pun on 'private parts')*
So he may fynde Goddes foyson there, — *God's plenty*
Of the remenant nedeth noght enquere.'
What sholde I moore seyn but this Millere
He nolde his wordes for no man forbere,
But tolde his cherles tale in his manere.
Me athynketh that I shal reherce it heere. — *I regret that I have to repeat it*
And therfore every gentil wight I preye,
Demeth noght for Goddes love that I seye
Of yvel entente, but for I moot reherse
Hir tales alle, be they bet or werse,
Or ellis falsen som of my matere.
And therfore, whoso list it noght yhere,
Turne over the leef and chese another tale;
For he shal fynde ynowe, grete and smale, — *of every sort*
Of storial thyng that toucheth gentilesse — *historically true, has to do with*
And eek moralitee and holynesse.
Blameth noght me if that ye chese amys.
The Millere is a cherl – ye knowe wel this;
So was the Reve and othere manye mo,
And harlotrye they tolden bothe two.
Avyseth yow, and put me out of blame; — *Think about it*
And eek men shal noght maken ernest of game. — *take a joke seriously*

The Miller's Tale

The Miller's Tale is a *fabliau*, that is, a tale of low sexual intrigue and trickery with a cast of characters that usually includes a petit-bourgeois husband, often old, a wife who has some degree of unfulfilled sexual appetite, and an intruder on the domestic scene who is usually a cleric or student or other religious. The latter role is 'doubled' in the brilliant double plot (of the predicted flood and the 'misdirected kiss') of the Miller's Tale. Tales such as this were popular in court and aristocratic circles (Boccaccio tells a number in the *Decameron*, with its idyllic courtly and garden setting) and are not necessarily to be thought of as lower-class entertainment. Chaucer's attribution of such tales to the 'cherles', on the basis that dirty stories are appropriate to the lower classes, may seem appropriate to a Victorian sensibility, but is in fact highly innovative. The Miller, however, is important only as a cover for Chaucer, giving him the freedom (maybe a freedom that it was necessary for him explicitly to win) to explore the rich comic potential of such stories. The Miller is soon forgotten: the voice is patrician (see 3268–70), lyrical, genially ruthless. Chaucer holds without flinching to the controlling ethos of *fabliau*: there are no things in life more important than survival and the satisfaction of appetite, and no more certain way of being assured of them than by being *smart*. *Fabliau* thus stands as the balanced opposite of 'romance', as the Miller's Tale stands juxtaposed to the Knight's Tale, which is also about the love of two men for the same woman: in *fabliau* the exhortation is not to be true, loyal, generous and courteous, but to be *clever*.

Whilom ther was dwellyng in Oxenford — *Once*
A riche gnof, that gestes heeld to bord, — *churl, lodgers, as boarders*
And of his craft he was a carpenter.
With hym ther was dwellynge a povre scoler,

3162–6 'I do not want to burden myself even with the thought that I might be a cuckold (even though my oxen might remind me of the horns cuckolds are supposed to wear); as long as I don't know, and as long as I get my share, where's the harm?'
3171–86 Chaucer excuses himself, in this beautifully ironical passage, for telling what we presume will be a low coarse tale by reminding us (cf. GP 725–42) of his obligation to be an accurate reporter of all that happened on the pilgrimage. He does not have a choice; but the reader does, and can turn the leaf if the prospect of scatology offends. Chaucer knows what kind of invitation this is.

the arts curriculum at university	Hadde lerned art, but al his fantasie
learn	Was turned for to leere astrologie,
(see n.)	And koude a certeyn of conclusions
analysis	To demen by interrogacions,
specific (astrologically significant)	If that men axed hym, in certein houres
	Whan that men sholde have droghte or ellis shoures,
	Or if men axed hym what shal bifalle
	Of every thyng – I may nat rekene hem alle.
courteous (gentle, 'handy')	This clerk was clepyd hende Nicholas.
secret, pleasure	Of derne love he koude and of solas,
cunning, secretive	And therto he was sleigh and ful pryvee
	And lyk a mayde meke for to see.
	A chambre hadde he in that hostelrie
	Allone withouten any compaignye,
daintily bedecked, sweet-smelling	Ful fetisly ydight with herbes swoote,
	And he hymself as sweete as is the roote
setwall (a gingery spice)	Of lycorys or any cetuale.
(Ptolemy's treatise on astrology)	His Almageste, and bookes grete and smale,
astrolabe, belonging to	His astrelabye, longynge for his art,
(see n.)	His augrym stones layen faire apart
	On shelves couched at his beddes heed,
linen-chest, coarse red cloth	His presse ycovered with a faldyng reed;
psaltery (kind of triangular harp)	And al above ther lay a gay sautrye
	On which he made a-nyghtes melodye
	So swetely that al the chambre roong;
	And *Angelus ad virginem* he soong,
the King's Tune (not identified)	And after that he soong the 'Kynges Note' –
	Ful often blissed was his murye throte.
	And thus this swete clerk his tyme spente
(see n.)	After his freendes fyndyng and his rente.
	This carpenter hadde wedded newe a wyf
	Which that he lovede moore than his lyf;
	Of eighteteene yeer she was of age.
	Jalous he was and heeld hire narwe in cage,
	For she was wilde and yong, and he was old
likely to be	And demed hymself been lyk a cokewold.
	He knew nat Catoun, for his wit was rude,
instructed that one	That bad man sholde wedde his similitude.
state in life	Men sholde wedden after hir estaat,
	For youthe and elde is often at debaat.
	But sith that he was fallen in the snare,
	He moste endure, as oother folk, his care.
	Fair was this yonge wyf, and therwithal
weasel, delicate and slender	As any wesele hir body gent and smal.
belt, with vertical stripes	A ceynt she werde, barred al of sylk,
apron	A barmclooth as whit as morne mylk

3193 'And knew a certain number of logical propositions'.

3210 **augrym stones**: stones with Arabic numerals (algorism) for use on an abacus.

3216 ***Angelus ad virginem***: 'The angel to the Virgin (came)', an Annunciation carol that has been thought comically to prefigure Nicholas's sudden accosting of Alison (3271–81).

3220 'According to what his friends provided and his income'.

3227 **Catoun**: Cato was the supposed author of a series of 'Distichs', short Latin verse apophthegms taught in elementary classes in grammar schools.

3233–70 Detailed descriptions of women were a common rhetorical trope of medieval poetry, usually formal and feature-by-feature. Chaucer's version of the convention is minutely observed, subtle, suggestive, comical and yet seductive ('the queen of a sailor's dreams').

loins, gore (sewn-in strip of cloth)	Upon hir lendes, ful of many a goore.
(see n.)	Whit was hir smok, and broyden al bifoore
around the neck-line	And eek bihynde, on hir coler aboute,
	Of col-blak silk, withinne and eek withoute.
ribbons, cap	The tapes of hir white voluper
same colour as	Were of the same sute of hir coler,
headband	Hir filet brood of sylk and set ful hye,
flirtatious	And sikerly she hadde a likerous iye;
closely plucked	Ful smale ypulled were hir browes two
sloe	And tho were bent and blake as is a sloo.
	She was ful moore blisful on to see
early-ripe pear	Than is the newe pere-jonette tree,
	And softer than the wolle is of a wether;
	And by her girdel heeng a purs of lether,
spangled with brass	Tasseled with silk and perled with latoun.
	In al this world, to seken up and doun,
imagine	There nys no man so wys that koude thenche
popsy	So gay a popelote or swich a wenche.
	Ful brighter was the shynyng of hir hewe
gold coin	Than in the Tour the noble yforged newe.
lively	But of hir soong, it was as loude and yerne
	As any swalwe sittyng on a berne.
	Therto she koude skippe and make game,
	As any kyde or calf folwynge his dame.
ale and honey drink, mead	Hir mouth was sweete as bragot or the meeth
	Or hoord of apples leyd in hey or heeth.
Skittish, high-spirited	Wynsynge she was as is a joly colt,
(see n.)	Loong as a mast and uprighte as a bolt.
low	A brooch she baar upon hir loue coler
raised centre of a shield	As brood as is the boos of a bokeler;
	Hir shoes were laced on hir legges hye.
primrose, a real poppet	She was a prymerole, a piggesnye,
lay	For any lord to leggen in his bedde,
	Or yet for any good yemen to wedde.
again	Now, sire, and eft, sire, so bifel the cas
	That on a day this hende Nicholas
have fun	Fil with this yonge wyf to rage and pleye,
	Whil that hir housbonde was at Osneye
full of tricks	(As clerkes ben ful subtil and ful queynte),
(see glossary)	And pryvely he caughte hire by the queynte
	And seyde, 'Ywys, but if ich have my wille,
secret, sweetheart, die	For derne love of thee, lemman, I spille.'
	And heeld hire harde by the haunchebones
at once	And seyde, 'Lemman, love me al atones
	Or I wol dyen, also God me save!'
(see n.)	And she sproong as a colt dooth in the trave
twisted	And with hir heed she wryed faste awey.
	She seyde, 'I wol nat kisse thee, by my fey!
	Wy, lat be, quod ich, lat be, Nicholas,

3238 Her smock (a partly visible undergarment) was embroidered at front and back.
3256 **Tour**: the Tower of London, where the mint was.
3264 **uprighte as a bolt**: straight as an arrow for a crossbow.
3274 Osney, very close to Oxford (and now part of it), with a house of Augustinian canons where John, as we hear later (3400, 3659), was doing some carpentering.
3282 **trave**: frame for holding a restive horse to be shod.

oh help	Or I wol crye "out, harrow!" and "allas!"
	Do wey youre handes for youre curteisye!'
	This Nicholas gan mercy for to crye
pressed his attentions so earnestly	And spak so faire and profred hym so faste
	That she hir love hym graunted atte laste
	And swoor hir ooth by Seint Thomas of Kent
	That she wolde been at his comaundement
opportunity	Whan that she may hir leyser wel espie.
	'Myn housbonde is so ful of jalousie
be on guard	That but ye waite wel and been pryvee
	I woot right wel I nam but deed,' quod she.
secretive	'Ye moste been ful derne as in this cas.'
	'Nay, therof care thee noght,' quod Nicholas.
badly employed his time	'A clerk hadde lutherly biset his while
	But if he koude a carpenter bigyle.'
	And thus they been acorded and ysworn
watch out for	To waite a tyme, as I have told biforn.
	Whan Nicholas hadde doon thus everydel
patted, loins	And thakked hire aboute the lendes wel,
	He kiste hir sweete and taketh his sautrye
	And pleyeth faste, and maketh melodye.
	Thanne fil it thus, that to the parissh chirche,
	Cristes owene werkes for to wirche,
holy day	This goode wyf wente on an haliday.
	Hir forheed shoon as bright as any day,
left	So was it wasshen whan she leet hir werk.
	Now was ther of that chirche a parissh clerk,
	The which that was yclepid Absolon.
Curled	Crul was his heer and as the gold it shoon
radiated out	And strouted as a fanne large and brode;
fine hair-parting	Ful streight and evene lay his joly shode.
complexion	His rode was reed, hise eyen greye as goos.
(see n.)	With Poules wyndow corven on his shoos,
elegantly	In hoses rede he wente fetisly.
in close-fitting fashion	Yclad he was ful smal and proprely
tunic, light blue	Al in a kirtel of a lyght waget –
laces for tying	Ful faire and thikke been the pointes set –
	And therupon he hadde a gay surplys
twig	As whit as is the blosme upon the rys:
young man	A murye child he was, so God me save.
	Wel koude he laten blood and clippe and shave
quittance (legal release of property)	And maken a chartre of lond or aquitaunce.
	On twenty manere koude he trippe and daunce
In the fashion	After the scole of Oxenforde tho,
jig	And with his legges casten to and fro
rebeck (kind of fiddle)	And pleyen songes on a smal rubible;
high treble	Therto he soong somtyme a loud quynyble,
guitar	And as wel koude he pleye on a gyterne.

3313 Absolon, or Absalom, was the son of David, and renowned in the Middle Ages as the epitome of male beauty (2 Samuel 14:26).

3318 'With a traceried window carved in lattice-work on the uppers of his shoes'.

3326 It was usual for parish clerks (who were not full-time holders of livings) to supplement their income by acting as amateur surgeons and barbers, and as scribes in the making out of legal documents for land-conveyancing.

In al the town nas brewhous ne taverne
That he ne visited with his solas, *pleasant company*
Ther any gaylard tappestere was. *merry barmaid*
But sooth to seyn he was somdel squaymous *squeamish*
Of fartyng, and of speche daungerous. *prissy*
This Absolon, that joly was and gay,
Gooth with a sencer on the haliday, *incense-burner*
Sensynge the wyves of the parisshe faste, *(see n.)*
And many a lovely look on hem he caste
And namely on this carpenteris wyf. *especially*
To looke on hire hym thoughte a murye lyf,
She was so propre and sweete and likerous, *nice, tasty-looking*
I dar wel seyn if she hadde been a mous,
And he a cat, he wolde hir hente anon. *pounce on*
This parisshe clerk, this joly Absolon,
Hath in his herte swich a love-longynge
That of no wyf ne took he noon offrynge –
For curteisye he seyde he wolde noon.
The moone, whan it was nyght, ful brighte shoon
And Absolon his gyterne hath ytake –
For paramours he thoghte for to wake – *For the sake of love, stay awake*
And forth he gooth, jolyf and amorous,
Til he cam to the carpenteres hous
A litel after cokkes hadde ycrowe,
And dressed hym up by a shot-wyndowe *(see n.)*
That was upon the carpenteris wal.
He syngeth in his voys gentil and smal, *high-pitched*
'Now, deere lady, if thy wille be,
I praye yow that ye wole rewe on me,' *have pity*
Ful wel acordant to his giternynge.
This carpenter awook and herde him synge
And spak unto his wyf and seyde anon,
'What, Alison! Herestow noght Absolon,
That chaunteth thus under oure boures wal?' *bedroom wall*
And she answerde hir housbonde therwithal,
'Yis, God woot, John, I here it everydel.'
This passeth forth; what wol ye bet than wel? *(what more would you have?)*
Fro day to day this joly Absolon
So woweth hire that hym is wo-bigon.
He waketh al the nyght and al the day;
He kembed his lokkes brode and made hym gay;
He woweth hire by meenes and brocage, *go-betweens and brokers*
And swoor he wolde been hir owene page; *personal servant*
He syngeth, brokkyng as a nyghtyngale; *warbling*
He sente hire pyment, meeth and spiced ale *spiced wine, mead*
And wafres pipyng hoot out of the gleede, *glowing coals*
And, for she was of towne, he profred meede – *money*
For som folk wol be wonnen for richesse

3341 'Eagerly carrying the censer up and down among the parish-wives'.

3358 'And set himself up by a shuttered window (hinged at the sides)'.

3380 **for she was of towne**. Absolon thinks that, since she is a townswoman, she will understand the practical value of cash in hand. The meaning is not 'of the streets'.

blows And som for strokes and som for gentilesse.
masterly skill Somtyme, to shewe his lightnesse and maistrye,
He pleyeth Herodes upon a scaffold hye.
But what availleth hym as in this cas?
She loveth so this hende Nicholas
go whistle That Absolon may blowe the bukkes horn;
He ne hadde for his labour but a scorn.
fool And thus she maketh Absolon hire ape
And al his ernest turneth til a jape.
Ful sooth is this proverbe, it is no lye,
sly one near at hand Men seith right thus: 'Alwey the neighe slye
far-off loved one to be unloved Maketh the ferre leeve to be looth.'
For thogh that Absolon be wood or wrooth,
Bycause that he fer was from hir sighte,
This neighe Nicholas stood in his lighte.
Now bere thee wel, thow hende Nicholas,
For Absolon may waille and synge 'allas.'
And so bifel it on a Saterday
This carpenter was goon til Osenay,
And hende Nicholas and Alisoun
Acorded been to this conclusioun,
trick That Nicholas shal shapen hem a wile
This sely jalous housbonde to bigile,
And if so be the game wente aright
She sholde slepen in his arm al nyght –
For this was hir desir and his also.
And right anoon, withouten wordes mo,
This Nicholas no lenger wolde tarie
But dooth ful softe unto his chambre carie
Bothe mete and drynke for a day or tweye
And to hir housbonde bad hire for to seye,
If that he axed after Nicholas,
She sholde seye she nyste wher he was:
Of al that day she seigh hym noght with iye –
She trowed that he was in maladye,
For, for no cry, hir mayde koude hym calle,
whatever happened He nolde answere for nothyng that myghte falle.
This passeth forth al thilke Saterday
That Nicholas stille in his chambre lay
ate and slept And eet and sleepe or dide what hym leste
Til Sonday that the sonne gooth to reste.
This sely carpenter hath greet mervaille
ail Of Nicholas, or what thyng myghte hym aille,
And seyde, 'I am adrad, by Seint Thomas,
It stondeth nat aright with Nicholas.
forbid, should die God shilde that he deyde sodeynly!
unstable This world is now ful tikel, sikerly.
I seigh today a corps yborn to chirche
on Monday That now a Monday last I seigh hym wirche.'
'Go up,' quod he unto his knave anoon,

3384 **Herodes**. A second reference to the mystery plays, this time to the play of King Herod and the Magi; Herod would be on a throne high on the scaffolding that formed the set. His ranting speeches were famous.

'Clepe at his dore, or knokke with a stoon.
Looke how it is, and tel me boldely.'
This knave gooth hym up ful sturdily
And at the chambre dore whil that he stood
He cryde and knokked as that he were wood,
'What, how! What do ye, maister Nicholay?
How may ye slepen al the longe day?'
But al for noght; he herde nat a word.
An hole he foond, ful lowe upon a bord,
Ther as the cat was wont in for to crepe,
And at that hole he looked in ful depe
And atte laste he hadde of hym a sighte.
This Nicholas sat evere capying uprighte, — *gaping straight up in the air*
As he had kiked on the newe moone. — *stared*
Adown he gooth and tolde his maister soone
In what array he saw this ilke man. — *state*
This carpenter to blessen hym bigan, — *cross himself*
And seyde, 'Help us, Seinte Frideswyde!
A man woot litel what hym shal bityde.
This man is falle, with his astromye, — *astronomy (maybe a malapropism)*
In som woodnesse or in som agonye. — *madness*
I thoghte ay wel how that it sholde be!
Men sholde noght knowe of Goddes privetee.
Ye, blessed be alwey a lewed man
That noght but oonly his bileve kan! — *faith*
So ferde another clerk with astromye: — *fared*
He walked in the feeldes for to prye — *gaze*
Upon the sterres, what ther sholde bifalle,
Til he was in a marle-pit yfalle – — *clay-pit*
He saw nat that! But yet, by Seint Thomas,
Me reweth sore of hende Nicholas. — *I feel sorry for*
He shal be rated of his studiyng, — *scolded for*
If that I may, by Jesus, hevene kyng!
Get me a staf, that I may underspore, — *lever up from under*
Whil that thow, Robyn, hevest up the dore.
He shal out of his studyyng, as I gesse.'
And to the chambre dore he gan hym dresse.
His knave was a strong carl for the nones — *fellow*
And by the haspe he haaf it up atones; — *heaved it off in one go*
Into the floor the dore fil anoon.
This Nicholas sat ay as stille as stoon
And evere caped up into the eyr.
This carpenter wende he were in despeyr — *thought*
And hente hym by the sholdres myghtily
And shook hym harde and cryde spitously, — *fiercely*
'What! Nicholay! What how! What, looke adoun! — *What ho!*

3449 Frideswide was a local Oxford saint, renowned for her healing powers.

3450–61 This little vignette of the carpenter's smug satisfaction in the contemplation of his own simple honest Christian faith and of the fate of clever-dicks like Nicholas reconciles us to the relishing of any indignity that may befall him (though he has his sympathetic moments, as at 3462, 3522–4). The story of the absent-minded **clerk** (3457–61) was a favourite.

3466 It seems too much of a coincidence that the stout servant's name is **Robyn** (like that of the Miller), and that he too has a talent for heaving doors off their hinges (cf. GP 550).

Awake and thenk on Cristes passioun!
I crouche thee from elves and fro wightes.' — *(see n.)*
Therwith the nyght-spel seyde he anon-rightes — *charm, straightway*
On foure halves of the hous aboute
And on the thresshfold of the dore withoute: — *threshold*
'Jesus Crist and Seinte Benedight, — *Benedict*
Blesse this hous from every wikked wight,
For the nyghtes nerye the white *pater-noster*! — *(see n.)*
Where wentestow, Seinte Petres suster?' — *did you go*
  And at the laste this hende Nicholas
Gan for to sike soore, and seyde, 'Allas! — *sigh deeply*
Shal al the world be lost eftsoones now?' — *again*
  This carpenter answerde, 'What seistow?
What! Thenk on God, as we doon, men that swynke.'
  This Nicholas answerde, 'Fecche me drynke,
And after wol I speke in pryvetee
Of certein thyng that toucheth me and thee.
I wol telle it noon oother man, certayn.'
  This carpenter gooth doun and comth agayn
And broghte of myghty ale a large quart,
And whan that eech of hem hadde dronke his part
This Nicholas his dore faste shette — *shut*
And doun the carpenter by hym he sette,
And seyde, 'John, myn hoost, lief and deere,
Thou shalt upon thy trouthe swere me heere — *word of honour*
That to no wight thou shalt this conseil wreye, — *betray*
For it is Cristes conseil that I seye,
And if thou telle it man, thou art forlore; — *tell it to anyone, lost*
For this vengeaunce thow shalt have therfore,
That if thow wreye me thow shalt be wood.'
  'Nay, Crist forbede it, for his holy blood!'
Quod tho this sely man, 'I nam no labbe, — *blabbermouth*
And, thogh I seye, I nam nat lief to gabbe. — *(see n.)*
Sey what thow wolt, I shal it nevere telle
To child ne wyf, by hym that harwed helle!' — *harried (despoiled)*
  'Now John,' quod Nicholas, 'I wol noght lye:
I have yfounde in myn astrologye,
As I have looked in the moone bright,
That now a Monday next, at quarter nyght, — *on, a quarter of the way through*
Shal falle a reyn, and that so wilde and wood
That half so greet was nevere Noees flood.
This world,' he seyde, 'in lasse than in an hour
Shal al be dreynt, so hidous is the shour. — *drowned*
Thus shal mankynde drenche, and lese hir lyf.' — *drown, lose*
  This carpenter answerde, 'Allas, my wyf!
And shal she drenche? Allas, myn Alisoun!'

3478–86 The carpenter uses both orthodox (exhortation to think on Christ's passion, the making of the sign of the cross) and less orthodox means (the magic charm or **nyght-spel** said around the house) to ward off evil spirits. The white *pater-noster* (version of the 'Our Father' prayer, 'white' because not 'black' magic) survives to recent times. Relatives of St Peter (3486) wander in and out of these conjurations.

3479 'I make the sign of the cross over thee (for protection) from elves and (unearthly) creatures'.

3485 'May the white *pater-noster* defend (us) from the night-dangers'.

3510 'And though I say it myself, I am not one to gab'.

3512 **harwed helle**. A reference to the 'Harrowing of Hell', the despoiling or 'harrying' of hell by Christ (in the brief interval between his crucifixion and the resurrection), that freed all of its inmates who had been faithful to the Law in their lives. It was a favourite subject for mystery plays.

For sorwe of this he fil almoost adoun,
And seyde, 'Is ther no remedie in this cas?'
before God 'Why, yis, for Gode,' quod hende Nicholas,
learning and good advice 'If thow wolt werken after loore and reed –
according to your own ideas Thow mayst noght werken after thyn owene heed;
For thus seith Salomon, that was ful trewe:
good advice, be sorry "Werk al by conseil, and thow shalt noght rewe."
And if thow werken wolt by good consayl,
I undertake, withouten mast or sayl,
Yit shal I save hire and thee and me.
Hastow nat herd how saved was Noe,
Whan that oure Lord hadde warned hym biforn
That al the world with water sholde be lorn?'
'Yis,' quod this carpenter, 'ful yore ago.'
'Hastow nat herd,' quod Nicholas, 'also
family The sorwe of Noe with his felaweshipe
Er that he myghte gete his wyf to shipe?
Hym hadde levere, I dar wel undertake,
black rams At thilke tyme, than alle his wetheres blake,
That she hadde had a ship hirself allone.
do you know And therfore, wostow what is best to done?
This axeth haste, and of an hastyf thyng
Men may noght preche or maken tariyng.
this dwelling-house 'Anoon go gete us faste into this in
brewing tub A knedyng-trogh or ellis a kymelyn
For eech of us, but looke that they be large,
float In which we mowen swymme as in a barge,
And han therinne vitaille suffisaunt
But for a day – fy on the remenaunt!
subside The water shal aslake and goon away
around 9 a.m. Aboute pryme upon the nexte day.
But Robyn may nat wite of this, thy knave,
Ne eek thy mayde Gille I may nat save:
Axe noght why, for thogh thou axe me
I wol noght tellen Goddes pryvetee.
(see n.) Suffiseth thee, but if thy wittes madde,
To han as greet a grace as Noe hadde.
Thy wyf shal I wel saven, out of doute.
about this matter Go now thy wey, and speed thee heer-aboute.
'But when thou hast for hire and thee and me
Ygeten us thise knedyng-tubbes thre,
Thanne shaltow hangen hem in the roof ful hye,
preparations That no man of oure purveiance espye.
And whan thow thus hast doon as I have seyd
And hast oure vitaille faire in hem yleyd
And eek an ax to smyte the corde atwo,
Whan that the water cometh, that we may go

3538–43 The story of Noah (Genesis 7) was the subject of perhaps the most popular of the mystery plays, where the apocryphal episode of 'Mrs' Noah's truculent opposition to the Ark-scheme made for vigorous comic relief. John the carpenter does not seem to have learnt much about theology from seeing the play.

3559 'unless you are going out of your mind'.

3563–82 The tumble of Nicholas's sentences, in this wonderful passage, conveys the imaginative energy with which he enters into his plots, solving the problems as he thinks of them, and ending with a rapturous vision of the world renewed for the lucky threesome. One has the impression that Nicholas takes more pleasure in clever plots than anything.

And breke an hole an heigh, upon the gable,
on the garden side Unto the gardyn-ward, over the stable,
That we may frely passen forth oure way
Whan that the grete shour is goon away –
Thanne shaltow swymme as murye, I undertake,
As dooth the white doke after hire drake.
Thanne wol I clepe, "How, Alison! How, John!
Be murye, for the flood wol passe anon."
And thou wolt seyn, "Hail, maister Nicholay!
Good morwe, I see thee wel, for it is day."
And thanne shal we be lordes al oure lyf
Of al the world, as Noe and his wyf.
 'But of o thyng I warne thee ful right:
Be wel avysed on that ilke nyght
That we been entred into shippes bord
That noon of us ne speke noght a word,
Ne clepe ne crye, but been in his prayere,
commandment For it is Goddes owene heste deere.
far apart Thy wyf and thow mote hange fer atwynne,
For that bitwixe yow shal be no synne,
Namoore in lookyng than ther shal in dede.
This ordinaunce is seyd: go, God thee spede!
Tomorwe at nyght, whan men been alle aslepe,
Into oure knedyng-tubbes wol we crepe
And sitten there, abidyng Goddes grace.
time Go now thy wey, I have no lenger space
To make of this no lenger sermonyng.
(see n.) Men seyn thus, "Seend the wise, and sey nothyng."
Thow art so wys, it nedeth thee nat teche:
Go save oure lyf, and that I thee biseche.'
 This sely carpenter gooth forth his wey –
Ful ofte he seyde 'Allas and weylawey' –
And to his wyf he tolde his privetee
And she was war and knew it bet than he,
ingenious plot was all about What al this queynte cast was for to seye.
acted But nathelees she ferde as she wolde deye,
And seyde, 'Allas! go forth thy wey anon,
Help us to scape or we been dede echon!
I am thy trewe verray wedded wyf –
Go, deere spouse, and help to save oure lyf.'
what, strong emotion Lo, which a greet thyng is affeccioun!
things they imagine Men may dyen of ymaginacioun,
So depe may impressioun be take.
This sely carpenter bigynneth quake;
Hym thynketh verrailiche that he may se
Noes flood come walwyng as the see
To drenchen Alisoun, his hony deere.
has a very woeful appearance He wepeth, waileth, maketh sory cheere;
sighs, groan He siketh with ful many a sory swogh.
He gooth and geteth hym a knedyng-trogh

3589–92 Tradition – conveniently for Nicholas – had it that there was no sexual intercourse on the Ark.

3598 'The wise will understand, though nothing is said' (proverbial: 'A word to the wise is enough').

And after that a tubbe and a kymelyn
And pryvely he sente hem to his in
And heeng hem in the roof in privetee.
With his — His owene hand he made laddres thre,
uprights (of the ladders) — To clymben by the ronges and the stalkes
rafters — Unto the tubbes hangyng in the balkes,
And hem vitailed, bothe trogh and tubbe,
big jug — With breed and chese and good ale in a jubbe,
Suffisynge right ynogh as for a day.
preparation — But er that he hadde maad al this array,
servant girl — He sente his knave and eek his wenche also
business — Upon his nede to Londoun for to go.
And on the Monday, whan it drogh to nyght,
He shette his dore withouten candel-lyght
arranged — And dressed alle thyng as it sholde be,
in no time — And shortly up they clomben alle thre;
(see n.) — They seten stille wel a furlong way.
(see n.) — 'Now, *Pater-noster*, clom!' seyde Nicholay,
And 'Clum!' quod John, and 'Clum!' seyde Alisoun.
This carpenter seyde his devocioun,
quietly he sits, prays — And stille he sit and biddeth his prayere,
might hear — Awaitynge on the reyn, if he it heere.
because of his weariness with work — The dede sleepe, for wery bisynesse,
Fil on this carpenter right as I gesse
Aboute corfew-tyme, or litel moore;
weariness of his spirit — For travaillyng of his goost he groneth soore
likewise he snores — And eft he routeth, for his heed myslay.
Doun of the laddre stalketh Nicholay
And Alisoun ful softe adoun she spedde:
Withouten wordes mo they goon to bedde
Ther as the carpenter is wont to lye –
Ther was the revel and the melodye!
And thus lyth Alisoun and Nicholas
In busynesse of myrthe and in solas
Til that the belle of laudes gan to rynge
And freres in the chauncel gonne synge.
This parissh clerk, this amorous Absolon,
That is for love alwey so wo-bigon,
Upon the Monday was at Osneye
With compaignye hym to disporte and pleye,
(see n.) — And axed upon caas a cloistrer
Ful pryvely after John the carpenter;
And he drogh hym apart out of the cherche,
And seyde, 'I noot; I saugh hym here noght werche
Sith Saterday; I trowe that he be went
For tymber ther oure abbot hath hym sent,
For he is wont for tymber for to go
(see n.) — And dwellen atte graunge a day or two;
Or ellis he is at his hous, certeyn.

3637 **a furlong way**: a couple of minutes – the time taken to go a furlong (an eighth of a mile).
3638 'Now say an "Our Father" and then hush'.
3655 **laudes**: the early morning service, second of the canonical 'hours'.
3661 'And asked in passing one of the canons of the nearby abbey'.
3668 **graunge**: outlying farm belonging to the abbey.

Where that he be I kan noght soothly seyn.'
This Absolon ful jolyf was and lyght, *light-hearted*
And thoghte, 'Now is tyme to wake al nyght,
For sikerly I saugh hym noght stirynge
Aboute his dore syn day bigan to sprynge.
'So mote I thryve, I shal at cokkes crowe
Ful pryvely knokken at his wyndowe
That stant ful lowe upon his boures wal. *bedroom's*
To Alison now wol I tellen al
My love-longynge, for yit I shal nat mysse
That at the leeste wey I shal hir kisse.
Som manere confort shal I have, parfay.
My mouth hath icched al this longe day:
That is a signe of kissyng at the leeste.
Al nyght me mette eek I was at a feeste. *I dreamed*
Therfore I wol go slepe an houre or tweye
And al the nyght thanne wol I wake and pleye.'
Whan that the firste cok hath crowe, anon
Up rist this joly lovere Absolon *rises*
And hym arrayeth gay, at point-devys. *with attention to every detail*
But first he cheweth grayn and likorys,
To smellen swete, er he hadde kembd his heer.
Under his tonge a trewe-love he beer,
For therby wende he to be gracious. *attractive*
He rometh to the carpenteres hous
And stille he stant under the shot-wyndowe –
Unto his brest it raughte, it was so lowe – *reached*
And softe he cogheth with a semy sown: *thin soft sound*
'What do ye, hony-comb, swete Alisoun,
My faire bryd, my swete cynamome? *bird*
Awaketh, lemman myn, and speketh to me!
Wel litel thynken ye upon my wo
That for youre love I swete ther I go.
No wonder is thogh that I swelte and swete: *swoon and sweat*
I moorne as dooth a lamb after the tete.
Ywis, lemman, I have swich love-longyng
That lyk a turtle trewe is my moornyng. *turtle-dove*
I may nat ete namoore than a mayde.'
'Go fro the wyndow, Jakke fool,' she sayde; *you idiot*
'As help me God, it wol nat be "com pa me." *come kiss me*
I love another, and elles I were to blame,
Wel bet than thee, by Jesu, Absolon.
Go forth thy wey, or I wol caste a stoon,
And lat me slepe, a twenty devele wey!' *in the name of twenty devils*
'Allas,' quod Absolon, 'and weilawey,

3670 All in all, about as helpful a reply as one normally gets in such circumstances.

3680, 3683 **at the leeste wey** ... **at the leeste**. The phrases will come to have a special appropriateness or point in the story, as will Absolon's squeamishness about farting (3337–8) and the repeated specification of the height above ground of the window (3358, 3676–7, 3695–6).

3690 **grayn**: grain of paradise (cardamom, a breath-sweetener).

3692 **trewe-love**: four-leaved sprig of herb paris (like a true-love knot).

3698–707 Some of Absolon's endearments – like **hony-comb** and **cynamome** – echo the language of the biblical Song of Songs (4:11–14), supposedly Solomon's love-song to his beloved, the erotic language of which was enthusiastically allegorized by medieval exegetes; but Absolon's unfortunate image of the lamb longing for the teat is all his own.

That trewe love was evere so yvel biset! [*ill-bestowed, or ill-circumstanced*]
Thanne kys me, syn that it may be no bet,
For Jesus love, and for the love of me.'
'Woltow thanne go thy wey therwith?' quod she.
'Ye, certes, lemman,' quod this Absolon.
'Thanne make thee redy,' quod she, 'I come anon.'
And unto Nicholas she seyde stille, [*softly*]
'Now hust, and thou shalt laughen al thy fille.' [*hush*]
This Absolon doun sette hym on his knees,
And seyde, 'I am a lord at alle degrees,
For after this I hope ther cometh moore.
Lemman, thy grace, and swete bryd, thyn oore!' [*mercy*]
The wyndow she undooth, and that in haste.
'Have do,' quod she, 'com of, and speed thee faste, [*get a move on*]
Lest that oure neghebores thee espye.'
This Absolon gan wipe his mouth ful drye.
Derk was the nyght as pych or as the cole,
And at the wyndow out she putte hir hole,
And Absolon, hym fil no bet ne wers [*better nor worse*]
But with his mouth he kiste hir naked ers
Ful savourly er he were war of this. [*With great relish*]
Abak he sterte and thoghte it was amys,
For wel he wiste a womman hath no berd.
He felte a thyng al rogh and longe yherd, [*haired*]
And seyde, 'Fy! allas! what have I do?'
'Tehee!' quod she, and clapte the wyndow to,
And Absolon gooth forth a sory paas. [*with sad steps*]
'A berd! A berd!' quod hende Nicholas,
'By Goddes corpus, this gooth faire and wel.' [*body*]
This sely Absolon herde everydel
And on his lippe he gan for anger byte
And to hymself he seyde, 'I shal thee quyte.'
Who rubbeth now, who froteth now his lippes [*rubs*]
With dust, with sond, with straw, with clooth, with chippes,
But Absolon, that seith ful ofte, 'Allas!
My soule bitake I unto Sathanas [*commit*]
But me were levere than al this town,' quod he,
'Of this despit awreken for to be. [*insult, avenged*]
Allas,' quod he, 'allas, I ne hadde ybleynt!' [*turned away*]
His hote love was coold and al yqueynt; [*quenched*]
For fro that tyme that he hadde kist hir ers
Of paramours he sette noght a kers, [*romantic love, cress*]
For he was heelyd of his maladye.
Ful ofte paramours he gan defye [*renounce*]
And weep as dooth a child that is ybete.
A softe paas he wente over the strete
Until a smyth men cleped daun Gerveys, [*To a blacksmith*]

3742 **A berd! A berd!** It is curious that Absolon's first impression that he has kissed someone with a beard has not been spoken about, but Nicholas seems to know about it.

3761–2 Gervase's smithy is a vivid addition to the sense of 'overpowering substantiality' (see the account of the tale in Muscatine, *Chaucer and the French Tradition*, p. 226) in the tale, the sense of everyday life pursuing its course (friars singing in the chancel, carpentry-work at Osney) in the background of the story, like the background of a fifteenth-century Netherlandish painting. The detail is also scrupulously accurate: blacksmiths often worked at night (and were the cause of many complaints among their neighbours) because the tools they were repairing or sharpening were needed next day.

did blacksmithing work with	That in his forge smythed plogh-harneys;
(see n.)	He sharpeth shaar and cultour bisily.
gently	This Absolon knokketh al esily
	And seyde, 'Undo, Gerveys, and that anon!'
	'What, who artow?' 'It am I, Absolon.'
cross	'What, Absolon! for Cristes swete tree,
early, bless (me)!	Why rise ye so rathe? Ey, benedicitee!
	What eyleth yow? Som gay gerl, God it woot,
(see n.)	Hath broght yow thus upon the viritoot.
St Neot	By Seinte Note, ye woot wel what I mene.'
took not a bit (bean) of notice	This Absolon ne roghte nat a bene
in reply	Of al his pley; no word agayn he yaf;
(see n.)	He hadde moore tow on his dystaf
	Than Gerveys knew, and seyde, 'Freend so deere,
fireplace	That hoote cultour in the chymenee heere,
lend	As lene it me; I have therwith to doone,
	And I wol brynge it thee agayn ful soone.'
	Gerveys answerde, 'Certes, were it gold,
gold coins all uncounted in a bag	Or in a poke nobles al untold,
	Thow sholdest have, as I am trewe smyth.
by Christ's foe (the devil)	Ey, Cristes foo! What wol ye do therwith?'
	'Therof,' quod Absolon, 'be as be may.
	I shal wel telle it thee another day'–
handle	And caughte the cultour by the colde stele.
	Ful softe out at the dore he gan to stele
	And wente unto the carpenteris wal.
	He cogheth first and knokketh therwithal
before	Upon the wyndow, right as he dide er.
	This Alison answerde, 'Who is ther
	That knokketh so? I warante it a theef.'
dear one	'Wy, nay,' quod he, 'God woot, my swete lief,
	I am thyn Absolon, my derelyng.
	Of gold,' quod he, 'I have thee broght a ryng –
	My moder yaf it me, so God me save;
engraved	Ful fyn it is and therto wel ygrave.
	This wol I yeven thee if thow me kisse.'
	This Nicholas was risen for to pisse
improve on the whole joke	And thoghte he wolde amenden al the jape:
	He sholde kisse his ers er that he scape.
	And up the wyndow dide he hastely
	And out his ers he putteth pryvely
	Over the buttok to the haunche-bon;
	And therwith spak this clerk, this Absolon,
	'Spek, swete herte, I noot noght wher thow art.'
	This Nicholas anoon leet fle a fart
thunder-blast	As greet as it hadde been a thonder-dent,
blinded	That with the strook he was almoost yblent,
	And he was redy with his iren hoot
	And Nicholas amydde the ers he smoot.

3763 'ploughshare and coulter (vertical blade set at the front of the plough)'.

3770 **upon the viritoot**: 'so early astir' (with some salacious innuendo).

3774 **tow on his dystaf**: 'flax on his distaff' (i.e. business in hand).

Off, hand's-breadth	Of gooth the skyn an hande-brede aboute:
arse	The hoote cultour brende so his toute,
pain	That for the smert he wende for to dye.
	As he were wood for wo he gan to crye,
	'Help! Water! Water! Help, for Goddes herte!'
	This carpenter out of his slomber sterte,
	And herde oon cryen 'water!' as he were wood
	And thoghte, 'Allas, now cometh Nowelys flood!'
	He sette hym up withoute wordes mo
	And with his ax he smoot the corde atwo
he did not stop	And down gooth al; he foond neither to selle
flooring	Ne breed ne ale til he cam to the celle
in a dead faint	Upon the floor, and there aswowne he lay.
Up jumped Alison	Up stirte hire Alison and Nicholay
	And cryden 'Out!' and 'Harrow!' in the strete.
	The neghebores, bothe smale and grete,
gawp at	In ronnen for to gauren on this man
	That yet aswowne lay bothe pale and wan,
broken	For with the fal he brosten hadde his arm.
(see n.)	But stonde he moste unto his owene harm;
overborne by (what the others said)	For whan he spak he was anon bore doun
By	With hende Nicholas and Alisoun.
	They tolden every man that he was wood:
	He was agast so of Nowelys flood
deluded imaginings, foolishness	Thurgh fantasie, that of his vanytee
	He hadde yboght hym knedyng-tubbes thre
	And hadde hem hanged in the roof above;
	And that he preyde hem, for Goddes love,
for company	To sitten in the roof, par compaignye.
	The folk gan laughen at his fantasye;
peer and gape	Into the roof they kiken and they cape
	And turned al his harm unto a jape,
	For what-so that this carpenter answerde,
would listen to his explanation	It was for noght: no man his reson herde.
overborne by sworn oaths	With othes grete he was so sworn adoun
	That he was holden wood in al the toun;
agreed	For every clerk anon-right heeld with oother.
	They seyde, 'The man was wood, my leeve brother',
	And every wight gan laughen at this stryf.
	Thus swyved was the carpenteris wyf
keeping guard	For al his kepyng and his jalousye,
	And Absolon hath kist hir nether iye,
	And Nicholas is scalded in the toute.
company	This tale is doon, and God save al the route!

{The Reeve's Prologue follows}

3811 This is a painful moment for Nicholas, but in the logic of *fabliau* he deserved it, since he tried to play the same trick twice, which is not the cleverness expected of him.

3815 This sublime moment, in which the reader, who has quite forgotten about old John up in his tub, suddenly sees how the two plots are to come together, has been much admired.

3818 **Nowelys**: 'Noah's', or 'Noel's' (John is confused).

3830 'He had to face up to his own discomfiture'.

3850–4 The distribution of punishments is comically apt (and 'morally' absurd), though we should be clear that the *swyving* of Alison is John's punishment, not hers. She gets what she wants, not what she deserves, because she stayed true to the demands of *fabliau*: be smart.

The Wife of Bath's Prologue and Tale

The Wife of Bath's Prologue

The Wife of Bath's Prologue begins without introduction or invitation and forms the first tale in the group of tales known as Fragment III, and also the first in the larger group concerning marriage that ends with the Franklin's Tale. Like the Pardoner, the Wife has a long quasi-autobiographical monologue before she tells her tale, which in turn grows directly out of the motives, purposes and consciousness she reveals. Her Prologue derives from the medieval convention of the allegorical 'confession' (usually of a personified vice) and employs the materials of traditional clerical anti-feminism; but the effect of Chaucer's powerful individual realization of the voice of the Wife is to make the 'confession' into a manifesto of woman's sovereignty, and also subtly to expose the foundations of medieval anti-feminism in celibate male prejudice, spite, fear and envy (see M. Carruthers, 'The Wife of Bath and the Painting of Lions', *PMLA* 94 [1979], 209–22). The Prologue deals first with questions of the status of marriage in relation to virginity (1–183) and then with the Wife's first three (184–450) and last two (451–828) husbands. It is a rhetorical tour de force, a torrent of eloquence that sweeps the reader up in its energy; it is also an exploration of the question of female empowerment and the roots of men's fear of women. The Wife secures financial independence by a series of prudent marriages, in which she plays upon her husbands' vanity, weakness and sporadic sexual desires to gain control of their estates; having gained power in a man's world, she struggles heroically to keep at bay a sense of loss. Her Prologue becomes in the end much more than a manifesto of female sovereignty.

written authority 'Experience, thogh noon auctoritee
Were in this world, is right ynogh for me
To speke of wo that is in mariage;
For lordynges, sith that I twelf yeer was of age,
in life (alive) Thonked be God that is eterne on lyve,
Housbondes atte chirche dore I have had fyve –
If I so ofte myghte han wedded be –
And alle were worthy men in hir degree.
But me was told, certeyn, noght longe agon is,
once That sith that Crist ne wente nevere but onys
To weddyng, in the Cane of Galilee,
That by the same ensample taughte he me
That I ne sholde wedded be but ones.
what Herke eek, lo, which a sharp word for the nones,
Bisyde a welle, Jesus, God and man,
reproof Spak in repreeve of the Samaritan:
"Thow hast yhad fyve housbondes," quod he,
"And that ilke man which that now hath thee
Is nat thyn housbonde," thus he seyde certeyn.
What that he mente therby I kan nat seyn,
Except that I ask But that I axe why that the fifthe man
Was noon housbonde to the Samaritan?
How manye myghte she han in mariage?
Yet herde I nevere tellen in myn age
Upon this nombre diffynycioun.
(see n.) Men may dyvyne and glosen up and doun
expressly But wel I woot, expres, withoute lye,

6 **atte chirche dore**. See GP 460n.

7 The Wife accepts that there may be reservations about the legitimacy of so many marriages, and goes on to refer to two of the scriptural passages used by theologians such as St Jerome (in his treatise in praise of virginity and chaste wifehood, the *Epistola adversus Jovinianum*) in their argument against second and further marriages: the wedding at Cana (John 2:1) and the meeting of Jesus with the woman of Samaria (John 4:18). She does not so much refute these arguments as allow them to dissolve in their own bizarre illogicality.

26 'Men may conjecture and apply every kind of interpretation'.

God bad us for to wexe and multiplye –
That gentil text kan I wel understonde.
Eek wel I woot he seyde that myn housbonde
leave, cleave (Matt. 19:5) Sholde lete fader and moder and take to me;
But of no nombre mencioun made he,
Of bigamye, or of octogamye;
bad things Why sholde men thanne speke of it vileynye?
take note of Lo here the wise kyng, daun Salomon:
I trowe he hadde wyves many oon –
permissible As wolde God it leveful were to me
To be refresshed half so ofte as he!
What a gift, with Which yifte of God hadde he for alle hise wyvys!
No man hath swich that in this world alyve is.
God woot, this noble kyng, as to my wit,
The firste nyght hadde many a murye fit
so happy was he to be alive With ech of hem, so wel was hym on lyve.
Blessed be God that I have wedded fyve!
Of whiche I have pyked out the beste,
Bothe of here nether purs and of here cheste.
Diverse scoles maken parfyt clerkes,
And diverse practyk in many sondry werkes
Maken the werkman parfyt sekirly;
schooling Of fyve husbondes scoleiyng am I –
Welcome the sixte, whan that evere he shal.
For sith I wol nat kepe me chaast in al,
Whan myn housbonde is fro the world agon,
Som Cristen man shal wedde me anon,
For thanne th'Apostle seith that I am free
with God's blessing To wedde, a Goddes half, where it liketh me.
He seith that to be wedded is no synne;
burn Bet is to be wedded than to brynne.
do I care What rekketh me theigh folk seye vileynye
cursed Of shrewed Lameth and his bigamye?
I woot wel Abraham was an holy man
as far as I know And Jacob eek, as fer as evere I kan,
And ech of hem hadde wyves mo than two,
And many another holy man also.
Where kan ye seye in any maner age
forbade That heighe God defended mariage
By expres word? I pray yow telleth me;
Or where comanded he virgynytee?
doubt I woot as wel as ye, it is no drede,
Th'Apostle, whan he speketh of maydenhede,
He seyde that precept therof hadde he noon.

28 This 'text' (Gen. 1:28) is not, of course, the one the Wife was supposed to be talking about: it has to do not with the multiplication of marriages but with the multiplication of the faithful by procreation – quite a different story. But she carries it off.

35 Solomon, used by the Wife as an example of the happy legitimacy of multiple marriage (simultaneous in his case, not consecutive, 1 Kings 11:3), was usually regarded by scriptural exegetes as a wise man who was led into folly by his weakness for women.

44a–f These lines do not appear in either Hg or El but it is presumed that they are original and dropped out of an early exemplar (see Textual Notes).

52–8 The Wife draws on or disputes various biblical texts (all cited by Jerome) in the course of her argument. Paul (1 Cor. 7:28) said it was better to marry than to burn (with unfulfilled lust); Lamech (Gen. 4:19–23) was acclaimed the first bigamist; Abraham (Gen. 12–25) and Jacob (Gen. 27–36) were patriarchs with at least two wives. Paul ('th'Apostle') is further cited (1 Cor. 7:1–25, but again from Jerome) in lines 64–5, 73, 81–4, 87–9.

Man may conseille a womman to be oon *single (a virgin)*
But conseillyng nys no comandement.
He put it in oure owene juggement;
For hadde God comanded maydenhede,
Thanne hadde he dampned weddyng with the dede, *condemned*
And certes, if ther were no seed ysowe,
Virgynytee, thanne wherof sholde it growe?
Poul dorste nat comanden, at the leeste,
A thyng of which his mayster yaf noon heeste. *commandment*
The dart is set up for virgynytee;
Cacche who-so may, who renneth best lat se.
  But this word is noght take of every wight, *applicable to*
But ther as God list yeve it of his myght. *pleases*
I woot wel that th'Apostle was a mayde, *virgin*
But nathelees, thogh that he wroot or sayde
He wolde that every wight were swich as he,
Al nys but conseil to virgynytee.
And for to been a wyf he yaf me leve
Of indulgence; so nys it no repreve *matter of reproach*
To wedde me if that my make dye, *mate*
Withouten excepcioun of bigamye – *objection on the grounds of*
Al were it good no womman for to touche *even though it were*
(He mente as in his bed or in his couche,
For peril is bothe fyr and tow t'assemble: *flax*
Ye knowe what this ensample may resemble). *parallel, signify*
This al and som: he heeld virgynytee *This is what it amounts to*
Moore parfit than weddyng in freletee – *frailty*
Freletee clepe I but if that he and she *unless*
Wolde leden al hir lyf in chastitee.
  I graunte it wel; I have noon envye, *resentment*
Thogh maydenhede preferre bigamye. *take precedence over, remarriage*
It liketh hem to be clene in body and goost; *spirit*
Of myn estat ne wol I make no boost, *way of life*
For wel ye knowe a lord in his houshold
Ne hath nat every vessel al of gold;
Somme been of tree and doon hir lord servyse. *wood*
God clepeth folk to hym in sondry wyse,
And everich hath of God a propre yifte – *special talent*
Som this, som that, as hym liketh shifte. *as it pleases God to provide*
  Virgynytee is greet perfeccioun
And continence eek with devocioun,
But Crist, that of perfeccion is welle,
Bad nat every wight he sholde go selle
Al that he hadde and yeve it to the poore,
And in swich wise folwe hym and his foore. *his footsteps*
He spak to hem that wol lyve parfitly –
And lordynges, by youre leve, that am nat I.
I wol bistowe the flour of al myn age
In th'actes and in fruyt of mariage.

75–6 Women are not commanded to be virgins; but being a virgin is a very good thing and whoever wants may strive for the prize it carries (Chaucer's phrasing is directly from Jerome).

99–101 The allusion to 2 Tim. 2:20 is again picked up from Jerome, but the point of the text is mis-taken (in Paul's epistle, the wooden vessels correspond to wicked people who are not valued by God) by conflating it with another text (lines 102–4) from 1 Cor. 7:7.

107–12 Jerome's allusion is to Matt. 19:21.

end Telle me also, to what conclusioun
Were membres maad of generacioun,
And of so parfit wys a wight ywroght?
Trusteth right wel, they were nat maad for noght!
Interpret, in every way Glose who-so wole, and seye bothe up and doun
That they were maked for purgacioun
Of uryne, and oure bothe thynges smale
Was eek to knowe a femelle from a male
And for noon oother cause – sey ye no?
Th'experience woot wel it is noght so.
Provided that So that the clerkes be nat with me wrothe,
I sey this: that they maked been for bothe –
function That is to seyn, for office and for ese
procreation Of engendrure, ther we nat God displese.
Why sholde men ellis in hir bokes sette
That man shal yelde to his wyf hir dette?
Now wherwith sholde he make his paiement
If he ne used his sely instrument?
Thanne were they maad upon a creature
To purge uryne and eek for engendrure.
bound But I seye noght that every wight is holde,
That hath swich harneys as I to yow tolde,
To goon and usen hem in engendrure;
(if they did) then, heed Thanne sholde men take of chastitee no cure.
Crist was a mayde and shapen as a man
And many a seynt sith that the world bigan,
Yet lyved they evere in parfit chastitee.
resent I nyl envie no virgynytee:
Lat hem be breed of pured whete-seed
be called And lat us wyves hote barly-breed –
And yet with barly-breed, Mark telle kan,
Oure Lord Jesu refresshed many a man.
In swich estat as God hath clepyd us
fastidious I wol persevere; I nam nat precius.
In wifhode wol I use myn instrument
As frely as my Makere hath it sent.
play hard to get If I be daungerous, God yeve me sorwe!
Myn housbonde shal it han bothe eve and morwe,
Whan that hym list com forth and paye his dette.
give up my right An housbonde wol I have – I wol nat lette –
slave Which shal be bothe my dettour and my thral
And have his tribulacion withal
Upon his flessh whil that I am his wyf.
I have the power duryng al my lyf
Upon his propre body, and nat he.
Right thus th'Apostle tolde it unto me
And bad oure housbondes for to love us wel.
sound doctrine Al this sentence me liketh everydel.'

129–30 It was accepted in the church's teaching on marriage that sexual intercourse, when required by one partner, was a duty laid on the other.

145 The barley-loaves are mentioned in John 6:9, not Mark (Chaucer's mistake, or the Wife's?).

154–60 The Wife manages to convert Paul's warnings (line 160, from Jerome) about the 'tribulation of the flesh', that is, the bodily pain and grief of the married state (1 Cor. 7:28), into a promise of sexual torment for her husband.

started Up stirte the Pardoner, and that anon;
'Now, dame,' quod he, 'by God and by Seint John!
Ye been a noble prechour in this cas.
I was aboute to wedde a wyf: allas!
Why, pay for it What sholde I bye it on my flessh so deere?
this year Yet hadde I levere wedde no wyf to-yeere!'
'Abyd!' quod she, 'my tale is nat bigonne.
Nay, thow shalt drynken of another tonne
Er that I go, shal savoure wors than ale.
And whan that I have toold thee forth my tale
Of tribulacion in maryage,
Of which I am expert in al myn age –
This is to seye, myself hath been the whippe –
choose Thanne maystow chese wheither that thow wolt sippe
open up Of thilke tonne that I shal abroche.
close Be war of it er thow to neigh approche,
For I shal telle ensamples mo than ten.
warned "Whoso that nyle be war by othere men,
By hym shal othere men corrected be."
Thise same wordes writeth Ptholome:
find Rede in his Almageste and take it there.'
'Dame, I wolde pray yow, if youre wyl it were,'
Seyde this Pardoner, 'as ye bigan,
Telle forth youre tale, spareth for no man,
practical knowledge And techeth us yonge men of youre praktyke.'
'Gladly,' quod she, 'syn it may yow lyke,
But that I praye to al this compaignye,
fancy If that I speke after my fantasye,
don't take offence at As taketh nat agrief of that I seye,
For myn entente nys but for to pleye.
Now, sire, thanne wol I telle yow forth my tale.
As evere moot I drynke wyn or ale,
I shal seye sooth: tho housbondes that I hadde,
As three of hem were goode and two were badde.
The thre men were goode and ryche and olde;
Unnethe myghte they the statut holde
In which that they were bounden unto me –
Ye woot wel what I mene of this, pardee!
As help me God, I laughe whan I thynke
How pitously a-nyght I made hem swynke!
faith, had no regard for it And by my fey, I tolde of it no stoor.
They hadde me yeven hir land and hir tresoor:
Me neded nat do lenger diligence
To wynne hir love or doon hem reverence.

163 The Pardoner's intervention serves to redirect the flow of the Wife's discourse back to what she had promised to talk about (the 'wo that is in mariage', line 3); it also brings together in suggestive conjunction the two most elaborately developed and extraordinary characters on the pilgrimage.

170 **thow**. The Wife addresses the Pardoner in the familiar or contemptuous second person singular, where he addresses her in the polite or formal plural. **tonne**. Jupiter has two tuns or barrels in his cellar, one full of good, the other of ill fortune.

182–3 The second-century Greek astronomer Ptolemy wrote an astronomical treatise called the *Almagest* to which various well-known apophthegms accrued in medieval Latin translations.

191 **As** is syntactically superfluous here, and without meaning, as elsewhere (e.g. 196 below).

198 **statut**: obligation to pay the marriage-debt.

204–6 We hear something in these lines of the manner in which the Wife used her sexual skills to wrest financial control from her husbands.

	They loved me so wel, by God above,
set no value on	That I ne tolde no deyntee of hir love!
constantly	A wys womman wol bisye hire evere in oon
	To gete hir love, ye, ther as she hath noon,
power	But sith I hadde hem hoolly in myn hond,
	And sith that they hadde yeven me al hir lond,
take trouble	What sholde I take kepe hem for to plese
Unless	But it were for my profit and myn ese?
	I sette hem so a-werk, by my fey,
Woe is me!	That many a nyght they songen "Weylawey!"
fetched	The bacon was nat fet for hem, I trowe,
	That som men han in Essex at Donmowe.
	I governed hem so wel after my lawe
eager	That ech of hem ful blisful was and fawe
	To brynge me gaye thynges fro the feyre.
	They were ful glad whan I spak to hem feyre,
scolded	For, God it woot, I chidde hem spitously.
	Now herkneth how I bar me proprely.
	Ye wise wyves that konne understonde,
accuse them wrongfully	Thus sholde ye speke and bere hem wrong on honde,
	For half so boldely kan ther no man
	Swere and lye as a womman kan.
for the benefit of wives	I sey nat this by wyves that ben wyse,
Except it be, act unadvisedly	But if it be whan they hem mysavyse.
knows what's good for her	A wys womman, if that she kan hir good,
deceive him into thinking	Shal bere hym an hond the cow is wood,
	And take witnesse of hir owene mayde
Who is on her side	Of hire assent. But herkneth how I sayde:
dotard, way of behaving	"Sire olde kaynard, is this thyn array?
	Why is my neghebores wyf so gay?
	She is honoured overal ther she goth;
decent clothes	I sitte at hoom; I have no thrifty cloth.
	What dostow at my neghebores hous?
	Is she so fair? Artow so amorous?
whisper	What rowne ye with oure mayde? Benedicite!
	Sire olde lechour, lat thy japes be!
	And if I have a gossib or a freend,
	Withouten gilt, ye chiden as a feend
	If that I walke or pleye unto his hous!
	Thow comest hoom as dronken as a mous
curse you!	And prechest on thy bench, with yvel preef!
	Thow seyst to me it is a greet mescheef
because of the expense	To wedde a povre womman, for costage;
high birth	And if that she be ryche, of heigh parage,
	Thanne seistow that it is a tormentrye

218 An old custom at Dunmow allowed for a prize of a side of bacon (the 'Dunmow flitch') to be given annually to a married couple who could persuade the judges that they had lived a year without quarrelling.

232 The allusion is to the story of the talking bird, or chough (**cow**), that tells the husband of the adultery of his wife, who then persuades him that the bird is crazy. Chaucer tells a variant of the story in the Manciple's Tale.

235–378 This long diatribe is skilfully assembled from the commonplaces of anti-feminist writing (especially Jerome, the *Roman de la Rose*, and the *Miroir de Mariage* of the French poet Deschamps, Chaucer's contemporary), the accusations levelled against women being turned by the Wife into a tirade against men.

bad humour	To suffre hir pryde and hir malencolye;
	And if that she be fair, thow verray knave,
lecher	Thow seist that every holour wol hire have;
	She may no while in chastitee abyde
	That is assayled upon ech a syde.
	"Thow seyst som folk desiren us for richesse,
	Somme for oure shape and somme for oure fairnesse
	And somme for she kan outher synge or daunce
	And somme for gentillesse and dalyaunce,
slender	Somme for hir handes and hir armes smale;
according to what you say	Thus goth al to the devel, by thy tale.
	Thow seyst men may nat kepe a castel wal,
	It may so longe assaylled been overal.
	"And if that she be foul thow seyst that she
	Coveiteth every man that she may se,
	For as a spaynel she wol on hym lepe,
do a deal with her	Til that she fynde som man hir to chepe;
no goose so grey (i.e. plain)	Ne noon so grey goos goth ther in the lake
mate	As, seistow, wol be withoute make,
control	And seyst it is an hard thyng for to wolde
willingly	A thyng that no man wole, his thankes, holde.
wretch	Thus seistow, lorel, whan thow goost to bedde,
	And that no wys man nedeth for to wedde,
aims for	Ne no man that entendeth unto hevene.
lightning	With wilde thonder-dynt and firy levene
shrivelled, broken to bits	Moote thy welked nekke be to-broke!
leaking	"Thow seyst that droppyng houses and eek smoke
	And chidyng wyves maken men to flee
	Out of hir owene houses; a, benedicitee!
	What eyleth swich an old man for to chide?
	"Thow seyst we wyves wil oure vices hyde
securely married	Til we be fast, and thanne we wol hem shewe –
malicious wretch	Wel may that be a proverbe of a shrewe!
	"Thow seist that oxen, asses, hors and houndes,
tested, times	They been assayed at dyverse stoundes,
basins, wash-bowls	Bacynes, lavours, er that men hem bye,
household equipment	Spoones, stooles and al swich housbondrye,
	And so be pottes, clothes and array;
trial	But folk of wyves maken noon assay
	Til they be wedded – olde dotard shrewe! –
	And thanne, seistow, we wil oure vices shewe.
	"Thow seist also that it displeseth me
	But if that thow wolt preise my beautee
gaze intently	And but thow powre alwey upon my face
	And clepe me 'faire dame' in every place,
	And but thow make a feeste on thilke day
	That I was born and make me fressh and gay,
nurse	And but thow do to my norice honour
chambermaid, bedchamber	And to my chambrere withinne my bour
kinsfolk	And to my fadres folk and his allyes –
	Thus seistow, olde barel-ful of lyes!
	"And yet of oure apprentice Janekyn,
curly	For his crispe heer, shynyng as gold so fyn,

And for he squyereth me bothe up and doun,
Yet hastow caught a fals suspecioun.
I wil hym nat, thogh thow were deed to-morwe!
(damn you) "But tel me this: why hidestow, with sorwe,
The keyes of thy cheste awey fro me?
It is my good as wel as thyn, pardee!
(see n.) What, wenestow make an ydiote of oure dame?
Now by that lord that called is Seint Jame,
Thow shalt noght bothe, thogh that thow were wood,
Be maister of my body and my good;
(i.e. despite all you can do) That oon thow shalt forgo, maugree thyne eyen.
What helpeth it of me enquere and spyen?
I trowe thow woldest lok me in thy chiste!
Thow sholdest seye, 'Wyf, go wher thee liste;
believe Taak youre disport; I nyl leve no talis.
I knowe yow for a trewe wyf, dame Alis.'
takes too keen an interest We love no man that taketh kepe or charge
be free Wher that we goon; we wol been at oure large.
"Of alle men yblessed moote he be,
The wise astrologen, Daun Ptholome,
That seith this proverbe in his Almageste:
'Of alle men his wisdom is hyeste
cares, in his control That rekketh nat who hath the world in honde.'
By this proverbe thow shalt understonde,
what need Have thow ynogh, what thar thee rekke or care
How myrily that othere folkes fare?
For certes, olde dotard, by youre leve,
Ye shal han queynte right ynogh at eve.
refuse He is to greet a nygard that wil werne
A man to lighte a candle at his lanterne;
He shal han never the lasse light, pardee.
Have thow ynogh, thee thar nat pleyne thee.
"Thow seist also that if we make us gay
With clothyng and with precious array
That it is peril of oure chastitee;
try to strengthen your case And yet – with sorwe! – thow most enforce thee
And seye thise wordes in th'Apostles name:
clothing 'In habit maad with chastitee and shame
Ye wommen shal apparaille yow,' quod he,
jewels 'And nat in tressed heer and gay perree,
As perlys, ne with gold, ne clothes ryche.'
instruction for reading a text After thy text ne after thy rubryche
I wol nat werke as muche as is a gnat.
"Thow seydest this, that I was lyk a cat;
singe For who-so wolde senge a cattes skyn,
dwelling-place Thanne wolde the cat wel dwellen in his in;
sleek And if the cattes skyn be slyk and gay,
She wol nat dwelle in house half a day,
But forth she wole er any day be dawed
a-caterwauling To shewe hir skyn and goon a-caterwawed.

311 'What, do you think to make a fool of our mistress (i.e. of me)?'

324–5 See 182–3n above.

341 I.e. Paul (1 Tim. 2:9, quoted in Jerome).

This is to seye, if I be gay, sire shrewe,
I wol renne out my borel for to shewe. *cheap clothing*
Sire olde fool, what helpeth thee t'espyen?
Thogh thow preye Argus with his hundred eyen
To be my warde-corps, as he kan best, *body-guard*
In feith he shal nat kepe me but me lest; *unless I please*
Yet koude I make his berd, as mote I thee! *deceive him, as I may thrive!*
"Thow seydest eek that ther ben thynges thre,
The whiche thynges troublen al this erthe,
And that no wight may endure the ferthe.
O leeve sire shrewe, Jesu shorte thy lyf! *dear*
Yet prechestow and seist an hateful wyf
Yrekened is for oon of thise myschaunces.
Been ther noone othere maner resemblaunces
That ye may likne youre parables to,
But if a sely wyf be oon of tho?
"Thow liknest eek wommanes love to helle,
To bareyne lond ther water may nat dwelle.
Thow liknest it also to wilde-fyr: *(see n.)*
The moore it brenneth, the moore it hath desyr *burns*
To consumen every thyng that brent wol be.
Thow seist, right as wormes shende a tree, *destroy*
Right so a wyf destroyeth hir housbonde;
This knowen they that been to wyves bonde."
Lordynges, right thus, as ye han understonde,
Bar I stifly myne olde housbondes on honde *Deceived … into thinking*
That thus they seyden in hir dronkenesse;
And al was fals, but that I took witnesse
On Janekyn and on my nece also.
O Lord! the pyne I dide hem and the wo, *suffering*
Ful giltelees, by Goddes swete pyne!
For as an hors I koude byte and whyne.
I koude pleyne – and I was in the gilt –
Or ellis often tyme I hadde been spilt. *ruined*
Whoso that first to mille comth, first grynt; *grinds*
I pleyned first, so was oure werre stynt. *finished*
They were ful glad to excusen hem ful blyve *hurriedly*
Of thyng of which they nevere agilte hir lyve. *were guilty in their lives*
Of wenches wolde I beren hem on honde,
Whan that for syk they myghte unnethe stonde. *sickness, hardly*
Yet tikled I his herte for that he
Wende that I hadde had of hym so greet chiertee! *fondness*
I swoor that al my walkyng out by nyghte
Was for to espye wenches that he dighte; *was having sex with*
Under that colour hadde I many a myrthe.
For al swich wit is yeven us in oure birthe;
Deceite, wepyng, spynnyng God hath yeve
To wommen kyndely whil they may lyve. *by nature*
And thus of o thyng I avante me: *boast*
At ende I hadde the bet in ech degree, *in all respects*
By sleighte or force or by som maner thyng,

373 **wilde-fyr**: Greek fire (a burning substance used in warfare).

grumbling	As by continuel murmur or grucchyng.
	Namely abedde hadden they meschaunce:
	Ther wolde I chide and do hem no plesaunce.
	I wolde no lenger in the bed abyde,
	If that I felte his arm over my syde,
ransom	Til he hadde maad his raunceon unto me;
	Thanne wolde I suffre hym do his nycetee.
	And therfore every man this tale I telle:
	Wynne whoso may, for al is for to selle;
	With empty hond men may none haukes lure.
profit	For wynnyng wolde I al his lust endure
	And make me a feyned appetit;
bacon (i.e. old dried meat)	And yet in bacoun hadde I nevere delit.
	That made me that evere I wolde hem chyde,
sat	For thogh the pope hadde seten hem bisyde,
dinner-table	I wolde noght spare hem at hir owene bord,
repaid	For by my trouthe I quytte hem word for word.
	As help me verray God omnipotent,
	Thogh I right now sholde make my testament,
	I ne owe hem nat a word that it nys quyt.
	I broghte it so aboute by my wit
yield	That they moste yeve it up, as for the beste,
	Or ellis hadde we nevere been in reste;
	For thogh he looked as a wood leoun,
purpose	Yet sholde he faille of his conclusioun.
'dearie'	Thanne wolde I seye, "Goode lief, taak keepe
	How mekely looketh Wilkyn, oure sheepe!
kiss	Com neer, my spouse, lat me ba thy cheke!
	Ye sholden be al pacient and meke
scrupulous	And han a swete spyced conscience,
Job's	Sith ye so preche of Jobes pacience.
Be patient	Suffreth alwey, syn ye so wel kan preche,
	And but ye do, certeyn we shal yow teche
	That it is fair to han a wyf in pees.
	Oon of us two moste bowen, doutelees,
	And sith a man is moore resonable
patient	Than womman is, ye mosten been suffrable.
	What eyleth yow to grucche thus and grone?
	Is it for ye wolde have my queynte allone?
	Wy, taak it al! Lo, have it everydel!
By St Peter, damn you!	Peter! I shrewe yow, but ye love it wel.
fair thing	For if I wolde selle my *bele chose*,
	I koude walke as fressh as is a rose;
	But I wol kepe it for youre owene tooth.
	Ye be to blame, by God! I sey yow sooth."
on a regular basis	Swiche manere wordes hadde we on honde.
	Now wol I speken of my ferthe housbonde.
	My ferthe housbonde was a revelour –
	This is to seyn, he hadde a paramour –
wild wantonness	And I was yong and ful of ragerye,
Untamed, magpie	Stibourne and strong, and joly as a pye.
	How koude I daunce to an harpe smale
	And synge, ywys, as any nyghtyngale,

	Whan I hadde dronke a draghte of swete wyn!
	Metellyus, the foule cherl, the swyn,
	That with a staf birafte his wyf hir lyf
	For she drank wyn, though I hadde been his wyf
frightened	He sholde nat han daunted me fro drynke!
	And after wyn on Venus moste I thynke,
	For al so siker as coold engendreth hayl,
greedy, lecherous	A likerous mouth moste han a likerous tayl.
drunk with wine	In wommen vynolent is no defence –
	This knowen lechours by experience.
	But – Lord Crist! – whan that it remembreth me
	Upon my yowthe and on my jolytee,
	It tikeleth me aboute myn herte roote.
good (a healing remedy)	Unto this day it dooth myn herte boote
	That I have had my world as in my tyme.
poison	But age, allas, that al wole envenyme,
	Hath me biraft my beautee and my pith.
	Lat go, farewel! The devel go therwith!
	The flour is goon, ther is namoore to telle:
bran	The bren as I best kan now moste I selle;
strive	But yet to be right murye wol I fonde.
	Now wol I tellen of my ferthe housbonde.
	I seye, I hadde in herte gret despit
	That he of any oother had delit;
paid back, St Judocus	But he was quyt, by God and by Seint Joce!
	I made hym of the same wode a croce –
	Nat of my body, in no foul manere,
	But certeynly I made folk swich chiere
	That in his owene grece I made hym frye
	For angre and for verray jalousye.
	By God, in erthe I was his purgatorie,
	For which I hope his soule be in glorie.
	For God it woot, he sat ful ofte and soong
pinched	Whan that his shoo ful bitterly hym wroong.
	Ther was no wight, save God and he, that wiste
tormented	In many wise how soore I hym twiste.
	He deyde whan I cam fro Jerusalem
	And lith ygrave under the roode beem,
	Al is his toumbe noght so curyus
that Darius	As was the sepulcre of hym Daryus,
	Which that Appellus wroghte subtilly;
waste	It nys but wast to burye hym preciously.
	Lat hym fare wel, God gyve his soule reste!
coffin	He is now in his grave and in his cheste.
	Now of my fifthe housbonde wol I telle –
	God lat his soule nevere come in helle!
greatest scoundrel	And yet was he to me the mooste shrewe:

460 A story familiar to Chaucer from a popular Latin collection of anecdotes and exempla such as the *Facta et dicta memorabilia* ('Memorable Deeds and Sayings') of Valerius Maximus (first century AD).

469–73 This beautiful passage was inspired by the lament of the old woman (*La Vieille*) in the *Roman de la Rose* (12932–48) for her lost youth and beauty.

496 He had a very respectable burial place under the transverse beam that supported the cross (**roode**) at the rood-screen separating the nave from the chancel.

498–9 The Jewish craftsman Appelles was reputed to have made an elaborate tomb for the Persian king Darius.

That feele I on my rybbes al by rewe — *one by one in a row*
And evere shal unto myn endyng day.
But in oure bed he was so fressh and gay
And therwithal so wel koude he me glose, — *flatter*
Whan that he wolde han my *bele chose*, — *wanted*
That thogh he hadde me bet on every bon — *beaten*
He koude wynne agayn my love anon.
I trowe I loved hym best for that he
Was of his love daungerous to me. — *coldly reserved*
We wommen han, if that I shal nat lye,
In this matere a queynte fantasye: — *strange and curious*
Wayte what thyng we may nat lightly have, — *Look for whatever, easily*
Therafter wol we crye al day and crave.
Forbede us thyng, and that desiren we;
Preesse on us faste, and thanne wol we fle. — *Entreat us earnestly*
With daunger oute we al oure chaffare; — *coy reserve, put out, merchandise*
Greet prees at market maketh deere ware, — *crowd, expensive*
And to greet cheepe is holden at litel prys: — *bargain, value*
This knoweth every womman that is wys.
My fifthe housbonde – God his soule blesse! –
Which that I took for love and no rychesse,
He somtyme was a clerk of Oxenford,
And hadde laft scole and wente at hom to bord
With my gossyb, dwellyng in oure town –
God have hir soule! Hir name was Alisoun.
She knew myn herte and eek my pryvetee — *secrets*
Bet than oure parysshe preest, so mote I thee! — *as I may thrive*
To hire biwreyed I my conseil al, — *revealed, secret*
For hadde myn housbonde pissed on a wal
Or doon a thyng that sholde have cost his lyf,
To hire and to another worthy wyf
And to my nece, which that I loved wel,
I wolde han toold his conseil everydel;
And so I dide ful often, God it woot,
That made his face often reed and hoot
For verray shame, and blamed hymself for he
Hadde toold to me so greet a pryvetee.
And so bifel that ones in a Lente –
So often tymes I to my gossyb wente,
For evere yet I lovede to be gay,
And for to walke in March, Averyll and May
From hous to hous to here sondry tales –
That Jankyn clerk and my gossyb dame Alys
And I myself into the feeldes wente.
Myn housbonde was at Londoun al that Lente:
I hadde the bettre leyser for to pleye — *leisure*
And for to se and eek for to be seye — *seen*
Of lusty folk – what wiste I wher my grace
Was shapen for to be, or in what place?
Therfore I made my visitacions

530 Both the Wife herself (320, 804) and her 'gossip' (530, 548) are called 'Alys' or (dim.) 'Alisoun'. If they are 'god-siblings', co-sponsored at baptism, this would be natural enough; but Chaucer is generally parsimonious with names.

	To vigilies and to processions,
	To prechyng eek and to thise pilgrymages,
	To pleyes of myracles and to mariages,
had on, gowns	And wered upon my gaye scarlet gytes.
	Thise wormes ne thise mothes ne thise mytes,
On peril of my soul, devoured	Upon my peril, frete hem never a del;
	And wostow why? For they were used wel.
	Now wol I tellen forth what happed me.
	I seye that in the feeldes walked we,
	Til trewely we hadde swich daliaunce,
as part of my forward planning	This clerk and I, that of my purveiaunce
	I spak to hym and seyde hym how that he,
	If I were wydewe, sholde wedde me.
boastfulness	For certeynly – I seye for no bobaunce –
	Yet was I nevere withouten purveiaunce
	Of mariage, n'of othere thynges eek:
	I holde a mouses herte noght worth a leek
run off to	That hath but oon hole for to sterte to,
	And if that faille thanne is al ydo.
deceived him into thinking	I bar hym on honde he hadde enchanted me –
mother, subtle trick	My dame taughte me that soutiltee –
dreamed	And eek I seyde I mette of hym al nyght,
flat on my back	He wolde han slayn me as I lay upright,
	And al my bed was ful of verray blood –
	But yet I hope that he shal do me good,
	For blood bitokeneth gold, as me was taught.
	And al was fals, I dremed of it right naught –
	But I folwed ay my dames loore,
	As wel of this as othere thynges moore.
	But now, sire, lat me se, what shal I seyn?
	A ha! by God, I have my tale ageyn.
bier	Whan that my fourthe housbonde was a-beere
I wept, anyhow	I weep, algate, and made sory cheere,
	As wyves mooten, for it is usage,
	And with my coverchief covered my visage;
provided beforehand with a mate	But for that I was purveyed of a make
	I wepte but smal, and that I undertake.
	To chirche was myn housbonde born a-morwe
	With neghebores that for hym maden sorwe,
	And Jankyn oure clerk was oon of tho.
	As help me God, whan that I saw hym go
	After the beere, me thoughte he hadde a payre
	Of legges and of feet so clene and fayre
keeping	That al myn herte I yaf unto his hoold.
	He was, I trowe, twenty wynter oold,
	And I was fourty, if I shal seye sooth –
youthful tastes	But yet I hadde alwey a coltes tooth,
	Gat-tothed I was, and that bicam me weel;
(birth)mark	I hadde the preynte of seynte Venus seel.

556 **vigilies**: feasts on the evenings before saints' days.

558 **pleyes of myracles**: miracle-plays (outdoor religious plays).

575–84 The frequency of these textual lacunae in Hg (see also 609–12, 619–26, 717–20, and Textual Notes) suggests some process of revision in the Prologue unrepresented in the earlier MS (though 717–20 look suspect).

585–6 Not for the first time (cf. 453, 480, 503, 525, 563) the Wife seems carried away by the flood of reminiscence.

As help me God, I was a lusty oon,
And fayr and ryche and yong and wel bigoon, *well set up*
And trewely, as myne housbondes tolde me,
I hadde the beste *quonyam* myghte be. *'whatsit' ('whatchamacallit')*
For certes I am al Venerien
In feelynge, and myn herte is Marcien:
Venus me yaf my lust, my likerousnesse,
And Mars yaf me my sturdy hardynesse. *boldness*
Myn ascendent was Taur, and Mars therinne –
Allas, allas! that evere love was synne!
I folwed ay myn inclinacioun
By vertu of my constellacioun;
That made me I koude noght withdrawe
My chambre of Venus from a good felawe.
Yet have I Martes mark upon my face *the (birth)mark of Mars*
And also in another privee place.
For God so wys be my savacioun, *As surely as God may be*
I ne loved nevere by no discrecioun
But evere folwed myn appetit,
Al were he short or long or blak or whit; *dark or fair*
I took no kepe, so that he liked me, *pleased*
How poore he was ne eek of what degree.
  What sholde I seye but at the monthes ende
This joly clerk Jankyn that was so hende *courteous*
Hath wedded me with greet solempnytee
And to hym yaf I al the lond and fee *property*
That evere was me yeven therbifore.
But afterward repented me ful sore;
He nolde suffre nothyng of my list. *allow, desire*
By God, he smoot me ones on the lyst, *ear*
For that I rente out of his book a leef,
That of the strook myn ere weex al deef.
Stibourne I was as is a leonesse
And of my tonge a verray jangleresse, *loud chatterbox*
And walke I wolde as I hadde doon biforn
From hous to hous, althogh he hadde it sworn; *sworn to forbid it*
For which he often tymes wolde preche,
And me of olde Romayn gestes teche, *stories*
How he Symplicius Gallus lafte his wif
And hire forsook for terme of al his lif, *to the end of*
Noght but for open-heveded he hir say *bare-headed*
Lokynge out at his dore upon a day.
  Another Romayn tolde he me by name
That for his wyf was at a someres game

609–20 The Wife declares herself to be the way she is because of her horoscope: when she was born, the zodiacal sign of Taurus was in the ascendant (i.e. the sun was passing through it), and Mars was in it in conjunction with Venus. This determines her nature and prevents her from behaving other than according to her nature; it is a shame that people do not realize this and simply think that 'love' (i.e. being highly sexed) is sinful. Medieval people had a high regard for astrology, but would not normally assume that planetary influences created more than a 'disposition' or **inclinacioun** (615) to particular forms of behaviour.

616 **constellacioun**: configuration of the heavenly bodies at one's birth.

621–6 The Wife's claim to an almost heroic sexual appetite may be deliberately outrageous; it is not fully in accord with her care elsewhere to make it clear that she was not an adulteress (485).

630–1 The Wife's big mistake: the money and property that she had accumulated from her marriages she was by no means obliged to alienate to her husband; it was a loving act, which she came to regret.

643 This story, like the one below (647), is from Valerius Maximus (see 460n, above).

knowledge	Withouten his wityng, he forsook hire eke.
	And thanne wolde he upon his Bible seke
(Ecclus. 25:26)	That ilke proverbe of Ecclesiaste
strictly	Where he comandeth and forbedeth faste
wander	Man shal nat suffre his wyf go roule aboute.
	Thanne wolde he seye right thus, withouten doute:
willow branches	"Whoso that buyldeth his hous al of salwes,
fallow fields	And priketh his blynde hors over the falwes,
pilgrimage shrines	And suffreth his wyf to go seken halwes,
	Is worthy to been hanged on the galwes!"
hawthorn-berry	But al for noght – I sette noght an hawe
saying	Of his proverbe n'of his olde sawe,
	N'I wolde nat of hym corrected be.
	I hate hym that my vices telleth me,
	And so doon mo, God woot, of us than I.
absolutely	This made hym with me wood al outrely;
submit to	I nolde noght forbere hym in no cas.
	Now wol I seye yow sooth, by Seint Thomas,
	Why that I rente out of his book a leef,
	For which he smoot me so that I was deef.
	He hadde a book that gladly, nyght and day,
	For his disport he wolde rede alway;
	He clepyd it "Valerie and Theofraste",
laughed	At which book he logh alwey ful faste.
	And eek ther was somtyme a clerk at Rome,
	A cardynal that highte Seint Jerome
	That made a book agayn Jovinian;
	In which book eek ther was Tertulan,
	Crisippus, Trotula and Helowys,
	That was abbesse nat fer fro Parys,
the Book of Proverbs	And eek the Parables of Salomon,
many a one	Ovydes Art, and bokes many on –
	And alle thise were bounden in o volume.
	And every nyght and day was his custume,
spare time	Whan he hadde leyser and vacacioun
	From oother worldly ocupacioun,
	To reden in this book of wikked wyves.
	He knew of hem mo legendes and lyves
	Than been of goode wyves in the Bible.
	For trusteth wel, it is an inpossible
	That any clerk wol speke good of wyves,
	But if it be of holy seintes lyves,
	N'of noon oother womman never the mo.
	Who peynted the leoun, tel me who?

655–8 This little quatrain of 'inadvisables' is cited as if it were a well-known jingle, but it is not elsewhere recorded.

669–81 Jankyn's 'book of wikked wyves' (685) is a not unrepresentative example of collections of anti-feminist and anti-marriage stories and *exempla* such as were popular among clerics as an aid to the celibate life. It includes the famous twelfth-century letter of 'Valerius to Rufinus' advising him not to marry (*Epistola Valerii ad Rufinum*) and the 'Golden Book of Marriage' (*Liber aureolus de nuptiis*) of Theophrastus, known only from being quoted by Jerome (674–5; see note to line 7 above); also others such as the early theologian Tertullian, the female gynaecologist Trotula from the great medical school at Salerno (she seems to have dropped in by mistake), and Héloïse, who dispraised marriage in her letters to Abélard.

680 **Ovydes Art**: Ovid's *Ars amatoria*, or 'Art of Love'.

692 A proverbial phrase, referring to the lion's question when he saw a picture of a peasant killing a lion with an axe. The view chosen depends on who is painting the picture. See M. Carruthers, 'The Wife of Bath and the Painting of Lions', *PMLA* 94 (1979), 209–22.

By God, if wommen hadden writen stories
As clerkes han, withinne hir oratories,
They wolde han writen of men moore wikkednesse
Than al the mark of Adam may redresse. *the male sex*
The children of Mercurie and Venus
Been in hir wirkyng ful contrarius:
Mercurie loveth wysdam and science *knowledge*
And Venus loveth riot and dispence:
And for hir diverse disposicioun
Ech faileth in ootheres exaltacioun,
And thus, God woot, Mercurie is desolat
In Pisces, wher Venus is exaltat,
And Venus faileth ther Mercurie is reysed.
Therfore no womman of no clerk is preysed.
The clerk, whan he is old and may noght do
Of Venus werkes worth his olde sho,
Thanne sit he doun and writ in his dotage
That wommen kan nat kepe hir mariage.
  But now to purpos why I tolde thee
That I was beten for a book, pardee!
Upon a nyght Jankyn, that was oure sire, *my husband*
Redde on his book as he sat by the fire
Of Eva first, that for hir wikkednesse
Was al mankynde broght to wrecchednesse,
For which that Jesu Crist hymself was slayn
That boghte us with his herte blood agayn.
Lo, heere expres of womman may ye fynde *explicitly*
That womman was the los of al mankynde. *ruin*
  Tho redde he me how Sampson loste his herys:
Slepynge, his lemman kitte it with hir sherys, *lady-love, cut*
Thurgh which tresoun loste he bothe his eyen.
  Tho redde he me, if that I shal nat lyen,
Of Hercules and of his Dianyre,
That caused hym to sette hymself afyre.
  Nothyng forgat he the sorwe and wo
That Socrates hadde with his wyves two,
How Xantippa caste pisse upon his heed.
This sely man sat stille as he were deed;
He wiped his heed, namoore dorste he seyn
But "Er that thonder stynte, comth a reyn!" *stops*
  Of Phasifpha, that was the queene of Crete,
For shrewednesse hym thoughte the tale swete;
Fy! spek namoore – it is a grisly thyng –
Of hire horrible lust and hir likyng.
  Of Clitermystra, for hir lecherye,

697–706 Clerks (under the influence of the planet Mercury, signifying knowledge and learning) and sexually active women (under Venus) are opposed in their very nature (see note to line 609 above) or **disposicioun** (701). Each is weakest where the other is strongest, as with the planets, where each is weakest in the zodiacal sign, such as Pisces (704), in which the other has its greatest power, or **exaltacioun** (702).

721–64 Stories well known from anti-feminist writings and other sources: Samson, betrayed by Delilah; Hercules, burnt to death in a fiery shirt given to him (unwittingly) by Deïaneira; Socrates, the model of husbandly patience; Pasiphae, who gave birth to the Minotaur after an amorous encounter with a bull; Clytemnestra, who had her husband Agamemnon murdered by her lover Aegisthus on his return from Troy; Amphioraus, betrayed by his wife Eriphyle; and other stories from the *Epistola Valerii*.

That falsly made hir housbonde for to dye,
He redde it with ful good devocioun.
He tolde me eek for what occasioun
Amphiorax at Thebes loste his lyf.
Myn housbonde hadde a legende of his wyf
brooch Eriphilem, that for an ouch of gold
Hath prively unto the Grekys told
Wher that hir housbonde hidde hym in a place,
sad fate For which he hadde at Thebes sory grace.
Of Lyvia tolde he me and of Lucie:
They bothe made hir housbondes for to dye,
That oon for love, that oother was for hate.
Lyvia hir housbonde, on an even late,
Empoysoned hath for that she was his fo;
Lucya, likerous, loved hir housbonde so
That for he sholde alwey upon hir thynke
She yaf hym swich a manere love-drynke
That he was deed er it were by the morwe.
always And thus algates housbondes han sorwe.
a certain Thanne tolde he me how that oon Latumyus
Compleyned unto his felawe Arrius
That in his gardyn growed swich a tree
On which he seyde how that hise wyves thre
out of spite Honged hemself for hertes despitus.
"O leeve brother," quod this Arrius,
"Yif me a plante of thilke blissed tree
And in my gardyn planted shal it be."
Of latter date of wyves hath he red
That somme han slayn hir housbondes in hir bed
have sex with And lete hir lechour dighte hire al the nyght
stretched out flat Whan that the corps lay in the floor upryght;
And somme han dryven nayles in hir brayn
Whil that they sleepe and thus they han hem slayn;
Somme han hem yeven poysoun in hir drynke.
imagine He spak moore harm than herte may bithynke,
And therwithal he knew of mo proverbes
Than in this world ther growen gras or herbes.
"Bet is," quod he, "thyn habitacioun
Be with a leoun or a foul dragoun
Than with a womman usyng for to chide.
Bet is," quod he, "hye in the roof abyde
Than with an angry wyf down in the hous.
They been so wikked and contrarious,
what They haten that hir housbondes loveth ay."
casts He seyde, "A womman cast hir shame away,
Whan she cast of hir smok", and forthermo,
"A fair womman, but she be chaast also,
Is lyk a gold ryng in a sowes nose."
Who wolde wene, or who wolde suppose,
pain The wo that in myn herte was, and pyne?

775–85 Proverbs from Ecclus. 15:16, Prov. 21:9, Jerome, and Prov. 11:22, respectively.

saw, finish — And whan I say he wolde nevere fyne
To reden on this cursed book al nyght,
snatched — Al sodeynly thre leves have I plyght
was reading — Out of his book, right as he radde, and eke
I with my fist so took hym on the cheke
That in oure fyr he fil bakward adown.
And he up stirte as dooth a wood leoun
And with his fest he smoot me on the heed
That in the floor I lay as I were deed.
And whan he say how stille that I lay,
He was agast and wolde have fled his way,
swoon, started awake — Til atte laste out of my swowgh I brayde:
"O! hastow slayn me, false theef?" I sayde,
"And for my land thus hastow mordred me?
Er I be deed yet wol I kisse thee."
And neer he cam and kneled faire adown,
And seyde, "Deere suster Alisoun,
As help me God, I shal thee nevere smyte!
blame — That I have doon it is thyself to wyte.
Foryeve it me, and that I thee biseke!"
straightway — And yet eftsoones I hitte hym on the cheke,
revenged — And seyde, "Theef, thus muchel am I wreke;
Now wol I dye, I may no lenger speke."
But at the laste, with muchel care and wo,
We fille acorded by us selven two.
He yaf me al the brydel in myn hond
To han the governance of hous and lond
And of his tonge and his hond also;
And made hym brenne his book anon right tho.
And whan that I hadde geten unto me
By maistrye al the soveraynetee,
And that he seyde, "Myn owene trewe wyf,
to the end — Do as thee lust the terme of al thy lyf;
Keepe thyn honour, and keepe eek myn estaat" –
After that day we hadden nevere debaat.
God help me so, I was to hym as kynde
As any wyf from Denmark unto Inde
And also trewe, and so was he to me.
I pray to God that sit in magestee,
So blesse his soule for his mercy deere.
Now wol I seye my tale, if ye wol heere.'
The Frere logh, whan he hadde herd al this;
'Now dame,' quod he, 'so have I joye or blys,
This is a long preamble of a tale!'
exclaim thus — And whan the Somnour herde the Frere gale,
'Lo,' quod the Somonour, 'Goddes armes two!
always be meddling — A frere wol entremette hym everemo.

811–25 This is not an undignified close, but the amity of their future proceeding, it should be noted, is not based on a reciprocal exchange of rights but on Jankyn's total capitulation to all Alysoun's demands. She is *kynde* and *trewe* to him for ever after, but he has to give up everything to her.

829–49 Friars and summoners were traditional professional rivals, though the Summoner here seems most offended by the Friar's verbal ostentation (**preamble**), which he mocks and parodies (837–8). The main reason for introducing their argument is to whet the reader's appetite for the violently abusive tales that they are to tell after the Wife has finished.

Loo, goode men, a flye and eek a frere
Wol falle in every dyssh and ech matere.
What spekestow of preambulacioun?
What! amble or trotte or pisse or go sit doun!
spoilest our fun — Thow lettest oure disport in this manere.'
'Ye, woltow so, sire Somnour?' quod the Frere;
'Now by my feith I shal er that I go
Telle of a somnour swich a tale or two
That al the folk shal laughen in this place.'
curse — 'Now ellis, Frere, I wol bishrewe thy face,'
Quod this Somnour, 'and I bishrewe me
But if I telle tales two or thre
Of freres er I come to Sydyngborne
mourn — That I shal make thyn herte for to morne,
For wel I woot thy pacience is gon.'
Oure Hoost cryde 'Pees! and that anon!'
And seyde, 'Lat the wromman telle hir tale.
Ye fare as folk that dronken ben of ale.
Do, dame, tel forth youre tale, and that is best.'
'Al reddy, sire,' quod she, 'right as yow lest,
If I have licence of this worthy Frere?'
'Yis, dame,' quod he, 'tel forth, and I wol heere.'

The Wife of Bath's Tale

The Wife of Bath's Tale is apparently a demonstration of her argument, that not only do women have an inalienable right to sovereignty in marriage, but men cannot themselves be happy until they recognize this fact. The story is derived from an old folk-tale of transformation, the story of the Loathly Hag, but is retold so as to enforce the Wife's argument: the knight's offence is specifically an offence against womankind; it is the intervention of women that saves him from death; and it is an old woman who gives him the answer to the question he has been set. Further, she explains patiently to him, on their wedding-night, not only the love and duty he owes to her as his wife but the whole basis, in respect for ideal values, of his vocation as a knight. She is then transformed into a beautiful woman. Is it the knight's transformation that makes possible her transformation? Or does she *choose* to be transformed when the knight has properly learnt his lesson? Questions of love, power, sexuality and the mutual respect due in human relationships, raised in the Wife's Prologue, are here further explored within the context of a traditional story. Study by S. Crane, in *PMLA* 102 (1987), 20–8.

In th'olde dayes of the kyng Arthour,
Of which that Britons speken greet honour,
full of supernatural creatures — Al was this land fulfild of fairye.
The elf-queene with hir joly compaignye
Daunced ful ofte in many a grene mede;
This was the olde opynyoun, as I rede –
I speke of manye hundred yerys ago.
But now kan no man se none elves mo,
For now the grete charitee and prayeres
Of lymytours and othere holy freres,

847 Sittingbourne, a town on the road to Canterbury half-way from London.

857 Chaucer rarely mentions Arthurian legend, and when he does he associates it with the tastes of women (Nun's Priest's Tale, VII.3212) or with fairy-tales, as here. To him it probably seemed old-fashioned, provincial and unsophisticated. The behaviour of the knight of the tale does not reflect much credit on the court of Arthur.

866–81 **lymytours**: friars licensed to beg in a particular area. The comic picture of the land filled with friars instead of fairies is obviously directed at the Friar, not so much to mock him as to arouse his attention: the Wife's remarks are quite salacious, especially the suggestion that friars have taken the place of the elf and incubus (demons who jumped out of the woods and raped women and left them pregnant).

find their way to That serchen every lond and every streem,
specks of dust As thikke as motes in the sonne-beem,
Blessynge halles, chambres, kichenes, boures,
Citees, burghes, castels, hye toures,
Villages, barns, stables Thropes, bernes, shipnes, dayeryes –
This maketh that ther been no fairyes.
For ther as wont to walken was an elf
Ther walketh now the lymytour hymself
early afternoons, mornings In undermelys and in morwenynges,
And seith his matyns and his holy thynges
assigned territory As he gooth in his lymytacioun.
Wommen may go saufly up and down:
In every bussh or under every tree
Ther is noon oother incubus but he,
And he ne wol doon hem but dishonour.
And so bifel that this kyng Arthour
young knight Hadde in his hous a lusty bachiler,
hawking by the riverside That on a day cam ridyng fro ryver,
And happed that, allone as he was born,
He say a mayde walkynge hym biforn,
despite all she could do Of which mayde anoon, maugree hir hed,
By verray force he rafte hir maydenhed.
For which oppressioun was swich clamour
suing for justice And swich pursuyte unto the kyng Arthour
That dampned was this knyght for to be deed
By cours of lawe and sholde han lost his heed –
Paraventure swich was the statut tho –
But that the queene and othere ladyes mo
So longe preyeden the kyng of grace
Til he his lyf hym graunted in the place
And yaf hym to the queene, al at hir wille,
cause to die To chese wheither she wolde hym save or spille.
The queene thanketh the kyng with al hir myght
And after this thus spak she to the knyght,
Whan that she saw hir tyme upon a day:
in such a state 'Thow standest yet,' quod she, 'in swich array
That of thy lyf yet hastow no suretee.
I graunte thee lyf if thow kanst tellen me
What thyng is it that wommen moost desiren:
iron (i.e. the executioner's axe) Be war, and keepe thy nekke-boon from iren!
straightaway And if thow kanst nat tellen me anon
Yet wol I yeve thee leve for to gon
search and learn A twelf-monthe and a day to seche and lere
An answere suffisant in this matere;
depart And seuretee wol I han, er that thow pace,
surrender Thy body for to yelden in this place.'
sighs Wo was this knyght and sorwefully he siketh;
But what! he may nat doon al as hym liketh,
chose And atte laste he chees hym for to wende
And come agayn right at the yeres ende
provide With swich answere as God wolde hym purveye;
And taketh his leve, and wendeth forth his weye.
He seketh every hous and every place

Where as he hopeth for to fynde grace
To lerne what thyng wommen love moost,
region But he ne koude arryven in no coost
Where as he myghte fynde in this matere
together Two creatures acordyng in-feere.
Somme seyden wommen loven best richesse,
Somme seyde honour, somme seyde jolifnesse,
Somme riche array, somme seyden lust abedde,
And ofte tyme to be widwe and wedde.
Somme seyde that oure herte is moost esed
Whan that we been yflatered and yplesed –
He gooth ful ny the sothe, I wol nat lye:
A man shal wynne us best with flaterye,
And with attendaunce and with bisynesse
ensnared Been we ylymed, bothe moore and lesse.
   And somme seyn that we loven best
For to be free and do right as us lest
And that no man repreve us of oure vice
foolish But seye that we be wise and nothyng nyce.
For trewely ther is noon of us alle,
sore spot If any wight wolde clawe us on the galle,
will not kick out That we nyl kike for he seith us sooth.
Assay and he shal fynde it that so dooth;
For be we never so vicious withinne
wish to be considered We wol be holden wise and clene of synne.
   And somme seyn that greet delit han we
able to keep a secret For to be holden stable and eek secree
And in o purpos stedefastly to dwelle
betray And nat biwreye thyng that men us telle –
rake-handle But that tale is nat worth a rake-stele.
hide Pardee, we wommen konne nothyng hele:
Witnesse on Mida – wol ye heere the tale?
   Ovyde, amonges othere thynges smale,
Seyde Mida hadde under his longe herys,
Growynge upon his heed, two asses erys,
defect The whiche vice he hidde as he best myghte
Ful sotilly from every mannes sighte,
That save his wyf ther wiste of it namo.
He loved hire moost and trusted hire also;
He preyed hire that to no creature
disfigurement She sholde tellen of his diffigure.
   She swoor him nay – for al this world to wynne,
She nolde do that vileynye or syn
To make hir housbonde han so foul a name;
She nolde nat telle it for hir owene shame.
would die But nathelees hir thoughte that she dyde
secret That she so longe sholde a conseil hyde;
swelled Hir thoughte it swal so soore aboute hir herte
of necessity, must escape That nedely som word hir moste asterte;
And sith she dorste nat telle it to no man,

951–82 In Ovid's story (*Met.* XI.174–93), it is King Midas's barber who knows his secret and cannot keep it. Her version of the story enables the Wife to make her point, though at the expense of reminding us of her own free-running tongue.

marsh	Doun to a marys faste by she ran –
	Til she cam there hir herte was afyre –
bittern (type of heron) booms	And as a bitore bombleth in the myre
	She leyde hir mouth unto the water down:
	'Biwrey me nat, thow water, with thy sown,'
	Quod she. 'To thee I telle it and namo:
	Myn housbonde hath longe asses erys two!
	Now is myn herte al hool, now is it oute.
	I myghte no lenger kepe it, out of doute.'
	Heere may ye se, thogh we a tyme abyde,
	Yet out it moot; we kan no conseil hyde.
	The remenant of the tale if ye wol heere,
learn	Redeth Ovyde, and ther ye may it leere.
	This knyght, of which my tale is specially,
	Whan that he say he myghte nat come therby –
	This is to seye, what wommen loven moost –
spirit	Withinne his brest ful sorweful was the goost.
	But hom he gooth, he myghte nat sojorne;
	The day was come that homward moste he torne.
	And in his wey it happed hym to ryde
	In al this care under a forest syde,
	Wher as he say upon a daunce go
	Of ladyes foure and twenty and yet mo;
eagerly	Toward the whiche daunce he drow ful yerne
	In hope that som wysdom sholde he lerne.
	But certeynly er he cam fully there
knew not	Vanysshed was this daunce, he nyste where.
was living	No creature say he that bar lyf
	Save on the grene he say sittynge a wyf –
	A fouler wight ther may no man devyse.
At the approach of	Agayn the knyght this olde wyf gan ryse,
	And seyde, 'Sire knyght, heer forth ne lyth no wey.
	Tel me what that ye seken, by youre fey!
	Paraventure it may the bettre be;
These	This olde folk konne muchel thyng,' quod she.
	'My leeve moder,' quod this knyght, 'certeyn
	I nam but deed but if that I kan seyn
	What thyng it is that wommen moost desire.
inform, pay you a reward	Koude ye me wisse I wolde wel quyte youre hyre.'
	'Plight me thy trouthe here in myn hand,' quod she,
	'The nexte thyng that I requere thee
	Thow shalt it do, if it lye in thy myght,
	And I wol telle it yow er it be nyght.'
	'Have heer my trouthe,' quod the knyght, 'I graunte.'
make boast	'Thanne,' quod she, 'I dar me wel avaunte
be your support	Thy lyf is sauf, for I wole stonde therby;
	Upon my lyf the queene wol seye as I.
	Lat see which is the prouddeste of hem alle
has on, decorative hairnet	That wereth on a coverchief or a calle

1011–12 She does not tell him what it is she will require of him in return, as she does in the traditional version of the story told for instance by Gower in his tale of Florent (*Confessio Amantis* I.1407–1861). This change is made so that, when he finds out, he is trapped (at the queen's court) and has no choice. He does not even get the chance to choose whether to behave honourably.

That dar seye nay of that I shal thee teche.
Lat us go forth withouten lenger speche.'
Tho rowned she a pistel in his ere — *whispered, message*
And bad hym to be glad and have no fere.

Whan they be comen to the court, this knyght
Seyde he hadde holde his day as he had hight — *promised*
And redy was his answere, as he sayde.
Ful many a noble wyf and many a mayde
And many a widwe – for that they ben wise –
The queene hirself sittyng as justise,
Assembled been this answere for to here,
And afterward this knyght was bode appere. — *bidden to*

To every wight comanded was silence
And that the knyght sholde telle in audience
What thyng that worldly wommen loven best.
This knyght ne stood nat stille as dooth a best — *beast*
But to his question anon answerde
With manly voys that al the court it herde:

'My lige lady, generally,' quod he, — *liege*
'Wommen desire to have sovereyntee
As wel over hir housbonde as hir love
And for to been in maistrie hym above.
This is youre mooste desir, thogh ye me kille.
Dooth as yow list: I am here at youre wille.'

In al the court ne was ther wyf ne mayde
Ne wydwe that contraryed that he sayde
But seyden he was worthy han his lyf.

And with that word up stirte that olde wyf
Which that the knyght say sittyng on the grene:
'Mercy,' quod she, 'my sovereyn lady queene!
Er that youre court departe, do me right.
I taughte this answere unto the knyght,
For which he plighte me his trouthe there,
The firste thyng that I wolde hym requere
He wolde it do, if it laye in his myght.
Bifore the court thanne preye I thee, sire knyght,'
Quod she, 'that thow me take unto thy wyf,
For wel thow woost that I have kept thy lyf.
If I seye fals, sey nay, upon thy fey!'

This knyght answerde, 'Allas and weilawey!
I woot right wel that swich was my biheste. — *promise*
For Goddes love, as chees a newe requeste! — *choose*
Taak al my good and lat my body go.' — *wealth*

'Nay, thanne,' quod she, 'I shrewe us bothe two! — *curse*
For thogh that I be foul, old and poore
I nolde for al the metal ne for oore
That under erthe is grave or lith above
But if thy wyf I were and eek thy love.'

'My love?' quod he, 'nay, my dampnacioun!
Allas, that any of my nacioun — *family*
Sholde evere so foule disparaged be!' — *disgraced*
But al for noght; th'ende is this, that he
Constreyned was, he nedes moste hir wedde;

And taketh his olde wyf and goth to bedde.
  Now wolden som men seye, paraventure,
That for my necligence I do no cure — *(see n.)*
To tellen yow the joye and al th' array
That at the feste was that ilke day.
To which thyng shortly answere I shal:
I seye ther nas no joye ne feste at al;
Ther nas but hevynesse and muche sorwe.
For prively he wedded hire on morwe
And al day after hidde hym as an owle,
So wo was hym his wyf looked so foule.
  Greet was the wo the knyght hadde in his thoght
Whan he was with his wyf abedde ybroght;
He walweth and he turneth to and fro.
His olde wyf lay smylynge everemo,
And seyde, 'O deere housbonde, benedicite!
Fareth every knyght thus with his wyf as ye?
Is this the lawe of kyng Arthures hous?
Is every knyght of his thus daungerous? — *of his (court)*
I am youre owene love and youre wyf;
I am she which that saved hath youre lyf,
And certes yet ne dide I yow nevere unright;
Why fare ye thus with me this firste nyght?
Ye faren lyk a man hadde lost his wit.
What is my gilt? For Goddes love, tel it
And it shal ben amended, if I may.'
  'Amended?' quod this knyght, 'Allas, nay, nay!
It wol nat ben amended neveremo.
Thow art so loothly and so old also
And therto comen of so lowe a kynde — *low-born*
That litel wonder is thogh I walwe and wynde. — *twist about*
So wolde God myn herte wolde breste!' — *break*
  'Is this,' quod she, 'the cause of youre unreste?'
  'Ye, certeynly,' quod he, 'no wonder is.'
  'Now, sire,' quod she, 'I koude amende al this,
If that me liste, er it were dayes thre,
So wel ye myghte bere yow unto me. — *Provided that, behave well*
  'But for ye speken of swich gentillesse
As is descended out of old richesse –
That therfore sholden ye be gentil men –
Swich errogaunce is nat worth an hen.
Looke who that is moost vertuous alway,
Pryvee and apert, and moost entendeth ay — *In private and in public*
To do the gentil dedes that he kan:
Taak hym for the gentileste man.
Crist wol we clayme of hym oure gentilesse, — *wishes that*

1074 'That it's because of my negligence that I take no trouble'.

1109–1216 The old wife takes up the knight's grievances (1100–1) in turn, adding poverty (1177), which he did not complain about, for good measure. The case concerning *gentillesse*, that 'noble is as noble does', is a medieval commonplace, given eloquent expression by Boethius in the *Consolation of Philosophy* (II, prose 6; III, prose 4); by Jean de Meun in the *Roman de la Rose* (6579–92, 11607–896); and by Dante in the *Convivio* (*Trattato* 4 and the *canzone* preceding). The prevalence of the sentiment did not much affect actual attitudes or behaviour towards people of rank.

Nat of oure eldres for hir old richesse.
For thogh they yeve us al hir heritage,
noble lineage For which we clayme to been of hir parage,
Yet may they nat biquethe for nothyng
To noon of us hir vertuous lyvyng,
That made hem gentil men ycalled be,
And (made that they) bade us And bad us folwen hem in swich degree.
'Wel kan the wise poete of Florence,
on this theme That highte Dant, speken in this sentence.
Lo, in swich maner rym is Dantes tale:
by the branches (of his family tree) "Ful selde up riseth by his braunches smale
Prowesse of man, for God of his goodnesse
Desires Wole that of hym we clayme oure gentilesse".
For of oure eldres may we nothyng clayme
(i.e. that is transient) But temporel thyng that man may hurte and mayme.
'Eek every wight woot this as wel as I,
If gentilesse were planted naturelly
Unto a certeyn lynage doun the lyne,
cease Pryvee and apert, thanne wolde they nevere fyne
To doon of gentilesse the faire office –
They myghte do no vileynye or vice.
'Taak fyr and bere it in the derkeste hous
Caucasus Bitwix this and the mount of Kaukasous
thence And lat men shette the dores and go thenne,
Yet wol the fyr as faire lye and brenne
As twenty thousand men myghte it biholde:
His office naturel ay wol it holde,
I stake my life on it Up peril of my lyf, til that it dye.
innate nobility 'Here may ye se wel how that genterye
Is nat annexed to possessioun,
what they should do Sith folk ne doon hir operacioun
according to its nature Alwey, as dooth the fyr, lo, in his kynde.
For God it woot men may wel often fynde
A lordes sone do shame and vileynye;
And he that wol han prys of his gentrye,
For he was born of a gentil hous
And hadde his eldres noble and vertuous,
And nyl hymselven do no gentil dedis
who is dead Ne folwen his gentil auncestre that deed is –
He nys nat gentil, be he duc or erl,
For vileynes synful dedes maken a cherl.
the gentility you claim, renown For gentilesse nys but renomee
goodness Of thyne auncestres for hir hye bountee,
a thing alien to Which is a straunge thyng for thy persone;
Thy gentilesse cometh fro God allone.
Thanne comth oure verray gentilesse of grace;
It was nothyng biquethe us with oure place.
'Thenketh how noble, as seith Valerius,
Was thilke Tullius Hostillius
That out of poverte roos to heigh noblesse.

1125–30 Close to Dante, *Purgatorio* 7.121–3.
1165–8 The story of Tullius Hostilius, legendary third king of Rome, is told by Valerius Maximus (see 460n, above); for Seneca, see Epistle 44.

Redeth Senek and redeth eek Boece:
there is no doubt Ther shul ye seen expres that no drede is
That he is gentil that dooth gentil dedis.
'And therfore, leve housbonde, I thus conclude:
low-born Al were it that myne auncestres weren rude,
Yet may the hye God – and so hope I –
Graunte me grace to lyven vertuously.
Thanne am I gentil whan that I bigynne
abandon To lyven vertuously and weyve synne.
'And ther as ye of poverte me repreve,
The hye God, on whom that we bileve,
voluntary In wilful poverte chees to lyve his lyf.
And certes every man, mayden or wyf
May understonde that Jesus, hevene kyng,
Ne wolde nat chese a vicious lyvyng.
honourable Glad poverte is an honeste thyng, certeyn;
This wol Senek and othere clerkes seyn.
is content with Whoso that halt hym payd of his poverte
I holde hym riche, al hadde he nat a sherte.
He that coveiteth is a povre wight
For he wolde han that is nat in his myght;
But he that noght hath, ne coveiteth have,
peasant Is riche, althogh we holde hym but a knave.
of its own accord Verray poverte, it syngeth proprely:
Juvenal seith of poverte, "Myrily
The povre man, whan he gooth by the weye,
Biforn the theves he may synge and pleye."
Poverte is hateful good and, as I gesse,
(see n.) A ful greet bryngere out of bisynesse,
improver A greet amendere eek of sapience
To hym that taketh it in pacience.
wretched Poverte is this, althogh it seme elenge:
Possessioun that no wight wol chalenge.
Poverte ful often, whan a man is lowe,
Enables him Maketh hymself and eek his God to knowe.
eyeglass Poverte a spectacle is, as thynketh me,
Thurgh which he may his verray freendes se.
And therfore, sire, syn that I noght yow greve,
Of my poverte namoore ye me repreve.
'Now, sire, of elde ye repreve me:
And certes, sire, thogh noon auctoritee
gentlemen Were in no book, ye gentils of honour
Seyn that men an old wight sholde doon favour
And clepe hym fader, for youre gentilesse:
authoritative writers (to support this) And auctours shal I fynden, as I gesse.
'Now ther ye seye that I am foul and old –
cuckold Thanne drede yow noght to been a cokewold,
age For filthe and elde, also mote I thee,
guardians Been grete wardeyns upon chastitee.

1177–1206 Voluntary and patient poverty were widely acclaimed by medieval writers, using both classical (e.g. Seneca, Epistle 2; Juvenal, Satire 10) and biblical (e.g. 2 Cor. 8:9) sources.

1196 'Something that is very effective in freeing one from care'.

what you take pleasure in But nathelees, syn I knowe youre delit,
I shal fulfille youre worldly appetit.
'Chees now,' quod she, 'oon of thise thynges tweye:
To han me foul and old til that I deye
And be to yow a trewe, humble wyf
And nevere yow displese in al my lyf;
Or ellis ye wol han me yong and fair
chance, resort (visits) And take youre aventure of the repair
That shal be to youre hous bycause of me –
Or in som oother place, may wel be.
whichever of the two Now chees yourselven wheither that yow liketh.'
considers carefully This knyght avyseth hym and soore siketh,
But atte laste he seyde in this manere:
'My lady and my love, and wyf so deere,
I putte me in youre wise governaunce:
Cheseth youreself which that may be moost plesaunce
And moost honour to yow and me also.
I do not care I do no fors the wheither of the two,
For as yow liketh it suffiseth me.'
'Thanne have I gete of yow maistrye,' quod she,
'Syn I may chese and governe as me lest?'
'Ye, certes, wyf,' quod he, 'I holde it best.'
'Kys me,' quod she, 'we be no lenger wrothe,
For by my trouthe I wol be to yow bothe –
This is to seyn, ye, bothe fair and good.
may die insane I prey to God that I mote sterven wood
as good But I to yow be also good and trewe
As evere was wyf syn that the world was newe.
in the morning And but I be to-morn as fair to sene
As any lady, emperice or queene
That is bitwix the est and eek the west,
Do with my lyf and deth right as yow lest.
curtain (round the bed) Cast up the curtyn, looke how that it is.'
And whan the knyght say verraily al this,
That she so fair was and so yong therto,
For joye he hente hire in his armes two,
His herte bathed in a bath of blisse.
in succession A thousand tyme a-rewe he gan hir kisse
And she obeyed hym in every thyng
That myghte do hym plesance or likyng.
And thus they lyve unto hir lyves ende
In parfit joye; and Jesu Crist us sende
Housbondes meke, yonge and fressh abedde –
outlive And grace t'overbyde hem that we wedde;
And eek I praye Jesu shorte hir lyves

1219–27 The question in the traditional story is, would you rather have me fair by day and foul by night, or foul by day and fair by night? The old wife's version gives no power to the husband to exercise a preference between two kinds of marital satisfaction (private and public) but only to choose between two ways in which his wife has the power to make him unhappy.

1230 The knight's form of address seems spontaneously generous and loving, not merely conciliatory, as if he has truly learnt his lesson; he has not yet, it should be noted, as he has in the analogues, had the encouragement of actually witnessing the effects of the promised transformation.

1255–6 The exact nature of this 'obedience' (whether merely sexual *complaisance* or something more) is left ambiguous, and goes with the raucous tone of the Wife's last lines (1257–64) in leaving a question mark hovering over the apparently happy ending of the story.

That noght wol be governed by hir wyves;
expenditure And olde and angry nygardes of dispence,
God sende hem soone verray pestilence!

{The Friar's Prologue follows}

The Franklin's Prologue and Tale

Fragment V began with the Squire's Tale, an oriental romance which looked as though it might go on for ever and which Chaucer left unfinished. Whether the Franklin's commendation of the Tale was intended to follow on smoothly from the Tale when Chaucer eventually got round to finishing it, or whether it is to be seen as an interruption, in which the Franklin, with the company's sanity in mind, pretends to believe that the Tale is really over, is not certain. He soon introduces preoccupations of his own – his anxiety about his son's wayward career and his admiration for *gentillesse*. The Host is scornful of the Franklin's pretensions to 'gentle' status (as a rich independent landowner, the Franklin has a claim to belong to this privileged class, but his status, like Chaucer's, is interestingly 'liminal'), but the Franklin's Tale turns out to be much preoccupied with questions of *gentillesse*.

The Words of the Franklin to the Squire, and of the Host to the Franklin

acquitted 'In feith, Squyer, thow hast thee wel yquyt
And gentilly. I preise wel thy wit,'
Quod the Frankeleyn: 'considerynge thy youthe,
commend you highly So feelyngly thow spekest, sire, I allow the!
In my judgement As to my doom ther is noon that is heere
Of eloquence that shal be thy peere,
If that thow lyve; God yeve thee good chaunce
And in vertu sende thee continuaunce,
pleasure For of thy speche I have gret deyntee.
I have a sone, and by the Trinitee
(see n.) I hadde levere than twenty pound worth lond,
Thogh it right now were fallen in myn hond,
He were a man of swich discrecioun
As that ye ben! Fy on possessioun
But if a man be vertuous withal!
rebuked I have my sone snybbed and yit shal,
chooses to pay no attention For he to vertu lusteth nat entende,
dice, spend But for to pleye at dees and to despende
lose And lese al that he hath is his usage.
servant-lad And he hath levere talken with a page
Than to commune with any gentil wight
Where he myghte lerne gentillesse aright.'
'Straw for youre gentillesse!' quod oure Hoost.
'What, Frankeleyn! Pardee, sire, wel thow woost
That ech of yow moot tellen atte leeste
promise A tale or two, or breken his biheste.'
'That knowe I wel, sire,' quod the Frankeleyn.
'I prey yow, haveth me nat in desdeyn,
Thogh to this man I speke a word or two.'
'Telle on thy tale withouten wordes mo.'

683 'I would rather have land yielding an annual income of twenty pound'.

686–7 Like the hag in WBT 1146–7, the Franklin says that having money and property is worth nothing unless a man is virtuous, and has true **gentillesse** and inward nobility of nature.

'Gladly, sire Hoost,' quod he, 'I wol obeye
Unto youre wyl; now herkneth what I seye.
I wol yow nat contrarien in no wise
As fer as that my wittes wole suffise.
I prey to God that it may plesen yow;
Thanne woot I wel that it is good ynow.'

The Franklin's Prologue

Bretons Thise olde gentil Britons in hir dayes
Of diverse aventures maden layes,
Composed in verse, original Rymeyed in hir firste Briton tonge,
Whiche layes with hir instrumentz they songe
Or ellis redden hem for hire plesaunce;
And oon of hem have I in remembraunce,
Which I shal seyn with good wyl as I kan.
a plain unlearned man But sires, bycause I am a burel man,
At my bigynnyng first I yow biseche
Have me excused of my rude speche.
I lerned nevere rethorik, certeyn;
Thyng that I speke it moot be bare and pleyn.
slept, Parnassus (home of the Muses) I sleepe nevere on the Mount of Parnaso,
Cicero Ne lerned Marcus Tullius Scithero.
doubt Colours ne knowe I none, withouten drede,
But swiche colours as growen in the mede,
Or ellis swiche as men dye or peynte.
too strange and esoteric Colours of rethoryk they ben to queynte;
My spirit feeleth nat of swich matere.
But if yow list, my tale shul ye heere.

The Franklin's Tale

The Tale is derived from the traditional story of 'the Damsel's Rash Promise', where a woman is rescued from the painful consequences of the promise-that-must-be-kept by another's unexpected act of generosity. Such stories act to reassure us that human truth and love and loyalty can dispel the illusions in which we ensnare ourselves through wilfulness and folly. Chaucer complicates this simple but powerful story-line by giving the Tale the aristocratic setting of medieval romance (partly influenced by the version of the story in Boccaccio's *Filocolo*: see R.R. Edwards, in *MP* 94 [1996–7], 141–62), by describing it (in the Prologue) as an old 'Breton lay' and placing it in a long-ago and apparently pre-Christian world (so that the issues of conduct can be developed in a more open and less swiftly resolvable way), and by representing the endangered heroine and her husband as partners in an ideal marriage. Within the Tale, he gives particular depth and interest to the portrayal of Dorigen, and a dramatic reality to her dilemma (for instance, the change in the terms of her promise) which threaten to throw the story off its romantic fairy-tale course. The Tale ends happily, but it is hard to know whether this is achieved at Dorigen's expense, by forcing her back into a position of marital subordination in which male solidarity is reasserted (see Aers, *Chaucer, Langland and the Creative Imagination*, pp. 160–9), or whether there is a subtler strength to her relationship with Arveragus which rests upon the power to surrender freedom as well as the power to exercise it (see J. Mann, 'Chaucerian Themes and Style in the Franklin's Tale', in B. Ford, ed., *The New Pelican Guide to English Literature*,

707–8 The Franklin's claim to speak of **gentillesse**, so brusquely rejected by the Host, is perhaps well demonstrated in the impeccably courteous way in which he 'puts down' the Host.

709–15 A classic statement of the origin of the 'Breton lay', from which a number of Middle English verse-romances known to Chaucer derive or claim to derive. The magical and romantic associations of the genre are useful to Chaucer here.

723–5 The Franklin's little joke, or 'modesty-topos': he claims to know nothing of the **Colours of rethoryk**, or figures and ornaments of speech, but of course the manner in which he makes his disclaimer shows that he is perfectly at ease with them.

Vol. I, Part 1 [Harmondsworth, 1982], pp. 133–53). There is also, despite the pagan setting, a religious dimension to the story in which the final question as to who was 'the mooste free' (1622) is intriguingly related to the question of who kept best the 'trouthe' (1479), since, as the Gospel says, it is 'the truth shall make you free' (John 8:32). The interpretation of the story in terms of the character of the teller, whether as a social upstart who bungles the whole idea of aristocratic marriage because of his bourgeois origins (Robertson, *A Preface to Chaucer*, pp. 470–2), or as a perfect gentleman who understands exactly what a thoroughly modern marriage should be (G.L. Kittredge, in *MP* 9 [1912], 435–67), seems to over-simplify the questions and issues that the Tale explores.

Armorica (ancient name of) Brittany	In Armorik, that called is Britayne,
did his utmost	Ther was a knyght that lovede and dide his payne
	To serve a lady in his beste wise;
chivalric exploit	And many a labour, many a gret emprise,
	He for his lady wroghte er she were wonne.
	For she was oon the faireste under sonne,
	And eek therto come of so heigh kynrede
	That wel unnethes dorste this knyght for drede
	Telle hire his wo, his peyne and his distresse.
	But atte laste she, for his worthynesse,
especially, obedience	And namely for his meke obeysance,
	Hath swich a pitee caught of his penance
	That prively she fel of his acord
	To taken hym for hir housbonde and hir lord –
	Of swich lordshipe as men han over hir wyves.
	And for to lede the moore in blisse hir lyves
	Of his fre wyl he swoor hire as a knyght
	That nevere in al his lyf he, day ne nyght,
	Ne sholde upon hym take no maistrye
show	Agayn hir wyl, ne kithe hire jalousye,
	But hire obeye and folwe hir wyl in al
	As any lovere to his lady shal,
	Save that the name of soveraynetee,
	That wolde he have for shame of his degree.
	She thonked hym, and with ful gret humblesse
since	She seyde, 'Sire, sith of youre gentilesse
so free a rein (so much freedom)	Ye profre me to have so large a reyne,
God would never wish	Ne wolde nevere God bitwix us tweyne,
For any fault of mine, war	As in my gilt, were outher werre or stryf.
	Sire, I wol be youre humble trewe wyf –
troth (pledged word of honour), break	Have heer my trouthe – til that myn herte breste.'
	Thus been they bothe in quiete and in reste.
for certain	For o thyng, sires, saufly dar I seye:
	That freendes everich oother moote obeye,
	If they wol longe holden compaignye.
exercise of force	Love wol nat be constreyned by maistrye:
	Whan maistrie comth, the God of Love anon

751–2 The marriage-arrangement may seem admirable to us, but it would have been against accepted practice in the Middle Ages, and Arveragus conceals it in order not to bring shame upon himself (and therefore upon his wife) in his status as a lord and his wife's lord. The distinction between the public and private spheres of action is characteristic of a 'shame-culture' (in which propriety and reputation are more important than the strict honesty and adherence to a moral code of a 'guilt-culture') and is not necessarily a form of hypocrisy, but it is potentially problematic.

761–90 Throughout this paragraph, Chaucer manoeuvres to find a language for the mutual forbearance and tolerance that seem required in any sensible and successful relationship. The words he uses are partly from the discourse of courtly love (though it is not only sexual relations that are being spoken about) and partly from the moral discourse of **pacience** and **suffraunce** (though it is human relations that are at issue, not moral obligations). There was as yet no other language: the words so commonplace to us (tolerance, mutual respect, etc.) had to be 'invented' (found).

Beteth his wynges, and farwel, he is gon!
Love is a thyng as any spirit free.
by nature Wommen, of kynde, desiren libertee,
servant And nat to been constreyned as a thral –
And so doon men, if I sooth seyen shal.
Looke who that moost is pacient in love,
(see n.) He is at his avantage al above.
Pacience is an heigh vertu, certeyn,
achieves For it venquysseth, as thise clerkes seyn,
accomplish Thynges that rigour sholde nevere atteyne.
At every (annoying) word, complain For every word men may nat chide or pleyne.
be patient, ('so help me') Lerneth to suffre, or ellis, so moot I gon,
whether Ye shul it lerne, wher-so ye wole or non.
For in this world, certeyn, ther no wight is
That he ne dooth or seith somtyme amys.
the influences of one's stars Ire, siknesse, or constellacioun,
balance of body-humours Wyn, wo, or chaungyng of complexioun
Causeth ful ofte to doon amys or speken.
avenged On every wrong a man may nat be wreken.
According to the occasion After the tyme moste be temperaunce
knows about self-control To every wight that kan on governaunce.
And therfore hath this wise worthy knyght,
promised her patient forbearance To lyve in ese, suffraunce hire bihight,
And she to hym ful wisly gan to swere
defect That nevere sholde ther be defaute in here.

Here may men seen an humble wys acord.
Thus hath she take hir servant and hir lord –
Servant in love and lord in mariage.
in the position of a servant Thanne was he bothe in lordshipe and servage –
in a superior kind of 'lordship' Servage? Nay, but in lordshipe above,
Sith he hath bothe his lady and his love –
His lady, certes, and his wyf also,
The which that lawe of love acordeth to.
And whan he was in this prosperitee,
Hom with his wyf he gooth to his contree,
Penmarch (on west coast of Brittany) Nat fer fro Pedmark, ther his dwellyng was,
Wher-as he lyveth in blisse and in solas.

unless Who koude telle but he hadde wedded be
The joye, the ese and the prosperitee
That is bitwix an housbonde and his wyf?
A yeer and moore lasted this blisful lyf,
Til that the knyght of which I speke of thus,
Kerru (a town in Brittany) That of Kairrud was clepid Arveragus,
Made his plans Shoope hym to goon and dwelle a yeer or twayne
In Engelond, that clepid was ek Britayne,
To seke in armes worshipe and honour –
For al his lust he sette in swich labour –
And dwelled ther two yeer, the book seith thus.

772 'He has the advantage of being in the superior position'.

791–8 The language of reciprocal relationship is here more witty and brilliant, playing rhetorically with the happy paradox of Arveragus's position as simultaneously the lord of his wife and the servant of his lady. Perhaps inevitably, the language here is more male-centred: Arveragus can eat his cake and have it too, but Dorigen is out of the picture.

803–5 These lines echo ironically similar lines in the Merchant's Tale (IV.1259–60), a mordant marriage-satire.

stop talking about
sighs
when it pleases them
afflicts
valued
sad state of mind
In course of time
engrave
inscribed
impression of their
continue, passionate grief
time of distress
have a stroll
imaginings
the high cliff
sailing-vessel
part
cured

Now wol I stynte of this Arveragus
And speke I wole of Dorigene his wyf,
That loveth hir housbonde as hire hertes lyf.
For his absence wepeth she and siketh,
As doon thise noble wyves whan hem liketh.
She moorneth, waketh, waileth, fasteth, pleyneth;
Desir of his presence hir so destreyneth
That al this wide world she set at noght.
Hir freendes, whiche that knowe hir hevy thoght,
Conforten hire in al that ever they may.
They prechen hire, they telle hire nyght and day
That causelees she sleeth hirself, allas!
And every confort possible in this cas
They doon to hire with al hir bisynesse,
Al for to make hire leve hir hevynesse.
By proces, as ye knowen everichoon,
Men may so longe graven in a stoon
Til som figure therinne emprinted be.
So longe han they conforted hire til she
Receyved hath, by hope and by resoun,
The emprintyng of hir consolacioun,
Thurgh which hir grete sorwe gan aswage:
She may nat alwey duren in swich rage.
And eek Arveragus in al this care
Hath sent hire lettres hom of his welfare
And that he wole come hastily agayn –
Or ellis hadde this sorwe hir herte slayn.
Hire freendes sawe hir sorwe gan to slake
And preyde hire on knees for Goddes sake
To come and romen hire in compaignye,
Awey to dryve hir derke fantasye;
And finally she graunted that requeste,
For wel she saw that it was for the beste.
Now stood hir castel faste by the see
And often with hir freendes walketh she
Hir to disporte upon the bank an heigh,
Wher-as she many a shipe and barge seigh
Seillynge hir cours, wher-as hem liste go.
But thanne was that a parcel of hir wo
For to hirself ful ofte, 'Allas!' seith she,
'Is ther no shipe, of so manye as I se,
Wol bryngen hom my lord? Thanne were myn herte
Al warisshed of hise bittre peynes smerte.'
Another tyme there wolde she sitte and thynke,
And caste hir eyen downward fro the brynke.
But whan she seigh the grisly rokkes blake,
For verray fere so wolde hir herte quake
That on hir feet she myghte hir noght sustene.
Thanne wolde she sitte adoun upon the grene

818 **whan hem liketh**. This has a dismissive sound, as if upper-class women fell to tears on cue like heroines in a melodrama. The next line, with its slightly sarcastic multiplication of verbs of grieving, reinforces the impression. The effect may be part of the 'colouring' of the Tale with residual traces of the Franklin's opinions – here a nervous breeziness about overdoing the expression of feeling.

And pitously into the see biholde
sad and grievous sighs And seyn right thus, with sorweful sikes colde:
providence (foresight) 'Eterne God, that thurgh thy purveiance
Ledest the world by certeyn governance,
In vain (for no purpose) In ydel, as men seyn, ye nothyng make.
diabolical But, Lord, thise grisly feendly rokkes blake,
chaos That semen rather a foul confusioun
Of werk than any fair creacioun
Of swich a parfit wys God and a stable,
Why han ye wroght this werk unresonable?
For by this werk, south, north, ne west, ne eest,
benefited Ther nys yfostred man, ne bryd, ne beest;
does harm It dooth no good, to my wit, but anoyeth.
Se ye nat, Lord, how mankynde it destroyeth?
An hundred thousand bodies of mankynde
although they cannot be remembered Han rokkes slayn, al be they nat in mynde –
Which mankynde is so fair part of thy werk
image That thow it madest lyk to thyn owen merk.
loving-kindness Thanne semed it ye hadde a greet chiertee
Toward mankynde; but how thanne may it be
That ye swiche menes make it to destroyen,
Whiche menes do no good, but evere anoyen?
I woot wel clerkes wol seyn as hem leste,
By argumentz, that al is for the beste,
Thogh I ne kan the causes nat yknowe.
But thilke God, that made wynd to blowe,
Look after my lord! As kepe my lord! This my conclusioun.
logical disputation To clerkes lete I al disputisoun.
But wolde God that alle thise rokkes blake
Were sonken into helle for his sake!
Thise rokkes sleen myn herte for the feere.'
Thus wolde she seyn, with many a pitous teere.
Hir freendes sawe that it was no disport
To romen by the see, but disconfort,
arranged And shopen for to pleyen somwher ellys.
springs They leden hire by ryvers and by wellys,
delightful And eek in othere places delitables;
backgammon They dauncen and they pleyen at ches and tables.
morning So on a day, right in the morwe-tyde,
Unto a gardyn that was ther bisyde,
arrangements In which that they hadde maad hir ordinance
food, provision Of vitaille and of oother purveiance,
They goon and pleye hem al the longe day.
And this was on the sixte morwe of May,
Which May hadde peynted with his softe shoures
This gardyn ful of leves and of floures;
skilfully And craft of mannes hond so curiously
Arrayed hadde this gardyn, trewely,

865–90 Debates about the existence of evil in the universe, and why God allows it, were familiar to Chaucer from Book IV of the *Consolation of Philosophy* (see *TC* II.621n) by Boethius (see also Book I, metre 5); the language of logical disputation is echoed in 886–90. But the rocks around the sea-coast, though on occasion inconvenient, are hardly a proof of God's lack of care for his creatures, except to a mind distempered by anxiety.

907–17 Gardens are traditionally a place of beauty and refreshment in medieval poetry, also of amorous flirtation – and dangerous temptation, as the allusion to the Garden of Eden (912) reminds us.

excellence	That nevere was ther gardyn of swich prys
the very Garden of Eden	But if it were the verray paradys.
	The odour of floures and the fresshe sighte
	Wolde han maked any herte lighte
too great	That evere was born, but if to greet siknesse
	Or to greet sorwe helde it in destresse,
	So ful it was of beautee with plesaunce.
	At after-dyner gonne they to daunce,
	And synge also, save Dorigen allone,
lament	Which made alwey hir compleynt and hir mone,
	For she ne saugh hym on the daunce go
	That was hir housbonde and hir love also.
must	But nathelees she moste a tyme abyde
allow her sorrow to be assuaged	And with good hope lete hir sorwe slyde.
	Upon this daunce, amonges othere men,
	Daunced a squier bifore Dorigen,
	That fressher was and jolier of array,
According to my judgement	As to my doom, than is the monthe of May.
	He syngeth, daunceth, passyng any man
	That is or was sith that the world bigan.
describe	Therwith he was, if men sholde hym discryve,
most handsome	Oon of the beste farynge man on lyve;
	Yong, strong, right vertuous, and riche and wys,
in high repute	And wel biloved, and holden in gret prys.
	And shortly if the sothe I tellen shal,
	Unwityng of this Dorigen at al,
	This lusty squier, servant to Venus,
	Which that yclepid was Aurelius,
	Hadde loved hire best of any creature
(good or bad) fortune	Two yeer and moore, as was his aventure,
	But nevere dorste he tellen hire his grevance:
(see n.)	Withouten coppe he drank al his penance.
	He was despeyred, nothyng dorste he seye –
reveal	Save in his songes somwhat wolde he wreye
	His wo, as in a general compleynyng:
	He seyde he lovede and was biloved nothyng,
	Of which matere made he many layes,
	Songes, compleyntes, roundels, vyrelayes,
	How that he dorste nat his sorwe telle,
	But langwissheth as a furye dooth in helle;
	And dye he moste, he seyde, as dide Ekko
	For Narcisus, that dorste nat telle hir wo.
	In oother manere than ye heere me seye
reveal	Ne dorste he nat to hire his wo biwreye,
	Save that, paraventure, somtyme at daunces,
follow their amorous rituals	Ther yonge folk kepen hir observaunces,
	It may wel be he looked on hir face
	In swich a wise as man that asketh grace;

942 **Withouten coppe**: 'Not in cupfuls' (i.e. he suffered abundantly).

948 **roundels** and **vyrelayes**: songs of love with fixed rhyming form and refrain. The number of different kinds of verse-form in which Aurelius pours forth the unutterableness of his love is one of a number of wry and ironic touches in this passage, suggestive of an uneasiness with high-flown passion (cf. 818n).

950 **a furye**: one of the Furies (goddesses of torment, Eumenides).

951–2 In classical legend, Echo was unable to tell her love for Narcissus and died of despair, leaving only her voice to deputize.

But nothyng wiste she of his entente.
Nathelees it happed, er they thennes wente,
Bycause that he was hir neghebour
And was a man of worshipe and honour,
And she had known him
And hadde yknowen hym of tyme yoore,
They fille in speche, and forth moore and moore
Unto his purpos drough Aurelius
And whan he saugh his tyme he seyde thus:
'Madame,' quod he, 'by God that this world made,
Provided that I thought, gladden
So that I wiste it myghte youre herte glade,
I wolde that day that youre Arveragus
Wente over the see that I, Aurelius,
come back
Hadde went ther nevere I sholde have come agayn.
For wel I woot my servyce is in vayn:
reward, breaking
My gerdon is but brestyng of myn herte.
have pity
Madame, reweth upon my peynes smerte,
For with a word ye may me sle or save.
buried
Here at youre feet God wolde that I were grave!
I ne have as now no leyser moore to seye;
cause me to die
Have mercy, swete, or ye wol do me deye!'
She gan to looke upon Aurelius;
'Is this youre wil,' quod she, 'and sey ye thus?
before, had in mind
Nevere erst,' quod she, 'ne wiste I what ye mente.
But now, Aurelie, I knowe youre entente,
By thilke God that yaf me soule and lyf,
Ne shal I nevere been untrewe a wyf
In word ne werk, as fer as I have wyt;
I wol been hys to whom that I am knyt.
Taak this for fynal answere as of me.'
But after that in pleye thus seyde she:
'Aurelie,' quod she, 'by heighe God above,
Yet wolde I graunte yow to been youre love,
Syn I yow se so pitously complayne.
the whole length of the Brittany coast
Looke what day that endelong Britayne
Ye remoeve alle the rokkes, stoon by stoon,
hinder
That they ne lette shipe ne boot to goon –
I seye, whan ye han maad the coost so clene
Of rokkes that ther nys no stoon ysene,
Thanne wol I love yow best of any man –
Have heer my trouthe – in al that evere I kan.'
'Is ther noon oother grace in yow?' quod he.
'No, by that Lord', quod she, 'that maked me!
For wel I woot that it shal nevere bityde.
Lat swiche folies out of youre herte slyde.
pleasure
What deyntee sholde a man han in his lyf
For to go love another mannes wyf,
That hath hir body whan so that hym liketh?'
Aurelius ful ofte soore siketh:
Wo was Aurelie whan that he this herde,

989–98 In Boccaccio, the lady promises to reward her suitor if he can make a garden bloom in January. In Chaucer, the promise is changed and, though made in play and in the conscious knowledge that its fulfilment is **an inpossible** (1009), draws its origin, and its bitter irony, from Dorigen's obsessive fears for her husband's safety. To save her love, she promises what would destroy it.

And with a sorweful herte he thus answerde:
an impossibility 'Madame,' quod he, 'this were an inpossible!
Thanne moot I dye of sodeyn deth horrible.'
And with that word he turned hym anon.
Then Tho coome hir othere freendes many oon
garden paths And in the aleyes romeden up and doun
this business And nothyng wiste of this conclusioun.
But sodeynly bigonne revel newe
Til that the brighte sonne loste his hewe;
horizon, taken away For th'orisonte hath reft the sonne his light –
This is as muche to seye as it was nyght –
And hom they goon in joye and in solas,
Save oonly wrecche Aurelius, allas!
He to his hous is goon with sorweful herte.
escape He seeth he may nat from his deeth asterte;
Hym semed that he felte his herte colde.
Up to the hevene hise hondes he gan holde,
knees And on his knowes bare he sette hym doun,
prayer And in his ravynge seyde his orisoun.
went abruptly For verray wo out of his wit he breyde.
He nyste what he spak, but thus he seyde;
With pitous herte his pleynt hath he bigonne
Unto the goddes, and first unto the sonne.
He seyde, 'Appollo, god and governour
Of every plaunte, herbe, tree and flour,
(see n.) That yevest after thy declynacioun
To ech of hem his tyme and his sesoun,
(see n.) As thyn herberwe chaungeth, lowe or heighe,
Lord Phebus, cast thy merciable eighe
lost On wrecche Aurelie which that am but lorn.
Lo, lord! My lady hath my deeth ysworn
unless Withouten gilt, but thy benygnytee
death-doomed Upon my dedly herte have som pitee.
For wel I woot, lord Phebus, if yow lest,
Ye may me helpen, save my lady, best.
vouchsafe (grant), describe Now voucheth sauf that I may yow devyse
helped How that I may been holpe and in what wyse.
bright 'Youre blisful suster, Lucyna the shene,
That of the see is chief goddesse and queene –
Thogh Neptunus have deitee in the see,
Yet empiresse aboven hym is she –
Ye knowen wel, lord, that right as hir desir
quickened into life Is to be quyked and lighted of youre fyr,
For which she folweth yow ful bisily,

1018 The rhetorical 'colour' of the previous line (*circumlocutio*) is self-consciously signalled, in a manner reminiscent of the tone of the Franklin's Prologue.

1031–79 Aurelius prays to Apollo, or Phoebus (god of the sun), to use his influence upon his sister Lucina (goddess of the moon, and therefore in control of the tides) so that the next time they are in opposition (i.e. when the moon is on the opposite side of the earth from the sun, which is one of the two times when tides are fullest), and the sun is in the sign of Leo (when the sun's power is strongest), an exceptional flood-tide may occur and the rocks be fully covered. He further prays that the sun may hold this position, with the moon at the full and in opposition, for fully two years; if this cannot be done, he prays in desperation that all the rocks may be sunk into the underworld, through the power of Lucina (Diana) in her capacity as Proserpina, goddess of the underworld.

1033 'according to your angle and position in the sky'.

1035 **herberwe**: astrological 'lodging' (position in the zodiac).

Right so the see desireth naturelly
To folwen hire, as she that is goddesse
Bothe in the see and ryvers moore and lesse.
Wherfore, lord Phebus, this is my requeste –
Do this myracle, or do myn herte breste – *make my heart break*
That now next at this opposicioun
Which in the signe shal be of the Lioun,
As preyeth hire so greet a flood to brynge *flood-tide*
That fyve fadme at the leeste it oversprynge *fathoms*
The hyeste rok in Armoryk Britayne;
And lat this flood endure yeris twayne.
Thanne certes to my lady may I seye,
"Holdeth youre heste, the rokkes been aweye." *Keep your promise*
'Lord Phebus, dooth this myracle for me.
Pray hire she go no faster cours than ye –
I seye this, prayeth youre suster that she go
No faster cours than ye thise yeris two.
Thanne shal she been evene at the fulle alway,
And spryng-flood lasten bothe nyght and day.
And but she vouche sauf in swich manere
To graunte me my soverayn lady deere,
Pray hire to synken every rok adown
Into hir owene dirke regioun
Under the ground ther Pluto dwelleth inne, *(god of the underworld)*
Or nevere mo shal I my lady wynne.
Thy temple in Delphos wol I bar-foot seke. *Delphi (in Greece)*
Lord Phebus, se the teerys on my cheke
And of my peyne have som compassioun.'
And with that word in swowne he fil adoun,
And longe tyme he lay forth in a traunce.
His brother, which that knew of his penaunce,
Up caughte hym and to bedde he hath hym broght.
Despeired in this torment and this thoght *mental anxiety*
Lete I this woful creature lye; *Leave*
Chese he for me wher he wol lyve or dye. *(see n.)*
Arveragus, with heele and greet honour, *prosperity*
As he that was of chivalrie the flour, *Being the one that*
Is comen hom, and othere worthy men.
O blisful artow now, thow Dorigen,
That hast thy lusty housbonde in thyn armes,
The fresshe knyght, the worthy man of armes,
That loveth thee as his owene hertes lyf.
Nothyng list hym to been ymagynatyf *to imagine to himself*
If any wight hadde spoke whil he was oute
To hire of love; he ne hadde of it no doute.
He noght entendeth to no swich matere, *pays no attention*
But daunceth, justeth, maketh hir good cheere.
And thus in joye and blisse I lete hem dwelle,
And of the syke Aurelius wol I telle.
In langour and in torment furyus

1086 'Let him choose for himself, as far as I am concerned, whether he live or die'. The tone is somewhat dismissive and unsympathetic (see 818n, 948n).

Two yeer and moore lay wrecche Aurelius,
Er any foot he myghte on erthe gon,
Ne confort in this tyme hadde he non,
Save of his brother, which that was a clerk.
He knew of al this wo and al this werk,
For to noon oother creature, certeyn,
Of this matere he dorste no word seyn.
Under his brist he baar it moore secree
Than evere dide Panfilus for Galathee.
on the outside — His brist was hool withoute for to sene
But in his herte ay was the arwe kene.
wound healed only on the surface — And wel ye knowe that of a sursanure
In surgerye is perilous the cure,
Unless — But men myghte touche the arwe or come therby.
His brother weepe and wayled pryvely,
he happened to remember — Til at the laste hym fil in remembrance
Orleans (at the university) — That whils he was at Orliens in France –
eager — As yonge clerkes that been lykerous
subjects of study, arcane — To reden artes that been curious
in every nook and cranny — Seken in every halke and every herne
Specialized branches of learning — Particuler sciences for to lerne –
He hym remembred that upon a day
At Orliens in studie a book he say
Of magyk naturel, which his felawe,
That was that tyme a bachiler of lawe,
Al were he ther to lerne another craft,
left — Hadde prively upon his desk ylaft;
Which book spak muchel of the operaciouns
day-by-day stations — Touchynge the eighte and twenty mansiouns
appertain — That longen to the moone – and swich folye
As in oure dayes is nat worth a flye,
according to our belief — For holy chirches feith, in oure bileve,
Ne suffreth noon illusioun us to greve.
And whan this book was in his remembraunce,
Anon for joye his herte gan to daunce
And to hymself he seyde pryvely:
cured — 'My brother shal be warisshed hastily;
For I am siker that ther be sciences
visual illusions — By whiche men make diverse apparences,
magicians — Swiche as thise subtile tregettours pleye.
For ofte at festes have I wel herd seye
That tregettours withinne an halle large
Have maad come in a water and a barge,
And in the halle rowen up and doun.
Somtyme hath semed come a grym leoun,
And somtyme floures sprynge as in a mede;

1110 Pamphilus and Galatea are the lovers in the thirteenth-century Latin poem of *Pamphilus de amore*; in a line cited in the margin of MS El, Pamphilus complains of the arrow of love that festers hidden in his breast.

1125 **magyk naturel** is the science of controlling and manipulating events by the use of astrological prediction (see GP 416n), as opposed to calling up spirits ('black' magic).

1131–2 Whether the contempt for astrological 'magic' is meant to be understood as the Franklin's – a kind of bourgeois we-know-better complacency – is a question Chaucer happily evades.

1142–51 Tricks like this are well documented in contemporary sources describing French court-entertainments (see R.S. Loomis, in *Speculum* 33 [1958], 242–55).

Somtyme a vyne, and grapes white and rede,
Somtyme a castel, al of lym and stoon,
they made it disappear And whan hem lyked, voyded it anoon:
Thus semed it to every mannes sighte.
'Now thanne conclude I thus, that if I myghte
fellow-student At Orliens som old felawe yfynde
That hadde this moones mansions in mynde,
in addition Or oother magyk naturel above,
He sholde wel make my brother han his love.
For with an apparence a clerk may make
To mannes sighte that alle the rokkes blake
Of Britaigne were yvoyded everichon,
And shippes by the brynke comen and gon,
And in swich forme enduren a day or two.
cured Thanne were my brother warisshed of his wo;
Thanne moste she nedes holden hir biheste,
Or ellis he shal shame hire at the leeste.'
What sholde I make a lenger tale of this?
Unto his brotheres bed he comen is,
And swich confort he yaf hym for to gon
To Orliens that he up stirte anon,
gone And on his wey forthward thanne he is fare
relieved In hope for to been lissed of his care.
Whan they were come almoost to that citee,
But if it were a two furlong or thre,
A yong clerk romynge by hymself they mette,
in a very proper manner, greeted Which that in Latyn thriftily hem grette
And after that he seyde a wonder thyng:
'I knowe,' quod he, 'the cause of youre comyng.'
And er they ferther any foote wente,
He tolde hem al that was in hir entente.
This Britoun clerk hym asked of felawes
days The whiche that he hadde knowe in olde dawes
And he answerde hym that they dede were,
For which he weepe ful ofte many a teere.
Doun of his hors Aurelius lighte anon
And with this magicien forth he is gon
Hom to his hous, and maden hem wel at ese.
Hem lakked no vitaille that myghte hem plese.
as the one that was there So wel arrayed hous as ther was oon
Aurelius in his lyf saw nevere noon.
He shewed hym, er he wente to soper,
Forestes, parkes ful of wilde deer:
Ther saw he hertes with hir hornes hye,
The gretteste that evere were seyn with eye,
He say of hem an hundred slayn with houndes
And somme with arwes blede of bittre woundes.
made to disappear He saw, whan voyded were thise wilde deer,
hawking ground by a river Thise fawconers upon a fair ryver,
That with hir hawkes han the heron slayn.

1175 **a wonder thyng**. One can think of various ways in which this apparently amazing act of telepathy could have been accomplished; it is nevertheless a very effective sales gimmick, as is the Latin salutation.

Tho saugh he knyghtes justyng in a playn;
And after this he dide hym this plesaunce –
That he hym shewed his lady on a daunce
On which hymself he daunced, as hym thoughte.
And whan this maister that this magyk wroughte
Saugh it was tyme, he clapte his handes two,
And farwel! al oure revel was ago.
And yet remoeved they nevere out of the hous
Whil they sawe al this sighte merveillous,
But in his studie, ther as his bookes be,
They sitten stille, and no wight but they thre.
To hym this maister called his squyer
And seide hym thus: 'Is redy oure soper?
Almoost an houre it is, I undertake,
Sith I yow bad oure soper for to make,
Whan that thise worthy men wenten with me
Into my studie, ther as my bookes be.'
'Sire,' quod this squyer, 'whan it liketh yow,
even if you want it right now It is al redy, thogh ye wol right now.'
'Go we thanne soupe,' quod he, 'as for the beste.
Thise amorous folk somtyme mote han hir reste!'
negotiation At after-soper fille they in tretee
sum, reward What somme sholde this maistres gerdoun be
To remoeven alle the rokkes of Britayne,
(rivers) Gironde, Seine And eek from Geround to the mouth of Sayne.
He raised difficulties He made it straunge, and swoor, so God hym save,
Lasse than a thousand pound he wolde nat have,
Ne gladly for that somme he wolde nat gon.
Aurelius, with blisful herte anon,
Answerde thus: 'Fy on a thousand pound!
This wyde world, which that men seye is round,
I wolde it yeve if I were lord of it.
fully made, in agreement This bargayn is ful dryve, for we ben knyt.
Ye shal be payed trewely, by my trouthe!
But looketh now, for no necligence or slouthe
Ye tarie us heer no lenger than to-morwe.'
as a pledge 'Nay,' quod this clerk, 'have heer my feith to borwe.'
To bedde is goon Aurelius whan hym leste
And wel-neigh al that nyght he hadde his reste.
What for his labour and his hope of blisse
respite His woful herte of penaunce hadde a lisse.
Upon the morwe, whan that it was day,
direct To Britayne tooke they the righte way,
Aurelius and this magicien bisyde,
dismounted And been descended ther they wolde abyde.
remind And this was, as thise bookes me remembre,
The colde, frosty seson of Decembre.
(see n.) Phebus wax old, and hewed lyk latoun,

1203 **clapte his handes**: to dispel the illusion and to summon the servants. The suggestion is that the clerk-magician has not been putting himself out to display his skills but just passing the time agreeably till dinner. Did Shakespeare remember these lines in *The Tempest* (IV.i.148)?

1228 That the world was round, or spherical, was taken for granted in the Middle Ages; but no one seemed much exercised to find out for certain.

1245–6 'The sun grew old (i.e. it was late in the year) and hued like copper alloy, that in his high summer position in the sky (in Cancer) …'

That in his hote declynacioun
burnished, rays Shoon as the burned gold with stremys brighte;
But now in Capricorn adoun he lighte,
Where as he shoon ful pale, I dar wel seyn.
The bittre frostes with the sleet and reyn
garden Destruyed hath the grene in every yerd.
sits Janus sit by the fyr, with double berd,
wild-ox horn And drynketh of his bugle-horn the wyn;
stands meat, boar Biforn hym stant brawen of the tusked swyn,
Noel And 'Nowel!' crieth every lusty man.
  Aurelius, al that evere he kan,
good cheer Dooth to this maister cheere and reverence
And preyeth hym to doon his diligence
To bryngen hym out of his peynes smerte,
Or with a swerd that he wolde slytte his herte.
pity   This subtil clerk swich routhe hadde of this man
all he knows how That nyght and day he spedde hym that he kan
(see n.) To wayten a tyme of his conclusioun,
This is to seyn, to make illusioun
illusion or conjuring trick By swich an apparence or jogelrye –
I ne kan no termes of astrologye –
think That she and every wight sholde wene and seye
That of Britayne the rokkes were aweye,
Or ellis they were sonken under grounde.
So at the laste he hath his tyme yfounde
tricks, contemptible exercise To maken his japes and his wrecchednesse
Of swich a supersticious cursednesse.
(see n.) His tables Tolletanes forth he broght,
Ful wel corrected, ne ther lakked noght,
(see n.) Neither his collect ne his expans yeris,
base-dates, paraphernalia Ne hise rootes, ne hise othere geris,
(see n.) As been his centris and hise argumentz
And hise proporcionels convenientz
For hise equacions in every thyng.
eighth sphere (of the fixed stars) And by his eighte speere in his wirkyng
had moved He knew ful wel how fer Alnath was shove
fixed constellation Fro the heed of thilke fixe Aries above,
observed That in the ninthe speere considered is;
Ful subtilly he kalkuled al this.
  Whan he hadde founde his firste mansioun,
(see n.) He knew the remenaunt by proporcioun,

1248 **Capricorn**: the zodiacal sign that the sun passes through in December.

1252 **Janus** is the god of entrances, and therefore of January; he looks backward and forward, and so has a **double berd**. The echo is of calendar-pictures in books of hours, which often show feasting-scenes for January. The passage as a whole (1245–55) is prompted by the garden in Boccaccio that must be made to bloom in January, but Chaucer turns it to wonderfully effective use as a seasonal turning-point in the narrative: deep in the midwinter of misfortune lies the promise of hope.

1263 'To look for a good time for his astrological operation'.

1270–96 The description of the magician's operations tumbles forth somewhat impatiently, as if the narrator were anxious not to be seen to know too much about such dubious practice (see 1264–6, 1271–2, 1292–3, and 1131–2n); but Chaucer's expertise on the subject is evident.

1273 **tables Tolletanes**: astronomical tables adapted for use in Toledo (Spain) in 1272.

1275 'his tables of planetary positions in multiple or single years'.

1277–9 'his tables and figures used in calculating planetary positions, and his tables for computing planetary motions for his divisions of the planetary sphere into astrological houses'.

1281 **Alnath**: a star in the constellation Aries.

1283 **ninthe speere**: the sphere of the Primum Mobile (see *PF* 59n).

1286 'by calculations derived from his astronomical tables'.

And knew the arisyng of his moone wel,
(see n.) And in whos face, and terme, and everydel;
And knew ful wel the moones mansioun
To be conformable Acordaunt to his operacioun,
And knew also hise othere observaunces
evil practices For swiche illusions and swiche meschaunces
As hethen folk useden in thilke dayes.
For which no lenger maked he delayes,
week But thurgh his magyk, for a wyke or tweye,
It semed that alle the rokkes were aweye.
still Aurelius, which that yet despeired is
Whether, have everything go wrong Wher he shal han his love or fare amys,
Awaiteth nyght and day on this myracle;
And whan he knew that ther was noon obstacle,
That voyded were thise rokkes everichon,
Doun to his maistres feet he fil anon,
And seyde, 'I, woful wrecche Aurelius,
Thonke yow, lord, and lady myn Venus,
helped That me han holpen fro my cares colde.'
And to the temple his wey forth hath he holde,
Wher as he knew he sholde his lady se.
And whan he saw his tyme, anon-right he,
fearful With dredful herte and with ful humble cheere,
Greeted Salued hath his soverayn lady deere:
true 'My righte lady,' quod this woful man,
'Whom I moost drede and love as I best kan,
And lothest were of al this world displese,
Were it not, distress Nere it that I for yow have swich disese
That I moste dyen heer at youre foot anon,
Noght wolde I telle how me is wo-bigon.
either, complain But certes outher moste I dye or pleyne:
Ye sleen me giltelees for verray peyne.
But of my deeth thogh that ye have no routhe,
Think hard Avyseth yow er that ye breke your trouthe.
Repenteth yow, for thilke God above,
Er ye me sleen bycause that I yow love.
promised For, madame, wel ye woot what ye han hight –
claim Nat that I chalange any thyng of right
Of yow, my sovereyn lady, but youre grace –
But in a gardyn yond, at swich a place,
promised Ye woot right wel what ye bihighten me;
And in myn hand your trouthe plighten ye
To love me best – God woot, ye seyden so,
Al be that I unworthy am therto.
Madame, I speke it for the honour of yow
Moore than to save myn hertes lyf right now.
I have do so as ye comaunded me;
And if ye vouche sauf, ye may go se.
promise Dooth as yow list; have youre biheste in mynde,
living For, quyk or deed, right ther ye shal me fynde.
lies In yow lyth al to do me lyve or deye:

1288 **face, terme**: names for sectors of the zodiacal sign.

But wel I woot the rokkes been aweye.'
astonished He taketh his leve, and she astoned stood;
In al hir face nas a drope of blood.
thought She wende nevere have come in swich a trappe.
'Allas,' quod she, 'that evere this sholde happe!
For wende I nevere by possibilitee
monstrous thing That swich a monstre or merveille myghte be!
It is agayns the proces of nature.'
And hom she gooth a sorweful creature;
For verray feere unnethe may she go.
She wepeth, wayleth, al a day or two,
And swowneth that it routhe was to se.
But why it was to no wight tolde she,
For out of towne was goon Arveragus.
But to hirself she spak, and seyde thus,
With face pale and with ful sorweful cheere,
In hire compleinte, as ye shal after heere:
complain 'Allas,' quod she, 'on thee, Fortune, I pleyne,
without my being aware of it That unwar wrapped hast me in thy cheyne,
For which t'escape woot I no socour,
Save oonly deeth or elles deshonour –
Oon of thise two bihoveth me to chese.
rather lose But nathelees, yet have I levere to lese
My lyf than of my body to have a shame,
Or knowen myselven fals, or lese my name,
discharged of my promise And with my deth I may be quyt, ywis.
Hath ther nat many a noble wyf er this,
And many a mayde, yslayn hirself, allas,
Rather than with hir body doon trespas?
'Yis, certes, lo, thise stories beren witnesse:
Whan thritty tirauntz, ful of cursednesse,
Hadde slayn Phidon in Atthenes atte feste,
to be arrested They comaunded his doghtren for t'areste
And bryngen hem biforn hem in despit
Al naked, to fulfille hir foul delit,
And in hir fadres blood they made hem daunce
Upon the pavement, God yeve hem meschaunce!
For which thise woful maydens, ful of drede,
Rather than they wolde lese hir maydenhede,
jumped They pryvely been stirt into a welle
drowned And dreynte hemselven, as the bokes telle.
caused to be enquired out and sought 'They of Mecene leete enquere and seke
Lacedaemon (Sparta) Of Lacedomye fifty maydens eke,
On whiche they wolden doon hir lecherye.
But was ther noon of al that compaignye

1355–1456 Dorigen's **compleinte** draws on Jerome's treatise *Adversus Jovinianum* (see WBP 7n), which is extensively quoted in the margins of MS El. Jerome, in the praise of womanly virtue that accompanies his generally anti-feminist tirade, cites many examples of maidens and wives who slew themselves rather than submit to rape, or after being raped; he also cites examples of wives, unthreatened by rape, who led notably blameless lives. Strictly speaking irrelevant to Dorigen's plight, these exemplary wives may indicate the drift of her mind (not to do anything drastic, but to be a faithful wife – and tell her husband). This would be to see her *compleinte* as a genuine soliloquy, in some way processing her anxieties; but its character as a rhetorical *tour de force* has also to be reckoned with, and the manner in which, representing Dorigen in this unlikely and operatic (and even comic) way, it distances the reader and prepares for the oblivions of the romance-ending.

That she nas slayn, and with a good entente
Chees rather for to dye than assente
ravished To been oppressed of hir maydenhede.
Why sholde I thanne to dye been in drede?
'Loo, eek, the tiraunt Aristoclides
called That loved a mayden, highte Stymphalides,
Whan that hir fader slayn was on a nyght,
directly Unto Dianes temple gooth she right,
clasped And hente the ymage in hir handes two,
Fro which ymage wolde she nevere go.
tear No wight ne myghte hir handes of it arace
very same Til she was slayn right in the selve place.
indignant scorn 'Now sith that maydens hadden swich despit
To been defouled with mannes foul delit,
Wel oghte a wyf rather hirselven sle
Than be defouled, as it thynketh me.
'What shal I seyn of Hasdrubales wyf,
deprived herself of That at Cartage birafte hirself hir lyf?
For whan she saw that Romayns wan the town,
She took hir children alle and skipte adown
Into the fyr, and chees rather to dye
Than any Romayn dide hire vileynye.
'Hath nat Lucresse yslayn hirself, allas,
raped At Rome, whan that she oppressed was
Of Tarquyn, for hir thoughte it was a shame
To lyven whan she hadde lost hir name?
Miletus The sevene maydens of Milesie also
Han slayn hemself for verray drede and wo
Galatia (or Gaul?) Rather than folk of Gawle hem sholde oppresse.
Mo than a thousand stories, as I gesse,
Koude I now telle as touchyng this matere.
Whan Habradate was slayn, his wyf so deere
Hirselven slow, and leet hir blood to glyde
In Habradates woundes depe and wyde,
And seyde, 'My body, at the leeste way,
if I can help it Ther shal no wight defoulen, if I may.'
'What sholde I mo ensamples her-of sayn?
Sith that so manye han hemselven slayn
Wel rather than they wolde defouled be,
I wol conclude that it is bet for me
To sleen myself than ben defouled thus.
I wol be trewe unto Arveragus,
Or rather sle myself in som manere,
As dide Democienis doghter deere
Bycause that she wolde nat defouled be.
Scedasus O Cedasus, it is ful gret pitee
To reden how thy doghtren deyde, allas,
cause That slowe hemself for swich maner cas.
As greet a pitee was it, or wel moore,
(see n.) The Theban mayden that for Nychanore

1432 **for Nychanore**: 'because of the conqueror Nicanor's desire for her'.

slew — Hirselven slow right for swich manere wo.
Another Theban mayden dide right so:
Macedonia, raped — For oon of Macedonye hadde hire oppressed,
made amends for — She with hir owene deeth hir maydenhed redressed.
What shal I seyn of Nyceratis wyf
That for swich cas birafte hirself hir lyf?
How trewe eek was to Alcebiades
His love, that rather for to dyen chees
Than for to suffre his body unburyed be.
what — Lo, which a wyf was Alceste,' quod she.
Homer — 'What seith Omer of goode Penelopee?
Al Grece knoweth of hir chastitee.
Pardee, of Laodomya is writen thus,
That whan at Troye was slayn Protheselaus,
Ne lenger wolde she lyve after his day.
The same of noble Porcia telle I may:
Withoute Brutus koude she nat lyve,
entirely — To whom she hadde al hool hir herte yeve.
The parfit wifhod of Arthemesye
all heathendom — Honoured is thurgh al the Barbarye.
(queen of Illyria) — O Teuta, queene, thy wyfly chastitee
To alle wyves may a mirour bee.
The same thyng I seye of Bilyea,
Of Rodogone and eek Valeria.'
  Thus pleyned Dorigene a day or tweye,
Purposynge evere that she wolde deye.
But nathelees, upon the thridde nyght,
Hom cam Arveragus, this worthy knyght,
And asked hire why that she weepe so soore;
And she gan wepen ever lenger the moore.
'Allas,' quod she, 'that evere was I born!
Thus have I seyd,' quod she, 'thus have I sworn' –
And tolde hym al as ye han herd bifore:
It nedeth nat reherce it yow namoore.
This housbonde with glad cheere in frendly wyse
Answerde and seyde as I shal yow devyse:
'Is ther oght ellis, Dorigen, but this?'
as surely as God may help me! — 'Nay, nay,' quod she, 'God help me so as wys!
if it were — This is to muche, and it were Goddes wille.'
  'Ye, wyf,' quod he, 'lat slepen that is stille.
It may be wel, paraventure, yet to-day.
Ye shul youre trouthe holden, by my fay!
For God so wisly have mercy upon me,
stabbed to death — I hadde wel levere ystiked for to be
For verray love which that I to yow have,
Than that . . . not — But if ye sholde youre trouthe kepe and save.
Trouthe is the hyeste thyng that man may kepe.'
burst suddenly into tears — But with that word he brast anon to wepe,
on pain — And seyde, 'I yow forbede, up peyne of deeth,

1442 Alceste chose to die in place of her husband Admetus.
1451 Artemisia built a great tomb to honour her husband Mausolus.
1455–6 Bilia was famed for her chastity and for not complaining of her husband's bad breath, while Rhodogone and Valeria refused to remarry after their husbands' death.

That nevere whil thee lasteth lyf ne breeth
To no wight tel thow of this aventure –
As I may best I wol my wo endure –
Ne make no contenance of hevynesse, *carry a sad face*
That folk of yow may demen harm or gesse.' *concerning you, imagine*
  And forth he clepyd a squyer and a mayde:
'Goth forth anon with Dorigen,' he sayde,
'And bryngeth hire to swich a place anon.'
They toke hir leve and on hir wey they gon,
But they ne wiste why they thider wente:
He nolde to no wight tellen his entente.
  Paraventure an heepe of yow, ywis, *lot*
Wol holden hym a lewed man in this, *stupid and ignorant*
That he wol putte his wyf in jupartie. *jeopardy*
Herkneth the tale er ye upon hire crie:
She may have bettre fortune than yow semeth; *(than you think)*
And whan that ye han herd the tale, demeth. *make your judgement*
  This squyer which that highte Aurelius,
On Dorigen that was so amorus,
Of aventure happed hir to meete *By chance*
Amydde the town, right in the quykkest strete, *busiest*
As she was boun to goon the wey forth-right *prepared, directly*
Toward the gardyn ther as she had hight.
And he was to the gardyn-ward also,
For wel he spyed whan she wolde go
Out of hir hous to any maner place.
But thus they meete, of aventure or grace,
And he salueth hire with glad entente *greets*
And asked of hire whiderward she wente;
And she answerde, half as she were mad,
'Unto the gardyn, as myn housbond bad,
My trouthe for to holde – allas, allas!'
  Aurelius gan wondren on this cas
And in his herte hadde greet compassioun
Of hire and of hire lamentacioun,
And of Arveragus, the worthy knyght,
That bad hir holden al that she had hight,
So looth hym was his wyf sholde breke hir trouthe;
And in his herte he caughte of this greet routhe,
Considerynge the beste on every syde,
That fro his lust yet were hym levere abyde *he would rather abstain*
Than doon so heigh a cherlyssh wrecchednesse *low-born miserable act*
Agayns franchise and alle gentillesse; *Against noble generosity*
For which in fewe wordes seyde he thus:
  'Madame, seyeth to youre lord Arveragus
That sith I se his grete gentillesse
To yow – and eek I se wel youre distresse –
That hym were levere han shame (and that were routhe)
Than ye to me sholde breke thus your trouthe,

1489 **swich a place** ('such-and-such a place') proves to be the garden (1504), a symbolically appropriate if not altogether convenient place for the keeping of the promise, which now seems to be understood as a single act of sex (cf. 997).

1493–8 The absence of these lines in Hg suggests they were added by Chaucer in revision as a further set of modulations from the anxious tensions of the Dorigen story to the cheerful romance-conclusion.

I have wel levere evere to suffre wo
Than I departe the love bitwix yow two.
give you back (release to you) I yow relesse, madame, into youre hond
(see n.) Quyt every serement and every bond
That ye han maad to me as her-biforn
Sith thilke tyme which that ye were born.
pledge My trouthe I plighte, I shal yow never repreve
Of no biheeste. And here I take my leve,
As of the treweste and the beste wyf
That evere yet I knew in al my lyf.
take warning from her promise But every wyf be war of hir biheste!
On Dorigene remembreth at the leste.
Thus kan a squyer doon a gentil dede
doubt As wel as kan a knyght, withouten drede.'
She thonketh hym upon hir knees al bare
gone And hom unto hir housbond is she fare
(heard me say) And tolde hym al as ye han herd me sayd;
sure, pleased And be ye siker, he was so wel apayd
That it were inpossible me to write.
What sholde I lenger of this cas endite?
Arveragus and Dorigene his wyf
In sovereyn blisse leden forth hir lyf.
Nevere eft ne was ther angre hem bitwene:
He cherisseth hire as thogh she were a queene,
And she was to hym trewe for everemoore.
Of thise two folk ye gete of me namoore.
has lost all his investment Aurelius, that his cost hath al forlorn,
Curseth the tyme that evere he was born:
'Allas!' quod he, 'allas, that I bihighte
weight Of pured gold a thousand pound of wighte
Unto this philosophre! How shal I do?
ruined I se namoore but that I am fordo.
Myn heritage moot I nedes selle
And been a beggere; here may I nat dwelle
And shamen al my kynrede in this place,
Unless But I of hym may gete bettre grace.
try But nathelees I wol of hym assaye
At certeyn dayes yeer by yeer to paye,
And thonke hym of his grete curteisye.
will not My trouthe wol I kepe, I nel nat lye.'
With herte soor he gooth unto his cofre
And broghte gold unto this philosophre
The value of fyve hundred pound, I gesse,
And hym bisecheth of his gentillesse
additional time to pay the balance To graunten hym dayes of the remenant,
boast And seyde, 'Maister, I dar wel make avant,
I fayled nevere of my trouthe as yit.
paid For sikerly my dette shal be quyt

1534 'Every oath and bond (considered to be) satisfactorily discharged'.

1541–2 These lines are spoken somewhat 'out of character', but 'character' in Chaucer is not such an impermeable container as to argue that they should be detached from Aurelius.

1549 **write**: a slip in dramatic consistency on Chaucer's part, not the only one in the *Canterbury Tales*.

Towardes yow, howevere that I fare
a-begging, tunic and nothing else To goon a-begged in my kirtel bare.
on provision of some security But wolde ye vouche sauf, upon seuretee,
grant me a respite Two yeer or thre for to respiten me,
Thanne were I wel, for elles moot I selle
Myn heritage; ther is namoore to telle.'
This philosophre sobrely answerde,
And seyde thus, whan he thise wordes herde:
'Have I nat holden covenant unto thee?'
'Yis, certes, wel and trewely,' quod he.
'Hastow nat had thy lady as thee liketh?'
'No, no,' quod he, and sorwefully he siketh.
'What was the cause? Tel me if thow kan.'
Aurelius his tale anon bigan
And tolde hym al as ye han herd bifore:
It nedeth nat to yow reherce it moore.
He seyde, 'Arveragus, of gentillesse,
Hadde levere dye in sorwe and in distresse
Than that his wyf were of hir trouthe fals.'
also The sorwe of Dorigen he tolde hym als,
How looth hir was to ben a wikked wyf,
And that she levere had lost that day hir lyf,
And that hir trouthe she swoor thurgh innocence:
before, illusion She nevere erst hadde herde speke of apparence.
'That made me han of hire so greet pitee;
And right as frely as he sente hir me
As frely sente I hire to hym agayn.
This is the whole story This al and som; ther is namoore to sayn.'
This philosophre answerde, 'Leeve brother,
Everich of yow dide gentilly til oother.
Thow art a squyer, and he is a knyght:
But God forbede, for his blisful myght,
But if a clerk koude doon a gentil dede
As wel as any of yow, it is no drede!
(see n.) 'Sire, I relesse thee thy thowsand pound,
had crept As thow right now were cropen out of the ground,
Ne nevere er now ne haddest knowen me.
For, sire, I wol nat take a peny of thee
the exercise of my art, labour For al my craft ne noght for my travaille.
Thow hast ypayed wel for my vitaille:
It is ynogh. And farewel, have good day!'
And took his hors and forth he goth his way.
Lordynges, this questioun than wol I aske now:
generous Which was the mooste free, as thynketh yow?
Now telleth me, er that ye ferther wende.
I kan namoore; my tale is at an ende.

1604–5 'Traffic in women' seems here the means of restoring male solidarity.

1613 **relesse thee**: 'return back to you' (release you from obligation for).

1622 The question is not only asked but also discussed in Boccaccio's *Filocolo* (where it is decided that the husband showed most *gentillesse*). Chaucer leaves the debate open, perhaps encouraging us to insert Dorigen as a possible outsider in the contest (since it is her honesty which triggers the denouement, and honesty is a kind of truth and generosity of spirit that makes for 'freedom').

The Pardoner's Prologue and Tale

The Introduction

The Host is much moved by the Physician's Tale, of how the Roman lord Virginius slew his daughter Virginia to save her from the lust of the judge Appius. He moralizes upon the Tale and misses the point in a characteristic way. He then calls upon the Pardoner to tell his tale; the two tales together form what is usually called Fragment VI of the *Tales*, the line-numbering of which is followed here.

Oure Hoost gan to swere as he were wood:
Alas! 'Harrow!' quod he, 'by nayles and by blood!
This was a fals cherl and a fals justise.
As shameful deeth as herte may devyse
Come to thise juges and hire advocatz!
All the same, innocent Algate this sely mayde is slayn, allas!
Allas, to deere boghte she beautee!
Wherfore I seye al day that men may se
gifts That yiftes of Fortune and of Nature
Been cause of deeth to many a creature.
Hir beaute was hir deth, I dar wel sayn.
Allas, so pitously as she was slayn!
Of bothe yiftes that I speke of now
benefit Men han ful ofte moore for harm than prow.
But trewely, myn owene maister deere,
This is a pitous tale for to heere.
it's no matter But nathelees, passe over, is no fors.
body I pray to God so save thy gentil cors,
(medical vessels) And eek thyne urynals and thy jurdones,
(medicines) Thyn ypocras, and eek thy galiones,
box, medicine And every boyste ful of thy letuarie –
God blesse hem, and oure lady Seinte Marie!
as I may thrive So mote I then, thow art a propre man,
Ronan And lyk a prelat, by Seint Ronyan!
technical language Seyde I nat wel? I kan nat speke in terme,
makest, grieve But wel I woot thow doost myn herte to erme,
That I almoost have caught a cardynacle.
medicine By corpus bones! but if I have triacle,
fresh and malty Or ellis a draghte of moyste and corny ale,
Or but I heere anon a murye tale,
Myn herte is lost for pitee of this mayde.
fair friend (perhaps mockingly) Thow *beel amy*, thow Pardoner,' he sayde,
funny stories 'Tel us som myrthe or japes right anon.'
  'It shal be doon,' quod he, 'by Seint Ronyon!
But first,' quod he, 'heere at this ale-stake
I wol bothe drynke and eten of a cake.'
gentlefolk   And right anon thise gentils gonne to crye,
filthiness 'Nay, lat hym telle us of no ribawdye!

313–14 The Host's determination to show off his knowledge of medical terms ends in disaster; the word he is after is *cardiacle* (a heart-attack). In the next line he garbles two oaths, 'by Corpus Christi' and 'by Goddes bones'.

320 **Ronyon**. Perhaps a mocking echo of the Host's garbled oath (there is sixteenth-century evidence of a word 'runnion' meaning 'male sexual organ').

323–8 Why the **gentils** are allowed to exercise censorship on this occasion, and not others, is not clear, unless it be to prepare for the rich retrospective irony of the Pardoner's offer of **som honeste thyng** as an alternative to **ribawdye**.

learn Telle us som moral thyng, that we may leere
wisdom Som wit, and thanne wol we gladly heere.'
'I graunte, ywis,' quod he, 'but I moot thynke
Upon som honeste thyng whil that I drynke.'

The Pardoner's Prologue

For the profession of the Pardoner, see GP 669n. Like the Wife of Bath, the Pardoner has a quasi-autobiographical monologue before he begins his tale, describing the practices by which he deceives his simple audiences into parting with their money. As with the Wife of Bath, Chaucer draws upon the convention of the confession of the allegorical vice-figure, in this case the figure of *Faus-Semblant* ('Hypocrisy') in *RR* 11065–11974. The outrageousness of the Pardoner's account of his evil-doing and perversion of his holy office can be associated with the allegory of its origin, but it comes to seem, because of the vividness of Chaucer's individual realization of the speaker, a part of his 'character'. Whether it is seen as an arrogant display of power on the part of one who knows the contempt in which he is held, or a boasting of 'normal' depravity on the part of one who is fearful of revealing his outcast state as a homosexual (see M. McAlpine, 'The Pardoner's Homosexuality and How it Matters', *PMLA* 95 [1980], 8–22), or a destabilization of traditional values by an untraditionally gendered person (see C. Dinshaw, 'Eunuch Hermeneutics', in *Chaucer's Sexual Poetics* [Madison, 1989]), is matter for debate. We may be observing, more simply, the atrophy of moral sensibility in one whose profession, systematically, year in and year out, is lying.

'Lordynges,' quod he, 'in chirches whan I preche
lofty and resonant I peyne me to han an hauteyn speche
And rynge it out as round as gooth a belle,
For I kan al by rote that I telle.
sermon-text, one and the same My theme is alwey oon, and evere was –
Radix malorum est cupiditas.
'First I pronounce whennes that I come
one and all And thanne my bulles shewe I, alle and some.
Oure lige lordes seel on my patente,
protect That shewe I first, my body to warente,
That no man be so boold, ne preest ne clerk,
Me to destourbe of Cristes holy werk.
And after that thanne telle I forth my tales;
Bulles of popes and of cardynales,
Of patriarkes and bisshopes I shewe,
And in Latyn I speke a wordes fewe
add spice to To saffron with my predicacioun
And for to stire hem to devocioun.
glass cases Thanne shewe I forth my longe cristal stones,
rags Ycrammed ful of cloutes and of bones –
think Relikes been they, as wenen they echon.
latten (brass alloy) Thanne have I in a latoun a shulder-bon
Which that was of an holy Jewes sheepe.
"Goode men," I seye, "tak of my wordes keepe:
If that this boon be wasshe in any welle,
If cow or calf or sheepe or oxe swelle
snake That any worm hath ete or worm ystonge,
Taak water of that welle and wassh his tonge,

334 'Cupidity is the root of all evils', from 1 Tim. 6:10.
336–7 The **bulles** are the papal authorization of the grant of indulgence, which could be directly obtained from other sources than the pope (see 342–3). The open letter or **patente**, with the seal of **oure lige lorde** (presumably the pope or bishop, rather than the king), is what authorizes the Pardoner to preach in a particular area (since he is not an ordained priest: see 391).

whole And it is hool anoon; and forthermoor,
Of pokkes and of scabbe and every soor
Shal every sheepe be hool that of this welle
Drynketh a draughte. Taak kepe eek what I telle:
householder, owns If that the goode-man that the bestes oweth
week Wol every wike, er that the cok hym croweth,
Fastynge, drynken of this welle a draghte,
As thilke holy Jew oure eldres taghte,
stock Hise bestes and his stoor shal multiplie.
'"And, sire, also it heeleth jalousie:
For thogh a man be falle in jalous rage,
soup Lat maken with this water his potage
mistrust And nevere shal he moore his wyf mystriste,
misdeed Thogh he the soothe of hir defaute wiste,
Al hadde she taken preestes two or thre.
mitten (glove for sowing seed) '"Heere is a miteyn eek that ye may se:
He that his hand wol putte in this mitayn,
He shal have multiplyyng of his grayn
Whan he hath sowen, be it whete or otes,
pence, groats (worth fourpence) So that he offre pens or ellis grotes.
'"Goode men and wommen, o thyng warne I yow:
If any wight be in this chirche now
That hath doon synne horrible, that he
confessed Dar nat for shame of it yshryven be,
Or any womman, be she yong or old,
That hath ymaked hir housbond cokewold,
Swich folk shal have no power ne no grace
To offren to my relikes in this place.
And whoso fyndeth hym out of swich blame
in God's name He wol come up and offre a Goddes name
absolve And I assoille him by the auctoritee
Which that by bulle ygraunted was to me."
trick 'By this gaude have I wonne, yeer by yeer,
(a mark is two-thirds of a pound) An hundred mark sith I was pardoner.
I stonde lyk a clerk in my pulpet
ignorant And whan that lewed peple is doun yset
I preche so as ye han herd bifore
And telle an hundred false japes more.
Thanne peyne I me to strecche forth the nekke
nod my head And est and west upon the peple I bekke
barn-roof As dooth a dowve sittyng on a berne.
briskly Myne handes and my tonge goon so yerne
That it is joye to se my bisynesse.
'Of avarice and of swich cursednesse
Is al my prechyng, for to make hem free
To yeven hir pens, and namely unto me.
obtain money For myn entente is nat but for to wynne
And nothyng for correccioun of synne.
I rekke nevere, whan that they been beryed,

387 **assoille**. The Pardoner, it should be emphasized, has no power to grant absolution (a sacrament that only an ordained priest can administer), only to give indulgences (remissions of earthly penance) to those who are truly penitent.

399 The joye of which the Pardoner speaks is an almost aesthetic delight in watching a supremely skilful practitioner at work.

a-blackberrying	Thogh that hir soules goon a-blakeberyed!
	For certes many a predicacioun
	Comth ofte tyme of yvel entencioun:
	Som for plesance of folk and flaterye,
	To been avanced by ypocrisie,
	And som for veyne glorie and som for hate.
argue against someone	For whan I dar noon oother weyes debate,
sharply	Thanne wol I stynge hym with my tonge smerte
escape	In prechyng, so that he shal nat asterte
	To been diffamed falsly, if that he
fellow-pardoners	Hath trespased to my bretheren or to me.
	For though I telle noght his propre name,
	Men shal wel knowe that it is the same
	By signes and by othere circumstances.
pay back	Thus quyte I folk that doon us displesances;
spit, colour (pretence)	Thus spete I out my venym under hewe
	Of holynesse, to seme holy and trewe.
describe	'But shortly myn entente I wol devyse:
	I preche of nothyng but for coveitise.
	Therfore my theme is yet and evere was
	Radix malorum est cupiditas.
against	Thus kan I preche agayn that same vice
	Which that I use, and that is avarice.
	But though myself be gilty in that synne,
turn away	Yet kan I maken oother folk to twynne
	From avarice and soore to repente –
	But that is nat my principal entente:
	I preche nothyng but for coveitise.
	Of this matere it oghte ynow suffise.
exemplary stories	'Thanne telle I hem ensamples many oon
	Of olde stories longe tyme agoon,
	For lewed peple loven tales olde –
	Swiche thynges kan they wel reporte and holde.
	What, trowe ye that whiles I may preche
because of how	And wynne gold and silver for I teche,
in voluntary poverty	That I wol lyve in poverte wilfully?
had it in mind	Nay, nay, I thoghte it nevere, trewely!
	For I wol preche and begge in sondry landes;
	I wol nat do no labour with myne handes
	Ne make baskettes and lyve therby,
without making a profit	Bycause I wol nat beggen ydelly.
	I wol none of the apostles countrefete;
wool(len clothes)	I wol have moneye, wolle, chese and whete,
lad	Al were it yeven of the poverest page
	Or of the povereste widwe in a village,
	Al sholde hir children sterve for famyne.
	Nay, I wol drynke licour of the vyne
	And have a joly wenche in every toun.

432 The eagerness with which the Pardoner disclaims any intention of doing good suggests that his anxious determination to do evil is something of a point of pride with him. This determination is further expressed in his obsessively insistent repetition of **I wol** (443–52).

447–8 The apostles were sent out to preach and told to take no thought for worldly things but simply to beg for their daily bread (Mark 6:7–10).

'But herkneth, lordynges, in conclusioun:
Youre likyng is that I shal telle a tale;
Now have I dronke a draghte of corny ale,
By God, I hope I shal yow telle a thyng
That shal by resoun been at youre likyng.
For thogh myself be a ful vicious man,
A moral tale yet I yow telle kan
Which I am wont to preche for to wynne.
Now holde youre pees! My tale I wol bigynne.'

The Pardoner's Tale

The Pardoner's Tale is in two parts: a sermon on the sins of the tavern (drunkenness, gluttony, gambling and swearing), prompted by the introduction of the riotous company from whom the three protagonists of the Tale are drawn; and the Tale proper, which functions as the sermon *exemplum*. The homily is forceful and lurid, and can be seen as apt to the extravagant rhetoric of one who wants, above all, to achieve a dramatic effect – though it is not uncharacteristic of medieval sermons. The Tale is told with outstanding economy and power, evocative of the real world and yet verging on allegory in the namelessness of the personages of the story and the belief of all of them that Death is literally a person. It is a traditional story, widely disseminated in western and eastern cultures. On the level of *exemplum*, or preacher's illustrative story, it is perfectly designed to convince the Pardoner's ignorant audience that greed for money is a (literally) deadly sin which they can avoid by giving their money to him. On another level, it reveals an automaton-like quality in the Pardoner, a death-like atrophy of sensibility in which he can think of nothing to do in the way of telling a story other than to do what he always does in his professional life. He seems to have no life but in the act of performance or in boasting about it, no awareness but of the act of will that drives his performance and that must for ever be reiterated. In some sense, he is 'dead'.

'In Flandres whilom was a compaignye
lived a life of — Of yonge folk that haunteden folye,
debauchery, gambling, brothels — As riot, hasard, stewes and tavernes,
guitars — Where as with harpes, lutes, and gyternes
dice — They daunce and pleyen at dees bothe day and nyght
And ete also and drynke over hir myght,
Thurgh which they doon the devel sacrifise
Withinne that develes temple in cursed wise
By superfluytee abhomynable.
Hir othes been so grete and so dampnable
That it is grisly for to heere hem swere.
tear in pieces — Oure blissed Lordes body they to-tere –
Hem thoughte that Jewes rente hym noght ynough –
And eech of hem at otheres synne lough.
dancing-girls — And right anon thanne coomen tombesteres
shapely and slender, fruit-girls — Fetys and smale, and yonge frutesteres,
cake-sellers — Syngeris with harpes, baudes, waufereres,
Whiche been the verray develes officers
To kyndle and blowe the fyr of lecherye,
That is annexed unto glotonye.
The holy writ take I to my witnesse
lechery — That luxure is in wyn and dronkenesse.

483–572 The material for the Pardoner's discourse on drunkenness and gluttony is drawn from a variety of sources: the Bible, for the stories of Lot (Gen. 19:30–6), Herod (Matt. 14:3–12) and Samson (Judges 13:5), and for Paul (1 Cor. 6:13) in lines 521–3; Jerome *Adversus Jovinianum* (see WBP 7n) for parts of 505–28 and 547–50; Seneca, Epistle 83, for lines 493–7; and, for lines 538–9, the *De miseria condicionis humanae* (written 1195 by Lotario dei Segni, later Pope Innocent III), a violent outburst against 'the misery of the human condition', of which Chaucer did a translation, now lost.

against nature Lo, how that dronken Loth unkyndely
Lay by his doghtres two, unwityngly:
So dronke he was he nyste what he wroghte.
Herodes, whoso wel the stories soghte,
Whan he of wyn was replet at his feste,
command Right at his owene table he yaf his heste
To sleen the Baptist John, ful giltelees.
Senec seith a good word doutelees:
He seith he kan no difference fynde
Bitwix a man that is out of his mynde
habitually drunk And a man which that is dronkelewe,
bad man But that woodnesse, yfallen in a sherewe,
Persevereth lenger than dooth dronkenesse.
O glotonye, ful of cursednesse!
ruin O cause first of oure confusioun!
O original of oure dampnacioun,
Til Crist hadde boght us with his blood agayn!
Lo, how deere, shortly for to sayn,
Aboght was thilke cursed vileynye!
Corrupt was al this world for glotonye.
Adam oure fader and his wyf also
Fro Paradys to labour and to wo
Were dryven for that vice, it is no drede.
For whil that Adam fasted, as I rede,
He was in Paradys, and whan that he
forbidden Eet of the frut defended on a tree,
Anon he was out cast to wo and peyne.
O glotonye, on thee wel oghte us pleyne!
O, wiste a man how manye maladies
Folwen of excesse and of glotonyes,
He wolde been the moore mesurable
Of his diete, sittyng at his table.
Allas, the shorte throte, the tendre mouth,
Maketh that est and west and north and south,
In erthe, in eyr, in water, men to swynke
To gete a gloton deyntee mete and drynke!
Of this matere, O Paul, wel kanstow trete:
belly "Mete unto wombe, and wombe eek unto mete,
Shal God destroyen bothe," as Paulus seith.
Allas, a foul thyng is it, by my feith,
To seye this word, and fouler is the dede,
(wines) Whan man so drynketh of the white and rede
That of his throte he maketh his pryvee
Thurgh thilke cursed superfluite.
The Apostle wepyng seith ful pitously,
"Ther walken manye of whiche yow toold have I –
I seye it now wepyng with pitous voys –
cross Ther been enemys of Cristes croys,
Of whiche the ende is deth; wombe is hir god!"
bag of guts O wombe! O bely! O stynkyng cod,
Fulfilled of dong and of corrupcioun!
At either ende of thee foul is the soun.
it is to provide food for you How greet labour and cost is thee to fynde!

Thise cokes, how they stampe and streyne and grynde
And turnen substance into accident
To fulfillen al thy likerous talent! *gluttonous inclination*
Out of the harde bones knokke they
The mary, for they caste nat awey *marrow*
That may go thurgh the golet softe and soote. *(Anything) that, sweetly*
Of spicerie of lief and bark and roote
Shal been his sauce ymaked by delit, *for his pleasure*
To make hym yet a newer appetit.
But certes he that haunteth swiche delices *delights*
Is deed, whil that he lyveth in tho vices.
  A lecherous thyng is wyn, and dronkenesse
Is ful of stryvyng and of wrecchednesse. *strife*
O dronke man, disfigured is thy face,
Sour is thy breeth, foul artow to embrace,
And thurgh thy dronke nose semeth the soun
As thogh thou seydest ay "Sampsoun, Sampsoun!"
And yet, God woot, Sampson drank nevere no wyn.
Thou fallest as it were a stiked swyn; *stuck pig*
Thy tonge is lost and al thyn honest cure, *care for decency*
For dronkenesse is verray sepulture
Of mannes wit and his discrecioun.
In whom that drynke hath domynacioun
He kan no conseil kepe, it is no drede. *secret*
Now kepe yow fro the white and fro the rede
And namely fro the white wyn of Lepe
That is to selle in Fissh-strete or in Chepe:
This wyn of Spaigne crepeth subtilly
In othere wynes growynge faste by,
Of which ther riseth swich fumositee
That whan a man hath dronken draghtes thre
And weneth that he be at hom in Chepe,
He is in Spaigne, right at the toune of Lepe –
Nat at the Rochel, ne at Burdeux toun –
And thanne wol he seyn "Sampson, Sampsoun!"

{The Pardoner continues with further examples against drunkenness and then goes on to gambling and swearing.}

But, sires, now wol I telle forth my tale.
  Thise riotoures thre of whiche I telle,
Longe erst er pryme ronge of any belle,
Were set hem in a taverne to drynke,
And as they sat they herde a belle klynke
Biforn a cors, was caryed to his grave.

539 The scholarly allusion, drawn directly from Innocent III's *De miseria*, is to the presence within an object of an inner informing reality (**substance**) and an outward set of signs by which it is recognized (**accident**); the cooks are perverting nature by converting the one into the other. An allusion to the doctrine of transubstantiation (the miraculous conversion of the substance of the communion wafer into the flesh of Christ as another substance, a 'real presence') and to the denial of this doctrine by Wyclif and his Lollard followers (who said that the 'accidents' of the bread remain), is possible.

562–72 An allusion to the selling in Fish Street and Cheapside of wines from La Rochelle and Bordeaux in south-west France (the best area for wine) that had been mixed with cheaper wines from **Lepe**, in southern Spain, producing a particularly heady concoction.

662 Long before the bell rang for the first service of the day (the first of the seven canonical 'hours'), about 6 a.m.

servant	That oon of hem gan callen to his knave:
Go quickly	"Go bet," quod he, "and axe redily
goes past by here	What cors is this that passeth heer forby,
	And looke that thow reporte his name wel."
lad	"Sire," quod this boy, "it nedeth never-a-del;
	It was me told er ye cam heer two houres.
	He was, pardee, an old felawe of youres
	And sodeynly he was yslayn to-nyght,
Blind drunk	Fordronke, as he sat on his bench upright.
	Ther cam a privee theef men clepeth Deeth
	That in this contree al the peple sleeth
	And with his spere he smoot his herte a-two
	And wente his wey withouten wordes mo.
	He hath a thousand slayn this pestilence,
	And, maister, er ye come in his presence,
	Me thynketh that it were necessarie
	For to be war of swich an adversarie.
	Beeth redy for to meete hym everemoore:
mother	Thus taughte me my dame; I sey namoore."
	"By seinte Marie!" seyde this taverner,
young lad	"The child seith sooth, for he hath slayn this yer,
From here	Henne over a myle, withinne a greet village,
farm-worker and serving boy	Bothe man and womman, child and hyne and page:
	I trowe his habitacioun be there.
wary	To been avysed greet wisdom it were,
	Er that he dide a man a dishonour."
	"Ye, Goddes armes!" quod this riotour,
	"Is it swich peril with hym for to meete?
(everywhere)	I shal hym seke by wey and eek by strete,
worthy	I make avow to Goddes digne bones!
all of one mind	Herkneth, felawes, we thre been al ones:
	Lat ech of us holde up his hand to oother
	And ech of us bicomen ootheres brother
	And we wol sleen this false traytour Deeth.
	He shal be slayn, he that so manye sleeth,
	By Goddes dignytee, er it be nyght!"
	Togidres han thise thre hir trouthes plyght
	To lyve and dyen ech of hem with oother,
brother by birth	As thogh he were his owene ybore brother.
	And up they stirte, al dronken in this rage,
	And forth they goon towardes that village
	Of which the taverner hadde spoke biforn,
	And many a grisly ooth thanne han they sworn
tore to pieces	And Cristes blessed body they to-rente –
seize	Deeth shal be deed if that they may hym hente!
	Whan they had goon nat fully half a myle,
	Right as they wolde han treden over a style,
	An old man and a povre with hem mette.

699 The rioters' determination to slay Death gives them the air of public-spirited vigilantes, but they are of course blasphemously usurping the role of Christ as the slayer of 'death', that is, eternal perdition. They fail to understand the difference between physical death (which is not the enemy of the good Christian but the stimulus to good deeds and the only possible gateway to heaven) and spiritual death, which they have already undergone. The text they need is Romans 8:13: 'If you live according to the flesh you will die, but if by the spirit you put to death the deeds of the body you will live'.

greeted	This olde man ful mekely hem grette
	And seyde thus, "Now, lordes, God yow se!"
	The proudeste of thise riotoures thre
in reply, churl, damn you	Answerde agayn, "What, carl, with sory grace!
completely wrapped up	Why artow al forwrapped save thy face?
	Why lyvestow so longe in so greet age?"
	This olde man gan looke in his visage
	And seyde thus: "For I ne kan nat fynde
	A man, thogh that I walked into Inde,
	Neither in citee ne in no village,
	That wolde chaunge his youthe for myn age;
	And therfore moot I han myn age stille,
	As longe tyme as it is Goddes wille.
	Ne Deeth, allas, ne wol nat have my lyf.
captive wretch	Thus walke I lyk a restelees caytyf
	And on the ground, which is my modres gate,
	I knokke with my staf bothe erly and late
Dear	And seye, 'Leeve moder, leet me in!
	Lo how I vanysshe, flessh and blood and skyn!
	Allas, whan shal my bones been at reste?
treasure-chest	Moder, with yow wolde I chaunge my cheste
	That in my chambre longe tyme hath be,
haircloth (shroud)	Ye, for an heyre clowt to wrappe me!'
	But yet to me she wol nat do that grace,
withered	For which ful pale and welked is my face.
	"But, sires, to yow it is no curteisye
offensive words	To speken to an old man vileynye
Unless	But he trespase in word or ellis in dede.
	In holy writ ye may yourself wel rede:
In the presence of, grey-haired	'Agayns an old man, hoor upon his heed,
stand up (in respect), advice	Ye shal arise'; wherfore I yeve yow reed,
	Ne dooth unto an old man noon harm now
	Namoore than that ye wolde men dide to yow
	In age – if that ye so longe abyde.
wherever you walk	And God be with yow wher ye go or ryde!
	I moot go thider as I have to go."
	"Nay, olde cherl, by God, thow shalt nat so,"
	Seyde this oother hasardour anon;
	"Thow partest nat so lightly, by Seint John!
	Thow speeke right now of thilke traytour Deeth
	That in this contree alle oure freendes sleeth;
spy	Have heer my trouthe, as thow art his espye,
pay for it	Tel wher he is or thow shalt it abye,
	By God and by the holy sacrament!
in league with him	For soothly thow art oon of his assent
	To sleen us yonge folk, thow false theef!"

720–38 The Old Man has been identified with Cain, doomed to wander the world for ever, or with the Wandering Jew, or with Death. He is an outcast soul (728), a restless prisoner in exile (see Romans 7:24), obscurely aware (721–6) of a promise of youth or new life which is denied to him (i.e. the exchange of the 'old Adam' of sin, crucified with Christ on the cross, for the 'new man' of grace: see Romans 6:6). He is likewise obscurely aware that he must 'die to the world' before he can be spiritually reborn, but he sees this as a literal death or re-entry into mother-earth (729–38); like Nicodemus he can only ask, bewildered, when Christ speaks of being reborn, 'How can a man be born when he is old? Can he enter a second time into his mother's womb and be born again?' (John 3:4). The Old Man is in some sense a physical manifestation of the Pardoner's spiritual state.

"Now, sires," quod he, "if that yow be so leef — *desirous*
To fynde Deeth, turn up this croked wey,
For in that grove I lafte hym, by my fey,
Under a tree, and there he wol abyde;
Nat for youre boost he wol hym nothyng hyde.
Se ye that ook? Right ther ye shal hym fynde.
God save yow that boghte agayn mankynde,
And yow amende!" Thus seyde this olde man.
And everich of thise riotoures ran
Til he cam to that tree, and ther they founde
Of floryns fyne of gold ycoyned rounde
Wel-ny an eighte busshels, as hem thoughte:
No lenger thanne after Deeth they soughte.
But ech of hem so glad was of the sighte,
For that the floryns been so faire and brighte,
That doun they sette hem by this precious hoord.
The worste of hem, he spak the firste word.
"Bretheren," quod he, "taak kepe what that I seye:
My wit is greet, thogh that I bourde and pleye. — *jest*
This tresor hath Fortune unto us yeven
In myrthe and jolitee oure lyf to lyven,
And lightly as it cometh so wol we spende.
Ey, Goddes precious dignytee! Who wende — *would have thought*
Today that we sholde han so fair a grace?
But myghte this gold be caried fro this place
Hoom to myn hous, or ellis unto youres –
For wel ye woot that al this gold is oures –
Thanne were we in heigh felicitee.
But trewely, by daye it may nat be:
Men wolde seyn that we were theves stronge — *arrant thieves*
And for oure owene tresor doon us honge. — *have us hanged*
This tresor moste ycaried be by nyghte
As wisly and as sleyly as it myghte.
Therfore I rede that cut amonges us alle — *advise, lots be drawn*
Be drawe and lat se wher the cut wol falle,
And he that hath the cut with herte blithe
Shal renne to the towne, and that ful swithe, — *very quickly*
And brynge us breed and wyn ful prively.
And two of us shal kepen subtilly
This tresor wel; and if he wol nat tarye,
Whan it is nyght we wol this tresor carye
By oon assent wher as us thynketh best."
That oon of hem the cut broghte in his fest — *fist*
And bad hem drawe and looke wher it wol falle;
And it fel on the yongeste of hem alle
And forth toward the town he wente anon.
And also soone as that he was agon
That oon of hem spak thus unto that oother:
"Thow knowest wel thow art my sworn brother;

766 **boghte agayn**: redeemed for a second time. The Old Man's sardonic reference is to the rioters' re-enactment of Christ's victory over death (see 699n).

772 The double meaning here (they do not seek it further – because without realizing it they have found it) is the hinge on which the tale's irony turns.

Thy profit wol I telle thee anon.
Thow woost wel that oure felawe is agon,
And heere is gold, and that ful greet plentee,
divided That shal departed been among us thre.
But nathelees, if I kan shape it so
That it departed were among us two,
Hadde I nat doon a freendes torn to thee?"
  That oother answerde, "I noot how that may be:
He woot how that the gold is with us tweye.
What shal we doon? What shal we to hym seye?"
a secret, villain "Shal it be conseil?" seyde the firste shrewe,
"And I shal tellen in a wordes fewe
What we shul doon and brynge it wel aboute."
  "I graunte," quod that oother, "out of doute,
betray That by my trouthe I wol thee nat biwreye."
  "Now," quod the firste, "thow woost wel we be tweye
And two of us shul strenger be than oon.
sat down Looke whan that he is set, that right anon
(have some horse-play) Arys as though thow woldest with hym pleye
stab And I shal ryve hym thurgh the sydes tweye
Whil that thow strogelest with hym as in game
And with thy daggere looke thow do the same;
And thanne shal al this gold departed be,
My deere freend, bitwixe thee and me.
Thanne may we bothe oure lustes al fulfille
And pleye at dees right at oure owene wille."
And thus acorded been thise sherewes tweye
To sleen the thridde, as ye han herd me seye.
  This yongeste, which that wente to the toun,
Ful ofte in herte he rolleth up and doun
The beautee of thise floryns newe and brighte.
"O Lord!" quod he, "if so were that I myghte
Have al this tresor to myself allone,
throne Ther is no man that lyveth under the trone
Of God that sholde lyve so myrie as I!"
And at the laste the feend, oure enemy,
buy Putte in his thoght that he sholde poyson beye
With which he myghte sleen his felawes tweye –
The reason being that, state of life For-why the feend foond hym in swich lyvynge
permission (from God) That he hadde leve hym to sorwe brynge.
plainly For this was outrely his ful entente,
To sleen hem bothe and nevere to repente.
  And forth he goth – no lenger wolde he tarye –
Into the toun unto a pothecarye,
And preyed hym that he hym wolde selle
kill Som poysoun that he myghte his rattes quelle;
yard And eek ther was a polcat in his hawe
That as he seyde his capons hadde yslawe,
avenge himself And fayn he wolde wreke hym, if he myghte,
On vermyn that destroyed hym by nyghte.

847–8 An important theological point: the Devil can only bring into mortal sin those from whom, because of their sinful life, God has withdrawn his grace.

	The pothecarie answerde, "And thow shalt have
	A thyng that, also God my soule save,
	In al this world ther is no creature
mixture	That ete or dronke hath of this confiture
amount	Nat but the montaunce of a corn of whete
lose	That he ne shal his lyf anoon forlete –
die	Ye, sterve he shal, and that in lasse while
at a walking pace	Than thow wolt goon a-paas nat but a myle,
	The poyson is so strong and violent."
seized	This cursed man hath in his hand yhent
	This poyson in a box and sith he ran
	Into the nexte strete unto a man
	And borwed hym large botels thre
	And in the two his poison poured he;
	The thridde he kepte clene for his drynke,
planned	For al the nyght he shoope hym for to swynke
	In cariyng of the gold out of that place.
accursed may he be	And whan this riotour, with sory grace,
	Hadde filled with wyn hise grete botels thre,
returns	To hise felawes agayn repaireth he.
preach	What nedeth it to sarmone of it moore?
planned	For right as they hadde cast his deeth bifore,
	Right so they han hym slayn and that anon.
	And whan that this was doon, thus spak that oon:
	"Now lat us sitte and drynke and make us merye
	And afterward we wol his body berye."
by chance	And with that word it happed hym, *par cas*,
	To take the botel ther the poyson was,
	And drank, and yaf his felawe drynke also,
died	For which anon they storven bothe two.
	But certes, I suppose that Avycen
set of rules, chapter of treatise	Wroot nevere in no canon ne in no *fen*
	Mo wonder signes of empoysonyng
	Than hadde thise wrecches two er hir endyng.
	Thus ended been thise homicides two
	And eek the false empoysonere also.
	O cursed synne of alle cursednesse!
treacherous	O traytours homicide, O wikkednesse!
lechery	O glotonye, luxure, and hasardrye!
	Thou blasphemour of Crist with vileynye
oaths, habit	And othes grete of usage and of pryde!
	Allas, mankynde, how may it bityde
	That to thy Creatour which that thee wroghte
redeemed thee	And with his precious herte-blood the boghte
	Thow art so fals and so unkynde, allas!
	Now, goode men, God foryeve yow youre trespas
guard	And ware yow fro the synne of avarice!
save	Myn holy pardoun may yow alle warisse,
(see n.)	So that ye offre nobles or starlynges,
	Or ellis silver broches, spones, rynges.

889 Avicenna was an Arabic scholar, and author of medical treatises.

895–915 The Pardoner goes into his closing professional routine, as he recognizes (915), even though the situation is different and his audience is not the usual congregation of simpletons. There is a suggestion of an automaton-like acting-out of a set performance.

907 'Provided that you offer gold coins or silver pennies'.

	Boweth youre heed under this holy bulle!
wool	Cometh up, ye wyves, offreth of youre wolle!
	Youre name I entre here in my rolle anon:
	Into the blisse of hevene shul ye gon.
absolve	I yow assoille, by myn heighe power,
	Ye that wol offre, as clene and eek as cler
	As ye were born. – And lo, sires, thus I preche.
physician	And Jesu Crist, that is oure soules leche,
	So graunte yow his pardoun to receyve,
	For that is best – I wol yow nat deceyve.
	But sires, o word forgat I in my tale:
bag	I have relikes and pardon in my male
	As faire as any man in Engelond,
	Whiche were me yeven by the popes hond.
	If any of yow wol of devocion
	Offren and han myn absolucioun,
	Com forth anon and kneleth here adoun
	And mekely receyveth my pardoun;
	Or ellis taketh pardoun as ye wende
	Al newe and fressh at every myles ende,
	So that ye offren, alwey newe and newe,
	Nobles or pens whiche that been goode and trewe.
	It is an honour to everich that is heer
competent	That ye mowe have a suffisant pardoner
	T'assoille yow in contree as ye ryde
chances, befall	For aventures whiche that may bityde.
	Paraventure ther may falle oon or two
	Doun of his hors and breke his nekke a-two:
what an excellent form of insurance	Looke which a seuretee is it to yow alle
	That I am in youre felaweship yfalle
	That may assoille yow, bothe moore and lasse,
	Whan that the soule shal fro the body passe.
suggest	I rede that oure Hoost heere shal bigynne,
	For he is moost envoluped in synne.
	Com forth, sire Hoost, and offre first anon
	And thow shalt kisse the relikes everychon,
even if you only give a groat	Ye, for a grote! Unbokele anon thy purs.'
may I be damned first!	'Nay, nay!' quod he, 'thanne have I Cristes curs!
as I may thrive (I swear)	Lat be,' quod he, 'it shal nat be, so thee ich!
drawers (under-breeches)	Thow woldest make me kisse thyn olde breech
	And swere it were a relyk of a seint,
arse-hole	Thogh it were with thy fondement depeynt!
	But, by the croys which that Seint Eleyne foond,
testicles	I wold I hadde thy coylons in myn hond.
Instead of, a sainted relic	Instide of relikes or of seintuarie
Let's have them cut off	Lat cutte hem of, I wol thee helpe hem carie:
turd	They shul be shryned in an hogges toord!'

919–45 The Pardoner's tone here, especially the reference to the unfortunate accidents that may befall (936), seems intended to amuse, as do his remarks at the Host's expense (941–5). His humour proves ill-judged.

946–55 The scatological violence of the Host's response is perhaps not inexplicable; whether it suggests that the Pardoner has or has not got testicles (see GP 691n) has been debated, inconclusively.

951 **Eleyne**: St Helena, discoverer of the True Cross.

955 The pig's turd is to act as the reliquary in which the Pardoner's testicles, thought of as the relics of a saint (following a famous joke in *RR* 7108–9), are to be enshrined and carried in procession before the people.

This Pardoner answerde nat a word:
So wrooth he was, no word ne wolde he seye.
'Now,' quod oure Hoost, 'I wol no lenger pleye
With thee, ne with noon oother angry man.'
But right anon the worthy Knyght bigan,
Whan that he saugh that al the peple lough,
'Namoore of this, for it is right ynough!
Sire Pardoner, be glad and murye of cheere;
And ye, sire Hoost, that been to me so deere,
I pray yow that ye kisse the Pardoner.
And Pardoner, I pray thee, drawe thee neer,
laugh And as we diden lat us lawe and pleye.'
rode Anon they kiste, and ryden forth hir weye.

Minor Poems

Adam Scriveyn

This little poem reminds one of the circumstances under which long texts were copied by a professional scribe and returned to the author for correction before being 'published' (e.g. sent to a prospective patron). Complaints about the carelessness of scribes are a topos among medieval authors. One imagines the poem being sent with a new batch of work to the scribe: its mock-ferocity bespeaks a certain familiarity. The poem appears in only one MS, TCC MS R.3.20 (p. 367), copied by the ubiquitous scribe and Chaucerian enthusiast John Shirley: see Lerer (1993), pp. 117–46.

scribe Adam scriveyn, if ever it thee bifalle
anew (again) Boece or Troylus for to wryten newe,
may you Under thy long lokkes thow most have the scalle
writing, accurately But after my makyng thow wryte more trewe:
must So ofte a-daye I mot thy werk renewe,
It to correcte and eke to rubbe and scrape,
haste And al is thorugh thy neglygence and rape.

Truth

Called in some MSS a 'Balade de Bon Conseyl', the poem called *Truth* by its modern editors is an unambiguously hortatory poem, echoing a classical and Boethian tradition of stoic rejection of worldly ambition and court corruption. In form it is a 'balade', that is, a poem of three seven-line or eight-line stanzas on the same rhymes with the last line of each stanza repeated as a refrain. Often such poems have an 'envoy' consisting of a further stanza in which the poem is addressed (sent, Fr. *envoyé*) to a particular recipient: such a stanza, addressed to one 'Vache', is added in one MS of *Truth* (BL MS Add. 10340, the one used here); the effect is to lighten and personalize the tone of the poem, especially through the comical aptness of the friend's name ('Cow') to the *beste* (18) urged forth from its stall. The poem, perhaps specially valued for its grand (and unChaucerian) simplicity (to which the remarkably large number of end-stopped lines contributes), was copied into 24 MSS.

Adam Scriveyn

1 **Adam**, as the scribe's real name, allows the comic implication that he repeats the primal sin of Adam, through whose fall language fell from its pristine truth; **scriveyn** is an occupational identification, hovering on becoming a surname.

2 **Boece or Troylus**. Chaucer's prose translation of Boethius's *Consolation of Philosophy* and his poem of *Troilus and Criseyde* were both completed by about 1386, which gives an earliest date for this poem. At the end of *TC* (V.1793–8) Chaucer expresses a similar (but more serious) concern about the accurate transmission of his text.

3 **scalle**: a very nasty oozing scabbiness of the scalp. Adam is to be punished with a scratching that will somehow compensate Chaucer for having to scratch out the scribe's mistakes.

6 **rubbe and scrape**. Writing on parchment (vellum), commonly used for most MSS at this period (paper was coming in slowly), could be scraped out with a sharp knife and the surface of the parchment rubbed smooth and used again.

crowd (at court)	Flee fro the prees and dwelle with sothfastnesse;
Match yourself to what you have	Suffyce unto thy thing, though it be smal,
hoarding, instability	For hord hath hate, and climbing tikelnesse,
(see n.)	Prees hath envye, and wele blent overal.
Seek enjoyment	Savour no more than thee bihove shal,
advise	Reule wel thyself, that other folk canst rede,
doubt	And trouthe thee shal delivere, it is no drede.
everything that's wrong	Tempest thee noght al croked to redresse
(Fortune and her wheel)	In trust of hir that turneth as a bal;
well-being	Much wele stant in litel besinesse.
(see n.)	Be war therfore to sporne ayeyns an al,
(see n.)	Stryve not as doth the crokke with the wal.
Exert control over, deeds	Daunte thyself, that dauntest otheres dede,
	And trouthe thee shal delivere, it is no drede.
What, obedience	That thee is sent, receyve in buxumnesse;
	The wrastling for the world axeth a fal.
	Her is non hoom, her nis but wildernesse:
	Forth, pilgrim, forth! Forth, beste, out of thy stal!
	Know thy contree, look up, thank God of al;
spirit	Hold the heye wey and lat thy gost thee lede,
	And trouthe thee shal delivere, it is no drede.

Envoy

	Therfore, thou Vache, leve thyn old wrecchednesse;
cease	Unto the world leve now to be thral.
	Crye him mercy, that of his hy goodnesse
	Made thee of noght, and in especial
	Draw unto him, and pray in general
reward	For thee, and eek for other, hevenlich mede,
	And trouthe thee shal delivere, it is no drede.

The Envoy to Scogan

An occasional poem, in the form of a double 'balade' without refrain (see *Truth*), in which Chaucer playfully warns his friend Scogan of the dire consequences of his rash decision to give up love, just because his lady will not have him. Henry Scogan (d. 1407) was in service at court in the 1390s, and later tutor to the sons of the future Henry IV: Chaucer may hint in the envoy at some favour Scogan may do him at court in return for the amusement he gets from the poem. The *Envoy* is an extraordinarily precocious example in English of the urbane epistolary style of Horace and the Augustan poets (see J. Norton-Smith, *Geoffrey Chaucer* [London, 1974], pp. 213–25); it draws its vitality from the self-mocking spirit of male camaraderie which is present at a different level of authorial 'reality' in the imagining of the Wife of Bath. The poem survives in three MSS: the present text is from Bodl.MS Fairfax 16; study by J. Scattergood, *NMS* 35 (1991), 92–101.

Truth

4 'The crowd is full of malice, and prosperity is deceitful'.

7 From John 8:32: 'And you shall know the truth, and the truth shall make you free'.

11 'Be careful therefore not to kick against a sharp awl' (because you'll do no good and only hurt yourself). Proverbial.

12 A crock (jug) only breaks if it is thrown against the wall. Proverbial.

17–18 The image of the world as a place of exile (for the soul), and the exhortation to man to abandon his lower nature (**Forth, beste, out of thy stal**) for his higher, are central to the Boethian inheritance of the poem (e.g. *Consolation* I, prose 5–6; II, prose 5; III, prose 12, etc.).

22 **thou Vache**. A punning reference to Sir Philip la Vache (1346–1408), a friend of Chaucer's who had perhaps fallen on hard times and to whom a Boethian remonstrance could be playfully directed.

To-broken been the statutz hye in hevene
That creat weren eternally to dure,
(the seven planets) Syth that I see the bryghte goddis sevene
May Mowe wepe and wayle and passion endure
As may in erthe a mortal creature.
Allas, fro whennes may thys thing procede,
sign of disorder Of which errour I deye almost for drede?

decreed By word eterne whilom was yshape
(see n.) That fro the fyfte sercle in no manere
Ne myghte a drope of teeres doun escape.
But now so wepith Venus in hir spere
That with hir teeres she wol drenche us here.
Allas! Scogan, this is for thyn offence:
Thow causest this diluge of pestilence.

goddess Hastow not seyd, in blaspheme of this goddis,
rashness Thurgh pride, or thrugh thy grete rakelnesse,
forbidden Swich thing as in the lawe of love forbode is –
That for thy lady saugh nat thy distresse
Therfore thow yave hir up at Michelmesse?
Allas, Scogan, of olde folk ne yonge
before Was never erst Scogan blamed for his tonge!

called upon, as a witness Thow drowe in skorn Cupide eke to record
Of thilke rebel word that thow hast spoken,
For which he wol no lenger be thy lord.
And, Scogan, though his bowe be nat broken,
revenged He wol nat with his arwes been ywroken
shape On the, ne me, ne noon of oure figure:
We shul of him have neyther hurt nor cure.

misfortune Now certes, frend, I dreed of thyn unhap,
vengeance Lest for thy gilt the wreche of Love procede
grey-haired On alle hem that ben hoor and rounde of shap,
That ben so lykly folk in love to spede.
reward Than shal we for oure labour have no mede;
But wel I wot thow wolt answere and saye,
'grey-beard loon' 'Lo, th'olde grisel lyst to ryme and playe!'

Nay, Scogan, say not so, for I m'excuse –
God helpe me so! In no rym, dowteles,
Ne thynke I never of slep to wake my muse,
That rusteth in my shethe stille in pees.
public While I was yong I put yt forth in prees,

The Envoy to Scogan

9 **fyfte sercle**: the sphere of Venus (counting from the outside inward).

14 **diluge of pestilence**: 'pestilential flood'. Venus's tears fall as a deluge of rain (a mock-heroic variation on the idea that the planets affect the weather).

19 Michaelmas is 29 September, the beginning of the autumn law-term.

31 **rounde of shap**. Chaucer often represents himself (as in the prologue to *Thopas*, *CT* VII.70) as tubby.

32 **folk** is the object of **spede**, the reference in **labour** being to the writing of love-poetry.

38–40 Thinking of his muse as a sword in its sheath (or a pen in its pen-case) allows Chaucer the salacious *double entendre*.

write in prose But al shal passe that men prose or ryme;
Take every man hys turn as for his tyme.

Envoy

Scogan, that knelest at the stremes hed
Of grace, of alle honour and worthynesse,
In th'ende of which strem I am dul as ded,
Forgete in solytarie wildernesse –
Yet, Scogan, thenke on Tullius kyndenesse:
Remember Mynne thy frend there it may fructyfye!
again, defy Far-wel, and loke thow never eft Love dyffye.

The Complaint of Chaucer to his Purse

When Henry IV became king, after the deposition of Richard II, on 30 September 1399, Chaucer anticipated that his royal annuity (half-yearly instalment due 29 September) would be confirmed and continue to be paid. He was on good terms with Henry, to judge from his receipt from him of a handsome gift of a scarlet gown in 1395–6, and of course the new king's late father had been John of Gaunt, duke of Lancaster, Chaucer's patron in the 1360s and 1370s. The annuity was indeed confirmed, though not till 16 February 1400 (in a document antedated to 13 October), but no actual payment of any kind was made until 21 February. It may be presumed that in the interim Chaucer composed this witty and slightly salacious begging poem (or added a flattering envoy to an already existing poem) and sent it to the new king. The poem is in the form of a balade (see *Truth*) with independent envoy. It appears in 11 MSS: the present text is from Bodl.MS Fairfax 16.

creature To yow, my purse, and to noon other wight
Complayne I, for ye be my lady dere.
I am so sory now that ye been lyght,
(see n.) For certes but yf ye make me hevy chere
I would as rather Me were as leef be layd upon my bere;
For which unto your mercy thus I crye –
Be hevy ageyn, or elles mot I dye.

before Now voucheth sauf this day or hyt be nyght
That I of yow the blisful soun may here
Or see your colour lyk the sonne bryght
(of gold coins; of hair), equal That of yelownesse hadde never pere.
rudder Ye be my lyf, ye be myn hertes stere –
Quene of comfort and of good companye,
Beth hevy ageyn, or elles moot I dye.

Now purse that ben to me my lyves lyght
And saveour as doun in this world here,
Out of this toune helpe me thurgh your myght,

43–6 Chaucer imagines Scogan at the fountain-head of grace, that is, at the court at Windsor (the main royal residence) on the upper Thames, and himself in exile on the lower Thames at Greenwich (both Windsor and Greenwich are named in MS glosses).

47 **Tullius**: Cicero, with reference to his book on friendship, *De Amicitia*, cited in *Rom* 5286.

The Complaint of Chaucer to his Purse

3–4 **lyght … hevy**. The word-play throughout is on the lightness or heaviness of his purse and the wantonness or seriousness (or pregnancy) of his lady. He cannot be light except that she be heavy. The joke is a familiar one, and fits with Chaucer's familiar image of himself as an unsuccessful lover; but for a royal pensioner the public purse, if not his own, was indeed a difficult lady to be wooed.

4 'unless you behave seriously toward me' ('become heavy').

13 **Quene of comfort**: a phrase used of the Virgin Mary in Chaucer's *ABC* poem to the Virgin (cf. **lyves lyght**, 15; **saveour**, 16).

17 **this toune**. Puzzling: possibly Greenwich, where Chaucer was living at the time and which he wished to get out of, back to London (he leased a house in the precincts of Westminster Abbey on 24 December 1399). But what **myght** has his purse to help him to do this if it is not his **tresorere**?

Syn that ye wole nat ben my tresorere,
(see n.) For I am shave as nye as is a frere.
But yet I pray unto your curtesye,
Beth hevy ageyn, or elles moot I dye.

Envoy

O conquerour of Brutes Albyon,
lineage Which that by lyne and free eleccion
true Been verray kyng, this song to yow I sende,
may And ye that mowen alle oure harme amende
Have mynde upon my supplicacion.

19 **shave as nye**: 'shaven-headed (tonsured) as closely (i.e. as bare of money)'.

22–3 Chaucer alludes skilfully and unobtrusively to the three arguments with which Henry IV sought to buttress his claim to the throne: he had conquered England; he was descended from Edward III; he had been 'elected' by acclamation. See P. Strohm, *Hochon's Arrow: The Social Imagination of Fourteenth-Century Texts* (Princeton, 1992), pp. 75–94. **Brutes Albyon**: the Albion of Brutus, who first came from Troy, according to the *Historia regum Britanniae* of Geoffrey of Monmouth, and conquered the land and gave it his name ('Britain').

William Langland (fl. 1375–1380), *The Vision of Piers Plowman*

Piers Plowman, or *The Visions of Will concerning Piers the Plowman and the Life of Do-Well, Do-Better and Do-Best*, to give the poem its more fully descriptive title, is one of the great religious poems in the English language, an urgent and powerful exploration of the meaning of Christian belief – in history, in the life of the community, and in the life of the individual. It is framed as a series of dreams, with waking episodes, in which the questing dreamer, Will, sees first the rottenness of a society ruled by money and the attempt at reform through the agency of Piers, the good honest Christian ploughman (the *Visio Willelmi*); and then, as that project unravels, returns to a more personal search for spiritual truth (the *Vita de Dowel*, etc.) which culminates in Christ and the climactic vision of the Crucifixion and the Harrowing of Hell. The poem circles at last back to its beginning in the modern world. Little is known of the author, named as William Langland in a flyleaf inscription in one MS, except what he tells us in Passus V (see below). He was certainly a man of wide if sporadic learning, vividly aware of the social and economic crises through which England was passing, and sharing passionately in the radical anticlericalism that also characterized the Lollard movement and that same desire to rid the church of institutionalized corruption. The poem, which was being composed through the 1370s and 1380s, survives in 51 MSS, representing three principal 'shapes' of the poem, conventionally called A, B and C (though some MSS are not easily so classified, and may partially represent other stages in the development of the poem): a shorter poem, dealing principally with the reform of community (A); a reworking of A, with a continuation in nine added *passus* ('steps' or 'stages') that almost trebles its length, to well over 7000 lines (B); and an unsystematic reworking of nearly the whole of B, designed to clarify its meaning and distance the author from the radical readings to which his poem had been subjected in 1381 (C). The existence of the poem in different versions adds to the impression it gives of a remembered experience of personal spiritual pilgrimage; at least, it is the product of a visionary's zeal to understand, to grasp, to know intuitively the inward truth of the truth of Christian revelation. Doubt, despair, intellectual restlessness, caustic wit, contempt for outward show, are both the obstacles and the instruments of this search for understanding. For a study of the significance of the poem's naming and narrative of its author, see A. Middleton, in Patterson (1990), pp. 15–82.

The poem is written in the unrhymed alliterative line that is the traditional metre of Old English verse. Lines fall usually into two half-lines, with strong caesura, each half-line having two stresses and a varying number of unstressed syllables. Alliteration falls usually on the first letter of the first three stressed syllables (*aa/ax*).

The following extracts are designed to represent some of the best evidences of Langland's poetic power and some of his different kinds of poetic procedure, and to give some sense, through insertion of narrative links, of the whole shape of the poem. The C-text, as Langland's last and fullest attempt to make himself heard, is the text represented, and the base-MS is San Marino, Huntington Library MS HM 143 (X), with emendations from BL MS Add.35157 (U), University of London Library MS V.88 (J), Huntington MS HM 137 (P) and other MSS as listed in D. Pearsall, *Piers Plowman: An Edition of the C-text* (London, 1978) and in the parallel-text edition of A.V.C. Schmidt (Vol. 1 [Text], London, 1995). Schmidt's edition will no doubt replace the great parallel-text edition of W.W. Skeat (2 vols, Oxford, 1886). The Athlone Press edition (A, ed. G. Kane [London, 1960]; B, ed. G. Kane and E.T. Donaldson [1975]; C, ed. G. Russell and G. Kane [1997]) presents radically emended texts. There are good introductions to the poem by E. Salter in *Piers Plowman: An Introduction* (Oxford, 1962) and in her Introduction to *Selections*, ed. E. Salter and D. Pearsall, York Medieval Texts (London, 1967); and by J. Simpson, *Piers Plowman: An Introduction to the B-text* (London, 1990). See also D. Aers, *Chaucer, Langland and the Creative Imagination* (London, 1980); J.A. Alford (ed.), *A Companion to Piers Plowman* (Berkeley and Los Angeles, 1988); essays collected in S. Justice and K. Kerby-Fulton (eds), *Written Work: Langland, Labor, and Authorship* (Philadelphia, 1997). The *Yearbook of Langland Studies* has an annual bibliography.

The Vision of Piers Plowman (C-Text)

Prologue, 1–94, 139–233 (end): The Field Full of Folk

In a somur sesoun whan softe was the sonne
I shope me into shroudes as I a shep were – *dressed, rough woollen garments*
In abite as an heremite unholy of werkes *(see n.)*

1 Going out on a May morning is a conventional prelude to an allegorical dream-vision (usually to do with love).

2 **shep**: 'shepherd', or possibly 'sheep', with suggestions of innocence (the apostles are to go out 'as lambs in the midst of wolves', Luke 10:3) or ironically self-critical connotation of purposeful disguise ('a wolf in sheep's clothing', Matt. 7:15).

3 'Dressed in the habit of a hermit, but not one dedicated to holy works'.

Wente forth in the world wondres to here,
And say many sellies and selkouthe thynges. — *marvels, extraordinary*
Ac on a May mornyng on Malverne hulles
Me biful for to slepe, for werynesse of-walked; — *exhausted with walking*
And in a launde as I lay, lened I and slepte, — *grassy clearing, reclined*
And merveylousliche me mette, as I may telle. — *I dreamed*
Al the welthe of the world and the wo bothe
Wynkyng, as hit were, witterliche I seigh hit; — *truly*
Of treuthe and tricherye, tresoun and gyle,
Al I say slepynge, as I shal telle.
  Estward I beheld aftir the sonne — *in the direction of*
And say a tour – as I trowed, Treuthe was there-ynne;
  Westward I waytede in a while aftir — *looked*
And seigh a depe dale – Deth, as I leue, — *believe*
Woned in tho wones, and wikkede spirites. — *dwelt, regions*
A fair feld ful of folk fond I ther bytwene
Of alle manere men, the mene and the pore,
Worchyng and wandryng as this world asketh.
  Somme putte hem to the plogh, playde ful selde,
In settynge and in sowynge swonken ful harde — *worked*
And wonne that this wastors with glotony destrueth. — *what*
And summe putte hem to pruyde and parayled hem ther-aftir — *dressed accordingly*
In continance of clothyng in many kyne gyse. — *outward show, kinds of way*
In preiers and penaunces putten hem mony,
Al for love of oure lord lyveden swythe harde
In hope to have a good ende and hevenriche blisse,
As ankeres and eremites that holdeth hem in here selles, — *anchorites*
Coveyten noght in contreys to cayren aboute — *wander*
For no likerous liflode here lycame to plese. — *dainty living, body*
  And summe chesen chaffare – thei cheveth the bettre, — *choose trade*
As it semeth to oure sighte that suche men ythryveth;
And summe murthes to make as mynstrels conneth, — *know how to*
Wolleth neyther swynke ne swete, bote sweren grete othes,
Fyndeth out foule fantasyes and foles hem maketh — *behave like fools*
And hath wytt at wille to worche yf thei wolde. — *at their command*
That Poule prechede of hem preve hit I myhte:
Qui turpiloquium loquitur is Luciferes knave.
  Bidders and beggers fast aboute yede — *Beggars*
Til here bagge and here bely was bretful ycrammed, — *brimful*
Fayteden for here fode and foughten at the ale. — *Begged falsely*
In glotonye tho gomes goth thei to bedde
And ryseth with rybaudrye tho Robardes knaves; — *robbers (a cant term, 'Bob's lads')*
Slep and also slewthe sueth suche ever. — *attend upon*
  Pilgrymes and palmers plighten hem togyderes — *bound*

6 **Malverne hulles**: in Worcestershire, near where Langland is thought to have been brought up.
14 **Estward**: towards the source of light (and Truth), towards Jerusalem (all Christian churches are oriented east).
19 **A fair feld**. 'The field is the world', says Christ, interpreting the parable of the tares (Matt. 13:38).
30 **eremites**: holy hermits (cf. 3 above) who keep their vow of stability of life and stay in their cells.
35 **mynstrels**, true and false, are a preoccupation in the poem, perhaps because Langland sees his own life, real and assumed, reflected in them, distorted.
40 'He who speaks filth…' (Eph. 5:4).
47 **palmers** carried a palm-leaf as a token of pilgrimage to the Holy Land; but the word had come to mean habitual pilgrim. The reference to pilgrims bonding together reminds us, like much else in this Prologue, of Chaucer (who certainly knew a version of *PP*).

To seke seynt Jame and seyntes of Rome,
Wenten forth on here way with many wyse tales
And hadde leve to lye aftir, al here lyf-tyme.
Eremites on an hep with hokede staves
Wenten to Walsyngham, and here wenches aftir;
lazy hulking fellows Grete lobies and longe that loth were to swynke
long gowns, known (as different) Clothed hem in copis to be knowe fram othere
And made hemself heremites, here ese to have.
I fonde ther of freris alle the foure ordres,
Prechyng the peple for profyt of the wombe,
And glosede the gospel as hem good likede;
doctors of theology For coveytise of copis contraryed somme doctours.
Mony of thise maistres of mendenant freres
Here moneye and marchandise marchen togyderes.
merchant Ac sith charite hath be chapman and chief to shryve lordes
marvels Mony ferlyes han falle in a fewe yeres,
unless And but holi chirche and charite choppe adoun suche shryvars
The moste meschief on molde mounteth up faste.
Ther prechede a pardoner as he a prest were
And brought forth a bulle with bischopis selys,
Sayde that hymself myhte assoylen hem alle
Of falsnesses of fastynges, of vowes ybrokene.
Lewed men leved hym wel and lykede his wordes
And comen and knelede to kyssen his bulles;
tapped them on the head He bounchede hem with his bulles and blered here yes
raked in, roll of papal parchment And raughte with his rageman rynges and broches.
Thus ye gyve youre gold glotons to helpe
give, lazy rascals And leneth hit lorelles that lecherye haunten!
(see n.) Were the bischop yblessed and worth bothe his eres
His seel sholde nought be ysent in deseyte of the people.
according to the bishop's will Ac it is nought by the bischop, I leve, that the boy precheth
divide For the parsche prest and the pardoner parten the selver
That the peple in parsches sholde have, yf thei ne were.
Parsons Persones and parsche prestis pleyned to the bischop
That here parsches were pore sithe this pestelence tyme,
To have a licence and a leve in Londoun to dwelle
And synge ther for symonye while selver is so swete.
bachelors of divinity Bischopes and bachelers, bothe maystres and doctours,
cure of souls, tonsure That han cure under Crist and crownyng in tokene –
cultivate Ben charged with holy chirche charite to tylie,
true That is lele love and lyfe among lered and lewed –

48 **seynt Jame**: Santiago (= St James) da Compostela, in north-west Spain.

52 **Walsyngham**: the shrine of Our Lady of Walsingham, in Norfolk.

56 **the foure ordres**. Dominicans, Franciscans, Carmelites and Austin friars.

58 **glosede**. Friars were the professional preachers of their day, and it was a familiar complaint against them that they twisted the interpretation of scripture ('glosede') for their own purposes and advantage.

61 **marchen**: 'go hand in hand' (or, 'have a common boundary').

66 **pardoner**. For pardoners, see GP 669n. Chaucer's portrait makes an interesting comparison: Langland is evidently more committed, vehement, enraged.

76 'Were the bishop truly blessed (in his vocation) and "worth his salt"'.

81–4 The depopulation of parishes through successive visitations of plague, beginning in 1349, meant a loss of tithes and income, and many priests went to London, where there was a living to be made saying masses for the souls of the rich dead (i.e. as chantry-priests).

85–94 Clerics had long formed the backbone of the royal administration (Chaucer was one of the first exceptions). For Langland, with his apostolic vision of the church's mission, it is a betrayal of a sacred office.

Leyen in Londoun in lenton and elles.
count Summe serven the kynge and his silver tellen,
Exchequer, make formal demand of In the Cheker and in the Chancerye chalengen his dettes
Of wardes and of wardemotis, wayves and strayves;
And summe aren as seneschalles and serven other lordes
pass judgement And ben in stede of stewardes and sitten and demen.

{Conscience has an intervention here condemning worldly priests before the poem turns to the question of authority in this field full of folk, this turbulent commonwealth: by what right does the king rule?}

Thenne cam ther a kyng, knyghthede hym ladde,
Myght of tho men made hym to regne.
'Natural Intelligence' And thenne cam Kynde Wytt and clerkes he made
For to counseillen the kyng and the commune save
And Conscience and Kynde Wit and knyghthed togedres
(see n.) Caste that the comunes sholde here comunes fynde.
devised Kynde Wytt and the comune contreved alle craftes
And for most profitable to the peple a plogh gonne thei make,
With lele labour to lyve while lif on londe lasteth.
Thenne Kynde Witt to the kynge and to the comune saide,
kingdom 'Crist kepe the, kynge, and thy kyneriche
grant And leve the lede so thy londe that Lewte the lovye
And for thy rightful ruylynge be rewardid in hevene.'
Conscience to clergie and to the kynge sayde,
'"Sum Rex, sum princeps" – neutrum fortasse deinceps!
O qui jura regis christi specialia regis,
Hoc ut agas melius, justus es, esto pius.
Nudum jus a te vestiri vult pietate.
Qualia vis metere talia grana sere.
Si seritur pietas de pietate metas.'
Conscience and the kynge into court wente
lawyers' caps Where hoved an hundrid in hoves of selke,
serjeants-at-law (barristers) Serjantz it semede that serveth at the barre,
Plededen for penyes and poundes be lawe
And nat for love of oure lord unlose here lyppes ones.
measure Thow myghtest betre meten myst on Malverne hilles
Than gete a mum of here mouth ar moneye were hem shewed!
crowd Then ran ther a route of ratones as hit were

89 **lenton**. Lent was the busiest time of the year for a conscientious priest.

92 Various kinds of revenue that the king's officials would be engaged in collecting: money from the estates of minors in the king's guardianship (**wardes**); the dues payable by city-wards, rendered at ward-meetings or **wardemotis**; and various kinds of lost property (**wayves**) and strayed animals (**strayves**) which, being unclaimed, passed into the king's possession.

140 If Langland is examining the basis of the monarchic contract, and the part in it of the three estates (knighthood, clergy, commons), this would be a conservatively orthodox statement. Revisions from B in this passage suggest that he intends to clarify his orthodoxy, or at least to remove the potential for any radical reading of the role of the commons.

141 The **clerkes** are the bishops and abbots who sit in parliament to advise the king.

144 'Made a plea that the commons should provide food for the whole community'.

150 **Lewte**: an important recurrent personification in the poem, perhaps 'loyalty to truth, the spirit of fair-dealing', or 'the love of law that is the law of love'.

153–8 The Latin verses (not original) give authority to the modest reminder of the king's responsibilities. '(You say) "I am king, I am prince" – but neither perhaps one day! You who administer the supreme laws of Christ the king, that you may do it better, be merciful, as you are just. Naked justice should be clothed by you in mercy. Sow as you would reap. If mercy is sown, may you reap mercy'.

159–65 The passage on lawyers shows the king something of the problem he faces as the chief administrator of justice.

166–216 The fable of the belling of the cat was a favourite exemplum. Here it shows the futility of trying to curb royal power, with perhaps particular reference to the Good Parliament of 1376 (the rats and the mice being the upper and lower houses) and its failure to curb the power of John of Gaunt (the cat).

	And smale muys with hem, mo then a thousend,
	Comen til a conseyl for here comune profyt.
	For a cat of a court cam whan hym likede
pounced on, seized	And overlep hem lightliche and laghte hem alle at wille
	And playde with somme perilously and putte hem ther hym lykede.
grumble	'And yf we groche of his game he wol greve us sore,
claws	To his clees clawe us and in his cloches us halde
	That us lotheth the lyf ar he lette us passe.
withstand	Myghte we with eny wyt his wille with-sytte
	We myhte be lordes a-lofte and lyve as us luste.'
	A ratoun of renown moste resonable of tonge
	Sayde, 'I have seyen grete syres in cytees and in townes
	Bere beyes of bryghte gold al aboute here nekkes
	And colers of crafty werk, bothe knyghtes and squieres.
	Wer ther a belle on here beygh, by Jesu, as me thynketh,
know, leave clear	Men myghte ywete where thei wente and here way roume.
	Ryght so,' quath the raton, 'reison me shewith
buy	A belle to byggen of bras other of bryghte sylver
	And knytten hit on a coler for oure comune profyt
	And hongen hit aboute the cattes halse, thanne here we mowe
rides	Wher he rit othere reste or rometh to pleye;
play (be in a good mood)	And yf hym lust for to layke than loke we mowe
	And apere in his presence the while hym pleye lyketh
(see n.)	And yf hym wratheth ben we war and his way roume.'
	Alle thise route of ratones to this resoun thei assentide,
	Ac tho the belle was ybrought and on the beygh hangid
	Ther ne was no raton of al the route for al the reame of Fraunce
	That derste have ybounde the belle aboute the kattes nekke
	Ne have hanged it aboute his hals al Yngelond to wynne;
considered	And leten here labour ylost and al here longe study.
	A mous that moche good couthe, as me tho thoughte,
Stepped quickly	Strok forth sturnely and stod byfore hem alle
	And to the route of ratones rehersede thise wordes:
	'Thogh we hadde ykuld the cat yut shulde ther come another
	To crache us and alle oure kynde thogh we crope under benches.
be	Forthy I conseile for oure comune profit lat the cat yworthe
	And be nevere so bold the belle hym to shewe.
	For I herde my syre sayn, sevene yer ypassed,
	"Ther the cat is but a kytoun the court is ful elynge."
	Wyttenesse at holy wryt, who-so kan rede:
	Ve terre ubi puer est Rex!
	I seye it for me,' quod the mous, 'I se so muche aftur,
	Shal never the cat ne kytoun be my conseil be greved
speak	Ne carpen of here colers that costede me nevere.
	And thogh hit costed my catel, byknowen I ne wolde
	But soffre and sey nought and that is the beste
misfortune, chastens	Til that meschief amende hem that many man chasteth.
	For many mannys malt we muys wolde distruye

179 **beyes**: the rich collars or necklaces worn by great lords and their liveried followers.

190 'And if he is in a bad mood we can be wary and get out of his way'.

205 **kytoun**: Richard II was nine years old when he succeeded to the throne on the death of his grandfather, Edward III.

207 'Woe to the land where a child is king' (cf. Eccl. 10:16).

And the route of ratones of reste men awake
ready at hand Ne were the cat of the court and yonge kitones toward;
free run For hadde ye ratones youre reik, ye couthe nat reule yow-selven.'
dream (What this meteles bymeneth, ye men that ben merye,
Devyne ye, for I ne dar, by dere god almyhten.)
Yut mette me more of mene and of riche,
important city men, villages As barones and burgeys and bondemen of thorpes,
Al I say slepynge as ye shal here heraftur:
Bothe bakeres and breweres, bochers and other,
Women-weavers, cloth-fullers Webbesteres and walkeres and wynners with handes,
As taylers and tanners and tulyers of the erthe,
ditchers As dykers and delvers that doth here dedis ylle
And dryveth forth here days with *'Dew vous save, dame Emme.'*
Cokes and here knaves cryede, 'Hote pyes, hote!
piglets Goode gees and grys! Ga we dyne, ga we!'
cried their wares Taverners til hem tolde the same:
Alsace 'Whit wyn of Oseye and wyn of Gascoyne,
Of the Reule and of the Rochele the roost to defye!'
times Al this I say sleping and sevyn sythes more.

{In Passus I, the lady Holy Church explains Will's vision to him, shows him how a right use of worldly goods would be in accord with God's Law, and answers his urgent entreaty, How may I save my soul? (I.80), which in a sense initiates the whole movement of the poem, with a preliminary outline of the doctrine of Charity. But Will wishes to understand more of the ways of the world, and is presented in Passus II–IV with the vision of maiden Meed, an allegorical portrayal of the corruption of every estate and activity of society through the influence of money. Meed is on the brink of marriage to Falsehood, or, as it might be, the incentive of financial gain (not in itself wicked) is to become an institutionalized form of corruption; but Theology insists that Meed is already betrothed to Truth, and the king, as her guardian, must adjudicate. So all must go to the king's court at Westminster.}

Passus III.1–67: Meed at Westminster

Now is Mede the mayde and namo of hem alle
Thorw bedeles and baylifs ybrouhte byfor the kyng.
The kyng callede a clerke – I can nat his name –
To take Mede the mayde and maken here at ese.
ask 'I shal asaye here mysulve and sothliche appose
What man of this world that here levest hadde,
And yf she worche wysely and by wys men consayl
I wol forgyve here alle gultes, so me God helpe.'
commanded Cortesliche the clerk thenne, as the kyng hyhte,
Took Mede by the myddel and myldeliche here brouhte
Into boure with blisse and by here gan sitte.
Ac there was myrthe and mynstracie Mede to plese;
Those many who That wendeth to Westmynstre worschipede here monye.
some of them Genteliche with joye the justices somme
Hastened, maiden Boskede hem to the bour ther this buyrde dwelte
And confortede here as they couthe, by the clerkes leve,
And sayden, 'Mourne nat, Mede, ne make thow no sorwe

223–32 The picture crowds and blurs, and dissolves in a chorus of street-cries.

227 'God save you , Dame Emma' (a line from a popular song).

232 '(Wine) from La Reole and La Rochelle (in the Bordeaux area of France) to help digest the roast'.

Passus III

1–8 The king regards Meed as a young ward who has got into bad company; he does not summon her immediately, which gives her ample time to go about her usual business.

advise	For we wol wisse the kyng and thy way shape
gladly	For to wedde at thy wille where the leef liketh
contrivance	For al Consciences cast and craft, as y trowe.'
thanked	Myldeliche Mede thenne mercyede hem alle
	Of here grete goodnesse and gaf hem uchone
Bowls	Coupes of clene gold, coppes of sylver,
	Rynges with rubees and othere riche yeftes,
(see n.)	The leste man of here mayne a motoun of gold.
taken	Whenne they hadde lauhte here leve at this lady Mede
	Thenne come clerkes to conforte here the same
bade	And beden here be blythe, 'For we beth thyn owene
	For to worche thy wille the while thou myhte dure.'
graciously	And Mede hendeliche behyhte hem the same,
truly	To lovye hem leeliche and lordes to make,
pence	'And purchace yow provendres while youre panes lasteth
buy	And bygge yow benefices, pluralite to have,
	And in the constorie at court do calle youre names.
ignorance hinder	Shal no lewedenesse lette the clerk that I lovye
promoted, acknowledged	That he ne worth furste vaunsed, for I am byknowe
hobble	There connynge clerkes shal clokke byhynde.'
	Thenne come ther a confessour ycoped as a frere,
	To Mede the mayde myldeliche he sayde:
both slept with thee	'Thogh lewed men and lered men haved layn by the bothe,
provided for	And Falshede yfonde the al this fourty wyntur,
horse-load of	I shal assoyle the mysulve for a seem whete
	And yut be thy bedman and brynge adoun Conscience
	Amonge kynges and knyhtes and clerkes and the lyke.'
	Thenne Mede for here mysdedes to this man knelede,
	Shrofe here of here synne, shameles, I leve,
gave, gold coin	Tolde hym a tale and toke hym a noble
message	For to ben here bedman and to bere wel here ernde
do down	Among knyhtes and clerkes, Conscience to turne.
then	And he assoilede here sone and sethen he sayde:
cost	'We han a wyndowe a-worchynge wol stande us ful heye;
	Wolde ye glase that gable and grave ther youre name
	In masse and in matynes for Mede we shal synge
	Solempneliche and softlyche as for a suster of oure ordre.'
	Loveliche that lady laghynge sayde:
	'I shal be youre frende, frere, and fayle yow nevere
	The whiles ye lovyen this lordes that lecherye haunteth
blame	And lacketh nat this ladyes that lovyeth the same.
frailty	Hit is but frelete of fleysche, ye fyndeth wel by bokes,
process of nature	And a cours of kynde wherof we comen alle.
harm	Ho may askape the sclaundre, the skathe myhte sone be mended;
none more easily forgiven	Hit is synne as of sevene noon sonner relesed.

25 '(Gave) the humblest of her followers a gold coin (stamped with a sheep)'.

34 Meed will get their names mentioned at the ecclesiastical consistory court, meaning that they will be in line for lucrative positions.

38–67 A vivid demonstration of the friar-confessor in action.

43 **bedman**: 'beadsman' (one who prays for another for money).

51–4 Friars often begged money for the improvement of their churches. Donors of glass could have their names inscribed in a corner of the window; they could also have prayers and masses said for them, and be enrolled in the 'letters of fraternity' of the order (54, 67, below), which entitled them to share in the spiritual benefits of the order's prayers and good works.

53 **Mede**. Modern capitalization obscures a neat pun.

59–62 A good example of the friars' *glosing* (Prol. 58n).

Haveth mercy,' quod Mede, 'on men that hit haunteth
roof — And I shal cuvere youre kyrke and youre cloistre make,
walls — Bothe wyndowes and wowes I wol amende and glase
And peynten and purtrayen ho payede for the makyng
man — That every seg shal se I am a sustre of youre ordre.'

{A long debate on the legitimacy of Meed ends with Conscience distinguishing carefully between improper reward (graft) and 'mesurable hyre'; a new age, with the king under the guidance of Conscience and Reason, seems about to begin. But first the conscience of the body politic must be purged by confession, and Will, in a passage new in C, makes first his own 'confession'. Whether autobiographically accurate in every detail or not, it places the author's 'life' squarely at the centre of the poem's meaning (see A. Middleton, 'William Langland's "Kynde Name": Authorial Signature and Social Identity in late 14th-century England', in Patterson {1990}, pp. 15–82). It combines contrition with pugnacious self-justification in a characteristic way.}

Passus V.1–104:
Will's 'apologia pro vita sua'

(see n.) — Thus I awakede, wot God, whan I wonede in Cornehull,
little cottage — Kytte and I in a cote, yclothed as a lollare,
esteemed, believe — And lytel ylet by, leveth me for sothe,
Amonges lollares of Londone and lewede ermytes,
composed verses about — For I made of tho men as resoun me tauhte.
  For as I cam by Conscience with Resoun I mette
health — In an hot hervest whenne I hadde myn hele
to live well — And lymes to labory with and lovede wel fare
And no dede to do but to drynke and to slepe.
questioned — In hele and in inwitt oon me apposede;
Romynge in remembraunce, thus Resoun me aratede.
assist in the service — 'Can thow serven,' he sayde, 'or syngen in a churche,
pile hay, haycock-makers — Or koke for my cokeres or to the cart piche,
(see n.) — Mowen or mywen or make bond to sheves,
head-reaper — Repe or been a rype-reve and aryse erly,
hedge-ward — Or have an horn and be hayward and lygge theroute nyhtes
field, pilferers — And kepe my corn in my croft fro pykares and theves?
Or shap shon or cloth, or shep and kyne kepe,
Heggen or harwen, or swyn or gees dryve,
kind of — Or eny other kynes craft that to the comune nedeth,
(see n.) — That thou betere therby that byleve the fynden?'
  'Sertes,' I sayde, 'and so me god helpe,
weak — I am to wayke to worche with sykel or with sythe
And to long, lef me, lowe to stoupe,
To wurche as a werkeman eny while to duyren.'
  'Thenne hastow londes to lyve by,' quod Resoun, 'or lynage ryche

Passus V

1 'when I lived in Cornhill' (a district of London).

2 **Kytte**; 'Kitty', a type-name for 'a wife' (see VII.304), but perhaps the author's wife's real name. Clerics in minor orders often had wives (and thereby spoilt their prospects of advancement). **lollare**: 'idle layabout' – perhaps with some awareness of the association with 'Lollard' (it is characteristic of Langland, as in Prol. 3, to associate himself with persons of doubtful religious life).

11 **aratede**. There are reminiscences, in Reason's aggressive interrogation, of the judicial procedures for implementing the Statutes of Labourers in the questioning of able-bodied unemployed or itinerant workers. But Reason and Conscience remain, of course, as allegorical interrogators of Langland's interior self as well as external agents.

14 'Mow, or stack the mown swathes, or make straw-binding for sheaves'.

21 'That you might improve thereby the life of those that provide for you'.

24 **to long**: 'too tall' (cf. Luke 16:3). Langland says his nickname is 'Longe Wille' in B.XV.152.

That fynde the thy fode? For an ydel man thow semest,
must spend A spendour that spene mot or a spille-tyme,
food, men's Or beggest thy bylyve aboute at men hacches
begs falsely Or faytest uppon Frydayes or feste-dayes in churches,
idlers' The whiche is lollarne lyf, that lytel is preysed
There ryhtfulnesse rewardeth ryht as men deserveth.
Reddet unicuique iuxta opera sua.
Or thow art broke, so may be, in body or in membre
Or ymaymed thorw som myshap, whereby thow myhte be excused?'
'When I yong was, many yer hennes,
My fader and my frendes fonde me to scole,
truly Tyl I wyste witterly what holy writ menede
And what is beste for the body, as the bok telleth,
provided that I persevere And sykerest for the soule, by so I wol contenue.
never And fond I nere, in fayth, seth my frendes deyede,
Lyf that me lykede but in this longe clothes.
And yf I be labour sholde lyven and lyflode deserven,
That laboure that I lerned beste therwith lyven I sholde.
In eadem vocacione in qua vocati estis.
up in the country And so I lyve yn London and opelond bothe;
tools The lomes that I labore with and lyflode deserve
Is *pater-noster* and my prymer, *placebo* and *dirige*,
And my sauter som tyme and my sevene psalmes.
These I say This I segge for here soules of suche as me helpeth,
vouchsafe And tho that fynden me my fode fouchen-saf, I trowe,
from time to time To be welcome when I come, other-while in a monthe,
Now with hym, now with here; on this wyse I begge
stomach alone Withoute bagge or botel but my wombe one.
'And also moreover me thynketh, syre Resoun,
Men, low-born men's Me sholde constrayne no clerc to no knaves werkes,
(Leviticus 21) For by the lawe of Levyticy that oure lord ordeynede,
tonsured, it stands to reason Clerkes ycrouned, of kynde understondynge,
Sholde nother swynke ne swete ne swerien at enquestes
vanguard of an army Ne fyhte in no faumewarde ne his foe greve.
Non reddas malum pro malo.
they are the heirs For hit ben eyres of hevene, alle that ben ycrouned,
choir And in quoer and in kyrkes Cristes mynistres.
Dominus pars hereditatis mee. Et alibi: Clemencia non constringit.
Hit bycometh for clerkes Crist for to serve
And knaves uncrounede to carte and to worche.
For sholde no clerke be crouned but yf he come were

32a 'He will repay every man according to what he has done' (Matt. 16:27).

36 **My fader**. According to a note in Dublin, Trinity College MS D.4.1, Langland was the son of Stacy de Rokayle, a country gentleman of Shipton-under-Wychwood in Oxfordshire. His father and his **frendes** (includes relatives) provided for his schooling, traditionally at the priory of Great Malvern (see Prol. 6); but **scole** probably means university, where he was supported until they died, leaving him, half-trained for a clerical vocation, to make a living as best he could.

41 **this longe clothes**, i.e. the dress of a cleric in minor orders.

43a '(Remain) in the state to which you are called' (cf. 1 Cor. 7:20).

46–7 The **prymer** is the basic private prayer-book for lay-people, a collection of psalms, prayers and services including the Office of the Dead (where the words *placebo* and *dirige* introduce prayers) and the seven penitential psalms. These are the 'tools' of Langland's trade, which is that of intercession by prayer for the souls of the living (l. 48) and the dead (to accelerate their progress through purgatory).

57 **swerien at enquestes**: 'give evidence on oath in courts of law'. Clerics (through 'benefit of clergy') were exempt from the normal processes of law.

58a 'Do not repay evil for evil' (cf. 1 Thess. 5:15).

60a 'The lord is the portion of my inheritance' (Ps. 15:5). And elsewhere: 'The quality of mercy is not strained' (proverbial).

Of frankeleynes and fre men and of folke ywedded.
Bondemen and bastardes and beggares children,
Thyse bylongeth to labory, and lordes kyn to serve
rank requires God and good men, as here degre asketh,
Somme to synge masses or sitten and wryten,
Advise Reden and resceyven that resoun ouhte to spene.
children 'Ac sythe bondemen barnes han be mad bisshopes
And barnes bastardes han be erchedekenes
shoemakers And soutares and here sones for sulver han be knyhtes
mortgaged their estates And lordes sones here laboreres and leyde here rentes to wedde,
For the ryhte of this reume ryden ayeyn oure enemyes
In confort of the comune and the kynges worschipe,
nuns, beggars 'And monkes and moniales, that mendenantes sholde fynde,
knights' estates Imade here kyn knyhtes and knyhtes-fees ypurchased,
Popes and patrones pore gentel blood refused
sanctuary And taken Symondes sones seyntwarie to kepe,
Lyf-holynesse and love hath be longe hennes,
And wol, til hit be wered out, or otherwyse ychaunged.
'Forthy rebuke me ryhte nauhte, Resoun, I yow praye,
For in my conscience I knowe what Crist wolde I wrouhte.
Preyeres of a parfit man and penaunce discret
most precious Is the levest labour that oure lord pleseth.
Non de solo,' I sayde, 'for sothe *vivit homo*,
Nec in pane et in pabulo, the pater-noster wittenesseth;
provides us with *Fiat voluntas dei* – that fynt us alle thynges.'
Quod Conscience, 'By Crist, I can nat se this lyeth;
steadfast Ac it semeth no sad parfitnesse in citees to begge,
(see n.) But he be obediencer to prior or to mynistre.'
acknowledge 'That is soth,' I saide, 'and so I beknowe –
wasted That I have ytynt tyme and tyme myspened;
made business deals Ac yut, I hope, as he that ofte hath ychaffared
And ay loste and loste, and at the laste hym happed
He bouhte suche a bargayn he was the bet evere,
at nothing And sette al his los at a leef at the laste ende,
came to him Suche a wynnyng hym warth thorw wordes of grace.
Simile est regnum celorum thesauro abscondito in agro.
Mulier que inuenit dragmam, etc.
So hope I to have of hym that is almyghty
A gobet of his grace, and bigynne a tyme
That alle tymes of my tyme to profit shal turne.'
hasten 'I rede the,' quod Resoun tho, 'rape the to bigynne
praiseworthy The lyf that is louable and leele to thy soule'–
'Ye, and contynue!' quod Conscience; and to the kyrke I wente.

70–81 This sentence is dependent upon **Ac sythe** up to l. 80. It describes, with a special vehemence, how money has perverted the divinely established hierarchy of the estates by encouraging social mobility.

79 **Symondes sones** are those who buy office in the church, and so are sons of Simon Magus, who tried to purchase with money the apostles' gift of laying on hands (Acts 8:18).

86–7 'Man does not live by bread and food alone' (cf. Matt. 4:4).

88 'God's will be done' (cf. Matt. 6:10).

89 **lyeth**: 'applies, is to the point'. Conscience, catching up **parfit** (84), points out sharply that Langland's theory of the perfect life is not what he practises.

91 'Unless he be someone licensed to beg by a prior or church official'.

98a 'The kingdom of heaven is like treasure hidden in a field' (Matt. 13:44). 'The woman that found a silver coin': a cue-reference to the parable (Luke 15:10) which illustrates the joy in heaven over the sinner that repents.

{Reason now preaches a sermon before the king, calling upon the people to amend their lives and to seek Saint Truth. The confessions of the Seven Deadly Sins follow. Langland personifies the Sins as individuals, and draws for their portrayal on a rich repertoire of sermon-material, a mass of vivid and circumstantial detail of urban and rural life, and a variety of dramatic, pictorial and iconographic techniques. Much goes beyond the possible experience of a single individual, and the Sins are not self-standing satirical 'characters' but individualized versions of different characteristic types of homiletic treatment of the vices in question. Pride leads off, followed by Envy and then Wrath.}

Passus VI. 103–69, 196–238, 350–441 (end): The Confession of the People

	Thenne awakede Wrathe, with two whyte eyes
running with mucus	And with a nivilynge nose, nippynge his lippes.
man	'I am Wrothe' quod that weye, 'wol gladliche smyte
	Bothe with stoon and with staf, and stele uppon myn enemye;
cunning plots, think up	To sle hym sleyliche sleythes I bythenke.
	Thogh I sitte this sevene yer I sholde nat wel telle
	The harm that I have do with hand and with tonge;
	Inpacient in alle penaunces, and pleyned as hit were,
grumbled, what he sends	On God, when me greved auht, and grochede of his sonde,
	As som tyme in somur and also in hervest,
blamed	But I hadde weder at my wille, I witte God the cause
	In alle manere angres that I hadde or felede.
	'Amonges alle manere men my dwellyng is som tyme,
glad	With lewed and lered that leef ben to here
behind his back or in his presence	Harm of eny man, byhynde or bifore.
lead	Freres folewen my fore fele tyme and ofte
	And preven inparfit prelates of holy churche;
parishioners	And prelates pleyneth on hem for they here parschiens shryuen
	Withoute licence and leve – and herby lyveth wrathe.
	Thus thei speke and dispute that uchon dispiseth other.
	Thus beggares and barones at debat aren ofte
grow strong	Til I, Wrathe, wexe an hey and walke with hem bothe.
Either, live	Or til they bothe be beggares and by spiritualte libbe
grow rich	Or alle riche and ryde, reste shal I nat, Wrathe,
	That I ne mot folowe this folk – my fortune is non other.
who is a nun	'I have an aunte to nonne and an abbesse;
swoon or die	Here were lever swowe or swelte then soffre eny payne.
	I have be cok in here kychene and the covent served,
	Mony monthes with hem and with monkes bothe.
vegetable-cook	I was the prioresse potager and other pore ladies,
soups of squabbling	And made hem joutes of jangelynge: "Dame Jone was a bastard,
	And dame Clarice a knyhtes douhter, a cokewolde was here syre,
filly (concubine), will be	And dame Purnele a prestis fyle – prioresse worth she nevere;
hen-house, accused	For she hadde childe in the chapun-cote she worth chalenged at the eleccioun."
	Thus sytte they, tho sustres, sum tyme, and disputen
liest	Til "thow lixt" and "thow lixt" be lady over hem alle;

Passus VI

103 **Wrathe** is the only sin who names himself; he speaks of himself not only as the embodiment of anger and an angry person, but also as a genderless stirrer-up of anger in others, a diabolical sower of discord.

118–21 Friars prove prelates to be imperfect in their lives (e.g. because they do not observe the friars' vow of poverty) while prelates criticize friars for poaching confessions.

123 **beggares and barones**, ironical terms for mendicants and possessioners.

And thenne awake I, Wrathe, and wolde be avenged.
And thenne I crye and crache with my kene nayles,
shows of behaviour Byte and bete and brynge forth suche thewes
That alle ladyes me lotheth that lovyeth eny worschipe.
'Amonges wyves and wydewes I am woned to sitte
Enclosed in pews Yparroked in pues; the persone hit knoweth
How lytel I lovye Letyse-at-the-style;
For she had haly-bred ar I, my herte gan change.
the one woman and the other Aftur mete aftirward she and she chydde
stirred them to anger And I, Wrath, was war, and wrathe on hem bothe,
Tyl ayther clepede other "hore" and on with the clawes
Til bothe here hedes were bar and blody here chekes.
don't bother 'Amonges monkes I myhte be, ac mony tyme I spare,
stern, doings For there aren many felle frekes myne aferes to aspye,
That is, priour and suppriour and oure *pater abbas*.
consult And yf I telle eny tales they taken hem togyderes
And don me faste Fridayes to bred and to water.
Yut am I chalenged in oure chapitre-hous as I a childe were
caned And balayshed on the bare ers and no brech bytwene.
dwell long I have no luste, lef me, to longe amonges monkes,
For I ete more fysch then flesche there, and feble ale drynke.
Ac other-while when wyn cometh and when I drynke late at even
I have a flux of a foul mouth wel fyve daies aftur,
And al that I wiste wykked by eny of oure covent
I cough hit up in oure cloystre, that al the covent wot hit.'
repeat 'Now repente,' quod Repentaunce, 'and reherce nevere
Secret Consayl that thow knowest, by continaunce ne by speche.
And drynke nat overdelycatly no to depe neyther,
That thy wil ne thy wit to wrathe myhte turne.
Be sober (1 Pet. 5:8) *Esto sobrius*,' he saide, and assoiled hym aftur,
pray, to be And bad hym bid to god, be his help to amende.

{Lechery makes a brief appearance, then Covetousness.}

describe Thenne cam Covetyse – I can hym nat descreve,
So hungrily and holow sire Hervy hym lokede.
thick-lipped He was bitelbrowed and baburlippid, with two blered eyes,
purse And as a letherne pors lollede his chekes,
lower, wobbled Wel sydere then his chyn ycheveled for elde;
And as a bondemannes bacoun his berd was yshave,
With his hood on his heved and his hat bothe,
torn jerkin In a tore tabard of twelve wynter age –
believe But yf a lous couthe lepe, I leve and I trowe,
cheap Welsh flannel He ne sholde wandre uppon that walch, so was hit thredbare.
wretch, confess 'I have be covetous,' quod this kaytif, 'I biknowe hit here.
For som tyme I served Symme-at-the-style
bound, see to And was his prentis yplyht, his profit to wayte.
pageful or two Furste I lerned to lye a leef other tweye;

146 **haly-bred** is ordinary (leavened) bread, blessed, and distributed after mass as a mark of Christian fellowship.

155 Friday was the usual day for the performance of penances. The contrast between monasteries and nunneries is striking.

197 **sire** is usually applied to a man in holy orders; the allusion in **Hervy** ('Harvey') has not been identified.

201 i.e. roughly hacked, with tufts of hair showing here and there.

206 This first part of Avarice's confession has to do largely with offences against lawful trading practice, especially the giving of fair weight and measure.

weigh	Wykkedliche to waye was my furste lessoun.
Weyhill (in Hampshire)	To Wy and to Wynchestre I wente to the fayre
commanded	With many manere marchandise, as my maister hyhte;
	Ne hadde the grace of gyle go among my ware,
	Hit hadde be unsold this sevene yer, so me god helpe!
(see n.)	'Thenne drow I me amonge drapers, my donet to lere,
stretch the edge of the cloth	To drawe the lyst along, the lenger hit semede.
striped cloths	Amonges the ryche rayes I rendrede a lessoun,
	To brochen hem with a bat-nelde and bande hem togyderes,
	Putte hem in pressoures and pynne hem ther-ynne,
reckoned out at	Til ten yerde other twelve tolde out threttene.
weaver	'My wyf was a webbe and wollene cloth made;
(see n.)	Sche spak to the spynnesteres to spynnen it oute.
weighed	The pound that she payede hem by peysed a quarter more
scales	Then myn owene auncel, when I wayed treuthe.
brewed, sell	'I bouhte here barly, she brew hit to sulle;
thin ale (penny a gallon), thick	Peny-ale and poddyng-ale she poured togederes,
	For laboreres and for louh folke that lay by hymsulve.
	Ac the beste ale lay in my bour and in my bedchaunbre
tasted	And ho-so bommede thereof he bouhte hit theraftur
(fourpence), true	A galon for a grote – and yut no grayth mesure
cupfuls (inexact measures)	When hit cam in coppe-mele; this crafte my wyf usede.
retailer	Rose the regrater was here ryhte name;
(see n.)	Sche hadde holde hokkerye this elevene wynter.'
	'Repentedestow nevere?' quod Repentaunce, 'ne restitucioun madest?'
lodged	'Yus, ones I was herberwed,' quod he, 'with an heep of chapmen;
bags	I ros and ryflede here males when they a-reste were.'
	'That was a ruful restitucioun,' quod Repentaunce, 'for sothe;
	Thow wolt be hanged heye therfore, here other in helle!'

{The interrogation of Covetousness continues at some length. The account of Gluttony that follows is unique in being presented, up to l. 421, as a continuous narrative.}

	Now bygynneth Glotoun for to go to shryfte
goes, reckoning (of sin)	And kayres hym to kyrke-ward, his conpte to shewe.
	Fastyng on a Friday forth gan he wende
Betty's	By Betene hous the brewestere, that bad hym good morwen,
whither	And whodeward he wolde the breuh-wyf hym askede.
	'To holy churche,' quod he, 'for to here masse,
then, sin	And sennes sitte and be shryve and synege no more.'
have a taste	'I have good ale, gossip Glotoun, woltow assaye?'
	'Hastow,' quod he, 'eny hote spyces?'
peony(-seeds)	'I have pepur and pyonie and a pound of garlek,
	A ferthyng-worth fenkelsedes, for fastyng-dayes I bouhte hit.'
	Thenne goth Glotoun in and Grete Othes aftur.
Cissy the shoemaker-woman	Sesse the souteres sat on the benche,

215 'to learn my donet' (elementary grammar-book).

218–19 The pieces of cloth are sewn together with loose stitches with a coarse needle and then pinned in stretching-frames.

222 **spynnen it oute**: 'spin out the yarn loosely' (so that it would go further).

233 **holde hokkerye**: 'carried on fraudulent retail-dealing'.

234 **restitucioun** (of ill-gotten gains) is the practical demonstration of sincerity of repentance in confessions of avarice. The sinner (deliberately?) misunderstands, and thinks it has to do with robbing people when they are *at rest*.

360 **fenkelsedes**: fennel-seeds (taken to get rid of wind).

Walt the warren-keeper	Watte the wernare and his wyf dronke,
	Tymme the tynekare and tweyne of his knaves,
horse-hirer	Hicke the hackenayman and Hewe the nedlare,
(a street of brothels)	Claryce of Cockes-lane and the clerc of the churche,
Prunella	Syre Peres of Prydie and Purnele of Flaundres,
hedge-warden	An hayward, an heremyte, the hangeman of Tybourne,
Davy the ditch-digger	Dawe the dikere, with a doseyne harlotes
bald-headed	Of portours and of pikeporses and of pilede toth-draweres,
(see n.)	A rybibour and a ratoner, a rakeare and his knave,
master reed-thatcher, dish-seller	A ropere and a redyng-kynge and Rose the disshere,
	Godefray the garlek-monger and Gryffyth the Walshe,
second-hand clothes dealers	And of uphalderes an heep, herly by the morwe
as a gift ('the first round')	Geven Glotoun with glad chere good ale to hansull.
	Clement the coblere cast of his cloke
nominated, sell	And to the newe fayre nempnede hit forth to sull.
threw in	Hicke the hackenayman hit his hod aftur
	And bade Bitte the bochere ben on his syde.
deal, appraise	There were chapmen ychose this chaffare to preyse,
	That ho-so hadde the hood sholde nat have the cloke,
arbitrators, compensate	And that the bettere thyng, be arbitreres, bote sholde the worse.
quickly, whispered	Tho rysen up rapliche and rouned togyderes
	And preisede this peniworths apart by hemsulve,
	And there were othes an heep, for on sholde have the worse.
	They couthe nat by here conscience acorden for treuthe
	Til Robyn the ropere aryse they bisouhte
(see n.)	And nempned hym for a noumper, that no debat were.
ostler	Hicke the hostiler hadde the cloke,
	In covenaunt that Clement sholde the coppe fulle,
	And have Hickes hood the hostiler and holde hym yserved;
soonest	And ho-so repentede hym rathest sholde aryse aftur
	And grete syre Glotoun with a galon of ale.
laughing and scowling	There was leyhing and louryng and 'lat go the coppe!'
start up anew	Bargaynes and bevereges bygan tho to awake,
from time to time	And seten so til evensong, and songen umbywhile,
	Til Glotoun hadde yglobbed a galoun and a gylle.
rumble	His gottes gan to gothly as two grydy sowes;
potful	He pissede a potel in a pater-noster whyle,
little trumpet, backbone's	He blew his rownd ruet at his rygebones ende,
	That alle that herde the horne helde here nose aftur
wished, sprig of briars	And wesched hit hadde be wasche with a weps of breres.
	He myhte nother steppe ne stande til he a staf hadde,
	And thenne gan he go lyke a glemans byche,
backwards	Sum tyme asyde and sum tyme arere,
catch birds	As ho-so layth lynes for to lacche foules.
	And when he drow to the dore, thenne dymmede his yes,

367 *Pridie*, in Latin, means 'the day before', and is the word in the communion service that a priest has to go back to if he makes a mistake in the prayers of consecration. It is very apt to a priest who has his mind on other things.

371 'A rubible-player and a ratcatcher, a street-sweeper and his lad'.

377 **the newe fayre** is a game of exchanges. The two 'players' offer objects for exchange, which are appraised by selected **chapmen**, and the winner of what they deem the more valuable object offers compensation to the other player (382). If there is further argument, an umpire is appointed (388). The game had a bad name, and was probably used as a form of confidence trick.

388 'And nominated him as umpire, so that there should be no debate'.

404 **a glemans byche**: popular entertainers often had a dog who took part in their act (like Launce in *The Two Gentlemen of Verona*).

stumbled	And thromblede at the thresfold and threw to the erthe,
	And Clement the coblere cauhte hym by the myddel
	And for to lyfte hym aloft leyde hym on his knees.
gave a lot of trouble	Ac Gloton was a greet cherl and greved in the luftynge
coughed, mess	And cowed up a caudel in Clementis lappe;
	Ys none so hungry hound in Hertfordshyre
leaving, smelt	Durste lape of that lyvynge, so unlovely hit smauhte.
	With alle the wo of this world his wyf and his wenche
	Baren hym to his bed and brouhten hym ther-ynne,
fit of sloth (hangover)	And aftur al this exces he hadde an accidie aftur;
	He sleep Saturday and Sonenday til the sonne yede to reste.
	Then gan he wake wel wanne and wolde have ydronke;
Who's got the bowl	The furste word that he spake was 'Who halt the bolle?'
conscience, reproached	His wif and his inwit edwitede hym of his synne;
	He wax ashamed, that shrewe, and shrofe hym as swythe
	To Repentaunce ryht thus: 'Have reuthe on me,' he saide,
created	'Thow lord that aloft art and alle lyves shope!
	'To the, God, I, Glotoun, gulty I me yelde
	Of that I have trespased with tonge, I can nat telle how ofte,
	Sworn "Godes soule and his sides!" and "So helpe me, God almyhty!"
a time	There no nede ne was, many sythe falsly;
noon	And over-sopped at my soper and som tyme at nones
digest	More then my kynde myhte deffye,
retch	And as an hound that eet gras so gan I to brake
what I might have kept in	And spilde that I aspele myhte – I kan nat speke for shame
	The vilony of my foule mouthe and of my foule mawe –
	And fastyng-dayes bifore none fedde me with ale
	Out of resoun, among rybaudes, here rybaudrye to here.
	'Herof, gode God, graunte me foryevenesse
wicked	Of all my luyther lyf in al my lyf-tyme
	For I vowe to verray God, for eny hungur or furste,
	Shal nevere fysch in the Fryday defyen in my wombe
	Til Abstinence myn aunte have yeve me leve –
	And yut have I hated here al my lyf-tyme.'

{Sloth brings up the rear of the Sins. Repentance, now acting as officiating priest, says a prayer on behalf of all sinners, and the people tumble forth in search of Saint Truth. But they do not know the way, and a palmer that they meet cannot help them. At this point Piers Plowman appears.}

Passus VII.182–308 (end): Piers Plowman and the Search for Saint Truth

	'Peter!' quod a plouhman, and putte forth his heved,
intimately	'I knowe hym as kyndely as clerk doth his bokes.
taught	Conscience and Kynde Wyt kenned me to his place,
promise	And maden me sykeren sethen to serven hym for evere,

441 Glutton's last words are a backward look at his old life. His penitence seems peremptory and mechanical, and the allegorical suggestion is that formal confession will not prove adequate to cleanse society as a basis for reform.

Passus VII

182 **Peter**: an oath, by St Peter, but also, appropriately enough, the baptismal form of the ploughman's own name, Piers (Peres). We imagine him (this is his first appearance) poking his head through the hedge which separates the highway from his half-acre.

Bothe to sowe and to sette the while I swynke myhte,
And to sowen his seed, suewen his bestes, — *attend to*
Withynne and withouten to wayten his profit. — *look after*
Ich have ybe his foloware al this fourty wynter
And yserved Treuthe sothly, somdel to paye. — *to his satisfaction*
In alle kyne craftes that he couthe devise — *kinds of*
Profitable as for the plouh, he putte me to lerne,
And, thogh I sey hit mysulf, I serve hym to paye.
I have myn huyre of hym wel and other-whiles more.
He is the presteste payere that eny pore man knoweth; — *promptest*
He with-halt non hewe his huyre over even. — *(see n.)*
He is as louh as a lombe and leel of his tonge, — *humble, true*
And ho-so wilneth to wyte where that Treuthe woneth,
I wol wissen yow wel ryht to his place.'
'Ye, leve Peres,' quod thise pilgrimes, and profrede Peres mede. — *reward*
'Nay, bi the perel of my soule!' Peres gan to swerie,
'I ne wol fonge a ferthynge, for seynt Thomas shryne! — *take*
Were it itolde Treuthe that I toke mede
He wolde love me the lasse a long tyme aftur.
Ac ho-so wol wende ther Treuthe is, this is the way theder:
Ye mote go thorw Mekenesse, alle men and wommen,
Til ye come into Conscience, yknowe of God sulve,
That ye lovye hym as lord leely above alle; — *So that*
That is to sey sothly, ye sholde rather deye
Thenne eny dedly synne do, for drede or for preyere.
And thenne youre neyhebores nexst in none wyse apayre — *harm*
Otherwyse then ye wolden they wrouhte yow alle tymes. — *(Or act towards them) otherwise*
And so goth forth by the brok, a brugge as it were, — *bridge*
Forto ye fynde a ford, youre-fader-honoureth; — *Until*
Wadeth in at that water and wascheth yow wel there
And ye shal lepe the lihtloker al youre lyf-tyme.
Honora patrem et matrem.
And thenne shalt thow se Swere-nat-but-if-it-be-for-nede-
And-nameliche-an-ydel-the-name-of-god-almyhty. — *in vain*
Thenne shalt thow come by a croft, ac com thow nat ther-ynne; — *small enclosed field*
The croft hatte Coveyte-nat-menne-catel-ne-here-wyves — *is called*
Ne-none-of-here-servauntes-that-nuye-hem-myhte; — *harm*
Loke thou bere nat there away, but yf hit be thyn owene.
Two stokkes there stondeth, ac stynte thow nat there; — *tree-stumps, pause*
Thei hatte Stele-nat and Sle-nat – stryk forth by bothe
And leveth hem on the luft hand and loke nat theraftur,
And hold wel the haliday heye til even.

196 'He withholds no servant his wages beyond the evening' (see Lev. 19:13).
203 **mede**: see Passus II–IV. Peres knows the difference between payment offered in advance (a form of bribery) and a fair wage for work done.
213–31 The gospel summary of OT law having been referred to (206–12: 'Love God, and your neighbour as yourself', Luke 10:27), the journey to Truth passes through a countryside dotted with allegorical reminders of the Ten Commandments (Ex. 20). What is made clear in this little allegory is that knowledge of Truth is based on a hard-won rectitude of life in obedience to Law, and that the journey to Christ is through the OT, which his teaching does not supersede but fulfils (Matt. 5:17).
216a 'Honour (your) father and mother (and you shall live long upon the earth)' (Ex. 20:12).

turn aside, hill | Thenne shaltow blenche at a berw, Bere-no-fals-witnesse,
fenced | Is frithed in with floreynes and othere fees monye;
Loke thow plokke no plonte there, for perel of thy soule.
Thenne shaltow se Say-soth-so-hit-be-to-done-
In-none-manere-elles-nat-for-no-mannes-preyre.
And so shaltow come to a court as cleer as the sonne.
manor | The mote is of Mercy, the manere in the myddes,
Good Sense, Wilfulness | And al the wallyng is of Wyt, for Wil ne sholde hit wynne.
crenellations, (human) nature | The carneles ben of Cristendom, that kynde to save,
Ybotresed with Bileve-so-or-thow-best-not-ysaved;
dwellings, roofed | And alle the hous been yheled, halles and chaumbres,
With no leed but with love, and with lele-speche.
obedience | The barres aren of buxumnesse, as bretherne of o wombe.
The brygge hatte Byde-wel-the-bet-may-thow-spede;
pillar (supporting the bridge) | Uche a piler is of penaunces and preyeres to seyntes;
The hokes aren almes-dedes that the yates hange on.
Grace hatte the gateward, a god man for sothe;
His man hatte Amende-yow, many man hym knoweth.
(password) | Tel hym this ilke tokene: "Treuthe wot the sothe,
I am sory of my synnes and so I shal evere,
commanded | And parformed the penaunce that the prest me hihte."
introduce you humbly before | Biddeth Amende-yow to meke yow to his maister Grace,
To opene and undo the hye gate of hevene
That Adam and Eve ayenes us alle shette.
Per Evam cunctis clausa est. et per Mariam virginem iterum patefacta est.
unlocked | A ful leel lady unlek hit of grace,
latch-key, sleep (i.e. in her womb) | And she hath the keye and the clycat, thogh the kynge slepe,
And may lede in that she loveth as here lef lyketh.
And yf Grace graunte the to go in in this wyse
own | Thow shalt se Treuthe sitte in thy sulve herte,
And solace thy soule and save the fram payne,
And charge Charite a churche to make
provide a sanctuary for | In thyne hole herte, to herborwe alle trewe
And fynde alle manere folke fode to here soules,
Yef love and leute and oure lawe be trewe:
Quodcumque petieritis in nomine meo, dabitur enim vobis.
Ac be war thenne of Wrath, that wikkede shrewe,
For he hath envye to hym that in thyn herte setteth
And poketh forth pruyde to preyse thysulven.
good deeds | The boldenesse of thy been-fetes maketh the blynd thenne;
wilt thou be, dew | So worth thow dryven out as deux, and the dore yclosed,
Ykeyed and yclyketed to close the withouten,
Perhaps, again | Hapliche an hundred wyntur ar thow eft entre.
(see n.) | Thus myhte thow lesen his love, to lete wel by thysulve,

232 **a court**: the castle of Truth, of man dwelling in God, built of and inhabited by the Christian virtues of the soul redeemed by Christ. Langland draws on the rich allegorical tradition of the castle of the soul or the body.

236 'This is the Catholic faith: which except a man believe faithfully, he cannot be saved' (the closing words of the Athanasian Creed, recited on some special feast-days instead of the Apostles' Creed).

250a 'Through Eve it was closed to all men, and through the Virgin Mary it was opened again' (from an antiphon sung at lauds between Easter and Ascension Day). The image of Mary as the gate of paradise and as the key-bearer of redemption is derived from patristic commentary on OT texts such as Ez. 44:2 and Ps. 117:20.

255 The journey to Truth ends in self-discovery, in the recognition of the spirit of Truth that dwells within (John 14:17).

260a 'Whatever you shall ask in my name shall be given to you' (cf. John 16:23).

267 **an hundred wyntur**, i.e. in purgatory. The castle of Truth is thought of throughout as the life of Truth and spiritual grace on earth, and also as heaven.

268 'because of the need to think well of yourself'.

And geten hit agayne thorw grace, ac thorw no gifte elles.
Ac ther ben sevene susteres that serven Treuthe evere
And aren porteres over the posternes that to that place bilongen.
That on hatte Abstinence and Umbletee another,
Charite and Chastite ben his chief maydenes,
Pacience and Pees muche peple thei helpe,
Generosity Largenesse that lady lat in ful monye
Non of hem alle helpe may in betere,
dungeons For she payeth for prisones in puttes and in peynes.
kin And ho is sib to this sevene, so me God helpe,
Is wonderliche welcome and fayre underfonge.
Ho is nat syb to this sevene, sothly to telle,
by my head (oath) Hit is ful hard, be myn heved, eny of yow alle
To geten ingang at eny gate, bote grace be the more.'
'By Crist,' quod a cutte-purs, 'I have no kyn there.'
'Ne I,' quod an apeward, 'by auht that I knowe!'
Let God know 'Wyte God,' quod a wafrestere, 'wiste I this for sothe,
Wolde I nevere forthere no fot for no frere prechynge!'
'Yus,' quod Peres the plouhman, and pokede hem alle to gode,
'Mercy is a mayden there hath myhte over hem alle,
And she is sib to alle synful, and here sone bothe.
expect And thorw the helpes of hem two, hope thou non other,
Thow myhte gete grace there, so thow go bytymes.'
'Ye, *villam emi*,' quod oon, 'and now I moste thedre
To loke how me liketh hit'; and tok his leve at Peres.
Another anon-riht nede he sayde he hadde
plough To falewe with five yokes, 'Forthy me bihoveth
without delay To goo with a good wil and graytheliche hem dryve.
Forthy I pray yow, Peres, parauntur yif ye meten
Treuth, telleth hym this, that I be excused.'
husbandman Thenne was oon hihte Actif, an husbande he semede:
skittish 'I have wedded a wyf, wel wantowen of maneres;
Were I seven nyhte fro here syhte, sighen she wolde
quickly, say And loure on me and lihtly chyde and sygge I lovede another.
Forthy, Peres the plouhman, I preye the telle hit Treuthe
I may nat come for a Kitte so she cleveth on me.
Uxorem duxi et ideo non possum venire.'
Quod Contemplacioun, 'By Crist, thogh I care soffre,
want Famyne and defaute, folwen I wol Peres.
Ac the way is ful wikked, but ho-so hadde a gyde
That myhte folowe us uch a fote for drede of mysturnynge.'

269 Grace is shown, in accordance with orthodox doctrine, to transcend, even to ignore, human desert, and salvation not to be 'won' or deserved through good works.

270 **sevene susteres**: the seven Christian virtues, developed in penitential literature as *remedia* for the seven deadly sins; to be distinguished from the three theological or spiritual virtues (Faith, Hope and Charity) and the four cardinal virtues, which together formed another series of seven.

285 **wafrestere**: female seller of cakes and confections. These cake-sellers were associated with taverns and had a bad reputation (cf. PardT 479n). This one thinks her prospects of entering heaven so remote, if you need to be on such close terms with the seven sisters, that she is going to give up the attempt.

292 ***villam emi***: 'I have bought a field' (Luke 14:18). In lines 292–304, dealing with those who excuse themselves from the pilgrimage, Langland paraphrases the answers of those who decline the invitation to the great supper (i.e. refuse to participate as Christ's disciples in the kingdom of heaven) in the parable of Luke 14:16–24.

299 **Actif**: the 'Active Life', to be understood here as the life of the common body of sinful humanity, as distinct from the life of those who follow Christ in renouncing the world and seeking perfection (Matt. 19:21), i.e. the Contemplative Life (305, below).

304a 'I have married a wife, and therefore I cannot come' (Luke 14:20).

Passus VIII. 1–79, 112–354 (end): The Ploughing of the Half-Acre

(dim. of Peter, 'Peterkin')	Quod Perkyn the plouhman, 'Be seynt Peter of Rome!
plough	Ich have an half-aker to erye by the heye waye;
	Haved ich y-ered this half-aker and ysowed hit aftur,
	I wol wende with yow and the way teche.'
delay, veil	'That were a long lettyng,' quod a lady in a sclayre,
	'What sholde we wommen worche the whiles?'
	'I preye yow, for youre profit,' quod Peres to the ladyes,
to prevent	'That somme sowe the sak for shedynge of the whete,
	And ye worthily wymmen with youre longe fyngres
fine silk	That ye on selk and on sendel sowe whan tyme is
Chasubles	Chesibles for chapeleynes churches to honoure.
	Wyves and wyddewes wolle and flex spynneth;
	Conscience conseyleth yow cloth for to make
	For profit of the pore and plesaunce of yowsulven.
give, unless	For I shal lene hem lyflode, but the lond faylle,
	As longe as I leve, for the lordes love of hevene.
	And alle manere men that by the molde is susteyned
properly	Helpeth hym worche wittiliche that wynneth youre fode.'
	'By Crist,' quod a knyhte tho, 'he kenneth us the beste;
the subject (or the plough-team)	Ac on the teme treuely ytauhte was I nevere.
	I wolde I couthe,' quod the knyhte, 'by Crist and his moder;
for fun	I wolde assaie som tyme for solace as hit were.'
	'Sikerliche, sire knyhte,' sayde Peris thenne,
	'I shal swynke and swete and sowe for us bothe
	And labory for tho thow lovest al my lyf-tyme,
	In covenant that thow kepe holy kerke and mysulve
ruin	Fro wastores and fro wikked men that this world struyen,
	And go hunte hardelyche to hares and to foxes,
	To bores and to bukkes that breketh adoun myn hegges,
train up	And afayte thy faucones to kulle the wylde foules
damage	For they cometh to my croft my corn to diffoule.'
began	Courteisliche the knyhte thenne comesed thise wordes:
	'By my power, Peres, I plyhte the my treuthe
	To defende the in fayth, fyhte thogh I sholde.'
	'And yut a poynt,' quod Peres, 'I preye yow of more:
harm	Loke ye tene no tenaunt but treuthe wol assente
fine	And when ye mersyen eny man late mercy be taxour
in spite of all Meed's power	And mekenesse thy mayster, maugre Mede chekes.
	And thogh pore men profre yow presentes and gyftes
lest perchance	Nym hit nat an-auntur thow mowe hit nauht deserve,
pay dearly for	For thow shalt yelden hit so may be or sumdel abuggen hit.
Mistreat	Misbede nat thy bondeman, the bette may the spede;

Passus VIII

2 **half-aker**: the average area of one of the strips into which the open field was divided (see 114, below). Before the pilgrimage to Truth can begin (in fact, it never begins, though the theme of pilgrimage is taken up in the dreamer's search for Dowel), Peres must see to the ploughing of the half-acre (i.e. he must attend to the economic necessities and social obligations of life). Peres gives instructions to all classes as to how they are to participate, according to their station, in the work of the Christian community which is represented through the ploughing. The reference of the allegory is chiefly political, social and economic, though there is a spiritual dimension also, of course, in so far as any allegory of the well-ordered community will adumbrate both the well-ordered soul and also the kingdom of heaven.

24–31 The commons provide for the whole community (see Prol. 144n), but the other estates too are expected to play their part in the social covenant. Knights are to defend the realm, and to hunt (to keep down vermin, not for fun).

Thogh he be here thyn underlynge, in hevene parauntur
will be sooner He worth rather reseyved and reverentloker sitte.
Amice, ascende superius.
hard to recognize At churche in the charnel cherles aren evele to knowe
Or a knyhte fro a knave or a quene fram a queene.
Hit bicometh to the, knyhte, to be corteys and hende,
Treuwe of thy tonge and tales loth to here
Bute they be of bounte, of batayles or of treuthe.
Hoold nat with non harlotes ne here nat here tales,
Ac nameliche at the mete suche men eschewe
they are, popular reciters For hit beeth the develes dysors to drawe men to synne.
church's Ne countreplede nat Conscience ne holy kyrke ryhtes.'
'I assente, by seynt Gyle,' sayde the knyht thenne,
'For to worche by thy wit and my wyf bothe.'
clothe 'And I shal parayle me,' quod Perkyn, 'in pilgrimes wyse
And wende with alle tho that wolden lyve in treuthe.'
And caste on hym his clothes of alle kyn craftes,
leggings, mittens His cokeres and his coffes, as Kynde Wit hym tauhte,
sower's seed-basket, neck And heng his hopur on his halse instede of a scryppe;
A buschel of breed-corn brouht was ther-ynne.
'For I wol sowen hit mysulf and sethe wol I wende
To pilgrimages, as palmeres don, pardon to wynne.
My plouh-pote shal be my pyk-staff and pyche a-to the rotes
ploughshare And helpe my coltur to kerve and clanse the forwes
And alle that helpen me erye or elles to wedy
Shal haue leve by oure lord to go and glene aftur me
despite whoever grudges it And maken hym merye ther-myde, maugrey ho bigruchen hit.
And alle kyne crafty men that conne lyve in treuthe
faithfully I shal fynde hem fode that fayfulleche libbeth,
brothels Save Jacke the jogelour and Jonet of the stuywes
dice- And Danyel the dees-playere and Denote the baude
And frere faytour and folk of that ordre,
That lollares and loseles lele men holdeth,
filthy And Robyn the rybauder for his rousty wordes.
Treuthe telde me ones and bad me telle hit forthere:
Deleantur de libro vivencium, I sholde nat dele with hem,
commanded For holy chirche is hote of hem no tythe to aske,
Quia cum justis non scribantur.
(see n.) They ben ascaped good auntur, now God hem amende!'

{Peres makes his last will and testament and sets out now to be 'a pilgrim at the plough' (the ploughing having now completely absorbed the pilgrimage).}

Now is Perkyn and this pilgrimes to the plouh faren;
To erien this half-aker holpen hym monye.

44a 'Friend, go up higher' (Luke 14:10), from the parable of the marriage-feast, telling how humility will be rewarded in heaven.

58 Peres puts on the clothes and carries the equipment, not of the professional pilgrim (see VII.161), but of the hard-working Christian. The ploughing still seems to be a preliminary to the pilgrimage, but it is beginning to absorb it.

64 **plouh-pote**: the stick that the ploughman carried for cleaning the blade of the plough of accumulated earth and roots.

77 'Let them be blotted out of the book of the living' (Ps. 68:28).

78a 'Because they may not be enrolled among the righteous' (Ps. 68:28).

79 **good auntur**: 'by lucky chance' (or what seems one).

112–13 Peres act as the (manorial) lord's reeve or farm-manager in directing the work of the people.

(see n.) Dikares and delvares digged vp the balkes;
pleased Therwith was Perkyn apayed and payede wel hem here huyre.
eagerly Other werkemen ther were that wrouhten ful yerne,
Uch man in his manere made hymsulve to done
And somme to plese Perkyn a-feelde pykede wedes.
(9 a.m.) At hey prime Peres leet the plouh stande
And oversey hem hymsulve; ho-so beste wrouhte
He sholde be huyred theraftur when hervest tyme come.
And thenne seet somme and songen at the ale
And holpe erye this half-aker with 'hey trollilolly!'
anger Quod Peres the plouhman al in puyre tene:
hasten 'But ye aryse the rather and rape yow to worche
Shal no grayn that here groweth gladyen yow at nede,
sorrow, take him who cares And thogh ye deye for deul, the devel have that reche!'
Tho were faytours aferd and fayned hem blynde
(see n.) And leyde here legges alery as suche lorelles conneth
And maden here mone to Peres how thei may nat worche:
'And we praye for yow, Peres, and for youre plouh bothe
That God for his grace youre grayn multiplye
And yelde yow of youre almesse that ye yeven us here.
We may nother swynke ne swete, suche sekenes us ayleth,
Ne none lymes to labory with, lord God we thonketh.'
'Youre preyeres,' quod Peres, 'and ye parfyt weren,
Myhte helpe, as I hope, ac hey Treuthe wolde
deceit, a-begging That no faytrye were founde in folk that goth a-beggeth.
Ye been wastours, I wot wel, and waste and devouren
work to produce What lele land-tilynge men leely byswynken.
Ac Treuthe shal teche yow his teme to dryve
Or ye shal ete barly breed and of the broke drynke,
But yf he be blynde or broke-legged or bolted with yren –
share Suche poore,' quod Peres, 'shal parte with my godes,
Bothe of my corn and of my cloth to kepe hem fram defaute.
And ankeres and eremytes that eten but at nones
And freres that flateren nat and pore folke syke,
What! I and myn wolle fynde hem what hem nedeth.'
get angry Thenne gan Wastor to wrath hym and wolde have yfouhte
And to Peres the plouhman profrede to fyhte
ill-tempered And bad hym go pisse with his plogh, pyvische shrewe!
threatened boastfully A Bretener cam braggyng, he bostede Peres also:
'Wolle thow, nulle thow,' quod he, 'we wol have oure wille,
And thy flour and thy flesch feche whenne us liketh
whoever grumbles And maken us murye thermyde, maugreye ho begrucheth.'
Peres the plouhman tho pleynede hym to the knyhte
To kepe hym and his catel as covenant was bitwene hem:
Revenge, cause harm 'Awreke me of this wastors that maketh this world dere;
They acounteth nat of corsynges ne holy kyrke nat dredeth.
For ther worth no plente,' quod Peres, 'and the plouh lygge.'

114 'Ditchers and diggers dug up the strips of unploughed land'.
120–1 One of the suggestions of spiritual allegory in this passus (see above, 2n); those to be hired at harvest-time are those judged worthy of the kingdom of heaven (harvest is a frequent figure for the Last Judgement, e.g. Matt. 13:39).
129 **alery**: twisted backwards (as if cut off at the knee).
149 **Wastor** is a portrait of the itinerant labourers (see 330, below) who drifted into beggary and became associated with discharged soldiers (probably the Breton of 152 is a former mercenary) as vagabonds.

nature Courteisliche the knyhte thenne, as his kynde wolde,
advised Warnede Wastour and wissede hym betere:
'Or I shal bete the by the lawe and brynge the in stokkes.'
wont 'I was nat woned to worche,' quod Wastour, 'and now wol I nat bygynne!'
And leet lyhte of the lawe and lasse of the knyhte
at the value of a pea And sette Peres at a pes to playne hym whare he wolde.
punish 'Now by Crist,' quod Peres the plouhman, 'I shal apayre yow alle,'
And houped aftur Hunger that herde hym at the furste.
'I preye the,' quod Peres tho, 'pur charite, sire Hunger,
Awreke me of this wastors, for the knyhte wil nat.'
Hunger in haste tho hente Wastour by the mawe
And wronge hym so by the wombe that al watrede his yes.
He boffetede the Bretoner aboute the chekes
That he lokede lyke a lenterne al his lyf aftur,
And beet hem so bothe he barste ner her guttes
(see n.) Ne hadde Peres with a pese-loof preyede hym byleve.
'Have mercy on hem, Hunger,' quod Peres, 'and lat me yeve hem benes,
horse, remedy And that was bake for bayard hit may be here bote.'
flew Tho were faytours afered and flowen into Peres bernes
And flapten on with flales fro morwen til even,
fierce That Hunger was nat hardy on hem for to loke.
For a potte ful of potage that Peres wyf made
An heep of eremytes henten hem spades,
Dug Sputeden and spradden donge in dispit of Hunger.
cut up, short tunics They corven here copes and courtepies hem made
And wenten as werkemen to wedynge and to mowynge
Al for drede of here deth, such duntes yaf Hunger.
cured Blynde and broke-legged he botened a thousend
healed, lungs (offal) And lame men he lechede with longes of bestes.
Prestes and other peple towarde Peres they drowe
And freres of alle the fyve ordres, alle for fere of Hunger.
For that was bake for bayard was bote for many hungry,
Dregs Drosenes and dregges drynke for many beggares.
humbled There was no ladde that lyvede that ne lowede hym to Peres
faithful servant To be his holde hewe thogh he hadde no more
allowance (of food) But lyflode for his labour and his lone at nones.
Tho was Peres proude and putte hem alle a-werke
In daubynge and in delvynge, in donge afeld berynge,
thatching, whittling of pegs In threschynge, in thekynge, in thwytinge of pynnes,
In alle kyne trewe craft that man couthe devyse.
Was no beggare so bold, but yf he blynd were,
oppose That durste withsitte that Peres sayde for fere of syre Hunger.
And Peres was proud therof and putte hem alle to swynke
And yaf hem mete and money as thei myhte deserve.
Tho hadde Peres pitee uppon alle pore peple

168 Peres's role here is a little blurred; his action is dramatically vivid but not entirely logical. Clearly Famine, though Peres might welcome him as a means of coercing recalcitrant workers, does not come because Peres calls, but because the harvest has been bad, owing to the slackness of the workers; unless, indeed, the suggestion is that Peres, as manager of the economy, is administering a sharp dose of deflation. Hunger, as a form of coercion, is finally ineffective as an agent of reformation.

174 **lyke a lenterne**: '(hollow-cheeked) like a (horn) lantern'.

176 'Had not Piers with a pease-pudding (made from dried peas) begged him to leave off'.

191 The fifth order of friars (cf. Prol. 54) is the order of Crutched or Cruciferous friars.

	And bade Hunger in haste hye hym out of contraye
yard (land)	Hom to his owene yerd and halde hym there evere.
revenged upon	'I am wel awroke of wastours thorw thy myhte.
	Ac I preye the,' quod Peres, 'Hunger, ar thow wende,
	Of beggares and biddares what beste be to done?
	For I wot wel, be Hunger went, worche thei wol ful ille.
Hardship	Meschef hit maketh they ben so meke nouthe
want, commands	And for defaute this folk folweth myn hestes.
	Hit is nat for love, leve hit, thei labore thus faste
	But for fere of famyen, in fayth,' sayde Peres.
	'Ther is no filial love with this folk, for al here fayre speche;
blood-brothers (in Christ)	And hit are my blody bretherne, for God bouhte vs alle.
	Treuthe tauhte me ones to lovye hem uchone
	And to helpe hem of alle thynges ay as hem nedeth.
	Now wolde I wyte ar thow wendest what were the beste,
compel	How I myhte amayster hem to lovye and to labory
	For here lyflode, lere me now, sire Hunger.'
	'Now herkene,' quod Hunger, 'and holde hit for a wysdom.
work for	Bolde beggares and bygge that mowe here breed byswynke,
	With houndes bred and hors breed hele hem when thei hungren
(see n.)	And abave hem with benes for bollyng of here wombe;
	And yf the gromes gruche bide hem go and swynke
	And he shal soupe swetere when he hit hath deserved.
injured	Ac yf thow fynde eny folke that fals men han apayred
	Conforte hem with thy catel for so comaundeth Treuthe,
give to	Loue hem and lene hem, and so lawe of kynde wolde:
	Alter alterius onera portate.
	And alle manere men that thow myhte aspye
	In mischief or in mal-ese, and thow mowe hem helpe,
perish	Loke by thy lyve lat hem nat forfare.
make use of	Yf thow hast wonne auht wikkedliche, wiseliche despene hit.
	Facite vobis amicos de mammona iniquitatis.'
	'I wolde nat greve God,' quod Peres, 'for al the good on erthe!
	Myhte I synneles do as thow sayst?' sayde Peres the plouhman.
promise	'Ye, I bihote the,' quod Hunger, 'or elles the bible lyeth.
	Go to oure bygynnynge tho god the world made,
	As wyse men han wryten and as witnesseth Genesis,
sweat	That sayth with swynke and with swot and swetynge face
Till the ground for	Bytulye and bytravayle trewely oure lyflode:
	In sudore and labore vultus tui vesceris pane tuo.

210 A recurrent question in Langland, and one in which he echoes an acute contemporary preoccupation with the problem of beggars, and able-bodied beggars in particular. Hunger argues that Peres, as manager of the economy (i.e. the state), has a responsibility to ensure that no one should starve, though no responsibility to maintain life beyond the meanest level. But the problem for a Christian community was in the conflict between economic realism (and the texts recommending discrimination in charity) and the clear exhortation of the gospels: 'Give to all who ask' (Luke 6:30). Discrimination between the deserving and the undeserving poor became more difficult in the late fourteenth century, when the fluidity of labour created by the Black Death (see 149, above, and 330, below) made it difficult to disentangle the problems of relieving poverty and of suppressing vagrancy.

226 'And feed them with beans as a deterrent to prevent the swelling of their bellies (with malnutrition)'.

231a 'Bear one another's burdens (and so fulfil the law of Christ)' (Gal. 6:2).

235 This may not seem in accord with the doctrine of restitution (VI.234n), but canon law accepted that illicitly acquired wealth could be used for charitable purposes and for paying tithes provided that there was no injured party to claim restitution.

235a 'Make friends for yourselves of the mammon of unrighteousness' (Luke 16:9), i.e. use ill-gotten wealth for good ends, and so benefit spiritually.

242a 'In labour and the sweat of your brow you shall eat your bread' (Gen. 3:19).

And Salomon the sage with the same acordeth:
The slowe caytif for colde he wolde no corn tylye; — *sluggard*
In somer for his sleuthe he shal have defaute
And go a-bribeth and a-beggeth and no man beten his hunger. — *relieve*
Piger propter frigus noluit arare; mendicabit in yeme et non dabitur ei.
Mathew maketh mencioun of a man that lente
His sulver to thre maner men and menyng they sholden
Chaffare and cheue therwith in chele and in hete, — *Trade, prosper, cold*
And that best labored best was alloued — *commended*
And ledares for here laboryng over al the lordes godes.
Ac he that was a wreche and wolde nat travaile
The lord for his lachesse and his luther sleuthe — *idleness*
Bynom hym al that he hadde and yaf hit to his felawe — *Took from*
That leely hadde ylabored, and thenne the lord sayde:
"He that hath shal have and helpe ther hym liketh — *(have) help*
And he that nauht hath shal nauht have and no man yut helpen hym
And that he weneth wel to have I wol hit hym bireve." — *take away from*
And lo, what the sauter sayth to swynkares with handes: — *psalter*
"Yblessed be al tho that here bylyve biswynketh — *living*
Thorw eny lele labour as thorw lymes and handes."
Labores manuum tuarum quia manducabis.
This aren evidences,' quod Hunger, 'for hem that wolle nat swynke
That here lyflode be lene and lyte worth here clothes.' — *little*
'By Crist,' quod Peres the plouhman tho, 'this proverbis I wol shewe
To beggares and to boys that loth ben to worche.
Ac yut I praye yow,' quod Peres, 'pur charite, syre Hunger,
Yf ye can or knowe eny kyne thynges of fisyk, — *kind of*
For somme of my servauntes and mysulf bothe
Of al a woke worche nat, so oure wombe greveth us.' — *For a whole week*
'I wot wel,' quod Hunger, 'what sekenesse yow ayleth.
Ye han manged over-moche – that maketh yow to be syke. — *eaten*
Ac ete nat, I hote, ar hunger the take
And sende the of his sauce to savery with thy lyppes. — *give a savour to*
And kepe som til soper tyme and site nat to longe
At noon ne at no tyme, and nameliche at the sopere
Lat nat sire Sorfeet sittien at thy borde,
And loke thou drynke no day ar thow dyne sumwhat.
And thenk that Dives for his delicat lyf to the devel wente
And Lazar the lene beggare that longede after croumes — *crumbs*
And yut hadde he hem nat, for I, Hunger, culde hym, — *killed*
And sethen I say hym sitte as he a syre were
In al manere ese and in Abrahames lappe.

246a 'Because of the cold the sluggard would not plough; he shall beg in the winter and it shall not be given to him' (Prov. 20:4). The Vulgate (canonical Latin translation of the Bible) reads *aestate*, 'summer', for *yeme* (i.e. *hieme*); this is the reading alluded to above (245) and of course the correct one in the context (no winter ploughing, no summer harvest). The reading *hieme* arises by sympathetic association of winter and deprivation.

247 The parable of the talents (Matt. 25:14–30).

261a 'You shall eat the labour of your hands' (Ps. 127:2).

268 **and mysulf bothe**. For Peres to include himself as a victim of over-eating is at first puzzling. Allegorically, it confirms the suggestion that Peres, for all his competence as a spiritual guide, has the flaws of common humanity, at least at this point.

278 The parable of the rich man (**Dives**) and Lazarus is told in Luke 16:19–31.

282 **in Abrahames lappe**, i.e. in Limbo with prospects of heaven, under the protection of Abraham, to whom, with all who showed faith (Gen. 15:6), God promised the inheritance of the kingdom of heaven.

power	And yif thow have pouer, Peres, I the rede,
cry out	Alle that grat in thy gate for Godes love aftur fode,
bread, things to go with bread	Part with hem of thy payne, of potage or of sowl,
Give	Lene hem som of thy lof thouh thow the lasse chewe.
latch-pickers (sneak-thieves)	And thouh lyares and lach-draweres and lollares knocke,
table be put away	Lat hem abyde til the bord be drawe ac bere hem none croumes
midday repast	Til alle thyne nedy neyhbores have none ymaked.
wager	And yf thow dyete the thus I dar legge myn eres
	That Fysik shal his forred hodes for his fode sulle
(see n.)	And his cloke of Callabre for his comune legge
	And be fayn, be my fayth, his fysik to leete
	And lerne to labory with lond lest lyflode hem fayle.
	Ther ar many luther leches ac lele leches fewe;
	They don men deye thorw here drynkes ar destyne hit wolde.'
	'By seynte Poul,' quod Peres, 'thow poyntest neyh the treuthe
repay	And leelyche sayst, as I leve, lord hit the foryeld!
	Wende nouthe when thow wold and wel thow be evere
	For thow hast wel awroke me and also wel ytauhte me.'
	'I behote the,' quod Hunger, 'that hennes ne wol I wende
	Ar I have ydyned be this day and ydronke bothe.'
pullets, buy	'I have no peny,' quod Peres, 'polettes for to begge,
little pigs	Ne nother goos ne gries but two grene cheses
curds	And a fewe croddes and craym and a cake of otes
children	And bred for my barnes of benes and of peses
	And yut I say, be my soule, I have no salt bacoun
(see n.)	Ne no cokeney, be Crist, colloppes to make.
little onions, scallions	Ac I have poret-plontes, parsilie and skalones,
small onions, chervils, half-red	Chibolles and chirvulles and cheries sam-rede,
	And a cow with a calf and a cart-mare
	To drawe afeld my donge the while the drouhte lasteth.
(1st August)	And by this lyflode we mote lyve til Lamasse-tyme
	And by that I hope to have hervest in my croftes;
	Thenne may I dyhte my dyner as me dere lyketh.'
fetched	Alle the pore peple tho pese-coddes fette;
	Benes and bake aples they brouhten in here lappe,
	And profrede Pers this present to plese with Honger.
	Hunger eet al in haste and askede aftur more.
	Pore folk for fere tho fedde Honger yerne
	With craym and with croddes, with cresses and othere erbes.
market	By that hit nyhed neyh hervest and newe corn cam to chepyng
dainteously	And thenne were folke fayn and fedde Hunger dentiesliche,
made	And thenne Gloton with gode ale garte Hunger slepe.
	And tho wolde Wastor nat worche bote wandren aboute,
	Ne no beggare eten bred that benes ynne were,
(see n.)	Bote of cler-matyn and coket and of clene whete,
	Ne noon halpenny ale in none wyse drynke
	Bote of the beste and of the brouneste that brewestares sullen.

292 'And pledge his cloak of Calabrian fur for his commons (food)'.
301–2 Hunger is the personification of real economic necessity as well as a temporary economic advisor. Here he must be fed on left-overs and the plainest seasonal foods during the difficult months before the harvest is in.
308 **cokeney**: little egg (lit. 'cock's egg'). **colloppes**: egg dishes.
327 'But only (bread) made of different kinds of white flour and of pure wheat'.

Laborers that han no lond to lyve on but here handes
Deynede noght to dyne a-day of nyhte-olde wortes;
please May no peny-ale hem pay ne no pece of bacoun
But hit be fresh flesch or fisch, yfried or ybake,
And that *chaut* or *pluchaut* for chillyng of his mawe.
at a high rate And but yf he be heyliche yhuyred elles wol he chyde
made to be, bewail And that he was werkeman ywrouhte warien the tyme.
begins Ayenes Catones consayle comseth he to gruche:
Paupertatis onus pacienter ferre memento.
And thenne he corseth the kyng and alle the kynges justices,
give instruction for Suche lawes to lerne, laboreres to greve.
Ac whiles Hunger was here maister ther wolde non chyde,
Ne stryve ayeynes his statuyt, he lokede so sturne.
  Ac I warne yow werkmen, wynneth whiles ye mowe,
For Hunger hiderwardes hasteth hym faste.
flood, chastise He shal awake thorw water, wastors to chaste,
And ar fewe yeres be fulfeld famyne shal aryse,
And so sayth Saturne and sente us to warne.
Thorw flodes and thorw foule wederes fruytes shollen fayle;
fetch away (kill) Pruyde and pestilences shal moche peple feche.
Thre shypes and a schef with an viii folwynge
(see n.) Shal brynge bane and batayle on bothe half the mone.
the plague And thenne shal deth withdrawe and derthe be justice
Davy the digger And Dawe the delvare dey for defaute
But yf God of his goodnesse graunte us a trewe.

Passus IX.1–186, 282–98: The Pardon sent from Truth

Treuthe herde telle her-of and to Peres sent
plough-team To taken his teme and tilien the erthe,
(see n.) And purchasede hym a pardoun *a pena et a culpa*,
heirs For hym and his ayres for evere to ben assoiled,
fallow-lands And bad hym holden hym at hom and eryen his leyes
And all that holpe hym to erye, to sette or to sowe
job Or eny maner mester that myhte Peres avayle,
Pardoun with Peres the plouhman perpetuelly he graunteth.
  Kynges and knyhtes that holy kyrke defenden
And ryhtfulliche in reumes ruylen the comune

330 The Black Death of 1349 created a labour shortage, and many bondmen and tied labourers left their villages to work as wage-labourers, often travelling about the country to get higher wages. The government introduced Statutes of Labourers in 1361 and succeeding years, in an attempt to freeze wages and inhibit the movement of labour, but the attempt was by no means uniformly successful, and the tension created by this move was a general cause of the Peasants' Revolt of 1381.

331–3 In an attempt to circumvent the provisions of the Statutes of Labourers concerning wages, employers often resorted to concealed payments in the form of meals.

334 ***chaut, pluchaut***, i.e. *chaud, plus chaud*, 'warm', 'warmer', words from French cooking parlance used here contemptuously (like ***manged*** in 271).

338 'Remember to bear patiently the burden of poverty' (*Distichs of Cato*, 1.21)

343–54 This prophecy, warning of the disasters that will happen unless God intervenes, has Langland's characteristic sense of apocalyptic urgency.

347 Saturn is the most malignant and powerful of all planetary influences.

350 There is presumably a cryptic date-reference here, such as is often found in this genre of vaguely menacing popular prophecy.

351 'Shall bring destruction and conflict in all parts of the world'.

Passus IX

1 **Treuthe** is God and God's law.

3 ***a pena et a culpa***: 'from the punishment and guilt (of sin)'.

5 **holden hym at hom**. The pilgrimage has been abandoned: most folk must do the world's work and receive the conditional promise of salvation (only Contemplation, it will be remembered, welcomed the pilgrimage in the first place, VII.305). Hence, perhaps, Peres's impatience with the pardon (291, below), and the beginning of a new search, a new 'pilgrimage'.

Han pardon thorw purgatorye to passe ful lyhtly,
With patriarkes and prophetes in paradis to sitten.
  Bishopis yblessed, yf they ben as they sholde, [*consecrated*]
Lele and ful of love and no lord drede,
Merciable to meke and mylde to the gode
And bitynge in badde men but yf they wol amende,
Drede nat for no deth to distruye by here power
Lechery amonges lordes and here luyther custumes,
And suche live as thei lereth men, oure lord Treuthe hem graunteth [*If*]
To be peres to the apostles, alle peple to reule [*equals*]
And deme with hem at domesday bothe quyke and dede.
  Marchauntes in the margine hadde many yeres,
Ac no *pena et a culpa* no Treuthe wolde hem graunte
For they holde nat here haliday as holi chirch hem hoteth,
And for they swere by here soule and God mote hem helpe [*(oaths, in indirect speech)*]
Ayen clene conscience for covetyse of wynnynge.
Ac under his secrete seal Treuthe sent hem a lettre
That bad hem bugge boldly what hem best likede [*buy*]
And sethe sullen hit ayeyn and save the wynnynges,
Amende meson-dewes therwith and myseyse men fynde [*(see n.)*]
And wyckede wayes with here god amende [*bad highways*]
And brugges to-brokene by the heye wayes
Amende in som manere wyse and maydenes helpe,
Pore peple bedredene and prisones in stokkes [*bedridden, prisoners*]
Fynde hem for Godes love, and fauntkynes to scole, [*children*]
Releve religion and renten hem bettere: [*(see n.)*]
'And I shal sende yow mysulve seynt Mihel myn angel
That no devel shal yow dere ne despeyre in youre deynge
And sethe sende youre soules ther I mysulve dwelle
And abyde ther in my blisse, body and soule for evere.'
Tho were marchauntes mury; many wopen for joye
And preyde for Peres the plouhman that purchased hem this bulles.
  Alle the peple hadde pardon ynow that parfitliche lyvede. [*plentiful*]
Men of lawe hadde lest that loth were to plede [*(see n.)*]
But they *pre manibus* were payed for pledynge at the barre. [*in hand (in advance)*]
Ac he that speneth his speche and speketh for the pore [*gives freely*]
That innocent and nedy is and no man harm wolde,
That conforteth suche in eny cas and coveyteth nat here yiftes
And for the love of oure lord lawe for hem declareth
Shal have grace of a good ende and greet joye aftur.
Beth ywar, ye wis men and witty of the lawe,
For whenne ye drawe to the deth and indulgences wolde have
His pardoun is ful petyt at his partynge hennes
That mede of mene men for here motynge taken. [*poor, pleading at law*]
For hit is symonye to sulle that sent is of grace,

22 **in the margine**, i.e. in the form of a marginal addendum in a legal document, presumably because merchants are not a separate estate of society. **many yeres**, i.e. of remission of punishment in purgatory (as in 11, above).

27 **under his secrete seal**. The personal or privy seal of a pope or king was used on documents not intended for public distribution. The church privately recognizes the propriety of trade so long as the profits are devoted to good causes and works of charity, but cannot openly sanction trade as such.

30 'Improve religious hospitals (*maisons de dieu*) therewith and provide for people in distress'.

36 'Assist members of religious orders and endow them better'.

37 **seynt Mihel**. St Michael was present at the moment of death to take the soul, if it were so decreed, from the grasp of devils who gathered to terrify the dying man and tempt him to despair of salvation.

44 'Lawyers had fewest years' remission that were reluctant to plead at the bar'.

And that is wit and water and wynde and fuyre the ferthe;
Thise foure sholde be fre to alle folk that hit nedede.
  Alle libbyng laborers that lyven with here handes
Lellyche and lauhfullyche, oure lord Treuthe hem graunteth
Pardoun perpetuel, riht as Peres the plouhman.
  Beggares and biddares beth nat in that bulle
Bote the sugestioun be sothe that shapeth hym to begge.
For he that beggeth or biddeth, but yf they have nede,
He is fals and faytour and defraudeth the nedy
And also gileth hym that gyveth and taketh agayne his wille.
willingly — For he that gyveth for Goddes love wolde nat gyve, his thankes,
Bote ther he wiste were wel grete nede
And most merytorie to men that he yeveth fore.
Catoun acordeth therwith: *Cui des, videto.*
  Wot no man, as I wene, who is worthy to have;
if we take — Ac that most neden aren oure neyhebores, and we nyme gode hede,
prisoners, dungeons, hovels — As prisones in puttes and pore folk in cotes,
landlords' — Charged with childrene and chief lordes rente;
What, put aside — That they with spynnyng may spare, spenen hit on hous-huyre,
gruels — Bothe in mylke and in mele, to make with papelotes
(see n.) — To aglotye with here gurles that greden aftur fode.
And hemsulve also soffre muche hunger,
And wo in wynter-tymes, and wakynge on nyhtes
space between beds — To rise to the reule to rokke the cradel,
comb (wool), patch (clothes) — Bothe to carde and to kembe, to cloute and to wasche,
And to rybbe and to rele, rusches to pylie,
That reuthe is to rede or in ryme shewe
The wo of this wommen that wonyeth in cotes;
And of monye other men that moche wo soffren,
(see n.) — Bothe afyngred and afurste, to turne the fayre outward,
(it) be known — And ben abasched for to begge and wollen nat be aknowe
What hym nedede at here neyhebores at noon and at eve.
  This I wot witterly, as the world techeth.
to others is needful — What other byhoveth that hath many childrene
And hath no catel but his craft to clothe hym and to fede,
many (children) to grasp — And fele to fonge ther-to and fewe panes taketh.
bread, special treat — There is payne and peny-ale as for a pytaunce ytake,
like roast venison — And colde flesche and fische as venisoun were bake.
mussels — Fridays and fastyng-days a ferthing-worth of moskeles
cockles — Were a feste with suche folk, or so fele cockes.
(true) alms — These are almesse, to helpe that han suche charges
hovel-dwellers, crippled — And to conforte such coterelles and crokede men and blynde.

56 **wit** (intellectual ability) is added to the elements as a gift (possessed by lawyers) that should be freely available to all.

61 Having dealt with the estates within society, Langland turns now to beggars and to a prolonged meditation upon the opposed injunctions of Cato (69, below) and the gospels (VIII.210n) in relation to almsgiving. Having spoken earlier of a discriminating charity (VIII.210, 288), he now makes it clear that charity must positively seek out the truly needy in order to fulfil the promise that God will provide whilst accepting the ban on beggary (162, below).

69 'Consider to whom you should give' (*Distichs of Cato*, sent. 17).

73–83 Poor widows left to bring up a family by themselves are members of the traditional 'deserving poor' who have fallen into poverty by mischance; Langland gives to their lives a grinding authenticity, but he does not see them as part of a chronically poor and underemployed urban class such as was coming into being in the London of his time.

76 'To fill the stomachs of their children that cry out for food'.

81 **rybbe**: scrape flax with a flat iron tool, to remove particles of core. **rele**: wind yarn onto a reel. **pylie**: peel rushes, so as to make rushlights from the pith. These are the most menial and poorly paid jobs, done part-time by people working at home on a piece-work basis.

85 'Both hungry and thirsty, to keep up a respectable outward appearance'.

(for whom) Ac beggares with bagges, the whiche brewhous ben here churches,
maimed But they be blynde or to-broke or elles be syke,
fall dead Thouh he falle for defaute that fayteth for his lyflode,
Reche ye nevere, ye riche, thouh suche lollares sterve.
health For alle that han here hele and here ye-syhte
And lymes to labory with, and lollares lyf usen,
Lyven ayen Goddes lawe and the lore of holi churche.
And yut ar ther othere beggares, in hele, as hit semeth,
Ac hem wanteth wyt, men and women bothe,
The whiche aren lunatyk lollares and lepares aboute,
(see n.) And madden as the mone sit, more other lasse.
Careth they for no colde ne counteth of non hete
And aren mevynge aftur the mone; moneyeles they walke,
With a good will, witteles, mony wyde contreyes,
Riht as Peter dede and Poul, save that they preche nat
Ne none muracles maken – ac many tymes hem happeth
To profecye of the peple, pleyinge, as hit were.
And to oure syhte, as hit semeth, seth God hath the myhte
To yeve uch a wyht wyt, welthe, and his hele,
And suffreth suche go so, it semeth, to myn inwyt,
Hit aren as his postles, suche peple, or as his prive disciples.
sends For he sent hem forth selverles in a somur garnement
Withoute bagge and bred, as the book telleth:
Quando misi vos sine pane et pera.
Barfoot and bredles, beggeth they of no man.
And thauh he mete with the mayre ameddes the strete,
no one He reverenseth hym ryht nauht, no rather then another.
Neminem salutaveritis per viam.
Suche manere men, Matheu us techeth,
We sholde have hem to house and helpe hem when they come.
Et egenos vagosque induc in domum tuam.
For hit aren merye-mouthed men, munstrals of hevene,
jesters And Godes boys, bourdyors, as the book telleth.
Si quis videtur sapiens, fiet stultus ut sit sapiens.
And alle manere munstrals, me wot wel the sothe,
receive, is appropriate To underfongen hem fayre byfalleth for the ryche,
belong For the lordes love or the ladyes that they with longen.
good humour Me suffreth al that suche sayen and in solace taketh,
And yut more to suche men me doth ar they passe:
Men gyveth hem giftes and gold for grete lordes sake.
Ryht so, ye ryche, yut rather ye sholde

98 **beggares with bagges**, as opposed to true beggars, who beg only for their daily needs (see V.52). **the whiche ... here**: 'whose'.
105 Langland introduces here a consideration of beggars who are able-bodied but feeble-minded. Since they are God's creatures they must be serving God's purposes (115): they are, in fact, his secret apostles (118), capable of uttering hidden wisdom in their foolishness (114). Langland draws on a number of biblical texts here, particularly Christ's exhortation of his disciples to a divine 'carelessness' of worldly considerations (Luke 9:1–5, 10:1–12) such as is characteristic of the 'lunatyk lollares'; and Paul's assertion that men of Christ must be fools to the world ('We are fools for Christ's sake', 1 Cor. 4:10).
108 'Grow mad according to the phases of the moon, more or less'.
120a 'When I sent you forth without bread or bag' (cf. Luke 22:35, alluding to Luke 9:3).
122–3 A characteristic piece of behaviour that Langland associates with himself in B.XV.5. Like other classes of society with which Langland shows a particular preoccupation – minstrels, hermits, beggars – the **lunatyk lollares** contain features of self-portraiture.
123a 'Salute no one on the road' (Luke 10:4).
125a 'And bring the homeless and the poor into your house' (Isa. 58:7). The reference to Matthew is generally to 25:31–46.
127a 'If anyone thinks that he is wise, let him become a fool that he may be wise' (1 Cor. 3:18).

Welcomen and worschipen and with youre gode helpen
Godes munstrals and his mesagers and his mery bordiours,
The whiche arn lunatyk loreles and lepares aboute,
hidden For vnder Godes secret seal here synnes ben kevered.
For they bereth none bagges ne boteles under clokes,
lollars' The whiche is lollarne lyf and lewede ermytes,
(see n.) That loken louhliche to lache men almesse,
In hope to sitte at even by the hote coles,
Unlouke his legges abrood or ligge at his ese,
back Reste hym and roste him and his rug turne,
dry (the pot) Drynke druie and depe and drawe hym thenne to bedde,
pleasure And whenne hym lyketh and luste, his leve is to ryse,
And when he is rysen, rometh out and right wel aspyeth
round Where he may rathest have a repast or a ronde of bacoun,
Sulver or sode mete and sum tyme bothe,
Lof other half-lof other a lompe of chese;
plans And caryeth hit hom to his cote and cast hym to lyvene
In idelnesse and in ese and by otheres travayle.
wanders And what freke on this folde fisketh aboute
in the manner of a beggar With a bagge at his bak a begyneld wyse,
in the event that he wanted to And can eny craft in cas he wolde hit use,
Thorw which craft he couthe come to bred and to ale
garment, cover And over-more to an hater to hele with his bonis,
And lyveth lyke a lollare, Goddes lawe hym dampneth.
tramps 'Forthy lollares that lyven in sleuthe and over-land strikares
Beth nat in this bulle,' quod Peres, 'til they ben amended,
Ne no beggare that beggeth, but yf they have nede.'
The bok banneth beggarie and blameth hit in this manere:
Junior fui, etenim senui. Et alibi: Infirmata est virtus mea in paupertate.
now Hit nedeth nat nouthe anoon for to preche
And lere this lewede men what this Latyn meneth,
For hit blameth all beggarie, be ye ful certayn.
For they lyve in no love, ne no lawe holden,
Ne weddeth none wymmen that they with deleth;
by nature Bringeth forth bastardes, beggares of kynde,
Or the bak or som bon they breke of here children
infants And gon and fayten with here fauntes for everemore aftur.
Ther aren mo mysshape amonges suche beggares
Then of many othere men that on this molde walken.
believe And tho that lyveth thus here lyf, leve ye non other,
Thai have no part of pardoun, ne of preyeres ne of penaunces.
grey-haired Ac olde and hore, that helples ben and nedy,
And wymmen with childe that worche ne mowe,
Blynde and bedredne and broken in here membres,

136 **mesagers**, like minstrels and **bourdyors** (127), had a bad reputation, but Langland is here engaged in establishing a vocabulary of spiritual paradox on the model of Paul's 'fools' (105n, above).
138 They have a special dispensation from God for their sins.
141 'That put on an appearance of humility in order to get men's alms'.
159 This brief intervention of Peres as interpreter is appropriate enough to him, but not easily reconcilable with the authorial exposition of the whole of the rest of the pardon, and with the suggestion (283, below) that Peres cannot read the Latin document.
162a 'I have been young, and now am old (and I have not seen the righteous forsaken nor his children begging bread)' (Ps. 36:25). And elsewhere: 'My strength is weakened through poverty' (Ps. 30:11). The latter text refers to 'beggary' rather than 'begging' and seems equivocal in this context.

(see n.) And alle pore pacient, apayed of Goddes sonde,
lepers As mesels and mendenantes, men yfalle in meschief,
As prisones and pilgrimes and parauntur men yrobbed
slandered Or bylowe thorw luther men and lost here catel after,
Or thorw fuyr or thorw flod yfalle into poverte,
That taketh thise meschiefes mekeliche and myldeliche at herte,
For love of here lowe hertes oure lord hath hem ygraunted
Here penaunce and here purgatorye uppon this puyre erthe
And pardon with the plouhman *a pena et a culpa*.

{The exposition of the terms of the pardon concludes with some remarks on false hermits and the laxity of bishops in disciplining them.}

'Peres,' quod a prest tho, 'thy pardon moste I rede,
For I can construe uch a word and kennen hit the an Englische.'
And Peres at his preyre the pardon unfoldeth
And I byhynde hem bothe byheld alle the bulle
In two lynes as hit lay and nat a lettre more,
And was ywryte ryhte thus in witnesse of Treuthe:
Qui bona egerunt ibunt in vitam eternam;
Qui vero mala in ignem eternum.
'Peter!' quod the prest tho, 'I kan no pardoun fynde,
behave well Bote "Dowel and have wel and God shal have thy soule
And do yvele and have evele and hope thow non othere
Bote he that evele lyveth evele shal ende."'
argued The prest thus and Perkyn of the pardon jangelede
looked And I thorw here wordes awoke and waytede aboute
And seyh the sonne in the southe sitte that tyme.
Meteles and moneyles on Malverne hulles
dream Musyng on this meteles a myle way I yede.

{In his musing, Will debates the value of pardons and indulgences, and concludes that, though they are not valueless, they are of far less importance than 'doing well', whatever that is.}

178 'All patient poor people who are content with what God sends'.
185 The idea that poverty and other mischiefs, patiently borne, are a form of earthly purgatory is a consoling thought for the poet meditating on the oppressions of poverty and the horrors of beggary. It provides a spiritual solution to a social and economic problem.
283 The suggestion is that Peres does not understand the Latin of the document. On the other hand, he clearly understands the spirit and purpose of the document – what Truth intends. Thus the conflict between the priest and Peres might well be seen to dramatize a contrast between the literal and the spiritual. Peres's impatience is with 'the letter that killeth' (2 Cor. 3:6).
288–9 'They that have done good shall go into life everlasting; and they that have done evil into everlasting fire' (from the Athanasian Creed).
290–3 The priest is right in recognizing that it is not a 'pardon' in the usual sense. On the other hand, he fails to realize that the promise of redemption which makes the first clause (*Qui bona*) possible, is itself a form of pardon, that which was bought on Calvary. Peres, however, had expected rather more of the pardon than it contained. He seems to have interpreted the promise of redemption as if it were the gift of redemption, as if, like a papal or royal pardon, it constituted in itself the act of forgiveness. (A famous episode in B, where Peres tears the pardon in anger and frustration, is omitted in C, probably because the scenario, though highly dramatic, is not logical: Peres, the servant of Truth, cannot tear Truth's pardon.) Peres, anyway, retires from active contact with the community, and the dreamer is left to wonder on his dreams, and to make sense of the pardon by beginning his search for the whole truth of *dowel*. This he will find in the refounding and reforming of the inner life of the individual, rather than of society as in the *Visio*. But this process of reform is not detached from the real world in which the individual must live. There is never that concentration on the inner life of contemplation which we find in the writings of the mystics.

Passus X.1–29
The Beginning of the Search for Dowel

Thus yrobed in russet I romede aboute
Alle a somur seson for to seke Dowel,
asked And fraynede ful ofte of folke that I mette
was dwelling Yf eny wiht wiste where Dowel was at ynne,
And what man he myhte be of mony men I askede.
Was nevere wihte in this worlde that me wisse couthe
man dwelt Where this leode longed, lasse ne more,
Til hit biful on a Fryday two freres I mette,
Friars Minors (i.e. Franciscans) Maystres of the Menores, men of gret witte.
greeted, courteously I haylsede hem hendly, as I hadde ylered,
And preyde hem, pur charite, ar they passede forthere
districts Yf they knewe eny contre other costes aboute
Wher that Dowel dwelleth, 'Dere frendes, telleth me,
world For ye ar men of this molde that moste wyde walken
And knowen contrees and courtes and many kynne plases,
poor men's cottages Bothe princes paleis and pore menne cotes,
And Dowel and Do-evele, where thei dwellen both.'
'Sothly,' saide the frere, 'he sojourneth with us freres
as I think And evere hath, as I hope, and evere wol hereaftur.'
began '*Contra*,' quod I as a clerk, and comsed to despute,
And saide sothly, '*Septies in die cadit justus*,
Fallyng fro joye, Jesu wot the sothe!
times, sins "Sevene sithe," sayth the bok, "synegeth day by day
man, (lives confidently) The rihtfulleste reng that regneth in erthe."
And ho-so synegeth,' I sayde, 'certes, he doth nat wel;
For ho-so synegeth, sikerly doth evele,
And Dowel and Do-evele may nat dwelle togyderes.
Ergo, he is nat alwey at hom amonges yow freres;
He is other-while elles-wher to wisse the peple.'

{Thus unpromisingly begins Will's search for Dowel, for the means to the inward reform of the individual. The quest takes the form first of all of a series of interviews with his own intellectual faculties (Thought, Wit) and then with personifications of learning (Study, Clergy, Scripture) who all give good but partial and somewhat incompatible explanations of the meaning of Dowel (and Dobet and Dobest). The dreamer falls into despair and a stupor of worldliness from which he is rescued by Imaginatyf (representing a more-than-intellectual capacity for understanding), who answers all his anxious questions about the role of learning in winning salvation by assuring him that he has been asking the wrong questions. The way to Dowel is through the preparation of the self, through humility and patience and voluntary submission to the will of God, for the advent of Charity. Patience and Liberum Arbitrium *(Free Will) are the guides on this new quest for the meaning of Charity, and the dreamer learns how man's growth towards Charity is thwarted by the devil's work. An act of divine grace is needed, in history and in the soul of man, and a New Law of mercy and truth. After many anticipations and prefigurations (in Piers Plowman and in the parable figure of the Good Samaritan) the stage is thus set for Christ's entry into the poem; the great drama of Redemption is at hand.}*

Passus X

1–2 Langland echoes the opening of the poem, thus preparing us for a pattern of meaning in the *Vita* whereby the events of the *Visio* are revisited at a deeper level of meaning. This, now, is not an aimless wandering, but a journey with a purpose.

20 ***Contra***: 'against', i.e. 'I dispute that', a term used in scholastic debate. The dreamer's presumption in arguing 'as a clerk' does not augur well for his humble readiness to receive spiritual illumination, though the friar's remark is admittedly provoking.

21 'The righteous man falls seven times a day (and rises again)' (Prov. 24:16). Will would have done well to look at the immediate context of his biblical quotation, instead of being so pleased with his clever pun ('Fallyng').

28 ***Ergo***, 'therefore', another technical term from scholastic disputation.

Passus XX.1–124, 269–476 (end): The Crucifixion and the Harrowing of Hell

	Wolleward and wetschod wente I forth aftur
uncaring, takes no heed	As a recheles renk that recheth nat of sorwe,
	And yede forth ylike a lorel al my lyf-tyme
desired again	Til I waxe wery of the world and wilnede efte to slepe
took it easy until lent	And lened me to lenten and long tyme I slepte.
	Of gurles and of *gloria laus* greetliche me dremede
	And how *osanna* by orgene olde folke songe.
	Oon semblable to the Samaritan and somdeel to Pers the plouhman
without boots, riding	Barfot on an asse bake botles cam prikynge
eager and lively	Withouten spores other spere – sprakeliche he lokede,
	As is the kynde of a knyhte that cometh to be dubbed,
gilt, knight's cut-away shoes	To geten here gult spores and galoches ycouped.
window	And thenne was Faith in a fenestre and criede 'A, *filii David*!'
adventurous knights	As doth an heraud of armes when auntrous cometh to joustes.
	Olde Jewes of Jerusalem for joye they songen,
	Benedictus qui venit in nomine domini.
asked of, goings-on signified	Thenne I afraynede at Fayth what al that fare bymente,
	And ho sholde jouste in Jerusalem? 'Jesus', he saide,
	And feche that the fende claymeth, Pers fruyt the plouhman.'
gave me a meaningful look	'Is Peres in this place?' quod I, and he prente on me:
'The free will of God'	'*Liberum-dei-arbitrium* for love hath undertake
in accordance with his noble birth	That this Jesus of his gentrice shal jouste in Pers armes,
coat of mail	In his helm and in his haberjon, *humana natura*,
recognized	That Crist be nat yknowe for *consummatus deus*;
pieces of plate armour, horseman	In Pers plates the plouhman this prikiare shal ryde,
blow, injure	For no dount shal hym dere as *in deitate patris*.'
	'Who shal jouste with Jesus,' quod I, 'Jewes, or scribz?'
only the devil	'Nay,' quod Faith, 'bote the fende, and Fals-dom-to-deye.
destroy	Deth saith he wol fordo and adown brynge
on land	Alle that lyveth or loketh, a londe or a watre.
as a pledge	Lyf saith he lyeth and hath leide his lyf to wedde,
	That for al that Deth can do, withynne thre dayes to walke
	And feche fro the fende Peres fruyt the plouhman,
	And legge hit ther hym liketh and Lucifer bynde

Passus XX

1 'Wearing a garment of rough wool next to the skin (as a form of penance) and with shoes full of water'.

6 ***gloria laus***, 'glory, praise', the chorus of the processional hymn on Palm Sunday, sung here by **gurles** ('children', in allusion to Matt. 21:15), as if welcoming Christ as king and redeemer to Jerusalem. Much of the opening of this passus is inspired by the liturgy for Holy Week.

7 ***osanna***: 'Hosanna', lit. 'Be our saviour, we pray', shouted by the faithful as Christ entered Jerusalem **on an asse bake** (Matt. 21:9) and sung repeatedly in the antiphons on Palm Sunday. **by orgene**: not 'to the organ' but 'in *organum*' ('in concert').

11 **a knyhte**. Jesus's combat with the devil was often imaged as a joust, to which Jesus comes as a newly dubbed knight.

13 It is apt that **Faith**, the true adherent of the Old Law (traditionally represented by Abraham), should welcome Jesus with the title of his royal Jewish inheritance (cf. Matt. 21:9).

15a 'Blessed is he who comes in the name of the lord' (Matt. 21:9), repeated in the antiphons for Palm Sunday.

18 **Pers fruyt the plouhman**: 'the fruit of Piers the Plowman', i.e. the apples of the Tree of Charity (Passus XVIII), which was in the care of Piers.

21 **in Pers armes**: 'in the coat-armour of Piers', i.e. the flesh (of ***humana natura***). Piers is momentarily seen as God incarnate, in his manhood. To say that Piers 'is' Christ would do scant justice to this subtle and creative handling of the mystery of the Incarnation.

23 ***consummatus deus***: 'supreme god'. There is an allusion here to the doctrine of the impassibility of the godhead, i.e. the insusceptibility to injury or suffering of God in his divine nature – which was why he had to become man.

25 ***in deitate patris***: 'in his divine nature as the father'.

27 **Fals-dom-to-deye**: 'the false judgement of death upon mankind'. The idea of the Crucifixion as a combat between Death and Life was familiar from Heb. 2:14–15 and from the sequence *Victimae Paschali laudes* sung on Easter Sunday.

(see n.)	And forbete adown and brynge bale deth for evere.
	O mors, mors tua ero, morsus!'
	Thenne cam Pilatus with moche peple, *sedens pro tribunali*,
(see n.)	To se how douhtyliche Deth sholde do, and demen ther beyre rihte.
	The Jewes and the justices ageyns Jesus they were,
	And alle the court cryede '*Crucifige!*' loude.
accuser (Matt. 26:61)	Thenne putte hym forth a pelour bifor Pilatus and saide:
	'This Jesu of oure Jewene temple japed and despised
destroy	To fordon hit on a day, and in thre dayes aftur
	Edefien hit eft newe – here he stant that saide hit –
	And yut maken hit as moche in alle manere poyntes,
	Bothe as longe and as large, a-loofte and o grounde,
	And as wyde as hit evere was; this we witnesseth alle.'
officer of the court	'*Crucifige!*' quod a cachepol, 'he can of wycchecraft.'
'Away with him' (John 19:15)	'*Tolle, tolle!*' quod another, and tok of kene thornes
	And bigan of grene thorn a garlond to make
	And sette hit sore on his heved, and sethe saide in envye,
'Hail, master' (cf. Matt. 27:29)	'*Ave, raby*,' quod that ribaud, and redes shotte up to his eyes;
	And nayled hym with thre nayles naked upon a rode
	And with a pole poysen putten up to his lippes
prevent, lengthen	And beden hym drynke, his deth to lette and his dayes lenghe,
clever	And saiden, 'Yf he sotil be, hymsulve now he wol helpe';
	And 'Yf thow be Crist – and Crist, Godes sone –
	Come adoun of this rode and thenne shal we leve
	That Lyf the loveth and wol nat late the deye.'
	'*Consummatum est*,' quod Crist, and comsed for to swone.
prisoner	Pitousliche and pale, as prisoun that deyeth,
	The lord of lyf and of liht tho leyde his eyes togederes.
	The daye for drede ther-of withdrouh and derke bicam the sonne;
split asunder	The wal of the temple to-cleyef evene al to peces,
was riven asunder	The hard roch al to-rof, and riht derk nyht hit semede.
(see n.)	The erthe to-quasche and quok as hit quyk were
din	And dede men for that dene cam oute of depe graves
	And tolde why the tempest so longe tyme durede:
	'For a bittur bataile,' the ded bodye saide;
destroys the other of them	'Lyf and Deth, in this derkenesse here oon fordoth her other,
for certain	Ac shal no wyht wyte witturlich ho shal have the maistry
	Ar a Soneday, about the sonne-rysynge,' and sank with that til erthe.
	Somme saide he was godes sone that so fayre deyede,
	Vere filius dei erat iste,
	And somme saide, 'He can of sorcerie; gode is that we assaie
before he be taken down	Wher he be ded or nat ded, down or he be taken.'
suffered	Two theves tho tholed deth that tyme
	Uppon cros bisyde Crist, so was the comune lawe.

34 'And destroy utterly and bring to an end for ever man's miserable subjection to Satan'.

34a 'O death, I will be thy death! (O hell, I will be thy) destruction' (Hos. 13:14), sung as an antiphon on Holy Saturday.

35 'sitting in the judgement seat' (Matt. 27:19).

36 'and judge the right of both of them (to victory)'.

50 Details such as this are Langland's only concession to the image of the suffering humanity of Christ, and the emotional identification with that humanity so characteristic of fourteenth-century spirituality (see Julian, Kempe, Nicholas Love, below). For Langland, Christ is Pantocrator, lord of life and conqueror of death.

53 A macabre joke on the part of the tormentors rather than an indication that they are agents of the devil in attempting to prevent Christ's death (see 335, below).

58 ***Consummatum est***: 'It is finished' (John 19:30), i.e. the work of redemption is complete.

64 'The earth was shaken to pieces and quaked as if it were alive'.

71a 'Truly this was the son of God' (Matt. 27:54).

	A cachepol cam and craked a-to her legges
	And here armes aftur, of evereche of tho theves.
	Ac was no boie so bold godes body to touche;
Nature granted	For he was knyht and kynges sone, Kynde foryaf that tyme
	That hadde no boie hardynesse hym to touche in deynge.
	Ac ther cam forth a blynde knyhte with a kene spere ygrounde,
lost	Hihte Longius, as the lettre telleth, and longe hadde lore his sihte;
waited in readiness	Bifore Pilatus and othere peple in the place he hoved.
Despite all he could do	Maugre his mony teth he was made that tyme
	Jouste with Jesus, this blynde Jewe Longius;
	For alle were they unhardy that hoved ther or stode
touch	To touche hym or to trinen hym or to taken hym down and graven hym,
bachelor of arms (aspirant knight)	Bote this blynde bacheler, that bar hym thorw the herte.
unbarred	The blod sprang down by the spere and unspered the knyhte eyes;
	Tho ful the knyhte uppon knees and criede Jesu mercy –
	'Ageyn my will hit was,' quod he, 'that I yow wounde made!'
Sorely I repent it	And syhed and saide, 'Sore hit me forthenketh;
	Of the dede that I have do I do me in youre grace.
body	Bothe my lond and my licame at youre likynge taketh hit,
	And have mercy on me, rightful Jesu!' and riht with that he wepte.
	Thenne gan Faith fouly the false Jewes to dispice,
miserable wretches	Calde hem caytyves, acorsed for evere:
	For this was a vyl vilanye; vengeaunce yow bifall
	That made the blynde bete the dede – this was a boyes dede!
	Corsede caytives! knyhthod was hit nevere
	To bete a body ybounde, with eny briht wepene.
despite	The gre yut hath he geten for al his grete woundes,
	For youre chaumpioun chivaler, chief knyht of yow alle,
weeping	Yelde hym recreaunt remyng, riht at Jesu wille.
(see n.)	For be this derkenesse ydo, Deth worth yvenkused,
villains	And ye, lordeyns, han lost, for Lyf shal have maistrie,
	And youre franchise that fre was yfallen is into thraldom,
prosper	And alle youre childerne cherles, cheve shal thei nevere,
cultivate	Ne have lordschipe in londe ne no londe tulye,
live	And as bareyne be, and by usure libbe,
forbids	The which is lif that oure lord in all lawes defendeth.
	Now ben youre gode dayes ydon, as Daniel of yow telleth,
split asunder	When Crist thorw croos overcam, youre kynedom sholde to-cleve.
	Cum veniat sanctus sanctorum, cessat, etc.'
marvellous happening	What for fere of this ferly and of the false Jewes
	I withdrow in that derkenesse to *descendit ad inferna*,

76–7 The breaking of their limbs was intended to hasten their death.

82 **Longius**, or Longinus, is the name given to the unnamed soldier of John 19:34 who in apocryphal legend becomes a Jew who is blind, healed and converted.

94 Longinus behaves like a knight defeated in a joust, yielding himself to his victorious opponent (though the yielding of his **licame** to Christ is also of course symbolic of conversion).

96 Faith again plays the part of a herald (cf. 15 above), declaring the outcome of the battle.

102 **gre**: 'honour of the day's battle'.

105 'For when the darkness is passed, Death will be vanquished'.

109 **lordschipe in londe**. Jews were prohibited by law in Christian countries from owning land, which is one reason why they had to turn to moneylending as a profession.

113a 'When the holy of holies comes, (your anointing) ceases'. This prophecy, derived from Dan. 9:24–7, is taken to allude to the new law of Christ's cross which supersedes the kingdom of the old law, and is symbolized in the tearing of the temple-curtain (which veiled the *sanctus sanctorum* of the old law) at the moment of Christ's death (Matt. 27:51).

115 ***descendit ad inferna***; 'he descended into hell' (from the Apostles' Creed).

And there I seyh sothly, *secundum scripturas*,
Out of the west, as hit were, a wenche, as me thouhte,
Cam walkynge in the way, to hellward she lokede.
Mercy hihte that mayde, a mylde thynge with-alle
maiden, modest — And a ful benyngne buyrde and buxum of speche.
Here suster, as hit semede, cam softly walkynge
intended (to go) — Evene oute of the eest, and westward she thouhte,
A comely creature and a clene, Treuthe she hihte;
For the vertue that her folewede, afered was she nevere.

{Mercy and Truth are soon joined by their sisters Peace and Righteousness, and the debate that follows, between the Four Daughters of God (deriving from a hint in Ps. 84:11), is of a kind that was frequently elaborated in the Middle Ages as an effective allegorical means of dramatizing and explaining the reconciliation of the old law of justice and the new law of mercy in the doctrine of the Atonement. Mercy will temper justice, and Christ will pay for Adam's sin.}

Be quiet a minute — 'Suffre we,' sayde Treuthe; 'I here and se bothe
commands, unbar — A spirit speketh to Helle and bit to unspere the gates.'
Attollite portas.
A vois loude in that liht to Lucifer saide:
'Princes', unbar — '*Princepes* of this place, prest undo this gates,
For here he cometh with croune, the kynge of all glorie!'
Thenne syhed Satoun and saide to Helle,
'Suche a lyht ayenes oure leve Lazar hit fette;
distress — Care and combraunce is come to us alle.
Yf this kyng come in, mankynde wol he fecche
And lede hit ther Lazar is and lihtliche me bynde.
spoken — Patriarkes and prophetes han parled her-of longe
That such a lord and a lihte shal lede hem all hennes.
(name for a demon), hand to me — Ac arise up, Ragamuffyn, and areche me all the barres
grandfather — That Belial thy beel-syre beet with thy dame,
stop — And I shal lette this lord and his liht stoppe.
blinded — Ar we thorw brihtnesse be blente, go barre we the gates.
chain up (the gates), chink — Cheke we and cheyne we and uch a chine stoppe
That no liht lepe in at lover ne at loupe.
shout out — Astarot, hote out, and have out oure knaves,
(another demon) — Coltyng and al his kyn, the castel to save.
Brimstone — Brumston boylaunt brennyng out cast hit
Al hot on here hedes that entrith ney the walles.
Setteth bowes of brake and brasene gunnes
blind — And sheteth out shot ynow his sheltrom to blende.
catapult — Set Mahond at the mangenel and mullestones throweth
hooks, impede — And with crokes and kalketrappes acloye we hem uchone!'

116 ***secundum scripturas***; 'according to the scriptures' (from the Nicene Creed).
270a 'Lift open (your) gates, (O princes)': from Nicodemus 18, the apocryphal gospel which was the main source of the popular medieval story of the Harrowing of Hell, Christ's descent into hell to release the souls of the righteous.
274 **Helle**. Hell is personified (Lat. *inferus*) in Nicodemus 19. He represents the power of hell, to which Satan himself is subject. Langland seems to identify hell with Lucifer, the fallen angel, where Satan is the totally corrupted spirit of evil, or devil.
275 **Lazar**: Lazarus, who was brought back from the dead by Christ (John 11:43).
286 **lover**: louver (slatted turret to let out smoke). **loupe**: loop-hole.
287 **Astarot**: Ashtaroth, another demon, originally the Phoenician moon-goddess. Hell, as in Milton, and in accordance with tradition, is staffed by pagan deities (including Mahomet, 293).
291 **bowes of brake**: cross-bows with a winding-mechanism to give tension.
292 Christ has no **sheltrom**, or body of troops, but to Satan's incurably literal way of thinking this is how he will conquer hell.
294 **kalketrappes**: 'caltrops', spiked iron balls used to impede and maim horses in battle. Satan now seems to assume that Christ is leading a cavalry charge.

'Lustneth,' quod Lucifer, 'for I this lord knowe;
Bothe this lord and this lihte, ys longe ygo I knewe hym.
harm, tricks — May no deth this lord dere, ne no develes quentyse,
And where he wol is his way – ac war hym of the perelles!
through sheer power — Yf he reve me of my rihte, he robbeth me of his maistrie.
For bi riht and by resoun the renkes that ben here
Body and soule beth myne, bothe gode and ille.
For hymsulve said hit, that sire is of hevene,
That Adam and Eve and all his issue
Sholde deye with dole and here dwelle evere
Yf they touched a tre or toke ther-of an appul.
Thus this lord of liht such a lawe made,
believe — And sethe he is a lele lord I leve that he wol nat
Rob — Reven us of oure riht, sethe resoun hem dampnede.
been in legal possession — And sethen we han ben sesed sevene thousand wynter,
(see n.) — And nevere was ther-ageyne and now wolde bigynne,
deceitful — Thenne were he unwrast of his word, that witnesse is of treuthe.'
'That is soth,' saide Satoun, 'bote I me sore doute,
For thow gete hem with gyle and his gardyn breke;
Against — Ageyne his love and his leve on his londe yedest,
Not in fourme of a fende bote in fourme of an addre
on her own — And entisedest Eve to eten by here one –
Ve soli! –
promised — And byhihtest here and hym aftur to knowe
As two godes, with god, bothe gode and ille.
deceived — Thus with treson and tricherie thow troyledest hem bothe
made, obedience, promises — And dust hem breke here buxumnesse thorw fals bihestes,
And so haddest hem out and hiddere at the laste.'
properly — 'Hit is nat graythly ygete ther gyle is the rote,
(the devil), tricked — And god wol nat be gylde,' quod Gobelyne, 'ne byjaped.
We han no trewe title to hem, for thy tresoun hit maketh.
Forthy I drede me,' quod the devel, 'leste Treuthe wol hem fecche.
And as thow bigyledest godes ymages in goynge of an addre,
in going about as a man — So hath god bigiled us alle in goynge of a weye.
man's — For god hath go,' quod Gobelyne, 'in gome liknesse
Thus thritty wynter, as I wene, and wente aboute and prechede.
I have assayled hym with synne, and som tyme ich askede
Whether — Where he were god or godes sone? He gaf me short answere.
walked unhindered, proper — Thus hath he trolled forth like a tydy man this two and thritty wynter;
contrived cunningly — And when I seyh hit was so, I sotiled how I myhte
Hinder — Lette hem that lovede hym nat, leste they wolde hym martre.
I wolde have lenghed his lyf, for I leved, yf he deyede,

299 my rihte. The theory of the 'devil's rights' was evolved to provide a legalistic framework for the act of Redemption. The devil was granted the right of legal possession (see 309, below) to the souls of all sinful men after the Fall. He might forfeit this right by 'abuse of power', that is, by attempting to seize a sinless soul; or it might be annulled by ransom, the offer of soul for soul. Langland alludes to both schemes of Redemption. See C.W. Marx, *The Devil's Rights and the Redemption in the Literature of Medieval England* (Cambridge, 1995).

310 'And (he) never raised any objections against that and now wants to start'.

316a 'Woe to him who is alone (when he falls)' (Eccl. 4:10).

327 The doctrine of the Atonement had to be justified in law according to the theory of the devil's rights (see note to 299 above), and for this purpose the Incarnation was interpreted as a piece of divine deception. The devil was to be trapped into forfeiting his rights by transgressing his agreement with God, namely, by compassing the death of a sinless soul, that of Jesus, whom the devil did not recognize as God. In accordance with this doctrine the temptation of Christ was interpreted as the devil's attempt to find out whether Christ was the Son of God.

335 The reference is to the dream that Satan sent to Pilate's wife, warning her to persuade her husband not to condemn Christ. The legend grew from Matt. 27:19 and was extensively developed in the mystery cycles.

That if his soule hider cam hit sholde shende us all.
For the body, whiles hit on bones yede, aboute was hit evere *it was always busy*
To lere men to be lele and uch man to lovye other;
The which lyf and lawe, be hit longe y-used,
Hit shal undo us develes and down bryngen us all.'
'And now I se where his soule cometh sylinge hidward *gliding*
With glorie and with gret lihte – god hit is, ich wot wel.
I rede we flee,' quod the fende, 'faste all hennes,
For us were bettere nat to be then abyde in his sihte.
For thy lesinges, Lucifer, we losten furst oure joye,
And out of hevene hidere thy pryde made us falle;
For we leved on thy lesynges, there loste we oure blisse.
And now, for a lattere lesing that thow lowe til Eve, *lied*
We han ylost oure lordschipe a londe and in helle.
Nunc princeps huius mundi, etc.'
Sethe that Satan myssaide thus foule *berated*
Lucifer for his lesynges, leve I none other
Bote oure lord at the laste lyares here rebuke
And wyte hem al the wrechednesse that wrouhte is her on erthe. *blame them for*
Beth ywar, ye wyse clerkes and ye witty men of lawe,
That ye belyen nat this lewed men, for at the laste David *deceive by lies*
Witnesseth in his writynges what is lyares mede: *reward*
Odisti omnes qui operantur iniquitatem; perdes omnes qui loquuntur mendacium.
(A litel I over-leep for lesynges sake, *digressed*
That I ne sygge nat as I syhe, suynde my teme!) *say, saw, following my subject*
For efte that lihte bade unlouke, and Lucifer answeride.
'What lord artow?' quod Lucifer. A voys aloude saide:
'The lorde of myhte and of mayne, that made alle thynges.
Dukes of this demme place, anon undoth this gates *dark*
That Crist may come in, the kynges sone of hevene.'
And with that breth helle brak with alle Belialles barres;
For eny wey or warde, wyde open the gates. *(see n.)*
Patriarkes and profetes, *populus in tenebris*, *'the people in darkness' (Isa. 9:2)*
Songen with seynt Johan '*Ecce agnus dei*!'
Lucifer loke ne myhte, so liht hym ablende;
And tho that oure lord lovede forth with that liht flowen. *issued forth*
'Lo! me here,' quod oure lord, 'lyf and soule bothe,
For alle synful soules to save oure bothe rihte. *(see n.)*
Myne they were and of me; I may the bet hem clayme.
Althouh resoun recordede, and rihte of mysulve,
That if they ete the appul alle sholde deye,
I bihihte hem nat here helle for evere.
For the dedly synne that they dede, thi deseite hit made;
With gyle thow hem gete agaynes all resoun.
For in my palays, paradys, in persone of an addere
Falsliche thow fettest there that me biful to loke, *watch over*
Byglosedest hem and bigiledest hem and my gardyn breke *Deceived*

349a 'Now the ruler of this world (shall be cast out)' (John 12:31).
356a 'Thou hatest all evil-doers; thou destroyest all who speak lies' (Ps. 5:7).
365 'For all that any man or guard could do, the gates open wide'.
367 'Behold, the lamb of God' (John 1:36).
371 **oure bothe rihte**: 'the rights of both of us' (i.e. Christ and Satan).

Ageyne my love and my leve. The olde lawe techeth
That gylours be bigiled and yn here gyle falle,
And ho-so hit out a mannes eye or elles his fore-teth
Or eny manere membre maymeth other herteth,
The same sore shal he have that eny so smyteth.
Dentem pro dente, et oculum pro oculo.
So lyf shal lyf lete ther lyf hath lyf anyented,
So that lyf quyte lyf – the olde lawe hit asketh.
(see n.) *Ergo*, soule shal soule quyte and synne to synne wende,
And al that men mysdede, I, man, to amenden hit;
what, destroyed And that deth fordede, my deth to releve
destroyed And bothe quykie and quyte that queynte was thorw synne,
And gyle be bigyled thorw grace at the laste,
Ars ut artem falleret.
So leve hit nat, Lucifer, ageyne the lawe I feche
Here eny synful soule sovereynliche by maistrie,
liege-servant Bote thorw riht and thorw resoun raunsome here myn lege.
Non veni solvere legem, sed adimplere.
what So that with gyle was gete, thorw grace is now ywonne,
And as Adam and alle thorw a tre deyede,
come back to life Adam and alle thorw a tre shal turne to lyve.
And now bygynneth thy gyle agayne on the to turne
And my grace to growe ay wydere and wydere.
taste The bitternesse that thow hast browe, now brouk hit thysulve;
Thou that That art doctour of deth, drynke that thow madest!
For I that am lord of lyf, love is my drynke,
And for that drynke today I deyede, as hit semede.
deep (bowl of) learning Ac I wol drynke of no dische ne of deep clergyse,
Bote of comune cuppes, alle cristene soules;
will be, bowl Ac thy drynke worth deth and depe helle thy bolle.
I still thirst I fauht so, me fursteth yut, for mannes soule sake,
'I thirst' (John 19:28) *Sicio.*
(sweet drinks) May no pyement ne pomade ne preciouse drynkes
thirst slake Moiste me to the fulle ne my furst slokke
(see n.) Til the ventage valle in the vale of Josophat,
And I drynke riht rype must, *resurrecio mortuorum.*
And thenne shal I come as kynge, with croune and with angeles,
And have out of helle alle mennes soules.
Fendes and fendekynes byfore me shal stande
And be at my biddynge, at blisse or at payne.
Ac to be merciable to men thenne my kynde asketh,
(see n.) For we beth brethrene of o blod, ac nat in baptisme alle.
full brothers (i.e. Christians) Ac alle that beth myn hole brethrene, in blod and in baptisme,
Shal nevere in helle eft come, be he ones oute.

385a 'Tooth for tooth, and eye for eye' (Ex. 21:24). Christ's concern is to prove that the new law is grounded in the fulfilment of the letter of the old, and to prove that no law is being broken.

386 'So a living man must lose his life wherever a man has destroyed a life'.

388 'Therefore one soul shall pay for another and one sin (crucifying Christ) go to balance another (eating the apple)'.

392a 'One cunning stratagem in order to deceive another': from the famous hymn *Pange lingua gloriosi* (as also the two 'trees' of 397–8).

395a 'I have not come to destroy the law, but to fulfil it' (Matt. 5:17).

403–12 From the image of the drink of death brewed by the devil, and the allusion to the bitter drink offered to Jesus on the cross (Matt. 27:48), grows this magnificent elaboration of the image of the drink of love and life, of Christ thirsting for man's love.

411 'Till the time of grape-harvest come in the vale of Jehoshaphat (taken as the future scene of the resurrection of mankind in accordance with the prophecy of Joel 3:2, 12–13), and I drink fully ripe new wine (of the) "resurrection of the dead"' (this phrase is from the Nicene Creed).

418 **brethrene of o blod**: blood-brothers, fellow human beings (through the Incarnation).

Tibi soli peccavi, et malum coram te feci.
His is nat used on erthe to hangen eny felones
(see n.) Oftur then ones, thogh they were tretours.
And yf the kynge of the kyngdom come in the tyme
suffer, judicial penalty Ther a thief tholie sholde deth other jewyse,
would require, gave, if Lawe wole he yove hym lyf and he loked on hym.
And I that am kynge over kynges shal come such a tyme
Ther that dom to the deth dampneth alle wikkede,
And if lawe wol I loke on hem hit lith in my grace
Where they deye or dey nat, dede they nevere so ille.
paid for (i.e. by repentance) Be hit enythyng abouhte, the boldeness of here synne,
I may do mercy of my rihtwysnesse and alle myn wordes trewe.
avenged on For holy writ wol that I be wreke of hem that wrouhte ille,
As *nullum malum impunitum, et nullum bonum irremuneratum.*
And so of alle wykkede I wol here take venjaunce.
And yut my kynde in my kene ire shal constrayne my will –
Domine, ne in furore tuo arguas me –
To be merciable to monye of my halve-bretherne.
thirsty and cold For blod may se blod bothe a-furst and a-cale
without taking pity Ac blod may nat se blod blede, bote hym rewe.
Audivi archana verba, que non licet homini loqui.
Ac my rihtwysnesse and rihte shal regnen in helle,
And mercy (shall reign over) And mercy al mankynde bifore me in hevene.
For I were an unkynde kyng bote I my kyn helpe,
And namliche at such a nede that nedes helpe asketh.
Non intres in judicium cum servo tuo.
Thus by lawe,' quod oure lord, 'lede I wol fro hennes
Tho ledis that I lovye and leved in my comynge.
lied Ac for the lesynge that thow low, Lucifer, til Eve,
pay Thow shal abyye bittere,' quod god, and bonde hym with chaynes.
corners Astarot and alle othere hidden hem in hernes;
They dorste nat loke on oure lord, the lest of hem alle,
Bote leten hym lede forth which hym luste and leve which hym likede.
Many hundret of angels harpeden tho and songen,
Culpat caro, purgat caro, regnat deus dei caro.
a song from the poets Thenne piped Pees of poetes a note:
'Aftur sharpest shoures,' quod Pees, 'most shene is the sonne;
Is no wedere warmere then aftur watri cloudes,
more precious Ne no love levere, ne no levere frendes,
Then aftur werre and wrake when love and pees ben maistres.
Was nevere werre in this world ne wikkedere envye
if he wanted to, laughter That Love, and hym luste, to louhynge it ne brouhte,
And Pees thorw pacience alle perelles stopede.'

420a 'Against thee alone have I sinned, and done what is evil in thy sight' (Ps. 50:6). Therefore Christ's forgiveness cancels the debt.

422 **Oftur then ones**: 'more often than once' (i.e. in cases of imperfect hangings).

430 Christ nearly gets carried away with his near-promise of universal salvation, but there is a reminder here of the more orthodox doctrine of the necessity of penitence.

433 '(It is a just judge who leaves) no evil unpunished, no good unrewarded': from the *De contemptu mundi* of Pope Innocent III.

435a 'O Lord, rebuke me not in thy anger' (Ps. 37:1).

438a 'I heard words which cannot be told, which man may not utter' (2 Cor. 12:4). Langland transfers Paul's words, of the man (evidently Paul himself) caught up into the third heaven, to his dreamer, suggesting that he is aware of the limits to which his vision of Christ's promise of mercy can be taken.

442a 'Enter not into judgement with thy servant' (Ps. 142:2).

451 'The flesh sins, the flesh atones for sin, the flesh of God reigns as God': from the hymn *Aeterne rex altissime*, sung on the vigil of Ascension day.

453–6 The lines translate a Latin proverb, which is quoted in some MSS.

Truce — 'Trewes,' quod Treuthe, 'thow tellest us soth, by Jesus!
Let us embrace — Cluppe we in covenaunt and uch of us kusse othere!'
argued — 'And lat no peple,' quod Pees, 'parseyve that we chydde,
For inposible is no thynge to hym that is almyhty.'
'Thow saist soth,' saide Rihtwisnesse, and reverentlich here custe,
and Peace (kissed) her — Pees, and Pees here, *per secula seculorum.*
Misericordia et veritas obviaverunt sibi; justicia et pax osculate sunt.
blew on a trumpet — Treuth trompede tho and song *Te deum laudamus*,
played on a lute — And thenne lutede Love in a loude note,
Ecce quam bonum et quam jocundum est, etc.
Til the day dawed thes damoyseles caroled
That men rang to the resureccioun, and riht with that I wakede
And calde Kitte my wyf and Calote my douhter:
'Arise, and go reverense godes resurrecioun,
And crepe to the cros on knees and kusse hit for a jewel
And rihtfullokest a relyk, noon richere on erthe.
For godes blessed body hit bar for oure bote,
And hit afereth the fende, for such is the myhte
May no grisly gost glyde ther hit shaddeweth!'

{From this high climax the poem returns to the world, and the vision of the establishment of Christ's Church on earth. But there is dissension within the Christian community, and the problems of distinguishing worldly greed from basic need seem as acute as ever. The dreamer has an inconclusive interview with Need.}

Passus XXII.51–109, 297–386 (end): The Coming of Antichrist

taken me to task — Whenne Nede hadde undernome me thus, anon I ful aslepe
dreamt — And mette ful merveylousely that in mannes fourme
Auntecrist cam thenne, and al the crop of treuthe
quickly, overturned — Turned hit tyd up-so-down, and overtulde the rote,
(see n.) — And made fals sprynge and sprede and spede menne nedes;
In uch a contrey ther he cam, kutte awey treuthe
made — And garte gyle growe there as he a god were.
Freres folewed that fende, for he yaf hem copes,
And religious reverensed hym and rongen here belles
And al the covent cam to welcome a tyraunt

465 ***per secula seculorum***, i.e. 'for ever and ever' (from the *Gloria patri*, said or sung at the end of prayers and psalms).
465a 'Mercy and truth have met together; righteousness and peace have kissed' (Ps. 84:11).
466 ***Te deum laudamus***: 'We praise thee as god' (sung at matins on Sundays).
467a 'Behold, how good and pleasant it is (for brothers to dwell in unity)' (Ps. 132:1).
469 The dreamer awakens to the ringing of the bells on Easter morning, a return to time which confirms in reality the truth of his vision.
470 **Kitte ... Calote**: these are type-names (see V.2n, above), but they could be real people.
472 'Creeping to the cross' (i.e. shuffling forwards on the knees), and kissing it, were enjoined as penitential and devotional exercises, especially for Good Friday.

Passus XXII
53 **Auntecrist** now follows up the first attack of Pride (XXI.336), which was temporarily thwarted by the digging of the moat of holiness. The presence of Antichrist, whose coming, it was believed, would precede the Second Coming, gives to this last passus a powerful apocalyptic quality, in which the pattern of contemporary events is read as a premonition of the Last Days.
54 Langland continues here with the imagery of the field and the harvest of grace (from Matt. 13:25) before turning to the allegory of the siege of Unity (Holy Church).
55 'And made falsehood spring up and spread and satisfy men's desires (for worldly things)'.
58 The friars are commonly identified with Antichrist in Wycliffite writings. In this passus, Langland focuses on the friars as the principal agents in the corruption of the Christian community.

And alle hise as wel as hym, save onelich foles;
The whiche foles were wel gladere to deye
Then to lyve lengere, sethe leautee was so rebuked
And a fals fende Auntecrist over all folke regnede.
And those — And that were mylde men and holy that no meschief dradden,
Defyede all falsenesse and folke that hit usede,
And what kyng that hem confortede, knowynge here gyle,
Thei corsede, and here consail, were hit clerk or lewed.
  Auntecrist hadde thus sone hondredes at his baner
boldly — And Pryde hit bar baldly aboute
for the sake of pleasure — With a lord that lyveth aftur likyng of body,
guide — That cam agen Conscience, that kepar was and gyour
proper Christians — Over kynde cristene and cardinale vertues.
  'I consail,' quod Conscience tho, 'cometh with me, ye foles,
Into Unite holi churche, and halde we us there.
And crye we to Kynde that he come and defende us
limbs (agents) — Foles fro this fendes lymes, for Peres love the plouhman;
And crye we on al the comune that thei come to Unite
fight — And there abyde and bikere ageyn Beliales childrene.'
  Kynde Conscience tho herde and cam oute of the planetes
foragers — And sente forth his forreours, feveres and fluxes,
Coughs and heart-attacks — Cowhes and cardiades, crampes and toth-aches,
(see n.) — Reumes and radegoundes and roynous scabbes,
Boils and bunions — Byles and boches and brennynge aguwes;
Frenesyes and foule eveles, forageres of Kynde,
preyed upon heads — Hadde ypriked and preyed polles of peple;
lost — Largeliche a legioun lees the lyf sone.
  There was 'Harow!' and 'Help! here cometh Kynde
With Deth that is dredful to undon us alle!'
The lord that lyvede aftur lust tho aloud cryede
(to) come — Aftur Conforte, a knyhte, come and beer his baner.
To arms! Every man for himself! — 'Alarme! alarme!' quod that lord, 'uch lyf kepe his owene!'
Thenne mette thise men, ar mynstrals myhte pype
And ar heroudes of armes hadden descreved lordes,
vanguard — Elde the hore; he was in the vawwarde
And bar the baner bifore Deth – bi riht he hit claymede.
kinds of — Kynde cam aftur hym with many kyne sores,
As pokkes and pestilences, and moche peple shente;
So Kynde thorw corupcions kulde ful mony.
dashed down — Deth cam dryvyng aftur and al to dust paschte
emperors — Kynges and knyhtes, caysers and popes.
Lered ne lewed he lefte no man stande
squarely — That he hitte evene, that evere stured aftur.
Many a lovly lady and here lemmanes knyhtes
died, blows — Swowened and swelte for sorwe of dethes duntes.

61 **foles** is used here, ironically (as often in Paul, e.g. 1 Cor. 4:10, see IX.105n, above), of faithful Christians.

70 **Pryde** bears the banner, as the chief of the seven deadly sins.

76 **Kynde**. Conscience calls on Nature to help, assuming that man's human nature, which he shares with Piers Plowman, or Christ incarnate (see XX.21), is itself a defence against evil. Nature's help takes an unexpected form.

80 **oute of the planetes**. The incidence of disease was thought to be controlled by planetary influences. Nature's allies in the fight against sin are disease, age and death, since these reminders of mortality most surely bring man to an understanding of the urgent need to seek salvation.

83 'Rheums and running sores and scurfy scabs'.

94 **descreved**: 'described', i.e. introduced the combatants by name and blazon.

100 **Deth cam dryvyng aftur**. Perhaps we should imagine a skeleton astride a horse (cf. Rev. 6:8).

	Conscience of his cortesye tho Kynde he bisouhte
be patient	To sese and soffre, and se wher they wolde
quietly	Leve pruyde priveyliche and be parfyt cristene.
	And Kynde sesede tho, to se the peple amende.

{But the respite is only temporary: Lechery and Covetousness and the other sins are soon at their old work, and Conscience is driven to desperation. He calls on Clergy for help, but only the friars respond, and their motives are corrupt. Since they have no regular income, they are dependent on the money they make by begging or by the practice of 'selling' confession (cf. Prol. 62).}

	In Unite holi church Conscience heeld hym
bolt	And made Pees porter to pynne the gates
Against, idle tittle-tattlers	Of all tale-tellares and titerares an ydel.
they, assault, mounted	Ypocrisye and hy an hard sawt they yeven.
	Ypocrisye at the gate harde gan fyhte
	And wounded wel wykkedly many a wys techare
	That with Conscience acordede and cardinal vertues.
	Conscience calde a leche that couthe wel shryve
	To salve tho that syke were and thorw synne ywounded.
prescribed	Shrift schupte scharp salve and made men do penaunses
	For here mysdedes that thei wrouht hadde,
(to ensure) that	And that Peres pardon were ypayd, *redde quod debes*.
	Somme liked nat this leche and letteres they sente
besieged city	Yf eny surgien were in the sege that softur couthe plastre.
	Sire Lyf-to-lyve-in-lecherye lay ther and groned;
	For fastyng of a Fryday he feerde as he wolde deye.
	'Ther is a surgien in the sege that softe can handele,
And (knows) more	And more of fysyk bi fer, and fayrer he plastereth;
	Oon frere Flatrere is fisicien and surgien.'
	Quod Contricion to Conscience, 'Do hym come to Unite,
	For here is many man hert thorw Ypocrisye.'
	'We han no nede,' quod Conscience, 'I wot no bettere leche
confessor	Then person other parsche prest, penytauncer or bischope,
	Save Pers the plouhman, that hath power over alle
(see n.)	And indulgence may do, but yf dette lette hit.
allow (what you want)	I may wel soffre,' sayde Conscience, 'sennes ye desiren,
fetched, you sick people	That frere Flaterare be fet and fisyk yow seke.'
	The frere herof herde and hyede faste
	To a lord for a lettre, leve to have to curen
	As a curatour he were, and kam with his lettre
letter of authorization	Baldly to the bishope and his breef hadde
	In contreys ther he cam confessiones to here;
	And cam ther Conscience was and knokked at the gate.
	Pees unpynned hit, was porter of Unite,
	And in haste asked what his wille were?
	'In fayth,' quod this frere, 'for profyt and for helthe,
Speak, hither	Karpe I wolde with Contricioun and therfore I cam heddre.'
	'He is syke,' saide Pees, 'and so ar many other;
recover	Ypocrisye hath herte hem – ful hard is yf thei kevere.'

308 ***redde quod debes***: 'pay back what you owe' (derived from Rom. 13:7), a key text for Langland, referring not only to the necessity of restitution as a prerequisite of pardon, but, in a larger sense, to the rendering of the debt of love to God and one's neighbour.

321 'And may grant indulgence, unless the non-payment of debt prevents it'.

'I am a surgien,' saide the frere, 'and salves can make;
Conscience knoweth me wel and what I can bothe.'
'I preye the,' quod Pees tho, 'ar thow passe forthere,
What hattest thow? I praye the, hele nat thy name.' *are you called, hide*
'Certes,' saide his felawe, 'sire *Penetrans-domos*.'
'Ye? go thy gate!' quod Pees, 'bi god, for al thi fisyk, *way*
Bote thow conne eny craft thow comest nat here-ynne!
I knewe such oon ones, nat eyhte wynter passed,
Cam ynne thus ycoped at a court ther I dwelte,
And was my lordes leche and my ladyes bothe.
And at the laste this lymytour, tho my lord was oute,
He salved so oure wymmen til some were with childe!'
Hende-speche heet Pees tho opene the gates: *Courteous-speech, commanded*
'Lat in the frere and his felawe and make hem fayere chiere.
He may se and here here, so may bifalle,
That Lyf thorw his lore shal leve Covetyse
And be adrad of Deth and withdrawe hym fro Pruyde
And acorde with Conscience and kusse here ayther other.' *kiss each other*
Thus thorw Hende-speche entred the frere
And cam to Conscience and corteyslich hym grette.
'Thow art welcome,' quod Conscience; 'can thow hele syke?
Here is Contricioun,' quod Conscience, 'my cosyn, ywounded;
Conforte hym,' quod Conscience, 'and tak kepe to his sores. *heed*
The plasteres of the persoun, and poudres, ben to sore,
And lat hem lygge over-longe and loth is to chaungen;
Fro lente to lente he lat his plastres byte.'
'That is over-longe,' quod this lymitour, 'I leve – I schal amenden hit';
And goth and gropeth Contricion and gaf hym a plastre
Of a pryve payement and 'I shal preye for yow,
And for hem that ye aren holde to, al my lyf-tyme, *beholden to*
And make yow my Ladye in masse and in matynes
Of freres of oure fraternite, for a litel sulver.'
Thus he goth and gedereth and gloseth ther he shryveth *makes specious interpretations*
Til Contricioun hadde clene foryete to crye and to wepe
And wake for his wikkede werkes, as he was woned bifore.
For confort of his confessour, Contricioun he lefte,
That is the sovereyne salve for alle kyne synnes. *all kinds of*
Sleuth seyh that, and so dede Pruyde,
And comen with a kene wil, Conscience to assaile.
Conscience cryede efte Clergie come help hym,
And bad Contricioun to come to helpe kepe the gate.
'He lyeth adreint,' saide Pees, 'and so doth mony othere; *drowned (in physic)*
The frere with his fisyk this folk hath enchaunted
And doth men drynke dwale, that men drat no synne.' *opiate, fears*

340 ***Penetrans-domos***. 'Among them (i.e. those whose presence will be perilous "in the last days") are those who *insinuate themselves into households*, and subdue to their purposes weak and foolish women' (2 Tim. 3:6). The apocalyptic prophecies of 2 Tim. 3:1–10 had long been associated with the coming of the friars in anti-mendicant writing.

346 **lymytour**: friar licensed to beg in a certain district (cf. WBT 866n).

351 **Lyf**. The central figure in the allegory of this passus ('Pride of Life').

359–61 The plasters of true shrift are the painful kind of poultices which 'draw' as they draw out the evil of a wound or sore; but these plasters have been left on too long (Contrition only confesses once a year, at Easter, the time of obligation) and the wound is reinfected.

366 **my Ladye**, i.e. make you as important in our prayers as Our Lady.

'By Crist,' quod Conscience tho, 'I wol bicome a pilgrime,
And wenden as wyde as the world regneth — *extends its power*
To seke Pers the plouhman, that Pruyde myhte destruye,
And that freres hadde a fyndynge, that for nede flateren — *And (might ensure) that*
And countrepledeth me, Conscience. Now Kynde me avenge, — *oppose*
And sende me hap and hele til I have Peres plouhman.' — *good fortune and health*
And sethe he gradde aftur Grace tyl I gan awake. — *cried out*

382 Conscience goes out to seek Piers Plowman, the founder of Holy Church, who last appeared in the poem as he left to till truth in all the world (XXII.336). In other words, the church's strength can only be restored by a return to the principles on which it was founded.
383 The church is threatened by the friars, whose lack of a **fyndynge**, or provision for their necessary livelihood, drives them into a flattering and false misuse of confession, which undermines the act of penance and destroys all hope for men of winning Piers's pardon.
386 This last episode – closely detailed, bitterly specific, dry, toneless, unheroic, almost comic – makes an extraordinary ending to a long Christian poem, as Langland focuses his vision of the world's ills with desperate clarity upon the friars. The ending is abrupt, but not hopeless: it is a beginning of a new search, with the nature and object of the quest now at last clearly identified.

The Letters of John Ball (1381)

These 'letters' appear in the chronicles of Thomas Walsingham (*Historia Anglicana*, ed. H.T. Riley, Rolls series, 2 vols [1863–4], 2.33–4) and Henry Knighton (*Chronicon*, ed. J.R. Lumby, Rolls series, 2 vols [1889–95], 2.138–40), and are presumed by them to allude to a conspiracy that was being fomented in the months before the Peasants' Revolt of June 1381. The single letter in Walsingham is said to be from John Ball, though spoken under a pseudonym; the five in Knighton, which overlap in interesting ways with the first and with each other, also mention John Ball, though again three are written or 'spoken' by allegorically ordinary working men with honest-sounding names. John Ball was a real person, a priest of St Mary's, in York, who was hanged for his part in the rising, and the letters, in their variant versions, are probably all to be attributed to him. They were presumably circulated as a rallying call to action, urged on by the desire to reform the commonwealth according to simple Christian principles; the several references to *Piers Plowman* (including those to Dowel and Dobet) suggest how Langland's poem may have appealed to a popular body of reforming opinion (one that Langland was not over-keen to be identified with). Other forms of verse-complaint and satire and protest-poem are incorporated too, including the poetic censure of 'The Abuses of the Age' in cryptic and laconic style, and there is much proverbial and gnomic language, and echoing of the themes of popular preaching. The chroniclers are somewhat puzzled by these pieces, which they insert into the Latin of their main text, all in prose, and want to think of them as the incoherent outpourings of a popular rabble. A different view (S. Justice, *Writing and Rebellion: England in 1381* [Berkeley and Los Angeles, 1994]) sees them as a deliberate attempt to appropriate the language of authority, of official letters, and to demonstrate power over the written instruments that a centralized bureaucracy was increasingly employing to control people's lives. The letters speak to a sense of brotherhood, an idealized notion of the Christian commonwealth, which can be discovered sporadically even in the mostly hostile contemporary accounts of the Peasants' Revolt. For once, by accident of inclusion, the people have a voice. For valuable discussion and critical edition, see R.F. Green, in B. Hanawalt (ed.), *Chaucer's England: Literature in Historical Context* (Minneapolis, 1992), pp. 176–200; for the Revolt, see R.B. Dobson, *The Peasants' Revolt of 1381* (1970; 2nd edn, London, 1983).

The Letter of John Ball in Walsingham's Chronicle

Walsingham tells us that this letter was found in the tunic of a man who was to be hanged for his part in the rising. John Ball later confessed to having written it, and others; he was executed on 15 July 1381. BL MS Cotton Tiberius C.viii, fol.174r.

Johon Schep, somtyme seynte Marie prest of York, and now of Colchestre, greteth wel Johan Nameles, and Johan the Mullere, and Johon Cartere, and biddeth hem that thei bee war of gyle in borugh, and stondeth togidre in Godes name, and biddeth Peres Ploughman go to his werk, and chastise wel Hobbe the Robbere, and taketh with yow Johan Trewman and alle hiis felawes, and no mo, and loke schappe you to on heved,[1] and no mo.

Johan the Mullere hath ygrounde smal, smal, smal;
The kynges sone of hevene schal paye for al.[2]
Be war or ye[a] be wo;
Knoweth your frend fro your foo;
Haveth ynow, and seith 'Hoo!'
And do wel and bettre, and fleth synne,
And seketh pees, and hold you therinne.
And so biddeth Johan Trewaman and alle his felawes.

1 'see you hold to a single main purpose'

2 The old proverb is well known from Longfellow: 'Though the mills of God grind slowly, yet they grind exceeding small.' This metaphor for inexorable coming justice provides the structure for Knighton's first letter.

THE LETTERS OF JOHN BALL IN KNIGHTON'S CHRONICLE

Knighton speaks of the first as Jack Miller's address to the assembled rebels, and of the fourth and fifth as letters of John Ball. BL MS Royal 13.E.ix, fol.287r.

1 Jakke Mylner asket help to turne hys mylne aright.
He hath grounden smal, smal:
The kinges sone of heven he schal pay for alle.
Loke thi mylne go aryght, with the foure sayles, and the post stande in stedefastnesse.
With ryght and with myght,
With skyl[3] and with wylle,
Lat myght helpe ryght;
And[4] skyl go before wille
And ryght befor myght,
Than goth oure mylne aryght.
And if myght go before ryght
And wylle before skylle,
Lo, than is oure mylne mys-adyght.

2 Jakke Carter prayes yowe alle that ye make a gode ende of that ye have begunnen, and doth wele and ay bettur and bettur, for at the even men heryeth[b] the day.[5] For if the ende be wele, than is alle wele. Lat Peres the Plowman, my brother, duelle at home and dyght us corne, and I wil go with yowe and helpe that I may to dyghte youre mete and youre drynke, that ye none fayle. Lokke that Hobbe Robbyoure be wele chastysede for lesyng of youre grace, for ye have gret nede to take God with yowe in alle youre dedes.[6] For nowe is tyme to be ware.

3 Jakke Trewman doth yow to understande
That falsnes and gyle havith regned to longe,
And trewthe hat bene sette under a lokke,
And falsnes regneth in everylk flokke.
No man may come trewthe to,
But he syng *si dedero*.[7]
'Speke, spende and spede', quoth Jon of Bathon.[8]
And therfore synne fareth as wylde flode,
Trew love is away, that was so gode,
And clerkus for welthe worche hem wo.
God do bote, for nowe[c] is tyme.

4 Jon Balle gretyth yow wele alle and doth yowe to understande he hath rungen youre belle.[9]
Nowe ryght and myght,
Wylle and skylle,
God spede every dele.[d]
Nowe is tyme, Lady, helpe to Jesu thi sone, and thi sone to his fadur, to mak a gode ende, in the name of the Trinite, of that is begunne. Amen, amen, pur charite, amen.

3 'reason'
4 'If'
5 'praise the day', i.e. 'look back with satisfaction on the day's work'.
6 This exhortation has a striking parallel in Knighton's account of the Revolt, which tells how rebels burning down the Savoy Palace threw a looter into the flames, saying that they were followers of truth and not robbers (Dobson, *The Peasants' Revolt* [1983], p. 184).
7 'if I shall give (I'll expect something in return)', a play on the words of Ps. 131:4 (Vg.), common in venality satire.
8 Success is in knowing when to speak and when not to (*spare* would make better sense than *spende*); the source of the quotation has not been identified.
9 i.e. summoned you to action

5 John Balle, seynte Marye prist, gretes wele alle maner men and byddes hem in the name of the Trinite, Fadur and Sone and Holy Gost, stonde manlyche togedyr in trewthe, and helpes trewthe, and trewthe schal helpe yowe.

Nowe regneth pride in pris
And covetys is hold wys
And leccherye withouten schame[e]
And glotonye withouten blame.
Envye regnith with tresone
And slouthe is take in grete sesone.[10]
God do bote, for nowe is tyme. Amen.

10 'taken to be always in season'

John Trevisa (d. 1402)

John Trevisa went up to Oxford in 1362, was a student and fellow at Exeter College and then, from 1369, fellow at Queen's Hall. He was expelled in 1379 in a dispute between different college factions, but soon reinstated. From 1387 until his death he divided his time between Oxford and Berkeley, in Gloucestershire, where he had been made vicar in 1374. At the request of Sir Thomas Berkeley (see R. Hanna, in *Speculum* 64 [1989], 878–916), he undertook a number of translations, including translations of two very large Latin prose works: the *Polychronicon*, or universal history, of Ranulph Higden, monk of Chester (d. 1364), completed in 1387; and the *De proprietatibus rerum* of Bartholomaeus Anglicus, the standard encyclopaedia of natural history (*c.* 1250), completed in 1397. Though his translations are not elegant, he assisted in the inauguration of the massive programme of transfer through which English, hitherto so culturally backward, assimilated to itself the body of European and Latin learning. Brief biography by D.C. Fowler (Aldershot, 1993); see also R. Waldron, 'Trevisa and the Use of English', *PBA* 74 (1988), 171–202.

Translation of Higden's *Polychronicon*

Higden's *Polychronicon*, which runs to 1352, was the favourite universal history in England during the fourteenth and fifteenth centuries and provided the basis for many continuation-narratives. The famous passage below, in which he comments on the changes introduced in the language of grammar-school instruction by his Cornish compatriots, is one of the rare occasions when Trevisa adds anything substantial to his original. His information is thought to mark a significant moment in the shift from a dominantly Anglo-Norman to a dominantly English culture. Trevisa's translation is edited, with Higden, by J.R. Lumby, Rolls series, 9 vols (1865–86); the passage below is in Sisam (1921), p. 148. Text from BL MS Cotton Tiberius D.vii (*c.* 1400). NB *a*, 'they'; *a*, *an*, 'in'; *buth*, 'are'; *here*, 'their'; *hy*, 'they'.

The languages of Britain (chap. 59)

As hyt ys yknowe houw meny maner people buth in this ylond, ther buth also of so meny people longages and tonges. Notheles Walschmen and Scottes, that buth noght ymelled with other nacions, holdeth wel-nygh here furste longage and speche, bote yef[1] Scottes, that were somtyme confederat and wonede with the Pictes, drawe somwhat after here speche. Bote the Flemmynges that woneth in the west syde of Wales habbeth yleft here strange speche, and speketh Saxonlych ynow. Also Englyschmen, theygh hy hadde fram the bygynnyng thre maner speche, southeron, northeron, and myddel speche in the myddel of the lond, as hy come of thre maner people of Germania,[2] notheles by commyxstion and mellyng, furst with Danes and afterward with Normans, in menye the contray longage ys apeyred,[3] and som useth strange wlaffyng, chyteryng, harryng and garryng grisbittyng.[4] This apeyryng of the burthtonge ys bycause of twey thinges. On ys for chyldern in scole, ayenes the usage and manere of al other nacions, buth compelled for to leve here oune longage and for to construe here lessons and here thinges a Freynsch, and habbeth suthe the Normans come furst into Engelond. Also gentil-men children buth ytaught for to speke Freynsch fram tyme that a buth yrokked in here cradel, and conneth speke and playe with a child hys[5] brouch; and oplondysch men wol lykne hamsylf to gentil-men and fondeth with gret bysynes for to speke Freynsch, for to be more ytold of.

[*Trevisa adds:* Thys manere was moche y-used tofore the furste moreyn,[6] and ys sethe somdel ychaunged. For Johan Cornwal, a mayster of gramere, chayngede the lore[7] in gramer-scole and construccion of Freynsch into Englysch; and Richard Pencrych lurnede that manere techyng of hym, and other men of Pencrych, so that now, the yer of oure Lord a thousond thre hondred foure score and fyve, of the secunde kyng Richard after the Conquest nyne, in al the gramer-scoles of Engelond childern leveth Frensch and

1 'except that'
2 i.e. the Angles, Saxons and Jutes (as Bede describes); but the three ME dialects do not correspond so exactly to these continental origins.
3 'the native language is corrupted'
4 'snarling and grating teeth-gnashing'
5 'child's' (an archaic way of forming the genitive)
6 The first invasion of plague (the Black Death) in 1349; there were many subsequent outbreaks of plague, somewhat less severe.
7 'teaching'

construeth and lurneth an Englysch, and habbeth therby avauntage in on syde and desavauntage yn another. Here avauntage ys that a lurneth here gramer yn lasse tyme than childern wer ywoned to do. Disavauntage ys that now childern of gramer-scole conneth no more Frensch than can here lift heele, and that ys harm for ham and a scholle[8] passe the se and travayle in strange londes, and in meny caas also.[9] Also gentil-men habbeth now moche yleft for to teche here childern Frensch.] Hyt semeth a gret wondur houw Englysch, that ys the burth-tonge of Englyschmen, and here oune longage and tonge, ys so dyvers of soon[10] in this ylond; and the longage of Normandy ys comlyng[11] of another lond and hath on maner soon among al men that speketh hyt aryght in Engelond. [Notheles ther ys as meny dyvers maner Frensch yn the rem of Fraunce as ys dyvers manere Englysch in the rem of Engelond.][12]

Also of the forseyde Saxon tonge, that ys deled in thre, and ys abyde scarslych with feaw uplondysch men, ys[a] gret wondur, for men of the est with men of the west, as hyt were under the same party of hevene, acordeth more in sounyng of speche than men of the north with men of the south. Therfore hyt ys that Mercii,[13] that buth men of myddel Engelond, as hyt were parteners of the endes, undurstondeth betre the syde longages, northeron and southeron, than northeron and southeron undurstondeth eyther other.

Al the longage of the Northumbres, and specialych at York, ys so scharp, slyttyng and frotyng[14] and unschape that we southeron men may that longage unnethe undurstonde. I trowe that that ys bycause that a buth nygh to strange men and aliens, that speketh strangelych, and also bycause that the kynges of Engelond woneth alwey fer fram that contray; for a buth more yturnd to the south contray, and, yef a goth to the north contray, a goth with gret help and strengthe.

The cause why a buth more in the south contray than in the north may be betre corn-lond, more people, more noble cytes and more profytable havenes.

8 'harm for them if they have to'

9 'many other circumstances'

10 'sound'

11 'strange-comer'

12 Trevisa's comment seems like something Higden should have thought of for himself.

13 'Mercians': an archaic name for 'midlanders', from the Anglo-Saxon 'middle kingdom' of Mercia.

14 'grating'. This paragraph is not a witness to fourteenth-century northern pronunciation; it is taken by Higden from the Prologue to Book 3 of William of Malmesbury's *Gesta Pontificum* (1125) – a good example of the eclecticism of medieval monastic chroniclers.

The Wycliffite Bible (*c.* 1380–*c.* 1400)

The translation of the Bible into English was considered by Wyclif and his followers to be a first step towards reforming the church and reducing and demystifying the role of the priesthood as the sole interpreters of the Latin scriptures. The translation itself was so bare and so literal that nothing in it could be construed as heretical except the fact of choosing to translate it. But this was enough, and ownership of the Wycliffite Bible was constituted evidence of heresy in the *Constitutions* of Archbishop Arundel in 1409. Nevertheless, many religious houses owned copies (Henry VI gave one, now Bodl.MS Bodley 277, to the London Charterhouse), and very many continued to be produced, not always in clandestine circumstances. Though the textual affiliations between the many manuscripts (over 250, in whole or part) are complex, there seem to have been an Earlier Version, begun about 1382, very literal, crabbed, and at times barely intelligible, and a Later Version, completed about 1395–7, more fluent, idiomatic and consistent. Wyclif's ideas about Bible translation inspired the original undertaking, though he almost certainly took no part. Names of some of those who took part are known, such as John Purvey and Nicholas Hereford, but their role was at most as collaborators in a large task of translation and revision that took many years.

The passages below are taken from the Later Version as it is represented in Bodl.MS Rawlinson 259 (facsimile, introd. by D.L. Brake [Portland, Oregon, 1986]). They are chosen so that they may be compared with the versions of Tyndale, below (though clear and careful, they lack Tyndale's sense of speech and sentence rhythm). The complete text of the Bible is edited by J. Forshall and F. Madden (Oxford, 1850). For discussion, see Hudson (1988), pp. 231–47; also M. Deanesly, *The Lollard Bible* (Cambridge, 1920), old but still interesting.

The parable of the great supper (Luke 14:12–24)

And he seide to hym that hadde bodun hym to the feeste: 'Whanne thou makist a mete or a soper, nyle thou clepe[1] thi freendis nether thi britheren nether cosyns nether neighboris, ne riche men, lest peraventure thei bidden thee ayen[2] to the feeste, and it be yoldun ayen to thee. But whanne thou makist a feeste, clepe pore men, feble, crokid and blynde, and thou schalt be blessid, for thei han not wherof to yelde to thee, for it schal be yoldun to thee in the risyng ayen of just men.

And whanne oon of hem that saten togidere at the mete hadde hyrd these thingis, he seide to hym: 'Blessid is he that schal ete breed in the rewme of God!' And he seide to hym: 'A man made a greet soper, and clepide many, and he sente his servaunt in the our of soper to seie to men that weren bedun to the feeste that thei schulden come, "for now alle thingis ben redi". And alle bigunne togidere to excuse hem. The firste seide: "I have bought a toun, and I have nede to go out and se it; I preie thee have me excusid."[3] And the tothir seide: "I have bought fyve yockis of oxun, and I go to preve hem; I preye thee have me excusid." And anothir seide: "I have weddid a wiif, and therfor I mai not come." And the servaunt turnede ayen and telde these thingis to his lord. Thanne the hosebondeman was wrooth, and seide to his servaunt: "Go out swithe into the grete stretis and the smale stretis of the citee and bringe ynne hidur pore men and feble, blynde and crokid." And the servaunt seide: "Lord, it is don as thou hast comaundid, and yit there is a voide place." And the lord seide to the servaunt: "Go out into weies and heggis, and constreyne men to entre, that myn hous be fillid. For I seie to you, that noon of tho men that ben clepid schal taste my soper."'

The nature of charity (1 Cor. 13)

If I speke with tungis of men and of aungels, and I have not charite, I am maad as bras sownynge or a symbale tynkynge. And if I have prophecie, and knowe alle mysteries and al kunnyng, and if I have al feith so that I move hillis fro her place, and I have not charite, I am nought. And if I departe alle my goodis into the metis of pore men, and if I bitake my bodi so that I brenne, and if I have not charite, it profitith to me nothing. Charite is pacient; it is benygne. Charite envyeth not. It doith not wickidli. It

1 'Do not invite'

2 'invite thee back'

3 Cf. *PP* C.VII.292–304, above, p. 199.

is not blowun. It is not coveitous. It sekith not the thingis that ben his owne. It is not stirid to wrathe. It thenkith not yvel. It joyeth not on wickidnesse, but it joyeth togidere to treuthe. It suffrith alle thingis. It bileveth alle thingis. It hopith alle thingis. It susteyneth alle thingis. Charite fallith nevere doun, whether profesies schulen be voidid, ethir langagis chulen ceesse, ethir science schal be distried. For a parti we knowun, and a parti we profesien. But whane that schal come that is parfit, that thing that is of parti schal be voidid. Whanne I was a litil child, I spak as a litil child, I undirstood as a litil child, I thoughte as a litil child. But whanne I was maad a man, I avoidide tho thingis that weren of a litil child. And we seen now in a myrour in derknesse, but thanne face to face. Now I knowe of parti, but thanne I schal knowe as I am knowun. And now dwellen feith, hope and charite, these thre; but the moost of these is charite.

'The *Gawain*-Poet' (fl. 1390)

BL MS Cotton Nero A.x (*c.*1400) contains unique copies of four poems in alliterative verse that are customarily ascribed to the same poet and presumed to have been written in the north-west midlands in the late fourteenth century. *Patience* and *Cleanness* are poems of homiletic exhortation based on biblical stories, and written in unrhymed alliterative verse, like *Piers Plowman*, but arranged in quatrains. *Pearl* is a vision-poem in rhymed alliterative stanzas in which the poet's recently deceased two-year-old daughter instructs him in the mysteries of faith and salvation. There are editions of all four poems by M. Andrew and R. Waldron, *The Poems of the Pearl Manuscript* (London, 1978), and (with simplified spelling) by A.C. Cawley and J.J. Anderson (London, 1976); studies by A.C. Spearing, *The Gawain-Poet* (Cambridge, 1970), E. Wilson, *The Gawain-Poet* (Leiden, 1976), S. Stanbury, *Seeing the Gawain-Poet: Description and the Act of Perception* (Philadelphia, 1991); essays by different hands in D. Brewer and J. Gibson (eds), *A Companion to the Gawain-Poet* (Cambridge, 1997).

Sir Gawain and the Green Knight

Medieval romance is the narrative of the fantasy-life of an idealized warrior-aristocracy dedicated to the love and service of ladies and to high-minded principles of truth, honour and courtesy. It bears some, but not much, relation to real life. Romance developed, both as a form of oral entertainment and as a literary art-form, in the French courts of the twelfth century. Its greatest exponent, unrivalled for the wit and sensitivity of his response to the tragic and comic dilemmas of the noble life, is Chretien de Troyes. The subject-matter of medieval romance was, dominantly, Arthurian, though with Arthur appearing less as a heroic king and battle-leader than as the head of a brilliant court of knights and ladies; it is the knights of the Round Table who have the adventures. These adventures serve to exemplify and confirm the values of knighthood by subjecting the protagonist to a series of tests, which it is the point of romance that he should succeed in. *Sir Gawain and the Green Knight* is the greatest of the English Arthurian romances, remarkable both for its evocation of the quality, the 'feel', of courtly life, and for the subtlety, irony and cool sympathy of its treatment of Gawain. Gawain comes to the poem with a centuries-old reputation for high courtesy and susceptibility to female charm, though the English poet initially plays down the latter and emphasizes Gawain's special role as a Christian knight: he bears a pentangle on his shield symbolic of Christian virtue and faith. The plot, characterized by sophisticated repetitions, patternings and symmetries, locks two traditional stories, the 'Exchange of Beheadings' plot and the 'Exchange of Winnings' plot, into a narrative trap in which Gawain is seemingly forced into ignoble compromise. He answers successfully a public challenge only to discover, to his bitter embarrassment, that his performance is to be assessed on the basis of his conduct in what he thought was a private affair. The poet's mastery of courtly dialogue enables him to explore the nuances of refined sensibility, of questions of both morality and taste, in a manner worthy of Chretien, while his mastery of the language of description enables him to convey a rich variety of physical sensation – the biting cold of a winter-journey, the furred and silken luxury of a warm hearth, the joy of the hunt – with unprecedented vigour and energy.

Gawain is written in a more formal and precious style of alliterative verse, with the sequences of long lines punctuated as irregular stanza-units by the 'bob and wheel' (a one-stress line and four three-stress lines, rhyming *ababa*). Standard edition by J.R.R. Tolkien and E.V. Gordon (rev. Norman Davis [Oxford, 1967]); important studies by L.D. Benson, *Art and Tradition in SGGK* (New Brunswick, NJ, 1965), J. Burrow, *A Reading of SGGK* (London, 1965), and J. Mann, 'Price and Value in *SGGK*', *EC* 36 (1986), 294–318.

[A very large and fearsome knight, all green, arrives at Arthur's court at Camelot in the midst of the New Year's Day feast, and demands that the Round Table show its prowess by nominating a knight to engage with him in a Christmas 'game'. The game is that one of Arthur's knights shall strike a blow at the Green Knight with the great axe that he carries, and come a twelve-month later to the Green Chapel to receive a similar blow. Fear of the strange challenger, if not of the apparently ridiculous terms of the challenge, strikes the court dumb and Arthur has to step forward himself to take up the axe, but Gawain saves everyone further embarrassment by volunteering himself, with the utmost courtesy, to strike the first blow. His head having been struck off, the Green Knight, to everyone's dismay, picks it up and rides forth, reminding Gawain of his promise. Fit 2 (the poem is divided into four fits, or units of narration) describes Gawain's preparations to depart on the following All Souls' Day (30 November), with especial emphasis on his carrying of a pentangle on his shield and coat-armour symbolic of devotion to Christ and the Virgin. He rides off into the wilderness, apparently in the direction of the Peak District in northern England, but finds

himself nowhere near his destination as Christmas Day dawns. He comes suddenly upon a marvellously beautiful castle, where he is warmly welcomed by the lord of the castle, his beautiful young wife, and an ancient crone who keeps her company. He is invited to stay over the Christmas holiday, and the lord will supply a guide to take him to the Green Chapel, which is nearby, on the appointed day. Meanwhile, he is to enjoy a game with his host on the last three days of the holiday: the lord will go out hunting each day, Gawain will stay at home and keep his wife company, and at the end of each day they will exchange whatever they have won during the day.}

Fit 3

	Ful erly bifore the day the folk up rysen;
	Gestes that go wolde hor gromes thay calden,
hurry, quickly, horses	And thay busken up bilyve blonkkes to sadel,
Prepare, pack their bags	Tyffen her takles, trussen her males,
Get themselves ready	Richen hem the rychest, to ryde alle arayde,
take hold of	Lepen up lyghtly, lachen her brydeles,
man	Uche wyye on his way ther hym wel lyked.
well-loved	The leve lorde of the londe was not the last
men	Arayed for the rydyng, with renkkes ful mony;
He ate	Ete a sop hastyly, when he had herde masse,
open field	With bugle to bent-felde he buskes bylyve.
By the time that, gleamed	By that any daylyght lemed upon erthe,
	He with his hatheles on hyghe horsses weren.
(see n.)	Thenne thise cacheres that couthe cowpled hor houndes,
	Unclosed the kenel dore and calde hem theroute,
(see n.)	Blwe bygly in bugles thre bare mote;
Hounds, loud	Braches bayed therfore and breme noyse maked,
(see n.)	And thay chastysed and charred on chasyng that went,
	A hundreth of hunteres, as I haf herde telle,
	Of the best.
(see n.)	To trystors vewters yod,
	Couples huntes of kest;
because of	Ther ros for blastes gode
noise	Gret rurd in that forest.
sound	At the first quethe of the quest quaked the wylde;
fled, went frantic	Der drof in the dale, doted for drede,
high ground, promptly	Hiyed to the hyghe, bot heterly thay were
Checked by the beaters, shouted out	Restayed with the stablye, that stoutly ascryed.
way	Thay let the herttes haf the gate, with the hyghe hedes,
fierce, antlers	The breme bukkes also with hor brode paumes,
forbidden in the close season	For the fre lorde hade defende in fermysoun tyme

1126–7 **rysen ... calden**. Intermixture of present historic and past tenses is usual, and contributes to a characteristically ambiguous sense of both immediacy and distance.

1138 **hatheles**: 'men'. Originally a word of more specific meaning ('man of noble birth or bearing'), *hathel* is one of many nouns (e.g. *burne, freke, lede, renke, schalke, tolke, wyye*) pressed into service as an alliterating synonym for 'man'. Many verbs of originally specific meaning are likewise used as alliterating synonyms for 'go' (e.g. *bowe, cach, fare, ferke, founde, wende, wynne*), and there are numerous adjectives and adverbs used for alliteration that are pleonastic except for a general effect of courtly eulogy ('courteous', 'fine', 'noble', 'proper').

1139 'Then these huntsmen, who knew their job, leashed in pairs their hounds'.

1141 **thre bare mote**: 'three single notes' (the signal for unleashing the hounds).

1143 'And they (the huntsmen) chastised and turned back those that went chasing off'.

1146–7 'The keepers of the hounds went to their hunting-stations, and the huntsmen threw off the leashes'. The expert knowledge that the poem displays of hunting techniques and terms is one of the ways in which it appeals to a courtly audience.

1150 **the wylde**: 'the wild creatures'. The use of adjectives as substantives is a characteristic feature of the style of the poet, especially with vocatives, e.g. **gay** (1213), **hende** (1252).

chase after	That ther schulde no man meve to the male dere.
	The hindes were halden in with 'hay!' and 'war!'
valleys	The does dryven with gret dyn to the depe slades.
were released, the slanting flight	Ther myght mon se, as thay slypte, slentyng of arwes;
turn in the wood, flew an arrow	At uche wende under wande wapped a flone,
bit deeply into, brown (hide)	That bigly bote on the broun with ful brode hedes.
	What! thay brayen and bleden, bi bonkkes thay deyen,
hounds, rush, quickly	And ay raches in a res radly hem folwes,
loud	Hunteres with hyghe horne hasted hem after,
	Wyth such a crakkande kry as klyffes haden brusten.
escaped	What wylde so atwaped wyyes that schotten
(see n.)	Was al to-raced and rent at the resayt,
After being harassed from, driven	Bi thay were tened at the hyghe and taysed to the wattres –
	The ledes were so lerned at the lowe trysteres,
seized	And the grehoundes so grete, that geten hem bylyve
pulled down	And hem to-fylched as fast as frekes myght loke,
Right there	Ther ryght,
carried away	The lorde for blys abloy
(see n.)	Ful oft con launce and lyght,
passed	And drof that day wyth joy
	Thus to the derk nyght.
enjoys sport, forest edge	Thus laykes this lorde by lynde-wodes eves,
lies	And Gawayn the god mon in gay bed lyges,
gleamed, walls	Lurkkes quyl the daylyght lemed on the wowes,
canopy	Under covertour ful clere, cortyned aboute.
dozed	And as in slomeryng he slode, sleyly he herde
quickly	A litel dyn at his dor, and derfly open;
	And he heves up his hed out of the clothes,
	A corner of the cortyn he caght up a lyttel,
looks warily	And waytes warly thiderwarde quat hit be myght.
	Hit was the ladi, loflyest to beholde,
stealthily	That drow the dor after hir ful dernly and stylle,
went, man	And bowed towarde the bed; and the burne schamed
craftily, let on	And layde hym doun lystyly and let as he slepte.
she, stole	And ho stepped stilly and stel to his bedde,
	Kest up the cortyn and creped withinne,
	And set hir ful softly on the bed-syde
surprisingly	And lenged there selly longe, to loke quen he wakened.
	The lede lay lurked a ful longe quyle,
Turned over in his mind	Compast in his concience to quat that cace myght
Be tending or	Meve other amount – to mervayle hym thoght.
	Bot yet he sayde in hymself: 'More semly hit were
through the course of conversation	To aspye with my spelle in space quat ho wolde.'

1168 'Was pulled down and torn (by hounds) at the receiving-station'.

1175 **con launce and lyght**: 'galloped and dismounted'. The auxiliary **con** (a form of *gan*, 'began') here implies repeated action, but it is commonly used (like *gan*) merely as a periphrastic form of the past tense (= 'did') as well as to mean 'began'.

1178–9 The structure of Fit 3 is that of a triple triptych (aba/aba/aba), with the accounts of the three temptations embedded within the descriptions of the beginnings and ends of the three hunts – of the deer, boar and fox. The lord hunts his quarry, while his lady hunts hers. The juxtapositions provide effective contrasts of pace and tempo as well as parallels of content; it is worth considering why it is the hunts that are split and not the bedroom scenes.

1180 **quyl**: 'while'. The frequent spelling *qu* for *wh* (cf. **quat**, 1186; **quen**, 1194; **quyle**, 1195) indicates the still strongly aspirated pronunciation of northern dialects. There are many other such northernisms in the poem, e.g. *a* for *o* (**halden**, 1158; **snawe**, 2234; **hame**, 2451), pres. part. in *-ande* (**crakkande**, 1166), and pres. pl. and imper. pl. in *-es* (**desyres**, 1257; **hyyes**, 1351; **displeses**, 2439), as well as a large northern and Scandinavian element in the vocabulary.

turned	Then he wakenede and wroth and to-hir-warde torned
	And unlouked his yye-lyddes and let as hym wondered
(see n.)	And sayned hym, as bi his sawe the saver to worthe,
	With hande.
	Wyth chynne and cheke ful swete,
blend	Bothe quit and red in blande,
speak	Ful lufly con ho lete,
	Wyth lyppes smal laghande.
	'God moroun, sir Gawayn,' sayde that gay lady,
careless, anyone	'Ye ar a sleper unslyye, that mon may slyde hider.
(see n.)	Now ar ye tan astyt bot true us may schape,
sure	I schal bynde yow in your bedde, that be ye trayst.'
uttered those jesting words	Al laghande the lady lauced tho bourdes.
	'Goud moroun, gay,' quoth Gawayn the blythe,
It shall be with me	'Me schal worthe at your wille, and that me wel lykes,
promptly, cry for mercy	For I yelde me yederly and yeye after grace;
in my opinion	And that is the best, be my dome, for me byhoves nede.'
jested in return	And thus he bourded ayayn with mony a blythe laghter.
	'Bot wolde ye, lady lovely, then leve me grante,
release, prisoner	And deprece your prysoun and pray hym to ryse,
dress myself	I wolde bowe of this bed and busk me better,
acquire, talk	I schulde kever the more comfort to karp yow wyth.'
	'Nay, for sothe, beau sir,' sayd that swete,
have plans for you	'Ye schal not rise of your bedde, I rych yow better:
pin you down, side	I schal happe yow here that other half als,
	And sythen karp wyth my knyght that I kaght have;
	For I wene wel, iwysse, sir Wowen ye are,
	That alle the worlde worchipes, quere-so ye ride.
courtesy	Your honour, your hendelayk is hendely praysed
By lords	With lordes, wyth ladyes, with alle that lyf bere.
on our own	And now ye ar here, iwysse, and we bot oure one;
men, gone far away	My lorde and his ledes ar on lenthe faren,
my ladies	Other burnes in her bedde, and my burdes als,
fastened, strong	The dor drawen and dit with a derf haspe.
	And sythen I have in this hous hym that al lykes,
use my time	I schal ware my whyle wel quyl hit lastes,
In conversation	With tale.
body	Ye ar welcum to my cors,
pleasure, take	Yowre awen won to wale;
sheer necessity	Me behoves of fyne force
	Your servaunt be, and schale.'
a better thing	'In god fayth,' quoth Gawayn, 'gayn hit me thynkkes,
	Thagh I be not now he that ye of speken;
	To reche to such reverence as ye reherce here
	I am wyye unworthy, I wot wel myselven.
if you thought fit	Bi God, I were glad and yow god thoght

1202 'And crossed himself, as if by his prayer to be the safer'.
1210 'Now you are captured in a trice, unless we can arrange a truce'.
1226 **Wowen**. Spellings with *W*- and *G*- are both possible in the languages from which Gawain's name is derived, and this is useful for an alliterative poet.
1237 **Ye ar welcum to my cors**. This sounds surprisingly forward, and a doubtful strategy of seduction. It probably could mean 'I am at your disposal', with such overtones as the hearer chooses to hear.

In word or deed	At sawe other at servyce that I sette myght
Your honoured self	To the plesaunce of your prys – hit were a pure joye.'
	'In god fayth, sir Gawayn,' quoth the gay lady,
excellence	'The prys and the prowes that pleses al other,
disparaged, courtesy	If I hit lakked other set at lyght, hit were littel dayntye;
there are, in plenty, rather, now	Bot hit ar ladyes innoghe that lever wer nowthe
courteous lord	Haf the, hende, in hor holde, as I the habbe here,
	To daly with derely your dayntye wordes,
Obtain, assuage	Kever hem comfort and colen her cares,
treasure	Then much of the garysoun other gold that thay haven.
I give praise to, rules the heavens	But I louve that ilk lorde that the lyfte haldes,
	I haf hit holly in my honde that al desyres,
	Thurghe grace.'
	Scho made hym so gret chere,
	That was so fayr of face;
pure	The knyght with speches skere
each	Answared to uche a cace.
reward	'Madame,' quoth the myry mon, 'Mary yow yelde,
generosity	For I haf founden, in god fayth, yowre fraunchis nobele.
(see n.)	And other ful much of other folk fongen for hor dedes,
	Bot the dayntye that thay delen for my disert nysen –
	Hit is the worchyp of yourself that noght bot wel connes.'
noble (lady)	'Bi Mary,' quoth the menskful, 'me thynk hit another;
multitude	For were I worth al the wone of wymmen alyve,
wealth	And al he wele of the worlde were in my honde,
negotiate, obtain	And I schulde chepen and chose to cheve me a lorde,
qualities	For the costes that I haf knowen upon the, knyght, here,
courtesy	Of bewte and debonerte and blythe semblaunt –
	And that I haf er herkkened and halde hit here trwe –
	Ther schulde no freke upon folde bifore yow be chosen.'
chosen (i.e. your husband)	'Iwysse, worthy,' quoth the wyye, 'ye haf waled wel better;
	Bot I am proude of the prys that ye put on me,
	And soberly your servaunt, my soverayn I holde yow,
reward	And yowre knyght I becom, and Kryst yow foryelde!'
chatted, many things	Thus thay meled of muchquat til mydmorn paste,
behaved as if she	And ay the lady let lyk as ho hym loved mych;
conducted himself, behaved	The freke ferde with defence, and feted ful fayre.
lady	'Thagh I were burde bryghtest,' the burde in mynde hade,
mind, grievous harm	'The lasse luf in his lode' – for lur that he soght
Without delay	Boute hone,
blow, strike down	The dunte that schulde hym deve,
	And nedes hit most be done.
	The lady thenn spek of leve,
	He granted hir ful sone.
glance	Thenne ho gef hym god day, and wyth a glent laghed,

1252 **Haf the**. The lady begins here to make use of the second person singular pronoun as a mark of growing intimacy. But this would not normally be thought polite usage in the best courtly company, and Gawain keeps carefully to the second plural.
1256 **that ilke lorde that the lyfte haldes**. These periphrases for the deity, usually in oaths and adjurations (e.g. 1292), are part of the poet's repertoire of alliterative variation and synonymy.
1265–7 'And others receive plenty of praise from other folk for their deeds, but the kind things they say about me are not at all to my deserving – it reflects honour upon yourself, that know only how to behave generously.'

stunned, severe	And as ho stod ho stonyed hym wyth ful stor wordes:
makes prosper	'Now he that spedes uche spech this disport yelde yow!
causes some thought	Bot that ye be Gawen, hit gos in mynde.'
	'Querfore?' quoth the freke, and freschly he askes,
manners	Ferde lest he hade fayled in fourme of his costes.
form of reasoning	Bot the burde hym blessed, and bi this skyl sayde:
rightly	'So god as Gawayn gaynly is halden,
	And cortaysye is closed so clene in hymselven,
	Couth not lyghtly haf lenged so long wyth a lady,
kiss	Bot he had craved a cosse bi his courtaysye,
hint, trifling remark	Bi sum towch of summe tryfle at sum tales ende.'
let it be	Then quoth Wowen: 'Iwysse, worthe as yow lykes;
befits	I schal kysse at your comaundement, as a knyght falles,
as a further reason	And firre, lest he displese yow, so plede hit no more.'
	Ho comes nerre wyth that, and caches hym in armes,
bends	Loutes luflych adoun and the leude kysses.
commend, each other	Thay comly bykennen to Kryst ayther other;
	Ho dos hir forth at the dore withouten dyn more;
prepares, hastens	And he ryches hym to ryse and rapes hym sone,
clothes	Clepes to his chamberlayn, choses his wede,
ready	Bowes forth, quen he was boun, blythely to masse.
awaited	And thenne he meved to his mete that menskly hym keped,
	And made myry al day til the mone rysed,
	With game.
received	Was never freke fayrer fonge
	Bitwene two so dyngne dame,
	The alder and the yonge;
together	Much solace set thay same.
gone, sports	And ay the lorde of the londe is lent on his gamnes,
	To hunt in holtes and hethe at hyndes barayne.
quantity, had set	Such a sowme he ther slowe bi that the sunne heldet,
assess	Of dos and of other dere, to deme were wonder.
	Thenne fersly thay flokked in, folk at the laste,
killed, heap	And quykly of the quelled dere a querrye thay maked.
	The best bowed therto with burnes innoghe,
fat	Gedered the grattest of gres that ther were,
meticulously	And didden hem derely undo as the dede askes.
formal testing of quality	Serched hem at the asay summe that ther were,
(thickness of flesh), worst	Two fyngeres thay fonde of the fowlest of alle.
(see n.)	Sythen thay slyt the slot, sesed the erber,
Cut it clear, tied up the organ	Schaved wyth a scharp knyf, and the schyre knitten.
cut off	Sythen rytte thay the foure lymmes and rent of the hyde,
belly	Then brek thay the baly, the boweles out token
Carefully	Lystily, for laucyng the lere of the knot.
throat, expertly separated	Thay gryped to the gargulun, and graythely departed

1294–5 Gawain can cope with the lady's importunacy, but not easily with the thought that he may have been perceived to fail in some point of formal courtesy; to feel thus would be to lose his identity, not to be Gawain.

1323–61 This description of the butchering or 'brittling' (breaking) of the slain deer is a *tour de force* of expertise in the craft and terms of venery, one of the distinguishing marks of aristocratic accomplishment. Basically, the task is to make neat packages for carriage and presentation and to get rid of the unpleasant bits.

1330 'Then they slit the hollow at the base of the throat and took hold of the first stomach'.

1331 Sealing off the upper stomach is an important first step, since its contents would be obnoxious if released.

1334 **for laucyng the lere of the knot**: 'for fear of undoing the fastening of the knot' (that sealed off the upper stomach).

gullet, tossed	The wesaunt fro the wynt-hole and walt out the guttes.
cut	Then scher thay out the schulderes with her scharp knyves,
Pulled them out	Haled hem by a lyttel hole, to have hole sydes.
cut open, pulled it apart	Sithen britned thay the brest and brayden hit in twynne.
	And eft at the gargulun bigynes on thenne,
(see n.)	Ryves hit up radly ryght to the byght,
neck-offal	Voydes out the avanters, and verayly therafter
membranes, loosen	Alle the rymes by the rybbes radly thay lauce.
(see n.)	So ryde thay of by resoun bi the rygge-bones
Right down, together	Evenden to the haunche, that henged alle samen,
	And heven hit up al hole and hwen hit of there –
designate	And that thay neme for the noumbles bi nome, as I trowe,
Properly	Bi kynde.
	Bi the byght al of the thyghes
flaps (of loose flesh), loosen	The lappes thay lauce bihynde;
	To hewe hit in two thay hyyes,
	Bi the bakbon to unbynde.
neck	Bothe the hede and the hals thay hwen of thenne,
backbone	And sythen sunder thay the sydes swyft fro the chyne,
	And the corbeles fee thay kest in a greve.
pierced	Thenn thurled thay ayther thik syde thurgh bi the rybbe,
hocks (upper parts), haunches	And henged thenne ayther bi hoghes of the fourches,
to have his due portion	Uche freke for his fee as falles for to have.
skin	Upon a felle of the fayre best fede thayr houndes
lining	Wyth the lyver and the lyghtes, the lether of the paunches,
	And bred bathed in blod blende ther-amonges.
Vigorously	Baldely thay blw prys, bayed thayr raches;
took, all packed up	Sythen fonge thay her flesch folden to home,
Sounding, loud notes	Strakande ful stoutly mony stif motes.
By the time that, company, come	Bi that the daylyght was done the douthe was al wonen
	Into the comly castel, ther the knyght bides
	Ful stille.
kindled	Wyth blys and bryght fyr bette,
	The lorde is comen ther-tylle;
	When Gawayn wyth hym mette,
nothing but happiness	Ther was bot wele at wylle.
hall, gather, household	Thenne comaunded the lorde in that sale to samen alle the meny,
come downstairs	Bothe the ladyes on loghe to lyght with her burdes.
hall-floor, men, commands	Bifore alle the folk on the flette frekes he beddes
	Verayly his venysoun to fech hym byforne;
merry mood	And al godly in gomen Gawayn he called,
tallies (tails), fine-grown	Teches hym to the tayles of ful tayt bestes,
fine fat flesh	Schewes hym the schyre grece schorne upon rybbes.
pleases, praise	'How payes yow this playe? Haf I prys wonnen?
thoroughly, deserved	Have I thryvandely thonk thurgh my craft served?'
spoils	'Ye, iwysse,' quoth that other wyye, 'here is wayth fayrest

1341 'Cuts it up swiftly right to the fork of the back legs'.

1344 'In the same way they strip off methodically (the membranes) along the backbone'.

1347 **noumbles**: 'numbles', the stomach and other offal that is left when the carcass is hewn away.

1355 **the corbeles fee**: 'the raven's fee' was a piece of gristle at the end of the breast-bone which was thrown into the thickets as a titbit for crows and ravens.

1362 **blw prys**: the horn sounded the kill, the capture of 'the prize'.

That I sey this seven yere in sesoun of wynter.'
'And al I gif yow, Gawayn,' quoth the gome thenne,
may claim 'For by acorde of covenaunt ye crave hit as your awen.'
'This is soth,' quoth the segge, 'I say yow that ilke;
dwelling That I haf worthyly wonnen this wones wythinne,
becomes Iwysse with as god wylle hit worthes to youres.'
He hasppes his fayre hals his armes wythinne,
devise And kysses hym as comlyly as he couthe avyse;
Take, winnings, got 'Tas yow there my chevicaunce, I cheved no more;
bestow it freely, more I vowche hit saf fynly, thagh feler hit were.'
lord of the house, many thanks 'Hit is god,' quoth the god mon, 'grant mercy therfore.
if you would tell me Hit may be such hit is the better and ye me breve wolde
good fortune Where ye wan this ilk wele bi wytte of yorselven.'
the agreement, ask 'That was not forward,' quoth he, 'frayst me no more;
Since, taken what is due to you For ye haf tan that yow tydes, trawe ye non other
Ye mowe.'
Thay laghed and made hem blythe
words, to be praised Wyth lotes that were to lowe;
immediately To soper thay yede asswythe,
Wyth dayntyes nwe innowe.

And sythen by the chymnee in chamber thay seten,
choice, brought Wyyes the walle wyn weghed to hem oft,
jesting, agree And efte in her bourdyng thay baythen in the morn
fulfil, agreement To fylle the same forwardes that thay byfore maden:
winnings What chaunce so bytydes, hor chevysaunce to chaunge,
new things, obtained, night What nwes so thay nome, at naght quen thay metten.
Thay acorded of the covenauntes byfore the court alle –
with jesting The beverage was broght forth in bourde at that tyme –
took Thenne thay lovelych leghten leve at the last,
hastened Uche burne to his bedde busked bylyve.
Bi that the coke hade crowen and cakled bot thryse,
leapt The lorde was lopen of his bedde, the leudes uchone,
quickly despatched So that the mete and the masse was metely delyvered,
company The douthe dressed to the wod, er any day sprenged,
To chace.
Loud, huntsmen Hegh with hunte and hornes
in due course Thurgh playnes thay passe in space,
Uncoupled among tho thornes
Hounds, (like mad) Raches that ran on race.

marsh Sone thay calle of a quest in a ker syde,
huntsman urged on, scented The hunt rehayted the houndes that hit fyrst mynged,
uttered, loud Wylde wordes hym warp wyth a wrast noyce.
The howndes that hit herde hastid thider swythe,
trail And fellen as fast to the fuyt, fourty at ones.
racket and din Thenne such a glaver ande glam of gedered raches
rocky hillsides Ros that the rocheres rungen aboute.
urged on Hunteres hem hardened with horne and wyth muthe;
pack rushed Then al in a semblee sweyed togeder
pool, forest, fearsome Bitwene a flosche in that fryth and a foo cragge.

1393–4 He will be the better able to appreciate Gawain's gift of his day's winning if he knows where he got it.

1430–2 The unidealizing and unconventional precision of such landscape description has made readers think they could identify the locale of the poem in the hills of the Peak District, near the poet's dialectal home.

wooded knoll	In a knot bi a clyffe at the kerre syde,
rocky hillside confusedly	Ther as the rogh rocher unrydely was fallen,
went on	Thay ferden to the fyndyng, and frekes hem after.
surrounded the crag	Thay umbekesten the knarre and the knot bothe,
until	Wyyes, whyl thay wysten wel wythinne hem hit were,
was declared to be there	The best that ther breved was wyth the blodhoundes.
	Thenne thay beten on the buskes and bede hym up ryse,
(see n.)	And he unsoundyly out soght, segges overthwert –
most marvellous, rushed	On the sellokest swyn swenged out there,
herd, solitary beast because of age	Long sythen fro the sounder that synglere for olde.
big, greatest of all	For he was borelych and brode, bor alther-grattest,
grunted	Ful grymme quen he gronyed – thenne greved mony,
rush, dashed	For thre at the fyrst thrast he thryght to the erthe,
charged, without injuring more	And sparred forth good sped boute spyt more.
	Thise other halowed 'hyghe!' ful hyghe, and 'hay! hay!' cryed,
quickly sounded the recall	Haden hornes to mouthe, heterly rechated.
	Mony was the miry mouthe of men and of houndes
	That buskkes after this bor with bost and wyth noyse,
kill	To quelle.
stands at bay	Ful oft he bydes the baye
pack, in their midst	And maymes the mute in-melle;
	He hurtes of the houndes, and thay
piteously	Ful yomerly yaule and yelle.
Men, press forward	Schalkes to schote at hym schowen to thenne,
Loosed at	Haled to hym of her arewes, hitten hym ofte;
(see n.)	Bot the poyntes payred at the pyth that pyght in his sheldes,
bristles	And the barbes of his browe bite non wolde,
smooth-shaven, shattered	Thagh the schaven schaft schyndered in peces,
bounced back	The hede hypped ayayn were-so-ever hit hitte.
hurt, unceasing	Bot quen the dyntes hym dered of her dryye strokes,
(see n.)	Then braynwod for bate on burnes he rases,
cruelly	Hurtes hem ful heterly ther he forth hyyes,
were afraid, drew hesitantly back	And mony arwed therat and on lyte drowen.
gallops	Bot the lorde on a lyght horce launces hym after,
battlefield	As burne bolde upon bent his bugle he blowes,
thickets	He rechated and rode thurgh rones ful thyk,
Pursuing, slanted down	Suande this wylde swyn til the sunne schafted.
pass	This day wyth this ilk dede thay dryven on this wyse,
	Whyle oure luflych lede lys in his bedde,
properly, bedclothes	Gawayne graythely at home in geres ful ryche
	Of hewe.
	The lady noght foryate,
greet	Com to hym to salue;
	Ful erly ho was hym ate
change	His mode for to remwe.
peeps	Ho commes to the cortyn and at the knyght totes,
	Sir Wawen her welcumed worthy on fyrst,

1438 'And he fiercely came dashing out against the men across his path'.

1456 'But the points were blunted at the toughness that was in his flanks'.

1461 'Then frenzied by the persistent attack he rushes on the men'.

eagerly	And ho hym yeldes ayayn ful yerne of hir wordes,
	Settes hir sofly by his syde, and swythely ho laghes,
delivered	And wyth a luflych loke ho layde hym thyse wordes:
	'Sir, yif ye be Wawen, wonder me thynkkes,
disposed	Wyye that is so wel wrast alway to god,
manners, appreciate	And connes not of compaynye the costes undertake,
one teaches, them	And if mon kennes yow hom to knowe, ye kest hom of your mynde.
quickly, taught thee	Thou has foryeten yederly that yisterday I taght te
truest of all teaching	Bi alder-truest token of talk that I cowthe.'
	'What is that?' quoth the wyghe. 'Iwysse, I wot never.
declare	If hit be sothe that ye breve, the blame is myn awen.'
taught, fair lady	'Yet I kende yow of kyssyng,' quoth the clere thenne,
good reception is anticipated	'Quere-so countenaunce is couthe, quikly to clayme;
	That bicumes uche a knyght that cortaysy uses.'
brave	'Do way,' quoth that derf mon, 'my dere, that speche,
refused	For that durst I not do, lest I devayed were;
denied	If I were werned, I were wrang, iwysse, yif I profered.'
By my faith	'Ma fay,' quoth the mery wyf, 'ye may not be werned;
	Ye ar stif innoghe to constrayne wyth strenkthe, if yow lykes,
	Yif any were so vilanous that yow devaye wolde.'
	'Ye, be God,' quoth Gawayn, 'good is your speche,
not thought well of, land, live	But threte is unthryvande in thede ther I lende,
	And uche gift that is geven not with goud wylle.
	I am at your comaundement, to kysse quen yow lykes;
take, abstain, think fit	Ye may lach quen yow lyst, and leve quen yow thynkkes,
In due course	In space.'
bends	The lady loutes adoun
	And comlyly kysses his face;
	Much speche thay ther expoun
love's grief	Of druryes greme and grace.
	'I wolde wyt at yow, wyye,' that worthy ther sayde,
If, annoyed, reason	'And yow wrathed not therwyth, what were the skylle
fresh	That so yong and so yepe as ye at this tyme,
far and wide	So cortayse, so knyghtyly, as ye are knowen oute –
praised	And of alle chevalry to chose, the chef thyng alosed
true game, doctrine	Is the lel layk of luf, the lettrure of armes;
striving	For to telle of this tevelyng of this trwe knyghtes,
title-heading, text	Hit is the tytelet token and tyxt of her werkkes,
ventured	How ledes for her lele luf hor lyves han auntered,
love, times of trial	Endured for her drury dulful stoundes,
taken revenge	And after venged with her valour and voyded her care,
(lady's) bower, their own virtues	And broght blysse into boure with bountees hor awen –
known as comeliest, age	And ye ar knyght comlokest kyd of your elde,
fame, honour, everywhere	Your worde and your worchip walkes ayquere,
on two separate occasions	And I haf seten by yourself here sere twyes,
proceed	Yet herde I never of your hed helde no wordes
belonged	That ever longed to luf, lasse ne more.
knowledgeable, obligations	And ye, that ar so cortays and coynt of your hetes,

1499 In the politest possible way, Gawain hints that the lady's ideas of courtly behaviour are a little 'provincial'.

1512–19 These lines seem to be parenthetical; but the syntax of the whole sentence (1508–24) is not perspicuous, and may be meant to suggest that the lady is out of her depth in this kind of conversation.

young, eagerly Oghe to a yonke thynk yern to schewe
And teche sum tokenes of trwe-luf craftes.
ignorant, renown, enjoys Why! ar ye lewed, that alle the los weldes,
stupid Other elles ye demen me to dille your dalyaunce to herken?
For schame!
alone I com hider sengel and sitte
To lerne at yow sum game;
Do teach Dos teches me of your wytte,
away from home Whil my lorde is fro hame.'

reward 'In goud faythe,' quoth Gawayn, 'God yow foryelde!
pleasure Gret is the gode gle and gomen to me huge
make your way That so worthy as ye wolde wynne hidere,
bother And pyne yow with so pover a mon, as play wyth your knyght
favour of any kind, gives With anys-kynnes countenaunce – hit keveres me ese.
task Bot to take the torvayle to myself to trw-luf expoun,
touch on, themes And towche the temes of tyxt and tales of armes
skill To yow that, I wot wel, weldes more slyght
such Of that art, bi the half, or a hundreth of seche
on earth As I am other ever schal, in erde ther I leve –
folly manifold, noble lady Hit were a foly felefolde, my fre, by my trawthe.
(see n.) I wolde yowre wylnyng worche at my myght,
obliged As I am hyghly bihalden, and evermore wylle
the Lord Be servaunt to yourselven, so save me Dryghtyn!'
questioned, tempted Thus hym frayned that fre and fondet hym ofte,
evil-doing For to haf wonnen hym to woghe, what-so scho thoght elles;
was to be seen Bot he defended hym so fayr that no faut semed,
Ne non evel on nawther halve, nawther thay wysten
Bot blysse.
played Thay laghed and layked longe;
At the last scho con hym kysse,
take Hir leve fayre con scho fonge,
And went hir waye, iwysse.

bestirs Then ruthes hym the renk and ryses to the masse,
prepared And sithen hor diner was dyght and derely served.
The lede with the ladyes layked alle day,
galloped Bot the lorde over the londes launced ful ofte,
Pursues, ill-fated, slopes Swes his uncely swyn, that swynges bi the bonkkes
bit And bote the best of his braches the bakkes in sunder
stood at bay, broke (his stand) Ther he bode in his bay, tel bawemen hit breken,
(see n.) And made hym, mawgref his hed, for to mwe utter,
fiercely, arrows, flew So felle flones ther flete when the folk gedered.
start aside, at times Bot yet the styffest to start bi stoundes he made,
exhausted Til at the last he was so mat he myght no more renne,
Bot in the hast that he myght he to a hole wynnes
river-bank, stream Of a rasse, bi a rokk ther rennes the boerne.
He gete the bonk at his bak, bigynes to scrape,
at the corners The frothe femed at his mouth unfayre bi the wykes,

1546 'I would wish to do what you want to the extent of my power'.
1550 This is the first clear statement that the lady's visits are part of a malevolent plot; the suggestion that she has personal motives of another kind is interesting.
1565 'And made him, in spite of all he could do, to move out into the open'.

grew tired	Whettes his whyte tusches. With hym then irked
	Alle the burnes so bolde that hym by stoden
harass him from afar	To nye hym on-ferum, bot nyghe hym non durst
danger	For wothe.
	He hade hurt so mony byforne
	That al thught thenne ful lothe
	Be more wyth his tusches torne,
frenzied	That breme was and braynwod bothe.
urging on his horse	Til the knyght com hymself, kachande his blonk,
	Sygh hym byde at the bay, his burnes bysyde.
	He lyghtes luflych adoun, leves his corsour,
Pulls	Braydes out a bryght bront and bigly forth strydes,
Goes, stream, fierce (beast)	Foundes fast thurgh the forth ther the felle bydes.
	The wylde was war of the wyye with weppen in honde,
Bristled up, ferociously, snorted	Hef hyghly the here, so hetterly he fnast
many, worse	That fele ferde for the freke, lest felle hym the worre.
straight at the man	The swyn settes hym out on the segge even,
	That the burne and the bor were bothe upon hepes
swiftest	In the wyghtest of the water. The worre hade that other,
measures his aim	For the mon merkkes hym wel, as thay mette fyrst,
(see n.)	Set sadly the scharp in the slot even,
hilt	Hit hym up to the hult, that the hert schyndered,
snarlingly, went down	And he yarrande hym yelde, and yedoun the water
quickly	Ful tyt.
seized	A hundreth houndes hym hent,
	That bremely con hym bite;
bank	Burnes him broght to bent
do (him)	And dogges to dethe endite.
'prize' (see 1362)	There was blawyng of prys in mony breme horne,
	Heghe halowyng on highe wyth hatheles that myght;
Hounds bayed at that beast	Brachetes bayeden that best, as bidden the maysteres,
strenuous	Of that chargeaunt chace that were chef huntes.
	Thenne a wyye that was wys upon wodcraftes
meticulously	To unlace this bor lufly bigynnes:
	Fyrst he hewes of his hed and on highe settes,
roughly, along the backbone	And sythen rendes hym al roghe bi the rygge after,
red-hot coals	Braydes out the boweles, brennes hom on glede,
	With bred blent therwith his braches rewardes,
slices up, slabs	Sythen he britnes out the brawen in bryght brode sheldes,
entrails, properly	And has out the hastlettes, as hightly bisemes;
also, fastens	And yet hem halches al hole the halves togeder,
pole	And sythen on a stif stange stoutly hem henges.
	Now with this ilk swyn thay swengen to home;
	The bores hed was borne bifore the burnes selven,
put paid to, stream	That him forferde in the forthe thurgh forse of his honde
	So stronge.
	Til he sey sir Gawayne
the time seemed long to him	In halle hym thoght ful longe;

1593 'Set firmly the sharp (sword) straight in the hollow at the base of the throat'.

promptly He calde, and he com gayn
dues His fees ther for to fonge.

noise The lorde ful lowde with lote laghed myry
in high good humour When he seye sir Gawayn; with solace he spekes.
household The goude ladyes were geten, and gedered the meyny;
slabs of flesh He schewes hem the scheldes and schapes hem the tale
ferocity Of the largesse and the lenthe, the lithernes alse,
fighting defence Of the were of the wylde swyn in wod ther he fled.
That other knyght ful comly comended his dedes,
excellence And praysed hit as gret prys that he proved hade;
For suche a brawne of a best, the bolde burne sayde,
never before Ne such sydes of a swyn segh he never are.
Thenne hondeled thay the hoge hed, the hende mon hit praysed,
(see n.) And let lodly therat, the lorde for to here.
game (catch) 'Now, Gawayn,' quoth the godmon, 'this gomen is your awen
(see n.) Bi fyn forwarde and faste, faythely ye knowe.'
'Hit is sothe,' quoth the segge, 'and as siker trwe
gains Alle my get I schal yow gif agayn, bi my trawthe.'
He hent the hathel aboute the halse and hendely hym kysses,
once again And eftersones of the same he served hym there.
'Now ar we even,' quoth the hathel, 'in this eventide,
Of alle the covenauntes that we knyt sythen I com hider,
Bi lawe.'
The lorde sayde: 'Bi saynt Gile,
Ye ar the best that I knowe;
You will be Ye ben ryche in a whyle,
If you carry on such trade Such chaffer and ye drowe.'

set up, upon trestles Thenne thay teldet tables trestes alofte,
Kesten clothes upon; clere lyght thenne
walls Wakned bi wowes, waxen torches;
hall Segges sette and served in sale al aboute.
noisy merriment, sprang Much glam and gle glent up therinne
hearth-floor, many Aboute the fyre upon flet, and on fele wyse
fine At the soper and after, mony athel songes,
part-songs, dance-songs As coundutes of Krystmasse and caroles newe,
With alle the manerly merthe that mon may of telle,
And ever oure luflych knyght the lady bisyde.
demonstration of affection Such semblaunt to that segge semly ho made,
secret stolen glances Wyth stille stollen countenaunce, that stalworth to plese,
astonished That al forwondered was the wyye, and wroth with hymselven;
(see n.) Bot he nolde not for his nurture nurne here ayaynes,
with delicacy Bot dalt with hir al in dayntye, how-se-ever the dede turned
might be misinterpreted Towrast.
Quen thay hade played in halle
them lasted As longe as hor wylle hom last,
To chambre he con hym calle,
And to the chemnee thay past.

1634 'And behaved with a show of horror thereat, that the lord might hear'.
1636 'By completed and binding agreement, certainly you know'.
1661 'But he would not, because of his good breeding, repulse her advances openly'.

chatted, renewed the decision again	Ande ther thay dronken and dalten, and demed eft nwe
do the same thing	To norne on the same note on Nwe Yeres even;
	Bot the knyght craved leve to kayre on the morn,
appointed time, should go	For hit was negh at the terme that he to schulde.
dissuaded, prevailed on him to stay	The lorde hym letted of that, to lenge hym resteyed,
give my word	And sayde, 'As I am trwe segge, I siker my trawthe
get, business	Thou schal cheve to the grene chapel thy charres to make,
Sir, first light, (9 a.m.)	Leude, on Nwe Yeres lyght, longe bifore pryme.
take	Forthy thow lye in thy loft and lach thyn ese,
covenant	And I schal hunt in this holt and halde the towches,
thee winnings, when, return	Chaunge wyth the chevisaunce, bi that I charre hider;
tested thee	For I haf fraysted the twys, and faythful I fynde the.
	Now "thrid tyme, throwe best" thenk on the morne;
think	Make we mery quyl we may and mynne upon joye,
unhappiness, obtain	For the lur may mon lach when-so mon lykes.'
readily, is to stay	This was graythely graunted and Gawayn is lenged;
	Blithe broght was hym drynk and thay to bedde yeden
	With light.
	Sir Gawayn lis and slepes
	Ful stille and softe al night;
attends to	The lorde that his craftes kepes
prepared	Ful erly he was dight.
mass	After messe a morsel he and his men token;
mount	Miry was the mornyng, his mounture he askes.
follow	Alle the hatheles that on horse schulde helden hym after
ready prepared, horses	Were boun busked on hor blonkkes bifore the halle yates.
Wonderfully, earth, frost	Ferly fayre was the folde, for the forst clenged,
made ruddy, rack of cloud	In rede rudede upon rak rises the sunne,
dispels, sky	And ful clere castes the clowdes of the welkyn.
unleashed (the hounds), forest	Hunteres unhardeled bi a holt syde,
in the woods, noise	Rocheres roungen bi rys for rurde of her hornes.
trail, was lurking	Summe fel in the fute ther the fox bade,
to and fro across, cunning practice	Trayles ofte a-traveres bi traunt of her wyles.
small hound	A kenet kryes therof, the hunt on hym calles;
panted	His felawes fallen hym to, that fnasted ful thike,
very track	Runnen forth in a rabel in his ryght fare,
scampers	And he fyskes hem bifore; thay founden hym sone,
pursued	And quen thay seghe hym with syght thay sued hym fast,
Barking, furiously	Wreyande hym ful weterly with a wroth noyse;
twists and turns, rough thicket	And he trantes and tornayees thurgh mony tene greve,
Doubles back, listens out	Havilounes and herkenes bi hegges ful ofte.
little hedge	At the last bi a littel dich he lepes over a spenny
at the edge of a wooded marsh	Steles out ful stilly bi a strothe rande,
Thought to have escaped	Went haf wylt of the wode wyth wyles fro the houndes.
gone, fine hunting-station	Thenne was he went, er he wyst, to a wale tryster,
fierce ones, rush, threatened	Ther thre thro at a thrich thrat hym at ones,
	Al graye.
drew back	He blenched ayayn bilyve
sharply, darted aside	And stifly start onstray;
on earth	With alle the wo on lyve
	To the wod he went away.

joy (for anyone) alive, listen to	Thenne was hit list upon lif to lythen the houndes,
pack, mingled	When alle the mute hade hym met, menged togeder.
grievous clamour	Suche a sorwe at that syght thay sette on his hede
	As alle the clamberande clyffes hade clatered on hepes.
	Here he was halawed when hatheles hym metten,
greeted, snarling	Loude he was yayned with yarande speche;
	Ther he was threted and ofte thef called,
hounds	And ay the titleres at his tayl, that tary he ne myght.
broke cover	Ofte he was runnen at when he out rayked,
turned, Reynard	And ofte reled in ayayn, so Reniarde was wyly.
in a procession	And ye! he lad hem bi lag-mon, the lorde and his meyny,
until mid-morning	On this maner bi the mountes quyle myd-over-under,
	Whyle the hende knyght at home holsumly slepes
	Withinne the comly cortynes, on the colde morne.
allowed herself	Bot the lady for luf let not to slepe
become blunted, was fixed	Ne the purpose to payre that pyght in hir hert,
briskly, made her way	Bot ros hir up radly, rayked hir theder
reaching	In a mery mantyle, mete to the erthe,
skins	That was furred ful fyne wyth felles wel pured;
fine	No hwef goud on hir hede, bot the hagher stones
Adorned, hair-net	Trased aboute hir tressour be twenty in clusteres;
blooming	Hir thryven face and hir throte throwen al naked,
	Hir brest bare bifore, and bihinde eke.
	Ho comes withinne the chambre dore and closes hit hir after,
Throws open	Wayves up a wyndow and on the wyye calles
briskly, jokingly reproached	And radly thus rehayted hym with hir riche wordes,
	With chere:
	'A! mon, how may thou slepe?
	This morning is so clere.'
slumber	He was in drowping depe,
	Bot thenne he con hir here.
deep, muttered	In drey droupyng of dreme draveled that noble,
troubled with, oppressive	As mon that was in mornyng of mony thro thoghtes,
on the appointed day, fate	How that destinee schulde that day dele hym his wyrde
man	At the grene chapel when he the gome metes
	And bihoves his buffet abide withoute debate more.
recovered	Bot quen that comly com he kevered his wyttes,
dreams, answers	Swenges out of the swevenes and swares with hast.
	The lady luflych com, laghande swete,
sweetly	Felle over his fayre face and fetly hym kyssed.
courteous	He welcumes hir worthily with a wale chere;
	He sey hir so glorious and gayly atyred,
	So fautles of hir fetures and of so fyne hewes,
Ardent welling-up	Wight wallande joye warmed his hert.
gentle, fell	With smothe smylyng and smolt thay smeten into merthe,
happiness	That al was blis and bonchef that breke hem bitwene,
joy	And wynne.
uttered	Thay lauced wordes gode,

1733 **for luf**. The poet had earlier (see line 1550) hinted, perhaps irresponsibly, at some movement of affection on the lady's part. Here her intention to seduce is momentarily masked as the effect she intends to convey.

1738 **hwef**: 'coif' (cap), a head-covering suitable for a married woman.

	Much wele then was therinne;
	Gret perile bitwene hem stode,
If, have not in mind	Nif Mary of hir knyght mynne.
noble, pressed, hard	For that prynces of pris depresed hym so thikke,
Urged, limit	Nurned hym so neghe the thred, that nede hym bihoved
accept, boorishly	Other lach ther hir luf other lodly refuse.
a churl	He cared for his cortaysye, lest crathayn he were,
the harm to himself	And more for his meschef yif he schulde make synne
man, dwelling, owned	And be traytor to that tolke that that telde aght.
	'God schylde,' quoth the schalk. 'That schal not befalle!'
little, deflected	With luf-laghyng a lyt he layd hym bysyde
	Alle the speches of specialtee that sprange of her mouthe.
	Quoth that burde to the burne, 'Blame ye disserve,
person	Yif ye luf not that lyf that ye lye nexte,
	Bifore alle the wyyes in the worlde wounded in hert,
Unless, sweetheart, dearer	Bot if ye haf a lemman, a lever, that yow lykes better,
plighted, noble lady	And folden fayth to that fre, festned so harde
break, wish, believe now	That yow lausen ne lyst – and that I leve nouthe,
	And that ye telle me that now trwly, I pray yow;
conceal	For alle the lufes upon lyve, layne not the sothe
	For gile.'
	The knyght sayde, 'Be sayn Jon,'
gently	And smethely con he smyle,
possess	'In fayth I welde right non,
at present	Ne non wil welde the quile.'
	'That is a worde,' quoth that wyght, 'that worst is of alle;
answered, seems sad to me	Bot I am swared for sothe, that sore me thinkkes.
go hence	Kysse me now comly, and I schal cach hethen;
mourn, woman	I may bot mourne upon molde, as may that much lovyes.'
Sighing, stooped	Sykande ho sweye doun and semly hym kyssed,
	And sithen ho severes hym fro and says as ho stondes:
	'Now, dere, at this departyng do me this ese,
	Gif me sumquat of thy gifte, thi glove if hit were,
think of	That I may mynne on the, mon, my mournyng to lassen.'
	'Now iwysse,' quoth that wyye, 'I wolde I hade here
most precious	The levest thing for thy luf that I in londe welde,
wonderfully	For ye haf deserved, for sothe, sellyly ofte
give	More rewarde bi resoun then I reche myght;
(see n.)	But to dele yow for drurye, that dawed bot neked.
	Hit is not your honour to haf at this tyme
keepsake	A glove for a garysoun of Gawaynes giftes;
on a quest, unfamiliar lands	And I am here an erande in erdes uncouthe,
bags, valuable	And have no men wyth no males with menskful thinges.
upsets, for love's sake	That mislykes me, lady, for luf at this tyme;

1802 Cf. 1810. The slipping into the second person singular is perhaps a sign that Gawain is relaxing, thinking that the worst is over (he has definitively refused her) and that he can afford to be a little nicer to her.

1805 'But to give you something as a love-token, that would avail but little (not be a good idea)'. According to this punctuation, Gawain wants to make a distinction between an 'official' present and a secret love-token. But he does not want to say this too bluntly, and so he obscures the issue by hinting that the distinction is between a more and a less valuable present; the glove would be not a secret love-token but a present of inappropriately low value, one that was of little worth (**that dawed bot neked**). As usual, modern punctuation forces a choice between valuable ambiguities of interpretation.

(see n.)	Iche tolke mon do as he is tan, tas to non ille
Nor be distressed	Ne pine.'
	'Nay, hende, of hyghe honours,'
lovesome under linen (i.e. lady)	Quoth that lufsum under lyne,
	'Thagh I nade oght of youres,
	Yet schulde ye have of myne.'
offered, ring	Ho raght hym a riche rynk of red golde werkes,
glittering	Wyth a starande ston stondande alofte,
shining	That bere blusschande bemes as the bryght sunne;
wealth	Wyt ye wel, hit was worth wele ful hoge.
refused	Bot the renk hit renayed, and redyly he sayde:
want, before God (i.e. by God)	'I wil no giftes, for Gode, my gay, at this tyme;
offer	I haf none yow to norne ne noght wyl I take.'
pressed it on, offer refuses	Ho bede hit hym ful bysily, and he hir bode wernes,
take	And swere swyfte by his sothe that he hit sese nolde;
refused	And ho sory that he forsoke, and sayde therafter:
	'If ye renay my rynk, to ryche for hit semes,
obliged	Ye wolde not so hyghly halden be to me,
belt, profits	I schal gif yow my girdel, that gaynes yow lasse.'
took hold of, was fastened around	He laght a lace lyghtly that leke umbe hir sydes,
Tied over	Knit upon hir kyrtel under the clere mantyle –
Made, trimmed	Gered hit was with grene sylke and with golde schaped,
(see n.)	Noght bot arounde brayden, beten with fyngres –
	And that ho bede to the burne, and blythely bisoght,
	Thagh hit unworthi were, that he hit take wolde,
refused, accept	And he nay that he nolde neghe in no wyse
	Nauther golde ne garysoun, er God hym grace sende
accomplish, mission	To acheve to the chaunce that he hade chosen there.
	'And therfore I pray yow displese yow noght,
efforts, consent	And lettes be your bisinesse, for I baythe hit yow never
	To graunte.
	I am derely to yow biholde
kind behaviour	Bicause of your sembelaunt,
in all eventualities	And ever in hot and colde
	To be your trwe servaunt.'
refuse	'Now forsake ye this silke,' sayde the burde thenne,
	'For hit is symple in hitself? And so hit wel semes.
	Lo! so hit is littel, and lasse hit is worthy.
properties	Bot who-so knew the costes that knit ar therinne,
value	He wolde hit prayse at more prys, paraventure;
girt	For quat gome so is gorde with this grene lace,
closely fastened around	While he hit hade hemely halched aboute
	Ther is no hathel under heven to-hewe hym that myght,
by any stratagem	For he myght not be slayn for slyght upon erthe.'
pondered	Then kest the knyght, and hit come to his hert

1811 'Each man must do as he is taken (as things fall out for him), don't take it amiss'.

1829 **girdel**: an item of clothing that would qualify as exactly the kind of token of secret love that Gawain was wary of earlier.

1833 'Embroidered, and decorated by hand, only around the edges' (i.e. it is **symple**, 1847).

1855–8 The alliterating words convey the contradiction at the heart of Gawain's impulse – to accept the girdle as a talisman is an excellent device but there is an element of sly secrecy about it, only unconsciously acknowledged, as well as covert self-justification: his **sleght** will be excusable in view of the **slyght** that the Green Knight had already practised on him, and that the lady has subtly reminded him of (1854).

assigned	Hit were a juel for the jopardy that hym jugged were
arrived at, doom, receive	When he acheved to the chapel, his chek for to fech,
	Myght he haf slypped to be unslayn, the sleght were noble.
(see n.)	Thenne he thulged with hir threpe and tholed hir to speke,
pressed	And ho bere on hym the belt and bede hit hym swythe,
	And he granted, and ho hym gafe with a goud wylle,
reveal	And bisoght hym for hir sake discever hit never
	Bot to lelly layne fro hir lorde. The leude hym acordes
	That never wyye schulde hit wyt, iwysse, bot thay twayne,
	For noghte.
	He thonkked hir oft ful swythe,
earnestly	Ful thro with hert and thoght.
three times	Bi that on thrynne sythe
hardy	Ho has kyst the knyght so toght.
	Thenne laches ho hir leve and leves hym there,
	For more myrthe of that mon moght ho not gete.
attires	When ho was gon, sir Gawayn geres hym sone,
dresses	Rises and riches hym in araye noble,
Puts away, gave	Lays up the luf-lace the lady hym raght,
carefully	Hid hit ful holdely ther he hit eft fonde.
briskly, takes	Sythen chevely to the chapel choses he the waye,
	Prevely aproched to a prest and prayed hym there
hear his confession	That he wolde lyste his lyf and lern hym better
go hence	How his sawle schulde be saved when he schuld seye hethen.
confessed, fully, revealed	There he schrof hym schyrly and schewed his mysdedes
lesser (i.e. venial)	Of the more and the mynne, and merci beseches,
	And of absolucioun he on the segge calles;
	And he asoyled hym surely and sette hym so clene
As if, appointed	As domesday schulde haf ben dight on the morn.
makes	And sythen he mace hym as mery among the fre ladyes,
	With comlych caroles and alle kynnes joye,
	As never he did bot that daye, to the derk nyght,
	With blys.
courteous treatment	Uche mon hade dayntye thare
	Of hym, and sayde, 'Iwysse,
	Thus myry he was never are,
	Syn he com hider, er this.'
let him stay, place of comfort	Now hym lenge in that lee, ther luf hym bityde!
engaged in his sports	Yet is the lorde on the launde, ledande his gomnes:
headed off	He has forfaren this fox that he folwed longe.
jumped, rascal	As he sprent over a spenny to spye the schrewe,
	Ther as he herd the howndes that hasted hym swythe,
running, thicket	Renaud com richande thurgh a roghe greve,
rush	And alle the rabel in a res ryght at his heles.

1859 'Then he bore patiently with her importunity and allowed her to speak'.

1863 **lelly layne**: 'loyally conceal'. Again the alliterating words emphasize the ambiguity: is it possible to be honest and true in the concealment of a secret for the lady's sake (and his own) that involves a breach of trust to the lord and specifically a breaking of the exchange of winnings agreement?

1876–84 This confession scene has caused some debate. It has been asked how Gawain can confess so fully and be absolved when he has already done something he is going to be ashamed of later. It may be that modern readers have an unrealistic notion of what a priest would be likely to be concerned about on such an occasion, and of what constitutes a 'confessable' sin. Yet the pentangle did put Gawain in a position of specially high moral responsibility.

wild creature	The wyye was war of the wylde and warly abides
thrusts	And braydes out the bryght bronde and at the best castes.
flinched, was about to go back	And he schunt for the scharp and schulde haf arered;
dog rushes	A rach rapes hym to, ryght er he myght,
	And ryght bifore the hors fete thay fel on hym alle
	And woried me this wyly with a wroth noyse.
	The lorde lyghtes bilyve and laches hym sone,
quickly	Rased hym ful radly out of the rach mouthes,
	Haldes heghe over his hede, halowes faste,
fierce	And ther bayen hym mony brath houndes.
	Huntes hyyed hem theder with hornes ful mony,
sounding the recall	Ay rechatande aryght til thay the renk seyen.
By the time that	Bi that was comen his compeyny noble,
	Alle that ever ber bugle blowed at ones
	And alle thise other halowed that hade no hornes.
cry	Hit was the myriest mute that ever mon herde,
uproar	The rich rurd that ther was raysed for Renaude saule
clamour	With lote.
	Hor houndes thay ther rewarde,
fondle, rub	Her hedes thay fawne and frote;
take	And sythen thay tan Reynarde
strip off	And tyrven of his cote.
made for	And thenne thay helden to home, for hit was niegh nyght,
Blowing, strong	Strakande ful stoutly in hor store hornes.
alighted, dear	The lorde is lyght at the laste at hys lef home,
	Fyndes fire upon flet, the freke ther-byside,
	Sir Gawayn the gode, that glad was withalle:
	Among the ladies for luf he ladde much joye.
wore, reached	He were a bleaunt of blwe that bradde to the erthe;
	His surkot semed hym wel, that softe was forred,
	And his hode of that ilke henged on his schulder;
Trimmed, ermine	Blande al of blaunner were bothe al aboute.
	He metes me this godmon inmyddes the flore,
good humour	And al with gomen he hym gret and goudly he sayde:
fulfil, agreement now	'I schal fylle upon fyrst oure forwardes nouthe,
gladly	That we spedly han spoken ther spared was no drynk.'
embraces	Then acoles he the knyght and kysses hym thryes
With as much relish and vigour	As saverly and sadly as he hem sette couthe.
happiness	'Bi Kryst,' quoth that other knyght, 'ye cach much sele
acquisition, goods, bargain	In chevisaunce of this chaffer, yif ye hade goud chepes.'
no matter, briskly	'Ye, of the chepe no charge,' quoth chefly that other,
openly, owed	'As is pertly payed the chepes that I aghte.'
	'Mary,' quoth that other mon, 'myn is bihynde,
	For I haf hunted al this day and noght haf I geten
	Bot this foule fox felle – the fende haf the godes!-
valuable	And that is ful pore for to pay for suche prys thinges
given, earnestly	As ye haf thryght me here thro, suche thre cosses
	So gode.'

1902 **schunt for the scharp**. Cf. 2280.
1905 **woried me**: *me* here is 'ethic dative' (cf. 1932, 2014, 2144, 2459), untranslatable but suggestive of intimacy of narrative tone.
1928 **bleaunt of blwe**: 'blue tunic'. Blue was well established as the colour of truth and faithfulness (commonly used for the Virgin's mantle), and wearing it is a rather self-conscious ostentation on Gawain's part, a kind of guiltily pre-emptive strike, like the offer to make the return of winnings first (1934).

'Inogh,' quoth sir Gawayn,
cross — 'I thonk yow, bi the rode,'
And how the fox was slayn
He tolde hym as they stode.

With merthe and mynstralsye, wyth metes at hor wylle,
Thay maden as mery as any men moghten.
words, jests — With laghyng of ladies, with lotes of bordes,
Gawayn and the godemon so glad were thay bothe,
(see n.) — Bot if the douthe had doted other dronken ben other.
Bothe the mon and the meyny maden mony japes,
come — Til the sesoun was seyen that thay sever moste;
Burnes to hor bedde behoved at the laste.
Thenne lowly his leve at the lorde fyrst
Takes — Foches this fre mon, and fayre he hym thonkkes
wonderful — 'Of such a selly sojorne as I haf hade here;
Your honour at this hyghe fest the hyghe kyng yow yelde!
I yef yow me for on of youres, if yowreself lykes;
get going — For I mot nedes, as ye wot, meve to-morne,
If you provide me, promised — And ye me take sum tolke to teche, as ye hyght,
way — The gate to the grene chapel, as God wyl me suffer
be dealt, judgement, destiny — To dele on Nw Yeres day the dome of my wyrdes.'
'In god faythe,' quoth the godmon, 'wyth a goud wylle
Al that ever I yow hyght halde schal I redy.'
Ther asyngnes he a servaunt to sett hym in the waye
conduct, delay — And coundue hym by the downes, that he no drech had,
travel, wood, by the shortest route — For to ferk thurgh the fryth and fare at the gaynest
thicket — Bi greve.
The lorde Gawayn con thonk,
show — Such worchip he wolde hym weve.
noble — Then at tho ladyes wlonk
The knyght has tan his leve,

With care and wyth kyssyng he carppes hem tille,
hearty, pressed — And fele thryvande thonkkes he thrat hom to have,
eagerly — And thay yelden hym ayayn yeply that ilk.
sighs — Thay bikende hym to Kryst with ful colde sykynges.
Sythen fro the meyny he menskly departes;
Uche mon that he mette, he made hem a thonke
special trouble — For his servyse and his solace and his sere pyne
with busy care — That thay wyth busynes had ben aboute hym to serve;
And uche segge as sory to sever with hym there
As if, dwelt, noble knight — As thay hade wonde worthyly with that wlonk ever.
Then with ledes and lyght he was ladde to his chambre
And blythely broght to his bedde to be at his rest.
Yif he ne slepe soundyly, say ne dar I,
think about — For he hade muche on the morn to mynne, yif he wolde,
In thoght.
Let hym lyye there stille,
nearly what — He has nere that he soght;

1956 '(Could not be more so) unless the company had gone crazy or been drunk'.

1961–2 Transition in mid-sentence from indirect to direct speech is common in ME.

And ye wyl a whyle be stylle,
I schal telle yow how thay wroght.

Fit 4

	Now neghes the Nw Yere and the nyght passes,
forces its way upon	The day dryves to the derk, as Dryghtyn biddes.
	Bot wylde wederes of the worlde wakned theroute,
	Clowdes kesten kenly the colde to the erthe,
bitter wind, torment	Wyth nyye innoghe of the northe the naked to tene.
(see n.)	The snawe snitered ful snart, that snayped the wylde;
whistling, blew in gusts	The werbelande wynde wapped fro the hyghe
	And drof uche dale ful of dryftes ful grete.
	The leude lystened ful wel, that ley in his bedde:
	Thagh he lowkes his liddes, ful lyttel he slepes;
time	Bi uch kok that crue he knwe wel the steven.
Quickly, got up	Deliverly he dressed up er the day sprenged,
	For there was lyght of a laumpe that lemed in his chambre.
promptly, answered	He called to his chamberlayn, that cofly hym swared,
coat of mail, saddle his horse	And bede hym bryng hym his bruny and his blonk sadel;
gets up, clothes	That other ferkes hym up and feches hym his wedes
dresses, in splendid style	And graythes me sir Gawayn upon a grett wyse.
ward off	Fyrst he clad hym in his clothes, the colde for to were,
carefully	And sythen his other harnays, that holdely was keped,
belly-armour, polished	Bothe his paunce and his plates, piked ful clene,
	The rynges rokked of the roust of his riche bruny;
at first	And al was fresch as upon fyrst, and he was fayn thenne
	To thonk.
put on	He hade upon uche pece,
splendid	Wyped ful wel and wlonk;
	The gayest into Grece
Bade the man	The burne bede bryng his blonk.
put	Whyle the wlonkest wedes he warp on hymselven –
(see n.)	His cote wyth the conysaunce of the clere werkes
set	Ennurned upon velvet, vertuus stones
inlaid, bound in, embroidered	Aboute beten and bounden, enbrauded semes,
skins	And fayre furred withinne wyth fayre pelures –
	Yet laft he not the lace, the ladies gifte:
	That forgat not Gawayn, for gode of hymselven.
When, broad hips	Bi he hade belted the bronde upon his balwe haunches,
arranged, love-token	Thenn dressed he his drurye double hym aboute,
wound, waist	Swythe swethled umbe his swange swetely that knyght:
well suited that fair (knight)	The gordel of the grene silke that gay wel bisemed,
royal, look at	Upon that ryol red clothe that ryche was to schewe.
its richness	But wered not this ilk wyye for wele this gordel,
	For pryde of the pendauntes, thagh polyst thay were,

2003 'The snow sleeted down full sharply, that stung the wild creatures'.

2018 Armour was rocked in a barrel of sand in order to remove the rust.

2026 'His surcoat with the badge (i.e. the pentangle) of fine workmanship'.

2027 **vertuus stones**: precious stones were thought to carry certain 'virtues' or powers, as of healing or protection.

2035–6 The green girdle is slung over the red cloth upon which the pentangle is embroidered.

glinted	And thagh the glyterande golde glent upon endes,
	Bot for to saven hymself when suffer hym byhoved,
(see n.)	To byde bale withoute dabate of bronde hym to were
	Other knyffe.
ready	Bi that the bolde man boun
Proceeds	Wynnes theroute bilyve;
household retainers	Alle the meyny of renoun
earnestly	He thonkkes ofte ful ryve.
ready	Thenne was Gryngolet graythe, that gret was and huge,
comfortably	And hade ben sojourned saverly and in a siker wyse:
gallop, being in such good condition	Hym lyst prik for poynt, that proude hors thenne.
goes up, inspects, coat	The wyye wynnes hym to and wytes on his lyre
	And sayde soberly hymself and by his soth sweres:
castle, honour	'Here is a meyny in this mote that on menske thenkkes,
The man that	The mon hem maynteines, joy mot thay have!
	The leve lady on lyve, luf hir bityde!
	Yif thay for charyte cherysen a gest
lord, repay	And halden honour in her honde, the hathel hem yelde
	That haldes the heven upon hyghe, and also yow alle!
live	And yif I myght lyf upon londe lede any quyle,
give	I schuld rech yow sum rewarde redyly, if I myght.'
	Thenn steppes he into stirop and strydes alofte;
slung	His schalk schewed hym his schelde – on schulder he hit laght,
Puts spurs to	Gordes to Gryngolet with his gilt heles,
springs forward	And he startes on the ston – stod he no lenger
	To praunce.
man	His hathel on hors was thenne
	That bere his spere and launce.
commend	'This kastel to Kryst I kenne:
May he give	He gef hit ay god chaunce!'
drawn	The brygge was brayde doun and the brode yates
	Unbarred and born open upon bothe halve.
bridge-planks	The burne blessed hym bilyve and the bredes passed,
	Prayses the porter bifore the prynce kneled,
(see n.)	Gef hym God and goud day, that Gawayn he save,
	And went on his way with his wyye one
get to, perilous	That schulde teche hym to tourne to that tene place
grievous blow	Ther the ruful race he schulde resayve.
passed	Thay bowen bi bonkkes ther boghes ar bare,
	Thay clomben bi clyffes ther clenges the colde.
clouds were high, threatening	The heven was up-halt, bot ugly ther-under;
lay damp, drizzled	Mist muged on the mor, malt on the mountes;
mist-cloak	Uch hille hade a hatte, a myst-hakel huge.
boiled and foamed	Brokes byled and breke bi bonkkes aboute,
(see n.)	Schyre schaterande on schores ther thay doun schowved.
Very tortuous, had to (go)	Wela wylle was the way ther thay bi wod schulden,

2041 'To abide death without resisting with a sword to defend himself'.

2045–6 There is no one there except for himself and his servant (the guide assigned to him, who acts as his squire). As often, the 'wheel' is anticipatory of the next stanza.

2073 '(Who, i.e. the porter) commended him to God, and wished him good day, praying that God save Gawain'.

2083 'Brightly splashing on the banks where they made their way down'.

Til hit was sone sesoun that the sunne ryses
That tyde.
Thay were on a hille ful hyghe,
The quyte snaw lay bisyde;
The burne that rod hym by
Bede his mayster abide.

led 'For I haf wonnen yow hider, wyye, at this tyme,
noted And now nar ye not fer fro that note place
looked out and asked for That ye han spied and spuryed so specially after.
Bot I schal say yow for sothe, sythen I yow knowe,
And ye ar a lede upon lyve that I wel lovy,
act according to, would be Wolde ye worch bi my wytte, ye worthed the better.
hasten The place that ye prece to ful perelous is halden:
dwells Ther wones a wyye in that waste, the worst upon erthe,
For he is stiffe and sturne and to strike lovies,
earth And more he is then any mon upon myddelerde
And his body bigger then the best fowre
That ar in Arthures hous, Hector, other other.
has made it his practice He cheves that chaunce at the chapel grene,
Ther passes non bi that place so proude in his armes
beats him down, blow That he ne dynges hym to dethe with dynt of his honde;
violent For he is a mon methles and mercy non uses,
For be hit chorle other chaplayn that bi the chapel rydes,
Monk other masse-prest other any mon elles,
pleasant, kill, alive Hym thynk as queme hym to quelle as quyk go hymselven.
Forthy I say the, as sothe as ye in sadel sitte,
have his way Com ye there, ye be kylled, may the knyght rede –
Trawe ye me that trwely, thagh ye had twenty lyves
To spende.
He has wonyd here ful yore,
field, strife, brought about On bent much baret bende;
Ayayn his dyntes sore
Ye may not yow defende.

Therefore, alone 'Forthy, goude sir Gawayn, let the gome one,
way, for God's sake And gos away sum other gate, upon Goddes halve!
land Cayres bi sum other kyth, ther Kryst mot yow spede.
promise, further And I schal hyye me hom ayayn, and hete yow fyrre
saints That I schal swere bi God and alle his gode halwes –
sacred relic "As help me God and the halydam!" and othes innoghe –
utter That I schal lelly yow layne, and lauce never tale
sought, for any man That ever ye fondet to fle for freke that I wyst.'
with forced politeness 'Grant merci,' quoth Gawayn, and gruchyng he sayde:
Good luck to you, would wish 'Wel worth the, wyye, that woldes my gode,
believe And that lelly me layne I leve wel thou woldes.
kept, faithfully, if I Bot helde thou hit never so holde, and I here passed,
Sought for fear Founded for ferde for to fle, in fourme that thou telles,
I were a knyght kowarde, I myght not be excused.
whatever may befall Bot I wyl to the chapel, for chaunce that may falle,

2124 **lelly yow layne**. Cf. 1863. The guide's offer, by contrast with the lady's, is easy for Gawain to deal with according to his usual code of chivalric behaviour, and to reject.

	And talk wyth that ilk tulk the tale that me lyste,
Whether it fall out as, fate	Worthe hit wele other wo, as the wyrde lykes
	Hit hafe.
formidable fellow	Thaghe he be a sturn knape
be master of, standing there armed	To stightel, and stad with stave,
	Ful wel con Dryghtyn schape
	His servauntes for to save.'
say so determinedly	'Mary!' quoth that other mon, 'now thou so much spelles
harm, take upon	That thou wylt thyn awen nye nyme to thyselven,
lose, hinder, have inclination	And the lyst lese thy lyf, the lette I ne kepe.
	Haf here thi helme on thy hede, thi spere in thi honde,
path	And ryde me doun this ilk rake bi yon rokke syde,
wild	Til thou be broght to the bothem of the brem valay.
flat meadow	Thenne loke a littel on the launde, on thi lyfte honde,
valley	And thou schal se in that slade the self chapel
massive, field	And the borelych burne on bent that hit kepes.
	Now fares wel, on Godes half, Gawayn the noble!
	For alle the golde upon grounde I nolde go wyth the
one foot further	Ne bere thi felawschip thurgh this fryth on fote fyrre!'
With that, turns	Bi that the wyye in the wod wendes his brydel,
	Hit the hors with the heles as harde as he myght,
	Lepes hym over the launde and leves the knyght there
	Al one.
	'Bi Goddes self,' quoth Gawayn,
weep	'I wyl nauther grete ne grone;
obedient	To Goddes wylle I am ful bayn,
committed	And to hym I haf me tone.'
spurs, picks up	Thenne gyrdes he to Gryngolet and gederes the rake.
Pushes, rocky bank, wood	Schowves in bi a schore at a schawe syde,
hillside	Rides thurgh the roghe bonk ryght to the dale.
looked	And thenne he wayted hym aboute, and wylde hit hym thoght,
shelter	And seye no syngne of resette bisydes nowhere,
steep	Bot hyghe bonkkes and brent upon bothe halve,
rugged crags, gnarled	And rughe knokled knarres with knorned stones;
clouds, jutting rocks, grazed	The skwes of the scowtes skayned hym thoght.
halted	Thenne he hoved and wythhylde his hors at that tyde
turned this way and that	And ofte chaunged his cher the chapel to seche.
very strange	He sey non suche in no syde, and selly hym thoght,
small hill	Save a lyttel on a launde a lawe as hit were,
smooth rounded mound, water	A balw berw bi a bonke the brymme bysyde,
rapids, stream, ran down	Bi a fors of a flode that ferked thare –
stream	The borne blubred therinne as hit boyled hade.
urges on, horse	The knyght kaches his caple and com to the lawe,
(lime-)tree, attaches	Lightes doun luflyly and at a lynde taches
noble steed	The rayne of his riche with a roghe braunche.
	Thenne he bowes to the berwe, aboute hit he walkes,
	Debatande with hymself quat hit be myght.

2137–8 Gawain has a number of remarks of this kind (cf. 2158–9, 2208–11), all expressive of noble-sounding resignation to God's will. Does he remember the magical properties of the girdle? As often in the poem, a screen closes over Gawain's private inner consciousness, despite many assurances that he has one.

	Hit hade a hole on the ende and on ayther syde
patches all over	And overgrowen with gresse in glodes aywhere,
nothing but	And al was holw inwith, nobot an olde cave,
determine	Or a crevisse of an olde cragge – he couthe hit noght deme
words	With spelle.
Ah!	'We! Lorde,' quoth the gentyle knyght,
	'Whether this be the grene chapelle?
	Here myght aboute mydnyght
devil, say	The dele his matynnes telle!'
desolate	'Now iwysse,' quoth Wowayn, 'wysty is here;
oratory	This oritore is ugly, with erbes overgrowen;
clothed	Wel bisemes the wyye wruxled in grene
Perform	Dele here his devocioun on the develes wyse.
(senses)	Now I fele hit is the fende, in my fyve wyttes,
stuck me with, appointment, destroy	That has stoken me this steven to strye me here.
may ill-luck	This is a chapel of meschaunce – that chekke hit bytyde!
	Hit is the corsedest kyrk that ever I com inne!'
	With heghe helme on his hede, his launce in his honde,
makes his way, roof, dwelling	He romes up to the roffe of tho rogh wones.
	Thene herde he of that hyghe hil, in a harde roche
	Biyonde the broke, in a bonk, a wonder breme noyse.
split	Quat! hit clatered in the clyff as hit cleve schulde,
grindstone, scythe	As one upon a gryndelston hade grounden a sythe.
(see n.)	What! hit wharred and whette as water at a mulne.
grievous	What! hit rusched and ronge, rawthe to here.
	Thenne 'Bi Godde,' quoth Gawayn, 'that gere, as I trowe,
(see n.)	Is ryched at the reverence me, renk, to mete
In due course	Bi rote.
do (as he will), Alas!	Let God worche! "We loo",
whit	Hit helppes me not a mote.
	My lif thagh I forgoo,
noise	Drede dos me no lote.'
	Thenne the knyght con calle ful hyghe:
is in charge, place, appointed time	'Who stightles in this sted, me steven to holde?
	For now is gode Gawayn goande ryght here.
let him come	If any wyye oght wyl, wynne hider fast
get done	Other now other never, his nedes to spede.'
	'Abyde,' quoth on on the bonke aboven over his hede,
promised you once	'And thou schal haf al in hast that I the hyght ones.'
with that noise, quickly, while	Yet he rusched on that rurde rapely a throwe
turned aside, come down	And wyth quettyng awharf, er he wolde lyght.
makes his way, out of	And sythen he keveres bi a cragge and comes of a hole,
crack in the rock, fierce-looking	Whyrlande out of a wro wyth a felle weppen,
Danish, sharpened, give back	A denes ax nwe dyght, the dynt with to yelde,
(see n.)	With a borelych bytte bende bi the halme,
on a whetstone	Fyled in a fylor, fowre fote large –
	Hit was no lasse, bi that lace that lemed ful bryght!

2203 'Why! it whirred and made a grinding sound like water at a mill'.
2206 'Is being prepared, with due respect, to meet me (as) a knight'.
2224 'With a gigantic blade that curved back by the handle'.
2226 **bi that lace**. The eye that is measuring apprehensively the size of the axe catches sight of the talisman that is supposed to give protection against it.

	And the gome in the grene gered as fyrst,
face	Bothe the lyre and the legges, lokkes and berde,
strides	Save that fayre on his fote he foundes on the erthe,
handle	Sette the stele to the stone and stalked bysyde.
	When he wan to the watter, ther he wade nolde,
boldly	He hypped over on hys ax and orpedly strydes,
fierce	Bremly brothe on a bent that brode was aboute,
	On snawe.
	Sir Gawayn the knyght con mete,
bowed	He ne lutte hym nothyng lowe;
	That other sayde, 'Now, sir swete,
keeping the appointed time, believe	Of steven mon may the trowe.
may God guard thee	'Gawayn,' quoth that grene gome, 'God the mot loke!
	Iwysse thou art welcom, wyye, to my place,
journey	And thou hast tymed thi travayl as true mon schulde.
made	And thou knowes the covenauntes kest us bytwene:
befell	At this tyme twelmonyth thou toke that the falled,
promptly, repay	And I schulde at this Nwe Yere yeply the quyte.
on our own	And we ar in this valay verayly oure one:
separate, sway (in combat)	Here ar no renkes us to rydde, rele as us likes.
	Haf thy helme of thy hede and haf here thy pay.
Make, offered	Busk no more debate then I the bede thenne
single stroke	When thou wypped of my hede at a wap one.'
gave me a soul	'Nay, bi God,' quoth Gawayn, 'that me gost lante,
grudge, no jot, harm	I schal gruch the no grwe for grem that falles.
limit yourself	Bot styghtel the upon on strok, and I schal stonde stylle
offer, resistance	And warp the no wernyng to worch as the lykes,
	Nowhare.'
bowed down	He lened with the nek and lutte
white flesh	And schewed that schyre al bare,
behaved, feared	And lette as he noght dutte:
cower	For drede he wolde not dare.
got ready	Then the gome in the grene graythed hym swythe,
	Gederes up hys grymme tole, Gawayn to smyte;
strength	With alle the bur in his body he ber hit on lofte,
Aimed a blow, injure fatally	Munt as maghtyly as marre hym he wolde.
hard, intended	Hade hit dryven adoun as drey as he atled
he who	Ther hade ben ded of his dynt that doghty was ever.
battle-axe, glanced	Bot Gawayn on that giserne glyfte hym bysyde
ground, destroy	As hit com glydande adoun on glode hym to schende
	And schranke a lytel with the schulderes for the scharp yrne.
sudden jerk, bright blade	That other schalk wyth a schunt the schene wythhaldes,
	And thenne repreved he the prynce with mony prowde wordes:
	'Thou art not Gawayn,' quoth the gome, 'that is so goud halden,
was afraid, army	That never arwed for no here by hylle ne be vale,
flinchest, fear	And now thou fles for ferde er thou fele harmes.
	Such cowardise of that knyght cowthe I never here.
flinched, fled, aimed a blow	Nawther fyked I ne flaghe, freke, quen thou myntest,
raised, objection	Ne kest no kavelacion in kynges hous Arthor.
flew, flinched	My hede flaw to my fote and yet flagh I never;
received	And thou, er any harme hent, arwes in hert.

I must	Wherfore the better burne me burde be called
	Therfore.'
flinched	Quoth Gawayn, 'I schunt ones,
	And so wyl I no more;
	Bot thagh my hede falle on the stones,
	I con not hit restore.
	'Bot busk, burne, bi thi fayth, and bryng me to the poynt:
quickly	Dele to me my destinee and do hit out of honde,
start aside	For I schal stonde the a strok and start no more
	Til thyn ax have me hitte – haf here my trawthe.'
	'Haf at the thenne,' quoth that other, and heves hit alofte,
glares, angrily, mad	And waytes as wrothely as he wode were.
touches	He myntes at hym maghtyly bot not the mon rynes,
quickly	Withhelde heterly his honde er hit hurt myght.
duly, flinched	Gawayn graythely hit bydes and glent with no membre,
tree-stump	Bot stode stylle as the ston other a stubbe auther
anchored, rocky	That ratheled is in roche grounde with rotes a hundreth.
speak	Then muryly efte con he mele, the mon in the grene:
	'So now thou has thi hert holle, hitte me bihoves.
(see n.)	Halde the now the hyghe hode that Arthur the raght,
	And kepe thy kanel at this kest, yif hit kever may!'
fiercely, anger	Gawayn ful gryndelly with greme thenne sayde:
fierce	'Wy, thresch on, thou thro mon! Thou thretes to longe;
think, grows fearful	I hope that thi hert arwe wyth thyn awen selven.'
	'For sothe,' quoth that other freke, 'so felly thou spekes,
in anticipation, delay, mission	I wyl no lenger on lyte lette thin ernde
	Right nowe.'
takes, stance	Thenne tas he hym strythe to stryke
puckers	And frounses bothe lyppe and browe;
he is unhappy	No mervayle thagh hym myslyke
expected	That hoped of no rescowe.
weapon	He lyftes lyghtly his lome and let hit doun fayre,
edge, blade	With the barbe of the bitte bi the bare nek.
struck hard	Thagh he homered heterly, hurt hym no more
nicked	Bot snyrt hym on that on syde, that severed the hyde.
(see n.)	The scharp schrank to the flesche thurgh the schyre grece
bright	That the schene blod over his schulderes schot to the erthe.
	And quen the burne sey the blode blenk on the snawe,
sprang, feet together	He sprit forth spenne-fote more then a spere lenthe,
	Hent heterly his helme and on his hed cast,
	Schot with his schulderes his fayre schelde under,
	Braydes out a bryght sworde and bremely he spekes –
	Never syn that he was burne borne of his moder
	Was he never in this worlde wyye half so blythe –
Cease, violent blows, offer	'Blynne, burne, of thy bur, bede me no mo!

2282–3 Gawain's reminder to the Green Knight of the unfairness of the test is couched in the mildest possible terms.

2297–8 'May the high order of knighthood, that Arthur bestowed upon you, protect you, and save your neck at this blow, if it may survive'.

2313 'The sharp blade sank into the flesh through the white skin-fat'.

2316 Gawain's glee at the unexpected reprieve is as spirited and humanly endearing as his earlier exasperation at the Green Knight's taunts (2300).

received	I haf a stroke in this sted withoute stryf hent
offer	And if thow reches me any mo I redyly schal quyte
repay promptly, be sure	And yelde yederly ayayn – and therto ye tryst –
fiercely	And foo.
is assigned	Bot on stroke here me falles –
appointed	The covenaunt schop ryght so,
	Festned in Arthures halles –
good sir, stop	And therfore, hende, now hoo!'

turned	The hathel heldet hym fro and on his ax rested,
ground	Sette the schaft upon schore and to the schaft lened
	And loked to the leude that on the launde yede,
boldly	How that doghty, dredles, dervely ther stondes
fearless	Armed, ful awles: in hert hit hym lykes!
speaks, loud voice	Thenn he meles muryly wyth a much steven
ringing voice	And wyth a rynkande rurde he to the renk sayde:
angry	'Bolde burne, on this bent be not so gryndel.
has mistreated	No mon here unmanerly the mysboden habbes,
behaved	Ne kyd bot as covenaunde at kynges kort schaped.
promised	I hyght the a strok and thou hit has, halde the wel payed;
	I relece the of the remnaunt of ryghtes alle other.
If I had not been dextrous, perhaps	Nif I deliver had bene, a boffet paraunter
more harshly, dealt, injury	I couthe wrotheloker haf waret, to the haf wroght anger.
threatened, playfully, just a feint	Fyrst I mansed the muryly with a mynt one,
ripped open, gash	And rove the wyth no rof sore – with ryght I the profered
agreement	For the forwarde that we fest in the fyrst nyght;
	And thou trystyly the trawthe and trwly me haldes,
	Al the gayne thow me gef, as god mon schulde.
The second feint	That other munt for the morne, mon, I the profered
gave back	Thou kyssedes my clere wyf – the cosses me raghtes.
offered	For bothe two here I the bede bot two bare myntes
injury	Boute scathe.
	Trwe mon trwe restore,
need, danger	Thenne thar mon drede no wathe.
there	At the thrid thou fayled thore,
take	And therfor that tappe ta the.

garment	For hit is my wede that thou weres, that ilke woven girdel:
gave	Myn owen wyf hit the weved, I wot wel for sothe.
ways of behaving	Now know I wel thy cosses and thy costes als,
	And the wowyng of my wyf – I wroght hit myselven.
	I sende hir to asay the, and sothly me thynkkes
(you are) the most faultless man	On the fautlest freke that ever on fote yede.
white pea, value	As perle bi the quite pese is of prys more,
	So is Gawayn, in god fayth, bi other gay knyghtes.
loyalty	Bot here yow lakked a lyttel, sir, and lewte yow wonted;
deceitful intrigue	Bot that was for no wylyde werke, ne wowyng nauther,
	Bot for ye lufed your lyf – the lasse I yow blame.'
	That other stif mon in study stod a gret whyle,

2368 **the lasse I yow blame**. From the point of view of the Gospel texts that his remark echoes ('For whoever would save his life will lose it; and whoever loses his life for my sake, he will save it', Luke 9:24), the Green Knight could not be more mistaken. But the poet is fond of teasing us with the ambiguously Christian implications of chivalric values.

(see n.)	So agreved for greme he gryed withinne.
streamed together	Alle the blode of his brest blende in his face
at what, said	That al he schrank for schome that the schalk talked.
first, earth, spoke	The forme worde upon folde that the freke meled:
Cursed be	'Corsed worth cowarddyse and covetyse bothe!
	In yow is vylany and vyse that vertue disstryes.'
loosens the fastening	Thenne he kaght to the knot and the kest lawses,
Flung angrily	Brayde brothely the belt to the burne selven:
false thing, bad luck befall it	'Lo! ther the falssyng, foule mot hit falle!
anxiety about	For care of thy knokke cowardyse me taght
consent to, my true nature	To acorde me with covetyse, my kynde to forsake,
generosity and loyalty	That is larges and lewte that longes to knyghtes.
	Now am I fawty and falce and ferde haf ben ever
	Of trecherye and untrawthe – bothe bityde sorwe
	And care!
confess, in private	I biknowe yow, knyght, here stylle,
conduct	Al fawty is my fare;
understand what you want me to do	Letes me overtake your wylle,
And another time	And efte I schal be ware.'

laughed	Thenn loghe that other leude and luflyly sayde:
	'I halde hit hardily hole, the harme that I hade,
cleared, faults	Thou art confessed so clene, beknowen of thy mysses,
openly visible	And has the penaunce apert of the poynt of myn egge.
polished clean, offence	I halde the polysed of that plyght and pured as clene
committed sin	As thou hades never forfeted sythen thou was fyrst borne.
	And I gif the, sir, the gurdel that is golde-hemmed.
	For hit is grene as my goune, sir Gawayn, ye maye
contest, rides out	Thenk upon this ilke threpe ther thou forth thrynges
	Among prynces of prys, and this a pure token
adventure	Of the chaunce of the grene chapel at chevalrous knyghtes.
	And ye schal in this Nwe Yer ayayn to my wones
we shall	And we schyn revel the remnaunt of this ryche fest
pleasantly	Ful bene.'
invited, pressingly	Ther lathed hym fast the lorde,
	And sayde, 'With my wyf, I wene,
	We schal yow wel acorde,
	That was your enmy kene.'

	'Nay, for sothe,' quoth the segge, and sesed his helme
takes	And has hit of hendely, and the hathel thonkkes:
stayed long enough, happiness	'I haf sojorned sadly – sele yow bytyde,
(see n.)	And he yelde hit yow yare that yarkkes al menskes!
commend, companion	And comaundes me to that cortays, your comlych fere,
	Bothe that on and that other, myn honoured ladyes,
trick, skilfully	That thus hor knyght wyth hor kest han koyntly bigyled.

2370 'So overcome with mortification that he cried out in anguish'.

2374 **covetyse** seems wide of the mark, and to interpret *covetyse* as 'covetousness of life' is strained. Gawain seems to be casting around for some 'official' sin of which he can confess himself to be guilty while he comes to terms with a subtler and more inward shame. He gets closer in 2383.

2394 The Green Knight speaks explicitly in terms of confession, penance and absolution, obliging us to think back to the earlier confession to the priest (1884) and of the relation between the two 'confession' scenes.

2410 'And may he repay it you fully that rewards all noble deeds!'

marvel, become mad	Bot hit is no ferly thagh a fole madde
brought	And thurgh wyles of wymmen be wonen to sorwe.
	For so was Adam in erde with one bygyled,
many different (women), in his turn	And Salamon with fele sere, and Samson eftsones –
Delilah engineered his fate, David	Dalyda dalt hym hys wyrde – and Davyth therafter
(see n.)	Was blended with Barsabe, that much bale tholed.
brought to grief, gain	Now these were wrathed wyth her wyles, hit were a wynne huge
believe, knew how	To luf hom wel and leve hem not, a leude that couthe.
(see n.)	For thes wer forne the freest, that folwed alle the sele
heaven's kingdom	Exellently of alle thyse other under heven-ryche
lived	That mused;
beguiled	And alle thay were biwyled
had to do with	With wymmen that thay used.
	Thagh I be now bigyled,
I ought to	Me think me burde be excused.
reward	'Bot your gordel,' quoth Gawayn, 'God yow foryelde!
wear, rich	That wyl I welde wyth goud wylle, not for the wynne golde,
belt (itself)	Ne the saynt ne the sylk ne the syde pendaundes,
costliness, worth, rich workmanship	For wele ne for worchyp, ne for the wlonk werkkes;
transgression	Bot in syngne of my surfet I schal se hit ofte
call to mind with remorse	When I ride in renoun, remorde to myselven
frailty, perverse	The faut and the fayntyse of the flesche crabbed,
(see n.)	How tender hit is to entyse teches of fylthe.
	And thus quen pryde schal me pryk for prowes of armes,
humble	The loke to this luf-lace schal lethe my hert.
But one thing	Bot on I wolde yow pray, displeses yow never:
been staying	Syn ye be lorde of the yonder londe ther I haf lent inne
	Wyth yow wyth worschyp – the wyye hit yow yelde
	That uphaldes the heven and on hygh sittes –
call, name	How norne ye yowre ryght nome, and thenne no more?'
	'That schal I telle the trwly,' quoth that other thenne,
am called	'Bertilak de Hautdesert I hat in this londe,
	Thurgh myght of Morgne la Faye, that in my hous lenges,
	And koyntyse of clergye, bi craftes wel lerned –
magical powers, acquired	The maystryes of Merlyn mony ho has taken,
had a love-affair, once	For ho has dalt drwry ful dere sumtyme
excellent learned man	With that conable klerk, that knowes alle your knyghtes
	At hame.
	Morgne the goddes
	Therfore hit is hir name;
Possesses, pride	Weldes none so hyghe hawtesse
	That ho ne con make ful tame.

2415 Gawain is stubbornly trying to miss the point. It wasn't the wiles of the lady that caused him to accept the girdle, but his own fear of the axe. Searching for some form of self-exculpation, he falls into the vein of the preacher. The four 'victims' are a traditional topos of this kind of anti-feminist tirade.

2419 'Was deceived by Bathsheba, that (i.e. David) suffered much misery'.

2422 'For these were four of the noblest, that were all favoured by good fortune'.

2436 'How susceptible it is to catch the disease-spots of sin'.

2446 **Morgne la Faye** is Arthur's half-sister (daughter of Ygerne by her first husband) and traditionally a causer of mischief in Arthurian legend. She seems to be brought in here rather mechanically to provide an 'explanation' for the story, but much has been made of her role as a female subverter of authority.

sent, in this guise, splendid	'Ho wayned me upon this wyse to your wynne halle
pride	For to assay the surquidrye, yif hit soth were
	That rennes of the grete renoun of the Rounde Table.
sent this marvel, rob you of	Ho wayned me this wonder your wyttes to reve,
caused	For to haf greved Gaynour and gart hir to dyye
terror, spookily	With glopnyng of that ilke gome that gostlych speked
	With his hede in his honde bifore the hyghe table.
	That is ho that is at home, the auncian lady –
your very aunt	Ho is even thyn aunt, Arthures half-suster,
daughter of the duchess, Uther	The duches doghter of Tyntagelle, that dere Uter after
is now royally renowned	Hade Arthur upon, that athel is nowthe.
entreat	Therfore I ethe the, hathel, to com to thyn aunt,
	Make myry in my hous – my meny the lovies,
wish	And I wol the as wel, wyye, bi my faythe,
	As any gome under God, for thy grete trauthe.'
said him no, on no account	And he nikked hym naye, he nolde bi no wayes.
embrace, commend	Thay acolen and kyssen and kennen ayther other
	To the prynce of paradise, and parten ryght there
cold (ground)	On coolde.
fine	Gawayn on blonk ful bene
	To the kynges burgh buskes bolde,
bright	And the knyght in the enker grene
	Whiderwarde-so-ever he wolde.
	Wylde wayes in the worlde Wowen now rydes
(of survival)	On Gryngolet, that the grace hade geten of his lyve.
lodged, in the open	Ofte he herbered in house and ofte al theroute,
(had) many an adventure on the way	And mony aventure in vale, and venquyst ofte,
intend, rehearse	That I ne tyght at this tyme in tale to remene.
	The hurt was hole that he hade hent in his nek,
gleaming	And the blykkande belt he bere ther-aboute,
Cross-wise like a baldric	Abelef as a bauderyk, bounden bi his syde,
	Loken under his lyfte arme, the lace, with a knot,
found out, guilt	In tokenyng he was tane in tech of a faute.
in one piece	And thus he commes to the court, knyght al in sounde.
arose joy, great (king)	Ther wakned wele in that wone when wyst the grete
a great thing	That gode Gawayn was commen – gayn hit hym thoght.
	The kyng kysses the knyght, and the quene alce,
trusty, greet	And sythen mony syker knyght that soght hym to haylce,
asked, (to their amazement)	Of his fare that hym frayned; and ferlyly he telles,
confesses, experiences	Biknowes alle the costes of care that he hade –
adventure, behaviour	The chaunce of the chapel, the chere of the knyght,
	The luf of the ladi, the lace at the last.
nick	The nirt in the nek he naked hem schewed
received	That he laght for his unleute at the leudes hondes
	For blame.
was distressed	He tened quen he schulde telle,
shame	He groned for gref and grame;

2460 Morgan's hatred of Guenevere is well established in Arthurian story, partly through suggestion of an incestuous relation between herself and Arthur.

2464 Morgan la Fay is Gawain's aunt because his mother, Bellicent, queen of Orkney, was another of Morgan's (and Arthur's) half-sisters.

2465 The duchess of Tintagel was Ygerne (wife of Gorlois), secretly visited in the night by king Uther, disguised, as part of Merlin's plan to engineer the birth of Arthur.

[*rushed*] The blod in his face con melle,
When he hit schulde schewe, for schame.

'Lo! lorde,' quoth the leude, and the lace hondeled,
[*band*] This is the bende of this blame I bere in my nek,
[*injury*] This is the lathe and the losse that I laght have
Of couardise and covetyse that I haf caght thare.
This is the token of untrawthe that I am tan inne,
And I mot nedes hit were wyle I may last.
[*(see n.)*] For mon may hyden his harme bot unhap ne may hit,
[*fixed, depart*] For ther hit ones is tached twynne wil hit never.'
The kyng comfortes the knyght, and alle the court als
Laghen loude therat and luflyly acorden
That lordes and ladis that longed to the Table,
Uche burne of the brotherhede, a bauderyk schulde have,
A bende abelef hym aboute of a bryght grene,
[*following suit (to match his)*] And that for sake of that segge in swete to were.
[*For doing that was agreed to be good for*] For that was acorded the renoun of the Rounde Table
And he honoured that hit hade evermore after,
[*recorded*] As hit is breved in the best boke of romaunce.
[*adventure took place*] Thus in Arthurus day this aunter bitidde,
The Brutus bokes therof beres wyttenesse.
Sythen Brutus the bolde burne bowed hider fyrst,
After the segge and the asaute was sesed at Troye,
Iwysse,
Mony aunteres here-biforne
Haf fallen suche er this.
[*Now he that*] Now that bere the croun of thorne,
He bryng us to his blysse!

Patience

Patience is based on the OT book of Jonah, a tiny 48-verse gem of story-telling centring on Jonah's prayer, from the whale's belly, of faith, penitence and submission to God's will, a penitential cry of faith inspired by Ps. 130 (*De profundis clamavi*, 'Out of the depths have I cried' – see the paraphrase by Wyatt, below) and Ps. 69. The story provides a narrative context for this prayer, and it is to this context that the poet devotes his powerful dramatic and graphic descriptive powers. All the persons and events are brought vividly to life, and a quality specially worth noting is the intimacy with which the OT God is portrayed as a person. His humanity has little to do, theologically, with the contemporary cult of the humanity of Christ (as in Nicholas Love, below), except in so far as both provide opportunity for rich imaginative amplification. Here God's humanity is that of a kind and patient yet irresistibly powerful lord: his actions, his forbearance, and the patient submission to his will that his love asks, would provide admirable models for secular lords and those who are to obey them. In addition to its homiletic function, reinforced by the poet's power of materializing the world of all its participants, the story of Jonah was also a favourite for typological interpretation, typology be-

2511 'For a man may hide what he has done wrong but he cannot unfasten it (from himself)'. For Gawain, the healing of the physical mark of his fault means that it is hidden, but now he must wear the girdle as a visible sign that the inward stain of sin is ineradicable. In Christian terms, this would not be true, if he were truly penitent, and the court's reaction suggests that Gawain is taking things to extremes. His shame induces a vehement self-contempt.

2522 The story closes by circling back to its opening, and with a reminder of the place of Arthurian legend in the long cycle of 'British' history as it began with the arrival of Brutus from Troy, as told in 'the Brutus bokes', or *Brut* histories deriving from Geoffrey of Monmouth's *Historia regum Britanniae* (1135).

2530 'Amen' has been added below the last line, and, below that, 'Hon y soyt qui mal pence'; both are in a more formal script and possibly a later hand. The motto of the Order of the Garter ('Shame be to him who evil thinks') was evidently inserted to draw attention to the resemblance between this story and the story of the founding of the Garter.

ing the name given to the technique of interpreting the OT, whilst allowing its truth as history, as a series of prefigurings or 'types' of the life of Christ and of the life of the Christian under the dispensation of grace. So the Flood was read as a type of Baptism, and the sacrifice of Isaac as a prefiguration of God's sacrifice of his only son. Jonah is both type and anti-type: like Christ he dwelt in darkness for three days and three nights before emerging alive, but unlike Christ he was disobedient and intractable to God's wishes. The poet reminds us now and then of the story's typological significance (e.g. 96, 294).

{The poem begins with a praise of patience and of patient poverty, with the Beatitudes (Matt. 5:3–10) as the text. The story of Jonah is proposed as an exemplum of patience.}

Jonah and the whale

within the borders of	Hit bitydde sumtyme in the termes of Jude
appointed, prophet to the Gentiles	Jonas joyned was therinne Jentyle prophete;
voice, came	Goddes glam to hym glod that hym unglad made,
noise, whispered	With a roghlych rurd rowned in his ere:
quickly, go, at once	'Rys radly,' he says, 'and rayke forth even;
Take	Nym the way to Nynyve wythouten other speche
words, spread	And in that cete my sawes soghe alle aboute
at that time	That in that place at the poynt I put in thi hert.
they are, place	For iwysse hit arn so wykke that in that won dwelles
	And her malys is so much I may not abide,
at once	Bot venge me on her vilanye and venym bilyve:
hasten, message	Now sweye me thider swyftly and say me this arende.'
noise, stopped, stunned	When that steven was stynt that stowned his mynde
petulantly	Al he wrathed in his wyt and wytherly he thoght:
bidding	'If I bowe to his bode and bryng hem this tale,
seized, troubles	And I be nummen in Nunive, my nyes begynes.
perfect	He telles me those traytoures arn typped shrewes:
take	I com wyth those tythynges, thay ta me bylyve,
Confine	Pynes me in a prysoun, put me in stokkes,
foot-shackle, tear	Wrythe me in a warlok, wrast out myn yyen.
	This is a mervayl message a man for to preche
accursed	Amonge enmyes so mony and mansed fendes,
Unless, gracious	Bot if my gaynlych God such gref to me wolde
punishment, sin	For desert of sum sake that I slayn were!
Come what may, nearer	At alle peryles,' quoth the prophete, 'I aproche hit no nerre.
will (betake) me, looks out for	I wyl me sum other waye that he ne wayte after:
go, Tarshish	I schal tee into Tarce and tary there a whyle
readily, disappeared	And lyghtly when I am lest he letes me alone.'
	Thenne he ryses radly and raykes bilyve,
Jaffa, grumbling, indignation	Jonas toward Port Japh, ay janglande for tene
suffer	That he nolde thole for nothyng non of those pynes,
indifferent, well-being	Thagh the Fader that hym formed were fale of his hele.
throne	'Oure Syre syttes,' he says, 'on sege so hyghe
worries	In his glowande glorye and gloumbes ful lyttel
	Thagh I be nummen in Nunnive and naked dispoyled,
cross, pitifully, villains	On rode rwly to-rent with rybaudes mony.'
	Thus he passes to that port his passage to seche,
voyage	Fyndes he a fayr schyp to the fare redy,
Makes a deal, payment to them	Maches hym with the maryneres, makes her paye
take, quickly	For to towe hym into Tarce as tyd as thay myght.
stepped, boards, tackle prepare	Then he tron on tho tres, and thay her tramme ruchen,

	Cachen up the cros-sayl, cables thay fasten,
Quickly, windlass	Wight at the wyndas weyen her ankres,
(see n.)	Spende spak to the sprete the spare bawelyne,
Haul at	Gederen to the gyde-ropes, the grete cloth falles.
(see n.)	Thay layden in on laddeborde and the lofe wynnes.
(swelling of the sail)	The blythe brethe at her bak the bosum he fyndes:
	He swenges me thys swete schip swefte fro the haven.
	Was never so joyful a Jue as Jonas was thenne,
the Lord, boldly	That the daunger of Dryghtyn so derfly ascaped:
that being	He wende wel that that wyy that al the world planted
	Hade no maght in that mere no man for to greve.
be patiently obedient	Lo the wytles wreche! For he wolde noght suffer,
	Now has he put hym in plyt of peril wel more.
foolish thought, turned over	Hit was a wenyng unwar that welt in his mynde,
gone, further	Thagh he were soght fro Samarye, that God sey no fyrre.
(see n.)	Yise, he blusched ful brode – that burde hym by sure:
taught, words	That ofte kyd hym the carpe that kyng sayde,
Worthy, dais	Dyngne David on des that demed this speche
(Ps. 94:8–9)	In a psalme that he set the sauter withinne:
Be sensible sometimes	'O foles in folk, feles otherwhyle
sometimes, far gone	And understondes umbestounde, thagh ye be stape in folye.
Think	Hope ye that he heres not that eres alle made?
made	Hit may not be that he is blynde that bigged uche yye!'
old age	Bot he dredes no dynt that dotes for elde,
hurrying	For he was fer in the flod foundande to Tarce.
quickly	Bot I trow ful tyd overtan that he were
shamefully	So that schomely to schort he schote of his ame.
	For the welder of wyt that wot alle thynges,
watches, stratagems	That ay wakes and waytes, at wylle has he slyghtes.
power	He calde on that ilk crafte he carf with his hondes –
the more angrily	Thay wakened wel the wrotheloker for wrothely he cleped:
	'Ewrus and Aquiloun that on est sittes
bidding, dark	Blowes bothe at my bode upon blo watteres!'
space, words	Thenne was no tom ther bytwene his tale and her dede,
eager, command	So bayn wer thay bothe two his bone for to wyrk.
	Anon out of the north-est the noys bigynes,
	When bothe brethes con blowe upon blo watteres.
cloud-racks, reddening	Rogh rakkes ther ros with rudnyng anunder;
roared, wonder	The see soughed ful sore, gret selly to here;
dark	The wyndes on the wonne water so wrastel togeder
wild, tossed	That the wawes ful wode waltered so highe
plunged, terrified	And efte busched to the abyme, that breed fysches
	Durst nowhere for rogh arest at the bothem.
sea	When the breth and the brok and the bote metten,
craft	Hit was a joyles gyn that Jonas was inne,
around, waves	For hit reled on roun upon the roghe ythes.
gale bore it abaft	The bur ber to hit baft, that braste alle her gere,
	Then hurled on a hepe the helme and the sterne;

104 'Swiftly fasten to the bowsprit the spare bow-line.'

106 'They put in (the oars) on the larboard side and gain the luff (i.e. advantage of the wind).'

117 'Yes, he (God) saw with eyes wide open – of that he (Jonah) might have been quite sure.'

133 **Ewrus and Aquiloun**: classical names (e.g. *Aeneid*, 1.52) for winds from, respectively, the south-east and the north-east.

137–52 Alliterative poets, with the means at their disposal for the vivid and onomatopaeic representation of violent activity, were particularly fond of describing storms at sea.

broke	Furst tomurte mony rop and the mast after;
collapsed	The sayl sweyed on the see – thenne suppe bihoved
ship	The coge of the colde water, and thenne the cry ryses.
	Yet corven thay the cordes and kest al theroute;
bale	Mony ladde ther forth lep to lave and to kest –
threatening, (that = *who)*	Scopen out the scathel water that fayn scape wolde –
heavy	For be monnes lode never so luther, the lyf is ay swete!
hurried business	Ther was busy over-borde bale to kest,
	Her bagges and her fether-beddes and her bryght wedes,
chests, casks	Her kysttes and her coferes, her caraldes alle,
vessel, relief	And al to lyghten that lome, yif lethe wolde schape.
noise	Bot ever was ilyche loud the lot of the wyndes
	And ever wrother the water and wodder the stremes.
exhausted with toil, remedy	Then tho wery for-wroght wyst no bote
called, helped	Bot uchon glewed on his god that gayned hym beste:
	Summe to Vernagu ther vouched avowes solemne,
holy, mighty	Summe to Diana devout and derf Neptune,
	To Mahoun and to Mergot, the mone and the sunne,
	And uche lede as he loved and layde had his hert.
wisest	Thenne bispeke the spakest, dispayred wel nere:
believe, traitor	'I leve here be sum losynger, sum lawles wrech
	That has greved his god and gos here amonge us.
perishes	Lo! al synkes in his synne and for his sake marres.
recommend, cast lots	I louve that we lay lotes on ledes uchone
befalls	And who-so lympes the losse, lay hym theroute.
	And quen the gulty is gon, what may gome trawe
heavens	Bot he that rules the rak may rwe on those other?'
	This was sette in asent, and sembled thay were,
Harried, corner, receive	Heryed out of uche hyrne to hent that falles.
steersman	A lodesmon lyghtly lep under haches
look for	For to layte mo ledes and hem to lote bryng.
	Bot hym fayled no freke that he fynde myght
lay asleep in a secret place	Saf Jonas the Jwe, that jowked in derne.
fled, roaring	He was flowen for ferde of the flode lotes
plank	Into the bothem of the bot and on a brede lyggede,
(see n.)	Onhelde by the hurrok, for the heven wrache,
snores	Slypped upon a sloumbe-slepe, and sloberande he routes.
poked, get up	The freke hym frunt with his fot and bede hym ferk up –
May Ragnel (a devil), chains	Ther Ragnel in his rakentes hym rere of his dremes!
clasped garment	Bi the haspede hater he hentes hym thenne
	And broght hym up by the brest and upon borde sette,
roughly	Arayned hym ful runyschly what raysoun he hade
onslaughts	In such slaghtes of sorwe to slepe so faste.
lots, severally	Sone haf thay her sortes sette and serelych deled,
fell	And ay the lote upon laste lymped on Jonas.
berated, quickly	Thenne ascryed thay hym skete and asked ful loude:
	'What the devel has thou don, doted wrech?
	What seches thou on see, synful schrewe,
crimes, hateful	With thy lastes so luther to lose us uchone?

165–7 **Vernagu** is a Saracen giant in the Charlemagne romances, where the heathen god **Mergot** (cf. Magog) is also to be found; **Mahoun** is Mahomet. Medieval writers frequently lump classical pagan deities and infidels together.

185 'Huddled up by the rudder-band, for fear of heaven's vengeance.'

	Has thou, gome, no governour ne god on to calle
are about to be	That thou thus slydes on slepe when thou slayn worthes?
come, seekest	Of what londe art thou lent, what laytes thou here,
errand	Whyder in worlde that thou wylt, and what is thyn arnde?
fate, decided	Lo, thy dom is the dyght for thy dedes ille:
	Do gyf glory to thy godde er thou glyde hens.'
	'I am an Ebru,' quoth he, 'of Israyl borne;
	That wyye I worchyp, iwysse, that wroght alle thynges,
	Alle the worlde with the welkyn, the wynde and the sternes,
single	And alle that wones ther-withinne, at a worde one.
	Alle this meschef for me is made at thys tyme,
	For I haf greved my God and gulty am founden.
throw	Forthy beres me to the borde and bathes me theroute –
Before (you do that), I believe	Er gete ye no happe, I hope, forsothe!'
showed, signs, understood	He ossed hym by unnynges that thay undernomen
fled, noble	That he was flawen fro the face of frelych Dryghtyn;
fear	Thenne such a ferde on hem fel and flayed hem withinne
hastened, alone	That thay ruyt hym to rowe and letten the rynk one.
Men hurried	Hatheles hyyed in haste with ores ful longe,
	Syn her sayl was hem aslypped, on sydes to rowe,
with all their might	Hef and hale upon hyght to helpen hymeselven.
labour	Bot al was nedles note – that nolde not bityde:
turbulence	In bluber of the blo flod bursten her ores.
	Thenne hade thay noght in her honde that hem help myght;
obtain	Thenne nas no coumfort to kever ne counsel non other
doom	But Jonas into his juis jugge bylyve.
	Fyrst thay prayen to the Prynce that prophetes serven
	That he gef hem the grace to greven hym never
innocent, should steep	That thay in baleles blod ther blenden her handes,
killed	Thagh that hathel wer his that thay here quelled.
Quickly, then	Tyd by top and bi to thay token hym synne;
terrible sea, threw	Into that lodlych loghe thay luche hym sone.
sooner thrown out	He was no tytter out-tulde that tempest ne sessed:
became peaceful	The se saghtled therwith as sone as ho moght.
	Thenne thagh her takel were torne that totered on ythes,
Strong currents	Styffe stremes and streght hem strayned a whyle,
(see n.)	That drof hem dryylych adoun the depe to serve,
more favourable one, carried, shore	Tyl a swetter ful swythe hem sweyed to bonk.
praising	Ther was lovyng on lofte, when thay the londe wonnen,
manner	To oure mercyable God, on Moyses wyse,
raised up	With sacrafyse upset and solempne vowes,
him alone, truly	And graunted hym on to be God and graythly non other.
	Thagh thay be jolef for joye, Jonas yet dredes;
happiness is in doubt	Thagh he nolde suffre no sore, his seele is on anter.
became, after	For what-so worthed of that wyye fro he in water dipped
if it were not for	Hit were a wonder to wene, yif holy wryt nere.
doomed	Now is Jonas the Jwe jugged to drowne;
battered	Of that schended schyp men schowved hym sone.
Fate	A wylde walterande whal, as Wyrde then schaped,

235 'That drove them relentlessly down to be at the mercy of the deep'.

242 **suffre no sore.** The poet constantly emphasizes (cf. 113, 276) that it is Jonah's lack of 'suffrance', or patience, that causes God's displeasure.

	That was beten fro the abyme, bi that bot flotte
	And was war of that wyye that the water soghte
swooped, gullet	And swyftely swenged hym to swepe and his swolw opened.
	The folk yet haldande his fete, the fysch hym tyd hentes;
tumbled down	Withouten towche of any tothe he tult in his throte.
sweeps	Thenne he swenges and swayves to the se bothem,
swirling currents	Bi mony rokkes ful roghe and rydelande strondes,
dazed	Wyth the mon in his mawe, malskred in drede –
suffered	As lyttel wonder hit was yif he wo dreyed,
had not	For nade the hyghe Heven-Kyng, thurgh his honde myght,
	Warded this wrech man in warlowes guttes,
believe	What lede moght leve bi lawe of any kynde
granted	That any lyf myght be lent so longe hym withinne?
	Bot he was sokored by that Syre that syttes so highe,
(he) were without hope	Thagh were wanles of wele in wombe of that fissche,
	And also dryven thurgh the depe and in derk walteres.
	Lorde! colde was his cumfort and his care huge
misfortune, hardship	For he knew uche a cace and kark that hym lymped,
seized	How fro the bot into the blober was with a best lached
its	And thrwe in at hit throte withouten thret more,
speck of dust, minster, jaws	As mote in at a munster-dor, so mukel wern his chawles.
slime and filth	He glydes in by the giles thugh glaym ande glette,
Tumbling, along a gut, road	Relande in by a rop, a rode that hym thoght,
	Ay hele over hed hourlande aboute,
came to a halt, cavernous hollow	Til he blunt in a blok as brod as a halle;
gropes	And ther he festnes the fete and fathmes aboute
	And stod up in his stomak that stank as the devel.
in slime and in filth	Ther in saym and in sorwe that savoured as helle
	Ther was bylded his bour that wyl no bale suffer.
looks, shelter	And thenne he lurkkes and laytes where was le best
	In uche a nok of his navel, bot nowhere he fyndes
safety, muck	No rest ne recoverer bot ramel ande myre
	In wych gut so-ever he gos – bot ever is God swete!
Lord	And ther he lenged at the last and to the lede called:
	'Now, Prynce, of thy prophete pite thou have!
	Thagh I be fol and fykel and falce of my hert,
Withdraw	Devoyde now thy vengaunce, thurgh vertu of rauthe;
scum	Thagh I be gulty of gyle, as gaule of prophetes,
things, truly	Thou art God, and alle gowdes ar graythely thyn owen.
	Haf now mercy of thy man and his mysdedes
	And preve the lyghtly a Lorde in londe and in water.'
hit upon a nook	With that he hitte to a hyrne and helde hym therinne,
	Ther no defoule of no fylthe was fest hym abute;
darkness	Ther he sete also sounde, saf for merk one,
hold	As in the bulk of the bote ther he byfore sleped.

251 Bible-illustrators enjoyed the drama and economy of this scene, with Jonah simultaneously being thrown overboard and swallowed by the whale; it is also the subject of one of the homely but effective illustrations in the *Gawain*-MS (fol.82r: facsimile, ed. I. Gollancz, EETS, OS 162 [1923]).

258 **warlowes**; 'devil-monster's'. The whale was feared as monstrous and also as a type of the devil. A whale's mouth is often portrayed in illustrations of the Last Judgement as the mouth of hell.

268 **As mote in at a munster-dor**. This famous image is perhaps the best example of the *Gawain*-poet's power of evoking vivid sensory impression – here of unimaginable immensity of space. The image also carries a significant theological meaning as a reminder that, though Jonah (like Christ when he died) appears to be entering hell and the power of the devil, he is actually entering the place from which he will rise again to life.

	So in a bouel of that best he bides on lyve
	Thre dayes and thre nyght, ay thenkande on Dryghtyn,
moderation	His myght and his merci, his mesure thenne:
	Now he knawes hym in care that couthe not in sele.
	Ande ever walteres this whal bi wyldren depe
rank pride	Thurgh mony a regioun ful roghe, thurgh ronk of his wylle;
	For that mote in his mawe mad hym, I trowe,
compared with, feel queasy	Thagh hit lyttel were hym wyth, to wamel at his hert;
	Ande as sayled the segge, ay sykerly he herde
great flood	The bygge borne on his bak and bete on his sydes.
soon	Then a prayer ful prest the prophete ther maked;
	On this wyse, as I wene, his wordes were mony:
	'Lorde, to the haf I cleped in cares ful stronge:
	Out of the hole thou me herde of hellen wombe;
voice	I calde, and thou knew myn uncler steven.
plunged	Thou diptes me of the depe se into the dymme hert,
torrent, around	The grete flem of thy flod folded me umbe;
currents, deep gulphs, deeps	Alle the gotes of thy guferes and groundeles powles,
currents	And thy stryvande stremes of stryndes so mony,
overwhelming flood, over me	In on daschande dam dryves me over.
	And yet I sayde as I seet in the se bothem:
Full of care	"Careful am I, kest out fro thy cler yyen
	And desevered fro thy syght; yet surely I hope
Again, tread in, belong	Efte to trede on thy temple and teme to thyselven."
until, stupefies (me)	'I am wrapped in water to my wo stoundes;
	The abyme byndes the body that I byde inne.
surging flood itself	The pure poplande hourle playes on my heved;
verge	To laste mere of uche a mount, man, am I fallen.
strongly	The barres of uche a bonk ful bigly me haldes,
reach, shore	That I may lache no lont, and thou my lyf weldes.
justice	Thou schal releve me, renk, whil thy ryght slepes,
	Thurgh myght of thy mercy that mukel is to tryste.
	'For when th'acces of anguych was hid in my sawle,
noble	Thenne I remembred me ryght of my rych Lorde,
pity	Prayande hym for pete his prophete to here,
	That into his holy hous myn orisoun moght entre.
spoken, men of learning	I haf meled with thy maystres mony longe day
truly	Bot now I wot wyterly that those unwyse ledes
trust	That affyen hym in vanyte and in vayne thynges
For a thing, their (hope of) mercy	For think that mountes to noght her mercy forsaken.
what truly is to be held to	Bot I devoutly avowe that verray bes halden,
become safe	Soberly to do the sacrafyse when I schal save worthe
perfect	And offer the for my hele a ful hol gyfte
hold good, commandest	And halde goud that thou me hetes: haf here my trauthe.'
	Thenne oure Fader to the fysch ferslych biddes
quickly, land	That he hym sput spakly upon spare drye.
shore	The whal wendes at his wylle and a warthe fyndes
vomits up	And ther he brakes up the buyrne as bede hym oure Lorde.
shore, filthy	Thenne he swepe to the sonde in sluched clothes:

305–36 This speech is the centre of the poem's religious meaning. It is what Jonah is *for* – so that he can demonstrate the capacity of human beings to understand God's will and respond to his love, even though, with ordinary humans like Jonah, there may be back-sliding later.

need Hit may wel be that mester were his mantyle to wasche!
gazed upon The bonk that he blosched to and bode hym bisyde
refused to go to Wern of the regiounes ryght that he renayed hade.
upbraids Thenne a wynde of Goddes worde efte the wyye bruxles:
(on no account) 'Nylt thou never to Nunive bi no kynnes wayes?'
give 'Yisse, Lorde,' quoth the lede, 'lene me thy grace
pleasure For to go at thi gre – me gaynes non other.'
'Ris, aproche then to prech – lo, the place here.
locked, let it loose Lo, my lore is in the loke, lauce hit therinne!'

{Jonah goes off to Nineveh as instructed, and preaches so successfully that the people are convinced that destruction is imminent because of their sinful ways. They put themselves to spectacular repentance, and God relents and withholds his promised vengeance. Jonah is disgusted at God's weak-mindedness and at the waste of his own time. He stumps out of town and takes sulky refuge from the burning sun in a makeshift shelter. During the night a woodbine vine grows and turns his shelter into a beautiful shady arbour, in which he settles contentedly. The next day the woodbine is all withered and gone, and he shouts out angrily against God. God compares what Jonah has lost with what Jonah was praying God should destroy of his own beloved creation. The poem, it is clear, is in the end as much about God's patience as about Jonah's.}

John Gower (d. 1408)

John Gower died in 1408, probably in his seventies. His life as a gentleman with landed interests and legal and business connections was spent in and around London. In 1398 he married, and moved his wife into the priory of St Mary Overy in Southwark, where he had been living, probably as a semi-invalid, for some years; he later became blind. Gower's earliest extant writing is in French, the *Mirour de l'Omme* (*c.* 1370), a very long poem combining estates satire (the mountain of social observation and critique from which Chaucer mined his General Prologue) with penitential treatise. His next major poem was in Latin, the *Vox Clamantis*, another work of estates satire to which Gower added, soon after 1381, an opening book containing his cruelly patrician animal allegory of the Peasants' Revolt. By this time Gower had become friends with Chaucer (see *TC* V.1856, above), and was influenced by him in choosing English for his major opus, the *Confessio Amantis*, begun about 1387 (at about the same time as the *Canterbury Tales*, another but quite different set of stories in a frame). This vast poem, in over 33,000 lines of short couplet, is framed in a Prologue and eight books as a lover's confession, the first six books and the last each focusing on one of the Seven Deadly Sins. In these books the lover (Amans) is instructed by his confessor, Genius, the priest of Venus, principally through stories demonstrating the appropriate sin or its avoidance. Book 7 is didactic and encyclopaedic, concerned with good government and the virtues of princes, and bears out the promise of the Prologue that the analysis of the sins of love is in some way relevant to an analysis of the 'division' that is the source of disorder in the larger community. The poem ends touchingly with the dismissal of the lover, Amans, now identified as John Gower and an old man, from the court of Venus.

Gower draws on a variety of classical and medieval sources, but especially Ovid, for his illustrative stories, and from many points of view his poem can be seen as a rich anthology of tales within a 'confessional' framework. We are always intrigued by the relation between the intrinsic meaning of the story, its imaginative and poetic power, and the extrinsic meaning it is given by its function in the exemplary structure and within the Latin apparatus through which Gower tries to reinforce the moral meaning of his poem. Many readers will find this relation playful, oblique, ironic, subversive; other readers will pay more attention to the frame of the poem, the Prologue and Book 7, and see the poem as the work of 'moral Gower', rigorously structured and seriously committed to a political and ethical programmatic design.

There are over 50 manuscripts of the *Confessio*, including fragments, and a notable proportion of these are de luxe and illustrated manuscripts. The standard edition is that of G.C. Macaulay, *English Works*, 2 vols (Oxford, 1900). There are selections (nearly half the poem) edited by R.A. Peck (New York, 1968) and useful collections of essays edited by A.J. Minnis (Cambridge, 1983), by P. Nicholson (Cambridge, 1991), and in *Medievalia* 16 (1993). The standard life and works is J.H. Fisher, *Moral Philosopher and Friend of Chaucer* (New York, 1964). The following extracts are based on Bodl.MS Fairfax 3, with variants from Bodl.MS Bodley 294. The first extract is an example of the delightful and quizzical playfulness of the frame-story, while the second is Gower's version of one of the most famously gruesome of Ovidian tales. Gower has a gift for carefully shaded and even-tempered poetic narrative; he can also draw the touchingly and poignantly human out of an apparently meaningless story of inhuman savagery.

Confessio Amantis

The lover's business (IV.1118–1223)

{The confessor Genius interrogates the lover Amans on sins of Idleness (a branch of Sloth, the subject of Book 4).}

Confessor
   Now, sone, tell me thanne so
What hast thou don of besischipe — *busy service*
To love and to the ladischipe — *honour*
Of hire which thi ladi is?

Book IV

1118 **sone ... thanne.** Final *-e*, when not elided before a vowel or initial *h*-, is always syllabic in Gower's verse (except in *hire*, 'her'), which is copied with exceptional care in the Fairfax as in other MSS.

	Amans
	Mi fader, evere yit er this
place	In every place, in every stede,
commanded	What so mi lady hath me bede,
	With al myn herte obedient
	I have therto be diligent.
	And if so is sche bidde noght,
	What thing that thanne into my thoght
be able to do	Comth ferst of that I mai suffise,
	I bowe and profre my servise,
	Somtime in chambre, somtime in halle,
	Riht as I se the times falle.
to hear	And whan sche goth to hiere masse,
pass by (without)	That time schal noght overpasse
	That I n'aproche hir ladihede
On the chance that	In aunter if I mai hire lede
and back	Unto the chapelle and ayein.
my way (of life)	Thanne is noght al mi weie in vein,
	Somdiel I mai the betre fare
	Whan I, that mai noght fiele hir bare,
	Mai lede hire clothed in myn arm.
	Bot afterward it doth me harm
	Of pure ymaginacioun,
reflection	For thanne this collacioun
	I make unto miselven ofte,
	And seie, 'Ha, lord, hou sche is softe,
slender	How sche is round, hou sche is smal!
	Now wolde God I hadde hire al
Without reserve on her part	Withoute danger at mi wille!'
sigh	And thanne I sike and sitte stille
Because	Of that I se mi besi thoght
useless	Is torned ydel into noght.
neglect	Bot for al that lete I ne mai,
	Whanne I se time another dai,
	That I ne do my besinesse
lady's	Unto mi ladi worthinesse.
train my mind	For I therto mi wit afaite
watch for	To se the times and awaite
	What is to done and what to leve;
with her permission	And so, whan time is, be hir leve,
bids	What thing sche bidt me don, I do,
	And wher sche bit me gon, I go,
call	And whanne hir list to clepe, I come.
	Thus hath sche fulliche overcome
die	Min ydelnesse til I sterve,
of necessity	So that I mot hire nedes serve,
	For, as men sein, nede hath no lawe.
of necessity	Thus mot I nedly to hire drawe:

1140–1 The sensual longing here is all the more strongly conveyed because of the quiet transparency of Gower's style.

1149 **danger** is an allegorical character in the *Roman de la Rose* (which generally is much in Gower's mind in this passage of charming love-nonsense, especially *RR* 2551–2716), and represents the lady's disdain or standoffishness or reserve.

1167 **nede hath no lawe**: an old legal maxim (*Necessitas non habet legem*); proverbial.

I serve, I bowe, I loke, I loute, — *keep watch, make a bow*
Min yhe folweth hire aboute.
What-so sche wole, so wol I:
Whan sche wol sitte, I knele by,
And whan sche stant, than wol I stonde;
Bot whan sche takth hir werk on honde
Of wevinge or enbrouderie,
Than can I noght bot muse and prie
Upon hir fingres longe and smale, — *slender*
And now I thenke and now I tale — *talk*
And now I singe and now I sike
And thus mi contienance I pike. — *(see n.)*
And if it falle, as for a time
Hir liketh noght abide bi me,
Bot besien hire on other thinges,
Than make I othre tariinges
To dreche forth the longe dai, — *while away miserably*
For me is loth departe away.
And thanne I am so simple of port — *humble in demeanour*
That for to feigne som desport
I pleie with hire litel hound
Now on the bedd, now on the ground,
Now with hir briddes in the cage;
For ther is non so litel page
Ne yit so simple a chamberere — *maidservant*
That I ne make hem alle chere,
Al for thei scholde speke wel.
Thus mow ye sen mi besi whiel, — *(round of activities)*
That goth noght ydeliche aboute.
And if hir list to riden oute
On pelrinage or other stede, — *pilgrimage, place*
I come, thogh I be noght bede, — *asked*
And take hire in min arm alofte
And sette hire in hire sadel softe
And so forth lede hire be the bridel,
For that I wolde noght ben ydel.
And if hire list to ride in char, — *carriage*
And thanne I mai therof be war,
Anon I schape me to ryde — *arrange it so that I*
Riht evene be the chares side;
And as I mai I speke among, — *from time to time*
And otherwhile I singe a song
Which Ovide in his bokes made,
And seide, 'O whiche sorwes glade, — *O what*
O which wofull prosperite
Belongeth to the proprete — *nature (that which is proper to)*
Of love, who-so wole him serve!
And yit ther-fro mai no man swerve,

1180 'And thus I assume an appropriately meaningful facial expression'.

1211–17 The attribution of the following sentiment to Ovid has probably to do with his general medieval reputation as the 'poet of love'. The oxymoron of **sorwes glade** and **wofull prosperite** is a medieval commonplace, elaborately done to death by Jean de Meun in *RR* 4292–4330 (*Rom.* 4703–56).

That he ne mot his lawe obeie.'
And thus I ryde forth mi weie
And am riht besi overal
With herte and with mi body al,
As I have said you hier tofore.
My goode fader, tell therfore
Of Ydelnesse if I have gilt.

Confessor
Mi sone, bot thou telle wilt
Oght elles than I mai now hiere,
Thou schalt have no penance hiere.

The Tale of Tereus and Procne (V.5546–6052)

The tale of Tereus illustrates the vice of 'Ravine' (Violent Theft), one of the branches of the sin of Avarice, which is the subject of Book V, by far the longest book of the *Confessio*. The tale is freely adapted from Ovid, *Met.* VI.424–674, where it is told with great panache and brilliance and much gory detail. (Chaucer tells the story in the *Legend of Good Women*, 2228–2393, perfunctorily and with evident distaste, and alludes to it in *TC* II.64–70, above.) Gower 'medievalizes' the story, adding prayers to the gods (as representing some sort of moral order) and drawing out where he can the pathos of the story and the place of the characters within a world of intelligible and humane values. At the beginning of the story, there is, as is usual in *Confessio* MSS, a short Latin prose summary of the tale and its moral, beginning *Hic ponit exemplum contra istos in amoris causa raptores* ('Here [Genius] presents a story as an example against those who commit violent theft on account of love'). The summary does not mention the sisters' revenge nor the final transformations.

Confessor
Nou list, mi sone, and thou schalt hiere,
So as it hath befalle er this,
In loves cause hou that it is
A man to take be ravine
The preie which is femeline.
royal
Ther was a real noble king
And riche of alle worldes thing
Which of his propre onheritance
Athenes hadde in governance,
wishes to know about this
And who-so thenke therupon,
His name was king Pandion.
Tuo douhtres hadde he be his wif
The whiche he lovede as his lif;
was called
The ferste douhter Progne hihte
And the secounde, as sche wel mihte,
Was cleped faire Philomene,
great suffering
To whom fell after mochel tene.
(see n.)
The fader of his pourveance
give advancement to
His doughter Progne wolde avance
And yaf hire unto mariage
A worthi king of hih lignage,
A noble kniht eke of his hond,
known
So was he kid in every lond.

1223 There is often wit in the contrast between *applied* and *implied* meaning in Gower. The lover's 'business' would more normally, of course, be thought a form of 'idleness'.

Book V

5563 **of his pourveance**: 'as part of his provision for the future'.

Of Trace he hihte Tereus:
The clerk Ovide telleth thus.
   This Tereus his wif hom ladde,
A lusti lif with hire he hadde; — *pleasant*
Til it befell upon a tyde
This Progne, as sche lay him besyde,
Bethoughte hir hou it mihte be
That sche hir soster myhte se,
And to hir lord hir will sche seide
With goodly wordes and him preide
That sche to hire mihte go;
And if it liked him noght so
That thanne he wolde himselve wende
Or elles be som other sende
Which mihte hire diere soster griete
And schape hou that thei mihten miete.
Hir lord anon to that he herde — *to what*
Yaf his acord, and thus ansuerde:
'I wole,' he seide, 'for thi sake
The weie after thi soster take
Miself, and bringe hire, if I may.'
And sche with that, there as he lay,
Began him in hire armes clippe — *embrace*
And kist him with hir softe lippe,
And seide, 'Sire, grant mercy.'
And he sone after was redy
And tok his leve for to go:
In sori time dede he so!
   This Tereus goth forth to schipe
With him and with his felaschipe;
Be see the rihte cours he nam — *By sea, direct, took*
Into the contre til he cam
Wher Philomene was duellinge,
And of hir soster the tidinge
He tolde, and tho thei weren glade
And mochel joie of him thei made.
The fader and the moder bothe
To leve here douhter weren lothe — *give up*
Bot if thei weren in presence; — *in attendance (i.e. were with her)*
And natheles at reverence — *out of respect (for)*
Of him that wolde himself travaile — *put to so much trouble*
Thei wolden noght he sholde faile
Of that he preide, and yive hire leve;
And sche, that wolde noght beleve, — *remain*
In alle haste made hire yare — *ready*
Toward hir soster for to fare
With Tereus, and forth sche wente.
   And he with al his hole entente,
Whan sche was fro hir frendes go,
Assoteth of hire love so — *Became infatuated*
His yhe myhte he noght withholde

5569 **Tereus** is trisyllabic throughout.

That he ne moste on hir beholde; *must*
And with the sihte he gan desire
And sette his oghne herte on fyre;
And fyr, whan it to tow aprocheth,
To him anon the strengthe acrocheth, *To it (the fire), increases*
Til with his hete it be devoured –
The tow ne mai noght be socoured. *saved*
And so that tirant raviner, *robber*
Whan that sche was in his pouer
And he therto sawh time and place,
As he that lost hath alle grace,
Foryat he was a wedded man
And in a rage on hire he ran
Riht as a wolf which takth his preie.
And sche began to crie and preie,
'O fader, O mi moder diere,
Nou help!' Bot thei ne mihte it hiere,
And sche was of to litel myht
Defense ayein so ruide a knyht *violent*
To make, whanne he was so wod *mad*
That he no reson understod,
But hield hire under in such wise
That sche ne myhte noght arise,
Bot lay oppressed and desesed *distressed*
As if a goshauk hadde sesed
A brid, which dorste noght for fere
Remue; and thus this tirant there *Make a move*
Beraft hire such thing as men sein
Mai neveremor be yolde ayein, *given back*
And that was the virginite:
Of such ravine it was pite.
Bot whan sche to hirselven com
And of hir meschief hiede nom *came to a full realization*
And knew hou that sche was no maide,
With wofull herte thus sche saide:
'O thou of alle men the worste,
Wher was ther evere man that dorste
Do such a dede as thou hast do?
That dai schal falle, I hope so,
That I schal telle out al mi fille
And with mi speche I schal fulfille *fill full*
The wyde world in brede and lengthe. *breadth*
That thou hast do to me be strengthe, *What, by force*
If I among the poeple duelle,
Unto the poeple I schal it telle;
And if I be withinne wall
Of stones closed, thanne I schal
Unto the stones clepe and crie
And tellen hem thi felonie;
And if I to the wodes wende,

5623 **tow**: tow, unspun textile fibre used to catch flame from a flint or tinder.

5644–6 Cf. *TC* III.1191–2, above.

from beginning to end Ther schal I tellen tale and ende
And crie it to the briddes oute
That thei schul hiere it al aboute.
For I so loude it schal reherce
That my vois schal the hevene perce
resound That it schal soune in goddes ere.
fear (of the gods) Ha, false man, where is thi fere?
O mor cruel than eny beste,
promise Hou hast thou holden thi beheste
Which thou unto my soster madest?
makest miserable O thou, which alle love ungladest
And art ensample of alle untrewe,
Nou wolde god mi soster knewe
Of thin untrouthe hou that it stod!'
  And he thanne as a lyon wod
(misfortune-bringing) With hise unhappi handes stronge
Hire cauhte be the tresses longe,
With whiche he bond ther bothe hire armes –
That was a fieble dede of armes! –
And to the grounde anon hire caste
And out he clippeth also faste
Hire tunge with a peire scheres.
So what with blod and what with teres
Out of hire yhe and of hir mouth,
unrecognizable He made hire faire face uncouth:
Sche lay swounende unto the deth,
hardly Ther was unethes eny breth.
cut out Bot yit whan he hire tunge refte,
A litel part therof belefte,
Bot sche withal no word mai soune
twitter, chatter Bot chitre and as a brid jargoune.
And natheles that wode hound
seized Hir bodi hent up fro the ground
And sente hir there as be his wille
Sche scholde abyde in prison stille
For everemo. Bot nou tak hiede
What after fell of this misdede.
  Whanne al this meschief was befalle,
may evil befall him! This Tereus – that foule him falle! –
drew Unto his contre hom he tyh;
And whan he com his paleis nyh
awaited His wif al redi there him kepte.
Whan he hir sih, anon he wepte,
did And that he dede for deceite,
For sche began to axe him streite,
'Wher is mi soster?' And he seide
gave a start That sche was ded; and Progne abreide,
woman As sche that was a wofull wif
(on the point of death) And stod betuen hire deth and lif
As a result that Of that sche herde such tidinge;
Bot for sche sih hire lord wepinge,

5709 Apparently the rape took place on the way to Thrace.

thought	She wende noght bot alle trouthe
	And hadde wel the more routhe.
	The perles weren tho forsake
In her case, taken	To hire, and blake clothes take;
	As sche that was gentil and kinde,
honour, memory	In worschipe of hir sostres mynde
burial	Sche made a riche enterement,
benefit	For sche fond non amendement
	To syghen or to sobbe more:
'under the gown' (i.e. concealed)	So was ther guile under the gore.
	Nou leve we this king and queene
	And torne ayein to Philomene,
first	As I began to tellen erst.
	Whan sche cam into prison ferst
seemed to	It thoghte a kinges douhter strange
	To maken so soudein a change
	Fro welthe unto so grete a wo,
	And sche began to thenke tho,
	Thogh sche be mouthe nothing preide,
	Withinne hir herte thus sche seide:
	'O thou, almyhty Jupiter,
sittest	That hihe sist and lokest fer,
dost tolerate	Thou soffrest many a wrong-doinge,
	And yit it is noght thi willinge.
	To thee ther mai nothing ben hid:
befallen	Thou wost hou it is me betid.
born	I wolde I hadde noght be bore,
	For thanne I hadde noght forlore
	Mi speche and mi virginite.
	Bot, goode lord, al is in thee
	Whan thou therof wolt do vengance
	And schape mi deliverance.'
continually from time to time	And evere among this ladi wepte
cared	And thoghte that sche nevere kepte
	To ben a worldes womman more,
	And that sche wissheth everemore.
	Bot ofte unto hir soster diere
	Hire herte spekth in this manere,
	And seide, 'Ha, soster, if ye knewe
situation, take pity	Of myn astat, ye wolde rewe,
	I trowe, and my deliverance
	Ye wolde schape, and do vengance
	On him that is so fals a man.
	And natheles, so as I can,
	I wol you sende som tokninge
	Wherof ye schul have knowlechinge
to you be hateful	Of thing I wot that schal you lothe,
	The which you toucheth and me bothe.'
quickly	And tho withinne a whyle als tyt
wove	Sche waf a cloth of selk al whyt

5745 The attributes ascribed to Jupiter, as to Venus and Cupid (5821) and Apollo (5846, 5863) later, are in part those of the Christian deity; the historical slippage is usual in medieval versions of classical stories.

With lettres and ymagerie
In which was al the felonie
Which Tereus to hire hath do;
And lappede it togedre tho — *folded it up*
And sette hire signet therupon
And sende it unto Progne anon. — *sent*
The messager which forth it bar
What it amonteth is noght war, — *signifies*
And natheles to Progne he goth
And privately takth hire the cloth
And wente ayein riht as he cam: — *went back*
The court of him non hiede nam. — *took*
Whan Progne of Philomene herde
Sche wolde knowe hou that it ferde — *went*
And opneth that the man hath broght — *what*
And wot therby what hath be wroght
And what meschief ther is befalle.
In swoune tho sche gan doun falle
And efte aros and gan to stonde, — *again*
And eft sche takth the cloth on honde,
Behield the lettres and th'ymages,
Bot ate laste, 'Of suche oultrages,'
Sche seith, 'wepinge is noght the bote,' — *remedy*
And swerth, if that she live mote,
It schal be venged otherwise. — *in some other way*
And with that sche gan hire avise — *to deliberate*
Hou ferst sche mihte unto hire winne
Hir soster, that no man withinne,
Bot only thei that were suore, — *sworn (to secrecy)*
It scholde knowe, and schop therfore — *arranged*
That Tereus nothing it wiste.
And yit riht as hirselven list
Hir soster was delivered sone
Out of prison, and be the mone — *by moonlight*
To Progne sche was broght be nyhte.
Whan ech of other hadde a sihte,
In chambre, ther thei were alone,
Thei maden many a pitous mone;
Bot Progne most of sorwe made,
Which sihe hir soster pale and fade
And specheles and deshonoured
Of that sche hadde be defloured; — *Because*
And ek upon hir lord sche thoghte,
Of that he so untreuly wroghte
And hadde his espousaile broke. — *marriage(-vow)*
Sche makth a vou it schal be wroke, — *avenged*
And with that word sche kneleth doun.
Wepinge in gret devocioun
Unto Cupide and to Venus
Sche preide, and seide thanne thus:
'O ye, to whom nothing asterte — *escape*
Of love mai, for every herte
Ye knowe, as ye that ben above

The god and the goddesse of love,
always till now Ye witen wel that evere yit
With al mi will and al my wit
Sith ferst ye schopen me to wedde,
That I lay with mi lord abedde,
according to my state in life I have be trewe in mi degre
And evere thoghte for to be
And nevere love in other place
Bot al only the king of Trace,
Which is mi lord and I his wif.
Bot nou allas this wofull strif!
in return That I him thus ayeinward finde
The most untrewe and most unkinde
a lady's That evere in ladi armes lay.
And wel I wot that he ne may
Amende his wrong, it is so gret,
esteemed For he to lytel of me let
Whan he myn oughne soster tok
And me that am his wif forsok.'
   Lo thus to Venus and Cupide
Sche preide, and furthermor sche cride
Unto Appollo the hiheste,
peace And seide, 'O myhti god of reste,
May you do Thou do vengance of this debat.
Mi soster and al hire astat
Thou wost, and hou sche hath forlore
Hir maidenhod, and I therfore
In al the world schal bere a blame
Of how Of that mi soster hath a schame
Because That Tereus to hire I sente:
And wel thou wost that myn entente
Was al for worschipe and for goode.
O lord, that yifst the lives fode
hear To every wyht, I prei thee hiere
Thes wofull sostres that ben hiere
hateful And let ous noght to the ben lothe:
We ben thin oghne wommen bothe.'
asks for vengeance   Thus pleigneth Progne and axeth wreche,
And thogh hire soster lacke speche,
To him that alle thinges wot
passionate Hire sorwe is noght the lasse hot.
Bot he that thanne had herd hem tuo,
Him oughte have sorwed everemo
For sorwe which was hem betuene.
With signes pleigneth Philomene
revenged And Progne seith, 'It schal be wreke,
That al the world therof schal speke.'
   And Progne tho seknesse feigneth,
Wherof unto hir lord sche pleigneth

5850–2 Procne seems as upset about her own loss of reputation (cf. 5840–2) as about the violation of her sister, just as Philomena lamented chiefly the loss of her 'astat' of virginity. The injury to the women as *persons* is only hinted at in Gower, but even the hints are an achievement of the poetic imagination, since women are, in medieval legal theory, functions of male agency, not agents in themselves. Gower himself earlier (V.5505–28) defined 'Ravine' as the seizure of other men's property without right and without payment.

might And preith sche moste hire chambres kepe
And as hir liketh wake and slepe.
And he hire granteth to be so;
And thus togedre ben thei tuo
That wolde him bot a litel good.
Nou herk hierafter hou it stod
happenings Of wofull auntres that befelle:
savagely cruel Thes sostres, that ben bothe felle –
because of them And that was noght on hem along
only because of Bot onliche on the grete wrong
Which Tereus hem hadde do –
Thei schopen for to venge hem tho.
  This Tereus be Progne his wif
A sone hath, which as his lif
He loveth, and Ithis he hihte:
His moder wiste wel sche mihte
Do Tereus no more grief
beloved Than sle this child, which was so lief.
Thus sche that was, as who seith, mad
overcome Of wo, which hath hir overlad,
feeling Withoute insihte of moderhede
Foryat pite and loste drede
And in hir chambre prively
This child withouten noise or cry
hewed Sche slou, and hieu him al to pieces,
And after with diverse spieces
all cut up The fleissh, whan it was so to-heewe,
stew Sche takth and makth therof a sewe
With which the fader at his mete
Was served, til he hadde him ete,
That he ne wiste hou that it stod
Bot thus his oughne fleissh and blod
against nature Himself devoureth ayein kinde,
unnatural As he that was tofore unkinde.
And thanne, er that he were arise,
struck with horror For that he scholde ben agrise,
To schewen him the child was ded
This Philomene tok the hed
Betwen tuo disshes, and al wrothe
Tho comen forth the sostres bothe
And setten it upon the bord.
  And Progne tho began the word,
And seide, 'O werste of alle wicke,
Of conscience whom no pricke
disturb, done Mai stere, lo, what thou hast do!
Lo hier ben nou we sostres tuo:
prey O raviner, lo hier thi preie
With whom so falsliche on the weie
Thou hast thi tirannye wroght.

5877 The understatement is characteristic of Gower.

5881–3 Gower is eager as always to stake out the story within a network of civilized moral values.

5910 Gower much reduces Philomena's part in these grisly scenes, forcing Procne to take on more of the action of revenge so that her sister will remain a passive victim and a proper subject for pathos and sympathy.

paid for (requited) Lo nou it is somdel aboght,
better it shall (be paid for) And bet it schal, for of thi dede
The world schal evere singe and rede
In remembrance of thi defame:
For thou to love hast do such schame
That it schal nevere be foryete.'
With that he sterte up fro the mete
And schof the bord unto the flor
And cauhte a swerd anon and suor
That thei scholde of his handes dye.
And thei unto the goddes crie
voice Begunne with so loude a stevene
That thei were herd unto the hevene,
And in a twinclinge of an yhe
The goddes, that the meschief syhe,
Here formes changen alle thre.
according to his condition Echon of hem in his degre
Was torned into briddes kinde:
Diverseliche, as men mai finde,
After th'astat that thei were inne,
set apart (distinguished) Here formes were set atwinne.
And as it telleth in the tale,
The ferst into a nyhtingale
Was schape, and that was Philomene,
Which in the wynter is noght sene,
For thanne ben the leves falle
And naked ben the buisshes alle.
For after that sche was a brid
Hir will was evere to ben hid
And for to duelle in prive place
That no man scholde sen hir face
made less For schame, which mai noght be lassed,
Of thing that was tofore passed
Whan that sche loste hir maidenhiede:
For evere upon hir wommanhiede,
had wished Thogh that the goddes wolde hire change,
remote and withdrawn She thenkth, and is the more strange,
keeps herself in seclusion And halt hir clos the wyntres day.
Bot whan the wynter goth away
And that Nature the goddesse
Wole of hir oughne fre largesse
With herbes and with floures bothe
The feldes and the medwes clothe,
And ek the wodes and the greves
covered Ben heled al with grene leves,
So that a brid hire hyde mai,
During Betwen Averil and March and Maii,
Sche that the wynter hield hir clos
For pure schame and noght aros,
Whan that sche seth the bowes thikke

5926 It is a peculiarity of the medieval handling of the story that Tereus's offence is spoken of as an offence against 'love'.

5935–6047 Gower develops the transformations, only briefly referred to in Ovid, with charm and tenderness, as if to mitigate the horror and to place it in a distanced world where human emotions and values are poeticized.

And that ther is no bare sticke
Bot al is hid with leves grene,
To wode comth this Philomene
And makth hir ferste yeres flyht,
Wher as sche singeth day and niht
And in hir song al openly
Sche makth hir pleignte and seith, 'O why,
O why ne were I yit a maide?'
For so these olde wise saide, *(wise men)*
Which understoden what sche mente,
Hire notes ben of such entente. *(meaning)*
And ek thei seide hou in hir song
Sche makth gret joie and merthe among, *(at times)*
And seith, 'Ha, nou I am a brid,
Ha, nou mi face mai ben hid:
Thogh I have lost mi maidenhede,
Schal no man se my chekes rede.'
Thus medleth sche with joie wo *(mingles)*
And with hir sorwe merthe also,
So that of loves maladie
Sche makth diverse melodie
And seith love is a wofull blisse,
A wisdom which can no man wisse, *(body of knowledge, get the hang of)*
A lusti fievere, a wounde softe: *(pleasant)*
This note sche reherceth ofte *(song)*
To hem whiche understonde hir tale.
Nou have I of this nyhtingale,
Which erst was cleped Philomene,
Told al that evere I wolde mene, *(intended to say)*
Bothe of hir forme and of hir note,
Wherof men mai the storie note. *(take note of)*
　And of hir soster Progne I finde
Hou sche was torned out of kinde *(from her (human) nature)*
Into a swalwe swift of winge,
Which ek in wynter lith swounynge,
Ther as sche mai nothing be sene; *(not at all)*
Bot whan the world is woxe grene
And comen is the somertide,
Than fleth sche forth and ginth to chide
And chitreth out in hir langage
What falshod is in mariage
And telleth in a maner speche
Of Tereus the spouse-breche. *(Tereus's marriage-violation)*
Sche wol noght in the wodes duelle,
For sche wolde openliche telle;
And ek for that sche was a spouse
Among the folk sche comth to house
To do thes wyves understonde
The falshod of hir housebonde, *(their)*
That thei of hem be war also,

5993 For the oxymoron, see above, IV.1211–17n. It seems singularly inappropriate to Philomena's experience.

For ther ben manye untrewe of tho.
Thus ben the sostres briddes bothe
And ben toward the men so lothe *hateful*
That thei ne wole of pure schame
Unto no mannes hand be tame,
For evere it duelleth in here mynde
Of that thei founde a man unkinde, *How, unnatural*
And that was false Tereus.
If such on be amonges ous
I not, bot his condicion *his type*
Men sein in every region *say*
Withinne toun and ek withoute
Nou regneth comunliche aboute. *prevails*
And natheles in remembrance
I wol declare what vengance
The goddes hadden him ordeined
Of that the sostres hadden pleigned: *For what*
For anon after he was changed
And from his oghne kinde stranged – *estranged*
A lappewincke mad he was, *lapwing, made*
And thus he hoppeth on the gras
And on his hed ther stant upriht
A creste in tokne he was a kniht.
And yit unto this dai men seith
The lappewincke hath lore his feith *lost*
And is the brid falseste of alle.

Bewar, mi sone, er thee so falle;
For if thou be of such covine *wicked and deceitful purpose*
To gete of love be ravine
Thi lust, it mai thee falle thus
As it befell of Tereus.

6047 Cf. *PF* 347.

Mandeville's Travels (*c.* 1390–1400)

Mandeville's Travels is not a travel-book but a compendium of information about countries in the east, some of it not entirely inaccurate, enlivened with local stories, legends and marvels. It begins with a lament that the Holy Land is still in infidel hands, and exhortations to a new crusade, but soon relaxes into a general guide for pilgrims to the holy places (chaps 1–14), with many digressions and excursions, and then to a general account of the lands of the east, including the kingdoms of the Great Khan (chaps 23–6) and of Prester John (chaps 30–2). It purports to have been written in 1356 by Sir John Mandeville (chap. 34), recounting journeys that he made beginning in 1322, but the original author, whoever he was (most likely not English, writing in Liège about 1357), could have got all his information from compilations of books of travel (such as that of Odoric of Pordenone) and books of marvels (such as those associated with the Alexander-romances) and general encyclopaedias (such as that of Vincent of Beauvais) without moving from his library. The *Travels* were enormously popular, were translated from the original French into most European languages, and survive in over 300 manuscripts, including nearly 40 in English (in several versions, the earliest about 1390), and many early printed editions. It was the most popular secular book of the late Middle Ages. The *Travels* provided a structure for late medieval understanding of the non-European world, not just its geography but its social and moral systems, including the faith of the Koran (chap. 15); the attitude of the narrator is surprisingly open and receptive to their differentness, taking his cue from a long tradition in which non-Christian peoples were not reviled for being heathen but admired for being virtuous despite being heathen. The work was known to Leonardo da Vinci and was in the hand-baggage of Christopher Columbus when he boarded ship in 1492 (it makes abundantly clear, e.g. chap. 20, that the earth is to be thought of as a sphere).

The success of the *Travels* was due to the straightforward personal tone and sense of authenticity communicated by references to the author's personal experience; to the lively, varied and swift-moving narrative, with always some new and amazing fact or story to relate; and to the absence of heavy didacticism. Much is fantasy, but we should not overestimate the credulity of its early readers: they know that these stories, many of them, are told to shock, startle, cause outrage and give pleasure, but they are not under any irritable modern compulsion to separate fact from fiction or cynically to disparage the latter. It is pleasing to them to hear that there is a hill called Ararat, seven miles high, in greater Armenia, where Noah's ship rested after the Flood and can still be seen from far off in clear weather (chap. 16), or that a little way from Mount Sion there is the tree on which Judas hanged himself when he had betrayed Christ (chap. 11). At the same time, such a narrative offers the opportunity to entertain descriptions of variant forms of religious belief, including heretical forms of the Christian faith, without the dangers normally attendant upon such freedom.

Extracts here are from BL MS Cotton Titus C.xvi (*c.* 1400), the base-MS of the standard edition of M.C. Seymour (Oxford, 1967); modern English translation by C.W.R.D. Moseley (Penguin, 1983); studies by M. Letts (London, 1949), J.W. Bennett (Oxford, 1954), M.C. Seymour (London, 1994), and I.M. Higgins, *Writing East: The 'Travels' of Sir John Mandeville* (Philadelphia, 1997).

The holy places west of Jerusalem (chap. 11)

[*An example of the kind of information that was readily available in guide-books for pilgrims to the Holy Land. They wanted their visit to be worthwhile, and so the itinerary was crowded, like a modern tourists' guide, with places of interest, many of them the product of piously happy invention. The passage shows Mandeville's skill in giving an air of authenticity through precise-sounding detail and through the calm objective detachment with which he lays side by side both natural and supernatural explanations of phenomena.*]

...Also fro Jerusalem toward the west is a fair chirche where the tree of the cros grew. And ii. myle fro thens is a faire chirche where oure Lady mette with Elizabeth whan thei weren bothe with childe, and Seynt John stered in his modres wombe and made reverence to his creatour that he saugh not.[1] And under the awtier of that chirche is the place where Seynt John was born. And fro that chirche is a myle to the castelle of Emaux, and there also oure Lord schewed him to ii. of his disciples after his resurrexioun.[2]...

Also fro Jerusalem ii. myle is the Mount Joye, a fulle fair place and a delicyous, and there lyth Samuel the prophete in a fair tombe. And men clepen it Mount Joye for it yeveth joye to pilgrymes hertes because

Chapter 11

1 See Luke 1:41.

2 See Luke 24:13.

that there men seen first Jerusalem. Also betwene Jerusalem and the Mount of Olyvete is the vale of Josaphath[3] under the walles of the cytee, as I have seyd before, and in the myddes of that vale is a lytille ryvere that men clepen *Torrens Cedron*. And aboven it overthwart lay a tre that the cros was made offe[4] that men yeden over onne. And faste by it is a litylle pytt in the erthe where the foot of the pileer is yit entered[5], and there was oure Lord first scourged, for he was scorged and vileynsly entreted[6] in many places.

Also in the myddel place of the vale of Josaphath is the chirche of oure Lady, and it is of xliiii. degrees[7] under the erthe unto the sepulchre of oure Lady. And oure Lady was of age whan sche dyed lxxii. yeer. And beside the sepulcre of oure Lady is an awtier where oure Lord foryaf Seynt Peter alle his synnes. And fro thens toward the west under an awtere is a welle that cometh out of the flomme[8] of Paradys. And wyteth wel that that chirche is fulle lowe in the erthe, and sum is alle withinne the erthe. But I suppose wel that it was not so founded, but for because that Jerusalem hath often-tyme ben destroyed and the walles abated[9] and beten doun and tombled into the vale, and that thei han so filled it[a] ayen and the ground enhaunced, and for that skylle[10] is the chirche so lowe within the erthe. And natheles men seyn there comounly that the erthe hath so growen[b] syth the tyme that oure Lady was there buryed. And yit men seyn there that it wexeth and groweth every day withouten dowte. In that chirche were wont to ben monkes blake that hadden hire abbot....

The people of Dundeya (chap. 22)

{These strangely shaped people are familiar in stories of the marvels of the east, and strewn about in the blank spaces of maps such as the Hereford Map. 'Dundeya' is commonly identified as the Andaman Islands, in the Indian Ocean.}

...The kyng of this yle is a ful gret lord and a myghty, and hath under him liiii. grete yles that yeven tribute to him. And in everych of theise yles is a kyng crowned, and alle ben obeyssant to that kyng. And he hath in tho yles many dyverse folk. In on of theise yles ben folk of gret stature as geauntes, and thei ben hidouse for to loke upon. And thei han but on eye, and that is in the myddylle of the front.[1] And thei eten nothing but raw flesch and raw fyssch. And in another yle toward the south duellen folk of foul stature and of cursed kynde, that han non hedes. And here eyen ben in here scholdres, and here mouth is croked as an hors-schoo, and that is in the myddes of here brest. And in another yle also ben folk that han non hedes, and here eyen and here mouth ben behynde in here schuldres. And in another yle ben folk that han the face all platt,[2] all pleyn withouten nese and withouten mouth. But thei han ii. smale holes all rounde instede of hire eyen, and hire mouth is platt also withouten lippes. And in another yle ben folk of foul fasceoun and schapp that han the lippe above the mouth so gret that whan thei slepen in the sonne thei keveren all the face with that lippe. And in another yle ther ben lityll folk as dwerghes,[3] and thei ben to so meche as[4] the pygmeyes. And thei han no mouth, but instede of hire mouth thei han a lytyll round hole. And whan thei schull eten or drynken thei taken thorgh a pipe or a penne[5] or such a thing and sowken it in, for thei han no tonge. And therfore thei speke not but thei maken a manner of hissynge as a nedder[6] doth. And thei maken signes on to another as monkes don,[7] be the whiche every of hem understondeth other.

And in another yle ben folk that han grete eres and longe that hangen doun to here knees. And in another yle ben folk that han hors feet. And thei ben stronge and myghty and swift renneres, for thei taken wylde bestes with rennyng and eten hem. And in another yle ben folk that gon upon hire hondes

3 **Josaphath**. The vale of Jehoshaphat was the scene of the future resurrection of mankind (*PP* XX.411n).

4 **a tre that the cros was made offe**. The wood of the Cross, and the trees that it was made from, were ubiquitous in apocryphal legend. (The unusual spellings **offe** and **onne** mark the predicative adverbial use of 'of' and 'on'.)

5 interred

6 treated

7 steps

8 river

9 reduced

10 reason

Chapter 22

1 forehead

2 flat

3 dwarfs

4 of the height of

5 a reed or a quill

6 snake

7 **as monkes don**, i.e. when they are keeping silence, as at meals, but have to communicate.

and on hire feet as bestes. And thei ben all skynned and fedred. And thei wole lepen als lightly into trees and fro tree to tree as it were squyrelles or apes. And in another yle ben folk that ben bothe man and womman, and thei han kynde of that on and of that other. And thei han but o pappe on the o syde, and on that other non. And thei han membres of generacioun of man and womman, and thei usen bothe whan hem list, ones[8] that on and another tyme that other. And thei geten children whan thei usen the membre of man, and thei bere children whan thei usen the membre of womman. And in another yle ben folk that gon allweys upon here knees ful merveyllously, and at every pas that thei gon it semeth that thei wolde fall. And thei han in every foot viii. toos. Many other dyverse folk of dyverse natures ben there in other yles abouten, of the whiche it were to longe to telle and therfore I passe over schortly....

The approach to the land of Prester John (chap. 30)

{Though rich, Prester John's kingdom is not frequented by merchants so much as the land of the Great Khan, for reasons that are explained in a passage of brave inventiveness.}

...And therfore, alle be it that men han gretter chep[1] in the yle of Prestre John, natheless men dreden the longe weye and the grete periles in the see in tho partyes. For in many places of the see ben grete roches of stones of the adamant, that of his propre nature draweth iren to him. And therfore there passen no schippes that han outher bondes[2] or nayles of iren within hem. And yif ther do, anon the roches of the adamantes drawen hem to hem, that never thei may go thens. I myself have seen o ferrom[3] in that see as though it hadde ben a gret yle fulle of trees and buscaylle[4] fulle of thornes and breres gret plentee. And the schipmen tolde us that alle that was of schippes that weren drawen thider be the adamauntes for the iren that was in hem; and of the roteness[5] and other thing that was within the schippes grewen such buscaylle and thornes and breres and grene grass and such maner of thing. And of the mastes and the seylle-yerdes it semed a grete wode or a grove. And suche roches ben in many places thereabouten. And therfore dur[6] not the marchauntes passen there but yif thei knowen wel the passages or elles that thei han gode lodesmen....

The fools of despair (chap. 31)

...Another yle is there fulle fair and gode and gret and fulle of peple, where the custom is such that the firste nyght that thei ben maryed thei maken another man to lye be hire wifes for to have hire maydenhode, and therfore[1] thei taken gret huyre[2] and gret thank. And ther ben certeyn men in every town that serven of non other thing, and thei clepen hem *cadeberiz*, that is to seyne 'the foles of wanhope'.[3] For thei of the contree holden it so gret a thing and so perilous for to have the maydenhode of a womman that hem semeth that thei that haven first the maydenhode putteth him in aventure of his lif. And yif the husbonde fynde his wif mayden that other next nyght after that sche scholde have ben leyn by of the man that is assigned therefore, peraunter for dronkeness or for sum other cause, the husbonde schalle pleyne upon him that he hath not don his deveer[4] in such cruelle wise as though the officere wolde have slayn him.[5] But after the firste nyght that thei ben leyn by, thei kepen hem so streytely that thei ben not so hardy to speke with no man. And I asked hem the cause whi that thei helden such custom. And thei seyden me that of olde tyme men hadden ben dede for deflourynge of maydenes that hadden serpentes in hire bodyes that stongen men upon hire yerdes,[6] that thei dyeden anon. And therfore thei helden that custom to make other men ordeynd therfore[7] to lye be hire wyfes for drede of deth, and to assaye the passage be another rather[c] than for to putte hem in that aventure[8]....

8 at one time

Chapter 30

1 bargains
2 bands
3 from afar
4 underbrush
5 rottenness
6 dare

Chapter 31

1 for that service
2 wages
3 despair
4 duty
5 I.e. as though the proxy-bridegroom, by not doing his duty, had intended cruelly to bring about the death of the husband.
6 penises
7 for that purpose
8 risk

The Brahmins (chap. 32)

{The story of the virtuous Brahmins is told in the Alexander-romances; it derives in part from real contact with India, but also from the legends of the Saturnian or Golden Age. The idea of a people living in virtue according to reason and natural law, without the corruptions of western civilization, provides some of the materials for accounts of paradise and of other-worldly Utopias such as More's (below). But the chief purpose is to rebuke Christian peoples for falling away from virtue despite the benefit of the Christian revelation, and to ask again the question that preoccupied many fourteenth-century writers (including Langland), concerning the fate of the righteous heathen.}

And beyonde that yle is another yle gret and gode and plentyfous, where that ben gode folk and trewe and of gode lyvynge after hire beleve and of gode feyth. And alle be it that thei ben not cristned ne have no perfyt lawe, yit natheles of kyndely[1] lawe thei ben fulle of alle vertue. And thei eschewen alle vices and alle malices and alle synnes. For thei ben not proude, ne coveytous, ne envyous, ne wrathfulle, ne glotouns, ne leccherous,[2] ne thei don to no man otherwise than thei wolde that other men diden to hem.[3] And in this poynt thei fullefillen the x. commandementes of God, and yif no charge of aveer[4] ne of ricchess. And thei lye not ne thei swere not for non occasioun, but thei seyn symply *ye* and *nay*.[5] For thei seyn he that swereth wil disceyve his neyghbore, and therefore alle that thei don thei don it withouten oth. And men clepen that yle the yle of Bragman, and somme men clepen it the lond of feyth. And thorgh that lond renneth a gret ryvere that is clept Thebe. And in generalle alle the men of tho yles and of alle the marches[6] thereabouten ben more trewe than in ony othere contrees thereabouten, and more rightfulle than othere in alle thinges. In that yle is no thef ne mordrere ne comoun womman[7] ne pore beggere, ne nevere was man slayn in that contree. And thei ben so chast and leden so gode life as that thei weren religious men. And thei fasten alle dayes. And because thei ben so trewe and so rightfulle and so fulle of alle gode condiciouns thei weren nevere greved with tempestes ne with thonder ne with leyt[8] ne with hayl ne with pestylence ne with werre ne with hunger ne with non other tribulacioun as we ben many tymes amonges us for oure synnes. Wherfore it semeth wel that God loveth hem and is plesed with hire creance[9] for hire gode dedes. Thei beleven wel in God that made alle thinges, and him thei worschipen. And thei preysen non erthely ricchess, and so thei ben alle rightfulle. And thei lyven fulle ordynatly and so sobrely in mete and drynk that thei lyven right longe, and the most part of hem dyen withouten sykness whan nature fayleth hem for elde.

And it befelle in kyng Alisandres tyme that he purposed him to conquere that yle and to maken hem to holden[10] of him. And whan thei of the contre herden it thei senten messangeres to him with lettres that seyden thus: 'What may ben ynow to that man to whom alle the world is insuffisant? Thou schalt fynde nothing in us that may cause the to werren ayenst us, for we have no ricchess ne none we coveyten, and alle the godes of oure contree ben in comoun. Oure mete that we susteyne withalle oure bodyes is oure ricchess. And instede of tresour of gold and sylver we maken oure tresoure of accord and pees and for to love every man other. And for to apparaylle with oure bodyes, we usen a sely litylle clout[11] for to wrappen in oure careynes.[12] Oure wyfes ne ben not arrayed for to make no man plesance but only covenable[13] [d] array for to eschewe folye. Whan men peynen hem to arraye the body for to make it semen fayrere than God made it, thei don gret synne, for man schold not devise ne aske gretter beautee than God hath ordeyned man to ben at his birthe. The erthe mynystreth to us ii. thinges, oure liflode[14] that cometh of the erthe that we lyve by, and oure sepulture after oure deth. We have ben in perpetuelle pees tille now that thou come to disherite us. And also we have a kyng nought[e] for to do justice to every man, for he schalle fynde no forfete[15] among us, but for to keep nobless and for to schewe that we ben

Chapter 32

1 natural

2 Only Sloth is omitted of the Seven Deadly Sins.

3 See Luke 6:31.

4 attach no importance to possession

5 **thei seyn symply *ye* and *nay*.** Their bemusement at any other practice reminds one of Swift's Houyhnhnms.

6 bordering lands

7 prostitute

8 lightning. An allusion to the belief that bad weather began with the Fall, a disharmony of the outer as of the inner elements.

9 belief

10 hold their land as vassals

11 a simple little cloth garment

12 bodies

13 suitable

14 sustenance

15 wrongdoing

obeyssant we have a kyng. For justice ne hath not among us no place, for we don to no man otherwise than we desiren that men don to us, so that rightwisness ne vengeance han nought to don amonges us, so that nothing thou may take fro us but oure gode pes, that alleweys hath dured among us.'

And whan kyng Alisandre had rad theise lettres, he thoughte that he scholde do gret synne for to trouble hem. And thanne he sente hem surteez[16] that thei scholde not ben aferd of him and that thei scholde kepen hire gode maneres and hire gode pees as thei hadden used before of custom. And so he let hem allone....

The Earthly Paradise (chap. 33)

...And beyonde the lond and the yles and the desertes of Prestre Johnes lordschipe in goynge streight towardes the est men fynde nothing but montaynes and roches fulle grete. And there is the derke regyoun where no man may see nouther be day ne be nyghte, as thei of the contree seyn. And that desert and that place of derknesse duren fro this cost[1] unto Paradys Terrestre, where that Adam oure formest fader and Eve weren putt, that dwelleden there but lytylle while, and that is towardes the est at the begynnynge of the erthe. But that is not that est that we clepe oure est on this half where the sonne riseth to us. For whanne the sonne is est in tho partyes toward Paradys Terrestre, it is thanne mydnyght in oure parties o this half for the roundeness of the erthe, of the whiche I have towched to you of before. For oure Lord God made the erthe alle rownd in the mydde place of the firmament. And there as mountaynes and hilles ben and valeyes, that is not but only of Noes Flode that wasted the softe ground and the tendre and felle doun into valeyes.[2] And the harde erthe and the roche abyden mountaynes whan the soft erthe and tendre wax nessche[3] thorgh the water and felle and becamen valeyes.

Of Paradys ne can I not speken propurly, for I was not there.[4] It is fer beyonde, and that forthinketh[5] me, and also I was not worthi. But as I have herd seye of wyse men beyonde, I schalle telle you with gode wille. Paradys Terrestre, as wise men seyn, is the highest place of erthe that is in alle the world,[6] and it is so high that it toucheth nygh to the cercle of the mone, there as the mone maketh hire torn.[7] For sche is so high that the Flode of Noe ne myght not come to hire that wolde have covered alle the erthe of the world alle abowte and aboven and benethen, saf Paradys only allone. And this Paradys is enclosed alle aboute with a walle, and men wyte not wherof[8] it is, for the walles ben covered alle over with mosse, as it semeth. And it semeth not that the walle is ston of nature ne of non other thing that the walle is. And that walle streccheth fro the south to the north, and it hath not but on entree, that is closed with fyre brennynge so that no man that is mortalle ne dar not entren. *{Description of the four rivers that flow out of Paradise (Gen. 2:10): Ganges, Nile, Tigris and Euphrates.}*

And ye schulle understonde that no man that is mortelle ne may not approchen to that Paradys. For be londe no man may go for wylde bestes that ben in the desertes and for the high mountaynes and grete huge roches that no man may passe by for the derke places that ben there, and that manye. And be the ryveres may no man go, for the water renneth so rudely and so scharply because that it cometh doun so outrageously from the high places aboven that it renneth in so grete wawes that no schipp may not rowe ne seyle ayenes it. And the water roreth so and maketh so huge noyse and so gret tempest that no man may here other in the schipp, though he cryede with alle the craft[9] that he cowde in the hieste voys that he myghte. Many grete lordes han assayed with gret wille many tymes for to passen be tho ryveres toward Paradys with fulle grete companyes, but thei myght not speden[10] in hire viage. And manye dyeden for weryness of rowynge ayenst tho stronge wawes. And many of hem becamen blynde and many deve[11] for the noyse of the water. And summe weren perisscht and loste withinne the wawes. So that no mortelle man may approche to that place withouten specyalle grace of God, so that of that place I can sey you no more. And therfore I schalle holde me stille and retornen to that that I have seen.

16 sureties

Chapter 33

1 region

2 All the processes of erosion and land-formation are attributed here to the effect of Noah's Flood.

3 soft

4 This is the most famous flatly authentic deadpan remark in the book.

5 grieves

6 **the highest place of erthe**. In Dante's *Purgatorio*, the Earthly Paradise is on the summit of the antipodean mountain of Purgatory.

7 orbit

8 of what material

9 strength

10 succeed

11 deaf

The Cloud of Unknowing (*c.* 1390–1400)

Written in the 1390s by an unknown author, *The Cloud of Unknowing* is a work of advanced instruction in the mystical life of contemplation, which it is extraordinary to find in the vernacular at such a date (it was translated into Latin in the late fifteenth century – an indication perhaps of its precocity). It is directed to a 24-year-old disciple by an expert contemplative: Walter Hilton, canon of Thurgarton in Nottinghamshire, author of *The Scale of Perfection*, and a prominent late fourteenth-century mystical writer, is often spoken of as a possible author. It expounds the *via negativa* (the 'negative way') of contemplation, an important strand in western mystical thought from the time of the *Mystica Theologia* of the fifth-century Pseudo-Dionysius: God is unknowable, cannot be understood or known, but only loved, and the soul must be emptied of all knowledge, and all desire to know, if it is to seek and love God and gain a foretaste of that union with God which is the nature of the bliss hereafter. The 'negative way' of contemplation is contrasted by the author with the active life of those in the world and also with the more elementary version of the contemplative life which is attached to the body and bodily imaginings of the divine and characterized by the outpouring of emotion (see headnotes to Julian of Norwich and Nicholas Love, below). The success of the work is in the frank and informal tone of address, as to an intelligent and reliable friend, the ruthlessly impeccable command of argument and syntax, and the power of vivid image and turn of phrase (particularly well illustrated below in the satire on false contemplatives).

Survives in 17 manuscripts; text here from BL MS Harley 674 (early fifteenth century). Ed. Phyllis Hodgson, EETS, OS 218 (1944); extract in Windeatt (1994), pp. 67–77; trans. C. Wolters (Penguin, 1961). Useful essays by J.A. Burrow, *EC* 27 (1977), 283–98, and A.J. Minnis, *Traditio* 39 (1983), 323–66.

{The prologue warns sternly that only those dedicated to the higher contemplative life should read the book, and none should read it in selections. In the opening chapters, the author explains that the life of perfection to which his disciple aspires is the highest form of Christian life, and exhorts him to persevere in it. He begins with a brief summary of his programme of instruction.}

The plan of campaign (chap. 3)

Lift up thin herte unto God with a meek steryng[1] of love; and mene himself, and none of his goodes. And therto loke thee lothe to thenk on ought bot on hymself, so that nought worche in thi witte ne in thi wille bot only himself. And do that in thee is[2] to foryete alle the creatures that ever God maad and the werkes of hem, so that thi thought ne thi desire be not directe ne streche to any of hem, neither in general ne in special. Bot lat hem be, and take no kepe[3] to hem.

This is the werk of the soule that moste plesith God. Alle seintes and aungelles han joie of this werk, and hasten hem to helpe it in al here might. Alle feendes ben wood whan thou thus dost, and proven for to felle[4] it in alle that thei kun. Alle men levyng in erthe ben wonderfuli holpen of[5] this werk, thou wost not how; ye, the soules in purgatori ben esed of theire peine by vertewe of this werk; thiself art clensid and maad vertewos by no werk so mochel. And yit it is the lightest werk of alle, when a soule is holpen with grace in sensible liste,[6] and sonnest done; bot elles[7] it is hard and wonderful to thee for to do.

Lette[8] not therfore, bot travayle therin tyl thou fele lyst.[9] For at the first tyme when thou dost it, thou fyndest bot a derknes, and as it were a cloude of unknowyng, thou wost never what, savyng that thou felist in thi wille a nakid entent unto God. This derknes and this cloude is, howsoever thou dost, bitwix thee and thi God, and letteth[10] thee that thou maist not see him cleerly by light of understonding in thi reson, ne fele him in swetnes of love in thin affeccion. And therfore schap thee to bide in this derknes as

Chapter 3

1 stirring

2 **do that in thee is**: a favourite phrase of fourteenth-century theologians (*facere quod in se est*), to allow credit to human striving toward salvation and God without trespassing, in the manner of the new Pelagian heretics, on the divine prerogative to refuse grace regardless of merit or desert.

3 heed

4 try to stop

5 **holpen of**: 'helped by'. The life of contemplation was explained to have use to others as a work of intercession and as a witnessing to God of man's desire for grace.

6 joy that can be felt

7 **elles**: 'otherwise', i.e. without the help of grace.

8 desist

9 desire

10 **letteth**: 'prevents'. But this preventing, according to the systematic 'paradoxing' of ordinary language which is characteristic of the negative way, is a good thing.

longe as thou maist, evermore criing after him that thou lovest; for yif ever schalt thou fele him or see him, as it may be here,[11] it behoveth alweis be in this cloude and in this derknes. And yif thou wilt besily travayle as I bid thee, I triste in his mercy that thou schalt come therto.

The cloud of unknowing and the cloud of forgetting (chaps 4–7)

{Chap. 4} ...And wene not, for I clepe it a derknes or a cloude, that it be any cloude congelid of the humours that fleen in the ayre, ne yit any derknes soche as is in thin house on nightes when thi candel is oute.[1] For soche a derknes and soch a cloude maist thou ymagin with coriouste of witte, for to bere before thin iyen in the lightest day of somer; and also, ayenswarde,[2] in the derkist night of wynter thou mayst ymagin a clere schinyng light. Lat be soche falsheed: I mene not thus. For when I sey derknes, I mene a lackyng of knowyng, as alle that thing that thou knowest not, or elles that thou hast foryetyn, it is derk to thee, for thou seest it not with thi goostly iye. And for this skile[3] it is not clepid a cloude of the eire, bot a cloude of unknowyng, that is bitwix thee and thi God.

{Chap. 5} And yif ever thou schalt come to this cloude and wone[1] and worche therin as I bid thee, thee behoveth, as this cloude of unknowyng is aboven thee, bitwix thee and thi God, right so put a cloude of foryetyng bineth thee, bitwix thee and alle the cretures that ever ben maad. Thee thinketh, paraventure, that thou art ful fer fro God, forthi that[2] this cloude of unknowing is bitwix thee and thi God? Bot sekirly, and[3] it be wel conseyved, thou art wel ferther fro hym when thou hast no cloude of foryetyng bitwix thee and alle the creatures that ever ben maad. As ofte as I sey 'alle the creatures that ever ben maad', as ofte I mene, not only the self creatures, bot also alle the werkes and the condicions of the same creatures. I oute-take not o[4] creature, whether thei ben bodily creatures or goostly, ne yit any condicion or werk of any creature, whether thei be good or ivel; bot schortly to sey, alle schuld be hid under the cloude of foryetyng in this caas.

For thof-al[5] it be ful profitable sumtyme to think of certeyne condicions and dedes of sum certein special creatures, nevertheles yit in this werke it profiteth lityl or nought; for-why[6] mynde or thinkyng of any creature that ever God maad, or of any of theire dedes outher, it is a maner of goostly light, for the iye of thi soule is openid on it and even ficchid[7] ther-apon, as the iye of a schoter is apon the prik[8] that he schoteth to. And o thing I telle thee, that alle thing that thou thinkest apon it is aboven thee for the tyme, and bitwix thee and thi God. And in so mochel thou art the ferther fro God that ought is in thi mynde bot only God.

Ye, and yif it be cortesye and semely to sey, in this werk it profiteth litil or nought to think of the kyndenes or the worthines of God, ne on oure Lady, ne on the seintes or aungelles in heven, ne yit on the joies in heven, that is to say, with a special beholding to hem, as thou woldest bi that beholding fede and encrees thi purpos.[9] I trowe that on no wise it schuld be so in this caas and in this werk. For thof-al it be good to think apon[a] the kindenes of God, and to love hym and preise him for hem, yit it is fer betyr to think apon the nakid beyng of him and to love him and preise him for himself.

{Chap. 6} But now thou askest me, and seiest: 'How schal I think on himself, and what is hee?' And to this I cannot answere thee bot thus: 'I wote never.'

For thou hast brought me with thi question into that same derknes and into that same cloude of unknowyng that I wolde thou were in thiself. For of alle other creatures and theire werkes – ye, and of the werkes of God self – may a man thorou grace have fulheed of knowing, and wel to kon[1] thinke on

11 in this life

Chapter 4

1 A constant problem in mystical writing was to avoid being understood literally, an especial danger when words with a simple primary literal sense were used. The most satisfactory words were those that had no literal referent, such as 'unknowing'.

2 conversely

3 reason

Chapter 5

1 dwell

2 because

3 if

4 I except not one creature

5 although

6 because

7 fixed

8 target

9 The rejection of the normal subjects of devotion and piety (even of the Passion, chap. 7 below) is designedly shocking and paradoxical, to emphasize the singleness of the soul's naked longing for God.

Chapter 6

1 be able to

hem; bot of God himself can no man thinke. And therfore I wol leve al that thing that I can think, and chese to my love that thing that I cannot think, for-whi[2] he may wel be loved, bot not thought. By love may he be getyn and holden, bot bi thought neither. And therfore, thof-al it be good sumtyme to think of the kyndnes and the worthines of God in special, and thof-al it be a light and a party of contemplacion, nevertheles in this werk it schal be casten down and keverid[3] with a cloude of foryetyng. And thou schalt step aboven it stalworthly, bot listely,[4] with a devoute and a plesing stering of love, and fonde[5] for to peerse that derknes aboven thee, and smyte apon that thicke cloude of unknowyng with a scharp darte of longing love, and go not thens for thing that befalleth.[6]

{Chap. 7} And yif any thought rise and wil prees algates aboven thee, bitwix thee and that derknes, and aske thee, seying, 'What sekist thou, and what woldest thou have?' sey thou that it is God that thou woldest have: 'Him I coveite,[1] him I seche, and noght bot him.' And yif he aske thee 'What is that God?' sey thou that it is God that maad thee and bought thee,[2] and that graciously hath clepid thee to his love. And in him sei thou kanst no skile.[3] And therfore sey, 'Go thou down ayein,' and treed him fast doun with a steryng of love, thof[b] he seme to thee right holy, and seme to thee as he wolde help thee to seke hym.

For paraventure he[4] wil bryng to thi minde diverse ful feire and wonderful pointes of his kyndnes, and sey that he is ful swete and ful lovyng, ful gracious and ful mercyful. And yif thou wilt here him, he coveiteth no beter, for at the last he wil thus jangle[5] ever more and more til he bring thee lower to the mynde of his Passion.[6] And there wol he lat the see the wonderful kyndnes of God; and if thou here him, he kepeth[7] no beter. For sone after he wil lat thee see thin olde wrechid leving;[8] and paraventure, in seing and thinkyng therof, he wil bryng to thi mynde som place that thou hast wonid in before this tyme. So that at the last, er ever wite thou,[9] thou schalt be scaterid thou wost never where. The cause of this scateryng is that thou herddist him first wilfully, answeredist him, resceivedist him and letest him allone.[10]

And yit nevertheles the thing that he seide was bothe good and holy – ye, and so holy, that what man or womman that wenith to come to contemplacion withoutyn many soche swete meditacions of theire owne wrechidnes, the Passion, the kyndenes and the grete goodnes and the worthines of God comyng before, sekirly he schal erre and faile of his purpos. And yit nevertheles it behoveth a man or a womman that hath longe tyme ben usid in theese meditacions, algates leve hem, and put hem and holde hem fer doun under the cloude of foryetyng, yif ever schal he peerse the cloude of unknowyng bitwix him and his God.

Therfore, what tyme that thou purposest thee to this werk, and felest bi grace that thou art clepid of God, lift than up thin herte unto God with a meek steryng of love; and mene God[c] that maad thee and bought thee, and that graciousli hath clepid thee to this werk; and resseive none other thought of God. And yit not alle theese, bot thee list,[11] for it suffiseth inough a naked entent directe unto God, withouten any other cause then himself.

And yif thee list have this entent lappid[12] and foulden in o worde, for thou schuldest have betir holde ther-apon, take thee bot a litil worde of o silable;[13] for so it is betir then of two, for ever the schorter it

2 because
3 covered
4 joyfully
5 strive
6 anything that happens

Chapter 7
1 desire
2 **that maad thee and bought thee**, i.e. no other attributes of God are present in the mind of the spiritual 'worker' than the bare facts that he is Maker and Redeemer, and has called.
3 hast no knowledge
4 **he** is still 'the agency of pious thought'.
5 chatter
6 **bring thee lower to the mynde of his Passion**. The contrast is striking here between the singleness of purpose of the *via negativa* and the aims and methods of meditation as encouraged by Love's *Mirror* (see below) and by the cult of affective devotion generally.
7 seeks after
8 **wrechid leving**: not the wretchedness of his way of life in particular, but the wretchedness of living in the world, in the exile from God to which the soul is temporarily assigned.
9 before ever you know it
10 left him to his devices
11 unless you want
12 wrapped
13 **a litil worde of o silable**. The purpose is to remove words from the field of cognitive understanding and to make them into empty signifiers of mindless stirring of love to God. The negative way is generally hostile to and suspicious of words, though recognizing their preliminary utility. Note the absence of reference to the Bible and interpretation of the Bible.

is the betir it acordeth with the werk of the spirite. And soche a worde is this worde GOD or this worde LOVE. Cheese thee whether[14] thou wilt, or another as the list, whiche that thee liketh best of o silable, and fasten this worde to thin herte, so that it never go thens for thing that bifalleth.

This worde schal be thi scheeld and thi spere, whether thou ridest on pees or on werre. With this worde thou schalt bete on this cloude and this derknes aboven thee. With this worde thou schalt smite doun al maner thought under the cloude of foryeting, in so mochel that yif any thought prees apon thee to aske thee what thou woldest have, answere him with no mo wordes bot with this o worde. And yif he profre thee of his grete clergie[15] to expoune thee that worde and to telle thee the condicions[16] of that worde, sey him that thou wilt have it al hole, and not broken ne undon.[17] And yif thow wilt holde thee fast on this purpos, sekir be thou[18] he wil no while abide. And whi? For thou wilt not late him fede him on soche swete meditacions touchid before.

{Following chapters are concerned to define the nature of the contemplative life in relation to the active life; to defend it against its detractors; and to explain the special gifts of the contemplative life, and the dangers to which it is open, especially among those who falsely pretend to it.}

False contemplatives (chap. 53)

Many wonderful contenaunces[1] folowen hem that ben disseyvid in this fals werk, or in any spice[2] therof, forby that[3] doth hem that ben Goddes trewe disciples – for thei ben evermore ful semely in alle here contenaunces, bodily or goostly. Bot it is not so of thees other. For who-so wolde or might beholde unto hem ther thei sitte in this tyme, and it so were that theire iye-liddes were open,[4] he schulde see hem stare as thei were wode, and therto loke as thei sawe the devil. Sekirly it is good thei be ware, for trewly the feende is not fer! Som sette theire iyen in theire hedes as thei were sturdy scheep betyn in the heed,[5] and as thei schulde diye anone. Som hangen here hedes on syde, as a worme were in theire eres. Som pipyn when thei schuld speke, as ther were no spirit in theire bodies: and this is the propre condicion of an ypocrite. Som crien and whinen in theire throte, so ben thei gredy and hasty to sey that thei think: and this is the condicion of heretikes, and of hem that with presumpcion and with curiouste[6] of witte wil alweys meynteyn errour....

For som men aren so kumbred in nice corious contenaunces in bodily beryng, that whan thei schal ought here,[7] thei writhen here hedes on side queyntely, and up with the chin; thei gape with theire mouthes as thei schuld here with hem, and not with here eres. Som, when thei schulen speke, poynten with here fyngres, or on theire fyngres, or on theire owne brestes, or on theires that thei speke to. Som kan nouther sit stille, stonde stylle ne ligge stille, bot yif thei be outher waggyng with theire fete or elles sumwhat doyng with theire handes. Som rowyn with theire armes in tyme of[8] here spekyng, as hem nedid for to swymme over a grete water. Som ben evermore smyling and leighing at iche other worde that thei speke, as thei weren gigelotes[9] and nice japyng jogelers lackyng kontenaunce.[10] Semeli cher were with sobre and demure beryng of body and mirthe in maner.

I say not that alle thees unsemely contenaunces ben grete synnes in hemself, ne yit alle thoo that done hem ben grete synners hemself. Bot I sey, if that thees unsemely and unordeinde[11] contenaunces ben governers of that man that doth hem, in so mochel that he may not leve hem whan he wile – than I sey that thei ben tokenes of pride and coryouste of witte, and of unordeynde schewyng and covetise of knowyng; and specyaly thei ben verrei tokenes of unstabelnes of herte and unrestfulnes of mynde, and

14 whichever
15 learning
16 qualities
17 expounded
18 you may be sure

Chapter 53

1 kinds of behaviour
2 species
3 in comparison with what
4 **theire iye-liddes**, i.e. those of the false contemplatives, with the implication that their eyes are not often open.
5 giddy sheep knocked on the head
6 **curiouste**. 'Curiosity' is a suspect impulse, suggesting a busy desire to search into that which is not man's business and which feeds only vanity.
7 listen to hear anything
8 in time with
9 wanton women
10 manners
11 uncontrolled

namely of the lackyng of the werk of this book. And this is only the skile[12] whi that I set so many of thees disceytes here in this writyng, for-whi that a goostly[13] worcher schal prove his werk by hem.

{A theme developed throughout the Cloud *is the inadequacy of language to communicate spiritual truth, and especially the deathly literalness of 'up' and 'down' and 'somewhere'.}*

Nowhere is everywhere (chap. 68)

And on the same maner, wher another man wolde bid thee gader thi mightes and thi wittes holich withinne thiself, and worschip God there – thof-al he sey ful wel and ful trewly, ye! and no man trewlier and[1] he be wel conseivid – yit for feerde[2] of disseite and bodely conceyvyng of his wordes, me list not byd thee do so. Bot thus wil I bid thee: Loke on no wyse that thou be withinne thiself; and schortly, withoutyn thiself wil I not that thou be, ne yit aboven, ne behynde, ne on o side ne on other.

'Wher than,' seist thou, 'schal I be? Nowhere, by thi tale!' Now trewly thou seist wel, for there wolde I have thee, for-whi nowhere bodely is everywhere goostly. Loke than besily that thi goostly werk be nowhere bodely, and than whersoever that that thing is, on the whiche thou wilfully worchest in thi mynde in substaunce, sekerly ther art thou in spirit, as verrely as thi body is in that place that thou art bodely. And thof-al thi bodely wittes kon fynde ther nothing to fede hem on, for hem think it nought that thou dost, ye! do on than this nought, elles that[3] thou do it for Goddes love. And lete[4] nought, therfore, bot travayle besily in that nought with a wakyng desire to wilne[5] to have God, that no man may knowe.[6] For I telle thee trewly that I had lever be so nowhere bodely, wrastlyng with that blynde nought, than to be so grete a lorde that I might when I wolde be everywhere bodely, merily pleying with al this ought[7] as a lorde with his owne.

Lat be this everiwhere and this ought, in comparison of this nowhere and this[d] nought. Reche thee never[8] yif thi wittys kon no skyle[9] of this nought, for-whi I love it moche the betir. It is so worthi a thing in itself that thei kon no skyle ther-apon. This nought may betir be felt then seen, for it is ful blynde and ful derk to hem that han bot lityl while lokid ther-apon. Nevertheles, yif I schal sothlier sey, a soule is more bleendid[10] in felyng of it for habundaunce of goostly light then for any derknes or wantyng of bodely lighte. What is he that clepith it nought? Sekirly it is oure utter[11] man, and not oure inner. Oure inner man clepith it Al; for of it he is wel lernid to kon skyle[12] of alle thinges, bodely or goostly, withouten any specyal beholdyng to any o thing by itself.

{The treatise ends with further explanations of the nature of the mystical experience of blind stirring towards God, and the uniqueness of each individual's experience of it.}

12 this alone is the reason
13 contemplative

Chapter 68

1 if
2 fear
3 as long as
4 slacken
5 desire
6 **that no man may knowe**. The unknowability of God (though he may be 'had') is a cardinal principle of negative theology.
7 everything
8 Never mind
9 have no knowledge
10 blinded
11 outward
12 have knowledge

Julian (Juliana) of Norwich (1342–c.1418)

Julian ('Juliana') of Norwich was born in 1342 and died soon after 1416. She was a devout woman who on 13 May 1373 had a series of sixteen visions, to meditation upon which she devoted the rest of her life, as she describes in her *Revelations of Divine Love*. The *Revelations*, or 'Showings', survive in two versions, an early shorter version from the 1380s and a later version from the 1390s (first copied out in full in 1413), much expanded with additional contemplative material, including the long and beautiful meditation upon the parable of the lord and the servant (chap. 51). During all this time, Julian was an anchoress, that is, a woman who had vowed before a bishop to live for ever in solitary prayer and contemplation in an anchorhold, a small building adjoining a church (in her case, St Julian's church in Norwich). It was a safer life for a woman than that of a hermit in the wilds. Money came from the anchoress's own family, from pious endowments and bequests, or from charitable contributions. Julian became quite famous, and was visited by many seeking spiritual comfort and advice, including Margery Kempe. Her 'Showings' were, for her, a gift granted to her by God, an experience of mystical self-transcendence, which it was her responsibility to think and write about in order to share with others the spiritual sustenance they gave to her. The Passion of Christ is central to her meditations, as the proof of God's love and of the certainty of the promise of salvation, and she shares much in the spirit of late medieval affective devotion, particularly in her passionate desire to identify physically and emotionally with the humanity of the suffering Christ. Julian writes with fervour, though with a less rhapsodic intensity than her northern predecessor, Richard Rolle, hermit of Hampole (d. 1349); her contemplations are always conducted according to a rational-seeming programme, moving step by step towards interpretative resolution. On the other hand, she is less austere, and reaches out more to her community of fellow-Christians, than the author of *The Cloud of Unknowing*, a treatise written for someone well advanced in the life of mystical contemplation, and more approachable than Walter Hilton (d. 1396), Augustinian canon of Thurgarton in Nottinghamshire. All are prominent in the fourteenth-century flowering of English mystical writing, and Rolle and Hilton also wrote in Latin; Julian, though presumably literate in Latin, wrote only in English, as was thought fitting to her education and status as a woman. She has something in common with Langland, particularly in her desire to 'chew over' more than once the material of her visions, but she has none of his interest in programmes of social and political reform.

The longer version (LV) of the *Revelations* survives only in seventeenth-century manuscripts written for English female religious in houses in and around Cambrai (Julian has a readership still today among the devout); the shorter version (SV) is extant in the unique BL MS Add.37790, of the mid-fifteenth century. Though SV was written closer to the time of the showings, and is extant in a more nearly contemporary manuscript, LV, more gracefully written and more famous, is preferred here. The extracts below are from LV as it is represented in BN MS fonds anglais 40. There are editions of SV by Frances Beer, MET 8 (Heidelberg, 1978), and in Windeatt (1994), pp. 181–213, and of both SV and LV by E. Colledge and J. Walsh, *A Book of Showings to the Anchoress Julian of Norwich*, 2 vols (Toronto, 1978). Studies by B.A. Windeatt, in *RES* 28 (1977), 1–17; N. Watson, in *Speculum* 68 (1993), 637–83; D.N. Baker, *Julian of Norwich's 'Showings': From Vision to Book* (Princeton, 1994); D. Aers and L. Staley, *The Powers of the Holy: Religion, Politics and Gender in Late Medieval English Culture* (University Park, PA, 1996), pp. 77–178; for a general study, see W. Riehle, *The Middle English Mystics* (London, 1981).

The Revelations of Divine Love (longer version)

The bodily sickness and the first revelation (chaps 3–4)

{Chap. 3} And when I was thirty yere old and a halfe, God sent me a bodily sicknes in the which I ley thre daies and thre nyghtes; and on the ferthe nyght I toke all my rightes of holie church, and went not to have leven[1] tyll day. And after this I lay two daies and two nightes, and on the third night I weened oftentymes to have passed, and so wenyd thei that were with me. And yet in this I felt a gret lothsomnes[2] to die, but for nothing that was in erth that me lyketh to leve for, ne for no payne that I was afrayd of, for

Chapter 3

1 expected not to have lived

2 reluctance

I trusted in God of his mercie. But it was for I would have leved to have loved God better and longer tyme, that I might by the grace of that levyng have the more knowing and lovyng of God in the blisse of heven. For me[a] thought all that tyme that I had leved heer so litle and so shorte in regard of that endlesse blysse. I thought, 'Good Lorde, may my levyng no longer be to thy worshippe?' And I understode in my reson and by the feelyng of my paynes that I should die. And I assentyd fully with all the will of myn hert to be at Gods will.

Thus I indured till day, and by then was my bodie ded from the middes downward, as to my feeling. Then was I holpen to be set upright, undersett[3] with helpe, for to have the more fredom of my hert to be at Gods will and thinkyng on God while my life laste. My curate was sent for to be at my ending, and before he cam I had set up[4] my eyen and might not speke. He set the crosse before my face, and sayd, 'I have brought the image of thy Saviour: looke therupon and comfort thee therwith.'

Me[b] thought I was well, for my eyen was sett upright into heven, where I trusted to come by the mercie of God. But nevertheles I assentyd to sett my eyen in the face of the crucyfixe, if I might, and so I dide, for me[c] thought I might longer dure to looke even-forth[5] then right up. After this my sight began to feyle. It waxid as darke aboute me in the chamber as if it had ben nyght, save in the image of the crosse, wherin held a comon light;[6] and I wiste not how. All that was beside[7] the crosse was oglye[8] and ferfull to me as it had ben much occupied with fiendes.

After this the over[9] part of my bodie began to die, so ferforth[10] that unneth I had anie feeling.[11] My most[12] payne was shortnes of breth and failyng of life. Then went[13] I[d] verily to have passed. And in this sodenly all my paine was taken from me and I was as hole,[14] and namely in the over parte of my bodie, as ever I was befor. I merveiled of this sodeyn change, for me[e] thought that it was a previe[15] working of God and not of kynd.[16] And yet by feeling of this ese I trusted never the more to have lived, ne the feeling of this ese was no full ese to me, for me thought I had lever[17] have ben delivred of this world, for my hert was wilfully set therto.

Then cam sodenly to my mynd that I should desyer the second wound of our Lordes gifte and of his grace, that my bodie might be fulfilled with mynd and feeling of his blessed passion, as I had before praied, for I would that his paynes were my paynes, with compassion and afterward langyng to God. Thus[f] thought me that I might, with his grace, have his woundes that I had before desyred. But in this I desyred never no bodily sight ne no maner schewing of God,[18] but compassion as me thought that a kynd[19] sowle might have with our Lord Jesu, that for love would become a dedly[20] man. With him I desyred to suffer, livyng in my dedly bodie, as God would give me grace.

{Chap. 4}[1] And in this sodenly I saw the reed bloud rynnyng downe from under the garlande, hote and freyshely, plentuously and lively,[2] right as it was in the tyme that the garland of thornes was pressed on his blessed hede. Right so, both God and man, the same that sufferd for me, I conceived truly and mightly that it was himselfe that shewed it me without anie mene.[3]

3 supported
4 fixed in an upward gaze
5 straight forward
6 persisted an ordinary daylight
7 Everything except
8 ugly
9 upper
10 to such an extent
11 LV omits at this point a vivid detail in SV: 'Myne handys felle downe on aythere syde, and also for unpowere my heede satylde downe on syde' (fol. 98r). Other personal details are omitted in LV (such as the mention of the 'childe' who came with the priest to her bedside), in accord with Julian's developing belief that her visions would be more useful to others if they were less 'her own'. Nevertheless, the description of her illness retains a clinically detailed exactness.
12 greatest
13 thought
14 whole (well)
15 secret
16 Julian examines the possibility that her recovery might have been a natural remission of her illness, but concludes, dispassionately, that it must have been a miracle.
17 would rather
18 Julian is insistent that she sought no special revelation, only a modest stimulus to the work of 'compassionate' meditation and a better natural understanding such as any person might desire.
19 natural human
20 was willing to become a mortal man

Chapter 4

1 The first vision is marked in the MS as beginning here. The vision is precise and carefully focused and carries the weight of centuries of meditation (focused especially in the *Meditationes vitae Christi* translated by Nicholas Love) on the bleeding body of Christ.
2 living
3 intermediary

And in the same shewing sodeinly the trinitie fulfilled my hert most of joy,[4] and so I understode it shall be in heven without end to all that shall come ther. For the trinitie is God, God is the trinitie. The trinitie is our maker, the trinitie is our keper, the trinitie is our everlasting lover, the trinitie is our endlesse joy and our blisse, by our Lord Jesu Christ and in our Lord Jesu Christ. And this was shewed in the first syght and in all, for wher Jesu appireth the blessed trinitie is understand,[5] as to my sight. And I sayd, '*Benedicite Dominus*'.[6] This I sayd for reverence in my menyng,[7] with a mightie voyce, and full gretly was I astonned for wonder and mervayle that I had that he that is so reverent and so dredfull[8] will be so homely[9] with a synnfull creature living in this wretched flesh.

Thus I toke it[10] for that tyme that our Lord Jesu of his curteys love would shewe me comfort before the tyme of my temptation; for me thought it might well be that I should, by the sufferance[11] of God and with his keping,[12] be tempted of fiendes before I should die. With this sight of his blessed passion, with the Godhede that I saw in my understanding, I knew well that it was strenght inough to me, ye, and to all creaturs livyng that should be saved, against all the fiendes of hell and against all ghostely enemies.

In this he brought oure Ladie sainct Mari to my understanding. I saw her ghostly in bodily lykenes, a simple mayden and a meeke, yong of age, a little waxen above a chylde, in the stature as she was when she conceivede. Also God shewed me in part the wisdom and the truth of her sowle, wherin I understode the reverent beholding that[13] she beheld her God that is her maker, mervayling with gret reverence that he would[14] be borne of her that was a symple creature of his makyng. For this was her mervaling, that he that was her maker would be borne of her that was made.[15] And this wisdome and truth, knowing the gretnes of her maker and the littlehede[16] of herselfe that is made, made her to say full meekely to Gabriell, 'Lo me here, Gods handmayden'.[17] In this syght I did understand verily that she is more then all that God made beneth her in worthines and in fullhede;[18] for above her is nothing that is made but the blessed manhode of Christ, as to my sight.

The second revelation (chap. 10)

And after this I saw with bodely sight in the face of the crucifixe that hyng before me, in the which I beheld contynually, a parte of his passion: dispyte,[1] spyttyng, sowelyng[2] and buffetyng, and manie languryng[3] paynes, mo than I can tell, and often chaungyng of colour. And one tyme I saw how halfe the face, begynnyng at the ere, over-yede[4] with drye bloud tyll it closyd into the myd face, and after that the other halfe be-closyd on the same wyse, and the whiles[5] it vanyssched in this party evyn as it cam.

This I saw bodely, swemly[6] and darkely, and I desyred more bodely light to have seen more clerly. And I was answeryde in my reson:[7] 'If God will shew thee more, he shal be thy light:[8] thou nedyst none but him.' For I saw him and sought him,[9] for we be now so blynde and so unwyse that we can never seke God till what tyme that he of his goodnes shewyth hym to us. And whan we see owght of hym graciously, then are we steryd by the same grace to seke with gret desyer to see hym more blessedfully. And thus I saw him and sought him, and I had hym and wantyd hym; and this is and should be our comyn workyng in this life, as to my syght.

4 This passage on the Trinity is the first major addition in LV, an acknowledgement by Julian, on maturer consideration, that any showing of Christ is necessarily a showing of the Trinity.
5 to be understood
6 'Blessed be the Lord'.
7 intention
8 awe-inspiring
9 intimate
10 understood
11 permission
12 protection
13 wherewith
14 was willing to
15 The joyous syntactical play on **maker** ... **makyng** ... **made** is as near as Julian wants to get to the ecstatic cadences of Rolle.
16 littleness
17 Luke 1:38.
18 abundance of merit

Chapter 10
1 **dispyte**: 'scorn'. See Matt. 26:67.
2 defiling
3 enfeebling
4 was covered over
5 meanwhile
6 frighteningly
7 **in my reson**. Julian constantly emphasizes that the power of vision is not in the bodily seeing but in the inward mental illumination of meaning provided through God's grace.
8 **he shal be thy light**. Ps. 27:1.
9 The desire to see God more clearly, the longing for union with God, and the experience, however momentary, of that union, are usually considered to be the defining characteristics of the mystical life.

One tyme my understandyng was lett down into the see-grounde,[10] and ther saw I hilles and dales grene, semyng as it were mosse be-growyng with wrake[11] and gravell. Then I understode thus: that if a man or woman wer there under the brode water, and he myght have syght of God, so as God is with a man contynually, he shoulde be safe in sowle and body and take no harme. And ovyr-passyng[12] he should have more solace and comforte then all this worlde may or can tell. For he will that we beleve that we see hym contynually, though that us thynke that it be but litle; and in the beleve he maketh us evyrmore to gett grace, for he will[13] be seen, and he will be sought, and he will be abyden, and he will be trustyd.

This secounde shewyng was so lowe and so little and so symple that my spirytes were in gret traveyle in the beholdyng, mornyng, dredfull and longyng; for I was sometyme in a feer wheder it was a shewyng or none.[14] And then dyverse tymes our Lord gafe me more syght, wherby that I understonde[15] truly that it was a shewyng. It was a fygur and a lyknes of our fowle blacke dede, which that our feyre bryght blessed Lord bare for our synne.

{The darkness of the sea-bottom, as Julian goes on to explain at length, is the figure of the darkness of sin in which man has fallen but in which he is still looked upon lovingly and preserved by God's grace (see Ps. 139:9–10).}

The seventh revelation (chap. 15)

And after thys he shewde a sovereyne gostely lykynge[1] in my soule. In thys lykyng I was fulfyllyde of the evyrlastyng suernesse, myghtely fastnyd without any paynefulle drede. This felyng was so glad and so goostely that I was all in peese, in eese and in reste, that ther was nothyng in erth that shulde have grevyd me.

This lastyd but a whyle, and I was turned and left to myselfe in hevynes and werynes of my life and irkenes[2] of myselfe, that unneth I could have pacience to lyve. Ther was no comfort ne none eese to my felyng but feyth, hope and cheryte: and these I had in truth but fulle lytylle in felyng.[3] And anon after thys oure blessyd Lorde gave me agane the comfort and the rest in soule, lykyng and suernesse so blyssydfully and so myghtely that no drede, ne sorow, ne no peyne bodely ne gostely that myght be sufferde shulde have dyssesyde[4] me. And than the payne sheweth ayen to my felyng, and than the joy and lykyng, and now that oon and now that other, dyverse tymes – I suppose about twenty tymes. And in the tyme of joy I myght have seyde with seynt Paule, 'Nothyng shall departe me fro the charyte of Crist.'[5] And in the payne I myght have seyd with seynt Peter, 'Lorde, save me, I peryssch!'[6]

This vision was shewde to lerne me at my understandyng that it is spedfulle[7] to some soules to feele on thys wyse, sometyme to be in comfort and sometyme for to fayle and to be lefte to themselfe. God wylle that we know that he kepyth us evyr in-lyke[8] suer, in wo and in wele; and for profyte of mans soule a man is somtyme left to hymselfe, allthogh hys synne is not evyr[9] the cause. For in this tyme I synned not wherefor[10] [a] I shulde be left to myselfe, for it was so sodeyne. Also I deservyd not to have this blyssydfulle felyng, but frely our Lorde giveth[b] it when he wylle, and sufferyth us in wo sometyme, and both is one love. For it is Goddes wylle that we holde us in comfort with alle oure myght; for blysse is lastyng without ende, and payne is passyng, and shall be brought to nowght to them that shall be

10 sea-bed
11 seaweed
12 surpassingly
13 wishes to
14 Julian has no interest in the content of the vision (suggested by Ecclus. 24:5), or in its strange and evocative power, such as a modern reader might have. For her, since Christ does not figure in it, it is a humdrum vision that she has to work on in order to draw out its fullness of meaning.
15 understood

Chapter 15
1 delight
2 weariness
3 The loss of the feeling of delight, the sterility and barrenness that follow, the mechanical operation of the faculties of being, are experiences that mystics often describe, and that have been compared with the dreariness described by Romantic poets such as Wordsworth and Keats when inspiration is withdrawn.
4 troubled
5 Rom. 8:35.
6 Matt. 8:25.
7 advantageous
8 alike
9 always
10 in so much as to cause it that

savyd.[11] Therfore it is not Goddes wylle that we folow the felyng of paynes in sorow and mowrnyng[c] for them, but sodaynly passe ovyr and holde us in the endlesse lykyng that is God.

The eighth revelation (chap. 16)

After thys Crist shewde a parte of hys passyon nere his dyeng. I saw the swete face as it were drye and blodeles with pale dyeng and deede pale, langhuryng[1] and than turned more deede into blew, and after in browne-blew,[2] as the flessch turned more depe dede. For his passion shewde to me most propyrly in his blessyd face, and namely in hys lyppes. Therin saw I these foure colours, tho that were before fressch and rody, lyvely and lykyng[3] to my syght. This was a peinfulle chaungyng, to se this depe dying, and also hys nose clongyn[4] [a] togeder and dryed, to my syght; and the swete body waxid browne and blacke, alle chaungyd and turned oute of the feyer,[5] fressch and lyvely coloure of hymselfe into drye dyeng. For that same tyme that oure blessyd Savyour dyed uppon the rode it was a dry sharp wynd, wonder colde as to my syght; and what tyme that the precyous blode was bled out of the swete body that myght passe therfro, yet ther was a moyster[6] in the swete flessch of Crist as it was shewde.[7] Blodlessehed and payne dryed within and blowyng of the wynde and colde comyng from without mett togeder in the swete body of Christ, and these foure dryed the flessch of Crist by prosses of tyme. And thoughe this peyne was bitter and sharp, yet it was fulle longe-lastyng, as to my syght. And the payne dryede uppe alle the lyvely spyrites of Cristes flessh. Thus I saw the swete flessch dry in my syght, parte after parte dryeng with mervelous payne. And as long as any spryte had lyfe in Cristes flessch, so long sufferde he. This long peyne semyde to me as if he had be sennyght[8] deede, dyeng at the poynt of out-passyng, alwey sufferyng the gret peyne. And ther[9] I say it semyd as he had bene sennyght deed, it specyfyeth that the swet body was so dyscolouryd, so drye, so clongyn, so dedly and so pytuous as he had bene sennyght deed, contynually dyeng. And me thought the dryeng of Cristes flessch was the most peyne and the last of his passion.

{The contemplation of the stage-by-stage decomposition of Christ's flesh occupies the whole of the next chapter.}

The thirteenth revelation (chap. 27): Sin is behovely

And after thys oure Lorde brought to my mynde the longyng that I had to hym before, and I saw nothyng lettyd[1] me[a] but synne, and so I behelde generally in us alle, and me thought yf synne had not be[2] we shulde alle have be clene and lyke to oure Lorde as he made us. And thus in my foly before thys tyme often I wondryd why, by the grete forseyng[3] [b] wysdom of God, the begynnyng of synne was not lettyd.[4] For then thoucht me that alle shulde have be wele.

Thys steryng[5] was moch to be forsaken, and nevyrthelesse mornyng and sorow I made therfore withoute reson and dyscrecion. But Jesu, that in this vysyon enformyd me of alle that me nedyd, answeryd by thys

11 **to them that shall be savyd**. Not in SV. Julian is careful in LV to specify always that the promise of grace is made only to those who are predestined to be saved.

Chapter 16

1 languishing

2 The precision of the observation, the almost clinical detail of the exact process of Christ's dying, is also a technique for grounding affective devotion in an experience of objective, reasoned, careful analysis, as if Julian were aware of the need to rid female devotion of a reputation for excited imaginings. She is also conscious, especially in SV, of the church's prohibition on women preaching or teaching in church (see 1 Cor. 14:34; 1 Tim. 2:12), and speaks of her visions in an almost ostentatiously unemotional manner.

3 pleasing

4 shrunken down

5 fair

6 moisture

7 **as it was shewde**. There is more than usual emphasis in this chapter on the fact that what Julian describes herself as seeing was precisely what she was shown; it has not at this point been made the subject of interpretation.

8 seven nights

9 where

Chapter 27

1 hindered

2 existed

3 foreseeing

4 Wondering on why sin was allowed into the world in the first place by an all-seeing God is a natural thing for an ordinary person (such as Langland's dreamer, *PP* A.XI.66) to do, but it is a foolish questioning of God's providence.

5 worrying thought

worde and seyde, 'Synne is behovely,[6] but alle shall be wele, and alle shall be wele, and alle maner of thynge shall be wele.' In this nakyd worde 'Synne' oure Lorde broughte to my mynde generally alle that is not good, and the shamfull despyte and the uttermost trybulation that he bare for us in thys lyfe, and hys dyeng and alle hys paynes, and passion of alle hys creatures gostly and bodely. For we be alle in part trobelyd, and we schal be trobelyd, folowyng our master Jesu, tylle we be fully[c] purgyd of oure dedely flessch and of alle oure inwarde affections whych be not very[7] good.

And the beholdyng of thys, with alle the paynes that evyr were or evyr shall be – with alle thys I understode the passion of Criste for the most payne and ovyr-passyng. And alle thys was shewde in a touch,[8] redely passyd ovyr into comfort. For oure good Lorde wolde not that the soule were aferde of this ogly syghte. But I saw not synne, for I beleve it has[d] no maner of substaunce, ne no part of beyng,[9] ne it myght not be knowen but by the payne that is caused therof. And thys payne is somthyng, as to my syghte, for a tyme, for it purgyth and makyth us to know oureselfe and aske mercy; for the passion of oure Lorde is comfort to us ayenst alle thys, and so is his blessyd wylle. And for the tender love that oure good Lorde hath to alle that shall be savyd, he comfortyth redely and swetly, menyng thus: 'It is true that synne is cause of alle thys payne, but alle shall be wele, and alle maner of thyng shall be wele.'

Theyse wordes were shewde fulle tendyrly, shewyng no maner of blame to me ne to none that shall be safe. Than were it gret unkyndnesse of me to blame or wonder on God of my synne, sythen he blamyth not me for synne.

And in theyse same wordes I saw an hygh mervelous prevyte[10] hyd in God, whych pryvyte he shall opynly make and shall be knowen to us in hevyn. In whych knowyng we shall verely se the cause why he sufferde synne to come, in whych syght we shall endlessely have joye.

Jesus as Mother (chap. 60)

{This chapter is part of the meditation on Revelation 14.}

Oure kynde moder, oure gracious modyr, for he wolde alle hole[1] become oure modyr in alle thyng, he toke the grounde of his werke full lowe and full myldely in the maydyns wombe.[2] And that shewde he in the furst,[3] wher he broughte that meke maydyn before the eye of my understondyng in the sympyll stature as she was whan she conceyvyd; that is to sey oure hye God, the sovereyn wysdom of all, in this lowe place he arayed hym and dyght hym all redy in oure poure flessch hymselfe to do the servyce and the office of moderhode in alle thyng. The moders servyce is nerest, rediest and suerest: nerest for it is most of kynd, redyest for it is most of love, and sekerest[4] for it is most of trewth. This office ne myght nor coulde nevyr none done to the full but he allone. We wytt that alle oure moders bere us to payne and to dyeng. A, what is that? But oure very moder Jesu, he alone beryth us to joye and to endlesse levyng, blessyd mot he be! Thus he susteyneth us within hym in love and traveyle into the full tyme that he wolde suffer the sharpyst throwes[5] and most[a] grevous paynes that evyr were or evyr shalle be, and dyed at the last. And whan he had done, and so borne us to blysse, yet myght not all thys make aseeth[6] to his mervelous love. And that shewd he in theyse hye ovyr-passyng wordes of love: 'If I myght suffer more I

6 **behovely**: 'necessary'. Julian's meditation on the necessity of sin is amplified through chaps 27–40; her words here inspired T.S. Eliot in *Little Gidding*.

7 truly

8 glimpse

9 **no part of beyng**. Julian's conclusion, arrived at with her customary beautiful spare lucidity, is the orthodox Augustinian explanation of sin as non-existence. The idea of evil as non-being, the non-presence of God's grace, was developed by Augustine as an alternative to the Manichean view that evil was an alternative principle of being.

10 secret

Chapter 60

1 wholly

2 The tradition in which Jesus is spoken of as God the Mother, to which Julian (in LV only) contributed so significantly, begins in the parallel between a mother's love for her child and Jesus's love for his creatures, and in the determination to take advantage of every affective agent through which devotion to Jesus may be stirred. It was a favourite topos of women's devotion (see C.W. Bynum, *Jesus as Mother: Studies in the Spirituality of the High Middle Ages* [Berkeley and Los Angeles, 1982]), though Julian herself is scrupulous never to attribute any of her insights to a woman's intuition.

3 **in the furst**. See chap. 4 above.

4 surest

5 throes

6 satisfaction

wold suffer more.' He myght no more dye, but he wolde not stynte werkyng.

Wherfore hym behovyth to fynde us,[7] for the deerworthy love of moderhed hath made hym dettour to us. The moder may geve her chylde sucke hyr mylke, but oure precyous moder Jesu, he may fede us wyth hymselfe, and doth[8] full curtesly and full tendyrly with the blessyd sacrament, that is precyous fode of very lyfe; and with all the swete sacramentes he susteynyth us full mercyfully and graciously, and so ment he in theyse blessyd wordys, where he seyde: 'I it am that holy chyrch prechyth the and techyth the.' That is to sey, 'All the helth and the lyfe of the sacramentys, alle the vertu and the grace of my worde, alle the goodnesse that is ordeynyd in holy chyrch to the, I it am.'

The moder may ley hyr chylde tenderly to hyr brest, but oure tender mother Jesu, he may homely lede us into his blessyd brest by his swet opyn syde[9] and shewe us there in perty[10] of the Godhed and the joyes of hevyn, with gostely suernesse of endlesse blysse. And that shewde he in the tenth[b] revelation, gevyng the same understandyng in thys swet worde where he seyth: 'Lo, how I love thee!' – beholdyng[c] into his blyssyd syde, enjoyeng.[11]

Thys feyer lovely worde 'Moder', it is so swete and so kynde in itselfe that it may not verely be seyde of none ne to none but of hym and to hym that is very mother of lyfe and of alle. To the properte of moderhede longyth kynd,[12] love, wysdom and knowyng, and it is God. For though it be so that oure bodely forth-bryngyng be but lytle, lowe and symple in regard of oure gostely forth-bryngyng, yet it is he that doth it in the creaturys by whom that it is done. The kynde lovyng moder that woot and knowyth the nede of hyr chylde, she kepyth it full tenderly, as the kynde and condycion of moderhed wyll. And evyr as it waxith in age and in stature she chaungyth her werkes, but not her love. And when it is wexid of more age, she sufferyth it that it be chastised in brekyng downe of vicis, to make the chylde receyve vertues and grace. This werkyng, with all that be feyer and good, oure Lord doth it in hem by whom it is done. Thus he is our moder in kynde by the werkyng of grace in the lower perty,[13] for love of the hyer. And he wylle that we knowe it, for he wylle have alle oure love fastenyd to hym. And in this I sawe that alle dett that we owe by Gods byddyng to faderhod and moderhod[14] is fulfyllyd in trew lovyng of God, whych blessyd love Cryst werkyth in us. And this was shewde in alle, and namly in the hye plentuous wordes wher he seyth: 'I it am that thou lovest.'

7 provide for us

8 doth so

9 **his swet opyn syde**. The wound in Christ's side was not just the source of the blood that flowed forth to feed his children (compare the favourite image of the pelican pecking at her own breast to feed her brood with her blood), but an opening through which the devout could enter into his being.

10 in part

11 rejoicing

12 belongs nature

13 **lower perty**: 'lower part', i.e. the body.

14 **Gods byddyng**: i.e. the Fifth Commandment, 'Honour thy father and thy mother' (Ex. 20:12).

The Alliterative *Morte Arthure*

The *Morte Arthure* is a heroic battle-poem telling of king Arthur's continental campaign against the Roman emperor Lucius, a campaign that began as revenge for the insult offered by the emperor in demanding tribute from England. Nearly at the gates of Rome, he is called back to England by news of Mordred's usurpation, and the poem ends with the death of Gawain and Arthur, as in Malory (see below). Where Malory mostly follows the French Vulgate, *Morte Arthure* represents the native Arthurian tradition, going back to Geoffrey of Monmouth, in which Arthur is a great king and conqueror, and the knights of the Round Table are the warriors in his battles (Launcelot is mentioned, but plays no part). It is a powerful retelling of the story, struggling to find, in its account of history, an explanation of events that will go beyond the exhausted moral platitudes of Fortune-tragedy (as in Lydgate's *Fall of Princes*); it rises at times to a stern eloquence. The poem is written in unrhymed alliterative verse, like *Piers* and *Gawain*, but, unlike those two poems, it exploits rather than restrains the tendency of the line to headlong onrush: alliteration is heavy and often runs for several lines on the same letter or letter-combination. The multiplication of synonyms and headily inventive diction that necessarily accompanies such practice gives at times an air of vivid concretion, though more as a trick of rhetoric than for the sake of realism. The result, as in the passage below, is a cultivated 'excess' of style which is self-conscious of an older story-telling manner.

The *Morte Arthure* survives unique in Lincoln Cathedral Library MS 91 (facsimile, introd. by D.S. Brewer and A.E.B. Owen [London, 1978]), one of the two manuscripts written by the Yorkshire scribe and compiler Robert Thornton (*c.* 1440). Editions by V. Krishna (New York, 1976) and (in regularized spelling) by L.D. Benson (Indianapolis, 1974); studies by W. Matthews, *The Tragedy of Arthur* (Berkeley, 1960) and by L. Patterson, in *Negotiating the Past* (Madison, WI, 1987), pp. 197–230.

Arthur's fight with the giant of St Michael's mount

{Just after landing in France, Arthur makes a detour to deal with a giant who is ravaging northeastern Brittany.}

full length, taking his ease	He lay lenand on lang, lugand unfaire,
thigh	The thee of a manns lymme lyfte up by the haunche.
buttocks, loins	His bakke and his bewschers and his brode lendes
warms, bonfire, breechless	He bekes by the bale-fyre, and breklesse hym semede.
pitiful meats	Thare ware rostes full ruyd, and rewfull bredes,
Men, skewered	Berynes and bestaile brochede togeders,
Cauldron	Cowle full cramede of crysmed childyre,
women, (on the spit)	Sum as brede brochede, and bierdes tham tournede.
	And than this comlych kyng, by cause of his pople,
anguish, field	His herte bledes for bale on bent whare he standes.
delays	Than he dressede on his schelde, schuntes no lengere,
	Braundeschte his bryghte swerde by the bryghte hiltes,
Goes, man	Raykes towarde the renke reghte with a ruyd wille
greets	And hyely hailses that hulke with hawtayne wordes:
	'Now, all-weldand God, that wyrscheppes us all,
woe	Giff the sorowe and syte, sotte, there thow lygges,
foulest creature	For the fulsomeste freke that fourmede was evere!
	Foully thow fedys the, the fende have thi saule!
cooking, churl	Here es cury unclene, carle, be my trowthe,
Refuse (chaff)	Caffe of creatours all, thow cursede wriche!
	Because that thow killide has thise cresmede childyre,
	Thow has marters made, and broghte oute of lyfe,
butchered	That here are brochede on bente and brittened with thi handes,
assign, deserved	I shall merke the thy mede, as thou has myche served,

1050–2 Arthur has already been told of the giant's eating habits, and of how he keeps women to feed his lusts and turn his spits.

has charge of	Thurghe myghte of seynt Mighell, that this monte yemes,
left dead	And for this faire ladye, that thow has fey levyde,
violated, ground	And thus forced on folde for fylth of thiselfen.
	Dresse the now, dogge-sone, the devell have thi saule!
	For thow shall dye this day thurghe dynt of my handes!'
gaped, glowered	Than glopned the gloton and glored unfaire;
bared his teeth	He grenned as a grewhounde with grysly tuskes;
glowering looks	He gaped, he groned faste, with grucchand lates,
anger, wrath	For grefe of the gude kynge that hym with grame gretes.
hair, forelock, matted	His fax and his fore-toppe was filterede togeders,
	And owte of his face come an halfe fote large.
	His frount and his for-heved all was it over
skin, frog, freckled	As the fell of a froske, and fraknede it semede;
Hook-nosed, grey	Huke-nebbyde as a hawke, and a hore berde,
covered with hair, eye-hollows	And herede to the hole-eyghne with hyngande browes;
Rough-skinned, certainly	Harske as a hunde-fisch, hardly who-so lukes,
	So was the hyde of that hulke hally al over.
Ears	Erne had he full huge, and ugly to schewe,
eyes	With eghne fulle horreble and ardaunt forsothe;
flounder, sneering	Flatt-mowthede as a fluke with fleryand lyppys,
filthy	And the flesche in his for-tethe fowly as a bere.
covered with soup	His berde was brothy and blake, that till his brest rechede,
Greasy, porpoise, carcass	Grassede as a mere-swyne with corkes full huge,
tangled	And all falterd the flesche in his foule lippys,
(see n.)	Ilke wrethe as a wolfe-hevede it wraythe owt at ones.
man	Bulle-nekkyde was that bierne and brade in the scholders,
Badger-, boar	Brok-brestede as a brawne with brustils full large,
oak, roughly furrowed	Ruyd armes as an ake with rusclede sydes,
loins, horrible, believe	Lym and leskes full lothyn, leve ye for sothe!
Shuffle-footed, man, stumbling	Schovell-foted was that schalke, and schaylande hym semyde,
knocking	With schankes unschaply, schowand togedyrs;
monster	Thykke thees as a thursse and thikkere in the hanche,
Fat, swine	Greesse growen as a galte, full gryslych he lukes.
truly	Who the lenghe of the lede lelly accountes,
	Fro the face to the fote was fyfe fadome large!
	Than stertes he up sturdely on two styffe schankes
	And sone he caughte hym a clubb all of clene yryn.
	He walde hafe kyllede the kyng with his kene wapen,
	But thurghe the crafte of Cryste yit the carle failede;
helmet-band	The creest and the coronall, the claspes of sylver,
	Clenly with his clubb he crassched doune at ones.
	The kyng castes up his schelde and covers hym faire
stout sword	And with his burlyche brande a box he hym reches;
Point-blank, forehead, alien	Full-butt in the frunt the fromonde he hittes,
penetrates	That the burnyscht blade to the brayne rynnes.
clutches at his face	He feyed his fysnamye with his foule hondes
strikes	And frappes faste at hys face fersely ther-aftyre.
steps back	The kyng chaunges his fote, eschewes a lyttill –
	Ne had he eschapede that choppe, chevede had evyll!

1069 Mont St-Michel is a rocky outcrop off the north-east coast of Brittany (attached to the mainland at low tide, like St Michael's Mount in Cornwall), a place of legends and marvels and later of saints and shrines.

1093 'Each fold (of the flesh he had been eating) twisted (out of his mouth) like a wolf's head' (?).

	He folowes in fersly and festenes a dynte
	Hye up on the hanche with his harde wapyn
buried	That he hillid the swerde halfe a fote large.
	The hott blode of the hulke unto the hilte rynnes;
intestines	Evyn into inmette the gyaunt he hyttes
	Just to the genitales and jaggede tham in sondre.
	Than he romyed and rored and ruydly he strykes
	Full egerly at Arthur, and on the erthe hittes,
sward (turf), swipes	A swerde-lenghe within the swarthe he swappes at ones
passing wind	That nere swounes the kynge for swoughe of his dynttes!
quickly, swiftly, strains	Bot yit the kyng sweperly full swythe he byswenkes,
groin	Swappes in with the swerde that it the swange brysted.
gore (excrement)	Bothe the guttes and the gorr gusches owte at ones,
is enslimed	That all englaymes the gresse on grounde ther he standes.
throws away, seizes	Than he castes the clubb and the kyng hentes;
	On the creste of the cragg he caughte hym in armes
	And encloses hym clenly to cruschen hys rybbes.
noble one	So hard haldes he that hende that nere his herte brystes.
	Than the balefull bierdes bownes to the erthe,
	Kneland and cryande, and clappide theire handes:
	'Criste comforte yone knyghte and kepe hym fro sorowe
kill him	And latte never yone fende felle hym o-lyve!'
monster, strong, rolls	Yitt es the warlow so wyghte, he welters hym under,
Angrily	Wrothely thai wrythyn and wrystill togeders,
those bushes	Welters and walowes over within thase buskes,
	Tumbelles and turnes faste and teres thaire wedes.
roll about	Untenderly fro the toppe thai tiltin togeders –
	Whilom Arthure over and other-while undyre –
	Fro the heghe of the hyll unto the harde roche;
flinch, before, ocean-edges	They feyne never ar they fall at the flode-merkes.
dagger	Bot Arthur with an anlace egerly smytes
	And hittes ever in the hulke up to the hiltes.
death-throe, fiercely, squeezes	The theeffe at the dede-thrawe so throly hym thrynges
	That three rybbys in his syde he thrystes in-sunder!
	Then sir Kayous the kene unto the kyng styrtes,
	Said, 'Allas! we are lorne, my lorde es confundede,
we have had evil luck	Over-fallen with a fende – us es foul hapnede!
must be lost, exiled	We mon be forfeted in faith and flemyde for ever!'
	Thay hafe up hys hawberke than and handiles ther-undyr
	His hyde and his haunche eke and his faire sydes,
	Bothe his bakke and his breste and his bryghte armes.
torn open	Thay ware fayne that they fande no flesche entamed,
day's work, these	And for that journee made joye, thir gentill knyghtes.
	'Now, certes,' sais sir Bedwere, 'it semes, be my Lorde,
	He sekes seyntes bot selden, the sorer he grypes,
pulls, holy body	That thus clekys this cor-sant owte of thir heghe clyffes
and enclose	To carye forthe siche a carle at close hym in silver!
fellow	Be Myghell, of syche a makk I hafe myche wondyre
	That ever owre soveraygne Lorde suffers hym in heven.

1152 Arthur's companions on this expedition, Kay and Bedevere, are in the oldest Celtic lineage of his knights.

1162 Someone who has so much trouble ('**the sorer he grypes**') in bringing down the holy corpse of a saint from the cliffs is not likely to want to repeat the operation. Bedevere facetiously treats the whole episode as a pilgrimage to the shrine of a saint.

If	And all seyntes be syche that serves oure Lorde,
	I shall never no seynt bee, be my fadyre sawle!'
says banteringly	Than bourdes the bolde kyng at Bedvere wordes,
	'This seynt have I soghte, so helpe me owre Lorde!
draw, pierce	Forthy brayd owte thi brande and broche hym to the herte:
sure, servant (of God)	Be sekere of this sergeaunt, he has me sore grevede!
	I faghte noghte wyth syche a freke this fyftene wyntyre.'

William Thorpe (fl. 1407)

William Thorpe, a Lollard priest, was informally examined before Thomas Arundel, archbishop of Canterbury, at the archbishop's castle at Saltwood, in Kent, on 7 August 1407. Arundel, who was also Henry IV's chancellor, and thus the principal officer of state in the kingdom, had made it his business to hunt out Lollards, and had caused to be enacted in 1402 a statute for the burning of heretics. Lollardy was a threat to the established church because it tended to diminish the prerogatives of priests and of the church as an institution. It saw the church as a community of believers rather than as a priesthood of the elite; it emphasized the importance of preaching above the ministry of the sacraments (the Lollard view on the eucharist – that the bread was symbolically but not in real substance transformed at the consecration – though it dissipated some of the specifically priestly power over the mystery, was not in itself a danger, but it was convenient for the purposes of theological examination); it opposed tithing and the excommunication of non-tithe-payers; and it did not regard oral confession to a priest as indispensable, emphasizing rather the contrition of the individual before God. Lollard belief at first seemed to offer attractive options for the state, in its theory of secular dominion and its programme for the disendowment of the church, but disestablishment was soon perceived to be generally detrimental to the stability of the state, and Lollardy was declared a heresy in part because it was believed to be seditious.

The appeal of Thorpe's *Testimony*, whatever its basis in historical reality (Thorpe tells us, lines 36–9, that he has tried to make it as accurate as possible a record of his conversation with Arundel, but no doubt polemic purpose has gilded the record), is, first, in the wit and astuteness of Thorpe's characterizations of himself and Arundel: Thorpe becomes the kind of *person* whose beliefs command respect and who in some sense 'performs' Christ, while Arundel makes the opposition seem disreputable – ignorant, foolish and brutal; and, second, in the skill with which Thorpe matches his own role to that of the persecuted saint (as well as Christ), patiently and in the end silently witnessing for the truth before the interrogation of the ungodly. Thorpe's technique of self-presentation is worth comparing with that of Margery Kempe, in a similar situation. See R. Copeland, 'William Thorpe and his Lollard Community: Intellectual Labor and the Representation of Dissent', in B.A. Hanawalt and D. Wallace (eds), *Bodies and Disciplines: Intersections of Literature and History in Fifteenth-Century England* (Minneapolis, 1996), pp. 199–221; also F.E. Somerset, in *MS* 58 (1996), 207–41.

The *Testimony* survives in English in a single MS of the early fifteenth century (Bodl.MS Rawlinson C.208)(R) and in a copy (A) printed on the continent about 1530 for the reformers, and popular with Protestant polemicists like Bale and Foxe; and in Latin in two MSS written around 1420–30 in Bohemia (where Thorpe seems to have fled to join the Hussites). See A. Hudson (ed.), *Two Wycliffite Texts*, EETS, OS 301 (1993). The following extract corresponds to lines 1994–2247 of her edition, with R corrected from A.

The Testimony of William Thorpe

{The examination begins with Thorpe asking and receiving permission to make a statement of belief. He acknowledges obedience to the holy church of Christ, but reserves the right to determine for himself who are true members of it. Arundel demands that he forswear Lollard opinions, inform on Lollards, and not preach. Thorpe refuses. Arundel produces a roll listing the heresies that Thorpe preached at Shrewsbury. Thorpe attacks his accusers and defends preaching in general, and at length (his answers tend to be windily eloquent in the set phrases of Lollard polemic), and variously answers the charges that he preached the following heresies: that the sacrament of the altar does not involve transubstantiation; that the worship of images is idolatry; that pilgrimages are worthless; that paying tithes is not an obligation; that all swearing is wrong; and that confession may be made to God only. The interrogation ends with repeated demands that Thorpe submit unconditionally to the authority of holy church.}

And the Archebischop seide than, 'Youre cursid sect is bysie and it joieth gretli to contrarie and to distrie the privylege and the fredam of holy chirche.'

And I seide, 'Ser, I knowe no men[a] that traveilen so bisily as this sect doith that ye depraven[1] to make reste and pees in holy chirche. For pride, covetyse and symonye, whiche disturblen moost holy chirche, this sect hatith and fleeth, and traveilith bysyli to move alle other men to don in lik manere. And mekenesse, wilful povert and charite, and free mynystrynge of every sacrament this sect loveth and

1 denigrate

usith, and is ful bisie to move alle other folkis to do so, for these vertues oonen[2] alle the membris of holi chirche to her hed, Crist.'

And than a clerk seide to the Archebischop, 'Ser, it is forth daies,[3] and ye have ferre for to ride tonyght. Therfore, sere, make an ende with him, for he wol noon make; but the moore, sere, that ye bisien you for to drawe him[b] towardis you, the more contumax[4] he[c] is maade and the ferther fro you.'

And than Malverne[5] seide to me, 'William, knele doun and preie my lord of grace, and leve alle thi fantasies and bicome a chyld of holi chirche.'

And I seide, 'Ser, I have preied the Archebischop ofte and yit I pree him, for the love of Crist, that he wole leeve his indyngnacioun that he hath ayens me, and that he wole suffre me aftir my cunnynge for to do myn office of presthode, as I am chargid of God to don it. For I coveite not ellis, no-but[6] to serve my God to his plesynge in the staate that I stonde inne and have take me to.'

And the Archebischop seide to me, 'If of good herte thou wolt submytte thee now here mekely to be reulid fro this tyme forth by my counseile, obeiynge thee wilfully[7] and lowely to myn ordynaunce, thou schalt fynde it moost profitable and best to thee for to do thus. Therfore tarie thou me now no lenger: graunte to do this that I have seide to thee now here schortly, eithir[8] denyen it utterli.'

And I seide to the Archebischop, 'Owen[9] we, sere, to bileven that Jesu Crist was and is very God and verry man?'

And the Archebischop seide, 'Ye.'

And I seide, 'Sere, owen we to bileve that al Cristis lyvynge and his techynge was trewe in every poynt?'

And he seide, 'Ye.'

And I seide, 'Sere, owen we to bileve that the lyvynge and the techynge of the apostlis of Crist and of alle the prophetis ben trewe, whiche ben writun in the bible for the helthe and salvacioun of alle Goddis peple?'

And he seide, 'Ye.'

And I seide, 'Sere, owen alle Cristen men and wymmen, aftir her kunnynge and her power, for to conforme alle her lyvynge to the lyvynge and techynge of Crist specialy, and also to the lyvynge and to the techinge of hise apostlis and of hise profetis, in alle thingis that ben plesynge to God and edificacioun of his chirche?'

And he seide, 'Ye.'

And I seide, 'Sere, owith the doctrine, the heestis either the counseil of ony liif[10] to be accept either obeied unto no-but[11] this doctrine, these heestis and this counseil moun[12] ben groundid in Cristis lyvynge and techinge speciali, either in the lyvynge and techinge of hise apostlis or of hise prophetis?'

And the Archebischop seide to me, 'Other doctrine owith not to be accept, neither we owen to obeie to ony mannys heeste or counseile, no-but we mowen[13] perseyve that this heeste or counseile[d] acordith with the lyvynge and techinge of Crist and of hise apostlis and prophetis.'

And I seide, 'Ser, is not al the lore, the heestis[e] and the counseilis of holy chirche meenes and heleful[f] remedies to knowe and to withstonde the privy suggestiouns and the aperte temptaciouns of the fend, and also heleful[g] meenes and remedies to haten and fleen pride and alle other dedly synnes and the braunchis of hem, and sovereyn meenes to purchace grace for to withstonde and overcome alle fleischly lustis and movyngis?'

And the Archebischop seide, 'Yis.'

And I seide, 'Sere, whatever thing ye or any other liif biddith either counseilith me to do acording to this forseid lore, aftir my kunnynge and my power, thorugh the helpe of God, I wole mekeli of alle myn herte obeie therto.'

2 unite

3 well on in the day

4 contumacious (wilfully disobedient to legal process)

5 John Malvern was physician to Henry IV, also a priest, and something of a specialist in these Lollard investigations.

6 except

7 voluntarily

8 or else

9 Thorpe turns the tables neatly, by putting the archbishop to a catechism. It is very unlikely that Arundel would in reality have tolerated such an obvious piece of gamesmanship. Elsewhere, we notice how carefully Thorpe avoids answering the archbishop's questions directly, so as not to become complicit in the assumptions on which they are based.

10 person

11 unless (in any case other than where)

12 are able to

13 unless we may

And the Archebischop seide to me, 'Submitte thee than now here wilfulli and mekeli to the ordenaunce of holi chirche whiche I schal schewe to thee.'

And I seide, 'Sere, acordingli as I have rehersid to you I wole be now redy to obeie ful gladli to Crist the heed of al holi chirche, and to the lore and to the heestis and to the counseilis of every plesynge membre of him.'

And than the Archebischop, smytyng with his fist fersli upon a copbord, spake to me with a grete spirit, seiynge, 'Bi Jesu, but if thou leeve suche addiciouns, obeiynge thee now here withouten ony accepcioun[14] to myn ordinaunce, or that[15] I go out of this place I schal make thee as sikir[16] as ony theef that is in Kent! And avise thee now what thou wolt do.'

And than, as if he hadde ben angrid, the Archebischop wente from the copbord where he stood to a wyndowe. And than Malverne and another clerk camen ner-hond to me and thei spaken to me manye wordis ful plesyngeli, and also other wise,[17] manassynge me and counseilynge me ful bisili to submytte me, either ellis, thei seiden, I schulde not ascape ponyschinge over[18] mesure. For I schulde, thei seiden, be degratid,[19] cursid and brent and so thanne dampned. 'But now,' thei seiden, 'thou maist exchewe[20] alle these myscheves if thou wolt submitte thee mekeli and wilfully to this worthi prelate that hath cure of thi soule.[21] And for the pitee of Crist,' thei seiden, 'bethinke thee how greete clerkis the bischop of Lyncoln,[22] Herforde and Purveie weren and yit ben, and also Bowland, that is a wel undirstondynge man, which alle foure have forsaken and revokiden al the lore and opynyouns that thou and sich other holden. Wherfore, sith ech of hem is myche wiser than art thou,[23] we counseile thee for the beste that bi ensaumple of these foure clerkis sue[24] thou hem, submittinge thee as thei diden.'

And oon of the Archebischopis clerkis seide than there that he hadde herde Nicol Herforde seie that, sith he forsoke and revokide alle the Lollers opynyouns, he hath had gretter savoure and more delite to holde ayens hem than evere he hadde to holde with hem whilis that he heeld with hem. And therfor Malverne seide to me, 'I undirtake, if thou wolt take to thee a preest, and schryve thee clene, and forsake alle siche opynyouns, and take thi penaunce of my lord here for the holding and techynge of hem, withinne schort tyme thou schalt be greetly confortid in this doynge.'

And I seide to these clerkis that thus bisili counseileden me to sue these forseide men, 'Seres, if Philip of Repingtoun, Nicol Herforde, Jon Purveye and Robert Bowland, of whom ye counseilen me to take ensaumple, hadden thei forsaken beneficis of temperal profit and of worldly worschip, so that thei hadden exchewid and alyened hem[25] fro alle occasiouns of covetise and of fleischly lustis and hadden taken hem to symple lyvynge and wilful poverte, thei hadden hereinne yovun[26] good ensaumple to me and to manye other for to have sued hem. But now, sith alle these foure men have schamefulli and sclaundrousli don contrarie, consentynge to resceyven and to have and holden temperal beneficis, lyvynge now more worldli and fleischly than thei diden biforehonde, confourmynge hem to the maneres of this world, I forsake hem hereinne and alle her sclaundrouse doynge. For I purpose with the helpe of God, in remissioun of alle my synnes and of my ful cursid lyvynge, to hate and fle privyli and apeertli[27] to sue these men, techinge and counseilinge whomevere I may for to late[28] and exchewe the wei that thei have chosen to goon inne, which wol lede hem into the worst ende, if in covenable[29] tyme thei repenten hem not, verili forsakinge and revokinge opinli the sclaundre that thei have put and every dai yit putten to Cristis chirche. For certis, so opin blasfemye and sclaundre as thei have spoken and don in her revokinge and forsakinge of truthe owith not, neither may, privyly be amendid deweli![30]

14 condition
15 before
16 securely imprisoned
17 **ful plesyngeli, and also other wise**: the 'good cop–bad cop' technique of interrogation, as Copeland (p. 201) calls it.
18 beyond
19 stripped of priestly orders
20 avoid
21 **cure**: 'spiritual care'. This is the very claim to which Thorpe makes **accepcioun**.
22 **the bischop of Lyncoln**: Philip Repingdon. He and Nicholas Hereford were the most celebrated of Wyclif's early followers. John Purvey is often associated with the later version of the Wycliffite translation of the Bible. Robert Bowland is less famous. All four were Lollards who had recanted (though Purvey later relapsed).
23 **ech of hem is myche wiser than art thou**. Thorpe had earlier named Repingdon, Hereford and Purvey among those he counted as his early instructors in Lollard belief.
24 follow
25 removed themselves
26 given
27 openly
28 leave
29 appropriate
30 properly

'Wherefore, seres, I preie you that ye bisien you not for to move me to sue these men in revokinge and forsakinge of treuthe, as thei have do and yit done;[31] whereinne bi open evydence thei terren[32] God to grete wrathe, and not oonli ayens hemsilf but also ayens alle thilke that favouren hem either counsenten to hem hereinne, either comounen with eny of hem, no-but into[33] her amendement. Forwhi here-biforehonde these men weren pursued of enemyes of treuthe, now thei have oblischid hem[34] by ooth for to sclaundren and pursuen Crist in his membris. Wherefore, as I triste stedefastly in the goodnesse of God, the worldly covetyse, the lusty[35] lyvynge and the slydinge fro treuthe of these renegatis schulen ben to me and to manye other men and wymmen ensaumple and evydence to stonde the more styflier bi the treuthe of Crist. For certis, right many men and wymmen marken and hideousen[36] the falsnesse and the cowardise of these forseide untrewe men, how that thei ben stranglid with beneficis and withdrawen from the treuthe of Goddis word, forsakinge to suffre therfore bodili persecucioun. For bi this unfeithful doynge, and apostasie of hem specially that ben greete lettrid men[37] and have knowlechide[38] opinly the treuthe, and now, either for plesynge[h] or[39] displesinge of tirauntis, have take hire[40] and temperal wagis to forsaken the treuthe and to holde ther-ayens, sclaundringe and pursuynge hem that coveiten to suen Crist in the weie of rightwesnesse, manye men and wymmen herfore ben now moved; but many herafter thorugh the grace of God schulen be moved herebi for to lerne the treuthe of God and to don theraftir and to stonde boldeli therbi.'

And thanne the Archebischop seide to his clerkis, 'Bisie you no lengir aboute him, for he and other such as he is ben confedrid so togidre that thei wolen not swere to ben obedient and to submitte hem to prelatis of holi chirche. For now, sith I stod here,[41] his felowe sent me word that he wol not swere to me. And, losel,[42] in that thing that in thee is thou hast bisied thee to lese[43] this yonge man – but blessid be God, thou schalt not have thi purpos of him! For he hath forsaken al thi lore, submyttinge him to be buxom[44] and obedient to the ordynaunce of holi chirche. And he wepith ful bittirly and cursith thee ful hertely for the venymouse techinge which thou schewedist to him, conseilynge him to done theraftir. And for thi fals counseilinge of him and of many other thou hast grete cause to be right sory, for longe tyme thou hast bisied thee for to perverte whomevere thou myghtist. And forthi as many dethis thou art worthi as thou hast yovun yvel counseilis! And therfore, by Jesu, thou schalt go thidir where Nychol Herforde and Joon Purveye weren herborwiden.[45] And I undirtake, or[46] this dai eighte daies thou schalt be right glad for to don whatever thing I bidde thee done. And, losel, I schal asaie if I can make thee there as sorewful as it was told to me that thou were glad of my laste goynge out of Yngelonde.[47] Bi seint Tomas, I schal turne thi joie into sorewe!'

And I seide, 'Sere, ther mai no liif[48] preve lawefulli that I joiede evere of the manere of youre outgoynge of this londe. But, sere, to seie the sothe, I was joieful that, whanne ye weren gon, the bischop of London, in whos[i] prison ye putten me and lafte me, fond in me no cause for to holden me no lengir in prisoun. But at the preers of my freendis he delyverede me to hem, axynge of me no manere of submittinge.'

And than the Archebischop seide to me, 'Wherfore that I wente out of Yngelonde is unknowe to thee.[49] But be[j] this thing wel knowe to thee: that God, as I woot wel, hath clepid me ayen[50] and brought me into this londe for to distrie thee and the fals sect that thou art of. And, bi God, I schal pursue you unto Acle,[51] so that I schal not leve oo stap[52] of you in this londe!'

And I seide to the Archebischop, 'Sere, the holi profete Jeremye[53] seide to the fals prophete Ananye,

31 still do
32 provoke
33 except with the purpose of
34 pledged themselves
35 pleasure-loving
36 abominate
37 **grette lettrid men**, i.e. Repingdon and the others, whose apostasy was very damaging to the movement.
38 professed
39 or for fear of
40 hire
41 **sith I stod here**. Arundel wants to emphasize how recently it was that Thorpe's unnamed fellow-Lollard was still refusing to swear obedience.
42 wretch
43 destroy
44 obedient
45 **herborwiden**: 'lodged', i.e. to the prison at Saltwood castle.
46 before
47 Arundel refers to his exile during the last years of Richard II, 1397–9.
48 person
49 none of your business
50 called me back
51 **Acle** is in east Norfolk (the furthest that one could be pursued before falling into the sea).
52 a single trace
53 Jer. 28:9.

"Whanne the word, that is the prophecie of a profet, is knowen or fulfillid, thanne it schal be knowen that the Lord sente that prophete in treuthe."'

And the Archebischop, as if he hadde not ben[k] quyetid with my seiinge, turnede him aweiward, and yede hidir and thidir, and seide, 'Bi God, I schal sette upon thi schynes a peire of pillers[54] that thou schalt be gladde to chaunge thi vois!'

Theese wordis and manye oon moo suche greet wordis weren there spoken to me, manassynge me and alle other of the same sect for to ben poniyschid and distryed unto the utmest. And thanne the Archebischop clepid to him a clerk and rowned[55] with him; and that clerk went than forth, and soone he broughte in thidir the constable of Saltwode castel.[56] And thanne the Archebischop rownede a good while with him, and thanne the constable wente forth thens. And than cam in to us dyverse seculers, and thei scorneden me on eche side, and thei manasseden me gretli,[57] and summe conseileden the Archebischop to brenne me annon, and summe other counseileden to drenche me in the see, for it was nygh-honde there. And oo clerk, stondinge besides me, knelide doun bifore the Archebischop, preeynge him that he wolde delyvere me to him for to seie matyns with him, and he wolde undirtake that withinne thre daies I schulde not ayenseie[58] ony thing that were comaundid me to do of[59] my prelate. And the Archebischop seide to him that he wolde ordeyne for[60] me himsilf. And than theraftir cam in thidir ayen the constable, and spak privyly to the Archebischop. And than the Archebischop comaundide the constable to lede me forth thens with him, and so he dide.

And so whanne we weren goon forth thens, I was sent aftir ayen. And whanne I cam inne ayen bifore the Archebischop, a clerke bad me knele doun and axe grace and submitte me lowely, and I schulde fynde it for the best. And I seide thanne to the Archebischop, 'Ser, as I have seide to you dyverse tymes todaie, I wole wilfuli and lowely obeye and submitte me to be obedient and buxsum ever aftir my kunnyng and my power to God and to his lawe, and to every membre of holy chirche as ferforth as I can perseyve that these membris acorden with her heed, Crist, and wolen teche, reule me or chastise me bi autorite specially of Goddis lawe.'

And the Archebischop seide, 'I wiste wel he wolde not withoute suche addiciouns submitte him.'

And thanne I was rebukid and scorned and manassid on ech side. And yit after this dyverse persoones crieden upon me to knele doun to submytte me. But I stood stille and spak no word. And thanne there weren spoke of me and to me many greete wordis, and I stood and herde hem curse and manasse and scorne me, but I seide nothing.[61]

And thanne a while theraftir the Archebischop seide to me, 'Wolt thou not submitte thee to the ordynaunce of holy chirche?'

And I seide, 'Sere, I wol ful gladly submytte me as I have schewid to you.'

And than the Archebischop bad the constable to have me forth thens anoon. And so thanne I was led forth and brought into a ful unhonest[l] prisoun where I cam nevere bifore. But, thankid be God, whanne alle men weren gon forth thenns from me, schittinge[62] after hem the prisoun dore, anoon therafter, I beynge thereinne bi mysilf, I bisiede me to thenke on God and to thanke him of his goodnesse. And I was thanne gretli confortid in alle my wittis, not oonli forthi that[63] I was than delyvered for a tyme fro the sight, fro the heeringe, fro the presence, fro the scornynge and fro the manassinge of myn enemyes, but myche more I gladid in the Lord forthi thorugh his grace he kepte me so, bothe amonge the flateryngis specialli, also amonge the manassingis of myn adversaries, that[m] withouten hevynesse and agrigginge[64] of my conscience I passid awei fro hem. For as a tree leyde upon another tree overthwert[65] on crosse wyse, so weren the Archebischop and hise three clerkis alwei contrarie to me and I to hem.[66]

{The Testimony *ends with a prayer.}*

54 leg-irons

55 whispered

56 **the constable**, as the representative of the secular arm, would have the power to punish Thorpe (by imprisoning, burning or – rather unlikely – throwing him in the sea) once he was 'degraded' and handed over by the church authorities.

57 Thorpe is well advanced now in his imaging of himself as Christ before his persecutors. 'The chief priests and the scribes stood by, vehemently accusing him. And Herod with his soldiers treated him with contempt and mocked him' (Luke 23:10–11). Thorpe conveys well the atmosphere of bustle and menace.

58 oppose

59 by

60 deal with

61 **I seide nothing**. Where Arundel wants an interrogation and an exercise of power, Thorpe wants a theatre in which he can play Jesus to Arundel's Caiaphas. 'And the high priest stood up and said, "Have you no answer to make? What is it that these men testify against you?" But Jesus was silent' (Matt. 26:62–3).

62 shutting

63 because

64 burdening

65 transversely

66 Thus they make the cross on which Thorpe is made to suffer.

Nicholas Love (fl. 1410)

The Mirror of the Blessed Life of Jesus Christ

Nicholas Love was prior of the recently founded Carthusian house at Mount Grace, in north Yorkshire, when he completed his translation of the *Meditationes vitae Christi* and offered it in 1410 to archbishop Arundel for approval. Arundel was pleased to give his blessing to a work of such blameless orthodoxy, the more especially since Love had incorporated many incidental attacks on Lollardy and an additional chapter affirming the orthodox view on the sacrament of the eucharist (see headnote to Thorpe, above). The Latin *Meditationes*, an extended prose meditation on the life of Christ, one of the most influential works of western spirituality, was composed in Italy in the mid-fourteenth century by the Franciscan Johannes de Caulibus (though long attributed to St Bonaventure). Its purpose was to encourage devotion to the humanity of Christ (see also Julian of Norwich, above), and so to evoke an emotional response of loving gratitude to God for the offer of redemption. Its method was to fill out the Gospel narrative of Christ's life with a wealth of affecting detail. The drama of the Passion is the high point of the narrative, with skilful evocation of the scene, invention of dramatically plausible incidents, constant apostrophe and invocation, and urgent calls to the reader to behold the unfolding of events with the mind's eye. The whole work, and these chapters in particular, had an enormous impact on late medieval devotion, and provided inspiration, subject-matter and vivid detail for the mystery plays, for songs and lyrics, for meditative and reflective poems of all kinds, and for pictorial illustration. The story of Christ's life as a whole is divided into seven days, intended to provide material for meditation for the seven days of Holy Week. The narrative for Friday, that of the Passion, is itself divided into chapters according to the seven canonical hours of matins, prime, tierce, sext, nones, vespers and compline; this section circulated also as a separate text, frequently translated into English in the fifteenth century. The success and popularity of Love's *Mirror* (it survives in 56 MSS and was printed nine times before the Reformation) is attributable to the skill of the translator in adapting his material for a simpler audience, and to the fluent, idiomatic and expressive nature of his prose, but beyond that to the skill of the original in offering so many dramatic and homely images of Christ's life for the mind to fasten upon, to the intimacy with the divine that it permits, and to the freedom it promises to individual readers, men and women, to find in the person and body of Christ a focus for their religious longings.

Ed. M.G. Sargent, Garland Medieval Texts 18 (New York and London, 1992); valuable study by E. Salter, *Nicholas Love's 'Myrrour of the Blessed Lyf of Jesu Christ'*, Analecta Cartusiana 10 (Salzburg, 1974); see also S. Oguro, R. Beadle and M.G. Sargent (eds), *Nicholas Love at Waseda: Proceedings of the International Conference 1995* (Cambridge, 1997). Text from CUL MS Add.6578, 82r–v, 87r–92v.

The purpose of this work (chap. 40)

Who-so desireth with the apostle Poule[1] to be joyful in the crosse of oure Lorde Jesu Criste and in his blessede passioun, he moste with bisy meditacion abide there-inne. For the grete misteries and alle the processe therof, if thei were inwardly consideret with alle the inwarde mynde and beholdyng of mannes soule, as I fully trowe, thei sholde bringe that beholdere into a newe state of grace. For to him that wolde serche the passioun of oure Lorde with alle his herte and alle his inwarde affeccion there shuld come many devout felynges and stirynges that he never supposede before, of the whech he shuld fele a newe compassion and a newe love, and have newe gostly confortes, thorh the whech he shold perceyve himself turned as it were into a newe astate of soule, in the which astate thoo forseide gostly felynges shold seme to him as an erneste and partie of the blisse and joy to come.

And fort gete this astate of the soule, I trowe, as he that is unkenyng[2] and blaberinge, that it behovede to sette therto alle the sharpenesse of mynde, with wakyng eyene of herte, puttyng aweye and levyng alle othere cures[3] and bisinesses for the tyme and makynge himself as[4] present in alle that befelle aboute that passion and crucifixion, affectuesly, bisily, avisily[5] and perseverantly, and not passing lightly or with tediouse hevynes bot with alle the herte and gostly gladnes.

Wherefore, if thou that redist or herest this boke hast here-before bisily taken hede to thoo thinges

Chapter 40

1 **Poule**: Gal. 6:14.

2 one that is ignorant

3 cares

4 as if

5 advisedly

that haven be writen and spoken of the blessede life of oure Lorde Jesu Criste into this tyme, miche more now thou shalt gedire alle thi mynde and alle the strengh of thi soule to thoo thinges that folowen of his blessede passion. For here specialy is shewed his hye charite, the which resonably shold alle holely enflaume and brenne oure hertes in his love.

The scourging (chap. 41)

And than, at the biddyng of Pylate that he sholde be scourget and beten, oure Lord was despoilet,[1] bonden to a pilere, and harde and sore scourget. And so stant he naked before hem alle, that fairest yonge manne of alle childrene[2] that ever were born, takyng paciently of thoo foulest wrecches the hardest and moste bitter strokes of scourges; and so is that moste innocent, faireste and clennest flesh, floure of alle mankynde, alle to-rent and full of woundes, rennyng out of alle sides that preciouse kynges blode, and so longe beten and scourget, with wounde upon wounde and brisoure[3] upon brisour, til bothe the lokeres and the smyters were werye; and then was he biden to be unbounden.

Sothely the pylere that he was bounden to yit scheweth the steppes[4] of his blode, as it is contened in stories.[5]

Take now here gude hede by inwarde meditacioun of alle his peynes abidyngly, and bot thou fynde thi herte melte into sorouful compassioun, suppose fully and halde that thou hast to hard a stonene[6] herte.

Thanne was fulfilled in dede that the prophete Ysaie[7] seide of him longe tyme before: 'We seene him in that tyme, and there was none semlynesse nor beutye in hym, and we helde him as foule as a leprose manne that were smiten doun and made lowe of God, wherfore we set no rewarde[8] of him.' O Lorde Jesu, who was he so fole-hardye that dorst despoile the? Bot who were thei miche worse hardy that dorst bynde the? Bot yit who were thei althere-worst[9] and moste foole-hardye that dorst so bitterly bete the and scourge the?

Bot sothely thou sonne of rihtwisnes at that tyme withdrowest thi bemes of liht, and therfore alle was in derkenes, and in the miht of wikkednes. For nowe alle thine enmyes bene more mihtye than thou, and that made thi love and oure malice. Cursed be that malice and wikkednes of sinne, wherfore thou were so tormented and pyned![10]

After he was unbounden fro that pilere thei ladden him so beten and nakede aboute be house[11] sekynge after his clothes that were cast in diverse places of hem that despoilede him. And here have compassion of him in so grete colde quakyng and tremelyng, for as the Gospelle witnesseth it was thanne harde colde.[12] And when he wolde have done on his clothes, sume of thoo moste wikkede withstoden[13] and comen to Pylate, and seide, 'Lorde, he this[14] made himself a kynge, wherfore let us clothe him and corone him as a kynge.' And then thei token an olde silken mantelle of redde, and kast on him, and maden a garlande of sharpe thornes and thrist upon his hede and putten in his hande a rede as a sceptre, and alle he paciently suffreth. And after, when thei knelede and saluede him in scorne, seyinge, 'Heile, kynge of Jewes!' he helde his pees and spake not.

Now beholde him with sorowe of herte, namely when thei smiten him grevously and oft-sithes[15] upon the hede, ful of sharpe thornes, the whech persede grevously into the brayne-panne and made it alle full of blode. And so thei scornede him as theih he wolde have reigned, bot that he miht not; and alle he suffreth as hir servante or knafe.[16]

O wrecches, how dredeful sal that hede apere at the laste to yow, the which ye smyten now so boldly!

And yit this sufficeth not to hir malice, but to more[17] reprove and scorn of him thei gederet alle hir

Chapter 41

1 stripped

2 **of alle childrene**. Cf. 'Thou art the fairest of the sons of men' (Ps. 45:2).

3 bruise

4 traces

5 **stories**: here, as often, a reference to the *Historia Scholastica* of the twelfth-century Petrus Comestor, the standard medieval companion to biblical history (see chap. 167, *PL* 198:1628).

6 made of stone

7 Isa. 53:2.

8 regard

9 worst of all

10 made to suffer

11 through the house

12 **it was thanne harde colde**: John 18:18.

13 objected

14 this man

15 oft-times

16 servant-lad

17 for the greater

wikkede companye, first to wondre upon him in the hous, and after thei brouht him out before Pylate, and alle the peple in that manere illudet with[18] the corone of thornes and that olde purpure vestiment.

Se now, for Goddes love, how he stant in that maner, hangyng the face doun towarde the erthe, before alle the grete multitude criyng and askyng of Pilate, 'Crucifye! Crucifie him!' and scornyng him that he wolde make him wisere than the princes and the Pharisees and the doctours of the lawe, and how his wisdome was turned into so grete folie at it[19] shewede in that tyme. And so not onely he suffrede grete paynes and sorow in his body within-forth, bot also many and foule obreydynges[20] and reproves without-forth.

The crucifixion (chap. 43)

Now forthermore maiht thou se whan oure Lord Jesus was come to that stinkyng hille of Calvarie how wikkedly thoo cursede werkemenne begunne to worche on alle sides that cruele werke.

Take hede now diligently with alle thi herte alle tho thinges that be now to come, and make the there present in thi mynde, beholdyng alle that shal be done ageynes thi Lorde Jesu and that bene spoken or done of him. And so with the innere eye of thi soule beholde sume settyng and ficching[1] the crosse fast into the erthe, sume makyng redye the nailes and the hameres to dryve hem with, othere makyng redy and settyng up laddres and ordeinyng other instrumentis that hem thouht nedeful, and other faste aboute to spoile[2] him and drawe of his clothes. And so is he now the thridde tyme spoiled and standeth nakede in siht of alle that peple, and so bene now the thridde tyme renued the brisours of the woundes in his scourgyng by the clevyng of the clothes to his flesh.

Now also first his modere seeth how he is so taken and ordeyned to the deth. Wherefore she, sorouful out of mesure and havyng shame to se him standyng alle naked – for thei laft him not so miche as hese pryve clothes – she went in haste to hir dere sone and clippede[3] him and girde him aboute the leendes[4] with the kerchefe of hir hede.

A, Lorde, in what sorowe is hir soule now? Sothely, I trowe that she miht not speke one worde to him for sorowe. Bot she miht do no more to him, nor help him; for if she miht, without doute she wolde.

Thanne was hir sone anone taken oute of hir handes in wode manere, and ladde to the fote of the crosse.

Now take hede diligently to the maner of crucifying.[5] There bene sette up tweyn laddres, one behynde and anothere before, at the lift arme of the crosse, upon the whech thoo wikked ministres gone up with nailes and hameres. Also another short laddre is sette before the crosse that lasteth[6] up to the place where his feete sholde be nailed.

Now take gude hede to alle that foloweth. Oure Lorde thanne was compelled and beden fort go up on that laddre to the crosse, and he mekely doth alle that thei beden him. And when he came up to the overest[7] ende of that short laddre, he turnede his bakke to the crosse and streyht out on-brede[8] thoo kynges armes, and his fairest handes gafe up to hem that crucifiede him, and than, liftyng up his lovely eyene to heven, seide to the Fadere in thees maner wordes: 'Lo, here I am, my dere Fadere, as thou woldest that I sholde lowe[9] myself unto the crosse for the savacioun of mankynde; and that is pleisyng and acceptable to me, and for hem I offre myself, the whech thou woldest sholde be my bretherne. Wherefore also, thou Fadere, take gladely this sacrifice for hem of me, and now hethen-forwarde[10] be plesed and wele-willed to hem for my love, and alle olde offense and trespasse forgive and wipe awey, and put aferre alle unclannes of sinne fro hem, for sothely I offre here now myself for hem and hir hele.'[11]

And than he that was on the laddere behynde the crosse taketh his riht hande and naileth it fast to the

18 made fun of
19 as that
20 upbraidings

Chapter 43
1 fixing
2 strip
3 embraced
4 loins
5 **the maner of crucifying.** The detailed and realistic reconstruction of the manner and technique of crucifying was central to the appeal of the narrative, and to the plays and pictures based upon it.
6 reaches
7 top
8 stretched out wide
9 humble
10 henceforth
11 salvation

crosse. And after, he that was on the lift side draweth with alle his miht the lift arme and hande, and driveth ther-thorh anothere grete naile. After, thei comen doun and taken awey alle the laddres, and so hangeth oure Lorde onely by thoo tweyn nailes smyten thorh his handes, without sustenance of the body, drawyng dounwarde peynfully thorh the weiht therof.

Herewith also another harlote renneth to, and draweth doun his feete with alle his miht, and another anone driveth a grete longe naile thorh bothe his feete joynede to other.

This is one maner of his crucifiyng, after the opinion of sume men.[12]

Othere there bene that trowen that he was not crucified in this manere, bot that, first liggyng the crosse[13] on the grounde, thei nailede him there-upon, and after, with him so hangyng, thei liften up the crosse and festen it doun in the erthe.

And if it were done in this manere, than maist thou se how vileynsly thei taken him as a ribaude[14] and kasten him doun upon the crosse, and than as wode thefes drowen on bothe sides[15] first his handes and after his feete, and so nailede him fast to the crosse, and after with alle hir miht liften up the crosse, with him hangyng, als hye as thei miht and than lete it falle doun into the morteise.

In the which falle, as thou may undurstande, alle the senewes to-breken,[16] to his sovereyn peyne. Bot whether so it be in one maner or in othere, sothe it is that oure Lorde Jesus was nailed harde upon the crosse, hande and foote, and so streyned and drawen that, as he himself seith by the prophete David,[17] thei[a] mihten telle and noumbre alle his bones.

Than rennen out of his blessed body thee[18] stremes of that holiest blode on alle sides abundantly fro tho grete woundes, and so is he constreyned and arted[19] that he may not meve bot his hede.

Wherefore, hangyng the body[20] onely by tho thre nailes, no doute bot that he suffreth so bitter sorowes and peynes that there may no herte thenke, nor tonge telle.

And yit moreovere he hangeth bytwix two thefes, of the whech that one blasfemeth and tempteth him to impacience. And therwith other[21] blasfemyng and skornyng seyen, '*Vaath*![22] this is he that destrueth the temple of God, and maketh it up ageyn in thre daies!' And other seiden, 'He made other safe bot he may not now save himself!' And mani othere reproves and scornynges thei seiden to him, as the Gospelle telleth.

And alle these reproves, blasfemies and despites ben done, seynge and heryng his most sorowful modere, whose compassioun and sorowe made him hir sone to have the more bitter peyne.

And on that othere halfe she hange[23] in soule with hir sone on the crosse and desirede inwardly rather to have died that tyme with him than to have lyved lengire.

And so stode the modere byside the crosse of hir sone, bytwix his crosse and the thefes crosse. She turnede never hir eyene fro him; she was full of anguysh, as he was also. And she preide to the Fadere at that tyme, with alle hir herte seying thus: 'Fadere, and God without ende, it was pleisyng to yow that my sone solde be crucified, and it is done. It is not now tyme to aske him of yow ageyn, bot ye seene now in what anguish is his soule. I beseke yow that ye wille ese his peynes: gode Fadere, I recommende unto yow, in alle that I may, my dere sone.'

And also he, hir sone, praiede for hir prively in himself, seying:

'Mi fadere, ye knawen how my modere is tormented for me. I sholde onely[24] be crucified and not shee, but lo now, she hangeth on the crosse with me. Mine owne crucifiynge sufficeth, for I bere the synnes of alle the peple. She hath not deservet any seche thinge. Wherfore I recommende hir to yow, that ye make hir peynes lesse.'

Thanne was with oure Lady John and Maudeleyn, the belovede disciplesse, and othere of his frendes by the crosse of oure Lord Jesu, the whech alle maden grete sorowe and wepten and miht not be conforted

12 The offer of a choice of methods is not to do with historical accuracy but with the purpose of multiplying details of possible techniques so as to add to the imagined sum of Christ's sufferings.

13 with the cross first lying

14 common criminal

15 **drowen on bothe sides**. The pulling of the hands and feet to fit the cross, like the dropping of the cross into the hole in the ground prepared for it (the mortise), are details that were seized on for graphic representation and dramatic business in, for instance, the York play of the Crucifixion.

16 broke to pieces

17 **David**: Ps. 22:17.

18 those

19 restricted

20 the body hanging

21 others

22 ***Vaath***, Lat. *vah* (Matt. 27:40), exclamation, 'Ah!'

23 hung

24 alone

in no manere of her belovede maister, bot ever was her sorow renued with his sorowe, authere[25] in reproves or in dedes, as it foloweth after.

The seven last words from the Cross (chap. 44)

Now hangeth oure Lorde Jesus on the crosse in grete peyne, and yit is he not ydul bycause of that peyne, bot he wrouht alle-waye and spake that was profitable for us.

Wherefore, so hangyng, he spake vii notable wordes,[1] that bene fonden writen in the Gospelle.

The first was in the tyme that thei crucifiede him, when he praiede for hem, seying thus, 'Fadere, forgive hem, for thei wite not what thei done' – the which worde was a worde of grete pacience, of grete love, and of unspekable beningnite.

The seconde was to his modere, seying thus, 'Woman, lo thi sone,' and also to John, 'Lo thi modere.' He clepede hir not at that tyme, 'Modere', lest she sholde thorh fervent tendirnes of love have bene more sorye.

The thridde was to the blessede thefe, seying, 'This day thou shalt be with me in paradise', whereinne his moost large mercye opunly is shewed.

The ferthe was when he seide, '*Helye, Helye, lama zabathanye*!'[2] that is to sey, 'My God, my God, whi hast thou forsake me?' as theih he seide in this sentence, 'My God, Fadere of heven, thou hast so miche loved the redempcion of the worlde that thou hast given me therfore[3] and, as it semeth, forsaken.'

Lorde Jesu, what confort was that forseide worde to alle thine enemies, and what disconfort to alle thi freendes? Sothely, as it semeth, ther was never worde that oure Lorde Jesus spake that gafe so miche boldenes to his enemyes, and so miche occasion to his frendes fort despeire that he was God, as that worde. For thei[b] undirstode it that tyme bot nakedly after the letter sowneth.[4] Bot oure Lord wolde shewe into the last ende that as he suffrede in body fully after the kynde of man, so also in his spekyng after the infirmite of man that he was verrey man, suspendyng for the tyme the use of alle the miht of the Godhede.[5]

The fyft worde was, 'I am threstye', the whech worde also was occasioun to his modere and John and other frendes of grete compassion and to his wikked enemyes of grete rejoycing and gladnes. For thouh it so be that it may be undirstande, that worde 'I thriste', gostely, to that entent that he thrested thanne the hele[6] of soules, neverles also in sothenes he thristede bodily bycause of the grete passing out of blode where-thorh he was alle drye within-forth and thristy.

And then thoo wikked devels lymes,[7] that ever caste[8] how thei miht moste nuye[9] him, token aisele[10] and galle and proferede him up to drinke.

O cursede wodenes of hem, that bene never filled with[11] malice, bot in alle tyme nuyen als miche as thei kunne or mowen![12]

The sixte worde was when he seide, '*Consummatum est*, it is alle endet', as theih he seide thus, 'Fadere, the obedience[13] that thou hast given me I have perfitely and fully done indede, and yit I am redy to do what-so thou bidde me. Bot alle that is writen of me is now fulfilled. Wherfore, if it be thi wille, clepe me now ageyn to the.'

And thanne seide the Fadere, 'Come now, my swete lovede sone, thou hast wele done alle thinges, and I wole not that thou be more tormented. And therfore come now, for I shal clippe the with myn armes and take the into my bosume.'

25 either

Chapter 44

1 **vii notable wordes**. The Seven Last Words from the Cross are a frequent theme of devotional meditation (see Duffy [1992], pp. 248–56). They are gathered from Luke 23:34, John 19:26, Luke 23:43, Matt. 27:46, John 19:28, John 19:30 and Luke 23:46.

2 ***Helye***, etc. In Matt. 27:46, the Hebrew is transliterated as 'Eli, Eli, lama sabachthani'.

3 for that purpose

4 **after the letter sowneth**: 'according as the literal sense appears to mean.' The meditation requires that the literal sense, and Christ's suffering as a man, be recognized, but the spiritual sense needs to be acknowledged too, so that the larger divine purpose in everything is not neglected.

5 The concentration of devotion on the humanity of Christ was made theologically possible by the doctrine of 'impassibility' (see *PP* XX.23n, above).

6 salvation

7 agents

8 contrived

9 torment

10 vinegar

11 never have their fill of

12 may

13 test of obedience

And after that tyme oure Lorde began to faile in siht in manere of diynge men, and wax alle pale, now stekyng[14] the eyene and now opunyng, and lowde[15] his hede now into one side and now into another side, failyng alle the strenghes, and alle the vaynes than voide.

And so at the last he putte the seventhe worde, with a stronge crye and wepynge teres seying thus: 'Fadere, I commende my spirite into thi handes', and therwith he yelte[16] the spirite, bowynge his hede upon his breeste towarde the Fadere as in maner of thonkyng that he clepede him to him, and givyng him his spirite.

At this crye than was converted Centurio,[17] there beynge, and seide, 'Sothely this manne was Goddes sone!' bycause that he sawh him, so criynge, dye. For other menne when thei dyen mowe not crie.[18] Wherfore he belevede in him.

Sothly this crie was so grete, as holi men seyne, that it was herde into helle.

O Lord God, in what state was that tyme his modere[19] soule, when she sawh him so peynfully faile, wepe and dye? Sothely I trowe that for the multitude of anguishes she was alle out of hirself and unfelable made, as half-dede, and that now mich more than what tyme she mette with him beringe the crosse, as it is seide.

What trowe we diden then Maudleyn, the trewe lovede disciplesse, what John his awne derlyng, and other tweyn sistres of oure Lady? Bot what miht thei do? Thei were alle full of sorowe and bitternes, and therfore thei wepten sore without remedye.

Lo, now hangeth oure Lorde on the crosse, dede, and alle that grete multitude goth awey towarde the cite, and his sorouful modere, with the foure forseide felawes, sette hir doun byside the crosse and beholdeth piteuously hir dere sone so ferd with, and abideth helpe fro God that she miht have him to hir and birye him.

Than also, if thou beholde wele thi Lorde, thou maiht have here matire ynouh of hye compassioun, seynge him so tormented, that fro the sole of the fote into the hiest part of the hede ther was in him none hole place nor membre without passioun.[20]

This is a piteuous siht and a joyful siht: a piteuous siht in him, for that harde passion that he suffrede for oure savacion, bot it is a likyng[21] siht to us, for the matire and the effecte that we have thereby of oure redempcioun. Sothely this siht of oure Lord Jesu hangyng so on the crosse, by devoute ymaginacioun of the soule, is so likyng to sume creatours that after longe exercise of sorouful compassioun thei felen sumtyme so grete likyng, not onely in soule bot also in the body, that thei kunne not telle, and that no man may knowe, bot onely he that by experience feleth it. And than may he wele sey with the Apostle, 'Betyde me never to be joyful bot in the crosse of my Lord Jesu Criste.'[22] Amen.

{Friday continues with the deposition and burial, and Saturday and Sunday with the resurrection, appearances of Christ to the disciples, and ascension.}

14 closing
15 drooped
16 yielded up
17 **Centurio**: apparently regarded as someone's name. See Matt. 27:54.
18 cry out
19 mother's
20 **passioun**: 'suffering'. This image of Christ with his body covered with wounds was a favourite subject for pictorial illustration and devotional contemplation.
21 pleasing
22 **the Apostle**: Paul, Gal. 6:14.

Thomas Hoccleve (1368–1426)

Thomas Hoccleve was born about 1368, and entered the office of the Privy Seal (part of the government administration) as a clerk in 1387. He stayed a Privy Seal scribe all his life: a formulary (set of *pro forma* letters to be used as models) survives that was written by him, and he also did freelance copying; many of his poems survive in fair copies that he made himself. He lived in London, always complaining of being poor through not having his salary paid on time, and always seeking patronage and advancement (his hopes of a benefice were dashed by his marriage). Early in his poetic career he wrote occasional and begging-poems, and did a translation of the *Epistre de Cupide* of the contemporary French poet Christine de Pizan which manages to make her defence of women against the false accusations of men sound slightly tongue-in-cheek. His time of greatest success was 1411–15. He wrote the *Regement of Princes* for the prince of Wales, and when Henry became king in 1413 Hoccleve was inspired to write a series of poems that are almost 'policy statements' for the new reign: these include a long and vehement diatribe against the Lollard Sir John Oldcastle when he escaped from imprisonment in 1415. Hoccleve suffered a mental breakdown in 1416, and drops from sight; late in life he tried to resuscitate his poetic career with an ad hoc collection of pieces (the '*Series*') that he may have hoped to present to Humphrey, duke of Gloucester. He died in 1426. Hoccleve may have known Chaucer personally, and his diction and metre are intimately Chaucerian, as are the fluent informality and conversational quality of his verse, especially in dialogue. But he adds to Chaucer's assumed air of earnest and eager bafflement, so successful in seducing the reader and disconcerting expectation, an edginess of his own, to create an unexpectedly subtle comic persona. The combination of the disaster-prone drama he makes of his personal life and the wit, resourcefulness and crisp, easy command of his verse makes him a much more endearing poet than Lydgate.

Minor Poems, ed. F.J. Furnivall and I. Gollancz, EETS, ES 61, 73 (rev. edn, J. Mitchell and I. Doyle, 1970); *Regement of Princes*, ed. F.J. Furnivall, EETS, ES 72 (1897); useful *Selections*, ed. M.C. Seymour (Oxford, 1981), and an important study by J.A. Burrow, 'Autobiographical Poetry in the Middle Ages: The Case of Thomas Hoccleve', *PBA* 68 (1982), 389–412; conference papers in C. Batt (ed.), *Essays on Thomas Hoccleve* (London, 1996).

La Male Regle de T. Hoccleve

Hoccleve's confession of his 'Badly Ruled Life' was written between 29 September 1405 and 26 March 1406 as a way of reminding Thomas Nevil, Lord Fournival, the sub-treasurer at the exchequer responsible for the payment of Hoccleve's annuity, that the instalment for Michaelmas 1405 had not been paid. It is a begging-poem, and the trick of it is to confess to his misspent youth and the wreck it has made of his health and purse, but to do so with such witty naiveté and such an affectation of bumbling good nature that the prospective patron will be tickled with vanity to be in a position to reward such an amusing and clever fellow. The poem is in Huntington Library MS HM 111 (a Hoccleve holograph), fols 19r–21r; it is included in Hammond (1927), pp. 60–6, and in Seymour, *Selections*, pp. 12–23; see Spearing (1985), pp. 110–20.

{He confesses to his neglect of the cardinal principles of good health and self-regulation, and describes vividly some of the ways he neglected them.}

Living it up in London

advised Reson me bad and redde as for the beste
at appropriate times To ete and drynke in tyme attemprely,
was inclined But wilful youthe nat obeie leste
advice, set no store Unto that reed, ne sette nat therby.
I take have of hem bothe outrageously
at inappropriate times And out of tyme – nat two yeer or three
But twenty wyntir past continuelly
dinner-table Excesse at borde hath leyd his knyf with me.

109 **take have**. Hoccleve's pentameter is syllabically very regular, but regularity is occasionally achieved by unidiomatic inversions of this kind or by 'wrenched stress' (e.g. 130).

The custume of my repleet abstinence, *customs-house*
My greedy mowth, receite of swich outrage, *receiver*
And hondes two, as woot my negligence,
Thus han me gyded and broght in servage
Of hire that werreieth every age – *harasses*
Seeknesse, I meene, riotoures whippe,
Habundantly that paieth me my wage,
So that me neithir daunce list ne skippe.

The outward signe of Bachus and his lure
That at his dore hangith day by day
Excitith folk to taaste of his moisture
So often that man can nat wel seyn nay.
For me, I seye I was enclyned ay
Withouten daunger thidir for to hye me, *Without being compelled*
But if swich charge upon my bak lay *Unless, responsibility*
That I moot it forbere as for a tyme,

Or but I were nakidly bystad *circumstanced*
By force of the penylees maladie;
For thanne in herte kowde I nat be glad
Ne lust had noon to Bachus hows to hie.
Fy! lak of coyn departith conpaignie,
And hevy purs with herte liberal
Qwenchith the thristy hete of hertes drie,
Wher chynchy herte hath therof but smal. *niggardly*

I dar nat telle how that the fressh repeir *coming into company*
Of Venus femel lusty children deere,
That so goodly, so shaply were and feir,
And so plesant of port and of maneere,
And feede cowden al a world with cheere,
And of atyr passyngly wel byseye, *good to look at*
At Poules Heed me maden ofte appeere
To talke of mirthe and to disporte and pleye.

Ther was sweet wyn ynow thurghout the hous
And wafres thikke, for this conpaignie *spiced cakes*
That I spak of been sumwhat likerous. *over-fond of fancy food*
Where as they mowe a draght of wyn espie, *may*
Sweet and in wirkynge hoot for the maistrie *above all others*
To warme a stomak with, therof they drank.
To suffre hem paie had been no courtesie:
That charge I took to wynne love and thank.

Of loves aart yit touchid I no deel: *no part*
I cowde nat, and eek it was no neede.
Had I a kus I was content ful weel,
Bettre than I wolde han be with the deede:

121 **signe of Bachus**. Taverns had a pole projecting out above the door with a 'bush' or garland on it. **lure** is the feathery knick-knack with which the falconer tempts back the hawk (as the bush lures the drinker).

133 Hoccleve's exclamation is comically inapt to his general protestation of remorse.

143 **Poules Heed**: 'Paul's Head', a tavern in the city just south of St Paul's.

know, doubt Theron can I but smal, it is no dreede.
When that men speke of it in my presence
burning coal For shame I wexe as reed as is the gleede.
serious meaning Now wole I torne ageyn to my sentence.

Of him that hauntith taverne of custume
At shorte wordes the profyt is this:
In double wyse his bagge it shal consume
And make his tonge speke of folk amis,
For in the cuppe seelden fownden is
That any wight his neigheburgh commendith.
Beholde and see what avantage is his
That God, his freend, and eek himself offendith.

But oon avantage in this cas I have:
I was so ferd with any man to fighte,
slander Cloos kepte I me, no man durste I deprave
whisperingly, aloud But rownyngly – I spak nothyng on highte.
my desire (to slander others) And yit my wil was good, if that I mighte
Without being prevented by For lettynge of my manly cowardyse,
weight That ay of strokes impressid the wighte,
So that I durste medlen in no wyse.

Wher was a gretter maister eek than I,
Or bet aqweyntid at Westmynstre Yate?
Among the taverneres namely
And cookes whan I cam eerly or late,
found fault, bill of purchase I pynchid nat at hem in myn acate
But paied hem as that they axe wolde;
always Wherfore I was the welcomere algate
And for a verray gentil man yholde.

And if it happid on the someres day
That I thus at the taverne hadde be,
Whan I departe sholde and go my way
wooed Hoom to the Privee Seel, so wowed me
disinclination (for work) Hete and unlust and superfluitee
To walke unto the brigge and take a boot
That nat durste I contrarie hem alle three
But dide as that they stired me, God woot.

(deep in mud) And in the wyntir, for the way was deep,
betook myself Unto the brigge I dressid me also
notice And ther the bootmen took upon me keep,
from long ago For they my riot kneewen fern ago.
With hem I was itugged to and fro,
So wel was him that I with wolde fare;

167–8 As with Chaucer, the comic pose is always likely to be dropped, to make space for some witty and unambiguously ironic observation.
188 **Hoom to the Privee Seel**. The office of the Privy Seal was in Westminster Hall, but the clerks did a lot of their work at Chester's Inn, their lodging in the Strand, just outside the city on the Westminster side.
190 **brigge**: here, 'wharf', i.e. St Paul's wharf, a short step from the tavern.

riotous living — For riot paieth largely everemo,
He styntith nevere til his purs be bare.

Othir than maistir callid was I nevere
company, in my hearing — Among this meynee in myn audience:
Me thoghte I was ymaad a man for evere.
So tikelid me that nyce reverence
That it me made largere of despense
intended to have — Than that I thoghte han been. O flaterie,
manner — The guyse of thy traiterous diligence
Is folk to mescheef haasten and to hie!

THE REGEMENT OF PRINCES

The *Regement of Princes* (*regiment*, 'right rule of conduct') is a poem in the genre of advice for princes (the 'Mirror for Princes') that was by now well known in Europe, having been established in the early fourteenth century in the *De regimine principum* of Giles of Rome (part-source for Hoccleve). Based on the pre-Macchiavellian assumption that the conduct of a prince was the moral life of his subjects writ large, such works exhorted princes to act in accordance with the highest moral principles, with exemplary stories to support the argument. Hoccleve wrote his translation for the prince of Wales, the future Henry V, in 1411–12. The prince was in a difficult situation during these last years of his father's reign, eager to take charge of an ailing administration but conscious of the power of his enemies (particularly archbishop Arundel, his father's principal advisor) and of the dangers of exceeding his authority. Whether he 'commissioned' the work or not, he saw what a good idea it was to be seen to be receptive to wholesome advice from a harmless nobody like Hoccleve (one of the clerks in the administration that the prince himself was running during his father's illness, 1410–11). He no doubt encouraged him and maybe gave some hints as to what he would like to see emphasized – his pious orthodoxy and fierceness against heretics especially, which were under scrutiny because of his ambiguous behaviour towards the Lollard Oldcastle, his former lieutenant in Wales. What Hoccleve got out of it was a measure of financial security for some years (his annuity, erratically paid in the past, began to be paid more promptly) and the opportunity of limited royal patronage for some short poems lauding the new reign. The *Regement* itself is run-of-the-mill, but is preceded by a Prologue well over half as long as the treatise proper (2107 of a total of 5463 lines) in which Hoccleve develops his own poetic persona (his simplicity and plain-spokenness give him added credibility as an advisor), works up some favourite themes, and practises some favourite techniques of self-narration and dialogue, in the process turning himself from a nobody into an obdurately unresigned somebody.

The *Regement* was very popular and survives in over 40 MSS, including two very early ones, BL MSS Arundel 38 and Harley 4866; the former is preferred here, with emendation from the latter, and also from BL MS Royal 17.D.vi. Recent studies of the poem by L. Scanlon, in Patterson (1990), pp. 216–47 (revised as a chapter of Scanlon [1994], pp. 298–322); D. Pearsall, in *Speculum* 69 (1994), 386–410; J. Simpson, in J. Boffey and P. King (eds), *London and Europe in the Later Middle Ages* (London, 1995), pp. 149–80.

The sleepless night and meeting with the old man

Musynge upon the restlees bysynesse
Whyche that thys troubly world hath ay on honde,
That other thyng than fruyt of byternesse
Ne yeldeth nought, as I can understonde,
At Chestres Yn ryght fast by the Stronde
As I lay in my bedde upon a nyght
Thought me berefte of slepe the force and myght.

THE REGEMENT OF PRINCES

5 **Chestres Yn**: Chester's Inn, on the Strand, where the clerks of the Privy Seal had their lodging and did much of their work. It was the London house of the bishop of Chester.

7 **Thought**, in the sense of 'anxious introspection, worry', is the villain of much of Hoccleve's poetry. It gives to the sleepless night of so many woebegone medieval lovers, and writers of dream-poems, a new edge of urgency and idiosyncratic meaning.

chap And many a day and nyght that wykkyd hyne
Had before vexid my pore goost
suffering So grevously that of anguysch and pyne
region No rycher man was nowhere in no coost.
Thys dar I seyn: may no wyght make his bost
That he wyth Thought was bet than I aqueyntyd,
made faint For to the deth he wel-nygh hath me feyntyd.

Bysily in my mynde I gan revolve
well-being The welthe unseur of every creature,
How lyghtly that Fortune it can dissolve
Whan that hyre lust that yt no lenger dure;
instability And of the brotelnesse of hyre nature
fear My tremblyng herte so grete gastnesse hadde
That my spyrites were of my lyf sadde.

Me fyl to mynde how that noght long agoo
royal Fortunes stroke doun threst estat real
Into meschef, and I tok heede also
Of many another lord that hadde a fal.
In mene estat eke sykernesse at al
saw Ne sawe I non, but I se at the laste
intended Where seuretee for to abyde hyr caste.

pitched In pore estat sche pighte hyr pavyloun
protect To kever here fro the storm of descendyng,
For sche knewe no lower descension
living Sauf onli deth, fro whyche no wyght levyng
Preserve Diffende hym may. And thus in my musyng
I destitute was of joye and good hope,
grasp And to myn ese nothyng coude I grope.

quickly For ryght as blyve ranne yt in my thought,
lose Thoghe pore I be, yit sumwhat lese I may.
Than demed I that seurte wolde nought
pleasure Wyth me abyde, yt ys not to here pay
There to sojourne as sche descende may.
unsure, livelihood And thus unsyker of my smal lyflode,
Thought leyde on me ful many an hevy lode.

I thought eke yf I into poverte crepe
Than am I entred into sikernesse;
But swyche seurete myght I ay waylle and wepe,
For poverte bredyth nought but hevynesse.
Alas, wher ys thys worldes stabilnesse?
Here up, here doun, heer honure, heer repreef,
Now hool, now seke, now bountee, now myscheef.

22–4 An allusion to the fall of Richard II in 1399, commonly referred to by Lancastrian poets as an accident of fortune and not the consequence of the new dynasty's scheming and ambition.
26 **mene estat**: middling or low estate, as distinct from that of lords. Hoccleve is working his way down the social hierarchy: **pore estat** (29) is lower still, and lowest.
29–33 The only stable kind of life, free from uncertainty, is poverty, where things cannot get worse. But, as Hoccleve goes on to remind us, poverty is already pretty bad.

And whan I hadde rollyd up and doun
waves Thys worldys stormy wawes in my mynde,
saw I sy wel povert was exclusioun
Of al welfare regnynge in mankynde,
And how in bokes thus I wryten fynde:
'The werste kynde of wrecchednesse ys
before this A man to han be weleful or thys.'

Alas, thoughte I, what sykernesse ys that
causes of annoyance To lyve ay seur of gref and of nusaunce?
What schal I do? Best ys I stryve not
weight Ageyn the peys of Fortunes balaunce,
fragile For wel I wot that hyre brotel constaunce
A wyght no whyle suffre can sojourne
state In o plyt; thus nat wyst I hou to turne.

For whanne a man weneth stonde most constant
Thanne ys he next to hys overthrowyng.
unstable So flyttyng ys sche and so variant
trust, smiling There ys no triste upon hyre fayre lawhyng:
After glad loke sche schapyth hyre to stynge.
changeableness I was adrad so of hyre gerynesse
That my lyf was but a dedly gladnesse.

This ylke nyght I walwyd to and fro
Sekyng Reste, but certeynly sche
Appeeryd nought, for Thoght, my cruel fo,
Chaced hadde hyre and sleepe away fro me.
And for I scholde not alone be,
Wakefulness Ageyn my lust Wach profrid hys servyse
And I admyttyd hym in hevy wyse.

So long a nyght ne felte I never non
As was that same to my jugement.
Who-so that thoughty ys, ys wo-begon;
The thoughtful wyght ys vessel of turment;
Ther nys no gref to hym equypolent.
digs down He graveth deppest of sikenesses alle:
Ful wo ys hym that in swyche thought ys falle!

What wyght that inly pensyf is, I trowe,
Hys most desyre ys to be solytarie.
That thys is soth, in my persone I knowe,
gnawing For evere whyl that fretynge adversarie
Myn herte made to hym trybutarie
In sowkynge of the fresschest of my blood,
grieve alone To sorwe soule me thoughte yt dede me good.

55–6 Hoccleve remembers *TC* III.1625–8, itself an echo of Boethius, *Consolation of Philosophy* II, prose 4, 5–9 (to which a marginal note in the MS refers).
60 **Fortunes balaunce**. Fortune, throughout this passage portrayed as the fickle goddess that rules man's life without regard to justness of desert (the medieval personification derives principally from Boethius), is here shown weighing man's destiny in a set of balances.

For the nature of hevynesse ys thys:
If yt habunde gretly in a wyght,
The place eischewyt he where-as joye ys, *avoids*
For joye and he not mow acorde aryght. *may*
As discordant as day ys unto nyght,
And honure adversarie is unto schame,
Is hevynesse so to joye and game.

Whan to the thoughtful wyght ys tolde a tale,
He herith yt as though he thennes were.
Hys hevy thoughtys hym so plukke and hale *drag*
Hydyr and thyder and hym greve and dere *injure*
That hys eres avayle hym nat a pere. *pear*
He understondeth nothyng what men seye,
So ben hys wyttys fer gon hem to pleye.

The smert of thought I by experience
Knowe as wel as any man doth lyvynge.
Hys frosty swoot and fyry hote fervence *sweat*
And troubly dremes, drempt al in wakynge,
My mazyd hed sleplees han of konnyng *understanding*
And wyt despoylyd, and so me be-japyd *played tricks on*
That after deth ful often have I gapyd. *yearned*

Passe over: whanne thys stormy nyght was gon
And day gan at my wyndowe in to prye,
I roos me up, for boote fonde I non
In myn unresty bed lengere to lye.
Into the felde I dressed me an hye *in haste*
And yn my woo I herte-depe gan wade,
As he that was bareyn of thoughtes glade.

By that I walkyd hadde a certeyne tyme,
Were yt an houre, I not, or more or lesse, *know not*
A pore old hore man cam walkyng by me, *grey-haired*
And seyde, 'Good day, syre, and God yow blesse!'
But I no word, for my seekly dystresse
Forbad myn eres usen hyre offyce,
For whyche thys old man helde me lewed and nyce,

Tyl he took hede to my drery chere
And to my deedly colour pale and wan.
Thanne thought he thus: 'Thys man that I se here
Al wrong ys wrestyd, by owght I se can.' *twisted*
He sterte unto me, and seyde, 'Sleepstow, man?
Awake!' and gan me schake wonder faste,
And with a sygh I answeered atte laste,

92 **hevynesse**. One of the special qualities of Hoccleve's writing is to convey not only an understanding of the debilitating anxieties of excessive introspection, but to make us *feel*, through his remorseless circling upon it, his obsessive gnawing on the bone of discontent, what it is like. These passages in the *Regement* seem to be forewarnings of the mental breakdown described in the *Complaint*.

105 **gon hem to pleye**. Cf. *Complaint*, 51.

121 Hoccleve has the knack of conveying spontaneity and immediacy, the very cadences of unrehearsed conversational narration, through trivial and meaningless details like this.

'A! who ys there?' 'I', quod thys olde greye,
'Am here', and he me tolde the manere
How he spak to me, as ye herd me seye.
'O man,' quoth I, 'for Cristis love dere,
If that thou wolt ought don at my preyere,
As go thy way, talke to me no more:
Thy wordes al anoyen me ful sore.

Go away 'Voyde fro me: me lyst no compaignye.
Encresse nought my gref: I have inow!'
suffer 'My sone, hast thou good lust thy sorwe drye
And mayst releved be? What man art thou?
according to my advice, benefit Wyrke after me: yt schal be for thy prow.
Thow n'art but yong and hast but lytel seen,
And ful seelde ys that yonge folk wyse ben.

'If that the lyke to ben esyd wel,
As suffre me wyth the to talke a whyle.
Art thou ought lettred?' 'Ye,' quod I, 'sumdel.'
Giles 'Blessyd be God! Than hope I, by seynt Gyle,
restore That God to the thy wyt schal reconsyle,
Whyche that me thynketh ys fer fro the went,
Thorgh the assaut of thy grevouse turment.

'Lettred folk han gretter discrecion
understand, what a man says And bet conceyve konne a mannes sawe,
And rather wol applye to reson
And from folye sonner hem withdrawe
Than he that nother can reson ne lawe
book-learning Ne lerned hath no maner letterure.
Plukke up thyn herte! I hope I schal the cure.'

'Cure, good man? Ye, thou art a fayre leche!
Cure thyself, that tremblest as thow gost,
For al thyn arte wol enden in thy speche.
It lyth not in thy power, pore gost,
To hele me; thow art as seke almost
show As I! First on thyself kythe thyn art,
is left And yf ought leve let me thanne have part.

'Go forth thy way, I the praye, or be stylle;
Thou dost me more anoye than thou wenest.
Thou art as ful of clap as ys a mylle;
annoyest Thou dost noght heer but grevest me and tenest.
Good man, thou wost but litel what thou menest.
harm In the lyth noght redresse my noysaunce –
But yit thou mayst be wel-wyllyd perchaunce.

139 **As** is often added like this before an imperative by Chaucer; it has no meaning, but is useful for metre.

155–60 This must be ironical.

173 Echoes Chaucer's *Book of the Duchess*, 1305: 'Thow wost ful lytel what thow menest.' The point of the echo is to contrast the politeness of the exchange between Chaucer and the man in black with Hoccleve's shocking impoliteness towards the old man (serving to emphasize how far sunk in depression he is).

It would have to be — 'It most be a gretter man of myght
Than that thou art that scholde me releve.'
'What, sone myn! thou felyst noght aryght:
To herkene me, what schal yt harme or greve?'
'Peter! good man, thogh we talke here tyl eve,
Al ys in veyne; thy myght may noght atteyne
To hele me, swych ys my woful peyne.'

'What that I may or can ne wost thou nought:
Boldly — Hardely, sone, tel on how hyt ys!'
burdensome — 'Man, at a word, yt ys encombrous thought
That causeth me thys sorwe and fare amys.'
'Now, sone, and yf ther nothying be but thys,
Do as I schal the seye, and thyn estat
unless — Amende I schal, but thou be obstinat,

'And wylfully rebelle and disobeye
teaching — And lyst not to my lore the conforme;
For in swyche cas what scholde I speke or seye
Or in my beste wyse the enforme?
reject, course of action — If thou it wayve, and take another forme
After thy chyldyssh mysruled conceyt,
Thou dost unto thyself harm and deceyt.'

{The old man assures Hoccleve that he really can help him, and warns that 'thought' can lead to evil, even to heresy. It was 'thought' that was the undoing of John Badby, the Lollard who was burnt in 1410 in the presence of the prince of Wales. The old man makes a quick check on Hoccleve's orthodoxy. He proceeds to a description of his own wild and misspent youth, confirming to Hoccleve that at least his advice comes from experience. Hoccleve apologizes for his rudeness and agrees to tell the old man what's wrong.}

Hoccleve's troubles

Whan I was set adown, as he me prayde,
'Telle on,' seyde he, 'how ys yt wyth the, how?'
And I began my tale, and thus I seyde:
'My lyge lord, the kyng whyche that ys now,
I fynde to me gracious inow.
God yelde him! he hath for my long servyse
Rewarded, appropriate — Guerdouned me in covenable wyse.

'In th'eschequer, he of hys special grace
Hath to me grauntyd an annuitee
Of twenti mark, whyle I have lyves space.
due sum — Myght I ay payd ben of that duetee,
It schold stonde wel inow wyth me.
these days — But payement ys hard to gete a-dayes,
puts, frights — And that me put in many foule affrayes.

180 **Peter! good man**, i.e. 'by St Peter'. MS Harley 4866 has in the margin (fol. 4r), in a seventeenth-century hand, 'Peter Goodman was perhaps som olde man wt whom hee consulted concerning his pension &c.'
816 **the kyng whyche that ys now**. Is this as respectful as it might be? The prince was not on good terms with his father, but observed every formal duty.
821–2 **an annuitee / Of twenti mark**. Hoccleve's annuity of £10, granted by Henry IV in 1399, was increased to £13.6s.8d. in 1409 (equivalent to 20 marks, which were not an accounting currency). With such an annuity, of course, Hoccleve was never anything like poor; but he had expensive tastes, ambitious plans, and rich friends (and his annuity had to be confirmed by the new king).

gets very difficult, before 'It goth ful streyte and scharpe or I yt have.
If I seur were of yit be satysfyed
Fro yeer to yere, thanne, so God me save,
My depe-rootyd gryef were remedyed
guided Souffysantly; but how I schal be gyed
Here-after, whan that I no lenger serve,
weighs me down with care, perish This hevyeth me, so that I wel-ny sterve.

'For syn that I now in myn age grene
hardly And beyng in court with gret peyne unneth
Am paid, in elde, and out of court, I wene
My purs for that may be a ferthyng schethe.
Lo, fader myn, thys dullyth me to deth.
Now God helpe al! for but he me socoure,
My futur yeres lyke ben to ben soure.

'Service, I wot wel, ys non heritage.
Whan I am out of court another day,
As I mot, whan upon me hastyth age
And that no lengure I laboure may,
cottage Unto my pore cote, yt ys no nay,
must withdraw I mot me drawe and myn fortune abyde
And suffre storm after the mery tyde.

demonstrate by experience 'There preve I schal the mutabilitee
Of thys wrecchyd worldes affeccion,
Whyche whan that youthe ys past begynneth flee.
pleasure Frendschype, adieu! Farwel, dileccion!
Age ys put out of youre proteccion;
Hys loke unlusty and hys impotence
Quencheth youre love and youre benevolence.

future misfortune 'That after-clappe in my mynde so deepe
Fixed I-fycchyd ys and hath swyche rote icaght
That al my joye and myrthe ys leyde to slepe:
loaded down My schyp ys wel-nye wyth dyspeyr ifraght.
They that nat conne lerned be ne taght
painful By swyche ensamples smerte as they han seyn
Me thynketh, certes, over-blynde been.

'Allas! I se reuthe and pitee exiled
Out of thys land; allas, compassioun!
Whan schol ye thre to us be reconsiled?
Youre absence ys my grevous passioun:
Resorte, I preye yow, to thys regioun.
O come ageyn! The lak of youre presence
Threatens Manaceth me to sterve in indigence.'

835 **in court**, i.e. in government employment, the court, or royal household, still being thought of as the national administration or 'civil service'.

841 Being a salaried government servant is not like having inherited wealth.

845 **pore cote**. Hoccleve was living in Chester's Inn in line 5, but now he seems to be anticipating living in a little hovel when he is no longer in government employ (or perhaps has already moved there, because of his marriage).

{Hoccleve digresses for a moment to lament the government's lack of provision for old soldiers. This reminds him again of his own situation.}

Hoccleve's hard life as a scribe

'In feyth, fader, my lyflode, byside
Th'annuitee of whyche above I tolde,
May nought excede yeerly in no tyde
sits around — Six marc – that syt to myn herte so colde,
Whan that I loke abouten and beholde
How scars yt ys if that that other faylle,
be glad — That I nat glade can but mourne and waylle.

'And as ferforth as I can deme or gesse
Whanne I at hom dwelle in my pore cote
slipping away of friends — I fynde schal as freendly slypernesse
rotted away — As tho men now doon whos frendschip is rote.
Nat wolde I rekke as mochel as a mote
Thogh I no more hadde of yeerly encrees
So that I myght ay payed be doutlees.

Two thirds — 'Two partes of my lyf and mochel more,
I seur am, past ben – I ne doute yt noght –
And yf that I scholde in my yeres hore
Forgo my duetee, that I have boght
Wyth my flessch and my blood, that hevy thoght
Whyche I drede ay schal fal, as I yt thynke,
quickly — Me hasteth blyve unto my pyttys brynke.

'Faylyng, fader, myn annuite,
'Hot-foot', trouble — Foot-hoot in me crepyth dysese and wo,
For they that han byfore knowen me,
If I lack the wherewithal — Faylyng good, me faile wol also:
Who no good has ys fer hys frendes fro.
(money) — In muck ys al thys worldes frendlyhede;
spirit — My goost ys wrapped in an hevy drede.

habit — 'If that I hadde of custome or thys tyme
Lyved in indigences wrecchednesse,
afflict — The lesse hereafter schuld yt syt by me;
But in myn age wrastle with Hardnesse,
That wyth hym stroglid nevere in grennesse
Of youth, that mutacion and chaunge
Anothir day me seme schulde al straunge.

being well-off — 'He that nevere knew the swetnesse of wele,
Thogh he yt lakke ay, lesse hym greve yt schal
many — Than hym that hath ben weleful yeerys fele,
felt — And in effect hath feeld no greef at al.
O povert! God me schylde fro thy fal.

935 **Six marc**. This was his salary, paid by the Keeper of the Privy Seal, as distinct from his annuity, a favour granted by the king.

937 **that other**, i.e. his annuity, when he ceases to be a government employee.

O deth, thy strook yit ys more agreable
To me than lyve a lyf so miserable.

'Six marc yeerly and no more than that,
Fader, to me me thynkyth ys ful lyte,
Consideryng how that I am nought
In housbondrye ilerned worth a myte. *farming*
Scarsely kowde I charre away the kyte *scare*
That me byreve wolde my pullaylle – *poultry*
And more axith housbondly governaylle. *management*

'Wyth plow can I nought medlen ne with harwe,
Ne woot nought what lond good ys for what corne;
And for to lade a cart or fylle a barwe, *load*
To whyche I never usyd was toforn,
My bakke unbuxum hath swyche thyng forsworn *unwilling*
At instaunce of wrytyng, hys werreour, *harasser*
That stowpyng hath hym spylt with hys labour. *broken*

'Many men, fader, weenen that wrytyng
No travaile ys, they hold hyt but a game: *hard work*
Art hath no foo but swyche folk unkunnyng. *Mastery of a craft, ignorant*
But who-so lyst dysporte hym in that same
Let hym continue and he schal fynde yt grame. *vexatious*
It ys wel gretter labour than yt semeth:
The blynde man of colours al wrong demeth.

'A wryter moot thre thynges to hym knytte,
And in tho may be noo disseveraunce:
Mynde, ye and hande, non may fro other flytte
But in hem moot be joynt continuance.
The mynde al hool wythouten variaunce
On ye and hand awayte moot alway
And they two eke on hym, yt ys no nay.

'Who-so schal wryte may nought holde a tale
Wyth hym and hym, ne synge thys ne that,
But al hys wyttys hoole grete and smale
There most appere and halden them therat. *must be present*
And syn he speke may ne synge nat,
But bothe two he nedys moot forbere,
Hys labour to hym ys th'elengere. *the more arduous*

'Thys artificers se I day by day *manual workers*
In the hootteste of al hyre bysynesse
Talken and singe and make game and play
And forth hyr labour passyth wyth gladnesse,
But we laboure in travayllous stilnesse:
We stowpe and stare upon the schepys skyn
And kepe must oure song and wordys in.

976–85 The declaration of incompetence at farming was part of a lettered man's *amour propre*. Cf. *PP* V.22–5, and Luke 16:3.

994 Proverbial.

'Wrytyng also doth grete anoyes three, *harms*
Of whyche ful fewe folkes taken hede,
Sauf we oureself, and thyse, lo, they be:
Stomak ys on, whom stowpyng out of drede *doubtless*
Annoyeth sore; and to oure bakkes nede
Moot yt be grevous; and the thrid, oure yen
Upon the whyte mochel sorwe dryen. *suffer*

'What man that thre and twenti yere and more
In wrytyng hath continuid, as have I,
I dar wel seyn it smertyth hym ful sore
In every veyn and place of hys body;
And yen most it greveth, trewely,
Of any craft that man can ymagyne:
Fader, in feyth, yt spilt hath wel-ny myne.

'Lo, fadir, tolde have I yow the substaunce
Of al my greef, so as that I can telle.
But wel I woot it hath ben greet penaunce
To yow wyth me so longe for to dwelle:
I am ryght sykyr it hath ben an helle,
Yow for to herken me thus jangle and clappe,
So lewdly in my termes I me wrappe. *particular forms of expression*

'But nathales tryste I your pacience
Receyve wol in gre my wordys alle, *graciously*
And what mys-seyd I have of negligence
Ye wole yt lete asyde slyppe and falle.
My fader dere, unto your grace I calle:
Ye woot my greef, now redeth me the beste,
Wythouten whom my gost can han no reste.'

'Now, sone myn, hastow al seyd and spoke
That the good lykyth?' 'Ye, fader, as now.' *for now*
'Sone, yf aught in thyn herte els be loke, *locked away*
Unloke yt blyve! Com of, what seystow?'
'Fader, I can no more telle yow
Than I before spoken have and seyd.'
'A Goddes half, sone, I am wel apayed.' *In God's name, satisfied*

{The old man tells Hoccleve not to worry so much about money; poverty is really a blessing. Hoccleve, unconvinced, laments how he lost his chance of a benefice by marrying, but the old man congratulates him on marrying for love and not money, with examples of the bad results of the latter. Hoccleve continues to moan about money, so the old man advises him to apply to the generosity of prince Henry by writing something for him, something like a treatise on the duties of a prince. Hoccleve agrees, and begins with a Proem in which he addresses the prince and explains his purpose.}

Chaucer is dead

Also byseche I that the altitude
Of your estat, thogh that thys pamfilet
Non ordre holde ne in hym include,

Nat greved be, for I can do no bet.
Anothir day, whan wyt and I be met –
Whyche longe ys to! – and han us freendly kyst,
Reveal — Discovere I wol that now ys nat wyst.

Nathales, swyche as ys my smal connyng,
as true — Wyth also trewe an herte I wol yt oute
As tho two dide, or evere clerk lyfynge.
But tremblynge ys my spyrit, out of doute,
That to parforme that I am aboute.
solid — Allas! the stuf of sad intelligence
Me faillyth to speke in so hye presence.

book-learning — Symple is my goost and scars my letterure
Unto your excellence for to write
in the hands of chance — Myn inward love, and yit in aventure
know — Wil I me putte, thogh I can but lyte.
make free — My dere mayster – God hys soule quyte! –
And fadir, Chaucer, fayn wolde han me taght,
But I was dul, and lerned lyte or naght.

Alas! my worthy mayster honorable,
Thys landes verray tresour and rychesse,
Deth, by thy deth, hath harme irreparable
vengeful harshness — Unto us don; hir vengeable duresse
Despoyled hath this land of the swetnesse
(Cicero) — Of rethorik, for unto Tullius
Was never man so lyk amonges us.

heir — Also, who was heir in philosophye
To Aristotle in our tonge but thou?
The steppes of Virgile in poesie
Thow filwedist eek. Men wot wel inow
That combre-world that thee, my mayster, slow.
Wolde I slayn were! Deth was to hastyf
rob — To renne on the and reve the thy lyf.

Deth hath but smal consideracion
Unto the vertuous, I have espyed –
proof of experience — No more, as schewyth the probacion,
villain, notorious — Than to a vycyous mayster losel, tried
heap (of such), mastered (by) — Among an heep. Every man ys maystried
Wyth here, as wel the poore as ys the ryche:
Leered and lewde eek standen al yliche.

2068 **tho two**, presumably 'wyt and I'.
2078 This line does indeed suggest that Hoccleve knew Chaucer personally; and elsewhere, the affectionate tone of his remembrance is different from Lydgate's tributes.
2084–90 Chaucer is praised for his command of rhetoric, philosophy and poetry, and compared with the great classical exponents of each. **Despoyled hath this land**. Chaucer is here spoken of as a national poet, as later (4978, below) he will be spoken of as the founder of the English literary language. These claims have become part of the Chaucer inheritance or legend, but it is important to recognize how Hoccleve (and Lydgate) were encouraged to make such claims by a regime anxious to encourage the English language as a form of national identity (Henry V was the first king since Anglo-Saxon times to use English in official correspondence) and to elevate Chaucer to the position of a great English national poet. **swetnesse / Of rethorik**. The art of rhetoric was associated with poetic composition and its figures of speech often spoken of as 'colours' of rhetoric (see FrankT 723–5) or forms of sugar and sweetness. One can detect in these stanzas something of Hoccleve's effort to show his own capacities for the 'high style' of rhetoric.
2091 **combre-world**: 'encumbrance to the world' (from *TC* IV.279).
2099 **Wyth here**. Unusually, Death is personified as a woman.

She myghte han taried hir vengeaunce a while
Til that sum man had egal to the be.
Nay, let be that! She knewe wel that thys ile
May nevere man forth brenge lyk to the,
And hyre office nedes do moot sche:
God bade hir soo, I truste, as for thi beste.
O maister, maister, God thy soule reste!

{Hoccleve proceeds now to his translation, from different sources, of his treatise on princely conduct. Various virtues are recommended – truth, justice, mercy, etc. – including wisdom in taking counsel, important enough in the context of his poem for Hoccleve to be prompted again to speak of Chaucer.}

A way to remember Chaucer

The first findere of our fayre langage
written on a similar matter Hath seyde in caas semblable, and othyr moo,
So hyly wel that yt ys my dotage
For to expresse or touche ony of thoo.
Allas! my fader fro the world ys goo,
My worthy mayster Chaucer, hym I mene.
Be thow advokett for hym, hevenes quene.

As thou wel knowyst, O blessyd Virgine,
Wyth lovyng herte and hye devocioun
In thyn honour he wroot ful many a lyne.
influence in promoting the cause O now thyn help and thy promocioun!
To God thy sone make a mocioun
How he thi servaunt was, mayden Marie,
(the love of Chaucer) And lat his love floure and fructifie.

extinguished Althogh his lyfe be queynt, the resemblaunce
Of him hath in me so fressh lyflynesse
That to putte othir men in remembraunce
Of his persone I have heere his lyknesse
Caused to be made Do make, to this ende, in sothfastnesse,
That thei that have of him lost thought and mynde
By this peynture may ageyn him fynde.

The ymages that in the chirche been
Maken folk thenke on God and on his seyntes
Whan the ymages thei beholden and seen,
not seeing them Where oft unsyte of hem causith restreyntes
Of thoughtes gode. Whan a thing depeynt is

2103 **Nay, let be that!** Hoccleve allows us to understand that he himself would not be an impossible candidate to be Chaucer's heir.
4979 **and othyr moo**: 'and other (writers) besides'. Being receptive to good advice is the theme of the *Tale of Melibee* (Chaucer's own tale) in the *CT*.
4985 The Prioress's Tale and Second Nun's Tale would come to mind, as well as the *ABC* poem to the Virgin.
4992–8 Hoccleve clearly intends a portrait of Chaucer to stand beside this stanza. In Arundel 38 the page that contained it has been cut out, but Harley 4866 retains the famous three-quarter-length marginal picture of Chaucer (frequently reproduced, as in Pearsall, *Life of Geoffrey Chaucer*; the resemblance to the equestrian portrait of Chaucer in the Ellesmere MS of the *CT* is striking). Two other MSS of the *Regement* have pictures. In addition to the purposes Hoccleve explains, the portrait also 'iconizes' Chaucer as the founding father of English national poetry, associating with him in this project both Hoccleve and prince Henry.
4999–5005 The comparison of the portrait of Chaucer to the 'remembrance' of holy figures and saints in church images is audacious, a beginning, literally, for 'Chaucer-worship'.

carved Or entailed, if men take of it heede,
Thoght of the lyknesse it wil in hym breede.

Yit some holden oppynyoun and sey
That none ymages schuld imaked be.
Thei erren foule and goon out of the wey!
Of trouth have thei scant sensibilite.
Passe over that! Now blessid Trinite,
Uppon my maystres soule mercy have;
For him, Lady, eke thi mercy I crave.

More othir thing wolde I fayne speke and touche
Heere in this booke, but suche is my dulnesse,
For that al voyde and empty is my pouche,
pleasure in the job, quenched That al my lust is queynt with hevynesse,
And hevy spirit comaundith stilnesse.
When I have spoken And have I spoke of pees I schal be stille.
God sende us pees, if that it be his wille.

THE 'SERIES'

This is the name given to a sequence of five poetic pieces that Hoccleve put together around 1421–2 in the hope of attracting a patron. It begins with a *Complaint* about the way he has been shunned since his illness (the mental breakdown of 1416), despite his complete recovery, and continues with a *Dialogue with a Friend*, in which Hoccleve's future poetic prospects are discussed, and his hope of enrolling Humphrey of Gloucester as a patron. Examples of his poetic skill follow: the *Tale of Jereslaus's Wife*, a story of a faithful and much put-upon woman, somewhat resembling the story of Constance in Chaucer's Man of Law's Tale; a versified treatise, *How to Learn to Die* (from the same programme of discipline as the *Dance Macabre*); and the *Tale of Jonathas*, a story (to balance the first) of a man deceived by a false woman. The *'Series'* survives, whole or part, in eight MSS, including one copied by Hoccleve himself (Durham UL MS Cosin V.iii.9) with a dedication to the countess of Westmorland; but the first quire is missing (a copy by John Stow, the sixteenth-century antiquary, fills its place), and the extracts below are taken from Bodl.MS Arch.Selden supra 53, with emendations from the Durham MS. There are studies by J. Burrow, 'Hoccleve's *Series*: Experience and Books', in Yeager (1984), pp. 259–73, and by J. Simpson, 'Madness and Texts: Hoccleve's *Series*', in Boffey and Cowen (1991), pp. 15–29.

The Complaint of Hoccleve

Hoccleve suffered some kind of mental breakdown in 1416, and he writes about it here with affecting intimacy. 'Madness' usually appears in medieval writing in the service of some moral or narrative theme (see P.B.R. Doob, *Nebuchadnezzar's Children: Conventions of Madness in ME Literature* [New Haven, 1974]): the madness inflicted by God on the sinful (Nebuchadnezzar), the madness of thwarted love (Lancelot, Tristan), the 'madness' of those who have no care of the world (Langland's 'lunatyk lollares'). It is rarely observed, least of all by the sufferer, as closely as it is here. It is a mark of Hoccleve's desperate honesty that he chooses at all to speak of such a subject, though he has of course a consolatory and self-serving moral to draw at the end. There are editions of the *Complaint* by J. Burrow in *English Verse 1300–1500* (London, 1977), pp. 265–80 (ll. 1–308), and in Seymour, *Selections*, pp. 75–87.

5006–12 Those who **erren foule** are the Lollards, who considered the presence of such images to be an encouragement to idolatry. Their belief was declared heretical, and made one of the points of interrogation in Lollard inquisitions, as with William Thorpe (see above). Hoccleve conveniently reminds us of his own and the prince's strict and pious orthodoxy.

autumn, gathered in Aftir that hervest inned had hise sheves
Michaelmas (29 September) And that the broun sesoun of Mihelmesse
Was come, and gan the trees robbe of her leves
That grene had ben and in lusty freisshenesse,
And hem into colour of yelownesse
dyed Had died and doun throwen undir foote,
That chaunge sanke into myn herte roote,

For freisshly broughte it to my remembraunce
That stablenesse in this worlde is ther noon:
without Ther is nothing but chaunge and variaunce.
well provided Howe welthi a man be or wel-begoon,
Endure it shal not, he shal it forgoon.
thrust Deeth undir foote shal him thriste adoun:
That is every wightes conclucioun,

avoid Whiche for to weyve is in no mannes myght,
Howe riche he be, stronge, lusty, freissh and gay.
And in the ende of Novembre uppon a night,
Sighynge sore as I in my bed lay,
For this and othir thoughtis wiche many a day
Byforne I tooke, sleep cam noon in myn ye,
So vexid me the thoughtful maladie.

saw I sy wel sithin I with siknesse last
Was scourgid, cloudy hath bene the favour
That shoon on me ful bright in times past.
The sunne abated and the dirke shour
poured, misery Hilded doun right on me and in langour
Me made swymme, so that my spirite
To lyve no lust had ne no delite.

swelled The greef aboute myn herte so sore swal
swelled, this way and that And bolned evere to and to so sore
That nedis oute I muste therwithal.
I thoughte I nolde kepe it cloos no more,
leave, grow old and grey Ne lete it in me for to eelde and hore;
And for to preve I cam of a womman,
burst I braste oute on the morwe and thus bigan.

Here endith my prolog and folwith my compleinte

Almyghty God, as liketh his goodnesse,
Vesiteth folke alday, as men may se,
With los of good and bodily sikenesse,
And amonge othir he foryat not me –
Witnesse uppon the wilde infirmite
Wiche that I hadde, as many a man wel knewe,
And wiche me oute of mysilfe caste and threwe.

1–6 The autumn-opening, intended to evoke the cheerful spring-opening of the GP, prepares us for a melancholy poem.
23 **cloudy**. Hoccleve recalls Chaucer's image of Fortune covering her bright face with a cloud (*CT* VII.2766).
34 i.e. to prove that he is a proper human being.

It was so knowen to the peple and kouthe
secret — That counseil was it noon ne not be might.
Howe it with me stood was in every mannes mouthe,
And that ful sore my frendis affright.
promised — They for myn helthe pilgrimages hight
And soughte hem, somme on hors and somme on foote –
cure — God yelde it hem! – to gete me my boote.

But although the substaunce of my memorie
Wente to pleie as for a certein space,
Yit the lorde of vertue, the kyng of glorie,
Of his highe myght and his benigne grace
Made it for to retourne into the place
Whens it came, which at Alle Halwe-messe
Was five yeere, neither more no lesse.

And evere sithin, thankid be God oure lord
Of his good and gracious reconsiliacioun,
My wit and I have bene of suche acord
before — As we were or the alteracioun
Of it was; but by my savacioun,
Sith that time have I be sore sette on fire
'martyrdom' — And lyved in greet turment and martire.

For though that my wit were hoom come ayein,
Men wolde it not so undirstonde or take.
With me to dele hadden they disdein:
A rietous persone I was, and forsake.
shaken off — Min oolde frendshipe was al overshake;
have converse — No wight with me list make daliaunce;
The worlde me made a straunge countinaunce,

Whiche that myn herte sore gan to tourment,
For ofte whanne I in Westmynstir Halle
And eke in Londoun amonge the prees went,
saw the faces fall, grow pale — I sy the chere abaten and apalle
Of hem that weren wonte me for to calle
To companie; her heed they caste awry
as if — Whanne I hem mette, as they not me sy.

As seide is in the Sauter might I sey:
'They that me sy fledden awey fro me'.
Foryeten I was, al oute of mynde awey,
affection — As he that deed was from hertis cherte.
To a lost vessel lickned mighte I be,

51 **Wente to pleie**: 'went to amuse itself elsewhere'. A placidly wry retrospect on the experience of self-forgetting. Cf. *Regement*, 105.

55 **Alle Halwe-messe**: 'All-Hallows-mass', i.e. All Saints' Day (1 November). Since his breakdown was in 1416, Hoccleve must be writing in 1421 at the end of November (see l. 17).

72 **Westmynstir Halle**: where the Privy Seal office was.

78 **the Sauter**. Ps. 31:11–12: 'I am the scorn of all my adversaries, a horror to my neighbours, an object of dread to my acquaintances; those who see me in the street flee from me. [12] I have passed out of mind like one who is dead; I have become like a broken (Vg. *perditum*, cf. 82 below) vessel.' One sees here, not the source of Hoccleve's experience, but the inspiration of much of the language he uses to talk about it.

82 **a lost vessel**: not a boat, but a household vessel, left lying unnoticed as people go about their business.

For manie a wight aboute me dwelling
Herde I me blame and putte in dispreisyng.

about me — Thus spake manie oone and seide by me,
'Although from him his siiknesse savage
Withdrawen and passed as for a time be,
Return, especially — Resorte it wole, namely in suche age
As he is of.' And thanne my visage
Bigan to glowe for the woo and fere:
unbeknown to them — Tho wordis, hem unwar, cam to myn eere.

excessive — 'Whanne passinge hete is,' quod thei, 'trustith this,
Assaile him wole ayein that maladie.'
And yit, parde, thei token hem amis:
Noon effecte at al took her prophecie.
Manie someris bene past sithen remedie
Of that God of his grace me purveide.
turned out — Thankid be God, it shoop not as thei seide.

whatever men — What falle shal, what men so deme or gesse,
To him that woot every hertis secree
ignorance — Reserved is. It is a lewidnesse
Men wiser hem pretende than thei be,
And no wight knowith, be it he or she,
Whom, howe ne whanne God wole him vesite:
little expect it — It happith often whanne men wene it lite.

thought — Somtime I wende as lite as any man
For to han falle into that wildenesse;
But God whanne him liste may, wole and can
Helthe withdrawe and sende a wight siiknesse.
certainty — Though man be wel this day, no sikernesse
promised — To hym behighte is that it shal endure.
God hurte nowe can, and nowe hele and cure.

smites — He suffrith longe but at the laste he smit:
Whanne that a man is in prosperite,
wise thing — To drede a falle comynge it is a wit.
Who-so that taketh hede ofte may se
This worldis chaunge and mutabilite
In sondry wise – howe, nedith not expresse:
To my mater streite wole I me dresse.

Men seiden I loked as a wilde steer,
And that was the way — And so my looke aboute I gan to throwe.
bore — Min heed to hie, anothir seide, I beer:
capricious — 'Ful bukkissh is his brayn, wel may I trowe.'
And seide the thridde – and apt is in the rowe
uninformed opinion — To site of hem that a resounles reed
stable seriousness — Can yeve – 'No sadnesse is in his heed.'

94 **token hem amis**: 'mistook themselves' (i.e. were mistaken).
124–6 Punctuated here as Hoccleve's sardonic aside on his third 'friend', this could be part of that friend's comment.

way of walking Chaunged had I my pas, somme seiden eke,
roe-deer For here and there forthe stirte I as a roo,
No staying still, no resting Noon abood, noon areest, but al brain-seke.
Another spake and of me seide also,
My feet weren ay wavynge to and fro
Whanne that I stonde shulde and with men talke,
cranny And that myn yen soughten every halke.

I leide an eere ay to as I by wente
deliberated And herde al, and thus in myn herte I caste:
'Of longe abidinge here I may me repente;
Lest that of hastinesse I at the laste
Answere amys, beste is hens hie faste,
conduct myself For if I in this prees amys me gye,
To harme wole it me turne and to folie.'

And this I demed wel and knewe wel eke:
What-so that evere I shulde answere or seie
They wolden not han holde it worth a leke.
Wherefore, as if Forwhy, as I had lost my tunges keie,
went on my way Kepte I me cloos and trussid me my weie
woebegone Droupinge and hevy and al woo-bistaad.
Smal cause hadde I, me thoughte, to be glad.

My spirites labouriden evere ful bisily
put on an assumed To peinte countenaunce, chere and look,
For that men spake of me so wondringly,
And for the verry shame and feer I qwook.
Though myn herte hadde be dippid in the brook
quite wet enough, sweat It weet and moist was ynow of my swoot,
Wiche was nowe frosty colde, nowe firy hoot.

And in my chaumbre at home whanne that I was
Mysilfe aloone, I in this wise wrought:
hurried I streite unto my mirrour and my glas
To loke howe that me of my chere thought,
If any othir were it than it ought,
For fain wolde I, if it had not bene right,
to the best of my knowledge Amendid it to my kunnynge and myght.

leap Many a saute made I to this mirrour,
Thinking, 'If that I looke in this manere
Amonge folke as I nowe do, noon errour
Of suspecte look may in my face appere.
This countinaunce, I am sure, and this chere,
If I it forthe use, is nothing reprevable
ways of understanding To hem that han conceitis resonable.'

133 He wouldn't look straight at people when they were talking to him.
157 **my mirrour**. Hoccleve's inspection of his own countenance in the mirror, to see how he might look to others, and how he might pull faces that would look convincingly sane, is a sign of unusual self-consciousness about 'madness' and 'identity' and the manner of their fashioning through the perceptions of others; it is also a scene of considerable comic pathos.
162–75 Like Chaucer, in *TC* (e.g. II.703–805), Hoccleve uses soliloquy to present opposing internal arguments.

And therwithal I thoughte thus anoon:
'Men in her owne cas bene blinde alday,
As I have herde seie manie a day agoon,
And in that same plite I stonde may. *plight*
Howe shal I do? Wiche is the beste way
My troublid spirit for to bringe in rest?
If I wiste howe, fain wolde I do the best.'

Sithen I recovered was, have I ful ofte
Cause had of anger and inpacience,
Where I borne have it esily and softe,
Suffringe wronge be done to me and offence
And not answerid ayen but kepte scilence,
Leste that men of me deme wolde and sein,
'Se howe this man is fallen in ayein.'

As that I oones fro Westminstir cam,
Vexid ful grevously with thoughtful hete, *fever of anguished thought*
Thus thoughte I: 'A greet fool I am
This pavyment a-daies thus to bete *daily*
And in and oute laboure faste and swete, *sweat*
Wondringe and hevinesse to purchace,
Sithen I stonde out of al favour and grace.'

And thane thoughte I on that othir side:
'If that I not be sen amonge the prees, *crowd of people*
Men deme wole that I myn heed hide
And am werse than I am, it is no lees.' *lie (untruth)*
O Lorde, so my spirit was restelees!
I soughte reste and I not it fonde,
But ay was trouble redy at myn honde.

[He continues to complain how unreasonable people are not to see that he has regained his senses. Life hardly seems worth living. But he reads a book of consolation, and grows to recognize God's will in all his tribulations. (The 'book of consolation' has been identified as the De lamentatione animae dolentis *of Isidore of Seville: see A.G. Rigg, in* Speculum *45 [1970], 564–74.)]*

Dialogue with a Friend

And, endid my Compleinte in this manere,
Oon knockid at my chaunbre dore sore
And criede alowde, 'Howe, Hoccleve! art thou here?
Open thi dore, me thinketh it ful yore
Sithen I the sy. What, man! for Goddis ore *mercy*
Come oute, for this quarter I not the sy,
By ought I woote.' And oute to hym cam I.

This man was my good frende of fern agoon *long ago*
That I speke of, and thus he to me seide:

178 **borne have**. A particularly awkward Hocclevian inversion – and seemingly quite unnecessary metrically.

'Thomas, as thou me lovest, telle anoon
What didist thou whanne I knockede and leide
So faste uppon thi dore.' And I obeide
Unto his wil: 'Come in,' quod I, 'and see.'
And so he dide, he streit wente in with me.

obscure To my good frende not thoughte I to make it queinte
conceal Ne my labour from him to hide or leine,
And right anoon I redde hym my Compleinte;
Since And that done, thus he seide, 'Sin we tweine
Ben here, and no mo folke, for Goddis peine,
Thomas, suffre me speke and be not wrooth,
For the to offende were me ful looth.

'That I shal seie shal be of good entente:
Hast thou maad this Compleint forth to goo
Amonge the peple?' 'Ye, frende, so I mente;
be careful What ellis?' 'Nay, Thomas, war, do not so!
desist If thou be wiis, of that mater, ho!
Reherse thou it not ne it awake;
Kepe al that cloos for thin honoures sake.

'Howe it stood with the leide is al aslepe;
Men han foryete it, it is oute of mynde.
do not care for That thou touche therof I not ne kepe.
advise Lat be – that reede I, for I can not finde
O man to speke of it in as good a kinde.
before As thou hast stonde amonge men or this day,
Stondist thou nowe.' 'A, nay,' quod I, 'nay, nay!

'Though I be lewide, I not so ferforthe dote;
I woote what men han seide and seien of me;
Her wordis have I not as yit forgote.
But greet mervaile have I of yow, that ye
instructed No bet of my Compleint avisid be,
Sithen, ma fey, I not redde it unto yow
So longe agoon, for it was but right now.

'If ye took hede, it maketh mencioun
hearing That men of me speke in myn audience
gloomily Ful hevily. Of youre entencioun
I thanke you, for of benevolence
opinion Woote I ful wel procedeth youre sentence;
But certis, good frende, that thing that I heere
Can I witnesse and unto it refeere.

17 **I redde hym my Compleinte**. A striking reminder that what we have been reading was a piece of writing and not, as we thought ('braste oute', 35), a conventionally 'written' report of a spontaneous utterance, in the familiar literary genre of the 'Complaint' (like Cresseid's Complaint, in Henryson's *Testament*, below). The writing in the original manuscript, furthermore, was the poet's own. Such self-conscious cross-referencing between the written and the spoken has a very modern air to it.

'And where-as that ye me counseile and rede
That for myn honour shulde I by no weie
mention Anything mynge or touche of my wildhede,
I unto that answere thus and seie:
weigh heavily Of Goddis strook, howe-so it peise or weie,
Ought no man to thinke repreef or shame;
His chastisinge hurtith no mannes name.

'Anothir thing ther meveth me also:
Sithen my seeknesse sprad was so wide
That men knewe wel howe it stood with me tho,
So wolde I nowe uppon that othir side
That it were known Wist were howe oure lorde Jesu, wich is gide
To al releef and may alle hertis cure,
Releved hath me, sinful creature.

'Had I be for an homicide iknowe
Or an extorcioner or a robbour,
known Or for a coin-clipper as wide yblowe
As was my seeknesse, or a werriour
Ayen the feith, or a false maintenour
(one who perverts the law) Of causes, though I had amendid me,
mentioned, foolishness Hem to han mynged had ben nicite.

'And whi? for tho proceden of freelte
Of man – himsilfe he brewith alle tho;
For sithen God to man yove hath liberte,
Wiche chese may for to do wel or no,
If he myschese he is his owene foo;
And to reherse his gilte wich him accusith
Honour seith nay, there he scilence excusith.

'But this is al another caas sothly:
This was the strook of God, he yaf me this;
And sithen he hath withdrawe it curteisly,
obliged Am I not holden tell it out? O yis!
Unless But if God had this thanke it were amis.
In feith, frende, make I thenke an open shrifte
And hide not what I had of his yifte.

'If that a leeche curid had me so –
As they lacken alle that science and might –
A name he shulde han had for everemo,
What cure he had doon to so seek a wight –
And yit my purs he wolde have made ful light!
But curteis Jesu of his grace pacient
Axith not but of gilte amendement.

'The benefice of God not hid be sholde.
Sithen of myn heele he yaf me the triacle
It to confesse and thanke hym am I holde,
For he in me hath shewid his miracle.
His visitacioun is a spectacle

In wiche that I biholde may and se,
Bet than I dide, howe greet a lord is he.'

{There follows a diatribe against coin-clipping, a practice that Hoccleve inveighs against more than once, but that comes in oddly here. The discussion then returns to his poetic plans for the future.}

John Lydgate (1371–1449)

John Lydgate was born in the village of Lydgate, in Suffolk, in 1371 and entered the nearby Benedictine abbey at Bury St Edmund's while still a boy. He was educated there, made his profession in 1387, and was ordained priest in 1397. He spent some years around 1406–8 studying at Gloucester College, the Benedictine house at Oxford. Here he became acquainted with the prince of Wales, who gave him his first major commission, the *Troy-Book*, in 1412. Lydgate had already, with Chaucer as his model, written a good deal of poetry, probably mostly of a conventionally courtly and allegorical nature (including perhaps two courtly vision-poems, *The Complaint of the Black Knight* and *The Temple of Glass*), but the patronage of the prince (who succeeded as Henry V in 1413) launched him on a career as a Lancastrian poet-propagandist, as well as a prolific translator and consolidator of the Chaucerian tradition. After the completion of the 30,000-line *Troy-Book* in 1420, he was very active in the writing of court-poems for ceremonial occasions, mummings (dumb-shows with verse commentary) for court and city, a 26,000-line translation of the French religious allegory of the *Pilgrimage of the Life of Man* (1426–8), coronation poems for the young Henry VI (1429), who had succeeded as an infant in 1422, as well as occasional poems of every kind for court and city patrons and devotional poems for pious patronesses. During this decade he spent much time out of the cloister. The 1430s saw him back at Bury on a permanent basis, much occupied from 1431 to 1438 on his vast 36,000-line translation of *The Fall of Princes* and at other times on the long saints' lives of *St Edmund* and *St Alban*. He died in 1449.

Lydgate has claims to be the most prolific poet in the English language, with some 140,000 lines of verse attributed to him. He was much admired in his day, but his verbosity, the inflation of his diction, the uneasiness of his syntax, and the unevenness of his metre are obstacles to pleasure, while the comparison with Chaucer, whom he imitates everywhere and even comically attempts to outdo, is inevitably painful. He has qualities – a certain massive stateliness in the long poems, an occasional neatness of touch in the shorter poems, and a capacity to rise to the occasion in poems of devotional celebration and rhapsody – but his main claim on us is the conveniently ample way in which he stands as a representative of nearly every important late medieval tradition of thinking and writing, and of the exhaustions, self-contradictions and transformations latent or potential in those traditions. Late medieval England can be understood through Lydgate – albeit in ways that Chaucer obliges us to unlearn.

Editions of the major works will be noted below. There are studies of the life and works by W.F. Schirmer, *John Lydgate: A Study in the Culture of the XVth Century*, trans. Ann E. Keep (London, 1961), and by D. Pearsall, *John Lydgate* (London, 1970), and extracts with valuable apparatus in Hammond (1927), pp. 77–187; see also D. Pearsall, *John Lydgate: A Bio-bibliography* (Victoria, BC, 1997).

The Troy-Book

The *Troy-Book* was begun in 1412 and finished in 1420. It was written at the request of Henry V, when prince of Wales, so that the greatest epic story of antiquity should be registered in English, as it was in Latin and French (Prol. 115). The commission was thus an early witness to Henry's desire to encourage the use of the English language as a stimulus to the sense of English nationhood, embodied in himself. Lydgate took as his source the Latin prose *Historia destructionis Troiae* of Guido della Colonna (1287), and thus outdid Chaucer on two counts: by treating the whole medieval story of Troy (see C.D. Benson, *The Medieval History of Troy in Middle English Literature* [Cambridge, 1980]), from the visit to Troy of Jason and the Argonauts to the arrival home of Ulysses, and not just an episode, as in *Troilus and Criseyde*; and by working from a Latin 'auctoritee' and not from a mere Italian romance. Lydgate says that Henry's other motive in commissioning the work was so that the prowess of old chivalry might be remembered and be an example to the present (Prol. 75–89). If this was Henry's hope, he was ill-advised to choose the Troy-story, or Lydgate to tell it, for the story is one of murderous intrigues and disasters from beginning to end. Lydgate finds himself much at home here, lavishly amplifying Guido's rhetoric and endlessly lamenting the cruelty and treachery of human beings, the mutability of worldly joy, the fickleness of Fortune, the transience of fame, even with a sort of fierce glee at the downfall of a pagan civilization (cf. *TC* V.1849–53). The passage below, new in Lydgate, is the climax of a succession of lamentations in Book 4.

Twenty MSS, including some finely illustrated and decorated, and two early prints; ed. H. Bergen, 4 vols, EETS, ES 97, 103, 106, 126 (1906–20), from BL MS Cotton Augustus A.iv.

Lamentation upon the fall of Troy (IV.7036–85)

Now farewel Troye, farwel for everemore!
too Farwel, allas, to cruel was thi fal!
Of the no more now I write shal.
For thi sake, in sothe, whan I take hede,
Of inward wo myn herte I fele blede,
And whan that I remembre in my thought
By ruyne how thou art brought to nought,
That whilom were so noble and so riche
That in this world I trowe noon was liche
fully equal Nor perigal, to speken of fairnesse,
To speke of knyghthod and of worthinesse,
As clerkes seien that thi bildyng knewe,
That al the world oughte for to rewe
On thi pitous waste walles wylde,
Whilom so rial whan men gan to bilde
Thin touris highe, and kyng Priamus
The first began, most riche and glorious,
royal seat, (Troy) And sette his se in noble Ylyoun.
O, who can write a lamentacioun
appropriate Convenient, O Troye, for thi sake?
Or who can now wepe or sorwe make,
Thi grete meschef to compleyne and crie?
Certis, I trowe, nat olde Jeremye,
That so bewepte the captivite
Of thilke noble rial chefe cite
its Jerusalem, and his destructioun,
With al the hole transmygracioun
Of the Jewes; nor thou, Ezechiel,
befell That wepe that tyme that the meschef fel
Unto the kyng ycalled Sedechie
In Babilon, and for thi prophesie
With stonys were cruelly yslawe;
cut in half Nor he that was departed with a sawe –
Ye, bothe two – that koude so compleyne;
Nor Danyel, that felte so gret peyne
For the kynges transmutacioun
prayer Into a beste, til thorugh the orisoun
Of Daniel he restored was
To mynde ageyn, and ete no more no gras.
Yet verrailly, though ye alle thre
With youre weping had alive be
And present eke at the destruccioun
Of this noble worthi royal toun,

7054–74 A notable example of the 'inexpressibility topos' (see E.R. Curtius, *European Literature and the Latin Middle Ages* [Bern, 1948; Eng. trans., 1953], pp. 159–62), a favourite device of amplification with Lydgate. The destruction of Jerusalem in 587 BC, as lamented by Jeremiah in his Lamentations, and by Ezechiel, with allusion to the downfall and death of Zedekiah, the last of the kings of Judah (Ez. 12, 17, 19; the story is more clearly told in Jer. 39, 52), makes an apt and powerful comparison. Daniel's interpretation of Nebuchadnezzar's dream (Dan. 4), during the Babylonian captivity that followed, is less apt. The reference to the death of Ezechiel by stoning and of another (unnamed) prophet (probably Isaiah is intended) by being sawn in half is hardly relevant at all, and is based on a passing comment in Heb. 11:37 on the fate of the OT prophets (Paul gives no names).

To have beweiled the meschef and the wo
done — And the slaughter at the sege do
On outher party in ful cruel wyse,
Alle youre teris myghte nat suffise
To have bewepte her sorwes everychon,
foes — Be tresoun wrought, as wel as be her foon!
Here-of no more, for it may nat availle.

THE SIEGE OF THEBES

Lydgate completed *The Siege of Thebes* in the summer of 1422, ready presumably to present it to Henry V on his victorious return from France after enforcing French compliance with the terms of the Treaty of Troyes (1420), which is alluded to at the end of the poem as inaugurating a new era of peace between the two realms. But Henry V died on campaign in France on 31 August, and the poem remains undedicated. In itself, the 4716-line *Siege* is a respectable rendering of the medievalized story of Thebes, beginning with the birth of Oedipus and ending with the razing of the city by Theseus (Lydgate alludes to the treatment of this episode in the Knight's Tale, but is clearly confident of improving, at least in length, on the example of his master). The praise of peace with which the poem ends is appropriate to the circumstances for which it was designed. In the Prologue to the *Siege* Lydgate represents himself as a pilgrim arriving at Canterbury, meeting up with Chaucer's pilgrims, and being asked to tell the first story on the return home. Lydgate's 'Canterbury Prologue' is interesting as a witness to the immense popularity of the *Canterbury Tales* and as an example of the eagerness with which Chaucer's followers strove to incorporate themselves into its fictional framework. Lydgate, in particular, shows a most unexpected desire to be comic in what he takes to be Chaucer's vein. But throughout the Prologue he imitates Chaucer sedulously, and enables us to understand something of the way Chaucer was understood in the fifteenth century, how he was 'encapsulated' in that understanding, and the extent to which our view of Chaucer is shaped by it.

There are 29 MSS of the *Siege*, including those in which it appears with the *Canterbury Tales* (it was also printed in the collected editions of Chaucer from 1561 to 1721); the Prologue here is taken from BL MS Arundel 119 (*c.*1430), with correction from MSS as cited in the edition by A. Erdmann and E. Ekwall, 2 vols, EETS, ES 108, 125 (1911, 1930). There is much on the medieval version of Thebes in A. Renoir, *The Poetry of John Lydgate* (London, 1967), and studies of Lydgate's poem by R.W. Ayers, in *PMLA* 73 (1958), 463–74, A.C. Spearing, in Yeager (1984), pp. 333–64, R.S. Allen, in Boffey and Cowen (1991), pp. 122–42, and L. Patterson, in J.N. Cox and L.J. Reynolds (eds), *New Historical Literary Study* (Princeton, 1993), pp. 69–107; see also Hammond (1927), pp. 118–23.

Prologue

(Aries) — Whan bright Phebus passed was the Ram,
(Taurus) — Myd of Aprille, and into Bole cam,
And Satourn old with his frosty face
(Virgo) — In Virgyne taken had his place,
Malencolik and slowgh of mocioun,

7084 **Be tresoun wrought**. The reference is to the betrayal of Troy by Antenor and others (IV.4538–66).

THE SIEGE OF THEBES

1–17 Lydgate's spring-opening far outdoes Chaucer's (in the GP) in elaboration. It even provides, through the astronomy, an exact date for his meeting with the pilgrims, 27 April (1421), which Lydgate thought an appropriate date for them to be setting off on their return journey if they left Southwark on 18 April (the date given in the Introduction to the Man of Law's Tale). Lydgate's further attempt to emulate Chaucer's marvellous opening sentence founders in disaster, and there is still no main verb in sight when the desperate editor has to call a halt after 45 lines.

1 This opening line (cf. GP 1) is an example of a favourite type of Lydgate line, the headless line, with unstressed syllable omitted at the line-beginning. Unobjectionable in itself, and on occasion, as here, it causes distress when used on a regular basis without rhetorical justification. Lydgate's attempts to write Chaucerian pentameter are not always or often successful.

3 This type of line, with unstressed syllable omitted at the caesura, is so unemendably common in Lydgate that it is called the 'Lydgate line'. On occasion it can be rhetorically effective and acceptable (e.g. 21), but Lydgate unfortunately uses it as a regular variant, with abrupt jolting effect.

5 **Malencolik**: one of the planetary aspects of Saturn (and the disposition of those under his sign).

And was also in th'oposicioun
Of Lucina, the mone, moyst and pale,
fall — That many shour fro hevene made avale;
Whan Aurora was in the morowe red,
And Jubiter in the Crabbes hed
set up — Hath take his paleys and his mansioun –
The lusty tyme and joly fressh sesoun
Whan that Flora, the noble myghty quene,
The soyl hath clad in newe tendre grene
mingled — With her floures craftyly ymeynt,
Braunch and bough with red and whit depeynt,
Floating, fragrance — Fletinge the bawme on hillis and on valys –
The tyme in soth whan Canterbury talys
(Were) completely told — Complet and told at many sondry stage
Of estatis in the pilgrimage,
according to — Everich man lik to his degre –
entertainment — Some of desport, some of moralite,
Some of knyghthode, love and gentillesse,
And some also of parfit holynesse,
And some also in soth of ribaudye
To make laughter in the companye
tolerated — (Ech admitted, for non wold other greve),
Lich as the Cook, the Millere and the Reve
Aquytte hemsilf, shortly to conclude,
Boystously in her teermes rude
bowl — Whan thei hadde wel dronken of the bolle,
bald head — And ek also with his pylled nolle
The Pardowner, beerdlees al his chyn,
(red-faced) — Glasy-eyed and face of cherubyn,
Tellyng a tale to angre with the Frere –
teach — As opynly the storie kan yow lere,
Word for word with every circumstaunce,
Echon ywrite and put in remembraunce
By hym that was, yif I shal not feyne,
Floure of poetes thorghout al Breteyne,
Which sothly hadde most of excellence
In rethorike and in eloquence
poetic work — (Rede his making, who list the trouthe fynde),
fade — Which never shal appallen in my mynde
But alwey fressh ben in my memoyre.
given praise — To who be yove pris, honure and gloyre
Of wel-seyinge first in oure language,
Chief registrer of this pilgrimage,

6 **oposicioun**. Planets are 'in opposition' when they are in the opposite sign of the zodiac. If Saturn is in Virgo, the Moon must be in Pisces, a 'watery' sign.

10–11 Jupiter is in Cancer; **mansioun** is an astronomical term for one of the 28 divisions of the ecliptic in which planets appear to 'reside'.

32–5 Lydgate's Pardoner has attributes of Chaucer's Summoner (the **face of cherubyn**, and the tale against the Friar), perhaps also of the miller of the Reeve's Tale (the **pylled nolle**, cf. *CT* I.4306), as well as the Pardoner's own eyes and beardless chin. Lydgate's memory seems to have been a little hazy: why didn't he check? But the tolerance he extends to Chaucer's low realism is noteworthy, given the constraints of his own and the usual medieval view of poetry.

39–57 Lydgate often introduces tributes to Chaucer, of unfeigned admiration and even affection (though he is unlikely ever to have met him). The praise is not specifically of Chaucer's poetry but more generally of Chaucer as a great poet, the founder and flower of English poetry, who therefore possesses above all the qualities associated with a great poet, namely sententiousness of utterance (authoritative pronouncement of general truths) and sweetness of rhetoric.

Al that was tolde foryeting noght at al,
Invented Feyned talis nor thing historial,
unfamiliar With many proverbe divers and unkouth,
telling, sweet Be rehersaile of his sugrid mouth,
Of eche thyng keping in substaunce
whole significance The sentence hool withoute variance,
Voyding the chaf, sothly for to seyn,
Enlumynyng the trewe piked greyn
sayings Be crafty writinge of his sawes swete,
Fro the tyme that thei deden mete
First the pylgrimes sothly everichon,
one by one At the Tabbard assembled on be on,
And fro Suthwerk, shortly for to seye,
To Canterbury ridyng on her weie,
Tellynge a tale, as I reherce can,
Lich as the Hoste assigned every man –
None so hardy his biddyng disobeye!
And this while that the pilgrymes leye
At Canterbury, wel logged on and all,
I not in soth what I may it call,
Chance Hap or fortune, in conclusioun,
That me byfil to entren into toun,
The holy seynt pleynly to visite,
fulfil Aftere siknesse my vowes to aquyte,
cloak In a cope of blak and not of grene,
On a palfrey, slender, long and lene,
With rusty brydel mad nat for the sale,
empty bag My man to-forn with a voide male;
Which of fortune took myn inne anon
Wher the pylgrymes were logged everichon,
The same tyme her governour, the Host,
Stonding in hall ful of wynde and bost,
Lich to a man wonder sterne and fers,
Which spak to me and seide anon, 'Daun Pers,
Daun Domynyk, Dan Godfrey or Clement,
Ye be welcom newly into Kent –
ornamental stud Thogh youre bridel have neither boos ne belle!
Besechinge you that ye wil me telle
part of the country First youre name and of what contre
Withoute more, shortely, that ye be,
That loke so pale, al devoyde of blood,
Upon youre hede a wonder thred-bar hood,
Wel araied for to ride late.'
I answerde my name was Lydgate,
'Monk of Bery, nygh fyfty yere of age,

49 **foryeting**. In accepting Chaucer's fiction of the earnest reporter, Lydgate of course consciously puts himself into a time-warp: the pilgrims are still there, and yet Lydgate is with them, and yet Chaucer has already written about them.

56 **piked greyn**: the grain with the husk and chaff removed. The imagery of grain and chaff (or fruit and chaff, as in Nun's Priest's Tale, *CT* VII.3443) was commonly used in contrasting the inner content of poetry and the disposable trimmings (such as poetry).

73 **blak** was the habit of monks of the Benedictine order.

82–3 Lydgate's Host imitates the patronizing form of address of Chaucer's Host to the Monk, *CT* VII.1929–30.

86 **Besechinge...** Such loosely related participial constructions are characteristic of Lydgate's often tiresome syntax (cf. 98).

91 **to ride late**, i.e. sensible attire to be wearing when robbers might be about.

Come to this toune to do my pilgrimage,
As I have hight – I have therof no shame.' *promised*
'Daun John,' quod he, 'wel broke ye youre name! *(see n.)*
Thogh ye be soul, beth right glad and light! *alone*
Preiyng you soupe with us tonyght,
And ye shal han mad at youre devis *fancy*
A gret puddyng or a rounde hagys,
A franch-mole, a tansey or a froyse.
To ben a monk sclender is youre koyse: *affliction*
Ye han be seke, I dar myn hede assure,
Or late fed in a feynt pasture. *meagre*
Lift up youre hed, be glad, take no sorowe!
And ye shal hom ride with us tomorowe,
I seye, whan ye rested han your fille.
Aftere soper slepe wol do non ille:
Wrappe wel youre hede with clothes rounde aboute;
Strong notty ale wol make you to route! *snore*
Tak a pylow that ye lye not lowe:
Yif nede be, spare not to blowe. *break wind*
To holde wynde, be myn opynyoun,
Wil engendre collik passioun
And make men to greven on her roppys *'innards'*
Whan thei han filled her mawes and her croppys. *gullets*
But toward nyght ete some fenel rede,
Annys, comyn or coriandre sede. *Anise, caraway*
And lik as I pouer have and myght
I charge yow rise not at mydnyght
Thogh it so be the moone shyne cler:
I wol mysilf be youre orloger *(alarm-)clock*
Tomorow erly whan I se my tyme,
For we wol forth parcel afore pryme – *a little before 9 a.m.*
A company, parde, shal do you good.
'What! look up, monk, for by kokkis blood
Thow shalt be mery, who-so that sey nay!
For tomorowe, anoon as it is day
And that it gynne in the est to dawe,
Thow shalt be bound to a newe lawe
Att goyng oute of Canterbury toune
And leyn aside thy professioun.
Thow shalt not chese nor thisilf withdrawe,
Yif eny myrth be founden in thy mawe,
Lyk the custom of this compenye;
For non so proude that dar me denye,
Knight nor knave, chanon, prest ne nonne,
To telle a tale pleynly as thei konne,
Whan I assigne and se tyme opportune.
And for that we our purpoos wil contune, *continue*

96 **broke**: 'enjoy, make use of', i.e. you do your name credit.

101 A **franch-mole** was another sort of haggis, or meat-pudding; a **tansey** was a tansy-flavoured savoury pancake; a **froyse** was a kind of fish-pancake. None of these would be gourmet cooking.

114 **collik passioun**: an anglicization of Latin *colica passio*, violent colic.

117–18 These are all aperients, recommended for the relief of flatulence. Lydgate seems unwilling to let go of his little joke: perhaps, like us, he is thinking about a similar problem he has with his poetry.

126 **kokkis**, i.e. God's, with euphemistic misspelling.

We wil homward the same custome use,
And thow shalt not platly the excuse. *plainly*
Be now wel war: stody wel tonyght!
But, for al this, be of herte light:
Thy wit shal be the sharper and the bet.'
And we anon were to soper set
And served wel unto oure plesaunce;
And sone after be good governaunce
Unto bed goth every maner wight.
And towarde morowe, anon as it was light,
Every pilgryme, bothe bet and wors,
As bad oure Hoste, toke anon his hors
Whan the sonne roos in the est ful clere,
Fully in purpoos to come to dynere
Unto Osspryng and breke ther oure fast.
And whan we weren from Canterbury past
Noght the space of a bowe draught, *bow-shot*
Our Hoost in hast hath my bridel raught *seized*
And to me seide, as it were in game,
'Come forth, Daun John, be your Cristene name, *to call you by your*
And lat us make some manere myrth or play:
Shet youre portoos, a twenty devel way! *Shut, portable breviary*
It is no disport so to patere and seie –
It wol make youre lippes wonder dreye. *dry*
Tel some tale and make therof no jape! *don't take it lightly*
For be my rouncy, thow shalt not eskape. *horse*
But preche not of non holynesse!
Gynne some tale of myrth or of gladnesse,
And nodde not with thyn hevy bekke. *nose*
Tell us some thyng that draweth to effekke *conduces to effect*
Only of joye – make no lenger lette!' *delay*
And whan I saugh it wolde be no bette
I obeyde unto his biddynge
So as the lawe me bonde in al thinge;
And as I coude, with a pale cheere,
My tale I gan anon, as ye shal here.'

Explicit Prologus. Incipit Pars Prima

The Life of Our Lady

The *Life of Our Lady* is less a chronological account of the Virgin's life than a compendium of Mariolatry, a series of meditations, celebrations and expositions for the Marian feasts of the liturgical year, composed in honour of the feast of Our Lady's Nativity (8 September), and loosely compiled in biographical order for monastic reading or pious meditation. It runs to nearly 6000 lines, in six books, but at the end has only got to the Purification,

141 **We wil homward the same custome use.** This of course was Chaucer's plan, as outlined in the GP (I.794), though not his original plan, which seems, from the evidence of the Parson's Prologue, to have ended with the arrival at Canterbury.

155 **Osspryng**: Ospringe is 10 miles west of Canterbury. Like Chaucer, Lydgate mentions places on the way to give an air of authenticity.

162 **a twenty devel way**: 'in the name of twenty devils', a common oath in Chaucer, e.g. Miller's Tale, *CT* I.3713.

169 **hevy bekke.** Portraits of Lydgate in presentation pictures (see Pearsall, *John Lydgate*, p. 47), and in the picture of the pilgrims leaving Canterbury in BL MS Royal 18.D.ii (a *Thebes* MS), show the monk with a rather prominent nose.

having treated at length of the Debate of the Four Daughters of God, the prophecies of Advent, the marvellous nature of the virgin birth, the worship of the name of Jesus, and the explanation of Candlemas. A number of manuscripts (including the Durham MS) have a rubric saying it was made at the 'excitacion and stirryng' of Henry V, but there is no dedication such as Lydgate would normally have provided in such circumstances, and the work, though not broken off, does not present a complete narrative. It was perhaps left on one side after Henry's sudden death in 1422. The most famous passages are rhapsodic invocations in Lydgate's most florid style, but the stanzas below are quieter, a meditation on the joy of the Virgin as she suckles her child. It may not be much to modern taste ('Gospels-as-pap' is what D. Daniell, *William Tyndale* [New Haven, 1994], p. 100, calls the more general phenomenon of affective devotion represented by Nicholas Love), but it is a good example of a widespread form of popular devotion. Nor is it mere self-indulgent sentimentalism, as Lydgate shows by working skilfully from the imagery of feeding and suckling to the introduction of the central theology of Mary as mediatrix of grace.

There are 47 MSS in all, including 43 complete; the text below is from Durham UL MS Cosin V.ii.16 (fols 66r–8r); the only modern edition is that of J.A. Lauritis et al., Duquesne Studies, Philological Series 2 (Pittsburgh, 1961).

The Commendation of Our Lady at the Nativity (III.1667–1806)

{Book 3 deals with the story of the Nativity, and the prophecies and marvels surrounding it. This is the last section.}

art pleased to grant to him	Glad mayst thou be, that sauf hym luste to vouche
little	With his rounde softe lippes lyte
	To have pleasaunce thy brestes for to touche,
suck, breasts	Only to souke thy blissede pappes white,
	And that hym luste so godely to delyte
	For his playe to have so moche blisse
	Evere among thy holy mouthe to kysse;
	And sodenly with childely chere jocounde
	Than anone thy white nek to enbrace
	With his softe tendre armes rounde,
	And than at onys fallen on thy face
full	And of his eyen, fulfillede of alle grace,
	A godely loke to the-warde to enclyne;
	And so furthe his chekes ley by thyne,
	And with his fyngres mouthe and eyen touche,
palms	His smale pawmes on thy chekes layne,
	His yonge face betwene thy pappes couche
earnest effort	And holde hym stille with all his besy payne
	And grype hem faste with his handes twayne –
	For ther-in was his hevenly repaste,
	Thy yonge sone whan hym lust to breke his faste.
nourishing	Ther was his foode and his norchyng pure,
cellar	Sothefaste seler of his sustynaunce,
cask	The tunne of lyfe that evere dyd endure
Alike	Ilyche fresshe unto his pleasaunce
	With sacrede lycoure of holy habundaunce,
	That noon but he may touche nor aproche,
him alone, to be broached	For it for hym was only set abroche.
	For in that licour was fulle remedye,
protection	Holy refute and pleynly medycyne

Ayayne the venyme brought in by envye
trickery Thorughe fals engyne and malyce serpentyne
Whan the snake made Adam for to dyne
Of the appulle that was intoxicate,
Falsely with God to make hym at debate.

But nowe the mylke of thy pappes tweyne,
medicine Benygne Lady, is to us tryacle,
springeth Whiche in thy brest sprenketh fro a vayne,
Ayenst dethe to be to us obstacle.
O how it is a passyng high myracle,
Thorugh Goddys myght alone and by nought elles,
Oute of a breste to see two smalle wellys

Of mayden mylke spryng as a ryver
To yefe hym drynke that is kyng of alle!
butler (wine-provider) O goode Lady, O hevenly boteler,
distress Whan we in myscheve to the clepe and calle,
Some drope of grace lat upon us falle
And to that seler make a redy waye
Wher thou alone of mercy beryst the keye.

And of grace lat be no scarsite,
Gode Lady, that art of grace welle,
For nowe this day in erthe is bore of the
The sothefaste God of hevyn, erthe and helle,
Whiche is comyn doune with us for to dwelle
And hath of the our mortalle kynde itake
Of alle our woo an ende for to make.

manna Some-tyme fro hevyn fel adoune the manne
To refresshe the hungrye in her nede
And that befelle in desert righte thanne
When Moyses the peple of our Lorde dyd lede.
But nowe this day, in erthe man to fede,
An humble mayde, to all that ben trwe,
In this desert hath brought furthe manna newe;

Whiche to angelis is the fode of lyfe,
To man repast of joye and of gladnesse,
Chefe recomforte and eke restoratyfe
To alle feble oppressed with sekenesse.
O gode Lady, O myrour of alle mekenesse,
water-spring Benygne floure of womanhode, the welle
In this desert wher-as we nowe dwelle,

healing-power Sende us this manne of sovereigne hertes hele
To our comforte and our consolacion,
And lat us grace in thy mercy fele
For our refute and our refection,

1723 **manne**: manna was fed to the Israelites in the desert in Ex. 16:31. The word is correctly spelt in l. 1729, but in rhyme Lydgate is not averse to the pun on 'manne' (Christ), as with **sonne** in ll. 1748–50 below.

And in this valye of confucion
Late thy grace fro the skyes rayne,
manna The manne of lyfe that we may attayne.

For thou alone art comforte synguler
know To alle tho that no refute konne;
This day also of mercy the ryver,
Fro whiche alle grace is to mankynde ronne,
The sterre also that hath brought furthe the sonne,
dwell The sonne of lyfe, in erthe for to wonne.
O mayde, O mother, doughter of thy sonne –

Whiche non, in sothe, sithe the worlde bygan,
Was bothe two, but thyselfe alone,
For who is he that remembre can,
Firste or laste, late or elles sone,
So bright a sonne spryngyng of so fayre a mone?
Saff this day the sonne of lyf moste shene
Fro the arose, and thou a mayden clene,

losing Withoute eclipsyng or leesyng of thy light,
For thou a mother and mayden bothe two,
In vertu aye yliche shene and bryght:
(Ecclus. 24:14) O fayre rose, O Rose of Jericho,
That hast this day God and man also
In Bedlem borne ayen the graye morowe,
The nyght to voyde of al our olde sorowe;

(Ecclus. 24:13) Nowe fayre cedre, cypresse of Syon,
Spryngyng light oute of Nazareth;
(Ps. 19:5) Chose chaumbre of wyse Salamon;
(Song of Songs 2:1) Flour of the felde swettest of holte and hethe,
Of whom the vertu saveth man fro dethe;
Of Syloe the water eke depurede
Wherby the lepre of Naaman was curede;

(Judith 15:9) Laude and glorye of Jerusalem
Thou namede art, of Israel gladnesse;
(2 Sam. 23:15) Holsome cysterne this day of Bedlem
thirst The thruste of David to staunche in destresse;
Of Paradyse the welle in sothefastnesse,
realms Physon that floweth into sondry remes
bedew The soyl to adewe with his sote stremes;

1744–64 The syntax of these lines is not perspicuous: it has an incantatory and invocatory character, as Lydgate winds up for the closing apostrophe and prayer.

1748 **sterre**. The star is a familiar image for Mary (especially *stella maris*, 'star of the sea'); here she is the star that brought forth (or, like the morning-star, heralded the advent of) the sun, but also the Son, of life; also the star that stood over the cradle of his nativity.

1750 **doughter of thy sonne**: a favourite paradox (since she is a human being, God is her father).

1758–60 The pure light of Mary's virginity was not lessened or eclipsed by motherhood.

1761–82 Lydgate gathers together here some of the typological OT images for Mary; in his *Balade in Commendation of Our Lady* he had translated a comprehensive list of them from the *Anticlaudianus* of Alain of Lille.

1765 In the Durham MS, a new chapter begins here, entitled 'Of likenesse of our lady in commendacion of hir' (*likenesse*, 'image').

1770 **Syloe**. Naaman the Syrian was cured of leprosy by bathing in the waters of the Jordan (2 Kings 5:1–19); Lydgate has got Siloe (Siloam) from John 9:7, the curing of the blind man.

1777 **Physon**: Pishon was one of the four rivers that flowed out of Eden in Gen. 2:11. See *Mandeville's Travels* (above), chap. 33.

(Ex. 3:17) The londe also of promyssyon
together flows with That mylke and hony bothe in-fere shedyth,
The soyle and grounde of our salvacion
With his herbes that fosterth us and fedeth –
rewards Nowe, blisset Mayde, whose mercy evere medyth
live Alle tho that levyn in thy servyce,
This highe feste so for us devyse

That in honour of thy sonne so dere
with true heart We may of hert rede, syng and pray;
And late the stremes of thyne eyen clere
bring on our way Thy servauntes, O Lady myne, conveye
To contynue fully tylle we deye
The to serve with hertly love and drede
As moste is plesyng to thy womanhede;

And this feste, of festes principalle,
Callede the feste of thy Natyvyte,
Make love and pees to regnen overe alle
And hertes joyne with perfyte unyte;
Voyde alle discorde and late no rancour be
In brestes closede by malice or envye,
But of thy grace so governe us and gye,

This highe feste in whiche thy sonne was borne,
Now this mydwynter, with full affection,
While Phebus shynyth in the Capricorne,
(That) we We may the serve with alle devocion;
And Lady myne, in fulle conclusion,
Nowe this monyth that called is Decembre
Upon thy servaunte faythefully remembre.

THE DANCE MACABRE

The earliest known 'Dance of Death' was carved in relief on the walls of the charnel-house of the church of the Holy Innocents in Paris in 1424, in the form of a series of sculpted panels showing Death as a skeleton or decomposing corpse laying his bony finger on the arm of figures representing the 'estates' of society, as if inviting them to join a dignified processional dance. Verse-inscriptions accompanied the panels, giving the words of Death's invitation and the reply of the victim. The place became a resort of fashionable society and hell-fire preachers. Lydgate saw the panels on his stay in Paris in 1426 (he was there in the entourage of the earl of Warwick, who had him writing an English verse-translation of *The Title and Pedigree of Henry VI*, the claim of the infant Henry VI to the throne of France) and there is no reason not to accept his story of how he came to write his translation of the French text. He expanded it with new stanzas of his own (it is the kind of text that is as easy to add to as to excerpt from) and subsequently, around 1430, did a revised version at the request of John Carpenter, town clerk of London, to be inscribed, with appropriate illustrations, on the walls of the cloister (pulled down in 1549) in the Pardon churchyard of St Paul's. The 15 MSS of Lydgate's poem that survive divide roughly into two versions, and what is called the A version may be the original version written in 1426, but the relationships are not simple. There are editions of the poem in Hammond (1927), pp. 124–42, and by F. Warren and B. White, EETS, OS 181 (1931), both following A. The extracts from A below are based on Bodl.MS Arch.Selden supra 53, with emendation from other MSS as cited in Warren and White.

1794 **thy Natyvyte.** Lydgate refers here to the feast in whose honour the poem was composed, though this part of the poem was evidently written in and for meditation in the Christmas season (**this mydwynter**, 1801) of the **highe feste** (1800) of Christ's Nativity.

The origin of the *Dance Macabre* is much debated. Lydgate evidently thinks it to be named after a person called 'Machabre' who uses it to provide instruction in proper attitudes to mortality and death (see 641–8, below). The likeliest explanation, of many, is that the word *macabre* (properly trisyllabic) is derived from a Hebrew word meaning 'grave-digger', and refers to a death-dance introduced by Jewish burial societies into France in the thirteenth century, a kind of undertakers' pantomime. Whatever its origin, the Dance was very popular in the fifteenth and sixteenth centuries, and provided material for much visual illustration, as well as texts, culminating in the famous series of woodcuts done by Hans Holbein the Younger to accompany a text published at Lyons in 1538. Often associated, as by Johan Huizinga in his influential book on *The Waning of the Middle Ages* (1926), with a general spirit of morbidity and decadence in the later Middle Ages, it was in fact no such thing, nor was there such a spirit widespread (see Duffy [1992], pp. 299–337). The Dance of Death follows firmly in the tradition of mortality literature, its purpose being to remind folk of the inevitability of death so that they can repent and reform in time (unlike the victims here). The threat of death is beneficial to man (see *PP* XX.80n, above). In Lydgate's poem, in which some of his natural verbosity is restrained by the French original and its strict eight-line 'ballade' stanza, and in which he achieves at times even a crisply aphoristic quality, the victims usually show, in their last line or couplet, how they have learnt their salutary lesson, while Death, so far from gloating, congratulates those who know the 'Art of Dying Well' (*Ars Moriendi* is the title of a favourite kind of late medieval treatise). The whole poem is worth comparing with Chaucer's General Prologue, from which no doubt many details derive, as from the general tradition of estates satire. Lydgate's poem, appropriately to his proverbial style of closure, is a kind of 'General Epilogue'. In the manner in which it stands, uniquely in English, for a whole world of late medieval sentiment and writing, it is what Lydgate is most valuable for.

Verba translatoris

O yee folkes, harde-hertid as a stone,
attention Wich to the worlde have al your advertence,
Liche as it shulde laste evere in oone,
Where is your witt? Wher is your providence
To se aforn the sodeine violence
Of cruel dethe, that be so wis and sage,
Wiche sleeth, allas, by stroke of pestilence
birth Bothe yong and olde, of lowe and hy parage?

Deeth sparith not lowe ne hy degre,
Popes, kynges, ne worthy emperours:
Whan thei shyne most in felicite
He can abate the fresshnes of her flours,
eclipse The brighte sonne clipsen with his shours,
seats Make hem plunge from her sees lowe;
Despite Magre the myght of alle these conquerours
Fortune hath hem from her whele ythrowe.

Considerith this, ye folkes that be wys,
memory And it enprentith in youre memorial,
Like th'ensaumple wiche that at Parys
I fonde depict oones in a wal
Ful notably, as I reherce shal;
Therof Frensshe clerkis takyng aqueintaunce
I toke on me to translatyn al
Oute of the Frensshe Machabrees Daunce.

By whos avys and counceil, at the leste
urging Thorugh her steryng and her mocioun,
I obeide unto her requeste
Therof to make a playn translacioun
with the intention In Englissh tonge, of entencioun

That proude folkes, wiche that be stout and bold,
As in a mirrour to-for in her resoun
Her ougly fine may cleerly ther bihold, *end*

By exaumple that thei in her ententis
Amende her lif in every manere age;
The wiche daunce at Seint Innocentis
Portreied is, with al the surpluage, *extra things*
To shewe this worlde is but a pilgrimage
Yove unto us our lyves to correcte; *Given*
And to declare the fyne of oure passage *final purpose*
Right anoon my stile I wole directe

{The translation begins. Death comes to the Pope, the Emperor and a number of other high-ranking persons, secular and ecclesiastical.}

Deeth to the Squier

Come forth, sir squier, right fresshe of youre aray,
That can of daunces al the newe gise; *fashion*
Though ye bare armes fressh horsed yisterday,
With spere and shelde, with youre unkouthe devise, *unusually striking coat of arms*
And toke on yow so many hy emprise,
Daunceth with us – it wil no bettir be:
Ther is no socour in no manere wise,
For no man may fro dethes stroke fle.

The Squier aunswerith

Sithen that dethe me holdith in his lace *noose*
Yet shal I speke o worde or I pace: *before I pass*
Adieu al myrthe, adieu nowe al solace,
Adieu my ladies, somtime so fressh of face,
Adieu beute, plesaunce and solace!
Of dethes chaunge every day is prime; *a new beginning*
Thinketh on youre soules or that deth manace, *before*
For al shal rote and no man wote what tyme.

Deeth to the Abbot

Come forth, sir abbot, with youre brode hatte,
Beeth not abaisshed, though ye have right. *good cause*
Greet is your hood, youre bely large and fatte:
Ye mote come daunce, though ye be nothing light.
Leve up youre abbey to some othir wight:
Youre eir is of age youre state to occupie!
Who that is fattest I have hym behight *promised*
In his grave shal sonnest putrefie.

The Abbot answerith

Of thi thretis have I noon envie *feeling of annoyance*
That I shal nowe leve al governaunce,
But that I shal as a cloistrer dye –

238 **Youre eir**. The satirical touch (abbots should not, but did, have heirs) is Lydgate's.

This doth to me passinge grete grevaunce.
Mi liberte nor my greet habondaunce
What may availe in any manere wise?
Yit axe I mercy with hertly repentaunce,
Though in diynge to late men hem avise. — *give thought*

Deeth to the Abbesse

And ye, my lady, gentil dame abbesse,
With youre mantels furred large and wide.
Youre veile, youre wymple passinge of greet richesse — *of surpassing*
And beddis softe ye mote nowe leie aside,
For to this daunce I shal be youre guyde,
Though ye be tendre and born of gentil blood.
While that ye lyve for youresilfe provide,
For aftir deeth no man hath no good.

The Abbesse answerith

Allas, that deeth hath thus for me ordeined
That in no wise I may it not declyne,
Though it so be ful ofte I have constreyned
Brest and throte my notes out to twyne, — *wind together*
My chekes round vernysshed for to shyne, — *painted with make-up*
Ungirt ful ofte to walke atte large. — *(Informally attired), at liberty*
Thus cruel dethe doth al estates fyne: — *end*
Who hath no ship mote rowe in bote or barge.

{Death comes to the Bailiff, the Astronomer, the Burgess and the Canon.}

Deeth to the Marchaunt

Ye riche marchaunt, ye mote loke hiderwarde,
That passid have many divers londe
On hors, on foot, havynge moste reward — *regard*
To lucre and wynnyng, as I undirstond.
But nowe to daunce ye mote yeve me youre honde,
For al youre labour ful litel availeth yow.
Adieu, veinglorie, bothe of fee and bonde! — *money and bonds*
No more coveite than thei that have ynow. — *enough*

The Marchaunt answerith

By manie an hil and many a straunge vale
I have traveilid with my marchandise;
Overe the see do carie many a bale — *caused to be carried*
To sundry iles, mo than I can devise,
My herte inwarde ay fret with covetise; — *devoured*
But al for nought – nowe deeth doith me constreine;
By wiche I seie, by recorde of the wise,
Who al embraceth litel shal restreine. — *keep*

Deeth to the Chartereux

Yeve me youre hond, with chekis dede and pale,

259–60 The echo of Chaucer's description of the Prioress in the GP is noticeable here, elsewhere somewhat coarsened and exaggerated; the Abbess is new in Lydgate.

264 The idea is of getting used to a reduced station in life, i.e. being dead.

Causid of wacche and longe abstinence, *keeping vigil*
Sir Chartereux, and youresilfe avale *humble*
Unto this daunce, with humble pacience.
To stryve ayein may be no resistence: *there-against*
Lenger to lyve set not youre memorie. *mind*
Though I be lothsom as in apparence
Above alle men deth hath the victorie.

The Chartereux answerith

Unto the worlde I was dede longe agone
By my ordre and my professioun,
Though every man, be he nevere so stronge,
Dredith to die, by kindly mocioun, *natural impulse*
Aftir his flesshly inclinacioun.
But plese it to God my soule for to borowe *ransom*
From fendis myght and from dampnacioun:
Some bene today that shulle not be tomorwe.

{Death comes to the Sergeant.}

Deeth to the Monke

Sir monke also, with youre blak habite,
Ye may no lenger holde here sojour;
Ther is no thing that may yow here respite
Ayein my myght yow for to socour. *Against*
Ye mote acounte, touching youre labour,
Howe ye have spent it, in dede, worde and thought.
To erthe and asshes turneth every flour:
The life of man is but a thing of nought.

The monke answerith

I hadde levere in the cloistre be *rather*
At my book and studie my service,
Wiche is a place contemplatif to se;
But I have spent my life in many vice
Liche as a fool, dissolut and nyce – *foolish*
God of his mercy graunt me repentaunce!
By chere outwarde harde is to devise:
Alle be not mery wich that men se daunce.

{Death comes to the Usurer, Physician, Amorous Squire and Gentlewoman Amorous.}

Deeth to the man of lawe

Sir advocate, short processe for to make,
Ye mote come plete afore the highe juge. *plead a suit*
Many a quarel ye have undirtake
And for lucre to do folke refuge, *help*
But my fraunchise is so large and huge *license to exercise power*

347 **Chartereux**: a monk of the strict Carthusian order, which was founded in 1086 from the mother-house at La Grande Chartreuse, in the French Alps.

353 **I was dede**. The strictest orders of monks vowed to remove themselves from the world as if they were already dead.

385 The monk's reply, though it seems very appropriate to Lydgate, is much as in the French.

That counceile none availe may but trouthe:
He skapith wisly of deeth the greet deluge
judgement
To-fore the doom who is not teint with slouthe.

The man of lawe answerith

Of right and resoun by naturis lawe
I can not putte ayein deeth no defence,
Ne by no sleighte me kepe ne withdrawe,
For al my wit and al my greet prudence,
To make apele from his dredful sentence;
Nothing in erthe may a man preserve
Ayeins his myght to make resistence.
May God reward
God quite al men like as thei deserve!

Deeth to the Jourrour

Maister jurrour, wiche that at assise
judicial enquiries, receive bribes
And atte shires questes dost embrace,
own ideas
Departist londe like to thi devise,
And who most yaf moste stode in thi grace.
The pore man loste londe and place:
For golde thou cowdest folkes disherite.
guilty
But nowe let se, with thi teinte face
acquit thyself
To-fore the juge howe thou canst the quite.

The Jourour answerith

Somtyme I was clepid in my cuntre
that was really something
The belle-wedir, and that was not a lite –
Nought loved but drad of lowe and hie degre,
indict
For whom me list by crafte I coude endite
reprieve
And hange the trewe and the theef respite:
Al the cuntre by my worde was lad.
But I dar sey, shortly for to write,
Of my dethe many a man is glad.

Deeth to the Minstral

O thou mynstral, that canst so note and pipe
Unto folkes for to do plesaunce,
By the right honde I shal anoone the gripe
With these other to goo upon my daunce:
There is no scape neither avoidaunce
On no side to contrarie my sentence,
keeping due proportion
For in musik, by craft and acordaunce,
(superior) knowledge
Who maister is sheweth his science.

The minstral answerith

This newe daunce is to me so straunge,
Wondir diverse and passingly contrarie,
This dredful fotyng doth so ofte chaunge
And the mesures so ofte-sithes varie,

481 **jurrour**. The medieval English juror's functions were wide, and included valuations and assessments for tax, with much opportunity for corrupt exercise of power.

490 **belle-wedir**: bell-wether (the sheep that leads the others).

495 **to write**: not an uncommon kind of lapse in written but supposedly spoken texts.

Wiche nowe to me is nothing necessarie –
escape If it were so that I myght asterte!
But many a man, if I shal not tarie,
Ofte daunceth but nothing of herte.

Deeth to the Tregetour

Maistir John Rikele, some-tyme tregetour
Of noble Harry, kyng of Engelond
And of Fraunce the mighty conquerour,
For alle the sleightes and turnyng of thin hond
Thou must come ner, this daunce to undirstond:
tricky calculations Nought may availe al thi conclusiouns,
For deeth, shortly, nouther on see ne lond
Is nought deceivid by none illusions.

The Tregetour answerith

What may availe magik natural
illusory appearance Or any craft shewid by apparence
Or (by calculation of) Or cours of sterres above celestial
Or of the hevene al the influence
Ayeins deeth to stonde at defence?
Sleight of hand Legerdemeyn nowe helpith me right nought.
Farewel, my craft and al suche sapience,
For deth moo maistris yit than I hath wrought.

Deeth to the Persoun

O sir curat, that bene nowe here present,
That had youre worldly inclinacioun,
Youre herte entire, youre studie and entent
voluntary offerings Moste on youre tithes and oblacioun,
behaviour Wiche shulde have bene of conversacioun,
Mirrour unto othir, light and exaumplarie.
Like youre desert shal be youre guerdoun,
And to eche labour dewe is the salarie.

The Persoun answerith

Maugre my wille I must condiscende,
living For deeth assailith every lifly thing
Here in this worlde. Who can comprehende
His sodein stroke and his unware comyng?
Farewele, tithis, and farewel, myn offryng!
I mote goo counte in ordre by and by
And for my shepe make a just rekenyng.
acquits Whom he aquyteth I holde he is happy.

Deeth to the laborer

Thou laborer, wiche in sorwe and peine
Hast lad thi life in ful greet travaile,

513 **John Rikele**. Lydgate unexpectedly introduces a real character (though his name has not yet been found in any record), John Rickhill, Henry V's juggler. A **tregetour** was a deviser of court entertainments (involving mechanical contraptions and optical illusions) as well as a conjuror and a juggler: see FrankT 1141.

516–18 **For alle the sleightes . . .** : sounds a little like Hamlet on 'poor Yorick'.

Thou moste eke daunce and therfore not disdeyne
For if thou do it may thee not availe;
And cause why that I thee assaile
Is oonly this, from thee to dissevere
The fals worlde, that can so folke faile.
He is a fool that weneth to lyve evere.

The laborer answerith

I have wisshed aftir deeth ful ofte,
Al be that I wolde have fled hym now.
I had levere to have leyn unsofte
In winde and reyn and have gone at plow
pick-axe, benefit
With spade and pikoys and labourid for my prow,
Dug
Dolve and diched and at the carte goon;
For I may seie and telle pleinly howe
In this worlde here ther is reste noon.

{Death comes to the Friar.}

Deeth to the childe

Litel enfaunte, that were but late yborn,
Shape in this worlde to have no plesaunce,
Thou must with other that goon here to-forn
fateful decree
Be lad in haste by fatal ordinaunce.
Lerne of newe to goo on my daunce:
Ther may noon age escape in soth therfroo.
Lete every wight have this in remembraunce:
Who lengest lyveth moost shal suffre woo.

The childe answerith

one single
A, A, A – o worde I can not speke,
I am so yonge, I was bore yisterday.
avenged
Deeth is so hasty on me to be wreke
And list no lenger to make no delay.
I cam but nowe and nowe I goo my way;
Of me no more no tale shal be told.
The wil of God no man withstonde may:
As sone dieth a yonge man as an old.

{Death comes to the Clerk.}

Deeth to the hermyte

Ye that have lived longe in wildernesse
And there contynued longe in abstinence,
get ready
At the laste yet ye mote yow dresse
Of my daunce to have experience,
For there-ayein is no resistence:
Take nowe leve of thin ermytage.
attend to, wise statement
Wherfore eche man adverte this sentence,
That this life here is no sure heritage.

The hermite answerith

Life in desert callid solitarie

May ayein dethe have no respite ne space;
At unset hour his comyng doth not tarie,
And for my part, welcome be Goddes grace!
Thonkyng hym with humble chere and face
Of al his yiftes and greet habondaunce,
Fynally affermynge in this place,
contentment with a sufficiency No man is riche that lackith suffisaunce.

Deeth ayein to the Hermite

That is wel seide, and thus shulde every wight
direct Thanke his God and alle his wittis dresse
To love and drede hym with al his herte and myght,
Seth deeth to ascape may be no sikernesse.
repays As men deserve, God quit of rightwisnesse
To riche and pore uppon every side.
A bettir lessoun ther can no clerke expresse
Than, til tomorwe is no man sure to abide.

The kyng ligging dede and eten of wormes

Ye folke that lokyn upon this portrature,
estates of society Biholdyng here alle the states daunce,
Seeth what ye bene and what is youre nature –
Mete unto wormes, not ellis in substaunce –
And have this mirrour evere in remembraunce
Howe I lie here, somtyme crownyd kyng,
To alle estates a trewe resemblaunce
end That wormes food is fyne of oure lyvyng.

Machabre the doctour

plainly Man is not ellis, platly for to thinke,
But as a winde wiche is transitorie,
Passinge ay forthe, whether he wake or winke,
Towarde this daunce – have this in memorie,
better Remembringe ay there is no bet victorie
In this life here than fle synne at the leste.
Than shul ye regne in paradys with glorie:
Happy is he that maketh in hevene his feste.

Yit ther be folke, mo than six or sevene,
Reckles of liif in many maner wise,
Like as there were helle none nor hevene.
Suche false errour lete every man dispice,
For hooly seintis and oolde clerkis wise
refute Writen contrarie, her falsnes to deface.
plan to act on To lyve wel, take this for best emprice:
Is moche worth, whan men shul hennes pace?

L'envoye de Translatour

together O ye, my lordis and maistres alle in fere,
By chance Of aventure that shal this daunce rede,

633 **this portrature**: a reminder that the text was designed to accompany pictures.

Lowly I preie with al myn herte entere
To correcte where-as ye see nede;
reward For nought ellis I axe for my mede
But goodly support of this translacioun,
come to the help of And with favour to sowpouaile drede
Benignely in youre correccioun.

according to my purpose Out of the Frensshe I drewe it of entente,
Not worde by worde but folwynge the substaunce,
And fro Paris to Engelonde it sente
Oonly of purpos yow to do plesaunce.
Rude of langage, I was not born in Fraunce:
Have me excusid, my name is John Lidgate.
Of her tunge I have no suffisaunce
Her corious metris in Englisshe to translate.

Here endith the daunce of Deeth

THE FALL OF PRINCES

The *Fall of Princes* was begun in 1431 at the request of Humphrey, duke of Gloucester, the powerful uncle of the young king, and completed in 1438. Humphrey had ambitions to earn a name as a European patron of letters and as the English representative of the new Italian humanist learning, but Lydgate was unresponsive to his hints of humanism, and tended to fall back on medieval commonplaces. He worked from a French prose translation by Laurent de Premierfait (1409) of the Latin prose of Boccaccio, *De casibus virorum illustrium* (1358), amplifying the already much amplified French and adding 'envoys' at the end of each chapter moralizing upon the fall and death of the personages. The 'fall of princes' was an age-old topos of mutability (there are examples in the *Roman de la Rose* and in Chaucer's Monk's Tale – eerily prophetic of the monk of Bury); its theme is the reiteration *ad infinitum* that all men and women, good and bad, deserving and undeserving, must die; it is a kind of vast biographical dictionary of the dead, arranged broadly chronologically. There is not much of a moral, it might be thought, to be drawn from a fate so universal, but Lydgate inevitably draws it, over and over again. There are moments of grandeur and pathos (as below), but the work is not continuously readable and perhaps was not intended to be so. There are 34 MSS, but at least as many more contain excerpts, as if readers recognized the practical use of this dictionary of universal biography. The poem is edited by H. Bergen, 4 vols, EETS, ES 121–4 (1918–19); see Scanlon (1994), pp. 322–50.

The letter of Canace to her brother (I.6882–6951, 7008–42)

The story of Canace and her incestuous love for her brother Macareus is alluded to briefly by Laurent in an addition to Boccaccio's *De casibus*. It derives from Ovid, *Heroides* XI, some version of which may have been known to Lydgate; more likely he knew the touching treatment of the story in Gower, *Confessio Amantis* III.143–336. For Gower, it was part of a serious debate about the blamelessness of brother–sister love according to 'natural law', and his main criticism is of the intemperate anger of the father Aeolus. Lydgate enters no debate, but exploits the pathos of the situation with skill and feeling (for him, pathos is sufficient in itself, needs no thought and has no consequence), lapsing into verbosity only in stanzas that are easily omitted without loss.

swoon, wake with a start Out of hir swouh whan she dede abraide,
course of action Knowyng no mene but deth in hir distresse,
To hir brother ful pitousli she saide:

660 **To correcte**. Lydgate often concludes with such pleas of ignorance and requests for correction. It is a traditional kind of 'modesty-topos' (though there is nothing modest about it).

'Cause of my sorwe, roote of myn hevynesse,
That whilom were cheef sours of my gladnesse,
Whan bothe our joies be will were so disposid *by desire*
Under o keie our hertis to be enclosid.

'Whilom thou were support and sekirnesse,
Cheef rejoisshing of my worldli plesaunce,
But now thou art the ground of my siknesse,
Welle of wanhope of my dedli penaunce, *despair*
Which have of sorwe grettest habundaunce
That ever yit hadde any creature,
Which mut for love the deth, alas, endure. *must*

'Thou were whilom my blisse and al my trust,
Sovereyn confort my sorwes to appese,
Spryng and well of al myn hertis lust
And now, alas, cheef roote of my disese.
But yif my deth myht do the any ese,
O brother myn, in remembraunce of tweyne,
Deth shal to me be plesaunce and no peyne.

'Mi cruel fader most unmerciable
Ordeyned hath – it needis mut be soo, *must*
In his rigour he is so untretable,
Al merciles he will that it be doo – *done*
That we algate shal deie bothe too;
But I am glad, sithe it may been noon other,
Thou art escapid, my best beloved brother.

'This is myn eende, I may it nat asterte, *escape*
O brother myn, there is no mor to seye,
Lowli besechyng with al myn hoole herte
For to remembre speciali, I preie,
Yif it befall my litil sone deie,
That thou maist aftir sum mynde upon us have,
Suffre us bothe be buried in o grave.

'I holde hym streihtli atwen myn armys tweyne: *tightly*
Thou and Nature leide on me this charge.
He gilteles with me mut suffre peyne,
And sithe thou art at fredam and at large
Lat kyndenesse our love nat so discharge
But have a mynde, where-ever that thou be,
Onys a day upon my child and me.

'On the and me dependith the trespace,
Touchyng our gilte and eke our gret offence,
But wellaway! most angelik of face,
Our yonge child in his pur innocence
Shal ageyn riht suffre dethis violence, *against*
Tendre of lymes, God wot, ful gilteles,
The goodli faire that lith heere specheles.

'A mouth he hath, but woordis hath he noone,
Can nat compleyne, alas, for non outrage,
Nor gruchith nat, but lith heer al aloone,
Stille as a lamb, most meek of his visage.
What herte of steel coude doon to hym damage
Or suffre hym deie, beholdyng the maneer
And look benygne of his tweyne eyen cleer?

vengeance 'O thou my fader, to cruel is thi wreche!
Hardere of herte than any tigre or leoun
To slen a child that lith withoute speche,
Void of al mercy and remissioun,
And on his mooder hast no compassioun,
His youthe considred, with lippis softe as silk,
Which at my brest lith still and souketh mylk.

'Is any sorwe remembrid be writyng
Unto my sorweful sihhes comparable?
Or was ther ever creature lyvyng
grief That felte of dool a thyng mor lamentable?
For counfortles and unrecuperable
Ar thilke hepid sorwes ful of rage
spirit Which han with wo oppressid my corage.

{She complains against her father's cruelty, the blindness of love, her loss of reputation.}

'Now farweel, brother, to me it doth suffise
To deie allone for our bothe sake,
And in my moste feithful humble wise,
Unto my deth-ward thouh I tremble and quake,
Of the for evere now my leve I take;
And onys a yeer forget nat but take heed
Mi fatal day this lettre for to reed.

'So shaltow han on me sum remembraunce,
Mi name enprentid in thi kalender
As a way of recording Be rehersaile of my dedli grevaunce:
Wear Were blak that day and mak a doolful cheer,
And whan thou comest and shalt approche neer
Mi sepulture, I pray the nat disdeyne
Upon my grave summe teris for to reyne.'

stunned with grief Writyng hir lettir, awappid and in dreede,
In hir riht hand hir penne gan to quake
And a sharp suerd to make hire herte bleede
handed In hir left hand hir fader hath hir take;
And most hir sorwe was for hir childes sake,
bosom Upon whos face, in hir barm slepyng,
Ful many a teer she wepte in compleynyng.

6945 Cf. Lam. 1:12, 'O all ye who pass by, look and see if there is any sorrow like my sorrow'. These words, spoken by Zion, personified, in captivity, were transferred by typology to Christ and represented as spoken by him from the Cross. There are many ME lyrics on the theme.

trembled Aftir al this, so as she stood and quook,
Hir child beholdyng, myd of hir peynes smerte,
Withoute abood the sharpe suerd she took
pierced And roof hirself evene to the herte.
Hir child fill doun, which myhte nat asterte,
Havyng non helpe to socoure hym nor save,
itself But in hir blood the silf began to bathe.

And thanne hir fader, most cruel of entent,
Bad that the child sholde anon be take,
Of cruel houndis in haste for to be rent
And be devoured, for his mooder sake.
Of this tragedie thus an eende I make,
Narration Processe of which, as men may reede and see,
Concludith on myscheef and furious cruelte.

Exclamation on the death of Cyrus (II.3921–41)

Cyrus, king of Persia, meets a suitably bloodthirsty end at the hands of queen Tomyris, whose son he has slain. She has Cyrus's head cut off and thrown in a bath of blood. Lydgate borrows his rhetoric ('Lo heer...') from Chaucer's *TC* (V.1849) and uses the 'topos of negation' ('there was no...') as his technique of amplification. The gloating is magnificent, but the insistence that Cyrus's death is God's punishment of a wicked tyrant reveals how uneasy a Christian writer was with anything but a Christian version of pagan history.

Lo heer, th'exequies of this myhti kyng!
Lo heer, the eende of his estat roiall!
Ther wer no flawmys nor brondis cleer shynyng
To brenne his bodi with fires funerall,
Nor observaunces nor offrynges marciall,
Nor tumbe of gold with stonys riche and fyne
Was non ordeyned that day to make his shryne.

Epitaphie ther was non rad nor sunge
Be no poete with ther poetries,
Nor of his tryumphes ther nas no belle runge,
Nor no weperis with sobbyng tragedies –
Non attendaunce but of his enmyes,
Which of hatrede in ther cruel rage
carcass Cast out his kareyn to beestis most savage.

Lo heer, of Cirus the fynal aventure,
Which of al Asie was whilom emperour!
Now lith he abject, withoute sepulture,
Of hih ne low he fond no bet favour.
end Lo heer, the fyn of al worldli labour,
Namli of tirantis which list nat God to dreede
But set ther lust in slauhtre, and blood to sheede!

EXCLAMATION ON THE DEATH OF CYRUS

3931 **weperis with sobbyng tragedies**. Lydgate, like many in the Middle Ages, thought that classical plays were read out by the author, with actors miming the characters' feelings (see his account of the theatres of ancient Troy, *Troy-Book* II.860–926).

3940 **Namli**, 'especially', means nothing, since death is universal; it reveals how inevitably a Christian writer substitutes eschatology for 'fall-of-princes' or Fortune-tragedy.

Letter to Gloucester

Humphrey of Gloucester was not such an assiduous patron for the *Fall of Princes* as Lydgate had hoped, and the following poem seems to have been written as a reminder to him. If the burst of patronal generosity celebrated in a paean of praise at the start of Book 3 was prompted by the poem, then it was indeed a success. It belongs to the genre of begging-poem (cf. Chaucer's *Purse*), and is quite cleverly designed to appeal to a man who wants to be thought clever, though it tends to exhaust rather than to exploit the witty potential of its images. It might be asked why a cloistered monk living a communal life needed money, and what he could have done with it, but monastic life and administration were becoming much more bound up with money in the fifteenth century, and Lydgate would have been able to purchase many privileges – a private study, books, servants. There are seven MSS, including BL MS Harley 2255, a 'Lydgate anthology' written for Lydgate's abbot at Bury, William Curteys; the poem is printed in Hammond (1927), pp. 149–50; in H.N. MacCracken (ed.), *The Minor Poems of John Lydgate*, Part 2, EETS, OS 192 (1934), pp. 665–7; and in J. Norton-Smith (ed.), *John Lydgate: Poems* (Oxford, 1966), pp. 1–3. For the use and variation of the refrain-line, and the function of the 'envoy', see Chaucer's *Truth*, above.

if — Riht myhty prynce, and it be your wille,
Condescende leiser for to take
letter of petition — To seen the content of this litil bille,
Which whan I wrot myn hand I felte quake,
Tokne of mornyng weryd clothys blake
arrears — Cause my purs was falle in gret rerage,
Lynyng outward, his guttys wer out-shake,
Oonly for lak of plate and of coignage.

I souhte leechys for a restoratiff,
In whom I fond no consolacioun;
Appotecaryes for a confortatiff –
Drug, medicinal compound — Dragge nor dya was noon in Bury toun.
Botme of his stomak was tournyd up-so-doun:
A laxatif did hym so gret outrage,
Made hym slendre by a consumpcioun,
Oonly for lak of plate and of coignage.

Ship was ther noon nor seilis reed of hewe –
contrary — The wynd froward to make hem ther to londe.
flood-tide — The flood was passyd and sodeynly of newe
A lowh ground-ebbe was faste by the stronde.
No maryneer durste take on honde
narrowness — To caste an ankir, for streihtnesse of passage;
customs revenue — The custom skars, as folk may undirstonde,
Oonly for lak of plate and of coignage.

Tower of London (the Royal Mint) — Ther was no tokne sent doun from the Tour:
weighing-balance — As any gossomer the countirpeys was liht.
fever — A fretyng etyk causyd his langour
daily recurring fever — By a cotidian which heeld hym day and nyht.
Sol and Luna wer clypsyd of ther liht;
imprint — Ther was no cros nor preent of no visage;

17–24 The imagery of this stanza is of 'his ship coming in', prompted by the design of gold coins (nobles), which bore on the obverse an image of a ship.

29 **Sol and Luna**, i.e. sun and moon, used as alchemical terms for gold and silver.

30 **cros ... visage**. Silver coins bore a cross on the face, or obverse, and a crowned male head on the reverse.

His lynyng dirk, ther wer no platys briht,
Oonly for lak and scarsete of coignage.

Harde to likke hony out of a marbil stoon,
For ther is nouthir licour nor moisture.
An ernest-grote, whan it is dronke and goon,
Bargeyn of marchauntys stant in aventure.
My purs and I be callyd to the lure
Of Indigence, our stuff leyd in morgage.
But ye, my lord, may al our soor recure — *cause to recover*
With a receyt of plate and of coignage.

Nat sugre-plate, maad by th'appotecarye – — *(a sweet medicinal lozenge)*
Plate of briht metal yevith a mery soun.
In Boklerys-bury is noon such letuary; — *(see n.)*
Gold is a cordial, gladdest confeccioun
Ageyn etiques of oold consumpcioun,
Aurum potabile for folk ferre ronne in age, — *Drinkable gold*
In quyntessence best restauracioun — *In its purest form (i.e. gold coins)*
With silver plate enprentyd with coignage.

L'Envoy

O seely bille, whi art thu nat ashamyd — *silly-innocent*
So malapertly to shewe out thy constreynt! — *impertinently, shortage*
But povert hath so nyh thy tonne attamyd — *emptied your cask*
That *nichil habet* is cause of thy compleynt.
A drye tisyk makith oold men ful feynt: — *phthisis*
Reediest weye to renewe ther corage
Is a fressh dragge, of no spycis meynt, — *healing drug, mixed*
But of a briht plate enpreentyd with coignage.

Thu mayst afferme as for thyn excus
Thy bareyn celle is sool and solitarye;
Of cros nor pyl ther is no reclus, — *nothing shut away*
Preent nor impressioun in al thy seyntuarye. — *reliquary*
To conclude breefly and nat tarye:
Ther is no noyse herd in thyn hermytage.
God sende soone a gladdere letuarye
With a cleer soun of plate and of coignage.

The Testament of Dan John Lydgate (lines 874–97)

The writing of a 'testament', in which a (usually repentant) poet looks back over his life, is something of a convention (there are examples by Jean de Meun and François Villon). It is usually assumed that such poems are writ-

35 **ernest-grote**. A bargain was sealed by payment of a groat as 'earnest-money'; it often got spent on drink in the tavern where the deal was made.
37–8 **Indigence** is imagined as drawing purses to it as hawks are drawn to the 'lure' (tempting-looking snack) on the falconer's hand.
40 **receyt**: (1) prescription for a remedy; (2) the remedy itself; (3) the act of receiving. All are relevant here.
43 **Boklerys-bury**: Bucklesbury, a street of grocers and apothecaries in London. **letuary**: electuary, thick syrupy medicine.
52 ***nichil habet***: 'he has nothing', the return made by a sheriff concerning a candidate for distraint who had nothing to distrain.
59 **pyl**: a pillar-shaped impression made by the stamping-iron on the reverse of a silver coin (see line 30).

ten late in life. Lydgate's *Testament* is in five sections: (1) meditation on the holy name of Jesus; (2) comparison of man's life to the seasons; (3) prayer to Jesus for mercy; (4) confessions of misspent youth: how the 14-year-old boy came upon a crucifix with the inscription *Vide* ('Behold'); (5) the meaning of *Vide* is unfolded. There are 14 MSS, of whole or part (some stanzas are painted in the Clopton chapel in Long Melford church); ed. H.N. MacCracken, *The Minor Poems of John Lydgate*, Part 1, EETS, ES 107 (1911), pp. 329–62.

{Jesus reminds man, in a detailed account of his trial and crucifixion ('Behold...'), of what he suffered for man's sake.}

Emprente thes thynges in thyn inward thought
And grave hem depe in thy remembraunce.
Thynke on hem weel, and forgete hem nowght:
Al this I suffred to do the allegeaunce, *relief*
And with my seyntes to yeve the suffisaunce.
In the hevenly court for the I do devyse
A place eternall, a place of all plesaunce,
For which my blood I gaf in sacryfice.

And more my mercy to putte att a preef *to the proof*
To every synnere that non ne shal it mysse,
Remembre how I gaf mercy to the theef,
Which hadde so longe trespaced and doon amys;
Went he not frely with me to paradise?
Have this in mynde, how it is my guyse
All repentaunt to bryng hem to my blysse,
For whom my blood I gaf in sacryfice.

Tarye no lenger toward thyn herytage,
Hast on thy weye and be of ryght good chere, *Hasten*
Go eche day onward on thy pylgrymage,
Thynke howe short tyme thou hast abyden here; *to abide*
Thy place is bygged above the sterres clere, *built*
Noon erthly palys wrought in so statly wyse.
Kome on, my frend, my brother most entere!
For the I offered my blood in sacryfice.

Margery Kempe (*c.* 1373–*c.* 1440)

Margery Kempe was born about 1373, the daughter of John Brunham, a prosperous citizen and sometime mayor of King's Lynn, in Norfolk, a thriving port and commercial centre. At 20 she married John Kempe, by whom she had 14 children. She was in a position to achieve a high degree of bourgeois respectability, but she was unhappy from the time of the birth of her first child, and at the age of about 40, having heard the call of God and been spoken to and encouraged by Christ, she turned against her life and its sexual and other constraints. She began a career of wandering around England, in which she shared her visionary experiences with others, and wept and cried out in church and at public preachings where Christ and his passion were remembered. She was constantly pursued and interrogated by the authorities, suspected of being a Lollard as well as an unruly woman, and had interviews with the archbishops of both York and Canterbury. At first her husband accompanied her on her wanderings, but she later went off on pilgrimage on her own to Italy, the Holy Land, Spain and, after his death (about 1431), to Germany. Late in life, in her 60s, she dictated to scribes (herself probably minimally literate, she was not unacquainted with the literature of spirituality) an account of her life, the non-autobiographical portions of which (mostly Jesus's speeches) were printed in the early sixteenth century. The MS containing the whole 'Book' was believed lost until rediscovered in 1934. First reactions to the Book when it was published in 1940 were often hostile to this noisy and unaccommodating woman, who was dismissed, for all the historical interest of her work, as a pathological hysteric. More recently, especially with the advent of feminist criticism, scholars have recognized not just the extraordinary courage of her life but the remarkable originality, psychological astuteness and single-minded purposefulness of her work, in which she attempts to justify her life as an independent unvowed religious woman, a kind of self-made secular saint. In doing so, she challenged the exclusively male authority of the church and violated every prohibition by which men in general try to keep women silent. Men were happy with female recluses like Julian ('I would thou were closed in a house of stone that there should no man speak with thee', said one old monk, speaking for many), but Margery Kempe, despite her perfect orthodoxy of belief, was determined to be neither silent nor reclusive.

Exactly what is her own in the Book and what is the scribes' cannot be known for certain, but there is general agreement that the story is hers in nearly all respects and, with some benefit of hindsight, broadly true (though its worth does not depend on this); where verifiable, it is historically accurate. The Book survives only in BL MS Add.61823; the standard edition is that of S.B. Meech and H.E. Allen, EETS 212 (1940); there is a translation by B. Windeatt (Penguin, 1985). The Book has prompted much good recent criticism, including S. Delany, 'Sexual Economics, Chaucer's Wife of Bath, and *The Book of Margery Kempe*' (1975), reprinted in *Writing Woman: Women Writers and Women in Literature, Medieval to Modern* (New York, 1983), pp. 76–92; S. Beckwith, 'A Very Material Mysticism: the Medieval Mysticism of Margery Kempe', in Aers (1986), pp. 34–57; D. Aers, 'The Making of Margery Kempe', in Aers (1988), pp. 73–116; K. Lochrie, *Margery Kempe and the Translations of the Flesh* (Philadelphia, 1991); L. Staley, *Margery Kempe's Dissenting Fictions* (University Park, PA, 1994).

The Book of Margery Kempe

Her first childbirth, and first vision of Christ (chap. 1)

Whan this creatur[1] was xx yer of age or sumdele mor, sche was maryed to a worschepful burgeys and was wyth chylde wythin schort tyme, as kynde[2] wolde. And aftyr that sche had conceyved sche was labowrd wyth grett accessys[3] tyl the chyld was born, and than, what for labowr sche had in chyldyng[4] and for sekenesse goyng beforn, sche dyspered of hyr lyfe, wenyng sche myght not levyn.[5] And than sche sent for hyr gostly fadyr,[6] for sche had a thyng in conscyens whech sche had nevyr schewyd beforn that tyme in alle hyr lyfe. For sche was evyr lettyd[7] be hyr enmy, the Devel, evyrmor seyng to hyr whyl sche was in good heele[8] hir nedyd no confessyon but don penawns be hirself aloone and all schuld be foryovyn, for God is mercyful inow.[9] And therfor this creatur oftyntymes dede greet penawns in fastyng bred and

Chapter 1

1 **this creatur**. This is how Kempe refers to herself throughout the Book, in a manner ostentatiously self-abasing, yet perhaps appropriate to a dictated script.

2 nature

3 bouts of illness

4 childbirth

5 thinking that she might not live

6 confessor

7 prevented

8 health

9 The notion that inward confession was sufficient for forgiveness, without oral confession to a priest, was regarded as dangerously close to heresy, and commonly associated with Lollardy.

watyr and other dedys of almes wyth devowt preyers, saf sche wold not schewyn it in confessyon. And whan sche was any tym seke or dysesyd the Devyl seyd in her mende[10] that sche schuld be dampnyd, for sche was not schrevyn of that defawt.[11]

Wherfor, aftyr that hir chyld was born, sche, not trostyng hir lyfe, sent for hir gostly fadyr, as iseyd beforn, in ful wyl to be schrevyn of alle hir lyfetym as ner as sche cowde. And whan sche cam to the poynt for to seyn that thing whech sche had so long conselyd,[12] hir confessour was a lytyl to hastye and gan scharply to undyrnemyn[13] hir er than sche had fully seyd hir entent, and so sche wold no mor seyn for nowt he myght do. And anoon, for dreed sche had of dampnacyon on the to[14] syde and hys scharp reprevyng on that other syde, this creatur went owt of hir mende and was wondyrlye vexid and labowryd wyth spyritys half yer, viii wekys and odde days. And in this tyme sche sey, as hir thowt, develys opyn her mowthys al inflaumyd wyth brennyng lowys[15] of fyr as thei schuld a[16] swalwyd hyr in, sumtyme rampyng at hyr, sumtyme thretyng her, sumtym pullyng hyr and halyng hir bothe nyght and day duryng the forseyd tyme. And also the develys cryed upon hir wyth greet thretyngys and bodyn[17] hir sche schuld forsake hir Crystendam, hir feyth, and denyin hir God, hys Modyr, and alle the seyntys in hevyn, hyr goode werkys and alle good vertues, hir fadyr, hyr modyr and alle hire frendys.

And so sche dede. Sche slawndred hir husbond, hir frendys and her owyn self, sche spak many a reprevows[18] worde and many a schrewyd[19] worde, sche knew no vertu ne goodnesse, sche desyryd all wykkydnesse: lych as the spyrytys temptyd hir to sey and do, so sche seyd and dede. Sche wold a fordon[20] hirself many a tym at her steryngys[21] and a ben damnyd wyth hem in helle, and into wytnesse therof sche bot[22] hir owen hand so vyolently that it was seen al hir lyfe aftyr. And also sche roof[23] hir skyn on hir body ayen[24] hir hert wyth hir nayles spetowsly,[25] for sche had noon othyr instrumentys, and wers sche wold a don saf[26] sche was bowndyn and kept wyth strength bothe day and nyght that sche myght not have hir wylle.

And whan sche had long ben labowryd in thes and many other temptacyons that men wend sche schuld nevyr a skapyd ne levyd,[27] than on a tym, as sche lay aloone and hir kepars[28] wer fro hir, owyr mercyful Lord Crist Jesu, evyr to be trostyd, worshypd be hys name, nevyr forsakyng hys servawnt in tyme of nede, aperyd to hys creatur whych had forsakyn hym in lyknesse of a man, most semly, most bewtyuows and most amyable that evyr myght be seen wyth mannys eye, clad in a mantyl of purpyl sylke, syttyng upon hir beddys syde, lokyng upon hir wyth so blyssyd a chere that sche was strengthyd in alle hir spyritys, seyd to hir thes wordys: 'Dowtyr, why hast thow forsakyn me, and I forsoke nevyr the?' And anoon as he had seyd thes wordys sche saw veryly how the eyr openyd as bryght as ony levyn,[29] and he stey[30] up into the eyr, not ryght hastyli and qwykly, but fayr and esly that sche myght wel beholdyn hym in the eyr tyl it was closyd ageyn.

And anoon the creature was stabelyd in hir wyttys and in hir reson as wel as evyr sche was beforn, and preyd hir husbond as so soon as he cam to hir that sche myght have the keys of the botery to takyn hir mete and drynke as sche had don beforn. Hyr maydens and hir kepars cownseld hym he schulde delyvyr hir no keys, for thei seyd sche wold but yeve awey swech good as ther was,[31] for sche wyst not what sche seyde, as thei wende.[32] Nevyrthelesse hir husbond, evyr havyng tendyrnes and compassyon of hir, comawndyd thei schulde delyvyr to hyr the keyys. And sche[a] toke hyr mete and drynke as hir bodyly strength wold servyn hir and knew hir frendys and hir meny[33] and all other that cam to hir to se how owyr Lord Jesu Cryst had wrowt hys grace in hir, so blyssyd mot he be that evyr is ner in tribulacyon.

10 mind
11 confessed of that fault
12 **conselyd**: 'concealed'. There have been various speculations as to what the unconfessed sin, preying upon her mind during post-partum depression, may have been.
13 reprove
14 that one
15 flames
16 should have
17 commanded
18 reproving
19 harsh
20 have done away with
21 their promptings
22 bit
23 tore
24 next to
25 savagely
26 worse she would have done except that
27 never have escaped nor lived
28 minders
29 flash of lightning
30 ascended
31 was there
32 thought
33 household

Whan men wenyn he wer fer[b] fro hem, he is ful nere be hys grace. Sythen[34] this creatur dede alle other ocupacyons as fel for hir to do, wysly and sadly[35] inow, saf sche knew not veryli the drawt[36] of owyr Lord.

{She continues to live many years with her husband, unsuccessful in her ambition to be chaste, unsuccessful in business, tempted to despair, but comforted by Christ.}

Her contract with her husband, 23 June 1413, on the road to Bridlington (chap. 11)

It befel upon a Fryday on Mydsomyr Evyn in ryght hot wedyr, as this creatur was komyng fro Yorke-ward beryng a botel wyth bere in hir hand and hir husbond a cake in hys bosom, he askyd hys wyfe this qwestyon, 'Margery, yf her come a man wyth a swerd and wold smyte of myn hed les than[1] I schulde comown kendly[2] wyth yow as I have do befor, seyth me trewth of yowr consciens – for ye sey ye wyl not lye – whethyr wold ye suffyr myn hed to be smet of or ellys suffyr me to medele wyth yow ayen as I dede sumtyme.' 'Alas, ser,' sche seyd, 'why meve[3] ye this mater and have we[4] ben chast this viii wekys?' 'For[5] I wyl wete the trewth of yowr hert.' And than sche seyd wyth gret sorwe, 'Forsothe I had levar se yow be slayn than we schuld turne ayen to owyr unclennesse.' And he seyd ayen, 'Ye arn no good wyfe.'

And than sche askyd hir husbond what was the cawse that he had not medelyd wyth hir viii wekys befor, sythen sche lay wyth hym every nyght in hys bedde. And he seyd he was so made aferde whan he wold a towchyd hir that he durst no mor don. 'Now, good ser, amend yow and aske God mercy, for I teld yow ner iii yer sythen that ye schuld be slayn sodeynly, and now is this the thryd yer, and yet[6] I hope I schal han my desyr.[7] Good sere, I pray yow grawnt me that I schal askyn, and I schal pray for yow that ye schul be savyd thorw the mercy of owyr Lord Jesu Cryst, and ye schul have mor mede in hevyn than yyf ye weryd an hayr or an haburgon.[8] I pray yow, suffer me to make a vow of chastyte in what bysshopys hand that God wele.' 'Nay,' he seyd, 'that wyl I not grawnt yow, for now may I usyn yow wythowtyn dedly synne and than myght I not so.' Than sche seyd ayen, 'Yyf it be the wyl of the Holy Gost to fulfyllyn that I have seyd, I pray God ye mote consent therto, and yf it be not the wyl of the Holy Gost, I pray God ye nevyr consent therto.'

Than went thei forth to Brydlyngton-ward in ryght hoot wedyr, the forn-seyd creatur havyng gret sorwe and gret dred for hyr chastite. And as thei cam be a cros,[9] hyr husbond sett hym down undyr the cros, clepyng his wyfe unto hym and seyng this wordys onto hir, 'Margery, grawnt me my desyr, and I schal grawnt yow yowr desyr. My fyrst desyr is that we schal lyn stylle togedyr in o bed as we han do befor; the secunde that ye schal pay my dettys er ye go to Jerusalem;[10] and the thrydde that ye schal etyn and drynkyn wyth me on the Fryday as ye wer wont to don.' 'Nay ser,' sche seyd, 'to breke the Fryday I wyl nevyr grawnt yow whyl I leve.'[11] 'Wel,' he seyd, 'than schal I medyl yow ageyn.'

Sche prayd hym that he wold yeve hir leve to make hyr praerys, and he grawntyd it goodlych. Than sche knelyd down besyden a cros in the feld and preyd in this maner wyth gret habundawns of teerys, 'Lord God, thou knowyst al thyng; thow knowyst what sorwe I have had to be chast in my body to the al this iii yer, and now myght I han my wylle and I dar not for lofe of the. For yyf I wold brekyn that maner of fastyng whech thow comawndyst me to kepyn on the Fryday wythowtyn mete or drynk, I schuld now han my desyr. But, blyssyd Lord, thow knowyst I wyl not contraryen thi wyl, and mekyl[12] now is my sorwe les than[13] I fynde comfort in the. Now blyssed Jesu, make thi wyl knowyn to me unworthy that I may folwyn theraftyr and fulfyllyn it wyth al my myghtys.' And than owyr Lord Jesu Cryst wyth gret swetnesse spak to this creatur, comawndyng hir to gon ayen to hir husbond and prayn

34 Afterwards
35 soberly
36 spiritual call

Chapter 11

1 smite off my head unless
2 **comown kendly**: 'commune according to nature', i.e. have sexual intercourse ('medele').
3 raise
4 when we have
5 Because
6 still
7 **my desyr**, i.e. that he will amend (not that he will be slain suddenly).
8 **an hayr or an haburgon**: a hair-shirt or a coat of chain-mail, either of which might be worn as a penance.
9 wayside cross
10 The money to pay her husband's debts probably came from a legacy from her father, who had died the previous year.
11 live
12 great
13 unless

hym to grawntyn hir that sche desyred. 'And he schal han that he desyreth. For, my derworthy dowtyr, this was the cawse that I bad the fastyn – for thou schuldyst the sonar opteyn and getyn thi desyr, and now it is grawntyd the.[14] I wyl no lengar thow fast, therfor I byd the in the name of Jesu ete and drynk as thyn husbond doth.'

Than this creatur thankyd owyr Lord Jesu Cryst of hys grace and hys goodnes, sythen ros up and went to hir husbond, seyng unto hym, 'Sere, yf it lyke yow, ye schal grawnt me my desyr, and ye schal have yowr desyr. Grawntyth me that ye schal not komyn in my bed, and I grawnte yow to qwyte yowr dettys er I go to Jerusalem. And makyth my body fre to God so that ye nevyr make no chalengyng in me to askyn no dett of matrimony[15] aftyr this day whyl ye levyn, and I schal etyn and drynkyn on the Fryday at yowr byddyng.' Than seyd hir husbond ayen to hir, 'As fre mot yowr body ben to God as it hath ben to me.'[16] Thys creatur thankyd God gretly, enjoyng[17] that sche had hir desyr, preyng hir husbond that thei schuld sey iii Pater Noster in the worshep of the Trinyte for the gret grace that he had grawntyd hem. And so they ded, knelyng undyr a cros, and sythen thei etyn and dronkyn togedyr in gret gladnes of spyryt. This was on a Fryday on Mydsomyr Evyn....[18]

Among the monks at Canterbury (chap. 13)

On a tyme, as this creatur was at Cawntyrbery in the cherch among the monkys, sche was gretly despysed and reprevyd for cawse sche wept so fast bothyn of the monkys and prestys and of seculer men ner al a day bothe afor-noon and aftyr-noon, also in so mech that[1] hyr husbond went away fro hir as[2] he had not a-knowyn hir and left hir aloon among hem, cheys hir[3] as sche cowde, for other comfort had sche noon of hym as[4] that day. So an eld monk, whech had ben tresowrer wyth the Qwen whyl he was in seculer clothyng,[5] a riche man, and gretly dred of mech pepyl,[6] toke hir be the hand, seying unto hir, 'What kanst thow seyn of God?' 'Ser,' sche seyth, 'I wyl bothe speke of hym and heryn of hym,' rehersyng the monk a story of Scriptur. The munke seyd, 'I wold thow wer closyd in an hows of ston that ther schuld no man speke wyth the.'[7] 'A, ser,' sche seyd, 'ye schuld meynteyn[8] Goddys servawntys, and ye arn the fyrst that heldyn[9] ayens hem. Owyr Lord amend yow.' Than a yong monke seyde to this creatur, 'Eythyr thow hast the Holy Gost or ellys thow hast a devyl wythin the, for that thou spekyst her to us it is Holy Wrytte, and that hast thou not of thiself.'[10] Than seyd this creatur, 'I pray yow, ser, yeve me leve to tellyn yow a tale.'[11] Than the pepyl seyd to the monke, 'Late hir sey what sche wyl.'

And than sche seyd, 'Ther was onys a man that had synned gretly ayens God and whan he was schrevyn hys confessowr inyoined hym in party[12] of penawnce that he schuld o yer hyer men[13] to chyde hym and reprevyn hym for hys synnes and he schuld yeven hem sylver for her labowr. And on a day he cam among many gret men as[14] now ben her, God save yow alle, and stod among hem as I do now among yow, despysyng hym as ye do me, the man lawhyng or smylyng and havyng good game at here wordys. The grettest maystyr of hem seyd to the man, "Why lawhyst thu, brothel,[15] and art thow[16]

14 Kempe 'realizes' (as we might say) that Jesus's reason for recommending fasting was so that she would have something to exchange when bargaining for her chastity. Like the Wife of Bath, with whom she is often compared, Kempe has a keen sense of the bargaining power of sexuality, though of course she attributes her human resourcefulness to divine intervention.

15 **dett of matrimony**. See WBP 129n, above.

16 Both husband and wife would appreciate the wry irony of this.

17 rejoicing

18 **on a Fryday**. We understand why Kempe wants to remind us of this.

Chapter 13

1 in so much that (by reason that)

2 as if

3 let her choose

4 as of

5 Servants of the crown often took the habit and retired with their pensions to the larger and more comfortable abbeys: this is most probably John Kynton, chancellor to queen Joanna, wife of Henry IV. He became a monk of Christ Church, Canterbury, in 1408 and died in 1416.

6 feared by many people

7 The old monk could be a bitter opponent of public female devotion and yet a supporter of enclosed anchoresses; his remark is not necessarily dismissive, nor a reference to imprisonment.

8 support

9 hold

10 **that hast thou not of thiself**. She cannot be speaking of Holy Writ on her own authority, since she is a woman, but must be either divinely or diabolically inspired. Julian was also aware of this problem.

11 **to tellyn yow a tale**. Kempe has, amongst much that she shares with the Wife of Bath, the capacity to use her powers of language to disarm her opponents or to make them look ridiculous.

12 as a part

13 for one year hire men

14 such as

15 wretch

16 when thou art

gretly despysed?" "A, ser, I have a gret cause to lawh, for I have many days put sylver owt of my purse and hyred men to chyde me for remyssyon of my synne, and this day I may kepe my sylver in my purs, I thank yow alle." Ryght so I sey to yow, worshepful serys, whyl I was at hom in myn owyn contre day be day wyth gret wepyng and mornyng, I sorwyd for I had no schame, skorne and despyte as I was worthy. I thank yow alle, serys, heyly[17] what fore-noon and aftyr-noon I have had resonably[18] this day, blyssed be God therof.'

Than sche went owt of the monastery, thei folwyng and crying upon hir, 'Thow schalt be brent, fals lollare.[19] Her is a cartful of thornys redy for the and a tonne[20] to bren the wyth.' And the creatur stod wythowtyn the yatys at Cawntyrbery, for it was in the evenyng, mech pepyl wonderyng on hir. Than seyd the pepyl, 'Tak and bren hir.' And the creatur stod stylle, tremelyng and whakyng[21] ful sor in hir flesch wythowtyn ony erdly comfort, and wyst not wher hyr husbond was become. Than prayd sche in hir hert to owyr Lord, thynkyng on this maner, 'Hedyr[22] cam I, Lord, for thi lofe. Blyssed Lord, help me and have mercy on me.'[23] And anon aftyr sche had mad hir prayerys in hir hert to owyr Lord, ther komyn tweyn fayr yong men and seyd to hir, 'Damsel, art thow non eretyke ne no loller?' And sche seyd, 'No, serys, I am neythyr eretyke ne loller.' Than thei askyd hir wher was hir in.[24] Sche seyd sche wyst never in what strete, nevyrthelesse it schuld be at a Dewchmannys[25] hows. Than this tweyn yong men browgt hir hom to hir ostel and made hir gret cher, preyng hir to pray for hem, and ther fond sche hyr husbond.

{Her peregrinations continue; she goes to see Julian of Norwich (chap. 18), receives many visits and promises of singular grace from Jesus, and journeys to the Holy Land and Rome. In Rome, Jesus speaks to her of his love for her.}

Wedded to the Godhead (chap. 36)

'Fastyng, dowtyr, is good for yong begynnars and discrete[1] penawns, namly that her gostly fadyr yevyth hem or injoyneth hem for to do. And for to byddyn many bedys[2] it is good to hem that can no bettyr do, and yet it is not parfyte. But it is a good wey to perfeccyon-ward. For I telle the, dowtyr, thei that arn gret fastarys and gret doers of penawnce thei wold that it schuld ben holdyn the best lyfe; also thei that yevyn hem to sey many devocyons thei wold han that the best lyfe; and thei that yevyn mech almes thei wold that that wer holdyn the best lyfe. And I have oftyn-tymes, dowtyr, teld the that thynkyng, wepyng and hy contemplacyon is the best lyfe in erthe. And thu schalt have mor meryte in hevyn for o yer of thynkyng in thi mende than for an hundryd yer of preyng wyth thi mowth, and yet thu wylt not levyn[3] me, for thu wilt byddyn many bedys whedyr I wil or not. And yet, dowtyr, I wyl not be displesyd wyth the whedir[4] thu thynke, sey or speke, for I am alwey plesyd wyth the. And yyf I wer in erde[5] as bodily as I was er I deyd on the cros, I schuld not ben aschamyd of the as many other men ben, for I schuld take the be the hande amongs the pepil and make the gret cher that thei schuldyn wel knowyn that I lovyd the ryght wel.

'For it is convenyent[6] the wyf to be homly[7] wyth hir husbond. Be he nevyr so gret a lorde and sche so powr a woman whan he weddyth hir, yet thei must ly togedir and rest togedir in joy and pes. Ryght so mot[8] it be twyx the and me, for I take non hed what thu hast be but what thu woldist be. And oftyn-tymes have I telde the that I have clene foryove the alle thy synnes. Therfore most I nedys be homly wyth the and lyn in thi bed wyth the. Dowtyr, thow desyrest gretly to se me, and thu mayst boldly, whan thu art in thi bed, take me to the as for thi weddyd husbond, as thy derworthy derlyng, and as for thy swete

17 heartily
18 in reasonable measure
19 Any unorthodox form of behaviour was likely to prompt accusations of Lollardy. The enthusiasm to have Kempe burnt is a reminder that the burning of heretics was now (William Sawtre, in 1401, was the first heretic to be burnt in England) an accepted and probably widely popular instrument of government policy.
20 large barrel
21 quaking
22 Hither
23 It is hard for Kempe to avoid giving the impression that God is to blame (as well as her husband) for her predicament.
24 inn
25 German's

Chapter 36
1 judicious
2 pray many prayers
3 believe
4 whatever
5 on earth
6 fitting
7 intimate
8 must

sone, for I wyl be lovyd as a sone schuld be lovyd wyth the modyr[9] and wil that thu love me, dowtyr, as a good wife owyth[10] to love hir husbonde. And therfor thu mayst boldly take me in the armys of thi sowle[11] and kyssen my mowth, myn hed and my fete as swetly as thow wylt. And as oftyn-tymes as thu thynkyst on me or woldyst don any good dede to me, thu schalt have the same mede in hevyn as yyf thu dedist it to myn owyn precyows body whech is in hevyn, for I aske no mor of the but thin hert for to lovyn me that lovyth the, for my lofe is evyr redy to the.' Than sche yaf thankyng and preysing to owr Lord Jesu Crist for the hy grace and mercy that he schewyd unto hir, unworthy wrech.

Thys creatur had divers tokenys in hir bodily heryng. On[12] was a maner of sownde as it had ben a peyr of belwys[13] blowyng in hir ere. Sche beyng abasshed therof was warnyd in hir sowle no fer[14] to have, for it was the sownd of the Holy Gost. And than owyr Lord turnyd that sownde into the voys of a dowe,[15] and sithyn he turnyd it into the voys of a lityl bryd whech is callyd a reedbrest, that song ful merily oftyn-tymes in hir ryght ere. And than schuld sche evyrmor han gret grace aftyr that sche herd swech a tokyn. And sche had been used to swech tokenys abowt xxv yer at the writyng of this boke. Than seyd owr Lord Jesu Crist to hys creatur, 'Be thes tokenys mayst thu wel wetyn that I love the, for thu art to me a very modir and to al the world for that gret charite that is in the, and yet I am cawse of that charite myself, and thu schalt have gret mede therfor[16] in hevyn.'

{In 1417 she goes on pilgrimage to Compostella, in Spain, returning thence to Bristol and so to Leicester, where she is examined before the mayor, referred to the bishop of Lincoln, and later brought before the archbishop of York.}

Before the archbishop of York (chap. 52)

...On the next day sche was browt into the Erchebischopys chapel,[1] and ther comyn many of the Erchebischopys meny,[2] despisyng hir, callyng hir 'loller' and 'heretyke', and sworyn many an horrybyl othe that sche schulde be brent. And sche, thorw the strength of Jesu, seyd ayen to hem, 'Serys, I drede me ye schul be brent in helle wythowtyn ende les than[3] ye amende yow of yowr othys sweryng, for ye kepe not the comawndementys of God. I wolde not sweryn as ye don for al the good of this worlde.' Than thei yedyn awey as thei had ben aschamyd. Sche than, makyng hir prayer in hir mende, askyd grace so to be demenyd[4] that day as was most plesawns to God and profyte to hir owyn sowle and good exampyl to hir evyn-Cristen.[5] Owr Lord, answeryng hir, seyd it schulde be ryght wel.

At the last the seyd Erchebischop cam into the chapel wyth hys clerkys and scharply he seyde to hir, 'Why gost thu in white?[6] Art thu a mayden?' Sche, knelyng on hir knes befor hym, seyd, 'Nay, ser, I am no mayden; I am a wife.' He comawndyd hys mene[7] to fettyn[8] a peyr of feterys and seyd sche schulde ben feteryd, for sche was a fals heretyke. And than sche seyd, 'I am non heretyke, ne ye schal non preve me.' The Erchebisshop went awey and let hir stondyn alone. Than sche mad hir prayers to owr Lord God almyghty for to helpyn hir and socowryn hir ageyn alle hir enmyis, gostly and bodily, a long while, and hir flesch tremelyd and whakyd[9] wondirly that sche was fayn to puttyn hir handys undyr hir clothis that it schulde not ben aspyed.

Sythyn the Erchebischop cam ageyn into the chapel wyth many worthy clerkys, amongys whech was

9 by the mother
10 ought
11 **of thi sowle**. These occasional reminders that Kempe is talking about the mystical celebration of spiritual love do not disguise the eroticism of the imaginings. Such eroticism (which had a long tradition in devotional writing, especially as deriving from allegorical meditation on the Song of Songs) disturbed some male writers, and Kempe's repeated **boldly** may allude to their criticism. Mystic marriages to the Persons of the Trinity, with much of the language and ritual of regular marriage-services, are frequent in the writing of female visionaries.
12 One
13 bellows
14 fear
15 dove
16 reward for it

Chapter 52
1 The archbishop from 1407 to 1423 was Henry Bowet, a zealous Lollard-hunter. His chapel, attached to his palace, was at Cawood, 9 miles south of York.
2 household
3 unless
4 to demean herself
5 fellow-Christians
6 Kempe had worn white for some years, as a symbol of the rededication of her chastity to Jesus. It created some stir, partly because of a contemporary association with an ostentatious white-clad sect of Flagellants.
7 followers
8 fetch
9 quaked

the same doctowr whech had examynd hir beforn and the monke that had prechyd ageyn hir a lityl tyme beforn in Yorke. Sum of the pepil askyd whedyr sche wer a Cristen woman or a Jewe; sum seyd sche was a good woman, and sum seyd nay. Than the Erchebischop toke hys see,[10] and hys clerkys also, iche of hem in hys degre,[11] meche pepil beyng present. And in the tyme whil the pepil was gaderyng togedyr and the Erchebischop takyn hys see, the seyd creatur stod al behyndyn, makyng hir preyerys for help and socowr ageyn hir enmiis wyth hy devocyon so long that sche meltyd al into teerys. And at the last sche cryed lowde therwith, that the Erchebischop and his clerkys and meche pepil had gret wondyr of hir, for thei had not herd swech crying beforn. Whan hir crying was passyd, sche cam beforn the Erchebischop and fel down on hir kneys, the Erchebischop seying ful boystowsly[12] unto hir, 'Why wepist thu so, woman?' Sche, answeryng, seyde, 'Syr, ye schal welyn[13] sum day that ye had wept as sor as I.'

And than anon, aftyr the Erchebischop put to hir the Articles of owr feyth, to the whech God yaf hir grace to answeryn wel and trewly and redily wythowtyn any gret stody so that he myght not blamyn[14] hir, than he seyd to the clerkys, 'Sche knowith hir feyth wel anow.[15] What schal I don wyth hir?' The clerkys seyden, 'We knowyn wel that sche can[16] the Articles of the feith, but we wil not suffyr hir to dwellyn among us, for the pepil hath gret feyth in hir dalyawnce,[17] and peraventur sche myght pervertyn summe of hem.' Than the Erchebischop seyd unto hir, 'I am evyl enformyd of the; I her seyn[18] thu art a ryght wikked woman.' And sche seyd ageyn, 'Ser, so I her seyn that ye arn a wikkyd man. And yyf ye ben as wikkyd as men seyn, ye schal nevyr come in hevyn les than[19] ye amende yow whil ye ben her.' Than seyd he ful boistowsly, 'Why, thow wreche, what sey men of me?'[20] Sche answeryd, 'Other men, syr, can telle yow wel anow.' Than seyd a gret clerke wyth a furryd hood, 'Pes, thu! speke of thiself and late hym ben.'

Sithyn seyd the Erchebischop to hir, 'Ley thin hand on the boke her beforn me and swer that thu schalt gon owt of my diocyse as sone as thu may.' 'Nay, syr,' sche sayd, 'I praye yow, yeve me leve to gon ageyn into Yorke to take my leve of my frendys.' Than he yaf hir leve for on day or too. Sche thowt it[c] was to schort a tyme, wherfor sche seyd ayen, 'Sir, I may not gon owt of this diocyse so hastily, for I must teryin[21] and spekyn wyth good men er I go, and I must, ser, wyth yowr leve, gon to Brydlyngton and spekyn wyth my confessor, a good man, the whech was the good Priowrys confessor that is now canonysed.'[22]

Than seyd the Erchebischop to hir, 'Thow schalt sweryn that thu ne schalt[d] techyn ne chalengyn[23] the pepil in my diocyse.'[24] 'Nay, syr, I schal not sweryn,' sche seyde, 'for I schal spekyn of God and undirnemyn[25] hem that sweryn gret othys wher-so-evyr I go unto the tyme that the Pope and Holy Chirche hath ordeynde that no man schal be so hardy to spekyn of God, for God almyghty forbedith not, ser, that we schal speke of hym. And also the Gospel makyth mencyon that whan the woman had herd owr Lord prechyd sche cam beforn hym wyth a lowde voys and seyd, "Blyssed be the wombe that the bar and the tetys that yaf the sowkyn."[26] Than owr Lord seyd ayen to hir, "Forsothe so ar thei blissed that heryn the word of God and kepyn it." And therfor, sir, me thynkyth that the Gospel yevyth me leve to spekyn of God.' 'A, ser,' seyd the clerkys, 'her wot we wel that sche hath a devyl wythinne hir, for sche spekyth of the Gospel.'[27] As-swythe[28] a gret clerke browt forth a boke and leyd[29] seynt Powyl for hys party ageyns hir that no woman schulde prechyn.[30] Sche, answeryng therto, seyde, 'I preche not, ser, I come in no pulpytt. I use but comownycacyon and good wordys, and that wil I do whil I leve.'[31]

10 official seat
11 according to his rank
12 roughly
13 wish
14 find fault with her
15 enough
16 knows
17 conversation
18 I hear say
19 unless
20 The archbishop always seems to say the wrong thing to help his case, and falls into all the traps, while Kempe says exactly the right thing to help hers. Obviously there was sharpening of the dialogue in the process of organized remembrance.
21 tarry
22 The famous prior John of Bridlington died in 1379 and was canonized in 1401.
23 publicly reprove
24 The archbishop seems desperate now to get her to agree to something, so that he can save face and get rid of her.
25 reprove
26 gave thee to suck (Luke 11:27).
27 **sche spekyth of the Gospel**. Not quite as absurd as it sounds: Lollard inquisitions often focus on unauthorized personal reading of the Gospels, in the vernacular, as evidence of heresy. The church wished to keep the Bible in Latin, and all interpretation under its own control.
28 Immediately
29 cited
30 Paul, 1 Cor. 14:34–5.
31 live

{She tells a story against corrupt priests, which the archbishop commends, and he dismisses her with his blessing. After 1417, she returns to live mostly in Lynn, performing various miracles, and nursing her husband in his last illness.}

Her husband's last illness (chap. 76)

It happyd on a tyme that the husbonde of the sayd creatur, a man in gret age passyng thre scor yer, as he wolde a comyn down of hys chambyr bar-foot and bar-legge, he slederyd or ellys faylyd of hys fotyng and fel down to the grownd fro the gresys,[1] and hys hevyd undyr hym grevowsly brokyn and bresyd,[2] in-so-meche that he had in hys hevyd v teyntys[3] many days whil hys hevyd was in holyng.[4] And, as God wold, it was knowyn to summe of hys neybowrys how he was fallyn downe of the gresys, peraventur thorw the dene and the luschyng[5] of hys fallyng. And so thei comyn to hym and fowndyn hym lying wyth hys hevyd undir hym, half on lyfe, al rowyd[6] wyth blood, nevyr lyke to a spokyn wyth preyst[7] ne with clerk but thorw hy grace and myracle. Than the sayd creatur, hys wife, was sent for, and so sche cam to hym. Than was he takyn up and hys hevyd was sowyd,[8] and he was seke a long tyme aftyr, that men wend that he schulde a be deed.

And than the pepil seyd yyf he deyd hys wyfe was worthy to ben hangyn for hys deth, for-as-meche as sche myght a kept[9] hym and dede not. They dwellyd not togedyr, ne thei lay not togedyr, for, as is wretyn beforn, they bothyn wyth on assent and wyth fre wil of her eithyr[10] haddyn mad avow to levyn chast. And therfor to enchewyn[11] alle perellys thei dwellyd and sojowryd in divers placys[12] wher no suspicyon schulde ben had of her incontinens, for first thei dwellyd togedir aftyr that thei had mad her vow, and than the pepil slawndryd hem and seyd thei usyd her lust and her likyng as thei dedyn beforn her vow-makyng. And whan thei wentyn owt on pilgrimage or to se and spekyn wyth other gostly creaturys, many evyl folke whos tongys wer her owyn hurt, faylyng[13] the dreed and lofe of owr Lord Jesu Crist, demtyn[14] and seydyn that thei went rathar to woodys, grovys or valeys to usyn the lust of her bodiis that the pepil schuld not aspyin it ne wetyn it. They, havyng knowlach how prone the pepil was to demyn evyl of hem, desiryng to avoydyn al occasyon, in-as-mech as thei myght goodly, be her good wil and her bothins[15] consentyng, thei partyd asundyr as towchyng to her boord and to her chambrys, and wentyn to boord in divers placys. And this was the cawse that sche was not wyth hym, and also that sche schulde not be lettyd fro hir contemplacyon.

And therfor, whan he had fallyn and grevowsly was hurt, as is seyd beforn, the pepil seyd yyf he deyid it was worthy that sche schulde answeryn for hys deth. Than sche preyid to owr Lord that hir husbond myght levyn a yer and sche to be deliveryd owt[16] slawndyr yyf it wer hys plesawns. Owr Lord seyd to hir mende, 'Dowtyr, thu schalt have thi bone,[17] for he schal levyn and I have wrowt a gret myrakyl for the that he was not ded. And I bydde the take hym hom and kepe hym for my lofe.' Sche seyd, 'Nay, good Lord, for I schal than not tendyn to the as I do now.' 'Yys, dowtyr,' seyd owr Lord, 'thu schalt have as meche mede[18] for to kepyn hym and helpyn hym in hys nede at hom as yyf thu wer in chirche to makyn thi preyerys. And thu hast seyd many tymys that thu woldist fayn kepyn me.[19] I prey the now kepe hym for the lofe of me, for he hath sumtyme fulfillyd thi wil and my wil bothe, and he hath mad thi body fre to me that thu schuldist servyn me and levyn chast and clene, and therfor I wil that thu be fre to helpyn hym at hys nede in my name.' 'A, Lord,' seyd sche, 'for thi mercy grawnt me grace to obeyn thi wil and fulfille thi wil and late nevyr my gostly enmys han no powyr to lett me fro fulfillyng of thi wil.'

Than sche toke hom hir husbond to hir and kept hym yerys aftyr as long as he levyd and had ful mech

Chapter 76

1 stairs
2 bruised
3 wound-dressings
4 healing
5 the din and the rushing noise
6 streaked
7 'never likely to have spoken with a priest', i.e. in order to receive the last rites before death.
8 stitched up
9 looked after
10 either of them
11 avoid
12 stayed in different places
13 lacking
14 deemed
15 both of them
16 out of
17 request
18 reward
19 look after

labowr wyth hym, for in hys last days he turnyd childisch ayen and lakkyd reson that he cowd not don hys owyn esement to gon to a sege,[20] or ellys he wolde not, but as a childe voydyd his natural digestyon in hys lynyn clothys ther he sat be the fyre or at the tabil, whethyr[21] it wer, he wolde sparyn no place. And therfor was hir labowr meche the mor in waschyng and wryngyng and hir costage in fyryng[22] and lettyd hir ful meche fro hir contemplacyon that many tymys sche schuld an yrkyd[23] hyr labowr saf sche bethowt hir how sche in hir yong age had ful many delectabyl thowtys, fleschly lustys and inordinat lovys to hys persone. And therfor sche was glad to be ponischyd wyth the same persone and toke it mech the mor esily and servyd hym and helpyd hym, as hir thowt, as sche wolde a don Crist hymself.

{She has many visions and intimate meetings with Jesus and his Mother; the first part of her Book is copied out; she later journeys to Germany with her daughter-in-law (1433).}

20 stool
21 whichever
22 expenses of maintaining a fire
23 should have grudged

Charles of Orleans (1394–1465)

Charles, duke of Orleans, was captured at Agincourt in 1415 and spent the next 25 years as a prisoner in England, returning to France in 1440. He was an important pawn in Anglo-French negotiations, and remained in contact with court circles in France, as well as making the acquaintance of members of the English nobility, including the duke of Suffolk, who was responsible for his detention from 1432 to 1436 (see below, 'Myn hertys joy'). He was a prolific poet in French, especially after his return to France, mostly love-poems in the fashionable forms of ballade and rondeau. There is also an English MS (BL MS Harley 682) in which many of his French poems appear in clever, metrically fluent yet oddly unidiomatic English translations, along with other poems not known to be translated from French. The poems are organized in a sequence similar to that called the 'Livre de prison' in Charles's own personal MS of his French poems (BN MS fr.25458). The English sequence, which it is plausible and convenient to ascribe to Charles himself, consists of: (1) a series of ballades, with narrative prologue and end-link, tracing the development of the poet's love for a lady until her untimely death; (2) after his renunciation of love, a series of (mostly) roundels making a 'banquet of song and dance' for lovers; (3) a long narrative section in rhyme royal describing how he was conscripted back into the service of Venus; (4) a series of ballades in honour of his new lady. The whole sequence resembles the compilations of love-lyrics within a narrative framework that were composed by Machaut and Froissart, and also the Petrarchan sonnet-sequence with implied narrative that was to become so popular in sixteenth-century England. The influence of Chaucer is evident in language and phraseology, though the syntax is often peculiar, partly because of the contortions involved in following the exacting rhyme-schemes of the French. The familiar themes and conventions of courtly lyric are skilfully manipulated, but there is also an individually confected poetic 'voice', in which colloquialisms, sharp questions, interpolated exclamations and staccato repetitions are used to convey the impression of strong feeling barely restrained by convention (in a manner somewhat anticipating Wyatt). It is probably not helpful to look in real life for the experiences described nor the ladies addressed in such poems.

The poems are edited, with continuous line-numbering (followed here only in the narrative section), by R. Steele and M. Day, EETS, OS 215, 220 (1941, 1946; repr. 1970); and by M.-J. Arn, *Fortunes Stabilnes: Charles of Orleans's English Book of Love*, MRTS 138 (Binghamton, NY, 1994). The French texts are edited by P. Champion (Paris, 1956). See A.C. Spearing, 'Prison, Writing, Absence: Representing the Subject in the English Poems of Charles d'Orleans', *MLQ* 53 (1992), 83–99.

Ballade 48: 'To longe, for shame...'

A May-day poem: gathering blossoms of may (flowering white hawthorn) was a May-day folk-custom that had been embraced at court as one of the seasonal rituals of the love-game (e.g. *TC* II.56). This is the standard ballade form (there are minor variations): three eight-line stanzas rhyming *ababbcbc*, with last-line refrain and four-line envoy. MS, fol. 33r; French text, Champion, p. 70.

To longe, for shame, and all to longe, trewly,
Myn hert, I se thee slepe in displesere.
Awake, this day, awake! O verry fy!
Lete us at wode go geder may in fere, *to the wood, gather, together*
To holde of oure oold custome the manere.
Ther shall we here the birdis synge and pley
Right as the wood therwith shulde forshyvere,
This joly tyme, this fresshe first day of May.

The god of love, this worldis god myghti,
Holdith this day his feste, to fede and chere
The hertis of us poore lovers hevy
Which only him to serve sett oure desere;

3 **O verry fy**: an odd and unidiomatic phrase ('O shame on you, really!').

7 **forshyvere**: 'shiver to pieces' (*PF* 493).

cover with leaves, dry and withered

Wherfore he doth affoyle the trees sere
With grene, and hath the soyle y-flowrid gay,
Only to shewe his fest to more plesere,
This joly tyme, this fresshe first day of May.

Myn hert, thou wost how daungere hath on whi
Doon thee endure full grevous paynes here,
Which doth the longe thus absent thi lady,
That willist most to ben unto hir nere;
Wherfore the best avise I kan thee lere
Is that thou drawe thee to disportis ay,
Thi trowbely sorow therwith to aclere,
This joly tyme, this fresshe first day of May.

from thee, cause to be absent

teach

My first in thought and last, my lady dere,
Hit axith more then this oon day leysere
To telle yow, loo, my greef and gret affray
That this wolde make myn hert a poore martere
This joly tyme, this fresshe first day of May.

asks, day's leisure

BALLADE 70: 'IN THE FOREST OF NOYOUS HEVYNES...'

An example of the poet's skill in manipulating the familiar conventions of allegorical place, personification and dialogue. MS, fols 46v–47r; French text, Champion, p. 88.

grievous sorrow

In the forest of Noyous Hevynes
As I went wandryng in the moneth of May,
I mette of Love the myghti gret goddes,
Which axid me whithir I was away.
I hir answerid, 'As Fortune doth convey
As oon exylid from joy, al be me loth,
That passyng well all folke me clepyn may
The man forlost that wot not where he goth.'

though it be hateful to me

call

Half in a smyle, ayen of hir humblesse
She seide, 'My frend, if so I wist, ma fay,
Wherfore that thou art brought in such distresse,
To shape thyn ese I wolde mysilf assay,
For here-tofore I sett thyn hert in way
Of gret plesere – I not who made thee wroth.
Hit grevith me thee see in suche aray,
The man forlost that wot not where he goth.'

in reply

by my faith

know not

to see thee

'Allas!' I seide, 'most sovereyne good princesse,
Ye knowe my case: what nedith to yow say?
Hit is thorugh Deth, that shewith to all rudesse,

because

17 **daungere** was used for any obstacle to a love-affair, such as the lady's fear and standoffishness, the suspicion of others, or the jealousy of a husband. **on whi**: 'wrongfully', a phrase used elsewhere in the English poems with the same sense, in the context of the translation, but of doubtful origin.

27 **loo** ('lo') is a favourite metrical filler.

BALLADE 70

6 **As** is often used as an expletive (meaningless word) with imperatives by Chaucer, but in these poems it is used also with other forms of the verb. **oon** is object of **convey**.

Hath fro me tane that I most lovyd ay,
In whom that all myn hope and comfort lay.
So passyng frendship was bitwene us both
That I was not, to fals Deth did hir day, *until, caused her to die*
The man forlost that wot not where he goth.

'Thus am I blynd, allas and welaway!
Al fer myswent, with my staf grapsyng wey, *groping for the way*
That nothyng axe but me a grave to cloth; *clothe*
For pite is that I lyve thus a day,
The man forlost that wot not where he goth.'

BALLADE 72: 'WHAN FRESSHE PHEBUS...'

A Valentine's day poem (cf. *PF* 309) with a difference. Rhymes of *-oft* and *-ought* in this poem show how unstable was the pronunciation of *-ough-* at the time (cf. MnE cough, through, slough). MS, fols 47v–48r; French text, Champion, p. 91.

Whan fresshe Phebus, day of seynt Valentyne,
Had whirlid up his golden chare aloft, *chariot*
The burnyd bemys of it gan to shyne *burnished*
In at my chambre where I slepid soft,
Of which the light that he had with him brought *By which light*
He wook me of the slepe of hevynes
Wherin forslepid I all the nyght dowtles
Upon my bed so hard of newous thought. *troubled*

Of which this day to parten there bottyne *divide, booty*
An oost of fowlis semblid in a croft *field*
Myn eye biside and pletid ther latyne *pleaded, (bird-)language*
To have with them, as Nature had hem wrought,
Ther makis for to wrappe in wyngis soft; *mates*
For which they gan so loude ther cries dresse *address*
That I ne koude not slepe in my distres
Upon my bed so hard of newous thought.

Tho gan I reyne with teeris of myn eyne
My pilowe, and to wayle and cursen oft
Mi destyny, and gan my look enclyne
These birdis to, and seide, 'Ye birdis ought
To thanke Nature – where-as it sittith me nought – *is appropriate to*
That han yowre makis to yowre gret gladnes,
Where I sorow the deth of my maystres *grieve for*
Upon my bed so hard of noyous thought.

Als wele is him this day that hath him kaught *(Als is expletive)*
A Valentyne that lovyth him, as I gesse,

27 Possibly reminiscent of PardT 736.

BALLADE 72
2 A direct echo of the lines with which the Squire's Tale breaks off, *CT* V.671–2 (lines often imitated in the fifteenth century).

facing page
27 **this comfort sole**: (1) 'without this comfort' (**sole** = alone from, deprived of), or (2) the **comfort** is the poetic soliloquy addressed to himself (possibly an anachronistic modern reading), or (3) emend 'this comfort] discomfort'. French reads, 'Seul me tendray de confort desgarny'.

Where-as this comfort sole I here me dresse
Upon my bed so hard of noyous thought.

ROUNDEL 35: 'TAKE, TAKE THIS COSSE...'

This is standard roundel form: (with lines repeated indicated by upper-case letters) ABba abAB abba AB. The scribe writes just the first two or three words of lines to be repeated. MS, fol. 77v; French text, Champion, p. 224, cited here for comparison: 'Prenez tost ce baiser, mon cuer, / Que ma maistresse vous presente, / La belle bonne jeune et gente, / Par sa tres grant grace et doulceur. / Bon guet feray sur mon honneur / Affin que danger riens n'en sente. / Prenez, etc. / Dangier toute nuyt en labeur / A fait guet or gist en sa tente; / Acomplissez brief vostre entente / Tandis qu'il dort, c'est le meilleur. / Prenez, etc.'

kiss, at once Take, take this cosse, atonys, atonys, my hert!
That thee presentid is of thi maystres –
The goodly fayre so full of lustynes –
Only of grace to lessen with thi smert.
pay attention But to myn honoure loke thou well avert
That Daunger not parseyve my sotilnes.
  Take, take this cosse, atonys, atonys, my hert!
  That thee presentid is of thi maystres.
Daunger wacchith al nyght in his shert
To spye me, in a gery currisshenes;
get ready So to have doon attones let se thee dresse
covered While in a slepe his eyen ben covert.
  Take, take this cosse, atonys, atonys, my hert!
  That thee presentid is of thi maystres.

ROUNDEL 37: 'I PRAYSE NOTHING...'

Four-stress lines. MS, fol. 78v; French text, Champion, p. 225.

value I prayse nothing these cossis dowche
appearance's sake Whiche geve are for a countenaunce
to be taken from one's And for to take with acqueyntaunce –
Though many folkis love to towche.
(see n.) A man may bie, out crosse or crowche,
Ynowe of them, gret habundaunce.
  I prayse nothing these cossis dowche
  Which geve are for a countenaunce.
you know what But wot ye whiche, I cherisshe moche
The prive cossis of plesaunce:
Alle othir whiche that come askaunce,
Ben goode to feste with straungeris soche.
  I prayse nothing these cossis dowche
  Which geve are for a countenaunce.

ROUNDEL 35
6 **Daunger** here (see note to Ballade 48.17 above) behaves like the jealous husband.
10 **gery currisshenes**: 'unpredictable ill-bred (cur-like) way'.

ROUNDEL 37
1 **dowche**: 'German' (cf. 'Dutch', *deutsch*). These are polite or ceremonial kisses; the French merely has 'telz baisiers'.
4 Many people who are not acquainted like exchanging kisses.
5 'A man may buy, without coins (marked with various forms of cross)'.
11 **askaunce**: 'on the side' (i.e. by the way, incidentally), or 'on the side of the face' (on the cheeks).

ROUNDEL 57: 'MY GOSTLY FADIR...'

The poet speaks to his father-confessor, as if in the confessional: the scene is that of Gower's *Confessio Amantis*, where Genius the Confessor does on one occasion ask Amans if he has ever 'stolen kisses' (V.6543–4). Four-stress lines. MS, fol. 88v; no French.

My gostly fadir, I me confesse
First to God and then to yow
you know how — That at a wyndow, wot ye how,
stole — I stale a cosse of gret swetnes;
Which don was out avisynes –
But hit is doon, not undoon, now.
        My gostly fadir, I me confesse
        First to God and then to yow.
But I restore it shall, dowtles,
may — Ageyn, if so be that I mow,
And that to God I make a vow
for the rest, forgiveness — And ellis I axe foryefnes.
      My gostly fadir, I me confesse
      First to God and then to yow.

Charles meets his new lady

In a dream, he sees Venus, who urges him to fall in love again; Fortune descends in a golden chariot, bearing a wheel on which there is a lady with whom he instantly falls in love. He wakes up, wanders off, and comes across a courtly group playing 'post and pillar' (a game of tag and running about from base to base and finishing up with someone you like, you hope). MS, fols. 122r–124v; no French.

Now was ther on had knowen me tofore
That me aspide and I ne wiste not how
torn to pieces — And in his corse he fel and had for-tore
His hose, at which full many of hem lough.
'Now laughe,' seide he, 'for some han pleid ynough!'
Which to me spake, 'I thank yow, frend, my fal,
For nad ye be I had hit not at al.

indeed — 'But nevyrtheles ye ar welcome, parde!
make room — So now gef rome, take here a pleyer in,
part in the game — For he shal pley his pagaunt now for me,
Though that his chekis be but passyng thyn.
Set forth, let se how fayre ye kan bigynne.'
'Nay, good cosyne,' seide I, 'therof no more.'
'Seynt Yve, ye shall! See, that myn hose is tore!'

seized — Bi hond he hent me so and to the place
solution — He drew me in. 'Is ther noon othir bote?'
Seide I. 'Noo, no, ye get no bettir grace.'
to (it), must — Quod I, 'Then must I to, that nedis mote.'
hasten — And so to renne I gan to make a foot

ROUNDEL 57

5 **out avisynes**: 'without premeditation' (i.e. not such a serious sin).

9 **restore**. Penitence is complete only if restitution is made, in this case the restoration of the stolen goods.

And wel I wot I ran not long abowt
Before, company Or that I on had towchid of the rowt.

And as the corse thus drove me here and there,
Unto my lady newe so streight I went,
fearful With gastful hert that quoke for verry fere
How me were best to uttir myn entent.
Yet at the last, on this porpose ybent,
When that ther stood no mo but she and I:
'A questioun wold I axe of yow, lady.'

'Of me?' quod she. 'Now, good, what thing is that?'
assure 'It is not small, madame, I yow ensewre!
was affected I put a case, if so myn hert it sat
To yow in love above eche creature,
reveal Told I it yow, wold ye it so diskever
And make of it a skoffe or yet a play,
perhaps, weigh down with anxiety In which, per cas, my liif so myght it way?'

'God helpe me, nay! Why, what erthely wight,
honourably That lovyd me unto myn honour evyr,
Sothely, me thynke I did him gret unright
dearer Without the more he were unto me lever.
Eek who wil skorne, skoffe on, for I will never;
is fitting For bett I wot in suche case how me sit
To doon, and ellis I had but litill witt.'

'Mercy, madame, for I stond in the case
That bothe my liif and deth doth on yow hong;
For certis, swete, but ye have on me grace,
receive As for my deth I must it nedis fong.
I kan not say that I have lovyd yow long
But well I wott I love yow so, my dere,
together That bothe ye are my joy and payne in fere.

'My payne are ye, only for fere and drede
complain to The which I have to playne yow of my greef;
And then my joy – that is yowre goodlihede
For to bihold, and shall while that I lyve.
make test Ther nys no more, but from this tyme do preve
whether In any thing where that I be yowre man,
slay And if ye othir fynde, so sle me than!

'This is hit all that I of yow desere,
spiritual That as yowre gostly child ye wold me take
And ye to ben my fayre shrift-fadir dere,
To here the poore confessioun that I make;
And that ye not my simpilnes forsake,

5265 He argues the same case as the second eagle in *PF* 470.
5275–8 There is evidently some enjoyment to be had from the erotic suggestiveness of the relationship of father-confessor and spiritual 'child'. Cf. Roundel 57, above, and Chaucer's Shipman's Tale, *CT* VII.131.

For half so moche I dar not to yow say
if — As that I wolde and these folk were away.

(see n.) — 'Eek not I eft from this tyme how aquaynt,
Without the helpe of yow, myn owne swet hert –
Allas! be war, yowre coloure gynnys faynt!
kerchief — Pynne up yowre kercher, kepe yowre face covert.
may — Ye mow say how the sonne hit doth yow smert.'
over-delicate — 'Bi my good soth, I holde yow nyse,' quod she,
And did right so, and syns seide unto me:

ill-bred behaviour — 'I trowe wel ye have my rewde haver sene,
excessively — The which ye prayse so cleyn out of mesure.
(see n.) — Gramercy yow therof and not yowre eyene,
For which yn me thei fynde no such figure
To cawse yow of so gret a payne endure.
But many suche as ye in wordis dy
graves — That passyng hard ther graffis ar to spy.

prevent — 'Also, to lett yow speke that may I not,
And when ye lust, so say me what ye wol;
But for to love, it cometh not in my thought,
Save only on which plesith me at full;
try to attract — Nor I cast not to me noon othir pull.
with honourable purpose — But in all that ye love in good entent
if I knew you meant otherwise — I thank yow, but wist I ye othir ment,

'God helpe me, so I shulde yow then eschew –
But then I gesse ye wolde myn honour more?'
without doubt — 'Now dredles, lo, madame, that is yet trew,
rather had I not, born — For lever nad I ben to liif ybore
Then that I shulde for any gref or soore
Enjoin you further — Wil ye more fer then ye may goodly graunt
Unto me, wrecche – durste I say, yowre servaunt?

each bit — 'But wold God ye knew myn hert eche deel!
Kan ye not rede?' 'Yes, so, so,' quod she.
'O what? Dere hert, though fer from yow I dwel,
permission to write — Yet wil ye graunt me writ to yow, parde,
And not disdayne yow on hit for to see
in reply — And send me so of hit sum word agayn
If that I shulde desire yow such a payn?

noisy crowd — 'The raket cometh –' 'I graunt it yow, writ on.'
And so anothir came and afore hir stood,
For which that I must nedis ben agoon.
Yit nevyrtheles me thought it did me good
cross — That she so moche knew of myn hert, bi the rood!

5282 'Also I do not know, further, how from this time to improve our acquaintance'.

5286 The skill and charm of this scene, trifling as it is, is in how much of growing intimacy is conveyed through dialogue alone, without narratorial explanation. It is a Chaucerian gift.

5291 'It's thanks to you (your inner perception) and not (merely) your eyes'.

5295 A familiar sardonic rebuff to male rhetoric; elsewhere, there are reminiscences of Criseyde's gentler techniques.

And so we ran a corse or two, no more,
Or that we must depart, unto my sore. *to my sore regret*

For Crepuscule, that revith day his light,
Gan in the west his clowdy mantel shake;
And for bicause I fastid, lo, that nyght,
From oon to oon of them my leve I take.
But lord! so that myn hert bigan to quake
When that I take shulde of my lady leve,
And for nothing it wold me not bileve. *leave (the trembling)*

She blusshid reed to see how that I ferde, *fared*
For as I kist I seide, 'Now welcome, sorow.'
'Ye made me gast,' quod she, 'y-shrympe your berd!
But may ye not abide here to tomorrow?'
'A, madame, no, farewel, seynt John to borow.' *be my surety*
'Bi holy God, I trowe bet that ye may
Ellis come and se us, lo, sum othir day?'

'Madame, a trouthe, I thanke yowre ladiship, *in truth*
It may me happe to se yow here this weke.'
Thus did I so depart the feleship
And gan me forth to my poor loggyng peke. *slink*
But all that nyght myn hert did rore and seke, *sigh*
For nought me nyst as what was best to do,
To speke or writ when next I came hir to.

But nevyrtheles to this purpos I felle,
That when I myght, for fere of forgetyng, *(her) forgetting (me)*
Bi mouth I wolde my mater to hir telle –
And lak of space to take it bi writyng.
For which that thus bigan my new servyng,
When that I fond my tymys of laysere, *leisure*
As sewith next, if it lust yow to here. *follows*

{The Ballades to his new lady follow.}

BALLADE 96: 'SYN HIT IS SO WE NEDIS MUST DEPART...'

A rather literal-minded reading of the conceit of the lovers' exchange of hearts, and an example of the easy fluency of the non-translated poems – of the ease too with which, despite anticipations of the Elizabethan sonneteers, they can decline into emptiness. MS, fols 130v–131r; no French.

Syn hit is so we nedis must depart
And when to mete the tyme in none-certayne,
Even to myn hert hit is as dethis dart,

5324 **Crepuscule**: 'Twilight'. The phrasing echoes FrankT 1017.
5333 **Ye made me gast**: 'You had me scared' (that his fit of trembling would betray their secret). **y-shrympe your berd**: 'may your beard shrivel' (playful exclamation).
5348 'And (equally) for lack of opportunity to put it to her in writing'.

BALLADE 96
2 **in none-certayne**: 'in uncertainty', from *TC* I.337.

The which, allas, me sleth for verry payne.
But syn so is infortune lust ordayne *is pleased to*
Suche fatall fate, wo worth the destene! *woe betide*
I yow biseche, to that we mete agayne, *until*
As take myn hert and lete yowris bide with me.

For most ynly myn hert as doth desire *inwardly*
To serven yow, ay beyng in yowre sight,
Withouten part of othir wage or hire; *partaking*
And I as moche agayne wille, if I myght, *wish*
Yowre hert tofore the hert of any wight
To have with me, all be I not worthy.
To eft we mete, now, good, this stevyne plight: *Until again, agreement*
As take myn hert and lete yowre bide with me. *yours*

Myn hert of right must cause yow on me thinke
And to revolve the trouthe of my servise,
And as for yowre, all wake I, slepe or wynke,
Yet must me doo to like myn entirprise *Yet it must cause me*
And more to take in gree myn owen jewise *be pleased with, judgement*
To do me thynke yowre goodnes and bewte. *think about*
And syn it is to yow no prejudice,
As take myn hert and lete yowre bide with me.

Thus mowe ye, lo, enesen me gretly, *may, ease*
And in no wise yowre honoure lessid be;
Wherfore I yow biseche even hertily,
As take myn hert and lete yowre bide with me.

9 **as** is expletive, as with the imperative in the refrain-line.

Anonymous Songs and Short Poems, Religious, Comic and Amatory

These poems are commonly called 'lyrics', and most are indeed intended to be sung (many of them are from BL MS Sloane 2593, a tiny early fifteenth-century song-book, presumably the repertoire of a travelling minstrel), but if 'lyric' carries its modern connotations (spontaneous expression of personal feeling, etc.) it is almost totally misleading as a term to describe them. They do not express personal feeling, nor do they have an individual 'voice'; they are part of a larger world of shared thought and experience, and without some knowledge of that world and its literary conventions they are almost meaningless. The function of the religious poems is to work witty and dramatic variations on familiar themes of Christian celebration, remembrance and lamentation, and of pious exhortation, so as to move people to firmer faith and virtuous lives. The non-religious poems are like little indices to sets of communal or popular beliefs and attitudes. The love-poems are not poems 'of' love but poems 'about' love, skilful embroideries upon conventional expectations.

Standard editions are those of C. Brown, *Religious Lyrics of the XVth Century* (Oxford, 1939), R.H. Robbins, *Secular Lyrics of the XIVth and XVth Centuries* (Oxford, 1952), and R.L. Greene, *The Early English Carols* (1935; 2nd edn, Oxford, 1977); there are selections by R.T. Davies (London, 1963), T. Silverstein (London, 1971), and D. Gray (Oxford, 1975), and excellent studies by R. Woolf, *The English Religious Lyric in the Middle Ages* (Oxford, 1968), and D. Gray, *Themes and Images in the Medieval English Religious Lyric* (London, 1972). For the music, see J. Stevens, *Mediaeval Carols*, Musica Britannica 4 (London, 1952).

'Adam lay ibowndyn...'

A song, remarkable for the lightness of touch with which it celebrates the paradox of the Fortunate Fall, or *felix culpa* (see *PP* C.VII.127), the 'happy sin' of apple-eating that made Christ and his mother necessary. It uses the technique of 'incremental repetition', familiar in ballad and popular song, in a sophisticated way to build up the little blocks of meaning that make the logic of the poem. When sung, it ends with a cascade of repetitions of *Deo gracias*, as if the singers can hardly contain their joy. The poem is in short three-stress lines (arranged here as long lines), close to ballad-metre, but retaining links still with the old four-stress long line from which ballad-metre derived. Unique text in BL MS Sloane 2593, fol. 11r.

Adam lay ibowndyn, bowndyn in a bond,
Fowre thowsand wynter thowt he not to long.

And al was for an appil, an appil that he tok,
As clerkes fyndyn wretyn in here book.

Ne hadde the appil take ben, the appil taken ben, — *Had not*
Ne hadde never our Lady a ben hevene qwen. — *have been*

Blyssid be the tyme that appil take was,
Therfore we mown syngyn '*Deo gracias*'. — *may, 'Thanks be to God'*

'I syng of a mayden...'

A brain and a subtle ear has gone into the making of this poem too (from the same MS, fol. 10v; same metre), celebrating the mystery of Christ's conception. Dew falling on grass, flower and spray (traditional imagery, deriving from OT texts such as Ps. 72:6) suggests ease, grace and delicacy generally (not progressive stages of insemination). The emphasis on Mary's freedom of choice, at the moment of the Annunciation, is theologically strictly proper.

'Adam lay ibowndyn...'

2 Adam thought he deserved his punishment. Four thousand years, or thereabouts, was the usual computation of the period from the Fall to the Incarnation.

matchless (mate-less) I syng-a of a mayden that is makeles,
chose Kyng of alle kynges to here sone she ches.

as silently He cam also stylle ther his moder was
As dew in Aprylle that fallyt on the gras.

He cam also stylle to his moderes bowr
As dew in Aprille that fallyt on the flour.

He cam also stylle ther his moder lay
As dew in Aprille that fallyt on the spray.

Moder and maydyn was never non but she:
Wel may swych a lady Godes moder be!

'THER IS NO ROSE...'

This well-known song is embroidered, in macaronic style, with Latin phrases from the sequence *Laetabundus* ('sequences' were prose texts originally developed in the twelfth century to provide verbal material for the increasingly elaborate musical decoration), celebrating God's gift of himself to man, and from Luke's account of the Nativity. It appears in a collection of carols in a battered roll (first half of the fifteenth century) such as might be carried about by a professional singer, TCC MS O.3.58.

Ther is no rose of swych vertu
As is the rose that bar Jesu.

Ther is no rose of swych vertu
As is the rose that bar Jesu;
Alleluya.

For in this rose conteynyd was
Heven and erthe in lytyl space,
'Thing to be marvelled at' *Res miranda.*

Be that rose we may weel see
That he is God in personys thre,
'In one substance' *Pari forma.*

The aungelys sungyn the sheperdes to:
'Glory to God on high' '*Gloria in excelsis deo*'.
Let us rejoice' *Gaudeamus.*

Leve we al this worldly merthe,
And folwe we this joyful berthe;
'Let us proceed' *Transeamus.*

'I SYNG OF A MAYDEN...'

1 **syng-a**. The **a** is usually omitted by editors; but it seems to be a singer's device to fill out the metre.

'THER IS NO ROSE...'

1 **rose**. The image of Mary as a rose originated in OT texts such as Ecclus. 24:18.

4–5 In Mary's womb was Christ, and thus the Trinity, and thus the whole of creation.

'LULLY, LULLA, THOW LITEL TINY CHILD...'

The scene is the massacre of the Innocents; the carol is sung by the women whose children are slain in the Nativity play performed by the Coventry Shearmen and Tailors. The text of the play, one of two plays surviving from the Coventry cycle of mystery-plays, was destroyed by fire in 1879, and is taken here from a copy made in 1825.

Lully, lulla, thow litel tiny child,
By, by, lully, lullay

O sisters two,
How may we do
For to preserve this day
This pore yongling
For whom we do singe
'By, by, lully, lullay'?

Lully, lulla, etc.

Herod the king
In his raging *mad anger*
Chargid he hath this day
His men of might
In his owne sight
All yonge children to slay.

Lully, lulla, etc.

That wo is me,
Pore child, for thee,
And ever morne and may
For thi parting
Nether say nor singe
'By, by, lully, lullay.'

Lully, lulla, etc.

'A GOD AND YET A MAN...'

A self-consciously witty poem on the paradoxes of the Christian faith, which defy human reason and can be understood only through faith; written on a flyleaf of Bodl.MS Rawlinson B.332 in a sixteenth-century hand.

A god and yet a man?
A mayde and yet a mother?
Witt wonders what witt can
Conceave this or the other.

A god, and can he die?
A dead man, can he live?
What witt can well replie?
What reason reason give?

God truth itselfe doth teach it;
Mans witt senkis too farr under
By reasons power to reach it.
Beleeve and leave to wonder!

'WHO CANNOT WEPE COME LERNE AT ME'

A dramatic *pieta* (scene of the 'Compassion of the Virgin', Mary weeping over Jesus brought down from the cross), with Mary torn between her own grief for her son and her grief at man's hard-heartedness and reluctance to be moved to love by Christ's sacrifice. The opening refrain alludes cryptically to the speaker's state of mind, and a chance meeting. The stanza is in the alliterative manner (four-stress lines, with strong caesura; a triplet of half-lines), but without regular alliteration. In two MSS; here from Manchester, John Rylands Library MS Lat.395 (fifteenth century, third quarter), fol. 120r–v.

Sodenly afraide,
Half wakyng, half slepyng,
And gretly dismayde –
A woman sat wepyng,

beauty, understanding — With favoure in hir face ferr passyng my reason,
reason — And of hir sore weepyng this was the encheson:
Hir son in hir lap lay, she seid, slayne by treason.
Yif wepyng myght rype be, it seemyd than in season.
'Jesu!' so she sobbid,
buffeted — So hir son was bobbid
And of his lif robbid,
Saying thies wordes, as I say thee:
'Who cannot wepe, come lerne at me.'

I said I cowd not wepe, I was so harde-hartid.
She answerd me with wordys shortly that smarted:
'Lo, nature shall move the; thou must be converted;
argued in reply — Thyne owne Fader this nyght is deed' – lo, thus she thwarted!
'So my son is bobbid
And of his lif robbid.'
Forsooth than I sobbid,
Veryfyng the wordes she seid to me:
'Who cannot wepe may lern at thee.'

pitifully — 'Now breke, hert, I the pray! this cors lith so ruly,
treated, 'Jewishly' — So betyn, so wowndid, entreted so Jewly.
What wight may me behold and wepe nat? Noon, truly,
To see my deed dere son lygh bleedyng, lo, this newly.'
Ever stil she sobbid,
So hir son was bobbid
And of his lif robbid,
Saying anew — Newyng the wordes, as I say thee:
'Who cannot wepe, com lern at me.'

'A GOD AND YET A MAN...'

12 **leave to wonder**: 'leave off wondering'. The sense of wonder was not cultivated by medieval churchmen; curiosity about the mysteries of faith and revelation was not encouraged. These last lines may derive from an earlier quatrain (Brown, *Lyrics*, p. 186) attributed to bishop Pecock (see below) at the time of his recantation.

On me she caste hir ey, said, 'See, man, thy brothir!'
She kissid hym and said, 'Swete, am I not thy modir?'
swooning In sownyng she fill there – it wolde be noon othir;
dead-looking I noot which more deedly, the toon or the tothir.
Yit she revived and sobbid,
So hir son was bobbid
And of his lif robbid –
'Who cannot wepe,' this was the laye,
And with that word she vanysht away.

'In a tabernacle of a toure...'

In this poem, called *Canticus amoris* ('Song of love') in the MS, the Virgin, appearing as the crowned queen of heaven, appeals for man's love, for herself and her son; she presents herself variously as man's sister, wife, mother, neighbour, friend and courtly mistress, weaving together elements from the Song of Songs and other devotional sources. The handling of stanza and alliteration shows polish, and it was a popular poem, appearing in eight MSS; text here from Bodl.MS Douce 322 (fifteenth century, second half), fol. 8v, with emendation from BL MS Add.37049.

canopied niche In a tabernacle of a toure,
As I stode musyng on the mone,
A crouned quene, most of honoure,
spiritual Apered in gostly syght ful sone.
on her own She made compleynt thus by hyr one
For mannes soule was wrapped in wo:
'I may nat leve mankynde allone,
'For I am sick with love' *Quia amore langueo.*

'I longe for love of man my brother,
advocate, clear him of I am hys vokete to voyde hys vyce;
I am hys moder, I can none other –
Why shuld I my dere chylde dispyce?
anger Yef he me wrathe in diverse wyse,
frailty Through flesshes freelte fall me fro,
Yet must me rewe hym tyll he ryse,
Quia amore langueo.

pray, await 'I byd, I byde in grete longyng,
I love, I loke when man woll crave,
I pleyne for pyte of peynyng;
Wolde he aske mercy, he shuld hit have.
Say to me, soule, and I shall save;
Byd me, my chylde, and I shall go;
Thow prayde me never but my son forgave,
Quia amore langueo.

'O wreche in the worlde, I loke on the,
I se thy trespas day by day,
With lechery ageyns my chastite,

'In a tabernacle of a toure...'

2 **musyng on the mone**. The moon was associated with the Virgin Mary, from texts in Song of Songs 6:10 and Rev. 12:1.

With pryde agene my pore aray.
My love abydeth, thyne ys away;
My love the calleth, thow stelest me fro.
Sue Sewe to me, synner, I the pray,
Quia amore langueo.

'Moder of mercy I was for the made;
Who nedeth it, man, but thow allone?
To gete the grace I am more glade
Than thow to aske hit – why wylt thou noon?
to one (request) When seyd I nay, tel me, tyll oon?
Forsoth never yet to frende ne foo!
When thou askest nought, than make I moone,
Quia amore langueo.

'I seke the in wele and wrechednesse,
I seke the in ryches and poverte;
Thow man, beholde where thy moder ys,
Why lovest thou me nat syth I love the?
Synful or sory howevere thow be,
no others So welcome to me there ar no mo:
I am thy suster, ryght trust on me,
Quia amore langueo.

'My childe ys outlawed for thy synne,
My barne ys bete for thy trespasse;
Yet prykketh myne hert that so ny my kynne
in distress Shuld be dysseased. O sone, allasse!
Thow art hys brother, thy moder I was;
Thow sokyd my pappe, thow lovyd man so;
Thow dyed for hym, myne hert thow has,
Quia amore langueo.

'Man, leve thy synne than for my sake;
would wish Why shulde I gyf the that thou nat wald?
And yet yef thow synne, som prayer take
told And trust in me as I have tald.
Am nat I thy moder called?
Why shulde I flee thee? I love the, lo!
I am thy frende, I helpe – behald,
Quia amore langueo.

'Now, sone,' she sayde, 'wylt thou sey nay
misdeed Whan man wolde mende hym of hys mys?
Thow lete me never in veyne yet pray.
Than, synfull man, see thow to thys:
What day thou comest, welcome thow ys,
even if, away Thys hundreth yere yef thow were fro.
embrace I take the ful fayne, I clyppe, I kysse,
Quia amore langueo.

52–6 She addresses Christ.
58–63 The rhymes on **called** here (MS wolde, tolde, beholde) show that the poem was originally written in a northern dialect, with long *a* for *o*.

'Now wol I syt and sey no more,
Leave off Leve, and loke with grete longyng;
Whan man woll calle, I wol restore;
offspring I love to save hym – he is myne hosprynge.
hang No wonder yef myne hert on hym hynge,
He was my neyghbore – what may I doo?
high honour (being made queen) For hym had I thys worshippyng,
And therfore *amore langueo.*

'Why was I crouned and made a quene?
Why was I called of mercy the welle?
Why shuld an erthly woman bene
So hygh in heven above aungelle?
For the, mankynde – the truthe I telle!
Thou aske me helpe, and I shall do
That I was ordeyned – kepe the fro helle,
Quia amore langueo.

'Nowe, man, have mynde on me for ever,
Loke on thy love thus languysshyng;
each other, separate Late us never fro other dissevere,
Myne helpe ys thyne oune, crepe under my wynge.
Thy syster ys a quene, thy brother ys a kynge,
entailed (to a particular heir) Thys heritage ys tayled – sone, come therto,
Take me for thy wyfe and lerne to synge
Quia amore langueo.'

THE CORPUS CHRISTI CAROL

A carol (song with burden or refrain) found in this version (there are others) in Oxford, Balliol College MS 354 (fol. 165v), the commonplace-book of Richard Hill, a London grocer, compiled 1503–36. The poem is mysterious: it suggests a *pieta*, Mary mourning for Jesus, as a knight fatally wounded in battle (cf. *PP* XX.11), but also a scene from an Arthurian Grail-legend (a dying 'Fisher King' who never dies). The lamentation of the refrain (suggesting a lullaby, soothing grief) seems unrelated; it may be a snatch of song, adapted to the older poem by the addition of lines 3–4, alluding to the alienation of the affections of Henry VIII from Katharine of Aragon by Anne Boleyn, whose badge was a white falcon: see R.L. Greene, in *MAE* 29 (1960), 10–21; 33 (1964), 53–60.

Lully, lulley, lully, lulley,
mate The fawcon hath born my mak away.

He bare hym up, he bare hym down,
He bare hym into an orchard brown.
Lully, etc.

In that orchard ther was an hall
rich dark cloth That was hangid with purpill and pall.
Lully, etc.

And in that hall ther was a bed,
Hit was hangid with gold so red.
Lully, etc.

And yn that bed ther lyth a knyght,
His wowndes bledyng day and nyght.
Lully, etc.

maiden By that beddes side ther kneleth a may
And she wepeth both nyght and day.
Lully, etc.

And by that beddes side ther stondith a ston,
'*Corpus Christi*' wretyn theron.
Lully, lulley, lully, lulley,
The fawcon hath born my mak away.

CHRIST TRIUMPHANT

Spoken by the dead Christ as if recovering from a fight, these lines warn of coming judgement, and are heavy with menace. This is a very different Christ from the humanized figure of devotional tradition. Text on an endleaf of a MS of Hoccleve's *Regement*, NLS MS Advocates' 19.1.11.

I have laborede sore and suffered deth,
And now I rest and draw my breth;
But I schall come and call ryght sone
(the Last Judgement) Hevene and erth and hell to dome;
And than schall know both devyll and man
What I was and what I am.

'FAREWELL, THIS WORLD...'

The speaker is dead and buried, in the body, and awaiting the 'particular judgement' (made at death), and in the meantime the soul offers advice and warning based on his experience. The first-person narration gives an unexpected twist to the lesson of mortality; otherwise the theme is that of Lydgate's *Dance Macabre*, to which the gnomic style of utterance may owe a debt (e.g. 7, cf. *Dance*, 360). Text from Oxford, Balliol College MS 354, fol. 199r.

Farewell, this world! I take my leve for ever;
I am arrested to appere afore Goddes face.
rather O merciful God, thou knowest I had lever
hour's Than all this worldes good to have an owr space
amends For to make asseth for my gret trespace.
My hert, alas, is broken for that sorow:
Som be this day that shall not be tomorrow!

This world, I see, is but a cherry fair;
in any case All thinges passeth, and so moste I algate.
throne This day I sat full royally in a chair
subtle Till sotil deth knocked at my gate
without warning And unavised he said to me 'Checkmate'.

'FAREWELL, THIS WORLD...'
2 **arrested**. 'This fell sergeant Death / Is strict in his arrest' (*Hamlet* V.ii.288–9).
8 **cherry fair**: a fair held in a cherry orchard for the sale of the fruit (which lasts only a brief season).
10 The speaker is represented as a king. Cf. *Dance Macabre*, 633.

(of soul from body) Lo how sodeinly he maketh a devorce!
And, wormes to fede, here he hath laid my corse.

Speke soft, ye folkes, for I am laid aslepe;
I have my dreme – in trust is mich treason.
From dethes hold fain wold I make a lepe
But my wisdom is turned into feble reason.
I see this worldes joy lasteth but a season.
Wold God I had remembred this beforne!
I say no more, but be ware of an horne!

This feckil world so false and so unstable
Promoteth his lovers for a litel while,
bauble But at the last he giveth them a bable
When his painted trouth is torned into gile.
set down Experience causeth me the trouth to compile,
began (to realize this) Thinking this – to late, alas, that I began!
For foly and hope disseiveth many a man.

time Farewell, my frendes! The tide abideth no man:
I moste departe hens, and so shall ye.
But in this passage the best song that I can
Is '*Requiem eternam*': I pray God grant it me.
(i.e. in purgatory) Whan I have ended all myn adversite,
Graunte me in paradise to have a mancion
He who That shed his blood for my redempcion.

'KYRIE, SO KYRIE'

A carol (song with burden) from the same song-book, BL MS Sloane 2593 (fol. 34r–v), as 'Adam lay ibowndyn', etc. It is an example of how the church service was often mischievously adapted for extra-curricular purposes in 'parish-clerk culture' (like that of the Latin Goliardic songs of the twelfth century). *Kyrie eleison* (Gk. 'Lord have mercy') is the opening of the Mass, and the song follows the order of service of the Christmas Mass, from *Kyrie*, through the reading of the Epistle and the singing of the *Sanctus* and *Agnus Dei* to the closing *Benedicamus* and *Deo gracias* (for a description of the Latin Mass, see Duffy [1992], pp. 91–130). It could be a little scene from the Miller's Tale, though 'Aleyson' here is more responsive to the attentions of the parish-clerk (called, conventionally, 'Jankyn', like the Wife of Bath's 'joly clerk' and fifth husband). The charm of the piece is that the girl is entirely won over by aesthetic appreciation of Jankyn's performance in church; he just does his job so well.

Kyrie, so kyrie,
sweetly Jankyn syngyt mirie,
(or 'Aleyson') With aleyson.

Yule As I went on Yol day in owre prosessyon
singing-tone Knew I joly Jankyn be his mery ton:
Kyrieleyson.

16 Not too clear, except the general sense that there is no trust to be placed in the illusion of life.
18 The speaker is unable to make use of his newly acquired wisdom.
21 **horne**: the trumpet that will announce the Last Judgement.
32 ***Requiem eternam***: 'Eternal rest (grant unto them, O Lord)', the opening of the Introit in the Mass for the Dead.

opening Introit	Jankyn began the offys on the Yol day
And still	And yit me thynkyt it dos me good, so merie gan he say
	Kyrieleyson.
Epistle	Jankyn red the Pystyl ful fayre and ful wel
good fortune	And yit me thynkyt it dos me good, as ever have I sel,
	Kyrieleyson.
'Holy'	Jankyn at the *Sanctus* crakit a merie note
	And yit me thinkyt it dos me good (I payid for his cote),
	Kyrieleyson.
	Jankyn crakit notes an hunderid on a knot
vegetables	And yit he hakkyt hem smaller than wortes to the pot,
	Kyrieleyson.
'Lamb {of God}'	Jankyn at the *Agnus* beryt the pax-brede;
winked, trod	He twynkelid but sayd nowt and on myn fot he trede,
	Kyrieleyson.
'Let us bless the Lord'	*Benedicamus Domino*, Cryst fro shame me schylde,
'Thanks be to God'	*Deo gracias* therto – alas, I go with chylde!
	Kyrieleyson.

'I HAVE A GENTIL COK...'

Also from BL MS Sloane 2593 (fol. 10v; same metre as 'Adam lay ibowndyn', etc.). The *double entendre* is unmistakeable, but left for the reader (or performer) to make out. The cock has something of the technicolour glamour of Chauntecler, in Chaucer's Nun's Priest's Tale, who also has a comb of red coral and azure legs (*CT* VII.2859–62).

	I have a gentil cok, crowyt me the day;
	He doth me rysyn erly my matyns for to say.
high lineage	I have a gentil cok, comyn he is of gret;
jet-black	His comb is of reed corel, his tayl is of get.
good stock	I have a gentyl cok, comyn he is of kynde;
indigo	His comb is of red corel, his tayl is of inde.
azure, delicate, slender	His leggis ben of asour so gentil and so smale,
white to the base of the spur	His sporis arn of sylvir qwyt into the worte-wale.
eyes	His eynyn arn of cristal lokyn al in aumbyr,
	And every nyght he perchit hym in myn ladyis chaumbyr.

'KYRIE, SO KYRIE'

13 **crakit**: breaks up the musical line into a string of short staccato notes, as was the fashion in the newer kind of polyphonic singing (cf. MillT 3377, where it is called 'brokkynge').

19 **pax-brede**: literally 'peace-board', a silver or gilt disc inscribed with a sacred image, usually of the Crucifixion, which was passed round for the congregation to kiss as a substitute for the priest's 'kiss of peace'; nothing to do with bread.

'I dar not seyn...'

BL MS Sloane 2593, fols 24v–25r.

falsehood How! hey! it is non les,
dare not speak I dar not seyn quan she seyth 'Pes!'

Ying men, I warne you everychon,
Old Elde wyvys tak ye non,
For I myself have on at hom:
I dar not seyn quan she seyth 'Pes!'

Quan I cum fro the plow at non,
broken In a reven dysh myn mete is don;
'our old woman' I dar not askyn our dame a spon –
I dar not seyn quan she seyth 'Pes!'

If I aske our dame bred,
She takyt a staf and brekit myn hed
makes me run And doth me rennyn undir the bed:
I dar not seyn quan she seyth 'Pes!'

for meat If I aske our dame fleysh,
She brekit myn hed with a dysh:
rush 'Boy, thou art not worth a reysh!'
I dar not seyn quan she seyth 'Pes!'

If I aske our dame chese,
'Boy,' she seyth, al at ese,
pea 'Thou art not worth half a pese.'
I dar not sey quan she seyth 'Pes!'

'Care away for evermore'

Bodl.MS Eng.poet.e.1 (second half of the fifteenth century), fol. 23r–v. The burden, which seems inexplicably hopeful, must have been brought in from elsewhere.

Care away, away, away,
Care away for evermore!

work or sweat for All that I may swynk or swet
My wyfe it wyll both drynk and ete;
If And I sey ought, she wyl me bete –
Full of care Carfull ys my hart therfor!

If I sey ought of hyr but good,
She loke on me as she war wod
And wyll me clout about the hod –
Carfull ys my hart therfor!

'I dar not seyn...'

4 **Elde wyvys.** Young men often married older wives with money, or widows (like the Wife of Bath) who had accumulated property from their dead husbands.

If she wyll to the gud ale ryde,
Me must trot all be hyr syde;
And whan she drynk I must abyde –
Carfull ys my hart therfor!

If I say, 'It shal be thus,'
She sey, 'Thou lyist, charll, iwus!
Wenest thou to overcome me thus?'
Carfull ys my hart therfor!

Yf ony man have such a wyfe to lede,
He schal know how *judicare* cam in the Crede;
reward Of hys penans God do hym mede!
Carfull ys my hart therfor!

THE SCHOOLBOY'S LAMENT

Oxford, Balliol College MS 354, fol. 252r.

Hay, hay, by this day,
What avayleth it me thowgh I say nay?

I wold fayn be a clarke,
hard job But yet hit is a strange werke;
The byrchyn twygges be so sharpe
Hit makith me have a faynt harte.
What avaylith it me thowgh I say nay?

On Monday in the mornyng whan I shall rise
custom At six of the clok hyt is the gise
without question To go to skole withowt avise –
I had lever go twenti myle twyse!
What avaylith it me thowgh I say nay?

My master lokith as he were mad:
'Wher hast thou be, thow sory lad?'
'Milked dukkes, my moder bad.'
downhearted Hit was no mervayle thowgh I were sad:
What vaylith it me thowgh I say nay?

My master pepered my ars with well good spede,
Hit was worse than fynkyll-sede;
He wold not leve till it did blede –
Myche sorow have he for his dede!
What vayleth it me thowgh I say nay?

'CARE AWAY FOR EVERMORE'

20 ***judicare***: 'to judge'. The Apostles' Creed has 'he shall come to judge the quick and the dead'. The speaker thinks husbands are getting their judgement already, and their penance too, and hopes God will recognize this.

THE SCHOOLBOY'S LAMENT

15 A pretty cheeky answer.

19 **fynkyll-sede**: fennel-seed, made into a sharp sauce.

I wold my master were a watt [*hare*]
And my boke a wyld catt
And a brase of grehowndes in his toppe: [*on top of that*]
I wold be glade for to se that!
What vayleth it me thowgh I say nay?

I wold my master were an hare
And all his bokes howndes were
And I myself a joly huntere:
To blow my horn I wold not spare!
For if he were dede I wold not care.
What vaylith me thowgh I say nay?

Against Blacksmiths

A metrical tour de force, in which an extravagant form of alliterative verse, with heavy alliteration (often *aa/aa*, sometimes *aaa/aa*; see headnotes to *PP* and *Gawain*), is used onomatopoeically and highly inventively. There are several ad hoc nominal compounds of the kind that were anciently traditional in alliterative verse. The speaker's annoyance is understandable, given that blacksmiths usually worked at night (like Gerveys in the Miller's Tale) on implements needed for the morrow; but he shows nevertheless an appreciation of the music of heavy metal. Unique text in BL MS Arundel 292 (a Norwich MS, *c.*1440), fol. 71v; ed. in Sisam (1921), p. 169; valuable study by E. Salter in *Literature and History* 5 (1979), 194–215.

Swarte smekyd smethes smateryd wyth smoke [*Black smoky*]
Dryve me to deth wyth den of here dyntes. [*din*]
Swech noys on nyghtes ne herd men never.
What knavene cry and clateryng of knockes! [*lads'*]
The cammede kongons cryen after 'Col, col!' [*crooked-nosed trolls, coal*]
And blowen here bellewys that al here brayn brestes. [*brain bursts*]
'Huf, puf!' seith that on, 'Haf, paf!' that other.
Thei spyttyn and spraulyn and spellyn many spelles, [*tell many stories*]
Thei gnawen and gnacchen, thei gronys togydere [*grind and gnash their teeth*]
And holdyn hem hote wyth here hard hamers. [*keep themselves warm*]
Of a bole-hyde ben here barm-fellys, [*leather aprons ('lap-skins')*]
Here schankes ben schakeled for the fere-flunderys. [*(see n.)*]
Hevy hamerys thei han that hard ben handled, [*wielded*]
Stark strokes thei stryken on a stelyd stokke. [*steel anvil*]
'Lus, bus! las, das!' rowtyn be rowe. [*they crash down in turn*]
Swech dolful a dreme the devyl it to-dryve! [*noise, drive away*]
The mayster longith a lityl and lascheth a lesse,
Twyneth hem tweyn and towchith a treble:
'Tik, tak! hic, hac! tiket, taket! tyk, tak!
Lus, bus! las, das! – swych lyf thei ledyn,
Alle clothe-merys: Cryst hem gyve sorwe!
May no man for bren-waterys on nyght han hys rest!

Against Blacksmiths

12 'Their legs are protected with iron greaves because of the sparks ("fire-flinders")'.

17–18 'The master-smith lengthens a little piece of metal and beats at a smaller one, twists them both together and strikes a treble note'.

21 **clothe-merys**; 'clothe-mares', providers of clothing and protective gear for war-horses.

22 **bren-waterys**: 'burn-waters', when they temper the red-hot metal in water.

'ALONE WALKYNG...'

From TCC MS R.3.19, fol. 160r, a famous post-1485 anthology of Chaucerian and sub-Chaucerian writing; like many other poems in the MS, this one is attributed hopefully to Chaucer. It is a poem of fixed form called a virelay, with concatenation ('chain-linking') of rhyme from stanza to stanza. It is a lover's complaint of unrequited love – the form that tends to monopolize courtly love-poetry – but it is gracefully handled, with a plangency that makes one think of Wyatt, writing not many years later.

Alone walkyng,
In thought pleynyng
And sore syghyng,
All desolate,
Me remembryng
Of my lyvyng,
My deth wysshyng
Bothe erly and late.

Infortunate
Ys soo my fate
That, wote ye whate,
Oute of mesure
My lyfe I hate.
Thus desperate
In suche pore estate
Do I endure.

Of other cure
Am I nat sure;
Thus to endure
Ys hard, certain.
Suche ys my ure, *customary experience*
I yow ensure;
What creature
May have more payn?

My trouth so pleyn
Ys take in veyn,
And gret disdeyn
In remembraunce.
Yet I full feyne
Wold me compleyne
Me to absteyne
From thys penaunce.

But in substaunce
Noon allegeaunce *alleviation*
Of my grevaunce
Can I nat fynde.
Ryght so my chaunce
With displesaunce
Doth me avaunce –
And thus an ende.

'Myn hertys joy...'

From Bodl.MS Fairfax 16, fols 323v–324r, an important MS (*c.*1440) of Chaucer (it contains, e.g., *PF*) and Chaucerian courtly verse. Fifteenth-century courtly love-poems are often in the form of epistles; this one claims to be a real letter, with a date and 'running-out-of-time' topos. Every word and phrase slots into place predictably, but with consummate ease. The poem is sometimes attributed to the duke of Suffolk (d. 1450), a powerful political figure who befriended Charles of Orleans (see above) while he was in prison in England. What is important for the understanding of the culture of courtly lyric is not whether it is by the duke (other poems are reliably attributed to him) but that it could well have been written by such a person.

Myn hertys joy, and all myn hole plesaunce,
Whom that I serve and shall do faythfully
Wyth trew entent and humble observaunce,
Yow for to plese in that I can treuly,
letter Besechyng yow thys lytell byll and I
May hertly, wyth symplesse and drede,
Be recomawndyd to your goodlyhede.

health And yf ye lyst have knowlech of my qwert,
I am in hele – God thankyd mot he be –
As of body, but treuly not in hert,
Nor nought shal be to tyme I may you se;
But thynke that I as treuly wyll be he
That for your ese shall do my payn and myght
As thogh that I were dayly in your syght.

time I wryte to yow no more for lak of space,
But I beseche the holy trinite
Yow kepe and save be support of hys grace,
And be your sheld from al adversyte.
Go, lytill byll, and say thou were wyth me
Of verey trouth, as thou canst wele remembre,
uprising At myn upryst, the fyft day of Decembre.

'Westren wynde...'

This snatch of verse, from BL MS Royal Appendix 58, fol. 5r, has always sent shivers of ecstasy down the backs of modern readers, but the narrative behind it is entirely up to the reader (this may be no small part of its success). Even its verbal felicity is 'accidental': line 2 has been much admired, but *smalle* is just the usual ME word for 'thin', and *can* is a variant spelling of *gan*, a past tense auxiliary like 'did'. The poem is evocative by default, perhaps the 'purest' kind of poetry. The syntax of the first two lines is ambiguous.

Westren wynde, when wyll thow blow,
The smalle rayne downe can rayne –
Cryst, if my love wer in my armys
And I yn my bed agayne!

Love-Poems (by Women?) from the Findern Manuscript

The 'Findern' manuscript (CUL MS Ff.1.6) is a late fifteenth-century household album from Derbyshire into which well-known poems and extracts from famous authors were copied by professional and amateur scribes, and also poems of original composition. The latter are customarily assumed to be all by men, and mostly written from the point of view of a man. However, a number of women's names (not attached to particular poems) are written in the manuscript ('Margery Hungerford', 'Fraunces Crucker', 'Elisabet Frauncys', 'Anne Schyrley') and it seems possible they may have been authors as well as readers. Indeed it has been claimed by S. McNamer, in *Viator* 22 (1991), 279–310, that female authorship of certain poems (she prints 15 in the appendix to her essay, including the five below), and not only those that purport to be spoken by women, can be determined from internal evidence: they are, she says, 'expressions of authentic female experience' (p. 296), in which the masculine 'game of love' (see headnote to Wyatt) is transformed into sad or anxious or joyful reality. Since they would thus be among the earliest poems in English presumed to be by women, the argument is tempting; tone and expression can be compared with the love-complaints of Charles of Orleans and Wyatt, and with the poems in which men write of absence ('Myn hertys joy', attributed to the duke of Suffolk) or write in the person of a woman lamenting such absence (Surrey, Poems 7 and 8).

There is a facsimile of Findern with introduction by R. Beadle and A.E.B. Owen (London, 1977), and a study by K. Harris, *TCBS* 8 (1983), 299–333; see also Barratt (1992), pp. 268–74.

1 (fol. 28v)

This is not about love-sickness, but real sickness; clumsily metred, stilted in diction, it yet speaks from the heart of anxious, passive waiting.

As in yow restyth my joy and comfort,
Youre dissese ys my mortal payne.
Sone God send me seche reporte
That may comfort myn hert in every vayne.
Ho but ye may me sustayne
Or of my gref be the remedy
But ye sone have amendement of yowre maledy?

Weche ys to me the heviest remembraunce
That ever can be thouht in any creature,
Myne hert hanggyng thus in balaunce
Tyl I have knowlege and verely sure
That God in yow hath lyst done thys cure
alleviation Of yowre dyssese to have allygaunce
And to be relevyd of all yowre grevaunce.

2 (fol. 56r)

What-so men seyn,
Love is no peyn
To them, serteyn,
Butt varians;
For they constreyn
Ther hertis to feyn,
Ther mowthis to pleyn
Ther displesauns

(Whych is indede
Butt feynyd drede,
So God me spede,
And dowbilnys),
offer Ther othis to bede
Ther lyvys to lede,
And proferith mede,
Newfangellnys.

For when they pray
Ye shall have nay,
What-so they sey:
Beware for sham!
For every daye
lie in wait for They waite ther pray
Wher-so they may
And make butt game.

Then semyth me
Ye may well se
(free with their promises) They be so fre
In evyry plase,
Hitt were pete
Butt they shold be
Beguiled Begelid, parde,
Withowtyn grase.

3 (fol. 69v)

My woofull hert, thus clad in payn,
Wote natt welle what do nor seyn:
Longe absens grevyth me so.

For lakke of syght nere am I sleyn,
All joy myne hert hath in dissedeyn:
Comfort fro me is go.

Then thogh I wold me owght complayn
Of my sorwe and grete payn,
Who shold comforte me do?

Ther is nothynge can make me to be fayn
Butt the syght of hym agayn
That cawsis my wo.

None butt he may me susteyn,
He is my comfort in all payn:
I love hym and no moo.

3.15 **I love hym and no moo**: written over 'my joy for well or w', perhaps to avoid the repetition of the rhyme-word (there are only two rhymes in the poem), as well as to replace the conventional phrasing with a downright declaration of love.

To hym I woll be trywe and playn,
And evyr his owne in serteyn
Tyll deth departe us to.

My hert shall I never fro hym refrayn:
I gave hitt hym withowte constrayn,
Evyr to contenue so.

4 (fol. 135r)

A cycle of four poems, lamenting the lover's/husband's absence, seeking forgiveness for complaining about it, complaining about being neglected, and rejoicing at his return. The speaker is identified as female, and the situation is characteristically that of the woman, as we see in several of the Paston letters. The four poems are in an unusual metrical form: each is of 13 lines, on two rhymes only, in stanzas of five, three and five lines, with the second rhyme of each poem picked up as one of the rhymes of the next. 'Welcome be ye' is placed first in the MS, but the rhyme-sequence (and the desire for a happy ending), argue that it should be put last (see Barratt [1992], p. 271: she suggests further that the 'lost line' of 'Welcome be ye' is a clue to the 51 lines of the whole cycle – and a 51-week absence).

(a) Come home, dere herte, from tarieng –
Kausith me to wepe, bothe weile and wring,
Also to lyve evere in distresse
So gret there may no wight expresse:
Al my joye ye torne to mournyng.

Sorowe is in myn herte digging –
would like to To dethe, I trowe, he would me bring
In woful trans withoute redresse.

Whanne I have of you sume tiding,
Gret joye I have, withoute failing,
Right as me ought with rightwisnesse;
But yet may not myn heveynesse
Depart from me til your comyng.

(b) To you, my joye and my worldly plesaunce,
fearful (of rebuke) I wol shrive me with dredful countenaunce
Of chiding, which your letter bereth wittenesse;
Therto constrained by my woful distresse,
Asking you absolucion and penaunce.

What wol ye more of me but repentaunce?
God wol himselve have therof suffisaunce:
Mercy I seke and aske aye foryevenesse.

(would that you knew) By seynt Martyn, and ye knew my grevaunce,
The whiche I suffred with long continuance,
uncaring Dreding ye were of my woos roghtlesse:
That was to me a grevous hevinesse,
Yet aske I mercy to be in pacience.

3.18 **Tyll deth departe us to**: the echo of the marriage-service goes with much else to suggest an affirmation of wifely devotion and fidelity.

(c) There may areste me no pleasance, — *stop me (grieving)*
And our be our I fele grevaunce. — *hour by hour*
I not to whom I may complaine,
For he that may my woo restreine
Wol have of me no remembrance.

Sith I am under his governaunce,
He shuld sett me suche ordinaunce
As I might have ease of my paine.

Me thinkith he might have conscience
And of my woos sum suffisance,
Considering that I am so plaine — *open and candid*
To him ever, with joye or paine:
Let him have therof repentance. — *compunction*

(d) Welcome be ye, my sovereine,
The cause of my joyfull peine,
For the while ye were away
Myn hert seyd noght but 'walaway'.

No more I do my mirthis fayne
But in gladnesse I swym and baine: — *bathe*
Ye have my mornyng dreven away.

Of your comyng I am so fayne
That mirthes done my sorow steine — *make pale*
And make amonge theim suche afray
That reste may they with me no day.
Gladnesse ye have brought me againe.

5 (fol. 138v)

Continuaunce
Of remembraunce
Withowte endyng
Doth me penaunce
And grete grevaunce
For your partynge.

So depe ye be
Graven, parde
Withyn myn hert
That afore mee
Ever I yow see
In thought covert.

Though I ne playn
My wofull payn
But bere yt styll;
It were in vayn
To sey agayn — *against*
Fortunes wyll.

Popular Ballads

Ballads are short narrative poems in 'ballad-metre' (quatrains of alternating four- and three-stress lines, rhyming *abcb*; see headnote to 'Adam lay ibowndyn', above), originally orally communicated, and rarely written down. They find only an accidental place in written culture, where they appear as the relics of popular and oral verse-making. The first three below survive in early MSS and show that the ballad was an authentic medieval form. The first, in particular, exhibits fully the formal characteristics that chiefly, after metre, distinguish traditional ballad: the use of incremental repetition, which originates in the repetitive mouthing needed by oral improvisers as they ponder the next segment of narrative song, and which survives to give ballads their peculiarly haunting empty cadences; and the abrupt handling of narrative (often communicated through unconnected dialogue), in which little is explained, though much suggested. Comprehensive edition by F.J. Child, *English and Scottish Popular Ballads*, 5 vols (Boston, 1888); modern survey by D.C. Fowler, *A Literary History of the Popular Ballad* (Durham, NC, 1968).

Saint Steven

Extant only in BL MS Sloane 2593 (fols 22v–23r), the early fifteenth-century song-book which is the source of many of the songs printed above. Though very early, and unusual for a ballad in being on a religious subject, this poem has the formal and stylistic character of a traditional ballad.

Saint Stevene was a clerk in kyng Herowdis halle
And servyd him of bred and cloth as every king befalle. *table-linen, would befit*

Stevyn out of kechoun cam with boris hed on honde;
He saw a sterre was fayr and bryght over Bedlem stonde.

He kyst adoun the boris hed and went into the halle:
'I forsak the, kyng Herowdis, and thy werkis alle!

'I forsak the, kyng Herowdis, and thy werkis alle;
Ther is a chyld in Bedlem born is betir than we alle.'

'What eylyt the, Stevene, what is the befalle? *aileth*
Lakkyt the eythir mete or drynk in kyng Herowdis halle?'

'Lakit me neythir mete ne drynk in kyng Herowdis halle;
Ther is a child in Bedlem born is betir than we alle.'

'What eylyt the, Stevyn, art thou wod or thou gynnyst brede? *become peevish*
Lakkyt the eythir gold or fe or ony ryche wede?' *payment, clothing*

'Lakyt me neythir gold ne fe ne non ryche wede;
Ther is a chyld in Bedlem born shal helpyn us at our nede.'

'That is also soth, Stevyn, also soth, iwys, *just as true*
As this capoun crowe shal that lyth here in myn dysh.'

That word was not so sone seyd, that word in that halle,
The capoun crew '*Christus natus est*' among tho lordis alle.

3 **boris hed**: a traditional Christmas dish. There are several 'boar's head carols' to accompany the ceremonial entry of the dish.

20 'Christ is born', from the service at matins on Christmas Day. The miracle of the cock is associated with several other saints too.

Rise up, (i.e. all of you) 'Rysyt up, myn turmentowris, be two and al be on,
And ledyt Stevyn out of this town and stonyt hym with ston.'

They took, on the road Tokyn he Stevene and stonyd hym in the way,
And therfore is his evyn on Crystis owyn day.

The Hunting of the Cheviot

Border raids were the means by which the frontier between Scotland and England was roughly stabilized during periods when there was not open warfare. The skirmishes between the earl of Northumberland's son Henry Percy (1364–1403), the 'Hotspur' of Shakespeare's *Henry IV Part 1*, and James, earl of Douglas (1358–88), became a favourite subject of popular ballad, and three ballad-poems survive that allude to the events leading up to Douglas's death at the battle of Otterburn (19 March 1388): *The Battle of Otterburn*, the most accurate version historically, more a simple heroic poem in ballad-metre than a ballad; *Chevy Chase*, the version that Joseph Addison read; and the present poem, which dates from the late fifteenth century, though extant only in a mid-sixteenth-century copy (with bizarre spelling, much emended in the present text), Bodl.MS Ashmole 48. In this version (probably the version that Sir Philip Sidney knew and admired: 'I must confess my own barbarousness, I never heard the old song of Percy and Douglas that I found not my heart moved more than with a trumpet', *Apology for Poetry*, ed. G. Shepherd, p. 118), events are removed from their actual history and placed in the early years of the reign of Henry IV (1399–1413), and the occasion of the battle becomes a deliberately provocative English hunting foray into the Cheviot Hills (which form the border between Scotland and England: 'The Cheviot' is the central hill-mass), rather than, as in reality, a Scottish raid into Northumberland. Historical accuracy is less important than the steeping of events in the poetic conventions of ballad. Edition by O. Arngart (Lund, 1973).

The First Fit

(came) out The Persy owt of Northomberlond
And avowe to God made he
That he wold hunte in the mowntayns
Of Cheviat within days thre,

That he wold hunte in the mowntayns
Of Cheviat within days thre
In spite of In the magger of doughty Doglas
And all that ever with him be.

The fattest hartes in all Cheviat, he sayd,
He wold kyll and cary them away.
in reply 'Be my feith,' sayd the doughty Doglas agayn,
prevent 'I wyll let that huntyng yf that I may.'

Bamborough Then the Persy owt of Banborow cam,
company With him a myghty meany,
With fifteen hondrith archeres bold of blood and bone,
They were chosen owt of shyers thre.

24 St Stephen's day is 26 December.

The Hunting of the Cheviot

1 **Persy** is used for MS *Perse* throughout.

5–6 The repetitions here and in 69–70, 101–2, 161–2, 265–6, are those inserted by J. Burrow, in his edition of the poem in *English Verse 1300–1500* (London, 1977), pp. 349–62, in order to preserve the quatrain-structure.

15 The metre of the ballads, particularly of those in early copies, is distinctly rough, whether through carelessness in transmission, or through metrical licences appropriate only to oral delivery, or – a particular problem here – through adaptation to written form through the addition of speech-prefixes (see the effect of this in lines 53, 67, 95, etc.).

	This began on a Monenday at morn,
	In Cheviat the hillys so hye;
	The chyld may rue that ys unborn,
	It was the more pite.
	The dryvers thorow the woodes went
	For to raise the deer;
let fly, open ground	Bowmen byckered upon the bent
bright	With ther broad arrows clear.
wild creatures	Then the wyld thorow the woodes went
different side	On every syde sere;
groves slipped	Grehondes thorow the grevis glent
	For to kyll ther deer.
high up	This began in Cheviat the hylls abone
	Erly on a Monenday;
hour	Be that it drew to the ower of none
	A hondrith fat hartes ded ther lay.
signal to gather	They blew a mote upon the bent,
from every direction	They sembled on sydis sere;
slaughtered game	To the quyrry then the Persy went
	To see the bryttlyng of the dere.
	He sayd, 'It was the Doglas promys
	This day to meet me here,
truly	But I wyste he wold faylle, verament' –
	A great oth the Persy swear.
	At the last a squyer of Northomberlond
side, near	Lokyd at his hand full ny:
	He was war a' the doughty Doglas comynge,
	With him a myghty meany,
coat of mail	Both with spear, bylle and brand,
	It was a myghty sight to se;
	Hardyer men both of hert nar hand
	Were not in Cristiante.
	They were twenti hondrith spearmen good
	Withoute any faile;
Tweed	They were born along be the watter o' Twide
Teviotdale	I' the bowndes of Tividale.
	'Leave of the bryttlyng of the dere,' he said,
	'And to your bows look ye tayk good hede,
	For never sith ye were on your mothers born
	Had ye never so mickle nede.'

19–20 This laconic kind of rueful foreshadowing is characteristic of ballad.

36 **bryttlyng**: 'breaking', in the formal manner that was an important part of hunt ritual; cf. *Gawain* 1323–61.

The doughty Doglas on a stede
He rode all his men beforn;
His armor glytteryd as dyd a glede, *burning coal*
A bolder barn was never born. *man*

'Tell me whos men ye are,' he says,
'Or whos men that ye be.
Who gave you leave to hunte in this Cheviat chays *chase (hunting-land)*
In the spyte of myn and of me?'

The first man that ever him an answer made
Yt was the good lord Persy:
'We wyll not tell the whos men we are,' he says,
'Nor whos men that we be.

'We wyll not tell thee whos men we are,
Nor whos men that we be;
But we wyll hunte here in this chays
In the spyte of thyn and of the.

'The fattest hartes in all Cheviat we have kylled
And cast to carry them away.' *plan*
'Be my troth,' sayd the doughty Doglas agayn, *in reply*
'Therfor the ton of us shall de this day.' *the one, die*

Then sayd the doughty Doglas
Unto the lord Persy:
'To kyll all thes giltles men, alas,
It were great pite.

'But, Persy, thow art a lord of land,
I am a yerl callyd within my contre: *an earl*
Let all our men upon a parti stand *stand apart*
And do the battel of the and of me.'

'Now Cristes cors on his crown,' said the lord Persy, *curse on his head*
'Whosoever therto says nay!
Be my troth, doughty Doglas,' he says,
'Thow shalt never se that day,

Neither in Ynglond, Scotland nar France,
Nor for no man of a woman born,
But – and fortune be my chance –
I dar meet him, oon man for oon.' *man for man*

Then bespake a squyer of Northomberlond, *up spoke*
Richard Wytheryngton was him name:
'It shall never be told in Sothe Ynglond,' he says, *South*
'To King Herry the Fourth for shame.

81–2 Their equality of rank must be formally recognized if they are to engage in single combat.

'I wat you ben great lordes twa,
I am a poor squyer of land:
I wyll never se my captayn fyght on a fylde
And stand myself lookande.

'I wyll never se my captayn fyght on a fylde
And stand myself lookande,
But whyle I may my weppon welde
I wyll not fayle both hert and hand.'

That day, that day, that dredful day!
The first fit here I fynde. *reach the end of*
And you wyll here any more o' the hunting o' the Cheviat
Yet ys ther more behynde. *to follow*

The Second Fit

The Ynglysh men had ther bowys ybent,
Ther hertes were good ynough.
The first of arrows that they shot off
Seven score spearmen they slough.

Yet bydys the yerl Doglas upon the bent,
A captayn good ynough,
And that was sene verament,
For he wrought hom both woo and wough. *injury*

The Doglas partyd his ost in thre
Lyk a chefe cheften of pryde;
With suer spears of mighty tre *wood*
They cum in on every syde,

Thorow our Ynglysh archery *Through*
Gave many a wound full wyde;
Many a doughty they garde to dy, *caused*
Which ganyd them no pryde.

The Ynglysh men let their bowes be
And pulde owt brandes that were bright;
It was a hevy syght to se
Bryght swordes on basnetes lyght. *helmets*

Thorow ryche maile and mynyplye *gauntlet (?)*
Many sterne they strok down streght: *brave warriors*
Many a freke that was full fre
Ther under foot dyd lyght. *fall*

106 **first fit**. A 'fit' is a division of a poem suitable for recitation at one sitting (cf. *Gawain*); the 'I' here suggests a minstrel-reciter – and indeed the ballad was very likely part of the stock-in-trade of 'Rychard Sheale', a Tamworth minstrel (fl. 1550), who is named in the MS.

121 **our Ynglysh archery**. As with the other poems on the battle, the point of view is English, though the Scots are treated as equally heroic and worthy of respect.

At last the Doglas and the Persy met
Lyk to captayns of myght and of mayn;
They swapte together tyll they both swat — *exchanged blows, sweated*
With swordes that wer of fyn myllayn. — *steel as made in Milan*

Thes worthy frekes for to fyght
Therto they were full fayn,
Tyll the blood owt of ther basnetes sprent — *spurted*
As ever dyd hail or rayn.

'Yelde the, Persy,' sayd the Doglas,
'And i'feith I shall the brynge
Wher thow shalt have a yerls wagis
Of Jamy our Scottish kynge.

'Thou shalt have thy ransom fre,
I hight the here this thing,
For the manfullyst man yet art thow
That ever I conqueryd in filde fightyng.'

'Nay,' sayd the lord Persy,
'I told it the beforn,
That I wold never yeldyd be
To no man of a woman born.'

With that ther cam an arrow hastely
Forth of a myghty wane; — *bow (?)*
Hit hath streken the yerl Doglas
In at the brest-bane.

Thorow liver and longes bathe
The sharp arrow ys gane,
That never after in all his lyf-days
He spake mo wordes but ane;

That never after in all his lyf-days
He spake mo wordes but ane,
That was, 'Fyght ye, my myrry men, whylys ye may,
For my lyf-days ben gane.'

The Persy leanyd on his brand
And saw the Doglas de; — *die*
He took the dede man by the hand
And sayd, 'Wo ys me for the!

'To have savyd thy lyf I wold have partyd with
My landes for yeares thre,
For a better man of hert nar of hand
Was nat in all the north contre.'

144 The first James was not crowned king in Scotland until 1424; but this is more of a generic Scottish king's name.

165–72 In the *Spectator* for 1711, Joseph Addison published two essays on *Chevy Chase* that foreshadow eighteenth-century romantic medievalism; he expresses particular admiration for the unaffected nobility of this tribute, as it appears in that version.

saw Of all that se a Scottish knyght,
Montgomery Was callyd Sir Hewe the Mongombyrry,
He saw the Doglas to the deth was dyght,
grasped He spendyd a spear o' trusti tree.

charger He rode upon a corsiere
Through a hondrith archery,
stopped, paused He never styntyd nar never blane
Tyll he cam to the good lord Persy.

He set upon the lord Persy
A dynt that was full sare;
With a suer spear of a mighty tre
Clean thorow the body he the Persy bare,

O' the tother syde that a man might se
A large cloth-yard and mare.
Two better captayns were nat in Cristiante
Then that day slain were thare.

An archer of Northomberlond
saw Say slain was the lord Persy.
strung He bar a bend bow in his hond
Was made of trusti tre.

An arrow that a cloth-yard was lang
drew To the hard stele halyd he,
A dynt that was both sad and sare
He set on Sir Hewe the Mongombyrry.

The dynt yt was both sad and sare
That he on Mongombyrry set;
The swan-fethers that his arrow bare
With his hert-blood they were wet.

Ther was never a freke one foot wold fle,
battle But still in stour dyd stand,
endure Hewyng on yche other whyle they myght dre
With many a balful brand.

This battel began in Cheviat
An ower befor the none,
And when even-song bell was rang
The battel was nat half-done.

went on fighting They toke on on ether hand
By the lyght of the mone;
Many had no strength for to stand
In Cheviat the hillys abone.

186 **cloth-yard**: the yard used in measuring cloth was the length of a long-bow arrow (36 inches).

Of fifteen hondrith archers of Ynglond
Went away but seventi and thre;
Of twenti hondrith spearmen of Scotlond
But even five and fifti.

But all were slayn Cheviat within,
They had no strenge to stand on hy;
The chyld may rue that ys unborn,
It was the more pite.

{Lists of the dead on either side are given, and report of the news being brought to the Scottish and English kings.}

This was the huntyng of the Cheviat –
That e'er began this spurn! *(Alas) that, fray*
Old men that knowen the grownd well ynough
Call it the battel of Otterburn.

At Otterburn began this spurn
Upon a Monenday;
Ther was the doughty Doglas slain,
The Persy never went away.

Ther was never a tyme on the March partyes
Sen the Doglas and the Persy met,
But yt ys mervel and the red blud runne not *When it was not a marvel if*
As the reane does in the stret. *rain*

Jesu Crist our balys bete *end our tribulations*
And to the blys us brynge.
Thus was the huntyng of the Cheviat –
God send us alle good endyng!

Robin Hood and the Monk

Robin Hood began his 'real' life, if he ever had one, as a local bandit and highway robber in south Yorkshire, one of a kind that won popularity because of their opposition to increasingly centralized bureaucratic control, especially tax-collecting, and the corruption that accompanied it. Some time in the fifteenth century he became associated with a legendary bad sheriff of Nottingham; his career began to ripen under the influence of models from chivalric romance, and he became the outlaw-hero of a so-called 'yeoman' class – sturdily independent, jealous of individual freedom, opposed to self-serving government officials and fat monks, yet pious, and generous to the poor. The cultural role that he served here, as in the ballad printed below, was to stand for certain values, and for the embodiment of those values in a certain class in a manner that bore little relation to historical reality but that it pleased all ranks of society to accept as their image of that reality. In subsequent centuries the image was further polished: he became not just a mirror-image of knighthood, but a knight himself, temporarily exiled; always now chivalrous to women, he was equipped with a lady-friend, and became a staunch upholder of the true king Richard against the upstart John. He becomes more purely a figure of romance, fulfilling escapist fantasies; but always he and his men have been available, like king Arthur and his knights, to serve the cultural purposes for which society needed them.

The earliest mention of Robin Hood is in *PP* (C.VII.11), the earliest documents (which may draw on earlier oral narratives) are the ballads and short playlets from the end of the fifteenth century, including the lengthy *Geste of Robyn Hode* printed about 1510. There is a wide selection of ballads and other texts included in the study by R.B. Dobson and J. Taylor, *The Rymes of Robyn Hode* (London,

285 **March partyes**: regions of the March, or borderlands.

1976), and a socio-cultural analysis, going up to modern times and films, by S. Knight, *Robin Hood: A Complete Study of the English Outlaw* (London, 1994).

The ballad below is found in CUL MS Ff.5.48 (fifteenth century, second half), fols 128v–135v. Robin Hood here is pious but ineffectual and the real hero is Little John, who is smart, resourceful, strongly independent but fiercely loyal, and brutally unsentimental. He seems to be occupying some of the positions of the clever folk-hero vacated by Robin as he moved upwards socially.

woods, bright In somer when the shawes be shene
And leves be large and long,
Hit is full mery in feyre foreste
To here the foulys song;

To se the dere draw to the dale
high And leve the hilles hee,
And shadow hem in the leves grene
Under the grene-wode tre.

Hit befel on Whitsontide,
Erly in a May mornyng,
The sun up feyre can shyne
And the briddis mery can syng.

'This is a mery mornyng,' seid Litull John,
By him (Christ) 'Be hym that dyed on tre;
A more mery man then I am one
Lyves not in Cristiante.

'Pluk up thi hert, my dere mayster,'
did say Litull John can sey,
'And thynk hit is a full fayre tyme
In a mornyng of May.'

'Ye, on thyng greves me,' seid Robyn,
'And does my hert mych woo:
That I may not no solem day
To mas nor matyns goo.

'Hit is a fourtnet and more,' seid he,
(i.e. at communion) 'Syn I my savyour see;
Today wil I to Notyngham,' seid Robyn,
'With the myght of mylde Marye.'

Then spake Moche, the mylner sun –
Evermore wel hym betyde!
sturdy 'Take twelve of thi wyght yemen,
Well weppynd, be thi side.
slay Such on wolde thiselfe slon
That twelve dar not abyde.'

'Of all my mery men,' seid Robyn,
'Be my feith I wil none have,

29 **Moche** (Much), the miller's son, is one of the few members of the band who are named.

But Litull John shall bere my bow,
Til that me list to drawe.'

'Thou shall bere thin own,' seid Litull Jon,
'Maister, and I wyl bere myne,
And we wyll shete a peny,' seid Litull Jon, *shoot for a penny-stake*
'Under the grene-wode lyne.' *linden-tree*

'I wil not shete a peny,' seyd Robyn Hode,
'In feith, Litull John, with the,
But ever for one as thou shetis,' seide Robyn,
'In feith I holde the thre.' *wager*

Thus shet thei forth, these yemen too,
Bothe at buske and brome,
Til Litull John wan of his maister
Five shillings to hose and shone. *to buy stockings and shoes*

A ferly strife fel them betwene *wondrous*
As they went bi the wey;
Litull John seid he had won five shillings
And Robyn Hode seid schortly nay.

With that Robyn Hode lyed Litul Jon *called a liar*
And smote hym with his hande;
Litul Jon waxed wroth therwith
And pulled out his bright bronde.

'Were thou not my maister,' seid Litull John,
'Thou shuldis by hit ful sore; *pay for*
Get the a man wher thou wilt,
For thou getis me no more.'

Then Robyn goes to Notyngham,
Hymselfe mournyng allone,
And Litull John to mery Scherwode –
The pathes he knew ilkone. *each one*

Whan Robyn came to Notyngham,
Sertenly withouten layn, *hiding the truth*
He prayed to God and myld Mary
To bryng hym out save agayn.

He gos into Seynt Mary chirch
And kneled down before the rode;
Alle that ever were the church within
Beheld wel Robyn Hode.

39 Little John holds to the old principles of the robber-band, and does not want to serve Robin in the capacity of a squire, or page.

46 Robin regards himself as odds-on favourite.

48 'Both at bush and broom-plant' (improvised targets).

65 **Scherwode**. Though originating further north, the story eventually settled in Sherwood Forest, in Nottinghamshire, a suitable place to take refuge in, to poach the king's deer, and to annoy the sheriff of Nottingham.

68 These 'fillers' are common in ballad, especially in the second line of the quatrain (cf. 80, 108, 172, etc.); they have something to do with the exigencies of an originally orally improvised narrative.

Beside hym stode a gret-hedid munke,
I pray to God woo he be!
Ful sone he knew gode Robyn,
As sone as he hym se.

Out at the durre he ran
Ful sone and anon;
Alle the gatis of Notyngham
barred He made to be sparred everychon.

'Rise up,' he seid, 'thou prowde schereff,
ready Buske the and make the bowne;
I have spyed the kynggis felon,
For sothe he is in this town.

'I have spyed the false felon,
As he stondis at his masse;
on account of thee Hit is long of the,' seide the munke,
If 'And ever he fro us passe.

'This traytur name is Robyn Hode,
Under the grene-wode lynde;
He robbyt me onys of a hundred pound –
Hit shall never out of my mynde!'

Up then rose this prowde schereff
quickly, ready And radly made hym yare;
Many was the moder son
To the kyrk with hym can fare.

eagerly thrust In at the durres thei throly thrast
plenty With staves ful gode wone;
'Alas, alas!' seid Robyn Hode,
'Now mysse I Litull John!'

But Robyn toke out a too-hond sworde
That hangit down be his kne;
Ther as the schereff and his men stode thyckust
Thedurwarde wolde he.

Thryes thorowout them he ran then,
For sothe as I yow sey,
And woundyt mony a moder son,
And twelve he slew that day.

His sworde upon the schireff hed
Sertanly he brake in too;
'The smyth that the made,' seid Robyn,
'I pray to God wyrke hym woo!

'For now am I weppynlesse,' seid Robyn,
against 'Alasse! agayn my wyll;

Unless
But if I may fle these traytors fro
I wot thei wil me kyll.'

{A portion of the poem is lost here. Evidently Robin is captured, and the news comes to his men.}

Sum fel in swonyng as thei were dede
And lay stil as any stone;
Non of theym were in her mynde
But only Litull Jon.

noisy wailing
'Let be your rule,' seid Litull Jon,
'For his luf that dyed on tre;
Ye that shulde be dughty men
Het is gret shame to se.

beset (i.e. in the past)
'Oure maister has been hard bystode
And yet scapyd away;
moaning
Pluk up your hertis and leve this mone
And harkyn what I shal say.

'He has servyd oure Lady many a day
certainly
And yet wil, securly;
Therfor I trust in hir specialy
No wyckud deth shal he dye.

'Therfor be glad,' seid Litul John,
'And let this mournyng be,
And I shal be the munkis gyde,
With the myght of mylde Mary.'

{A few lines lost: Little John is joined by Much, the miller's son, whose uncle's house looks out on the highway.}

Forth then went these yemen too,
together
Litul John and Moche on-fere,
Much's uncle's
And lokid on Moch emys hows –
The hye-way lay full nere.

Litul John stode at a wyndow in the mornyng
from an upper storey
And lokid forth at a stage;
He was war wher the munke came ridyng,
And with hym a litul page.

'Be my feith,' seid Litul John to Moch,
tidings
'I can the tel tithyngus gode;
I se wher the munke cumys rydyng,
I know hym be his wyde hode.'

They went into the way, these yemen bothe,
courteous, gracious
As curtes men and hende;

137 **the munkis gyde**. Little John speaks ironically. Evidently, they had heard that the monk was to bear the news of Robin's capture to the king.

asked Thei spyrred tithyngus at the munke,
As they hade bene his frende.

'Fro whens come ye?' seid Litull Jon,
Tel us tithyngus, I yow pray,
Of a false owtlay callid Robyn Hode
Was takyn yisterday.

'He robbyt me and my felowes bothe
Of twenti marke in serteyn;
If that false owtlay be takyn,
For sothe we wolde be fayn.'

'So did he me,' seid the munke,
'Of a hundred pound and more;
I layde furst hande hym apon –
Ye may thonke me therfore!'

'I pray God thanke you,' seid Litull John,
'And we wil when we may;
We wil go with you, with your leve,
And bryng yow on your way,

'For Robyn Hode has many a wilde felow,
I tell you in certeyn;
If thei wist ye rode this way,
In feith ye shulde be slayn.'

As thei went talking be the way,
The munke and Litull John,
John toke the munkis horse be the hede
Ful sone and anon.

Johne toke the munkis horse be the hed,
For sothe as I yow say;
So did Much the litull page,
For he shulde not scape away.

(part round the throat) Be the golett of the hode
John pulled the munke down;
John was nothyng of hym agast,
He lete hym falle on his crown.

Litull John was sore agrevyd
haste And drew owt his swerde in hye;
This munke saw he shulde be ded,
Lowd mercy can he crye.

'He was my maister,' seid Litull John,
to harm 'That thou has browght in bale;
Shall you never cum at our kyng,
For to telle hym tale.'

John smote of the munkis hed,
No longer wolde he dwell;
So did Moch the litull page
For ferd lest he wolde tell. *fear*

Ther thei beryed hem bothe
In nouther mosse nor lyng, *heath*
And Litull John and Much in-fere
Bare the letturs to oure kyng.

[When Litull John cam to the kyng]
He knelid down upon his kne:
'God yow save, my lege lorde,
Jesus yow save and se!

'God yow save, my lege kyng!'
To speke John was full bolde;
He gaf hym the letturs in his hond,
The kyng did hit unfold.

The kyng the letturs red anon,
And seid, 'So mot I the, *as I may thrive*
Ther was never yoman in mery Inglond
I longut so sore to se.

'Wher is the munke that these shuld have brought?'
Oure kyng can say;
'Be my trouth,' seid Litull John,
'He dyed after the way.' *back on*

The kyng gaf Moch and Litul Jon
Twenti pound in sertayn,
And made theim yemen of the crown
And bade theim go agayn. *return*

He gaf John the seel in hand
The sheref for to bere,
To bryng Robyn hym to
And no man do hym dere. *injury*

John toke his leve at oure kyng,
The sothe as I yow say;
The next way to Notyngham *nearest*
To take, he yede the way.

Whan John came to Notyngham
The gatis were sparred ychon; *barred*
John callid up the porter,
He answerid sone anon.

'What is the cause,' seid Litul Jon,
'Thou sparris the gates so fast?'

'Because of Robyn Hode,' seid the porter,
'In depe prison is cast.

'John and Moch and Wyll Scathlock,
For sothe as I yow say,
Thei slew oure men upon our wallis
attack And sawten us every day.'

asked Litull John spyrred after the schereff
And sone he hym fonde;
He oppyned the kingus prive seel
And gaf hym in his honde.

Whan the scheref saw the kyngus seel
He did of his hode anon;
'Wher is the munke that bare the letturs?'
He seid to Litull John.

pleased with 'He is so fayn of hym,' seid Litul John,
'For sothe as I yow say,
He has made hym abot of Westmynster,
A lorde of that abbay.'

The scheref made John gode chere
And gaf hym wyne of the best;
At nyght thei went to her bedde
And every man to his rest.

When the scheref was on slepe,
Dronken of wyne and ale,
Litul John and Moch, for sothe,
Toke the way unto the jale.

Litul John callid up the jayler
And bade hym rise anon;
He seyd Robyn Hode had brokyn prison
And out of hit was gon.

The porter rose anon sertan
As sone as he herd John calle;
Litul John was redy with a swerd
And bare hym to the walle.

'Now wil I be porter,' seid Litul John,
'And take the keyes in honde.'
He toke the way to Robyn Hode
And sone he hym unbonde.

He gaf hym a gode swerd in his hond,
His hed with for to kepe,

239 **Wyll Scathlock**, better groomed, became Will Scarlet.

And ther as the walle was lowyst
Anon down can thei lepe.

Be that the cok began to crow,
The day began to spryng,
The scheref fond the jaylier ded;
The comyn bell made he ryng. *common (town) bell*

He made a crye thorowowt al the town, *proclamation*
Wheder he be yoman or knave,
That cowthe bryng hym Robyn Hode, *He that*
His warison he shuld have. *reward*

'For I dar never,' said the scheref,
'Cum before oure kyng,
For if I do, I wot serten
For sothe he wil me heng.'

The scheref made to seke Notyngham *search*
Bothe be strete and stye, *alley*
And Robyn was in mery Scherwode
As light as lef on lynde.

Then bespake gode Litull John, *up spoke*
To Robyn Hode can he say,
'I have done the a gode turne for an evyll –
Quyte the whan thou may! *Even the scores*

'I have done the a gode turne,' seid Litull John,
'For sothe as I yow say:
I have brought the under grene-wode lyne –
Farewel and have gode day!'

'Nay, be my trouth,' seid Robyn Hode,
'So shall hit never be;
I make the maister,' seid Robyn Hode,
'Of alle my men and me.'

'Nay, be my trouth,' seid Litull John,
'So shall hit never be;
But lat me be a felow,' seid Litull John,
Non oder kepe I be.' *care*

Thus John gate Robyn Hod out of prison,
Sertan withoutyn layn;
Whan his men saw hym hol and sounde,
For sothe they were full fayne.

They filled in wyne and made hem glad
Under the levys smale
And yete pasties of venyson, *ate*
That gode was with ale.

Than worde came to oure kyng
How Robyn Hode was gon
And how the scheref of Notyngham
Durst never loke hym upon.

Then bespake oure cumly kyng
In an angur hye:
'Litull John has begyled the schereff,
In faith so has he me!

'Litul John has begyled us bothe,
And that full wel I se,
Or ellis the schereff of Notyngham
Hye hongut shulde he be.

'I made hem yemen of the crowne
And gaf hem fee with my hond;
safe-conduct I gaf hem grith,' seid oure kyng,
'Thorowout all mery Inglond.

'I gaf theym grith,' then seid oure kyng,
'I say, so mot I the;
For sothe soch a yeman as he is on
In all Inglond ar not thre.

'He is trew to his maister,' seid our kyng,
'I sey, be swete seynt John;
He lovys better Robyn Hode
Then he dose us ychon.

'Robyn Hode is ever bond to hym
place where he stays Bothe in strete and stalle;
Speke no more of this mater,' seid oure kyng,
'But John has begyled us alle!'

Thus endys the talkyng of the munke
And Robyn Hode, iwysse;
God that is ever a crowned kyng
Bryng us all to his blisse!

Reginald Pecock (*c.* 1392/5–*c.* 1460?)

Pecock was made bishop of St Asaph in 1444 and bishop of Chichester in 1450. He had by then already written his two best-known works: *The Follower to the Donet* (*c.* 1454), a more advanced supplement to his *Donet* (*c.* 1440), an introduction to the chief truths of the Christian religion, cast in the form of a dialogue between a father and son (the *Donet* was the basic Latin grammar); and *The Repressor of Overmuch Blaming of the Clergy* (*c.* 1449), a defence of the clergy against attacks by 'Bible men', as he calls them (i.e. the Lollards). In the second part of this work, he takes up six of the arguments of the Lollards against the established church, and deals with them in turn: their opposition to images (in the extract below), pilgrimages, clerical endowment, ecclesiastical hierarchy, papal authority and the religious orders. He states the arguments of the Lollards first, as clearly and coherently as he can, and then refutes them by a process of reasoning. Later, in his *Book of Faith* (1456), he came close to arguing that faith can be established by rational argument. This was too much for the church authorities, and the Yorkists, now all-powerful, were not in favour: subjects of this kind were still not appropriate to be written of in English. He was brought for examination before archbishop Bourgchier in 1457 and condemned for heretical opinions. Given a choice between abjuration and burning, he abjured, and made a public recantation at St Paul's Cross on Sunday 4 December 1457 (see the poem, p. 389, above). He assented to the burning of his books, resigned his bishopric, and went to live in confinement at Thorney abbey in Cambridgeshire. Pecock's mistake was to suppose that 'reason' had anything to do with questions of heretical opinion, and that entering into rational debate with the Lollards would do anything other than appear to make him complicit in their assumptions. His confidence in the power of reason was naive (in relation to the realities of power), as was his evident pleasure in his powers as a controversialist. Yet he wrote the first original philosophically ratiocinative prose in English, complex and pedantically precise but never in the slightest degree confusing. Text from CUL MS Kk.4.26, fol. 53; ed. C.Babington, 2 vols, Rolls series (London, 1860); short biography by W. Scase (Aldershot, 1996); see also Hudson (1988), pp. 55–8, 440–3. In the passage below, Pecock is arguing against the Lollard view that the use of images in church is a form of idolatry (see Hoccleve, *Regement*, 5006–12n, above).

The Repressor of Overmuch Blaming of the Clergy

Images not a form of idolatry

Peple in havyng and using ymagis sett up in the chirche doon noon ydolatrie by hem. Forwhi ydolatrie is nevere doon save whanne a man takith a creature for his God and worschipith thilk creature as for his God; but so doith no man with eny ymage now in Cristendoom, aftir that the man is come into yeeris of discrecioun and is passid childhode, and which is not a natural fool. Forwhi, if of eny of hem it be askid, whether this ymage is God in heven, which made al thing and which was ever withoute bigynnyng and was therfore eer this ymage was maad, he wole seie anoon that this ymage is not he, but that this ymage is the ymage of him. And thanne, if this man take not this ymage as for his God, certis he wole not therwith worschipe him as his God, neither he wole yeve to him the worschip which he knowith to be dew to God oonli, neither he wole be aknowe[1] that the ymage is his God. Forwhi theryn he dide repugnaunce[2] in sum maner, or ellis certis cause is not likeli to be founde whi he schulde so do tho thingis togidere. And therfore as for drede of ydolatrie, that is to seie, lest peple be ydolatreris in having and using ymagis, doom of resoun hath not for to weerne[3] and reprove ymagis to be had and usid.

The strengthe of this argument stondith upon the very knowing what ydolatrie is. And sithen ydolatrie is nothing ellis than what is now seid to be, the argument now maad muste needis have his entent.[4] Ful ofte have I herd men and wommen unwiseli juge and diffame ful scherpli weel-nygh alle Cristene[5] to be ydolatrers, and al for the havyng and using of ymagis. And yit whanne it hadde be askid of hem what ydolatrie is, forsothe thei couthe not seie neither feele what it is in his trouthe,[6] though thei schulden have wonne therbi al the worldis blis or the blis of heven. And whether this was not an horrible abhomynacioun and a vile stinking presumpcioun, hem for to so sturdili bi manye yeeris juge and diffame bothe the clergi and weel-nygh al the lay party of Goddis chirche in so greet a cryme, which thei

1 will he acknowledge
2 acted with inconsistency
3 rational judgement has no cause to forbid
4 necessarily prevail
5 Christians
6 understand what it truly is

couthen neither myghten prove to be doon – forwhi thei wisten not what thing thilk cryme is, and therfore thei myghten not knowe whether it was doon or not doon – and whether such peple be able and worthi to be admyttid into the homeli[7] reding of Holi Writt, eer thei be weel adauntid[8] and weel schamed of her folie and of her unwisdom and pride, seie[9] whoevere schal this heere. And I trowe he may not ayens this seie and holde, if he have eny quantite of discrecioun. Manye lesingis I have herd hem lie, how thei knowen that persoones reulen hem amys in bilyvyng fonnedli[10] aboute ymagis; but whanne profris of greet meene (ye, of .xl. pound and of more) hath be mad to hem for to bringe forth .ii. or .iii. of suche persoones, thei couthen bringe forth noon of hem.

Peraventure thei wolen seie thus: Manye hundridis of men clepiden this ymage the Trinyte, and thei clepen this ymage Crist, and this ymage the Holi Goost, and this ymage Marie, and this ymage Seint Petir, and this ymage Seint Poul, and so forth of othere, and thei wolden not so clepe but if thei feeliden and bileeveden withinne-forth as thei clepen withoute-forth, for ellis thei weren double.[11] Wherfore alle tho hundridis bileeven amys aboute tho ymagis. Herto it is ful light for to answere. Whanne I come to thee in thi parisch chirche thou wolt peraventure seie to me thus, 'Lo, here lieth my fadir and there lieth my grauntfadir, and in the other side lieth my wif' – and yit thei liggen not there, but oonli her boonys liggen there. If I come to thee into thin halle or chaumbir thou wolt peraventure seie to me in descryvyng the storie peintid or wovun in thin halle or chaumbre, 'Here ridith King Arthur, and there fightith Julius Cesar, and here Hector of Troie throwith doun a knyt', and so forth. For though thou thus seie, thou wolte not holde thee[12] for to seie theryn amys. Schal I therfore bere thee an hoond[13] that thou trowist thi fadir and thi grauntfadir and thi wiif for to lyve and dwelle in her sepulcris, or schal I bere thee an hond that thou trowist Artur and Julius Cesar and Hector to be quyk[14] in thi clooth, or that thou were double in this so reuling of speche? I trowe thou woldist seie I were uncurteis, or ellis unwiis and folisch, if I schulde beere thee so an honde, if it likid thee for to so speke. And if this be trewe it folewith that as weel thou art uncurteis, or ellis thou art to be excusid of uncurtesie bi thi greet folie and madnes, if thou bere me an hond that al the world ful of clerkis and of othere lay men weenen summe ymagis to be God, and summe ymages to be quyke seintis, or that thei ben double and gileful if thei clepen an ymage of God bi the name of God, and an ymage of a seint bi the name of a seint.

But, for more clereli this same answere to be undirstonde, it is to wite[15] that if figuratiif spechis weren not allowid to be had in uce, that the ymage or the likenes of a thing mai be clepid bi the name of the thing of which he is ymage and likenes, and that the parti of a thing mai be clepid under and bi the name of his hool (as that men seien thei han lyved .xl. wynteris, meenyng therbi that thei han lyved forti yeeris), certis thi chalenge myghte weel procede and have his entent. But ayenward[16] it is so that such figuratiif and unpropre speche, for to clepe the ymage of a thing bi and undir the name of the thing of which he is ymage, hath be in famose uce[17] and hath be allowid bothe of Holi Scripture and of alle peplis. And therfore, though men in such woned[18] figuratiif speche seie, 'Here at this autir is the Trinyte, and there at thilk auter is Jesus, and yondir is the Holi Goost, and ther-bi is Marie with Seint Peter', and so forth, it nedith not that therfore be seid that thei meenen and feelen that this ymage is the Trinyte, or that thilk ymage is verili Jesus, and so forth of othere, but that these ymagis ben the liknessis or the ymagis of hem.

7 at home
8 put down
9 let him say
10 foolishly
11 guilty of duplicity
12 consider yourself
13 maintain against you
14 alive
15 (clearly) to be understood
16 on the contrary
17 a matter of commonly known practice
18 accustomed

The Paston Letters

Letters in the vernacular rarely survive from the fifteenth century, but there are one or two collections (e.g. Stonor, Cely, Plumpton), and the Paston Letters and Papers are a uniquely valuable hoard. The earliest is 1425, the latest just after 1500, and the letters, both to and from members of the Paston family of Norfolk, relate to all the activities of a prosperous, ambitious and extensive family. Many of them are to and from the male heads of the family (John I, 1421–66, John II, 1442–79, and John III, his brother, 1444–1504) when they were in London about the family's business, especially the business of protecting the family's interest in the estate of Sir John Fastolf (d. 1459) from rival claimants. The letters below are all from women, and relate to two family crises. The first was when Margery (*c.* 1448–*c.* 1479), daughter of John I and his formidable wife Margaret (*c.* 1420–84), fell in love with Richard Calle, the family bailiff, and contracted a secret marriage with him. The family, especially the mother, did everything they could to prevent such an unsuitable marriage, including putting pressure on the bishop of Norwich who was called in to interview the parties and determine whether a binding contract had been entered into (personal exchange of vows in the proper form, though unwitnessed, could constitute civil marriage). Margaret's letter reveals the cruel anger that could be felt when parental ambitions and wishes in such matters were flouted, especially when there was so much else to worry about. Margery, meanwhile, comes over as a woman of independence and spirit; and she had her way in the end. The other letters concern a love-match between John Paston III and Margery Brews, and are from Margery and her mother. This was not an unsuitable match, but it ran into financial problems. The letters are touching in their tale of true love (rewarded, for they married before the year was out), but their women's discourse is already coopted into the coldly financial calculations and blackmailing strategies surrounding marriage.

The letters are couched in a mixture of formal phrases and direct colloquial speech; they were dictated to family clerks or chaplains, who acted as scribes because the women were not used to writing. The scribe of the first letter is Margaret's younger son Edmund, whose spelling is highly inventive, and much modified here.

Complete edition by N. Davis, 2 vols (Oxford, 1971); also *Selections* (Oxford, 1958) and *Selections in Modern Spelling* (Oxford, 1963) by the same editor; see also Barratt (1992), pp. 238–61. Texts from BL MSS Add.34889 (83v–84r), 27445 (105r) and 43490 (22r–24r).

Margaret Paston to her son Sir John Paston II, 10/11 September 1469

I grete yow wel and send yow Goddys blyssyng and myn, letyng yow wete that, on Thurysday last was, my moder and I were wyth my lord of Norwych and desyerd hym that he woold no more do in the matere towchyng yowr syster tyl that ye and my brothere, and othere that wern executors to yowr fader, myhte beyn here togeder, for they had the rule of her as weel as I. And he sayde playnly that he had be requeryd so oftyn for to exameyn her that he myhte not, nor woold, no lengare delay yt, and chargyd me in peyn of cursyng that sche schuld not be deferred but that sche schuld apere beforn hym the nexte day. And I sayd pleynly that I woold nowder bryng her nor send her. And than he sayd that he woold send for her hymsylfe, and chargyd that sche schuld be at her lyberte to cume whan he sent for her. And he seyd be hys trowthe that he woold be as sory for her and sche ded not welle as he wold be and sche were ryht nere of hys kyn, bothe for my moderys sake and myn and othere of her frenddys, for he woost welle that her demenyng had stekyd soore at owr hartys.

My moder and I informyd hym that we kowd never onderstond be her sayyng, be no language that ever sche had to hym, that neythere of hem were bownd to othere, but that they myht chese bothe.[1] Than he seyd that he woold sey to her as wele as he kowde before that he exameynd her; and so yt was told me be dyverse persones, that he ded as welle and as pleynly as sche had be ryhte nere to hym, whych were to long to wryte at thys tyme. Hereaftyr ye shalle wete, and who were laberers therein. The chanselere was not so gylty therein as I weend he had ben.

On Fryday the bysschope sent for her be Asschefeld and othere that arn ryht sory of her demenyng. And the bysschop seyd to her ryht pleynly, and put her in rememberawns how sche was born, what kyn and frenddys that sche had, and schuld have mo yf sche were rulyd and gydyd aftyre them; and yf sche

1 They were both free to choose, and not bound.

ded not, what rebuke and schame and los yt schuld be to her, yf sche were not gydyd be them, and cause of foresakyng of her for any good or helpe or kownfort that sche schuld have of hem; and seyd that he had hard sey that sche loved seche on that her frend were not plesyd wyth that sche schuld have, and therefore he bad her be ryht wel avysyd how sche ded; and seyd that he woold undyrstond the worddys that sche had seyd to hym, wheythere yt mad matramony or not.

And sche rehersyd what sche had seyd, and seyd yf thoo worddys mad yt not sure, sche seyd boldly that sche wold make it surer or than[2] sche went thens. For sche sayd sche thowht in her conschens sche was bownd, whatsoevere the worddys wern. Thes lewd wordys greve me and her grandam as myche as alle the remnawnte. And than the bysschop and the chawnselere bothe seyd that there was neythere I nere no frend of hers wold reseyve her.

And than Calle was exameynd aparte be hymsylfe, that her worddys and hys acordyd, and the tyme and where yt schuld a be don.[3] And than the bysschop sayd that he supposyd that there schuld be fownd othere thynggys ageyns hym that myhte cause the lettyng thereof,[4] and therefore he sayd he wold not be to hasty to geve sentens thereupon, and sayd that he wold geve overe day[5] tyl the Wodynsday or Thursday aftyre Mykylmes, and so yt tys delayyd. They woold an had here wyl parformyd in haste, but the bysschop seyd he woold non otherewyse than he had sayd.

I was wyth my moder at her plase whan sche was exameynd and whan I hard sey what her demenyng was, I chargyd my servantys that sche schuld not be reseyved in myn hows. I had yeven her warnyng: sche myhte a be ware afore yf sche had a be grasyows. And I sent to on or too more that they schuld not reseyve her yf sche cam. Sche was browhte ageyn to my place for to a be reseyved, and Ser Jamys tolde them that browhte her that I had chargyd hem alle, and sche schuld not be reseyved. And soo my lord of Norwych hath set her at Rogere Bestys to be there tyl the day before-sayd – God knowyth ful evel ageyn hys wyl and hys wyvys, yf they durst do otherewyse! I am sory that they arn acumryd[6] wyth her, but yet I am better payed[7] that sche is there for the whyle than sche had ben in othere place, because of the sadnes[8] and god dysposysion of hymsylfe and hys wyfe, for sche schal not be soverd there to pleye the brethele.[9]

I pray yow and requere yow that ye take yt not pensyly,[10] for I wot wele yt goth ryht nere yowr hart, and so doth yt to myn and to othere. But remembyre yow, and so do I, that we have lost of her but a brethele, and set yt the les to hart. For and sche had be good, whatsoevere sche had be yt schuld not a ben as it tys, for and he[11] were ded at thys owyre sche schuld nevere be at myn hart as sche was. As for the devors[12] that ye wrete to me of, I suppose what ye ment, but I charge yow upon my blyssyng that ye do not, nere cause non othere to do, that schuld offend God and yowr conschens. For and ye do, or cause for to be do, God wul take vengawns thereupon, and ye schuld put yowrsylfe and othere in gret joparte. For wott yt wele, sche schal ful sore repent her lewdnes hereaftyre, and I pray God sche mute[13] soo. I praye yow, for myn hartys ese, be ye of a good cownfort in alle thynngys. I trust God schal helpe ryht wele, and I pray God so do in all owre maters.

I wuld ye toke hed yf there were any labore mad in the kort of Cawntyrbery for the lewd matere foresayd.

But yf the Duke be purveyd for,[14] he and hys wyse kownsel schalle lese thys cuntre. Yt tys told me that he seth that he wul not spare to do that he is purposyd for no duke in Ynglond.[15] God helpe at nede.

2 before

3 have been done

4 The bishop thinks that if other reasons can be found for preventing the marriage, things will be less awkward.

5 postpone his decision

6 encumbered

7 pleased

8 soberness

9 fool

10 sadly

11 Richard Calle

12 divorce

13 may do

14 'unless something is done about the Duke'. The duke of Norfolk was threatening to attack and seize Caister castle, one of the disputed estates (he did so the next week).

15 The duke of Clarence had offered to mediate.

ELIZABETH BREWS TO JOHN PASTON III, FEBRUARY 1477

Ryght wurschypfull cosyn, I recommande me unto yowe, etc. And I sent myn husbonde a bill of the mater that ye knowe of, and he wrote another bill to me agayn towchyng the same mater; and he wold that ye schuld go unto my maistresse yowr modur and asaye if ye myght gete the hole twenty pound[1] into yowr handes, and then he wolde be more gladd to marye wyth yowe[2] and will gyffe yowe an hundred pound. And cosyn, that day that sche is maryed my fadur will gyffe hyr fifty merk. But and we acorde I schall gyffe yowe a grettur tresure, that is a wytty[3] gentylwoman, and, if I sey it, bothe good and vertuos. For if I schuld take money for hyr I wold not gyffe hyr for a thousend pound. But cosyn, I trust yowe so meche that I wold thynke hyr wele besett on yowe and ye were worthe meche more.

And cosyn, a lytull aftur that ye were gon, come a man fro my cosyn Derby and broght me wurde that suche a chance fell that he myght not com at the day that was set, as I schall let yowe undyrstond more pleynly when I speke wyth yowe. But cosyn, and it wold please yowe to com agayn what dey that ye will set, I dar undyrtake that they schall kepe the same day; for I wold be glad that, and myn husbond and ye myght acorde in thys maryage, that it myght be my fortune to make an ende in thys mater betwene my cosyns and yowe, that yche of yowe myght love other in frendely wyse.

And cosyn, if thys byll please not yowr entent, I pray yowe that it may be brent. No more unto yowe at thys tyme, but almyghty Jesus preserve yowe.

THE SAME, ABOUT 9 FEBRUARY 1477

Cosyn, I recommande me unto yowe, thankyng yowe hertely for the grette chere that ye made me and all my folkys the last tyme that I was at Norwych. And ye promysyd me that ye wold never breke the mater to Mergery unto suche tyme as ye and I were at a poynt.[1] But ye hafe made hyr suche advokett for yowe that I may never hafe rest nyght ner day for callyng and cryeng uppon to brynge the saide mater to effecte.

And cosyn, uppon Fryday is Sent Volentynes Day, and every brydde chesyth hym a make; and yf it lyke yowe to com on Thursday at nyght, and so purvey yowe that ye may abyde ther tyll Monday, I trust to God that ye schall so speke to myn husbonde, and I schall prey that we schall bryng the mater to a conclusyon. For cosyn, it is but a sympill oke that is cut down at the firste stroke; for ye will be resonabill, I trust to God, whech hafe yowe ever in hys mercyfull kepyng.

MARGERY BREWS TO JOHN PASTON III, FEBRUARY 1477

Ryght reverent and wurschypfull and my ryght wele-beloved Voluntyne, I recommande me unto yowe full hertely, desyring to here of yowr welefare, whech I beseche almyghty God long for to preserve unto hys plesure and yowr hertys desyre. And yf it please yowe to here of my welefare, I am not in good heele of body ner of herte, nor schall be tyll I here from yowe. For ther wottys no creature what peyn that I endure, And for to be deede I dare it not discure.[1] And my lady my moder hath labored the mater to my fadure full delygently, but sche can no more gete than ye knowe of, for the whech God knowyth I am full sory.

But yf that ye loffe me, as I tryste verely that ye do, ye will not leffe me therfor. For if that ye hade not

1 'xx li [*librae*]' in the original. All money sums are thus expressed, the scribal form, in the midst of the chattiness, acknowledging the impersonal imperative of the economic.

2 'to come to a marriage agreement with you'. The occlusion of the female party is striking.

3 intelligent

1 in agreement

1 'And even on pain of death I cannot reveal it.' This rhyming couplet may be a quotation, or an original composition. There may be more attempts at rhymed composition later in the letter.

halfe the lyvelode that ye hafe, for to do the grettyst labure that any woman on lyve[2] myght, I wold not forsake yowe. And yf ye commande me to kepe me true where-ever I go, iwyse I will do all my myght yowe to love and never no mo. And yf my freendys say that I do amys, thei schal not me let[3] so for to do. Myn herte me byddys evermore to love yowe truly over all erthely thing. And yf thei be never so wroth, I tryst it schall be bettur in tyme commyng.

No more to yowe at this tyme, but the holy Trinite hafe yowe in kepyng. And I besech yowe that this bill be not seyn of non erthely creature safe only yourselfe. And thys lettur was indyte at Topcroft wyth full hevy herte.

THE SAME

Ryght wurschypfull and wele-belovyd Volentyne, in my moste umble wyse I recommande me unto yowe, etc. And hertely I thanke yowe for the letture whech that ye sente me be John Bekurton, wherby I undyrstonde and knowe that ye be purposyd to com to Topcroft in schorte tyme, and wythowte any erand or mater but only to hafe a conclusyon of the mater betwyx my fadur and yowe. I wolde be most glad of any creature on lyve so that the mater myght growe to effect. And theras ye say, and ye com and fynde the mater no more toward[1] then ye dyd afortyme, ye wold no more put my fadur and my lady my moder to no cost ner besenesse for that cause a good whyle afture, wheche causyth myn herte to be full hevy; and yf that ye com and the mater take to non effecte, then schuld I be meche more sory and full of hevynesse.

And as for myselfe, I hafe don and undyrstond in the mater that[2] I can or may, as God knowyth. And I let yowe pleynly undyrstond that my fader wyll no more money parte wythall in that behalfe but an hundred pound and fifty marke, whech is ryght far fro the acomplyshment of yowr desyre. Wherfor, yf that ye cowde be content wyth that good and my por persone, I wold be the meryest mayden on grounde. And yf ye thynke not yowrselfe so satysfyed, or that ye myght hafe mech more good, as I hafe undyrstonde be yowe afor, good, trewe and lovyng Volentyne, that ye take no such labure uppon yowe as to com more for that mater, but let it passe and never more to be spokyn of, as I may be yowr trewe lover and bedewoman[3] duryng my lyfe.

No more unto yowe at thys tyme, but almyghty Jesus preserve yowe, bothe body and sowle.

2 alive
3 prevent

1 forward
2 what
3 woman who prays for you

Sir John Fortescue (*c.* 1395–*c.* 1477)

Sir John Fortescue was prominent in the political affairs of his day, Chief Justice (1442) and briefly Chancellor under Henry VI, and a faithful Lancastrian after Henry VI was deposed in 1461. He went into exile in France, from where he urged support for Henry's 're-adeption'. During this time he wrote his Latin treatise, *De laudibus legum Anglie* ('In praise of the laws of England'), in the form of a dialogue between himself, as Chancellor, and prince Edward, the heir-apparent. He returned to England with queen Margaret and prince Edward in 1471, but the attempt to reinstate Henry VI failed and Fortescue was imprisoned. After being pardoned and released, he adapted a treatise that he had written for Henry VI, in English, *The Governance of England*, and readdressed it to Edward IV. The substance of the two treatises is similar: both are attempts to show that absolute rule by the king according to such laws as he makes for himself (*jus regale*) is less just than rule by a king according to laws that his people have assented to (*jus politicum et regale*). The English system (supposed to be the latter) is favourably compared with the French (the former). But Fortescue is perhaps less interested in the justice of the 'constitutional' system (as it came to be called) than in its greater promise of stability. The Wars of the Roses provided him with ample evidence of the devastation wrought when a king is weak, and the praise of the English political system provided somewhat of a cover for his very practical recommendations, in *The Governance*, for its improvement through the strengthening of monarchic authority: the insistence that the king must have adequate guaranteed revenues (and greater than any magnate), that no rewards should be granted from royal revenue-sources (e.g. lands), and that a permanent council should be appointed and paid (i.e. not a council of magnates) to advise on the granting of gifts and offices and to assist in the deliberation of policy. *The Governance* has its philosophical roots in Aquinas, but it is distinctly more pragmatic and specific than earlier discussions of kingship in the *De regimine principum* tradition (e.g. Hoccleve), as well as brisk and forthright in the manner of a man with a good mind speaking. Under the title, 'Of the difference between an absolute and limited monarchy', it played an important part in English political discussion during the seventeenth and eighteenth centuries. See *The Governance of England*, ed. C. Plummer (Oxford, 1885); modern translations of both treatises in *On the Laws and Governance of England*, ed. S. Lockwood (Cambridge, 1997). Text from Bodl.MS Laud 593 (chaps 2 and 3).

The Governance of England

Jus regale *and* Jus politicum et regale

{Chap. 2}{In the earliest realms there was only 'royal' rule.} But aftirwarde, whan mankynde was more mansuete,[1] and bettir disposid to vertu, grete comunaltes, as was the felowshippe that came into this lande with Brute,[2] willynge to be unite and made[3] a body pollitike callid a reawme, havynge an hed to governe it – as, aftir the saynge of the philisopher,[4] every comunalte unyed of mony parties must nedis have an hed – than thai[a] chese the same Brute to be ther hed and kynge. And thai and he, upon this incorperacion, institucion and onynge of hemself into a reaume, ordenyd the same reaume to be ruled and justified by suche lawes as thai all wolde assent unto; wich lawe therfore is callid *polliticum*, and bicause it is ministrid bi a kynge, it is callid *regale*....

{Chap. 3} And how so be it that the Frenche kyng reignith uppon his peple *dominio regali*, yet seynt Lowes, sometyme kynge ther,[5] nor eny of his progenitors sette never tayles[6] or other imposicion uppon the peple of that lande withowt the assent of the .iii. estates, wich whan thai bith assembled bith like to the courte of the parlement in Ingelonde. And this ordre kepte many of his successours into late dayis, that Ingelonde men made suche warre in Fraunce that the .iii. estates durst not come togedre. And than for that cause and for gret necessite wich the French kynge hade of good[7] for the defence of that lande, he toke upon hym to sett tayles and other imposicions upon the comouns withowt the assent of the .iii.

1 civilized

2 Brutus, who left Troy after it was sacked by the Greeks, sailed west, and founded Britain – the originary story of Britain, first told by Geoffrey of Monmouth, and here adapted as the foundation narrative of the monarchic contract.

3 united and made into

4 Aristotle (commonly so called), in the *Politics*; but it is a common saw.

5 Louis IX, king of France 1226–70.

6 taxes

7 money

estates; but yet he wolde not sett any such charges, nor hath sette, uppon the nobles of his lande for fere of rebillion. And bicause the commons ther, though thai have grucched, have not rebellid or beth hardy to rebelle,[8] the French kynges have yerely sithyn sette such charges upon them, and so augmented the same charges, as the same comouns be so impoveryesshid and distroyed that thai mowe unneth leve.[9]

Thai drinken water, thai eyten apples, with brede right browne made of rye; thai eyten no flesshe but yf it be right seldon a litle larde, or of the entrales and heydes of bestis slayn, for the nobles and marchauntes of the lande ete such catalle as thai brede. And the comouns weren no wolen, but yf it be a povere cote undir thair uttermest garnement, made of grete[10] caunvas, and callid a frokke. Thair hausyn beth of lyke caunvas, and passyn not thair kne, wherfore thai beth gartered and ther theis[11] bare. Thair wyfes and childeren gone barefote; thai mowe in non other wyse leve. For somme of thaim that were wont to pay to his lorde for his tenement, wich he hiryth by the yere, a scute,[12] payith nowe to the kyng over that scute .v. scutes. Wher-thurgh thai be arted[13] bi necessite so to wacch, labour and grubbe in the erthe for thair sustenance that thair nature is wasted and the kynde of hem broght to noght. Thai gon crokyd and ben feble, not able to fight nor to defende the realme; nor thai have wepens, nor money to bie thaim wepen withall. But verely thai liven in the most extreme poverte and miserie, and yet dwellyn thai in on the[b] most fertile reaume of the worlde. Wer-thurgh the French kyng hath not men of his owne reaume able to defende it, except his nobles, wich beyren non such imposicions, and therfore thai ben right likely of thair bodies;[14] bi wich cause the said kynge is compellid to make his armeys and retenues for the defence of his lande of straungers, as Scottes, Spaynardes, Arrogoners, men of Almeyn and of other nacions, or ellis all his enmyes myght overrenne hym; for he hath no defence of his owne except his castels and fortresses. Lo, this is the frute of his *jus regale*!

Yf the reaume of Englonde, wich is an ile, and mey not lyghtly geyte soucor of other landes, were rulid undir such a lawe, and undir such a prince, it wolde be than a pray to all other nacions that wolde conqwer, robbe or devouir it; wich was previd in the tyme of the Bretouns,[15] when the Scottes and the Pyctes so bete and oppressid this lande that the peple therof sought helpe of the Romayns, to whom thai hade be tributori. And when thai coude not be defende be thaym,[16] thai sought helpe of the duke of litle Bretayn, and thai grauntid therfore to make his brother Constantyne ther kynge. And so he was made kynge here, and reigned many yeres, and his childirren aftir hym, of wich gret Artour was one of thair issue.

But, blessyd be God, this lande is rulid undir a bettir lawe; and therfore the peple therof be not in such peynurie, nor therby hurt in thair persons, but thai bith in welthe, and have all thinges necessarie to thair sustenance of nature. Wherfore thai ben myghty and able to resiste the adversaries of this reaume and to beete other reaumes that do or wolde do them wronge. Lo, this is the fruyt of *jus polliticum et regale*, undre wich we live.

8 As Fortescue says elsewhere (chap. 13), 'It is not poverte that kepith Frenchmen fro rysinge, but it is cowardisse and lakke of hartes and corage, wich no Frenchman hath like unto a Englyshman.' In the context, this might not seem an entirely tactful thing to tell an English king.

9 may hardly live

10 thick

11 thighs

12 French crown

13 forced

14 A sneer at the French nobles.

15 The story of Constantine of Brittany ('little Britain') coming to help the Britons ('Bretouns') fight against the Scots and Picts is told by Geoffrey of Monmouth.

16 defended by them

Sir Thomas Malory (*c.* 1410–1471)

The Arthurian legends, as they had developed from Celtic and other earlier origins from the twelfth century onwards, were the principal materials of medieval chivalric romance (see *Gawain and the Green Knight*, above). The characteristic form of Arthurian romance did not concern itself with the conquests and achievements of king Arthur as a national hero (such as we see him in the alliterative *Morte Arthure*, above) but with the fortunes in love and war of the knights of the Round Table. It was Gawain, Lancelot, Perceval, Tristram, Yvain, who acted as protagonists in the romances that spread from France and flourished in every European vernacular. A massive prose compilation of Arthurian legends was made in France in the thirteenth century, and given a strong religious slant by its monastic authors: the story of the Grail was given a central role, Galahad replaced Lancelot (his father) as the ideal knight, and the failure of Lancelot and others in the quest of the Grail made the basis of a critique of secular chivalry. It was this compilation, known as the Vulgate version of the legend, that dominated Arthurian story-telling during the next centuries, and it was what Sir Thomas Malory chose as the basis for his own collection of Arthurian stories when he found himself, after a chequered military career and service with the earl of Warwick, with unwonted time on his hands as he lay in prison in London in the 1460s, convicted of various offences but perhaps chiefly a victim of the partial justice of the time. His idea was to make a memorial of true chivalry for the example of these modern fallen days. He may have begun his translating work with a prose version, suitably truncated, of the alliterative *Morte Arthure*, but large-scale prose compilations of whole bodies of legend (Troy, Jason, Alexander) were fashionable in Burgundy, to which English literary culture was tending to look for its models, and Malory followed the fashion in working with the Vulgate.

His *Morte D'Arthur* was known only in the version printed by Caxton in 1485 until in 1934 a manuscript was discovered in Winchester college (now BL MS 59678) which clearly stood in a much closer relation to Malory's original. It showed that Caxton, in his desire to present Malory's work as the complete, continuous and definitive English version of the whole Arthurian story (see his Preface, below), had somewhat misrepresented the work by editing out internal text-divisions and numbering the work in 21 books, broken up into chapters with new headings, and by thus obscuring the separateness of Malory's original eight books, viz. (1) The Tale of king Arthur (his coming to the throne and early conquests); (2) The war against Rome (drawn from the alliterative *Morte*); (3) the early adventures of Sir Lancelot; (4) Sir Gareth; (5) Sir Tristram; (6) the Grail; (7) the ill-fated love of Lancelot and Guenevere; and (8) the death of Arthur. Eugene Vinaver, whose life's work was to be the editing and explication of the Winchester MS, argued that the book-structure revealed by the MS gave insight into Malory's essential originality as a narrative writer: what he had done was to unweave the interlaced strands of the Vulgate, with its polyphonic narrative of multitudes of parallel and interlocking adventures, and to draw out the tellable tales of single heroes, with a beginning, a directed movement, and an end. In other words, he invented the novel. Vinaver's arguments are pleasing and persuasive, and certainly borne out in the handling of the last two books, but there are many who would demur, pointing out that Malory takes great pleasure in interlaced narrative in Book 1 and in the enormously long Book 5, which should not therefore be regarded as failures; that the books, though separate, are sequential, and build up powerfully to the telling of the one grand story of rise, flourishing and fall; and that Malory works hard to bind the whole together by prophetic anticipation and backward reference and also by the consistency with which he elevates Lancelot and concentrates upon him as both the epitome of chivalric idealism and the chief agent of its destruction.

Malory has a powerful sense of the tragic, both the tragedy of a noble ideal betrayed and the personal tragedy of a divided loyalty. It is the battle fought in his narrative between the sense of tragedy, of human beings as the agents of their own destiny, and the residual pietism of his sources – that the downfall of a secular chivalry is inevitable, and necessary to demonstrate that the true goal for human beings to strive after is a spiritual one – that provides the structural dynamic and dramatic intensity of Malory's work. His narrative techniques are transparent, and permit no distraction from this concentration upon the fateful significance of events: simple but evocatively repetitive diction; stylized colloquial syntax and intonation; the minimum of descriptive visualization; character expressed through gesture, direct speech and dialogue rather than through analysis or comment; very rare intervention by the narrator, and that mostly of a laconic and impersonal kind. Malory's success is to seem less an author than the unmediating medium through which the whole story of Arthur is written unforgettably into English prose.

Edition with full apparatus by E. Vinaver, 3 vols (Oxford, 1947; rev. edn, 1967; 3rd edn, rev. P.J.C. Field, 1990); single volume (Oxford, 1954; rev. edn, 1971); facsimile of Winchester MS, introd. by N.R. Ker, EETS, SS 4; facsimile of Caxton's 1485 print, introd. by P. Needham (London, 1976); modern-spelling edn of Caxton's text, ed. J. Cowen, 2 vols (Penguin, 1969); *Life and Times* by P.J.C. Field (Cambridge, 1993); studies by S. Knight (Sydney, 1969), P.J.C. Field (London, 1970), E. Pochoda (Chapel Hill, NC, 1971), M. Lambert (New Haven, 1975), L.D. Benson (Cambridge, MA, 1977), F.

Riddy (Leiden, 1987); collected essays in J.A.W. Bennett (ed.), *Essays on Malory* (Oxford, 1963), R.M. Lumiansky (ed.), *Malory's Originality* (Baltimore, 1964), E. Archibald and A.S.G. Edwards, *Companion to Malory* (Cambridge, 1997). See also J. Mann, *The Narrative of Distance, The Distance of Narrative, in Malory* (London, 1991); S. Knight, *Arthurian Literature and Society* (London, 1983).

The following extract represents almost the whole of the last Book; it is based on the Winchester MS (fols 449r–484v), with corrections mostly from Caxton, and the last pages (missing from the MS) supplied from the same source.

Morte D'Arthure

The moste pyteuous tale of the Morte Arthure saunz Gwerdon (Vinaver's Book 8)

{Life at Arthur's court has been disturbed, since the return of the knights from the Grail-quest, by the intrigues and complications caused by Lancelot's adulterous liaison with Guenevere.}

The accusation and rescue of Guenevere

In May, whan every harte floryshyth and burgenyth – for, as the season ys lusty to beholde and comfortable, so man and woman rejoysyth and gladith of somer commynge with his freyshe floures, for wynter wyth hys rowghe wyndis and blastis causyth lusty men and women to cowre and to syt by fyres – so thys season hit befelle in the moneth of May a grete angur and unhappy that stynted nat tylle the floure of chyvalry of the worlde was destroyed and slayne.

And all was longe uppon two unhappy knyghtis[1] whych were named sir Aggravayne and sir Mordred,[2] that were brethirn unto sir Gawayne.[3] For thys sir Aggravayne and sir Mordred had ever a prevy hate unto the quene, dame Gwenyver, and to sir Launcelot, and dayly and nyghtly they ever wacched uppon sir Launcelot.

So hyt myssefortuned sir Gawayne and all hys brethirne were in kynge Arthurs chambir, and than sir Aggravayne seyde thus opynly, and nat in no counceyle,[4] that manye knyghtis myght here: 'I mervayle that we all be nat ashamed bothe to se and to know how sir Launcelot lyeth dayly and nyghtly by the quene. And all we know well that hit ys so, and hit ys shamefully suffird of us all that we shulde suffir so noble a kynge as kynge Arthur ys to be shamed.'

Than spake sir Gawayne and seyde, 'Brothir, sir Aggravayne, I pray you and charge you, meve[5] no such maters no more afore me, for wyte you well, I woll nat be of youre counceyle.'

'So God me helpe,' seyde sir Gaherys and sir Gareth, 'we woll nat be knowyn of[6] your dedis.'

'Than woll I!' seyde sir Mordred.

'I lyve[7] you well,' seyde sir Gawayne, 'for ever unto all unhappynes, sir, ye woll graunte. And I wolde that ye leffte all thys,[a] and make you nat so bysy, for I know,' seyde sir Gawayne, 'what woll falle of hit.'

'Falle whatsumever falle may,' seyde sir Aggravayne, 'I woll disclose hit to the kynge.'

'Nat be my counceyle,' seyde sir Gawayne, 'for, and ther aryse warre and wrake[8] betwyxte sir Launcelot and us,[b] wyte you well, brothir, there woll many kynges and grete lordis holde with sir Launcelot. Also, brothir sir Aggravayne,' seyde sir Gawayne, 'ye muste remembir how oftyntymes sir Launcelot hath rescowed the kynge and the quene; and the beste of us all had bene full colde at the harte-roote had nat sir Launcelot bene bettir than we, and that hath he preved hymselff full ofte. And as for my parte,' seyde sir Gawayne, 'I woll never be ayenste sir Launcelot for one dayes dede, that was whan

1 due to two misfortune-bringing knights

2 **sir Mordred** is strictly speaking not the brother but the half-brother of Gawain, having the same mother (Morgawse, Arthur's half-sister) but not the same father (king Lot of Orkney). Mordred's father is Arthur.

3 **sir Gawayne** has an up-and-down career in Malory, not because he has a complex character or because he changes, but because the stories in which he appears have different origins and cast him in different roles. Generally he has been shown to have a rather inflated reputation, both as a fighter and as a servant of ladies, but in this last Book he emerges as the warrior-knight of the older tradition, leader of a powerful court-faction.

4 secrecy

5 bring up

6 party to

7 believe

8 strife

he rescowed me frome kynge Carados of the Dolerous Towre and slew hym and saved my lyff. Also, brother sir Aggravayne and sir Mordred, in lyke wyse sir Launcelot rescowed you bothe and three score and two from sir Tarquyne. And therefore, brothir, me thynkis suche noble dedis and kyndnes shulde be remembirde.'

'Do ye as ye lyste,' seyde sir Aggravayne,[c] 'for I woll layne[9] hit no lenger.'

So wyth thes wordis cam in sir Arthur.

'Now, brothir,' seyde sir Gawayne, 'stynte youre stryff.'

'That woll I nat,' seyde sir Aggravayne and sir Mordred.

'Well, woll ye so?' seyde sir Gawayne. 'Than God spede you, for I woll nat here of youre talis, nothir be of youre counceile.'

'No more woll I,' seyde sir Gaherys.

'Nother I,' seyde sir Gareth, 'for I shall never say evyll by that man that made me knyght.'[10]

And therewythall they three departed makynge grete dole.

'Alas!' seyde sir Gawayne and sir Gareth, 'now ys thys realme holy destroyed and myscheved, and the noble felyshyp of the Rounde Table shall be disparbeled.'[11]

So they departed. And than kynge Arthure asked them what noyse[12] they made.

'My lorde,' seyde sir Aggravayne, 'I shall telle you, for I may kepe hit no lenger. Here ys I and my brothir sir Mordred brake unto my brothir sir Gawayne, sir Gaherys and to sir Gareth – for thys ys all, to make hit shorte – we know all[13] that sir Launcelot holdith youre quene, and hath done longe; and we be your syster sunnes,[14] we may suffir hit no lenger. And all we wote that ye shulde be above sir Launcelot, and ye ar the kynge that made hym knyght, and therefore we woll preve hit that he is a traytoure to youre person.'

'Gyff hit be so,' seyde the kynge, 'wyte you well, he ys non othir. But I wolde be lothe to begyn such a thynge but I myght have prevys[15] of hit, for sir Launcelot ys an hardy knyght, and all ye know that he ys the beste knyght amonge us all, and but if[16] he be takyn with the dede he woll fyght with hym that bryngith up the noyse, and I know no knyght that ys able to macch hym. Therefore, and hit be sothe as ye say, I wolde that he were takyn with the dede.'

For, as the Freynshe booke seyth,[17] the kynge was full lothe that such a noyse shulde be uppon sir Launcelot and his quene; for the kynge had a demyng of hit,[18] but he wold nat here thereoff, for sir Launcelot had done so much for hym and for the quene so many tymes that wyte you well the kynge loved hym passyngly well.

'My lorde,' seyde sir Aggravayne, 'ye shall ryde to-morne an-huntyng, and doute ye nat, sir Launcelot woll nat go wyth you. And so whan hit drawith towarde nyght ye may sende the quene worde that ye woll ly oute all that nyght, and so may ye sende for your cookis. And than, uppon payne of deth, that nyght we shall take hym wyth the quene, and we shall brynge hym unto you, quycke or dede.'

'I woll well,' seyde the kynge. 'Than I counceyle you to take with you sure felyshyp.'

'Sir,' seyde sir Aggravayne, 'my brothir sir Mordred and I woll take wyth us twelve knyghtes of the Rounde Table.'

'Beware,' seyde kynge Arthure, 'for I warne you, ye shall fynde hym wyght.'[19]

'Lat us deale!'[20] seyde sir Aggravayne and sir Mordred.

So on the morne kynge Arthure rode an-huntyng and sente worde to the quene that he wolde be oute all that nyght. Than sir Aggravayne and sir Mordred gate to them twelve knyghtes and hyd hemselff in

9 conceal

10 **that man that made me knyght**. The Tale of Gareth (Book 4) told how Lancelot befriended and encouraged Gareth when he was newly come to court and of no reputation.

11 dispersed

12 rumour of accusation

13 we all know

14 **syster sunnes**: this relationship was regarded as a specially close one in older Germanic societies.

15 proofs

16 unless

17 **as the Freynshe booke seyth**. Malory often introduces this asseveration of authority when he has some tricky or doubtful point of narrative or attribution of motive to negotiate, or indeed when he wants to say something of his own that is *not* in the French.

18 **the kynge had a demyng**. Arthur's behaviour in much of the French-derived romance is not noble or kingly or warrior-like; as the foil to Lancelot, and as his cuckold, he is bound to appear feeble. But in not acting upon his **demyng**, or suspicion, he has the interests of his kingdom in mind; it is not mere weakness.

19 strong

20 leave us to deal with it

a chambir in the castell of Carlyle. And thes were ther namys:[21] sir Collgrevaunce, sir Mador de la Porte, sir Gyngalyne, sir Mellyot de Logris, sir Petipace of Wynchylse, sir Galleron of Galoway, sir Melyon de la Mountayne, sir Ascomore, sir Gromore Somer Joure, sir Cursesalyne, sir Florence, and sir Lovell. So thes twelve knyghtes were with sir Mordred and sir Aggravayne, and all they were of Scotlonde, other ellis of sir Gawaynes kynne, othir well-wyllers[d] to hys brothir.

So whan the nyght cam sir Launcelot tolde sir Bors how he wolde go that nyght and speke wyth the quene.

'Sir,' seyde sir Bors, 'ye shall nat go thys nyght be my counceyle.'

'Why?' seyde sir Launcelot.

'Sir, for I drede me ever of sir Aggravayne that waytith[22] uppon you dayly to do you shame and us all. And never gaff my harte ayenste no goynge that ever ye wente to the quene so much as now, for I mystruste that the kynge ys oute thys nyght from the quene. Therefore I drede me sore of som treson.'

'Have ye no drede,' seyde sir Launcelot, 'for I shall go and com agayne and make no taryynge.'

'Sir,' seyde sir Bors, 'that me repentis,[23] for I drede me sore that youre goyng thys nyght shall wratth[24] us all.'

'Fayre neveawe,' seyd sir Launcelot, 'I mervayle me much why ye say thus, sytthyn the quene hath sente for me. And wyte you well I woll nat be so much a cowarde but she shall undirstonde I woll se her good grace.'

'God spede you well,' seyde sir Bors, 'and sende you sounde and sauff agayne!'

So sir Launcelot departed and toke hys swerde undir hys arme, and so he walked in hys mantell, that noble knyght, and put hymselff in grete jouparte. And so he past on tylle he cam to the quenys chambir, and so lyghtly[25] he was had into the chambir.

For, as the Freynshe booke seyth, the quene and sir Launcelot were togydirs. And whether they were abed other at other[26] maner of disportis, me lyste nat thereof make no mencion, for love that tyme was nat as love ys nowadayes.[27] But thus as they were togydir there cam sir Aggravayne and sir Mordred wyth twelve knyghtes with them of the Rounde Table, and they seyde with grete cryyng and staryng[28] voyce, 'Thou traytoure,[29] sir Launcelot, now ar thou takyn!'

And thus they cryed wyth a lowde voyce, that all the courte myght hyre hit. And thes fourtene knyghtes all were armed at all poyntis, as they shulde fyght in a batayle.

'Alas!' seyde quene Gwenyver, 'now ar we myscheved bothe!'

'Madame,' seyde sir Launcelot, 'ys ther here ony armour within your chambir[e] that myght cover my body wythall? And if there be ony, gyff hit me and I shall sone stynte ther malice, by the grace of God!'

'Now, truly,' seyde the quyne, 'I have none armour nother helme, shylde, swerde, nother speare, wherefore I dred me sore oure longe love ys com to a myschyvus ende. For I here by ther noyse ther be many noble knyghtes, and well I wote they be surely armed, and ayenst them ye may make no resistence. Wherefore ye ar lykly to be slayne, and than shall I be brente! For and ye myght ascape them,' seyde the quene, 'I wolde nat doute but that ye wolde rescowe me in what daunger that I ever stood in.'

'Alas!' seyde sir Launcelot, 'in all my lyff thus was I never bestad[30] that I shulde be thus shamefully slayne, for lakke of myne armour.'

But ever sir Aggravayne and sir Mordred cryed, 'Traytour knyght, com oute of the quenys chambir! For wyte thou well thou art besette so that thou shalt nat ascape!'

21 **ther namys**. Such roll-calls of names are frequent in Malory: they have their own evocative clangour and their own significance in their context (some here are old enemies of Lancelot, and others are of the Scottish faction), but they are also part of Malory's apparatus of historical authenticity and veracity. They are all set off in a more formal script and written in red in the MS.

22 spies

23 causes regret

24 harm

25 quickly

26 or at other

27 **love that tyme was nat as love ys nowadayes**. Malory alludes to an earlier episode, where he drew a contrast between the faithful (and possibly chaste) love of old and the lechery and casual affairs of modern times. The implication here is that the lovers were not in bed, which gives a greater dignity to their immediate situation – though their relationship in the past has been clearly shown to be adulterous. It is as if Malory wanted to idealize and ennoble and chasten their love as the destruction it has wrought draws near.

28 wild

29 **Thou traytoure**. The use of the second person singular as a mark of insolent familiarity and contempt (or of special intimacy, as in some of Guenevere's more impassioned outbursts to Lancelot) should be noted throughout Malory's conversational exchanges.

30 in a situation

'A, Jesu mercy!' seyd sir Launcelot, 'thys shamefull cry and noyse I may nat suffir, for better were deth at onys than thus to endure thys payne.'

Than he toke the quene in hys armys and kyssed her and seyde, 'Moste nobelest Crysten quene, I besech you, as ye have ben ever my speciall good lady, and I at all tymes your poure knyght and trew unto my power, and as I never fayled you in ryght nor in wronge sytthyn the firste day kynge Arthur made me knyght, that ye woll pray for my soule if that I be slayne. For well I am assured that sir Bors, my nevewe, and all the remenaunte of my kynne, with sir Lavayne and sir Urre, that they woll nat fayle you to rescow you from the fyer. And therefore, myne owne lady, recomforte youreselff, whatsomever com of me, that ye go with sir Bors, my nevew, and they all woll do you all the plesure that they may, and ye shall lyve lyke a quene uppon my londis.'

'Nay, sir Launcelot, nay!' seyde the quen. 'Wyte thou well that I woll nat[f] lyve longe aftir thy dayes. But and ye be slayne I woll take my dethe as mekely as ever ded marter take hys dethe for Jesu Crystes sake.'

'Well, madame,' seyde sir Launcelot, 'syth hit ys so that the day ys com that oure love muste departe, wyte you well I shall selle my lyff as dere as I may. And a thousandfolde,' seyde sir Launcelot, 'I am more hevyar for you than for myselff! And now I had levir than to be lorde of all Crystendom that I had sure armour uppon me, that men myght speke of my dedys or[31] ever I were slayne.'

'Truly,' seyde the quene, 'and hit myght please God, I wolde that they wolde take me and sle me and suffir you to ascape.'

'That shall never be,' seyde[g] sir Launcelot. 'God deffende me from such a shame! But, Jesu Cryste, be thou my shylde and myne armoure!'

And therewith sir Launcelot wrapped hys mantel aboute hys arme well and surely; and by than they had getyn a grete fourme[32] oute of the halle, and therewith they all russhed at the dore.

'Now, fayre lordys,' seyde sir Launcelot, 'leve youre noyse and youre russhynge, and I shall sette opyn thys dore, and than[h] may ye do with me what hit lykith you.'

'Com of, than,' seyde they all, 'and do hit, for hit avaylyth the nat to stryve ayenste us all! And therefore lat us into thys chambir, and we shall save thy lyff untyll thou com to kynge Arthur.'

Than sir Launcelot unbarred the dore, and with hys lyffte honde he hylde hit opyn a lytyll that but one man myght com in at onys. And so there cam strydyng a good knyght, a much man and a large, and hys name was called sir Collgrevaunce of Goore. And he wyth a swerde strake at sir Launcelot myghtyly, and so he put asyde the stroke, and gaff hym such a buffette uppon the helmet that he felle grovelyng wythin the chambir dore. Than sir Launcelot with grete myght drew the knyght within the chambir dore. And than sir Launcelot, wyth helpe of the quene and her ladyes, he was lyghtly[33] armed in Coligrevaunce armoure. And ever stood sir Aggravayne and sir Mordred, cryyng, 'Traytoure knyght! Com forthe oute of the quenys chambir!'

'Sires, leve youre noyse,' seyde sir Launcelot, 'for wyte you well, sir Aggravayne, ye shall nat preson me thys nyght! And therefore, and ye do be my counceyle, go ye all from thys chambir-dore and make you no suche cryyng and such maner of sclaundir as ye do; for I promyse you be my knyghthode, and ye woll departe and make no more noyse, I shall as to-morne appyere afore you all and before the kynge, and than lat hit be sene whych of you all, other ellis ye all, that woll deprave me[34] of treson. And there shall I answere you, as a knyght shulde, that hydir I cam to the quene for no maner of male-engyne,[35] and that woll I preve and make hit good uppon you wyth my hondys.'

'Fye uppon the, traytour,' seyde sir Aggravayne and sir Mordred, 'for we woll have the magre thyne hede[36] and sle the, and we lyste! For we let the wyte we have the choyse of kynge Arthure to save the other sle the.'

'A, sirres,' seyde sir Launcelot, 'ys ther none other grace with you? Than kepe[37] youreselff!'

And than sir Launcelot sette all opyn the chambir dore, and myghtyly and knyghtly he strode in amonge them. And anone at the firste stroke he slew sir Aggravayne, and anone aftir twelve of hys

31 before
32 bench
33 swiftly
34 find me guilty
35 evil intention
36 despite all you can do
37 guard

felowys. Within a whyle he had layde them down colde to the erthe, for there was none of the twelve knyghtes myght stonde sir Launcelot one buffet. And also he wounded sir Mordred, and therewithall he fled with all hys myght.

And than sir Launcelot returned agayne unto the quene and seyde, 'Madame, now wyte you well, all oure trew love ys brought to an ende, for now wyll kyng Arthur ever be my foo. And therfore, madam, and hit lyke you that I may have you with me, I shall save you from all maner adventures daungers.'

'Sir, that ys nat beste,' seyde the quene, 'me semyth, for now ye have don so much harme hit woll be beste that ye holde you styll with this. And if ye se that as to-morne they woll putte me unto dethe, than may ye rescowe me as ye thynke beste.'

'I woll well,' seyde sir Launcelot, 'for have ye no doute, whyle I am a man lyvyng I shall rescow you.'

And than he kyste her, and ayther of hem gaff othir a rynge, and so the quene he leffte there and wente untyll hys lodgynge.

Whan sir Bors saw sir Launcelot he was never so glad of hys homecomynge.

'Jesu mercy!' seyde sir Launcelot, 'why be ye all armed? What meanyth thys?'

'Sir,' seyde sir Bors, 'aftir ye were departed from us we all that ben of youre blood and youre well-wyllars were so adremed[38] that som of us lepe oute of oure beddis naked, and som in ther dremys caught naked swerdys in ther hondis. And therefore,' seyde sir Bors, 'we demed there was som grete stryff on honde, and so we demed that ye[i] were betrapped with som treson; and therefore we made us thus redy, what nede that ever ye[j] were in.'

'My fayre nevew,' seyde sir Launcelot unto sir Bors, 'now shall ye wyte all that thys nyght I was more harde bestad[39] than ever I was dayes of my lyff. And thanked be God, I am myselff ascaped ther daungere.' And so he tolde them all how and in what maner, as ye have harde toforehande. 'And therefore, my felowys,' seyde sir Launcelot, 'I pray you all that ye woll be of harte good, and helpe me in what nede that ever I stonde, for now ys warre comyn to us all.'

'Sir,' seyde sir Bors, 'all ys wellcom that God sendyth us, and as we have takyn much weale[40] with you and much worshyp, we woll take the woo with you as we have takyn the weale.'

And therefore they seyde, all the good knyghtes, 'Loke ye take no discomforte, for ther ys no bondys[41] of knyghtes undir hevyn but we shall be able to greve them as muche as they us, and therefore discomforte nat youreselff by no maner. And we shall gadir togyder all that we love and that lovyth us, and what that ye woll have done shall be done. And therefore lat us take the wo and the joy togydir.'

'Grauntmercy,' seyde sir Launcelot, 'of youre good comforte, for in my grete distresse, fayre nevew, ye comforte me gretely. But thus, my fayre nevew, I wolde that ye ded, in all haste that ye may, for hit ys far dayes past:[42] that ye woll loke in ther lodgynge that ben lodged nyghe here aboute the kynge, whych woll holde with me and whych woll nat.[43] For now I wolde know whych were my frendis fro my fooes.'

'Sir,' seyde sir Bors, 'I shall do my payne, and or hit be seven of the clok I shall wyte of such as ye have dout fore, who that woll holde with you.'

Than sir Bors called unto hym sir Lyonel, sir Ector de Marys, sir Blamour de Ganys, sir Gahalantyne, sir Galyhodyn, sir Galyhud, sir Menaduke, sir Vyllyers the Valyaunte, syr Hebes le Renowne, sir Lavayne, sir Urre of Hungry, sir Neroveus, sir Plenoryus (for thes two were knyghtes that[k] sir Launcelot wan uppon a brydge, and therefore they wolde never be ayenst hym), and sir Harry le FyzLake, and sir Selyses of the Dolerous Towre, sir Mellyas de Lyle, and sir Bellangere le Bewse that was sir Alysaundir le Orphelyne sone;[l] bycause hys modir was kyn unto sir Launcelot, he hylde wyth hym. So cam sir Palomydes and sir Saphir, hys brothir; sir Clegis, sir Sadok, sir Dynas and sir Clarryus of Cleremount.

So thes two-and-twenti knyghtes drew hem togydirs, and by than[44] they were armed and on horsebak they promysed sir Launcelot to do what he wolde. Than ther felle to them, what[45] of Northe Walys and of Cornwayle, for sir Lamorakes sake[46] and for sir Trystrames sake, to the numbir of a seven score knyghtes.

38 afflicted by bad dreams
39 beset
40 good
41 bands
42 far on in the day
43 Malory's romance-making is backed by a keen sense of political realities: this kind of negotiation of shifting affiliations was as much part of the Wars of the Roses as war itself.
44 when
45 fell in with them, what with those of
46 **sir Lamorake** has little independent history in romance, but in Malory he is raised to third place, after Lancelot and Tristram, in the prowess-ranking.

Than spake sir Launcelot: 'Wyte you well, I have bene ever syns I cam to thys courte well-wylled unto my lorde Arthur and unto my lady quene Gwenyver, unto my power. And thys nyght bycause my lady the quene sente for me to speke with her, I suppose hit was made by treson; howbeit I dare largely excuse her person, natwithstondynge I was thereby nerehonde slayne, but as[47] Jesu provyded for me.'

And than that noble knyght sir Launcelot tolde hem how he was harde bestad in the quenys chambir, and how and in what maner he ascaped from them. 'And therefore wyte you well, my fayre lordis, I am sure there nys but warre unto me and to myne. And for cause I have slayne thys nyght sir Aggravayne, sir Gawaynes brothir, and at the leste twelve of hys felowis, and for thys cause now am I sure of mortall warre. For thes knyghtes were sente by kynge Arthur to betray me, and therefore the kyng woll in thys hete and malice jouge the quene unto brennyng, and that may nat I suffir that she shulde be brente for my sake. For and I may be harde and suffirde and so takyn,[48] I woll feyght for the quene, that she ys a trew lady untyll[49] her lorde. But the kynge in hys hete, I drede, woll nat take me as I ought to be takyn.'

'My lorde sir Launcelot,' seyde sir Bors, 'be myne advyce, ye[m] shall take the woo wyth the weall. And sytthyn hit ys fallyn as hit ys, I counceyle you to kepe[50] youreselff, for and ye woll kepe[n] youreselffe, there ys no felyshyp of knyghtes crystynde that shall do you wronge. And also I woll counceyle you, my lorde, that my lady quene Gwenyver, and she be in ony distres, insomuch as she ys in payne for youre sake, that ye knyghtly rescow her; for and ye ded ony other wyse all the worlde wolde speke you shame to the worldis ende. Insomuch as ye were takyn with her, whether ye ded ryght othir wronge, hit ys now youre parte to holde wyth the quene, that she be nat slayne and put to a myschevous deth. For and she so dye, the shame shall he evermore youres.'

'Now Jesu deffende me from shame,' seyde sir Launcelot, 'and kepe and save my lady the quene from vylany and shamefull dethe, and that she never be destroyed in my defaute! Wherefore, my fayre lordys, my kyn and my fryndis,' seyde sir Launcelot, 'what woll ye do?'

And anone they seyde all with one voyce, 'We woll do as ye woll do.'

'Than I put thys case unto you,' seyde sir Launcelot, 'that my lorde, kynge Arthure, by evyll counceile woll to-morn in hys hete put my lady the quene unto the fyre and there to be brente: than, I pray you, counceile me what ys beste for me to do.'

Than they seyde all at onys with one voice, 'Sir, us thynkis beste that ye knyghtly rescow the quene. Insomuch as she shall be brente, hit ys for youre sake; and hit ys to suppose, and ye myght be handeled,[51] ye shulde have the same dethe, othir ellis a more shamefuller dethe. And, sir, we say all that ye have rescowed her from her deth many tymys for other mennes quarels; therefore us semyth hit ys more youre worshyp that ye rescow the quene from thys quarell, insomuch that she hath hit for your sake.'

Than sir Launcelot stood stylle and sayde, 'My fayre lordis, wyte you well I wolde be lothe to do that thynge that shulde dishonour you or my bloode; and wyte you well I wolde be full lothe that my lady the quene shulde dye such a shamefull deth. But and hit be so that ye woll counceyle me to rescow her, I must do much harme or I rescow her, and peradventure I shall ther destroy som[o] of my beste fryndis. And if so be that I may wynne the quene away, where shall I kepe her?'

'Sir, that shall be the leste care of us all,' seyde sir Bors, 'for how ded the moste noble knyght sir Trystram? By youre good wyll, kept nat he with hym La Beall Isode nere three yere in Joyous Garde, the whych was done by youre althers[52] avyce? And that same place ys youre owne, and in lyke wyse may ye do, and ye lyst, and take the quene knyghtly away with you, if so be that the kynge woll jouge her to be brente. And in Joyous Garde may ye kepe her longe inowe untyll the hete be past of the kynge, and than hit may fortune you to brynge the quene agayne to the kynge with grete worshyp, and peradventure ye shall have than thanke for youre bryngyng home where othir may happyn to have magre.'[53]

'That ys hard for to do,' seyde sir Launcelot, 'for by sir Trystram I may have a warnynge: for whan by meanys of tretyse sir Trystram brought agayne La Beall Isode unto kynge Marke from Joyous Garde, loke ye now what felle on the ende, how shamefully that false traytour kyng Marke slew hym as he sate harpynge afore hys lady, La Beall Isode. Wyth a grounden glayve[54] he threste hym in behynde to the

47 had not
48 'If I may be heard, and allowed (to speak) and (my offer to fight) accepted'.
49 unto
50 guard
51 laid hands on
52 of all of you
53 enmity
54 sharp-ground spear

harte, whych grevyth sore me,' seyde sir Launcelot, 'to speke of his dethe, for all the worlde may nat fynde such another knyght.'

'All thys ys trouthe,' seyde sir Bors, 'but ther ys one thyng shall corrayge you and us all: ye know well that kynge Arthur and kynge Marke were never lyke of condycions, for ther was never yet man that ever coude preve kynge Arthure untrew of hys promyse.'

But so, to make shorte tale, they[p] were all condiscended[55] that, for bettir othir for wars, if so were that the quene were brought on that morne to the fyre, shortely they all wolde rescow her. And so by the advyce of sir Launcelot they put hem all in a wood as nyghe Carlyle as they myght, and there they abode stylle to wyte what the kynge wold do.

Now turne we agayne, that whan sir Mordred was ascaped from sir Launcelot he gate hys horse and cam to kynge Arthur sore wounded and all for-bled,[56] and there he tolde the kynge all how hit was, and how they were all slayne save hymselff alone.

'A, Jesu, mercy! How may thys be?' seyde the kynge. 'Toke ye hym in the quenys chambir?'

'Yee, so God me helpe,' seyde sir Mordred, 'there we founde hym unarmed, and anone he slew sir Collgrevaunce and armed hym in hys armour.' And so he tolde the kynge from the begynnyng to the endynge.

'Jesu, mercy!' seyde the kynge, 'he ys a mervaylous knyght of proues! And alas,' seyde the kynge, 'me sore repentith that ever sir Launcelot sholde be ayenste me, for now I am sure the noble felyshyp of the Rounde Table ys brokyn for ever, for wyth hym woll many a noble knyght holde. And now hit ys fallen so,' seyde the kynge, 'that I may nat with my worshyp but my quene muste suffir dethe,'[57] and was sore amoved.

So than ther was made grete ordynaunce in thys ire, and the quene muste nedis be jouged to the deth. And the law was such in tho dayes that whatsomever they were, of what astate or degre, if they were founden gylty of treson there shuld be none other remedy but deth, and othir the menour other[58] the takynge wyth the dede shulde be cause of their hasty jougement. And ryght so was hit ordayned for quene Gwenyver: bycause sir Mordred was ascaped sore wounded, and the dethe of thirtene knyghtes of the Rounde Table, thes previs and experyenses caused kynge Arthure to commaunde the quene to the fyre and there to be brente.

Than spake sir Gawayn and seyde, 'My lorde Arthure, I wolde counceyle you nat to be over-hasty, but that ye wolde put hit in respite,[59] thys jougemente of my lady the quene, for many causis. One ys thys: thoughe hyt were so that sir Launcelot were founde in the quenys chambir, yet hit myght be so that he cam thydir for none evyll. For ye know, my lorde,' seyde sir Gawayne, 'that my lady the quene hath oftyntymes ben gretely beholdyn unto sir Launcelot, more than to ony othir knyght; for oftyntymes he hath saved her lyff and done batayle for her whan all the courte refused the quene. And peradventure she sente for hym for goodnes and for none evyll, to rewarde hym for his good dedys that he had done to her in tymes past. And peraventure my lady the quene sente for hym to that entente that sir Launcelot sholde a[60] com prevaly to her, wenyng that hyt had be beste in eschewyng of slaundir; for oftyntymys we do many thynges that we wene for the beste be, and yet peradventure hit turnyth to the warste. For I dare sey,' seyde sir Gawayne, 'my lady your quene ys to you both good and trew. And as for sir Launcelot, I dare say he woll make hit good uppon ony knyght lyvyng that woll put uppon hym vylany or shame, and in lyke wyse he woll make good for my lady the quene.'

'That I beleve well,' seyde kynge Arthur, 'but I woll nat that way worke with sir Launcelot, for he trustyth so much uppon hys hondis and hys myght that he doutyth[61] no man. And therefore for my quene he shall nevermore fyght, for she shall have the law. And if I may gete sir Launcelot, wyte you well he shall have as shamefull a dethe.'

'Jesu defende me' seyde sir Gawayne, 'that I never se hit nor know hit.'

'Why say you so?' seyde kynge Arthur. 'For, perde, ye have no cause to love hym! For thys nyght last

55 agreed
56 weak from loss of blood
57 In the French original, the *Mort Artu*, and in the English stanzaic romance of *Le Morte Arthur*, which Malory is also using in this Book, it is Arthur's barons who condemn Guenevere to the fire. In Malory it is Arthur who does so, not out of revenge or pique, but because of his adherence, before all things, to the rule of law as something beyond the king's personal will.
58 either the evidence of behaviour or
59 postpone it
60 should have
61 fears

past he slew youre brothir sir Aggravayne, a full good knyght, and allmoste he had slayne youre othir brother, sir Mordred, and also there he slew thirtene noble knyghtes. And also remembir you, sir Gawayne, he slew two sunnes of youres, sir Florens and sir Lovell.'

'My lorde,' seyde sir Gawayne, 'of all thys I have a knowleche, whych of her dethis sore repentis me. But insomuch as I gaff hem warnynge and tolde my brothir and my sonnes aforehonde what wolde falle on the ende, and insomuche as they wolde nat do be my counceyle, I woll nat meddyll me theroff, nor revenge me nothynge of ther dethys; for I tolde them there was no boote to stryve with sir Launcelot. Howbeit I am sory of the deth of my brothir and of my two sunnes, but they ar the causars of ther owne dethe; for oftyntymes I warned my brothir sir Aggravayne, and I tolde hym of the perellis.'

Than seyde kynge Arthur unto sir Gawayne, 'Make you redy, I pray you, in youre beste armour, wyth youre brethirn, sir Gaherys and sir Gareth,[q] to brynge my quene to the fyre and there to have her jougement.'

'Nay, my moste noble kynge,' seyde sir Gawayne, 'that woll I never do, for wyte you well I woll never be in that place where so noble a quene as ys my lady dame Gwenyver shall take such a shamefull ende. For wyte you well,' seyde sir Gawayne, 'my harte woll nat serve me for to se her dye, and hit shall never be seyde that ever I was of youre counceyle for her deth.'

'Than,' seyde the kynge unto sir Gawayne, 'suffir your brethirn sir Gaherys and sir Gareth to be there.'

'My lorde,' seyde sir Gawayne, 'wyte you well they wyll be lothe to be there present bycause of many adventures[62] that ys lyke to falle, but they ar yonge and full unable to say you nay.'

Than spake sir Gaherys and the good knyght sir Gareth unto kynge Arthur, 'Sir, ye may well commaunde us to be there, but wyte you well hit shall be sore ayenste oure wyll. But and we be there by youre strayte commaundement, ye shall playnly holde us there excused: we woll be there in pesyble wyse, and beare none harneyse of warre uppon us.'

'In the name of God,' seyde the kynge, 'than make you redy, for she shall have sone her jugemente.'

'Alas,' seyde sir Gawayne, 'that ever I shulde endure to se this wofull day!'

So sir Gawayne turned hym and wepte hartely, and so he wente into hys chambir. And so the quene was lad furthe withoute[63] Carlyle, and anone she was dispoyled into[64] her smokke. And than her gostely fadir[65] was brought to her to be shryven of her myssededis. Than was ther wepyng and waylynge and wryngyng of hondis of many lordys and ladyes; but ther were but feaw in comparison that wolde beare ony armoure for to strengthe[66] the dethe of the quene.

Than was ther one that sir Launcelot had sente unto, whych wente to aspye what tyme the quene shulde go unto her deth. And anone as he saw the quene dispoyled into her smok and shryvyn, than he gaff sir Launcelot warnynge anone. Than was ther but spurryng and pluckyng up of horse, and ryght so they cam unto the fyre. And who that stoode ayenste them, ther were they slayne, full many a noble knyght. For there was slayne sir Bellyas le Orgulus, sir Segwarydes, sir Gryfflet, sir Braundyles, sir Agglovale, sir Tor, sir Gauter, sir Gyllymer, sir Raynold (three brethirn), and sir Damas, sir Priamus, sir Kay le Straunge, sir Dryaunt, sir Lambegus, sir Hermynde, sir Pertolyp, sir Perymones (two brethern whych were called the Grene Knyght and the Rede Knyght).

And so in thys russhynge and hurlynge, as sir Launcelot thrange[67] here and there, hit mysfortuned hym to sle sir Gaherys and sir Gareth, the noble knyght, for they were unarmed and unwares. As the Freynsh booke sayth, sir Launcelot smote sir Gaherys and sir Gareth uppon the brayne-pannes, wherethorow that they were slayne in the felde. Howbeit in very trouth sir Launcelot saw them nat.[r] And so were they founde dede amonge the thyckyste of the prees.

Than sir Launcelot, whan he had thus done, and slayne and put to flyght all that wolde wythstonde hym, than he rode streyt unto quene Gwenyver and made caste a kurdyll[68] and a gown uppon her, and than he made her to be sette behynde hym and prayde her to be of good chere. Now wyte you well the quene was glad that she was at that tyme ascaped from the deth, and than she thanked God and sir Launcelot.

62 chance happenings
63 outside
64 stripped to
65 confessor
66 show support for
67 forced his way
68 kirtle

And so he rode hys way wyth the quene, as the Freynshe booke seyth, unto Joyous Garde, and there he kepte her as a noble knyght shulde. And many grete lordis and many good knyghtes were sente hym, and many full noble knyghtes drew unto hym. Whan they harde that kynge Arthure and sir Launcelot were at debate many knyghtes were glad, and many were sory of their debate.

The vengeance of Sir Gawain

Now turne we agayne unto kynge Arthure, that whan hit was tolde hym how and in what maner the quene was taken away from the fyre, and whan he harde of the deth of his noble knyghtes, and in especiall sir Gaherys and sir Gareth, than he sowned[1] for verry pure sorow. And whan he awooke of hys swoughe, than he sayde, 'Alas, that ever I bare crowne uppon my hede! For now have I loste the fayryst felyshyp of noble knyghtes that ever hylde Crystyn kynge togydirs. Alas, my good knyghtes be slayne and gone away fro me, that now within thys two dayes I have loste nygh forty knyghtes and also the noble felyshyp of sir Launcelot and hys blood, for now I may nevermore holde hem togydirs with my worshyp. Now, alas, that ever thys warre began!

'Now, fayre felowis,' seyde the kynge, 'I charge you that no man telle sir Gawayne of the deth of hys two brethirne, for I am sure,' seyde the kynge, 'whan he hyryth telle that sir Gareth ys dede, he wyll go nygh oute of hys mynde. Merci Jesu,' seyde the kynge, 'why slew he sir Gaherys and sir Gareth? For I dare sey, as for sir Gareth, he loved sir Launcelot of all men erthly.'

'That ys trouth,' seyde som knyghtes, 'but they were slayne in the hurlynge as sir Launcelot thrange in the thyckyst of the prees. And as they were unarmed he smote them and wyst nat whom that he smote and so unhappely they were slayne.'

'Well,' seyde Arthure, 'the deth of them woll cause the grettist mortall warre that ever was, for I am sure that whan sir Gawayne knowyth hereoff that sir Gareth ys slayne, I shall never have reste of hym tyll I have destroyed sir Launcelottys kynne and hymselff bothe, othir ellis he to destroy me. And therefore,' seyde the kynge, 'wyte you well, my harte was never so hevy as hit ys now. And much more I am soryar for my good knyghtes losse than for the losse of my fayre quene; for quenys I myght have inow,[2] but such a felyship of good knyghtes shall never be togydirs in no company. And now I dare sey,' seyde kynge Arthur, 'there was never Crystyn kynge that ever hylde such a felyshyp togydyrs. And alas, that ever sir Launcelot and I shulde be at debate! A, Aggravayne, Aggravayne!' seyde the kynge, 'Jesu forgyff hit thy soule, for thyne evyll wyll that thou haddist and sir Mordred, thy brothir, unto sir Launcelot hath caused all this sorow.'

And ever amonge thes complayntes the kynge wepte[a] and sowned.

Than cam there one to sir Gawayne and tolde how the quene was lad away with sir Launcelot, and nygh a four-and-twenti knyghtes slayne.

'A, Jesu, save me my two brethirn!' seyde sir Gawayne. 'For full well wyst I,' sayde sir Gawayne, 'that sir Launcelot wolde rescow her, othir ellis he wolde dye in that fylde; and to say the trouth he were nat of worshyp but if he had rescowed the quene, insomuch as she shulde have be brente for his sake. And as in that,' seyde sir Gawayne, 'he hath done but knyghtly, and as I wolde have done myselff and I had stonde in lyke case. But where ar my brethirn?' seyde sir Gawayne. 'I mervayle that I se nat of them.'

Than seyde that man, 'Truly, sir Gaherys and sir Gareth be slayne.'

'Jesu deffende!' seyd sir Gawayne. 'For all thys worlde I wolde nat that they were slayne, and in especiall my good brothir sir Gareth.'

'Sir,' seyde the man, 'he ys slayne, and that ys grete pite'.

'Who slew hym?' seyde sir Gawayne.

'Sir Launcelot,' seyde the man, 'slew hem both.'

'That may I nat beleve,' seyde sir Gawayne, 'that ever he slew my good brother sir Gareth, for I dare say my brothir loved hym bettir than me and all hys brethirn and the kynge bothe. Also I dare say, an[3]

1 swooned

2 **quenys I myght have inow**. This is not a very chivalrous remark, but Arthur has long been in the habit of representing himself as a man who places his duties as king higher than his personal feelings.

3 if

sir Launcelot had desyred my brothir sir Gareth with hym, he wolde have ben with hym ayenste the kynge and us all. And therfore I may never belyeve that sir Launcelot slew my brethern.'

'Veryly, sir,' seyde the man, 'hit ys noysed that he slew hym.'

'Alas,' seyde sir Gawayne, 'now ys my joy gone!'

And than he felle downe and sowned, and longe he lay there as he had ben dede. And whan he arose oute of hys swoughe he cryed oute sorowfully and seyde, 'Alas!'

And forthwith he ran unto the kynge, criyng and wepyng, and seyde, 'A, myne uncle kynge Arthur! My good brothir sir Gareth ys slayne, and so ys my brothir sir Gaherys, whych were two noble knyghtes.'

Than the kynge wepte and he bothe, and so they felle on sownynge. And whan they were revyved, than spake sir Gawayne and seyde, 'Sir, I woll goo and se my brother sir Gareth.'

'Sir, ye may nat se hym,' seyde the kynge, 'for I caused hym to be entered[4] and sir Gaherys bothe, for I well undirstood that ye wolde make overmuche sorow, and the syght of sir Gareth shulde have caused youre double sorow.'

'Alas, my lorde,' seyde sir Gawayne, 'how slew he my brothir sir Gareth? I pray you telle me.'

'Truly,' seyde the kynge, 'I shall tell you as hit hath bene tolde me: sir Launcelot slew hym and sir Gaherys both.'

'Alas,' seyde sir Gawayne, 'they beare none armys ayenst hym, neyther of them bothe.'

'I wote nat how hit was,' seyde the kynge, 'but as hit ys sayde, sir Launcelot slew them in the thyk prees[5] and knew tham nat. And therefore lat us shape a remedy for to revenge ther dethys.'

'My kynge, my lorde, and myne uncle,' seyde sir Gawayne, 'wyte you well, now I shall make you a promyse whych I shall holde be my knyghthode, that from thys day forewarde I shall never fayle[6] sir Launcelot untyll that one of us have slayne that othir. And therefore I requyre you, my lorde and kynge, dresse you unto the warres, for wyte you well, I woll be revenged uppon sir Launcelot; and therfore, as ye woll have my servyse and my love, now haste you therto and assay youre frendis. For I promyse unto God,' seyde sir Gawayn, 'for the deth of my brothir sir Gareth I shall seke sir Launcelot thorowoute seven kynges realmys, but I shall sle hym, other ellis he shall sle me.'

'Sir, ye shall nat nede to seke hym so far,' seyde the kynge, 'for as I here say, sir Launcelot woll abyde me and us all wythin the castell of Joyous Garde. And muche pepie drawyth unto hym, as I here say.'

'That may I ryght well belyve,' seyde sir Gawayne. 'But my lorde,' he sayde, 'assay your fryndis and I woll assay myne.'

'Hit shall be done,' seyde the kyng, 'and as I suppose I shall be bygge[7] inowghe to dryve hym oute of the bygyst toure of hys castell.'

So than the kynge sente lettirs and wryttis thorowoute all Inglonde, both the lengthe and the brede, for to assomon all hys knyghtes. And so unto kynge Arthure drew many knyghtes, deukes, and erlis, that he had a grete oste, and whan they were assembeled the kynge enfourmed hem how sir Launcelot had beraffte hym hys quene. Than the kynge and all hys oste made hem redy to ley syege aboute sir Launcelot where he lay within Joyous Garde.

And anone sir Launcelot harde thereof and purveyde hym off many good knyghtes, for with hym helde many knyghtes,[b] som for hys owne sake and som for the quenys sake. Thus they were on bothe partyes well furnysshed and garnysshed of all maner of thynge that longed unto the warre. But kynge Arthurs oste was so grete that sir Launcelottis oste wolde nat abyde hym in the fylde. For he was full lothe to do batayle ayenste the kynge; but sir Launcelot drew hym unto hys stronge castell with all maner of vytayle plente, and as many noble men as he myght suffyse within the towne and the castell.

Than cam kynge Arthure with sir Gawayne wyth a grete oste and leyde syge all aboute Joyus Garde, both the towne and the castell. And there they made stronge warre on bothe partyes, but in no wyse sir Launcelot wolde ryde oute of the castell of longe tyme; and nother he wold nat suffir none of hys good knyghtes to issew oute, nother of the towne nother of the castell, untyll fiftene wykes were past.

So hit felle uppon a day that sir Launcelot loked over the wallys and spake on hyght unto kynge Arthure and to sir Gawayne: 'My lordis bothe, wyte you well all thys ys in vayne that ye make at thys

4 interred

5 dense crowd

6 abandon pursuit of

7 strong

syge, for here wynne ye no worshyp, but magre[8] and dishonoure. For and hit lyste me to com myselff oute and my good knyghtes, I shulde full sone make an ende of thys warre.'

'Com forth,' seyde kynge Arthur unto sir Launcelot, 'and thou darste, and I promyse the I shall mete the in myddis of thys fylde.'

'God deffende me,' seyde sir Launcelot, 'that ever I shulde encounter wyth the moste noble kynge that made me knyght.'

'Now, fye uppon thy fayre langayge!' seyde the kynge, 'for wyte thou well and truste hit, I am thy mortall foo and ever woll to my deth-day; for thou hast slayne my good knyghtes and full noble men of my blood, that shall I never recover agayne. Also thou hast layne be my quene and holdyn her many wynters, and sytthyn, lyke a traytoure, taken her away fro me by fors.'

'My moste noble lorde and kynge,' seyde sir Launcelot, 'ye may sey what ye woll, for ye wote well wyth youreselff I woll nat stryve. But thereas ye say that I have slayne youre good knyghtes, I wote well that I have done so, and that me sore repentith; but I was forced to do batayle with hem in savyng of my lyff, othir ellis I muste have suffirde hem to have slayne me. And as for my lady quene Gwenyver, excepte youre person of your hyghnes and my lorde sir Gawayne, there nys no knyght undir hevyn that dare make hit good[9] uppon me that ever I was traytour unto youre person. And where hit please you to say that I have holdyn my lady, youre quene, yerys and wynters, unto that I shall ever make a large[10] answere, and prove hit uppon ony knyght that beryth the lyff, excepte your person and sir Gawayne, that my lady, quene Gwenyver, ys as trew a lady unto youre person as ys ony lady lyvynge unto her lorde, and that woll I make good with my hondis. Howbeyt hit hath lyked her good grace to have me in favoure and cherysh me more than ony other knyght; and unto my power agayne[11] I have deserved her love, for oftyntymes, my lorde, ye have concented that she sholde have be brente and destroyed in youre hete, and than hit fortuned me to do batayle for her, and or I departed from her adversary they confessed there untrouthe, and she full worsshypfully excused. And at suche tymes, my lorde Arthur,' seyde sir Launcelot, 'ye loved me and thanked me whan I saved your quene from the fyre, and than ye promysed me for ever to be my good lorde. And now me thynkith ye rewarde me evyll for my good servyse. And, my lorde, me semyth I had loste a grete parte of my worshyp in my knyghthod and I had suffird my lady, youre quene, to have ben brente, and insomuche as she shulde have bene brente for my sake; for sytthyn I have done batayles for youre quene in other quarels than in myne owne quarell, me semyth now I had more ryght to do batayle for her in her ryght quarell. And therefore, my good and gracious lorde,' seyde sir Launcelot, 'take your quene unto youre good grace, for she ys both tru and good.'

'Fy on the, false recreayed[12] knyght!' seyde sir Gawayn. 'For I lat the wyte my lorde, myne uncle kynge Arthur, shall have hys quene and the bothe, magre thy vysayge,[13] and sle you bothe and save you whether[14] hit please hym.'

'Hit may well be,' seyde sir Launcelot, 'but wyte thou well, my lorde sir Gawayne, and me lyste to com oute of thys castell ye shuld wyn me and the quene more harder than ever ye wan a stronge batayle.'

'Now, fy on thy proude wordis!' seyde sir Gawayne. 'As for my lady the quene, wyte thou well I woll never say her shame. But thou, false and recrayde knyght,' seyde sir Gawayne, 'what cause haddist thou to sle my good brother sir Gareth, that loved the more than me and all my kynne? And alas, thou madist hym knyght thyne owne hondis! Why slewest thou hym that loved the so well?'

'For to excuse me,' seyde sir Launcelot, 'hit boteneth[15] me nat, but by Jesu, and by the feyth that I owghe unto the hyghe order of knyghthode, I wolde with as a good a wyll have slayne my nevew, sir Bors de Ganys! And alas, that ever I was so unhappy,' seyde sir Launcelot, 'that I had nat seyne sir Gareth and sir Gaherys!'

'Thou lyest, recrayed kyght,' seyde sir Gawayne, 'thou slewyst hem in the despite of me. And therfore wyte thou well, sir Launcelot, I shall make warre uppon the, and all the whyle that I may lyve be thyne enemy!'

'That me repentes,' seyde sir Launcelot, 'for well I undirstonde hit boteneth me nat to seke none

8 ill-will
9 prove by combat
10 unqualified
11 to the extent of my power in return
12 recreant
13 despite you
14 whichever
15 avails

accordemente whyle ye, sir Gawayne, ar so myschevously sett. And if ye were nat, I wolde nat doute to have the good grace of my lorde kynge Arthure.'

'I leve well, false recrayed knyght, for thou hast many longe dayes overlad[16] me and us all, and destroyed many of oure good kyghtes.'

'Sir, ye say as hit pleasith you,' seyde sir Launcelot, 'yet may hit never be seyde on me and opynly preved that ever I be forecaste[17] of treson slew no goode knyght as ye, my lorde sir Gawayne, have done; and so ded I never but in my deffence, that I was dryven therto in savyng of my lyff.'

'A, thou false knyght!' seyde sir Gawayne: 'that thou menyst by sir Lamorak. But wyte thou well, I slew hym!'

'Sir, ye slew hym nat youreselff,' seyde sir Launcelot, 'for hit had ben overmuch for you, for he was one of the beste knyghtes crystynde of his ayge. And hit was grete pite of hys deth!'

'Well, well, sir Launcelot,' seyde sir Gawayne, 'sytthyn thou enbraydyst[18] me of sir Lamorak, wyte thou well I shall never leve the tyll I have the at suche avayle[19] that thou shalt nat ascape my hondis.'

'I truste you well inowgh,' seyde sir Launcelot. 'And ye may gete me, I gett but lytyll mercy!'

But the Freynsh booke seyth kynge Arthur wolde have takyn hys quene agayne and to have bene accorded with sir Launcelot, but sir Gawayne wolde nat suffir hym by no maner of meane. And so sir Gawayne made many men to blow uppon[20] sir Launcelot, and so all at onys they called hym 'false recrayed knyght'.

But whan sir Bors de Ganys, sir Ector de Marys and sir Lyonell harde thys outecry they called unto them sir Palomydes and sir Lavayne and sir Urre wyth many mo knyghtes of ther bloode, and all they wente unto sir Launcelot and seyde thus: 'My lorde, wyte you well we have grete scorne of the grete rebukis that we have harde sir Gawayne sey unto you; wherefore we pray you and charge you as ye woll have oure servyse, kepe us no lenger wythin thys wallis, for we lat you wete playnly we woll ryde into the fylde and do batayle wyth hem. For ye fare as a man that were aferde, and for all your fayre speche hit woll nat avayle you, for wyte you well sir Gawayne woll nevir suffir you to accorde wyth kynge Arthur. And therfore fyght for youre lyff and ryght, and ye[c] dare.'

'Alas,' seyde sir Launcelot, 'for to ryde oute of thys castell and to do batayle I am full lothe.'

Than sir Launcelot spake on hyght unto kyng Arthur and sir Gawayne: 'My lorde, I requyre[21] you and beseche you, sytthyn that I am thus requyred and conjoured to ryde into the fylde, that neyther you, my lorde kyng Arthur, nother you, sir Gawayne, com nat into the fylde.'

'What shall we do than?' seyde sir Gawayne. 'Is nat thys the kynges quarell to fyght wyth the? And also hit ys my quarell to fyght wyth the because of the dethe of my brothir, sir Gareth.'

'Than muste I nedys unto batayle,' seyde sir Launcelot. 'Now wyte you well, my lorde Arthur and sir Gawayne, ye woll repent hit whan-somever I do batayle wyth you.'

And so than they departed eythir from othir; and than aythir party made hem redy on the morne for to do batayle, and grete purveyaunce was made on bothe sydys. And sir Gawayne lat purvey many knyghtes for to wayte uppon[22] sir Launcelot for to oversette hym and to sle hym. And on the morn at underne[23] kynge Arthure was redy in the fylde with three grete ostys.[24]

And than sir Launcelottis felyshyp com oute at the three gatis in full good aray; and sir Lyonell cam in the formyst batayle, and sir Launcelot cam in the myddyll, and sir Bors com oute at the thirde gate. And thus they cam in order and rule as full noble knyghtes. And ever sir Launcelot charged all hys knyghtes in ony wyse to save kynge Arthure and sir Gawayne.

Than cam forth sir Gawayne from the kyngis oste and profirde to juste. And sir Lyonel was a fyers knyght, and lyghtly he encountred with hym, and there sir Gawayne smote sir Lyonell thorowoute the body, that he daysshed to the erth lyke as he had ben dede. And than sir Ector de Marys and other mo bare hym into the castell.

And anone there began a grete stowre[25] and much people were slayne; and ever sir Launcelot ded what he myght to save the people on kynge Arthurs party. For sir Bors and Sir Palomydes and sir Saffir

16 oppressed
17 by plotting
18 upbraidest
19 advantage
20 defame
21 request
22 lie in wait for
23 9 a.m.
24 armies
25 battle

overthrew many knyghtes, for they were dedely knyghtes, and sir Blamour de Ganys and sir Bleoberys, wyth sir Bellyngere le Bewse, thes six knyghtes ded much harme. And ever was kynge Arthur aboute sir Launcelot to have slayne hym, and ever sir Launcelot suffird hym and wolde nat stryke agayne. So sir Bors encountirde wyth kynge Arthur, and sir Bors smote hym, and so he alyght and drew hys swerde and seyd to sir Launcelot, 'Sir, shall I make an ende of thys warre?' (For he mente to have slayne hym.)

'Nat so hardy,' seyde sir Launcelot, 'uppon payne of thy hede, that thou touch hym no more! For I woll never se that moste noble kynge that made me knyght nother slayne nor shamed.'

And therewithall sir Launcelot alyght of hys horse and toke up the kynge and horsed hym agayne, and seyd thus: 'My lorde the kynge, for Goddis love, stynte thys stryff, for ye gette here no worshyp and I wolde do myne utteraunce.[26] But allwayes I forbeare you, and ye nor none off youres forberyth nat me. And therefore, my lorde, I pray you remembir what I have done in many placis, and now am I evyll rewarded.'

So whan kynge Arthur was on horsebak he loked on sir Launcelot; than the teerys braste oute of hys yen, thynkyng of the grete curtesy that was in sir Launcelot more than in ony other man. And therewith the kynge rod hys way and myght no lenger beholde hym, saiyng to hymselff, 'Alas, alas, that yet thys warre began!'

And than aythir party of the batayles[27] wythdrew them to repose them, and buryed the dede and serched[28] the wounded men, and leyde to ther woundes soffte salves; and thus they endured that nyght tylle on the morne. And on the morne by undirn they made them redy to do batayle, and than sir Bors lad the vawarde.[29]

So uppon the morn ther cam sir Gawayne, as brym[30] as ony boore, wyth a grete spere in hys honde; and whan sir Bors saw hym he thought to revenge hys brother, sir Lyonell, of the despite sir Gawayne gaff hym the other day; and so, as they that knew aythir other, feautred[31] ther spearis, and with all ther myght, of ther horsis and themselff, so fyersly they mette togydirs and so felonsly[32] that aythir bare other thorow, and so they felle bothe to the bare erthe.

And than the batayle joyned, and there was much slaughter on bothe partyes. Than sir Launcelot rescowed sir Bors and sent hym into the castell. But neyther sir Gawayne nother sir Bors dyed nat of ther woundis, for they were well holpyn.[33]

Than sir Lavayne and sir Urre prayde sir Launcelot to do hys payne and feyght as they do: 'For we se that ye forbeare and spare, and that doth us much harme. And therfore we pray you spare nat youre enemyes no more than they do you.'

'Alas,' seyde sir Launcelot, 'I have no harte to fyght ayenste my lorde Arthur, for ever me semyth I do nat as me ought to do.'

'My lorde,' seyde sir Palomydes, 'thoughe ye spare them never so much all thys day they woll never[d] can you thanke;[34] and yf they may gete you at avayle[35] ye ar but a dede man.'

So than sir Launcelot undirstoode that they seyde hym trouthe. Than he strayned hymselff more than he ded toforehonde, and by cause of hys nevew sir Bors was sore wounded he payned hymselff the more. And so within a lytyll whyle, by evynsong-tyme, sir Launcelottis party the bettir stood, for ther horsis wente in blood past the fyttlokkes, there were so many people slayne.

And than for verry pite sir Launcelot withhylde hys knyghtes and suffird kynge Arthurs party to withdraw them insyde. And so he withdrew hys meyny into the castell, and aythir partyes buryed the dede and put salve unto the wounded men. So whan sir Gawayne was hurte, they on kynge Arthurs party were nat so orgulus[36] as they were toforehonde to do batayle.

So of thys warre that was betwene kynge Arthure and sir Launcelot hit was noysed thorow all Crystyn realmys, and so hit cam at the laste by relacion unto the Pope. And than the Pope toke a consideracion of the grete goodnes of kynge Arthur and of the hyghe proues off sir Launcelot, that was called the moste nobelyst knyght of the worlde. Wherefore the Pope called unto hym a noble clerke that at that tyme was

26 utmost
27 armies
28 tended
29 vanguard
30 fierce
31 couched
32 malevolently
33 helped
34 be grateful
35 advantage
36 boastful

there presente (the Freynsh boke seyth hit was the bysshop of Rochester), and the Pope gaff hym bulles[e] undir leade, and sente hem unto the kynge, chargyng hym uppon payne of entirdytynge[37] of all Inglonde that he take hys quene agayne and accorde with sir Launcelot.

So whan thys bysshop was com unto Carlyle he shewed the kynge hys bullys, and whan the kynge undirstode them he wyste nat what to do: but full fayne he wolde have bene acorded with sir Launcelot, but sir Gawayn wolde nat suffir hym. But to have the quene he thereto agreed, but in no wyse he wolde suffir the kynge to accorde with sir Launcelot; but as for the quene, he consented. So the bysshop had of the kynge hys grete seale[38] and hys assuraunce, as he was a trew and anoynted kynge, that sir Launcelot shulde go sauff and com sauff and that the quene shulde nat be seyde unto of[39] the kynge, nother of none other, for nothynge done of tyme past. And of all thes appoyntementes the bysshop brought with hym sure wrytynge to shew unto sir Launcelot.

So whan the bysshop was com to Joyous Garde, there he shewed sir Launcelot how he cam from the Pope with wrytynge unto kyng Arthur and unto hym. And there he tolde hym the perelis, gyff he wythhelde the quene from the kynge.

'Sir, hit was never in my thought,' seyde sir Launcelot, 'to withholde the quene from my lorde Arthur, hut I kepe her for thys cause: insomuche as she shulde have be brente for my sake, me semed hit was my parte to save her lyff and put her from that daungere tyll bettir recover[40] myght com. And now I thanke God,' seyde sir Launcelot, 'that the Pope hathe made her[f] pease. For God knowyth,' seyde sir Launcelot, 'I woll be a thousandefolde more gladder to brynge her agayne than ever I was of her takyng away, wyth thys[41] I may be sure to com sauff and go sauff, and that the quene shall have her lyberte, and never for nothyng that hath be surmysed afore thys tyme that she never from thys stonde in no perell. For ellis,' seyde sir Launcelot, 'I dare adventure me to kepe her from an harder showre[42] than ever yet I had.'

'Sir, hit shall nat nede you,' seyde the bysshop, 'to drede thus muche, for wyte yow well, the Pope muste be obeyed, and hit were nat the Popis worshyp nother my poure honesty to know you distressed nother the quene, nother in perell nother shamed.'

And than he shewed sir Launcelot all hys wrytynge bothe from the Pope and kynge Arthur.

'Thys ys sure ynow,' seyde sir Launcelot. 'For full well I dare truste my lordys owne wrytyng and hys seale, for he was never shamed of hys promyse. Therefore,' seyde sir Launcelot unto the bysshop, 'ye shall ryde unto the kynge afore and recommaunde me unto hys good grace, and lat hym have knowlecchynge that this same day eyght dayes, by the grace of God, I myselff shall brynge the quene unto hym. And than sey ye to my moste redouted kynge that I woll sey largely for the quene[43] that I shall none excepte,[44] for drede nother for feare, but the kynge hymselff and my lorde sir Gawayne; and that ys for the kyngis love more than for hymselff.'

So the bysshop departed and cam to the kynge to Carlehyll, and tolde hym all how sir Launcelot answerd hym; so that made the teares falle oute at the kyngis yen. Than sir Launcelot purveyed hym an hondred knyghtes, and all well clothed in grene velvet, and their horsis trapped in the same to the heelys, and every knyght hylde a braunche of olyff in hys honde in tokenyng of pees. And the quene had four-and-twenti jantillwomen folowyng her in the same wyse. And sir Launcelot had twelve coursers folowyng hym, and on every courser sate a yonge jantylman; and all they were arayed in whyght velvet with sarpis of golde aboute their quarters,[45] and the horse[46] trapped in the same wyse down to the helys, wyth many owchys,[47] isette with stonys and perelys[48] in golde, to the numbir of a thousande. And in the same wyse was the quene arayed, and sir Launcelot in the same, of whyght clothe of golde tyssew.

And ryght so as ye have harde, as the Freynshe booke makyth mencion, he rode with the quene from

37 **entirdytynge**: interdict. There was historical precedent for this: in 1208–13 all England was placed under an interdict (that is, in effect, 'excommunicated') during the reign of king John. The respect accorded here to the Pope's authority is a relic of the originally monastic authorship of the French Vulgate cycle.

38 **grete seale**. The Great Seal of the kingdom was applied to documents of the highest importance and was the king's public guarantee of their authenticity.

39 reproached by

40 rescue

41 provided

42 battle

43 **sey largely for the quene**: speak freely on behalf of the queen (against all her accusers).

44 exempt

45 chains of gold hanging to their thighs

46 horses

47 clasps

48 pearls

Joyus Garde to Carlehyll. And so sir Launcelot rode thorowoute Carlehylle, and so into the castell, that all men myght beholde hem. And there was many a wepyng ien.

And than sir Launcelot hymselff alyght and voyded[49] hys horse, and toke adowne the quene, and so lad her where kyng Arthur was in hys seate; and sir Gawayne sate afore hym, and many other grete lordys.

So whan sir Launcelot saw the kynge and sir Gawayne, than he lad the quene by the arme, and than he kneled downe and the quene bothe. Wyte you well, than was there many a bolde knyght wyth kynge Arthur that wepte as tendirly as they had seyne all ther kynne dede afore them!

So the kynge sate stylle and seyde no worde. And whan sir Launcelot saw hys countenaunce he arose up and pulled up the quene with hym, and thus he seyde full knyghtly: 'My moste redouted kynge, ye shall undirstonde, by the Popis commaundemente and youres I have brought to you my lady the quene, as ryght requyryth. And if ther be ony knyght, of what degre that ever he be off, except your person, that woll sey or dare say but that she ys trew and clene to you, I here myselff, sir Launcelot du Lake, woll make hit good uppon hys body that she ys a trew lady unto you.[50]

'But, sir, lyars ye have lystened, and that hath caused grete debate betwyxte you and me. For tyme hath bene, my lorde Arthur, that ye[g] were gretly pleased with me whan I ded batayle for my lady youre quene; and full well ye know, my moste noble kynge, that she hath be put to grete wronge or[51] thys tyme. And sytthyn hyt pleased you at many tymys that I shulde feyght for her, therefore[h] me semyth, my good lorde, I had more cause to rescow her from the fyer whan she sholde have ben brente for my sake.

'For they that tolde you tho talys were lyars, and so hit felle uppon them: for by lyklyhode, had nat the myght of God bene with me, I myght never have endured with fourtene knyghtes, and they armed and afore purposed, and I unarmed and nat purposed; for I was sente unto my lady, youre quyne, I wote nat for what cause, but I was nat so sone within the chambir-dore but anone sir Aggravayne and sir Mordred called me traytoure and false recrayed knyght.'

'Be my fayth, they called the ryght!' seyde sir Gawayne.

'My lorde sir Gawayne,' seyde sir Launcelot, 'in ther quarell they preved nat hemselff the beste, nother in the ryght.'

'Well, well, sir Launcelot,' seyde the kynge, 'I have gyvyn you no cause to do to me as ye have done, for I have worshipt[52] you and youres more than ony othir knyghtes.'

'My lorde,' seyde sir Launcelot, 'so ye be nat displeased, ye shall undirstonde that I and myne have done you oftyntymes bettir servyse than ony othir knyghtes have done, in many dyverce placis; and where ye have bene full hard[i] bestadde dyvers tymes, I have rescowed you from many daungers; and ever unto my power I was glad to please you and my lorde sir Gawayne. In justis and in turnementis and in batayles set, bothe on horsebak and on foote, I have oftyn rescowed you, and you, my lorde sir Gawayne, and many mo of youre knyghtes in many dyvers placis.

'For now I woll make avaunte,' seyde sir Launcelot. 'I woll that ye all wyte that as yet I founde never no maner of knyght but that I was over-harde for hym and I had done myne utteraunce, God graunte mercy! Howbeit I have be macched with good knyghtes, as sir Trystram and sir Lamorak, but ever I had favoure unto them and a demyng what they were. And I take God to recorde, I never was wrothe nor gretly hevy wyth no good knyght and I saw hym besy and aboute to wyn worshyp; and glad I was ever whan I founde a good knyght that myght onythynge endure me on horsebak and on foote. Howbeit sir Carados of the Dolerous Toure was a full noble knyght and a passynge stronge man, and that wote ye, my lorde sir Gawayne; for he myght well be called a noble knyght whan he be fyne[53] fors pulled you oute of your sadyll and bounde you overthwarte[54] afore hym to hys sadyll-bow. And there, my lorde sir Gawayne, I rescowed you and slew hym afore your syght. Also I founde youre brothir, sir Gaherys, and sir Terquyn ledyng hym bounden afore hym; and there also I rescowed youre brothir and slew sir Terquyn and

49 left

50 Throughout this exchange, Lancelot holds to the letter of the chivalric code in asserting that the right of his claim, and the truth of the queen, will be proved by his success in combat with any challenger. But his knowledge that the claim is untrue, and that the might given by God to those who fight in a just cause is being used not to defend the right but to make wrong into right, brings the whole institution of the Round Table into jeopardy.

51 before

52 honoured

53 sheer

54 across

delyverde three score and four of my lorde Arthurs knyghtes oute of hys preson.[55] And now I dare sey,' seyde sir Launcelot, 'I mette never wyth so stronge a knyght nor so well-fyghtyng as was sir Carados and sir Tarquyn, for they and I faught to the uttermest. And therfore,' seyde sir Launcelot unto sir Gawayne, 'me semyth ye ought of ryght to remembir this; for, and I myght have youre good wyll, I wold truste to God for to have my lorde Arthurs good grace.'

'Sir, the kynge may do as he wyll,' seyde sir Gawayne, 'but wyte thou well, sir Launcelot, thou and I shall never be accorded whyle we lyve, for thou hast slayne three of my brethyrn. And two of hem thou slew traytourly and piteuously, for they bare none harneys ayenste the, nother none wold do.'

'Sir, God wolde they had ben armed,' seyde sir Launcelot, 'for than had they ben on lyve.[56] And for Gareth, I loved no kynnesman I had more than I loved hym, and ever whyle I lyve,' seyde sir Launcelot, 'I woll bewayle sir Gareth hys dethe, nat all only for the grete feare I have of you, but for many causys whych causyth me to be sorowfull. One is that I made hym knyght; another ys, I wote well he loved me aboven all othir knyghtes; and the third ys, be was passyng noble and trew, curteyse and jantill and well condicionde. The fourth ys, I wyste well, anone as I harde that Sir Gareth was dede, I knew well that I shulde never aftir have youre love, my lorde sir Gawayne, but everlastyng warre betwyxt us. And also I wyste well that ye wolde cause[j] my noble lorde kynge Arthur for ever to be my mortall foo. And as Jesu be my helpe, and be[57] my knyghthode, I slewe never sir Gareth nother hys brother be my wyllynge, but alas that ever they were unarmed that unhappy day.

'But this much I shall offir me to you,' seyde sir Launcelot, 'if hit may please the kyngis good grace and you, my lorde sir Gawayn: I shall firste begyn at Sandwyche, and there I shall go in my shearte, barefoote; and at every ten myles ende I shall founde and gar make[58] an house of relygious, of what order that ye woll assygne me, with an holye covente to synge and rede day and nyght in especiall for sir Gareth sake and sir Gaherys. And thys shall I perfourme from Sandwyche unto Carlyle; and every house shall have suffycyent lyvelod.[59] And thys shall I perfourme[k] whyle that I have ony lyvelod in Crystyndom, and there ys none of all thes religious placis but they shall be perfourmed, furnysshed and garnysshed with all thyngis as an holy place ought to be. And thys were fayrar and more holyar and more profyte to ther soulis than ye, my moste noble kynge, and you, sir Gawayne, to warre uppon me, for therby shall ye gete none avayle.'

Than all the knyghtes and ladyes that were there wepte as they were madde, and the tearys felle on kynge Arthur hys chekis.

'Sir Launcelot,' seyde sir Gawayne, 'I have ryght well harde thy langayge and thy grete proffirs. But wyt thou well, lat the kynge do as hit pleasith hym, I woll never forgyff the my brothirs dethe, and in especiall the deth of my brothir sir Gareth. And if myne uncle, kynge Arthur, wyll accorde wyth the, he shall loose my servys, for wyte thou well,' seyde sir Gawayne, 'thou art bothe false to the kynge and to me.'

'Sir,' seyde sir Launcelot, 'he beryth nat the lyff that may make hit good! And ye, sir Gawayne, woll charge me with so hyghe a thynge, ye muste pardone me, for than nedis must I answere you.'[60]

'Nay, nay,' seyde sir Gawayne, 'we ar past that as at thys tyme, and that causyth the Pope, for he hath charged myne uncle the kynge that he shall take agayne his quene and to accorde wyth the, sir Launcelot, as for thys season, and therefore thou shalt go sauff as thou com. But in this londe thou shalt nat abyde past a fiftene dayes, such somons I gyff the, for so the kynge and we were condescended[61] and accorded ar[62] thou cam. And ellis,' seyde sir Gawayn, 'wyte thou well, thou shulde nat a comyn here but if hit were magre thyne hede.[63] And if hit were nat for the Popis commaundement,' seyde sir Gawayne, 'I shulde do batayle with the myne owne hondis, body for body, and preve hit uppon the that thou hast ben both false unto myne uncle, kynge Arthur, and to me bothe; and that shall I preve on thy body, whan thou art departed fro hense, wheresomever that I fynde the!'

55 The calling to mind of the deeds of the past serves Lancelot's immediate purpose, and also strengthens the integrity of the whole story as the heroic narrative of sir Lancelot (the 'Lancelotiad').

56 **for than had they ben on lyve**, i.e. Lancelot would have recognized them, in their armour and coats of arms, and forborne to kill them.

57 by

58 cause to be built

59 possessions (endowment)

60 **nedis must I answere you**, i.e. by challenging you to single combat in order to determine the truth or otherwise of your accusation.

61 agreed

62 before

63 at your own peril

Than sir Launcelotte syghed, and therewith the tearys felle on hys chekys, and than he seyde thus: 'Moste nobelyst Crysten realme, whom I have loved aboven all othir realmys! And in the I have gotyn a grete parte of my worshyp, and now that I shall departe in thys wyse, truly me repentis that ever I cam in thys realme, that I shulde be thus shamefully banysshyd, undeserved and causeles! But Fortune ys so varyaunte, and the wheele so mutable,[64] that there ys no constaunte abydynge. And that may be preved by many olde cronycles, as of noble Ector of Troy and Alysaunder, the myghty conquerroure, and many mo other: whan they were moste in her royalte,[65] they alyght passyng lowe. And so faryth hit by me,' seyde sir Launcelot, 'for in thys realme I had worshyp, and be me and myne all the hole Rounde Table hath bene encreced more in worshyp, by me and myne, than ever hit was by ony of you all.

'And therfore wyte thou well, sir Gawayne, I may lyve uppon my londis as well as ony knyght that here ys. And yf ye, my moste redoutted kynge, woll com uppon my londys with sir Gawayne to warre uppon me, I muste endure you as well as I may. But as to you, sir Gawayne, if that ye com there, I pray you charge me nat wyth treson nother felony, for and ye do I muste answere you.'

'Do thou thy beste,' seyde sir Gawayne, 'and therefore hyghe the faste that thou were gone! And wyte thou well we shall sone com aftir, and breke thy strengyst castell that thou hast, uppon[66] thy hede!'

'Hyt shall nat nede that,' seyde sir Launcelot, 'for and I were as orgulous sette as ye ar, wyte you well I shulde mete you in myddys of the fylde.'

'Make thou no more langayge,' seyde sir Gawayne, 'but delyvir the quene from the, and pyke the lyghtly oute of thys courte!'

'Well,' seyde sir Launcelot, 'and I had wyste of thys shortecomyng, I wolde a advysed me twyse or that I had com here. For and the quene had be so dere unto me as ye noyse her, I durste have kepte her from the felyshyp of the beste knyghtes undir hevyn.'

And than sir Launcelot seyde unto quene Gwenyver in hyryng of the kynge and hem all, 'Madame, now I muste departe from you and thys noble felyshyp for ever. And sytthyn hit ys so, I besech you to pray for me, and I shall pray for you. And telle ye me, and if ye be harde bestad by ony false tunges, but lyghtly,[67] my good lady, sende me worde; and if ony knyghtes hondys undir the hevyn may delyver you by batayle, I shall delyver you.'

And therewithall sir Launcelot kyssed the quene, and than he seyde all opynly, 'Now lat se whatsomever he be in thys place that dare sey the quene ys nat trew unto my lorde Arthur, lat se who woll speke, and he dare speke.'

And therewith he brought the quene to the kynge, and than sir Launcelot toke hys leve and departed. And ther was nother kynge, duke, erle, barowne, nor knyght, lady nor jantyllwoman, but all they wepte as people oute of mynde, excepte sir Gawayne. And whan thys noble knyght sir Launcelot toke his horse to ryde oute of Carlehyll, there was sobbyng and wepyng for pure dole of hys departynge.

And so he toke his way to Joyous Garde, and than ever afftir he called hit 'the Dolerous Towre'. And thus departed sir Launcelot from the courte for ever.

And so whan he cam to Joyous Garde he called hys felyshyp unto hym and asked them what they wolde do. Than they answerde all hole togydirs with one voyce, they wold do as he wolde do.

'Than, my fayre felowys,' seyde sir Launcelot, 'I muste departe oute of thys moste noble realme. And now I shall departe, hit grevyth me sore, for I shall departe with no worship; for a fleymed[68] man departith never oute of a realme with no worship. And that ys to me grete hevynes, for ever I feare aftir my dayes that men shall cronycle uppon me that I was fleamed oute of thys londe. And ellis, my fayre lordis, be ye sure, and I had nat drad shame, my lady quene Gwenyvere and I shulde never have departed.'

Than spake noble knyghtes, as sir Palomydes and sir Saffyr, hys brothir, and sir Bellynger le Bewse, and sir Urre with sir Lavayne, with many other: 'Sir, and ye woll so be disposed to abyde in thys londe we woll never fayle you; and if ye lyste nat abyde in thys londe, ther ys none of the good knyghtes that here

64 **the wheele** of Fortune was pictured as a kind of giant spinning-wheel which was turned by the goddess Fortune and onto which were bound those who lived their lives in the world, suffering the bitter arbitrariness, now up, now down, of its continuous revolutions. The 'Nine Worthy', amongst them Hector and Alexander, were often cited as an exemplum of the power of Fortune over even the greatest of heroes.

65 splendour

66 I swear upon

67 quickly

68 exiled

be that woll fayle you, for many causis. One ys, all we that be nat of your bloode shall never be wellcom unto the courte. And sytthyn hit lyked us to take a parte with you in youre distres in this realme, wyte you well hit shall lyke us as well to go in othir contreyes with you and there to take suche parte as ye do.'

'My fayre lordys,' seyde sir Launcelot, 'I well undirstond you, and as I can, I thanke you. And ye shall undirstonde, suche lyvelode as I am borne unto I shall departe with you in thys maner of wyse: that ys for to say, I shall departe[69] all my lyvelode and all my londis frely amonge you, and myselff woll have as lytyll as ony of you; for, have I sufficiaunte that may longe[70] unto my person, I woll aske none other ryches nother aray. And I truste to God to maynteyne you on my londys as well as ever ye were maynteyned.'

Than spake all the knyghtes at onys: 'Have he shame that woll leve you! For we all undirstonde, woll be[1] never quyett in thys realme but ever debate and stryff now the felyshyp of the Rounde Table ys brokyn. For by the noble felyshyp of the Rounde Table was kynge Arthur upborne, and by ther nobeles the kynge and all the realme was ever in quyet and reste. And a grete parte,' they sayde all, 'was because of youre moste nobeles, sir Launcelot.'

'Now, truly I thanke you all of youre good sayinge! Howbeit I wote well that in me was nat all the stabilite of thys realme, but in that I myght I ded my dever.[71] And well I am sure I knew many rebellyons in my dayes that by me and myne were peased;[72] and that I trow we all shall here of in shorte space, and that me sore repentith. For ever I drede me,' seyde sir Launcelot, 'that sir Mordred woll make trouble, for he ys passyng envyous and applyeth hym muche to trouble.'

And so they were accorded to departe wyth sir Launcelot to hys landys. And to make shorte thys tale, they trussed[73] and payed all that wolde aske them; and hole an hondred knyghtes departed with sir Launcelot at onys, and made their avowis they wolde never leve hym for weale ne for woo.

{Lancelot returns to France, and keeps his promise to his followers by rewarding them with lands and titles. Urged on by Gawain, Arthur leaves England under the regency of Mordred and crosses to France to besiege Lancelot in his castle at Benwick. Lancelot tries to avoid battle but in the end Gawain's taunts force him to take up the challenge of single combat.}

The combat of Lancelot and Gawain

Than hit befelle uppon a day that sir Gawayne cam afore the gatis, armed at all pecis, on a noble horse, with a greate speare in hys honde, and than he cryed with a lowde voyce and seyde, 'Where art thou now, thou false traytour, sir Launcelot? Why holdyst thou thyselff within holys and wallys lyke a cowarde? Loke oute, thou false traytoure knyght, and here I shall revenge uppon thy body the dethe of my three brethirne!'

And all thys langayge harde sir Launcelot every deale. Than hys kynne and hys knyghtes drew aboute hym, and all they seyde at onys unto sir Launcelot, 'Sir, now muste you deffende you lyke a knyght, othir ellis ye be shamed for ever, for now ye be called uppon[1] treson hit ys tyme for you to styrre! For ye have slepte over-longe, and suffirde overmuche.'

'So God me helpe,' seyde sir Launcelot, 'I am ryght hevy at sir Gawaynes wordys, for now he chargith me with a grete charge. And therfore I wote as well as ye I muste nedys deffende me, other ellis to be recreaunte.'

Than sir Launcelot bade sadyll hys strongest horse and bade let fecche hys armys and brynge all to the towre of the gate. And than sir Launcelot spake on hyght unto the kynge and seyde, 'My lorde Arthur, and noble kynge that made me knyght! Wyte you well I am ryght hevy for youre sake that ye thus sewe uppon[2] me. And allwayes I forbeare you, for and I wolde be vengeable I myght have mette you in myddys the fylde or thys tyme and thereto have made your boldiste knyghtes full tame. And now I have forborne you and suffirde you halff a yere, and sir Gawayne, to do what ye wolde do. And now I may no lenger suffir to endure, but nedis I muste deffende myselff, insomuch as sir Gawayn hath becalled me of

69 share
70 be appropriate
71 duty
72 subdued
73 equipped

The combat of Lancelot and Gawain
1 accused of
2 pursue

treson; whych ys gretly ayenste my wyll that ever I shulde fyghte ayenste ony of youre blood, but now I may nat forsake hit, for I am dryvyn therto as beste tylle a bay.'[3]

Than sir Gawayne seyde unto sir Launcelotte, 'And thou darste do batayle, leve thy babelynge and com off, and lat us ease oure hartis!'

Than sir Launcelot armed hym and mownted uppon hys horse, and aythir of them gate greate spearys in their hondys. And so the oste withoute stoode stylle all aparte, and the noble knyghtes of the cite cam a greate numbir, that whan kynge Arthur saw the numbir of men and knyghtes he mervaylde and seyde to hymself, 'Alas, that ever sir Launcelot was ayenst me! For now I se that he hath forborne me.'

And so the covenaunte was made, there sholde no man nyghe hem nother deale wyth them tylle the tone were dede other yolden.

Than sir Launcelot and sir Gawayne departed a greate way in sundir, and than they cam togydirs with all ther[a] horse myghtes as faste as they myght renne, and aythir smote othir in myddis of ther shyldis. But the knyghtes were so stronge and ther spearys so bygge that ther horsis myght nat endure ther buffettis, and so ther horsis felle to the erthe. And than they avoyded ther horsys and dressed ther shyldis afore them. Than they cam togydirs and gaff many sad[4] strokis on dyverse placis of ther bodyes, that the bloode braste oute on many sydis.

Than had sir Gawayne suche a grace and gyffte that an holy man had gyvyn hym, that every day in the yere, from undern tyll hyghe noone, hys myght encresed tho three owres as much as thryse hys strength.[5] And that caused sir Gawayne to wynne grete honoure. And for hys sake kynge Arthur made an ordynaunce that all maner off batayles for ony quarels[6] that shulde be done afore kynge Arthur shulde begynne at undern; and all was done for sir Gawaynes love, that by lyklyhode if sir Gawayne were on the tone parte, he shulde have the bettir in batayle whyle hys strengthe endured three owrys. But ther were that tyme but feaw knyghtes lyvynge that knewe thys advauntayge that sir Gawayne had, but kynge Arthure all only.

So sir Launcelot faught wyth sir Gawayne, and whan sir Launcelot felte hys myght evermore encrese, sir Launcelot wondred and drad hym sore to be shamed; for, as the Freynshe booke seyth, he wende, whan he felte sir Gawaynes double hys strengthe, that he had bene a fyende and none earthely man. Wherefore sir Launcelot traced and traverced, and coverde hymselff with hys shylde, and kepte hys myght and hys brethe duryng three owrys. And that whyle sir Gawayne gaff hym many sad bruntis,[7] that all knyghtes that behylde sir Launcelot mervayled how he myght endure hym, but full lytyll undirstood they that travayle that sir Launcelot had to endure hym.

And than whan hit was past noone sir Gawaynes strengthe was gone and he[b] had no more but hys owne myght. Whan sir Launcelot felte hym so com downe, than he strecched hym up and strode nere sir Gawayne and seyde thus: 'Now I fele ye have done youre warste! And now, my lorde sir Gawayn, I muste do my parte, for many a grete and grevous strokis I have endured you thys day with greate payne.'

And so sir Launcelot doubled hys strokis and gaff sir Gawayne suche a stroke uppon the helmet that sydelynge[8] he felle downe uppon hys one syde. And sir Launcelot withdrew hym from hym.

'Why wythdrawyst thou the?' seyde sir Gawayne. 'Turne agayne, false traytoure knyght, and sle me oute! For and thou leve me thus, anone as I am hole I shall do batayle with the agayne.'

'Sir,' seyde sir Launcelot, 'I shall endure you, be Goddis grace! But wyte thou well, sir Gawayne, I woll never smyte a felde knyght.'

And so sir Launcelot departed and wente unto the cite. And sir Gawayne was borne unto kynge Arthurs pavylon, and anone lechys were brought unto hym of the beste, and serched and salved hym with souffte oynementis. And than sir Launcelot seyde, 'Now have good day, my lorde the kynge! For wyte you welle ye wynne no worshyp at thes wallis, for and I wolde my knyghtes oute brynge, there shulde many a douty man dye. And therefore, my lorde Arthur, remembir you of olde kyndenes, and howsomever I fare, Jesu be youre gyde in all placis!'

'Now, alas,' seyde the kynge, 'that ever thys unhappy warre began! For ever sir Launcelot forbearyth me in all placis, and in lyke wyse my kynne, and that ys sene well thys day, what curtesy he shewed my neveawe, sir Gawayne.'

3 beast to bay
4 heavy
5 Gawain's **grace and gyffte** – that his strength waxes threefold till noon – is a relic of his origin in myth as a sun-god.
6 **batayles for ony quarels**: single combats to settle grievances or disputes between a challenger and defendant.
7 blows
8 sideways

Than kynge Arthur felle syke for sorow of sir Gawayne, that he was so sore hurte, and bycause of the warre betwyxte hym and sir Launcelot. So aftir that they on kynge Arthurs party kepte the sege with lytyll warre wythoute-forthe, and they within-forthe kepte their wallys and deffended them whan nede was.

Thus sir Gawayne lay syke and unsounde three wykes in hys tentis with all maner of lechecrauffte that myght be had. And as sone as sir Gawayne myght go and ryde, he armed hym at all poyntis and bestroode a styff courser and gate a grete speare in hys honde, and so he cam rydynge afore the chyeff gate of Benwyke. And there he cryed on hyght and seyde, 'Where art thou, sir Launcelot? Com forth, thou false traytoure knyght and recrayed, for I am here, sir Gawayne, that woll preve thys that I say uppon the!'

And all thys langayge sir Launcelot harde and sayde thus: 'Sir Gawayne, me repentis of youre fowle sayinge, that ye woll nat cease your langayge. For ye wote well, sir Gawayne, I know youre myght and all that ye may do, and well ye wote, sir Gawayne, ye may nat greatly hurte me.'

'Com downe, traytoure knyght,' seyde he, 'and make hit good the contrary wyth thy hondys! For hit myssehapped me the laste batayle to be hurte of thy hondis, therefore, wyte thou well, I am com thys day to make amendis, for I wene this day to ley the as low as thou laydest me.'

'Jesu deffende me,' seyde sir Launcelot, 'that ever I be so farre in youre daunger[9] as ye have bene in myne, for than my dayes were done. But, Gawayne,'[10] seyde sir Launcelot, 'ye shall nat thynke that I shall tarry longe, but sytthyn that ye unknyghtly calle me thus of treson, ye shall have bothe youre hondys fulle of me.'

And than sir Launcelot armed hym at all poyntis and mounted uppon his[c] horse and gate a grete speare in hys honde and rode oute at the gate. And bothe ther ostis were assembled, of them withoute and within, and stood in aray full manly, and bothe partyes were charged to holde hem stylle to se and beholde the batayle of thes two noble knyghtes.

And than they layde their spearys in ther restis and so cam togydir as thundir. And sir Gawayne brake hys speare in an hondred peces to hys honde, and sir Launcelot smote hym with a gretter myght, that sir Gawaynes horse feete reysed,[11] and so the horse and he felle to the erthe. Than sir Gawayne delyverly[12] devoyded hys horse and put hys shylde afore hym, and egirly drew hys swerde and bade sir Launcelot, 'Alyght, traytoure knyght!' and seyde, 'Gyff a marys[13] sonne hath fayled me, wyte thou well a kyngis sonne and a quenys sonne shall nat fayle the!'

Than sir Launcelot devoyded hys horse and dressed hys shylde afore hym and drew hys swerde, and so cam egirly togydirs and gaff many sad strokis, that all men on bothe partyes had wondir.

But whan sir Launcelot felte sir Gawaynes myght so mervaylously encres, he than wythhylde hys corayge[14] and hys wynde, and so he kepte hym undir coverte of hys myght and of hys shylde: he traced and traverced here and there to breake sir Gawaynys strokys and hys currayge. And ever sir Gawayne enforced hymselff wyth all hys myght and power to destroy sir Launcelot, for, as the Freynshe booke sayth, ever as sir Gawaynes myght encresed, ryght so encreced hys wynde and hys evyll wyll.

And thus he ded grete payne unto sir Launcelot three owres, that he had much ado to defende hym.[15] And whan the three owres were past, that he felte sir Gawayne was com home to his owne propir strengthe, than sir Launcelot sayde, 'Sir, now I have preved you twyse that ye ar a full daungerous knyght and a wondirfull man of hys myght! And many wondir dedis have ye done in youre dayes,[d] for by youre myght encresyng ye have desceyved many a full noble knyght. And now I fele that ye have done youre myghty dedis, and now, wyte you well, I muste do my dedis!'

And than sir Launcelot strode nere sir Gawayne and doubled hys strokis, and ever sir Gawayne deffended hym myghtyly, but nevertheles sir Launcelot smote such a stroke uppon hys helme and uppon the olde wounde that sir Gawayne sanke downe and sowned. And anone as he ded awake he waved and foyned[16] at sir Launcelot as he lay, and seyde, 'Traytoure knyght, wyte thou well I am nat yet slayne. Therefore com thou nere me and performe[e] thys batayle to the utteraunce!'

9 power to hurt
10 **Gawayne**. The omission of 'sir' (if it is not a scribal error) is an unexpected though pardonable rudeness on Lancelot's part.
11 reared up
12 nimbly
13 mare's
14 fighting energy
15 himself
16 thrust

'I woll no more do than I have done,' seyde sir Launcelot. 'For whan I se you on foote I woll do batayle uppon you all the whyle I se you stande uppon youre feete; but to smyte a wounded man that may nat stonde, God defende me from such a shame!'

And than he turned hym and wente[f] hys way towarde the cite, and sir Gawayne evermore callyng hym 'traytoure knyght', and seyde, 'Traytoure knyght! Wyte thou well, sir Launcelot, whan I am hole I shall do batayle with you agayne, for I shall never leve the tylle the tone of us be slayne!'

Thus as thys syge endured and as sir Gawayne lay syke nerehande a moneth, and whan he was well recovirde and redy within three dayes to do batayle agayne with sir Launcelot, ryght so cam tydyngis unto kynge Arthur frome Inglonde that made kynge Arthur and all hys oste to remeve.

The last battle and the death of Arthur

As sir Mordred was rular of all Inglonde, he lete make lettirs as thoughe that they had com from beyonde the see, and the lettirs specifyed that kynge Arthur was slayne in batayle with sir Launcelot. Wherefore sir Mordred made a parlemente, and called the lordys togydir, and ther he made them to chose hym[a] kynge. And so was he crowned at Caunturbyry, and hylde a feste there fiftene dayes.

And aftirwarde he drew hym unto Wynchester, and there he toke quene Gwenyver, and seyde playnly that he wolde wedde her (which was hys unclys wyff and hys fadirs wyff). And so he made redy for the feste, and a day prefyxte that they shulde be wedded; wherefore quene Gwenyver was passyng hevy. But she durst nat discover her harte, but spake fayre, and aggreed to sir Mordredys wylle.

And anone she desyred of sir Mordred to go to London to byghe all maner thynges that[b] longed to the brydale. And bycause of her fayre speche sir Mordred trusted her and gaff her leve; and so whan she cam to London she toke the Towre of London, and suddeynly in all haste possyble she stuffed hit with all maner of vytayle, and well garnysshed hit with men, and so kepte hit.

And whan sir Mordred wyst thys he was passynge wrothe oute of mesure. And shorte tale to make, he layde a myghty syge aboute the Towre and made many assautis, and threw engynnes unto them, and shotte grete gunnes. But all myght nat prevayle, for quene Gwenyver wolde[1] never, for fayre speache nother for foule, never to truste unto sir Mordred to com in hys hondis agayne. Than cam the bysshop of Caunturbyry, whych was a noble clerke and an holy man, and thus he seyde unto sir Mordred: 'Sir, what woll ye do? Woll ye firste displease God and sytthyn shame youreselff and all knyghthode? For ys nat kynge Arthur youre uncle, and no farther but youre modirs brothir, and uppon her he hymselffe begate you, uppon hys owne syster? Therefore how may ye wed youre owne fadirs wyff? And therefor, sir,' seyde the bysshop, 'leve thys opynyon, other ellis I shall curse you with booke, belle and candyll.'[2]

'Do thou thy warste,' seyde sir Mordred, 'and I defyghe the!'

'Sir,' seyde the bysshop, 'wyte you well and I shall nat feare me to do that me ought to do. And also ye noyse that my lorde Arthur ys slayne, and that ys nat so, and therefore ye woll make a foule warke in thys londe.'

'Peas, thou false pryste!' seyde sir Mordred, 'for and thou chauffe[3] me ony more, I shall stryke of thy hede!'

So the bysshop departed, and ded the cursynge in the moste orguluste[4] wyse that myght be done. And than sir Mordred sought the bysshop off Caunturbyry for to have slayne hym. Than the bysshop fledde, and tooke parte of hys good with hym, and wente nyghe unto Glassyngbyry.[5] And there he was a preste-ermyte in a chapel, and lyved in poverte and in holy prayers; for well he undirstood that myschevous warre was at honde.

Than sir Mordred soughte uppon quene Gwenyver by lettirs and sondis,[6] and by fayre meanys and foule meanys, to have her to com oute of the Towre of London; but all thys avayled nought, for she answerd hym shortely, opynly and pryvayly, that she had levir sle herselff than to be maryed with hym.

The last battle and the death of Arthur

1 was willing

2 **booke, belle and candyll**: referring to the closing of the Bible, the ringing of the bell and the quenching of the candle as formal excommunication was pronounced.

3 enrage

4 proudly defiant

5 **Glassyngbyry**. Glastonbury was the holiest site of Arthurian England, reputed to be where Joseph of Arimathaea (an ancestor of Lancelot) brought the Holy Grail.

6 messengers

Than cam ther worde unto sir Mordred that kynge Arthure had areysed the syge from sir Launcelot and was commynge homwarde wyth a greate oste to be avenged uppon sir Mordred, wherefore sir Mordred made wryttes unto all the baronny of thys londe. And muche people drew unto hym; for than was the comyn voyce amonge them that with kynge Arthur was never othir lyff but warre and stryff, and with sir Mordrede was grete joy and blysse. Thus was kynge Arthur depraved,[7] and evyll seyde off; and many there were that kynge Arthur had brought up of nought, and gyffyn them londis, that myght nat than say hym a good worde.

Lo ye all Englysshemen, se ye nat what a myschyff here was?[8] For he that was the moste kynge and nobelyst knyght of the worlde, and moste loved the felyshyp of noble knyghtes, and by hym they all were upholdyn, and yet myght nat thes Englyshemen holde them contente with hym. Lo thus was the olde custom and usayges of thys londe, and men say that we of thys londe have nat yet loste that custom. Alas! thys ys a greate defaughte of us Englysshemen, for there may no thynge us please no terme.[9]

And so fared the peple at that tyme: they were better pleased with sir Mordred than they were with the noble kynge Arthur, and muche people drew unto sir Mordred and seyde they wold abyde wyth hym for bettir and for wars. And so sir Mordred drew with a greate oste to Dovir, for there he harde sey that kyng Arthur wolde aryve, and so he thought to beate hys owne fadir fro hys owne londys. And the moste party of all Inglonde hylde wyth sir Mordred, for the people were so new-fangill.

And so as sir Mordred was at Dovir with hys oste, so cam kyng Arthur wyth a greate navy of shyppis and galyes and carykes,[10] and there was sir Mordred redy awaytyng uppon hys londynge, to lette[11] hys owne fadir to londe uppon the londe that he was kynge over.

Than there was launchyng of greate botis and smale, and full of noble men of armys; and there was muche slaughtir of jantyll knyghtes, and many a full bolde barown was layde full lowe, on bothe partyes.

But kynge Arthur was so currageous that ther myght no maner of knyght lette hym to lande, and hys knyghtes fyersely folowed hym. And so they londed magre sir Mordredis hede, and all hys power, and put sir Mordred abak and all hys people.

So whan thys batayle was done, kynge Arthure let serche[12] hys people that were hurte and dede. And than was noble sir Gawayne founde in a greate boote, liynge more than halff dede. Whan kyng Arthur knew that he was layde so low he wente unto hym and so fownde hym. And there the kynge made greate sorow oute of mesure, and toke sir Gawayne in hys armys, and thryse he there sowned. And than whan he was waked, kyng Arthur seyde, 'Alas! sir Gawayne, my syster son, here now thou lyghest, the man in the worlde that I loved moste. And now ys my joy gone. For now, my nevew, sir Gawayne, I woll discover me unto you, that[c] in youre person and in sir Launcelot I moste had my joy and myne affyaunce. And now have I loste my joy of you bothe, wherefore all myne erthely joy ys gone fro me!'

'A, myn uncle,' seyde sir Gawayne, 'now I woll that ye wyte that my deth-dayes be com. And all I may wyte[13] myne owne hastynes and my wylfulnesse, for thorow my wylfulnes I was causer of myne owne dethe; for I was thys day hurte and smytten uppon myne olde wounde that sir Launcelot gaff me, and I fele myselff that I muste nedis be dede by the owre of noone. And thorow me and my[d] pryde ye have all thys shame and disease,[14] for had that noble knyght, sir Launcelot, ben with you, as he was and wolde have ben, thys unhappy warre had never ben begunne; for he, thorow hys noble knyghthode and hys noble bloode, hylde all youre cankyrde enemyes in subjeccion and daungere.[15] And now,' seyde sir Gawayne, 'ye shall mysse sir Launcelot. But alas that I wolde nat accorde with hym! And therefore,[e] fayre unkle, I pray you that I may have papir, penne, and inke, that I may wryte unto sir Launcelot a letter wrytten with myne owne honde.'[16]

So whan paper, penne and inke was brought, than sir Gawayne was sette up waykely by kynge Arthure, for he was shryven a lytyll afore. And than he toke hys penne and wrote thus, as the Freynshe booke

7 defamed

8 Malory's normal style is reticence and understatement: this is one of his rare intrusions into the narrative.

9 for a long time

10 carracks

11 prevent

12 caused to be tended

13 blame

14 distress

15 fear of his power

16 The text of the letter is supplied by Malory, so that he can stress the personal responsibility that Gawain takes for his actions; in the French there are only the usual lamentations about fate and fortune. The importance of the letter is indicated, most unusually, by an ornamental heading or rubric in the margin of the MS.

makith mencion: 'Unto the, sir Launcelot, floure of all noble knyghtes that ever I harde of or saw be my dayes, I, sir Gawayne, kynge Lottis sonne of Orkeney, and systirs sonne unto the noble kynge Arthur, sende the gretynge, lattynge the to have knowlecche that the tenth day of May I was smytten uppon the olde wounde that thou gaff me afore the cite of Benwyke,[17] and thorow that wounde I am com to my dethe-day. And I woll that all the worlde wyte that I, sir Gawayne, knyght of the Table Rounde, soughte thy[f] dethe, and nat thorow thy deservynge, but myne owne sekynge. Wherefore I beseche the, sir Launcelot, to returne agayne unto thys realme and se my toumbe and pray som prayer, more other les, for my soule. And thys same day that I wrote this same sedull[18] I was hurte to the dethe, whych wounde was fyrste gyffyn of thyn honde, sir Launcelot; for of a more nobelar man myght I nat be slayne.

'Also, sir Launcelot, for all the love that ever was betwyxte us, make no taryyng, but com over the see in all the goodly haste that ye may, wyth youre noble knyghtes, and rescow that noble kynge that made the knyght, for he ys full straytely bestad[19] wyth an false traytoure whych ys my halff-brothir, sir Mordred. For he hath crowned hymselff kynge, and wolde have wedded my lady, quene Gwenyver; and so had he done, had she nat kepte the Towre of London with stronge honde. And so the tenth day of May last past my lorde kynge Arthur and we all londed uppon them at Dover, and there he put that false traytoure, sir Mordred, to flyght. And so hit there mysfortuned me to be smytten uppon the strooke that ye gaff me of olde.

'And the date of thys lettir was wrytten but two owrys and an halff afore my dethe, wrytten with myne owne honde and subscrybed with parte of my harte blood. And therfore I requyre[20] the, moste famous knyght of the worlde, that thou wolt se my tumbe.'

And than he wepte, and kynge Arthur both, and sowned. And whan they were awaked bothe, the kynge made sir Gawayne to resceyve hys sacrament, and than sir Gawayne prayde the kynge for to sende for sir Launcelot and to cherysshe hym aboven all othir knyghtes.

And so at the owre of noone sir Gawayne yelded up the goste. And than the kynge lat entere[21] hym in a chapell within Dover castell. And ther yet all men may se the skulle of hym, and the same wounde is sene that sir Launcelot gaff in batayle.[22]

Than was hit tolde the kynge that sir Mordred had pyght[23] a new fylde uppon Bareon Downe.[24] And so uppon the morne kynge Arthur rode thydir to hym, and there was a grete batayle betwyxt hem, and muche people were slayne on bothe partyes. But at the laste kynge Arthurs party stoode beste, and sir Mordred and hys party fledde unto Caunturbyry.

And than the kynge let serche all the downys for hys knyghtes that were slayne and entered them; and salved them with soffte salvys that full sore were wounded. Than much people drew unto kynge Arthur, and than they sayde that sir Mordred warred uppon kynge Arthure wyth wronge.

And anone kynge Arthure drew hym wyth his oste downe by the see-syde westewarde, towarde Salusbyry. And there was a day assygned betwyxte kynge Arthur and sir Mordred, that they shulde mete uppon a downe besyde Salesbyry and nat farre from the see-syde. And thys day was assygned on Monday aftir Trynyte Sonday, whereof kynge Arthur was passyng glad that he myght be avenged uppon sir Mordred.

Than sir Mordred araysed muche people aboute London, for they of Kente, Southsex[25] and Surrey, Esax, Suffolke and Northefolke helde the moste party with sir Mordred. And many a full noble knyght drew unto hym and also the kynge; but they that loved sir Launcelot drew unto sir Mordred.

So uppon Trynyte Sunday at nyght kynge Arthure dremed a wondirfull dreme, and in hys dreme hym semed that he saw uppon a chafflet a chayre,[26] and the chayre was faste to a whele,[27] and theruppon sate

17 It is important to Gawain's sense of self-esteem and 'worship' that he should claim to have died, even at one remove, by the hand of Lancelot.

18 document

19 sorely pressed

20 request

21 inter

22 The presence of Gawain's skull in Dover Castle is mentioned in Caxton's Preface (see below) as a proof of the historical veracity of the Arthurian story.

23 encamped upon

24 Barham Down, 6 miles south-east of Canterbury.

25 **Southsex**: Sussex. It is often thought that Malory uses such place-names in allusion to contemporary wars and allegiances: these southeastern counties, for instance, were an important source of support for the Yorkist party during the Wars of the Roses.

26 upon a platform a throne

27 For the wheel of Fortune, see note above.

kynge Arthure in the rychest[g] clothe of golde that myght be made. And the kynge thought there was undir hym, farre from hym, an hydeous depe blak watir, and therein was all maner of serpentis and wormes and wylde bestis fowle and orryble. And suddeynly the kynge thought that the whyle turned up-so-downe, and he felle amonge the serpentis, and every beste toke hym by a lymme. And than the kynge cryed as he lay in hys bed, 'Helpe! helpe!'

And than knyghtes, squyars and yomen awaked the kynge, and than he was so amased that he wyste nat where he was. And than so he awaked[28] untylle hit was nyghe day, and than he felle on slumberynge agayne, nat slepynge nor thorowly wakynge.

So the kyng semed[29] verryly that ther cam sir Gawayne unto hym with a numbir of fayre ladyes wyth hym. So whan kyng Arthur saw hym he seyde, 'Wellcom, my systers sonne, I wende ye had bene dede! And now I se the on lyve, much am I beholdyn unto Allmyghty Jesu. A, fayre nevew, what bene thes ladyes that hyder be com with you?'

'Sir,' seyde sir Gawayne, 'all thes be ladyes for whom I have foughten for, whan I was man lyvynge. And all thes ar tho that I ded batayle for in ryghteuous quarels, and God hath gyvyn hem that grace at ther grete prayer, bycause I ded batayle for them[h] for ther ryght, that they shulde brynge me hydder unto you. Thus much hath gyvyn me leve God for to warne you of youre dethe: for and ye fyght as to-morne with sir Mordred, as ye bothe have assygned, doute ye nat ye shall be slayne, and the moste party of youre people on bothe partyes. And for the grete grace and goodnes that Allmyghty Jesu hath unto you, and for pyte of you and many mo other good men there shall be slayne, God[i] hath sente me to you of hys speciall grace to gyff you warnyng that in no wyse ye do batayle as to-morne, but that ye take a tretyse[30] for a moneth-day. And proffir you largely,[31] so that to-morne ye put in a delay. For within a moneth shall com sir Launcelot with all hys noble knyghtes, and rescow you worshypfully, and sle sir Mordred and all that ever wyll holde wyth hym.'

Than sir Gawayne and all the ladyes vanysshed, and anone the kynge called uppon hys knyghtes, squyars and yomen, and charged them wyghtly[32] to fecche hys noble lordis and wyse bysshoppis unto hym. And whan they were com the kynge tolde hem of hys avision: that sir Gawayne had tolde hym and warned hym that, and he fought on the morn, he sholde be slayne. Than the kynge commaunded sir Lucan the Butlere and hys brothir sir Bedyvere the Bolde, with two bysshoppis wyth hem, and charged them in ony wyse[33] to take a tretyse for a moneth-day wyth sir Mordred: 'And spare nat, proffir hym londys and goodys as much as ye thynke resonable.'

So than they departed and cam to sir Mordred where he had a grymme oste of an hondred thousand, and there they entretyd sir Mordred longe tyme. And at the laste sir Mordred was aggreed for to have Cornwale and Kente by[34] kynge Arthurs dayes; and afftir that all Inglonde, after the dayes of kynge Arthur.[35]

Than were they condescende[36] that kynge Arthure and sir Mordred shulde mete betwyxte bothe ther ostis, and everych of them shulde brynge fourtene persons. And so they cam wyth thys worde unto Arthur. Than seyde he, 'I am glad that thys ys done'; and so he wente into the fylde.

And whan kynge Arthur shulde departe he warned all hys oost[j] that, and they se ony swerde drawyn, 'Loke ye com on fyersely and sle that traytoure, sir Mordred, for I[k] in no wyse truste hym'.

In lyke wyse sir Mordred warned hys oste that 'And ye se ony maner of swerde drawyn, loke that ye com on fyersely and so sle all that ever before you stondyth, for in no wyse I woll nat truste for thys tretyse'. And in the same wyse seyde sir Mordred unto hys oste, 'For I know well my fadir woll be avenged uppon me.'

And so they mette as ther poyntemente was, and were agreed and accorded thorowly. And wyne was fette,[37] and they[l] dranke togydir. Ryght so cam oute an addir of a lytyll hethe-buysshe, and hit stange a

28 lay awake
29 thought
30 truce
31 be prepared to make a generous offer of terms
32 directly
33 at all costs
34 during
35 Mordred is offered what he may well, as Arthur's only acknowledged son, think to be his due. He remains a shadowy figure in Malory, not ignoble, and the beneficiary of an older Scottish tradition in which his claim to the throne was much stronger. The cunning Machiavel of Tennyson and the psychopath of T.H. White are far in the future.
36 agreed
37 fetched

knyght in the foote. And so whan the knyght felte hym so stonge, he loked downe and saw the adder; and anone he drew hys swerde to sle the addir, and thought none othir harme. And whan the oste on bothe partyes saw that swerde drawyn, than they blewe beamys,[38] trumpettis and hornys, and shoutted grymly, and so bothe ostis dressed hem[39] togydirs. And kynge Arthur toke hys horse and seyde, 'Alas, this unhappy day!' and so rode to hys party, and sir Mordred in lyke wyse.

And never syns was ther never seyne a more dolefuller batayle in no Crysten londe, for there was but russhynge and rydynge, foynynge and strykynge, and many a grym worde was ther spokyn of aythir to othir, and many a dedely stroke. But ever kynge Arthure rode thorow-oute the batayle[40] of sir Mordred many tymys and ded full nobely, as a noble kynge shulde do, and at all tymes he faynted[41] never. And sir Mordred ded hys devoure[42] that day and put hymselffe in grete perell.

And thus they fought all the longe day, and never stynted tylle the noble knyghtes were layde to the colde erthe. And ever they fought stylle tylle hit was nere nyght, and by than was ther an hondred thousand leyde dede uppon the erthe. Than was kynge Arthure wode wroth oute of mesure, whan he saw hys people so slayne from hym. And so he loked aboute hym and cowde se no mo of all hys oste and good knyghtes leffte no mo on lyve but two knyghtes: the tone was sir Lucan de Buttler and hys brother, sir Bedwere; and yette they were full sore wounded.

'Jesu mercy!' seyde the kynge, 'where ar all my noble knyghtes becom? Alas, that ever I shulde se thys doleful day! For now', seyde kynge Arthur, 'I am com to myne ende. But wolde to God,' seyde he, 'that I wyste now where were that traytoure sir Mordred that hath caused all thys myschyff.'

Than kynge Arthur loked aboute and was ware where stood sir Mordred leanyng uppon hys swerde amonge a grete hepe of dede men. 'Now gyff me my speare,' seyde kynge Arthure unto sir Lucan, 'for yondir I have aspyed the traytoure that all thys woo hath wrought.'

'Sir, latte hym be,' seyde sir Lucan, 'for he ys unhappy.[43] And yf ye passe this unhappy day ye shall[m] be ryght well revenged. And, good lord, remembre ye of your nyghtes dreme and[n] what the spyryte of sir Gawayne tolde you tonyght, and yet God of hys grete goodnes hath preserved you hyddirto. And for Goddes sake, my lorde, leve of thys, for, blyssed be God, ye have won the fylde: for yet we ben here three on lyve, and with sir Mordred ys nat one on lyve. And therfore if ye leve of now, thys wycked day of desteny ys past!'

'Now tyde[44] me dethe, tyde me lyff,' seyde the kyng, 'now I se hym yondir alone, he shall never ascape myne hondes! For at a bettir avayle shall I never have hym.'

'God spede you well!' seyde sir Bedyvere.

Than the kynge gate his speare in bothe hys hondis and ran towarde sir Mordred, cryyng and saying, 'Traytoure, now ys thy dethe-day com!'

And whan sir Mordred saw kynge Arthur he ran untyll hym with hys swerde drawyn in hys honde, and there kyng Arthur smote sir Mordred undir the shylde, with a foyne[45] of hys speare, thorow-oute the body more than a fadom. And whan sir Mordred felte that he had hys dethys wounde he threste hymselff with the myght that he had upp to the burre[46] of kyng Arthurs spear, and ryght so he smote hys fadir, kynge Arthure, with hys swerde holdynge in both hys hondys, uppon the syde of the hede, that the swerde perced the helmet and the tay[47] of the brayne. And therewith Mordred daysshed downe starke dede to the erthe.

And noble kynge Arthure felle in a swoughe to the erthe, and ther he sowned oftyntymys, and sir Lucan and sir Bedwere offtetymys hove hym up. And so waykly betwyxte them they lad hym to a lytyll chapell nat farre from the see, and whan the kyng was there, hym thought hym resonabely eased.

Than harde they people crye in the fylde. 'Now go thou, sir Lucan,' seyde the kyng, 'and do me to wyte what betokyns that noyse in the fylde.'

So sir Lucan departed, for he was grevously wounded in many placis; and so as he yode[48] he saw and

38 trumpets
39 arrayed themselves for battle
40 army
41 flinched
42 duty
43 cause of ill-luck
44 betide
45 thrust
46 hand-guard
47 outer membrane
48 went

harkened by the moonelyght how that pyllours[49] and robbers were com into the fylde to pylle and to robbe many a full noble knyght of brochys and bees[50] and of many a good rynge and many a ryche juell. And who that were nat dede all oute, there they slewe them for ther harneys and ther ryches.

Whan sir Lucan undirstood thys warke he cam to the kynge as sone as he myght and tolde hym all what he had harde and seyne. 'Therefore, be my rede,'[51] seyde sir Lucan, 'hit ys beste that we brynge you to som towne.'

'I wolde hit were so,' seyde the kynge, 'but I may nat stonde, my hede worchys so. A, sir Launcelot!' seyde kynge Arthure, 'thys day have I sore myssed the! And alas, that ever I was ayenste the! For now have I my dethe, whereof sir Gawayne me warned in my dreame.'

Than sir Lucan toke up the kynge the tone party and sir Bedwere the othir parte, and in the lyfftyng up the kynge sowned, and in the lyfftynge sir Lucan felle in a sowne, that parte of hys guttis felle oute of hys body, and therewith the noble knyght hys harte braste. And whan the kynge awoke he behylde sir Lucan, how he lay fomyng at the mowth and parte of his guttes lay at hys fyete.

'Alas,' seyde the kynge, 'thys ys to me a fulle hevy syght, to se thys noble deuke so dye for my sake, for he wold have holpyn me that had more nede of helpe than I! Alas, that he wolde nat complayne hym, for hys harte was so sette to helpe me. Now Jesu have mercy uppon hys soule!'

Than sir Bedwere wepte for the deth of hys brothir.

'Now leve thys mournynge and wepyng, jantyll knyght,' seyde the kyng, 'for all thys woll nat avayle me. For wyte thou well, and I myght lyve myselff, the dethe of sir Lucan wolde greve me evermore. But my tyme passyth on faste,' seyde the kynge. 'Therefore,' seyde kynge Arthur unto sir Bedwere, 'take thou here Excaliber, my good swerde, and go wyth hit to yondir watirs syde; and whan thou commyst there, I charge the throw my swerde in that water,[52] and com agayne and telle me what thou syest there.'

'My lorde,' seyde sir Bedwere, 'youre commaundement shall be done, and lyghtly brynge you worde agayne.'

So sir Bedwere departed. And by the way he behylde that noble swerde, and the pomell and the hauffte was all precious stonys. And than he seyde to hymselff, 'If I throw thys ryche swerde in the water, thereof shall never com good, but harme and losse.' And than sir Bedwere hyd Excalyber undir a tre, and so as sone as he myght he cam agayne unto the kynge and seyde he had bene at the watir and had throwen the swerde into the watir.

'What sawe thou there?' seyde the kynge.

'Sir,' he seyde, 'I[o] saw nothyng but wawis and wyndys.'

'That ys untruly seyde of the,' seyde the kynge. 'And therefore go thou lyghtly agayne, and do my commaundemente; as thou art to me leve[p] and dere, spare nat, but throw hit in.'

Than sir Bedwere returned agayne and toke the swerde in hys honde; and yet hym thought synne and shame to throw away that noble swerde. And so effte[53] he hyd the swerde and returned agayne and tolde the kynge that he had bene at the watir and done hys commaundement.

'What sawist thou there?' seyde the kynge.

'Sir,' he seyde, 'I sy nothynge but watirs wap and wawys wanne.'[54]

'A, traytour unto me and untrew!' seyde kyng Arthure; 'now hast thou betrayed me twyse! Who wolde wene that thou that hast bene to me so leve and dere, and also named so noble a knyght, that thou wolde betray me for the ryches of thys swerde? But now go agayn lyghtly; for thy longe taryynge puttith me in grete jouperte of my lyff, for I have takyn colde. And but if thou do now as I bydde the, if ever I may se the, I shall sle the myne owne hondis, for thou woldist for my rych swerde se me dede.'

Than sir Bedwere departed and wente to the swerde and lyghtly toke hit up, and so he wente unto the watirs syde. And there he bounde the gyrdyll[55] aboute the hyltis, and threw the swerde as farre into the watir as he myght. And there cam an arme and an honde above the watir, and toke hit and cleyght[56] hit,

49 **pyllours**: pillagers. This scene is symbolic and graphically expressive of the return of lawlessness to the land that Arthur had tamed. Malory, characteristically, leaves the scene to speak for itself.

50 bracelets

51 advice

52 Arthur knows that he must repeat, in reverse, the procedure by which he first received the sword Excalibur at the hands of the Lady of the Lake (the 'sword in the stone' was a different sword, kept for ceremonial purposes, and not used in battle).

53 again

54 waters lap and dark waves

55 strap

56 clasped

and shoke hit thryse and braundysshed, and than vanysshed with the swerde into the watir.

So sir Bedyvere cam agayne to the kynge and tolde hym what he saw.

'Alas,' seyde the kynge, 'helpe me hens, for I drede me I have taryed over-longe.'

Than sir Bedwere toke the kynge uppon hys bak and so wente with hym to the watirs syde. And whan they were there, evyn faste by the banke hoved a lytyll barge wyth many fayre ladyes in hit, and amonge hem all was a quene, and all they had blak hoodis. And all they wepte and shryked whan they saw kynge Arthur.

'Now put me into that barge,' seyde the kynge.

And so he ded sofftely, and there resceyved hym three ladyes with grete mournyng.[57] And so they sette hem downe, and in one of ther lappis kyng Arthure layde hys hede. And than the quene seyde, 'A, my dere brothir! Why have ye taryed so longe from me? Alas, thys wounde on youre hede hath caught overmuch coulde!'

And anone they rowed fromward the londe, and sir Bedyvere behylde all tho ladyes go frowarde hym. Than sir Bedwere cryed and seyde, 'A, my lorde Arthur, what shall becom of me now ye go from me and leve me here alone amonge myne enemyes?'

'Comforte thyselff,' seyde the kynge, 'and do as well as thou mayst, for in me ys no truste for to truste in. For I muste into the vale of Avylyon to hele me of my grevous wounde. And if thou here nevermore of me, pray for my soule!'

But ever the quene and ladyes wepte and shryked, that hit was pite to hyre. And as sone as sir Bedwere had loste the syght of the barge he wepte and wayled, and so toke the foreste and wente all that nyght.

And in the mornyng he was ware, betwyxte two holtis hore,[58] of a chapell and an ermytage. Than was sir Bedwere fayne,[59] and thyder he wente, and whan he cam into the chapell he saw where lay an ermyte grovelynge on all four, faste there by a tumbe was newe gravyn. Whan the ermyte saw sir Bedyvere he knewe hym well, for he was but lytyll tofore bysshop of Caunturbery that sir Mordred fleamed.[60]

'Sir,' seyde sir Bedyvere, 'what man ys there here entyred[61] that ye pray so faste for?'

'Fayre sunne,' seyde the ermyte, 'I wote nat veryly, but by demynge. But thys same nyght, at mydnyght, here cam a numbir of ladyes and brought here a dede corse and prayde me to entyre hym. And here they offird an hondred tapers, and they gaff me a thousande besauntes.'

'Alas!' seyde sir Bedyvere, 'that was my lorde[q] kynge Arthur whych lyethe here gravyn in thys chapell.'

Than sir Bedwere sowned, and whan he awooke he prayde the ermyte that he myght abyde with hym stylle, there to lyve with fastynge and prayers: 'For from hens woll I never go,' seyde sir Bedyvere, 'be my wyll,[62] but all the dayes of my lyff here to pray for my lorde Arthur.'

'Sir, ye ar wellcom to me,' seyde the ermyte, 'for I know you bettir than ye wene that I do: for ye ar sir Bedwere the Bolde, and the full noble duke sir Lucan de Butlere was your[r] brother.'

Than sir Bedwere tolde the ermyte all as ye have harde tofore, and so he belaffte[63] with the ermyte that was beforehande bysshop of Caunturbyry. And there sir Bedwere put uppon hym poure clothys, and served the ermyte full lowly in fastyng and in prayers.

Thus of Arthur I fynde no more wrytten in bokis that bene auctorysed,[64] nothir more of the verry sertaynte of hys dethe harde I never rede, but thus was he lad away in a shyp wherein were three quenys: that one was kynge Arthur syster, quene Morgan le Fay, the tother was the quene of North Galis, and the thirde was the quene of the Waste Londis. Also there was dame Nynyve, the chyff lady of the lake, whych had wedded sir Pellyas, the good knyght; and thys lady had done muche for kynge Arthure. (And thys dame Nynyve wolde never suffir sir Pelleas to be in no place where he shulde be in daungere of hys lyff, and so he lyved unto the uttermuste of hys dayes with her in grete reste.)

Now more of the deth of kynge Arthur coude I never fynde but that thes ladyes brought hym to hys grave, and such one was entyred there whych the ermyte[s] bare wytnes that sometyme was bysshop of Caunturbyry. But yet the ermyte knew nat in sertayne that he was veryly the body of kynge

57 The **three ladyes** are named later. Their role is partly to echo the appearance of the three Maries at the Crucifixion and Resurrection.

58 gray woods

59 glad

60 sent into exile

61 interred

62 voluntarily

63 remained

64 **auctorysed**: of authority. Malory adds here his own account, from non-French sources, of the circumstances of Arthur's death and the legend of his survival.

Arthur; for thys tale sir Bedwere, a knyght of the Table Rounde, made hit to be wrytten.[65]

Yet som men say in many partys of Inglonde that kynge Arthure ys nat dede, but had by the wyll of oure Lorde Jesu into another place; and men say that he shall com agayne, and he shall wynne the Holy Crosse. Yet I woll nat say that hit shall be so, but rather I wolde sey: here in thys worlde he chaunged hys lyff.[66] And many men say that there ys wrytten uppon the tumbe thys:

HIC JACET ARTHURUS, REX QUONDAM REXQUE FUTURUS.[67]

And thus leve I here sir Bedyvere with the ermyte that dwelled that tyme in a chapell besydes Glassyngbyry, and there was hys ermytage. And so they lyved in prayers and fastynges and grete abstynaunce.

And whan quene Gwenyver undirstood that kynge Arthure was dede and all the noble knyghtes, sir Mordred and all the remanaunte, than she stale away with fyve ladyes with her, and so she wente to Amysbyry. And there she lete make herselff a nunne, and wered whyght clothys and blak, and grete penaunce she toke uppon her as ever ded synfull woman in thys londe. And never creature coude make her myry, but ever she lyved in fastynge, prayers, and almes-dedis, that all maner of people mervayled how vertuously she was chaunged.

The death of Guenevere and of Lancelot

Now leve we the quene in Amysbery, a nunne in whyght clothys and blak – and ther she was abbas and rular, as reson wolde – and now turne we from her and speke we of sir Launcelot du Lake, that whan he harde in hys contrey that sir Mordred was crowned kynge in Inglonde and made warre ayenst kyng Arthur, hys owne fadir, and wolde lette hym to londe in hys owne londe (also hit was tolde hym how sir Mordred had leyde a syge aboute the Towre of London, bycause the quene wold nat wedde hym), than was sir Launcelot wrothe oute of mesure and seyde to hys kynnesmen, 'Alas! that double traytoure, sir Mordred, now me repentith that ever he ascaped my hondys, for much shame hath he done unto my[a] lorde Arthure. For I fele by thys dolefull letter that sir Gawayne sente me, on whos soule Jesu have mercy, that my lorde Arthur ys full harde bestad. Alas,' seyde sir Launcelot, 'that ever I shulde lyve to hyre of that moste noble kynge that made me knyght thus to be oversette with hys subjette in hys owne realme! And this dolefull lettir that my lorde sir Gawayne hath sente me afore hys dethe, praynge me to se hys tumbe, wyte you well hys doleffull wordes shall never go from my harte, for he was a full noble knyght as ever was born, and in an unhappy owre was I born that ever I shulde have that myssehappe to sle firste sir Gawayne, sir Gaherys, the good knyght, and myne owne frynde sir Gareth, that was a full noble knyght. Now, alas, I may sey I am unhappy that[b] ever I shulde do thus. And yet, alas, myght I never have hap[1] to sle that traytoure, sir Mordred!'

'Now leve youre complayntes,' seyde sir Bors, 'and firste revenge you of the dethe of sir Gawayne, on whos soule Jesu have mercy! And hit woll be well done that ye se hys tumbe, and secundly that ye revenge my lorde Arthur and my lady quene Gwenyver.'

'I thanke you,' seyde sir Launcelot, 'for ever ye woll my worshyp.'[2]

Than they made hem redy in all haste that myght be, with shyppis and galyes, with hym and hys oste to pas into Inglonde. And so at the laste he cam to Dover, and there he landed with seven kyngis, and the numbir was hedeous to beholde.

Than sir Launcelot spyrred[3] of men of Dover where was the kynge becom. And anone the people tolde hym how he was slayne and sir Mordred to, with an hondred thousand that dyed uppon a day; and how sir Mordred gaff kynge Arthur the first batayle there at hys londynge, and there was sir Gawayne slayne.

65 Bedevere's role in providing the written record (and also in being momentarily unfaithful, like Peter, to his lord) echoes that of the apostles.

66 **he chaunged hys lyff**: the phrasing is deliberately enigmatic.

67 'Here lies Arthur, the once and future king.' Written in red, in a formal hand, in the MS. That Arthur was buried in Glastonbury was a belief well established in England: his skeleton was ceremonially disinterred (and found to be that of an unusually tall man) in the presence of Henry II and reburied, according to Giraldus Cambrensis, writing 1193–9. The legend that he would one day return was likewise cherished, appearing first in written form in the *Brut*, or chronicle of Britain, of the English poet Layamon (*c.* 1250).

The death of Guenevere and of Lancelot

1 the good fortune

2 want what is most honourable for me

3 asked

'And uppon the morne sir Mordred faught with the kynge on Baram Downe and there the kyng put sir Mordred to the wars.'[4]

'Alas,' seyde sir Launcelot, 'thys is the hevyest tydyngis that ever cam to[5] my harte! Now, fayre sirres,' seyde sir Launcelot, 'shew me the tumbe of sir Gawayne.'

And anone he was brought into the castel of Dover, and so they shewed hym the tumbe. Than sir Launcelot kneled downe by the tumbe and wepte, and prayde hartely for hys soule. And that nyght he lete make a dole,[6] and all[c] that wolde com of the towne or of the contrey they had as much[7] fleyssh and fysshe and wyne and ale, and every man and woman he dalt to twelve pence, com whoso wolde. Thus with hys owne honde dalte he thys money, in a mournyng gown; and ever he wepte hartely and prayde the people to pray for the soule of sir Gawayne.

And on the morn all the prystes and clarkes that myght be gotyn in the contrey and in the town were there, and sange massis of Requiem. And there offird first sir Launcelot, and he offird an hondred pounde,[8] and than the seven kynges offirde, and every of them offirde fourty pounde. Also there was a thousand knyghtes, and every of them offirde a pounde; and the offeryng dured fro the morne to nyght.

And there sir Launcelot lay two nyghtes uppon hys tumbe, in prayers and in dolefull wepynge. Than, on the thirde day, sir Launcelot called the kyngis, deukes and erlis, with the barownes and all hys noble knyghtes, and seyde thus: 'My fayre lordis, I thanke you all of youre comynge into thys contrey with me. But wyte you well all, we ar com to late, and that shall repente me whyle I lyve, but ayenste deth may no man rebell. But sytthyn hit ys so,' seyde sir Launcelot, 'I woll myselffe ryde and syke my lady, quene Gwenyver. For, as I here sey, she hath had grete payne and muche disease, and I here say that she ys fledde into the weste. And therfore ye all shall abyde me here, and but if I com agayne within thes fyftene dayes, take youre shyppis and youre felyship, and departe into youre contrey, for I woll do as I sey you.'

Than cam sir Bors and seyde, 'My lorde, sir Launcelot, what thynke ye for to do, now for to ryde in thys realme? Wyte you well ye shall do fynde feaw fryndis.'

'Be as be may as for that,' seyde sir Launcelot. 'Kepe you stylle here, for I woll furthe on my journey, and no man nor chylde shall go with me.'

So hit was no boote to stryve, but he departed and rode westirly; and there he sought a seven or eyght dayes. And at the laste he cam to a nunry, and anone quene Gwenyver was ware of sir Launcelot as she walked in the cloyster. And anone as she saw hym there, she sowned thryse, that all ladyes and jantyllwomen had worke inowghe to hold the quene from the erthe. So whan she myght speke she called her ladyes and jantillwomen to her, and than she sayde thus: 'Ye mervayle, fayre ladyes, why I make thys fare.[9] Truly,' she seyde, 'hit ys for the syght of yondir knyght that yondir stondith. Wherefore I pray you calle hym hyddir to me.'

Than sir Launcelot was brought before her; than the quene seyde to all tho ladyes, 'Thorow thys same man and me hath all thys warre be wrought, and the deth of the moste nobelest knyghtes of the worlde; for thorow oure love that we have loved togydir ys my moste noble lorde slayne. Therefore, sir Launcelot, wyte thou well I am sette in suche a plyght to gete my soule helthe. And yet I truste, thorow Goddis grace and thorow hys passion of hys woundis wyde, that aftir my deth I may have a syght of the blyssed face of Cryste Jesu, and on Doomesday to sytte on hys ryght syde;[10] for as synfull as ever I was now ar seyntes in hevyn. And therefore, sir Launcelot, I requyre the and beseche the hartily, for all the love that ever was betwyxt us, that thou never se me no more in the visayge. And I commaunde the, on Goddis behalff, that thou forsake my company. And to thy kyngedom loke thou turne agayne, and kepe well thy realme from warre and wrake,[11] for as well as I have loved the heretofore, myne harte woll nat serve now to se the; for thorow the and me ys the floure of kyngis and knyghtes[d] destroyed. And therfore go thou

4 worse

5 to in this line is supplied, having been lost in one of the worm-holes which are frequent in these last pages of the MS. Most of the letters and words that are lost are able to be confidently supplied by conjecture.

6 distribution of gifts

7 an equal amount of

8 The colossal sums offered in pious observance, like the somewhat treacly piety of these last episodes (all added to the original Arthurian material by the compilers of the Vulgate cycle), have an obvious relation to the monastic origins of the cycle.

9 behave thus

10 **on hys ryght syde**, i.e. on the side allocated to those who are to be saved.

11 strife

to thy realme, and there take ye a wyff, and lyff with hir wyth joy and blys. And I pray the hartely to pray for me to the everlastynge Lorde that I may amende my mysse-lyvyng.'

'Now, my swete madame,' seyde sir Launcelot, 'wolde ye that I shuld turne agayne unto my contrey and there to wedde a lady? Nay madame, wyte you well that shall I never do, for I shall never be so false unto you of that I have promysed. But the selff desteny that ye have takyn you to, I woll take me to, for the pleasure of Jesu, and ever for you I caste me[12] specially to pray.'

'A, sir Launcelot, if ye woll do so and holde thy promyse! But I may never beleve you,' seyde the quene, 'but that ye woll turne to the worlde agayne.'

'Well, madame,' seyde he, 'ye say as hit pleasith you, for yet wyste ye me never false of my promyse. And God deffende but that I shulde forsake the worlde as ye have done! For in the queste of the Sankgreall I had that tyme forsakyn the vanytees of the worlde, had nat youre love bene. And if I had done so at that tyme with my harte, wylle and thought, I had passed all the knyghtes that ever were in the Sankgreall[13] excepte syr Galahad, my sone. And therfore, lady, sythen ye have taken you to perfeccion, I must nedys take me to perfection, of ryght. For I take recorde of God, in you I have had myn erthly joye, and yf I had founden you now so dysposed, I had caste me to have had you into myn owne royame. But sythen I fynde you thus desposed, I ensure you faythfully I wyl ever take me to penaunce and praye whyle my lyf lasteth, yf that I may fynde ony heremyte, other graye or whyte,[14] that wyl receyve me. Wherfore, madame, I praye you kysse me, and never no more.'[15]

'Nay,' sayd the quene, 'that shal I never do, but absteyne you from suche werkes.'

And they departed; but there was never so harde an herted man but he wold have wepte to see the dolour that they made, for there was lamentacyon as they had be stungyn wyth sperys, and many tymes they swouned. And the ladyes bare the quene to hir chambre.

And syr Launcelot awok, and went and took his hors, and rode al that day and al nyght in a forest, wepyng. And atte last he was ware of an ermytage and a chappel stode betwyxte two clyffes, and than he herde a lytel belle rynge to masse. And thyder he rode and alyght, and teyed his hors to the gate, and herd masse.

And he that sange masse was the bysshop of Caunterburye. Bothe the bysshop and sir Bedwer knewe syr Launcelot, and they spake togyders after masse. But whan syr Bedwere had tolde his tale al hole, syr Launcelottes hert almost braste for sorowe, and sir Launcelot threwe hys armes abrode, and sayd, 'Alas! who may truste thys world?'

And than he knelyd doun on his knee and prayed the bysshop to shryve hym and assoyle hym; and than he besought the bysshop that he myght be hys brother. Than the bysshop sayd, 'I wyll gladly', and there he put an habyte upon syr Launcelot. And there he servyd God day and nyght with prayers and fastynges.

Thus the grete hoost abode at Dover. And than sir Lyonel toke fyftene lordes with hym and rode to London to seke sir Launcelot; and there syr Lyonel was slayn and many of his lordes. Thenne syr Bors de Ganys made the grete hoost for to goo hoome ageyn, and syr Boors, syr Ector de Maris, syr Blamour, syr Bleoberis, with moo other of syr Launcelottes kynne, toke on hem to ryde al Englond overthwart and endelonge to seek syr Launcelot.

So syr Bors by fortune rode so longe tyl he came to the same chapel where syr Launcelot was. And so syr Bors herde a lytel belle knylle that range to masse, and there he alyght and herde masse. And whan masse was doon, the bysshop, syr Launcelot and sir Bedwere came to syr Bors, and whan syr Bors sawe sir Launcelot in that maner clothyng, than he preyed the bysshop that he myght be in the same sewte. And so there was an habyte put upon hym, and there he lyved in prayers and fastyng.

And wythin halfe a yere there was come syr Galyhud, syr Galyhodyn, sir Blamour, syr Bleoberis, syr Wyllyars, syr Clarrus, and sir Gahallantyne. So al these seven noble knyghtes there abode styll. And whan they sawe syr Launcelot had taken hym to suche perfeccion they had no lust[e] to departe but toke such an habyte as he had.

12 intend

13 **Sankgreall**. This is the last word of the text in the Winchester MS (apart from the catchword 'except'), the last few pages being missing. The remainder of the text is supplied here from Caxton's print.

14 **other graye or whyte**: either Franciscan or Carmelite.

15 This whole scene of their last meeting, potentially awash with sentimentality, is handled with beautiful restraint by Malory (compare Henryson's handling of the meeting between Troilus and Cresseid in the *Testament*).

Thus they endured in grete penaunce syx yere. And than syr Launcelot took th'abyte of preesthode of the bysshop, and a twelve-monthe he sange masse. And there was none of these other knyghtes but they redde in bookes and holpe for to synge masse, and range bellys, and dyd lowly al maner of servyce. And soo ther horses wente where they wolde,[16] for they toke no regarde of no worldly rychesses; for whan they sawe syr Launcelot endure suche penaunce in prayers and fastynges they toke no force what payne they endured, for to see the nobleste knyght of the world take such abstynaunce that he waxed ful lene.

And thus upon a nyght there came a vysyon to syr Launcelot and charged hym, in remyssyon of his synnes, to haste hym unto Almysbury: 'And by thenne thou come there, thou shall fynde quene Guenever dede. And therfore take thy felowes with the, and purvey them of an hors-bere, and fetche thou the cors of hir, and burye hir by her husbond, the noble kyng Arthur.'

So this avysyon came to Launcelot thryse in one nyght. Than syr Launcelot rose up or day and tolde the heremyte. 'It were wel done,' sayd the heremyte, 'that ye made you redy and that ye dysobeye not the avysyon.'

Than syr Launcelot toke his seven felowes with hym, and on fote they yede from Glastynburye to Almysburye, the whyche is lytel more than thirty myle, and thyder they came within two dayes, for they were wayke and feble to goo.

And whan syr Launcelot was come to Almysburye within the nunerye, quene Guenever deyed but halfe an oure afore. And the ladyes tolde syr Launcelot that quene Guenever tolde hem al or she passyd that syr Launcelot had ben preest nere a twelve-monthe, 'and hyder he cometh as faste as he may to fetche my cors, and besyde my lord kyng Arthur he shal berye me.'

Wherefore the quene sayd in heryng of hem al, 'I beseche Almyghty God that I may never have power to see syr Launcelot wyth my worldly eyen!'

'And thus,' said al the ladyes 'was ever hir prayer these two dayes tyl she was dede.'

Than syr Launcelot sawe hir vysage, but he wepte not gretelye, but syghed. And so he dyd al the observaunce of the servyce hymself; bothe the dyryge[17] and on the morne he sange masse. And there was ordeyned an hors-bere, and so wyth an hondred torches ever brennyng aboute the cors of the quene and ever syr Launcelot with his eyght felowes wente aboute the hors-bere, syngyng and redyng many an holy oryson, and frankensens upon the corps encensed.

Thus syr Launcelot and his eyght felowes wente on foot from Almysburye unto Glastynburye; and whan they were come to the chapel and the hermytage, there she had a dyryge wyth grete devocyon. And on the morne the heremyte that somtyme was bysshop of Canterburye sange the masse of Requyem wyth grete devocyon, and syr Launcelot was the fyrst that offeryd, and than al his eyght felowes. And than she was wrapped in cered clothe of Raynes,[18] from the toppe to the too, in thirtyfolde; and after she was put in a webbe[19] of leed, and than in a coffyn of marbyl.

And whan she was put in th'erth syr Launcelot swouned, and laye longe stylle, whyle the hermyte came and awaked hym, and sayd, 'Ye be to blame, for ye dysplese God with suche maner of sorow-makyng.'

'Truly,' sayd syr Launcelot, 'I trust I do not dysplese God, for he knoweth myn entente: for my sorow was not, nor is not, for ony rejoysyng of synne, but my sorow may never have ende. For whan I remembre of hir beaulte and of hir noblesse, that was bothe wyth hyr kyng and wyth hyr, so whan I sawe his corps and hir corps so lye togyders, truly myn herte wold not serve to susteyne my careful body. Also whan I remembre me how by my defaute and myn orgule[20] and my pryde that they were bothe layed ful lowe, that were pereles that ever was lyvyng of Cristen peopie, wyt you wel,' sayd syr Launcelot, 'this remembred, of there kyndenes and myn unkyndenes, sanke so to myn herte that I myght not susteyne myself.' So the Frensshe book maketh mencyon.

Thenne syr Launcelot never after ete but lytel mete, nor dranke, tyl he was dede, for than he seekened more and more and dryed and dwyned[21] awaye. For the bysshop nor none of his felowes myght not make hym to ete and lytel he dranke, that he was waxen by a kybbet[22] shorter than he was, that the

16 **ther horses wente where they wolde**. An expressive detail added by a man who knows that the separation of the warrior-knight from his horse is the end of his life in the world.

17 **dyryge**: *dirige*, the first word of the antiphon in the Office of the Mass for the Dead.

18 waxed cloth of Rennes

19 sheet

20 pride

21 withered and wasted

22 cubit (a foot and more)

peple coude not knowe hym.[23] For evermore, day and nyght, he prayed, but somtyme he slombred a broken slepe. Ever he was lyeng grovelyng on the tombe of kyng Arthur and quene Guenever, and there was no comforte that the bysshop, nor syr Bors, nor none of his felowes coude make hym, it avaylled not.

Soo wythin syx wekys after, syr Launcelot fyl seek and laye in his bedde. And thenne he sente for the bysshop that there was heremyte, and al his trewe felowes. Than syr Launcelot sayd wyth drery steven,[24] 'Syr bysshop, I praye you gyve to me al my ryghtes[25] that longeth to a Crysten man.'

'It shal not nede you,' sayd the heremyte and al his felowes. 'It is but hevynesse of your blood. Ye shal be wel mended by the grace of God to-morne.'

'My fayr lordes,' sayd syr Launcelot, 'wyt you wel my careful body wyll into th'erthe, I have warnyng more than now I wyl say. Therfore gyve me my ryghtes.'

So whan he was howselyd and enelyd[26] and had al that a Crysten man ought to have, he prayed the bysshop that his felowes myght bere his body to Joyous Garde. (Somme men say it was Anwyk, and somme may say it was Bamborow.)[27] 'Howbeit,' sayd syr Launcelot, 'me repenteth sore, but I made myn avowe somtyme that in Joyous Garde I wold be buryed. And bycause of[28] brekyng of myn avowe, I praye you al, lede me thyder.'

Than there was wepyng and wryngyng of handes among his felowes. So at a seson[29] of the nyght they al wente to theyr beddes, for they alle laye in one chambre. And so after mydnyght, ayenst day, the bysshop that ther was hermyte[f], as he laye in his bedde aslepe, he fyl upon a grete laughter. And therwyth al the felyshyp awoke and came to the bysshop and asked hym what he eyled.

'A, Jesu mercy!' sayd the bysshop, 'why dyd ye awake me? I was never in al my lyf so mery and so wel at ease.'

'Wherfore?' sayd syr Bors.

'Truly,' sayd the bysshop, 'here was syr Launcelot with me, with mo angellis than ever I sawe men in one day. And I sawe the angellys heve up syr Launcelot unto heven, and the yates of heven opened ayenst hym.'

'It is but dretchyng of swevens,'[30] sayd syr Bors, 'for I doubte not syr Launcelot ayleth nothynge but good.'

'It may wel be,' sayd the bysshop. 'Goo ye to his bedde, and than shall ye preve the soth.'

So whan syr Bors and his felowes came to his bedde they founde hym starke dede; and he laye as he had smyled, and the swettest savour aboute hym that ever they felte. Than was there wepyng and wryngyng of handes, and the grettest dole they made that ever made men.

And on the morne the bysshop dyd his masse of Requyem, and after the bysshop and al the nine knyghtes put syr Launcelot in the same hors-bere that quene Guenevere was layed in tofore that she was buryed. And soo the bysshop and they al togydere wente wyth the body of syr Launcelot dayly, tyl they came to Joyous Garde; and ever they had an hondred torches brennyng aboute hym.

And so within fyftene dayes they came to Joyous Garde. And there they layed his corps in the body of the quere,[31] and sange and redde many saulters and prayers over hym and aboute hym. And ever his vysage was layed open and naked, that al folkes myght beholde hym; for suche was the custom in tho dayes that al men of worshyp shold so lye wyth open vysage tyl that they were buryed.

And ryght thus as they were at theyr servyce, there came syr Ector de Maris that had seven yere sought al Englond, Scotlond and Walys, sekyng his brother, syr Launcelot. And whan syr Ector herde suche noyse and lyghte in the quyre of Joyous Garde, he alyght and put his hors from hym and came into the quyre. And there he sawe men synge and wepe, and al they knewe syr Ector, but he knewe not them.

Than wente syr Bors unto syr Ector and tolde hym how there laye his brother, syr Launcelot, dede. And than syr Ector threwe hys shelde, swerde and helme from hym, and whan he behelde syr Launcelottes

23 **that the peple coude not knowe hym.** It is important for the narrative of spiritual transcendence that Lancelot should not only be reformed but that he should become unrecognizable in his former person: he must be made nothing, so that he can be made whole.

24 voice

25 rites (sacrament of extreme unction)

26 given communion and anointed

27 Alnwick and Bamborough are castles in Northumberland. Malory added the names, perhaps in allusion to his own experience fighting there in the Wars of the Roses.

28 to avoid

29 an appropriate time

30 illusion of dreams

31 chancel

vysage he fyl doun in a swoun. And whan he waked it were harde ony tonge to telle the doleful complayntes that he made for his brother.

'A, Launcelot!' he sayd, 'thou were hede of al Crysten knyghtes! And now I dare say,' sayd syr Ector, 'thou sir Launcelot, there thou lyest, that thou were never matched of erthely knyghtes hande. And thou were the curtest[32] knyght that ever bare shelde. And thou were the truest frende to thy lovar that ever bestrade hors, and thou were the trewest lover, of a synful man,[33] that ever loved woman, and thou were the kyndest man that ever strake wyth swerde. And thou were the godelyest persone that ever cam emonge prees of knyghtes, and thou was the mekest man and the jentyllest that ever ete in halle emonge ladyes, and thou were the sternest knyght to thy mortal foo that ever put spere in the reeste.'[34]

Than there was wepyng and dolour out of mesure.

Thus they kepte syr Launcelotes corps on-lofte fyftene dayes, and than they buryed it with grete devocyon. And than at leyser they wente al with the bysshop of Canterburye to his ermytage, and there they were togyder more than a monthe.

Than syr Costantyn that was syr Cadores sone of Cornwayl was chosen kyng of Englond, and he was a ful noble knyght, and worshypfully he rulyd this royame. And than thys kyng Costantyn sent for the bysshop of Caunterburye, for he herde saye where he was. And so he was restored unto his bysshopryche and lefte that ermytage, and syr Bedwere was there ever stylle heremyte to his lyves ende.

Than syr Bors de Ganys, syr Ector de Maris, syr Gahalantyne, syr Galyhud, sir Galyhodyn, syr Blamour, syr Bleoberys, syr Wyllyars le[g] Valyaunt, syr Clarrus of Cleremounte, al these knyghtes drewe them to theyr contreyes. Howbeit kyng Costantyn wold have had them wyth hym, but they wold not abyde in this royame. And there they al lyved in their cuntreyes as holy men.

And somme Englysshe bookes maken mencyon that they wente never oute of Englond after the deth of syr Launcelot – but that was but favour of makers.[35] For the Frensshe book maketh mencyon – and is auctorysed[36] – that syr Bors, syr Ector, syr Blamour and syr Bleoberis wente into the Holy Lande, there as Jesu Cryst was quycke and deed.[37] And anone as they had stablysshed theyr londes (for, the book saith, so syr Launcelot commaunded them for to do or ever he passyd oute of thys world), there[h] these foure knyghtes dyd many bataylles upon the myscreantes, or Turkes. And there they dyed[i] upon a Good Fryday for Goddes sake.

Here is the ende of the hoole[j] book of kyng Arthur and of his noble knyghtes of the Rounde Table, that whan they were hole togyders there was ever an hondred and forty. And here is the ende of *The Deth of Arthur*.

I praye you all jentylmen and jentylwymmen that redeth this book of Arthur and his knyghtes from the begynnyng to the endyng, praye for me whyle I am on lyve that God sende me good delyveraunce.[38] And whan I am deed, I praye you all praye for my soule.

For this book was ended the ninth yere of the reygne of kyng Edward the Fourth, by syr Thomas Maleore, knyght, as Jesu helpe hym for hys grete myght as he is the servaunt of Jesu bothe day and nyght. *{Caxton has a final colophon in which he explains the title of the work (it is called 'Le Morte Darthur' even though it treats of the whole story of Arthur) and his own work in putting Malory into books, chapters and print.}*

32 most courteous

33 **the trewest lover, of a synful man**, i.e. the truest that a man could be in love though still burdened with the sin inseparable from living in the world.

34 Sir Ector's lament for Lancelot is Malory's innovation; it is done in exclusively secular chivalric terms, as if Malory wanted to make this final acknowledgement of his admiration for the ideals of secular chivalry in the midst of the unavoidable odours of piety and sanctification.

35 biased opinion of poets

36 has authority

37 lived and died

38 **God sende me good delyveraunce**. The appeal to be delivered from prison has a special poignancy, since in this year (1470) Malory had just been excluded for the fourth time from a general pardon granted to Lancastrians by Edward IV.

William Caxton (*c.* 1422–1492)

Printing with movable type was first perfected in Europe by Johann Gutenberg at Mainz in the 1440s; it was Caxton who, in 1476, introduced printing into England. He went originally to the continent as a merchant, and took up printing and publishing as essentially another form of business venture (to some extent it remained so for him), in Cologne and then in Bruges. The business was so successful that he returned to England and set up a printing press at Westminster, and proceeded to turn out, over the next 16 years, over 100 printed titles, many of them large works (*Canterbury Tales*, Malory), and some of them his own translations (*Eneydos*). His tastes, and his calculation of the tastes of his predominantly well-off customers, were conservative, with a particular inclination to romance, established English poets, encyclopaedic works, and works of moral and didactic instruction. In fact, he mostly went on printing the kinds of work that had achieved most success in the thriving manuscript-copying industry. Unlike his assistant and successor, Wynkyn de Worde, he had little sense of the commercial possibilities of popular printing. Nevertheless, Caxton played a key role in helping to create a taste and an audience for printed books, in shaping the sense of an English literary tradition, and in standardizing the English language and English spelling. The standard works are by N.F. Blake: *Caxton and his World* (London, 1969); (ed.) *Caxton's Own Prose* (London, 1973); (ed.) *Selections* (Oxford, 1973); *William Caxton* (Aldershot, 1993) – a short biography.

Prologue to Malory's Morte D'Arthur

This prologue raises two main questions about Arthurian romance – its historical veracity and its value as moral example. Caxton answers them tactfully, somewhat against the trend of the most sophisticated contemporary thinking, but in such a manner as to encourage or at least not to alienate any potential reader or customer. But his own enthusiasm for chivalric romance, despite its increasingly dated image, gleams through his inflated publisher's prose and his inveterate word-doublings, and he did a good deal of work on Malory's original (see headnote to Malory) in order to shape it to a unified whole and to clarify its moral message. His enthusiasm was rewarded, for only weeks after the print left the press (31 July 1485) Richard III was defeated and killed at Bosworth Field (22 August) and the victorious Henry VII not only claimed Arthurian descent for the Tudors but named his eldest son (b. 1486) Arthur. With the Reformation, though, Malory's great work began to suffer from Protestant attacks on its glorification of 'open manslaughter and bold bawdry' (Ascham, below), and it was not reprinted until modern times.

After that I had accomplysshed and fynysshed dyvers hystoryes, as wel of contemplacyon as of other hystoryal and worldly actes of grete conquerours and prynces and also certeyn bookes of ensaumples and doctryne, many noble and dyvers gentylmen of thys royame of Englond camen and demaunded me many and oftymes wherfore that I have not do made and enprynte[1] the noble hystorye of the Saynt Greal and of the moost renomed Crysten kyng, fyrst and chyef of the thre best Crysten and worthy, kyng Arthur, whyche ought moost to be remembred emonge us Englysshemen tofore al other Crysten kynges. For it is notoyrly knowen thorugh the unyversal world that there been .ix. worthy and the best that ever were: that is to wete, thre paynyms, thre Jewes and thre Crysten men *{namely, as Caxton recounts, Hector, Alexander and Julius Caesar; Joshua, David and Judas Maccabeus; and Arthur, Charlemagne and Godfrey of Boulogne}*.

The sayd noble jentylmen instantly requyred me t'emprynte th'ystorye of the sayd noble kyng and conquerour, kyng Arthur, and of his knyghtes, wyth th'ystorye of the Saynt Greal and of the deth and endyng of the sayd Arthur, affermyng that I ought rather t'enprynte his actes and noble feates than of Godefroye of Boloyne or ony of the other eyght, consyderyng that he was a man borne wythin this royame and kyng and emperour of the same and that there ben in Frensshe dyvers and many noble volumes of his actes and also of his knyghtes. To whome I answerd that dyvers men holde oppynyon that there was no suche Arthur and that alle suche bookes as been maad of hym ben but fayned and fables bycause that somme cronycles make of hym no mencyon ne remembre hym noothynge ne of his knyghtes.

1 'caused to be made and printed'. These many gentlemen who press in at Caxton's office to demand that he print certain things are a generic fiction of his prologues.

Wherto they answerd, and one in specyal sayd, that in hym that shold say or thynke that there was never suche a kyng callyd Arthur myght wel be aretted[2] grete folye and blyndenesse, for he sayd that there were many evydences of the contrarye.

Fyrst, ye may see his sepulture in the monasterye of Glastyngburye; and also in *Polycronycon*[3] in the .v. book, the syxte chappytre, and in the seventh book, the .xxiii. chappytre, where his body was buryed and after founden and translated into the sayd monasterye. Ye shal se also in th'ystorye of Bochas, in his book *De Casu Principum*,[4] parte of his noble actes and also of his falle; also, Galfrydus in his Brutysshe book recounteth his lyf.[5] And in dyvers places of Englond many remembraunces ben yet of hym and shall remayne perpetuelly and also of his knyghtes. Fyrst, in the abbey of Westmestre at saynt Edwardes shryne remayneth the prynte of his seal in reed waxe closed in beryll, in whych is wryton *Patricius Arthurus Britannie, Gallie, Germanie, Dacie Imperator*. Item, in the castel of Dover ye may see Gauwayns skulle and Cradoks mantel, at Wynchester the Rounde Table,[6] in other places Launcelottes swerde and many other thynges. Thenne al these thynges consydered there can no man resonably gaynsaye but there was a kyng of thys lande named Arthur, for in al places Crysten and hethen he is reputed and taken for one of the .ix. worthy and the fyrst of the thre Crysten men. And also he is more spoken of beyonde the see, moo bookes made of his noble actes than there be in Englond, as wel in Duche, Ytalyen, Spaynysshe and Grekysshe as in Frensshe. And yet[7] of record remayne in wytnesse of hym in Wales in the toune of Camelot[8] the grete stones and mervayllous werkys of yron lyeng under the grounde and ryal vautes, which dyvers now lyvyng hath seen. Wherfor it is a mervayl why he is no more renomed in his owne contreye, sauf onelye it accordeth to the word of God, whyche sayth that no man is accept for a prophete in his owne contreye.[9] Thenne al these thynges forsayd aledged,[10] I coude not wel denye but that there was suche a noble kyng named Arthur and reputed one of the .ix. worthy, and fyrst and chyef of the Cristen men.

And many noble volumes be made of hym and of his noble knyghtes in Frensshe which I have seen and redde beyonde the see, which been not had in our maternal tongue. But in Walsshe ben many and also in Frensshe and somme in Englysshe, but nowher nygh alle. Wherfore suche as have late ben drawen oute bryefly into Englysshe I have, after the symple connyng that God hath sente to me, under the favour and correctyon of al noble lordes and gentylmen, enprysed[11] to enprynte a book of the noble hystoryes of the sayd kynge Arthur and of certeyn of his knyghtes after a copye unto me delyverd. Whyche copye Syr Thomas Malorye dyd take oute of certeyn bookes of Frensshe and reduced it into Englysshe. And I accordyng to my copye have doon sette it in enprynte to the entente that noble men may see and lerne the noble actes of chyvalrye, the jentyl and vertuous dedes that somme knyghtes used in tho dayes by whyche they came to honour, and how they that were vycious were punysshed and ofte put to shame and rebuke; humbly bysechyng al noble lordes and ladyes wyth al other estates of what estate or degree they been of that shal see and rede in this sayd book and werke that they take the good and honest actes in their remembraunce and to folowe the same, wherin they shalle fynde many joyous and playsaunt hystoryes and noble and renomed actes of humanyte, gentylnesse and chyvalryes. For herein may be seen noble chyvalrye, curtosye, humanyte, frendlynesse, hardynesse, love, frendshyp, cowardyse, murdre, hate, vertue and synne. Doo after the good and leve the evyl and it shal brynge you to good fame and renommee. And for to passe the tyme thys book shal be plesaunte to rede in. But for to gyve fayth and byleve that al is trewe that is conteyned herin, ye be at your lyberte. But al is wryton for our doctryne and for to beware that we falle not to vyce ne synne, but t'excersyse and folowe vertu, by whyche we may come and atteyne to good fame and renomme in thys lyf and after thys shorte and transytorye lyf to come unto everlastyng blysse in heven, the whyche he graunte us that reygneth in heven, the blessyd Trynyte. Amen. *{Caxton concludes by giving a summary of the work.}*

2 ascribed

3 See Trevisa, above.

4 See Lydgate, *Fall of Princes*, above.

5 Geoffrey of Monmouth, author of the *Historia regum Britanniae*, and originator of the story of the foundation of Britain by the Trojan Brutus; English derivatives of his work were called *Brut* histories.

6 There is indeed a Round Table at Winchester, dating from the fourteenth century.

7 still

8 Probably Caerleon, in south Wales.

9 Luke 4:24.

10 confirmed

11 undertaken

PROLOGUE TO ENEYDOS

This prologue (c.1490) dramatizes vividly some of the real problems Caxton faced in printing works for a linguistically heterogeneous audience. His complaint about the diversity of English echoes Chaucer's, in *TC* V.1793, though of course printing worked in course of time to homogenize at least the non-spoken language. He complains also of the difficulty of writing an English that is neither too plain nor too fancy. It was a problem that poets like Hawes and Skelton faced and did not solve. Prose, in the hands of writers like More and Cavendish, managed much better.

After dyverse werkes made, translated and achieved, havyng noo werke in hande, I sittyng in my studye where as laye many dyverse paunflettis and bookys, happened that to my hande cam a lytyl booke in Frenshe whiche late was translated oute of Latyn by some noble clerke of Fraunce, whiche booke is named *Eneydos*, made in Latyn by that noble poete and grete clerke Vyrgyle. Whiche booke I sawe over and redde therin how after the generall destruccyon of the grete Troye Eneas departed berynge his olde fader Anchises upon his sholdres, his lityl son Yolus on his honde, his wyfe wyth moche other people folowynge; and how he shypped and departed, wyth all th'ystorye of his adventures that he had er he cam to the achievement of his conquest of Ytalye, as all alonge[1] shall be shewed in this present boke. In whiche booke I had grete playsyr bycause of the fayr and honest termes and wordes in Frenshe, whyche I never sawe tofore lyke, ne none so playsaunt ne so wel ordred. Whiche booke, as me semed, sholde be moche requysyte to noble men to see as wel for the eloquence as the historyes, how wel that[2] many honderd yerys passed was the sayd booke of *Eneydos* wyth other werkes made and lerned dayly in scolis, specyally in Ytalye and other places;[3] whiche historye the sayd Vyrgyle made in metre.

And whan I had advysed me in this sayd boke, I delybered and concluded to translate it into Englysshe, and forthwyth toke a penne and ynke and wrote a leef or tweyne whyche I oversawe agayn to corecte it. And whan I sawe the fayr and straunge termes therin, I doubted that it sholde not please some gentylmen whiche late blamed me, sayeng that in my translacyons I had over-curyous termes whiche coude not be understande of comyn peple and desired me to use olde and homely termes in my translacyons. And fayn wolde I satysfye every man, and so to doo toke an olde boke and redde therin; and certaynly the Englysshe was so rude and brood that I coude not wele understande it. And also my lorde abbot of Westmynster ded do shewe to me late certayn evydences wryton in olde Englysshe for to reduce it into our Englysshe now usid. And certaynly it was wreton in suche wyse that it was more lyke to Dutche[4] than Englysshe: I coude not reduce ne brynge it to be understonden. And certaynly our langage now used varyeth ferre from that whiche was used and spoken whan I was borne, for we Englysshemen ben borne under the domynacyon of the mone, whiche is never stedfaste but ever waverynge, wexynge one season and waneth and dyscreaseth another season.

And that comyn Englysshe that is spoken in one shyre varyeth from another. In so moche that in my dayes happened that certayn marchauntes were in a shippe in Tamyse[5] for to have sayled over the see into Zelande. And for lacke of wynde thai taryed atte forlond and wente to lande for to refreshe them. And one of theym named Sheffelde, a mercer, cam into an hows and axed for mete and specyally he axyd after eggys. And the goode wyf answerde that she coude speke no Frenshe. And the marchaunt was angry, for he also coude speke no Frenshe, but wolde have hadde egges; and she understode hym not. And thenne at laste another sayd that he wolde have eyren; then the good wyf sayd that she understod hym wel.[6] Loo! what sholde a man in thyse dayes now wryte, 'egges' or 'eyren'? Certaynly it is harde to playse every man bycause of dyversite and chaunge of langage.

For in these days every man that is in ony reputacyon in his countre wyll utter his commynycacyon and maters in suche maners and termes that fewe man shall understonde theym. And som honest and

1 at length
2 although
3 Virgil's *Aeneid* was an important set book in grammar-school Latin instruction in England too. Caxton seems to think this might put people off.
4 Low German.
5 The river Thames.
6 **egges** was the regular plural in the north, where Master Sheffield came from; **eyren** was the southern form.

grete clerkes have ben wyth me and desired me to wryte the moste curyous termes that I coude fynde. And thus bytwene playn rude and curyous I stande abasshed. But in my judgemente the comyn termes that be dayli used ben lyghter to be understonde than the olde and auncyent Englysshe. And for as moche as this present booke is not for a rude uplondyssh man to labour therin ne rede it, but onely for a clerke and a noble gentylman that feleth and understondeth in faytes[7] of armes, in love and in noble chyvalrye, therfor in a meane bytwene bothe I have reduced and translatyd this sayd booke into our Englysshe not over-rude ne curyous but in suche termes as shall be understanden by Goddys grace accordynge to my copye. And yf ony man wyll entermete[8] in redyng of hit and fyndeth suche termes that he cannot understande, late hym goo rede and lerne Vyrgyll or the *Pystles* of Ovyde, and ther he shall see and understonde lyghtly all, yf he have a good redar and enformer.[9] For this booke is not for every rude and unconnynge man to see, but to clerkys and very gentylmen that understande gentylnes and scyence. *{Caxton concludes by praying that Master John Skelton, 'poete laureate', may oversee and correct the translation, which is presented thus to prince Arthur, eldest son of Henry VII.}*

7 feats
8 engage
9 Caxton suggests that those who do not understand his translation should go back to the original – which they will not understand, since they are clearly not the right kind of educated reader in the first place.

Robert Henryson (*c.* 1430–*c.* 1505)

Robert Henryson was admitted as a Master of Arts (that is, as someone already holding a degree from elsewhere) to the newly founded University of Glasgow in 1462, and was a schoolmaster at Dunfermline, and probably a notary public, before his death around 1505. Otherwise, nothing is known for certain of his life. Like Dunbar and the other Scots poets represented in the present volume he wrote in the dialect of English called 'Middle Scots' that developed as a primarily literary language in the fifteenth century. He and his fellow-poets are often called the 'Scottish Chaucerians' (see D. Fox, in Brewer [1966], pp. 164–200), and certainly they owe much to Chaucer in their choice of subject-matter, metre, style and vocabulary, but the label does scant justice to their originality. Henryson, in particular, is almost the equal of Chaucer as a narrative poet, though in a more restricted sphere. His manner is laconic, in contrast to the general trend among fifteenth-century poets, and his output is small: apart from the *Fables* and the *Testament of Cresseid*, there are only the Scottish *pastourelle* of *Robene and Makyne*, the learned and witty version of the story of *Orpheus and Eurydice*, and some powerful short moral and mortality poems. The definitive edition is by D. Fox (Oxford, 1981); there are *Selections*, ed. C. Elliott (2nd edn, Oxford, 1974), and *Selected Poems of Henryson and Dunbar*, ed. P. Bawcutt and F. Riddy (Edinburgh, 1992); studies by J. MacQueen (Oxford, 1967) and D. Gray, *Robert Henryson* (Leiden, 1979).

Middle Scots shares many forms and spellings with northern English (long *a* for *o*, *quh-* for *wh-*) but has features of its own, notably the spellings with *i* of the long vowels (*mair*, 'more', *greit*, 'great', *befoir*, 'before', *tuik*, 'took'), of *u* for *o* (*luf*, 'love') and *ch* for *gh* (*licht*, 'light'). Note *bot*, 'but', but *but*, 'without'; *into*, *intill*, 'in, within'.

The Testament of Cresseid

Chaucer refused to judge Criseyde, except by allowing her words and actions to speak for themselves. His refusal to judge was an act of great human and poetic significance, as Henryson recognizes by bringing Chaucer's heroine to the bar of judgement. For him, there is no alternative to an eschatological frame of reference: Cresseid must be punished so that she can be saved. The punishment is carefully chosen – Cresseid's leprosy (this is Henryson's invention) is cruelly appropriate to her pride in her beauty – and the administration of it is carefully legitimated in relation to an apparatus of quasi-divine surveillance. Cresseid is not punished for being unfaithful to Troilus, but for blaspheming against the gods. This is like looking for the exact letter of the law under which someone who is 'known' to be guilty can be convicted. The gods are not Christian gods, of course, nor do they stand for the Christian God, but they operate in a manner uncannily similar to what goes under the name of divine justice. But the fearful machine that Henryson constructs to destroy Cresseid physically is not the instrument of her repentance and salvation: she learns nothing from it except to complain against her misfortune and warn others to learn by it. It may, though, prepare her for 'grace', again with bitter allusion to the bruising of the body in inquisitional torture that 'softens' the victim into receptivity, as well as to the more comforting idea that lepers were chosen by God to be close to him through their suffering. Her progress through misery is at any rate untouched by self-knowledge until she meets Troilus, in a scene of overwhelming yet totally unsentimental poignancy. Only then does she recognize her offence, understanding having been bestowed not by punishment and suffering but by the recognition of what Troilus's love was and is. It is an extraordinary moment, and it shows how deeply Henryson had absorbed the ethos of Chaucer's poem whilst ostensibly correcting its morality: with all its powerful Christian overtones and implications, the *Testament* is seen to rest on the assertion of the 'holiness of the heart's affections', or rather on a system of organizing those affections to the exclusive benefit of men. Troilus is the unflawed representative of an ideal code of love which Cresseid betrayed. The simplicity of the conclusion is so at odds with the intensity of the engagement with Cresseid's fate – an engagement which is all the more deepened because we recognize the spuriousness of the narrator's sympathetic noise-making – that it is not surprising that the poem stirs an enigmatic response. It has above all the quality of concentrated poetic intensity that makes every word fraught with meaning – what volumes are spoken in 'And mair' (72) of stale and forced lust – and the contribution of every minor character part of the passion with which we read: the tenderness and stoic resignation of Calchas, or of the 'lipper lady', are like balm to the bruising administered by the poem.

The *Testament* was written before 1492, but there are no early MSS; the most important source for the text is the Edinburgh print (1593) of Henry Charteris (C), followed here with emendation from other prints and MSS as cited in the valuable edition of D. Fox (Edinburgh and London, 1968). There are influential essays by D. Duncan, *EC* 11 (1961), 128–35; A.C. Spearing, *Speculum* 37 (1962), 208–25; L. Patterson, *PQ* 52 (1973), 696–714; Spearing (1985), pp. 165–87.

	Ane doolie sessoun to ane cairfull dyte
	Suld correspond and be equivalent:
	Richt sa it wes quhen I began to wryte
intense(ly cold)	This tragedie – the wedder richt fervent,
	Quhen Aries in middis of the Lent
caused	Schouris of haill gart fra the north discend,
	That scantlie fra the cauld I micht defend.
	Yit nevertheles within myne oratur
(the sun)	I stude, quhen Titan had his bemis bricht
hidden under cover	Withdrawin doun and sylit under cure,
	And fair Venus, the bewtie of the nicht,
	Uprais and set unto the west full richt
	Hir goldin face, in oppositioun
	Of God Phebus, direct discending doun.
burst	Throwout the glas hir bemis brast sa fair
	That I micht se on everie syde me by:
	The northin wind had purifyit the air
scattered	And sched the mistie cloudis fra the sky;
	The froist freisit, the blastis bitterly
	Fra Pole Artick come quhisling loud and schill
remove	And causit me remufe aganis my will.
trusted, love's	For I traistit that Venus, luifis quene,
promised	To quhome sumtyme I hecht obedience,
	My faidit hart of lufe scho wald mak grene,
	And therupon with humbill reverence
	I thocht to pray hir hie magnificence –
prevented	Bot for greit cald as than I lattit was
	And in my chalmer to the fyre can pas.
Though love be hot	Thocht lufe be hait, yit in ane man of age
	It kendillis nocht sa sone as in youtheid,
	Of quhome the blude is flowing in ane rage;
sexual desire (is) dull	And in the auld the curage doif and deid
remedy	Of quhilk the fyre outward is best remeid:
medicine (e.g. aphrodisiacs)	To help be phisike quhair that nature faillit
both, tried	I am expert, for baith I have assaillit.
mended, basked in its warmth	I mend the fyre and beikit me about,
	Than tuik ane drink, my spreitis to comfort,
	And armit me weill fra tha cauld thairout.
	To cut the winter nicht and mak it schort
little book	I tuik ane quair – and left all uther sport –

1 The appropriateness of a dismal season to a doleful poem is part of the rhetoric of decorum that more usually dictated spring-openings for happy love-poems.

5 It is a surprise to find that the 'doolie sessoun' is actually spring (the sun was in Aries from 12 March to 11 April). Perhaps it is a Scottish spring, or a 'real' spring, for a story of what love 'really' is, as distinct from the fictions of the poets.

8 **myne oratur**: a small chapel, dedicated to the service of Venus. (Venus is also the evening star.)

27 Not quite the image we have of the devoted servant of Venus; but the narrator is old, and unfulfillable lusts have to give way to more practical considerations.

Writtin be worthie Chaucer glorious
Of fair Cresseid and worthie Troylus.

And thair I fand, efter that Diomeid
Taken (as his mistress) Ressavit had that lady bricht of hew,
went How Troilus neir out of wit abraid
And weipit soir with visage paill of hew;
Because of which despair For quhilk wanhope his teiris can renew,
Until hope Quhill esperance rejoisit him agane.
one time… (another time), lived Thus quhyle in joy he levit, quhyle in pane.

promise Of hir behest he had greit comforting,
Traisting to Troy that scho suld mak retour,
Quhilk he desyrit maist of eirdly thing,
Because Forquhy scho was his only paramour.
Bot quhen he saw passit baith day and hour
return Of hir ganecome, than sorrow can oppres
His wofull hart in cair and hevines.

Of his distres me neidis nocht reheirs,
For worthie Chauceir in the samin buik,
In gudelie termis and in joly veirs,
whoever Compylit hes his cairis, quha will luik.
keep myself awake (serving Venus) To brek my sleip ane uther quair I tuik,
In quhilk I fand the fatall destenie
Of fair Cresseid, that endit wretchitlie.

Quha wait gif all that Chauceir wrait was trew?
Nor I wait nocht gif this narratioun
authoritative, made up Be authoreist, or fenyeit of the new
Be sum poeit throw his inventioun,
Maid to report the lamentatioun
And wofull end of this lustie Creisseid,
suffered, death And quhat distres scho thoillit, and quhat deid.

Quhen Diomeid had all his appetyte,
And mair, fulfillit of this fair ladie,
whole Upon ane uther he set his haill delyte
formal letter of divorce And send to hir ane lybell of repudie
And hir excludit fra his companie.
Than desolait scho walkit up and doun,
openly promiscuous And sum men sayis, into the court, commoun.

O fair Cresseid, the flour and A *per se*
destined by fortune Of Troy and Grece, how was thow fortunait
To change in filth all thy feminitie
spotted And be with fleschelie lust sa maculait

64 Henryson pretends to take seriously Chaucer's earnest avowals of fidelity to the historical source.

78 A *per se*: letter standing first in the alphabet by its own nature, i.e. 'paragon'.

78–91 The narrator's 'sympathy' seems suspect: there is more of the fervent exhausting relish of aged impotence (see the syntax of 79–83) at the exposure of rampant female sexuality, while the explanation of Cresseid's fall as the result of bad luck, and scandalous talk, is shallow.

early and late And go amang the Greikis air and lait,
harlot-like So giglotlike takand thy foull plesance!
I have pietie thow suld fall sic mischance!

Yit nevertheles, quhatever men deme or say
frailty In scornefull langage of thy brukkilnes,
I sall excuse als far furth as I may
Thy womanheid, thy wisdome and fairnes,
such The quhilk Fortoun hes put to sic distres
As hir pleisit, and nathing throw the gilt
malicious talk, ruined Of the – throw wickit langage to be spilt!

This fair lady, in this wyse destitute
Of all comfort and consolatioun,
Richt privelie, but fellowschip, on fute,
Disagysit passit far out of the toun
Ane myle or twa, unto ane mansioun
where (was) Beildit full gay, quhair hir father Calchas
Quhilk than amang the Greikis dwelland was.

Quhen he hir saw, the caus he can inquyre
sighing Of hir cumming; scho said, siching full soir:
After 'Fra Diomeid had gottin his desyre
He wox werie and wald of me no moir.'
Quod Calchas, 'Douchter, weip thow not thairfoir:
Peraventure all cummis for the best.
Welcum to me: thow art full deir ane gest!'

according as, then This auld Calchas, efter the law was tho,
Wes keiper of the tempill as ane preist
In quhilk Venus and hir sone Cupido
dwelling, nearest to them War honourit, and his chalmer was thame neist,
sorrow enough To quhilk Cresseid, with baill aneuch in breist,
Usit to pas, hir prayeris for to say,
Until, feast-day Quhill at the last, upon ane solempne day,

As custome was, the pepill far and neir
Befoir the none unto the tempill went
devout With sacrifice, devoit in thair maneir.
dejected, mind Bot still Cresseid, hevie in hir intent,
Into the kirk wald not hirself present,
For giving of the pepill ony deming
Of hir expuls fra Diomeid the king,

Bot past into ane secreit orature,
Quhair scho micht weip hir wofull desteny.
Behind hir bak scho cloisit fast the dure
haste And on hir kneis bair fell doun in hy.
Upon Venus and Cupide angerly

87 Cf. *TC* V.1097–9.
101–2 There are several moments in the poem where Henryson's famous conciseness is specially and startlingly effective: this is one of them.

Scho cryit out, and said on this same wyse:
'Allace, that ever I maid yow sacrifice!

'Ye gave me anis ane devine responsaill — *once, response*
That I suld be the flour of luif in Troy;
Now I am maid ane unworthie outwaill — *outcast*
And all in cair translatit is my joy.
Quha sall me gyde? Quha sall me now convoy, — *look after*
Sen I fra Diomeid and nobill Troylus
Am clene excludit, as abject odious? — *one cast out*

'O fals Cupide, is nane to wyte bot thow — *blame*
And thy mother, of lufe the blind goddes!
Ye causit me alwayis understand and trow
The seid of lufe was sawin in my face, — *sown*
And ay grew grene throw your supplie and grace; — *assistance*
But now, allace, that seid with froist is slane,
And I fra luifferis left and all forlane!' — *abandoned*

Quhen this was said, doun in ane extasie,
Ravischit in spreit, intill ane dreame scho fell,
And be apperance hard, quhair scho did ly, — *heard*
Cupide the king ringand ane silver bell,
Quhilk men micht heir fra hevin unto hell;
At quhais sound befoir Cupide appeiris — *whose*
The sevin planetis, discending fra thair spheiris,

Quhilk hes power of all thing generabill, — *able to be generated*
To reull and steir be thair greit influence — *steer*
Wedder and wind, and coursis variabill. — *(i.e. not the fixed stars)*
And first of all Saturne gave his sentence, — *judgement*
Quhilk gave to Cupide litill reverence,
Bot as ane busteous churle on his maneir — *rough*
Come crabitlie with auster luik and cheir. — *ill-naturedly*

His face fronsit, his lyre was lyke the leid, — *wrinkled, complexion, lead*
His teith chatterit and cheverit with the chin, — *shivered*
His ene drowpit, how sonkin in his heid, — *eyes, hollow sunken*
Out of his nois the meldrop fast can rin, — *mucus*
With lippis bla and cheikis leine and thin; — *blue*
The ice-schoklis that fra his hair doun hang — *icicles*
Was wonder greit and as ane speir als lang.

135 **the blind goddes**. It is usually Cupid who is blind.

137 **seid of lufe**: 'seed of love'. This unusual image will return as a bitter memory when we hear the details of Cresseid's punishment.

147 **the sevin planetis**. The classical deities were well known to medieval writers from their reading of classical literature and were regarded as poetic fictions or at most euhemeristic; but they were 'domesticated' and their power made intelligible within a Christian frame of reference by being interpreted as planetary influences. Such influences were widely regarded as determining a person's character or 'disposition', though not compelling any course of action (*pace* the Wife of Bath, WBP 615–18). They are still poetically represented as gods and goddesses, with features drawn from classical myth as well as from astrological lore. The classic study is J. Seznec, *The Survival of the Pagan Gods* (New York, 1953); see also J. Mann, 'The Planetary Gods in Chaucer and Henryson', in Morse and Windeatt (1990), pp. 91–106.

156 **His teith chatterit**. Saturn is a 'cold' planet, of malevolent influence. The description of the planetary deities is done as a pageant, a deliberately poetic *tour de force* which acts within the narrative to impress us with the ineluctability and impassivity of the circumstances that shape human destiny.

Atovir his belt his lyart lokkis lay
Felterit unfair, ovirfret with froistis hoir,
His garmound and his gyte full gay of gray,
His widderit weid fra him the wind out woir.
Ane busteous bow within his hand he boir,
Under his girdill ane flasche of felloun flanis
Fedderit with ice and heidit with hailstanis.

Down over, grey-streaked
Matted, sprinkled, hoar-frost
cloak and gown
threadbare, caused to billow out
sheaf, deadly arrows
tipped

Than Juppiter, richt fair and amiabill,
God of the starnis in the firmament
And nureis to all thing generabill –
Fra his father Saturne far different,
With burelie face and browis bricht and brent,
Upon his heid ane garland wonder gay
Of flouris fair, as it had bene in May.

stars
nourisher
handsome, forehead, smooth

His voice was cleir, as cristall wer his ene,
As goldin wyre sa glitterand was his hair,
His garmound and his gyte full gay of grene
With goldin listis gilt on everie gair;
Ane burelie brand about his middil bair,
In his richt hand he had ane groundin speir,
Of his father the wraith fra us to weir.

hems, gore (cloth-panel)
(he) bore
sharp-ground
ward off

Nixt efter him come Mars, the god of ire,
Of strife, debait and all dissensioun,
To chide and fecht als feirs as ony fyre,
In hard harnes, hewmound and habirgeoun,
And on his hanche a roustie fell fachioun,
And in his hand he had ane roustie sword,
Wrything his face with mony angrie word.

armour, helmet and coat of mail
blood-rusted savage broad-sword
Contorting

Schaikand his sword befoir Cupide he come,
With reid visage and grislie glowrand ene,
And at his mouth ane bullar stude of fome,
Lyke to ane bair quhetting his tuskis kene,
Richt tuilyeour-lyke but temperance in tene.
Ane horne he blew with mony bosteous brag,
Quhilk all this warld with weir hes maid to wag.

bubble stood
boar
brawler-like, without, anger
violent blast
war, shake

Than fair Phebus, lanterne and lamp of licht,
Of man and beist, baith frute and flourisching,
Tender nureis, and banischer of nicht;
And of the warld causing, be his moving
And influence, lyfe in all eirdlie thing,
Without comfort of quhome of force to nocht
Must all ga die that in this warld is wrocht.

(of) both, blossom
perforce

As king royall he raid upon his chair,
The quhilk Phaeton gydit sum tyme unricht.

rode, chariot

205 **Phaeton** borrowed the horses of the sun (his father, Apollo) and came to grief.

bare The brichtnes of his face quhen it was bair
Nane micht behald for peirsing of his sicht.
This goldin cart with fyrie bemis bricht
Four yokkit steidis full different of hew
feeding-stop or wearying through But bait or tyring throw the spheiris drew.

sorrel-red The first was soyr, with mane als reid as rois,
Callit Eoye, into the orient;
was called The secund steid to name hecht Ethios,
Quhitlie and paill, and sumdeill ascendent;
intense(ly hot) The thrid Peros, richt hait and richt fervent;
The feird was blak, callit Phlegonie,
sea Quhilk rollis Phebus doun into the sey.

Venus was thair present, that goddes gay,
Hir sonnis querrell for to defend, and mak
foolishly fancy Hir awin complaint, cled in ane nyce array,
The ane half grene, the uther half sabill-blak,
combed, parted With hair as gold kemmit and sched abak.
Bot in hir face semit greit variance,
At times… Quhyles perfyte treuth and quhyles inconstance.

dissembling Under smyling scho was dissimulait,
glances Provocative with blenkis amorous,
And suddanely changit and alterait,
Angrie as ony serpent vennemous,
stinging Richt pungitive with wordis odious.
take heed Thus variant scho was, quha list tak keip,
With ane eye lauch and with the uther weip,

tokening, sexual love In taikning that all fleschelie paramour,
Quhilk Venus hes in reull and governance,
Is sumtyme sweit, sumtyme bitter and sour,
Richt unstabill and full of variance,
Mingled Mingit with cairfull joy and fals plesance,
Now hait, now cauld, now blyith, now full of wo,
withered and gone Now grene as leif, now widderit and ago.

With buik in hand than come Mercurius,
Richt eloquent and full of rethorie,
With polite termis and delicious,
make a report With pen and ink to report all reddie,
Composing Setting sangis and singand merilie;
up over His hude was reid, heklit atouir his croun,
old fashion Lyke to ane poeit of the auld fassoun.

syrupy medicines Boxis he bair with fyne electuairis
And sugerit syropis for digestioun,
Spycis belangand to the pothecairis,

210 **spheiris** are the invisible intangible concentric spheres in which the planets have their orbits.
212 **Eoye**. Henryson's names for the four horses of the sun are ultimately from Ovid, *Met.* II.153–4: Eous, Aethon, Pyrois and Phlegon.
244 **heklit**: 'hackled' (like a cock's comb).

With mony hailsum sweit confectioun;
Doctour in phisick, cled in ane skarlot goun,
And furrit weill, as sic ane aucht to be –
Honest and gude, and not ane word culd lie.

Nixt efter him come Lady Cynthia,
The last of all and swiftest in hir spheir;
equipped — Of colour blak, buskit with hornis twa,
And in the nicht scho listis best appeir;
Bluish-grey — Haw as the leid, of colour nathing cleir,
For all hir licht scho borrowis at hir brother
Titan, for of hirself scho hes nane uther.

Hir gyte was gray and full of spottis blake
quite plainly — And on hir breist ane churle paintit full evin
Beirand ane bunche of thornis on his bak,
no nearer — Quhilk for his thift micht clim na nar the hevin.
these — Thus quhen thay gadderit war, thir goddes sevin,
chose — Mercurius thay cheisit with ane assent
'speaker' (presiding chairman) — To be foir-speikar in the parliament.

(so fortunate as) — Quha had bene thair and liken for to heir
eloquent — His facound toung and termis exquisite
practice, learn — Of rethorick the prettick he micht leir,
In a few words, (how to) write — In breif sermone ane pregnant sentence wryte.
doffing — Befoir Cupide veiling his cap a lyte,
He asks, summons — Speiris the caus of that vocatioun,
set forward his accusation — And he anone schew his intentioun.

'Lo,' quod Cupide, 'quha will blaspheme the name
Of his awin god, outher in word or deid,
insult — To all goddis he dois baith lak and schame
And suld have bitter panis to his meid.
I say this by yone wretchit Cresseid,
The quhilk throw me was sumtyme flour of lufe,
Me and my mother starklie can reprufe,

'Saying of hir greit infelicitie
I was the caus, and my mother Venus
Ane blind goddes hir cald that micht not se,
With sclander and defame injurious.
living — Thus hir leving unclene and lecherous
throw back — Scho wald returne on me and my mother,
granted (i.e. to Cresseid) — To quhome I schew my grace abone all uther.

'And sen ye ar all sevin deificait,
Participant of devyne sapience,
This greit injure done to our hie estait

252 **culd**, as past tense of *can*, can likewise form the past tense of other verbs (= 'did').

254 **swiftest in hir spheir**, because her sphere, being nearer to the earth, is smaller.

261 **ane churle**: the old story of the 'man in the moon' as a thief banished there because he stole a bundle of thorns (Peter Quince puts him in his play of Pyramus and Thisbe in *A Midsummer Night's Dream*, V.i.253).

289 The gods have a part, as planetary influences, in the divine will: it is not just a classical poetic charade.

retribution Me think with pane we suld mak recompence.
Was never to goddes done sic violence –
speak As weill for yow as for myself I say –
Thairfoir ga help to revenge, I yow pray!'

Mercurius to Cupide gave answeir
Sir And said, 'Schir King, my counsail is that ye
Refer yow to the hiest planeit heir
And tak to him the lawest of degre
decide upon The pane of Cresseid for to modifie:
As god Saturne, with him tak Cynthia.'
'I am content,' quod he, 'to tak thay twa.'

Than thus proceidit Saturne and the Mone
considered Quhen thay the mater rypelie had degest:
For the dispyte to Cupide scho had done
And to Venus, oppin and manifest,
In all hir lyfe with pane to be opprest
And torment sair with seiknes incurabill,
And to all lovers be abhominabill.

took charge of This duleful sentence Saturne tuik on hand
And passit doun quhair cairfull Cresseid lay
And on hir heid he laid ane frostie wand.
Than lawfullie on this wyse can he say:
'Thy greit fairnes and all thy bewtie gay,
Thy wantoun blude, and eik thy goldin hair,
Heir I exclude fra the for evermair.

'I change thy mirth into melancholy,
Quhilk is the mother of all pensivenes;
Thy moisture and thy heit in cald and dry;
Thyne insolence, thy play and wantones
distress To greit diseis; thy pomp and thy riches
In mortall neid; and greit penuritie
Thow suffer sall and as ane beggar die.'

ill-tempered O cruell Saturne, fraward and angrie,
judgement, too Hard is thy dome and to malitious!
On fair Cresseid quhy hes thow na mercie,
Quhilk was sa sweit, gentill and amorous?
Withdraw thy sentence and be gracious –
act As thow was never: sa schawis throw thy deid,
vindictive Ane wraikfull sentence gevin on fair Cresseid.

Than Cynthia, quhen Saturne past away,
Out of hir sait discendit doun belyve

312 **lawfullie**: 'according to correct legal procedure'. There is much technical legal language in these stanzas.

318 **cald and dry**: the combination of elemental qualities that produces the 'humour' melancholy (see GP 333n), which in turn, as the source of black bile, causes leprosy. Leprosy was often thought of – and Henryson may have had this in mind in assigning it as Cresseid's punishment – as a form of venereal disease (there is a preliminary hint of this in l. 81).

323–9 The narrator's indignant apostrophe to Saturn carries little weight, since the qualities he asks to be taken in extenuation (326) are the very qualities that led to her fall. The narrator is not just a Chaucerian *naif*; he is vulgar and shallow, like Cresseid.

(formally) read a document — And red ane bill on Cresseid quhair scho lay,
Contening this sentence diffinityve:
'Fra heit of bodie I the now depryve
remedy — And to thy seiknes sall be na recure
Bot in dolour thy dayis to indure.

eyes, mingled — 'Thy cristall ene mingit with blude I mak,
rough and hoarse — Thy voice sa cleir unplesand hoir and hace,
lovely complexion — Thy lustie lyre ovirspred with spottis blak,
greyish — And lumpis haw appeirand in thy face:
Quhair thow cummis, ilk man sall fle the place.
Thus — This sall thow go begging fra hous to hous
leper — With cop and clapper lyke ane lazarous.'

This doolie dreame, this ugly visioun
Brocht to an end, Cresseid fra it awoik,
And all that court and convocatioun
rose — Vanischit away. Than rais scho up and tuik
reflection — Ane poleist glas and hir schaddow culd luik;
And quhen scho saw hir face sa deformait,
woeful, knows — Gif scho in hart was wa aneuch, God wait!

Weiping full sair, 'Lo, quhat it is,' quod sche,
move and provoke — 'With fraward langage for to mufe and steir
Our craibit goddis – and sa is sene on me!
My blaspheming now have I bocht full deir;
behind me — All eirdlie joy and mirth I set areir.
Allace, this day! allace, this wofull tyde
Quhen I began with my goddis for to chyde!'

When — Be this was said, ane chyld come fra the hall
To warne Cresseid the supper was reddy;
First knokkit at the dure, and syne culd call:
'Madame, your father biddis yow cum in hy:
prone on the ground — He hes mervell sa lang on grouf ye ly,
somewhat — And sayis your beedes bene to lang sumdeill;
The goddis wait all your intent full weill.'

Quod scho, 'Fair chyld, ga to my father deir
And pray him cum to speik with me anone.'
And sa he did, and said, 'Douchter, quhat cheir?'
'Allace!' quod scho, 'Father, my mirth is gone!'
'How sa?' quod he, and scho can all expone,
As I have tauld, the vengeance and the wraik
For hir trespas Cupide on hir culd tak.

He luikit on hir uglye lipper face,
The quhylk befor was quhite as lillie flour;
Wringand his handis, oftymes he said, allace!
lived — That he had levit to se that wofull hour!

339 **spottis blak**. Cf. 260. Cresseid takes on, grotesquely disfigured, the physical features of her two judges.

343 **cop and clapper**. Lepers carried a cup for alms and a clapper or rattle to warn of their approach.

For he knew weill that thair was no succour
To hir seiknes, and that dowblit his pane.
Thus was thair cair aneuch betuix thame twane!

Quhen thay togidder murnit had full lang,
known Quod Cresseid, 'Father, I wald nat be kend:
go Thairfoir in secreit wyse ye let me gang
Unto yone spitall at the tounis end,
And thidder sum meit for cheritie me send
live, earth To leif upon, for all mirth in this eird
cruel fate Is fra me gane – sic is my wikkit weird!'

beaver-hat (worn by Calchas) Than in ane mantill and ane bawer-hat,
With cop and clapper, wonder prively,
gate He opnit ane secreit yet and out thairat
Convoyit hir, that na man suld espy,
Unto ane village half ane myle thairby,
Delyverit hir in at the spittaill-hous
alms And daylie sent hir part of his almous.

Sum knew hir weill and sum had na knawledge
Of hir becaus scho was sa deformait,
boils With bylis blak ovirsprad in hir visage
And hir fair colour faidit and alterait.
lamentation Yit thay presumit, for hir hie regrait
quiet And still murning, scho was of nobill kin;
With better will thairfor they tuik her in.

The day passit and Phebus went to rest,
The cloudis blak ovirquhelmit all the sky.
God wait gif Cresseid was ane sorrowfull gest,
fare and lodging Seing that uncouth fair and harbery!
prepared But meit or drink scho dressit hir to ly
In ane dark corner of the hous allone,
And on this wyse weiping scho maid hir mone:

The Complaint of Cresseid

(thing soaked in) 'O sop of sorrow, sonkin into cair!
wretched O cative Creisseid! For now and ever mair
Gane is thy joy and al thy mirth in eird;
made pale and bare Of all blyithnes now art thou blaiknit bair;
heal Thair is na salve may saif the of thy sair!
Cruel Fell is thy fortoun, wickit is thy weird,
(see n.) Thy blys is baneist and thy baill on breird!
grant, buried Under the eirth God gif I gravin wer,
hear it Quhair nane of Grece nor yit of Troy micht heir'd!

382 **spitall**. Leper-houses, or 'hospitals', were often set up on the edges of towns, to keep lepers isolated.

407–69 The Complaint, in a nine-line stanza on two rhymes, is a formal poetic *tour de force*. Its extreme stylistic elaboration creates a 'distance' between Cresseid and the reader, who is left free to see that her moralizing upon her abject condition is the product of self-pity, not self-knowledge. Nevertheless, it is a powerful warning of mortality in the tradition of the *memento mori*, given added pungency by being delivered by a walking corpse (lepers were regarded as legally and in effect dead).

413 'Thy bliss is banished and thy distress beginning to increase'.

luxuriously furnished	'Quhair is thy chalmer wantounlie besene,
(see n.)	With burely bed and bankouris browderit bene?
evening refreshment	Spycis and wyne to thy collatioun,
goblets	The cowpis all of gold and silver schene,
	The sweit-meits servit in plaittis clene
saffron sauce, flavour	With saipheron sals of ane gude sessoun?
	Thy gay garmentis with mony gudely goun,
fine linen, brooch	Thy plesand lawn pinnit with goldin prene?
	All is areir thy greit royall renoun!
these plants	'Quhair is thy garding with thir greissis gay
	And fresche flowris quhilk the quene Floray
part	Had paintit plesandly in everie pane,
	Quhair thou was wont full merilye in May
gather, as soon as	To walk and tak the dew be it was day,
blackbird and song-thrush	And heir the merle and mawis mony ane,
go	With ladyis fair in carrolling to gane
	And se the royall rinkis in thair array,
smallest part	In garmentis gay garnischit on everie grane?
	'Thy greit triumphand fame and hie honour,
creatures	Quhair thou was callit of eirdlye wichtis flour,
overturned	All is decayit, thy weird is welterit so:
	Thy hie estait is turnit in darknes dour.
dwelling	This lipper ludge tak for thy burelie bour,
straw	And for thy bed tak now ane bunche of stro,
choice	For waillit wyne and meitis thou had tho
mouldy, perry (pear-cider)	Tak mowlit brid, peirrie and ceder sour;
Except for	Bot cop and clapper now is all ago.
	'My cleir voice and courtlie carrolling,
	Quhair I was wont with ladyis for to sing,
raucous, rook	Is rawk as ruik full hiddeous, hoir and hace;
excelling	My plesand port, all utheris precelling,
worthy	Of lustines I was hald maist conding –
	Now is deformit the figour of my face:
person	To luik on it na leid now lyking hes.
Immersed in sorrow, sighing	Sowpit in syte, I say with sair siching,
Lodged, folk	Ludgeit amang the lipper leid, "Allace!"
	'O ladyis fair of Troy and Grece, attend
	My miserie, quhilk nane may comprehend,
fickle	My frivoll fortoun, my infelicitie,
	My greit mischeif, quhilk na man can amend.
	Be war in tyme, approchis neir the end,
	And in your mynd ane mirrour mak of me:
	As I am now, peradventure that ye
	For all your micht may cum to that same end,
worse	Or ellis war, gif ony war may be.

416–33 The place whose loss Cresseid laments, in a version of the *Ubi sunt* ('Where are…?') topos, is reminiscent of Venus's temple in the *PF*.

417 'With sumptuous bed and finely embroidered seat-covers'.

429 **tak the dew**. Washing in early-morning dew was thought to make a woman beautiful.

452–69 Quite missing the point, Cresseid generalizes her condition as the inevitable result of mutability and ageing.

'Nocht is your fairnes bot ane faiding flour,
Nocht is your famous laud and hie honour
Bot wind inflat in uther mennis eiris; — *puffed*
Your roising reid to rotting sall retour. — *rosy*
Exempill mak of me in your memour — *memory*
Quhilk of sic thingis wofull witnes beiris:
All welth in eird away as wind it weiris. — *passes away*
Be war thairfoir, approchis neir the hour:
Fortoun is fikkill quhen scho beginnis and steiris.' — *gets moving*

Thus chydand with hir drerie destenye,
Weiping scho woik the nicht fra end to end;
Bot all in vane – hir dule, hir cairfull cry,
Micht not remeid nor yit hir murning mend.
Ane lipper lady rais and till hir wend — *rose, went to her*
And said, 'Quhy spurnis thow aganis the wall
To sla thyself and mend nathing at all? — *destroy*

'Sen thy weiping dowbillis bot thy wo, — *Since*
I counsall the mak vertew of ane neid:
Go leir to clap thy clapper to and fro — *learn*
And leif efter the law of lipper leid.' — *live*
Thair was na buit, bot furth with thame scho yeid — *remedy, went*
Fra place to place, quhill cauld and hounger sair — *until*
Compellit hir to be ane rank beggair.

That samin tyme, of Troy the garnisoun, — *garrison*
Quhilk had to chiftane worthie Troylus,
Throw jeopardie of weir had strikken doun — *fortune of war*
Knichtis of Grece in number mervellous;
With greit tryumphe and laude victorious
Agane to Troy richt royallie thay raid — *rode*
The way quhair Cresseid with the lipper baid. — *waited*

Seing that companie come, all with ane stevin — *voice*
Thay gaif ane cry and schuik coppis gude speid, — *with vigour*
Said, 'Worthie lordis, for Goddis lufe of hevin,
To us lipper part of your almous-deid!' — *give a share*
Than to thair cry nobill Troylus tuik heid,
Having pietie, neir by the place can pas — *pity*
Quhair Cresseid sat, not witting quhat scho was.

Than upon him scho kest up baith hir ene –
And with ane blenk it come into his thocht — *glance*
That he sumtime hir face befoir had sene;
Bot scho was in sic plye he knew hir nocht – — *state*
Yit than hir luik into his mynd it brocht
The sweit visage and amorous blenking
Of fair Cresseid, sumtyme his awin darling.

475 **spurnis**. Kicking against a wall was a proverbial image of useless rebellion.

489 This last meeting of Troilus and Cresseid is a sad reprise of the scene in *TC* where he first rode past her house (II.610).

supposing if	Na wonder was, suppois in mynd that he
Interpreted her appearance	Tuik hir figure sa sone – and lo, now quhy:
image, perchance	The idole of ane thing in cace may be
	Sa deip imprentit in the fantasy
	That it deludis the wittis outwardly,
condition	And sa appeiris in forme and lyke estait
	Within the mynd as it was figurait.
	Ane spark of lufe than till his hart culd spring
	And kendlit all his bodie in ane fyre;
hot fever, a fit of sweating	With hait fewir ane sweit and trimbling
until	Him tuik, quhill he was reddie to expyre –
	To beir his scheild his breist began to tyre.
	Within ane quhyle he changit mony hew,
	And nevertheles not ane ane uther knew.
	For knichtlie pietie and memoriall
	Of fair Cresseid ane gyrdill gan he tak,
	Ane purs of gold and mony gay jowall,
throw	And in the skirt of Cresseid doun can swak,
	Than raid away and not ane word he spak,
	Pensive in hart, quhill he come to the toun,
oft-times	And for greit cair oft-syis almaist fell doun.
	The lipper folk to Cresseid than can draw
	To se the equall distributioun
	Of the almous, bot quhen the gold thay saw
whisper	Ilk ane to uther prevelie can roun,
	And said, 'Yone lord hes mair affectioun,
	However it be, unto yone lazarous
	Than to us all – we knaw be his almous.'
idea	'Quhat lord is yone,' quod scho, 'have ye na feill,
	Hes done to us so greit humanitie?'
	'Yes,' quod a lipper man, 'I knaw him weill:
	Schir Troylus it is, gentill and fre.'
	Quhen Cresseid understude that it was he,
pang	Stiffer than steill thair stert ane bitter stound
	Throwout hir hart, and fell doun to the ground.
revived	Quhen scho ovircome, with siching sair and sad,
and bitter cries of 'alas!'	With mony cairfull cry and cald ochane:
beset	'Now is my breist with stormie stoundis stad,
bewildered	Wrappit in wo, ane wretch full will of wane!'
	Than swounit scho oft or ever scho culd refrane,
	And ever in hir swouning cryit scho thus:
	'O fals Cresseid and trew knicht Troylus!

505–11 The explanation of Troilus's perception is well in accord with medieval views of the deluding power of fantasy, or imagination. The difference, of course – and perhaps Henryson is making a point about the power of imagination – is that in this case the perception is correct.

518 Why does not Cresseid recognize Troilus? It may be that leprosy has affected her sight; or it may suggest, allegorically, that she never truly knew him.

loyalty 'Thy lufe, thy lawtie and thy gentilnes
I countit small in my prosperitie,
So elevait I was in wantones
And clam upon the fickill quheill sa hie.
All faith and lufe I promissit to the
in itself Was in the self fickill and frivolous:
O fals Cresseid and trew knicht Troylus!

'For lufe of me thow keipt gude continence,
dealings with others Honest and chaist in conversatioun.
Of all wemen protectour and defence
reputation Thou was, and helpit thair opinioun –
My mynd in fleschelie foull affectioun
Was inclynit to lustis lecherous:
Fy, fals Cresseid! O trew knicht Troylus!

'Lovers be war and tak gude heid about
Quhome that ye lufe, for quhome ye suffer paine:
I lat yow wit thair is richt few thairout
in return Quhome ye may traist to have trew lufe agane –
Test it out Preif quhen ye will, your labour is in vaine.
Thairfoir I reid ye tak thame as ye find,
steadfast, weathercock For thay ar sad as widdercok in wind.

'Becaus I knaw the greit unstabilnes,
Brittle, within Brukkill as glas, into myself, I say –
Anticipating Traisting in uther als greit unfaithfulnes,
faith Als unconstant and als untrew of fay –
Though, know Thocht sum be trew, I wait richt few ar thay:
praise Quha findis treuth lat him his lady ruse!
Nane but myself as now I will accuse.'

Quhen this was said, with paper scho sat doun,
And on this maneir maid hir testament:
commit 'Heir I beteiche my corps and carioun
toads With wormis and with taidis to be rent;
My cop and clapper and myne ornament
And all my gold the lipper folk sall have
Quhen I am deid, to burie me in grave.

'This royall ring set with this rubie reid
as a love-token Quhilk Troylus in drowrie to me send
leave To him agane I leif it quhen I am deid
death, known To mak my cairfull deid unto him kend.
Thus I conclude schortlie and mak ane end:
My spreit I leif to Diane quhair scho dwellis,
uninhabited woods with pools To walk with hir in waist woddis and wellis.

550 **the fickill quheill** of Fortune is turned continually by the goddess so that those who are bound to it rise and fall arbitrarily.
574 This is the moment of self-knowledge to which the poem has been directed.
587 **Diane**. By leaving her soul to Diana, goddess of chastity, Cresseid formally relinquishes the service of Venus.

'O Diomeid, thou hes baith broche and belt
Quhilk Troylus gave me in takning
swooned to death Of his trew lufe!' And with that word scho swelt.
took off And sone ane lipper man tuik of the ring,
Then Syne buryit hir withouttin tarying.
To Troylus furthwith the ring he bair
And of Cresseid the deith he can declair.

Quhen he had hard hir greit infirmitie,
Hir legacie and lamentatioun,
And how scho endit in sic povertie,
swooned He swelt for wo and fell doun in ane swoun;
ready For greit sorrow his hart to brist was boun,
Siching full sadlie, said, 'I can no moir:
Scho was untrew and wo is me thairfoir.'

tombstone Sum said he maid ane tomb of merbell gray
And wrait hir name and superscriptioun
And laid it on hir grave quhair that scho lay,
statement In golden letteris, conteining this ressoun:
'Lo, fair ladyis, Cresseid of Troyis toun,
Sumtyme countit the flour of womanheid,
Under this stane, lait lipper, lyis deid.'

little poem Now, worthie wemen, in this ballet schort,
Maid for your worschip and instructioun,
admonish Of cheritie I monische and exhort,
Ming not your lufe with fals deceptioun.
Beir in your mynd this schort conclusioun
here-before Of fair Cresseid, as I have said befoir;
Sen scho is deid, I speik of hir no moir.

The Fables

The *Fables* are drawn partly from the Latin collection of fables attributed to Aesop (very well known to a schoolmaster, since it was a Latin school-text) and partly from the thirteenth-century French *Roman de Renart*, a satiric and scurrilous animal-epic in which Reynard out-foxes everyone. The genre is that of beast-fable, in which animals talk, think and act like humans but live partly animal lives (rather like humans). The continual flickering movement between animal and human perspectives is exploited for its intrinsic comicality, while the general displacement of the point of view makes for an acidly objective commentary on human foibles and weaknesses. Comedy of this kind, which Jonson and Fielding would have found much to their taste, is the appeal of several of the *Fables*. But the ostensibly primary purposes of beast-fable are moral and satiric, and Henryson attaches a *Moralitas* to each of his fables in which he expounds its allegorical meaning in relation to human existence. These meanings are not always strikingly profound nor self-evident, and there are times when one suspects that Henryson is interrogating as much as asserting the relation between story and *Moralitas*. If there is a question about that relation, it has to do, in the grimmer tales, not with the semiotics of narrative, but with the possibility of justice. There is much of the law in Henryson (who had some legal training), of legal motifs and legal language, and a kind of sardonic admiration for the efficiency with which the law works to the benefit of the powerful who manipulate it. There is something of this in Henryson's attitude to divine justice too. The lack of

589 The **broche** plays a key part in *TC* in finally convincing Troilus that Criseyde has gone over to Diomede (see III.1371, V.1040, 1661, 1681).

rapport between story and *Moralitas* in some of the fables, between the human compassion of the former and the lofty distance of the latter, seems to speak to an awareness of this brutal disjunction between pity and justice.

The earliest surviving text of the *Fables* is the Bassandyne print of 1571 (B), which is followed below with emendation from other witnesses as cited in Fox (1981) and with his continuous line-numbering. In this as in other complete texts the 13 fables are arranged in an order which seems to be planned (Fox, pp. lxxv–lxxxi), but the basis of the plan is not explained and Henryson may have left it for the reader to work out. What is clear is an increasing sense of darkness in the work: he begins with a group of fairly light-hearted fables, including the tale of 'The Town Mouse and the Country Mouse' (No. 2) and Nos 3 and 4 as below. In No. 8, 'The Preaching of the Swallow', he outlines the principles of God's government as they operate to the benefit of his creatures if they are prudent (see J. Burrow, in *EC* 25 [1975], 25–37). The last three tales, including Nos 11 and 12 as below, are increasingly grim, and No. 12 ends with a long and passionate outburst against the oppressions of great lords.

The Cock and the Fox

This is the story that Chaucer tells with such a pyrotechnic display of learned and mock-heroic allusion in the Nun's Priest's Tale. Henryson's version is self-consciously independent of Chaucer (though almost exclusively indebted to him), with the bourgeois genre-scene in which the hens become reconciled to the loss of their lord as the comic high point.

Though	Thocht brutall beistis be irrationall,
	That is to say, wantand discretioun,
each one	Yit ilk ane in thair kyndis naturall
	Hes mony divers inclinatioun.
fierce	The bair busteous, the wolf, the wylde lyoun,
deceitful, full of tricks	The fox fenyeit, craftie and cawtelows,
	The dog to bark in nicht and keip the hows.
	Sa different thay ar in properteis
	Unknawin unto man and infinite,
having, many	In kynd haifand sa fell diversiteis,
write	My cunning it excedis for to dyte.
	Forthy as now I purpose for to wryte
(see n.)	Ane cais I fand quhilk fell this ather yeir
	Betuix ane fox and gentill Chantecleir.
in a village in those	Ane wedow dwelt intill ane drope thay dayis,
distaff	Quhilk wan hir fude of spinning on hir rok,
	And na mair had, forsuth, as the fabill sayis,
	Except of hennis scho had ane lyttill flok,
	And thame to keip scho had ane jolie cok
spirited	Richt curageous, that to this wedow ay
Marked the divisions of night	Devydit nicht and crew befoir the day.
	Ane lyttill fra this foirsaid wedowis hows
(see n.)	Ane thornie schaw thair wes, of grit defence,
	Quhairin ane foxe, craftie and cautelous,
	Maid his repair and daylie residence;
	Quhilk to this wedow did grit violence

397–407 The irrationality and infinite diversity of animals and the tendency of different species to have fixed characteristics make them apt as figures for humankind.

409 'A case I found which befell a year or two back'.

410 **Chantecleir** ('Sing-clear') is the cock's name in Chaucer, but Henryson has his own names for the fox and hens.

419 'A thorny wood there was, affording excellent protection'.

stealing In pyking of pultrie baith day and nicht,
And na way be revengit on him scho micht.

fox This wylie tod, quhen that the lark couth sing,
farmstead Full sair hungrie unto the toun him drest,
(into = *in*) Quhair Chantecleir, into the gray dawing,
Worn out by his night's work Werie for nicht, wes flowen fra his nest.
pondered Lowrence this saw and in his mynd he kest
stratagems The jeperdies, the wayis and the wyle
Be quhat menis he micht this cok begyle.

Dissimuland into countenance and cheir,
On kneis fell and smyland thus he said:
'Gude morne, my maister, gentill Chantecleir!'
jerk With that the cok start bakwart in ane braid.
Sir 'Schir, be my saull, ye neid not be effraid,
Nor yit for me to start nor fle abak:
I come bot heir service to yow to mak.

'Wald I not serve to yow, it wer bot blame,
As I have done to yowr progenitouris.
Your father full oft fillit hes my wame
And send me meit fra midding to the muris.
cares And at his end I did my besie curis
To hald his heid and gif him drinkis warme,
Then, dear creature Syne at the last the sweit swelt in my arme.'

giggled 'Knew ye my father?' quod the cok, and leuch.
'Yea, my fair sone, I held up his heid
died, birch bough Quhen that he deit under ane birkin beuch,
Syne said the Dirigie quhen that he wes deid.
enmity Betuix us twa how suld thair be ane feid?
trust Quhame suld ye traist bot me, your servitour,
That to your father did sa grit honour?

'Quhen I behald your fedderis fair and gent,
hackle, comb Your beik, your breist, your hekill and your kame –
Schir, be my saull and the blissit sacrament,
My hart is warme, me think I am at hame!
belly To mak yow blyith I wald creip on my wame
dark In froist and snaw, in wedder wan and weit,
grey-streaked And lay my lyart loikkis under your feit.'

This fenyeit fox, fals and dissimulate,
cavil (minor complaint) Maid to this cok ane cavillatioun:
'Ye ar, me think, changit and degenerate
Fra your father of his conditioun:
Of craftie crawing he micht beir the croun,
toes For he wald on his tais stand and craw.
no lie This is na le – I stude beside and saw.'

442 'And sent me food from the farmyard dungheap to the moorlands', i.e. sired chickens that the fox stole. The speech is full of *double entendres*.

449 **Dirigie**, from Lat. *dirige*, 'direct', the first word of an antiphon in the Office for the Dead, often used to denote the whole office (cf. MnE 'dirge').

With that the cok, upon his tais hie,
Kest up his beik and sang with all his micht.
Quod schir Lowrence, 'Weill said, sa mot I the:
Ye ar your fatheris sone and air upricht! — *rightful heir*
Bot of his cunning yit ye want ane slicht, — *trick*
For,' quod the tod, 'he wald – and haif na dout – — *don't doubt me*
Baith wink and craw and turne him thryis about.' — *close his eyes*

The cok, inflate with wind and fals vanegloir,
That mony puttis unto confusioun,
Traisting to win ane grit worschip thairfoir,
Unwarlie winkand walkit up and doun
And syne to chant and craw he maid him boun – — *ready*
And suddandlie, be he had crawin ane note, — *by the time that*
The fox wes war and hint him be the throte, — *seized*

Syne to the woid but tarie with him hyit, — *without delay*
Of countermaund haifand bot lytill dout. — *fear*
With that Pertok, Sprutok and Toppok cryit;
The wedow hard and with ane cry come out. — *heard*
Seand the cace, scho sichit and gaif ane schout, — *situation*
'How, murther, reylok!' with ane hiddeous beir; — *robbery, noise*
'Allace, now lost is gentill Chantecleir!'

As scho wer woid, with mony yell and cry, — *mad*
Ryvand hir hair, upon hir breist can beit, — *Tearing,* (can = *'did'*)
Syne paill of hew, half in ane extasye,
Fell doun for cair in swoning and in sweit. — *sweating-fit*
With that the selie hennis left thair meit
And quhill this wyfe wes lyand thus in swoun
Fell of that cace in disputatioun.

'Allace!' quod Pertok, makand sair murning,
With teiris grit attour hir cheikis fell, — *down over, (that) fell*
'Yone wes our drowrie and our dayis darling, — *sweetheart*
Our nichtingall and als our orlege bell, — *clock*
Our walkryfe watche, us for to warne and tell — *wakeful*
Quhen that Aurora with hir curcheis gray — *(dawn-goddess), kerchiefs*
Put up hir heid betuix the nicht and day.

'Quha sall our lemman be? Quha sall us leid? — *sweetheart*
Quhen we ar sad, quha sall unto us sing?
With his sweit bill he wald brek us the breid –
In all this warld wes thair ane kynder thing?
In paramouris he wald do us plesing — *sexual love*
At his power, as nature did him geif. — *give*
Now efter him, allace, how sall we leif?' — *live*

Quod Sprutok than, 'Ceis, sister, of your sorrow:
Ye be to mad, for him sic murning mais. — *you make*
We sall fair weill, I find Sanct Johne to borrow: — *take as security*
The proverb sayis, "Als gude lufe cummis as gais".
I will put on my haly-dayis clais — *clothes*

in preparation for And mak me fresch agane this jolie May,
Syne chant this sang: "Wes never wedow so gay!"

in fear 'He wes angry and held us ay in aw
And woundit with the speir of jelowsy.
bedroom-fun Of chalmer-glew, Pertok, full weill ye knaw,
Waistit he wes, of nature cauld and dry.
Since Sen he is gone, thairfoir, sister, say I,
sorrow Be blyith in baill, for that is best remeid:
Let quik to quik, and deid ga to the deid!'

pretended Than Pertok spak, that feinyeit faith befoir,
without love In lust but lufe that set all hir delyte,
know, such 'Sister, ye wait of sic as him ane scoir
Wald not suffice to slaik our appetyte.
promise, rid of him I hecht yow be my hand, sen ye ar quyte,
week, if Within ane oulk, for schame and I durst speik,
man, breeches To get ane berne suld better claw oure breik!'

smugly Than Toppok lyke ane curate spak full crous:
'Yone wes ane verray vengeance from the hevin!
dissolute He wes sa lous and sa lecherous,
Leave off, wenches ('kitties') Seis coud he nocht with kittokis ma than sevin.
balance Bot rychteous God, haldand the balandis evin,
Smytis rycht sair, thocht he be patient,
Adulteraris that will thame not repent.

'Prydefull he wes, and joyit of his sin,
cared, enmity And comptit not for Goddis favour nor feid,
expected, rule, flourish Bot traistit ay to rax and sa to rin
Until Quhill at the last his sinnis can him leid
To schamefull end and to yone suddand deid.
Thairfoir it is the verray hand of God
seized by That causit him be werryit with the tod!'

Quhen this wes said, the wedow fra hir swoun
(small hunting) dogs Start up on fute and on hir kennettis cryde,
'How, Birkye! Berrie! Bell! Bawsie Broun!
Rip-thicket, Run-well Rype-schaw! Rin-weil! Curtes! Nuttieclyde!
without grumbling Togidder all but grunching furth ye glyde!
Reskew my nobill cok or he be slane
Or ellis to me se ye cum never agane!'

(see n.) With that but baid thay braidet over the bent,
As fyre of flint thay over the feildis flaw;
quickly Full wichtlie thay throw wood and wateris went

515 Henryson alludes to a favourite theme of anti-feminist satire – the merry lives and insatiable sexual appetites of widows. Chaucer worked his own variations on it, with the Wife of Bath, and Dunbar, in *The Two Married Women and the Widow* (below), more or less did it to death.

519 **cauld and dry**: this combination of humours (see *Testament*, 318n) signified melancholy and miserable unfitness for love.

530 It is a stroke of genius to make one of the hens a moralist who sounds like Henryson on a bad day.

546–7 A string of dogs' names is usual at this point, as in Nun's Priest's Tale, VII.3383. Some of the names here are very inventive, and might be imperatives.

551–3 A little outbreak of mock-heroic alliterative poeticism.

551 'With that, without delay, they dashed over the open ground'.

And ceissit not Schir Lourence quhill thay saw.
Bot quhen he saw the kennettis cum on raw, — *in a string*
Unto the cok in mynd he said, 'God sen — *Would to God*
That I and thow wer fairlie in my den!'

Then said the cok, with sum gude spirit inspyrit,
'Do my counsall, and I sall warrand the. — *protect*
Hungrie thow art and for grit travell tyrit,
Richt faint of force and may not ferther fle:
Swyith turne agane and say that I and ye — *Quickly*
Freindis ar maid and fellowis for ane yeir;
Than will thay stynt – I stand for it – and not steir.' — *guarantee, stir*

This tod, thocht he wes fals and frivolus,
And had frawdis, his querrell to defend, — *tricks*
Desavit wes be menis richt mervelous –
For falset failyeis ay at the latter end. — *falsehood comes to grief*
He start about and cryit as he wes kend: — *instructed*
With that the cok he braid unto a bewch. — *sprang, bough*
Now juge ye all quhairat Schir Lowrence lewch! — *(see n.)*

Begylit thus, the tod under a tre
On kneis fell, and said: 'Gude Chantecleir,
Cum doun agane and I, but meit or fe, — *wages*
Sal be your man and servand for ane yeir.'
'Nay, fals theif and revar – stand not me neir! — *robber*
My bludy hekill and my nek sa bla — *black-and-blue*
Hes partit freindschip for ever betwene us twa.

'I wes unwyis that winkit at thy will,
Quhairthrow almaist I loissit had my heid.'
'I wes mair fule,' quod he, 'coud nocht be still, — *more foolish*
Bot spake to put my pray into pleid.' — *(see n.)*
'Fair on, fals theif! God keip me fra thy feid!' — *Off with you, enmity*
With that the coke over the feildis tuke his flicht,
And in at the wedowis lewer couth he licht. — *did he alight*

Moralitas

Now, worthie folk, suppose this be ane fabill
And ouerheillit wyth typis figurall, — *covered over*
Yit may ye find ane sentence richt agreabill — *suitable*
Under thir fenyeit termis textuall.
To our purpose this cok weill may we call
Nyse proud men, woid and vaneglorious — *mad*
Of kyn and blude, quhilk ar presumpteous.

558 **inspyrit**, i.e. it is not a reply to the fox, who did not speak aloud.
571 'You tell me what Mr Fox had to laugh about now!'
582 'But opened my mouth and so made my prey a subject of debate' (i.e. gave up my power over it).
585 **lewer**: louver (slatted turret for escape of smoke).
586–9 Beast-fables were conventionally thought of as having a literal (**textuall**) sense, invented (**fenyeit**) and untrue, and a moral-allegorical meaning, similar to the way in which OT stories were interpreted as allegorical 'types' or 'figures' of Christ and the Christian revelation.

Fy, puft-up pryde, thow is full poysonabill!
Quha favoris the on force man haif ane fall. *perforce must*
Thy strenth is nocht, thy stule standis unstabill –
Tak witnes of the feyndis infernall
Quhilk houndit doun wes fra that hevinlie hall
To hellis hole and to that hiddeous hous
Because in pryde thay wer presumpteous.

This fenyeit foxe may weill be figurate *deceitful, used as a figure for*
To flatteraris with plesand wordis quhyte, *white (specious)*
With fals mening and mynd maist toxicate, *poisonous*
To loif and le that settis thair haill delyte. *praise and lie*
All worthie folk at sic suld haif despyte,
For quhair is thair mair perrellous pestilence
Nor gif to learis haistelie credence? *Than to, liars*

This wickit mynd and adullatioun,
Of sucker sweit haifand the similitude, *sugar*
Bitter as gall and full of fell poysoun *destructive*
To taist it is, quha cleirlie understude. *whoever*
Forthy as now, schortlie to conclude,
Thir twa sinnis, flatterie and vaneglore, *These*
Ar vennomous – gude folk, fle thame thairfoir!

The Fox and the Wolf

The practice of confession was central to the experience of the medieval Christian and a key element in the church's exercise of control over the minds of the faithful. Abuse of the practice was a serious matter, but was widespread, and the high comedy of this fable is an index to some of the forms it took: confession undertaken out of fear rather than penitence, with no intention of breaking the habit of sin, nor of performing penance; and absolution administered with indulgence, especially by friars who were susceptible to flattery or bribes and had no continuing pastoral responsibility. Somehow, amidst all the animal energies and high spirits, it is not easy to remember how serious it all was, though Henryson reminds us, in the three heavy stanzas of the *Moralitas*.

Leif we this wedow glaid, I yow assure, *Leave*
Of Chantecleir, mair blyith than I can tell,
And speik we of the fatal aventure
And destenie that to this foxe befell,
Quhilk durst na mair with miching intermell *pilfering, engage in*
Als lang as leme or licht wes of the day,
Bot bydand nicht full styll lurkand he lay, *awaiting*

Quhill that Thetes, the goddes of the flude, *sea*
Phebus had callit to the harbery, *night's lodging-place*
And Hesperous put up his cluddie hude, *(the evening star)*
Schawand his lustie visage in the sky.
Than Lourence luikit up, quhair he couth ly, *from where he lay*
And kest his hand upon his ee on hicht, *(shaded his eyes)*
Merie and glade that cummit wes the nicht.

Out of the wod unto ane hill he went
Quhair he micht se the tuinkling sternis cleir
And all the planetis of the firmament,

Thair cours and eik thair moving in thair spheir,
Sum retrograde and sum stationeir,
And of the zodiak in quhat degre
Thay wer ilk ane. As Lowrence leirnit me, *each one, taught*

Than Saturne auld wes enterit in Capricorne,
And Juppiter movit in Sagittarie,
And Mars up in the Rammis heid wes borne,
And Phebus in the Lyoun furth can carie;
Venus the Crab, the Mone wes in Aquarie,
Mercurius, the god of eloquence,
Into the Virgyn maid his residence. *Virgo*

But astrolab, quadrant or almanak, *Without*
Teichit of nature be instructioun,
The moving of the hevin this tod can tak, *ascertain*
Quhat influence and constellatioun *stellar influence*
Wes lyke to fall upon the eirth adoun,
And to himself he said, withoutin mair,
'Weill worth the, father, that send me to the lair. *Good befall you, to learning*

'My destenie and eik my weird I wait, *fate, know*
My aventure is cleirlie to me kend; *fortune*
With mischeif myngit is my mortall fait
My misleving the soner bot gif I mend; *unless*
It is reward of sin, ane schamefull end.
Thairfoir I will ga seik sum confessour
And schryiff me clene of my sinnis to this hour.

'Allace,' quod he, 'richt waryit ar we thevis: *cursed*
Our lyif is set ilk nicht in aventure, *in jeopardy*
Our cursit craft full mony man mischevis, *injures*
For ever we steill and ever ar lyke pure; *alike poor*
In dreid and schame our dayis we indure,
Syne "Widdinek" and "Crakraip" callit als, *(see n.)*
And till our hyre hangit up be the hals.' *for our reward*

Accusand thus his cankerit conscience,
Into ane craig he kest about his ee,
So saw he cummand, ane lyttill than frome thence,
Ane worthie doctour in divinitie,
Freir Wolff Waitskaith, in science wonder sle, *'Do-harm', knowledge, clever*
To preiche and pray was new cummit fra the closter,
With beidis in hand, sayand his Pater Noster. *prayer-beads*

Seand this wolff, this wylie tratour tod *Seeing*
On kneis fell, with hude into his nek: *(see n.)*

632 **retrograde**: refers to the planet's apparent motion in its sphere in relation to the zodiac, that is, east to west instead of west to east.
634 **As Lowrence leirnit me**. The narrator imagines himself present, learning the story as it happens, like Chaucer in the *CT* (cf. 694–6).
635–41 A sky-chart for all seven planets: the fox's expertise as an astrologer enables him to miss the point more resoundingly (649–53): man's destiny is *not* written in the stars.
661 'Then also called "Gallows-neck" and "Crack-rope"'.
671 **into his nek**: 'around his neck' (i.e. bare-headed in humility).

	'Welcome, my gostlie father under God',
bow, inclination of the head	Quod he, with mony binge and mony bek.
	'Ha,' quod the wolff, 'schir Tod, for quhat effek
behaviour	Mak ye sic feir? Ryse up, put on your hude!'
do it	'Father,' quod he, 'I haif grit cause to du'de:
sure	'Ye are mirrour, lanterne and sicker way
	Suld gyde sic sempill folk as me to grace;
coarse cloth cowl	Your bair feit and your russet coull of gray,
	Your lene cheik, your paill and pietious face,
	Schawis to me your perfite halines;
once	For weill wer him that anis in his lyve
good fortune	Had hap to yow his sinnis for to schryve.'
poor simple, smiled	'Na, selie Lowrence,' quod the wolf, and leuch,
	'It plesis me that ye ar penitent.'
robbery and theft	'Of reif and stouth, schir, I can tell aneuch,
	That causis me full sair for to repent.
	Bot father, byde still heir upon the bent,
	I yow beseik, and heir me to declair
	My conscience, that prikkis me sa sair.'
set	'Weill,' quod the wolff, 'sit doun upon thy kne.'
knelt	And he doun bair-heid sat full humilly
	And syne began with 'Benedicitie'.
aside	(Quhen I this saw, I drew ane lytill by,
is fitting	For it effeiris nouther to heir nor spy
seal (promise of confidentiality)	Nor to reveill thing said under that seill.)
in this way, spoke	Unto the tod this-gait the wolf couth mele:
	'Art thow contrite and sorie in thy spreit
do it	For thy trespas?' 'Na, schir, I can not du'id.
	Me think that hennis ar sa honie sweit
	And lambes flesche that new ar lettin bluid,
make a decision	For to repent my mynd can not concluid,
	Bot of this thing, that I haif slane sa few.'
	'Weill,' quod the wolf, 'in faith thow art ane schrew.
Since, repent	'Sen thow can not forthink thy wickitnes,
	Will thow forbeir in tyme to cum, and mend?'
If, live	'And I forbeir, how sall I leif, allace,
	Haifand nane uther craft me to defend?
	Neid causis me to steill quhair-ever I wend:
am ashamed, dig	I eschame to thig, I can not wirk, ye wait,
	Yit wald I fane pretend to gentill stait.'

679 **gray**. The wolf is a Grey Friar (Franciscan).

693 **Benedicitie**: the *Benedicite* ('Bless ye'), a prayer recited before confession.

702–3 Echoes famous lines in the Scottish epic of *Wallace* (c.1475) by 'Blind Hary', where the hero is asked by a priest if he repents his life of killing: 'Than Wallace smyld a litill at his langage. / "I grant," he said, "part Inglismen I slew, / In my quarell me thocht nocht halff enew..." ' (XII.1384–6).

704 Friar Wolf's repeated 'Weill' is not quite the stinging reproof one might expect.

707–9 There was a whole debate in medieval canon law, put in a comically different context here, about the neediness of poor people and beggars and their right to steal food in cases of desperate need. See 731, below, and *PP* VIII.210, XXII.1–50.

710 Like Langland (*PP* V.24) and Hoccleve (*Regement*, 976–85) in similar situations, the fox alludes to Luke 16:3.

'Weill,' quod the wolf, 'thow wantis pointis twa
Belangand to perfyte confessioun;
To the thrid part of penitence let us ga:
accept penitential discipline Will thow tak pane for thy transgressioun?'
'Na, schir, considder my complexioun,
Seikly and waik, and off my nature tender;
Lo, will ye se, I am baith lene and sklender.

'Yit nevertheles I wald, swa it wer licht,
Schort, and not grevand to my tendernes,
a little bit Tak part of pane, fulfill it gif I micht,
To set my selie saull in way of grace.'
'Thow sall,' quod he, 'forbeir flesch untill Pasche
To tame this corps, that cursit carioun,
grant And heir I reik the full remissioun.'

'I grant thairto, swa ye will giff me leif
To eit puddingis, or laip ane lyttill blude,
paunch-meats (tripe, etc.), taste Or heid, or feit, or paynchis let me preif,
lack In cace I falt of flesch into my fude.'
In case of great need 'For grit mister I gif the leif to du'de
week Twyse in the oulk, for neid may haif na law.'
reward 'God yeild yow, schir, for that text weill I knaw.'

Quhen this wes said, the wolf his wayis went;
went, sea The foxe on fute he fure unto the flude;
To fang him fisch haillelie wes his intent.
surging angry waves Bot quhen he saw the walterand wallis woude,
astonished, a horrified stare All stonist still into ane stair he stude,
stayed And said, 'Better that I had biddin at hame
Than Nor bene ane fischar, in the Devillis name!

must 'Now man I scraip my meit out of the sand,
For I haif nouther boittis, net nor bait.'
As he wes thus for falt of meit murnand,
sustenance, seek Lukand about, his leving for to lait,
troop of goats Under ane tre he saw ane trip of gait.
little hollow Than wes he blyith, and in ane hewch him hid,
And fra the gait he stall ane lytill kid.

Syne over the heuch unto the see he hyis
And tuke the kid be the hornis twane
And in the watter outher twyis or thryis
He dowkit him, and till him can he sayne,
'Ga doun, schir Kid, cum up, schir Salmond, agane,'
Quhill he wes deid, syne to the land him drewch
And of that new-maid salmond eit anewch.

714 The **thrid part** of penitence is 'satisfaction', that is, performing some act of penance or restitution that shows true penitence.
723 **untill Pasche**: not too severe a penance, since the time before Easter was Lent, when everyone was supposed to give up meat.
731 **neid may haif na law**. Proverbial.
751 The kid is 'baptised' and is **new-maid** as a Christian fish, suitable for a Christian to eat when fasting. There is allusion here to some of the fine distinctions that were made in ecclesiastical regulations about what was and was not a fish, in the attempt to broaden the Friday menu.

Thus fynelie fillit with young tender meit,
hiding-place Unto ane derne for dreid he him addrest,
Under ane busk, quhair that the sone can beit,
warm To beik his breist and bellie he thocht best;
And rekleslie he said, quhair he did rest,
belly Straikand his wame aganis the sonis heit,
(see n.) 'Upon this wame set wer ane bolt full meit.'

Quhen this wes said, the keipar of the gait,
Cairfull in hart his kid wes stollen away,
look On everilk syde full warlie couth he wait,
Quhill at the last he saw quhair Lowrence lay.
arrow Ane bow he bent, ane flane with fedderis gray
drew He haillit to the heid and, or he steird,
pinned The foxe he prikkit fast unto the eird.

'Now,' quod the foxe, 'allace and wellaway!
Spiked Gorrit I am, and may na forther gane;
Me think na man may speik ane word in play
Bot now-on-dayis in ernist it is tane.'
herdsman, seized The hird him hynt and out he drew his flane
And for his kid and uther violence
got some of his own back He tuke his skyn and maid ane recompence.

Moralitas

unforeseen This suddand deith and unprovysit end
Of this fals tod, without contritioun,
Exempill is exhortand folk to amend,
For dreid of sic ane lyk conclusioun;
For mony gois now to confessioun
weep Can not repent nor for thair sinnis greit
Because thay think thair lustie lyfe sa sweit.

custom and habit Sum bene also throw consuetude and ryte
Vanquished Vincust with carnall sensualitie:
Suppose thay be as for the tyme contryte,
Can not forbeir nor fra thair sinnis fle.
in the character Use drawis nature swa in propertie
of necessity, must Of beist and man that neidlingis thay man do
accustomed As thay of lang tyme hes bene hantit to.

Be war, gude folke, and feir this suddane schoit,
Quhilk smytis sair withoutin resistence.
take note Attend wyislie and in your hartis noit,
Aganis deith may na man mak defence.

760 'It would be perfect justice if an arrow went straight through my stomach'. In his euphoric state, the fox remembers laughingly all the mumbo-jumbo of sin and punishment that he has just been play-acting.

768–71 The heroes of northern saga are expected to make some nonchalant 'death-quip' as they die; this of the fox's takes the prize for insouciance.

776–94 Readings in the copy-text here (at 776, 778, 779, 794) show Protestant revision. Protestants were presumably happy with the comic parody of the confessional, but not with serious exhortation to confession.

792 A line that would be at home in Lydgate's *Dance Macabre*.

Ceis of your sin, remord your conscience, *examine remorsefully*
Do wilfull pennance here, and ye shall wend, *voluntary*
Efter your deith, to blis withouttin end.

The Wolf and the Wether

Qwhylum thair wes, as Esope can report, *Once upon a time*
Ane scheipheird duelland be ane forrest neir,
Quhilk had ane hound that did him grit comfort:
Full war he wes to walk his fauld, but weir, *sheep-fold, without doubt*
That nouther wolf nor wildcat durst appeir,
Nor foxe on feild nor yit no uther beist,
Bot he thame slew or chaissit at the leist.

Sa happinnit it – as everilk beist man de – *must die*
This hound of suddand seiknes to be deid;
Bot than, God wait, the keipar of the fe *livestock*
For verray wo woxe wanner nor the weid: *paler than a weed*
'Allace!' quod he, 'now se I na remeid
To saif the selie beistis that I keip,
For with the wolf weryit beis all my scheip!' *worried, will be*

It wald have maid ane mannis hart sair to se
The selie scheipirdis lamentatioun:
'Now is my darling deid, allace!' quod he;
'For now to beg my breid I may be boun, *ready*
With pyikstaff and with scrip to fair of toun; *bag, go out of*
For all the beistis befoir that bandonit bene *have been cowed*
Will schute upon my beistis with ire and tene!' *rush, anger*

With that ane wedder wichtlie wan on fute: *quickly got up*
'Maister,' quod he, 'mak merie and be blyith;
To brek your hart for baill it is na bute. *sorrow, remedy*
For ane deid dogge ye na cair on yow kyith: *don't show yourself sorrowful*
Ga fetche him hither and fla his skyn off swyth, *flay*
Syne sew it on me – and luke that it be meit, *well-fitting*
Baith heid and crag, bodie, taill and feit. *neck*

'Than will the wolf trow that I am he,
For I sall follow him fast quharever he fair. *goes*
All haill the cure I tak it upon me *Entirely, charge*
Your scheip to keip at midday, lait and air: *early*
And he persew, be God I sall not spair *If*
To follow him as fast as did your doig,
Swa that I warrand ye sall not want ane hoig.' *be missing one young sheep*

Than said the scheipheird: 'This come of ane gude wit;
Thy counsall is baith sicker, leill and trew; *reliable, faithful*
Quha sayis ane scheip is daft, that lieit of it.'
With that in hy the doggis skyn off he flew *flayed*
And on the scheip rycht softlie couth it sew.
Than worth the wedder wantoun of his weid: *foolishly proud*
'Now of the wolf,' quod he, 'I have na dreid.'

In all thingis he counterfait the dog,
For all the nycht he stude and tuke na sleip
Swa that weill lang thair wantit not ane hog.
watchful Swa war he wes and walkryfe thame to keip
That Lowrence durst not luke upon ane scheip,
For, and he did, he followit him sa fast
That of his lyfe he maid him all agast.

Was nowther wolf, wildcat nor yit tod
those Durst cum within thay boundis all about
rough ground and smooth Bot he wald chase tham baith throw rouch and snod.
Those harmful, such fear Thay bailfull beistis had of their lyvis sic dout,
For he wes mekill and semit to be stout,
death That everilk beist thay dreid him as the deid,
wood Within that woid that nane durst hald thair heid.

Yit happinnit thair ane hungrie wolf to slyde
open field Out-throw his scheip quhair that lay on ane le:
'I sall have ane,' quod he, 'quhatever betyde,
before I die Thocht I be werryit, for hunger or I de!'
clutch, seized With that ane lamb intill his cluke hint he.
rest The laif start up, for thay wer all agast –
But God wait gif the wedder followit fast!

(when released) Went never hound mair haistelie fra the hand
quickly, roe-deer Quhen he wes rynnand maist raklie at the ra
Than, moorland and stream Nor went this wedder baith over mois and strand,
bush nor hillside And stoppit nouther at bank, busk nor bra,
Bot followit ay sa ferslie on his fa,
impetus, covered With sic ane drift, quhill dust and dirt overdraif him,
And maid ane vow to God that he suld have him.

With that the wolf let out his taill on lenth,
evening For he wes hungrie and it drew neir the ene,
endeavoured And schupe him for to ryn with all his strenth,
From the time that Fra he the wedder sa neir cummand had sene.
feared for, if He dred his lyfe and he overtane had bene:
Thairfoir he spairit nowther busk nor boig,
For weill he kennit the kenenes of the doig.

To mak him lycht he kest the lamb him fra,
leapt, drove, pool Syne lap over leis and draif throw dub and myre.
'Na,' quod the wedder. 'in faith we part not swa:
It is not the lamb, bot the, that I desyre!
I sall cum neir, for now I se the tyre.'
broken-down stone wall (?) The wolf ran till ane rekill stude behind him –
dogged his steps Bot ay the neirar the wedder he couth bind him.

Sone efter that he followit him sa neir
fright, fouled Quhill that the wolf for fleidnes fylit the feild,
Then, track Syne left the gait and ran throw busk and breir
woodland-thickets And schupe him fra the schawis for to scheild.
without cease, refuge He ran restles, for he wist of na beild;

The wedder followit him baith out and in,
Quhill that ane breir-busk raif rudelie off the skyn. *tore*

The wolf wes wer and blenkit him behind *aware, glanced*
And saw the wedder come thrawand throw the breir, *thrusting*
Syne saw the doggis skyn hingand on his lind: *around his loins*
'Na,' quod he, 'is this ye, that is sa neir?
Richt now ane hound and now quhyte as ane freir! *(a Carmelite friar)*
I fled over-fer and I had kennit the cais: *if, known the situation*
To God I vow that ye sall rew this rais! *race/course of action*

'Quhat wes the cause ye gaif me sic ane katche?' *chase*
With that in hy he hint him be the horne:
'For all your mowis ye met anis with your matche, *tricks, for once*
Suppois ye leuch me all this yeir to scorne. *Even if, get me laughed at*
For quhat enchessoun this doggis skyn have ye borne?' *reason*
'Maister,' quod he, 'bot to have playit with yow:
I yow requyre that ye nane uther trow.'

'Is this your bourding in ernist than?' quod he; *jesting*
'For I am verray effeirit and on flocht; *afraid, in a flutter*
Cum bak agane and I sall let yow se.'
Than quhar the gait wes grimmit he him brocht: *befouled*
'Quhether call ye this fair play or nocht,
To set your maister in sa fell effray *terrible fright*
Quhill he for feiritnes hes fylit up the way! *Until, fear*

'Thryis, be my saull, ye gart me schute behind – *made me shoot out*
Upon my hoichis the senyeis may be sene: *hocks, signs*
For feiritnes full oft I fylit the wind.
Now is this ye? Na, bot ane hound I wene!
Me think your teith over-schort to be sa kene.
Blissit be the busk that reft yow your array,
Ellis, fleand, bursin had I bene this day!' *bursted (by his bowels)*

'Schir,' quod the wedder, 'suppois I ran in hy,
My mynd wes never to do your persoun ill: *intention*
Ane flear gettis ane follower commounly, *One in flight*
In play or ernist – preif quha-sa-ever will;
Sen I bot playit, be gracious me till
And I sall gar my freindis blis your banis; *cause*
Ane full gude servand will crab his maister anis.' *(is allowed to) annoy*

'I have bene oftymis set in grit effray,
Bot, be the rude, sa rad yit wes I never *cross, terrified*
As thow hes maid me with thy prettie play.
I schot behind quhen thow overtuke me ever – *kept catching up with me*
Bot sikkerlie now sall we not dissever!' *part*

2558 **Maister**. This looks like calculated polite flattery on the wether's part, but it also prepares for the *Moralitas*, where the wolf represents the class of lords and masters.

2584 **I schot behind**. The wolf is more upset about his little accident than anything, and returns to it again and again; it seems that he cannot get over the needless indignity of it. (He is a gentleman, after all.)

	Than be the crag-bane smertlie he him tuke,
asunder	Or ever he ceissit, and it in schunder schuke.

Moralitas

	Esope that poete, first father of this fabill,
fitting	Wrait this parabole, quhilk is convenient
suitable	Because the sentence wes fructuous and agreabill,
furnishing an example	In moralitie exemplative prudent;
riddles of interpretation	Quhais problemes bene verray excellent,
(see n.)	Throw similitude of figuris, to this day,
	Gevis doctrine to the redaris of it ay.
	Heir may thow se that riches of array
poor	Will cause pure men presumpteous for to be:
(see n.)	Thay think thay hald of nane, be thay als gay,
	Bot counterfute ane lord in all degre.
situation in life	Out of their cais in pryde thay clym sa hie
no place	That thay forbeir thair better in na steid,
pulls	Quhill sum man tit thair heillis over thair heid.
some others go too far	Richt swa in service uther sum exceidis,
If, success	And thay haif withgang, welth and cherising,
disparage	That thay will lychtlie lordis in thair deidis,
	And lukis not to thair blude nor thair ofspring.
knows, state of affairs, prevail	Bot yit nane wait how lang that reull will ring;
	Bot he wes wyse that bad his sone considder:
benches, slippery	'Bewar in welth, for hall-benkis ar rycht slidder!'
estate	Thairfoir I counsell men of everilk stait
	To knaw thameself and quhome thay suld forbeir
	And fall not with thair better in debait,
Even if	Suppois thay be als galland in thair geir:
is proper, strife	It settis na servand for to uphald weir,
	Nor clym sa hie quhill he fall of the ledder:
Only	Bot think upon the wolf and on the wedder!

The Wolf and the Lamb

This fable has the second longest *Moralitas*, a cry of indignation against the oppressions of great lords and others, one in a long line of medieval complaints against the social evils and abuses of the time. The simple honest farmer or poor labourer is generally the victim and hero (cf. *PP*). Such complaints, though they may be vividly responsive to particular kinds of contemporary economic oppression, do not envisage structural reform, rather a return to an ideal world where the different estates live in harmony under the benevolent rule of a wise and just king.

2588–94 A stanza of high-flown allegorical theory unhappily reminiscent of Lydgate (who also wrote a set of Aesopic fables).

2593 'Through aptness of figurative application'.

2597 'They think they have no feudal obligation, if they can go as gay'.

2611 **thair better**. How is the wolf the 'better', or social superior, of the wether, except in being able to tear him limb from limb when he wants? The moral of the story, 'Know your place', unravels as one thinks back over the brilliant inventiveness of the fable that purports to exemplify it. Stories told as Henryson tells them will not allow themselves to be stuffed into moral pigeon-holes; there seems a particular uneasiness in the relation of fable and *Moralitas* when the reference is to social rather than religious obligation.

	Ane cruell wolf, richt ravenous and fell,
	Upon ane tyme past to ane reveir
rocky hillside, pool	Descending from ane rotche unto ane well;
	To slaik his thrist, drank of the watter cleir.
by chance	Swa upon cace ane selie lamb come neir,
	Bot of his fa the wolf nathing he wist,
	And in the streme laipit to cule his thrist.
	Thus drank thay baith, bot not of ane intent:
	The wolfis thocht wes all on wickitnes,
	The selie lamb wes meik and innocent.
	Upon the rever in ane uther place
	Beneth the wolf he drank ane lytill space,
While	Quhill he thocht gude, belevand thair nane ill.
	The wolf him saw and rampand come him till,
bared	With girnand teith and awfull angrie luke,
miserable	Said to the lamb, 'Thow cative wretchit thing,
defile	How durst thow be sa bald to fyle this bruke,
	Quhar I suld drink, with thy foull slavering?
a charitable deed, hang	It wer almous the for to draw and hing,
	That suld presume with thy foull lippis vyle
To muddy	To glar my drink and this fair watter fyle!'
	The selie lamb, quaikand for verray dreid,
leave	On kneis fell and said, 'Schir, with your leif,
Even though, lied	Suppois I dar not say thairof ye leid,
prove	Bot, be my saull, I wait ye can nocht preif
grieve	That I did ony thing that suld yow greif;
	Ye wait alswa that your accusatioun
Is lacking in	Failyeis fra treuth and contrair is to ressoun.
I (myself)	'Thocht I can nocht, nature will me defend,
(see n.)	And of the deid perfyte experience:
must of itself	All hevie thing man of the self discend,
Unless, by force	Bot gif sum thing on force mak resistence;
go upward	Than may the streme on na way mak ascence
	Nor ryn bakwart. I drank beneth yow far:
worse	*Ergo*, for me your bruke wes never the war.
	'Alswa, my lippis, sen that I wes ane lam,
Touched	Tuitchit nathing that wes contagious,
	Bot sowkit milk from pappis of my dam,
also	Richt naturall, sweit and als delitious.'
severely precise	'Weill,' quod the wolf, 'thy language rigorus
by nature	Cummis the of kynd: swa thy father before
(see n.)	Held me at bait, baith with boist and schore.
angered, warned him	'He wraithit me, and than I culd him warne,
if I had the use of my head	Within ane yeir, and I brukit my heid,

2645 'And an accurate understanding of the facts (will also defend me)'.

2657 'Held me in debate, both with threatening and menacing behaviour'.

revenged	I suld be wrokkin on him or on his barne
offensive and obstreperous arguing	For his exorbetant and frawart pleid:
	Thow sall doutles for his deidis be deid.'
	'Schir, it is wrang that for the fatheris gilt
innocent, harmed	The saikles sone suld punist be or spilt.
heard	'Haif ye not hard quhat Halie Scripture sayis,
Dictated	Endytit with the mouth of God almycht?
weight (of responsibility)	Of his awin deidis ilk man sall beir the pais,
	As pane for sin, reward for werkis rycht.
blame	For my trespas, quhy suld my sone have plycht?
wrong	Quha did the mis, lat him sustene the pane.'
wranglest	'Yaa!' quod the wolf. 'Yit pleyis thow agane?
	'I let the wit, quhen that the father offendis,
exempt	I will refuse nane of his successioun,
	And of his barnis I may weill tak amendis
generation	Unto the twentie degre descending doun.
	Thy father thocht to mak ane strang poysoun
	And with his mouth in my watter did spew.'
	'Schir,' quod the lamb, 'thay twa ar nouther trew.
if	'The law sayis, and ye will understand,
	Thair suld na man, for wrang nor violence,
	His adversar punis at his awin hand
	Without proces of law and evidence;
Which (i.e. the opponent)	Quhilk suld have leif to mak lawfull defence,
with reference to that be summoned	And thairupon summond peremtourly
state his case	For to propone, contrairie or reply.
Appoint, lawful, appear	'Set me ane lauchfull court: I sall compeir
true	Befoir the lyoun, lord and leill justice,
pledge	And be my hand I oblis me rycht heir
submit to	That I sall byde ane unsuspect assyis.
the way things are done now	This is the law, this is the instant gyis;
undertake	Ye suld pretend thairfoir ane summondis mak
In preparation for	Aganis that day, to gif ressoun and tak.'
	'Na,' quod the wolf, 'thou wald intruse ressoun
robbery, remain in possession	Quhair wrang and reif suld duell in propertie.
	That is ane poynt and part of fals tressoun,
make	For to gar reuth remane with crueltie.

2663 One could see this coming, and it is hard not to feel a twinge of sympathy for the wolf. The narrative communicates something of the exasperation that powerful men feel when faced with objections based on coolly rational argument: the 'law' is part of the problem, as they see it, not the solution.

2665 **Halie Scripture**. The lamb appeals to Ezek. 18:20. The wolf retorts (2672–5) with Ex. 20:5 (where God's wrath, however, extends only to the third and fourth generations, not the twentieth).

2679–82 The allusion is to the common legal maxim, 'No man ought to be judge in his own cause' (Whiting M244).

2687 **lyoun**. The lion has something of the role hopefully assigned to the king (below, 2775) as the ideal administrator of justice.

2689 **unsuspect**: 'impartial'. The qualification reminds one of William Thorpe's constant reiteration of similar reservations in his own submission to the church (see p. 310, above). The wolf's objection to 'reason' being brought in to questions of power (2693) likewise resembles the contempt of the archbishop of York's clerks for Margery Kempe's talk of the gospels (p. 375, above).

2695 **tressoun**. The medieval history of the law of treason shows how it was always in the interest of those in power to have treason defined as whatever action was contrary to their interest. The wolf reduces this to absurdity.

Be Goddis woundis, fals tratour, thow sall de
For thy trespas, and for thy fatheris als!'
With that anone he hint him be the hals. *seized, neck*

The selie lamb culd do nathing bot bleit:
Sone wes he hedit – the wolf wald do na grace; *beheaded*
Syne drank his blude and of his flesche can eit
Quhill he wes full, syne went his way on pace. *apace*
Of his murther quhat sall we say, allace?
Wes not this reuth, wes not this grit pietie,
To gar this selie lamb but gilt thus de?

Moralitas

The pure pepill this lamb may signifie, *poor*
As maill-men, merchandis and all laboureris, *tenant-farmers, tradesmen*
Of quhome the lyfe is half ane purgatorie,
To wyn with lautie leving, as efferis. *(see n.)*
The wolf betakinnis fals extortioneris
And oppressouris of pure men, as we se,
Be violence, or craft in facultie. *aptitude in cunning*

Thre kynd of wolfis in this warld now rings: *reign*
The first ar fals perverteris of the lawis,
Quhilk under poleit termis falset mingis, *polished, falsehood*
Lettand that all wer gospell that he schawis; *Letting on, alleges*
Bot for ane bud the pure man he overthrawis, *bribe*
Smoirand the richt, garrand the wrang proceid – *Smothering, making*
Of sic wolfis hellis fyre sall be thair meid!

O man of law, let be thy subteltie,
With nice gimpis and fraudis intricait, *subtle points*
And think that God in his divinitie
The wrang, the richt, of all thy werkis wait.
For prayer, price, for hie nor law estait, *payment*
Of fals querrellis se thow mak na defence:
Hald with the richt, hurt not thy conscience.

Ane uther kynd of wolfis ravenous
Ar mychtie men, haifand full grit plentie, *having*
Quilkis ar sa gredie and sa covetous
Thay will not thoill the pure in pece to be: *suffer*
Suppois he and his houshald baith suld de
For falt of fude, thairof thay gif na rak, *lack, heed*
Bot over his heid his mailling will thay tak. *rented farm*

O man but mercie, quhat is in thy thocht?
War than ane wolf, and thow culd understand! *Worse, if*
Thow hes aneuch, the pure husband richt nocht *farmer*
Bot croip and crufe upon ane clout of land. *standing-crop, hovel, patch*
For Goddis aw, how durst thow tak on hand – *fear of God*

2710 'To win with truth a living, as is fitting'.

well-off	And thow in barn and byre sa bene and big –
rented farm, make him dig	To put him fra his tak and gar him thig?
	The thrid wolf ar men of heritage,
loan	As lordis that hes land be Goddis lane,
leases, tenant-farmers	And settis to the mailleris ane village,
tenant's fine/fee (is) paid	And for ane tyme gressome payit and tane;
	Syne vexis him, or half his terme be gane,
	With pykit querrellis for to mak him fane
	To flit or pay his gressome new agane.
must lend	His hors, his meir, he man len to the laird,
carrying	To drug and draw in cairt or in cariage;
	His servand or his self may not be spaird
labour	To swing and sweit withoutin meit or wage;
This is	Thus how he standis in labour and bondage
farm-income	That scantlie may he purches by his maill
cabbage-broth	To leve upon dry breid and watter-caill.
	Hes thow not reuth to gar thy tennentis sweit
stomach	Into thy laubour, with faynt and hungrie wame,
	And syne hes lytill gude to drink or eit
family	With his menye, at evin quhen he cummis hame?
afraid	Thow suld be rad for richteous Goddis blame,
	For it cryis ane vengeance unto the hevinnis hie
without food or wages	To gar ane pure man wirk but meit or fe.
	O thow grit lord, that riches hes and rent,
	Be nocht ane wolf, thus to devoir the pure!
	Think that nathing cruell nor violent
	May in this warld perpetuallie indure.
be sure of	This sall thow trow and sikkerlie assure:
In return for oppressing	For till oppres, thow sall haif als grit pane
As if	As thow the pure with thy awin hand had slane.
	God keip the lamb, quhilk is the innocent,
	From wolfis byit – I mene extortioneris;
	God grant that wrangous men of fals intent
Be revealed, as is fitting	Be manifestit, and punischit as effeiris;
	And God, as thow all rychteous prayer heiris,
May (you) save	Mot saif our king, and gif him hart and hand
banish	All sic wolfis to banes out of the land.

2760–2 Payment of fair wages due to labourers was backed by biblical injunction, e.g. Deut. 24:15, Jas. 5:4.

2775 **our king**. The king was commonly appealed to as the ideal arbiter of justice (as in *PP*), but not in his person as a particular contemporary king. There is no occasion to find allusion here to either James III (1460–88) nor his more energetic successor James IV (1488–1513).

William Dunbar (*c.* 1456–*c.* 1515)

William Dunbar is the most notable exponent in English of the art of poetry as it was recommended and taught by the medieval rhetoricians – the clothing of familiar ideas in a new and brilliant dress of style, verbal luxuriance, elaborate figuration of syntax, precise attention to verbal music and sound-effects. He is the master of all the techniques of poetry, even to the point of verbal riot in the exuberant display of that command, and although his themes are generally commonplace and his own individual voice can scarce be heard above the noise of style, it hardly seems to matter. His poetic career centred on the years he spent at the court of James IV (1488–1513) from about 1500 until the king's death at Flodden. James tried to encourage a court culture around himself, mostly of a showy and sycophantic kind, and Dunbar, a university-trained cleric (BA St Andrews, 1477) and priest (ordained 1503), was one of the recipients of his patronage. Much of his poetry is occasional in nature, comic, satirical, abusive, petitionary, or celebratory in relation to court events. Virtuoso stylistic display is his strength, not engagement with narrative or ideas; tonal effects range from hectic glee to exhausted cynicism, but there is something missing in the middle.

Edition by J. Kinsley (Oxford, 1979); *Selected Poems of Henryson and Dunbar*, ed. P. Bawcutt and F. Riddy (Edinburgh, 1992); life and works by P. Bawcutt, *Dunbar the Makar* (Oxford, 1992); studies by E. Morgan, in *EC* 2 (1952), 138–58, and J. Leyerle, in *UTQ* 31 (1962), 316–38; see also L. Fradenburg, *City, Marriage, Tournament: Arts of Rule in Late Medieval Scotland* (Madison, WI, 1991).

Meditation in Winter

Winter brings gloom and thoughts of mortality, as it did for Hoccleve in his *Complaint*; Age and Death offer invitations that cannot be refused, as in Lydgate's *Dance Macabre*. Dunbar gives novelty to an old topos by dramatizing it as a little allegorical inner debate. Text from Cambridge, Magdalene College MS Pepys 2553 (the Maitland Folio MS, 1570–85), pp. 318–19, with lines 1–21 supplied from the Reidpeth transcript of Maitland, made in 1622.

Into thir dirk and drublie dayis — *In these, overcast*
Quhone sabill all the hevin arrayis
With mystie vapouris, cluddis and skyis,
Nature all curage me denyis — *heart (for)*
Of sangis, ballattis and of playis. — *poems*

Quhone that the nycht dois lenth in houris
With wind, with haill and havy schouris,
My dulie spreit dois lurk for schoir; — *doleful, cowers under the threat*
My hairt for languor dois forloir — *becomes forlorn*
For laik of Symmer with his flouris.

I waik, I turne, sleip may I nocht;
I vexit am with havie thocht.
This warld all ovir I cast about — *consider*
And ay the mair I am in dout — *anxiety*
The mair that I remeid have socht. — *remedy*

I am assayit on everie syde: — *assailed*
Dispair sayis ay, 'In tyme provyde
And get sum thing quhairon to leif, — *live*
Or with grit trouble and mischeif
Thow sall into this court abyd.' — *(i.e. James's court)*

Than Patience sayis, 'Be not agast:
Hald hoip and treuthe within the fast
And lat Fortoun wirk furthe hir rage, — *work off*

Quhome that no rasoun may assuage
hour-glass Quhill that hir glas be run and past.’

And Prudence in my eir sayis ay,
hold on to what ‘Quhy wald thow hald that will away?
crave what, no length of time Or craif that thow may have no space,
Thow tending to ane uther place,
day’s journey A journay going everie day?’

And than sayis Age, ‘My friend, cum neir,
distant with me, request And be not strange, I the requeir:
Cum, brodir, by the hand me tak;
reckoning Remember thow hes compt to mak
Of all thi tyme thow spendit heir.’

gates Syne Deid castis upe his yettis wyd,
These open Saying, ‘Thir oppin sall the abyd;
Although Albeid that thow wer never sa stout,
stoop Undir this lyntall sall thow lowt:
Thair is nane uther way besyde.’

For feir of this all day I drowp:
chest No gold in kist, nor wyne in cowp,
No ladeis bewtie nor luiffis blys,
prevent May lat me to remember this,
How glaid that ever I dyne or sowp.

Yit, quhone the nycht begyynis to schort,
It dois my spreit sum pairt confort
Of thocht oppressit with the schowris.
Cum, lustie Symmer, with thi flowris,
live That I may leif in sum disport!

Christ in Triumph

The moment is the one that Langland celebrates in *PP* (XX.450), the triumph of the risen Christ and the Harrowing of Hell. The poem has the character of a fanfare blazing out to welcome the triumphant hero on his return from hell. There is no development, no argument: the stanzas consist of structures of half-lines, lines or groups of lines in reiterated apposition to the statement made in the repeated refrain. The impression is of overwhelming power: if the poem were one stanza longer, it would be too much. Text from NLS MS Adv.1.1.6 (the Bannatyne MS), fol. 35.

Done is a batell on the dragon blak;
Our campioun Chryst confoundit hes his force.
gates The yettis of hell ar brokin with a crak;
The signe triumphall rasit is of the croce.

Meditation in Winter

46–50 If winter comes, can spring be far behind? Dunbar manages to give a bitter twist to the traditional consolation, making it sound like a catching at straws in the face of the realization of the inevitable.

Christ in Triumph

1 **dragon blak**. Satan is the ‘great dragon’ and ‘ancient serpent’ (see line 10) in Rev. 12:9, and in Rev. 20:2 it is told how he will be bound and thrown into a pit for 1000 years – a passage taken to refer to the Harrowing of Hell. The poem is rich in allusion to biblical images and types of Christ triumphant.

4 Many paintings of the time (e.g. that of Piero della Francesca) show the risen Christ with the banner of the Resurrection, a red cross on a white background.

tremble	The divillis trymmillis with hiddous voce;
ransomed	The saulis ar borrowit and to the blis can go.
	Chryst with his blud our ransonis dois indoce:
	Surrexit Dominus de sepulchro.
Beaten down	Dungin is the deidly dragon Lucifer,
	The crewall serpent with the mortall stang,
bared ('ajar')	The auld kene tegir with his teith on char,
ambush, lain	Quhilk in a wait hes lyne for us so lang,
claws	Thinking to grip us in his clowis strang;
	The merciful Lord wald nocht that it wer so,
fail, attempt to seize his prey	He maid him for to felye of that fang:
	Surrexit Dominus de sepulchro.
	He for our saik that sufferit to be slane
offered	And lyk a lamb in sacrifice wes dicht
	Is lyk a lyone rissin up agane,
reared	And as gyane raxit him on hicht.
(the dawn), radiant	Sprungin is Aurora radius and bricht,
Aloft, (the sun)	On loft is gone the glorius Appollo,
	The blisful day depairtit fro the nycht:
	Surrexit Dominus de sepulchro.
	The grit victour agane is rissin on hicht
	That for our querrell to the deth wes woundit;
	The sone that wox all paill now schynis bricht
having cleared away	And dirknes clerit, our fayth is now refoundit;
bell-ringing	The knell of mercy fra the hevin is soundit,
	The Cristin ar deliverit of thair wo,
	The Jowis and thair errour ar confoundit:
	Surrexit Dominus de sepulchro.
brought to an end	The fo is chasit, the battell is done ceis,
jailers fled and put to flight	The presone brokin, the jevellouris fleit and flemit;
war	The weir is gon, confermit is the peis,
emptied	The fetteris lowsit and the dungeoun temit,
	The ransoun maid, the presoneris redemit;
won	The feild is win, ourcumin is the fo,
guarded	Dispulit of the tresur that he yemit:
	Surrexit Dominus de sepulchro.

THE GOLDEN TARGE

The spring-time seasonal opening had a long history in the medieval allegorical love-vision, from the *Roman de la Rose* through the French poets to Chaucer and his followers, and here it finally explodes in a flamboyant pyrotechnic display. Dunbar alludes to all the conventions of the form, but carries the Lydgatian rhetoric of

7 **indoce**: 'endorse'. The Atonement is made legal by a document which Christ signs with his blood.

8 'The Lord has risen from the tomb', a verse said in the Mass on Easter Day.

10 **the mortall stang**. 'The sting of death is sin' (1 Cor. 15:56), as administered by the serpent in the Garden of Eden.

19 **lyone**. Christ is the lion of the tribe of Judah (Gen. 49:9) who has returned to triumph over its enemies (Rev. 5:5).

20 **gyane**. Christ is called a 'giant' because Ps. 19:5 speaks of the sun rising like a giant to run its course.

27 **wox all paill**. The sun was eclipsed at the moment of Christ's death (*PP* XX.61).

'enamelled' and 'aureate' language to the point where all nature, sun and sky, leaf and flower, seems hypostatized in bejewelled splendour. The impression is of a form of heraldic decoration or, with a subtler sense of colour values, of a brilliant manuscript miniature. The allegorical 'story' that follows is the merest gesture, but the close is worth having for Dunbar's explicit statement of the 'official' view of poetry and of the English poetic tradition. Text from the print of Chepman and Myllar (1508); study by D. Fox, *ELH* 26 (1959), 311–34; see also Spearing (1993), pp. 240–8.

day-star, began	Ryght as the stern of day begouth to schyne,
were the evening-star and moon	Quhen gone to bed war Vesper and Lucyne,
rose, rose-bush	I raise, and by a rosere did me rest.
of the morning	Up sprang the goldyn candill matutyne,
	With clere depurit bemes cristallyne,
	Glading the mery foulis in thair nest;
Before, cap, clad	Or Phebus was in purpur cape revest
	Up raise the lark, the hevyns menstrale fyne,
in a morning	In May, intill a morow myrthfullest.
	Full angellike thir birdis sang thair houris
within	Within thair courtyns grene, into thair bouris
	Apparalit quhite and rede wyth blomes suete.
Enamelled	Anamalit was the felde wyth all colouris;
shook	The perly droppis schake in silvir schouris
Until, dewy fragrance, flow	Quhill all in balme did branch and levis flete.
weep	To part fra Phebus did Aurora grete:
	Hir cristall teris I saw hyng on the flouris,
	Quhilk he for lufe all drank up wyth his hete.
	For mirth of May, wyth skippis and wyth hoppis,
uppermost shoots	The birdis sang upon the tender croppis
intricate	With curiouse note, as Venus chapell clerkis.
buds	The rosis yong, new spreding of thair knopis,
beryl (crystal-clear)	War powdrit brycht with hevinly beriall droppis
	Throu bemes rede birnyng as ruby sperkis.
	The skyes rang for schoutyng of the larkis;
(see n.)	The purpur hevyn, ourscailit in silvir sloppis,
Gilded over	Ourgilt the treis, branchis, lef and barkis.
rushes	Doun throu the ryce a ryvir ran wyth stremys,
(see n.)	So lustily agayn thai lykand lemys
water-surface	That all the lake as lamp did leme of licht,
was reflected	Quhilk schadowit all about wyth twynkling glemis
boughs	That bewis bathit war in secund bemys
	Throu the reflex of Phebus visage brycht.
	On every syde the hegies raise on hicht;
bream	The bank was grene, the bruke was full of bremys,
gravel (on the river-bed), stars	The stanneris clere as stern in frosty nycht.

10 **houris**: prayers appropriate to the canonical hours. The song of birds was often represented figuratively as a version of the divine office (cf. 21 below).

16 Aurora, goddess of the dawn, weeps to part from Phebus, the sun, after their brief early-morning assignation.

20 **tender croppis**: echoing GP 7.

23 **powdrit**: 'powdered', a heraldic term for the scattering of a charge on the 'field' (cf. **felde**, 13). Heraldic names for colours are also used (line 41; also **purpur**, 7).

26 'The purple (i.e. scarlet) sky, sprinkled over (as if with fish-scales) with little trailing clouds'.

29 'So cheerfully reflecting back those pleasant gleams'.

The cristall air, the sapher firmament,
The ruby skyes of the orient
Kest beriall bemes on emerant bewis grene.
garden The rosy garth depaynt and redolent
noble red With purpur, azure, gold and goulis gent
Arayed was by dame Flora the quene
So nobily that joy was for to sene.
The roch agayn the rivir resplendent
flame As low enlumynit all the leves schene.

Quhat throu the mery foulys armony
And throu the ryveris soun rycht ran me by
On Florais mantill I slepit as I lay,
Quhare sone into my dremes fantasy
I saw approch, agayn the orient sky,
A saill als quhite as blossum upon spray,
ship's topcastle Wyth merse of gold brycht as the stern of day,
approached Quhilk tendit to the land full lustily
As falcoun swift desyrouse of hir pray.

hard at hand, blooming And hard on burd unto the blomyt medis
sedge Amang the grene rispis and the redis
(the vessel) Arrivit sche, quharfro anon thare landis
beautifully dressed Ane hundreth ladyes, lusty into wedis,
Als fresch as flouris that in May upspredis,
caul (hair-net) In kirtillis grene, withoutyn kell or bandis;
glittering Thair brycht hairis hang gleting on the strandis
bound round In tressis clere, wyppit wyth goldyn thredis;
slender With pappis quhite and mydlis small as wandis.

Discrive I wald, bot quho coud wele endyte
(the ladies) How all the feldis wyth thai lilies quhite
glitter Depaynt war brycht, quhilk to the hevyn did glete?
Noucht thou, Omer, als fair as thou coud wryte,
For all thine ornate stilis so perfyte;
Nor yit thou, Tullius, quhois lippis suete
flowed with terms of rhetoric Of rethorike did into termes flete.
inadequate Your aureate tongis both bene all to lyte
give an account of For to compile that paradise complete.

{The ship disembarks its crew of gods and goddesses, who sing, dance and soon discover the dreamer hiding. He is subjected to a full-scale allegorical siege, in which the Golden Targe (shield) of Reason at first protects him from the assaults of Beauty and Venus. Eventually overcome by 'Perilous Presence', he is made happy, then miserable, then woken up by the noise of the departing ship's gunfire salute (a remarkably modern touch).}

rhetoricians O reverend Chaucere, rose of rethoris all,
As in oure tong ane flour imperiall

67, 69 Homer and Cicero are conventional paragons of excellence in eloquence and rhetoric, conceived of as ornateness of language and expression. The 'sweetness' of rhetoric is often spoken of, almost as if it were a form of honey; its power of gilding everything (a power that Dunbar literalizes in this poem) is called aureation, a quality of style much admired in Lydgate.

253 The poem has been a display-piece, in which Dunbar shows his command of every convention of the Chaucerian love-vision, names every deity in the classical pantheon, and assembles every possible personification from the *Roman de la Rose* tradition (he manages to mention 47 in all), and it is appropriate that he should now take his

continued overleaf

rose That raise in Britane, evir (quho redis rycht)
Thou beris of makaris the tryumph riall:
enamelled, heavenly Thy fresch anamalit termes celicall
This mater coud illumynit have full brycht.
Was thou noucht of oure Inglisch all the lycht
Surmounting eviry tong terrestriall
Als fer as Mayes morow dois mydnycht?

O morall Gower and Ludgate laureate,
Your sugurit lippis and tongis aureate
Bene to oure eris cause of grete delyte;
Your angel mouthis most mellifluate
Oure rude langage has clere illumynate
And fair ourgilt oure spech, that imperfyte
set out Stude, or your goldyn pennis schupe to write.
This ile before was bare and desolate
writing Of rethorike or lusty fresch endyte.

book Thou lytill quair, be evir obedient,
Humble, subject and symple of entent,
knowledgeable Before the face of eviry connyng wicht.
wasted I knaw quhat thou of rethorike hes spent:
Of all hir lusty rosis redolent
Is non into thy gerland sett on hicht;
Be ashamed Eschame tharof, and draw the out of sicht.
Rude is thy wede, disteynit, bare and rent –
Wele aucht thou be aferit of the licht!

THE TREATISE OF THE TWO MARRIED WOMEN AND THE WIDOW

This poem has more words for '(man with) floppy penis' than one could believe existed in the language: carnival mockery of that 'sary lume'. Like several of Dunbar's poems, it is almost too much. Ideas from the clerical anti-feminist tradition that Chaucer, in his portrayal of the Wife of Bath and in the Merchant's Tale, placed under the prism of a wry and ironic scrutiny – the voracious and indiscriminate sexual appetite of women, their natural facility in lying, cheating, deceiving, scolding and nagging, their eagerness to jump out of the arms of their enfeebled and exhausted husbands into those of any handy young blade – here find hyperbolical expression. The format – a series of confessions, in the convention of the *chanson de mal mariée* ('Song of the Unhappily Wedded Woman') – enables Dunbar to heap up a huge midden of abusive sex-talk. As with a lot of such writing, the wives, with their vitality and sense of fun, come off better than the husbands, who are, old and young, mostly drooling and impotent, and who of course don't get much chance to speak. Impotence is the obsessive fantasy, as a kind of consequence of the fantasy of women's insatiable sexual appetite. It is all very preposterous, but it has some

place, with becoming modesty, in the great tradition of English poetry. He echoes terms of praise that had long been familiar among Chaucer's followers (see the remarks of Lydgate and Hoccleve above), particularly in the emphasis on his powers of ornate rhetoric (see *Thebes* 39–57n).

257 **anamalit**; 'enamelled' (cf. 13), which conveys well the characteristic medieval idea of rhetoricated style as a kind of non-transparent glossy surface fixative applied to content – any content, it seems. It is a topos of praise, required by medieval poetic aesthetic, quite unrelated to observation of Chaucer's poetry. As it happens, Dunbar's poem is an exact example of what he praises poetry for, and the same words (*anamalit, ourgilt, enlumynit*) are used to describe the beauty of nature as are used to describe the beauty of poetic style.

262 **morall Gower**. Chaucer's phrase, *TC* V.1856. Gower and Lydgate were customarily grouped in a triad with Chaucer as the founding fathers of English poetry. A myth of the kind was needed, to legitimize English poetry and give it a status comparable to French and Italian, and it soon became accepted (and became, in being accepted, 'true').

271 For the humble address to the 'little book', cf. *TC* V.1786. Dunbar, in thus seeking to establish his place in the poetic tradition, sets his sights high.

authentically ugly moments. The metre that Dunbar chooses for his *tour de force* – the unrhymed alliterative long line with regular and often heavy alliteration and with the insistent percussive beat of the late northern and Scottish alliterative manner – is suitably whirling and extravagant, giving the impression at times of being nearly but not quite out of control. The whole scene is witnessed by the narrator from a secret hiding-place: what is he doing there, we might ask, except being a peeping Tom? He deserves all he gets: perhaps they saw him coming. Text from the print of 1508, with lines 1–103, missing by loss of leaves, supplied from Cambridge, Magdalene College MS Pepys 2553 (the Maitland Folio MS, 1570–85), pp. 82–96. Studies by R. Pearcy, *Speculum* 55 (1980), 58–74, and Spearing (1993), pp. 249–67.

	Apon the Midsummer evin, mirriest of nichtis,
	I muvit furth till ane meid, as midnicht wes past,
garden	Besyd ane gudlie grein garth, full of gay flouris,
	Hegeit of ane huge hicht with hawthorne treis,
	Quhairon ane bird on ane bransche so birst out hir notis
bough heard	That never ane blythfullar bird was on the beuche hard.
What with	Quhat throw the sugarat sound of hir sang glaid
health-giving	And throw the savour sanative of the sueit flouris,
(see n.)	I drew in derne to the dyk to dirkin efter mirthis;
made damp, made a din	The dew donkit the daill, and dynnit the feulis.
holly-tree	I hard, under ane holyn hevinlie grein hewit,
loud	Ane hie speiche at my hand with hautand wourdis:
	With that in haist to the hege so hard I inthrang
hidden, pleasant	That I was heildit with hawthorne and with heynd leveis.
prickles, intertwined	Throw pykis of the plet thorne I presandlie luikit
	Gif ony persoun wald approche within that plesand garding.
	I saw thre gay ladeis sit in ane grein arbeir,
arrayed in	All grathit into garlandis of fresche gudlie flouris:
wire	So glitterit as the gold wer thair glorius gilt tressis,
	Quhill all the gressis did gleme of the glaid hewis.
Combed, elegantly parted	Kemmit was thair cleir hair, and curiouslie sched,
Over, bright	Attour thair schulderis doun schyre schyning full bricht,
(see n.)	With curches cassin thair-abone of kirsp cleir and thin.
	Thair mantillis grein war as the gress that grew in May sessoun,
Fastened	Fetrit with thair quhyt fingaris about thair fair sydis.
wonderful	Of ferliful fyne favour war thair faceis meik,
	All full of flurist fairheid as flouris in June,
	Quhyt, seimlie and soft as the sweit lillies,
opened-out	Now upspred upon spray as new spynist rose,
verdure	Arrayit ryallie about with mony riche vardour,
enamelled	That nature full nobillie annamalit with flouris
all kinds of, courteous person	Of alkin hewis under hevin that ony heynd knew,
	Fragrant, all full of fresche odour fynest of smell.
	Ane cumlie tabil coverit wes befoir tha cleir ladeis,
	With ryalle cowpis apon rawis, full of ryche wynis.
these noble creatures	And of thir fair wlonkes whit, tua weddit war with lordis,
behaviour	Ane wes ane wedow, iwiss, wantoun of laitis.
	And as thai talk at the tabill of mony taill sindry

1 **Midsummer evin**, the night of 23–4 June, a time of great revelry, when whole villages were reported to take to the woods and 'scarce a maiden returned undefiled'.

9 'I approached in secret to the fence in order to lie hidden on the look-out for amusement'.

17–25 The contrast between the refined elegance of the ladies' appearance and the coarseness of their conversation is part of the antifeminist image of women as whited sepulchres, as well as comically incongruous in itself.

23 'With kerchiefs of fine and delicate fabric thrown over (their hair)'.

quaffed, strong, pour	They wauchtit at the wicht wyne and waris out wourdis,
coherently	And syn thai spak more spedelie and sparit no matiris.
Reveal, wedded	'Bewrie,' said the wedo, 'ye woddit wemen ying,
	Quhat mirth ye fand in maryage, sen ye war menis wyffis;
carelessly entered-upon	Reveill gif ye rewit that rakles conditioun,
man alive	Or gif that ever ye luffit leyd upon lyf mair
Than	Nor thame that ye your fayth hes festinit for ever,
	Or gif ye think, had ye chois, that ye wald cheis better.
	Think ye it nocht ane blist band that bindis so fast
one bit, alone	That none undo it a deill may, bot the deith ane?'
a fine woman, at once, manner	Than spak ane lusty belyf with lustie effeiris:
	'It that ye call the blist band that bindis so fast
misery	Is bair of blis and bailfull and greit barrat wirkis.
ask	Ye speir, had I fre chois, gif I wald cheis bettir?
Chains	Chenyeis ay ar to eschew, and changeis ar sueit;
for once	Sic cursit chance till eschew, had I my chois anis,
escape	Out of the chenyeis of ane churle I chaip suld for evir.
(see n.)	God gif matrimony wer made to mell for ane yeir!
nuisance	It war bot merrens to be mair, bot gif our myndis pleisit.
	It is agane the law of luf, of kynd and of nature,
	Togidder hartis to strene that stryveis with uther.
than men, by far	Birdis hes ane better law na bernis, be meikill,
enjoys, mate	That ilk yeir with new joy joyis ane maik
takes, mate, unspoiled	And fangis thame ane fresche feyr, unfulyeit and constant,
worn-out	And lattis thair fulyeit feiris flie quhair thai pleis.
custom, land	Cryst gif sic ane consuetude war in this kith haldin!
	Than weill war us wemen that evir we war born:
	We suld have feiris as fresche to fang quhen us likit,
impotent, tickets-of-leave	And gif all larbaris thair leveis quhen thai lak curage.
	'Myself suld be full semlie in silkis arrayit,
Dainty, ladylike	Gymp, jolie and gent, richt joyus and gentryce.
	I suld at fairis be found, new faceis to se,
	At playis and at preichingis and pilgrimages greit,
crowd	To schaw my renone royaly quhair preis was of folk,
beauty	To manifest my makdome to multitude of pepill
abroad	And blaw my bewtie on breid quhair bernis war mony,
	That I micht cheis and be chosin and change quhen me lykit.
choose, out of all	Than suld I waill ane full weill our all the wyd realme
	That suld my womanheid weild the lang winter nicht;
fitter than any other	And quhen I gottin had ane grome ganest of uther,
Fresh	Yaip and ying in the yok ane yeir for to draw,
once, tested	Fra I had preveit his pith the first plesand moneth,
look around	Than suld I cast me to keik in kirk and in markat
	And all the cuntre about, kyngis court and uther,
	Quhair I ane galland micht get aganis the nixt yeir,
	For to perfurneis furth the werk quhen failyeit the tother –

56 'God grant that marriage were made for the purpose of having sex for a year!'

58 The law of **kynd** (nature) was recognized by medieval churchmen as unfortunately necessary for procreation, and admitted under the constraint of matrimony; only scandalously wicked women such as La Vieille (an old bawd) in the *Roman de la Rose* would advocate free love.

60–3 Cf. *PF* – where Chaucer, however, does not draw attention to this advantage of the birds' practice.

62 Parts of the MS are now stained and illegible, and the readings of early editors have to be relied upon; **constant** here seems hardly appropriate.

70–1 Like much in the first wife's harangue, this is reminiscent of the WBP (555–9).

lively fellow, at the ready	A forky fure ay furthwart and forsy in draucht,
worn out	Nother febill nor fant nor fulyeit in labour,
	But als fresche of his forme as flouris in May –
take, cause to bud	For all the fruit suld I fang, thocht he the flour burgeoun.
weakling, hairy caterpillar churl	'I have ane wallidrag, ane worme, ane auld wobat carle,
worn-out boar	A waistit wolroun, na worth bot wourdis to clatter;
A 'bum', phlegm	Ane bumbart, ane dron-bee, ane bag full of flewme,
monster, shit-shooter	Ane skabbit skarth, ane scorpioun, ane scutarde behind;
scratch, cause of disgust	To se him scart his awin skyn grit scunner I think.
ogre (?)	Quhen kissis me that carybald, than kyndillis all my sorrow:
bristles, fierce boar	As birss of ane brym bair his berd is als stif,
sorry tool	Bot soft and soupill as the silk is his sary lume –
blameless	He may weill to the syn assent, but sakles is his deidis!
slime, eyes, besmeared	With gore his tua grym ene ar gladdereit all about,
clogged up, mud	And gorgeit lyk tua gutaris that war with glar stoppit.
ghoul	Bot quhen that glowrand gaist grippis me about
	Than think I hiddowus Mahowne hes me in armes:
making of the sign of the cross	Thair ma na sanyng me save fra that auld Sathane,
though, completely	For thocht I croce me all cleine, fra the croun doun,
embrace	He wil my corse all beclip and clap to his breist.
'shack-rag'	Quhen schaiffyn is that ald schaik with a scharp rasour,
twisted, bruises	He schovis on me his schevill mouth and schendis my lippis,
hedgehog, scratches	And with his hard hurcheone skyn sa heklis he my chekis
live coal, jaws	That as a glemand gleyd glowis my chaftis:
pain	I schrenk for the scharp stound, bot schout dar I nought
fear	For schore of that auld schrew – schame him betide!
love-glances, bogey	The luf-blenkis of that bogill, fra his blerde ene,
smirked, cast down my spirits	As Belzebub had on me blent abasit my spreit,
wretch, villainous nether lip	And quhen the smy on me smyrkis with his smakes molet,
(see n.)	He fepillis like a farcy aver that flyrit one a gillot.
voice	'Quhen that the sound of his saw sinkis in my eris,
annoyance	Than ay renewis my noy or he be neir cumand;
(see n.)	Quhen I heir nemmyt his name, than mak I nyne crocis
encumbrance, moronic churl	To keip me fra the cummerans of that carll mangit,
jealousy, qualities	That full of eldnyng is and anger and all evill thewis.
mangy tom-cat	I dar nought luke to my luf for that lene gib,
contrivances	He is sa full of jelusy and engyne fals,
	Ever ymagynyng in mynd materis of evill,
Devising and planning ways	Compasand and castand casis a thousand
trick, at tryst with	How he sall tak me with a trawe at trist of ane othir.
peep at, lad	I dar nought keik to the knaip that the cop fillis
jealousy	For eldnyng of that ald schrew that ever on evill thynkis;
	For he is waistit and worne fra Venus werkis
satisfy, needs	And may nought beit worth a bene in bed of my mystirs,

85 **forsy in draucht**: 'a good strong puller', alluding to the yoked farmhorse of l. 79.

89–92 A brief example of the technique of the Scottish *flyting*, the heaping of abusive names upon an opponent as part of an exchange of bravura invective, as in Dunbar's *The Flyting of Dunbar and Kennedie* (or as between Falstaff and prince Hal in *Henry IV, Part* 1, II.v.246–54).

101 **Mahowne**: Mahomet, often used, since all non-Christian religions were lumped together, as a name for the devil.

105–10 Echoes Chaucer's description of old January in the Merchant's Tale, as does much in this description of the classic figure of fun called the *senex amans* ('aged lover').

114 'He sticks out his lower lip like a diseased old cart-horse leering at a mare'. This comically arcane line wins a certain kind of poetic prize, communicating its meaning before one understands any one of its key words, almost like a structuralist exercise in syntactical substitution.

117 'When I hear his name mentioned, I make the sign of the cross nine times'.

because he has become impotent	He trowis that young folk I yerne, yeild for he gane is,
have the itch, prick	Bot I may yuke all this yer or his yerd help.
	'Ay quhen that caribald carll wald clym one my wambe,
(see n.)	Than am I dangerus and daine and dour of my will:
	Yit leit I never that larbar my leggis ga betueene
defile, grope	To fyle my flesche na fumyll me without a fee gret.
penis, poorly	And thoght his pen purly me payis in bed,
	His purse pays richely in recompense efter!
worthless	For or he clym on my corse, that carybald forlane,
(see n.)	I have conditioun of a curche of kersp alther-fynest,
dyed-in-grain scarlet	A goun of engranyt claith, right gaily furrit,
	A ring with a ryall stane, or other riche jowell –
antique fumbling, stark mad	Or rest of his rousty raid, thoght he wer rede wod.
bribes	For all the buddis of Johne Blunt, quhen he abone clymis,
long wait, feeble	Me think the baid deir abboucht, sa bawch ar his werkis.
	And thus I sell him solace, thoght I it sour think:
	Fra sic a syre God yow saif, my sueit sisteris deir!'
opinion	Quhen that the semely had said her sentence to end,
laughed aloud, jests	Than all thai leuch apon loft with latis full mery
passed	And raucht the cop round about full of riche wynis
joked	And ralyeit lang, or thai wald rest, with ryatus speche.
noble lady, uttered	The wedo to the tothir wlonk warpit ther wordis:
it falls to you, without feigning	'Now, fair sister, fallis yow but fenying to tell,
honoured	Sen man ferst with matrimony yow menskit in kirk
fared	How haif ye farne, be your faith? Confese us the treuth:
bless or curse	That band to blise or to ban, quhilk yow best thinkis?
faithful	Or how ye like lif to leid into lell spousage?
then, examine	And syne myself ye exem on the samyn wise
	And I sall say furth the soth, dissymyland no word.'
	The plesand said, 'I protest, the treuth gif I schaw,
trustworthy	That of your toungis ye be traist.' The tothir twa grantit:
higher	With that sprang up hir spreit be a span hechar.
	'To speik,' quoth scho, 'I sall nought spar – ther is no spy neir:
long catalogue (of woes)	I sall a ragment reveil fra rute of my hert,
sore, festered	A roust that is sa rankild quhill risis my stomok.
filled with pus	Now sall the byle all out brist that beild has so lang,
breast, burden	For it to beir one my breist wes berdin our-hevy.
outburst	I sall the venome devoid with a vent large
swelling	And me assuage of the swalme that suellit wes gret.
whore-master	'My husband wes a hur-maister, the hugeast in erd,
	Tharfoir I hait him with my hert, sa help me our Lord!
fresh	He is a young man ryght yaip, bot nought in youth flouris,
	For he is fadit full far and feblit of strenth.
	He wes as flurising fresche within this few yeris,
fallen away, exhausted	Bot he is falyeid full far and fulyeid in labour.
	He has bene lychour so lang quhill lost is his natur.
tool, feeble	His lume is waxit larbar and lyis into swoune:

131–44 Cf. WBP 409–16.
132 'Then I am coldly standoffish and disdainful and wilfully stubborn'.
138 'I make it a condition that I receive a kerchief of the finest fabric of all'.
142 **Johne Blunt**: proverbial name for a simpleton, used in an 'impossibility-topos'.
162–7 Repetition of the same thought in different words was an acknowledged ornament of style in medieval rhetoric.

(see n.)	Wes never sugeorne wer set na on that snaill tyrit,
weeks, 'knock', once	For efter sevyn oulkis rest it will nought rap anys.
for wife	He has bene waistit apone wemen or he me wif chesit
	And in adultre, in my tyme, I haif him tane oft.
cocky	And yit he is als brankand with bonet one syde
winking at	And blenkand to the brichtest that in the burgh duellis,
	Alse curtly of his clething and kemmyng of his hair
	As he that is mare valyeand in Venus chalmer.
	He semys to be sumthing worth, that syphyr in bour;
	He lukis as he wald luffit be, thoght he be litill of valour.
foolish, urinates	He dois as dotit dog that dankys on all bussis
	And liftis his leg apon loft, thoght he nought list pische.
	He has a luke without lust and lif without curage;
the manner without the power	He has a forme without force, and fessoun but vertu,
useless	And fair wordis but effect, all fruster of dedis.
illusory appearance	He is for ladyis in luf a right lusty schadow,
in the dark, in the act, droopy	Bot into derne, at the deid, he sal be drup fundin.
jests, uproarious noise	He ralis and makis repet with ryatus wordis,
boasting of his sexual successes	Ay rusing him of his radis and rageing in chalmer,
boldly	Bot God wait quhat I think quhen he so thra spekis
suits, extravagantly, speak	And how it settis him so syde to sege of sic materis,
Unless, some evening, assay	Bot gif himself, of sum evin, myght ane say amang thaim –
	Bot he nought ane is, bot nane, of naturis possessoris.
	'Scho that has ane auld man nought all is begylit:
no worse than	He is at Venus werkis na war na he semys.
thought, chose, jet	I wend I josit a gem, and I haif geit gottin;
found (to be)	He had the glemyng of gold and wes bot glase fundin.
as soon as	Thought men be ferse, wele I fynde, fra falye ther curage,
jealousy	Thar is bot eldnyng or anger ther hertis within.
	Ye speik of berdis on bewch: of blise may thai sing
free to take a mate	That on Sanct Valentynis day ar vacandis ilk yer:
depart	Hed I that plesand prevelege to part quhen me likit,
	To change and ay to cheise agane, than chastite, adew!
companion	Than suld I haif a fresch feir to fang in myn armys:
until he becomes impotent	To hald a freke quhill he faynt may foly be calit.
	'Apone sic materis I mus at mydnyght full oft
	And murnys so in my mynd I murdris myselfin;
toss	Than ly I waikand for wa and walteris about,
Cursing, wicked	Wariand oft my wekit kyn that me away cast
(see n.)	To sic a craudoune but curage that knyt my cler bewte
When there are, kingdom	And ther so mony kene knyghtis this kenrik within.
	Than think I on a semelyar, the suth for to tell,
Than, by seven times, sigh	Na is our syre be sic sevin – with that I sych oft.
empty	Than he ful tenderly dois turne to me his tume person
floppy penis	And with a yoldin yerd dois yoik me in armys,
	And sais, "My soverane sueit thing, quhy sleip ye no betir?
fever, ails	Me think ther haldis yow a hete, as ye sum harme alyt."

176 'Taking a rest (from sex) was never a worse waste of time than with that tired-out old snail'.

186 This is the image given in Chaucer's Parson's Tale (*CT* X.858), as one of the twigs of lechery on the tree of sin, for the old lecherous dotard who goes through all the motions of flirting long after he has lost the urge.

198 **naturis possessoris**: those who have healthy sexual appetites.

215 'To such a sexless coward, that tied up and hid away my fine beauty'.

	Quoth I, "My hony, hald abak, and handill me nought sair;
ache	A hache is happinit hastely at my hert-rut."
don't actually faint	With that I seme for to swoune, though I na swerf tak,
deceive, fellow	And thus beswik I that swane with my sueit wordis.
jaundiced eye	I cast on him a crabit ee quhen cleir day is cummyn
pretend, glares round	And lettis it is a luf-blenk quhen he about glemys:
really meant in anger	I turne it in a tender luke that I in tene warit
kindly	And him behaldis hamely with hertly smyling.
young girl, endure any poking	'I wald a tender peronall that myght na put thole,
erect penises	That hatit men with hard geir for hurting of flesch,
	Had my gud man to hir gest, for I dar God aver
(see n.)	Scho suld not stert for his straik a stray breid of erd!
	And syne I wald that ilk band that ye so blist call
until his back finally gave out	Had bund him so to that bryght quhill his bak werkit,
	And I wer in a beid broght with berne that me likit –
(see n.)	I trow that bird of my blis suld a bourd want!'

{The widow says she will tell how experience has taught her to manage successfully the business of being a wife, chiefly by bullying, flattering and deceiving her husbands (she has had two) into submission, meanwhile taking young lovers. Widowhood has brought her nothing but happiness and chances to carry on more openly, in what we might call her salon.*}*

sport	'Bot yit me think the best bourd, quhen baronis and knyhtis
	And othir bachilleris blith blumyng in youth
resort to my house	And all my luffaris lele my lugeng persewis
	And fyllis me wyne wantonly with weilfair and joy.
One whispers, one cracks jokes	Sum rownis and sum ralyeis and sum redis ballatis,
talks wildly	Sum raiffis furth rudly with riatus speche,
complains (of love)	Sum plenis and sum prayis, sum prasis mi bewte,
pats	Sum kissis me, sum clappis me, sum kyndnes me proferis,
bows	Sum kerffis to me curtasli, sum me the cop giffis,
within (into an inner room)	Sum stalwardly steppis ben with a stout curage
thrust, fist	And a stif standand thing staiffis in mi neiff.
(see n.)	And mony blenkis ben our, that but full fer sittis,
thrive	That mai for the thik thrang nought thrif as thai wald;
welcome	Bot with my fair calling I comfort thaim all,
	For he that sittis me nixt, I nip on his finger;
	I serf him on the tothir syde on the samin fasson,
	And he that behind me sittis, I hard on him lene,
	And him befor, with my fut fast on his I stramp,
far without	And to the bernis far but sueit blenkis I cast.
	To every man in speciall speke I sum wordis
	So wisly and so womanly quhill warmys ther hertis.
living man, low	'Thar is no liffand leid so law of degre
warm-hearted	That sall me luf unluffit, I am so loik-hertit,
inclined, skin	And gif his lust so be lent into my lyre quhit
lie, be in danger	That he be lost or with me lig, his lif sall not danger.
take pity on	I am so mercifull in mynd and menys all wichtis,

234 'She would not start (make a sudden movement of pain or surprise) a straw's breadth of ground for any thrust of his'.

238 'I believe that woman would be lacking anything to jest about concerning my happiness'.

487 'And one who sits full far outside may look within from a distance'.

God (the Lord Sabaoth)	My sely saull sal be saif, quhen Sabot all jugis.
learn, innocent little girls	Ladyis, leir thir lessonis and be no lassis fundin:
	This is the legeand of my lif, thought Latyne it be nane!'
	Quhen endit had hir ornat speche, this eloquent wedow,
laughed, rest, praised	Lowd thai lewch all the laif and loffit hir mekle,
	And said thai suld exampill take of her soverane teching
	And wirk eftir hir wordis, that woman wes so prudent.
cooled	Than culit thai ther mouthis with confortable drinkis
chatted, intimately	And carpit full cummerlik with cop going round.
passed	Thus draif thai out that deir nyght with danceis full noble
dawn	Quhill that the day did up daw and dew donkit flouris.
	The morow myld wes and meik, the mavis did sing,
	And all remuffit the myst and the meid smellit.
	Silver schouris doune schuke as the schene cristall
wood	And berdis shoutit in schaw with ther schill notis:
	The goldin glitterand gleme so gladit ther hertis,
music, boughs	Thai maid a glorius gle amang the grene bewis.
sough, valley	The soft sowch of the swyr and soune of the stremys,
	The sueit savour of the sward, singing of foulis
	Myght confort ony creatur of the kyn of Adam
gone completely cold	And kindill agane his curage, thoght it wer cald sloknyt.
rose	Than rais ther ryall rosis in ther riche wedis
went, shrub-blossoms	And rakit hame to rest throu the rise blumys,
	And I all prevely past to a plesand arber
pastime	And with my pen did report ther pastance most mery.
	Ye auditoris most honorable, that eris has gevin
unusual	Onto this uncouth aventur, quhilk airly me happinnit:
	Of ther thre wantoun wiffis that I haif writtin heir,
choose	Quhilk wald ye waill to your wif, gif ye suld wed one?

'Timor mortis conturbat me'

It is impossible to read this best known of Dunbar's poems ('The Lament for the Makers') without sharing, for a moment, his grim perturbation. The very remorselessness of the catalogue of 'estatis' and names has a cumulative effect: the consolation is almost an afterthought. There is a difference, though, from medieval mortality-poems such as Lydgate's *Dance Macabre*, and it registers some influence of Renaissance ideas: names are introduced of real poets, who are thereby rescued from the oblivion of death because they were poets. Dunbar too must die (93–5), but in doing so he will join their company. Text from the 1508 print of *Two Married Women*.

health	I that in heill wes and gladnes
	Am trublit now with gret seiknes
	And feblit with infermite:
	Timor mortis conturbat me.
	Our plesance heir is all vane-glory,
	This fals warld is bot transitory,

504 **legeand**. The widow describes her life as a 'legend', that is, like a saint's legend, a story of suffering crowned in glory. The word is similarly used by the wife in Chaucer's Shipman's Tale, *CT* VII.145.

527–30 It was a convention to end poems that dealt with questions of love with a *demande d'amour* addressed to the audience (e.g. FrankT 1621).

'Timor mortis conturbat me'

4 'The fear of death troubles me' (a sentence from the Office of the Dead, used elsewhere also as a refrain in mortality-poems).

frail, sly The flesch is brukle, the fend is sle:
Timor mortis conturbat me.

The stait of man dois change and vary,
Now sound, now seik, now blith, now sary,
Now dansand mery, now like to dee:
Timor mortis conturbat me.

sure No stait in erd heir standis sickir;
willow-branch As with the wynd wavis the wickir,
Wavis this warldis vanite:
Timor mortis conturbat me.

death Onto the ded gois all estatis,
powerful lords Princis, prelotis and potestatis,
Baith riche and pur of al degre:
Timor mortis conturbat me.

on the battlefield He takis the knyhtis into feild
Anarmyt undir helme and scheild –
every battle Victour he is at all melle:
Timor mortis conturbat me.

(i.e. Death) That strang unmercifull tyrand
Takis on the moderis breist sowkand
The bab full of benignite:
Timor mortis conturbat me.

battle He takis the campion in the stour,
The capitane closit in the tour,
The lady in bour full of bewte:
Timor mortis conturbat me.

puissance He sparis no lord for his piscence,
Na clerk for his intelligence;
stroke His awfull strak may no man fle:
Timor mortis conturbat me.

Art-magicianis and astrologgis,
Rethoris, logicianis and theologgis –
clever arguments Thame helpis no conclusionis sle:
Timor mortis conturbat me.

greatest In medicyne the most practicianis,
Lechis, surrigianis and phisicianis,
deliver Thameself fra ded may not supple:
Timor mortis conturbat me.

poets, rest I se that makaris amang the laif
grave Playis heir ther pageant, syne gois to graif:

37 **Art-magicianis**: contrivers of magical illusions, like Lydgate's *tregetour* (*Dance Macabre*, 513; cf. FrankT 1143).

45 **makaris**: 'makers', a term tending to be reserved for vernacular poets, where classical poets are always 'poets'.

46 **pageant**: the term commonly used for the short plays performed on wagons in the guild-cycles of mystery-plays.

profession Sparit is nocht ther faculte:
Timor mortis conturbat me.

He has done petuously devour
The noble Chaucer, of makaris flour,
The Monk of Bery, and Gower, all thre:
Timor mortis conturbat me.

The gud Syr Hew of Eglintoun,
And eik Heryot, and Wyntoun,
(i.e. Scotland) He has tane out of this cuntre:
Timor mortis conturbat me.

poisoned That scorpion fell has done infek
Maister Johne Clerk and James Afflek,
Fra balat making and tragidie:
Timor mortis conturbat me.

seized Holland and Barbour he has berevit;
Allace! that he nocht with us levit
Schir Mungo Lokert of the Le:
Timor mortis conturbat me.

Clerk of Tranent eik he has tane,
Adventures That maid the 'Anteris of Gawane';
Schir Gilbert Hay endit has he:
Timor mortis conturbat me.

He has Blind Hary and Sandy Traill
Slaine with his schour of mortall haill,
Quhilk Patrik Johnestoun myght nought fle:
Timor mortis conturbat me.

(power of) writing He has reft Merseir his endite,
about love That did in luf so lifly write,
So schort, so quyk, of sentence hie:
Timor mortis conturbat me.

He has tane Roull of Aberdene,
And gentill Roull of Corstorphin –
Two bettir fallowis did no man se:
Timor mortis conturbat me.

whispered In Dunfermelyne he has done roune
With Maister Robert Henrisoun;

50 For the triad of English worthies, cf. *Golden Targe*, 262. Chaucer appears here at line 50 of a 100-line poem, at what numerologists would call its 'sovereign mid-point' (see A.C. Spearing, *RES* 33 [1982], 247–61). All of the rest of the 'makaris' named are Scottish, some of them well-known poets, such as John Barbour (author of *The Bruce*), Sir Gilbert Hay (author of *The Buik of Alexander*), Blind Harry (*Wallace*) and Henryson; others are less well-known poets and writers, such as Walter Kennedy, Dunbar's *flyting*-opponent, and the chronicler Andrew of Wyntoun, while some are known only from the mention of their names here or in similar contexts. A few are quite mysterious, and have provided tempting identities for the anonymous authors of a number of late medieval northern and Scottish poems (e.g. 65–6).

63 Sir Mungo Lockhart of Lanarkshire, not known as a poet.

65–6 This poem, and its author, have been variously identified.

71 Johnston was a producer of interludes for James IV's court.

75 Cf. GP 306.

81 **done roune**: 'whispered'. Death does not invite his victims to dance, as he does in Lydgate, but he varies his approach; the suggestion here, whatever influence rhyme has had, is subtle.

Schir Johne the Ros enbrast has he:
Timor mortis conturbat me.

all And he has now tane, last of aw,
Gud gentill Stobo and Quintyne Schaw,
pity Of quham all wichtis has pete:
Timor mortis conturbat me.

Gud Maister Walter Kennedy
In poynt of dede lyis veraly –
Gret reuth it wer that so suld be!
Timor mortis conturbat me.

brothers Sen he has all my brether tane,
let me alone live He will naught lat me lif alane:
Perforce, must On forse I man his nyxt pray be:
Timor mortis conturbat me.

death Sen for the ded remeid is none,
make ready Best is that we for dede dispone,
live Eftir our deid that lif may we:
Timor mortis conturbat me.

Quoth Dunbar quhen he wes sek.

86 **Stobo**: John Reid, king's secretary (d. 1505), so called from his village of origin.

Gavin Douglas (*c.* 1475–1522)

Like Henryson and Dunbar, and like Skelton in England, Gavin Douglas was university-educated (at St Andrews and perhaps also at Paris), but unlike them he was born into a powerful family and rose swiftly in the church to become bishop of Dunkeld in 1506. After the disastrous defeat of the Scots and the death of James IV at the battle of Flodden in 1513, Douglas became increasingly involved in politics and died in exile in London. While still a young man he wrote *The Palace of Honour* (1501), an impressive *rifacimento* of medieval themes, allegorical, moral and encyclopaedic, inspired by a lofty conception of the poet's vocation. His masterpiece is his translation of Virgil's *Aeneid*, which he completed in 1513. Virgil was the poet of poets for the Middle Ages, and the exemplar of poetic diction and style in manuals of eloquence. The interpretation of his fourth Eclogue as a prophecy of the coming of Christ made him a kind of Christian by special proleptic grace, and gave to the praise of the 'pius' Aeneas an anticipatory significance; the founding of Rome by Aeneas had a special place in the divine scheme of things since it was into the Roman Empire at the height of its power that Christ chose to be born. Douglas's view of Virgil is not much touched by the Renaissance: he praises Virgil, as was customary, for his rhetoric, his 'scharp sugurate sang' (Book I, Prologue, 29), and for his 'sentence', for 'under the clowdis of dyrk poecy / Hyd lyis thar mony notabill history' (193–4); he moralizes at length in the Prologue to Book IV on the 'lufe inordinat' of Dido; and he included in his translation the sequel (describing Aeneas's marriage to Lavinia and his apotheosis) composed by Mapheus Vegius in 1428 and called Book XIII, much to the disgust of Renaissance purists (for a study of this book, see D.J. Pinti, in *JMRS* 23 [1993], 323–44). But his translation is magnificent: the extract given below, one of Virgil's most dramatic and terrible scenes, may be compared with Surrey's translation of the same passage (below) as well as with the Latin of *Aeneid*, II.544–58. Douglas's triumph is a triumph of diction and muscular idiomatic syntax, and one in which he reflects the central strengths of the Scots tradition, especially by contrast with the English poetry of the period (e.g. Hawes, Skelton), that is, its capacity to absorb both literary and colloquial elements into a coherent poetic language of supple vigour and beauty. Douglas also offers, in his own Prologues to each book, discussions of poetry and style, of Virgil, of the work of the translator, and, on three occasions, independent bravura passages of seasons and landscape description, of winter (VII), of May (XII) and of a summer night (XIII). In their precision of evocative detail, their sense of space and perspective, of light and shade, and of the busy life of the labourer, these descriptions, though drawing on much that is traditional in medieval poetry of the seasons, are quite incomparable in the use they make of those traditions. Two are given below, VII and XIII, the second continuing with the lively and humorous interview with Mapheus and a summer-morning scene. A comparison can be made with late medieval northern calendar-pictures (the representation of the twelve labours of the months opposite the calendar in books of hours), where, as in Douglas, the delight in landscape is inseparable from the recognition of human life and work within the landscape, and the landscape-picture is further framed within the astronomical information that gives it its place in the larger universe of immutable forms (see D. Pearsall and E. Salter, *Landscapes and Seasons of the Medieval World* [London, 1973], pp. 139–60, 200–5). But Douglas also points forward to the fuller emancipation of northern landscape-painting, in Bruegel and others, from the religious themes that had traditionally governed representation of nature: the first snowy winters were painted because it was winter-time when Christ was born into a world of cold and privation; the first nocturnes were painted because it was night-time when Christ endured his dark night of the soul in Gethsemane. But in sixteenth-century northern painting, and in Douglas, winter-time and night-time became themselves the subject.

The *Aeneid*-translation is extant in five early MSS and a print of 1553; the present text is based on TCC MS O.3.12 of *c.* 1515 (35v–36v, 130r–131r, 304v–307r). Edition by D.F.C. Coldwell, STS, Third Series, 25, 27–8, 30 (1950–7); *Selections*, ed. D.F.C. Coldwell (Oxford, 1964); study by P. Bawcutt, *Gavin Douglas* (Edinburgh, 1996), and of the *Aeneid*-translation by A.E.C. Canitz, in *M&H* 17 (1989), 81–99.

AENEID-TRANSLATION

Book II, chapter 9

Into this nixt cheptour ye may attend
Of Priam, kynge of Troy, the fatale end.

ask	'Peraventur of Priamus wald ye speir
How befell	Quhou tyd the chance. Hys fait, gif ye lyst, heir:
	Quhen he the cite saw takyn and downbet,
gate	And of his palyce brokyn every yet,
also, foes	Amyd the secret closettis eik hys fays,
grey-beard, takes	The auld grayth, al for nocht, to hym tays
coat of mail which, long past	Hys hawbryk quhilk was lang furth of usage,
trembling	Set on his schulderis trymlyng than for age;
without assistance	A sword but help about hym beltis he
die	And ran towart hys fays, reddy to de.
palace courtyard	Amyd the clos, under the hevyn al bayr,
	Stude thar that tyme a mekil fair altare,
Near which	Neyr quham thar grew a rycht ald lawrer tre
way	Bowand towart the altare a litill wie,
(household) gods, cover	That with his schaddow the goddis dyd ourheld.
refuge	Hecuba thyddir with hir childer for beild
	Ran al in vane and about the altare swarmys,
Embracing	Brasand the godlyke ymage in thar armys,
doves, each one	As for the storm dowis flokkis togidder ilkane.
	Bot quhen scho saw how Priamus has tane
as though	His armour, so as thocht he had beyn ying:
foolish, wretched	"Quhat fulych thocht, my wrachit spows and kyng,
such	Movis the now syk wapynnys forto weld?
such protection	Quhidder hastis thou?" quod sche. "Of na sik beld
need	Have we now mystir, nor syk diffendouris as the.
fitting	The tyme is nocht ganand tharto, we se:
Even if	In cace Hectour war present heir, my son,
	He mycht nocht succur Troy, for it is won.
	Quharfor I pray the syt doune and cum hydder
save	And lat this altare salve us al togidder,
at once	Or than atanys al heir lat us de."
semblance (of dignity)	Thus said scho and with sik sembland as mycht be
without any show of force	Hym towart hir has brocht, but ony threte,
old (man)	And set the auld doune on the haly sete.
	Bot lo, Polytes, ane of Priamus sonnys,
	Quhilk from the slauchter of Pyrrus away run is,
	Throw wapynnys fleyng and his ennemys all,
passages	Be lang throwgangis and mony voyd hall:
	Woundit he was and come to seik reskew.
	Ardently Pyrrus gan him fast persew,
sharp-ground, stretched forth	With grondyn lance at hand so neir furthstrekit,
(see n.)	Almaist the hed hym twichit and arekit,

1 Aeneas, having fled from Troy, has landed in Carthage, where he is narrating the story of the sack of Troy to the spellbound Dido, queen of Carthage.

36 Pyrrhus is the son of Achilles, and his mood is specially vengeful because of the death of his father at the gates of Troy.

42 'That the head (of the lance) almost touched and reached him'.

Until	Quhil at the last, quhen he is cummyn, I weyn,
eyes	Befor his faderis and his moderis eyn,
	Smate hym down ded in thar sycht quhar he stude;
spirit, yielded up	The gaist he yald with habundans of blude.
halfway	Priamus than, thocht he was halfdeill ded,
anger	Mycht nocht conteyn his ire nor wordis of fed,
	Bot cryis furth: "For that cruell offens
	And owtragyus fuyl-hardy violens,
pity, above	Gif thar be piete in the hevin abone
this that	Quhilk takis heid to this at thou has done,
May the gods suitably repay thee	The goddis mot condyngly the foryeld,
According to, reward	Eftir thi desert rendring sik gaynyeld,
	Causit me behald myne awyn child slane, allace,
defiled	And with hys blude fylit the faderis face.
by whom, feigns	Bot he quhamby thou fenys thiself byget,
	Achil, was not to Priam sa hard set,
moved to shame	For he, of rycht and faith eschamyt eik,
	Quhen that I come hym lawly to beseik,
	The ded body of Hector rendrit me,
	And me convoyit hame to my cite."
the old man feebly, without	Thus sayand, the ald waykly, but fors or dynt,
slight piercing	A dart dyd cast, quhilk with a pyk gan stynt
	On his harnes, and in the scheild dyd hyng
	But ony harm or other dammagyng.
Since, so	Quod Pyrrus, "Sen always thou saist swa,
go (i.e. die)	To Pellyus son, my fadir, thou most ga.
	Beir hym this message, ramembir weil thou tell
	Him al my warkis and dedis sa cruell –
completely	Schaw Neoptolemus is degenerit cleyn.
anger	Now salt thou de." And with that word in teyn
The old man trembling	The ald trymlyng towart the altare he drew,
	That in the hait blude of his son, sched new,
Was drenched	Fundrit; and Pyrrus grippis hym by the hayr
	With his left hand, and with the other al bayr
	Drew furth his schynand swerd, quhilk in his syde
(He) plunged	Festynnyt and onto the hyltis dyd he hyde.
	Of Priamus thus was the finale fait –
	Fortone heir endit his gloryus estait,
Seeing, (Troy)	Seand Ilion al byrn in fyris brown
tumbled	And Troys wallis fall and tumlyt down.
(which) once over	That ryal prince, umquhile our Asya
many, also	Apon sa feil pepil and realmys alswa
Reigned, shore	Ryngnyt in welth, now by the cost lyis ded
No more than	Bot as a stok and of-hakkit his hed,

63 With Douglas, 63–88, compare *Aeneid*, II.544–58:

Sic fatus senior, telumque imbelle sine ictu
coniecit, rauco quod protinus aere repulsum
et summo clipei nequiquam umbone pependit.
Cui Pyrrhus: 'Referes ergo haec et nuntius ibis
Pelidae genitori; illi mea tristia facta
degeneremque Neoptolemum narrare memento;
nunc morere.' Hoc dicens altaria ad ipsa trementem
traxit et in multo lapsantem sanguine nati,
implicuitque comam laeva, dextraque coruscum
extulit ac lateri capulo tenus abdidit ensem.
Haec finis Priami fatorum; hic exitus illum
sorte tulit, Troiam incensam et prolapsa videntem
Pergama, tot quondam populis terrisque superbum
regnatorem Asiae. Iacet ingens litore truncus,
avolsumque umeris caput et sine nomine corpus.

71 Neoptolemus is another name for Pyrrhus.

A corps but lyfe, renown or other fame,
Onknawyn of ony wight quhat was his name.'

Prologue to Book VII

bright, eye	As bryght Phebus, scheyn soverane hevynnys e,
mansions	The opposit held of hys chymmys hie,
summer's	Cleir schynand bemys and goldyn symmyris hew
copper, entirely	In laton cullour alteryng haill of-new,
Showing, sign	Kythyng no syng of heyt be hys vissage,
	So neir approchit he his wyntir stage;
	Reddy he was to entyr the thrid morn
	In clowdy skyis undre Capricorn.
Although	All-thocht he be the hart and lamp of hevyn,
grew, gleaming golden light	Forfeblit wolx hys lemand gylty levyn,
sphere	Throu the declynyng of hys large round speir.
reigns	The frosty regioun ryngis of the yer,
	The tyme and sesson bittir, cald and paill,
wintry (Lat. brumalis)	Tha schort days that clerkis clepe brumaill,
fierce, direction	Quhen brym blastis of the northyn art
	Ourquhelmyt had Neptunus in his cart,
	And all to-schaik the levis of the treis,
tossing about, stormy	The rageand storm ourweltrand wally seys.
furiously	Ryveris ran reid on spait with watir broune,
streams	And burnys hurlys all thar bankis doune,
surf roaring, such noise	And landbrist rumland rudely with sik beir,
	So lowd ne rumyst wild lyoun or ber;
Sea-monsters, porpoises, whales	Fludis monstreis, sik as meirswyne or quhalis,
low, descend	Fro the tempest law in the deip devalis.
in the west	Mars occident, retrograde in his speir,
	Provocand stryfe, regnyt as lord that yer;
Rainy	Rany Oryon with his stormy face
Blew about, in his course	Bewavit oft the schipman by hys race;
Ill-natured	Frawart Saturn, chill of complexioun,
whose, dearth	Throu quhais aspect darth and infectioun
	Beyn causyt oft, and mortal pestilens,
degrees	Went progressyve the greis of his ascens;
	And lusty Hebe, Junoys douchtir gay,
despoiled	Stude spulyeit of hir office and array.
soaked, wet	The soyl ysowpit into watir wak,
clouds	The firmament ourcast with rokis blak,
yellowy-brown	The grond fadyt, and fawch wolx all the feildis,
smooth, are covered	Montane-toppis slekit with snaw ourheildis;

87–8 Virgil has only 'sine nomine corpus'. Douglas makes considerable use of the extensive commentary on Virgil by the Dutch humanist Ascensius (1501), who here gets carried away with some rather irrelevant medieval reflections on death.

Prologue to Book VII

7–8 It is the morning of 15 December, three days after the winter solstice (12 December in the early sixteenth century).

25 Mars is moving apparently backward through the zodiac, i.e. from east to west, contrary to the order of the signs – an unfortunate situation for a very unfortunate planet. These lines (25–34) show the roots of Douglas's landscape-description in traditional kinds of literary seasons-setting and astronomical periphrasis.

27 The appearance of the constellation Orion in the sky was associated with storm and rain.

29 **Frawart Saturn.** Cf. Henryson, *Testament*, 151–68.

33–4 Hebe was goddess of youth (and spring-time) and cupbearer to the gods; her office was taken over by Ganymede, associated with the winter-sign of Aquarius.

rocks, whinstone	On raggit rolkis of hard harsk quhyn-stane
fissured cliffs shone	With frosyn frontis cauld clynty clewis schane.
barren	Bewte was lost, and barrand schew the landis,
hoar, patterned over	With frostis hair ourfret the feldis standis.
(see n.)	Seir bittir bubbis and the schowris snell
open field	Semyt on the sward a symylitude of hell,
Bringing back, place	Reducyng to our mynd in every sted
age, death	Gousty schaddois of eild and grisly ded.
gloomy shadows	Thik drumly skuggis dyrknyt so the hevyn,
threw, lightning	Dym skyis oft furth warpit feirfull levyn,
Flashes, fierce blast	Flaggis of fire, and mony felloun flaw,
downpours, biting	Scharpe soppys of sleit and of the snypand snaw.
dismal, damp	The dolly dichis war all donk and wait,
flooded	The law valle flodderit all with spait,
level	The plane stretis and every hie way
pools, puddles	Full of floschis, dubbis, myre and clay.
(see n.)	Laggerit leyis wallowit farnys schew,
showed, wizened	Browne muris kythit thar wysnyt mossy hew,
hillside, valley-bottom, pallid	Bank, bra and boddum blanchit wolx and bar.
rough	For gurl weddir growit bestis hair.
wave	The wynd maid waif the red wed on the dyke,
In flood, pools, brook	Bedowyn in donkis deip was every sike.
Over, here and there	Our craggis and the front of rochis seir
icicles	Hang gret ische-schouchlis lang as ony speir.
	The grond stud barrant, widderit, dosk or gray,
grasses, withered	Herbis, flowris and gersis wallowyt away.
boughs bare	Woddis, forestis, with nakyt bewis blowt,
wood	Stude stripyt of thar weid in every howt.
(north wind)	So bustuusly Boreas his bugill blew,
timidly	The deyr full dern doun in the dalis drew;
bramble-clusters	Smale byrdis, flokkand throu thik ronys thrang,
chirping	In chyrmyng and with cheping changit thar sang,
hiding-places and nooks	Sekand hidlis and hyrnys thame to hyde
season	Fra feirfull thuddis of the tempestuus tyde;
waterfalls roar, (lime-)tree	The watir-lynnys rowtis, and every lynd
roared, rushing	Quhislit and brayt of the swouchand wynd.
	Puyr lauboraris and bissy husbandmen
wet	Went wait and wery draglit in the fen.
shepherd-lads	The silly scheip and thar litil hyrd-gromys
broom-bushes	Lurkis undre le of bankis, woddis and bromys;
domesticated	And other dantit grettar bestiall,
settled	Within thar stabillis sesyt into stall,
Such, kine	Sik as mulis, horssis, oxin and ky,
Fatted, boars	Fed tuskyt barys and fat swyne in sty,
	Sustenyt war by mannys governance
summer's	On hervist and on symmeris purvyance.
Everywhere	Wyde-quhar with fors so Eolus schowtis schill
frozen	In this congelit season scharp and chill,

41 A line much admired, like 59 below. The success of both lines is in the use of alliteration, so subtly subdued amid the crash and grind of surrounding lines.

43 'Persistently returning bitter squalls and the harsh showers'.

44 **a symylitude of hell**. Douglas slips back into an older stereotype of winter.

55 'Meadows covered in mire are seen with withered ferns.'

85 **Eolus**: Aeolus (ruler of the winds).

fresh	The callour ayr, penetratyve and puyr,
Benumbing	Dasyng the blude in every creatur,
Made (them) seek, comforting	Maid seik warm stovis and beyn fyris hoyt,
under-waistcoat	In dowbill garmont cled and wily-coyt,
	With mychty drink and metis confortyve,
	Agane the stern wyntir for to stryve.
Having eaten, warmed	Repatyrrit weil, and by the chymnay bekyt,
stretched	At evin be-tyme downe a-bed me strekyt,
Wrapped	Warpit my hed, kest on clathis thrynfald,
	For til expell the peralus persand cald...

{Waking up the next morning to the 'chil wyntir cald', the poet returns to the work of translation.}

Prologue to Book XIII

Heir begynnys the Proloug in the Threttene and last Buk of Eneados ekit to Virgill be Mapheus Vegius

summer's	Towart the evyn, amyd the symmyris heit,
	Quhen in the Crab Appollo held hys sete,
	Duryng the joyus moneth tyme of June,
	As gone neir was the day and supper doyn,
briskly	I walkyt furth abowt the feildis tyte,
Which	Quhilkis tho replenyst stud full of delyte,
livestock	With herbys, cornys, catal, and frute treis,
	Plente of stoir, byrdis and byssy beys
emerald	In amerant medis fleand est and west,
	Eftir laubour to tak the nychtis rest.
sky	And as I lukit on the lift me by,
	All byrnand red gan walxin the evyn sky:
all on fire	The son enfyrit haill, as to my sight,
	Quhirlit about hys ball with bemys brycht,
	Declynand fast towart the north indeid,
dark	And fyry Phegon, his dun nychtis steid,
Dipped	Dowkit hys hed sa deip in fludis gray
	That Phebus rollis doun undir hell away;
(the evening-star)	And Esperus in the west with bemys brycht
	Upspryngis, as for-rydar of the nycht.
river-meadows	Amyd the hawchis, and every lusty vaill,
fresh, fall	The recent dew begynnys doun to scaill,
soothe, shone	To meys the byrnyng quhar the son had schyne,
	Quhilk tho was to the neddir warld declyne:
grass-blade's	At every pilis poynt and cornys croppis
dew-drops, gleaming crystal	The techrys stude, as lemand beryall droppis,
wholesome, entirely without	And on the hailsum herbis, cleyn but wedis,
flower-buds	Lyke cristal knoppis or smal silver bedis.
began, be quenched	The lyght begouth to quynchyng owt and faill,
descend	The day to dyrkyn, declyne and devaill;
vapours, damp chill mist	The gummys rysis, doun fallis the donk rym,

Prologue to Book XIII

16 **Phegon**, properly Phlegon, one of the four horses of the sun (Apollo Phebus). See Henryson, *Testament*, 212n.

shadows	Baith heir and thar scuggis and schaddois dym.
bat	Upgois the bak with hir pelit ledderyn flycht,
	The lark discendis from the skyis hycht,
compline (evensong), manner	Syngand hir complyng sang, efter hir gys,
	To tak hir rest, at matyn hour to rys.
valley	Owt our the swyre swymmys the soppis of myst,
border	The nycht furthspred hir cloke with sabill lyst,
	That all the bewte of the fructuus feld
shade, covered	Was with the erthis umbrage cleyn ourheld;
frith (woodland)	Baith man and beste, fyrth, flude and woddis wild
Wrapped, were concealed	Involvyt in tha schaddois warryn syld.
(that) fly	Still war the fowlis fleis in the air,
stock, settled down	All stoir and catall seysit in thar lair,
	And everything quharso thame lykis best
Prepares	Bownys to tak the hailsum nychtis rest
	Eftir the days laubour and the heyt.
	Clos warryn all and at thar soft quyet,
Without stirring	But sterage or removing, he or sche,
Either	Owder best, byrd, fysch, fowle, by land or sey.
go about	And schortlie, everything that doith repar
	In firth or feild, flude, forest, erth or ayr,
brushwood, luxuriant bushes	Or in the scroggis or the buskis ronk,
marshes, these dank pools	Lakis, marrasis or thir pulys donk,
	Astabillit lyggis still to slepe, and restis;
Beside (are)	Be the smaill byrdis syttand on thar nestis,
midges, restless	The litill mygeis and the vrusum fleys,
ants	Laboryus emmotis and the bissy beys;
	Als weill the wild as the taym bestiall,
	And every othir thingis gret and small,
Except	Owtak the mery nychtgaill, Philomeyn,
	That on the thorn sat syngand fra the spleyn;
longing to hear	Quhais myrthfull notis langyng for til heir,
Into a garden	Ontill a garth undir a greyn lawrer
walked presently, seat	I walk onon, and in a sege down sat,
	Now musyng apon this and now on that.
pole	I se the poill and eik the Ursis brycht
Lucina (the moon)	And hornyt Lucyn castand bot dym lycht
shone	Becaus the symmyr skyis schayn sa cleir;
	Goldyn Venus, the mastres of the yeir,
	And gentill Jove, with hir participate,
	That bewtuus bemys sched in blyth estait;
reclined	That schortly, thar as I was lenyt doun,
	For nychtis silens and this byrdis soun
slid	On sleip I slaid, quhar sone I saw appeir
(who) said	Ane agit man, and said, 'Quhat dois thou heir
	Undyr my tre, and willyst me na gude?'

33 **pelit ledderyn**: 'peeled [without hair] leathern'. The epithets are extraordinary in their precision, as is the coincidence by which William Collins also speaks of the bat flying 'on leathern wing' in his *Ode to Evening*, 10. Douglas is not close to the eighteenth-century landscape-poets, but there are some suggestive comparisons to be made.

62 **fra the spleyn**: 'out of sad distress' (the spleen was the seat of melancholy). For the cause of Philomena's distress, see her story as told by Gower, above. Her song is **mery**, 'sweet', **myrthfull**, 'giving pleasure', not 'merry'.

67 **Ursis**: 'Bears', i.e. the constellations of the Great and Little Bear.

peered furtively — Me thocht I lurkit up under my hude
old (man) — To spy this ald, that was als stern of spech
As he had beyn ane medicyner or lech,
And weill persavit that hys weid was strange,
Tharto so ald that it had not beyn change,
In my opinion — Be my consait, fully that fourty yeir,
in several places — For it was threidbair into placis seir.
Wide, suitably — Syde was this habyt, round, and closyng meit,
stretched — That strekit to the grund doun our his feit;
And on his hed of lawrer-tre a crown,
Lyke to sum poet of the ald fasson.
Me thocht I said to hym with reverens,
'Fader, gif I have done you ony offens,
I sall amend, gif it lyis in my mycht;
Bot suythfastly, gyf I have perfyte sycht,
To my judgement — Onto my doym I saw you nevir ayr,
(And) gladly — Fayn wald wyt quhen, on quhat wys or quhar
Agaynst you trespassit ocht have I.'
'Weill,' quod the tother, 'wald thou mercy cry
forgive — And mak amendis, I sal remyt this falt,
uncomfortable — Bot other-ways that sete sal be ful salt.
Knawis thou not Mapheus Vegius, the poet,
That onto Virgillis lusty bukis sweit
added — The thretteyn buke ekit Eneadan?
same, not at all pleased with you — I am the sammyn, and of the nathyng fayn,
That hes the tother twelf into thy tong
Translait of-new – thai may be red and song
All over, vernacular tongue — Our Albyon ile into your vulgar leid –
Bot to my buke yit lyst the tak na heid.'
'Mastir,' I said, 'I heir weill quhat yhe say
And in this cace of perdon I you pray –
Not that I have you onything offendit
Bot rathir that I have my tyme mysspendit
So lang on Virgillis volume for to stair
And laid on syde full mony grave mater
treatise — That, wald I now write in that trety mor,
Quhat suld folk deym bot all my tyme forlor?
(see n.) — Als, syndry haldis, fader, trastis me,
without — Your buke ekit but ony necessite,
As to the text accordyng never-a-deill
Mair than langis to the cart the fift quheill.
in such large terms — 'Thus, sen yhe beyn a Cristyn man, at large
Lay na sik thing, I pray you, to my charge;
It may suffys Virgill is at ane end!
know, known — I wait the story of Jerom is to you kend,
struck, beaten in — Quhou he was dung and beft intill hys sleip
heathens' — For he to gentilis bukis gaif sik keip.

90 Douglas addresses Mapheus in the respectful second person plural, where Mapheus uses the familar and rather contemptuous singular.
115 'Also, some people consider, father, believe me'.
122–4 St Jerome, the fourth-century translator of the Bible from Hebrew and Greek into Latin (the 'Vulgate' Bible of the Middle Ages), was learned in classical literature, and tells in his Epistle 22 of the dream in which he was tormented for spending time on classical writers that he should spend on Christian. It was a familiar crisis of conscience among the early Church Fathers, whose education was all in the classics.

Ful scharp repreif to sum is write, ye wist,
In this sentens of the haly Psalmyst:
"Thai ar corruppit and maid abhominabill
In thar studeyng thyngis onprofitabill!"
(see n.) Thus sair me dredis I sal thoill a heit
neglected For the grave study I have so long forleit.'
villain 'Ya, smy!' quod he, 'wald thou eschape me swa?
before In faith we sall nocht thus part or we ga!
excuses, escape Quhou think we he essonyeis hym to astart,
As all for consciens and devoit hart,
Fenyeand hym Jerom for to contyrfeit
Where, soaked, sweat Quhar-as he lyggis bedovyn, lo, in sweit?
I lat the wyt I am nane hethyn wight
gone And gif thou has afortyme gayn onrycht,
heathen Followand sa lang Virgill, a gentile clerk,
Quhy schrynkis thou with my schort Cristyn wark?
though, see For thocht it be bot poetry we say
are both two moral My buke and Virgillis morall beyn bath tway.
Grant Len me a fourteyn-nycht, howevir it be,
that begot me Or be the faderis sawle me gat,' quod he,
buy dearly 'Thou salt deir by that evir thou Virgill knew!'
And with that word doun of the sete me drew,
Then, rushing attack Syne to me with hys club he maid a braid
blows, back And twenty rowtis apon my riggyng laid,
Until, 'God' Quhill 'Deo, Deo, mercy!' dyd I cry,
right And be my ryt hand strekit up in hy
Promised Hecht to translait his buke in honour of God
(God + 12 = 13) And hys Apostolis twelf, in the numbir od.
He, glaid tharof, me by the hand uptuke,
Syne went away, and I for feir awoik
glanced And blent abowt to the north-eist weill far,
Saw gentill Jubar schynand, the day-star,
sign (constellation) And Chiron, clepit the syng of Sagittary,
proceed That walkis the symmyrris nycht, to bed gan cary.
fades Yondyr doun dwynys the evyn sky away
And upspryngis the brycht dawyng of day
In, away Intill ane other place nocht far in-sundir
That to behald was plesans and half wondir.
die out Furth quynchyng gan the starris, on be on,
That now is left bot Lucifer allon.
describe fittingly And forthirmor to blason this new day,
singing Quha mycht discryve the byrdis blisfull bay?
Swiftly, wing Belyve on weyng the bissy lark upsprang
To salus the blyth morrow with hir sang;
Sone our the feildis schynys the lycht cleir,
Welcum to pilgrym baith and lauborer.
Quickly, farm-labourers, reeve Tyte on hys hynys gaif the greif a cry,
at once, go to 'Awaik on-fut, go till our husbandry!'
herdsman, lad And the hyrd callis furth apon hys page,

127–8 Adapted from Ps. 14:1.
129 'Thus I am sorely afraid that I shall suffer a heating (get into hot water)'.
133 **Quhou think we**: 'What can we think of how…' with the implied answer 'Not much'. Douglas's excuses have indeed been pretty lame, and are swiftly demolished by Mapheus (137–40).

'Do dryve the catall to thar pasturage.'
The hynys wife clepis up Katheryn and Gill:
'Ya, dame,' said thai, 'God wait, with a gude will!'
powdered The dewy greyn, pulderit with daseis gay,
Schew on the sward a cullour dapill gray;
The mysty vapouris spryngand up full sweit,
Maist confortabill to glaid all manis spreit.
groves Tharto thir byrdis syngis in the schawys,
As menstralis playng 'The joly day now dawys!'
agreement Than thocht I thus: I will my cunnand kepe,
slacker I will not be a daw, I will not slepe,
I will compleit my promys schortly thus
Maid to the poet master Mapheus,
make an end of work And mak upwark heirof and cloys our buke
then That I may syne bot on grave materis luke;
For thocht hys stile be nocht to Virgill lyke,
know, please many Full weill I wayt my text sall mony like,
Since in accord Sen eftir ane my tung is and my pen,
unlearned men Quhilk may suffys as for our vulgar men.
fame or glory Quha-evir in Latyn hes the bruyt or glor,
I speke na wers than I have doyn befor.
know, (to be) different Lat clerkis ken the poetis different
take heed And men onletterit to my wark tak tent,
touching, together Quhilk, as twiching this thretteynt buke in-feir,
Begynnys thus, as furthwith followis heir.

182 A popular song of the time.
189–96 Those who are unlearned in Latin will appreciate my vernacular translation of Mapheus as much as my translation of Virgil, since like them I write and speak in the same language (191). For those who have Latin, and know the difference between the two poets, my own translation is no worse than it was before.

Stephen Hawes (d. after 1521)

Stephen Hawes was a groom of the chamber in the court of Henry VII. He admired the poetry of Lydgate, wrote a number of Lydgatian poems in the genre of moralized love-allegory and courtly allegory, and also a *Joyful Meditation* on the coronation of Henry VIII (1509). His reputation rests on his long allegorical romance, *The Pastime of Pleasure* (1506), dedicated to Henry VII, a romance of chivalry crossed with the allegorical narrative of the pilgrimage of human life (an influential earlier example is Deguileville's poem of that name, which was translated by Lydgate). The materials are stale, but the blend is new, and the poem a stumbling step towards *The Faerie Queene* (Spenser probably knew Hawes's poem). New also in Hawes, and perhaps reflecting Renaissance ideas concerning the importance of formal education for princes (see A.B. Ferguson, *The Indian Summer of English Chivalry* [Durham, NC, 1960], pp. 66–8), is the emphasis on the education of the hero, Graunde Amour, in the Seven Liberal Arts. He spends well over half the poem in the Tower of Doctrine receiving instruction in the basic university arts curriculum, before a brief spell in the Tower of Chivalry prepares him more directly for the allegorical fights through which he wins his lady, La Bell Pucell. Hawes has a talent for narrative and for the exploitation of conventional moral and descriptive motifs, but his imitation of the Lydgatian high style produces only a tawdry display of aureation, and his metre is halting. Hawes's ideas about poetry are exactly those of his Scottish contemporary Dunbar, but the difference in the success with which they put them into execution is striking.

Pastime of Pleasure, ed. W.E. Mead, EETS, OS 173 (1928); *Minor Poems*, ed. F.W. Gluck and A.B. Morgan, EETS, 271 (1974); see A.S.G. Edwards, *Stephen Hawes* (Boston, 1983). Text from the print of 1517.

The Pastime of Pleasure

[*Dedication*]

Ryght myghty prynce and redoubted soverayne,
Saylynge forth well in the shyppe of grace
Over the wawes of this lyfe uncertayne   *waves*
Ryght towarde heven to have dwellynge place,
Grace doth you guyde in every doubtfull cace:
Your governaunce doth evermore eschewe
The synne of slouthe, enemy to vertewe.

Grace stereth well, the grace of God is grete,
Whiche you hath brought to your ryall se   *royal seat*
And in your ryght it hath you surely sette
Above us all to have the soveraynte,
Whose worthy power and regall dygnyte
All our rancour and our debate gan ceace   *did cease*
And hath to us brought bothe welthe, reste and peace.

From whom dyscendeth by the ryghtfull lyne
Noble prynce Henry to succede the crowne,
That in his youthe doth so clerely shyne
In every vertu, castynge the vyce adowne.
He shall of fame attayne the hye renowne;
No doubte but grace shall hym well enclose,
Whiche by trewe ryght sprange of the reed rose.

15–21 Hawes probably has the young prince Henry in mind as a possible beneficiary of the poem's extensive educational programme for princes, and as a future patron.

21 **the reed rose**: the emblem of the house of Lancaster. Henry VII claimed the throne by right of descent from John of Gaunt and, further, through the union of the red rose with the white through his marriage to Elizabeth of York, daughter of Edward IV. But his Lancastrian claim was thin, and needed constant reaffirmation, as here, and buttressing through the association with Henry V (29), who was, conveniently, Lydgate's patron.

Your noble grace and excellent hyenes
For to accepte I beseche ryght humbly
This lytell boke, opprest with rudenes,
Without rethorycke or colour crafty. *skilful rhetorical figures*
Nothynge I am experte in poetry
As is the monke of Bury, floure of eloquence,
Whiche was in the tyme of grete excellence

Of your predecessour, the fifth kynge Henry,
Unto whose grace he dyde present
Ryght famous bokes of parfyte memory
Of his faynynge with termes eloquent, *invention*
Whose fatall fyccyons are yet permanent, *(see n.)*
Grounded on reason; with clowdy fygures
He cloked the trouthe of all his scryptures. *writings*

The lyght of trouthe I lacke connynge to cloke;
To drawe a curtayne I dare not to presume,
Nor hyde my mater with a mysty smoke,
My rudenes connynge doth so sore consume.
Yet as I may I shall blowe out a fume *vaporous cloud*
To hyde my mynde underneth a fable,
By covert colour well and probable; *hidden figurative meaning*

Besechynge your grace to pardon myne ignoraunce,
Whiche this fayned fable, to eschewe ydlenesse,
Have so compyled now without doubtaunce
For to present to your hye worthynesse.
To folowe the trace and all the parfytenesse *footsteps*
Of my mayster Lydgate, with due exercyse,
Suche fayned tales I do fynde and devyse.

For under a colour a truthe may aryse, *figure of speech*
As was the guyse in olde antyquyte
Of the poetes olde a tale to surmyse
To cloke the trouthe, of theyr infyrmyte,
Or yet on joye to have moralyte.
I me excuse yf by negligence
That I do offende for lacke of scyence.

How Graunde Amour met with Fame

Whan Phebus entred was in Gemyny, *(Gemini)*
Shynynge above in his fayre golden spere, *sphere*
And horned Dyane than but one degre *(the moon)*
In the Crabbe hadde entred fayre and clere;

33 'Whose prophetically true fictions are still always relevant'.
34–5 Hawes repeats this description of poetry, as essentially allegorical in form and moral in substance, whenever he has the opportunity. He speaks for instance of 'Invention', the first part of Rhetoric, as 'Clokynge a trouthe with colour tenebrous' (712); the poets of old 'Pronounced trouthe under cloudy fygures / By the invencyon of theyr fatall scryptures' (720–1).
53–4 These lines are not clear (Hawes seems to take rather literally his recommendation that poetry should be cloudy and vaporous). The sense, perhaps, is that classical poets invented tales whose underlying true meaning they sometimes failed to understand, through infirmity of (pagan) ignorance, and sometimes appreciated in full.

Whan that Aurora dyde well appere
purified In the depured ayre and cruddy fyrmament,
Forth than I walked without impedyment

Into a medowe bothe gaye and gloryous
Whiche Flora depaynted with many a colour
pleasure-giving Lyke a place of pleasure most solacyous,
Giving off Encensynge out the aromatyke odoure
Of Zepherus brethe, whiche that every floure
vaporous exhalation Through his fume doth alwaye engendre.
So as I went amonge the floures tendre

By sodayne chaunce a fayre pathe I founde,
On whiche I loked and ryght ofte I mused,
And than all aboute I behelde the grounde,
With the fayre pathe whiche I sawe so used.
My chaunce or fortune I nothynge refused
But in the pathe forth I went a pace
To knowe whyther and unto what place

likelihood It wolde me brynge, by ony symylytude.
So forth I wente, were it ryght or wronge,
Tyll that I sawe, of ryall pulcrytude,
Before my face, an ymage fayre and stronge
With two fayre handes stretched out alonge
dividing Unto two hye-wayes there in pertycyon;
And in the ryght hande was this dyscrypcyon:

'This is the streyght waye of contemplacyon
enduring Unto the joyfull toure perdurable.
Who that wyll walke unto that mancyon
He must forsake all thynges varyable,
With the vayne-glory so moche deceyvable;
And though the waye be harde and daungerous,
The laste ende therof shall be ryght precyous.'

And in the other hande ryght fayre wryten was:
'This is the waye of worldly dygnyte
Of the actyfe lyfe, who wyll in it passe,
Unto the toure of fayre Dame Beaute.
Fame shall tell hym of the waye in certaynte
Unto La Bell Pucell, the fayre lady excellent,
Above all other in clere beaute splendent.'

I behelde ryght well bothe the wayes twayne
And mused oft whiche was best to take.

62 **cruddy**: 'curd-like in appearance', referring to the torn rack of white clouds. Hawes is fond of neologisms, and occasionally, as here, he hits the target.

63–4 The run-on rhyme royal stanza, a rare device for special effect in Chaucer, is commonplace in Hawes, who has little understanding of the structural integrity of the stanza.

68–9 The general imitation of Chaucer (GP) and Lydgate (*Thebes*) here becomes unluckily specific (cf. GP 3–4).

83 **two hye-wayes**. Allegorical narrators are often faced with a parting of the ways, and a life-deciding choice (e.g. *PF* 125). The nature of the choice here, between the Active and Contemplative lives (the life of virtuous action in the world and the life of spiritual contemplation withdrawn from the world) shows how close Hawes is to the tradition of moral allegory exemplified in *PP* (e.g. C.VII.299–308).

The one was sharpe, the other was more playne,
And unto myselfe I began to make
A sodayne argument, for I myght not slake
Of my grete musynge of this ryall ymage
And of these two wayes so moche in usage.

For this goodly pycture was in altytude
Nyne fote and more, of fayre marble stone,
Ryght well favoured and of grete fortytude,
Though it were made full many yeres agone.
Thus stode I musynge myselfe all alone
By ryght longe tyme, but at the last I went
The actyfe waye with all my hole entent.

{He comes to another nine-foot statue pointing the way to the Tower of Doctrine, but he becomes weary and falls asleep.}

death-like Thus as I satte in a deedly slombre,
trumpet, royal Of a grete horne I herde a ryall blast,
With whiche I awoke and hadde a grete wondre
From whens it came – it made me sore agast!
I loked aboute: the nyght was well nere past
And fayre golden Phebus in the morowe graye
With cloudes reed began to breke the daye.

far-off I sawe come rydynge in a valaye ferre
A goodly lady envyronned aboute
With tongues of fyre as bryght as ony sterre,
flared That fyry flambes ensensed alwaye out,
fear Whiche I behelde and was in grete doubt.
Her palfraye swyfte rennynge as the wynde,
With two whyte grehoundes that were not behynde –

Whan that these grehoundes had me so espyed,
With faunynge chere of grete humylyte
In goodly hast they fast unto me hyed.
I mused why and wherfore it shoulde be,
way But I welcomed them in every degre.
They leped ofte and were of me ryght fayne:
permitted, in return I suffred them and cherysshed them agayne.

Theyr colers were of golde and tyssue fyne,
Wherin theyr names appered by scrypture
Of dyamondes that clerely do shyne;
The lettres were graven fayre and pure.
made an earnest effort To rede theyr names I dyde my besy cure:
The one was Governaunce, the other named Grace.
happening Than was I gladde of al this sodayne cace.

161 **two whyte grehoundes** were often used as supporters with the arms of Henry VII and Henry VIII: their names (174) make a nice compliment.

And than the lady with fyry flame
Of brennynge tongues was in my presence
Upon her palfraye, whiche hadde unto name
Pegase the swyfte, so fayre in excellence,
Whiche somtyme longed with his premynence
To kynge Percyus, the sone of Jubyter,
through On whom he rode by the worlde so fer.

To me she sayde she mervayled moche why
That her grehoundes shewed me that favour.
What was my name? she axed me treuly,
To whom I sayde it was La Graunde Amour –
'Besechynge you to be to me socour
To the Toure of Doctryne, and also me tell
Your propre name and where you do dwell?'

'My name,' quod she, 'in all the worlde is knowen,
Called Yclipped Fame in every regyon;
For I my horne in sondry wyse have blowen
After the dethe of many a champyon,
And with my tonges have made aye mencyon
Of theyr grete actes, agayne to revyve,
In flammynge tongues for to abyde on lyve.

{Fame gives examples of those who have won fame, such as Hercules, acting always for 'the comyn proffet' (241) and the sake of 'the comyn-welthe' (252). The greyhounds lead Graunde Amour to the Tower of Doctrine, which has features of the palaces of eastern emperors such as are described in Mandeville's Travels *(chap. 23).}*

nearer Than to the toure I drewe nere and nere
And often mused of the grete hyghnes
four-square Of the craggy rocke, whiche quadrant dyde appere;
But the fayre toure, so moche of rychesse,
Was all about sexangled, doubtles,
'Gargoyled' Gargeylde with grehoundes and with many lyons
Made of fyne golde, with dyvers sundry dragons.

The lytell turrets with ymages of golde
Aboute was set, whiche with the wynde aye moved
Upon their own revolving shafts With propre vyces that I dyde well beholde;
hovered Aboute the toures in sondry wyse they hoved
With goodly pypes in theyr mouthes i-tuned,
That with the wynde they pyped a daunce
Called 'Love of noble pleasure' Yclyped 'Amour de la hault pleasaunce'.

{Instruction at the Tower of Doctrine begins with Grammar and Logic, briefly, and then, at great length, Rhetoric, with its five divisions, Invention, Disposition, Elocution (Style), Pronunciation and Delivery.}

179 The winged horse Pegasus sprang from the blood of Medusa when her head was struck off by Perseus, but the horse's subsequent career was in association with Bellerophon, not Perseus.

191 **Fame**, with her trumpet and flaming tongues of fire telling of the deeds of heroes (her half-sister Rumour is 'painted full of tongues' in *Henry IV, Part 2*), wakes Graunde Amour from his sleep of sloth ('Fame is the spur…'). The medieval view of Fame was generally more circumspect: in Chaucer's *House of Fame* she is a fickle goddess, emblematic of the mutability of the world and the uncertainty of worldly fame (see P. Boitani, *Chaucer and the Imaginary World of Fame* [Cambridge, 1984]).

And than the thyrde parte is Elocucyon.
Whan Invencyon hath the purpose wrought
And set it in ordre by Dysposycyon,
avails Without this thyrde parte it vayleth ryght nought:
Though it be founde and in ordre brought,
Yet Elocucyon with the power of Mercury
adorns, copiously The mater exorneth ryght well facundyously

In fewe wordes swete and sentencyous,
hard to construe Depaynted with golde, harde in construccyon,
artful (skilled in art) To the artyke eres swete and dylycyous.
food The golden rethoryke is good refeccyon
And to the reder ryght consolacyon.
As we do golde from coper puryfy,
So Elocucyon doth ryght well claryfy

sweet The dulcet speche from the langage rude,
Tellynge the tale in termes eloquent.
vulgar The barbary tongue it doth ferre exclude,
appropriate Electynge wordes whiche are expedyent
In Latyn or Englysshe after the entent,
Encensynge out the aromatyke fume
Our langage rude to exyle and consume.

But what avayleth evermore to sowe
The precyous stones amonge gruntynge hogges?
Pig-swill, suitable Draffe unto them is more meter, I trowe.
Let an hare and swyne be amonge curre-dogges,
Though to the hares were tyed grete clogges,
beast The gentyl best they wyll regarde nothynge
chase after But to the swyne take course of rennynge.

{In the Tower of Music, Graunde Amour meets La Bell Pucell, who, after appropriate displays of reluctance, accepts him as her knight. He completes his education with Geometry, Arithmetic and Astronomy, passes to the Tower of Chivalry (where emphasis is again placed on the duty of the knight to fight for 'the comyns sake', 3374) and emerges to begin his quest. He fights against a giant with three heads (Falsehood, Imagination and Perjury) and another with seven heads (Dissimulation, Delay, etc.) and eventually wins his lady. The story of his subsequent life is passed over briefly so that he can die (in the first person) and offer himself, in the manner of 'Farewell this world' (see above), as an exemplar of mortality, the transitoriness of life, the inevitability of death, and the mutability of all earthly fame.}

904 The classical art of Rhetoric was taken over in the Middle Ages as the art of poetry, with overwhelming emphasis on Elocution (Style), mostly in the forms of lists of tropes and figures of speech, with examples. For a brief account of the background to Hawes's account of Rhetoric, see R. Copeland, in *MLQ* 53 (1992), 57–82.

908 **founde**. Latin *inventio*, referring to the first stage of rhetorical composition, the gathering of materials (what later poets would attribute to the activity of 'Imagination' – a thoroughly suspect faculty in Hawes), is derived from *invenio*, 'find'.

909 For the association of Mercury with eloquence, cf. Henryson, *Testament*, 240.

911–24 The high style of eloquence is the product of a kind of alchemical process in which diction is purged of its impurities and metamorphosed to a hard gem-like state or to gold (hence the term 'aureate'). True eloquence is the philosophers' stone.

922 **Latyn**. Hawes is referring to the wholesale adoption of Latin words into English, a feature of the aureate style as practised by Lydgate and himself.

923–4 True eloquence is a purifying fire that sends out sweet-smelling exhalations to get rid of and burn away the grossness of ordinary language.

925–6 See Matt. 7:6. In this stanza, Hawes may be attacking popular rhymesters generally, or possibly Skelton, a court-contemporary, more particularly.

O mortall folke, you may beholde and se
How I lye here, somtyme a myghty knyght.
The ende of joye and all prosperyte
Is dethe at last, through his course and myght.
After the day there cometh the derke nyght,
For though the day be never so longe
At last the belles ryngeth to evensonge.

And myselfe, called La Graunde Amoure,
Sekynge adventure in the worldly glory
For to attayne the ryches and honoure,
Dyde thynke full lytell that I sholde here ly
Tyll dethe dyde marke me full ryght pryvely. *mark me (as one destined to die)*
Lo! what I am and where to you must:
Lyke as I am so shall you be all dust.

{Fame parades the Nine Worthy, but Time declares her triumph over all, only to be contradicted by Eternity. Hawes finally takes leave of his poem.}

Go, lytell boke, I pray God the save
From mysse-metrynge by wronge impressyon,
And who that ever lyst the for to have
That he perceyve well thyne entencyon
For to be grounded withoute presumpcyon
As for to eschewe the synne of ydlenes.
To make suche bokes I apply my besynes,

Besechynge God for to gyve me grace
Bokes to compyle of morall vertue,
Of my mayster Lydgate to folowe the trace,
His noble fame for to laude and renue
Whiche in his lyfe the slouthe dyde eschewe,
Makynge grete bokes to be in memory:
On whose soule I pray God have mercy.

5474 **beholde and se**. The stanzas (which recall Lydgate's *Dance Macabre*) are accompanied by a woodcut showing decaying corpses in open coffins in the manner of many late medieval tombs.

5804 Hawes imitates *TC* V.1795–6, adapting Chaucer's plea for accurate transmission of his text and metre to the age of print.

John Skelton (*c.* 1460–1529)

John Skelton was educated at Cambridge and then at Oxford, where he received a kind of honorary degree in rhetoric that enabled him to call himself 'laureate' (he accumulated a number of other such degrees during his lifetime). He finished a prose translation of the Latin encyclopaedia of Diodorus Siculus in 1488 and entered the royal service in the same year. He was ordained in 1498 at a time when he was already tutor to prince Henry, for whom a career in the church was planned; Skelton was sacked when Henry's eldest brother Arthur died in 1502 and Henry became heir to the throne, with different educational needs. In 1504 Skelton became rector of Diss, in Norfolk, whence he tried persistently to return to court, especially after the prince succeeded as Henry VIII in 1509. In 1512 he secured the title of 'King's Orator' and began to write quantities of satirical and propagandist anti-French and anti-Scottish verse and, in the early 1520s, a series of attacks on Cardinal Wolsey. He lived mostly in London, though still rector at Diss, where he retired about 1523; he died in 1529.

Skelton is to some extent a new kind of English poet – university-trained, expert in Latin, secular in his interests and in his interpretation of his clerical vocation. His two ambitions were to be accepted in England and Europe as a laureate poet, like Petrarch (both Caxton and Erasmus praised him effusively), and, through success in that ambition, to be 'in' at court. His poetry is generally reckoned to be more or less successful in so far as it is involved in these ambitions (i.e. the more, the less). Skelton also writes at a moment when the role of the English poet is in transition, and when the high courtly style deriving from Chaucer is on the verge of disintegration. His poetic career could be seen as a search for a new kind of secular poetic style (see S. Fish, *John Skelton's Poetry* [New Haven, 1965]): his most notable innovation, his 'Skeltonics' (short lines rhymed helter-skelter), had great success as a vehicle for apparently casual and offhand running tirades of a whimsical and satirical nature, but it had no imitators. Skelton's themes are varied: every poem seems like a new beginning, in a new genre and style, except for the presence always of the urge towards self-promotion, which is an inseparable part of his poetic identity even when it is self-promotion masquerading as self-parody. Whether his themes are personal or political, he always strives to be up-to-the-minute and topical, which gives his poetry an appealing and lively impression of modernity. It is all restless and unsettling, a rag-bag of clichés and prejudices shaken together with such inventive wit and so many gratuitous scraps of erudition that hectic uncertainty becomes the norm of expectation. This may not be inapt to the England of these early Tudor years.

Complete Poems, ed. J. Scattergood (Penguin, 1983); *Selections*, ed. R.S. Kinsman (Oxford, 1969); studies by A.R. Heiserman, *Skelton and Satire* (Chicago, 1961), Fish (see above), Walker (see below), D. Lawton, 'Skelton's Use of *Persona*', *EC* 30 (1980), 9–28, B. Sharratt, 'John Skelton: Finding a Voice – Notes after Bakhtin', in Aers (1986), pp. 192–222, and Hadfield (1994), 23–50.

The Bowge of Court

This is a dream-allegory with a difference – peopled by personifications, in the old style, but having nothing to do with the courtly-love or didactic-religious themes of traditional allegory. It is a court-allegory, not a courtly allegory, having as its subject the pains, (few) pleasures, anxieties and dangers of life at court (the title, from French *bouche de court*, refers to the free rations, or 'mouthfuls', often of indifferent quality, provided to those in the royal household), as they had been long the matter of classical Horatian and Renaissance Italian satire. The first-person narrator, Drede, is not the Everyman figure of moral allegory or drama, but a particular vulnerable suppliant at the gates of preferment; he learns no moral lesson nor way of salvation, but he does learn something about the sinister and powerful realities of court-life and, at best, how to be ahead of the game. Though the poet's identity is almost swallowed in the paranoid fears of his dream-persona, Drede, this might be Skelton's ambition, too, as he begins his career at court: the poem was written in 1498, and is part of that ambition (court-people enjoy court-satire and relish their reputation for glamorous wickedness). Text from the Wynkyn de Worde print of 1499. Studies by Spearing (1985), pp. 261–5; S. Dickey, *YES* 22 (1992), 238–54; J. Simpson, in E. Maslen (ed.), *The Timeless and the Temporal: Writings in Honour of John Chalker* (London, 1993), pp. 58–79.

Virgo In autumpne, whan the sonne *in Vyrgyne*
By radyante hete enryped hath our corne;

1–16 The opening is a skilful valedictory evocation of the English poetic tradition, echoing the seasons-description of Chaucer and Lydgate (and the syntax of the latter!), with the autumn-variation of Hoccleve, and the moral-rhetorical view of poetry as craftily sententious in the manner of Hawes.

Whan Luna, full of mutabylyte,
As emperes the dyademe hath worne
Of our pole artyke, smylynge halfe in scorne
At our foly and our unstedfastnesse;
The tyme whan Mars to werre hym dyde dresse;

I, callynge to mynde the greate auctoryte
Of poetes olde, whyche, full craftely,
Under as coverte termes as coude be,
Can touche a trouthe and cloke it subtylly
Wyth fresshe utteraunce full sentencyously –
Dyverse in style, some spared not vyce to wyte, *chastise*
Some of moralyte nobly dyde endyte,

Wherby I rede theyr renome and theyr fame *opine*
May never dye, but evermore endure –
I was sore moved to aforce the same, *attempt*
But Ignoraunce full soone dyde me dyscure *betray*
And shewed that in this arte I was not sure;
For to illumyne, she sayde, I was to dulle, *write brilliantly*
Avysynge me my penne awaye to pulle *put away*

And not to wryte, for ho-so wyll atteyne,
Excedynge ferther than his connynge is, *understanding*
His hede may be harde, but feble is his brayne –
Yet have I knowen many suche er this!
But of reproche surely he may not mys
That clymeth hyer than he may fotynge have:
What and he slyde downe, who shall hym save?

Thus up and down my mynde was drawen and cast
That I ne wyste what to do was beste,
So sore enweried that I was, at the laste,
Enforsed to slepe and for to take some reste;
And to lye downe as soone as I me drest, *prepared*
At Harwyche porte slumbrynge as I laye
In myne hostes house called Powers Keye,

Me thoughte I sawe a shyppe, goodly of sayle,
Come saylynge forth into that haven brood,
Her takelynge ryche and of hye apparayle.
She kyste an anker and there she laye at rode; *cast, riding at anchor*
Marchauntes her borded to see what she had lode. *was loaded with*
Therein they founde royall marchaundyse,
Fraghted with plesure to what ye coude devyse. *Loaded*

4 **dyademe**: the Corona Borealis, seen around the moon in the northern sky from April to December.

16–18 Poets often talk at the beginnings of poems about their uncertainty as to their poetic vocation; the ensuing poem shows that they have no need to be so modest.

35 **Powers Keye**. There was a house or inn on the quay at Harwich, owned by a John Power.

36 **a shyppe**. The ship was a traditional image for the state, or for the church, and was to be used for satirical purposes, as here, in the *Narrenschiff*, or 'Ship of Fools', of Sebastian Brant (1494), translated into English by Alexander Barclay.

{The poet (whose name turns out to be Drede) boards the ship, which is called 'The Bowge of Court' and has Fortune at the helm. He meets some of the passengers, including Favell (Flattery), who practises his art and takes his leave.}

Than thanked I hym for his grete gentylnes.
But, as me thoughte, he ware on hym a cloke
That lyned was with doubtfull doublenes;
Me thoughte of wordes that he had full a poke – *bag*
His stomak stuffed ofte tymes dyde reboke. *belch back*
Suspycyon, me thoughte, mette hym at a brayde, *all of a sudden*
And I drewe nere to herke what they two sayde.

'In fayth,' quod Suspecte, 'spake Drede no worde of me?'
'Why? What than? Wylt thou lete men to speke? *prevent*
He sayth he can not well accorde with the.'
'Twysh!' quod Suspecte, 'go playe; hym I ne reke!' *Tush! care about*
'By Cryste,' quod Favell, 'Drede is a soleyne freke! *sullen fellow*
What, lete us holde him up, man, for a whyle.' *leave him be*
'Ye, so,' quod Suspecte, 'he may us bothe begyle.'

And whan he came walkynge soberly,
Wyth 'Hom' and 'Ha' and with a croked loke,
Me thoughte his hede was full of gelousy,
His eyen rollynge, his hondes faste they quoke;
And to me-warde the strayte waye he toke. *direct*
'God spede, broder!' to me quod he than,
And thus to talke with me he began:

'Ye remembre the gentylman ryghte nowe
That communed with you, me thought, a praty space? *a fair time*
Beware of him, for, I make God avowe,
He wyll begyle you and speke fayre to your face.
Ye never dwelte in suche another place,
For here is none that dare well other truste –
But I wolde telle you a thynge, and I durste!

'Spake he, a'fayth, no worde to you of me?
I wote, and he dyde, ye wolde me telle.
I have a favoure to you, wherof it be, *liking, for whatever reason*
That I muste shewe you moche of my counselle,
But I wonder what the devyll of helle
He sayde of me, whan he with you dyde talke?
By myne avyse, use not with him to walke.

'The soveraynst thynge that ony man may have
Is lytyll to saye and moche to here and see;
For, but I trusted you, so God me save,
I wolde nothynge so playne be.
To you only, me thynke, I durste shryve me, *confess my inmost thoughts*
For now am I plenarely dysposed *fully*
To shewe you thynges that may not be disclosed.'

181–2 **Suspycyon** is neatly represented here, as someone Drede is suspicious of and also as an aspect of his own behaviour.

212 Proverbial: see Whiting H 264.

{'This and thus it is' is all his secret. Drede next meets Hervy Hafter, con-man and trickster, who does his 'spiel', checks out the newcomer, and takes his leave.}

Wyth that, as he departed so fro me,
Anone ther mette with him, as me thoughte,
strangely attired A man, but wonderly besene was he.
haughty He loked hawte, he sette eche man at noughte;
His gawdy garment with scornys was all wrought;
With indygnacyon lyned was his hode;
(God's) He frowned as he wolde swere by Cockes blode.

bit, disdainful He bote the lyppe, he loked passynge coye;
disfigured His face was belymmed as bees had him stoung;
It was no tyme with him to jape nor toye.
Envye hath wasted hys lyver and his loung;
Hatred by the herte so had hym wroung
That he loked pale as asshes to my syghte.
unwieldy carcase Dysdayne, I wene, this comerous carkes hyghte.

To Hervy Hafter than he spake of me,
And I drewe nere to harke what they two sayde.
'Now,' quod Dysdayne, 'as I shall saved be,
pleased I have grete scorne and am ryghte evyll apayed.'
Than quod Hervy, 'Why art thou so dysmayde?'
'By Cryste,' quod he, 'for it is shame to saye,
To see Johan Dawes, that came but yesterdaye,

'How he is now taken in conceyte,
This Doctour Dawcocke – Drede, I wene he hyghte.
By Goddis bones, but yf we have som sleyte,
It is lyke he wyll stonde in our lyghte!'
'By God,' quod Hervy, 'and it so happen myghte!
Lete us, therfore, shortely at a worde
Fynde some mene to caste him over the borde.'

'By him that me boughte,' than quod Dysdayne,
I wonder sore he is in suche conceyte.'
hide 'Turde!' quod Hafter, 'I wyll the nothynge layne,
There muste for hym be layde some prety beyte.
We tweyne, I trowe, be not withoute dysceyte:
Fyrste pycke a quarell and fall oute with hym then,
And so outface hym with a carde of ten.'

Forthwith he made on me a prowde assawte,
angered With scornfull loke mevyd all in moode.
He wente aboute to take me in a fawte:
He frounde, he stared, he stamped where he stoode.
I loked on hym, I wende he had be woode.

288 **He bote the lyppe**. Detail such as this, here and in 190–3 above, takes us directly to *PP* (see C.VI.104, above) and the origins of this kind of vivid personal description in the iconographic portraiture of the Seven Deadly Sins.

301 **Johan Dawes**: like **Dawcocke** (below, 303), a popular name for a stupid ignorant person (lit. male jackdaw).

315 See Whiting C 36: 'play confidently on not a very high card, bluff'.

He set the arme proudly under the syde,
And in this wyse he gan with me to chyde:

'Remembrest thou what thou sayd yesternyght?
Wylt thou abyde by the wordes agayne?
By God, I have of the now grete dyspyte;
in every possible way I shall the angre ones in every vayne!
low-born rustic It is greate scorne to see suche an hayne
As thou art, one that cam but yesterdaye,
tricks to win mastery With us olde servauntes suche maystryes to playe.

a person of reputation in the world 'I tell the, I am of countenaunce.
What wenest I were? I trowe thou knowe not me.
By Goddis woundes, but for dysplesaunce,
Of my querell soone wolde I venged be!
But, no force, I shall ones mete with the:
Come whan it wyll, oppose the I shall,
Whatsomever aventure therof fall.

kitchen-drudge 'Trowest thou, drevyll, I saye, thou gawdy knave,
take pleasure That I have deynte to see the cherysshed thus?
By Goddis syde, my sworde thy berde shall shave!
for once, subdued, indeed Well, ones thou shalt be chermed, iwus:
(I give nothing for) Naye, strawe for tales, thou shalt not rule us;
We be thy betters, and so thou shalt us take,
Or we shall the oute of thy clothes shake!'

Wyth that came Ryotte, russhynge all at ones,
shabbily pretentious A rusty gallande, to-ragged and to-rente,
set of dice And on the borde he whyrled a payre of bones,
Four three two '*Quater treye dews!*' he clatered as he wente.
have a go at 'Nowe have at all, by Saynte Thomas of Kente!'
cast, never And ever he threwe, and kyst I wote nere what;
His here was growen thorowe-oute his hat.

dressed in a new-fangled way Thenne I behelde how he dysgysed was:
His hede was hevy for watchynge over-nyghte,
His eyen blered, his face shone lyke a glas;
His gowne so shorte that it ne cover myghte
His rumpe, he wente so all for somer lyghte;
trimmed, strip His hose was garded with a lyste of grene,
torn Yet at the knee they were broken, I wene.

His cote was checked with patches rede and blewe;
close-fitting jacket Of Kyrkeby Kendall was his shorte demye;
And ay he sange, 'In fayth, Decon, thou crewe.'
tight His elbowe bare, he ware his gere so nye,
His nose a-droppynge, his lyppes were full drye;

321 A stereotyped theatrical gesture of proud and scornful rebuke.
350 A proverbial way of describing a down-at-heel spendthrift (Whiting H 22).
359 **Kyrkeby Kendall**, in Westmorland, where a cheap green cloth was made ('Kendal green').
360 Evidently a line from a popular song. **Decon**, i.e. Dickon, dim. of Richard.

short sword And by his syde his whynarde and his pouche –
coin (with a cross on it) The devyll myghte daunce therin for ony crowche!

(see n.) Counter he coude *O lux* upon a potte.
ostrich An eestryche fedder of a capons tayle
He set up fresshely upon his hat alofte.
Let's have a wild revel, run on 'What, revell route!' quod he, and gan to rayle
How ofte he hadde hit Jenet on the tayle,
dainty Of Felyce fetewse and lytell prety Cate,
latch-gate (obscenely) How ofte he knocked at her klycked-gate.

What sholde I tell more of his rebaudrye?
I was ashamed so to here hym prate.
He had no pleasure but in harlotrye.
'Ay,' quod he, 'in the devylles date,
What art thou? I sawe the nowe but late.'
'Forsothe,' quod I, 'in this courte I dwell nowe.'
'Welcome,' quod Ryote, 'I make God avowe.

'And, syr, in fayth, why comst not us amonge
To make the mery, as other felowes done?
Thou muste swere and stare, man, al daye longe,
And wake all nyghte and slepe tyll it be none.
Thou mayst not studye or muse on the mone.
This worlde is nothynge but ete, drynke and slepe,
And thus with us good company to kepe.

(see n.) 'Plucke up thyne herte upon a mery pyne,
a farthing's-worth, at the ale And lete us laugh a placke or tweyne at nale.
What the devyll, man, myrthe was never syne!
set What, lo, man, see here of dyce a bale:
A brydelynge caste for that is in thy male!
have a go at, board Now have at all that lyeth upon the burde.
Fye on this dyce, they be not worth a turde!

hazard (a dice-game) 'Have at the hasarde or at the dosen browne,
Or els I pas a peny to a pounde!
Now wolde to God thou wolde leye money downe!
quickly Lorde, how that I wolde caste it full rounde!
Ay, in my pouche a buckell I have founde:
nor coin marked with a cross The armes of Calyce I have, no coyne nor crosse.
lucky I am not happy, I renne ay on the losse!

365 'He could sing the descant to *O lux beata Trinitas* (a hymn sung at Vespers) when he had a potful of ale'.
369 **Jenet** could be 'jennet', a small horse, or 'Janet'.
375 **in the devylles date**: proverbial, a parodic form of *anno Domini*, 'in the year (date) of the Lord', but here just an oath, 'in the devil's name'.
386 **upon a mery pyne**: 'in a merry frame of mind', referring to the tuning of an instrument by means of a pin or peg.
388 **myrthe was never syne**. Cf. WBP 614. For the emendation, see Gray (1985), p. 487.
390 **A brydelynge**: 'a last throw', while the bridles are put on the horses ready for departure.
393 **the dosen browne**: 'the full dozen'? (a throw at dice?).
394 **pas**: make a bet in the dice-game called 'passage'.
398 **armes of Calyce**: coins carrying the arms of the city were minted in Calais in the fifteenth century, but would now be obsolete and as useless as the old buckle he has just found.

brothel quarter
'Now renne muste I to the stewys syde
To wete yf Malkyn, my lemman, have gete oughte.
I lete her to hyre that men may on her ryde;
Her harnes easy ferre and nere is soughte.
By Goddis sydes, syns I her thyder broughte,
She hath gote me more money with her tayle
Bordeaux
Than hath some shyppe that into Bordews sayle.

'Had I as good an hors as she is a mare,
I durste aventure to journey thorugh Fraunce.
Who rydeth on her, he nedeth not to care,
compactly framed
For she is trussed for to breke a launce.
(small horse), kick skittishly
It is a curtel that well can wynche and praunce;
plead on oath
To her wyll I nowe all my poverte lege.
And tyll I come, have here myne hat to plege.'

{Drede's education in the ways of the court is continued by Disdain, Dissimulation and Deceit (the bewildering multiplicity of similar-sounding names is part of Skelton's technique, as in his allegorical play of Magnificence, *of suggesting the quicksand uncertainties and dangers of court-life). Fearful for his safety in this world of claustrophobic menace, he makes to leap overboard and, with that, wakes up.}*

THE BOOK OF PHILIP SPARROW

The occasion of this poem, written about 1505, is the death of a pet sparrow belonging to Jane Scrope, a young woman living with her sisters and widowed mother in lodgings at Carrow Abbey, a Benedictine house near Norwich (not far from Diss). Jane laments her loss in extravagantly learned terms, working in many allusions to the Mass for the Dead (17–833); Skelton continues *in propria persona* (if one can imagine such a thing) with some beautiful and most improper 'Commendations' (a term usually reserved for poems or prayers in memory of the departed or in praise of the Virgin) of Jane (845–1267). With these hostages given to poetic pretension (the poem has classical models too, in Catullus's lament for Lesbia's dead sparrow, and Corinna's lament for her dead parrot in Ovid's *Amores* II.vi), Skelton can develop his most winning vein of comedy and burlesque, commenting astutely in passing on poetic style and the English poetic tradition, and touching riskily on female adolescent sexual fantasy. One secret of the poem is how Jane provides him with a voice to explore unexpected kinds of wit and feeling; another is the audacious blending throughout of Christian and classical allusion, in a manner that would hardly have been countenanced, except in Latin, in the Middle Ages. The short couplets run on as if unhindered, offering neither resistance to nor constraint upon the poet's characteristic energies, but the effect is delicate, sparkling, cascade-like, not that of a wild rampage. Text from Kele's print of *c.*1545; studies by S. Schibanoff, *PMLA* 101 (1986), 832–47; Spearing (1993), pp. 268–82; C.R. Daileader, *PQ* 75 (1996), 391–409.

Pla ce bo,
Who is there, who?
Di le xi,
Dame Margery,
Fa, re, my, my.

401 **Malkyn**: a familiar name for a woman of the lower classes (dim. of Matilda or Mary). Cf. *PP* C.I.180.
403 **harnes**. Cf. WBP 136.

THE BOOK OF PHILIP SPARROW
1–5 ***Placebo***, 'I shall please [the Lord]' (Vg. Ps. 114:9, cf. AV Ps. 116), is the first word of the opening antiphon of Vespers of the Office for the Dead. ***Dilexi***, 'I have loved [the Lord]' (Vg. Ps. 114:1), begins the first psalm of that office. (The openings of the second, third, fourth and fifth antiphons and psalms are similarly quoted in lines 64–6, 95–7, 143–5 and 183–5 below.) The division of the syllables suggests the setting out of the text with music, for the reader to sing, and ***Fa, re, my, my*** the tune (in tonic solfa notation). **Dame Margery** was a senior nun at St Mary's Carrow; she leads the office and answers the poet's questions.

Wherfore and why, why?
For the sowle of Philip Sparowe,
That was late slayn at Carowe
Among the Nones Blake.
For that swete soules sake,
And for all sparowes soules
Set in our bede-rolles, — *prayer-rolls*
Pater noster qui,
With an *Ave Mari*,
And with the corner of a Crede,
The more shal be your mede. — *reward*
 When I remembre agayn
How mi Philyp was slayn,
Never halfe the payne
Was betwene you twayne,
Pyramus and Thesbe,
As than befell to me.
I wept and I wayled,
The tearys downe hayled,
But nothynge it avayled
To call Phylyp agayne
Whom Gyb our cat hath slayne.
 Gyb, I saye, our cat,
Worrowyd her on that — *that one*
Which I loved best.
It can not be exprest
My sorowfull hevynesse,
But all without redresse;
For within that stounde, — *moment*
Halfe slumbrynge, in a sounde — *swoon*
I fell downe to the grounde.
 Unneth I kest myne eyes — *With difficulty*
Towarde the cloudy skyes;
But whan I dyd beholde
My sparow dead and colde,
No creature but that wolde
Have rewed upon me,
To behold and se
What hevynesse dyd me pange:
Wherewith my handes I wrange
That my senaws cracked — *sinews*
As though I had ben racked,
So payned and so strayned
That no lyfe well-nye remayned.
 I syghed and I sobbed,
For that I was robbed
Of my sparowes lyfe.
O mayden, wydow and wyfe,

13–15 Prayers to be said for the soul of the departed. **corner of a Crede**: the portion of the Creed on the first page of the Primer, or basic prayer-book.
21 **Pyramus and Thesbe** were the lovers separated by a wall in Ovid, *Met.* IV.55–166 (and in Chaucer's *Legend of Good Women* and Shakespeare's *A Midsummer Night's Dream*).
29 **Worrowyd her on**: 'Worried' (bit into the throat of and shook to death).

Of what estate ye be,
Of hye or lowe degre,
Great sorowe than ye myght se,
And lerne to wepe at me!
gnaw at Such paynes dyd me frete
That myne hert dyd bete,
My vysage pale and dead,
Wanne, and blewe as lead:
The panges of hatefull death
Well-nye had stopped my breath.
Heu, heu, me,
That I am wo for the!
Ad dominum, cum tribularer, clamavi.
Of God nothynge els crave I
But Phyllypes soule to kepe
swamp From the marees depe
Of Acherontes well,
river That is a flode of hell,
And from the great Pluto,
The prynce of endles wo;
And from foule Alecto,
blackish-blue With vysage blacke and blo;
hag (as in 'night-mare') And from Medusa, that mare,
That lyke a fende doth stare;
snakes And from Megeras edders,
For rufflynge of Phillips fethers,
And from her fyry sparklynges,
For burnynge of his wynges;
And from the smokes sowre
Of Proserpinas bowre;
And from the dennes darke
Wher Cerberus doth barke,
frighten Whom Theseus dyd afraye,
vanquish Whom Hercules dyd outraye,
As famous poetes say;
From that hell-hounde
That lyeth in cheynes bounde,
With gastly hedes thre,
To Jupyter pray we
That Phyllyp preserved may be!
Amen, say ye with me!
Do mi nus,
Helpe nowe, swete Jesus!
Levavi oculos meos in montes.
Wolde God I had Zenophontes,

57 **lerne to wepe at me**: echoes the lamentation of Mary over the dead Christ (as in 'Who cannot wepe', p. 390 above).

61 **blewe**: 'blackish-blue', an epithet often used to describe the colour of Christ's skin as he died on the cross.

64, 66 'Woe, woe is me' (Vg. Ps. 119:5). 'In my distress I cried out unto the Lord' (Vg. Ps. 119:1).

70–91 **Acherontes** is Acheron, one of the rivers of the underworld (Hades). **Pluto** and **Proserpina** were king and queen of Hades. **Alecto** and **Megaera** were two of the snake-headed Furies. **Medusa** was a Gorgon, whose **stare** turned men to stone. **Theseus** went to Hades to rescue **Hercules**, one of whose twelve 'labours' was to capture **Cerberus**, the three-headed dog who guarded the entrance to the underworld.

95, 97 'Lord' (Vg. Ps. 120:5). 'I lifted up my eyes to the hills' (Vg. Ps. 120:1).

98 **Zenophontes**. Xenophon was a Greek philosopher-historian and pupil of Socrates.

Or Socrates the wyse,
technique
To shew me their devyse
Moderatly to take
This sorow that I make
For Phyllip Sparowes sake!
So fervently I shake,
I fele my body quake,
So urgently I am brought
sad
Into carefull thought.
  Like Andromach, Hectors wyfe,
Wax wery of her lyfe
Whan she had lost her joye,
Noble Hector of Troye,
In lyke maner also
Encreaseth my dedly wo,
For my sparowe is go.
It was so prety a fole,
It wold set on a stole,
schooling
And lerned after my scole
know his place (behave himself)
For to kepe his cut,
With 'Phyllyp, kepe your cut!'
  It had a velvet cap
And wold syt upon my lap
And seke after small wormes
And somtyme white bred-crommes;
And many tymes and ofte
Betwene my brestes softe
It wolde lye and rest –
decorous and well behaved
It was propre and prest.
  Somtyme he wolde gaspe
Whan he sawe a waspe;
A fly or a gnat,
He wold flye at that;
prettily
And prytely he wolde pant
Whan he saw an ant;
Lord, how he wolde pry
After the butterfly!
Lord, how he wolde hop
grasshopper
After the gressop!
And whan I sayd, 'Phyp, Phyp,'
Than he wold lepe and skyp,
And take me by the lyp.
slay
Alas, it wyll me slo,
That Phillyp is gone me fro!
  Si in i qui ta tes
Alas, I was evyll at ease!
De pro fun dis cla ma vi,
Whan I sawe my sparowe dye!
  Nowe, after my dome,
Dame Sulpicia at Rome,

143, 145 'If [thou, Lord, shouldest mark] iniquities' (Vg. Ps. 129:3). 'Out of the depths have I cried' (Vg. Ps. 129:1).

148 **Sulpicia**, a Roman poetess of the first century.

Whose name regystred was
Forever in tables of bras,
Because that she dyd pas — *surpass*
In poesy to endyte
And eloquently to wryte,
Though she wolde pretende
My sparowe to commende,
I trowe she coude not amende
Reportynge the vertues all
Of my sparowe royall.
For it wold come and go,
And fly so to and fro;
And on me it wolde lepe
Whan I was aslepe,
And his fethers shake,
Wherewith he wolde make
Me often for to wake,
And for to take him in
Upon my naked skyn,
God wot, we thought no syn.
What though he crept so lowe?
It was no hurt, I trowe.
He dyd nothynge, perde,
But syt upon my kne.
Phyllyp, though he were nyse,
In him it was no vyse;
Phyllyp had leve to go
To pyke my lytell too;
Phillip myght be bolde
And do what he wolde;
Phillip wolde seke and take
All the flees blake
That he coulde there espye
With his wanton eye.
O pe ra,
La, soll, fa, fa,
Confitebor tibi, Domine, in toto corde meo.

...I toke my sampler ones
Of purpose, for the nones,
To sowe with stytchis of sylke
My sparow whyte as mylke,
That by representacyon
Of his image and facyon, — *appearance*
To me it myght importe
Some pleasure and comforte
For my solas and sporte.
But whan I was sowing his beke,
Me thought my sparow did speke

183, 185 '[O Lord, forsake not] the works [of thine own hands]' (Vg. Ps. 137:8). 'I will praise thee, Lord, with my whole heart' (Vg. Ps. 137:1).

And opened his prety byll,
Saynge, 'Mayd, ye are in wyll
Agayne me for to kyll!
Ye prycke me in the head!'
With that my nedle waxed red,
Me thought, of Phyllyps blode.
hair Myne hear ryght upstode,
fright And was in suche a fray
My speche was taken away.
I kest downe that there was,
And sayd, 'Alas, alas,
How commeth this to pas?'
My fyngers, dead and colde,
Coude not my sampler holde;
My nedle and threde
I threwe away for drede.
The best now that I maye
Is for his soule to pray:
   A porta inferi,
Good Lorde, have mercy
Upon my sparowes soule,
Wryten in my bede roule!

...Vengeaunce I aske and crye,
By way of exclamacyon,
On all the hole nacyon
Of cattes wylde and tame;
God send them sorowe and shame!
That cat specyally
That slew so cruelly
My lytell prety sparowe
That I brought up at Carowe.
churlish   O cat of carlyshe kynde,
fiend The fynde was in thy mynde
destroyed Whan thou my byrde untwynde!
I wold thou haddest ben blynde!
The leopardes savage,
The lyons in theyr rage,
(I wish they might) Myght catche the in theyr pawes,
And gnawe the in theyr jawes!
Libya The serpents of Lybany
Myght stynge the venymously!
The dragones with their tonges
Might poyson thy lyver and longes!
The mantycors of the montaynes
Myght fede them on thy braynes!
   Melanchates, that hounde

239 'From the gate of hell [deliver him]', alluding to Matt. 16:8: 'the gates of hell [i.e. the powers of the devil] shall not prevail'.

282–323 The curses called down upon the cat are one of the great rhetorical tirades of the poem.

294 **mantycors**. The manticore was a fabulous monster, having the body of a lion, the head of a man, the quills of a porcupine and the stinging tail of a scorpion.

296 **Melanchates** was the first of Actaeon's hounds to bite him after he had been turned into a stag by Diana because he saw her bathing (Ovid, *Met.* III.232).

That plucked Actaeon to the grounde,
Gave hym his mortall wounde,
Chaunged to a dere,
The story doth appere –
Was chaunged to an harte:
So thou, foule cat that thou arte,
The selfe same hounde
Myght the confounde,
That his owne lorde bote, — *bit*
Myght byte asondre thy throte!
Of Inde the gredy grypes — *India, griffins*
Myght tere out all thy trypes!
Of Arcady the beares
Might plucke awaye thyne eares!
The wylde wolfe Lycaon
Byte asondre thy backe-bone!
Of Ethna the brennynge hyll
That day and night brenneth styl,
Set in thy tayle a blase
That all the world may gase
And wonder upon the.
From Occyan the great se
Unto the Iles of Orchady, — *Orkney*
From Tyllbery fery — *Tilbury (on the Thames estuary)*
To the playne of Salysbery!
So trayterously my byrde to kyll
That never ought the evyll wyll! — *bore thee*
Was never byrde in cage
More gentle of corage
In doynge his homage
Unto his soverayne.
Alas, I say agayne,
Deth hath departed us twayne: — *separated*
The false cat hath the slayne!
Farewell, Phyllyp, adew:
Our Lorde thy soule reskew!
Farewell without restore, — *(hope of) restoration*
Farewell for evermore!
And it were a Jewe,
It wolde make one rew
To se my sorow new.
These vylanous false cattes
Were made for myse and rattes
And not for byrdes smale.
Alas, my face waxeth pale
Tellynge this pyteyus tale,
How my byrde so fayre,
That was wont to repayre — *make his way*
And go in at my spayre — *opening in a gown*

311 **Lycaon**, king of Arcadia, was turned into a wolf by Jupiter because he offered him a sacrifice of human flesh (Ovid, *Met.* I.163).
318 **Occyan** is the great ocean that encircles all the lands of the earth in medieval maps. The shift to homely Tilbury in 320 is the epitome of Skelton's mock-heroic technique in the poem, the abrupt puncturing of rhetorical inflation.

panel of a skirt

And crepe in at my gore
Of my gowne before,
Flyckerynge with his wynges –
Alas, my hert it stynges,
Remembrynge prety thynges!
Alas, myne hert it sleth,
My Phyllyppes dolefull deth!
Whan I remembre it,
How pretely it wolde syt
Many tymes and ofte
Upon my fynger aloft.
I played with him tytell-tattyll,
And fed him with my spattyl,
With his byll betwene my lippes –
It was my prety Phyppes!
Many a prety kusse
Had I of his swete musse.
And now the cause is thus:
That he is slayne me fro,
To my gret payne and wo.
  Of fortune this the chaunce
Standeth on varyaunce:
Oft tyme after pleasaunce
Trouble and grevaunce.
No man can be sure
Allway to have pleasure,
As well perceyve ye maye
How my dysport and play
From me was taken away
By Gyb, our cat savage,
That in a furyous rage
Caught Phyllyp by the head
And slew him there starke dead.
  Kyry, eleyson,
  Christe, eleyson,
  Kyry, eleson.

{Jane summons all the birds of the air and elsewhere (an enormous list, 386–570) to help her weep. Deciding that Philip must have a proper epitaph, she consults the store of books she has read (another enormous list, 607–768) but concludes that she is not learned enough to write one herself.}

buckets, bags

Though I have enrold
A thousand new and old
Of these historious tales,
To fyll bougets and males
With bokes that I have red,
Yet I am nothyng sped,
And can but lytell skyll
Of Ovyd or Virgyll,
Or of Plutharke,

378–80 'Lord have mercy, Christ have mercy, Lord have mercy': the opening of the Mass.

756–66 These classical writers can be looked up in an encyclopaedia (where Skelton himself found most of them).

Or Frauncys Petrarke,
Alcheus or Sapho,
Or such other poetes mo,
As Linus and Homerus,
Euphorion and Theocritus,
Anacreon and Arion,
Sophocles and Philemon,
Pyndarus and Symonides,
Philistion and Phorocides;
These poetes of auncyente,
They ar to diffuse for me.
   For as I tofore have sayd,
I am but a yong mayd,
And can not in effect
My style as yet direct
choice With Englysh wordes elect.
Our naturall tong is rude
made fresh And hard to be enneude
With pullysshed termes lusty.
Our language is so rusty,
So cankered and so full
awkwardnesses Of frowardes, and so dull,
That if I wolde apply
To wryte ornatly
I wot not where to fynd
Termes to serve my mynde.
   Gowers Englysh is olde
reckoned And of no value told;
His mater is worth gold
And worthy to be enrold.
well read   In Chauser I am sped,
His tales have I red;
His mater is delectable,
Solacious and commendable;
approved His Englysh well alowed,
put to good use So as it is enprowed,
For as it is enployd
superfluous There is no Englysh voyd
At those dayes moch commended.
And now men wold have amended
His Englyssh, whereat they barke
spoil, do And mar all they warke.
Chaucer, that famus clerke,
His termes were not darke,
But plesaunt, easy and playne –
No worde he wrote in vayne.
   Also John Lydgate

774–83 Complaints about the rusticity of the English tongue (compared with Latin) are commonplace in the late medieval and early Renaissance period (e.g. Hawes, *Pastime*, 918).

784–812 Gower, Chaucer and Lydgate were enshrined in the pantheon of English poetry in the later fifteenth century (see Dunbar, *Golden Targe*, 262). It is unusual for independent critical comments to be made (only Jane could do it), and most unusual for them to be so astute.

784–7 The contrast between mouldy old words and worthy moral content became a commonplace of Renaissance and neo-classical commentary on Chaucer, as well as Gower.

style Wryteth after an hyer rate:
difficult It is dyffuse to fynde
meaning he intended The sentence of his mynde.
distinctive manner Yet wryteth he in his kynd,
No man that can amend
Those maters that he hath pende.
Yet some men fynde a faute
too pretentiously And say he wryteth to haute.
  Wherfore hold me excused
If I have not well perused
Myne Englyssh halfe-abused;
Though it be refused,
At its true value In worth I shall it take
And fewer wordes make.
  But for my sparowes sake,
Yet as a woman may
My wyt I shall assay
An epytaphe to wryght
In Latyne playne and lyght,
Whereof the elegy
Foloweth by and by.

Flos volucrum formose, vale!
Philippe, sub isto
Marmore iam recubas
Qui mihi carus eras.
Semper erunt nitido
Radiantia sydera celo;
Impressusque meo
Pectore semper eris.

{Skelton now speaks in his own poetic persona (the verse seems to have slipped a gear), calling on the Muses to inspire him in his commendation of Jane's surpassing beauty, and reproaching those who accuse him of wasting his time on trifles.}

Now Phebus me ken
To sharpe my pen
And lede my fyst,
As hym best lyst,
That I may say
Honour alway
Of womankynd.
Trouth doth me bynd
And loyalte
Ever to be
Their true bedell
To wryte and tell
How women excell
In noblenes,

826–33 'Fair flower of birds, farewell. Philip, beneath that marble now thou liest, that wert dear to me. For ever the stars will shine in the bright sky, and for ever thou shalt be graven upon my heart.'

980 **bedell**: beadle (officer who makes a proclamation).

As my maistres,
Of whom I thynk
With pen and ynk
For to compyle
composition Some goodly style.
For this most goodly floure,
This blossome of fresh coloure,
So Jupyter me socoure,
She flourissheth new and new
In beaute and vertew:
Hac claritate gemina
O gloriosa femina,
Legem pone michi, domina, in viam justificationum tuarum!
Quemadmodum desiderat cervus ad fontes aquarum.
  How shall I report
All the goodly sort
Of her fetures clere,
That hath non erthly pere?
Her favour of her face
Made fresh Ennewed all with grace,
Confort, pleasure and solace,
Myne hert doth so enbrace
And so hath ravyshed me
Her to behold and se
That in wordes playne
I cannot me refrayne
To loke on her agayne.
Alas, what shuld I fayne?
It wer a plesaunt payne
With her aye to remayne.
shining   Her eyen gray and stepe
Causeth myne hert to lepe;
With her browes bent
She may well represent
Fayre Lucres, as I wene,
Or els fayre Polexene,
Or els Caliope,
Or els Penolope.
For this most goodly floure, etc.
  The Indy saphyre blew
make bright Her vaynes doth ennew;
The orient perle so clere,
complexion The whytnesse of her lere;
cheeks The lusty ruby ruddes
Resemble the rose buddes;

994–7 'Twin-born to this bright fame [of beauty and virtue], O glorious woman.' 'Instruct me, lady, in the way of thy just laws' (Vg. Ps. 118:33). 'As pants the hart for water-brooks' (Vg. Ps. 41:1). Note the substitution (by emendation on the basis of the use of the word in later citations proved by rhyme) of *domina* for *domine* ('O Lord') whereby Jane is elevated to the position of God as well as equal (*gemina*) with the Virgin (*gloriosa femina*). Skelton repeats lines 989–97 as a kind of refrain, varying the last two Latin lines with further citations from Vg. Ps. 118 (as employed in the *Ordo Commendationis Animae*, the Office for the Commendation of the Soul of the Departed: see I.A. Gordon, in *MLR* 29 [1934], 389–96). The refrain-lines are included here in the line-numbering, but not cited.

1014 **eyen gray**. In poetry, gray eyes were thought to be a special sign of beauty (cf. GP 152).

1019–21 Polyxena, daughter of Priam, was beloved of Achilles; Calliope was the Muse of epic poetry; Penelope was Ulysses' wife.

Her lyppes soft and mery
Blooming Emblomed lyke the chery –
It were an hevenly blysse
Her sugred mouth to kysse.
   Her beautye to augment
Dame Nature hath her lent
A warte upon her cheke,
Who-so lyst to seke;
In her vysage a skar
That semyth from afar
Lyke to the radiant star,
beauty adorned All with favour fret,
So properly it is set.
She is the vyolet,
The daysy delectable,
The columbyn commendable
gillyflower This jelofer amyable.
For this most goodly floure, etc.
   And whan I perceyved
grasped its significance Her wart, and conceyved,
It cannot be denayd
placed But it was well convayd,
And set so womanly
And nothynge wantonly
But ryght conveniently
appropriately And full congruently,
As Nature cold devyse,
In most goodly wyse.
Who-so lyst beholde,
It maketh lovers bolde
To her to sewe for grace,
Her favoure to purchase.
mark   The sker upon her chyn
Inscribed Enhached on her fayre skyn
Whyter than the swan,
It wold make any man
To forget deadly syn
Her favour to wyn.
For this most goodly floure, etc.
   Soft, and make no dyn,
For now I wyll begyn
extol To heve in remembraunce
Her goodly dalyaunce
pastime And her goodly pastaunce:
So sad and so demure,
Behavynge her so sure,
With wordes of pleasure
(see n.) She wold make to the lure

1050–3 The flower-comparisons are in imitation of those usually applied, by typology from OT sources, to the Virgin (see Lydgate, *Life of Our Lady*, III.1761–82n, above).

1074 **It maketh lovers bolde**: being a mark of imperfection, it makes her more humanly accessible (than the Virgin).

1100 **make to the lure**: 'bring to the lure', in falconry, to attract (the hawk back to the fist) with a bait.

And any man convert
To gyve her his hole hert.
She made me sore amased
Upon her whan I gased,
Me thought min hert was crased,
Myn eyne were so dased.
For this most goodly floure, etc.
to reinforce what she said — And to amende her tale,
was pleased to condescend — Whan she lyst to avale
And with her fyngers smale
And handes soft as sylke
Whyter than the mylke,
so full of life — That are so quyckely vayned,
Wherwyth my hand she strayned,
Lorde, how I was payned!
Unneth I me refrayned,
So completely, subdued — How she me had reclaymed
enrolled in service — And me to her retayned,
(From) embracing — Enbrasynge therewithall
Her goodly myddell small
With sydes longe and streyte.
To tell you what conceyte
I had than in a tryce
The matter were to nyse;
And yet there was no vyce
Nor yet no vyllany,
But only fantasy.
For this most goodly floure, etc.
But whereto shulde I note
peep — How often dyd I tote
Upon her prety fote?
It raysed myne hert rote
To se her treade the grounde
With heles short and rounde.
unmistakeably — She is playnly expresse
Egeria, the goddesse,
And lyke to her image,
Depicted — Emportured with corage,
A lovers pylgrimage.
Ther is no beest savage
Ne no tyger so wood
But she wolde chaunge his mood,
radiant — Such relucent grace
Is formed in her face.
For this most goodly floure, etc.
So goodly as she dresses,
So proprely she presses
The bryght golden tresses
Of her heer so fyne,
bright — Lyke Phebus beames shyne.

1148 **raysed myne hert rote**. For the sexual suggestiveness of this phrase, see WBP 471.

1152 **Egeria**, a faithful wife, in Ovid, *Met.* XV.547.

Wherto shuld I disclose
The garterynge of her hose?
a matter of imagining
It is for to suppose
How that she can were
Gorgiously her gere:
clothes
Her fresshe habylementes
With other implementes
To serve for all ententes,
Lyke Dame Flora, quene
Of lusty somer grene.
For this most goodly floure, etc.
Her kyrtell so goodly lased,
enclosed
And under that is brased
Such pleasures that I may
Neyther wryte nor say.
Yet though I wryte not with ynke
prevent
No man can let me thynke,
For thought hath lyberte,
Thought is franke and fre;
To thynke a mery thought
It cost me lytell nor nought.
Wolde God myne homely style
Were pullysshed with the fyle
Of Ciceros eloquence,
To prayse her excellence!
For this most goodly floure, etc.
Omnibus consideratis,
Paradisus voluptatis
Hec virgo est dulcissima.
My pen it is unable,
My hand it is unstable,
My reson rude and dull
To prayse her at the full,
Goodly maystres Jane,
Sobre, demure Dyane;
Jane this maystres hyght,
The lode-star of delyght,
Dame Venus of all pleasure,
fountain-head
The well of worldly treasure;
surpass
She doth excede and pas
In prudence dame Pallas.
For this most goodly floure, etc.
Requiem eternam dona eis, Domine,
With this psalme, *Domine, probasti me,*
Shall sayle over the see

1197 **Neyther wryte nor say.** The delicately modest skirting of indelicacy is a convention of medieval catalogue-descriptions of women: *taceo de partibus infra*, 'I am silent on the parts below', is the way one rhetorician puts it. Of course, it is disingenuous, for the effect is to emphasize the sexual suggestiveness, especially as the poet's fancy follows the route of Philip's adventurous flickerings (the poet becomes the pet).

1216–18 'All things considered, this sweetest of all girls is a paradise of delights'.

1230 **Pallas** (Athena) was the Greek goddess of wisdom, as Diana and Venus were the goddesses of chastity and love.

1238 'Give them eternal rest, O Lord' (the Introit in the Mass for the Dead). This sentence is the subject of 'Shall sayle' in 1240.

1239 'O Lord, thou hast searched me' (Vg. Ps. 138:1).

With *Tibi, Domine, commendamus*,
On pylgrimage to Saynt Jamys,
For shrympes and for pranys *prawns*
And for stalkynge cranys.
And where my pen hath offendyd
I pray you it may be amendyd
By discrete consyderacyon
Of your wyse reformacyon;
I have not offended, I trust,
If it be sadly dyscust. *soberly considered*
It were no gentle gyse
This treatyse to despyse
Because I have wrytten and sayd
Honour of this fayre mayd.
Wherefore shulde I be blamed
That I Jane have named
And famously proclamed?
She is worthy to be enrolde
With letters of golde.
Car elle vault.
Per me laurigerum Britonum Skeltonida vatem
Laudibus eximiis merito hec redimita puella est,
Formosam cecini, qua non formosior ulla est;
Formosam potius quam commendaret Homerus.
Sic juvat interdum rigidos recreare labores,
Nec minus hoc titulo tersa Minerva mea est.
Rien que playsere.

{Skelton later added a conjuration of Philip, in the name of Hercules, Saul and others, to come and explain why his poem should have caused offence (presumably to Jane and her mother!).}

THE TUNNING OF ELINOR RUMMING

Women did most of the ale-brewing in the Middle Ages (see *PP* VI.225, above); it was not a respectable trade, and women were abused and scorned for doing it. Alewives had a bad reputation, and were accused of cheating customers and being spreaders of malicious gossip (there was a genre of poems on the subject); alehouses were places where women ruled and so everything went to pot. Skelton's poem, written about 1517, begins with a description of Elinor Rumming as a low-life grotesque, and continues, in the lines quoted below, with her customers and her ale-making and 'tunning' (putting the beer in barrels). All the housewives of the district, grotesque and pathetic drabs, drunken and deranged slatterns, come flying to the alehouse, bringing anything but money to pay – household utensils, treasured heirlooms, junk, bric-a-brac. The alehouse becomes a universal pawn-shop where everything is converted into ale, a lawless form of exchange among women loosed ('unbrased') from the bonds of propriety and male control. The poem accommodates itself readily to a clerical view of women that moves without self-question from idealizing fantasy about delicate young virgins to disgust at nauseating old hags. But the exuberance of the poem's energy and inventiveness mitigates our unease,

1241 'We commend ourselves to thee, O Lord', the final prayer of the *Ordo Commendationis Animae*.

1242 The shrine of **Saynt Jamys** was in Compostella, in north-west Spain. The saint's emblem, and the souvenir that pilgrims brought back, was a scallop-shell, which is what prompted Skelton to think of shrimps and prawns.

1260 'Because she is worthy'.

1261–7 'Through me, Skelton, laureate poet of the Britons, this maiden is deservedly crowned with choice praises. I have sung of the fair maiden, than whom none is more fair, (who is) more fair than any that Homer might commend. Thus is it pleasant to take recreation from time to time from hard labours, nor is the goddess of wisdom in any way slighted by this inscription. Only to please.'

and one could even find something carnivalesque and Rabelaisian, in the style of Bakhtin, something subversive of conventional attitudes, in its picture of female solidarity and resourcefulness. That might spoil the fun, though. Text from Richard Lant's print of *c.* 1545. Valuable study by E. Fowler, in *Spenser Studies* 10 (1992), 245–73.

...Primus passus

And this comely dame,
I understande, her name
Is Elynour Rummynge
At home in her wonnynge; *dwelling*
And, as men say,
She dwelt in Sothray
In a certayne stede
Bysyde Lederhede.
She is a tonnysh gyb, *fat ('tun-like') old bag*
The devyll and she be syb. *kin*
  But to make up my tale,
She breweth noppy ale *heavy*
And maketh thereof port-sale *public sale*
To travellars, to tynkers,
To sweters, to swynkers,
And all good ale-drynkers,
That wyll nothynge spare
But drynke tyll they stare
And brynge them selfe bare
With, 'Now away the mare *melancholy*
And let us sley care!' –
As wyse as an hare!
  Come who-so wyll
To Elynoure on the hyll,
With 'Fyll the cup, fyll!'
And syt there by styll, *by the still*
Erly and late.
Thyther cometh Kate,
Cysly and Sare,
With theyr legges bare,
And also theyr fete
Hardely full unswete, *Certainly*
With theyr heles dagged, *covered with muck*
Theyr kyrtelles all to-jagged,
Theyr smockes all to-ragged,
With tytters and tatters, *rags*
Brynge dysshes and platters,
With all theyr myght runnynge
To Elynour Rummynge
To have of her tunnynge.
She leneth them on the same, *provides*

Primus passus The best-known poem in *passus* is *PP*, to which Skelton may jokingly allude. Glutton's tavern (VI.350, above) is worth comparing: Langland's tavern is a den of vice, a moral allegory in a vividly real place; Skelton's alehouse is a fantasy, a burlesque of social and economic realities.

98 **Lederhede**: Leatherhead, in Surrey. There was a real 'Alianora Romyng', an alewife, fined for selling short measure, in Leatherhead in 1525.

112 Hares were proverbially crazy ('wod as an hare').

And thus begynneth the game.
   Some wenches come unlased,
Some huswyves come unbrased
With theyr naked pappes
That flyppes and flappes,
It wygges and it wagges
Lyke tawny saffron bagges;
A sorte of foule drabbes
All scurvy with scabbes.
Some be flybytten,
piebald Some skewed as a kytten;
shoe-rag Some with a sho-clout
Bynde theyr heddes about;
hair-band Some have no here-lace,
Theyr lockes aboute theyr face,
Theyr tresses untrust,
All full of unlust;
straw-coloured Some loke strawry,
the colour of coarse undyed cloth Some cawry-mawry,
dirty old ewes Full untydy tegges
Lyke rotten egges.
Suche a lewde sorte
To Elynour resorte
From tyde to tyde.
Abyde, abyde,
And to you shall be tolde
Howe hyr ale is solde
(see n.) To mawte and to molde.

Secundus passus

Some have no mony
That thyder commy,
For theyr ale to pay;
bad business That is a shreud aray!
Elynour swered, 'Nay,
Ye shall not bere awaye
Myne ale for nought,
By hym that me bought!'
   With 'Hey, dogge, hay,
Have these hogges away!'
With 'Get me a staffe,
grain The swyne eate my draffe!
Stryke the hogges with a clubbe,
They have dronke up my swyllyng-tubbe!'
crowd For, be there never so moche prese,
table on raised dais These swyne go to the hye dese,
The sowe with her pygges;
waggles The bore his tayle wrygges,
rubs His rumpe also he frygges

159 **To mawte and to molde**: 'to become malty (i.e. "green", not properly brewed) or mouldy'. Either way, the beer is no good.

161 **commy**: 'come'. Skelton often uses this childish babble-language to convey contempt.

Agaynst the hye benche.
With 'Fo, ther is a stenche!
Gather up, thou wenche.
Seest thou not what is fall?
Take up dyrt and all,
And bere out of the hall.
God gyve it yll prevynge *ill-luck*
Clenly as yvell chevynge!' *As sure as ill-fortune*
  But let us turne playne, *directly*
There we lefte agayne, *left off*
For, as yll a patch as that, *great a nuisance*
The hennes ron in the mashfat; *excrete, mashing-vat*
For they go to roust,
Streyght over the ale-joust, *ale-vat*
And donge, whan it commes, *drop dung*
In the ale-tunnes.
Than Elynour taketh
The mashe-bolle and shaketh *mash-bowl*
The hennes donge awaye
And skommeth it into a tray *skims it off*
Where as the yeest is
With her maungy fystis.
And somtyme she blennes *mixes*
The donge of her hennes
And the ale togyder,
And sayth, 'Gossyp, come hyder,
This ale shal be thycker,
And floure the more quycker; *ferment*
For I may tell you
I lerned it of a Jewe
Whan I began to brewe
And I have found it trew.
Drinke now whyle it is new:
And ye may it broke, *digest*
It shall make you loke
Yonger than ye be
Yeres two or thre,
For ye may prove it by me.
Behold,' she sayd, 'and se
How bright I am of ble! *complexion*
Ich am not cast away,
That can my husband say,
Whan we kys and play
In lust and in lykyng.
He calleth me his whytyng,
His mullyng and his mytyng, *sweetie, dearie*
His nobbes and his conny, *darling, bunny*
His swetyng and his honny,
With "Bas, my prety bonny, *Give me a kiss*
Thou art worth good and monny." *goods and money*
This make I my falyre fonny *Thus, 'feller' foolish-fond*
Tyll that he dreme and dronny; *drowse*
For after all our sport

Than wyll he rout and snort. *snore*
Than swetely togither we ly,
As two pygges in a sty.'
To cease me semeth best
And of this tale to rest
And for to leve this letter
Bicause it is no better;
And bicause it is no swetter,
We wyll no farther ryme
Of it at this tyme,
But we wyll turne playne
Where we left agayne....

COLIN CLOUT

Skelton wrote a series of satires against Cardinal Wolsey, Henry VIII's chief minister, in 1521–2, criticizing him for abrogating to himself so much of the royal power, and abusing him for being vain and wealthy and of low birth. They include the ostentatiously learned and cryptic bird-allegory of *Speak, Parrot* in rhyme royal and two poems in Skeltonics. *Colin Clout* is spoken in the person of the plain honest rustic who travels the country and simply reports what everyone is saying – an effective device for establishing credibility (Spenser later used Colin Clout for similar purposes). *Why Come Ye Not to Court?*, completed in November 1522 ('To whyche court? / To the kynges courte? / Or to Hampton Court?' 402–4, is the point of the title), is more personal and virulent in its abuse of Wolsey, as if Skelton were annoyed that no one was listening. The poems have been praised for their courage and outspokenness, and Wolsey was certainly a powerful man, but the reality seems rather that Skelton thought, wrongly as it turned out, that he would gain favour with the king by attacking Wolsey (see G. Walker, *John Skelton and the Politics of the 1520s* [Cambridge, 1988]). The king was no doubt amused by his old tutor's antics, and enjoyed any irritation that Wolsey might feel, but he had no intention of abandoning his loyal and energetic minister (who was useful in taking the blame for unpopular decisions made by the king), and Skelton soon changed his tune, without anyone seeming much bothered. The idea of Skelton as a brave upholder of political and ecclesiastical probity and civil and poetic liberties betrays a misunderstanding of the realities of court-life and court-patronage (a year after *Why Come Ye*, Skelton was friends with Wolsey and writing anti-Scottish satire at his request). The anti-Wolsey satires are time-serving, politically shallow and inconsistent: but this does not affect the pleasure we take (and Skelton took) in the skilful handling of the weapons of satire and invective, nor has it prevented Skelton's attacks having had, in the longer view of history, a damaging effect on Wolsey's reputation. Text from Thomas Godfray's edition of c.1530.

What can it avayle
To dryve forth a snayle
Or to make a sayle
Of a herynges tayle?
To ryme or to rayle,
To wryte or to indyte,
Other for delyte *Either*
Or elles for despyte?
Or bokes to compyle
Of dyvers maner style,
Vyce to revyle
And synne to exyle?
To teche or to preche

COLIN CLOUT

1–4 These are ridiculous *impossibilia*, illustrating how difficult it is trying to reform the realm through satirical writing.

As reason wyll reche? *direct*
'Sey this and sey that:
His heed is so fat *(he's a fathead)*
He wottyth never what
Ne whereof he speketh.
He cryeth and he creketh, *croaks*
He pryeth and he preketh, *pricks (with irritation)*
He chydeth and he chatters,
He prayeth and he patters,
He clyttreth and he clatters, *chatters*
He medleth and he smatters, *is a busybody, blathers*
He gloseth and he flatters.' *speaks to deceive*
Or yf he speke playne,
Than he lacketh brayne:
'He is but a foole;
Let hym go to scole!
A thre-foted stole
That he may downe sytte,
For he lacketh wytte.'
And yf that he hytte
The nayle on the hede
It standeth in no stede: *does no good*
'The devyll,' they say, 'is dede,
The devyll is dede!'
   It may well so be,
Or elles they wolde se
Otherwyse, and fle
From worldly vanyte
And foule covytousnesse
And other wretchednesse,
Fyckell falsenesse,
Varyablenesse,
With unstablenesse.
And yf ye stande in doute
Who brought this ryme aboute,
My name is Collyn Cloute.
I purpose to shake oute
All my connynge bagge, *bag of knowledge*
Lyke a clerkely hagge. *(male-)hag*
For though my ryme be ragged,
Tattered and jagged,
Rudely rayne-beaten,
Rusty and mothe-eaten,
Yf ye take well therwith
It hath in it some pyth.

15 Not clear: perhaps a mocking imitation of the way he rails on and on.

16–25 How honest plain speaking is despised and dismissed.

37 **The devyll is dede**. Proverbial (Whiting D 187): 'the worst is over, good times are here!'.

49 **Collyn** is an old name for a humble rustic person, and **Cloute** means 'rag'.

{Having established his credentials, Colin tells how he hears reports from all quarters among lay-people concerning the ignorance of the clergy and the corruption of the church, and the neglectfulness of church leaders. The people are particularly incensed at the suppression of certain small nunneries (by Wolsey) in 1521–2.}

And all the faute they lay
In you prelates, and say
Ye do them wronge and no ryght
To put them thus to flyght:
No matyns at mydnyght,
Boke and chalys gone quyte;
lead-roofs Plucke away the leedes
Over theyr heedes,
And sell away theyr belles
And all that they have elles.
Thus the people telles,
Rayles lyke rebelles,
(see n.) Redes shrewdly and spelles,
And with foundacyons melles,
And talkes lyke tytyvylles
wills of the deceased Howe ye breke the dedes wylles,
Turne monasteries into water-mylles,
Of an abbey ye make a graunge –
Your workes, they say, are straunge –
So that theyr founders soules
(see n.) Have lost theyr bede-roules,
The money for theyr masses
Spent among wanton lasses;
Theyr dyriges are forgotten,
Theyr founders lye there rotten –
But where theyr soules dwell
meddle Therwith I wyll nat mell!
What coude the Turke do more
With all his false lore –
Saracen Turke, Sarazyn or Jewe?
I reporte me to you.

{The accusations circle more and more closely upon the great prelates, meaning Wolsey (who is not named).}

where it pleases them In matters that them lyke
They shewe them polytyke,
Pretendyng gravyte
authority And seygnyoryte,
With all solempnyte,

414–15 'Take things amiss and tell false stories, and meddle in the affairs of endowed religious institutions'. Colin's criticism of the views of the people he reports, his desire not to accept their criticisms, strengthens his claim to be an objective reporter.

416 **tytyvylles**. Originally, Titivillus was a lesser devil asssigned to collect words mumbled or mis-said by the priest in the office, or words said in malice or envy by others, and write them down to be brought in evidence at the Last Judgement. The word came to mean any malicious or evil-minded person.

418 This is what happened at Broomhall, in Berkshire, suppressed 5 December 1521 (there were two nuns in residence at the time).

419 Proverbial (cf. Whiting A 4). Skelton incorporates much material from traditional anticlerical satire.

422 **bede-roules**: 'prayer-rolls' (lists of people to be prayed for).

425 **dyriges**: prayers for the souls of the dead (MnE 'dirge'), from *dirige*, 'lead [me, O Lord]' (Ps. 5:8), the first word of the first antiphon in matins of the Office of the Dead.

427–8 If their souls (in purgatory) were not being prayed for, there was no knowing where they might end up.

To show themselves above reproach For theyr indempnyte;
For they wyll have no losse
coin (marked with a cross) Of a peny nor of a crosse
farm-lands Of theyr predyall landes
That cometh to theyr handes;
venture And as farre as they dare set,
All is fysshe that cometh to the net;
Buyldynge royally
Theyr mancyons curyously
With turrettes and with toures,
With halles and with boures,
Stretchynge to the sterres,
With glasse wyndowes and barres;
Hangynge aboute the walles
rich velvets Clothes of golde and paules,
Arras (tapestries) Arayse of ryche aray,
Fresshe as flours in May,
With Dame Dyana naked,
Howe lusty Venus quaked
And howe Cupyde shaked
His dart and bent his bowe
shoot from a crouching position For to shote a crowe
At her tyrly tyrlowe;
And howe Parys of Troy
Daunced a *lege moy*,
Made lusty sporte and joy
With Dame Helyn the quene;
all together With suche storyes bydene
decorated Theyr chambres well sene,
With tryumphes of Cesar
And of his Pompeyus warre,
Of renowne and of fame
By them to gette a name.
Howe all the worlde stares
chariots Howe they ryde in goodly chares
Conveyde by olyfauntes
With lauryat garlantes,
And by unycornes
With theyr semely hornes;
Upon these beestes rydynge
Naked boyes strydynge,
With wanton wenches wynkyng!
Nowe trewely, to my thynkyng,
That is a speculacyon
And a mete meditacyon

934 **Buyldynge royally**: refers especially to Wolsey's palace at Hampton Court, west of London.

940–68 The tapestries at Hampton Court were famous, especially those based on the *Trionfi* (Triumphs) of Petrarch (allegories of Fame, Death, Love, etc. shown as victory-processions). Three still remain *in situ*, one of which shows the Triumph of Renown, with Caesar and Pompey, and the chariot of Fame drawn by elephants, another the Triumph of Death, with unicorns and putti.

949 **tyrly tyrlowe**: a nonsense-refrain, used as a euphemism.

951 ***lege moy***: apparently the name of some kind of dance (a corruption of 'le jeu de mai'?).

969–79 These are not, of course, Skelton's views; like Wolsey, he would have found these classical themes not at all repugnant to his clerical vocation. But he knew that there was popular and bourgeois outrage at Wolsey's ostentation, and that Colin could voice it, and that the king might take heed of such a voice.

For prelates of estate,
Theyr courage to abate
From worldly wantones,
Theyr chambre thus to dresse
With suche perfytenesse
And all suche holynesse –
Howebeit they let downe fall
Theyr churches cathedrall!
   Squyre, knyght and lorde
find fault with
Thus the churche remorde:
With all temporall people
(= the church)
They renne agaynst the steple,
Thus talkynge and tellynge
meddling (in non-church affairs)
Howe some of you are mellynge.
swelling (with ostentation)
Yet softe and fayre for swellynge –
Beware of a quenes yellynge!
   It is a besy thynge
For one man to rule a kynge
Alone, and make rekenynge
To governe over all
And rule a realme royall
By one mannes wytte.
Fortune may chaunce to flytte,
And whan he weneth to sytte
Yet may he mysse the quysshon!...

Make ye no murmuracyon
Though I wryte after this facyon;
Though I, Collyn Clout,
whole crowd
Amongest the hole rout
Of you that clerkes be,
Take upon me
Thus copyously to wryte:
I do it nat for no despyte.
Wherfore take no dysdayne
At my style rude and playne,
For I rebuke no man
That vertuous is. Why than
Wreke ye your anger on me?
For those that vertuous be
Have no cause to say
That I speke out of the way.
   Of no good bysshop speke I,
denounce
Nor good preest I escrye,
Good frere nor good chanon,
Good nonne nor good canon,

987 Proverbial (Tilley S 601), but possibly also an allusion to queen Katharine's public criticism of Wolsey's policies.
996 Proverbial (Whiting C 641).
1095–1115 Colin's defence of his outspokenness – that he speaks no ill of the virtuous, and that he makes no attacks on named persons – is the traditional defence of the moral satirist and critic of society, from Horace to Pope.
1097–8 **chanon, canon**. A distinction may be intended between, respectively, *regular* canons, such as the Augustinian canons, living in a community like monks, and *secular* canons, attached to a church to perform its offices.

Good monke nor good clerke,
Nor of no good werke;
But my recountynge is
Of them that do amys
In spekynge and rebellynge,
In hyndrynge and dysavaylynge [*damaging*]
Holy churche our mother,
One agayne another. [*against*]
To use suche despytynge [*scornful criticism*]
Is all my hole wrytynge;
To hynder no man,
As nere as I can,
For no man have I named.
Wherfore shulde I be blamed?
Ye ought to be ashamed
Agaynst me to be gramed, [*angered*]
And can nat tell no cause why,
But that I wryte trewly.

{Ends with a mock-account of the outrage of his victims and their call for him to be arrested.}

The Garland of Laurel

The Garland of Laurel was first printed by Richard Fakes in 1523, but it was mostly written around 1495, when the poet was at Sheriff Hutton castle, in Yorkshire (see Skelton's headnote, below), in the company of the countess of Surrey (see 769) and her ladies. The poem represents Skelton's lifelong preoccupation with his poetic reputation: there are not many poems of 1600 lines that are so single-minded in their adherence to the subject of the author's own excellence as a poet. Chaucer was concerned to record his place among the poets of the past; Skelton is obsessed with doing so. Many of the set-piece descriptions, such as those of the palace and garden of Fame, are like the 'writing-samples' to go with his application for poetic immortality, while the vast list of his writings (the later ones inserted just before publication) constitutes the bibliography attached to his curriculum vitae. But nothing is entirely single-minded in Skelton: there is self-mockery as well as self-promotion, much beauty as well as much showy brilliance, and some new skills displayed (in the graceful scene at the castle) as well as impressive exercises in traditional forms. Edition by F.W. Brownlow (Newark, DE, 1990); studies by Spearing (1976), pp. 211–18, D.A. Loewenstein, *Neoph.* 68 (1984), 611–22, and J. Scattergood, in Morse and Windeatt (1990), pp. 122–38.

A ryght delectable tratyse upon a goodly Garlande or Chapelet of Laurell by Mayster Skelton, Poete Laureat, studyously dyvysed at Sheryfhotten Castell, in the foreste of Galtres, wherein ar comprysyde many and dyvers solacyous and ryght pregnant allectyves of syngular pleasure, as more at large it doth apere in the proces folowynge.

Eterno mansura die dum sidera fulgent,
Equora dumque tument, hec laurea nostra virebit:
Hinc nostrum celebre et nomen referetur ad astra,
Undique Skeltonis memorabitur alter Adonis.

1106 **one agayne another**. Colin diplomatically associates the critics of the church's corruption with the agents of that corruption, as working against each other, but both to the detriment of the church.

The Garland of Laurel
Eterno ... Adonis 'While the stars shine remaining in everlasting day, and while the seas swell, this our laurel shall be green: our famous name shall be echoed to the skies, and everywhere Skelton shall be remembered as another Adonis.' (Can this be serious?)

Raising up Arectyng my syght towarde the zodyake,
The sygnes twelve for to beholde afarre,
(see n.) When Mars retrogradant reversed his bak,
circuit Lorde of the yere in his orbicular,
Put up his sworde, for he cowde make no warre,
(the moon), fully And whan Lucina plenarly did shyne,
Scorpione ascendynge degrees twyse nyne;

In place alone then musynge in my thought
How all thynge passyth as doth the somer flower,
evidences On every halfe my reasons forthe I sought
How oftyn fortune varyeth in an howre,
Now clere wether, forthwith a stormy showre –
All things considered All thynge compassyd, no perpetuyte,
But now in welthe, now in adversyte.

So depely drownyd I was in this dumpe,
Oppressed by constraint, mind Encraumpysshed so sore was my conceyte,
That, me to rest, I lent me to a stumpe
Of an oke, that somtyme grew full streyghte,
A myghty tre and of a noble heyght,
Whose bewte blastyd was with the boystors wynde,
His levis loste, the sappe was from the rynde.

thickly wooded Thus stode I in the frythy forest of Galtres,
Soaked, filthy mud, wetland Ensowkid with fylt of the myry mose,
exhausted with running Where hartis belluyng, embosyd with distres,
at liberty Ran on the raunge so longe that I suppose
Few men can tell now where the hynde calfe gose.
set on Faire fall that forster that so well can bate his hownde!
basic matter But of my purpose now torne we to the grownde.

Whylis I stode musynge in this medytatyon,
In slumbrynge I fell and halfe in a slepe;
And whether it were of ymagynacyon,
Or of humors superflue, that often wyll crepe
Into the brayne by drynkyng over-depe,
prophetically fateful influence Or it procedyd of fatall persuacyon –
I can not tell you what was the occasyon –

became aware of my surroundings But sodeynly at ones, as I me advysed,
As one in a trans or in an extasy
tent-pavilion, decorated I sawe a pavylyon wondersly disgysede,
Garnysshed fresshe after my fantasy,

1–35 The opening is a revisitation of a familiar medieval poetic landscape: the astronomical dating (*CT*, *Thebes*), the melancholy musing on the mutability of life (Hoccleve), dreams and speculation on the causes of dreams (*PP*, *PF*).

3 **retrogradant**: going backward (apparently) in the zodiac.

5 A familiar medieval conflation of planet and classical deity (cf. Henryson's *Testament*), in which the retrograde motion of Mars the planet is represented as the withdrawal from battle of Mars the god of war. A date of 8 May 1495 has been deduced from the horoscope of 1–7.

22 **Galtres** is the forest that formerly stretched north of York, surrounding Sheriff Hutton castle, now a small but spectacular ruin, standing on its slight eminence. It can without superfluity be called a '**frythy**' forest, since a forest was a large tract of open country with trees and woods, suitable for hunting, not a continuously treed terrain.

25–7 There is so much good hunting of the hart that the young hinds hardly seem worth pursuing; the foresters have an easy job.

32 **superflue**: 'superfluity'. An excess of a certain humour, such as black bile (melancholy), was often diagnosed as a cause of dreams (as by Pertelot in Chaucer's Nun's Priest's Tale, *CT* VII.2923–36).

Enhachyde with perle and stones preciously, — *Set*
The grounde engrosyd and bet with bourne golde, — *(see n.)*
That passynge goodly it was to beholde.

Within that, a prynces excellente of porte; — *bearing*
But to recounte her ryche abylyment, — *clothing*
And what estates to her did resorte, — *high-ranking people*
Therto am I full insuffycyent.
A goddesse inmortall she dyd represente:
As I harde say, Dame Pallas was her name,
To whome supplyed the royall Quene of Fame. — *made supplication*

The Quene of Fame to Dame Pallas

'Prynces moost pusant, of hygh pre-emynence, — *puissant*
Renownyd lady above the sterry hevyn,
All other transcendyng, of very congruence — *with absolute appropriateness*
Madame regent of the scyences sevyn,
To whos astate all noblenes most leven, — *trust for support*
My supplycacyon to you I arrect, — *offer*
Whereof I beseche you to tender the effecte. — *attend to the point at issue*

'Not unremembered it is unto your grace
How you gave me a ryall commaundement
That in my courte Skelton shulde have a place,
Bycause that he his tyme studyously hath spent
In your servyce; and to the accomplysshement
Of your request, regestred is his name
With laureate tryumphe in the courte of Fame.

'But, good madame, the accustome and usage
Of auncient poetis, ye wote full wele, hath bene
Themselfe to embesy with all there holl corage, — *busy, whole*
So that there workis myght famously be sene,
In figure wherof they were the laurell grene. — *wear*
But, how it is, Skelton is wonder slak, — *whatever the reason*
And, as we dare, we fynde in hym grete lak.

'For, ne were onely he hath your promocyon, — *if it were not that, support*
Out of my bokis full sone I shulde hym rase; — *erase*
But sith he hath tastid of the sugred pocioun
Of Elyconis well, refresshid with your grace, — *Helicon's spring (sacred to the Muses)*
And wyll not endevour hymselfe to purchase
The favour of ladys with wordis electe, — *carefully chosen*
It is sittynge that ye must hym correct.' — *appropriate*

41 'The groundwork-material enriched and inlaid with burnished gold'.

53 **scyences sevyn**: the Seven Liberal Arts (grammar, logic, rhetoric, astronomy, arithmetic, geometry and music), the curriculum for the first university degree.

69 **Skelton is wonder slak**. But we are reassured to find that it is only his reluctance to push himself forward (not the first thing we would have thought of), and not his lack of poetic ability, that prevents his advancement.

Dame Pallas to the Quene of Fame

'The sum of your purpos, as we ar advysid,
Is that our servaunt is sumwhat to dull…' — *lacking in spirit*

{The two ladies debate Skelton's qualifications for the laurel crown, and all the poets of the past are summoned to the judgement, including Gower, Chaucer and Lydgate, who offer polite words of encouragement to Skelton. He is conducted by Occupation, Fame's registrar, to the palace of Fame and then into a beautiful garden and finally he is shown into the presence of the countess of Surrey.}

Thus talkyng we went forth in at a postern gate.
Turnyng on the ryght hande, by a windyng stayre, — *spiral staircase*
She brought me to a goodly chaumber of state,
Where the noble Cowntes of Surrey in a chayre
Sat honorably, to whom did repaire
Of ladys a bevy with all dew reverence:
'Syt downe, fayre ladys, and do your diligence!

'Come forth, jentylwomen, I pray you,' she sayd,
'I have contryvyd for you a goodly warke,
And who can worke beste now shall be asayde. — *tested*
A coronell of lawrell with verduris light and darke
I have devysyd for Skelton, my clerke,
For to his servyce I have suche regarde,
That of our bownte we wyll hym rewarde.

'For of all ladyes he hath the library, — *record in books*
Ther names recountyng in the court of Fame;
Of all gentylwomen he hath the scruteny, — *vote in his favour*
In Fames court reportynge the same;
For yet of women he never sayd shame,
But if they were counterfettes that women them call, — *call themselves*
That list of there lewdnesse with hym for to brall.'

With that the tappettis and carpettis were layd, — *tapestry-mats*
Whereon theis ladys softly myght rest,
The saumpler to sow on, the lacis to enbraid; — *braid together*
To weve in the stoule sume were full preste, — *embroidery-frame, ready*
With slayis, with tavellis, with hedellis well drest; — *prepared*
The frame was browght forth with his wevyng pin –
God geve them good spede there warke to begin!

Sume to enbrowder put them in prese, — *made themselves busy*
Well gydyng ther glowtoun to kepe streit theyr sylk, — *needle*
Sum pirlyng of golde theyr worke to encrese — *(see n.)*
With fingers smale and handis whyte as mylk;
With 'Reche me that skane of tewly sylk' — *dark red*

769 **Cowntes of Surrey**. Elizabeth (d. 1497), wife of the first earl of Surrey (d. 1524), and grandmother of the poet Surrey.

791 Slays, tavels (bobbins) and heddles are instruments used in weaving. Fine weaving and needlework were a major activity of upper-class ladies, sometimes functional, as here and in *PP* VIII.9 (above), and sometimes recreational, as in Gower, *Confessio* IV.1175 (above).

796 'Some winding gold threads into the cord in order to advance their work'.

ball of thread And 'Wynde me that botowme of such an hew' –
Grene, rede, tawny, whyte, purpill and blew;

work on a broken (varied) background Of broken warkis wrought many a goodly thyng,
(see n.) In castyng, in turnynge, in florisshyng of flowris,
With burris rowth and bottons surfillyng,
In nedill-wark raysyng byrdis in bowris,
busied With vertu enbesid all tymes and howris;
And truly of theyr bownte thus were they bent
careful planning To worke me this chapelet by goode advysemente.

{He must now show his poetic credentials with poems in honour of the ladies of the household. This is one of them.}

To maystres Margaret Hussey

Mirry Margaret,
the daisy (or 'marguerite') As mydsomer flowre,
Jentill as fawcoun
Or hawke of the towre:
With solace and gladnes,
Moche mirthe and no madnes,
All good and no badnes,
So joyously,
So maydenly,
So womanly
Her demenyng
In every thynge,
Far, far passynge
That I can endyght,
Or suffice to wryght
Of mirry Margarete,
As mydsomer flowre,
Jentyll as fawcoun
Or hawke of the towre:
As pacient and as styll
And as full of good wyll
As fayre Isaphill;
Coriander Colyaunder,
Swete pomaunder,
Good Cassaunder;
Stedfast of thought,
Wele made, wele wrought;
Far may be sought
Before Erst that ye can fynde

802–3 'In making knots at the end of cords, in twisting, in adding flourishes to flowers, with raised rings and embroidering of button-like knots'.

1006–7 The falcon and the hawk were thought of as birds of high and gentle breeding, as in Chaucer's *PF*. **of the towre**: 'of towering flight'.

1025 **Isaphill**: Hypsipyle, who saved her father Thoas, king of Lemnos, and sought after her children after being deserted by Jason (see Chaucer, *Legend of Good Women*, 1396).

1027 **pomaunder**: pomander (Fr. *pomme d'ambre*), a bag or ball of spices and aromatic substances, carried for the perfume or to keep plague away.

1028 **Cassaunder**: Cassandra, usually associated with prophecies of the doom of Troy, though a steadfast and strong-minded daughter, hardly seems appropriate in the context. Perhaps a sweet-smelling plant like cassia was intended, or a precious stone like *cassedoine* (chalcedony).

So corteise, so kynde
As mirry Margarete,
This midsomer flowre,
Jentyll as fawcoun
Or hawke of the towre.

{At last he comes into the presence of the Queen of Fame, to whom the book of his writings is presented.}

With that, of the boke losende were the claspis.
ornamental strap-work The margent was illumynid all with golden railles
purply-blue And byse, enpicturid with gressoppes and waspis,
With butterflyis and fresshe pecoke-taylis,
Enflorid with flowris and slymy snaylis,
(see n.) Envyvid picturis well towchid and quikly.
It wolde have made a man hole that had be ryght sekely,

To beholde how it was garnysshyd and bounde,
Encoverde over with golde of tissew fyne;
metal bosses on the cover The claspis and bullyons were worth a thousande pounde;
balays-rubies With balassis and charbuncles the borders did shyne;
With *aurum musicum* every other lyne
Was wrytin; and so she did her spede,
Occupacyon, immediatly to rede.

{There follows a huge list of Skelton's works, some extant, some not, and some perhaps made up ('The Balade of the Mustarde Tarte'? 1245). He wakes up, and ends with some Skeltonics and a cascade of Latin and French envoys and epigraphs.}

1157 **The margent was illumynid**. There was a fashion in late medieval book-illumination for filling the borders of pages with *trompe-l'œil* bugs and butterflies, exquisitely drawn and coloured.

1161 'Vividly lifelike pictures, well-painted and in a lively fashion'.

1167 ***aurum musicum***: 'mosaic gold' (bisulphide of tin, or 'bronze-powder', used for gold lettering).

The First English Life of Henry V (1513)

In the early months of 1412, the prince of Wales was much at odds with his father, Henry IV. The prince had been effectively in control of the government for a period of about 18 months during his father's ill-health, January 1410 to November 1411, and had pursued his own policies with great energy. His father, on his recovery and after mobilizing his support, dismissed his eldest son from the Council, and the prince, over the next few months, watched with alarm as his father pursued what the prince thought disastrous policies in France. The king meanwhile suspected that his son was trying to rebel against him, oppose his policy, and seize the crown. On 23 September 1412 the prince appeared at Westminster and, having taken the sacrament, requested a private audience with his father. He was dressed in an extraordinary fashion. The story that follows became famous in Stow's *Annales*, but it first appeared in *The First English Life of King Henry the Fifth*, written in 1513 by an anonymous author who translated most of the work from the *Vita Henrici Quinti* (*c.* 1439) of Titus Livius, but who interpolated material derived from the presumably written record of the reminiscences of James Butler, Earl of Ormonde (1392–1452), a close follower of Henry V. Whether it is an accurate record or not (parts of it are so bizarre that it seems that it must be, though we know that the sixteenth century saw much invention of stories celebrating Henry V, as by Elyot, below), it is difficult to imagine a more spectacular act of theatrical self-representation, or one in which the prince or his biographer so fully anticipated the skills in self-representation that have come to be associated with Tudor monarchs. It is worth recalling that the *First English Life* was written for Henry VIII, as a model for his kingly guidance, in the English language, as he too was about to invade France. The *First English Life* is edited by C.L. Kingsford (Oxford, 1911); text from Bodl.MS Bodley 966.

The prince of Wales presents himself to his father, Henry IV

But when this noble prince was advertised of his fathers jealosie and mistrust by some his secret friends of the kings Councell, he disguised[1] himselfe in a gowne of blewe satten or damaske made full of iletts[2] or holes, and at everie ilet the needle wherewith it was made hanginge there by the thridde of silke; and aboute his arme he wore a doggs collor sett full of S.S.[3] of goulde, and the teretts[4] of the same also of fine gold.[5]

And thus apparrelled, with greate companie of lords he came to the kinge his father, who at that time lay at Westminster; where at his comminge, by his owne commaundement, not one of his companie durst advance himselfe further then the fire in the hall, notwithstandinge they were greatlie and ofte desired to the contrarie by the lords and greate estats of the kings courte. And that[6] the prince had commaunded to give the lesse occasion of mistrust to the kinge his father; but he himselfe, accompanied of the kings house[7] only, passed forth to the kinge his father, to whome after due salutacions he desired to show the intent of his minde in secrett manner. Then the kinge caused himselfe to be borne in his chaire (because he was diseased and might not goe) into his secrett chamber, where, in the presence of three or foure persons in whome the kinge had his most confidence, he commaunded the prince to shewe the effect of his minde. Then the prince, kneelinge downe before his father, saide to him these words:

'Most redoubted lorde and father, I ame this time come to your presence as your liegeman and as your sonn naturall, in all things to obey your Grace as my soveraigne lord and father. And whereas I understande that you have me in suspecte of my behavour against your Grace, and that you feare I would usurp your crowne against the pleasure of your highnes: Of my conversacion[8] your Grace knoweth that if you weare in feare of any man within your realme, of what estate so-ever he were, my duty were to the endainger of my life to punish that person, thereby to araise[9] that sore from your harte. And then howe much rather ought I to suffer death, to bringe your Grace, that hath bene and yet be the most hardie and renowned kinge of the worlde, from that feare that ye have of me, that ame your naturall sonn and liegeman. And to that intent I have this day by confession and by receavinge my maker[10] prepared myselfe. And therefore,

1 Not 'disguised' but 'prepared himself as for a "disgysing"' (a form of court masque or entertainment).

2 eyelets

3 The collar of SS's intertwined was the principal item in the Lancastrian livery.

4 rings

5 The suggestion, it will be seen, is of high estate deliberately undone and made vulnerable, of innate nobility deliberately humbled without loss of dignity.

6 that was what

7 household (i.e. his immediate servants).

8 behaviour and character

9 erase

10 taking communion

most redoubted lorde and father, I desyre you in your honnor of God, for the easinge of your harte, heere tofore your knees, to slaye me with this dagger.' And at that worde with all reverence he delivered to the kinge his dagger, saying, 'My lord and father, my life is not so desirous to me that I would live one daye that I shoulde be to your displeasure, nor I covet not so much my life as I doe your pleasure and wellfare. And in your thus doinge here in the presence of those lords, and before God and the daye of Judgement, I cleerelie forgive you my death.'

At these words of the prince, the[a] kinge, taken with compassion of harte, caste from him the dagger and imbraced the prince and kissed him, and with effusion of teares saide unto him, 'My right deere and hartelie beloved sonn, it is of troth that I partlie had you in suspect, and as I now perceave undeserved on your part, but seeinge this your humilitie and faithfullness I shall neither slay you nor frome hencefoorth anie more have you in mistrust, for no reporte that shal be made unto me. And thereof[b] I assure you uppon myne honnour.'

And thus by his greate wisdome was the wrongfull imaginacion of his fathers hart utterlie avoyded, and himselfe restored to the kings former grace and favour.

Sir Thomas More (1478–1535)

Born in London in 1478, More was trained as a lawyer, but came early under the influence of the new humanism (essentially the rediscovery or rereading of the Latin and Greek classics as the means to the understanding of a *different* and living culture, non-Christian yet admirable) through Colet and the Dutch scholar Erasmus, whom he first met in 1499. He contemplated a career in the church, even as a monk, but in 1504 he married Jane Colt (after her death, he married Alice Middleton in 1511) and began a rapid rise in the legal profession and in public life. He became an MP, a judge, and in 1517 a member of the King's Council; he was knighted in 1521. His house at Chelsea, meanwhile, became the place where the scholars of the new learning gathered to share their reading in the Greek and Latin classics and their Renaissance imitators, forming a kind of European humanist intellectual 'court' such as England had never known. In the 1520s, as the king's secretary, he acted for him in his public debate with Martin Luther, and in 1529, upon the fall of Wolsey, he was made Lord Chancellor. Henry VIII had decided to put away queen Katharine and marry Anne Boleyn, and he hoped that More's reputation for probity of conscience, even if he declined his support, would give respectability to his undertaking. More meanwhile avoided the 'great question' and occupied himself with endless rancorous refutations of the position of Tyndale on Bible-translation, the church and the priesthood. Then, when papal approval for his divorce was not forthcoming, and Henry decided to have himself declared head of the church in England, More at first temporized, and attempted to distance his public responsibilities from his private beliefs, but he eventually resigned the Chancellorship in 1532. The next two years were spent trying to find a lawful means of squaring his conscience with his duties and loyalties as a subject (and his desire to remain alive), but in 1534 he refused to swear support for the Act of Succession (declaring Henry's children by Anne Boleyn to be heirs to the throne), on the grounds that it assumed the legality of Henry's divorce and of his assumption of supremacy in the English church; he was imprisoned in the Tower, tried, and, on 1 July 1535, executed. He was canonized in 1935.

Complete Works, Yale edition (New Haven, 1963–); biographies by R.W. Chambers (London, 1935) and R. Marius (New York, 1984); surveys of scholarship by Q. Skinner, *Past and Present* 38 (1967), 153–68, and A.J. Geritz, *ELR* 22 (1992), 112–40; *Essential Articles for the Study of Thomas More*, ed. R.S. Sylvester and G.P. Marc'hadour (Hamden, CT, 1977).

The History of King Richard III

Written between 1514 and 1518, the *History* has been called the first true historical writing in English, but in truth it is less a piece of historical biography than a vivid and brilliantly sustained calumny, part of the campaign of vilification through which the Tudors demonized Richard and legitimated their dynasty after his defeat and death at Bosworth in 1485. More took material from eye-witness reports (as from his patron, Cardinal Morton) and from earlier chronicles, as well as inspiration from the Roman historians Sallust, Suetonius and Tacitus for his dramatic and imaginative representation of history, but the witty and sardonic tone, the theatricalizing irony that makes Richard both monstrous and ridiculous as well as dangerous, is his own. It is his account of Richard, as transmitted through the Chronicles of Richard Grafton (1543) and Edward Hall (1548), that shaped Shakespeare's version of the story; two of the episodes below are dramatized in *Richard III*, but hardly made more dramatic.

Text from William Rastell's edition of More's *Works* (1557); edition by R.S. Sylvester, in Vol. 2 of the Yale edition (New Haven, 1963). For discussion, see Anderson (1984), pp. 75–109.

The fall of lord Hastings

{In the Tower, 13 June 1483, the Council is deliberating on the arrangements for the coronation of the 12-year-old king Edward V.}

These lordes so sytting togyther comoning[1] of thys matter, the protectour came in among them, fyrst aboute ix. of the clock, saluting them curtesly and excusyng hymself that he had ben from them so long, saieng merely that he had bene aslepe that day. And after a little talking with them, he sayd unto the

1 communing (discussing)

bishop of Elye,[2] 'My lord, you have very good strawberies at your gardayne in Holberne. I require[3] you let us have a messe[4] of them.' 'Gladly, my lord,' quod he; 'woulde God I had some better thing as redy to your pleasure as that.' And therwith in al the hast he sent hys servant for a messe of strauberies. The protectour sette the lordes fast in comoning, and therupon, prayeng them to spare hym for a little while, departed thence.

And sone, after one hower, betwene x. and xi. he returned into the chamber among them, al changed with a wonderful soure angrye countenaunce, knitting the browes, frowning and froting[5] and knawing on hys lippes, and so sat him downe in hys place – al the lordes much dismaied and sore merveiling of this maner of sodain chaunge, and what thing should him aile. Then when he had sitten still a while, thus he began: 'What were they worthy to have, that compasse and ymagine the distruccion of me, being so nere of blood unto the king and protectour of his riall person and his realme?'

At this question, al the lordes sat sore astonied, musyng much by whome thys question should be ment, of which every man wyst himselfe clere.[6] Then the lord chamberlen,[7] as he that for the love betwene them thoughte he might be boldest with him, aunswered and sayd that thei wer worthye to be punished as heinous traitors whatsoever they were. And al the other affirmed the same. 'That is,' quod he, 'yonder sorceres my brothers wife and other with her' (meaning the quene).[8] At these wordes many of the other lordes were gretly abashed that favoured her, but the lord Hastinges was in his minde better content that it was moved by her[9] then by any other whom he loved better, albeit hys harte somewhat grudged that he was not afore made of counsell[10] in this mater as he was of the taking of her kynred and of their putting to death, which were by his assent before devised to be byhedded at Pountfreit this selfe-same day (in which he was not ware that it was by other devised that himself should the same day be behedded at London).

Then said the protectour, 'Ye shal al se in what wise that sorceres and that other witch of her counsel, Shoris wife, with their affynite, have by their sorcery and witchcraft wasted my body.' And therwith he plucked up hys doublet-sleve to his elbow upon his left arme, where he shewed a werish[11] withered arme and small, as it was never other.[12] And thereupon every mannes mind sore misgave them, well perceiving that this matter was but a quarel.[13] For wel thei wist that the quene was to wise to go aboute any such folye. And also if she would, yet wold she of all folke leste make Shoris wife of counsaile, whom of al women she most hated, as that concubine whom the king her husband had most loved. And also no man was there present but wel knew that his arme[a] was ever such since his birth.

Natheles the lorde chamberlen (which fro the death of king Edward kept Shoris wife, on whome he somwhat doted in the kinges life, saving, as it is sayd, he that while forbare her, of reverence towarde hys king, or els of a certaine kinde of fidelite to hys frende) aunswered and sayd, 'Certeinly, my lorde, if they have so heinously done, thei be worthy heinouse punishement.' 'What!' quod the protectour, 'thou servest me, I wene, with iffes and with andes! I tel the thei have so done, and that I will make good on thy body, traitour.' And therwith, as in a great anger, he clapped his fist upon the borde a great rappe. At which token given, one cried 'Treason!' without the chambre. Therwith a dore clapped, and in come there rushing men in harneys as many as the chambre might hold. And anon the protectour sayd to the lorde Hastinges, 'I arest the, traitour.' 'What, me, my lorde?' quod he. 'Yea, the, traitour!' quod the protectour. And another let flee[14] at the lorde Standley,[15] which shronke at the stroke and fel under the

2 John Morton, bishop of Ely, was later archbishop of Canterbury and from 1493 a cardinal; More was a page in his household and gives a flattering portrait of him in *Utopia*.

3 request

4 dish

5 rubbing

6 innocent

7 **the lord chamberlen** is William, lord Hastings, a powerful man in the service and counsels of Edward IV.

8 **the quene**. Richard saw the queen, Elizabeth, mother of Edward V, as a principal obstacle to his plans, and had already arranged, with the connivance of Hastings, for the members of her family and affinity to be seized and beheaded at Pontefract castle.

9 that the matter was raised concerning her

10 taken into the secret

11 deformed

12 I.e. as if it had not always been like that.

13 **but a quarel**: only a pretext for a quarrel.

14 fly

15 Sir William Stanley, was reputed a friend of Hastings, but in the manner of the time he kept in favour, betraying Richard finally at Bosworth, only to be executed at last for treason by Henry VII in 1495.

table, or els his hed had ben clefte to the tethe; for as shortely[16] as he shranke yet ranne the blood aboute hys eares.

Then were they al quickly bestowed in diverse chambres, except the lorde chamberlen, whom the protectour bade spede and shryve hym apace, for 'By saynt Poule,' quod he, 'I wil not to dinner til I se thy hed of!' It boted him not[17] to aske why, but hevely he toke a priest at adventure,[18] and made a short shrift, for a longer would not be suffered, the protectour made so much hast to dyner, which he might not go to til this wer done for saving of his othe. So was he brought forth into the grene beside the chappel within the the Tower and his head laid down upon a long log of timbre and there striken of, and afterward his body with the hed entred[19] at Windsore beside the body of kinge Edward, whose both soules our Lord pardon.

Shore's wife

{To give colour to his accusations, Richard orders a brief persecution of Shore's wife (her name was Jane, or, as more recent research suggests, Elizabeth, but we are never told this in contemporary accounts). More's portrait made her famous enough for Shakespeare to need to allude to her only briefly. It is, in its own terms (that is, patronizing, loftily superior, as of a connoisseur examining a specimen), a notably generous and touching piece of writing.}

Now then by and bi, as it wer for anger, not for covetise, the protector sent into the house of Shores wife (for her husband dwelled not with her) and spoiled her of al that ever she had, above the value of ii. or iii. marks, and sent her body to prison. And when he had a while laide unto her, for the maner sake,[1] that she went about to bewitch him, and that she was of counsel with the lord chamberlein to destroy him – in conclusion, when that no colour could fasten upon these matters, then he layd heinously to her charge the thing that herself could not deny, that al the world wist was true, and that natheles every man laughed at to here it then so sodainly so highly taken, that she was nought[2] of her body. And for thys cause (as a goodly continent prince clene and fautles of himself, sent oute of heaven into this vicious world for the amendement of mens maners) he caused the bishop of London to put her to open penance, going before the crosse in procession upon a Sonday with a taper in her hand. In which she went in countenance and pace demure so womanly, and albeit she were out of al array save her kyrtle only;[3] yet went she so fair and lovely, namelye while the wondering of the people caste a comly rud[4] in her chekes (of whiche she before had most misse)[5] that her great shame wan her much praise among those that were more amorous of her body then curious of her soule. And many good folke also, that hated her living,[6] and glad wer to se sin corrected, yet pitied thei more her penance then rejoyced therin, when thei considred that the protector procured it more of a corrupt intent then ani vertuous affeccion.

This woman was born in London, worshipfully frended, honestly brought up and very wel maryed (saving somewhat to sone), her husbande an honest citezen, yonge and goodly and of good substance.[7] But forasmuche as they were coupled ere she wer wel ripe, she not very fervently loved for whom she never longed; which was happely[8] the thinge that the more easily made her encline unto the kinges appetite when he required her. Howbeit the respect of his royaltie, the hope of gay apparel, ease, plesure and other wanton welth, was able soone to perse a softe tender hearte. But when the king had abused her, anon her husband (as he was an honest man and one that could his good),[9] not presuming to touch a kinges concubine, left her up to him altogether. When the king died, the lord chamberlen toke her, which in the kinges daies, albeit he was sore ennamored upon her, yet he forbare her, either for reverence or for a certain frendly faithfulnes.

Proper she was and faire; nothing in her body that you wold have changed, but if you would have

16 quickly
17 was no use
18 at random
19 interred

Shore's wife

1 accused her, for the appearance's sake
2 sinful (naughty)
3 stripped of all her clothes except only her petticoat
4 redness
5 lack
6 way of life
7 Her marriage to William Shore was annulled (*c.* 1476) because of his impotence.
8 perhaps
9 knew what was good for him

wished her somewhat higher. Thus say thei that knew her in her youthe, albeit some that now se her (for yet she liveth) deme her never to have ben wel-visaged – whose jugement semeth me somwhat like as though men should gesse the bewty of one longe before departed by her scalpe taken out of the charnel-house, for now is she old, lene, withered and dried up, nothing left but ryvilde[10] skin and hard bone. And yet being even such, who-so wel advise[11] her visage might gesse and devise which partes, how filled, wold make it a faire face.

Yet delited not men so much in her bewty as in her plesant behaviour, for a proper wit had she, and could both rede wel and write, mery in company, redy and quick of aunswer, neither mute nor ful of bable, sometime taunting without displesure and not without disport... *{more on king Edward's concubines}*... in whom the king therfore toke speciall pleasure. For many he had, but her he loved, whose favour, to sai the trouth (for sinne it wer to belie the devil), she never abused to any mans hurt, but to many a mans comfort and relief. Where the king toke displeasure she would mitigate and appease his mind; where men were out of favour she wold bring them in his grace. For many that had highly offended, she obtained pardon; of great forfetures[12] she gate men remission. And finally, in many weighty sutes she stode many men in gret stede, either for none or very smal rewardes, and those rather gay then rich, either for that she was content with the dede selfe well done, or for that she delited to be suid unto and to show what she was able to do wyth the king, or for that wanton women and welthy be not alway covetouse.

I doubt not some shal think this woman to sleight a thing to be written of and set amonge the remembraunces of great matters; which thei shal specially think that happely shal esteme her only by that thei now see her. But me semeth the chaunce so much the more worthy to be remembred, in how much she is now in the more beggerly condicion, unfrended and worne out of acquaintance, after good substance, after as gret favour with the prince, after as gret sute and seking to with al those that those days had busynes to spede, as many other men were in their times, which be now famouse only by the infamy of their il dedes. Her doinges were not much lesse, albeit thei be muche lesse remembred because thei were not so evil. For men use, if they have an evil turne, to write it in marble, and who-so doth us a good tourne, we write it in duste: which is not worst proved by her, for at this daye she beggeth of many at this daye living that at this day had begged if she had not bene.

The duke of Buckingham has Richard acclaimed king

{The duke has made a long and brilliant speech, putting forward Richard's claim to the throne and touching on the bastardy of Edward IV's children, even of Edward himself.}

When the duke had saied, and looked that the people (whome he hoped that the mayer had framed[1] before) shoulde, after this proposicion made, have cried 'King Richarde! King Richard!' all was husht and mute, and not one word aunswered therunto. Wherewith the duke was mervailously abashed, and taking the maier nerer to him, with other that were about him privey to that matter, saied unto them softlye, 'What meaneth this, that this peple be so stil?' 'Sir,' quod the mayer, 'parcase they perceyve you not well.'[2] 'That shal we mende,' quod he, 'if that wyll helpe.' And by and by, somewhat louder, he rehersed them the same matter againe in other order and other wordes, so wel and ornately, and natheles so evidently and plaine, with voice, gesture and countenance so cumly and so convenient, that every man much mervailed that herd him, and thought that they never had in their lives heard so evill a tale so well tolde. But were it for wonder or feare, or that eche looked[b] that other shoulde speake fyrste, not one woorde was there aunswered of all the people that stode before, but al was as styl as the midnight, not so much as rowning[3] among them, by whych they myght seme to comen[4] what was best to do.

{The Recorder speaks to the people, but cannot stir them.}

10 shrivelled
11 might look upon
12 penalties

The duke of Buckingham has Richard acclaimed king
1 put in the right frame of mind
2 perhaps they do not understand you properly
3 whispering
4 discuss

Wherupon the duke rowned unto the mayer and sayd, 'Thys is a marvelouse obstinate silence.' And therewith he turned unto the peple againe with these wordes: 'Dere frendes, we cume to move you to that thing which peradventure we not so greately neded but that the lordes of thys realme and the comens of other parties might have suffised, saving that we such love bere you and so muche sette by you that we woulde not gladly do withoute you that thing in which to be parteners is your weale[5] and honour, which as it semeth eyther you se not or way[6] not. Wherfore we require[7] you give us aunswer one or other whether you be mynded as all the nobles of the realme be to have this noble prynce now protectour to be your kyng or not.'

At these wordes the people began to whisper among themselfe secretely, that the voyce was neyther loude nor distincke, but as it were the sounde of a swarme of bees, tyl at the last in the nether ende of the hal a bushement[8] of the dukes servantes and Nashefeldes, and other longing[9] to the protectour, with some prentises and laddes that thrust into the hal amonge the prese, began sodainelye at mennes backes to crye owte as lowde as their throtes would gyve,[10] 'King Rycharde! Kinge Rycharde!' and threwe up their cappes in token of joye. And they that stode before cast back theyr heddes mervailing thereof, but nothing they sayd.

And when the duke and the maier saw thys maner, they wysely turned it to theyr purpose, and said it was a goodly cry and a joyfull to here, every man with one voice, no manne sayeng nay. 'Wherfore, frendes,' quod the duke, 'sins that we parceive it is al your hole mindes to have this noble man for your king, whereof we shall make his grace so effectuall reporte that we doubte not but it shall redounde unto your great weal and commoditye,[11] we require ye that ye tomorow go with us and we with you unto his noble grace to make oure humble request unto him in maner before remembred.' And therewith the lordes came downe, and the company dissolved and departed, the more part al sad, som with glad semblaunce that wer not very mery.

{The play-acting continues next day (15 June 1483) at Baynard's Castle, where Richard is persuaded to assume the crown.}

With this there was a great shout, crying 'Kyng Richarde! King Rychard!' And then the lordes went up to the kyng (for so was he from that time called) and the people departed, talkyng diversly of the matter, every man as his fantasye gave[12] hym. But muche they talked and marveiled of the maner of this dealing, that the matter was on both partes made so straunge, as though neither had ever communed with other thereof before, when that themself wel wist there was no man so dul that heard them but he perceived well inough that all the matter was made betwene them.[13] Howbeit somme excused that agayne,[14] and sayde all must be done in good order though, and menne must sommetime for the manner sake not be a-knowen[15] what they knowe. For at the consecracion of a bishop every man woteth well by the paying for his bulles[16] that he purposeth to be one, and though[17] he paye for nothing elles. And yet must he be twise asked whether he wil be bishop or no, and he muste twyse say naye, and at the third tyme take it as compelled therunto by his owne wyll. And in a stage play all the people know right wel that he that playeth the sowdayne[18] is percase a sowter.[19] Yet if one should can[20] so lyttle good, to shewe out of seasone what acquaintance he hath with him, and calle him by his owne name whyle he standeth in his magestie, one of his tormentors[21] might hap to breake his head, and worthy[22] for marring of the play.

5 welfare
6 value
7 request
8 planted group
9 belonging
10 allow
11 advantage
12 prompted
13 **made**: 'previously worked out'. The people, in More's account, seem aware that they are being conned, but this may be a clever man's gloss on events. Buckingham's cunning, like Richard's (one is tempted to call it Machiavellian, but *The Prince*, though written in 1513, was not published until 1532), is the matter of More's invention as much as of history, offering us some evidence of what More contributed to Shakespeare's understanding of statecraft.
14 in its turn
15 for the appearance's sake not seem cognizant of
16 **bulles**: papal writs securing his election.
17 even though
18 sultan
19 cobbler
20 know
21 the sultan's executioners
22 serve him right

And so they said that these matters be 'kynges games',[23] as it were stage-playes, and for the more part plaied upon scafoldes – in which pore men be but the lokers-on. And thei that wise be wil medle no farther. For they that sometyme step up and playe with them, when they cannot play their partes, they disorder the play and do themself no good.

Utopia

Book 1 is a conversation between cautious, sceptical More and an imaginary alter ego, the impassioned idealist Raphael Hythlodaeus ('the archangel of expert nonsense'), a New World traveller recently returned from Utopia (a term coined by More, Gk.'no-place', punning on *eutopia*, 'happy place'), concerning what constitutes good government. It contains a serious and considered attack on the use of capital punishment for theft and on the whole idea of private property. Book 2 is Hythlodaeus's description of Utopia, a 'best-commonwealth exercise' conducted according to the rules set by Aristotle in his *Politics* and Plato in his *Republic*, very different from the Golden Age imagining of Boethius or Montaigne (and, following him, Gonzalo in *The Tempest*, III.ii), and at a different level of political sophistication from the moralized and dogmatic 'Mirrors for Princes' of the Middle Ages. Educated men had long amused themselves with fantasies of egalitarianism and rational government, but More's *Utopia* is worked out in some detail. Based on the principle that pleasure is the goal of life and the most pleasurable life is the life of virtue (Christian virtue, inevitably, for the most part), it is a world of elected city-governments, planned towns, collectivized farming, in which time, work and recreation are strictly controlled and money abolished.

But the 'best commonwealth', given the Christian view of the secular state, is bound to be flawed, and it may be that More included much that was distasteful (e.g. restrictions on the movement of citizens and on free speech, opportunistic and aggressive foreign policy) because it demonstrated this as much as because it was necessary to the logic of the commonwealth or because More didn't think distasteful some of the things that we do (e.g. bondmen and slaves do the dirty work, such as animal-slaughtering, which is considered 'inhuman'). The treatise, in fact, is essentially ambiguous, as can be seen from the speaker's name, and full of contradictions and inconsistencies, part of a tradition, to which Lucian (*The Golden Ass*) and Erasmus (*The Praise of Folly*) contributed (as well as Swift, later), in which serious matters are treated playfully and ironically. More is playing with speculations, experimenting with logical but impossible deductions, rather than proposing alternative political solutions to the economic and social problems he so plainly perceives. He has moved a little away from the medieval position – that the miseries of social and economic injustice and inequality, including the oppressions under which the poor labour, are part of the punishment of the fallen world and the suffering necessary to prepare for the life hereafter (see Henryson, *The Wolf and the Lamb*) – but he has no programme of political reform. The work may in the end be as interesting for what it reveals as for what it says: Greenblatt (1980, pp. 11–73) points out how striking it is that a man whose life was a battle to preserve private integrity in the face of many temptations to compromise, while shaping a public self that he could live with, should portray the annulment of the private self as a happy achievement.

More's *Utopia* is in Latin and was written 1515–16, while the author was deciding whether the service of the king, which he declares in Book 1 to be the good man's highest duty, was a possible service for a man of conscience; it was first published in Louvain in 1516. The earliest English translation, used in the extracts below, is by Ralph Robinson (1551): lively but not unfaithful, this translation has represented More in English literary tradition; it brings to us in the English of his time the most important piece of writing by a very important English writer.

Latin and modern English translation in Vol. 4 of the Yale edition, ed. E. Surtz and J.H. Hexter (New Haven, 1965); studies by J.H. Hexter, *More's Utopia: The Biography of an Idea* (Princeton, 1952); A.R. Heiserman, *PMLA* 78 (1963), 163–74; Halpern (1991), pp. 136–75; S. Bruce, *PQ* 75 (1996), 267–86. Robinson's translation, ed. J. Rawson Lumby (Cambridge, 1883), with text from the second edition of 1556, as here (though with omission of many superfluous final e's).

23 **'kynges games'**. Politics is a form of theatre, says More, who himself was not only fond of acting (he used, when young, to leap in among the players of an interlude and extemporize a part) but also a consummate role-player on the rotten boards of the Tudor political stage.

Restrictions on travel among the Utopians

{Like much else in Utopia, *the restraint on ordinary freedom to move about and the determination to have no place where a man may be private (may be 'himself') makes perfect logical sense, given the premises (of a rationally ordered commonwealth), but it is also alarmingly familiar from the practice of some modern states.}*

But if any be desierous to visite either theyr frendes dwelling in another citie, or to see the place itself, they easelie obteyne licence of their siphograuntes and tranibores,[1] onlesse there be some profitable let.[2] No man goeth out alone, but a companie is sente furth together with their princes letters, which do testifie that they have licence to go that journey, and prescribeth also the day of their retourne. They have a wageyn geven them, with a common bondman, which driveth the oxen and taketh charge of them; but onles they have women in their companie, they sende home the wageyn againe, as an impediment and a let.[3] And though they carye nothyng furth with them, yet in all their jorney they lack nothing, for whersoever they come they be at home. If they tary in a place longer then one daye, than there every one of them falleth to his owne occupation, and be very gentilly enterteined of the workemen and companies of the same craftes. If any man of his owne heade and without leave walke out of his precinct and boundes, taken without the princes letters, he is broughte againe for a fugitive or a runaway with great shame and rebuke, and is sharpely punished. If he be taken in that fault againe, he is punished with bondage.

If any be desirous to walke abrode into the feldes or into the countrey that belongeth to the same citie that he dwelleth in, obteining the good wil of his father and the consente of his wife, he is not prohibited. But into what part of the contrei soever he commeth he hath no meat geven him until he have wrought out his fore-nones taske, or dispatched so muche work as there is wont to be wrought before supper. Observing this law and condition, he may go whether[4] he wil within the boundes of his own citie. For he shal be no les profitable to the citie then if he were within it.

Now you se how litle liberte they have to loiter; how they can have no cloke or pretence to ydlenes. There be neither wine-tavernes, nor alehouses, nor stewes, nor any occasion of vice or wickednes, no lurking corners, no places of wycked counsels or unlawfull assembles. But they be in the presente sighte and under the eies of every man; so that of necessitie they must either apply their accustomed labours or els recreate themselves with honest and laudable pastimes.

How the Utopians regard gold

{The Utopians have abolished money and have found a way of making gold seem valueless.}

They eate and drinke in earthen and glasse vesselles, which indede be curiouslye and properlie made, and yet be of very small value; of golde and sylver they make commonly chaumber-pottes and other vesselles that serve for moste vile uses, not onely in their common halles but in every mans private house. Furthermore of the same mettalles they make greate chaines, fetters and gieves wherin they[a] tie their bondmen. Finally, whosoever for any offense be infamed,[1] by their eares hange rynges of golde, upon their fyngers they weare rynges of golde and aboute their neckes chaines of golde, and in conclusion their heades be tied aboute with gold. Thus by al meanes possible thei procure to have golde and silver among them in reproche and infamie. And these mettalles, which other nations do as grevously and sorowefullye forgo[2] as in a manner their owne lives, if they should altogethers at ones be taken from the Utopians, no man there would thinke that he had lost the worth of one farthing. *{Diamonds and other precious stones, similarly, are regarded as children's baubles.}*

Restrictions on travel among the Utopians

1 **siphograuntes and tranibores**: officials of the Utopian state. More is childishly fond of making up these comical-sounding names.

2 good reason for preventing it

3 hindrance

4 whither

How the Utopians regard gold

1 disgraced

2 are as grieved to be deprived of

These lawes and customes, which be so farre differente from al other nations, how divers fantasies also and myndes they do cause dydde I never so playnelie perceave as in the ambassadoures of the Anemolians.[3] These ambassadoures came to Amaurote whiles I was there.[4] And because they came to entreate of great and weightie matters, those three citizens apece oute of everie citie were comen thether before them.[5] But all the ambassadours of the nexte countreis, which had bene there before and knewe the fashions and maners of the Utopians, amonge whom they perceaved no honoure geven to sumptuous apparell, silkes to be contemned, golde also to be infamed and reprochful, were wont to come thether in verie homelye and simple araie. But the Anemolianes, because they dwell farre thence and had very litle aquaintaunce with them, hearing that they were all apparelled alike, and that verie rudely and homely; thinking them not to have the thinges which they did not weare; being therfore more proude then wise, determyned in the gorgiousnes of their apparel to represente verye goddes, and wyth the brighte shyning and glisteryng of their gay clothing to dasell the eyes of the silie poore Utopians.

So there came in .iii. ambassadours with .c. servauntes all apparelled in chaungeable colours,[6] the moste of them in silkes, the ambassadours themselves (for at home in their owne countrey they were noblemen) in cloth of gold, with great cheines of gold, with golde hanging at their eares, with gold ringes upon their fingers, with brouches and aglettes[7] of gold upon their cappes, which glistered ful of peerles and precious stones – to be short, trimmed and adourned with al those thinges which among the Utopians were either the punishement of bondmen or the reproche of infamed persones or elles trifels for yonge children to playe withal.

Therefore it wolde have done a man good at his harte to have sene how proudelye they displeyed their pecockes fethers, how muche they made of their paynted sheathes, and how loftely they set forth and advaunced themselfes, when they compared their gallaunte apparrell with the poore rayment of the Utopians (for al the people were swarmed forth into the stretes). And on the other side it was no lesse pleasure to consider how muche they were deceaved, and how farre they missed of their purpose, being contrary-wayes taken then they thought they should have bene. For to the eyes of all the Utopians, excepte very fewe, which had bene in other countreys for some resonable cause, all that gorgeousness of apparrel semed shamefull and reprocheful, insomuche that they most reverently saluted the vilest and most abject of them for lordes, passing over the ambassadoures themselfes without any honour, judging them by their wearing of golden cheynes to be bondmen. Yea, you shoulde have sene children also, that had caste away their peerles and pretious stones, when they sawe the like sticking upon the ambassadours cappes, digge and pushe their mothers under the sides, saing thus to them: 'Loke, mother, how great a lubbor doth yet were peerles and precious stoones, as though he were a litel child stil!' But the mother – yea, and that also in good earnest: 'Peace, sone!' saith she; 'I thinke he be some of the ambassadours fooles.'

How the Utopians wage war

{The ruthless pragmatism of Utopian tactics is a logical product of More's 'thought-experiment', differing from normal unprincipled practice only in the laudable goal pursued.}

Their chief and principall purpose in warre is to obteine that thyng which if they had before obteined they woulde not have moved battell. But if that be not possible, they take so cruell vengeaunce of them which be in the faulte that ever after they be aferde to do the like. This is their chiefe and principall intent, which they immediatlie and first of al prosequute and set forwarde, but yet so, that they be more circumspecte in avoiding and eschewyng jeopardies then they be desierous of prayse and renowne.

Therefore, immediatlye after that warre is ones solemnelie denounced,[1] they procure many

3 **Anemolians**: from the Greek word for 'windy' (i.e. vain and boastful).

4 **Amaurote** is the capital city of Utopia.

5 **those three**: the three appointed, as explained earlier, to represent each city on such occasions.

6 parti-coloured (raiment)

7 pendants

How the Utopians wage war

1 proclaimed

proclamations signed with their owne commen seale to be set up privilie at one time in their enemies lande, in places moste frequented. In these proclamations they promisse greate rewardes to hym that will kill their enemies prince, and somewhat lesse giftes, but them verye greate also, for everye heade of them whose names be in the saide proclamations conteyned (they be those whom they count their chiefe adversaries, next unto the prince). Whatsoever is prescribed unto him that killeth any of the proclaimed persons, that is dubled to him that bringeth any of the same to them alive – yea, and to the proclaimed persones themselves, if they wil chaunge their mindes and come in to them, taking their partes,[2] they profer the same greate rewardes, with pardone and suertie of their lives.

Therefore it quickely commeth to passe that their enemies have all other men in suspicion, and be unfaithfull and mistrusting among themselves one to another, living in great feare and in no lesse jeopardie. For it is well knowen that divers times the most part of them (and speciallie the prince himself) hath bene betraied of them in whom they put their moste hope and trust, so that there is no maner of act nor dede that giftes and rewardes do not enforce men unto. And in rewardes they kepe no measure,[3] but, remembring and considering into how great hasarde and jeopardie they cal them, endevoure themselves to recompence the greatnes of the daunger with like great benefites. And therefore they promise not only wonderful greate abundaunce of golde but also landes of greate revenues lieng in most safe places among their frendes. And their promisses they perfourme faythfully withoute any fraude or covyne.[4]

This custome of bying and sellyng adversaryes among other people is dysallowed as a cruel acte of a base and a cowardyshe mynde. But they in this behalfe thinke themselfes muche prayseworthy, as who lyke wyse men by this meanes dispatche greate warres withoute any battell or skyrmyshe. Yea, they counte it also a dede of pytye and mercye, bicause that by the deathe of a fewe offenders the lyves of a greate numbre of innocentes, as well of their oune men as also of their enemies, be raunsomed and saved, which in fighting shoulde have bene sleane. For they do no lesse pytye the base and common sorte of their enemies people then they do their owne, knowing that they be driven and enforced to warre againste their willes by the furyous madnes of their princes and heades.

The superiority of the Utopian commonwealth

{Much of Utopia *is tongue-in-cheek, or more ambiguously ironical, but at the end the powerful picture of the inequality, oppression and sordid greed of the English 'commonwealth' makes Utopia seem, again, 'Utopian'.}*

Now I have declared and described unto you, as truelye as I coulde, the fourme and ordre of that commenwealth, which verely in my judgment is not only the beste but also that which alone of good right maye claime and take upon it the name of a commenwealth or publique weale. For in other places they speake stil of the commenwealth, but every man procureth his owne private gaine. Here, where nothing is private, the commen affaires be earnestlye loked upon. And truely on both partes they have good cause so to do as they do. For in other countreys who knoweth not that he shall sterve for honger onles he make some severall[1] provision for himself, though the commenwealthe floryshe never so muche in ryches? And therefore he is compelled even of verye necessitie to have regarde to himself rather then to the people, that is to saye, to other.

Contrary-wyse there, where all thinges be commen to every man, it is not to be doubted that any man shal lacke anything necessary for his private uses, so that[2] the commen storehouses and bernes be sufficientlye stored. For there nothing is distributed after a nyggyshe[3] sorte, neither there is any poore man or begger. And though no man have anything, yet everye man is ryche. For what can be more riche then to lyve joyfully and merely,[4] without al griefe and pensifenes; not caring for his owne lyving,[5] nor vexed or troubled with his wifes importunate complayntes, nor dreadyng povertie to his sonne nor

2 their side
3 set no limits
4 treachery

The superiority of the Utopian commonwealth
1 separate
2 provided that
3 niggardly
4 merrily
5 earning a living

sorrowyng for his doughters dowrey? Yea, they take no care at all for the lyvyng and wealthe[6] of themselfes and al theirs, of their wyfes, their chyldren, their nephews, their childrens chyldren, and all the succession that ever shall followe in their posteritie. And yet besydes this there is no lesse provision for them that were ones labourers and be now weake and impotent then for them that do now laboure and take payne.

Here now woulde I see yf any man dare be so bolde as to compare with this equytie the justice of other nations, among whom I forsake God if I can fynde any signe or token of equitie and justice. For what justice is this, that a ryche goldesmythe, or an usurer, or, to be shorte, any of them which either do nothing at all or els that whych they do is such that it is not very necessary to the commonwealth, should have a pleasaunte and a welthie lyving, either by idlenes or by unnecessarye busines, when in the meanetyme poore labourers, carters, yronsmythes, carpenters and plowmen, by so greate and continual toyle as drawing and bearing beastes be skant able to susteine – and againe so necessary toyle that without it no commonwealth were able to continewe and endure one yere – should yet get so harde and poore a lyving and lyve so wretched and miserable a lyfe that the state and condicion of the labouring beastes maye seme muche better and welthier?[7] For they be not put to so continuall laboure, nor their lyving is not muche worse – yea, to them muche pleasaunter, takyng no thoughte in the meane season for the tyme to come. But these seilye poore wretches be presently[8] tormented with barreyne and unfrutefull labour, and the remembraunce of their poore indigent and beggerlye olde age kylleth them up. For their dayly wages is so lytle that it will not suffice for the same daye, muche lesse it yeldeth any overplus that may daylye be layde up for the relyefe of olde age.

Is not this an unjust and an unkynde publyque weale, whych gyveth great fees and rewardes to gentlemen, as they call them, and to goldsmythes and to suche other, which be either ydle persones or els onlye flatterers and devysers of vayne pleasures; and on the contrary parte maketh no gentle provision for poore plowmen, coliars, laborers, carters, yronsmythes and carpenters, without whom no commenwealthe can continewe? But after it hath abused the labours of their lusty and flowring age, at the laste when they be oppressed with olde age and syckenes, being nedye, poore and indigent of all thinges, then forgettyng their so manye paynefull watchinges,[9] not remembring their so manye and so greate benefites, recompenseth and acquyteth[10] them moste unkyndly with myserable death. And yet besides this the riche men, not only by private fraud but also by commen lawes, do every day pluck and snatche awaye from the poore some parte of their daily living. So whereas it semed before unjuste to recompense with unkindnes their paynes that have bene beneficiall to the publique weale, now they have to this their wrong and unjuste dealing (which is yet a muche worse pointe) geven the name of justice – yea, and that by force of a lawe.

Therfore when I consider and way[11] in my mind all these commenwealthes which nowadayes anywhere do florish, so God helpe me I can perceave nothing but a certein conspiracy of riche men procuring their owne commodities[12] under the name and title of the commenwealth. They invent and devise all meanes and craftes, first how to kepe safely, without feare of lesing, that[13] they have unjustly gathered together, and next how to hire and abuse the worke and laboure of the poore for as litle money as may be. These devises, when the riche men have decreed to be kept and observed under coloure of the comminaltie, that is to saye, also of the pore people, then they be made lawes. But these most wicked and vicious men, when they have by their unsatiable covetousnes devided among themselves al those thinges which woulde have sufficed all men, yet how farre be they from the welth and felicitie of the Utopian commenwealth? Out of the which, in that all the desire of money with the use thereof is utterly secluded[14] and banished, how greate a heape of cares is cut away! How great an occasion of wickednes and mischiefe is plucked up by the rotes! For who knoweth not that fraud, theft, ravine,[15] brauling, quarelling, brabling,[16] strife, chiding, contention, murder, treason, poisoning, which by daily punishmentes are rather revenged then refrained,[17] do dye when money dieth? And also that feare, griefe, care, laboures and watchinges do perish even the very same moment that money perisheth? Yea, poverty itself, which only semed to lacke money, if money were gone, it also would decrease and vanishe away.

6 sustenance and well-being
7 better off
8 at the present time
9 wakeful nights
10 requites
11 weigh
12 advantages
13 losing, what
14 excluded
15 robbery
16 arguing
17 restrained

A DIALOGUE OF COMFORT AGAINST TRIBULATION

In prison, at the last, intermittently deprived of writing materials and books, much in horror of bodily pain and harassed by threats of death by torture, visited by his wife and favourite daughter Margaret with temptations to compromise, More awaited trial. He wrote in 1534, during the early months of his imprisonment (he later wrote a *History of the Passion*), the *Dialogue of Comfort*, in which his own circumstances are figured in a dialogue between old Anthony and young Vincent, his nephew, as they contemplate, in Budapest in 1528, the sacking of the city by the Turks and the violent end that awaits all its Christian inhabitants. Though unrevised and structurally a sprawl, the *Dialogue* is perhaps the fullest representation of More's knowledge, beliefs and interests. There is much of the traditional consolation of reason and faith, in the line of Seneca and Boethius and others (Book 1), many moral and exemplary stories, some of them quite funny (Book 2), and in Book 3 the focusing upon the immediate perils of violent death. Though very much the long-awaited climax of the work, with a significance deepened by the circumstances of its composition, these last chapters remain calm and measured, slightly pedantic (the dialogue-form contributes to the air of detachment), breaking out only calculatedly in exclamation. Such was More's demeanour as he went to his execution.

Edition by L.L. Martz and F. Manley, Yale edition, Vol. 12 (New Haven, 1976); text from Oxford (Bodleian Library), Corpus Christi College MS D.37, in a contemporary hand with corrections in a slightly later hand.

How the Christian prepares himself to die for his faith

{Vincent puts the view that a man would do all he could to avoid a violent and painful death, even making temporary recantation, so that he might repent after and die a natural death. Anthony replies:}

{Book 3, Chapter 24} ...'By my trouth, cosyn, me thinketh that the deth which men call comonly naturall ys a violent deth to every man whom yt fetcheth hens by force agaynst his will – and that ys every man which whan he dieth ys loth to dye and fayne wold yet live lenger yf he might.

'Howbeit, how small the payne ys in the naturall deth, cosyn, fayne wold I wit who hath told you. As far as I can perceve, those folke that comonly depart of ther natural deth have ever one desease and sicknes or other, wherof yf the payne of that whole weke or twayne in which they lye pynyng in their bed were gatherid together into so short a tyme as a man hath his payne that dieth a violent deth, it wold, I wene, make dowble the payne that that is. So that he that naturally dieth ofter suffreth more payne than lesse, though he suffreth it in a lenger tyme; and than wold many a man be more loth to suffre so long lyngeryng in payne than with a sharper to be soner rid.

'And yet lieth many a man mo dayes than one in well nere as great payne contynually as is the payne that with the vyolent deth riddith the man in lesse than halfe an howre, except a man wold wene that, whereas the payne ys greate to have a knyfe to cut his flesh on the owtside fro the skynne inward, the payne wold be mich lesse yf the knyfe myght begyn on the inside and cut fro the myddes outward.[1]

'Some we here in their deth-bed complayne that they thinke they fele sharpe knyfes cut a-two their hart-strynges; some crye out and thynke they fele within the brayne-pan their hed prickyd even full of pynnys; and they that lye in a plurisie thynke that every tyme they cough they fele a sharpe swerd swapp them to the hart.

{Chapter 25} 'Howbeit, what shuld we neade to make any such comparison betwene the naturall deth and the violent for the matter that we be in hand with here? We may put yt out of dowt that he which for fere of the violent deth forsakith the fayth of Christ putteth hymselfe in the perell to fynd his naturall deth more paynefull a thowsand tymes. For his naturall deth hath his everlastyng payne so sodaynly knyt unto it that ther is not one moment of an hower betwene, but th'end of the tone is the begynnyng

1 More was not certain at this point that he was not to suffer a traitor's death by disembowelling. In thus making explicit (even though at one remove) his consciousness of his own approaching torment, More reveals the difference, whether personal or cultural, between himself and Boethius, who was likewise faced with the certainty of a painful and violent death. More is the inheritor of a Christian tradition in which such fearful self-examination was sanctioned by Christ's example; Boethius, though a Christian, observes the Stoic tradition and keeps his 'self' to himself and his consolation to the high abstract ground of philosophy.

of the tother, that after never shall have end. And therfor was yt not without great cause that Christ gave us so good warnyng before, when he said, as S.Luke in the xii chapitre rehersith: "I say to you that are my frendes, be not aferde of them that kill the body and which, whan that ys done, are able to do no more. But I shall shew you whom you shuld feare: feare hym which when he hath kyllid hath in his power forther to cast hym whom he kylleth into everlastyng fyre. So I say to you, be aferd of hym."[2]

'God meaneth not here that we shuld nothyng dreade at all any man that can but kyll the bodye, but he meanyth that we shuld not in such wise dreade any such that we shuld for dreade of them displease hym that can everlastyngly kyll both body and soule, with a deth ever dying and that yet never dye. And therfor he addith and repetith in th'end agayne the feare that we shuld have of hym, and sayth: "So I say to you, fere hym."

'Oh good God, cosyn! yf a man wold well waye those wordes and let them syncke as they shuld do downe depe into his hart, and often bethynke hymselfe theron, yt wold, I dowt not, be able ynough to make us set at nowght all the greate Turkes threttes and esteme hym not at a straw, but well content to endure all the payne that all the world wold put uppon us, for so short while as all they were able to make us dwell therin, rather then by the shrynkyng fro those paynes – though never so sharpe, yet but short – to cast ourselfe into the payne of hell, an hundred thowsand tymes more intollerable, and whereof there shall never come an end. A wofull deth is that deth in which folke shall evermore be dying and never can ones be ded, wherof the scripture sayth: "They shall call and cry for deth, and deth shall flye from them."[3]

'O, good Lord! yf one of them[4] were now put in choyse of the bothe, they wold rather suffre the whole yere together the most terrible deth that all the Turkes in Turkey could devise than the deth that they lye in for the space of halfe an howre. In how wrechid foly fall than those faythlesse or feble-faythed folke, that to avoyd the payne so farre the lesse and so short fall in the stede therof into payne a thowsand thowsand tymes more horrible, and of which terrible tourment they be sure they shall never have end.'

2 Luke 12:5. More also quotes the Latin. **be aferd of hym**, i.e. of God.

3 Rev. 9:6.

4 **one of them**, i.e. one of those who cried for death in the scriptural passage.

Sir Thomas Elyot (*c.* 1490–1546)

Educated, like More, at Oxford and the Inns of Court, Elyot was a member of the 'More circle' at his house in Chelsea, where he met many of the new humanists, such as Thomas Linacre (who taught him Greek), shared in the inspiration of the new learning, and had his picture painted, like More, by Hans Holbein the Younger. He served under Wolsey, but was out of office by 1530, and in retirement wrote *The Governor*, a book of political, moral and educational counsel which essentially sets out, 'in our vulgare tunge', a way of life for the Tudor governing class, 'the fourme of a juste publike weale' (Proem) – the subject that More had addressed more playfully in *Utopia*. The 'publike weale' is defined as 'a body lyvyng, compacte or made of sondry astates and degrees of men, whiche is disposed by the ordre of equite and governed by the rule and moderation of reason' (Book 1, chap. 1) – but it is of course an absolute monarchy, and the governors are noblemen. Book 1 concentrates on education, including music, painting, poetry and dancing, as the means to the knowledge of virtue and the proper conduct of government, while Books 2 and 3, on the model of the old 'Mirrors for Princes' (e.g. Hoccleve's *Regement*), list the virtues needed by rulers, with examples from Greek and Roman history and literature of those virtues in operation. It thus advocates as practice the principal doctrine of the new humanism – that a good classical education is the means to the making of good men and good governors (the foundation of the English educational system for the next 400 years). The change in the concept of the governing class (anticipated to some extent in Hawes) is radical: fighting and love-making were what a chivalric knight, the predecessor of the 'governor', was trained for, and Chaucer's Squire would have seen little of Latin. Now a career in the public service, such as that of Sir Thomas Wyatt (or More, who is Elyot's model), does not necessarily involve fighting and is, in part, what would have been done in the past by the clergy. Elyot draws attention to the fact that he writes in 'our vulgare tunge', conscious that this might leave him open to criticism from purists, but it is our good fortune that he did so: like many Tudor humanists, he writes excellent, current, idiomatic, unaffected English prose without seeming to try.

First printed by Berthelet, 1531 (facsimile, ed. R.C. Alston, Menston [1970]; modernized edition by S.E. Lehmberg, Everyman [1962]), the book was frequently reprinted and widely known: Shakespeare read it, and it was one of the books set for the young James VI of Scotland (the future James I) to study.

The Book named The Governor

The importance of beginning Latin early

Some olde autours holde opinion that before the age of seven yeres a chylde shulde nat be instructed in letters, but those writers were either Grekes or Latines, amonge whom all doctrine and sciences were in their maternall tonges, by reason wherof they saved all that longe tyme whiche at this dayes is spente in understandyng perfectly the Greke or Latyne. Wherfore it requireth nowe a longer tyme to the understandyng of bothe. Therfore that infelicitie of our tyme and countray compelleth us to encroche somewhat upon the yeres of children, and specially of noblemen, that thay may sooner attayne to wisedome and gravitie than private persones, consideryng, as I have saide, their charge and example, whiche above all thynges is most to be estemed.

Natwithstandyng, I wolde nat have them inforced by violence to lerne, but accordynge to the counsaile of Quintilian to be swetely allured therto with praises and suche praty gyftes as children delite in; and their fyrst letters to be paynted or lymned in a pleasaunt maner, wherein children of gentyl courage have moche delectation. And also there is no better allectyve[1] to noble wyttes than to induce them into a contention with their inferiour companions, they somtyme purposely suffring the more noble children to vainquysshe and as it were gyvyng to them place and soveraintie, though indede the inferiour chyldren have more lernyng.

But there can be nothyng more convenient than by litle and litle to trayne and exercise them in spekyng of Latyne, infourmyng them to knowe first the names in Latine of all thynges that cometh in syghte and to name all the partes of theyr bodies, and gyvynge them somewhat that they covete or desyre in most gentyl maner to teache them to aske it agayne in Latine. And if by this meanes they may

1 encouragement

be induced to understande and speke Latine it shall afterwarde be lasse grefe to them in a maner to lerne anything where they understande the langage wherin it is writen...

Hit shall be expedient that a noblemannes sonne in his infancie have with hym continually onely suche as may accustome hym by litle and litle to speake pure and elegant Latin; semblably[2] the nourice and other women aboute hym, if it be possible, to do the same, or at the leste way that they speke none Englisshe but that whiche is cleane, polite, perfectly and articulately pronounced, omittinge no lettre or sillable, as folisshe women often-times do of a wantonnesse, wherby divers noblemen and gentilmennes chyldren (as I do at this daye knowe) have attained corrupte and foule pronuntiation.

This industry used in fourminge litel infantes, who shall dought but that they (nat lackyng naturall witte) shall be apt to receyve lerninge whan they come to mo yeres? And in this wise maye they be instructed without any violence or inforsynge, using the more parte of the time until they come to the age of .vii. yeres in suche disportis as do appertaine to chldren, wherin is no resemblance or similitude of vice.

Why gentlemen's children are seldom properly educated

[Pride, avarice, parental negligence and insufficiency of good teachers are blamed for the poor state of education among the upper classes.]

The seconde occasion wherfore gentylmens children seldome have sufficient lernynge is avarice, for where[1] theyr parentes wyll nat adventure to sende them farre out of theyr propre[2] countrayes, partely for feare of dethe, whiche perchance dare nat approche them at home with theyr father, partely for expence of money, whiche they suppose wolde be lasse in theyr owne houses or in a village with some of theyr tenantes or frendes – havyng seldome any regarde to the teacher, whether he be well-lerned or ignorant. For if they hire a scholemaister to teche in theyr houses, they chiefely enquire with howe small a salary he will be contented and never to inserche howe moche good lernynge he hath and howe amonge well-lerned men he is therin estemed; usinge therin lasse diligence than in takynge servantes, whose service is of moche lasse importance and to a good scholemaister is nat in profite to be compared. A gentilman, er he take a cooke into his service, he wyll firste diligently examine hym, howe many sortes of meates, potages and sauces he can perfectly make, and howe well he can season them that they may be bothe pleasant and nourishynge. Yea, and if it be but a fauconer, he wyll scrupulously enquire what skyll he hath in feedyng (called diete) and kepyng of his hauke from all sickenes, also how he can reclaime her and prepare her to flight. And to suche a cooke or fauconer whom he findeth expert he spareth nat to gyve moche wages with other bounteous rewardes. But of a scholemaister, to whom he will committe his childe to be fedde with lernynge and instructed in vertue, whose lyfe shall be the principall monument of his name and honour, he never maketh further enquirie but where he may have a scholemaister and with howe litle charge. And if one be perchance founden well-lerned but he will nat take paynes to teache without he may have a great salary, he than speketh nothing more or els saith: 'What! Shall so moche wages be gyven to a scholemaister whiche wolde kepe me two servauntes?' To whom maye be saide these wordes, that by his sonne being wel-lerned he shall receive more commoditie and also worship than by the service of a hundred cokes and fauconers.

An illustration of the virtue of placability

[Prince Hal was the addressee of Hoccleve's Regement*; now he has become the model for other princes to emulate. Elyot's story, for which there is no known source (though it follows the pattern of other inspired inventions concerning the prince's riotous youth) is alluded to and is important in the political structure of Shakespeare's* Henry IV, Part 2 *(esp. V.ii.108–12). It is one of the few stories in* The Governor *that is not drawn from classical sources; elsewhere Elyot translates the story of Titus and Gisippus from Boccaccio's* Decameron, *one of the earliest imitations of Boccaccio since Chaucer.]*

2 likewise

1 wherefore
2 own

The moste renomed prince, kynge Henry the fifte, late kynge of Englande, durynge the life of his father was noted to be fierce and of wanton courage. It hapned that one of his servantes, whom he well favored, for felony by hym committed was arrayned at the Kynges Benche; wherof he being advertised and incensed by light persones aboute hym, in furious rage came hastily to the barre where his servant stode as a prisoner and commaunded hym to be ungyved[1] and sette at libertie, whereat all men were abasshed – reserved[2] the Chiefe Justice, who humbly exhorted the prince to be contented that his servaunt mought be ordred[3] accordyng to the auncient lawes of this realme; or if he wolde have hym saved from the rigour of the lawes that he shuld optaine if he moughte of the kynge his father his gracious pardone, wherby no lawe or justice shulde be derogate.[4] With whiche answere the prince, nothynge appeased but rather more inflamed, endevored hymselfe to take away his servaunt. The juge, consideringe the perilous example and inconvenience that moughte therby ensue, with a valiant spirite and courage commaunded the prince upon his alegeance to leve the prisoner and departe his way, with whiche commandment the prince, being set all in a fury, all chafed and in a terrible maner came up to the place of jugement, men thinkyng that he wolde have slayne the juge or have done to hym some damage; but the juge, sittyng styll without movynge, declarynge the majestie of the kynges place of jugement, and with an assured and bolde countenance, hadde to the prince these wordes folowyng:

'Sir, remembre yourselfe! I kepe here the place of the king your soveraigne lorde and father, to whom ye owe double obedience, wherfore eftsones in his name I charge you desiste of your wilfulnes and unlaufull entreprise, and from hensforth gyve good example to those whiche hereafter shall be your propre subjectes. And nowe for your contempt and disobedience go you to the prisone of the Kynges Benche, whereunto I committe you, and remayne ye there prisoner untill the pleasure of the kyng your father be further knowen.'

With whiche wordes beinge abasshed, and also wondrynge at the mervailous gravitie of that worshipful Justice, the noble prince, layinge his waipon aparte, doinge reverence, departed and wente to the Kynges Benche, as he was commaunded. Wherat his servant, disdainyng, came and shewed to the kynge all the hole affaire. Wherat he, a-whiles studienge, after, as a man all ravisshed with gladnesse, holdyng his eien and handes up towarde heven, abrayded,[5] sayinge with a loude voice: 'O mercifull God! howe moche am I above all other men bounde to your infinite goodnes, specially for that ye have gyven me a juge who feareth nat to ministre justice, and also a sonne who can suffre semblably and obey justice!'

1 unfettered
2 with the exception of
3 disciplined
4 diminished
5 burst out

William Tyndale (1494–1536)

Bible-translation was Tyndale's life's work, to which, after being educated at Oxford (MA 1515), he early determined to devote himself. The Bible had been translated in full once before, by the followers of Wyclif in the late fourteenth century, but that version had been suppressed as heretical, and Bible-translation was still so regarded; portions of the Bible did of course appear in English translation in widely available works such as Love's *Mirror*, but only as part of a set priestly programme of instruction and persuasion. Tyndale did not get the support he had hoped for in London and his project fell under suspicion of heresy (even though there were already printed Bibles in other vernaculars) and of contamination by the new Lutheranism that was coming into England from 1520. So he left England in 1524 and went to Cologne, where he published his fragment of the Gospel of St Matthew (1525), then to Worms, where he published his first New Testament (1526), and thence to Antwerp. There he worked indefatigably at his translations, revising his NT and adding most of the first half of the OT before having them printed and smuggled into England, meanwhile engaging in vigorous debate with More and others about Bible-translation, the priesthood and the church. The NT was done from the Greek (something that had been pioneered by Erasmus), the OT from the Hebrew (a much rarer accomplishment). Tyndale's great gift as a translator was to be able to use the English of his time to convey the sense of the Hebrew and Greek in an idiomatic and memorable way. In this, his work marks an advance on the Wycliffite version (see above, where corresponding passages have been chosen for comparison), though the extent to which the earlier version anticipated Tyndale in phrasing and syntax should not be underestimated. But it was Tyndale who provided the English text from which other translators worked: nine-tenths of the NT in the Authorized Version (1611) is Tyndale's. Tyndale's other great gift was to recognize the transformation that had taken place, as a result of printing, in the power of the disseminated word (see Greenblatt [1980], pp. 74–114). Persecution of those in possession of Tyndale's translations in England began in 1526, and burning in 1531 (the books had been burned for some time). Betrayed by an associate who was in the service of the Catholic Emperor Charles V, Tyndale was arrested in 1535, charged with heresy (i.e. being a Lutheran), and burnt in Antwerp in 1536. See D. Daniell, *William Tyndale: A Biography* (New Haven, 1994); also P. Collinson, in *Reformation* 1 (1996), 72–97. For an introduction to the historical background of these religious conflicts, see A.G. Dickens, *The English Reformation* (London, 1974), C. Cross, *Church and People 1450–1660: The Triumph of the Laity in the English Church* (London, 1976), and (from a different point of view) Duffy (1992).

The Prologue to the New Testament

This is Tyndale's first known piece of writing: it was printed with a fragment of the Gospel of Matthew in Antwerp in 1525. Most of the Prologue is worked up from Luther's Prologue to his NT (1522), but these opening paragraphs are Tyndale's own, and packed with NT echoes. Calm though his tone may be, in explaining that to have the scriptures in the vernacular is such an obvious necessity that it hardly needs arguing, the implications of what he says are explosive – especially the renaming of the church as 'the congregacion', the body of all believers, and not the priesthood of the elite (priests are always called 'seniors' or 'elders' in this newly charged vocabulary). Tyndale's suggestion, always, is that the 'bare text' of scripture, made available in a language that all can understand, will carry the truth home to all honest hearts, but he himself makes sure that the truth is the 'right' truth by adding extensive interpretative prologues and a stream of tendentious annotations. Text from the facsimile edition of A.W. Pollard (Oxford, 1926).

I have here translated, brethern and susters moost dere and tenderly beloved in Christ, the Newe Testament, for youre spirituall edyfyinge, consolacion and solas; exhortynge instantly[1] and besechynge those that are better sene[2] in the tonges then I, and that have hyer gyftes of grace to interpret the sence of the scripture and meanynge of the spyrite then I, to consydre and pondre my laboure, and that with the spyrite of mekenes. And yf they perceyve in eny places that I have not attayned the very sence of the tonge or meanynge of the scripture, or have not geven the right Englysshe worde, that they put to there handes to amende it, remembrynge that so is there duetie to doo. For we have not receyved the gyftes of God for oureselves only, or for to hyde them, but for to bestowe them unto the

1 urgently

2 versed

honouringe of God and Christ and edyfyinge of the congregacion, which is the body of Christ.

The causes that moved me to translate I thought better that other shulde ymagion then that I shulde rehearce them; moreover I supposed yt superfluous, for who ys so blynde to axe why lyght shulde be shewed to them that walke in dercknes, where they cannot but stomble, and where to stomble ys the daunger of eternall dammacion? other so despyghtfull that he wolde envye eny man (I speake nott his brother) so necessary a thinge? or so bedlem-madde[3] to affyrme that good is the naturall cause of yvell and derknes to procede oute of lyght, and that lyinge shulde be grounded in trouth and verytie, and nott rather clene contrary – that lyght destroyeth dercknes and veritie reproveth all manner lyinge?

THE NEW TESTAMENT

The New Testament is Tyndale's masterpiece: it contains some of the finest prose-writing in the English language. The following passages are infinitely familiar from the 1611 version which, apart from a word or two here and there, is all Tyndale. Text from the transliteration of the 1534 Antwerp edition by N.H. Wallis (Cambridge, 1938). There are modernized editions by D. Daniell of the NT (New Haven, 1989) and of the OT (New Haven, 1992).

The parable of the great supper (Luke 14:12–24)

An example of Tyndale's incomparable ease and clarity in a simple narrative passage. For Langland's use of the parable, see above, *PP* VII.192–204.

Then sayde he also to him that had desyred him to diner: 'When thou makest a diner or a supper, call not thy frendes nor thy brethren, nether thy kinsmen nor yet ryche neghbours, lest they bidde the agayne,[1] and a recompence be made the. But when thou makest a feast, call the poore, the maymed, the lame and the blynde, and thou shalt be happy,[2] for they cannot recompence the. But thou shalt be recompensed at the resurreccion of the juste men.'

When one of them that sate at meate also hearde that, he sayde unto him: 'Happy is he that eateth breed in the kyngdome of God!' Then sayd he to him: 'A certayne man ordened a greate supper, and bade many, and sent his servaunt at supper-tyme to saye to them that wer bidden, "Come, for all thinges are now redy." And they all at once beganne to make excuse. The fyrst sayd unto him: "I have bought a ferme, and I must nedes goo and se it; I praye the have me excused." And another sayd: "I have bought fyve yooke of oxen, and I goo to prove them; I praye the have me excused." The thyrde sayd: "I have maried a wyfe, and therfore I cannot come." And the servaunt went and brought his master worde therof. Then was the good man of the housse displeased, and sayd to his servaunt: "Goo out quickly into the stretes and quarters of the cite and bringe in hidder the poore and the maymed and the halt and the blynde." And the servaunt sayd: "Lorde, it is done as thou commaundedst, and yet ther is roume." And the lorde sayd to the servaunt: "Go out into the hye-wayes and hedges, and compell them to come in, that my housse maye be filled. For I saye unto you, that none of those men which were bidden shall tast of my supper."'

The nature of love (1 Cor. 13)

Though I spake with the tonges of men and angels, and yet had no love, I were even as soundinge brasse or as a tynklynge cymball. And though I coulde prophesy, and understode all secretes and all knowledge – yee, yf I had all fayth so that I coulde move mountayns oute of ther places, and yet had no love, I were nothynge. And though I bestowed all my gooddes to fede the poore, and though I gave my body even that I burned, and yet had no love, it profiteth me nothinge.

3 mad as a person in a bedlam (Bethlehem) hospital

THE NEW TESTAMENT

1 invite you back

2 well-fortuned

Love suffreth longe, and is corteous. Love envieth not. Love doth not frowardly, swelleth not, dealeth not dishonestly, seketh not her awne, is not provoked to anger, thynketh not evyll, rejoyseth not in iniquite; but rejoyseth in the trueth, suffreth all thynge, beleveth all thynges, hopeth all thynges, endureth in all thynges. Though that prophesyinge fayle, other[1] tonges shall cease, or knowledge vanysshe awaye, yet love falleth never awaye.

For oure knowledge is unparfect, and oure prophesyinge is unperfet. But when that which is parfect is come, then that which is unparfet shall be done awaye. When I was a chylde, I spake as a chylde, I understode as a childe, I ymagened as a chylde. But as sone as I was a man I put awaye childesshnes. Now we se in a glasse even in a darke speakynge, but then shall we se face to face. Now I knowe unparfectly, but then shall I knowe even as I am knowen. Now abideth fayth, hope, and love, even these thre; but the chefe of these is love.

THE OBEDIENCE OF A CHRISTIAN MAN

This lengthy treatise (1528) was written to calm fears that the Lutheran reforms involved some rejection of authority, and to reaffirm the obedience of the Christian to the king and secular state (Henry VIII found much to approve in the treatise). The extracts below, taken from the Antwerp edition of 1535, return to the subject of Bible-translation, explaining why the need for such translation is a matter of plain common sense (fols xv–xvi), and in the second (fol. lxiii), after giving examples of false and self-serving interpretations of scripture by John Fisher, bishop of Rochester, why the prelates oppose it. In a later passage (fol. lxxxv), after describing how kings are the prisoners of priestly hypocrites, Tyndale turns aside to a familiar catalogue of priestly absurdities that set his blood boiling and his pen singing.

That the scripture ought to be in the English tongue

The sermons which thou readist in the Actes of the Apostles, and all that the apostles preached, were no doute preached in the mother tonge. Why then might thei not be written in the mother tonge? As yf one of us preach a good sermon, why may it not be written? S.Hierom[1] also translated the bible into his mother tonge. Why maye not we also? Thei wil saye it cannot be translated into our tonge, it is so rude. It is not so rude as thei ar false lyers! For the Greke tonge agreeth moare with the English then with the Latyne. And the properties of the Hebrue tonge agreeth a thousande tymes moare with the Englysh then with the Latyne. The maner of speaking is both one, so that in a thousande places thou neadest not but to translat it into the Englysh worde for worde, when thou must seke a compasse[2] in the Latyne, and yet shalt have moch worke to translate it wel-faveredly, so that it have the same grace and swetnesse, sence and pure understandinge with it in the Latyne as it hath in the Hebrue. A thousande partes better maye it be translated into the English then into the Latyne. Yee, and except my memory fayle me and that I have forgotten what I redde when I was a child, thou shalt finde in the Englesh cronycle how that kynge Adelstone caused the holy scripture to be translated into the tonge that then was in Englonde, and how the prelates exhorted him therto.[3]

1 or

THE OBEDIENCE OF A CHRISTIAN MAN

1 St Jerome (d. 420) translated the Bible into Latin from Greek (the NT from the original, the OT from an earlier Greek translation). His Bible, known as the Vulgate (since Latin was at that time the vernacular or 'vulgar' tongue), was the 'authorized version' of the Middle Ages.

2 find a roundabout way of putting it

3 There is a translation of the Gospels into Anglo-Saxon, made in the late tenth century, but it is not known to have to do with Athelstan, who was king 925–40. Tyndale gets his story from the twelfth-century Anglo-Latin Chronicle of England by William of Malmesbury.

Why they will not have the scripture in English

But evere after this maner wise perverte they the hole scripture and all doctours, wrestinge them unto their abhominable purpose cleane contrary to the meanynge of the texte and to the circumstaunces that goo before and after. Which develish falsheed lest the laye-men shuld perceave is the veri cause[1] why that thei will not sofre the scripture to be had in the Englysh tonge, nether any worke to be made that shulde bringe the people to knowleage of the trueth.

Blind mouths

'Ye blinde gydes', saith Christe, 'ye strayne out a gnat and swallow a camell' (Math.xxiii). Doo not oure blinde gides also stomble at a straw and lepe over a blocke, makinge narrow consciences at trifyls and at maters of weght none att all? Yf any of them happen to swalow his spital or ani of the water wherewith he wesheth his mouth ther he goo to masse, or towch the sacramente with his nose, or if the asse forgett to breath on him,[1] or happen to handle it with ony of his fyngers which are not anoynted, or saye *Alleluia* instede of *Laus tibi domine* or *Ite missa est* instede of *Benedicamus domino*, or poure to moch wine in the chalice, or reade the Gospell without light, or make not his crosses aright, how trembleth he, how feareth he! What an horrible sinne is committed! 'I cry God merci!' saith he, 'and thou, mi gostli fader!' But to hold an whore or another mans wife, to bie a benefice, to set one realme at variaunce with another and to cause .xx. thousande to die on a daye is but a trifle and a pastime with them.

1 **the veri cause**. For polemic force, Tyndale makes the case very simply. One would have to recognize too the church's interest as an institution in preserving the clerical monopoly on reading and interpreting the Bible.

1 **if the asse forgett to breath on him**: breathing on the bread (**him**) was part of the preparation of the sacrament; is **the asse** the priest?

Simon Fish (*c.* 1500–1531)

Fish's famous tract, in which he imagines the beggars of the land crying out against the ravenous greed of the church, had great influence in its time and after. For all its half-humorous exaggerations and hectic eloquence, and even though it mostly repeated criticism of church abuses that had been current since the time of Chaucer and Langland and before, it helped shape opinion when opinion was still capable of being shaped, and, Foxe reports (see below), was read with approval (and no doubt some amusement) by the king and Anne Boleyn. It was condemned by the bishop of London, and spurred More to a reply: in his *Supplication of Souls*, the souls of those in purgatory (whose existence Fish denied, declaring it to be a money-making scam invented by the church in order to extract money from people for saying prayers for their relatives supposedly consigned there) cry out in anguish at the inevitable prolongation of their suffering if Fish's views prevail. In after years, Fish's tract was incorporated complete into Foxe's *Book of Martyrs* (1563: see below, also for Foxe's account of Fish's life), which assured its place as one of the classic documents of the English Reformation. Text from print of 1529; ed. F.J. Furnivall, EETS, ES 13 (London, 1871).

A Supplication for the Beggars (1529)

To the king, oure sovereygne lorde, most lamentably compleyneth theyre wofull mysery unto youre highnes youre poore daily bedemen,[1] the wretched hidous monstres on whom scarcely for horror any iye dare loke, the foule unhappy sorte of lepres and other sore people, nedy, impotent, blinde, lame and sike, that live onely by almesse, howe that theyre nombre is daily so sore encreased that all the almesse of all the wel-disposed people of this youre realme is not halfe ynough for to susteine them, but that for verey constreint they die for hunger. And this most pestilent mischief is comen uppon youre saide poore beedmen by the reason and[2] there is, yn the tymes of youre noble predecessours passed, craftily crept ynto this your realme another sort, not of impotent but of strong, puissaunt and counterfeit-holy and ydell beggers and vacabundes whiche syns the tyme of theyre first entre by all the craft and wilinesse of Satan are nowe encreased under your sight, not onely into a great nombre but also ynto a kingdome. These are not the herdes[3] but the ravinous wolves going in herdes clothing, devouring the flocke – the bisshoppes, abbottes, priours, deacons, archedeacons, suffraganes,[4] prestes, monkes, chanons, freres, pardoners and somners. And who is abill to nombre this idell ravinous sort whiche, setting all laboure aside, have begged so importunatly that they have gotten ynto theyre hondes more then the therd part of all youre realme? The goodliest lordshippes, maners, londes and territories are theyrs. Besides this, they have the tenth part of all the corne, medowe, pasture, grasse, wolle, coltes, calves, lambes, pigges, gese and chikens, over and bisides the tenth part of every servauntes wages, the tenth part of the wolle, milke, hony, waxe, chese and butter. Ye, and they loke so narowly uppon theyre proufittes that the poore wyves must be countable to theym of every tenth eg, or elles she gettith not her ryghtes at Ester,[5] shal be taken as an heretike. Hereto have they theire foure offering daies. Whate money pull they yn by probates of testamentes, privy tithes, and by mennes offeringes to theyre pilgremages and at theyre first masses? Every man and childe that is buried must pay sumwhat for masses and diriges[6] to be song for him, or elles they will accuse the dedes[7] frendes and executours of heresie. Whate money get they by mortuaries,[8] by hearing of confessions (and yet they wil kepe therof no counceyle),[9] by halowing of churches, altares, super-altares, chapelles and belles, by cursing[10] of men and absolving theim agein for money? What a multitude of money gather the pardoners in a yere? Howe moche money get the somners by extorcion yn a yere, by assityng[11] the people to the commissaries court and afterward releasing th'apparaunce for money? Finally, the infinite nombre of

1 **bedemen**: beadsmen (those who pray for your welfare)
2 that
3 shepherds
4 suffragan bishops (i.e. auxiliary bishops)
5 I.e. will not be allowed to take communion, enjoined on all Christians once a year, at Easter, at least.
6 **diriges**: see Henryson, *Cock and Fox*, 449n.
7 dead person's
8 Bequests of money to the parish church to pay tithes omitted in the lifetime of the deceased.
9 secret
10 excommunicating
11 summoning. For the activities of summoners, see GP 623n.

begging freres: whate get they yn a yere? Here, if it please your grace to marke, ye shall se a thing farre out of joynt. {*Fish explains further how the church is parasitical upon the commonwealth, corrupts its women, threatens the king's authority. The religious orders should be dissolved, their members put to work, priests allowed to marry, the scriptures translated into English, etc.*}

William Roper (1496–1577)

William Roper was in service in More's household from 1518 and married his daughter Margaret in 1521. He was very close to More, and the *Life* is an intimate record of the man, hagiography at one remove rather than biography, but compelling in its details and in the picture it gives of More's enigmatic, tense, teasing, self-veiling manner. The prose is plain and dramatic, and Roper has the gift of leaving the narrative to speak for itself. He wrote up the *Life* around 1557 during the reign of Mary, when circumstances were more propitious for a man who had remained in the service of the state. It circulated in manuscript and was not published until 1626; it was used by Nicholas Harpsfield, who was writing at the same time the authorized biography of More, and who incorporated much of it word for word into his *Life* (ed. E.V. Hitchcock and R.W. Chambers, EETS, OS 186, 1932). Much is taken verbatim into Robert Bolt's successful play, *A Man for All Seasons* (1960).

Roper's *Life* survives in 13 MSS; edition by E.V. Hitchcock, EETS, OS 197 (London, 1935); text below from BL MS Harley 6254 (pp. 27–39). Chambers has a famous introduction ('On the Continuity of English Prose from Alfred to More and his School') to the edition of Harpsfield (separately published as EETS, OS 191A, 1932) in which he makes the claim that the prose of More and Roper is the continuation of an unbroken tradition of English prose that goes back to Anglo-Saxon times. For 'biographical truth', see Anderson (1984), pp. 40–51.

The Life of Sir Thomas More

{Richard Rich, the newly made King's Solicitor, and a creature of Thomas Cromwell (Rich was later Lord Chancellor, 1547–51), is sent with others to the Tower to carry away More's books. (Roper was not present on this occasion, but he had eye-witness reports.)}

The testimony of master Rich

And while Sir Richard Southwell and master Palmer were busye in the trussing uppe of his bookes, master Rich, pretending freindly talke with him, amonge other things of a sett course,[1] as it seemed, saide thus unto him: 'Forasmuch as it is well knowen, master More,[a] that you are a man bothe wise and well learned as well in the lawes of the realme as otherwise, I pray you therefore, sir, lett me be so bold as of good will to putte unto you this case. Admitt there were, sir,' quoth he, 'an acte of parliament that all the realme should take me for kinge. Wold not you, master More, take me for kinge?'

Yes, sir,' quoth Sir Thomas More, 'that I wold.'

'I put the case further,' quoth master Riche, 'that there were an acte of parliament that all the realme should take me for pope. Wold you not then, master More, take me for pope?'

'For awneswer,' quoth Sir Thomas More, 'to your firste case: the parliament may well, master Riche, medle with the state of temporall princes. But to make awneswer to your other case, I will put you this case: suppose the parliament wold make a lawe that God shold not be God. Wold you then, master Riche, say that God were not God?'

'No, sir,' quoth he, 'that wold I not, sith no parliament maye make any such lawe.'

'No more,' said Sir Thomas More, as master Riche reported of him, 'could the parliament make the kinge supreame head of the churche.'

Uppon whose onlye reporte[2] was Sir Thomas More indicted of treason uppon the statute by which it was made treason to denye the kinge to be supreame head of the churche. Into which indictment were putt thes haynouse wordes – 'Maliciously, trayterouslye and diabolically'.

When Sir Thomas More was brought from the Tower to Westminster Hall to awneswer the indictment, and at the Kings Bench barre before the judges theruppon arraigned, he openly told them that he wold uppon that indictment have abidden in lawe, but that[3] he therby shoulde have bine driven to confesse of himself the matter indeede, which was the deniall of the kings supremacye, which he protested was

1 of a conventional nature
2 report alone
3 have abided by (i.e. been content to submit to) the law, except that

untrue. Wherefore he therto pleaded not giltye, and so reserved unto himself advantage to be taken of the body of the matter, after verdicte, to avoid that indictment; and moreover added that[b] if thos only[4] odious tearmes, 'Maliciously, traiterouslye and diabolicallye,' were put out of the indictment, he sawe nothinge therein justlye to charge him.[5]

And for proof to the jury that Sir Thomas More was guilty of this treason, master Rich was called forth to give evidence unto them uppon his oath, as he did. Against whom, thus sworne, Sir Thomas More began in this[c] wise to say: 'If I were a man, my lordes, that did not regarde an othe, I need not, as it is well knowen, in this place, at this tyme, nor in this case, to stand here[d] as an accused person. And if this othe[e] of yours, master Riche, be true, then pray I that I never see God in the face, which I wold not say, were it otherwise, to winne the whole world.' Then recites he to the whole courte the discourse of all theyr communicacion in the Tower, accordinge to the truthe, and said: 'In good faithe, master Riche, I am more sorye for your perjurye then for my owne perill. And yow shall understand that neyther I, nor no man els to my knowledge, ever tooke you to be a man of such creditt as in any matter of importaunce I, or any other, would at anye tyme vouchsaf to communicate with you. And I, as you knowe, of no small while have bine acquainted with yow and your conversacion,[6] who have knowen you from your youth hitherto;[7] for we longe dwelled both in one parishe together, where, as your self can tell (I am sory you compell me so to say), you were esteemed very light of your tongue, a greate dicer, and of no comendable fame. And so in your house at the Temple,[8] wheare hath bine your cheif bringing uppe, were you likewise accompted.

'Can it therefore seeme likely unto your honorable lordshipps that I wold, in so weyghty a cause, so unadvisedlye overshootte myself as to trust master Rich, a man of me alwaies reputed for one of so litle truth as your lordshipps have heard, so farre above my soveraigne lord the kinge, or any of his noble councellors, that I wold unto him utter the secreates of my consciens towchinge the kings supremacye – the speciall pointe and only marke at my handes so longe sought for, a thinge which I never did, nor never wold, after the statute thereof made, reveale either to the kings highnes himself or to any of his honorable councell, as (it is not unknowne to your honors) at sundry and severall times sent from his graces owne person unto the Tower unto me for none other purpose? Can this in your judgments, my lordes, seeme likely to be true? And yet[f] if it had bine so indeed, my lords, as master Riche hath sworne, seing it was spoken but in familiar frendly secreate[9] talk, nothing affirminge, and only in puttinge of cases, without other displeasaunt circumstances, it cannot justly be taken to be spoken maliciouslye; and where there is no malice, there can be no offence.'

{More continues with precise legal arguments, but, finding that it is determined he shall be found guilty, in the end he declares openly his belief that the Act of Supremacy is unlawful. He is forthwith condemned. His journey to the scaffold, five days later, was the occasion of a whole series of famous bons mots, *reported in Roper's* Life, *in the fine tradition of nonchalance in the face of death. The best is his remark to the Lieutenant of the Tower as he climbed the rickety scaffold (MS, p. 47): 'I pray you, master Leiuetenaunte, see me salf uppe, and for my cominge downe let me shifte for myself.'}*

4 if only those

5 More adduces here in his defence the common legal formula that where there is no malice there is no injury. More's general argument is that he would have been willing to stand to the indictment (understanding that he could plead in defence that it was not treason so to deny the king's supremacy) but that the wording of the indictment forced him, if he did not plead not guilty, to confess that he had denied the king's supremacy, which was not the case.

6 behaviour

7 up to now

8 **the Temple**, i.e. the Middle Temple, one of the Inns of Court.

9 private

Sir David Lindsay (*c.* 1486–1555)

Sir David Lindsay of the Mount was tutor to the young James V (1512–42), who succeeded as an infant after Flodden (1513); he later served in diplomatic and heraldic offices at court, and became Lyon king-of-arms in 1542. Most of Lindsay's poetry bears evidence of his strong consciousness of his political, moral and didactic responsibilities as a poet, as well as of his Reformation sympathies. The *Dream of Sir David Lindsay* (1528) is a vision of hell, heaven and earth and the sad state of Scotland, designed as a 'Mirror for Princes'; the *Complaint to the King* (1528) laments the disorderly and corrupt state of the church; the *Testament and Complaint of the Papyngo* (1530) records the advice given by a dying pet parrot to kings, nobles and clergy, ending, with savage aptness, with the dead parrot being torn to pieces by her executors; the *Dialogue between Experience and a Courtier*, better known as *The Monarch* (1554), is a racy exposition of world history from Fall to Doomsday, contrasting the ancient empires with the spiritual monarchy of Christ. There is also *A Pleasant Satire of the Three Estates*, Lindsay's best-known work, a long and whirling satirical morality-play, put on before the king and court in 1540, full of comic ribaldry as well as fierce anticlerical invective. *Squire Meldrum*, by contrast with all these, is a poem with no ambition but to please.

Works, ed. D. Hamer, STS, 3rd series, 1, 2, 6, 8 (1931–6). See C. Edington, *Court and Culture in Renaissance Scotland: Sir David Lindsay of the Mount* (Amherst, MA, 1994).

Squire Meldrum

William Meldrum was a Fifeshire laird (like Lindsay) who fought with the Scottish army in France in 1513, gaining a reputation as a brave and spirited captain. When he returned to Scotland, he fell in love with the widowed lady of Gleneagles, with whom he settled to live *paramours*, but the liaison earnt him the jealous enmity of her violent neighbour Sir John Stirling, who had him assaulted and nearly killed (1517). He lived thereafter a quiet life (his lady married someone else), got to know Lindsay well, and died in 1553. The poem in which his life and exploits are narrated (presumably completed 1553–4) is therefore both a real-life biography and a chivalric romance, a very superior genre, as Lindsay explains in his prologue, and one for which he had Scottish precedent in Barbour's *Bruce* and Harry's *Wallace*. It is a poem of superb vigour and panache, swiftly narrated in short couplets, with a sense of fun and many lyrical touches; it is a delight throughout. Edition by J. Kinsley (London and Edinburgh, 1959); study by F. Riddy, *YES* 4 (1974), 26–36. Text from the 1594 print of Henry Charteris.

Prologue

Quho that antique stories reidis
Considder may the famous deidis
Of our nobill progenitouris,
Quhilk suld to us be richt mirrouris,
Thair verteous deidis to ensew *follow*
And vicious leving to eschew.
Sic men bene put in memorie *Such*
That deith suld not confound thair glorie:
Howbeit thair bodie bene absent,
Thair verteous deidis bene present.
  Poetis, thair honour to avance,
Hes put thame in rememberance:
Sum wryt of preclair conquerouris, *illustrious*
And sum of vailyeand empriouris,
And sum of nobill michtie kingis
That royallie did reull thair ringis; *realms*

1–10 Lindsay explains that the stories of the chivalric heroes of the past are valuable as a memorial of their noble deeds and as an example to the present. This is the traditional justification of such narratives: see the opening of the alliterative *Morte Arthure* and of Lydgate's *Troy-Book*, and Caxton's preface to Malory.

And sum of campiounis and of knichtis
That bauldlie did defend thair richtis,
battle Quhilk vailyeandlie did stand in stour
For the defence of thair honour;
And sum of squyeris douchtie deidis,
warlike That wounders wrocht in weirlie weidis;
Sum wryt of deidis amorous,
As Chauceir wrait of Troilus
How that he luiffit Cressida,
Of Jason and of Medea.
With help of Cleo I intend,
Provided that Sa Minerve wald me sapience send,
Ane nobill Squyer to discryfe,
Quhais douchtines during his lyfe
I knaw myself: thairof I wryte,
And all his deidis I dar indyte;
And secreitis that I did not knaw
That nobill Squyer did me schaw.
Sa I intend the best I can
Descryve the deidis and the man,
Quhais youth did occupie in lufe
Full plesantlie without reprufe;
Quhilk did as monie douchtie deidis
As monie ane that men of reidis
Quhilkis poetis puttis in memorie
For the exalting of thair glorie.
Quhairfoir I think, sa God me saif,
rest He suld have place amangis the laif,
fall into obscurity That his hie honour suld not smure,
Considering quhat he did indure
Oft-times for his ladeis sake.
know I wait Sir Lancelote du Lake,
Quhen he did lufe King Arthuris wyfe,
Faucht never better with sword nor knyfe
For his ladie in no battell,
Nor had not half so just querrell.
The veritie quha list declair,
His lufe was ane adulterair,
And durst not cum into hir sicht
owl Bot lyke ane houlet on the nicht.
With this Squyer it stude not so:
His ladie luifit him and no mo;
Husband nor lemman had scho none,
And so he had hir lufe alone.
I think it is no happie lyfe,
seduce Ane man to jaip his maisteris wyfe,
As did Lancelote: this I conclude,
Of sic amour culd cum na gude.

26 Chaucer tells the story of Jason and Medea in the *Legend of Good Women*.

27 **Cleo**: Clio is the Muse of history, appropriate to Lindsay's claim for the historical authenticity of his narrative.

53–64 Lindsay reproves Lancelot's adultery all the more energetically because he knows that his own hero's love-life needs tactful handling. Meldrum did not marry his lady, because she was too close in kinship, and their clandestine 'marriage', affirmed by exchange of vows and rings, remained unofficial.

{After early adventures in Ireland (1513), Meldrum goes off to Picardy, where he joins the Scottish army fighting on the side of the French, and engages in single combat, lovingly and expertly described, with the English champion Talbart at Montreuil. The war over, he makes ready to return to Scotland.}

The sea-fight

	And quhen the schip was reddie maid,
ship-road (anchorage)	He lay bot ane day in the raid
Until	Quhill he gat wind of the south-eist.
	Than thay thair ankeris weyit on haist
	And syne maid saill, and fordwart past
	Ane day at morne; till at the last
	Of ane greit saill thay gat ane sicht,
showed	And Phoebus schew his bemis bricht
In	Into the morning richt airlie.
	Than past the skipper richt spedelie
topcastle (platform at mast-head)	Up to the top with richt greit feir
war	And saw it wes ane man-of-weir,
	And cryit, 'I see nocht ellis, perdie,
must either fight	Bot we mon outher fecht or fle!'
	The Squyer wes in his bed lyand
	Quhen he hard tell this new tydand.
artillery	Be this the Inglis artailye
attack	Lyke hailschot maid on thame assailye
tore	And sloppit throw thair fechting saillis
(see n.)	And divers dang out ouir the waillis.
	The Scottis agane, with all thair micht
	Of gunnis, than thay leit fle ane flicht,
	That thay micht weill see quhair they wair;
	Heidis and armes flew in the air.
low	The Scottis schip scho wes sa law
discharged	That monie gunnis out ouir hir flaw,
	Quhilk far beyond thame lichtit doun.
	Bot the Inglis greit galyeoun
Before against	Fornent thame stude lyke ane strang castell,
	That the Scottis gunnis micht na way faill
hit	Bot hat hir ay on the richt syde
breach	With monie ane slop, for all hir pryde,
buffeted	That monie ane beft wer on thair bakkis.
rose, smoke	Than rais the reik, with uglie crakkis
sea	Quhilk on the sey maid sic ane sound
	That in the air it did redound,
	That men micht weill wit on the land
	That shippis wer on the sey fechtand.
pilot	Be this the gyder straik the shippis
grappling-irons	And ather on uther laid thair clippis;
	And than began the strang battell.
adversary	Ilk man his marrow did assaill:

723 **fechting saillis**: the reduced sails of a ship going into action.
724 'And blew several men over the gunwales [stout timbers forming the sides around the deck]'.
729–37 This is the familiar explanation of the success of Drake's ships against the galleons of the Spanish armada in 1588. Much in this magnificent description of the sea-battle has an archetypal familiarity, perhaps from Hollywood films; Meldrum bears more than a passing resemblance to Douglas Fairbanks.
743 **straik**: caused to lose forward impetus by lowering the sails.

Sa rudelie thay did rushe togidder
That nane micht hald thair feit for slidder; [*slipperiness*]
Sum with halbert and sum with speir,
Bot hakbuttis did the greitest deir. [*(kind of gun), damage*]
Out of the top the grundin dartis [*sharp-ground*]
Did divers peirs out-throw the hartis. [*pierce*]
Everie man did his diligence
Upon his fo to wirk vengence,
Ruschand on uther routtis rude [*violent blows*]
That ouir the waillis ran the blude.
  The Inglis Capitane cryit hie,
'Swyith yeild yow, doggis, or ye sall die! [*Quickly*]
And do ye not, I mak ane vow
That Scotland sal be quyte of yow.'
Than pairtlie answerit the Squyar, [*boldly*]
And said, 'O tratour tavernar, [*innkeeper (insultingly)*]
I lat the wit thow hes na micht
This day to put us to the flicht!'
Thay derflie ay at uther dang: [*violently, struck*]
The Squyer thristit throw the thrang
And in the Inglis schip he lap [*leapt*]
And hat the Capitane sic ane flap [*hit, blow*]
Upon his heid till he fell doun,
Welterand intill ane deidlie swoun. [*Staggering around*]
  And quhen the Scottis saw the Squyer
Had strikkin doun that rank rever [*proud pirate*]
They left thair awin schip standand waist [*empty*]
And in the Inglis schip in haist
They followit all thair capitane,
And sone wes all the Sutheroun slane.
Howbeit thay wer of greiter number,
The Scottismen put thame in sic cummere [*distress*]
That thay wer fane to leif the feild,
Cryand 'Mercie!' than did thame yeild.
  Yit wes the Squyer straikand fast
At the Capitane; till at the last,
Quhen he persavit no remeid,
Outher to yeild or to be deid,
He said, 'O gentill capitane,
Thoill me not for to be slane! [*Allow*]
My lyfe to yow sal be mair pryse
Nor sall my deith, ane thowsand syse; [*Than, times*]
For ye may get, as I suppois,
Thrie thowsand nobillis of the Rois [*(coins stamped with a rose)*]
Of me and of my companie:
Thairfoir I cry yow loud mercie.
Except my lyfe, nothing I craif:
Tak yow the schip and all the laif. [*rest*]
I yeild to yow baith sword and knyfe:
Thairfoir, gude maister, save my lyfe!'

776 **the Sutheroun**: 'the Southerners', an insulting way of talking about the English.

The Squyer tuik him be the hand
made — And on his feit he gart him stand
And treittit him richt tenderly.
And syne unto his men did cry
strict — And gaif to thame richt strait command
To straik no moir, bot hald thair hand.
separated the combatants — Than baith the capitanes ran and red,
And so thair wes na mair blude shed.

{Back in Scotland, Meldrum finds himself staying in the castle of a rich widow, with whom he falls desperately in love.}

The wooing of the lady of Gleneagles

This Ladie ludgit neirhand by
heard — And hard the Squyer prively
With dreidfull hart makand his mone,
full of care, (sighing) yawn — With monie cairfull gant and grone.
pity — Hir hart fulfillit with pietie,
Thocht scho wald haif of him mercie,
And said, 'Howbeit I suld be slane,
He sall have lufe for lufe agane.
Wald God I micht with my honour
Have him to be my paramour!'
This wes the mirrie tyme of May
Quhen this fair Ladie, freshe and gay,
Start up to tak the hailsum air,
slippers — With pantonis on hir feit ane pair,
Airlie into ane cleir morning
Befoir fair Phoebus uprysing,
Kirtill alone, withouttin clok,
unlocked — And saw the Squyeris dure unlok.
Scho slippit in or ever he wist
chest — And fenyeitlie past till ane kist
And with her keyis oppinnit the lokkis
made as if — And maid hir to take furth ane boxe:
Bot that was not hir erand thair!
With that this lustie young Squyar
Saw this Ladie so plesantlie
Cum to his chalmer quyetlie,
damask — In kyrtill of fyne damais broun,
Hir goldin traissis hingand doun.
Hir pappis wer hard, round and quhyte,
Quhome to behald wes greit delyte;
skin — Lyke the quhyte lillie wes hir lyre,
Hir hair was like the reid gold wyre;
hose — Hir schankis quhyte withouttin hois,
Quhairat the Squyer did rejois;
And said than, 'Now *vailye quod vailye*,
sally — Upon the Ladie thow mak ane sailye!'

935 The scene is reminiscent of the lady's morning visits in *Gawain and the Green Knight*.

951 ***vailye quod vailye***: 'come what may' (Fr. *vaille que vaille*).

elegant Hir courlyke kirtill was unlaist
embraced And sone into his armis hir braist,
And said to hir, 'Madame, gude morne:
Help me, your man that is forlorne!
Without ye mak me sum remeid,
Withouttin dout I am bot deid;
must Quhairfoir ye mon releif my harmes.'
took With that he hint hir in his armes
And talkit with hir on the flure;
Syne quyetlie did bar the dure.
'Squyer,' quod scho, 'quhat is your will?
Think ye my womanheid to spill?
Na, God forbid, it wer greit syn.
My lord and ye wes neir of kyn:
Quhairfoir I mak yow supplicatioun,
Go forth Pas and seik ane dispensatioun;
Than sall I wed yow with ane ring,
live Than may ye leif at your lyking.
For ye ar young, lustie and fair,
also, heir And als ye ar your fatheris air.
Thair is na ladie in all this land
May yow refuse to hir husband.
And gif ye lufe me as ye say,
obtain a dispensation Haist to dispens the best ye may;
And thairto yow I geve my hand –
I sall yow take to my husband.'
Quod he, 'Quhill that I may indure
I vow to be your serviture,
Bot I think greit vexatioun
To tarie upon dispensatioun.'
Than in his armis he did hir thrist
And aither uther sweitlie kist
belly And wame for wame thay uther braissit;
With that hir kirtill wes unlaissit.
Than Cupido with his fyrie dartis
Inflammit sa thir luiferis hartis
Thay micht na maner of way dissever
Nor ane micht not part fra ane uther,
Bot like woodbind thay wer baith wrappit.
deposited Thair tenderlie he hes hir happit
Full softlie up intill his bed:
Judge ye gif he hir schankis shed!
'Allace,' quod scho, 'quhat may this mene?'
covered, eyes And with hir hair scho dicht hir ene.
I cannot tell how thay did play,
Bot I beleve scho said not nay.
heard say He pleisit hir sa, as I hard sane,

968 **ane dispensatioun**, from the church, available for ready cash, that would allow them to marry even though within the proscribed degrees of consanguinity.
991 **like woodbind**. Cf. *TC* III.1231.
994 **hir schankis shed**: 'parted her legs', a familiar euphemistic expression.
999 **as I hard sane**. The familiar phrase has a special ring to it, since Lindsay was indeed listening to what his old friend told him. No doubt they took particular pleasure in these reminiscences of youthful ardours.

That he was welcum ay agane.
Scho rais and tendirlie him kist
And on his hand ane ring scho thrist,
love-token And he gaif hir ane lufe-drowrie,
Ane ring set with ane riche rubie,
In takin that thair lufe for ever
these two Suld never frome thir twa dissever.
And than scho passit unto hir chalmer
amber And fand hir madinnis, sweit as lammer,
Sleipand full sound; and nothing wist
How that thair Ladie past to the kist.
Quod thay, 'Madame, quhair have ye bene?'
Quod scho, 'Into my gardine grene
To heir thir mirrie birdis sang.
I lat yow wit, I thocht not lang
Though Thocht I had taryit thair quhill none.'
Quod thay, 'Quhair wes your hois and schone?
Quhy yeid ye with your bellie bair?'
Quod scho, 'The morning wes sa fair:
(i.e. Judas) For be him that deir Jesus sauld
I felt na wayis ony maner of cauld.'
sweat Quod thay, 'Madame, me think ye sweit.'
Quod scho, 'Ye see I sufferit heit;
flow abundantly The dew did sa on flouris fleit
That baith my lymmis ar maid weit.
Thairfoir ane quhyle I will heir ly,
sweet Till this dulce dew be fra me dry.
go make Ryse and gar mak our denner reddie.'
'That sal be done,' quod thay, 'my Ladie.'
Efter that scho had tane hir rest
Scho rais and in hir chalmer hir drest
mass And efter mes to denner went.
Than wes the Squyer diligent
sundry To declair monie sindrie storie
Worthie to put in memorie.

{*The rest of the poem recounts his defence of her lands against the highland raider Macfarlane, and the treacherous ambush laid for him by Stirling, whose men hack at his legs from behind ('Yit quhen his schankis wer schorne in sunder, / Upon his kneis he wrocht greit wounder', 1349–50). Fearfully wounded, he parts heart-rendingly from his lady, to whom he remains forever faithful, and, having learnt so much about medicine during his convalescence, becomes himself a renowned surgeon, as well as under-sheriff of Fife. An elaborate poetic* Testament *is appended.*}

George Cavendish (*c.* 1499–*c.* 1562)

Cardinal Wolsey, in his pomp when Skelton attacked him in 1521–2, could never overcome the hostility of Anne Boleyn, who persuaded the king, much against his inclinations, it appears (for he had always found Wolsey loyal and useful), to put him out of office in 1529. He retired to York, where he was archbishop, but was summoned back to London to stand trial and died on the way at Leicester Abbey on 29 November 1530. George Cavendish was his gentleman-usher and closest servant, but his *Life* is not a work of devotion: it bears the marks of an attempt to shape the narrative to show the inevitable fall of a great prince of church and state through worldly living and proud ostentation, but the richness of the detail, the packing of the narrative with known circumstance, the supple, sinewy, economical and forceful prose, make it alive always to the complex political realities of Wolsey's career. Cavendish did another version of Wolsey's life, very brief, in his *Metrical Visions*, a fall-of-princes poem in the style of Lydgate, full of windy rhetoric. Wolsey is the first to appear, and the only churchman; the rest are queens, lords, hangers-on and other casualties of the reigns of Henry VIII and Edward VI. In literary terms, the poem and the prose biography together are an epitome of the time: the embarrassment of English verse – empty, clichéd, pompous, monotonous, unmusical – before high themes, against the crisp, direct, unforced ease of English prose. Both works were written 1554–8, and survive in Cavendish's autograph, BL MS Egerton 2402 (for the extracts below, see fols 85v–87r, 99r–100r).

The Life and Death of Cardinal Wolsey

Ed. R.S. Sylvester, EETS, OS 243 (1959); modernized version by R.S. Sylvester and D.P. Harding (New Haven, 1962); studies by R.S. Sylvester, *SP* 57 (1960), 44–71; Anderson (1984), pp. 27–39.

Wolsey's last journey

{Wolsey has been summoned back to London. His host at Sheffield castle, the venerable earl of Shrewsbury, tries to persuade him that the king means him well.}

'Wherfore I wold advyse you to pluke uppe your hart and be not agast of your ennemyes, who I assure you have you in more dout[1] than ye wold thynke, perceyvyng that the kyng is fully mynded to have the heryng of your case byfore his owen person. Nowe, sir, if ye can be of good chere I dout not but this journey whiche ye shall take towardes his highnes shal be myche to your avauncement and an overthrowe of your ennemyes. The kyng hath sent for you by that worshypfull knyght, master Kyngeston, and with hym four and twenti of your old servauntes, whiche be nowe of the gard to defend you ayenst your onknowen ennemyes, to th'entent that ye may savely come unto his majestie.'

'Sir,' quod my lord, 'as I suppose, master Kyngeston is Constable of the Tower?'

'Yea, what of that?' quod th'erle. 'I assure you he is oonly appoynted by the kyng for[2] oon of your frendes and for a discrett gentilman as most worthy to take uppon hym the save-conduct of your person, for without faylle the kyng favoreth you myche more and beryth towardes you a specyall secrett favor ferre otherwyse than ye do take it.'

'Well, sir,' quod my lord, 'as God wyll, so be it. I am subject to fortune, and to fortune I commytt myself, beyng a trewe man redy to accepte suche ordynance as God hath provydyd for me, and ther an end. Sir, I pray you, where is master Kyngeston?'

'Mary,' quod th'erle, 'if ye wyll, I woll send for hym, who wold most gladly se you.'

'I pray you than,' quod he, 'send for hym.'

At whos message he came incontynent[3] and as sone as my lord espied hym commyng into the gallery he made hast to encounter hym. Master Kyngeston came towardes hym with myche reverence; at his approche he kneled down and saluted hym on the kynges behalf; whom my lord, bare-heded, offred to take uppe, but he still kneled. Than quod my lord, 'Master Kyngeston, I pray you stand uppe and leve your knelyng unto a very wretche replett with mysery, not worthy to be estemed but for a vile abjecte[4]

1 fear
2 as being
3 without delay
4 degraded person

uttirly cast away without desert.[5] And therfore, good master Kyngeston, stand uppe, or I woll myself knele down by you.'[6]

With that master Kyngeston stod uppe, sayeng with humble reverence, 'Sir, the kynges majestie hath hym commendyd unto you.'

'I thanke his hyghnes,' quod my lord, 'I trust he be in helthe and mery, the whiche I beseche God long contynewe.'

'Yea, without dout,' quod master Kyngeston. 'And sir, he hath commaundyd me first to sey unto you that you shold assure yourself that he beryth you as myche good wyll and favour as ever he dyd, and wyllyth you to be of good chere. And where report hath byn made unto hym that ye shold commytt ayenst his royall majestie certyn haynous crymes, whiche he thynkyth to be untrewe, yet for the mynystracion of justice in suche casis requysit and to avoyd all suspecte parcyallytie, can do no lesse at the least than to send for you to your triall, mystrustyng nothyng your trowthe and wysdome but that ye shal be able to acquyt yourself ayenst all complayntes and accusacions exibyted ayenst you; and to take your journey towardes hym at your owen pleasure, commaundyng me to be attendaunt uppon you with mynestracion of dewe reverence, and to se your person preserved from all dammage and inconvenyences that myght ensewe, and to elect all suche your old servauntes (nowe his)[7] to serve you by the way, who hath most experyence of your diett.[8] Therfore, sir, I beseche your grace to be of good chere, and whan it shall be your good pleasure to take your journey I shall geve myn attendaunce.'

'Master Kyngeston,' quod my lord, 'I thanke you for your good newes. And sir, herof assure yourself that if I ware as able and lustie as I have byn but of late I wold not fayle to ride with you in post.[9] But sir, I am disseased with a fluxe that makyth me very weke. But master Kyngeston, all thes confortable wordes whiche ye have spoken be but for a purpose to bryng me in a fooles paradice. I knowe what is provydid for me.[10] Notwithstandyng, I thanke you for your good will and paynes taken about me, and I shall with all spede make me redy to ride with you tomorowe.'

And thus they fill into other commynycacion, bothe th'erle and master Kyngeston, with my lord, who commaundyd me to forse[11] and provyde that all thynges myght be made redy to departe the morowe after.

I caused all thynges to be thrust uppe[12] and made in redynes as fast as they could convenyently. Whan nyght came that we shold goo to bed, my lord waxed very syke thoroughe his newe desease, the whiche caused hym contynually from tyme to tyme to goo to the stolle all that nyght, insomyche from the tyme that his desease toke hym unto the next day he had above five and fifti stoolles, so that he was that day very weke. The matter that he avoyded[13] was wonderous blake, the whiche phisicions call *colour adustum*.[14] And whan he perceyved it, he sayd unto me, 'If I have not,' quod he, 'some helpe shortly yt will cost me my lyfe.' With that I caused oon doctor Nicholas, a phisicion beyng with th'erle, to loke uppon the grosse matter that he avoyded, uppon sight wherof he determyned howe he shold not lyve past four or fyve dayes.

Yet notwithstandyng, he wold have ridden with master Kyngeston that same day if th'erle of Shrewsbury had not byn.[15] Therfore in consideracion of hys infirmyte they caused hym to tary all that day. And the next day he toke his journey with master Kyngeston and the gard. And as sone as they espied ther old master in suche a lamentable estate, lamented hym with wepyng eyes, whom my lord toke by the handes and dyvers tymes by the way as he rode he wold talke with them, sometyme with oon and sometyme with another. At nyght he was lodged at an howse of th'erle of Shrewsburys called Hardwyke Hall,[16] very evyll at ease. The next day he rode to Nothyngham, and ther lodged that nyght more sykker. And the next day we rode to Leycester Abbey and by the way he waxed so sykke that he was dyvers tyme lykly to have fallen from his mewle.

5 without deserving

6 **I woll myself knele down.** We watch the struggle within Wolsey, as the habits of testy authority give way to the ironic recognition of the new realities and the extravagant display of the courtesies perceived to be required of the newly wise and penitent self.

7 **(nowe his).** In the midst of Kingston's courtesies, this is a cruel reminder.

8 daily regime

9 at the fastest pace

10 Wolsey believed that he was destined for the Tower. He was right.

11 plan ahead (foresee)

12 packed up (trussed up)

13 excreted

14 ***colour adustum***, usually 'choler adust', a 'melancholic' disease.

15 been there to intervene

16 Hardwick Hall, near Nottingham (not the more famous house in Derbyshire).

And beyng nyght or we came to the abbey aforeseyd, where at his commyng in at the gates the abbott of the place with all his covent mett hym with the light of many torches, whom they right honorably receyved with great reverence. To whom my lord sayd, 'Father abbott, I am come hether to leave my bones among you.' Whom they brought on his mewle to the stayers foote of his chamber, and there lighted. And master Kyngeston than toke hym by the arme and led hym uppe the stayers (who told me afterward that he never caried so hevy a burden in all his lyfe). And as sone as he was in his chamber he went incontynent[17] to his bedd very sykke.

This was uppon Satorday at nyght, and there he contynued sykker and sykker. Uppon Monday in the mornynge, as I stode by his beddes side about eight of the clocke, the wyndowes beyng cloose shett, havyng waxe lightes burnyng uppon the cupbord, I behyld hym, as me semed, drawyng fast to hys end. He perceyved my shadowe uppon the wall by his beddes side. Asked who was there, 'Sir, I am here,' quod I. 'Howe do you?' quod he to me. 'Very well, sir, if I myght se your grace well.' 'What is it of the clocke?' quod he to me. 'Forsothe, sir,' quod I, 'it is past eight of the clocke in the mornyng.' 'Eight of the clocke?' quod he, 'that cannot be' (rehersyng dyvers tyme, 'Eight of the clocke? Eight of the clocke?'). 'Nay, nay,' quod he at the last, 'it cannot be eight of the clocke, for by eight of the clocke ye shall loose your master, for my tyme drawyth nere that I must depart owt of this world.'[18]

Metrical Visions

Ed. A.S.G. Edwards (Columbia, SC, 1980).

The Complaint of Cardinal Wolsey

{Wolsey speaks in the first person and gives a moralized account of the splendours and miseries of his life, ending with his death at Leicester (85–217).}

'Lo, nowe may you se what it is to trust
become nothing In worldly vanytes that voydyth with the wynd,
For deathe in a moment consumyth all to dust.
No honor, no glory that ever man cowld fynd
But Tyme with hys tyme puttyth all owt of mynd;
obscures For Tyme in breafe tyme duskyth the hystory
Of them that long tyme lyved in glory.

'Where is my tombe that I made for the nones,
Wrought of fyne copper that cost many a pound
To couche in my carion and my rotten bones?
All is but vaynglory, nowe have I found,
And small to the purpose whan I am in the ground.
What doth it avaylle me, all that I have,
Seyng I am deade and layed in my grave?

'Farewell Hampton Court, whos founder I was!
(York Place) Farewell Westmynster Place, nowe a palace royall;
Farewell the Moore, lett Tynnynainger passe;
Farewell in Oxford my Colege Cardynall;

17 immediately

18 Wolsey died the next day, Tuesday 29 November 1530, though not before uttering, or being said to have uttered, some famous 'last words': 'If I had served God as dyligently as I have don the kyng, he wold not have gevyn me over in my gray heares'.

Metrical Visions

234 Moor Park, in Hertfordshire, and Tyttenhanger, nearby. The rhetoric of 'Farewell', as of 'Where are...' (*ubi sunt*) and 'What avayllyth...', is part of the traditional apparatus of *De casibus* complaint.

Farewell in Ipsewiche my scole grammaticall.
Yet ones farewell I say, I shall you never se:
Your somptious byldyng what nowe avaylleth me?

'What avayllyth my great aboundaunce?
What is nowe laft to helpe me in thys case?
Nothyng at all, but dompe in the daunce
Among deade men to tryppe on the trace. *dance according to the dance-steps*
And for my gay howsis nowe have I this place
To lay in my karcas wrapt in a shete,
Knytt with a knott att my hed and my feete.

'What avayllyth nowe my fether-beddes soft,
Shetes of Raynes, long, large and wyde, *Rennes (in France)*
And dyvers devysis of clothes chaynged oft?
Or vicious chapleyns walkyng by my syde,
Voyde of all vertue, fulfilled with pryde, *full of pride*
Whiche hath caused me by report of suche fame
For ther myslyvyng to have an yll name?

'This is my last complaynt, I can say you no moore,
But farewell, my servaunt, that faythefull hath be. *(i.e. Cavendish)*
Note well thes wordes,' quod he, 'I pray the therfore,
And wright them thus playn as I have told them the –
All whiche is trewe, thou knowest it well, parde!
Thou fayllededst me not untill that I dyed.
And nowe I must depart: I may no lenger byde.'

235 Cardinal College, founded 1524, passed to the king in 1531 and was renamed Christ Church in 1547.

241 **dompe**: 'dismayed, in the dumps'. **in the daunce**. Cavendish draws on the familiar imagery of the dance of death (as in Lydgate's *Dance Macabre*).

246–52 This stanza is lifted almost verbatim from Lydgate, *Fall of Princes* III.3760–6.

Sir Thomas Wyatt (1503–1542)

Thomas Wyatt was born in the family home at Allington Castle in Kent in 1503, son of a faithful and well-rewarded court-servant of Henry VII. He went up to Cambridge in 1517 and married in 1520, thereafter distinguishing himself at court both in tournament and in diplomatic work. He was Marshal of Calais 1528–32, and officiated as Chief Ewer at the coronation of Anne Boleyn after her marriage to Henry VIII in 1533. It is fairly certain that Wyatt had had an affair with Anne Boleyn before this, but the king, if he knew, seems not to have held it against him, and Wyatt's brief imprisonment in the Tower in 1536 (where he may have seen the execution of queen Anne) was for other reasons. He returned to favour immediately, was loaded with honours and offices, and was made ambassador to Spain in 1537. Returning to England in 1539, he witnessed the execution in 1540 of Thomas Cromwell, his friend and patron, who had been Henry's chief minister since 1533 and had superintended his divorce from Katharine of Aragon and the passing of the Act of Supremacy (1534). Soon afterwards, at the instigation of an old enemy, Edmund Bonner, bishop of London, Wyatt was again arrested, on a range of charges, and all his goods confiscated, but he defended himself eloquently and was soon released. He was restored to favour and office, and was a vice-admiral of the royal fleet when he caught a fever and died in 1542. His son, Sir Thomas Wyatt the Younger, was executed for conspiring against queen Mary in 1554.

Wyatt introduced Petrarch and the Petrarchan sonnet into English (though Chaucer knew Petrarch's poetry and had translated one of the sonnets in *TC* I.400–20), wrote satires, psalm-paraphrases and some epigrams and short poems about court-life, but he is most famous for his love-lyrics. These poems, with their monotone plangency of theme and cadence, can be fully understood only if we have in mind how many of them were set to music and if the social assemblies in which they had their first real or imagined existence are re-created in our historical imagination: the darkening candle-lit panelled palace-chamber, 'with many ladies present. The whole scene comes before us. The poet did not write for those who would sit down to *The Poetical Works of Wyatt*. We are having a little music after supper' (Lewis [1954], p. 230; see J. Stevens, *Music and Poetry in the Early Tudor Court* [London, 1961]). The songs get their charge from the imagined occasion: the covert allusions, the sly glances, debates, intrigues, spiteful bantering, the games of love that might turn suddenly dangerous, especially with someone like Henry VIII around. The game is given cultural pre-eminence in the central game of life: all kinds of power-struggles, rivalries and jealousies are metaphorized through its rituals. They are love-poems, little dramas from the game of love, seeking a public form for private feeling, but they are also poems in which love is a figure for talking about the self, newly vulnerable in this volatile court-society, about ambition, pride, the anxiety of integrity, temptation, the necessity of play-acting. Most of the poems are complaints of love disdained, neglected, deceived or betrayed, in which Wyatt develops his individual voice – manly, bravely defiant, honest, plain-speaking, bewildered by deceit, painfully inducted into unforeseen subtleties of suffering. He pays little attention to the woman, almost never describes her, almost never writes of happiness in love: his poetic eye is all on himself in pain, and on himself writing poems about himself.

Wyatt's songs and sonnets were many of them printed in Tottel's influential collection of *Songs and Sonnets* (1557), but they are chiefly found in manuscript in early Tudor song-books and poetical miscellanies, the latter including BL MS Egerton 2711, Wyatt's own manuscript, with some texts and corrections in his own hand, and the Devonshire MS (BL MS Add.17492), a court-album of the 1530s. The poems use a wide variety of stanza-forms, most of them long established in popular and courtly song-lyric, and owe a deep debt to the medieval traditions of love-complaint: in fact, several of the poems in the Devonshire MS consist of cannibalized extracts from the love-poems of Chaucer, Hoccleve and others. But Wyatt, unlike Skelton, has no hesitation in rejecting the old aureate Lydgatian 'literary' style and diction in favour of simpler manner; the courtier-gentleman, confident of the superiority of his cultural status (Wyatt is the first such poet in English who is not a mere dabbler), did not suffer the schizophrenic uneasiness of the learned poet-clerk on the margins of preferment. 'The first reformers of our vulgar Poesie' is what Puttenham calls Wyatt and Surrey in his *Arte of English Poesie* (1589), no doubt conscious of their aristocratic origins, and so they have come to be customarily regarded, with all the neglect that this has reinforced of their medieval inheritance.

But Wyatt, at least, *is* different. In introducing Petrarch into England, he brought to English love-poetry, including his own, a range of powers, resonances and instrumental effects that it had not had since Chaucer; a chamber-music ensemble replaced a fiddle. Metrically, his poetry, especially the sonnets, is full of experimentation with wrenched stress, clashing stress and held stress – often difficult, but evidently with a purpose of conveying strong feeling almost bursting the bonds of conventional expression (cf. Donne) and also with some intention, in imitation of Italian, of trying to break some of the tyranny of stress in English metre. In other ways, too, Wyatt is an innovator: in comparison with Charles of Orleans, for instance, he has the character of a 'real' person. Some of this is because he is, historically, a more real person: more is known about him. But it is also because he is more sophisticated, ingenious and aggressive in creating himself, inventing himself, as a poetic persona. Charles's poetic persona is a painted picture, conventionally coloured, in two dimensions; Wyatt's is a bold sculpted relief, surprising, individual, dramatic. It is not that Wyatt, as a person, was like that: the differences between Charles and Wyatt are not, primarily, differences in their historical nature as people, but in the different uses, within the historical circumstances in which they found themselves, to which they put poetry. Wyatt, at the centre of his historical stage, chiselled out a poetic persona against the grain, under stress, through his knottily personal and idiosyncratic structures of narrative and argumentation; Charles was, by comparison, a marginal figure.

Wyatt's special claim is that he gives a distinctive voice to the lover's conventional complaint, creating a voice that we come to recognize, and inducing us to read a poem as if it were a record of experiences we might have had. The 'I' of the poem comes to invite us, not just to interpret or understand, to match or remember or compare, but to re-experience the experience of the poem – and since the poems are so short, we can do this over and over again. There is a real sense of involvement in the drama. At the same time we know that these poems are fictions, and recognize and enjoy the rhetoric by which we are tempted to forget that; and we know, too, if we think about it, that we are participating with a monomaniac in an exercise in which the existence of the second person is posited, grammatically, so to speak, but not allowed. We are co-fanatics.

Poems 1–19 and 31–2 are from the Egerton MS, 20–7 from the Devonshire MS, 28 from the Arundel Castle MS and 29–30 from Tottel's *Songs and Sonnets*. *Collected Poems*, ed. K. Muir and P. Thomson (Liverpool, 1969); ed. R.A. Rebholz (New Haven, 1981); *Life and Letters*, ed. K. Muir (Liverpool, 1963); see P. Thomson, *Sir Thomas Wyatt and his Background* (Stanford, 1964); also Greenblatt, 'Power, Sexuality, and Inwardness in Wyatt's Poetry', in Greenblatt (1980), pp. 115–56; Spearing (1985), pp. 278–310.

I

In his sonnets, Wyatt follows the Petrarchan rhyme-scheme in the octave (*abba abba*) but varies the sestet (usually *cddcee*) with the effect of creating a final couplet, as in rhyme royal, and thus preparing the way for the 'Shakespearian' sonnet. 'The longe love' is based on Petrarch's Sonnet 107, given below, which was also translated by Surrey (see below). The conceit is of the poet blushing and then, because his lady is displeased at this open display of love, growing pale. Love, in this characteristically Petrarchan allegorical narrative of the inner self, is thought of as the poet's master. For a detailed study of this sonnet, see M. Holahan, in *ELR* 23 (1993), 46–80.

The longe love, that in my thought doeth harbar
  And in myn hert doeth kepe his residence,
  Into my face preseth with bolde pretence
And therin campeth, spreding his baner.
teaches She that me lerneth to love and suffre,
  And willes that my trust and lustes negligence
modesty Be rayned by reason, shame and reverence,
With his hardines taketh displeasur;
Wherewithall unto the hertes forrest he fleith,
  Leving his entreprise with payn and cry,
And ther him hideth and not appereth.
What may I do when my maister fereth

9 **forrest**. The idea of the forest of the heart, with its suggestion of a hunt as well as a military campaign, is Wyatt's addition.

Amor, che nel penser mio vive e regna
e 'l suo seggio maggior nel mio cor tene,
talor armato ne la fronte vene;
ivi si loca et ivi pon sua insegna.
Quella ch'amare e sofferir ne 'nsegna,
e vol che 'l gran desio, l'accesa spene,
ragion, vergogna e reverenza affrene,
di nostro ardir fra se stessa si sdegna.
Onde Amor paventoso fugge al core,
lasciando ogni sua impresa, e piange e trema;
ivi s'asconde e non appar piu fore.
Che poss'io far, temendo il mio signore,
se non star seco infin a l'ora estrema?
che bel fin fa chi ben amando more.

But in the feld with him to lyve and dye?
For goode is the lif, ending faithfully.

2

Based on Petrarch's Sonnet 155. According to legend, *Noli me tangere* ['Do not touch me', imitating Christ's words to Mary Magdalen in the garden after the resurrection, John 20:17] *quia Caesaris sum* was said to be inscribed on the collar of one of Caesar's hinds, found in the forest many years after his death. Wyatt uses Petrarch's allegory of Laura to allude, strikingly, to Anne Boleyn, who attracted the king's attention as early as 1526.

wishes Who-so list to hunt, I knowe where is an hynde,
But as for me, helas, I may no more –
The vayne travaill hath weried me so sore;
I ame of theim that farthest commeth behinde.
Yet may I by no meanes my weried mynde
Drawe from the diere, but as she fleeth afore
leave off Fayntyng I folowe. I leve of therefore,
Sins in a nett I seke to hold the wynde.
Who list her hunt, I put him owte of dowbte,
As well as I may spend his tyme in vain:
And graven with diamonds in letters plain
There is written her fair neck rounde abowte,
'*Noli me tangere*, for Cesars I ame,
And wylde for to hold, though I seme tame.'

3

Farewell, Love, and all thy lawes for ever:
Thy bayted hookes shall tangill me no more.
Senec and Plato call me from thy lore
well-being To perfaict welth my wit for to endever.
In blynde error when I did persever,
Thy sherpe repulse that pricketh ay so sore
Hath taught me to sett in tryfels no store
dearer And scape forth, syns libertie is lever.
Therefore farewell: goo trouble yonger hertes
And in me clayme no more authorite;
special power With idill youth goo use thy propertie
fragile And theron spend thy many brittil dertes;
For hetherto though I have lost all my tyme,
I wish Me lusteth no lenger rotten boughes to clymbe.

4

Based on Petrarch, Sonnet 154. The lover strives to escape the memory of his beloved but is thwarted at every turn by Love, his master.

full laden My galy charged with forgetfulnes
Thorough sharpe sees in wynter nyghtes doeth pas
Twene rock and rock, and eke myn enemy, alas,

That is my lorde, sterith with cruelnes,
(see n.) And every owre a thought in redines,
an unimportant matter As tho that deth were light in suche a case;
An endles wynd doeth tere the sayll apase
fear to trust Of forced sighes and trusty ferefulnes.
A rayn of teris, a clowde of derk disdain,
Hath done the weried cordes great hinderaunce,
Entangled Wrethed with errour and eke with ignoraunce.
The starres be hid that led me to this pain;
Drowned is reason that should me confort,
And I remain dispering of the port.

5

Freely adapted from an Italian madrigal by Dragonetto Bonifacio (*c.* 1535). In the MS, this poem is followed by the lady's reply, in another hand, not by Wyatt, an example of the social context in which these poems 'lived'. The lady says that any man who can be called with a 'beck' cannot be very serious about love. For women 'answering back' in the Devonshire MS, see E. Heale, in *MLR* 90 (1995), 296–313.

Madame, withouten many wordes
One day, (say yes) Ons, I am sure, ye will or no;
jests And if ye will, then leve your bordes
And use your wit and shew it so,

nod And with a beck ye shall me call;
And if of oon that burneth alwaye
Ye have any pitie at all,
Aunswer him faire with yea or nay.

Yf it be yea, I shal be fayne;
If it be nay, frendes as before;
Ye shall anothre man obtain
And I myn owne and yours no more.

6

The woman is imagined as a herd of wild creatures (her 'desires') that may be tamed for a while but will return to their natural ways (this view of women is common in the Middle Ages, e.g. Chaucer, Manciple's Tale, *CT* IX.160–82); the image, with the scene of dalliance in the second stanza, and the possible allusion to Anne Boleyn, gives a powerful erotic charge to the poem.

They fle from me that sometyme did me seke
With naked fote stalking in my chambre.
I have sene theim gentill, tame and meke
That nowe are wyld and do not remembre
in my power That sometyme they put theimself in daunger
To take bred at my hand; and nowe they raunge
Besely seking with a continuell chaunge.

Poem 4

5 'And every (stroke of the) oar a (sad) thought in readiness'.

Thancked be fortune, it hath ben othrewise
Twenty tymes better – but ons in speciall,
thin, in a pleasing way In thyn arraye after a pleasaunt gyse,
When her lose gowne from her shoulders did fall
slender And she me caught in her armes long and small,
Therewithall swetely did me kysse,
And softely saide, 'Dere hert, howe like you this?'

It was no dreme: I lay brode waking.
But all is torned thorough my gentilnes
Into a straunge fasshion of forsaking,
And I have leve to goo of her goodenes,
And she also to use new-fangilnes.
But syns that I so kyndely am served,
I would fain knowe what she hath deserved.

7

A rondeau (see Charles of Orleans, above).

indeed (par dieu) What no, perdy, ye may be sure!
(bait for a trained hawk) Thinck not to make me to your lure
With wordes and chere so contrarieng,
weighing against each other Swete and sowre contrewaing;
To much it were still to endure.
betrayed, use Trouth is trayed where craft is in ure;
care But though ye have had my hertes cure,
Trow ye I dote withoute ending?
What no, perdy!

try Though that with pain I do procure
what For to forgett that ons was pure,
Within my hert shall still that thing,
Unstable, unsure, and wavering,
remedy Be in my mynde withoute recure?
What no, perdy!

8

Lachrymose and 'manfully' honest ('Play who that can that part') in a characteristic vein, this poem unexpectedly explodes in a cascade of rhetorical fireworks in the last stanza, with word-play, repetition and permutation (of the same word through different parts of speech), all of them prescribed figures in the rhetorical arts of poetry. The fireworks include repetitions of the word 'suche' (27, 29, 31), in line 29 altered to 'souche' by a later hand, probably indicating a quibble on the name of Mary Souche, one of Jane Seymour's maids of honour.

Poem 6

15 In the version of Wyatt's poems printed by Tottel in 1557, an attempt was made to smooth and regularize his metre according to more conventional canons of taste. This line, where the omission of unstressed syllables and consequent clash of stress communicates well the shock of realization, is smoothed to 'It was no dreame, for I lay broade awakyng'. Similarly, **straunge**, in the much-admired line 17, with its pained drawing-out of the stress, is smoothed in Tottel to 'bitter'.

20 kyndely: 'naturally', according to the fickle creature's nature; or, ironically, 'kindly'.

Marvaill no more all-tho
  The songes I syng do mone,
For othre lif then wo
  I never proved none. *experienced*
And in my hert also
  Is graven with lettres diepe
A thousand sighes and mo,
  A flod of teres to wepe.

How may a man in smart *sharp pain*
  Fynde mater to rejoyse?
How may a mornyng hert
  Set forth a pleasaunt voise?
Play who that can that part:
  Nedes must in me appere
How fortune overthwart *opposed*
  Doeth cause my mornyng chere.

Perdy, there is no man
  If he never sawe sight
That perfaictly tell can
  The nature of the light.
Alas, how should I then,
  That never tasted but sowre,
But do as I began,
  Continuelly to lowre?

But yet perchaunce som chaunce
  May chaunce to chaunge my tune;
And when suche chaunce doeth chaunce
  Then shall I thanck fortune;
And if I have suche chaunce,
  Perchaunce ere it be long
For suche a pleasaunt chaunce
  To syng som plaisaunt song.

9

The simple formal structure, the simple diction, the perfect control of syntax, give this very characteristic poem its effectiveness. The stanza-form is not used elsewhere by Wyatt.

Tho I cannot your crueltie constrain
For my good will to favor me again,
  Tho my true and faithfull love
  Have no power your hert to move,
Yet rew upon my pain.

Tho I your thrall must evermore remain
And for your sake my libertie restrain,
  The greatest grace that I do crave
  Is that ye would vouchesave
To rew upon my pain.

Tho I have not deserved to obtain
So high reward but thus to serve in vain,
  Tho I shall have no redresse,
  Yet of right ye can no lesse
But rew upon my pain.

But I se well that your high disdain
Wull no wise graunt that I shall more attain;
  Yet ye must graunt at the last
  This my powre and small request:
Rejoyse not at my pain.

10

To wisshe and want and not obtain,
To seke and sew ese of my pain, *sue for relief*
Syns all that ever I do is vain,
  What may it availl me?

All-tho I stryve both dey and howre
Against the streme with all my powre,
If fortune list yet for to lowre,
  What may it availl me?

If willingly I suffre woo,
If from the fyre me list not goo,
If then I burne, to plaine me so *complain*
  What may it availl me?

And if the harme that I suffre
Be runne to farr owte of mesur, *too far*
To seke for helpe any further
  What may it availl me?

What tho eche hert that hereth me plain
Pitieth and plaineth for my payn?
If I no les in greif remain,
  What may it availl me?

Ye, tho the want of my relief
Displease the causer of my greife,
Syns I remain still in myschiefe, *distress*
  What may it availl me?

Suche cruell chaunce doeth so me threte
Continuelly inward to fret,
Then of relese for to trete
  What may it availl me?

Fortune is deif unto my call,
My torment moveth her not at all,

And though she torne as doeth a ball,
  What may it availl me?

For in despere there is no rede; — *wise advice (to be found)*
To want of ere, speche is no spede; — *Where there is no ear, benefit*
To linger still alyve as dede
  What may it availl me?

11

This *ottava rima* stanza was probably written in October 1532, when Wyatt went over to Calais in Anne Boleyn's train, just before her marriage to Henry VIII.

Some-tyme I fled the fyre that me brent,
  By see, by land, by water and by wynd,
And now I folow the coles that be quent — *quenched*
  From Dovor to Calais against my mynde.
Lo how desire is both sprong and spent!
  And he may se that whilom was so blynde, — *once*
And all his labor now he laugh to scorne, — *may laugh*
Mashed in the breers that erst was all to-torne. — *Enmeshed, torn to pieces*

12

This *ottava rima* epigram, with its curious conceit of the lover exploding with desire like a bombard with a cannon-ball stuck in it, is based on a *strambotto* by the Italian Petrarchan poet Serafino Aquilano (1466–1500).

The furyous gonne in his rajing yre,
  When that the bowle is rammed in to sore — *cannon-ball*
And that the flame cannot part from the fire, — *firing (of the ball)*
  Cracketh in sonder and in the ayer doeth rore
The shevered peces. Right so doeth my desire,
  Whose flame encreseth from more to more,
Whych to lett owt I dare not loke nor speke:
So now hard force my hert doeth all to-breke.

13

The variation in the refrain is particularly effective in this savagely (and pettily) vindictive imagining of the disdainful lady herself disdained in her later years.

My lute, awake! perfourme the last
Labor that thou and I shall wast,
  And end that I have now begon;
For when this song is sung and past,
  My lute, be still, for I have done.

Poem 10

31 **as doeth a ball.** The image is of Fortune's wheel, the turning of which, in relation to human life, is perceived, as usual, as both arbitrary and hostile.

As (easily) As to be herd where ere is none,
lead (metal) to engrave As lede to grave in marbill stone,
My song may perse her hert as sone;
Should we then sigh, or sing, or mone?
No, no, my lute, for I have done.

The rokkes do not so cruelly
Repulse the waves continuelly
suit (petition) As she my suyte and affection,
So that I am past remedy:
Whereby my lute and I have done.

Prowd of the spoyll that thou hast got
(Cupid's arrow) Of simple hertes thorough loves shot,
By whom, unkynd, thou hast theim wone,
Thinck not he hath his bow forgot,
All-tho my lute and I have done.

Vengeaunce shall fall on thy disdain,
That makest but game on ernest pain;
Thinck not alone under the sonne
(see n.) Unquyt to cause thy lovers plain,
All-tho my lute and I have done.

you may lie Perchaunce the lye wethered and old,
The wynter nyghtes that are so cold,
Playnyng in vain unto the mone:
Thy wisshes then dare not be told!
pleases Care then who lyst, for I have done.

And then may chaunce the to repent
The tyme that thou hast lost and spent
To cause thy lovers sigh and swoune;
Then shalt thou knowe beaultie but lent,
And wisshe and wante as I have done.

Now cesse, my lute, this is the last
Labour that thou and I shall wast,
And ended is that we begon;
Now is this song both sung and past;
My lute be still, for I have done.

14

The first part of each line, missing from Egerton on account of a torn leaf, is supplied here from Devonshire.

determined *In eternum* I was ons determed
For to have lovid and my minde affermed
That with my herte it shuld be confermed
In eternum.

24 'To cause thy lovers to complain without being paid back'.

Forthwith I founde the thing that I myght like
And sought with love to warme her hert alike,
For, as me thought, I shulde not se the like
In eternum.

(see n.) To trase this daunse I put myself in prese;
Vayne hope ded lede and bad I should not cese
To serve, to suffer and still to hold my pease
In eternum.

progressed rapidly With this furst rule I fordred me apase,
That, as me thought, my trowthe had taken place
With full assurans to stond in her grace
In eternum.

before It was not long or I by proofe had found
That feble bilding is on feble grounde,
For in her herte this worde ded never sounde:
In eternum.

cast *In eternum* then from my herte I kest
That I had furst determined for the best;
Now in the place another thought doeth rest,
In eternum.

15

The echo of the last words of the stanza (a trick derived from Serafino) creates emphasis but also an effect of a mind distracted ('...except my life, my life, my life', *Hamlet* V.ii.218).

complain Hevyn and erth and all that here me plain
Do well perceve what care doeth cause me cry,
Save you alone to whom I cry in vain:
'Mercy, madame, alas, I dy, I dy!'

Yf that you slepe, I humbly you require
slacken Forbere a while and let your rigour slake,
Syns that by you I burne thus in this fire:
To here my plaint, dere hert, awake, awake!

Syns that so oft ye have made me to wake
In plaint and teres and in right pitious case,
Displease you not if force do now me make
To breke your slepe, crieng 'Alas, alas!'

It is the last trouble that ye shall have
Of me, madame, to here my last complaint.

Poem 14

5 **the thing**. One imagines the caustic response to Wyatt's choice of words of the lady who replied to 'Madame, withouten many wordes', above.

5–7 The rhymes – variations on the meaning and function of the same word – are an example of *rime riche*.

9 'To follow the steps of this dance I went out among the throng'.

23 **another thought** might be to give up women altogether, and/or to turn the mind to higher things.

Pitie at lest your poure unhappy slave,
For in dispere, alas, I faint, I faint!

It is not now, but long and long ago
to (the best of) I have you served as to my powre and myght
As faithfully as any man myght do,
Clayming of you nothing of right, of right,

preserve Save of your grace only to stay my lif,
That fleith as fast as clowd afore the wynde;
For syns that first I entred in this stryf
An inward deth hath fret my mynde, my mynd.

Yf I had suffered this to you unware,
Myn were the fawte and you nothing to blame,
But syns you know my woo and all my care
Why do I dy? Alas, for shame, for shame!

I know right well my face, my lowke, my teeres,
Myn iyes, my wordes and eke my driery chiere
Have cryd my deth full oft unto your eres –
Hard Herd of belefe it doeth appere, appere!

A better prouff I se that ye would have
How I am dede; therefore when ye here tell
Beleve it not, all-tho ye se my grave.
Cruell, unkynd! I say farewell, farewell!

16

A neat series of paradoxes, putting the worn oxymorons of heat and cold, life and death, to a fresh para-logical employment in demonstrating the omnipotence of love in defying reason.

To cause accord or to agre
Two contraries in oon degre
And in oon poynct, as semeth me,
To all mans wit it cannot be:
It is impossible.

Of hete and cold when I complain
And say that hete doeth cause my pain,
When cold doeth shake me every vain
And both at ons, I say again
It is impossible.

That man that hath his hert away,
(i.e. in his heart) If lyf lyveth there, as men do say,
one That he hert-les should last on day

Poem 15

20–1 Courtly love-poetry often uses religious language and ideas (e.g. *TC*). Like the Christian praying to God, the lover asks his lady nothing as of right, only her grace, in seeking not to die (eternally). There are many flaws in the analogy, as any lady of Wyatt's acquaintance would have been willing to point out.

Alyve and not to torne to clay,
   It is impossible.

whatever anyone says

Twixt lyf and deth, say what who sayth,
There lyveth no lyf that draweth breth;
They joyne so nere and eke, i'feith,
To seke for lif by wissh of deth
   It is impossible.

closely

Yet love that all thing doeth subdue,
Whose power ther may no lif eschew,
Hath wrought in me that I may rew
These miracles to be so true,
   That are impossible.

17

The unfinished third stanza and obscure last lines suggest this is an early draft.

sue
dismayed

Th'answere that ye made to me, my dere,
   When I did sewe for my poore hartes redresse,
Hath so apalld my countenaunce and my chere
   That yn this case I am all comfortlesse,
   Sins I of blame no cawse can well expresse.

freed (quit)

I have no wrong when I can clayme no right;
   Nowght tane me fro wher I nothing have had:
Yet of my wo I cannot so be quyte,
   Namely, sins that another may be glad
   With that that thus in sorowe maketh me sad.

Another? Why? Shall lyberty be bond?
Fre hart may not be bond but by desert.
...

make claim

Nor none can clayme, I say, by former graunte
   That knowith not of any graunt at all;
And by deserte I dare well make avaunte
   Of faythfull will ther is nowher that shall
   Bere you more trowthe, more redy at your call.

revoke
jest

Now, good, then call agayne that frendly worde
   That sleith your frende in saving of his payne,
And say, my dere, that it was sayde in borde:
   Late or too sone, let that not rule the gayne
   Wherwith free will doth trew deserte retayne.

Poem 17

18–19 The 'friendly' answer was evidently, 'Spare your pains: I cannot love you'.

21–2 Apparently means, 'Don't take advantage of the right that free will has to hinder true desert'.

18

This sonnet, later than the sonnets from Petrarch, and more assured in syntax and metre, has many echoes of Chaucer (e.g. *TC* II.112), and makes a simple comparison with Charles of Orleans's Ballade 48, above. Charles's evocation of the May-day celebration of love as a contrast to the sadness of his absence from his lady is a conventionally poetic 'turn' on the convention. Wyatt, recalling wryly that he always seems to be in prison on May-day (as he was in 1534 and 1536), gives that edge of individual reality to the convention that makes his poetry different.

You that in love finde lucke and habundaunce
  And live in lust and joyful jolitie,
  Arise, for shame! Do away your sluggardie!
Arise, I say, do May some observaunce!
Let me in bed lye dreming in mischaunce
  Let me remembre the haps most unhappy
  That me betide in May most comonly,
As oon whom love list litil to avaunce.
Sephame saide true that my nativitie
  Mischaunced was with the ruler of the May:
He gest, I prove, of that the veritie! — *I find to be true*
  In May my welth and eke my lif, I say, — *well-being*
Have stonde so oft in suche perplexitie:
Rejoyse! Let me dreme of your felicitie.

19

In Wyatt's own hand, with many corrections made *currente calamo*. His spelling is kept here. Says Lewis (1954, p. 229), he 'hurls line after line at us in a sullen monotony of passion'.

What rage is this? what furour of what kynd?
What powre, what plage, doth wery thus my mynd?
Within my bons to rancle is assind
  What poyson, plesant swete?

Lo, se myn iyes swell with contynuall terys;
The body still away sleples it weris;
My fode nothing my faintyng strenght reperis,
  Nor doth my lyms sustayne.

In diepe wid wound the dedly strok doth torne
To curid skarre that never shall retorne. — *healed*
Go to, tryumphe, reioyse thy goodly torne!
  Thi frend thow dost opresse.

Opresse thou dost, and hast off hym no cure,
Nor yett my plaint no pitie can procure.
Fiers tygre fell, hard rok withowt recure, — *remedy*
  Cruell rebell to love!

Poem 18

9 Edward Sephame is recorded as having cast a horoscope for Edward VI.

One day

Ons may thou love, neuer belovffd agayne:
So love thou still and not thy love obttayne;
So wrathfull love with spites of just disdayne
May thret thy cruell hert.

20

The story is of a passionate falling-out, from which his mistress so swiftly recovers that the lover is doubtful of her stability of purpose. The stanza-form imitates insistent plaintive questioning falling back into bewilderment and exhaustion; resolution comes through the variation in the refrain.

Is it possible
so great a quarrel
That so hye debate,
intensity
So sharpe, so sore, and of suche rate,
Shuld end so sone and was begone so late?
Is it possible?

Is it possible –
So cruell intent,
So hasty hete and so sone spent,
From love to hate, and thence for to relent?
Is it possible?

Is it possible
That eny may fynde
Within oon hert so dyverse mynd,
To change or torne as wether and wynd?
Is it possible?

Is it possible
To spye it in an iye
What, at dice
That tornys as oft as chance on dy?
The trothe whereof can eny try?
Is it possible?

It is possible
For to torne so oft,
To bryng that lowyst that was most aloft,
And to fall hyest yet to lyght soft:
It is possible!

All is possible,
Who-so lyst beleve;
Trust therfore fyrst, and after preve,
As men wedd ladyes by lycence and leve:
All is possible.

16–19 'Can such changeableness be detected in a person's eye? Can truth of purpose be put to any test?'

24 i.e. to retain equanimity after what seems like a disaster.

29 i.e. As men put their trust in ladies when they marry them (and find out what they are really like afterwards).

21

Similar technique: persistent incredulous hopeless questioning answered in the hollow adjuration of the refrain.

And wylt thow leve me thus?
Say nay, say nay, for shame,
To save the from the blame
Of all my grefe and grame; *sorrow*
And wylt thow leve me thus?
Say nay, say nay!

And wylt thow leve me thus,
That hath lovyd the so long,
In welthe and woo among? *prosperity*
And is thy hart so strong
As for to leve me thus?
Say nay, say nay!

And wylt thow leve me thus,
That hath gevyn the my hart,
Never for to depart
Nother for payn nor smart? *Neither*
And wylt thow leve me thus?
Say nay, say nay!

And wylt thow leve me thus
And have no more pytye
Of hym that lovyth the?
Helas thy cruelte!
And wylt thow leve me thus?
Say nay, say nay!

22

A much-loved poem, the perfect brief and simple distillation of Wyatt's stoic pose and plaintive music; the variation on the refrain is hauntingly effective.

Forget not yet the tryde entent
Of suche a truthe as I have ment,
My gret travayle so gladly spent *labour*
Forget not yet.

Forget not yet when fyrst began
The wery lyfe ye know syns whan,
The sute, the servys none tell can, *love-suit, reckon up*
Forget not yet.

Forget not yet the gret assays, *trials*
The cruell wrong, the skornfull ways,
The paynfull pacyence in denays, *refusals*
Forget not yet.

Forget not yet, forget not thys,
How long ago hath ben and is
The mynd that never ment amys,
Forget not yet.

acknowledged (lover)

Forget not then thyn owne aprovyd,
The whyche so long hath the so lovyd,
Whose stedfast faythe yet never movyd,
Forget not thys.

23

The lute is the innocent instrument through which the lady's perfidy is made known. Don't blame my lute, and don't blame me, because I only speak the truth; blame yourself.

Blame not my lute for he must sownde
Of this or that as liketh me;
For lak of wytt the lute is bownde
To gyve suche tunes as plesith me.
Tho my songes be sumewhat strange
And spekes suche wordes as toche thy change, (*touch upon*)
Blame not my lute.

My lute, alas, doth not ofende
Tho that perfors he must agre
To sownde such tunes as I entende
To sing to them that hereth me;
Then tho my songes be somewhat plain (*direct in meaning*)
And tocheth some that use to fayn, (*are accustomed to*)
Blame not my lute.

My lute and strynges may not deny,
But as I strike they must obay;
Brake not them than so wrongfully
But wreke thyself some wyser way; (*avenge*)
And tho the songes whiche I endight
Do qwytt thy change with rightfull spight, (*requite your unfaithfulness*)
Blame not my lute.

Spyght askyth spight and changing change
And falsyd faith must nedes be known;
The faute so gret, the case so strange,
Of right it must abrode be blown.
Then since that by thyn own desart
My songes do tell how trew thou art,
Blame not my lute.

Blame but theself that hast mysdon
And well desarvid to have blame;
Change thou thy way, so evyl bygon,
And then my lute shall sownde that same.
But if tyll then my fyngeres play

According to your deserving

By thy desart their wontyd way,
Blame not my lute.

Farwell, unknown, for tho thow brake
My strynges in spight with gret desdayn,
Yet have I fownde owt for thy sake
Stringes for to strynge my lute agayne;
And if perchance this folysh ryme
Do make the blushe at any tyme,
Blame not my lute.

24

This is the same stanza as 'Forget not yet', but with internal rhyme; the effect of the short lines thus formed is that the lover is so desolated by the lady's unfaithfulness that he is expiring in short breaths.

What shulde I saye
Sins faithe is dede
And truthe awaye
From you is fled?
Shulde I be led
With doblenesse?
Naye, naye, mistresse!

I promiside you,
And you promiside me
To be as true
As I wolde be;
But sins I se
Your doble herte,
Farewell, my perte!

Though for to take
It is not my minde
But to forsake
One so unkind,
And as I finde
So will I truste –
Farewell, unjuste!

deny (that)

Can ye saye naye
But you saide
That I allwaye
Shulde be obeide?
And thus betraide

Before I knew

Or that I wiste –
Farewell, unkiste!

38–9 i.e. he has found another mistress.

14 **my perte**: 'my part (in all this affair)', or possibly 'loss' (Fr. *perte*).

25

Satisfied to have 'possessed' the lady who has thrown him over, resigned to contempt of women as being fickle by nature (30), the lover, moaning as always 'She done me wrong', cuts here an unlovely figure.

Spight hath no powre to make me sadde
 Nor scornefulnesse to make me playne; *complain*
It doth suffise that ons I had,
 And so to leve it is no payne.
 Let theim frowne on that leste doth gaine, *obtain least*
Who ded rejoise must nedes be glad;
 And tho with wordis thou wenist to rayne, *think to have power*
It doth suffise that ons I had.

Sins that in chekes thus overthwart *rebuffs, perverse*
 And coyly lookis thou dost delight,
It doth suffise that myne thou wart,
 Tho change hath put thy faithe to flight.
 Alas, it is a pevishe spight
To yelde thiself and then to part.
 But since thou setst thi faithe so light,
It doth suffise that myne thou wart.

And since thy love doth thus declyne
 And in thy herte suche hate doth grow,
It doth suffise that thou wart myne,
 And with good will I quite it soo. *repay*
 Some-tyme my frende, farewell my foo:
Since thou change, I am not thyne.
 But for relef of all my woo
It doth suffise that thou wart myne.

Prayeng you all that heris this song
 To judge no wight, nor none to blame;
It doth suffise she doth me wrong
 And that herself doth kno the same.
 And tho she change, it is no shame:
Their kinde it is and hath bene long.
 Yet I proteste she hath no name: *reputation for ill-doing*
It doth suffise she doth me wrong.

26

The usual Wyattian theme – the faithless mistress, the faithful lover – done in beautifully laconic style.

Wyth serving still *being always a faithful lover*
 This have I wone:
For my godwill
 To be undone;

And for redresse
 Of all my payne,

Disdaynefulnes
I have againe;

And for reward
Of all my smarte,
unheard
Lo, thus unharde
I must departe!

Wherefore all ye
That after shall
By fortune be,
As I am, thrall,

Example take
What I have won:
Thus for her sake
To be undone.

27

A 'sonnet' with four-stress lines. His lady has told him to be patient.

I abide and abide and better abide –
And after the olde proverbe – the happie daye;
And ever my ladye to me doth saye,
'Let me alone and I will provyde.'
prolong the time
I abide and abide and tarrye the tyde,
you may (but not me)
And with abiding spede well ye maye:
Thus do I abide, I wott, allwaye,
Neither
Nother obtayning nor yet denied.
Aye me! this long abidyng
Semith to me as who sayeth
A prolonging of a dieng dethe
Or a refusing of a desyred thing.
Moche ware it bettre for to be playne
Then to saye 'abide' and yet shall not obtayne.

28

An adaptation of a well-known chorus from the *Thyestes* (ll. 391–403) of Seneca (also translated by Marvell and Cowley), with a familiar theme – the miseries and hypocrisies of court-life and the pleasures of being away from it.

wishes, slippery
Stond who-so list upon the slipper toppe
Of courtes estate, and lett me here rejoyce,
live my life, hindrance
And use me quyet without lett or stoppe,
unappetising
Unknowen in courte, that hath suche brackishe joyes.
In hidden place so lett my dayes forth passe
That when my yeares be done, withouten noyse
course of life
I may dye aged after the common trace.

Poem 27

2 'He hasteth well that wisely can abide'.

head
For hym death greep'th right hard by the croppe
That is moche knowen of other, and of himself, alas,
bewildered, fearful
Doth dye unknowen, dazed, with dreadfull face.

29

Throughout the world, if it wer sought,
Faire wordes ynough a man shall finde:
a good bargain
They be good chepe, they cost right nought,
Their substance is but onely winde.
But well to say and so to mene,
That swete acord is seldom sene.

30

In court to serve decked with freshe aray,
tasting
Of sugred meates felyng the swete repast,
banquets
The life in bankets and sundry kindes of play
Amid the presse of lordly lokes to waste
Hath with it joynde oft-times such bitter taste
hold to
That who-so joyes such kinde of life to holde
In prison joyes, fettred with cheines of gold.

31. Satire 1

Wyatt wrote three 'satires' (poems of social commentary containing criticism of the follies of society), the second of them a version of the fable of the Town Mouse and the Country Mouse. They are all in *terza rima*, an Italian form (the metre of Dante's *Divina Commedia*) not used in English since Chaucer's brief experiment in the *Complaint to his Lady*. Satire 1 is adapted from Satire 10 (in *terza rima*) of the Italian Luigi Alamanni (1495–1556), and written while Wyatt was banished from court in 1536 and living at Allington Castle; it is addressed to a friend at court. Like most writers of urban and court-satire, from Horace on, Wyatt is the plain, straightforward, country-loving man who cannot dissemble, flatter or act a part at court. He cannot 'fashion himself' (19) other than he is. The claim, of course, makes the way clear for a subtler and more enduring kind of self-fashioning. From the Egerton MS; lines 1–52, missing in Egerton, are supplied from the Devonshire MS (lines 28–30 from CCCC MS 168).

Myne owne John Poynz, since ye delight to know
The cause why that homeward I me drawe
And fle the presse of courtes wher-so they go,
Rather then to lyve thrall, under the awe
Of lordly lokes, wrappid within my cloke,
pleasure
To will and lust lerning to set a lawe:
It is not for becawse I skorne or moke
The powar of them to whom Fortune hath lent
Charge over us, of right, to strike the stroke;
But true it is that I have allwais ment
Lesse to estime them then the common sort,
Of owtward thinges that juge in their intent

Poem 31

7–9 A careful way of acknowledging the power of those who are set in authority (and responsible for his exile from court).

Withowt regarde what doth inwarde resort.
  I grawnt sumtime that of glorye the fyer
Doth touche my hart: me lyst not to report *(see n.)*
Blame by honowr and honour to desyer.
But how may I this honour now atayne
That cannot dy the coloure blak a lyer? *dye*
  My Poynz, I cannot frame my tonge to fayne,
To cloke the trothe for praise withowt desart
Of them that lyst all vice for to retayne. *desire*
I cannot honour them that settes their part
With Venus and Baccus all their lyf long,
Nor hold my pece of them all-tho I smart.
I cannot crowche nor knele to do so grete a wrong
To worship them lyke God on erthe alone,
That ar as wolfes thes sely lambes among. *innocent*
I cannot with my wordes complayne and mone
And suffer nought, nor smart wythout complaynt,
Nor torne the worde that from my mouthe is gone. *turn back*
I cannot speke and loke lyke a saynct,
Use wiles for witt and make deceyt a pleasure,
And call craft counsell, for proffet styll to paint. *colour things falsely*
I cannot wrest the law to fill the coffer
With innocent blode to fede myself fat,
And doo most hurt where most help I offer.
  I am not he that can alow the state
Of him Cesar and dam Cato to dye, *damn*
That with his dethe dyd skape owt of the gate
From Cesares handes (if Lyve do not lye)
And wold not lyve whar lyberty was lost,
So did his hert the common-wele aplye. *(see n.)*
  I am not he suche eloquence to boste
To make the crow in singing as the swan,
Nor call the lyon of cowarde bestes the moste
That cannot take a mows as the cat can;
And he that dieth for hungar of the gold,
Call him Alessaundre; and say that Pan
Passith Apollo in musike manyfold;
Prayse Syr Thopas for a nobyll tale
And skorne the story that the Knyght told;
Praise him for counceill that is droncke of ale; *for being a wise advisor*
Grynne when he laugheth that bereth all the swaye,
Frowne when he frowneth and grone when he is pale;
On othres lust to hang both nyght and daye –
None of these poyntes would ever frame in me; *form part of the way I behave*
My wit is nought, I cannot lerne the waye.

15–16 'I don't want to (be one of those who) attach blame to honour and (yet themselves) desire honour'.

38 **him Cesar**: 'that Caesar' (for the idiom, see WBP 498). **Cato**: Cato the Younger committed suicide rather than submit to Caesar; he was praised as a great hero and patriot (and appears in Chaucer's *PF*). His story is told by the Roman historian Livy.

42 **the common-wele aplye**: 'devote itself to the common good, or commonwealth' (a preoccupation also of the *PF*).

48 **Alessaundre**. Alexander had the reputation of one who died a hero and conqueror, not a greedy land-grabber.

50–1 Chaucer's *Sir Thopas* is a parody of the inane triviality of popular minstrel-romance, his Knight's Tale a serious tale of love and destiny. It is hard to believe that there were people who had read Chaucer and who didn't understand this.

And much the lesse of thinges that greater be,
tricks of rhetoric That asken helpe of colours of devise
(see n.) To joyne the mene with eche extremitie,
With the neryst vertue to cloke alwaye the vise,
(see n.) And (as to purpose likewise it shall fall)
To presse the vertue that it may not rise –
As dronkenes good felloweship to call;
The frendly foo with his dowble face,
Say he is gentill and courtois therewithall;
Flattery And say that Favell hath a goodly grace
In eloquence; and crueltie to name
'Zele-of-Justice', and chaunge in tyme and place;
And he that sufferth offence withoute blame
Call him pitefull, and him true and playn
That raileth rekles to every mans shame;
Say he is rude that cannot lye and fayn;
The letcher a lover; and tirannye
To be the right of a prynces reigne.
I cannot, I – no, no, it will not be!
This is the cause that I could never yet
value Hang on their slevis that weigh, as thou maist se,
slice of luck A chippe of chaunce more then a pownde of witt.
This maketh me at home to hunte and hawke
And in fowle weder at my booke to sitt;
In frost and snowe then with my bow to stawke –
No man doeth marke where-so I ride or goo;
In lusty lees at libertie I walke,
these novelties (at court) And of these newes I fele nor wele nor woo,
Sauf that a clogg doeth hang yet at my hele –
No matter No force for that, for it is ordered so
That I may lepe both hedge and dike full well.
I am not now in Fraunce to judge the wyne,
savoury, taste With saffry sauce the delicates to fele;
Nor yet in Spaigne, where oon must him inclyne,
Rather then to be, owtewerdly to seme –
I meddill not with wittes that be so fyne!
prevents, judge Nor Flaunders chiere letteth not my sight to deme
Of black and white, nor taketh my wit awaye
With bestlynes they beeste do so esteme;
as prey (sacrifice) Nor I am not where Christe is geven in pray
For mony, poison and traison – at Rome
A commune practise used nyght and daie.
But here I am in Kent and Christendome
Emong the Muses where I rede and ryme;
Where if thou list, my Poynz, for to come,
Thou shalt be judge how I do spend my tyme.

60 i.e. to pretend that things are the same when they are actually different.

62 i.e. as will often happen in the pursuit of that same purpose.

84 **lusty lees**: 'pleasant fields' (an echo of *TC* II.752).

86 Wyatt was confined to his estate during the period of his banishment; he jokes that it does not stop him exercising his horse (88).

94 **Flaunders chiere**. Flemings had long had a reputation in England as heavy drinkers (the Pardoner's Tale is set in Flanders). Substituted for *Germania* in Alamanni.

98 **at Rome**: in Tottel's miscellany, published in 1557, during the reign of queen Mary, changed to 'of some'.

100 **in Kent and Christendome**. Kent, in this proverbial phrase, becomes jokingly the only place in Europe that is truly Christian.

32. Paraphrase of Ps. 130: *De profundis clamavi*

The verse-paraphrase of the Seven Penitential Psalms in *terza rima*, with linking verse commentary on the model of Aretino, was probably made during the uneasy period while Wyatt waited to see what would happen to him after the execution of his patron Cromwell in 1540. These Psalms (6, 32, 38, 51, 102, 130, 143, in AV numbering) were specially well known and frequently translated (especially Ps. 51) and commented upon in Middle English, because of their importance in confessional activity (see *PP* V.47, above). Wyatt's more immediate model is the paraphrase of the Penitential Psalms with commentary by the Italian Pietro Aretino, first published in 1536. Wyatt's Psalm-paraphrases, like his love-poems, have an intense inwardness which Greenblatt (1980, pp. 115–27) argues cannot be separated from the great public crisis of the period and the debate about religious doctrine and the nature of power (p. 119). This version of Ps. 130 is something of a rhetorical *tour de force* of amplification.

From depth of sin and from a diepe dispaire,
From depth of deth, from depth of hertes sorow,
From this diepe cave of darknes diepe repayre, *darkness's, resort*
The have I cald, O Lord, to be my borow. *guarantee of release*
Thow in my voice, O Lord, perceyve and here
My hert, my hope, my plaint, my overthrow,
My will to ryse, and let by graunt apere
That to my voyce thin eres do well entend. *listen*
No place so farr that to the is not nere,
No depth so diepe that thou ne maist extend
Thin ere therto – here then my wofull plaint!
For, Lord, if thou do observe what men offend
And putt thy natyf mercy in restraint,
If just exaction demaund recompense,
Who may endure, O Lord? Who shall not faynt
At such acompt? Dred, and not reverence, *accounting*
Shold so raigne large. But thou sekes rather love,
For in thi hand is mercys resedence,
By hope wherof thou dost our hertes move.
I in the, Lord, have set my confydence:
My sowle such trust doth evermore aprove.
Thi holy word of eterne excellence,
Thi mercys promesse that is alway just,
Have bene my stay, my piller and pretence. *defence*
My sowle in God hath more desyrus trust *earnest*
Then hath the wachman lokyng for the day,
By the relefe to quenche of slepe the thrust. *thirst*
Let Israel trust unto the Lord alway,
For grace and favour arn his propertie: *characteristic attribute*
Plenteous ransome shall come with hym, I say,
And shall redeme all our iniquitie.

12–15 'Use every man after his desert, and who should scape whipping?' (*Hamlet* II.ii.532).

17 **Shold so raine large**: 'Would in such a case largely dominate people's minds'.

John Leland (*c.* 1506–1552)

John Leland, already keeper of the king's books, was made 'king's antiquary' (a new post) in 1533 and sent round England and Wales to inspect the libraries of the monasteries and make a record of their contents. The first act for the suppression of the smaller religious houses was made in 1536, and the larger monasteries were taken over in the next six years – their inmates expelled, their treasures carted away, their lands and endowments confiscated or distributed to royal servants, their buildings given over to use as stone-quarries. The flow of wealth to the royal exchequer was enormous, the destruction unimaginable. Leland, meanwhile, had spent six years on his journeyings, and a further six organizing his notes. He was a lover of books, was amazed at the treasures he found, stood in awe, he says, as he entered the library of the great abbey of Glastonbury; he was a loyal servant of the king, but was appalled by the impending destruction, even though much of what was to be discarded, as he dutifully recorded, was Romish rubbish. He fell into a deep melancholy from which he never recovered, and left only notebooks recording his journeys. It was left to John Bale, the voluminous and vehement Protestant polemicist and dramatist, to sort through and publish some of his friend's remains and to reissue the brief report of his activities that Leland had written for Henry VIII in 1546, larding it out with his own anti-Papist invective (1549). In this report, his 'New Year's Gift', Leland tries to make out of the destruction of the past a new monument for the future to England's national history and greatness (for Bale's own contribution to this project, see Hadfield [1994], pp. 51–80). The impossibility of his task overcame him – indeed it overcomes the reader, as one mighty project is piled upon another – but he anticipated three and more centuries of historical scholarship in the service of the (newly self-conscious) nation-state. Text from the 1549 edition, with Bale's additions omitted.

A New Year's Gift to Henry VIII

... Wherfor, after that I had perpended the honest and profytable studyes of these hystoryographers, I was totallye enflamed wyth a love to se throughlye all those partes of thys your opulent and ample realme that I had redde of in the aforsayd wryters. In so muche that, all my other occupacyons intermytted, I have so traveled in your domynions both by the see-coastes and the myddle partes, sparynge neyther labour nor costes by the space of these .vi. yeares past, that there is almost neyther cape nor baye, haven, creke or pere, ryver or confluence of ryvers, breches,[1] washes, lakes, meres, fenny waters, mountaynes, valleys, mores, hethes, forestes, woodes, cyties, burges, castels, pryncypall manor places, monasteryes and colleges, but I have seane them and noted in so doynge a whole worlde of thynges verye memorable.

Thus instructed, I trust shortly to se the tyme that, like as Carolus Magnus[2] had among his treasures thre large and notable tables[3] of sylver, rychelye enameled, one of the syte and descripcion of Constantynople, another of the site and figure of the magnificent citie of Rome, and the third of the descripcion of the worlde, so shall your majestie have thys your worlde and impery of Englande so sett forth in a quadrate table of sylver (yf God sende me lyfe to accomplyshe my beginning), that your grace shall have ready knowledge at the fyrst sighte of many right delectable, fruteful and necessary pleasures by contemplacion therof as often as occasyon shall move yow to the syghte of it.

And because that it may be more permanent and farther knowne then to have it engraved in sylver or brasse, I entend by the leave of God, within the space of .xii. moneths folowyng, such a descripcion to make of your realme in wryttinge that it shall be no mastery after for the graver or painter to make the lyke by a perfect example.

Yea, and to wade further in thys matter, whereas now almost no man can wele gesse at the shaddow of the auncyent names of havens, ryvers, promontories, hilles, woodes, cities, townes, castelles, and varyete of kyndes of people, that Cesar, Livi, Strabo, Diodorus, Fabius Pictor, Pomponius Mela, Plinius, Cornelius Tacitus, Ptolomeus, Sextus Rufus, Ammianus Marcellinus, Solinus, Antoninus and dyverse other make mencyon of, I trust so to open this wyndow that the lyght shal be seane so long (that is to say, by the space of a whole thousand yeares) stopped up,[4] and the old glory of your renoumed Britaine to reflorish through the worlde.

1 valleys opening to the sea
2 Charlemagne
3 tablets
4 For 1000 years, says Leland, the monasteries have prevented this knowledge from being disseminated (though they alone, he might have added, have preserved it).

This done, I have matter at plenty already prepared to this purpose, that is to saye, to wryte an hystorie, to the whiche I entende to adscribe this title, *De antiquitate Britannica*, or els, *Civilis historia*. And this worke I entende to dyvyde into so many bokes as ther be shires in Englande and shyres and great dominions in Wales. So that I esteme that thys volume wyl enclude a fyfty bokes, wherof eche one severally shall conteyne the beginninges, encreases and memorable actes of the chiefe townes and castelles of the province allotted to it.[5]

Then I entende to dystrybute into syx bokes suche matter as I have already collected concernynge the isles adjacent to your noble realme and undre your subjeccion. Wherof .iii. shal be of these isles, Vecta, Mona and Menavia, somtime kingedomes.[6]

And to superadde a worke as an ornament and a ryght comely garlande to the enterpryses aforesayd, I have selected stuffe to be distributed into thre bokes, the which I purpose thus to entytle, *De nobilitate Britannica*. Whereof the fyrst shal declare the names of kynges and quenes wyth theyr chyldren, dukes, earles, lordes, capitaynes and rulers in this realme to the commynge of the Saxons and their conquest; the seconde shal be of the Saxons and Danes to the vyctorye of kyng Willyam the greate; the thirde from the Normannes to the reygne of youre most noble grace, descendynge lyneally of the Brytayne, Saxon and Norman kynges. So that all noble men shal clerely perceyve theyr lyneal parentele.[7]

Now yf it shal be the pleasure of almyghty God that I maye lyve to perfourme these thynges that be alreadye begonne, and in a greate forwardnesse, I trust that thys your realme shall so wele be knowne, ones paynted with hys natyve colours, that the renoume therof shal geve place to the glory of no other regyon. And my great laboures and costes, procedinge from the moste habundaunt fountayne of your infinite goodnesse towardes me, your pore scholar and most humble servaunt, shall be evydently seane to have not only pleased but also profyted the studyouse, gentil and equal reders. This is the briefe declaracyon of my laboriouse journey, taken by mocyon of your hyghnesse, so much studyeng at all houres about the frutefull preferrement of good letters and auncyent vertues.

Christ contynue your most royall estate and the prosperyte, wyth succession in kyngely dygnyte of your dere and worthylye beloved sonne, prynce Edwarde, grauntynge yow a numbre of pryncely sonnes by the moste gracyouse, benygne and modest lady, your quene Cataryne.[8]

5 Leland anticipates the county histories of antiquarians over the next 300 years, beginning with John Speed and William Camden.

6 The isles of Wight, Anglesey and Man.

7 Here Leland anticipates the volumes devoted (e.g. by Sir William Dugdale) to *The Baronage of England*, and the *Complete Peerage* of 'G.E.C[okayne]'.

8 **Cataryne**: Henry VIII's last queen, Catharine Parr. The prospect of further issue was by now, a year before the king's death, a polite fiction.

Henry Howard, Earl of Surrey (1517–1547)

Henry Howard inherited the courtesy-title of earl of Surrey when his father Thomas became third duke of Norfolk in 1524. He married Lady Frances Vere, daughter of the earl of Oxford, in 1532, and had a spectacular career at court, where he was long a favourite of the king. He distinguished himself in tournament and on campaign at home and abroad, and was made Knight of the Garter in 1541. Impatient and headstrong, he found himself briefly in prison on three occasions for challenging or striking other members of the court or for generally riotous behaviour. His campaigning in France 1545–6 was not a success: he was wounded, rebuked by the king for taking unnecessary risks, and lost an important battle. During the last few months of his life, back in England, he was rash enough to court the enmity of the king's current favourites and was arrested, charged with treason, and executed on 19 January 1547 (his father, due to be executed at dawn on 28 January, was reprieved after the king's death during the night).

Surrey was of higher rank than Wyatt (whose poetry he admired, but whom he hardly knew well), but belonged to the same aristocratic milieu, and his poems served many of the same occasions and functions. But, though his name has been linked with Wyatt's since Puttenham elected them founding fathers of English poetry, he is a much lesser poet. He worked in many of the same genres, including the Petrarchan love-sonnet, but his output is smaller, more varied and occasional, and the passion behind the love-poems is less intense. They are poems about love rather than *of* love – equable, easy, elegant, untormented, sweetly melancholy. Where Wyatt hammers at the doors of disdain and denial, Surrey waits patiently, amuses himself with patterns, drifts off onto other subjects, meditates. Things don't seem to *matter* quite so much, and the smoothness and regularity of his versification, at first a relief after the strenuous challenges of Wyatt, can veer towards monotony. Yet his elegances, seeming easy, are hard won and worth treasuring: his diction is effortless and unstrained, his syntactical cadences carefully measured, and he is a metrical innovator of the first importance. He smooths out the Petrarchan sonnet to a more comfortable English fluency, introducing the 'English' or 'Shakespearian' sonnet of alternate-rhyming quatrains plus final couplet, and he also wrote the first true blank verse in English, in his translation of Books II and IV of the *Aeneid*. Surrey's poems in 'Poulter's measure' (introduced, but used sparingly by Wyatt), have not won him so many admirers: he uses it quite frequently (as in his translations of *Ecclesiastes*, chaps 1–4, and of four of the Psalms), finding in it a music that few others hear.

Poems, ed. E. Jones (Oxford, 1964). Of the poems below, nos 1, 2, 5, 6, 7 and 11 are from Tottel's *Songs and Sonnets* (1557), 3, 4, 9, 10, 12 and 13 are from BL MS Add.36529, and no. 8 is from BL MS Add.28635; the *Aeneid*-translation is from Tottel's print of 1557. See Spearing (1985), pp. 310–26.

I

An example of Surrey's special ease and control of syntax: the first sentence unfolds over its three stanzas with perfect lucidity.

When ragyng love with extreme payne
   Most cruelly distrains my hart;
When that my teares, as floudes of rayne,
   Beare witnes of my wofull smart;
When sighes have wasted so my breath
That I lye at the poynte of death,

I call to minde the navye greate
   That the Grekes brought to Troye towne,
And how the boysteous windes did beate
   Their shyps and rente their sayles adowne,
Till Agamemnons daughters bloode
Appeasde the goddes that them withstode;

11 The Greek leader Agamemnon was told that he must sacrifice his daughter Iphigenia if the Greeks were to win favourable winds to Troy.

And how that in those ten yeres warre
Full manye a bloudye dede was done,
And manye a lord that came full farre
There caught his bane, alas, to sone, *destruction*
And many a good knight overronne,
Before the Grekes had Helene wonne.

Then thinke I thus: sithe suche repayre,
So longe time warre of valiant men,
Was all to winne a ladye fayre,
Shall I not learne to suffer then,
And thinke my life well spent to be
Servyng a worthier wight than she?

Therfore I never will repent,
But paynes contented stil endure,
For like as when, rough winter spent,
The pleasant spring straight draweth in ure, *comes into being*
So after ragyng stormes of care
Joyful at length may be my fare.

2

Freely adapted from Petrarch, Sonnet 266, on two rhymes only. Surrey tends, as here, to choose Petrarch sonnets where he can develop a single thought or conceit in an even flow of lines, without too much counter-movement or conflict. There is a touch of archaism ('eke'), and many echoes of the phrasing of medieval English spring-descriptions ('soote season', 'spray now springes'); the contrast of springtime joy with the poet's unhappiness in love is also conventional in ME love-poetry.

The soote season, that bud and blome furth bringes, *sweet*
With grene hath clad the hill and eke the vale;
The nightingale with fethers new she singes;
The turtle to her make hath tolde her tale. *turtledove, mate*
Somer is come, for every spray now springes;
The hart hath hong his olde hed on the pale; *antlers, fence*
The buck in brake his winter cote he flinges; *thickets*
The fishes flote with newe repaired scale.
The adder all her sloughe awaye she slinges;
The swift swalow pursueth the flyes smale;
The busy bee her honye now she minges; *has mind of*
Winter is worne that was the flowers bale. *harm*
And thus I see among these pleasant thinges
Eche care decayes, and yet my sorow springes.

3

Translated from Petrarch, Sonnet 111.

Set me wheras the sonne doth perche the grene, *pierce*
Or wher his beames may not dissolve the ise;
In temprat heat where he is felt and sene;

With prowde people, in presence sad and wyse;
Set me in base or yet in highe degree,
In the long night or in the shortyst day,
In clere weather or wher mysts thikest be,
In loste yowthe or when my haires be grey;
Set me in earthe, in heaven, or yet in hell,
In hill, in dale, or in the fowming floode,
at liberty Thrawle or at large, alive whersoo I dwell,
Sike or in healthe, in yll fame or in good:
Yours will I be, and with that onely thought
fortune Comfort myself when that my hap is nowght.

4

Translated from Petrarch, Sonnet 107, also translated by Wyatt ('The longe love', see above). Surrey's version is smoother, more consistent, less arresting.

reign Love, that doth raine and live within my thought
And buylt his seat within my captyve brest,
Clad in the armes wherin with me he fowght
Oft in my face he doth his banner rest.
But she that tawght me love and suffre paine,
My doubtfull hope and eke my hote desire
(taught me) to With shamfast looke to shadoo and refrayne,
Her smyling grace convertyth streight to yre.
And cowarde love than to the hert apace
Taketh his flight where he doth lorke and playne
His purpose lost, and dare not show his face.
For my lordes gylt thus fawtless byde I payne,
Yet from my lorde shall not my foote remove:
Sweet is the death that taketh end by love.

5

Adapted from Petrarch, Sonnet 129, inspired in its turn by the beautiful nocturne preceding Dido's complaint in *Aeneid* IV.522–8.

Alas, so all thinges nowe do holde their peace,
Heaven and earth disturbed in nothing;
wind The beastes, the ayer, the birdes their song do cease,
chariot The nightes chare the starres aboute doth bring.
Calme is the sea, the waves worke lesse and lesse:
So am not I, whom love, alas, doth wring,
Bringing before my face the great encrease
Of my desires, whereat I wepe and syng
In joye and wo as in a doutfull ease;
For my swete thoughtes sometyme do pleasure bring,

Poem 4

13 He continues the image of Love as a military commander, with himself as a faithful foot-soldier who will not desert his lord.

Poem 5

5 Did Keats, in his sonnet, 'Bright star', remember this striking personification of the waves 'working' in describing 'the moving waters at their priestlike task / Of pure ablution round earth's human shores'?

But by and by the cause of my disease
  Geves me a pang that inwardly doth sting,
When that I thinke what griefe it is againe
To live and lacke the thing should ridde my paine.

6

Geve place, ye lovers, here before
  That spent your bostes and bragges in vain:
My ladies beawtie passeth more
  The best of yours, I dare well sayn,
Than doth the sonne the candle-light
Or brightest day the darkest night;

And thereto hath a trothe as just
  As had Penelope the fayre,
For what she saith, ye may it trust
  As it by writing sealed were.
And vertues hath she many moe
Than I with pen have skill to showe.

I coulde rehearse, if that I wolde,
  The whole effect of Natures plaint
When she had lost the perfit mold,
  The like to whom she could not paint:
With wringing handes howe she dyd cry,
And what she said – I know it, I.

I knowe she swore with ragyng mind,
  Her kingdom onely set apart, *alone excepted*
There was no losse, by lawe of kind,
  That could have gone so nere her hart.
And this was chiefly all her payne:
She coulde not make the lyke agayne.

Sith Nature thus gave her the prayse
  To be the chiefest worke she wrought,
In faith, me thinke some better waies
  On your behalfe might well be sought
Then to compare, as ye have done,
To matche the candle with the sonne.

7

Surrey ventriloquizes his wife's experience (perhaps in 1543 or 1545) of love and longing for her absent husband (Dorigen, in the Franklin's Tale, is bound to be in our minds); inevitably, he imagines it as a secondary experience of love, sentiment moulding itself to the person and activity of the male beloved. The closing triplet and final pentameter of the stanza draw out the anguish very satisfactorily. One of the extant copies of the poem is in the hand of Mary Shelton, whose lover Thomas Clere was with Surrey in France.

15 **lost the perfit mold**: a variant of the topos of surpassing beauty in which Nature breaks the mould, e.g. 'Natura il fece, e poi ruppe la stampa' ('Nature made him, and then broke the mould'), Ariosto, *Orlando Furioso* (1516), X.84.

O happy dames, that may embrace
   The frute of your delight,
Help to bewaile the wofull case
   And eke the heavy plight
Of me, that wonted to rejoyce   *was wont*
The fortune of my pleasant choyce:
Good ladies, help to fill my moornyng voyce!   *swell out*

In ship, freight with rememberance   *laden*
   Of thoughtes and pleasures past,
He sailes that hath in governance
   My life, while it wil last,
With scalding sighes, for lack of gale,
Furdering his hope, that is his sail,
Toward me, the swete port of his avail.   *disembarkation*

Alas, how oft in dreames I se
   Those eyes that were my food,
Which somtime so delited me
   That yet they do me good;
Wherwith I wake with his returne
Whose absent flame did make me burne.
But when I find the lacke, Lord how I mourne!

When other lovers in armes acrosse   *embracing*
   Rejoyce their chief delight,
Drowned in teares to mourne my losse
   I stand the bitter night
In my window, where I may see
Before the windes how the cloudes flee.
Lo, what a mariner love hath made me!

And in grene waves when the salt flood
   Doth rise by rage of wind,
A thousand fansies in that mood
   Assayle my restlesse mind.
Alas, now drencheth my swete fo,   *drowns*
That with the spoyle of my hart did go,
And left me – but, alas, why did he so?

And when the seas waxe calme againe,
   To chase fro me annoye,
My doubtfull hope doth cause me plaine:
   So dreade cuts of my joye.   *off*
Thus is my wealth mingled with wo,   *well-being*
And of ech thought a dout doth growe:
Now he comes – will he come? alas, no, no!

8 **freight with rememberance**: remembering Petrarch, Sonnet 154, and Wyatt's translation ('My galy charged with forgetfulnes', above).

33 **swete fo**: a conventional oxymoron for the beloved ('foe', because love causes pain).

8

This poem, a pleasant, and more intimate and homely, and quite touching amplification of the theme of 'O happy dames', is an example of Surrey's skill with 'Poulter's measure', rhymed couplets of alexandrines and fourteeners (playfully so called in allegation that poultry-dealers gave irregular measure). It is not unmusical, but the pause in the alexandrine is difficult to get the hang of. The sing-song simplicity was maybe thought appropriate to a woman's musings.

Good ladies, you that have your pleasure in exyle,
Take up your refrain — Stepp in your foote, come take a place and mourne with me awhyle;
And suche as by their lords do sett but lytle pryce,
concerns — Lett them sitt still, it skills them not what chaunce come on the dyce.
But you whom love hath bound, by order of desyre,
To love your lordes, whose good desertes none other wold requyre,
Come you yet once agayne and sett your foote by myne,
Whose wofull plight and sorowes great no tongue may well defyne.
well-being — My lord and love, alas, in whom consystes my wealth,
Hath Fortune sent to passe the seas, in haserd of his health.
He whom — That I was wont for to embrace, content in mynde,
Ys now amyd the foming floods, at pleasure of the wynde.
There God hym well preserve and safely me hym send;
Without whiche hope my lyf, alas, were shortly at an ende;
Whose absence yet, although my hope doth tell me plaine
With short returne he comes anon, yet ceasith not my paine.
The fearefull dreames I have oft-tymes they greeve me so
That then I wake and stand in dowbt yf they be trew or no.
Somtyme the roring seas, me seemes, they grow so hye
That my sweete lorde in daunger greate, alas, doth often lye.
Another tyme, the same doth tell me he is come
And playng where I shall hym fynd with T. his lytle sonne.
life-giving — So forthe I go apace to see that lyfsome sight,
And with a kysse me thinckes I say, 'Now wellcome home, my knight!
Welcome, my sweete, alas, the staye of my welfare;
Thy presence bringeth forthe a truce betwixt me and my care'.
kisses me back — Then lyvely doth he looke and saluith me agayne,
And saith, 'My deare, how is it now that you have all this payne?'
Wherewith the heavie cares that heapt are in my brest
Breake forth and me dischargeth cleane of all my great unrest.
But when I me awayke and fynde it but a dreame,
The angwyshe of my former woe beginneth more extreme
hardly — And me tourmenteth so that unneth may I fynde
place where — Some hydden where to stille the gryfe of my unquyet mynd.
Thus every waye you see with absence how I burne,
And for my wound no cure there is but hope of some retourne,
Save when I feele by sower how sweete is felt the more,
It doth abate some of my paynes that I abode before;
And then unto myself I saye, 'When that we two shall meete,
But lyttle tyme shall seeme this payne, that joye shall be so sweete'.
direct — Ye wyndes, I you convart, in chiefest of your rage,
That you my lord me safely send, my sorowes to asswage;
And that I may not long abyde in suche excesse,
Do your good will to cure a wight that lyveth in distresse.

22 **T. his lytle sonne**: Thomas Howard, born 1536.

9

Surrey is imprisoned at Windsor, as in Poem 10, but the occasion provokes here a more stilted and conventional series of reactions; the last line is good.

When Windesor walles sustained my wearied arme,
   My hand my chyn, to ease my restless hedd,
Ech pleasant plot revested green with warm,   *reclothed*
   The blossomed bowes with lustie veare yspred,   *spring*
The flowred meades, the weddyd birds so late   *so recently wed*
   Myne eyes discovered. Than did to mynd resort
The jolly woes, the hateles shorte debate,
   The rakhell life that longes to loves disporte.   *reckless, belongs*
Wherwith, alas, myne hevy charge of care
   Heapt in my brest brake forth against my will,
And smoky sighes that overcast the ayer.
   My vapored eyes such drery teares distill
The tender spring to quicken wher thei fall,
And I half bent to throwe me down withall.

10

Surrey spent part of his boyhood (1530–2) at Windsor in the company of the king's natural son, Henry Fitzroy (a courtesy title for such offspring), duke of Richmond (he married Surrey's sister and died in 1536). Back at the castle in 1537, in prison, after being committed for striking Sir Edward Seymour within the court-precincts, he remembers his happy life there and grieves for his friend. His poem, in the 'heroic quatrain' (like Gray's *Elegy*), is unaffectedly evocative of a golden world of youth and youthful friendship. It is constructed, like Poem 11, very simply, in the form of a list of attributes, extensively qualified with epithets, phrases and clauses.

So crewell prison howe could betyde, alas,   *could there happen to be*
   As prowde Wyndsour, where I in lust and joye   *pleasure*
With a kinges son my childishe yeres did passe,   *youthful*
   In greater feast then Priams sonnes of Troye;

Where eche swete place retournes a tast full sowre –
   The large grene courtes, where we wer wont to hove,   *linger*
With eyes cast upp unto the maydens towre,
   And easy syghes, such as folke drawe in love;

The stately sales, the ladyes bright of hewe,   *rooms*
   The daunces short, long tales of great delight,
With wordes and lookes that tygers could but rewe,
   Where eche of us did plead the others right;

The palme-playe, where, dispoyled for the game,   *hand-tennis, stripped*
   With dased eyes oft we by gleames of love
Have mist the ball and got sight of our dame
   To bayte her eyes which kept the leddes above;   *attract, frequented the roof-walks*

Poem 10

4 Priam, king of Troy, had fifty sons whom he feasted, according to Homer.

11 **that tygers could but rewe**, i.e. ferociously passionate language.

The graveld ground, with sleves tyed on the helme,
  On fomynge horse, with swordes and frendly hertes,
With chere as though the one should overwhelme, *demeanour*
  Where we have fought and chased oft with dartes.

With sylver drops the meades yet spred for rewthe,
  In active games of nymbleness and strengthe
Where we dyd strayne, trayled by swarmes of youthe,
  Our tender lymes, that yet shot up in lengthe;

The secret groves, which ofte we made resound
  Of pleasaunt playnt and of our ladyes prayse,
Recording soft what grace eche one had found,
  What hope of spede, what dred of long delayes;

The wyld forest, the clothed holtes with grene, *woods*
  With raynes avald and swift ybrethed horse, *reins held loosely*
With crye of houndes and mery blastes bitwen,
  Where we did chase the fearfull hart a-force;

The voyd walles eke, that harbourd us eche night –
  Wherwith, alas, revive within my brest
The swete accord, such slepes as yet delight,
  The pleasaunt dremes, the quyet bedd of rest,

The secret thoughtes imparted with such trust,
  The wanton talke, the dyvers chaunge of playe, *playful exchange*
The frendshipp sworne, eche promyse kept so just,
  Wherwith we past the winter nightes awaye.

And with this thought the blood forsakes my face,
  The teares berayne my cheke of dedly hewe;
The which, as sone as sobbing sighes, alas,
  Upsupped have, thus I my playnt renewe: *swallowed*

'O place of blisse, renewer of my woos,
  Geve me accompt wher is my noble fere, *account, companion*
Whom in thy walles thou didest eche night enclose –
  To other lief, but unto me most dere.' *To others dear*

Eache stone, alas, that doth my sorowe rewe,
  Retournes therto a hollowe sound of playnt.
Thus I alone, where all my fredome grew, *nobility of behaviour*
  In pryson pyne with bondage and restraynt,

And with remembraunce of the greater greif,
To bannishe the lesse I fynde my chief releif.

20 **with dartes**. One recalls Pandarus's story of himself and Troilus at this sport (*TC* II.513).

32 **a-force**, from Fr. *chasse à forcer*, to run down (game) to the death (as opposed to shooting it).

53 **the greater greif**, i.e. the memory of lost happiness (cf. *TC* III.1625–8), and the death of his friend.

11 Epitaph for Wyatt

Probably the first of Surrey's poems to be printed, this epitaph appeared in a small volume of tributes brought out soon after Wyatt's death in 1542. The first line (based on the first line of an earlier Latin epitaph), with its subtly suggested chiasmic repetition, has a classical poise that seems new in English verse.

alive W. resteth here, that quick could never rest,
because of the disdain (of others) Whose heavenly giftes encreased by disdayn
And vertue sank the deper in his brest –
from envious malice Such profit he by envy could obtain:

A hed, where wisdom misteries did frame,
Whose hammers bet styll in that lively brayn
anvil As on a stithe where that some work of fame
Was dayly wrought to turne to Britaines gayn;

both (qualities) A visage stern and myld, where bothe did grow
Vice to contemne, in vertue to rejoyce,
Amid great stormes whom grace assured so
To lyve upright and smile at Fortunes choyce;

A hand that taught what might be sayd in ryme,
robbed That reft Chaucer the glory of his wit –
unfinished for want of time A mark the which, unparfited for time,
Some may approche but never none shall hit;

A toung that served in forein realmes his king,
Whose courteous talke to vertue did enflame
Eche noble hart – a worthy guide to bring
Our English youth by travail unto fame;

passion An eye whose judgement none affect could blinde,
Frendes to allure and foes to reconcile,
Whose persing loke did represent a mynde
With vertue fraught, reposed, voyd of gyle;

A hart where drede was never so imprest
To hyde the thought that might the trouth avance,
lofty In neyther fortune loft nor yet represt –
To swell in wealth or yeld unto mischance;

A valiant corps, where force and beawty met –
Happy, alas to happy, but for foes! –
Lived and ran the race that Nature set,
Of manhodes shape where she the molde did lose.

innocent But to the heavens that simple soule is fled,
Which left with such as covet Christ to know
Witnesse of faith that never shall be ded,
Sent for our helth, but not received so.

32 **the molde did lose**: the topos developed in Poem 6, above.

Thus, for our gilt, this jewel have we lost:
spirit The earth his bones, the heavens possesse his gost.

12

Sardanapalus is the subject of this powerful sonnet, with its magnificently scornful last line; his wicked life and degenerate kingship were a favourite medieval horror-story, e.g. Gower, *Confessio Amantis* VII.4313; Lydgate, *Fall of Princes* II.2234.

Th'Assyrans king, in peas with fowle desyre
  And filthy luste that staynd his regall harte,
In warr that should sett pryncely hertes afyre
  Vanquyshd dyd yeld for want of martyall arte.
compared with kisses The dent of swordes from kysses semed straunge,
shield   And harder then hys ladyes syde his targe;
From glotton feastes to sowldyers fare a chaunge,
weight   His helmet far above a garlandes charge;
scarce Who scace the name of manhode dyd retayne,
  Drenched in slouthe and womanishe delight,
spirit Feble of sprete, unpacyent of payne;
  When he had lost his honor and hys right,
in time of, made pale Prowde tyme of welthe, in stormes appawld with drede,
Murdred hymselfe to shew some manfull dede.

13

A translation of Martial's epigram, 10.47; pleasant recommendations to the quiet life (cf. Wyatt's Satire 1) which Surrey in his own life spectacularly failed to follow.

Marshall, the thinges for to attayne
  The happy life be thes, I finde:
The riches left, not got with payne;
  The frutfull grownd; the quyet mynde;
The equall frend – no grudge nor stryf,
  No charge of rule nor governance;
Without disease the helthfull life;
continence   The howshold of contynuance;
The meane dyet, no delicate fare;
  Wisdom joyned with simplicitye;
The night discharged of all care,
  Where wyne may beare no soverainty;
The chast wife wyse, without debate;
  Such sleapes as may begyle the night;
Contented with thyne owne estate,
  Neyther wisshe death nor fear his might.

Aeneid-translation, II.654–729

The Death of Priam

Surrey used Douglas's translation extensively, and, to facilitate comparison, their translations of the same passage (*Aeneid* II.506–58) are given here and above. Surrey is occasionally more fluent in his phrasing, but Douglas is everywhere more powerful; the two poets have a different reading of Virgil as well as different kinds of poetic ability. Jones, in his perceptive account of Surrey's translation (*Poems*, pp. xiv–xx), considers that he is at his best in translating speeches.

Perhaps Parcase yow wold ask what was Priams fate.
fortune When of his taken town he saw the chaunce
And the gates of his palace beaten down,
His foes amid his secret chambers eke,
Th'old man in vaine did on his sholders then,
cuirass Trembling for age, his curace long disused,
His bootelesse swerd he girded him about,
And ran amid his foes ready to die.
  Amid the court under the heven all bare
A great altar there stood, by which there grew
An old laurel tree, bowing therunto,
(household) gods Which with his shadow did embrace the gods.
Here Hecuba with her yong daughters all
About the altar swarmed were in vaine,
Like doves that flock together in the storme,
The statues of the gods embracing fast.
But when she saw Priam had taken there
His armure, like as though he had ben yong,
'What furious thought, my wretched spouse,' quod she,
'Did move thee now such wepons for to weld?
Why hastest thow? This time doth not require
Such succor, ne yet such defenders now –
No, though Hector my son were here againe!
Come hether; this altar shall save us all,
Or we shall dye together.' Thus she sayd,
Wherwith she drew him back to her, and set
The aged man down in the holy seat.
  But lo, Polites, one of Priams sons,
Escaped from the slaughter of Pyrrhus,
Comes fleing through the wepons of his foes,
Searching all wounded the long galleries
And the voyd courtes; whom Pyrrhus all in rage
deal Followed fast to reach a mortal wound,
in the act And now in hand well-nere strikes with his spere;
Who fleing forth till he came now in sight
Of his parentes, before their face fell down,
Yelding the ghost with flowing streames of blood.
  Priamus then, although he were half ded,
Might not kepe in his wrath nor yet his words,

654 Aeneas, having fled from Troy, has landed in Carthage, where he is narrating the story of the sack of Troy to the spellbound Dido, queen of Carthage.

682 Pyrrhus is the son of Achilles, and his mood is specially vengeful because of the death of his father at the gates of Troy.

But cryeth out: 'For this thy wicked work,
And boldnesse eke such thing to enterprise,
If in the heavens any justice be
That of such things takes any care or kepe,
According thankes the gods may yeld to thee,
And send thee eke thy just deserved hyre
That made me see the slaughter of my childe
And with his blood defile the fathers face.
But he by whom thow fainst thyself begot,
Achilles, was to Priam not so stern;
For lo, he tendring my most humble sute
The right and faith, my Hectors bloodlesse corps
Rendred for to be layd in sepulture,
And sent me to my kingdome home againe.'
  Thus sayd the aged man, and therewithall
Forcelesse he cast his weake unweldy dart,
where it struck
Which, repulst from the brasse where it gave dint,
Without sound hong vainly in the shieldes bosse.
  Quod Pyrrhus: 'Then thow shalt this thing report.
(Peleus)
On message to Pelide my father go:
Shew unto him my cruel dedes, and how
has become unnaturally perverted
Neoptolem is swarved out of kinde.
Now shalt thow dye,' quod he. And with that word
To the altar
At the altar him trembling gan he draw
Wallowing through the blodshed of his son;
And his left hand all clasped in his heare,
With his right arme drewe forth his shining sword,
Which in his side he thrust up to the hilts.
end
  Of Priamus this was the fatal fine,
The wofull end that was alotted him,
When he had seen his palace all on flame,
With ruine of his Troyan turrets eke.
That royal prince of Asie, which of late
Reignd over so many peoples and realmes,
Like a great stock now lieth on the shore;
His hed and sholders parted ben in twaine,
A body now without renome and fame.

693–4 Priam's outrage is much more strongly conveyed by Douglas.

704 Surrey's borrowing of 'right and faith' from Douglas is unsatisfactorily integrated into the sentence.

710 **Without sound**. Virgil says the spear clanged and hung idly; Douglas omits mention of the clanging (perhaps wondering how it could do both).

714 Neoptolemus is another name for Pyrrhus.

728–9 Surrey follows Douglas in his additions to Virgil.

Hugh Latimer (1491–1555)

Hugh Latimer was appointed bishop of Worcester in 1516 but became a follower of Lutheranism and resigned his bishopric in 1539 rather than assent to the Six Articles. He resumed preaching in 1549, after the accession of Edward VI (1547), and often preached public sermons at St Paul's Cross. With the accession of Mary he was brought to trial, and burnt in 1555 (see the account by Foxe, below). The 'Sermon on the Plougher,' preached at St Paul's Cross on Friday 18 January 1549, is a vigorous and eloquent example of the traditional type of popular sermon in which the preacher, addressing the different estates of society, analyses the ill state of the realm. It is a form of preaching with which *Piers Plowman*, soon to be published for the first time in printed form by Robert Crowley (1550), with a Protestant preface, has many affinities. Latimer argues that prelates must be ploughers (see *PP* VIII.2n): their ploughing is preaching, and the neglect of it ruins the commonwealth. At the end, the preacher gives an extraordinary twist to the image of the 'faithful ploughman'. Text from the print of 1549, issued a few weeks after the sermon was delivered.

Sermon on the Plougher

... But nowe for the defaulte of unpreachyng prelates, me thinke I coulde gesse what myghte be sayed for excusynge of them: they are so troubeled wyth lordelye lyvynge, they be so placed in palacies, couched in courtes, ruffelynge[1] in theyr rentes, daunceynge in theyr dominions, burdened with ambassages, pamperynge of theyr panches lyke a monke that maketh his Jubilie,[2] mounchynge in their maungers, and moylynge[3] in their gaye manoures and mansions, and so troubeled wyth loyterynge in theyr lordeshyppes, that they canne not attende it. They are otherwyse occupyed, somme in the kynges matters, some are ambassadoures, some of the Pryvie Counsell, some to furnyshe the courte, some are lordes of the parliamente. some are presidentes and some comptroleres of myntes. Well, well.

Is thys theyr duetye? Is thys theyr offyce? Is thys theyr callyng? Should we have ministers of the church to be comptrollers of the myntes? Is thys a meete[4] office for a prieste that hath cure of soules?[5] Is this hys charge? I woulde here aske one question. I would fayne knowe who comptrolleth the devyll at home in his parishe, whyle he comptrolleth the mynte? If the apostles mighte not leave the office of preaching to be deacons, shall one leave it for myntyng?...

Let the priest preache, and the noble-men handle the temporall matters. Moyses was a mervelous man, a good man. Moyses was a wonderful felowe, and dyd his dutie, beinge a maried man.[6] We lacke such as Moyses was. Well, I woulde al men woulde loke to their dutie, as God hath called them,[7] and then we shoulde have a florishyng Christian commune-weale.

And nowe I would aske a straung question. Who is the most diligent bishoppe and prelate in al England, that passeth al the reste in doinge his office? I can tel, for I knowe him, who it is; I knowe hym well. But nowe I thynke I se you lysting and hearkening that I shoulde name him. There is one that passeth al the other, and is the most diligent prelate and precher in al England. And wyl ye knowe who it is? I wyl tel you. It is the Devyl. He is the moste dyligent preacher of al other, he is never out of his diocese, he is never from his cure, ye shall never fynde hym unoccupyed, he is ever in his parishe, he keepeth residence at al tymes, ye shall never fynde hym out of the waye. Cal for him when you wyl, he is ever at home, the diligenteste preacher in all the realme. He is ever at his ploughe, no lordynge nor loytringe can hynder hym; he is ever appliynge his busynes, ye shal never fynde hym idle, I warraunte you. And his office is to hinder religion, to mayntayne supersticion, to set up idolatrie, to teache al kynde of popetrie;[8] he is readye as can be wished for to sette forthe his ploughe, to devise as manye wayes as can be to deface and obscure Godes glory. Where the Devyl is residente and hath his plough goinge,

1 **ruffelynge in theyr rentes**: 'swaggering in clothes bought with their rents'. Latimer's fancy alliteration mocks the preening self-indulgence of prelates.

2 fiftieth anniversary

3 busying themselves

4 suitable

5 **cure of soules**: pastoral responsibility for the care of the souls of his parishioners.

6 **beinge a maried man**: 'even though he was a married man' (a jibe at the enforced celibacy of the Roman clergy).

7 See 1 Cor. 7:20, and *PP* V.43a.

8 popery

there, awaye wyth bokes, and up wyth candelles; awaye wyth bibles and up wyth beades;[9] awaye wyth the lyghte of the Gospel, and up wyth the lyghte of candelles, yea, at noone-dayes. Where the Devyll is residente, that he maye prevaile, up wyth al superstition and idolatrie, sensing,[10] peintynge of ymages, candles, palmes, asshes,[11] holye water, and newe service of mennes inventing, as though man could invent a better waye to honoure God wyth then God himselfe hath apointed. Downe with Christes crosse, up with purgatory picke-purse, up wyth hym, the popishe pourgatorie, I meane. Awaye wyth clothinge the naked, the pore and impotent, up wyth deckynge of ymages and gaye garnishinge of stockes and stones;[12] up wyth mannes traditions and his lawes, downe with Gods traditions and hys most holy worde; downe wyth the olde honoure dewe to God, and up wyth the new gods honour; let al things be done in Latine.[13] There muste be nothynge but Latine, not as much as *Memento, homo, quod cinis es, et in cinerem reverteris* – 'Remembre, man, that thou arte asshes, and into asshes thou shalte returne.' Whiche be the wordes that the minister speaketh to the ignoraunte people when he gyveth them asshes upon Asshe Wensdaye, but it muste be spoken in Latine. Goddes worde may in no wyse be translated into Englyshe. Oh that our prelates woulde be as diligente to sowe the corne of good doctrine as Sathan is to sowe cockel and darnel![14] And this is the devilyshe ploughinge, the which worcketh to have thinges in Latine, and letteth[15] the fruteful edification...

9 prayer-beads (rosaries)

10 **sensing**: use of incense (see MillT 3341).

11 **asshes**: the practice of smearing ashes on the foreheads of penitents on Ash Wednesday.

12 The idea that image-worship distracted people from Christian charity was a commonplace among Lollards. Much of Protestant polemic is inevitably reminiscent of Lollard views, whether or not it is indebted to them. See Thorpe, Pecock, pp. 308, 423, above.

13 Latin is the 'new god'.

14 **cockel and darnel**: weeds growing amongst the corn. The orthodox church had formerly applied this same image to the Lollards.

15 hinders

Roger Ascham (1515–1568)

Roger Ascham was educated at Cambridge and became one of the most famous humanist scholars of his day. He was briefly tutor to the young princess Elizabeth (1548–50) and later, after serving as an ambassadorial secretary at the court of the emperor Charles V, he was Latin secretary to both queen Mary and queen Elizabeth. He maintained an extensive Latin correspondence with scholars on the continent, and reminds us, in his Preface to *Toxophilus* (1545), that English, for all its triumphs, was still thought, among scholars, a vulgar language, much inferior to Latin and Greek, and very vulnerable to vulgar attempts at enrichment. Yet he writes this treatise on archery in English, and the language seems to encourage him in a wonderful lightness and ease, and an extraordinarily fresh acuteness of observation, especially in the description of the play of the wind on the snow on the open Yorkshire fields. He is here almost a precursor of the indefatigably observant amateur natural historians of the eighteenth century. In *The Schoolmaster* (1570), he pleads for a more humane treatment of schoolboys (against the regular practice of severe beating), believing the purpose of education to be the inculcation of good manners and virtues as well as learning (for an analysis of Tudor schooling, see Halpern [1991], pp. 19–100). His attack on the corrupting influence of Italian books carries him into his famous diatribe against Malory. *English Works*, ed. W.A. Wright (Cambridge, 1904), containing reprints of the first printed texts, by Edward Whitchurch (1545) and John Daye (1570), as followed here.

Toxophilus, or, The School of Shooting

Why he writes in English (from the Preface)

... If any man woulde blame me, eyther for takynge such a matter in hande, or els for writing it in the Englyshe tongue, this answere I maye make hym, that whan the beste of the realme thinke it honest for them to use, I, one of the meanest sorte, ought not to suppose it vile for me to write. And though to have written it in another tonge had bene bothe more profitable for my study and also more honest for my name, yet I can thinke my labour wel bestowed yf, with a little hynderaunce of my profyt and name, maye come any fourtheraunce to the pleasure or commoditie of the gentlemen and yeomen of Englande, for whose sake I tooke this matter in hande. And as for the Latin or Greke tonge, everythyng is so excellently done in them that none can do better; in the Englysh tonge, contrary, everythinge in a maner so meanly, bothe for the matter and the handelynge, that no man can do worse. For therin the least learned, for the moste parte, have ben alwayes moost redye to wryte. And they whiche had leaste hope in Latin have bene moste boulde in Englyshe, when surelye every man that is moste ready to taulke is not moost able to wryte.

He that wyll wryte well in any tongue muste folowe thys councel of Aristotle, to speake as the common people do, to thinke as wise men do; and so shoulde every man understande hym and the judgement of wyse men alowe hym. Many English writers have not done so, but, usinge straunge wordes, as Latin, French and Italian, do make all thinges darke and harde. Ones I communed with a man whiche reasoned the Englyshe tongue to be enryched and encreased thereby, sayinge: 'Who wyll not prayse that feaste where a man shall drinke at a diner bothe wyne, ale and beere?' 'Truely,' quod I, 'they be all good, every one taken by hymselfe alone, but if you putte Malvesye and sacke, read wyne and white, ale and beere and al in one pot, you shall make a drynke neyther easie to be knowen nor yet holsom for the bodye.'

The wind on the snow

To se the wynde, with a man his eyes, it is unpossible, the nature of it is so fyne and subtile, yet this experience of the wynde had I ones myselfe, and that was in the great snowe that fell .iiii. yeares agoo. I rode in the hye-waye betwixt Topcliffe-upon-Swale and Borowebridge,[1] the waye beyng sumwhat trodden afore by waye-fayrynge men. The feeldes on bothe sides were playne,[2] and laye almost yearde-depe with

1 These are places in north Yorkshire, where Ascham was born, and where he visited frequently.

2 flat

snowe; the nyght afore had ben a litle froste, so that the snowe was hard and crusted above. That morning the sun shone bright and clere, the winde was whistelinge alofte, and sharpe accordynge to the tyme of the yeare. The snowe in the hye-waye laye lowse and troden wyth horse feete: so as the wynde blewe it toke the lowse snow with it and made it so slide upon the snowe in the felde (whyche was harde and crusted by reason of the frost overnyght) that therby I myght se verye wel the hole nature of the wynde as it blewe that daye. And I had a great delyte and pleasure to marke it, whyche maketh me now far[3] better to remember it.

Sometyme the wynd would be not past .ii. yeardes brode, and so it would carie the snowe as far as I could se. Another tyme the snow woulde blowe over halfe the felde at ones. Sometyme the snowe woulde tomble softly, by and by it would flye wonderfull fast. And thys I perceyved also, that the wind goeth by streames and not hole togither. For I should se one streame wythin a score on me,[4] than the space of .ii. score no snow would stirre, but after so muche quantitie of grounde another streame of snow at the same very tyme should be caryed lykewyse, but not equally. For the one would stande styll when the other flew apace, and so contynewe, somtyme swiftlyer, sometime slowlyer, sometime broder, sometime narrower, as far as I coulde se. Nor it flewe not streight, but sometyme it crooked thys waye, sometyme that waye, and somtyme it ran round aboute in a compase. And somtyme the snowe wold be lyft clene from the ground up into the ayre, and by and by it would be al clapt to the grounde as though there had bene no winde at all, streightway it woulde rise and flye agayne.

And that whych was the moost mervayle of al, at one tyme .ii. driftes of snowe flewe, the one out of the west into the east, the other out of the north into the east. And I saw .ii. windes, by reason of the snow, the one crosse over the other, as it had bene two hye-wayes. And agayne I shoulde here the wynd blow in the ayre, when nothing was stirred at the ground. And when all was still where I rode, not verye far from me the snow should be lifted wonderfully. This experience made me more mervaile at the nature of the wynde than it made me conning in the knowlege of the wynd; but yet therby I learned perfitly that it is no mervayle at al thoughe men in a wynde lease theyr length in shooting, seying[5] so many wayes the wynde is so variable in blowynge.

The Schoolmaster

How Italian books and Arthurian romances corrupt the young

There be in man two speciall thinges: mans will, mans mynde. Where will inclineth to goodnes, the mynde is bent to troth; where will is caried from goodenes to vanitie, the mynde is sone drawne from troth to false opinion. And so the readiest way to entangle the mynde with false doctrine is first to intice the will to wanton livyng. Therfore when the busie and open Papistes abroad could not by their contentious bookes turne men in England fast enough from troth and right judgement in doctrine, than the sutle and secrete Papistes at home procured bawdie bookes to be translated out of the Italian tonge, whereby over-many yong willes and wittes allured to wantonnes do now boldly contemne all severe bookes that sounde to[1] honestie and godlines.

In our forefathers tyme, whan Papistrie, as a standyng poole, covered and overflowed all England, fewe bookes were read in our tong, savyng certaine bookes of chevalrie, as they sayd, for pastime and pleasure, whiche, as some say, were made in monasteries by idle monkes or wanton chanons:[2] as one for example, *Morte Arthure*, the whole pleasure of which booke standeth in two speciall poyntes, in open mans-slaughter and bold bawdrye. In which booke those be counted the noblest knightes that do kill most men without any quarell and commit fowlest advoulteries by sutlest shiftes:[3] as Sir Launcelote

3 feel
4 within twenty yards of me
5 seeing that

The Schoolmaster
1 have to do with
2 Ascham gives a wildly inaccurate account of pre-Reformation literacy and reading practice; but as long as he can abuse these books as both immoral *and* Catholic, he is happy.
3 The Scots Protestant Lindsay likewise condemns Lancelot's adultery (*Squire Meldrum*, 54, above).

with the wife of king Arthure his master; Syr Tristram with the wife of king Marke his uncle; Syr Lamerocke with the wife of king Lote, that was his owne aunte. This is good stuffe, for wise men to laughe at, or honest men to take pleasure at! Yet I know when Gods bible was banished the court and *Morte Arthure* received into the princes chamber. What toyes the dayly readyng of such a booke may worke in the will of a yong jentleman or a yong mayde, that liveth welthelie and idlelie, wise men can judge, and honest men do pitie.

And yet ten *Morte Arthures* do not the tenth part so muche harme as one of these bookes made in Italie and translated in England. They open, not fond and common wayes to vice, but such subtle, cunnyng, new and diverse shiftes to cary yong willes to vanitie and yong wittes to mischief, to teach old bawdes new schole-poyntes, as the simple head of an Englishman is not able to invent nor never was hard of in England before, yea, when Papistrie overflowed all. Suffer these bookes to be read and they shall soone displace all bookes of Godly learnyng.

A Mirror for Magistrates (second edition, 1563)

John Wayland, having brought out a printed edition of Lydgate's *Fall of Princes*, saw the opportunity, about 1554, for a sequel. He enlisted the services of a group of poets and versifiers, under the supervision of William Baldwin, a respected writer and scholar, in the putting together of a compilation of similar 'tragedies', based on a roll-call of the famous unfortunate of English history from the late fourteenth century (where the *Fall* left off) up to near-contemporary times. There was no shortage of materials, since to be famous and dead were the sole requirements for admission, and there was no danger, even in the reign of Mary, in the dissemination of such a toothless version of history. The *Mirror* eventually came out in 1559, with different tragedies by different hands (including George Ferrers, Thomas Chaloner, Thomas Phaer and Thomas Churchyard), and Baldwin replacing 'Bochas' as the person to whom the unfortunates addressed their complaints. More tragedies were added in 1563, 1578 and 1587: the 1563 edition included the long Induction that Thomas Sackville, co-author of the verse-tragedy of *Gorboduc* (1561), later a prominent court-servant of Elizabeth (Lord Buckhurst 1567, earl of Dorset 1604), wrote for his tragedy of the duke of Buckingham. This lurid and facilely accomplished piece, once much admired, is mostly Virgilian pastiche, inspired by the description of Aeneas's descent into Hades in *Aeneid* VI, as translated by Douglas and Surrey (see above). Many of the conventions of medieval dream-allegory are also present (seasonal setting, metrical form), and there are ghoulish echoes of the *PF*. These death-throes of the medieval high style, even as they anticipate its renewal and recuperation in Spenser's *Faerie Queene*, make a striking contrast with the plainer and tougher styles of the poems of Wyatt in Tottel's *Songs and Sonnets*, published just a few years before (1557). But one at least of the *Mirror*'s hacks refused to acquiesce as limply as Lydgate in the moral lessons of 'fall of princes' Fortune-tragedy, or merely to indulge in contentless poeticizing. The tragedy of lord Hastings, as it is told by a precocious young lawyer, John Dolman, reflects upon omens, chance, fate and predestination in a manner that both Chaucer (Dolman seems to know the Nun's Priest's Tale) and Shakespeare would have found interesting. Edition by L.B. Campbell (Cambridge, 1938); text from the print of 1563. Studies by L.B. Campbell, *Tudor Conceptions of History and Tragedy in* A Mirror for Magistrates (Berkeley, 1936); A. Hadfield, *LSE* 23 (1992), 127–56; Hadfield (1994), pp. 81–107.

THE INDUCTION TO THE COMPLAINT OF HENRY, DUKE OF BUCKINGHAM, BY THOMAS SACKVILLE (1536–1608)

The wrathfull winter prochinge on apace
With blustring blastes had al ybared the treen,
And olde Saturnus with his frosty face
With chilling colde had pearst the tender green,
The mantels rent, wherein enwrapped been
The gladsom groves that nowe laye overthrowen,
The tapets torne, and every blome downe blowen. *'tapestries'*

The soyle that earst so seemely was to seen
Was all despoyled of her beauties hewe,
And soot freshe flowers, wherwith the sommers queen *sweet*
Had clad the earth, now Boreas blastes downe blewe; *the north wind's*
And small fowles flocking in theyr song did rewe
The winters wrath, wherwith eche thing defaste
In woful wise bewayld the sommer past.

Hawthorne had lost his motley lyverye,
The naked twigges were shivering all for colde,
And dropping downe the teares abundantly
Eche thing, me thought, with weping eye me tolde
The cruell season, bidding me withholde

1–21 This gloomy variant on the medieval seasons-opening (cf. Skelton's *Garland of Laurel*) uses much antique-sounding language (**treen**, **ybared**, cf. **yeding**, 208, formed from a ME past tense) as well as heavily archaic alliteration.

Myselfe within, for I was gotten out
Into the fieldes where as I walkte about.

{The seasonal opening continues with elaborate astronomical allusion.}

And sorowing I to see the sommer flowers,
The lively greene, the lusty leas forlorne,
The sturdy trees so shattered with the showers,
The fieldes so fade that floorisht so beforne,
It taught me wel all earthly thinges be borne
To dye the death, for nought long may time last:
The sommers beauty yeeldes to winters blast.

gleams Then looking upward to the heavens leames
With nightes starres thicke powdred everywhere,
Which erst so glistened with the golden streames
That chearefull Phebus spred downe from his sphere,
Beholding darke oppressing day so neare,
brought back The sodayne sight reduced to my minde
The sundry chaunges that in earth we fynde;

That musing on this worldly wealth in thought,
Which comes and goes more faster than we see
The flyckering flame that with the fyer is wrought,
My busie minde presented unto me
noblemen Such fall of pieres as in this realme had be,
That ofte I wisht some would their woes descryve,
To warne the rest whom Fortune left alive.

{He meets the ghastly goddess Sorrow, who is come to warn princes that their pomp and power is but transient. She conducts him down to the pit of Avernus.}

An hydeous hole al vaste, withouten shape,
Of endles depth, orewhelmde with ragged stone,
Wyth ougly mouth and grisly jawes doth gape,
And to our sight confounds itselfe in one.
proceeding Here entred we and, yeding forth, anone
An horrible lothly lake we might discerne
As blacke as pitche, that cleped is Averne –

A deadly gulfe where nought but rubbishe growes,
effluent With fowle blacke swelth in thickned lumpes that lyes,
Which up in the ayer such stinking vapors throwes
That over there may flye no fowle but dyes,
Choakt with the pestilent savours that aryse.
Hither we cum, whence forth we still dyd pace,
In dreadful feare amid the dreadfull place.

And first within the portche and jawes of Hell
Sate diepe Remorse of Conscience, al besprent
With teares, and to herselfe oft would she tell
stop Her wretchednes, and cursing never stent
To sob and sigh, but ever thus lament

With thoughtful care, as she that all in vayne
Would weare and waste continually in payne.

Her iyes unstedfast rolling here and there
Whurld on eche place, as place that vengeaunce brought,
So was her minde continually in feare,
Tossed and tormented with the tedious thought
Of those detested crymes which she had wrought,
With dreadful cheare and lookes throwen to the skye,
Wyshyng for death, and yet she could not dye.

{Dread, Revenge, and other allegorical inhabitants of Avernus are described, and the portrayal all around of the miserable fate of the princes of the past, and the fall of Troy.}

But Troy, alas, me thought, above them all
It made myne iyes in very teares consume,
When I beheld the wofull werd befall *fate*
That by the wrathfull wyl of gods was come;
And Joves unmooved sentence and foredoome
On Priam kyng and on his towne so bent
I could not lyn but I must there lament. *cease*

And that the more sith destinie was so sterne
As force perforce there might no force avayle
But she must fall; and by her fall we learne
That cities, towres, wealth, world and al shal quayle.
No manhoode, might nor nothing mought prevayle,
Al were there prest ful many a prynce and piere *vigorously engaged*
And many a knight that solde his death full deere.

Not wurthy Hector, wurthyest of them all,
Her hope, her joye, his force is nowe for nought.
O Troy, Troy, there is no boote but bale! *nothing for it but destruction*
The hugie horse within thy walles is brought:
Thy turrets fall, thy knightes, that whilom fought
In armes amyd the fyeld, are slayne in bed,
Thy gods defylde and all thy honour dead.

The flames upspring and cruelly they crepe
From wall to roofe, til all to cindres waste.
Some fyer the houses where the wretches slepe,
Sum rushe in here, sum run in there as fast:
In everywhere or sworde or fyer they taste. *either sword or*
The walles are torne, the towers whurld to the ground:
There is no mischiefe but may there be found.

Cassandra yet there sawe I howe they haled
From Pallas house, with spercled tresse undone, *dishevelled*
Her wristes fast bound, and with Greeks rout empaled; *surrounded*

435–76 The fall of Troy is one of the great themes of medieval lamentation, as in Lydgate's *Troy-Book* (see above), which Sackville raids freely, as well as the *Aeneid*-translations of Douglas and Surrey. The portrayal of these events in the form of paintings on the shield of Mars (*Warre*) imitates *Aeneid* VII.625, and there are many echoes too of the description of the temple of Mars in Chaucer's Knight's Tale.

And Priam eke in vayne howe he did runne
To armes, whom Pyrrhus with despite hath done
To cruel death, and bathed him in the bayne
Of his sonnes blud before the altare slayne.

But howe can I descryve the doleful sight
That in the shylde so livelike fayer did shyne,
Sith in this world I thinke was never wyght
Could have set furth the halfe not halfe so fyne?
I can no more but tell howe there is seene
hot coals Fayer Ilium fal in burning red gledes downe
And from the soyle great Troy, Neptunus towne.

{Crossing Acheron, they come at last to the centre of Hades.}

Thence cum we to the horrour and the hel,
realm The large great kyngdomes and the dreadful raygne
Of Pluto in his trone where he dyd dwell,
The wyde waste places and the hugye playne,
The waylinges, shrykes and sundry sortes of payne,
The syghes, the sobbes, the diepe and deadly groane,
Earth, ayer and all resounding playnt and moane.

Here pewled the babes and here the maydes unwed
With folded handes theyr sory chaunce bewayled;
Here wept the gyltles slayne, and lovers dead,
That slewe themselves when nothyng els avayled;
A thousand sortes of sorrowes here that wayled
together With sighes and teares, sobs, shrykes and all yfere,
That, oh alas! it was a hel to heare.

{At this point, as the Induction sinks into exhaustion, the duke of Buckingham steps forward to lament his life and the service he did to Richard III.}

The tragedy of lord Hastings, by John Dolman (*c.*1540–*c.*1602)

{Hastings, after telling the story of his life, recounts the omens and forewarnings that preceded and accompanied his last journey to the Tower to attend the meeting called by Richard III to discuss the coronation of the new king.}

What should we thinke of sygnes? They are but happs.
How maye they then be sygnes of afterclaps?
Doth every chaunce forshew or cause some other,
Or endyng at itselfe extendth no furder?
As th'overflowyng floude some mount doth choake,
Unless But to his ayde some other floude hit yoake:
So yf with sygnes thy synnes once joyne, beware,
(see n.) Els wherto chaunces tend nere curyous care.

476 Sackville, copying Douglas, misses the sense: 'And fra [rooted out from] the soyll gret Troy, Neptunus town, / Ourtumlyt to the grond' (Book 2, chap. 10, 114–15).

496 'were not a matter for earnest enquiry'

revenge — Had not my synne deserved my death as wreake,
bowing its head — What myght my myrth have hurt? or horses becke?
Or Hawardes bitter scoffe? or Hastinges talke?
reckon — What meane then foole astrologers to calke
That twyncklyng sterres flyng down the fixed fate,
And all is guyded by the sterrye state?
duty — Perdye, a certayne taxe assygned they have
To shyne, and tymes divyde, not fate to grave.

But graunt they somwhat gyve: is at one instant
Of every babe the byrth in heaven so skannd
(i.e. the planets) — That they that restlesse roll and never staye
Should in his lyfe beare yet so vyolent swaye,
That not his actions onely next to byrth
But even last fyne and death be sweyed therwith?
Howe may one mocion make so sundry effectes?
Or one impression tend to such respectes?

deferred — Some rule there is yet. Els, whye were differrd
plagues — Tyll nowe these plages, so long ere now deserved?
Yf for they are tryfles, they ne seeme of care:
But toyes with God the statelyest scepters are.
too plainly, foreordained — Yet in them to playne doth appere foresett
The certayne rule and fatall lymytes sett.
Yet thinke we not this sure foresettyng fate
But Gods fast provydence for eche pryncely state.

And hath he erst restraynd his provydence,
Or is he nygard of his free dispence?
Or is he uncertayne foresett dryfts to dryve
That not Dame Chaunce but he all goods may gyve?
A heathen god they hold whoe Fortune keepe
To deale them happs whyle God they ween asleepe.
introduce — Mock-godds they are and many gods induce
Whoe Fortune fayne to father theyr abuse.

should have — Howe so it be, hit mought have warned me;
But what I could not, that in me see ye,
Whoe runne in race the honour lyke to wynn,
Whose fayrest forme nought maye deforme but synne.
Alas, when most I dyd defye all dread
By syngle heare deaths sworde hong over my head.
For herk the end and lysten now my fall:
This is the last, and this the fruit of all.

{He describes the meeting at the Tower, from which he was taken to execution (as told by More, above, in Richard III*, Dolman's source), and ends with moralizing reflections upon his fall.}*

498–9 He refers to omens already recounted – his affair with mistress Shore, the hesitation of his horse before the Tower, Howard's jibe, as Hastings stops to talk to a priest, that he does not yet (but soon will) need a priest, and the warnings of Hastings, his pursuivant.

515–16 God's idea of what are trifles is not the same as ours.

528 Dolman's knotted syntax can be difficult, but this line is a triumph.

534 The allusion is to the sword of Damocles.

John Foxe (1517–1587)

Acts and Monuments of Martyrs

John Foxe became a Fellow of Magdalen College, Oxford, in 1543, but was expelled from the university for his religious views. He became tutor to the children of the earl of Surrey (the poet), but was forced into exile during the reign of Mary. He published a Latin 'Book of Martyrs' while abroad, and translated it and continued expanding and revising it after returning to England on the accession of Elizabeth and being appointed to a prebendary at Salisbury. His vast work, published in 1563 as *Acts and Monuments of these latter and perilous days, touching matters of the church...* (etc.), is a chronological inventory of those martyred by the Roman church as heretics from the year 1000, the bulk of the attention being given to the Protestant martyrs of the reigns of Henry VIII and Mary. His work was considered to be so important that when the second edition came out in 1570 (*The Ecclesiastical History containing the Acts and Monuments of Martyrs...*) it was ordered that a copy be put beside the Bible in cathedral and other churches. In its two large folio volumes, with marginal summaries and dates, indices, illustrations and variation of typeface, it is a magnificent piece of book-production. The work continued to be expanded and reprinted for 300 years after Foxe's death. Text here from the second edition (John Daye, 1570), II.1152–3, 1937–9. Modernized text, ed. S.R. Cattley, 8 vols (London, 1837–41); studies by J.F. Mozley (London, 1940), W. Haller (New York, 1963), W.W. Wooden (Boston, 1983) and J.R. Knott, *Discourses of Martyrdom in English Literature, 1563–1694* (Cambridge, 1993), pp. 11–116.

The first extract, concerning Simon Fish (see above), is not an account of a martyrdom: it shows Foxe in his quieter vein, shaping a narrative to his great purpose, lacing the account with the specific details and dates that give authenticity, and representing the villains, Wolsey and More, as vain and petty rather than as monsters of bigotry. The portrait of Henry VIII is interesting: it shows Foxe working with a variety of source-materials, but also (surely) adding some inventive touches of his own, making the king into a benevolently god-like observer of what is happening, all-powerful and yet blameless (as indeed must be the case, given that he was the queen's father). The second extract has Foxe at his more usual work of fortifying the resolve of the Protestant state by keeping the Marian persecutions vividly in mind. Hugh Latimer, former bishop of Worcester (see above), and Nicholas Ridley, bishop of London, had been prominent in the cause of Protestantism during the reign of Edward VI, and it was important that an example should be made of them now that Catholicism was restored. It is perhaps the most famous of Foxe's many martyrdoms, which derive their power from simplicity and homely touches rather than from ranting. Foxe allows the terrible story to tell itself as if it were the plain record, as indeed it may well mostly be, since although he may have relied uncritically upon eye-witness and other reports (if they were of the right persuasion), he did not engage in wholesale fabrication.

Concerning Simon Fish

After that the light of the Gospel, workyng mightely in Germanie, began to spread his beames here also in England, great styrre and alteration folowed in the harts of many, so that colored hypocrisie and false doctrine and painted holynes began to be espyed more and more by the readyng of Gods word. The authoritie of the Bishop of Rome and the glory of his Cardinals was not so high but such as had fresh wittes, sparcled with Gods grace, began to espy Christ from Antichrist, that is, true sinceritie from counterfait religion. In the number of whom was the sayd Master Symon Fish, a gentleman of Grayes Inne.[1]

It happened the first yeare that this gentleman came to London to dwell, which was about the yeare of our Lord 1525, that there was a certaine play or interlude made by one Master Roo of the same Inne, gentleman, in which play partly was matter agaynst the Cardinal Wolsey. And where none durst take upon them to play that part, whiche touched the sayd Cardinall, this foresayd Master Fish tooke upon him to do it; wherupon great displeasure ensued agaynst him upon the Cardinals part; in so much as he, beyng pursued by the sayd Cardinall, the same night that this tragedie was playd, was compelled of force to voyde his owne house, and so fled over the sea unto Tyndall.[2] Upon occasion wherof, the next yeare folowyng, this booke[3] was made (beyng about the yeare 1527) and so not long after, in the yeare (as

1 One of the Inns of Court, where lawyers were trained.

2 William Tyndale (see above) was in Antwerp working on his Bible-translations.

3 viz. *A Supplication for the Beggars*.

I suppose) 1528, was sent over to the Lady Anne Bulleyne, who then lay at a place not farre from the court. Which booke, her brother seyng in her hand, tooke it and read it, and gave it her agayne, willyng her earnestly to give it to the kyng, which thyng she so dyd. This was, as I gather, about the yeare of our Lord 1528. The kyng, after he had receaved the booke, demaunded of her, who made it. Wherunto she aunswered and sayd, a certaine subject of his, one Fish, who was fled out of the realme for feare of the Cardinall. After the kyng had kept the booke in his bosome iii. or iiii. dayes, as is credibly reported, such knowledge was given by the kynges servantes to the wife of the sayd Symon Fishe that she might boldly send for her husband, without all perill or daunger. Whereupon she, thereby beyng incouraged, came first and made sute to the kyng for the safe returne of her husband. Who, understandyng whose wife she was, shewed a marvelous gentle and chearefull countenaunce towardes her, askyng where her husband was. She aunswered, 'If it like your grace, not farre off.' Then sayth he, 'Fetch him, and he shall come and go safe without perill, and no man shal do him harme'; saying moreover that hee had much wrong that hee was from her so long (who had bene absent now the space of two yeares and a half). In the whiche meane tyme the Cardinall was deposed, as is afore shewed, and Master More set in his place of the Chauncellourshyp.

Thus Fishes wife, beyng emboldened by the kynges wordes, went immediatly to her husband, beyng lately come over and lying prively within a myle of the court, and brought him to the kyng (which appeareth to be about the yeare of our Lord 1530). When the kyng saw him, and understode he was the authour of the booke, he came and embraced him with loving countenaunce; who after long talke, for the space of iii. or iiii. houres, as they were ridyng together on huntyng, at length dimitted him and bad him take home his wife, for she had taken great paynes for him. Who aunswered the kyng agayne and sayd he durst not so do, for feare of Syr Thomas More, then Chauncellour, and Stoksley, then Byshop of London. This seemeth to be about the yeare of our Lord 1530.

The kyng, takyng his signet of his finger, willed hym to have him recommended to the Lord Chauncellour, chargyng him not to bee so hardy to worke him any harme. Master Fishe, receivyng the kynges signet, went and declared hys message to the Lord Chauncellour, who tooke it as sufficient for his owne discharge, but he asked him if he had anythyng for the discharge of his wife; for she a litle before had by chaunce displeased the friers, for not sufferyng them to say their gospels in Latine in her house, as they did in others, unlesse they would say it in English. Whereupon the Lord Chauncellour, though he had discharged the man, yet leavyng not his grudge towardes the wife, the next mornyng sent his man for her to appeare before hym; who, had it not bene for her young daughter, which then lay sicke of the plague, had bene lyke to come to much trouble. Of the which plague her husband, the sayd Master Fish, deceasing within halfe a yeare, she afterward maryed to one Master James Baynham, Syr Alexander Baynhams sonne, a worshypful knight of Glostershyre. The which foresaid Master James Baynham, not long after, was burned, as incontinently after, in the processe of this story, shall appeare.[4]

And thus much concernyng Symon Fishe, the author of the booke of beggars, who also translated a booke called the Summe of the Scripture out of the Dutch.

{Foxe goes on to tell another story, from a different source, of how the book came into the king's hands – how it was brought to him by merchants returning from overseas:} The whole booke beyng read out, the kyng made a long pause, and then sayd, 'If a man should pull downe an old stone wall and begyn at the lower part, the upper part thereof might chaunce to fall upon his head.' And then he tooke the booke and put it into his deske and commaunded them uppon their allegiance that they should not tell to any man that he had sene the booke. The copie of the foresayd booke, intituled of the Beggars, here ensueth.

The behaviour of doctor Ridley and master Latimer at the time of their death (16 October 1555)

{Latimer and Ridley have been brought to Oxford to be interrogated and invited to recant. At the last, condemned to the stake, they are made to listen to a sermon by doctor Richard Smith, university professor of divinity, in which they are, at one point, denounced as heretics.}

4 James Bainham was brought to trial for heresy and made submission, but he later recanted his submission and was burned.

At which place they lifted up both their handes and eyes to heaven, as it were callyng God to witnes of the truth. The which countenance they made in many other places of his sermon, where as they thought he spake amisse. He ended with a very short exhortation to them to recant and come home agayne to the church and save their lyves and soules, which els were condemned. His sermon was scant in all a quarter of an houre.[1]

Doctor Ridley sayd unto master Latymer, 'Will you begyn to aunswere the sermon, or shall I? Master Latymer sayd, 'Begyn you first, I pray you.' 'I will,' sayd master Ridley.[2]

Then, the wicked sermon being ended, doctor Ridley and master Latimer kneeled downe upon their knees towardes my lord Williams of Tame, the vice-chauncellour of Oxford, and divers other commissioners appointed for that purpose, who sat upon a forme thereby; unto whom master Ridley sayd, 'I besech you, my lord, even for Christes sake, that I may speake but two or three wordes.' And whilest my lord bent his head to the maior and vice-chauncellour, to know (as it appeared) whether he might geve hym leave to speake, the bayliffes and doctor Marshall ran hastely unto hym and with theyr handes stopped his mouth, and sayd, 'Master Ridley, if you wil revoke your erroneous opinions, and recant the same, you shall not onely have libertie so to do but also the benefite of a subject, that is, have your lyfe.' 'Not otherwise?' said master Ridley. 'No,' quoth doctor Marshall; 'therefore if you will not so do, then there is no remedy but you must suffer for your desertes.' 'Well,' quoth master Ridley, 'so long as the breath is in my body, I will never deny my Lord Christ and his knowen truth: Gods will be done in me!' And with that he rose up, and sayd with a loude voyce, 'Well then, I commit our cause to Almighty God, which shall indifferently judge all.' To whose saying, master Latimer added his old posie,[3] 'Well! there is nothyng hid but it shal be opened.' And he sayd hee could aunswere Smith well inough, if he might be suffered.

Incontinently[4] they were commaunded to make them ready, which they with all meekenes obeyed. Master Ridley tooke his gowne and his tippet,[5] and gave it to his brother-in-law master Shepside, who all his tyme of emprisonment, although he might not bee suffered to come to hym, lay[6] there at hys own charges to provide hym necessaries, which from tyme to tyme he sent hym by the serjeant that kept hym. Some other of hys apparell, that was litle worth, he gave away; other the bayliffes tooke.

He gave away, besides, divers other small things to gentlemen standyng by, and divers of them pitifully weepyng: as to syr Henry Ley he gave a new groate, and to divers of my lord Williams's gentlemen some napkyns, some nutmegs, and races[7] of gynger; hys diall,[8] and such other thinges as he had about hym, to everyone that stode next hym. Some plucked the pointes off hys hose.[9] Happy was he that might get any ragge of hym!

Master Latimer gave nothyng, but very quietly suffered hys keeper to pull of hys hose and his other aray, which to looke unto was very simple. And beyng stripped into his shrowde, he seemed as comely a person to them that were there present as one should lightly see; and whereas in hys clothes he appeared a withered and crooked sely old man, he now stode bolt upryght, as comely a father as one might lightly behold.

Then master Ridley, standyng as yet in hys trusse,[10] sayd to his brother, 'It were best for me to go in my trusse still.' 'No,' quoth hys brother, 'it will put you to more payne: and the trusse will do a poore man good.' Whereunto master Ridley said, 'Be it, in the name of God', and so unlaced himselfe. Then, beyng in his shirt, he stode uppon the foresayd stone and held up his handes, and sayd, 'Oh heavenly Father, I geve unto thee most hartie thankes for that thou hast called me to bee a professour[11] of thee, even unto death. I besech thee, Lord God, take mercy uppon thys realme of England, and deliver the same from all her enemies.'

1 A short sermon would be scorned by Protestants, who placed a high value on preaching.

2 Ridley throughout takes the lead: he was more of a scholar, and Latimer was older, and growing very tired.

3 **posie**: motto, saying. The remark that follows seems to have been a catchphrase of Latimer's.

4 immediately

5 **tippet**: scarf of cloth attached to the head-dress. Foxe has a note to say that it was nothing like the rich silk tippets affected by Catholic priests.

6 lodged

7 roots

8 **diall**: watch. This distribution of personal possessions was part of the ritual of preparation for the stake.

9 **pointes**: tagged laces that attached the hose to the doublet.

10 close-fitting breeches

11 one who professes (bears witness to the truth of)

Then the smith tooke a chaine of iron, and brought the same about both doctor Ridleyes and master Latimers middles; and, as he was knocking in a staple, doctor Ridley tooke the chayne in his hand, and shaked the same, for it did gyrd in[12] his belly, and, looking aside to the smith, said, 'Good fellow, knocke it in hard, for the flesh wyll have his course.' Then his brother did bring hym gunpouder in a bag, and would have tyed the same about his necke. Master Ridley asked what it was. His brother sayd, 'Gunpowder.' 'Then,' sayd hee, 'I take it to be sent of God; therefore I wyll receive it as sent of him. And have you any,' said he, 'for my brother?' (meaning master Latimer). 'Yea sir, that I have,' quoth his brother. 'Then geve it unto hym,' sayd he, 'betyme, lest ye come to late.' So his brother went and carryed of the same gunpouder unto master Latymer.

In the meane time doctor Ridley spake unto my lord Wyllyams, and sayd, 'My lord, I must be a suter unto your lordship in the behalfe of divers poore men, and especially in the cause of my poore sister: I have made a supplication to the queenes majesty in their behalfes. I besech your lordship, for Christes sake, to be a meane[13] to her grace for them. My brother here hath the supplication, and will resort to your lordship to certify you hereof. There is nothing in all the world that troubleth my conscience, I prayse God, this onely excepted: whyles I was in the see of London, divers poore men took leases of me and agreed with me for the same. Now I heare say the bishop that now occupyeth the same roome wyll not allow my grauntes unto them made, but contrary unto all law and conscience hath taken from them their livinges, and will not suffer them to enjoy the same. I beseech you, my lord, bee a meane for them: you shall do a good dede, and God wyll reward you.'

Then they brought a fagot, kindled with fyre, and layd the same downe at doctor Ridleyes feete. To whom master Latymer spake in this maner: 'Be of good comfort, master Ridley, and play the man. We shall this day lyght such a candle, by God's grace, in England, as I trust shall never be put out.'[14]

And so the fier being geven unto them, when doctor Ridley saw the fire flaming up towards hym, he cryed with a wonderfull loud voyce, '*In manus tuas, Domine, commendo spiritum meum: Domine recipe spiritum meum!*'[15] And after, repeated this latter part often in English, 'Lord, Lord, receave my spirite', master Latimer crying as vehemently on the other syde, 'Oh Father of heaven, receave my soule!' who receyved the flame as it were embrasing of it. After that he had strooked hys face with his handes and as it were bathed them a litle in the fier, he soone died, (as it appeareth) with very litle payne or none. And thus much concernyng the end of thys old and blessed servaunt of God, master Latimer, for whose laborious travailes, fruitfull life and constant death the whole realme hath cause to geve great thankes to Almightie God.

But master Ridley, by reason of the evill making of the fire unto hym, because the woodden fagottes were layd about the gosse,[16] and over-hye built, the fyre burned first beneath, being kept downe by the wood; which when he felt, he desired them for Christes sake to let the fyre come unto him. Which when his brother-in-law heard, but not well understoode, entending to rid him out of hys payne (for the which cause he gave attendaunce), as one in such sorrow not well advysed what he did, heaped fagots uppon him, so that he cleane covered him, which made the fire more vehement beneath, that it burned cleane all hys neather partes before it once touched the upper; and that made him leape up and downe under the fagots, and often desyre them to let the fyre come unto hym, saying, 'I cannot burne.' Which indeede appeared wel; for, after his legges were consumed by reason of his struggling through the payne (whereof he had no release, but onely his contentation in God),[17] he shewed that syde towardes us[18] cleane, shirt and all untouched with flame. Yet in all this torment he forgat not to cal unto God stil, having in his mouth, 'Lord have mercy upon me,' intermedling his cry, 'Let the fyre come unto me, I cannot burne.' In which paynes he laboured till one of the standers-by with his bill[19] pulled of the fagots above, and where he sawe the fire flame up, he wrested[20] himselfe unto that syde. And when the flame touched the gunpowder, he was seene styrre no more, but burned on the other syde, fallyng downe at master Latimers

12 press too tightly upon

13 intercessor

14 These, the most famous lines in Foxe, were added in the 1570 edition, it is not known from what source. They are in the tradition of 'last words' (cf. Wolsey, More).

15 'Into thy hands, O Lord, I commend my spirit; Lord, receive thou my spirit.'

16 **gosse**: gorse (brushwood used for kindling).

17 acquiescence in the will of God

18 **us**. Foxe's account was taken from the eye-witness report of Ridley's brother-in-law.

19 **bill**: a spear with a curved axe-head. Several are shown in the woodcut accompanying the text at p. 1938.

20 twisted

feete: which, some sayd, happened by reason that the chayne loosed; others sayd that he fell over the chayne by reason of the poyse of his body and the weakenes of the neather limmes. Some said that before he was lyke to fall from the stake he desired them to hold him to it with their billes. However it was, surely it moved hundreds to teares, in beholding the horrible sight, for I thinke there was none that had not cleane exiled all humanitie and mercy which would not have lamented to behold the furye of the fire so to rage upon their bodies....

Well, dead they are, and the reward of this world they have already. What reward remaineth for them in heaven, the day of the Lordes glory, when he cometh with hys sayntes, shall shortly, I trust, declare.

George Gascoigne (1539–1578)

George Gascoigne was educated at Cambridge and as a lawyer, tried unsuccessfully to attach himself at court, fought in campaigns in the (Protestant) Low Countries against the Spanish, and eventually settled to a career as a writer. He was representative of a new breed of professional writer – gentlemen with education and not much money who took advantage of the financial and career opportunities offered by the printing press and who tried also to create a network of patrons to sustain them in difficult times. Gascoigne and his friends (such as Nicholas Breton and George Whetstone) were thus different from Wyatt and Surrey: they wrote fashionable love-poems, but also much in more public genres. Gascoigne wrote poems upon set moral and proverbial themes, flattering poems to prospective patrons, commendatory verses for his friends' publications (as they for his), travel poems, verses for royal pageants, a poem on his experience of war in the Low Countries, plays and translations of plays, and much prose in various genres. *Works*, ed. J.W. Cunliffe, 2 vols (London, 1907–10).

The Steel Glass

The Steel Glass (1576) is Gascoigne's most famous poem, an 'estates-satire', much influenced by Chaucer and Langland, in which he criticizes in turn the corruption of the several classes of society. The poet is a plain, honest-dealing man who, instead of showing vanity and folly in a flattering mirror, will show them for what they are in a mirror of steel, which never lies ('true as steel'). His style is deliberately plain, in the manner that C.S. Lewis (1954) called 'drab'; blank verse is used for the first time in a non-translated poem (cf. Surrey), though the lines are so systematically end-stopped that the rhyme seems almost obtrusively absent. In the extracts below, the appeal to knights and gentlemen to serve their country echoes, after two centuries, many of Langland's preoccupations (e.g. *PP* I.90–100, VIII.23–53), though it is responsive too to Tudor ideas of the role in local government of the knightly class, while the introduction of the Plowman (as one of those whom good priests are bidden to pray for) shows the direct influence of *Piers Plowman*, popular in Protestant England after being printed for the first time by Robert Crowley in 1550. Text from the first edition (1576).

Exhortation to knights, squires and gentlemen

O knights, O squires, O gentle blouds yborne,
You were not borne al onely for yourselves:
Your countrie claymes some part of al your paines.
There should you live and therin should you toyle
To hold up right and banish cruel wrong,
To help the pore, to bridle back the riche,
To punish vice, and vertue to advaunce,
To see God servde and Belzebub suprest.
You should not trust lieftenaunts in your rome — *place*
And let them sway the scepter of your charge,
Whiles you meanewhile know scarcely what is don,
Nor yet can yeld accompt if you were callde.
  The stately lord, which woonted was to kepe
A court at home, is now come up to courte,
And leaves the country for a common prey
To pilling, polling, brybing and deceit – — *pillaging, thieving*
Al which his presence might have pacified,
Or else have made offenders smel the smoke! — *(feel the pain of punishment)*
And now the youth which might have served him
In comely wise, with countrey clothes yclad,
And yet therby bin able to preferre — *to be recommended*
Unto the prince and there to seke advance,
Is faine to sell his landes for courtly cloutes, — *clothes*
Or else sits still and liveth like a loute

(Yet of these two the last fault is the lesse).
young shoots And so those imps which might in time have sprong
Alofte, good lord, and servde to shielde the state
Are either nipt with such untimely frosts
pruned Or else growe crookt bycause they be not proynd.

Pray for ploughmen

Now these be past, my priests, yet shal you pray
For common people, eche in his degree,
That God vouchsafe to graunt them al his grace.
say my prayers Where should I now beginne to bidde my beades,
Or who shal first be put in common place?
My wittes be wearie and my eyes are dymme,
I cannot see who best deserves the roome.
Stand forth, good Peerce, thou Plowman by thy name....
   Behold him, priests, and though he stink of sweat
Disdaine him not, for shal I tel you what?
Such clime to heaven before the shaven crownes.
But how? Forsooth, with true humilytie.
Not that they hoord their grain when it is cheape,
Nor that they kill the calfe to have the milke,
Nor that they set debate betwene their lords
ploughing By earing up the balks that part their bounds;
Nor for because they can both crowche and creep
(The guilefulst men that ever God yet made)
When as they meane most mischiefe and deceite;
Nor that they can crie out on landelordes lowde
raise, jot And say they racke their rents an ace to high,
When they themselves do sel their landlordes lambe
For greater price then ewe was wont be worth
(I see you, Peerce, my glasse was lately scowrde!) –
But for they feed with frutes of their gret paines
Both king and knight and priests in cloyster pent.
Therefore I say that sooner some of them
Shal scale the walles which leade us up to heaven
Than corn-fed beasts, whose bellie is their God,
Although they preach of more perfection.

The Spoil of Antwerp

By contrast with *The Steel Glass*, this description of the sack of the rich city of Antwerp (1576), besieged and taken with ease by a small force of well-trained Spanish troops, with slaughter of 17,000 of its inhabitants, is writing of a new kind. Gascoigne is the eye-witness, communicating the actuality, the confusion, the hectic tumble of experience, in an efficient, colloquial, graphic prose and in a manner befitting the first real 'war-reporter'. The characterization and self-characterization is vivid, the eye (and prejudices) of the professional soldier much in evidence. Text from the printed tract of 1576 (which includes a map of Antwerp).

1029 Cf. *PP* XI.292–8. In the following lines, the true honest Peerce Plowman is contrasted with the greedy and self-seeking husbandman.

1034 **balks**: ridges separating ploughed land (see *PP* VIII.114n, above).

The seizing of the town

The castle[1] had all this while played at the towne and trenches with thundring shot, but now, upon a signall geven, ceased to shoote any more, for feare to hurt their owne men: wherin I noted their good order, which wanted no direction in their greatest furye. The Wallonnes and Almaynes[2] which served in the trenches defended al this while very stoutly, and the Spanyerds, with their Almaynes, contynewed the charge with such valure that in fyne[3] they won the counterscarf[4] and presently scaled the trenches with great fury. The Wallonnes and Almaines, having long resysted without any fresh reliefe or supplye (many of them in this mene-while being slayne and hurte), were not able any longer to repulse the Spanyerds; so that they entred the trenches about twelve of the clock and presently pursued their victory down every streate. In their chase, as faste as they gained any crosse-streate, they flanked the same with their musquets untill they saw no longer resistance of any power, and then proceeded in chase, executing all such as they overtooke. In this good order they charged and entred; in this good order they proceded; and in as good order their lackeyes and pages followed with firebrands and wyldfyre, setting the houses on fyre in every place where their maysters had entred.

The Wallonnes and Almaynes which were to defend the town, being growen into some security by reason that their trenches were so high as seemed invincible, and lacking sufficient generals and directors, were found as far out of order as the Spanyerds were to be honored for the good order and direction which they kepte. For those which came to supplye and relieve the trenches came stragling and loose. Some came from the furdest side of the towne, some that were nearer came very fearefully, and many out of their lodginges, from drinking and carousing, who would scarsely beleeve that any conflicte was begonne, when the Spanyerdes nowe mette them in the streates to put them out of doubt that they dallyed not. To conclude, their carelesnesse and lack of foresyght was such that they had never a *Corps du gard* to supply and relieve their trenches, but only one in the market-place of the town, whiche was a good quarter of a myle from their fortifycations; and that also was of Almaynes who, when they spied the Spanyerds, did gently kneele down, letting their pykes fall, and crying *'Oh lieve Spaniarden! lieve Spaniarden!'*[5]

Now I have set downe the order of their entrye, approch, charge and assaulte, together with their proceeding in victory, and that by credible report, both of the Spanyerdes themselves and of others who served in their company, let me also say a litle of that which I sawe executed. I was lodged in the Englishe house *ut supra*,[6] and had not gone abroade that morning by reason of weighty businesse which I had in hand the same day. At dinner-tyme the marchauntemen of my countrey, whiche came out of the towne and dined in my chamber, told me that a hote scarmouch[7] was begon in the castle-yeard, and that the furye thereof stil increased. Aboute the middest of dinner, newes came that the shot was so thick as neyther ground, houses nor people could be discearned for the smoke thereof, and, before dinner were fully ended, that the Spaniardes were like to win the trenches. Whereat I stept from the table and went hastily up into a high tower of the sayd English house, from whence I might discover fyre in fower or five places of the towne, towardes the castle-yeard, and thereby I was wel assured that the Spanyerds indeede were entred within the trenches. So that I came down and tooke my cloake and sword, to see the certainty thereof, and as I passed toward the Bource[8] I met many, but I overtoke none. And those which I mette were no townsmen, but souldyeres, neither walked they as men which use traffique[9] but ran as men whiche are in feare. Wherat being somwhat greved, and seeing the townsemen stand every man before his doore with such weapons as they had, I demaunded of one of them, what it mente? Who aunswered me in these wordes: *'Helas, mounsieur, il n'y a poynt de ordre, et voila la ruine de ceste ville!' 'Aiez courage, mon amy!'* quoth I, and so went onwardes yet towards the Bowrce, meeting all the way more and more which mended[10] their pace. At last a Wallon trompeter on horsback (who seemed to be but a boy of yeres) drew his sworde and layd about him, crying, *'Ou est que vous enfuiez, canaille? Faisons teste, pour le honeur de la*

1 siege-castle (wooden tower to fire from into the city)
2 Walloons and Germans (there are German mercenaries fighting on both sides)
3 in the end
4 exterior slope of the defensive ditch
5 'dear Spaniards!'
6 ***ut supra***: 'as (explained) above'. The English merchants and other businessmen had their own 'hotel'.
7 **scarmouch**: 'skirmish' (cf. *TC* II.611).
8 central banking and commerce building
9 go about their business
10 quickened

patrie!' Wherewith fyfty or three score of them turned head and wente backewardes towardes the Bource, the which encouraged mee (*per companie*) to proceede.

But alas, this comforte indured but a while, for by that time I came on the farder syde of the Bource I might see a great trowpe comming in greater haste, with their heads as close togeather as a skoule of yong frye[11] or a flocke of sheepe; who met me on the farder side of the Bource toward the market-place, and having their leaders formost (for I knewe them by their javelines, bore-speares and staves) bare me over backwardes and ran over my belly and my face, long time before I could recover on foote. At last, when I was up, I looked on every syde and, seeing them ronne so fast, began thus to bethinke me: What in Gods name doe I heare, which have no interest in this action, synce they who came to defend this town are content to leave it at large, and shift for themselves? And whilest I stoode thus musing, another flocke of flyers came so fast that they bare me on my nose and ran as many over my backe as erst had marched over my guttes. In fine, I gotte up, like a tall fellow, and wente with them for company, but their haste was such as I could never overtake them, until I came at a broad crosse-streate which lyeth betweene the English house and the sayd Bource. There I overtooke some of them, groveling on the ground and groning for the last gaspe, and some other which turned backwards to avoyd the tickling of the Spanishe musquets, who had gotten the ends of the sayd broad crosse-streate and flanked it both wayes. And there I stayde a whyle till, hearing the shot increase and fearing to bee surprysed wyth suche as mighte follow in tayle of us, I gave adventure[12] to passe through the sayde crosse-streate and (without vaunte be it spoken) passed through five hundred shotte before I could recover the English house...

11 fish

12 took a chance

Edmund Spenser (1552–1599)

The Shepherd's Calendar

The Shepherd's Calendar is Spenser's first published work (1579), though his name was not attached to it until the folio edition of his works in 1611. Like Virgil, he begins his poetic career with a sequence of twelve pastorals or eclogues: Spenser adds an extra touch of rusticity by having them follow, month by month, the round of the shepherd's year, as if in a shepherd's almanac. In pastoral the shepherd is a figure for the poet, the lover or the pastor, and their concerns are less with sheep than with themselves, poetry, love and public affairs. Pastoral provides poetic occasions, authorial distance, licence to speak of contentious issues in the authentic voice of natural truth and simplicity, pleasure in the uncorrupted world of natural beauty – and the opportunity of tapping into one of the richest veins of classical and western poetry. Spenser enhances the Virgilian effect by arranging for the provision of scholarly apparatus and annotations (attributed to 'E.K.', perhaps his friend Edward Kirke) such as editions of Virgil were customarily equipped with for scholars. Some of the eclogues are love-laments; some are occasions for song, panegyric and celebration; some (E.K.'s 'moral' eclogues) are written in a tradition of ecclesiastical satire that consciously goes back to Chaucer and Langland, both of whom were regarded as anticipating Protestantism in their anticlerical satire. It is Spenser's polite way (with Chaucerian mock-humility, he attributes the whole *Calendar* to one 'Immerito' – see A.M. Esolen, in *SP* 87 [1990], 285–311) of declaring his place in the tradition of English poetry, of restoring poetry to the centre-stage of public life, and thus preparing for the *Faerie Queene*. *January* alone is included here, as sounding the first strains of a new voice in English poetry. It harks back to Chaucer and Langland, in its occasionally archaic vocabulary and thick alliteration, but there is a quality of self-conscious and near-comic hyperbole in the imitations, and in the occasional fustian of the winter-descriptions (purposeful poeticizing, by contrast with Sackville's hollow pastiche), that declares Spenser's independence and distance from his predecessors and also his more complex characterization of the lover/poet's hopes, fears and anxieties. Text from the first edition (1579). Important studies of the *Calendar* by R. Helgerson, in *PMLA* 93 (1978), 893–911; L. Montrose, in *TSLL* 21 (1979), 34–67, and in *ELH* 50 (1983), 415–59; J.N. King, in Lewalski (1986), pp. 369–98; P. Alpers, in Greenblatt (1988), pp. 163–80; L. Staley Johnson, *The Shepheardes Calender* (University Park, PA, 1990); Halpern (1991), pp. 176–214; and of *January* by H. Berger, in *Helios* 10 (1983), 139–60.

January

'In this fyrst Aeglogue Colin Cloute, a shepheardes boy complaineth him of his unfortunate love, being but newly (as semeth) enamoured of a countrie lasse called Rosalinde; with which strong affection being very sore traveled, he compareth his carefull case to the sadde season of the yeare, to the frostie ground, to the frozen trees, and to his owne winterbeaten flocke. And lastlye, fynding himselfe robbed of all former pleasaunce and delights, hee breaketh his pipe in peeces and casteth himselfe to the ground.'

A shepeheards boye (no better doe him call),
When winters wastful spight was almost spent,
All in a sunneshine day, as did befall,
Led forth his flock, that had bene long ypent.
So faynt they woxe and feeble in the folde
That now unnethes their feete could them uphold.

All as the sheepe, such was the shepeheards looke,
For pale and wanne he was, alas the while!
Perhaps May seeme he lovd, or els some care he tooke:
he knew how to Well couth he tune his pipe and frame his stile.
Then Tho to a hill his faynting flocke he ledde
And thus him playnde, the while his shepe there fedde.

'Ye gods of love, that pitie lovers payne
(If any gods the paine of lovers pitie),

Looke from above, where you in joyes remaine,
And bowe your eares unto my doleful dittie.
And Pan, thou shepheards god, that once didst love,
Pitie the paines that thou thyselfe didst prove.

Thou barrein ground, whome winters wrath hath wasted,
Art made a myrrhour to behold my plight:
Whilome thy fresh spring flowrd and after hasted
Thy sommer prowde with daffadillies dight,
And now is come thy wynters stormy state,
Thy mantle mard wherein thou maskedst late.

Such rage as winters reigneth in my heart,
My life-bloud friesing with unkindly cold;
Such stormy stoures do breede my balefull smart *fits of anguish*
As if my yeare were wast and woxen old.
And yet, alas, but now my spring begonne,
And yet, alas, yt is already donne.

You naked trees, whose shady leaves are lost,
Wherein the byrds were wont to build their bowre,
And now are clothd with mosse and hoary frost
Instede of bloosmes wherwith your buds did flowre,
I see your teares that from your boughes doe raine,
Whose drops in drery ysicles remaine.

All so my lustfull leafe is drye and sere,
My timely buds with wayling all are wasted;
The blossome which my braunch of youth did beare
With breathed sighes is blowne away and blasted,
And from mine eyes the drizling teares descend,
As on your boughes the ysicles depend.

Thou feeble flocke, whose fleece is rough and rent,
Whose knees are weake through fast and evill fare,
Mayst witnesse well by thy ill governement
Thy maysters mind is overcome with care.
Thou weake, I wanne; thou leane, I quite forlorne;
With mournyng pyne I, you with pyning mourne.

A thousand sithes I curse that carefull hower *times*
Wherein I longd the neighbour towne to see,
And eke tenne thousand sithes I blesse the stoure *moment of pain*
Wherein I sawe so fayre a sight as shee.
Yet all for naught: such sight hath bred my bane.
Ah, God, that love should breede both joy and payne!

It is not Hobbinol wherefore I plaine,
Albee my love he seeke with dayly suit.

55–60 'In thys place seemeth to be some savour of disorderly love, which the learned call *paederastice*: but it is gathered beside his meaning'. E.K.'s note goes on at some length to distinguish between noble Platonic love, as of Socrates for Alcibiades, and the 'execrable and horrible sinnes of forbidden and unlawful fleshlinesse'. The learned note seems the occasion of the stanza, rather than vice versa.

His clownish gifts and curtsies I disdaine,
home-made cakes His kiddes, his cracknelles and his early fruit.
Ah, foolish Hobbinol, thy gifts bene vayne:
Colin them gives to Rosalind againe.

I love thilke lasse (alas, why doe I love?)
And am forlorne (alas, why am I lorne?)
Shee deignes not my good will, but doth reprove,
And of my rurall musick holdeth scorne.
Shepheards devise she hateth as the snake,
And laughes the songes that Colin Clout doth make.

Wherefore my pype, albee rude Pan thou please,
Yet for thou pleasest not where most I would,
And thou unlucky Muse, that wontst to ease
My musyng mynd, yet canst not when thou should,
pay for Both pype and Muse shall sore the whyle abye!'
So broke his oaten pype, and downe dyd lye.

faded, bring down By that the welked Phoebus gan availe
cart His weary waine, and nowe the frosty night
draw over Her mantle black through heaven gan overhaile;
Which seene, the pensife boy, halfe in despight,
sun-wearied Arose, and homeward drove his sonned sheepe,
Whose hanged heads did seeme his carefull case to weepe.

61–2 'A pretty Epanorthosis in these two verses, and withall a Paronomasia or playing with the word' (E.K.). The scholarly pedantry is not entirely ironic. For other rhetorical figures, see 13–14, 29–30, 47–8.

66 Colin Clout seems to have been introduced as a rustic personage by Skelton (see above).

78 The final alexandrine anticipates that of the nine-line stanza of the *Faerie Queene*.

Textual Variants

CHAUCER

PARLIAMENT OF FOWLS. (MS Gg.4.27, 481r–490v.) 5. Astonyeth F] Gg ther. 7. flete Ff] Gg slete. 29. make F] Gg make of. 33. therynne F (theryn)] Gg thereon. 50. here F] Gg now. 57. lytel F] Gg *om.* 65. disseyvable] Gg was sumdel d. 77. of Ff] Gg *om.* 80. th'erthe F] Gg there. 82. hir F] Gg his. 84. his MSS] Gg *om.* 85 faylen MSS] Gg folwyn. 88. bed F] Gg self. 110. to-torn F] Gg byforn. 123. gate F] Gg gatis. 124. iwriten MSS (F writen)] Gg iwrete. 132. of-caste F] Gg ouercaste . 137. Ther F] Gg That. tre F] Gg yit. 138. the F] Gg *om.* 143. with F] Gg whi. 155. iwriten] Gg writyn. 170. went in F] Gg that as. 175. joye Ff] Gg sothe. 185. that MSS] Gg ther. 204. aire F] Gg erthe. 216. touchede MSS] Gg couchede. 221 by force MSS] Gg before. 299. sonne F] Gg sunnys. 303. of F] Gg *om.* 324. the F] Gg *om.* 326. of which F] Gg *om.* no F] Gg myn. 345. chough F] Gg crowe. 354. of hewe F] Gg and newe. 358. ever F] Gg most. 368. of F] Gg *om.* 400. ye F] Gg they. 401. yow F] Gg ye. 404. sorest F] Gg soryest. 436. she F] Gg he. 438. knette F] Gg arette. 444. the F] Gg hire. 450. and F] Gg *om.* 461. to F] Gg in. 462. she F] Gg the. 471. But as F] Gg That. 507. the charge nowe F] Gg no charg howe. 516. synge F] Gg fynde. 518. uncommytted F] Gg onquit. 520. behynde F] Gg *om.* 524. of F] Gg on. 533. thanne F] Gg *om.* 551. hir F] Gg he. 560. hire F] Gg hym. 562. hire F] Gg his. 563. She F] Gg He. 569. she F] Gg he. 577. turtil F] Gg tersel (*so* 583). 594. goos MSS] Gg doke (*over erasure*). 596. fy F] Gg sey. 614. wormes F] Gg werm. 622. or F] Gg and. 627. ryght F] Gg *om.* 645. ryght F] Gg that. 658. hem F] Gg hym. 663. quyte F] Gg what. 680. thy MSS] Gg *om.* 682. longe MSS] Gg large. 684. smale MSS] Gg smal. 689. synge MSS] Gg ben.

TROILUS AND CRISEYDE. **Book II**. (MS Corpus 61, 27r–46r.) 35. no J] Cp *om.* 61. that hym J] Cp hym. 86. the J] Cp the fayre. 90. goode J] Cp good. 128. swiche J] Cp swych. 204. frendlieste MSS] Cp frendliest. 206. felawshipe MSS] Cp felawship. 212. namelich Cl] Cp namlich. 216. herde J] Cp herd. 220. it MSS] Cp *om.* 224. yow J] Cp thow. 248. fremde MSS] Cp frende. 276. faste J] Cp fast. 279. thoughte J] Cp thought. 309. Now J] Cp And. 323. deyen J] Cp deye. 328. gilteles MSS] Cp giltles. 334. fulle Cl] Cp ful. 338. listeth J] Cp list. 349. ther Cl] Cp *om.* 383. goode MSS] Cp good. 426. for me J] Cp *om.* 441. bothe Cl] Cp both. 487. yow though J] Cp youre thought. bothe J] Cp both. 488. o J] Cp a. 519. softely J] Cp softly. 553. newe J] Cp new. 588. yet Cl] Cp *om.* 597. so J] Cp *om.* 598. ne J] Cp no. 603. wax MSS] Cp was. 610. thoughte Cl] Cp thought. 641. myghte Cl] Cp myght. 646. herde J] Cp herd. 669. firste Cl] Cp first. 670. ne MSS] Cp *om.* 677. herte MSS] Cp *om.* 701. thoughte MSS] Cp thought. 704. yit J] Cp that. 713. to J] Cp *om.* 737. this MSS] Cp this ilk. 778. moste J] Cp moost. 780. or J] Cp and. 781. that J] Cp the. 801. that J] Cp *om.* 851. righte MSS] Cp right. 852. alle J] Cp al. 860. hym J] Cp it. 871. deere J] Cp deer. 904. eye J] Cp heye. 914. unto J] Cp til. **Book III**. (MS Corpus 61, 71v–92v.) 507. ilke Cl] Cp ilk. 525 an Cl] Cp and. 529. bothe J]

Cp both. 535. hereupon eke J] Cp hereup. 559. moste J] Cp most. 623. The J] Cp At the. 631. goode Cl] Cp good. 655. bedde J] Cp bed. 696. alle MSS] Cp al. 699. And J] Cp As. 722. O J] Cp *om.* 758. thus J] Cp *om.* 759. trappedore J] Cp trapdore. 763. myghte MSS] Cp myght. 781. worthieste J] Cp worthiest. 866. that J] Cp *om.* 876. that J] Cp *om.* 892. myghte J] Cp myght. 917. al J] Cp *om.* 928. hadde grace Cl] Cp a grace hadde. 942. ben bothe J] Cp beth both. 950. ese J] Cp eseth. 955. beste J] Cp best. 956. sodeynliche MSS] Cp sodeynlich. 958. koude Cl] Cp kouth. 963. trouthe J] Cp trouth. 977. oother J] Cp *om.* 996. deere J] Cp deer. 1009. goode J] Cp good. 1012. wolde J] Cp wold. 1024. thus ye J] Cp thi (*gap left*). 1025. busshel venym J] Cp busshe (*gap left*) evyn. 1027. heighe Cl] Cp heigh. 1049. that J] Cp *om.* 1066. liste J] Cp list. 1106. is J] Cp *om.* 1110. dere J] Cp deer. 1137. sike Cl] Cp sik. 1142. it J] Cp *om.* 1166. alle J] Cp al. 1193. but J] Cp *om.* 1211. iwys J] Cp I was. 1214. moste J] Cp most. 1216. ofte J] Cp oft. 1220. assaied was J] Cp w.a. 1223. bothe J] Cp both. 1228. *so* J; Cp *om.* 1294. I J] Cp *om.* 1296. wommanliche Cl] Cp wommanlich. 1299. nat J] Cp *om.* 1331. myne J] Cp myn. 1368. entrechaungeden J] Cp entrechaunged. 1375. cretche MSS] Cp tecche. 1385. ther J] Cp that. 1387. wolde J] Cp wold. 1404. a J] Cp *om.* 1438. and thyn Cl] Cp and. 1473. myn J] Cp *om.* 1552. he J] Cp she. 1553. eft J] Cp ofte. 1573. smyteth J] Cp smyten. 1576–82. *so* Cl; Cp *om.* **Book V.** (MS Corpus 61, 131v–137v, 148r–150r.) 885. on-lyve J] Cp lyve. 900. lye J] Cp he. 910. dorste J] Cp dorst. 956. ilke J] Cp ilk. 991. then J] Cp *om.* 992. nevere er I MSS] Cp I n.e. 993. werke J] Cp werk. 1012. sothe J] Cp soth. 1033. hymselven J] Cp hymself. 1035. sothe J] Cp soth. 1781. false Cl] Cp fals. 1782. wit J] Cp *om.* 1791. pace Cl] Cp space. 1796. the J] Cp the this. 1798. I MSS] Cp *om.* 1800. for J] Cp *om.* 1809. eighthe J (viij)] Cp seventhe. 1839. thilke J] Cp thilk. 1857. and to the J] Cp and to.

THE CANTERBURY TALES. **General Prologue.** (Hengwrt MS, 2r–12v.) 43. KNYGHT: modern editions use capitals to mark the introduction of each new pilgrim, following the wording of the marginal rubrication in HgEl. 60. arivee] HgEl armee (for this emendation, see E.T. Donaldson, in *Medieval Studies in Honor of Lillian H. Hornstein* [New York, 1977], pp. 99–110). 95. make and wel El] Hg wel make and. 120. seinte] HgEl seint (for this emendation, see E.T. Donaldson, in *SN* 21 [1949], 122–30). 131. ne fille El] Hg fille. brest El] Hg brist. 132. ful muchel El] Hg muchel. lest El] Hg list. 161. ther El] Hg *om.* 196. ywroght El] Hg wroght. 207. is a El] Hg any. 375. weere they El] Hg t.w. 485. ypreved MSS] HgEl proeved. 509. Seinte] HgEl seint (see textual note to GP 120). 516. to synful men noght MSS] HgEl n.t.s.m. 603. ne El] Hg *om.* 637–8. *so* El; Hg *om.* 660. him MSS] HgEl *om.* 756. lakkede MSS] HgEl lakked. **Miller's Prologue and Tale.** (Hengwrt MS, 41r–50v.) 3120. al El] Hg a. 3155–6. *so* El; Hg *om.* 3183. and othere manye El] Hg eek a.o. 3205. ydight El] Hg dight. 3304. aboute El] Hg upon. 3329. Oxenforde MSS] HgEl Oxenford. 3343. carpenteris El] Hg carpenters (*so* 3356, 3359, 3694, 3787, 3850; perhaps pronounced with four syllables?). 3422. the El] Hg *om.* 3429. yborn El] Hg born. 3431–2. *reversed* Hg. 3477. what(3) El] Hg *om.* 3482. of El] Hg on. 3483. Seinte] HgEl seint (see textual note to GP 509). 3518. Noees El] Hg Nowelis. 3576. hire El] Hg his. 3577. wol I El] Hg woltow. 3590. bitwixe El] Hg bitwix. 3621. that El] Hg *om.* 3697. softe El] Hg ofte. 3721–2. *so* El; Hg *om.* 3750. I El] Hg *om.* 3810. amydde El] Hg in. 3811. handebrede El] Hg handbrede. 3828. yet El] Hg *om.* **Wife of Bath's Prologue and Tale.** (Hengwrt MS, 58r–73v.) 44a–f. *so* MSS; HgEl *om.* (see Donaldson, as cited in textual note to GP 60). 120. maked MSS] HgEl maad. 215. so El; Hg *om.* 231. womman] HgEl wyf. 303. Janekyn El] Hg Jankyn (*so* 383). 306. a El] Hg *om.* 368. maner MSS] HgEl *om.* 385. giltelees MSS] HgEl giltlees. 393. beren El] Hg bern. 397. al El] Hg *om.* 431. Goode] HgEl good. 452. speken El] Hg speke. 575–84. *so* El; Hg *om.* 604. seynte] HgEl seint (see textual note to GP 509). 609–12. *so* El; Hg *om.* 619–26. *so* El; Hg *om.* 717–20. *so* El; Hg *om.* 717. that Jesu MSS] El *om.* 792. hym El] Hg *om.* 836. ech MSS] HgEl *om.* 838. pisse MSS] HgEl pees (see Donaldson, as cited in textual note to GP 60). 895. preyeden MSS] HgEl preyden. 899. *so* El; Hg *om.* 927. seyden El] Hg *om.* 955. whiche MSS] HgEl which. 1129. goodnesse El] Hg prowesse. 1161. a El] Hg *om.* 1191. it syngeth El] Hg is synne. 1199. this El] Hg thyng. **Franklin's Tale.** (Hengwrt MS, 137v, 153v–165r.) 675. Frankeleyn El] Hg Marchant (*so* 696, 699: the link is mis-adapted in Hg as the Prologue to the Merchant's Tale). 699. Frankeleyn El] Hg Marchant certeyn. 721. on El] Hg in. 770. seyen El] Hg seyn. 853. to El] Hg of. 956. yonge MSS] HgEl yong. 965. his MSS] HgEl this. 987. answere El] Hg *om.* 1003. in El] Hg *om.* 1004. go

El] Hg *om.* 1020. wrecche El] Hg wrecched. 1120. artes MSS] HgEl artz. 1269. they El] Hg *om.* 1318. giltelees MSS] HgEl giltlees. 1358. elles MSS] HgEl *om.* 1406. that MSS] HgEl *om.* 1443. seith El] Hg *om.* 1455–6. *so* El; Hg *om.* 1493–8. *so* El; Hg *om.* **Pardoner's Prologue and Tale.** (Hengwrt MS, 195r–203v.) 297–8. *so* MSS; HgEl *om.* 430. maken El] Hg make. 540. thy El] Hg the. 661. riotoures MSS] HgEl riotours (so 716, 768). 710. that El] Hg *om.* 796. the MSS] HgEl *om.* 817. how El] Hg *om.* 820. tellen El] Hg telle. 882. that El] Hg *om.* 913. heighe MSS] HgEl heigh. 941. heere El] Hg *om.* 954. thee helpe MSS] Hg thee; El with thee. 964. ye El] Hg *om.*

MINOR POEMS. **Truth.** (BL MS Add.10340, 41r.) 2. unto thy thing MSS] A thin owen thing. 7. thee MSS] A *om.* (*so* 14, 21) 28. thee] A *om.* **Scogan.** (Bodl.MS Fairfax 16, 41r.) 3. bryghte MSS] F bryght. 27. oure MSS] F youre. **Purse.** (Bodl.MS Fairfax 16, 193r–v.) 25. oure MSS] F myn.

PIERS PLOWMAN. (MS HM 143, 1r–106v.) **Prologue.** 5. sellies U] X selles. 15. I U(y)] X *om.* 21. wandryng U] X wondryng. 26. of U] X and. 44. tho U] X the. 61. marchen P] X maken. 69. of fastynges P] X and f. 141. and...made P] X *om.* 142. *from* B-text; X *om.* 143. And...Wit P] X *om.* 146. to the peple P] X *om.* 147. With P] X And with. 182–4. way...other of P] X beygh war. 188. hym P] X us. 193. no raton P] X non. 203. to U] X *om.* 217. reik MSS] X ryot. 225. of the MSS] X the. 233. *so* U; X *om.* **Passus III.** 5. here U] X at here. 41. And U] X *om.* 60. a U] X *om.* **Passus V.** 35. yong U] X yong yong. 81. or U] X *om.* 84. discret U] X desirede. **Passus VI.** 118. fore U] X lore (*over erasure*). 136. cote U] X coke. 137. tho U] X *om.* 143. I am woned U] X than woned I. 149. clawes J] X clothes. 167. wrathe U] X wreche. 222. it J] X *om.* 223. that she U] X tho he. 224. owene *so B-text*; X *om.* 234. -ow J] X *om.* 377. hit U] X *om.* 402. be U] X *om.* 420. word P] X *om.* 441. hated J] X chasted. **Passus VII.** 185. sykeren U (sekeron)] X sykerenesse. 208. as P] X *om.* 219. nat P] X *om.* 223. Two U] X tho. 225. nat P] X *om.* 236. thow U] X two. 240. thow U] X they. 254. in in P] X in. 260. be P] X *om.* 261. that P] X nat that. 277. puttes U] X places. 301. sighen U] X shien[de]. 305. *so* U] X *om.* **Passus VIII.** 2. waye U] X *om.* 5. a lady U] X that lady. 10. sowe P] X to sowe. 20. on the teme P] X in tyme. 22. assaie U] X *om.* 46. fro P] X or. 166. pes U] X mase. 226. abave U] X bane. 228. when he U] X when. 278. Dives U] X on. 283. have U] X *om.* 307. say P] X sayde. 313. Lamasse J] X lowe masse. 333. fresh U] X *om.* **Passus IX.** 38. deynge U (dying)] X doynge. 46. that U] X *om.* 48. here U] X he. 68. to U] X and to. 88. I U] X he. 133. gyveth U] X syneth. 137. arn U] X *om.* 141. That U] X *om.* 144. him U] X *om.* 157. an hater J] X han after. 291. God U] X *om.* 294. and U] X and the. **Passus X.** 7. leode *so B-text*] X *om.* 8. on a U] X in. **Passus XX.** 74. Two U] X Tho. 76. cam and U] X of tho theves cam a. 87. trinen U] X turnen (*over erasure*). 284. blente U] X brente. 285. Cheke we MSS] X Cheke. 288. castel] X car. 294. with P (whith)] X *om.* acloye P] X and cloye. 297. ne no J] X ne do. 338. be U] X *om.* 342. gret U] X *om.* 347–8. there loste...lesing MSS] X *om.* 359. and Lucifer answeride MSS] X *om.* 379. thow *so B-text*] X *om.* 382. be MSS] X *om.* yn U] X *om.* 386. lete U] X lede. 392. be MSS] X *om.* 412. I *so B-text*] X *om.* 431. I U] X or. 435. in U] X and. 440. al *so B-text*] X and. 444. ledis MSS] X *om.* 458. it ne MSS] X *om.* **Passus XXII.** 51. me MSS] X *om.* 55. spede U] X speke. 62. The whiche foles MSS] X *om.* 300. hy] X they. 363. goth and] X goth.

LETTERS OF JOHN BALL. a. ye] the. b. heryeth] heryth. c. nowe] nowye. d. dele] ydele. e. outen schame *suppl.*

TREVISA. a. ys] and ys.

SIR GAWAIN AND THE GREEN KNIGHT. (BL MS Cotton Nero A.x, 106–124v.) 1208. gay] fayr. 1265. for *suppl.* 1281. as ho] a. 1295. costes] castes. 1304. firre] fire. 1315. Was] With. 1333. boweles] bales. 1334. the lere] & lere. 1406. What] That. 1440. synglere] wight. 1441. borelych and *suppl.* brode] MS b[....] (*smudged*). 1444. sparred] *near-illegible.* 1580. and *suppl.* 1623. lote] lote and. 1639. hent *suppl.* 1696. castes] costes. 1700. a-traveres] atrayteres. 1719. list upon lif] lif upon list. 1738. hwef] hwes. 1752. dele hym *suppl.* 1755. com *suppl.* 1770. prynces] prynce. 1799. if] of. 1815. nade] hade. 1825. swyfte by] swyftel. 1861. ho *suppl.* 1878. lyste] lyfte. 1906. laches] caches. hym] by. 2105. dynges] dynnes. 2177. of] and. 2187. Here] He. 2337. rynkande] rykande. 2343. Nif] Iif. 2448. has *suppl.* 2472. and kennen *suppl.* 2506. in *suppl.* 2511. mon] non.

PATIENCE. (BL MS Cotton Nero A.x, 83v–87v.)

122. ye] he. in folye] fole. 189. hater *suppl.* 240. on] un. 259. leve] lyve. 294. thre nyght] the nyght. 313. sayde] say. 348. non] mon.

GOWER, CONFESSIO AMANTIS. (Bodl.MS Fairfax 3, 68r–69r, 113r–115v.) 5769. tyt B] F tyd. 6020. hir B] F here.

MANDEVILLE'S TRAVELS. a. so filled it] ben so filled. b. growen] ben cloven. c. rather *suppl.* d. covenable] comnable. e. nought] nought only.

CLOUD OF UNKNOWING. a. apon] MS onpon. b. thof] MS for thof. c. God] MS God love. d. nowhere and this] MS *om.*

JULIAN, REVELATIONS. **Chap. 3.** a. me] my. b. Me] My. c. me] my. d. I] it. e. me] my. f. Thus] This. **Chap. 15.** a. wherefor] were for. b. giveth] gaveth. c. mowrnyng] mownyng. **Chap. 16.** a. clongyn] cloeggeran. **Chap. 27.** a. me] my. b. forseyng] forseyde. c. fully] fulle. d. has] had. **Chap. 60.** a. throwes and most] thornes and. b. tenth] ix. c. beholdyng] beholde.

MORTE ARTHURE. (Lincoln MS 91, 64v–65v.) 1056. Braundeschte] braundesche. 1079. come] fome. 1101. gryslych] grylych.

WILLIAM THORPE. (Bodl.MS Rawlinson C.208, 81v–91v.) a. men A] R man. b. him A] R *om.* c. he A] R *om.* d. no-but...counseile A] R *om.* e. heestis A] R heest. f, g. heleful A] R helpful. h. plesynge A] R plesyngis. i. in whos A] R whos. j. be A] R bi. k. ben A] R *om.* l. unhonest A] R honest. m. that A] R *om.*

LOVE'S MIRROR. a. thei] MS that thei. b. thei *suppl.*

HOCCLEVE. **Regement of Princes.** (BL MS Arundel 38, 1r–4r, 15v–16r, 17v–19v, 38r–v, 90v; 4990–5019 from Harley 4866, where a leaf is cut out of Arundel, with the portrait.) 14. nygh R] A ne. 27. at the R] A at. 59. stryve H] A stryf. 71. This] A Thus. 83. sikenesses R] A seekenesse. 98. hevynesse R] A hevynes. 117. dressed H] A dresse. 127. drery H] A drere. 135. the R] A *om.* 141. compaignye H] A compaygne. 154. assaut MSS] A assent. 167. As I H] A As. 193. beste H] A best. 195. mysruled H] A mysruel. 830. depe R] A deep. 833. ny H] A ne. 936. abouten H] A abowte. 949. duetee R] A dutee. 965. chaunge H] A chonge. 966. straunge H] A stronge. 1003. and H] A and wyth. 1004. al H] A of al. 1027. yen R] A than. trewely] A trewly. 1039. mysseyd H] A myseyd. 2073. is H] A as. 2075. in H] A *om.* 2077. soule H] A soul. 2082. hath H] A *om.* 2087. heir] A hier. 4985. thou H] A now. 4997. lost R] H lest. 5014. suche R] H schuch. **Series.** (Bodl.MS Arch.Selden supra 53, 76r–79v, 83v–85r.) **(Complaint).** 71. Whiche D] S With. 126. yeve D] S he yeve. 127. my D] S me. **(Dialogue).** 4. it D] S *om.* 81. tell *suppl.*

LYDGATE. **Troy-Book.** (BL MS Cotton Aug.A.iv, 134v.) 7048. oughte] ought. 7057. grete] gret. 7062. transmygracioun] transmutacioun. 7064. wepe] were. 7070. felte] felt. 7082. myghte] myght. **Siege of Thebes.** (BL MS Arundel 119, 1r–3v.) 43. trouthe] trouth. 58. deden] ded. 66. while] whil. 109. with *suppl.* 110. make] mak. to *suppl.* 112. spare] spar. 114. collik] collis. 151. bothe] both. 163. It *suppl.* 165. no] a. 167. preche] prech. **Life of Our Lady.** (Durham UL MS Cosin V.ii.16, 66r–68r.) 1675. to *suppl.* 1678. eyen] eyne. 1679. to *suppl.* 1681. eyen] eyne. 1682. smale] smal. 1683. yonge] yong. 1687. yonge] yong. 1690. tunne] tune. 1699. for *suppl.* 1707. alone *suppl.* 1716. scarsite] scarste. 1724. hungrye] hungre. 1725. righte] right. 1730. angelis] angel. 1740. and our] and. 1741. valye] vale. 1745. alle] al. 1763. graye] gray. 1771. curede] purede. 1777. floweth] foloweth. 1785. highe] high. 1788. eyen] eyne. 1794. of thy] of the. 1795. regnen] regne. 1806. servaunte] men. **Dance Macabre.** (Bodl.MS Arch.Selden supra 53, 148r–158v.) 13. brighte] bright. 24. Machabrees] Machabres. 220. with] a. 233. brode] brood. 262–4. to walke...barge *suppl.* 335. fee] free. 391. is *suppl.* 476. al (2) *suppl.* 485. loste] lost. 487. teinte] teint. 504. sheweth] shewe. science] sentence. 580. Be] By. 638. I] ye. 656. hennes] hens. **Fall of Princes.** (Bodl.MS Bodley 263, pp.85–6, 135.) I.6888. enclosid] onclosid. 6912. hoole] hool. 6919. gilteles] giltles (*also* 6929). 6921. kyndenesse] kyndnesse. 6925. gilte] gile. eke *suppl.* 6946. comparable] incomparable. 7025. hir (1)] his. 7031. sharpe] sharp. 7033. myhte] myht. 7041. as *suppl.* **Letter to Gloucester.** (BL MS Harley 2255, 45v–47r.) 58. celle] soyl. **Testament.** (BL MS Harley 218, 71v–72r.) 876. weel *suppl.* 887. mynde] mende.

MARGERY KEMPE. (BL MS Add.61823.) a. sche] MS *om.* b. fer] MS for. c. it] MS is. d. ne schalt] MS schalt.

CHARLES OF ORLEANS. **Roundel 57**. 11. to *suppl.* **(Narrative)**. 5220. ne wiste *suppl.* 5244. porpose] poor posse. 5259. sit] set. 5288. unto] to. 5290. of *suppl.* 5292. yn] ny. 5293. cawse] sawse. 5324. Crepuscule] Crepusculus. **Ballade 96**. 14. worthy] worthe. 25. enesen] enese.

ANONYMOUS SONGS AND SHORT POEMS. **In a tabernacle**. 14. Through] D Though. 15. me A] D we. 31. Sewe] D Shewe. 34. man A] D but man. 50. My barne A] D Mankynde. bete A] D bette. thy A] D hys. 53. thy A] D hys. 55. thow A] D he. 60. And A] D or. 75. man A] D a man. 90. thus] D thys. **Farewell, this world**. 23. for] but for. 24. the *suppl.* **I have a gentil cok**. 1. cok] cook (*so* 3,5). the *suppl.* **Myn hertys joy**. 16. holy] only.

FINDERN POEMS. 1.7. have *suppl.* 4.7. would] woul. 5.13. Though] Thought.

BALLADS. **Saint Steven**. 4. sterre] storre. **The Hunting of the Cheviot**. 17. Monenday] Monday. 45. bylle] brylly. 100. lookande] and loocke on. 104. fayle *suppl.* 129. mynyplye] myne ye ple. 196. set] sat. 198. on] of. 209. on on] on. 278. e'er] tear. 285. partyes] partes. **Robin Hood and the Monk**. 107. them] at them. 157. callid Robyn Hode *suppl.* 187. sore] so. 203. *line supplied*. 211. the letturs red] r.t.l. 237. the *suppl.*

FORTESCUE. a. thai *suppl.* b. the *suppl.*

MALORY, MORTE D'ARTHUR. **(Accusation and rescue)**. a. all thys *suppl.* b. and us *suppl.* c. Aggravayne] Gawayne. d. well- *suppl.* e. your chambir] you. f. nat *suppl.* g. seyde] seyde seyde. h. than] that. i, j. ye] we. k. that] than. l. sone *suppl.* m. ye] yf ye. n. kepe *suppl.* o. som] ther som. p. they] the. q. Gareth] Gawayne. r. nat *suppl.* **(Vengeance of Gawain)**. a. wepte] wepte amonge. b. for...knyghtes *suppl.* c. ye *suppl.* d. never *suppl.* e. hym bulles *suppl.* f. her] he. g. ye] he. h. therefore] and therefore. i. hard] had. j. cause *suppl.* k. from Sandwyche...perfourme *suppl.* l. woll be] was. **(Combat of Lancelot and Gawain)**. a. ther] the. b. he *suppl.* c. his *suppl.* d. dayes] dedis. e. performe] profounde. f. hym and wente *suppl.* **(The last battle)**. a. hym] a. b. that] than. c. that] than. d. my *suppl.* e. therefore] ther. f. thy dethe] my dethe. g. in the rychest *suppl.* h. for them] wyth them. i. God] for god. j. oost *suppl.* k. I *suppl.* l. they *suppl.* m. ye shall] yshall. n. good lord...dreme and *suppl.* o. I] he. p. leve] lyff. q. lorde] londe. r. your] you. s. the ermyte] ermyte. **(Death of Lancelot)**. a. my] thy. b. that] ther. c. and all] of all. d. knyghtes *suppl.* e. lust] last. f. that ther] then. g. le] de. h. there] and. i. dyed] dede. j. hoole] booke.

HENRYSON. **Testament of Cresseid**. 6. gart] can. 48. esperance] Esperus. 164. gyte] gyis (*also* 178, 260). 205. unricht] upricht. 216. Phlegonie] Philologie. 218. gay] *om.* 222. With] Quhyte. 275. or] in. 290. injure] injurie. 328. throw] thow. 337. mingit] minglit. 363. beedes] prayers. 382. spitall] hospitall. 479. Go] To. 480. leif] leir. 491. come] thai come. 523. he *suppl.* 544. ever *suppl.* **Fables**. 399. kyndis] kynd. 405. unto] to. and] and sa. 407. it excedis] is excludit. 410. and] and ane. 430. jeperdies] jeperdie. 433. smyland] simuland. 466. is] wes. 474. inflate] infect. 477. winkand] wawland. 482. countermaund] that cryme. 486. reylok] hay. 494. of] in. 523. that] with. 524. that] he. hir] his. 527. yow *suppl.* ye ar] he is. 533. Seis...with] He had quod scho. 536. Adulteraris] For adulterie. 546. Birkye] Berk. Bell *suppl.* 570. unto a] out of the. 581. coud nocht be] to be sa. 582. Bot spake] Quhairthrow. 609. fell *suppl.* 616. fatal] subtell. 618. miching] waitting. 621. Thetes *suppl.* 631. thair (3)] the. 648. the (1)] my. 649. wait] ken. 651. fait] men. 665. thence] hence. 680. and *suppl.* 697. mele] kneill. 729. falt of] fall no. into] unto. 736. walterand] water and. 737. All stonist] Astonist all. 741. For] And. net nor] nor net. 769. gane] gang. 772. The...hynt] He harlit him. 776. contritioun] provisioun. 778. conclusioun] confusioun. 779. gois...confessioun] now hes gude professioun. 780. Can] Yit. repent] repentis. 791. noit] be noit. 794. Do...here] Obey unto your god. 2474. that *suppl.* 2476. wichtlie] wrechitlie. 2537. till ane rekill] still quhill ane strand. 2632. this] and. 2667. pais] prais. 2697. Goddis] his. 2701. hedit] deid. 2703. syne] and. 2716. poleit] poete. 2750. cairt] court. 2760. be rad] dreid. 2769. with] had with. 2771. I mene] and men.

DUNBAR. **Meditation in Winter**. 24. Quhome] MS Quhone. 28. no] MS mo. **Golden Targe**. 274. hes] P may. **Two Married Women**. 2. till ane meid] MS allane neir. 36. whit] MS with. 65. born] MS b... 66. feiris] MS freiris. 69. gentryce] MS gent. 98. gore his] MS goreis. 102. sanyng] MS sanyne. 124. How] P Ho. 127. waistit] P wistit. 141. wod] P wmyod. 150. to *suppl.* 175. into] P in tho. 176. wer set] P werse. 183. As] P

And. 186. dankys] P danys. 492. sittis *suppl.* 495. speciall] P speiall. 500. lig] P lak. 516. schill] P still. ***'Timor mortis'***. 26. Takis] P Tak. 59. tragidie] P trigide.

HAWES. **Pastime of Pleasure**. 13. gan] and. 14. And *suppl.* 28. the *suppl.* 154. cloudes] cloude. 184. grehoundes] grehounde. 917. So] So that. 922. or] or in. 5813. renue] remeue.

SKELTON. **Bowge of Court**. 13. wyte] wrythe. 14. moralyte] mortalyte. 19. I *suppl.* 22. ho] he. 25. many *suppl.* 31. enweried] enwered. 186. Twysh] Twyst. 187. a *suppl.* 191. Hom] Whom. 198. communed] commaunde. praty space] party spake. 289. bees] byes. 294. carkes] carbes. 329. maystryes] maysters. 388. syne] one. 403. harnes] harmes. 413. here] here is. **Philip Sparrow**. 89. From] For. 163. fethers] fether. 169. though] thought. 290. The] These. 362. his] this. 773. elect] clere. 996. *domina*] *domine*. 1054. For *suppl.* 1205. pullysshed] publysshed. 1231. For *suppl.* 1244. stalkynge] stalke. 1261. *vatem*] *latem*. 1263. *cecini*] *pocecini*. **Elinor Rumming**. 224. mytyng] nytyng. **Colin Clout**. 8. despyte] to desyte. 56. mothe] moche. 414. Redes] Rede. 416. talkes] talke. 1093. Have] Hath. 1114. gramed] greved. **Garland of Laurel**. 6. plenarly] plenary. 26. now *suppl.* 53. scyences] scyence. 54. leven] lene. 68. they] the. the] they. 767. a *suppl.* 771. a bevy] above. 776. coronell] cronell.

FIRST ENGLISH LIFE. a. the] and the. b. thereof] therefore.

MORE. **Richard III**. a. arme] harme. b. looked] looke. **Utopia**. a. they] the.

ROPER'S LIFE OF MORE. a. More] Moore (*et sic passim*). b. that *suppl.* c. this] thus. d. here *suppl.* e. othe *suppl.* f. yet *suppl.*

WYATT. **Poem 1**. 6. lustes] lust. **Poem 3**. 11. thy] they. **Poem 4**. 8. sighes] sightes. 10. weried] wered. 13. confort] consort. **Poem 5**. 8, 9. yea] & (*perhaps standing for a nod of assent*). **Poem 7**. 6. trayed] tryed. **Poem 13**. 4, 39. sung] song. 27. nyghtes] nyght. **Poem 17**. 19. sleith] seith. 22. doth *suppl.* **Poem 23**. 11. hereth] herth. 20. Do] To. 40. folysh] folys. **Poem 24**. 18. *line supplied*. **Poem 25**. 6. must] most. 15. setst] seiste. **Poem 28**. 2. estate] estates. 4. Unknowen] Unknowe. 8. For] From. **Poem 31**. 15. touche my] twyche me. 19. frame my tonge] from me tune. 27. That] Thar. 32. wiles] willes. 44. in *suppl.* 45. cowarde] cowardes. 52. droncke] drounkin. 54. he is] is.

SURREY. **Poem 8**. 7. you] yove. 11. content in mynde] contentyd myndes. 12. wynde] wyndes. 15–16. *supplied from Tottel*. 34. stille] steale. **Poem 10**. 49. stone *suppl.* **Poem 13**. 8. contynuance] cotynuance.

Glossary of Common Hard Words

NB *i/y*, *c/k*, are treated as interchangeable.

ac *conj.* but, and
after *prep.* according to
agayn, ayen *prep.* against; *adv.* again, back, in reply
al *conj.* although, even if
alday *adv.* always, all the time
algate(s) *adv.* always, at any rate
als, also *adv., conj., prep.* as, also
and *conj.* and, if
ane *indef. art. (Scot.)* a, an
anon, anoon *adv.* straightway
ar *conj.* before
as *adv.* often used, with no meaning, to introduce an imperative
assoille *v.* absolve
atones *adv.* at once
atte *prep.* at the
ay *adv.* always
ayen *see* **agayn**
baar, bar *v.* bore, carried
be *prep.* by
been, ben *v.* be, been
behight *v. pa. t.* promised
benedicite(e) *interj.* bless you (an oath)
bere *v.* bear (**beren on honde**, accuse falsely)
bet *adj., adv.* better
biforn *adv., prep.* before
biheste *n.* promise
bilyve, blyve *adv.* quickly
bokeler *n.* buckler, small shield
bot *conj.* but
bowe *v.* go, move
boye, boie *n.* boy, lad, fellow, rascal
breme *adj.* fierce, loud, wild
burde *n.* woman
burne *n.* man
but *prep. (Scot.)* without
but if *conj.* unless, if...not
can *v.* can, knows how to
carp, karp *v.* talk
catel *n.* property, wealth, estate
cayre, kayre *v.* go
chees(e), chese *v., v. pa. t.* choose, chose
cherl *n.* churl, villain, low-class person
cleped *v.* called
clerc, clerk *n.* learned man, scholar, student, priest
cokewold *n.* cuckold
conseil *n.* secret
corage *n.* spirit, heart
dan, daun *n.* sir, master, lord
dangerous, daungerous *adj.* disdainful, haughty, standoffish, (affecting to be) hard to get
degree *n.* social rank
doute *n.* doubt (**out of doute**, doubtless, without doubt)
drede *n.* doubt (**out of drede**, doubtless, without doubt)
dredfull *adj.* frightening, fearful
ech, echon *pron.* each, each one
eek, eke *adv.* also
eft, efte *adv.* again
elde *n.* age
elles *adv.* otherwise, else
endite *v.* compose

ensamples *n. pl.* examples, exempla (illustrative stories)
erst *adv.* first
everich *adj.* every, each
everichon *pron.* each one, every one
everydeel *adv.* every bit, all, all over
fang *v.* receive, take
fay, fey *n.* faith (**by my fey**, truly)
faytour *n.* false beggar, vagabond, malingerer
fele *adj.* many
fil, fille *v. pa. t.* fell
finde, fynde *v.* provide for
folde *n.* earth
fonge *v.* receive, take
forthy *adv.* therefore
forwhy *conj.* because
fowel *n.* bird
freke *n.* man
fro *prep.* from
ful *adv.* very
fyn, fyne *n.* end, conclusion
geere, gere *n.* equipment, utensils
gentil *adj.* of noble birth, noble (sometimes ironically)
gome *n.* man
goost, gost *n.* spirit
gossib, gossip *n.* fellow-sponsor at child's baptism, bosom-friend, confidant
greet, gret, grete *adj.* great (**gretter, gretteste**)
grote *n.* groat (silver coin worth fourpence)
han *v.* have
harrow *interj.* help! woe, alas!
hathel *n.* man, knight, lord
heed *n.* head
heeng, heng *v.* hung, hanged
heigh *adj.* high
hem *pron.* them
hende *adj.* courteous
hente *v.* catch, take, seize
hight(e) *v. pa. t.* was called; promised
hir, her, hor *adj.* their
hir, hire *adj., pron.* her
ho *pron.* she
hom *pron.* them
hulles *n. pl.* hills
hym *pron.* him, himself; them
ilk, ilke *adj.* same
innoghe, innowe, ynogh *adj., adv.* plenty, in plenty
into, intill *prep. (Scot.)* in, within
inwit, inwytt *n.* active conscience
iwysse, ywis *adv.* indeed
jupartie *n.* risk, jeopardy
kan *v.* knows how to, can
keep, kep *n.* heed (in **take keep**, take heed)
knave *n.* servant, servant lad, boy, workman, low-born man
koude *v.* knew how to, could
kouthe, kowthe *adj.* well known, famous
kynde *n.* nature
lache *v.* take, seize, get
lede, leude *n.* man
leere, lere *v.* learn
leeve, leve *adj.* dear
lele *adj.* true, loyal, faithful
lemman *n.* sweetheart ('sweetie'), lover, mistress (a somewhat popular but not vulgar term)
lenger *adv.* longer
lesynge *n.* lie (untruth)
lest, list, lust *n.* pleasure
lest, leste *v.* pleased (**hym leste**, it pleased him)
let *v.* hinder, prevent
leve, leeve *adj.* dear
levere *adv.* rather
lewed *adj.* uneducated, ignorant, simple, stupid
lewte *n.* loyalty, adherence to law, justice
liketh *v.* pleases (**yow liketh**, it pleases you)
liste *v.* pleased (**hym liste**, it pleased him)
lite *adj.* little
lordynges *n. voc.* sirs, good sirs
lorel *n.* lazy worthless fellow
losel *n.* wastrel
lust *n.* pleasure, desire
luther, luyther *adj.* wicked
make *n.* mate
mensk *adj.* noble, honourable
meschief *n.* misfortune, trouble, harm, plight
ming *v.* mix, mingle
mo *pron.* more
mochel *adv.* much, greatly
molde *n.* earth
moot, moote, mooten *v.* must, may
morwe *n.* morning, morrow
moste, mot *v.* must
mowe *v.* may
muchel *adv.* much, greatly
namely *adv.* especially, particularly
namo *pron.* no more, no others
nat, noght *adv.* not
neer *adv.* nearer
nice, nyce *adj.* foolish

nis, nys *v.* is not
no-but *conj.* unless, except that
nolde *v.* would not, did not wish to
nones, nonys *in* **for the nones**, for the occasion, at that time
noon *pron.* no one, none
noot *v.* know not
ny *adv.* near
o, oo, oon *pron.* one, a certain, a single
of *adv.* off
ones, onis *adv.* once
or *prep., conj.* before
other *conj.* or
outher *conj.* either
overal *adv.* everywhere
panes *n. pl.* pence
pardee *interj.* indeed
pay *n.* pleasure, satisfaction
pay *v.* please
plain *v.* complain
pleyn *adj., adv.* full, fully, plain, plainly
preve *n.* prove, demonstrate
propre *adj.* own
pryvee *adj.* secret, discreet
pryvete *n.* secret, secrets
queynte *adj.* strange, curious, ingeniously contrived; as *n.* a curious and interesting device or ornament, a woman's external sex organ (a less vulgar word than 'cunt', which was available in the fourteenth century)
quhilk *pron. (Scot.)* which
quhill *conj. (Scot.)* until
quite, quyte *v.* repay, pay back, requite
rede *v.* advise
reed *n.* advice
renk *n.* man
renne *v.* run
rent, rente *n.* income
ribaudes, rybaudes *n. pl.* rascals, scurrilous tale-tellers
right, ryght *adv.* quite, very, completely, exactly
sad *adj.* sober, serious, steady, steadfast
sall *v. (Scot.)* shall
sauf *adj.* safe
saugh, say, seigh *v.* saw
schalke *n.* man
scho *pron.* she
segge *n.* man
sely *adj.* blessed, innocent, simple, hapless, silly
semely *adj.* fitting, suitable, proper
semely, semyly *adv.* in a fitting or appropriately elegant manner
sen *conj. (Scot.)* since
sethen, sithen *adv.* then, afterwards
seye, seyn *v.* say
sheene, shene *adj.* bright, shiny
shende *v.* destroy
shrew(e) *n.* ill-disposed person, scold, scoundrel
siker *adj.* sure, certain
sikerly *adv.* truly, indeed
sith, sithen *conj.* since
skile *n.* reason, knowledge
smal *adj.* slender
somdel *adv.* somewhat
sooth *adj.* true
sothly *adv.* truly
sterve *v.* die, starve
stinte *v.* stop
suld *v. (Scot.)* should
swevene *n.* dream
swich *adj.* such
swynk *n.* work
swynke, swynken *v.* work
swythe, swythely *adv.* very, very much, quickly
swyve *v.* have sex with (a woman) (not as vulgar as 'fuck', which was available in the fourteenth century)
sy *v. pa. t.* saw
syn *conj.* since
than, thanne *adv.* then
thar *v.* need
that *pron.* what
thee, theen *v.* thrive (**so moot I thee**, as I may thrive)
ther as *conj.* where
thilke *adj.* that same
this, thise *adj., pron.* these
tho *adj., pron.* those
tho *conj.* when, then
thocht *conj. (Scot.)* though
thoughte *v.* seemed (**me t., it t. me**, it seemed to me)
thries *adv.* thrice
til *prep.* to
tolke, tulke *n.* man
travaile *n., v.* work, labour
trowe *v.* believe, think
uche *adj.* each
unnethe(s) *adv.* hardly, with difficulty, scarcely
verray *adj.* true, absolute, real, genuine
vileynye *adv.* rudeness, coarseness, bad things

vitaille *n.* victuals, food
wait *v. (Scot.)* know
weene, wene *v.* suppose, think, imagine
wel, weel *adv.* well
whan, whanne *conj.* when
wif, wyf *n.* wife, woman
wight *n.* person, creature
wisse *v.* guide, direct, advise
wiste *v.* knew
wit *n.* wisdom, intelligence
withal, withalle *adv.* also, indeed
witterly *adv.* truly, certainly
wol *v.* will
wolde *v.* would, wished, would wish
wone *v.* dwell
wood, wode *adj.* mad, crazy
woot, wot *v.* know, knows
worthe *v.* be, become
wyghe, wyye *n.* man, creature
yaf *v.* gave
ye *n.* eye (pl. **yen**)
ye *interj.* yea, indeed
yede *v. pa. t.* went
yerne *adv.* eagerly
yeve, yive *v.* give, given
yis *adv.* yes indeed (emphatic form, in response to negative questions, of **ye**)
yut *adv.* yet

Index

Note particularly references to themes and topics collected under the following entries: astrology and astronomy; authors, narrators and authorial self-representation; church and religion; death and mortality; drama; Fortune and destiny; landscape and seasons-description; language; Lollards and Lollardy; love and love-poetry; medicine and medical terms; metre and verse-form; music; mysticism and affective devotion; politics and government; style and rhetoric; women and marriage.